The Scrapbook History
of Baseball

The Scrapbook History of Baseball

BY

Jordan A. Deutsch, Richard M. Cohen,
Roland T. Johnson and David S. Neft

BOBBS-MERRILL

Indianapolis/New York

ISBN 0-672-52028-1
Library of Congress Catalog Card Number: 75-4335
Manufactured in the United States of America

First printing

Library of Congress Cataloging in Publication Data
Main entry under title:

The scrapbook history of baseball.

   1. Baseball—History—Miscellanea.   I. Deutsch, Jordan A.
GV862.5.S35   796.357'09   75-4335
ISBN 0-672-52028-1

ACKNOWLEDGMENTS

The authors would like to express their deep appreciation to the following individuals, institutions, libraries, and newspapers who were so cooperative in extending their time and facilities during the preparation of this book:

Mark Swayne, *Visual and Technical Coordinator*
Nancy McCormack, *Technical Consultant*
Bill Loughman, *Research Advisor*

Baseball Hall of Fame:
Jack Redding, *Librarian*
Cliff Kachline, *Historian*

Football Hall of Fame:
Jim Campbell, *Historian*

M-K Super Pictures, Inc.

Microfilm Corporation of America:
Dick Schmidt
Pat Hochstetler

Hartford Public Library, Reference and General Reading Department:
Josephine Sale, *Head*
Martha Nolan, *Assistant Head*
Dorothy Brickett, Ann Casey, Rosalie Fawcett, Carol Fitting, Shirley Kiefer, Fernando Labault, Beverly Loughlin, Betty Mullendore, Gene Seymour, *Research Assistants*

Library of Congress Annex, Serial Division:
Katherine Gould, *Assistant Head, Reference Section*
Paul Boswell, Henry Brzezanski, Porter Humphrey, William Laing, Anne Lewis, Susan Miller, Jean Sansobrino, Joan Sullivan, *Reference Librarians*
Norman Chase, William Moten, *Deck Attendants*

The staff of the newspaper collection of the New York Public Library Annex

The staff of the newspaper division of the Danbury Public Library

The authors would also like to thank those newspapers who were good enough to allow the use of their material even though it could not be incorporated in this edition:

Atlanta Constitution, Cleveland Press, Columbus Dispatch, Houston Chronicle, Indianapolis News, Indianapolis Star, Milwaukee Sentinel, Minneapolis Tribune, Philadelphia Bulletin, Rochester Democrat & Chronicle, San Diego Union, San Francisco Chronicle, St. Louis Globe Democrat, St. Louis Post-Dispatch.

Design and production: Helen Barrow, Rosalie Barrow, Libra Graphics, Inc. and Irving Perkins

The authors' wives: Thea Deutsch, Nancy Cohen, Judy Johnson, Naomi Neft—a special thanks for their faith and cooperation throughout the project.

All comments and inquiries on this book should be sent to:
SPORTS PRODUCTS, INC.
632 North Mountain Road
Newington, Conn. 06111

Foreword

MY VERY EARLIEST memory of my Old Man is of him sitting in the kitchen, waiting for supper (they always called it "supper" in the Midwest; "dinner" was something that Clark Gable and Carole Lombard had), reading the sports page and muttering. My mother, hanging over the sink, knew from long experience that it was time to keep her mouth shut. The Old Man was getting his daily dose of bad news. He was a White Sox fan, who grew up on the South Side in the very shadow of Comiskey Park. He had seen it all. How many ball fans can honestly say that they were a fan of the only team ever to actually throw a World Series? My Old Man was only a kid himself at that time, but it scarred him for life, and it was a truly symbolic beginning to a notably disappointment-ridden baseball fan career. He was a fanatic, and a fitting epitaph to his life could well have been:

SOX DROP TWO TO YANKS.

He hated the Yanks, naturally. There was something about the cool, diabolical professionalism of the Bombers that incensed every follower of the White Sox, who throughout my father's entire baseball-watching career had absolutely none of those traits. True, there were occasional highlights, such as the day Luke Appling fouled seventeen consecutive pitches off Eldon Auker, the submariner, and then tripled off the right field wall on the eighteenth. True, he died on third, but you can't win 'em all. In fact, that particular cliché was used in reverse by the White Sox fans: *You can't lose 'em all*. Although some seasons they nearly pulled it off.

The names of the White Sox luminaries of my Old Man's day still stick in the back recesses of my memory; names rich and redolent, indeed ripe with White Sox-edness: "Banana Nose" Zeke Bonura, "Luscious Luke" Appling, "Iron Mike" Kreevich, "Bullfrog Bill" Dietrich, also known, perhaps more accurately, as "Wild Bill" Dietrich, "Ripper" Radcliff, an outfielder who once prostrated himself in the grass of left field to stop a ground ball and prove to the fans that he could actually keep one from getting to the wall (it took a bad hop at the last minute, skipped right over him, and went into the bullpen for a triple), "Jungle Jim" Rivera, a true primitive who entertained his fans in the bleachers by long, involved arguments with loud-mouthed yahoos who were trying to instruct him in the finer points of outfielding.

The spirit of this roistering crowd of athletes was beautifully epitomized by the time Banana Nose Zeke, a lumbering, good-natured, heavy-hitting first baseman with a fielding range of roughly eight to eleven inches on either side of the bag, one day announced to the truly long-suffering manager (a special hero to the White Sox nuts, Jimmy Dykes) that he couldn't make the road trip to the East Coast because "som'pin's wrong with my back. I got a bad crick in it, or som'pin, and the doctor says I gotta rest for at least the next two weeks." Dykes, always eager to try anything that might, just conceivably *might,* win a game or two before September, agreed. The team left town without Banana Nose.

Two days later, Dykes unexpectedly reappeared in Chicago. He was called back on business. A group of friends took him out to dinner at a hotel that was famous for its Conga band. Halfway through his steak, who does he spot leading the Conga line, whooping it up and moving better than he ever had around first base but Guess Who?

The next day the newspapers read:

Dykes fines Banana Nose Bonura for Conga Dancing when the player was supposed to have been recovering from injuries. The first baseman stated: "I don't know what he's so sore about. I was just working out the crick in my back."

It was items like this that made the Old Man mutter over his nightly meat loaf and mashed potatoes.

My Old Man would have loved this collection of historic newspaper reports that in some ways are a highly significant social history of most of the 20th Century. There is something so satisfying and fascinating about reading the immediate, on-the-spot stories of long-forgotten ball games that is impossible to explain. Single lines leap out:

Joe DiMaggio, Sensational Rookie Making his big league debut came through with three hits [May 4, 1936],

or

The first night game of baseball in Brooklyn started in a circus atmosphere Wednesday night and resulted in Johnny Vander Meer's second no-hit game in a week as the Cincinnati Reds won 6-0 [June 16, 1938].

That must have been some night! Practically every page of this magnificent collection says as much about the America of its time as the editorial pages ever did. Branch Rickey's great comment on Jackie Robinson's historic entry into baseball:

"If some players quit, they'll be back after a year or two in a cotton mill,"

says it all. Or take September 23, 1949 when

Bill Veeck, the Cleveland Indians president, wearing a top hat, drove a horse-drawn hearse in a "pre-game funeral procession." Manager Lou Boudreau and his coaches were pall bearers. They carried their 1948 Pennant flag to the outfield and buried it. The epitaph on the cardboard headstone read "1948 Champs." [They were out of the race in 1949.] While Veeck wiped his eyes as they circled the field, 35,000 fans howled.

They don't make 'em like that any more. They just don't.

They're all here in these pages, alive, slugging, booting ground balls, winning, losing, making predictions, getting fired, going off to war, and even sometimes coming back. It is always Summer in these pages, and the Pennant Races of 1924, 1932, 1941, 1950 still hang in the balance.

JEAN SHEPHERD

BASE BALL.

Wholesome Revolution in the Professional Code.

A New National League Organized.

Playing Rules for the Centennial Year.

The leading professional clubs have by their representatives lately taken a step which seems calculated to work some needed improvements in the whole system or code of professional ball playing. The movement lately developed was first agitated in the East, and was taken up heartily by the best men in the West. Messrs. W. A. Hulbert and Chas. A. Fowle, in their capacity as a committee appointed by the Chicago, Cincinnati, Louisville and St. Louis clubs, issued a call under date of Jan. 23 to the leading Eastern clubs to meet at New York, and consider matters of interest to the game, with especial reference to correcting existing abuses and forming a new association.

The Convention

met at the Grand Central Hotel, New York, on Wednesday morning, the Mutual, Boston, Hartford, Athletic, Chicago, St. Louis, Louisville and Cincinnati clubs being represented. The Western clubs came prepared with drafts of constitution and by-laws. The clubs represented formally withdrew from the old association, and a new organization was resolved upon, to be called the National League of Professional Base Ball Clubs, instead of an Association of Players, as before. Under the constitution adopted, the entrance fee of each club is fixed at $100, instead of $10 as heretofore. No club shall ever be admitted from a city of less than 75,000 inhabitants, except by unanimous vote, or from any city within five miles of any club in the league, thus giving to the league club virtually full proprietary rights over the city to which it belongs. No visiting club, member of the League, shall play any club in a city, or within five miles of a city, in which there is a league club except the league club, but this does not prohibit a league club from playing another club belonging to the same city. For instance, no club of the league, such as the Mutual or Chicago, can go to Philadelphia and play the Philadelphia Club in that city, the latter club not belonging to the league, but the Athletic, if it so desires, can play with the Philadelphia a friendly game, as both clubs belong there. The penalty for a violation of this rule is the expulsion of the offending club from the league. The league, in the preamble adopted, declares that as base ball has depreciated in the estimation of the public, principally because of dishonest and incompetent clubs, it is for the interest of the game, public and players, for an entirely new system to be devised which will keep out all

Dishonest and Incompetent Clubs

and players; therefore this organization is effected. To prevent bad feeling and sectional differences, as the foundation and intent of the league is harmony and unity, which can only be obtained by making it a whole in everything, a change in the mode of the election of officers is necessary. Every one will have an equal chance, each club having but one vote on any matter; the names of the clubs are placed in a box and five drawn out. The delegates of those clubs form the board of directors, and have exclusive charge of all the affairs of the league, thus doing away with all judiciary, championship and other committees, as all duties formerly devolving upon them are now to be performed by the board. The board elect their president, also a person to act as secretary and treasurer, the latter not to be a member of any club, and really but a clerk, who shall take care and charge of all papers and business documents of the league, and be pledged to divulge none of its affairs without permission. He is to receive not less than $300 nor more than $500 per annum, and be under bonds. The clubs which form the board of directors for this year, as drawn, are the Hartford (president), Boston, St. Louis, Mutual and Louisville. This board has conclusive control of all the general business and interests of the league. In case of disputes arising upon the construction, interpretation or violation of the playing rules only,

The President Shall Appoint Three Arbitrators,

not members of the board, and within fifteen days the complaining club must file with the secretary their complaint, with the affidavits of witnesses, and the other club shall state their case, or there may be a mutual statement made of the difficulty. The secretary must forward the statements to the first arbitrator, who indorses his opinion and sends the papers to the second arbitrator, who doing likewise sends them to the third, who with similar action sends them to the secretary. The majority decision is sent to the contesting clubs, and there is no appeal. The arbitrators are not restricted as to the penalty which may be inflicted upon the club or players found to be in fault, and the costs of the arbitration are to be borne equally by the clubs litigant.

The Rules on Players

and regarding contracts are greatly changed. A club in the league can make a contract with a player for the succeeding year at any time. It must be signed by the player and an officer of the club and a witness. A copy is to be sent at once to the secretary to file, and he at once notifies all other clubs, who are bound thenceforward to have no negotiation with such player for that season, thus preventing revolving. The penalty for violation is the expulsion of both player and club. If any player is released during his contract, the club releasing him is bound to send to the secretary a statement of the fact, and also that there is nothing against his character as a player to prevent his being re-engaged. If his release bears no such indorsement it shall be taken for granted that the player has been expelled or dismissed for cause that will prevent his re-engagement, and it is not necessary to send to the club to ascertain this, the absence of the indorsement being *prima facie* evidence. No player shall be engaged by any club until his record shall be found clear on the secretary's book, under penalty of the club taking him being expelled. No player expelled for dishonesty shall ever be readmitted, and if a club engages him the club shall be expelled. In case of a club being expelled there shall be no reconsideration of the vote at any time. These stringent rules will make both clubs and players careful. The championship series will be ten games, five on the grounds of each club, and in case of a tie or postponed game it may be played over, but this is not necessary. If a player on a nine dies after a game has been arranged, the game can be postponed by either contestant; but postponement, outside of weather or unavoidable accident, can be had for no other cause.

The Base Ball Season

shall begin on March 15th and end on Nov. 15th. The championship emblem shall cost $100, and be a national flag, bearing the date, name of club, and the word "champion." The board of directors shall meet on the first Monday of December of each year and hear all cases coming before it. The convention meets on the following Thursday, at a city at least 50 miles from a station of any club in the league. One rule adopted was that a player, being released either by agreement or disbandment of a club, can play after twenty days.

The revised playing rules were presented by Harry Wright, who was chairman of a committee appointed at the meeting of the old association in March last for that purpose. They were adopted as recommended by the committee with but few modifications. Some of

The Changes Introduced

are radical and much needed. A foul fly is now to be in play as soon as caught if it is caught before touching the ground. Base runners may return to their bases on foul grounders without being put out. This removes the danger of base runners being sacrificed by being caught running on a hit which they were prevented by the calls of the audience or of the other players from hearing called "foul" by the umpire. The effect will be to make the batsman hit out more freely when there is a man on first base, and will also give the base-runner more confidence as he will be sure to take more chances if he knows that he can return safely on a ball hit foul to the ground. The batsman is to be declared out for making one "foul strike" *i. e.*, stepping outside the lines of his position *when he hits the ball*. The rule regarding pitching is unaltered except in requiring that the hand must pass *below* the hip when the ball is being delivered. The batsman is to have more license given him by having under some circumstances a fourth "strike" before being declared out. In this way—all ball players know that after a man has had "two strikes" called on him he will hit at almost anything, for fear of having a "third" called. It is now provided that after "two strikes" have been called a striker may let a "good ball" pass him without having a "third strike" called, but the pitcher is to be informed and the striker is to be warned that it is a "good ball" by the umpire's so calling. This gives the batsman a chance to "settle" himself, and he must then strike at or hit the next "good ball," or have "three strikes" called. Some of the laws heretofore placed under the head of "playing rules" are now transferred to the constitution, which also embraces the old championship code. Mr. N. E. Young of Washington was chosen secretary and treasurer of the league. The constitution and playing rules will be officially published by him as soon as practicable.

The Action of the Convention

was thoroughly harmonious and unanimous. Although the course taken may bear hard upon the minor clubs, yet it seems to be the only one left to the clubs interested to protect their very existence. The lovers of the game can now depend upon seeing championship contests between first-class clubs only, and stockholders and managers may reasonably expect a good attendance at all matches instead of empty benches at about one-third or one-half of the games arranged.

OPENING OF THE LEAGUE SERIES OF BASE-BALL MATCHES.

THE BOSTONS OPEN THE BALL WITH THE ATHLETICS, AND SCORE A VICTORY BY ERRORS OF THE LATTER—A GOOD BEGINNING.

PHILADELPHIA, PA., April 22.—The first championship game of the season was played here this afternoon between the Bostons and Athletics, in the presence of about 3000 spectators. The weather was cloudy, but favorable. O'Rourke made his reappearance with the Bostons in this game. The Athletics were slightly favorites in the betting. A wild throw by Sutton gave the Bostons their first run in the second inning, the good batting of Coons and Hall scoring one for the Athletics in the same inning. The Bostons added two more in the third inning by a difficult catch, missed by Fisler, followed by O'Rourke's two-baser, and a safe hit by Murnan. The Bostons scored one run in their first inning by the good batting and base-running of Wright. The Athletics tied in the sixth inning, Fisler, Coons and Hall being credited with clean hits, and Meyerle getting a base on called balls. Safe hits by Murnan and Schafer in ninth inning, and a muff by Fouser, who was then playing second base, gave the Bostons two more runs and the victory, as the Athletics could only score one run, that being earned by Knight's splendid two-base hit. Two men were on the bases when Sutton [the weak spot of the Athletics in this game] went out at first base on a feeble hit to Josephs. McGinley was hit in the eye by a foul in the seventh inning, but pluckily played through. The Bostons won by their superior fielding and base-running, the Athletics excelling at the bat. The contest was very exciting. McLean umpired impartially and satisfactorily. Following is the score:

BOSTON.	R	1B	PO	A	E	ATHLETIC.	R	1B	PO	A	E
G. Wright, s.s.	2	1	2	2	0	Force, s.s.	0	1	0	4	1
Leonard, 2b.	0	2	0	4	1	Eggler, c.f.	0	0	4	1	1
O'Rourke, c.f.	1	2	0	0	0	Fisler, 1b.	1	3	11	0	1
Murnan, 1b.	1	2	8	0	0	Meyerle, 2b.	1	1	3	2	1
Schafer, 3b.	1	1	1	0	1	Sutton, 3b.	0	0	0	1	2
McGinley, c.	1	0	8	0	3	Coons, c.	2	2	1	2	3
Manning, r.f.	0	0	4	0	0	Hall, l.f.	0	2	1	0	0
Parks, l.f.	0	0	3	0	1	Fouser, r.f.	0	0	3	1	2
Josephs, p.	0	0	1	1	1	Knight, p.	1	1	1	3	2
Totals	6	8	27	7	7	Totals	5	10	27	14	13

Boston..................0 1 2 0 1 0 0 0 0 2—6
Athletic.................0 1 0 0 3 0 0 1—5

Runs earned—Athletic, 2; Boston, 1. First base by errors—Athletic, 3; Boston, 6. Bases on balls—Boston, 2; Athletic, 1. Umpire—William McLean. Time of game—2 hours 5 minutes.

The GLOBE-DEMOCRAT yesterday morning announced the fact that the St. Louis Base Ball Club intended accomplishing the greatest feat in the annals of the game, if sharp play could bring about the result prayed for, which was nothing less than the whitewashing of the famous Hartford nine for the third consecutive time. They did it, and thereby covered themselves with glory and sent their admirers into ecstacies. A large crowd was present to witness the discomfiture of the Dark Blues. In the matter of the toss, luck for the first time in a long while deserted McGeary, which was considered a favorable omen for Hartford, but, as the sequel showed, failed to prove such. St. Louis won the game in the first two innings by the fine batting of Clapp and Blong, and four unfortunate errors by their opponents. In the last seven innings Bond was so

WELL SUPPORTED

that the Browns could not possibly increase their score. Bradley's pitching, and the magnificent backing given it by the fielders, won the day for St. Louis. For the first time in the annals of the League, nine innings were played without a single base hit being placed to the credit of one of the teams. The Hartford's utterly failed to do anything whatever with Bradley's twisters. Weak infield hits and easy flies were the order of the afternoon on their side, and a chance for an out was rarely missed. Bradley has good reason to be proud of his record. His associates, especially Clapp, whose beautiful batting was a marked feature of the game, did fairly off Bond's curves, and thereby won the game. Three such games as have been played during the past week by the St. Louis and Hartford Clubs

HAVE NEVER BEEN WITNESSED,

the scores being 2 to 0, 3 to 0, and 2 to 0, all in favor of St. Louis. They will be placed on record as the most wonderful struggles in the history of the national pastime. When it is stated that until last Tuesday Hartford had not been whitewashed this season, and that for twenty-seven consecutive innings they were retired by the Browns without scoring, and almost in one-two-three order, some idea of the magnificent manner in which they must have fielded the stinging hits of such men as Burdock, Higham, Ferguson, and the other Blue Legs can be formed.

THE SCORE.

ST. LOUIS.	R	1B	PO	A	E	HARTFORD.	R	1B	PO	A	E
Cuthbert, l.f.	0	0	2	0	0	Remsen, c.f.	0	0	3	0	0
Clapp, c.	1	3	3	0	3	Burdock, 2b.	0	0	3	0	0
McGeary, 2b.	0	0	3	5	0	Higham, r.f.	0	0	1	0	0
Pike, c.f.	0	1	1	0	0	Ferguson, 3b.	0	0	2	1	0
Battin, 3b.	0	0	2	3	1	Carey, s.s.	0	0	3	0	3
Blong, r.f.	1	1	0	0	0	Bond, p.	0	0	0	0	1
Bradley, p.	0	0	3	1	0	York, l.f.	0	0	3	0	1
Dehlman, 1b.	0	1	16	0	1	Mills, 1b.	0	0	11	0	1
Pearce, s.s.	0	0	3	2	1	Harbidge, c.	0	0	4	3	1
Total	2	6	27	11	6	Total	0	0	27	7	4

Innings	1	2	3	4	5	6	7	8	9	
St. Louis	1	1	0	0	0	0	0	0	0	—2
Hartford	0	0	0	0	0	0	0	0	0	—0

Runs earned—None.
Time of game—1 hour 50 minutes.
Umpire—Mr. Daniels, of Hartford.

BASE-BALL.

THE CLOSE OF THE LEAGUE CAMPAIGN.

Though some of the Western clubs are still playing with outside nines, the regular league campaign has ended, and the several positions in the pennant race are now definitely settled. For the first time in the history of the regular professional clubs of the country Chicago bears off the championship honors; and after a tough struggle at the close Hartford comes in for second place; St. Louis being obliged to content herself with third position, though the style in which she handled her Chicago rivals by defeating them in ten out of sixteen games showed that she had the ability to do better had not a corrupt element, combined with weak management, acted against her success in the campaign. The hitherto invincible Boston team is this season obliged to be content with fourth place, while last on the list of the contesting nines stands the experimental team of Cincinnati, the badly-managed Athletics not being far ahead of them, and the unreliable Mutuals further down on the record than ever before, though they had the material at command to have placed them at least a good third. Thus closes the championship campaign of 1876, the inaugural year of the League Association and the most unsatisfactory one take it altogether, the professional clubs have yet had. One club of the eight in the league finishes in bankruptcy; another suspends operations before the season's close; a third winds up the worst defeated professional nine that has ever entered the lists; while all but two—the Chicago and Boston clubs—close the season with worse than empty treasuries, being hundreds of dollars in debt. In many respects the managerial season of 1876 has been one of blunders. The high tariff of 50 cents was one mistake, but it was not so fatal to pecuniary success as was that of engaging suspected players, under the mistaken idea that the new laws, if never so stringent, would prevent any more crooked work.

Club.	Chicago	Hartford.	St. Louis	Boston.	Louisville.	Mutual.	Athletic.	Cincinnati.	Games won.	Games drawn.	Games played.	Games unplayed
Chicago....	—	6	4	9	7	7	10	9	52	0	66	4
Hartford....	4	—	7	9	7	9	4	6	46	1	68	2
St. Louis...	6	4	—	6	6	8	7	8	45	0	64	6
Boston....	1	2	4	—	5	8	9	10	39	6	69	6
Louisville..	1	1	4	5	—	5	6	8	30	3	69	4
Mutual.....	1	4	1	2	3	—	7	1	21	1	57	13
Athletic....	1	0	1	0	1	2	—	4	14	1	60	10
Cincinnati..	0	1	2	0	2	1	3	—	9	0	65	5
Games lost	14	21	19	30	36	35	45	56	256	6	518	45

June 14

FIRST MEETING THIS SEASON OF THE BOSTON AND ST. LOUIS CLUBS—A SCORE IN WHICH THE ERRORS ARE THE PRINCIPAL FEATURE.

Charity must be broad indeed to cover the sins of the first game of the season between the Boston and St. Louis clubs. Never was there a professional game played which was so full of disgusting muffs, disgraceful fumbles and loose and slovenly playing. The Bostons played the first three innings without an error, but in the very opening of the fourth Leonard muffed a ball thrown him by Merrill, and from that point onward it was a race to see who could make the most mistakes. Leonard, having the more opportunities, easily led the score in spite of frantic efforts on the part of Schafer and George Wright. Leonard had no less than nine errors in six innings, and the rest succeeding in running the total up to 25. Most of this was while the St. Louis nine were posting McBride out to right field—on the fourth inning for six first bases and four runs; on the fifth, four bases and five runs; and in the sixth for eight bases and seven runs. Although there was a two-base hit in each inning, only four of these runs were earned. Manning then went in to pitch, and though the St. Louisans got three runs, only one of them was after a base hit, and none were earned. The Bostons made very little headway against Bradley, getting one run in the fourth inning on errors of Blong and Clapp, and in the

fifth on passed balls, two in the seventh and two in the ninth on errors of Clapp, Mack and McGeary.

This sad exhibition was witnessed by about 800 people, only half of whom waited to see the whole of it.

The score follows:—

BOSTON.	AB	R	1B	PO	A	E	ST. LOUIS.	AB	R	1B	PO	A	E
G. Wright, s.s.	5	0	0	6	3	3	Cuthbert, l.f.	7	1	4	2	0	1
Leonard, 2b.	5	1	1	4	5	9	Clapp, c.	6	1	3	6	2	5
O'Rourke, c.f.	4	0	2	0	0	0	McGeary, 2b.	6	3	4	3	2	2
Murnan, 1b.	4	0	1	9	0	2	Pike, c.f.	6	3	3	1	0	0
Manning, r.f.	4	0	0	2	0	0	Battin, 3b.	6	3	3	1	0	0
Morrill, c.	4	0	0	5	2	3	Blong, r.f.	6	2	1	1	0	1
Schafer, 3b.	4	1	1	2	2	3	Bradley, p.	6	4	3	0	6	3
Whitney, l.f.	4	2	1	3	0	0	Dehlman, 1b.	6	2	2	11	0	0
McBride, p.	4	2	2	0	1	3	Mack, s.s.	6	2	1	1	3	4
Totals	38	6	8	27	13	24	Totals	55	20	23	27	14	16

Boston.................0 0 0 1 1 0 2 0 2—6
St. Louis..............1 0 0 4 5 7 0 0 3—20

Earned runs—St. Louis, 4. First base on called balls—Boston, 4; St. Louis, 3. On other errors—Boston, 3; St. Louis, 4. Left on bases—Boston, 4; St. Louis, 5. Struck out—Wright 2, Murnan, Morrill and Dehlman once each. Two-base hits—Pike 2, Murnan and Battin once each. Wild pitch—McBride, 1. Passed balls—Morrill, 2; Clapp, 4. Time of game, 2:44. Umpire, A. G. Hodges, of the Suffolk club.

BATTING RECORD FOR 1876.

Rank.	Name and Club.	Games played.	Total times at bat.	Total base hits made.	Percentage of base hits to times at bat.
1.	Barnes, Chicago......................	66	342	137	.400
2.	Hall, Athletic......................	60	276	98	.355
3.	Peters, Chicago......................	66	318	111	.349
4.	McVey, Chicago......................	63	310	107	.345
5.	Anson, Chicago......................	66	321	110	.342
6.	Andrus, Chicago......................	8	38	13	.342
7.	Clinton, Louisville......................	16	65	22	.338
8.	Meyerle, Athletic......................	55	259	87	.335
9.	White, Chicago......................	66	311	104	.334
10.	Hines, Chicago......................	63	304	99	.325
11.	Higham, Hartford......................	67	314	102	.324
12.	Devlin, Louisville......................	68	304	94	.312
13.	Pike, St. Louis......................	61	290	90	.310
14.	Spalding, Chicago......................	66	298	91	.305
15.	O'Rourke, Boston......................	70	327	100	.305
16.	Clapp, St. Louis......................	64	306	91	.297

THE CINCINNATI CLUB IN TROUBLE.—A dispatch from Cincinnati, O., dated June 16, says: "The Cincinnati Club, which was to have started on its Eastern tour to-morrow night, is, financially speaking, in trouble. Mr. Keck refuses to do more for it, and has called a meeting of the club and those interested in it for Monday, to announce its disbandment. Eight or ten of our wealthy citizens will invest $10,000 in the club to reorganize and play it this season, and by next season have it so that the men will work together. It will yet be a club to be proud of."

THE CHAMPIONSHIP RECORD.
The League Campaign.

Things are not running smoothly in League-club circles, and it is hardly likely that they will do so as long as that demoralizing rule of allowing players to engage themselves to other clubs in the midst of an exciting season is kept in force. This has been the entering-wedge of every club difficulty the League has had to contend with since its organization, from the year that the Chicago Club broke up the Philadelphia nine to the present time. The latest working of the mischievous system is cropping out in Louisville. According to *The Courier-Journal* of July 10, McManus and McGeary were in that city on Monday, the 9th, endeavoring to secure Devlin, Snyder and Hall for next year's St. Louis nine. If these engagements have been made, the result may be the practical breaking-up of the Louisville nine; for, though the players may be kept together until the end of the season, the power to discipline is in a measure lost, and the result of their play is likely to show this. This trouble and the breaking-up of the Cincinnati, together with the failure to place the new Cincinnati nine on a legal footing, will materially affect the interests of the League clubs. In view of the uncertainty of the status of the new Cincinnati nine, we are obliged to put on record two tables of the League-pennant games, viz., one showing the record with the games of the new and old Cincinnati nines included, and the other showing the record as it will be likely to be counted in November. The failure of the League to take action upon the Cincinnati Club's position at a special meeting is anything but in accordance with their profession of fair-dealing with the baseball public. Why does not the president of the Chicago Club—the "Boss of the League," as a Western paper calls him—attend to this important matter? Surely, he must be aware of the fact that it is not right to leave the Cincinnati Club's position in doubt. Either they are a League-club team, or they are not. If not, then their games are of no account. Why do not the new managers of the Cincinnati Club call for a show of League hands on the question of their position?

Sept. 27

That Sell Out.
[From the Pittsburg Gazette.]

The Alleghenys and Syracuse Stars played yesterday at Union Park, and the latter won by a score of 1 to 0. They made their run in the ninth inning. The gate receipts did not amount to $100, which shows that selling tournament games don't pay. Base ball is dead in this city unless something is done to wipe out the disgrace that now justly clings to the Allegheny Club. In a conversation which our reporter had last night with two Allegheny players, they frankly stated that the game in Chicago on Saturday was sold, and named the men who sold it. It is unnecessary to mention them here, but they have always been looked upon, and undoubtedly are, among the best players in the club. The other players keenly feel the position in which they are placed by the action of their colleagues, and one of them, who has already signed with another club for next season, says that even if he could get his release from it, nothing could now induce him to remain here. He depends largely upon base ball for his living, and says he can not afford to have the name of belonging to a club that plays crooked games. He claims to be an honest player, and no doubt is. He says that he was offered money to assist in the selling of the Chicago game on Saturday, but refused. There is great indignation among the lovers of the game in this city over the conduct of the Alleghenys, and the stockholders and directors of the nine express themselves as determined to institute a rigid investigation, and make public every dishonorable act which they can ascertain was committed, no matter by whom, and no matter who may be hurt. The only way left for the redemption of the Allegheny club, and its restoration to public confidence, is by the summary expulsion of the players who sold out, and the resignation of those alleged to have been implicated and financially interested to a large extent in the sale. And the Syracuse Stars are no better than the Alleghenys. They sold out on Friday to the Indianapolis Club, and the latter in buying is as bad as any of the rest. Last night a Star player said to the writer: "We wanted to beat Nolan's team the worst kind on Friday, but couldn't do it, because two of our nine were playing for the other side." The sale on Friday was even more palpable than the one on Saturday.

THE CLOSE OF THE LEAGUE SEASON.

The League-pennant race for 1877 has ended, and the result, in brief, is that Boston is first, Louisville second, Brooklyn third, St. Louis fourth, Chicago fifth, and Cincinnati last. Never before in the history of professional playing has the contest for the palm of supremacy been so close or so exciting as it has been this season. Up to the very last month of the season was it doubtful as to which club would lead, and almost the last week of the season was the final issue settled. This is just as it should be. The success of the Boston nine against such strong opponents shows the vital importance of thorough harmony in the working of a nine together. Some people may attribute the victory of the "Reds" to this or that particular advantage they possessed in the individual playing strength of their team; but if they do this they will err sadly. Their victory was due to the fact that as a team they excelled all others in having earnest and reliable men in each position, and a team which worked together with more united effort than any other in the League. Some will say that it was Bond's pitching that did it. To such it may be said, where would Bond's pitching have been without Brown's splendid catching? and where would the pitching and catching have been but for the earnest, united and effective support in the field? Then, too, there is another feature in which the Boston team excelled all opponents, and that was in strategic batting and base-running. Taking these things into due consideration, and in combination with the excellent discipline of the nine, it is not surprising that the Boston Club won the pennant against field teams equally as strong in the individual skill of the players, but lacking in the essentials of harmony, discipline and integrity of play.

Last on the list comes the Cincinnati Club with their season of experiments from May to October, the wonder being that they have managed to excel their record of 1876, which they have done by six games. Without further comment at the present time, we proceed to give the statistics of the League season of 1877, showing the games won and lost by each nine up to Oct. 7, when the season practically ended. The table below gives the record of all the games played, exclusive, of course, of exhibition contests:

	Boston	Louisville	Hartford	St. Louis	Chicago	Cincinnati	Games Won
Boston	..	8	7	6	10	11	42
Louisville	4	..	6	10	8	7	35
Hartford	5	6	..	7	4	9	31
St. Louis	6	2	7	..	5	8	28
Chicago	2	4	4	8	..	8	26
Cincinnati	1	5	3	3	3	..	15
Games lost	18	25	27	32	33	42	177

By the above table Boston leads by a majority of seven, Louisville taking second place by a lead of four, and Brooklyn third by the same figure. St. Louis leads Chicago by two games, while Cincinnati scores but fifteen victories to nine in 1876. Throwing out the Cincinnati Club contests as illegal, as they unquestionably are, the record of the season stands as follows:

	Boston	Louisville	Hartford	St. Louis	Chicago	Games Won
Boston	..	8	7	6	10	31
Louisville	4	..	6	10	8	28
Hartford	5	6	..	5	8	24
St. Louis	6	2	7	..	4	19
Chicago	2	4	4	8	..	18
Games lost	17	20	24	29	30	120

By the above it will be seen that Boston leads Louisville by three games only, and St. Louis excels Chicago by but one game, the Louisvilles being second by a lead of four over Brooklyn as in the first table. "And the first shall be last" is applicable to the Chicago nine of 1877.

THE CINCINNATI CLUB.

The career of this club during 1877 has thus far been a chequered one; but the promise is that in 1878 the Queen City will be represented by an organization which will be a worthy successor of the model professional club of 1869. *The Cincinnati Enquirer* of Aug. 7 says: "The present Board of Directors forming the Cincinnati Ball Club Association have already begun their arrangements for a brilliant season of baseball in Cincinnati next year. Four men have been engaged for the club of 1878, namely, Jones, Pike, Addy, and Gerhardt. The rest of the nine will be filled up with the best men it is possible to get at reasonable salaries. Last year there were but few professional players who wanted to come to Cincinnati to play. This year the reverse is the case. Baseball men recognize the fact that the new club is on a permanent basis, and that next season in Cincinnati promises to be more successful than in any city in the Union. The club will consist of eleven men, who will be engaged carefully and cautiously. No man addicted to liquor or who is not in the habit of conducting himself as a gentleman, need apply. The directors want a club that they can send away from home without having a watch placed over them; who will act and look like gentlemen all the time; who will be a credit to Cincinnati; and in which the city may take a pride as representative men. No matter what may be the player's abilities as a professional, his social record must be unquestionable, else he need not apply for a position on the Cincinnati nine." This is the right way to go to work, undoubtedly. Professional club-managers of ability and reputation have learned by bitter and costly experience that character is as essential in a ball-player as skill or a practical knowledge of the game.

DISHONEST BASE-BALL PLAYERS.

LOUISVILLE, Ky., Nov. 2.—The examination of the players of the Louisville Base-ball Club for alleged "crookedness" was conducted by an able lawyer, and has resulted in the expulsion of A. H. Nichols, James A. Devlin, George W. Hall, and William Craver. Hall, Devlin, and Nichols confessed to having received bribes for selling games. The first two told the whole story and begged for mercy at the hands of the Directors. Nichols gave the information which led to the discovery of the nefarious practice. Craver proclaims his innocence. He was expelled for general misconduct. Devlin acknowledges having "stood in" with Hall, and in his statement of "crooked" transactions relates how he swindled the latter out of the proceeds of their dishonesty. McCloud, a New-York gambler or pool-seller, is the name of the party who is known to have paid them for "throwing" games. This is not the first time Craver has been expelled for dishonest practices.

An audience of 8000 people, comprising the best families in the city, were witnesses of the first League game of the season on the new and beautiful grounds of the Providence Club at Providence, R. I., yesterday afternoon. Many ladies graced the occasion with their presence, both in stylish equippages with liveried servants and in the grand stand. The grounds are spacious and are fitted with every convenience both for players and spectators. There was a large delegation present from this city, including several members of the Common Council, and the utmost interest was manifested by all. Play was called at 3.10, with the Providence boys at the bat.

BOSTONS.

	AB.	R.	1B.	RB.	PO.	A.	E.
G. Wright, s. s.	4	0	1	1	1	8	0
Leonard, l. f.	4	1	1	1	2	0	0
O'Rourke, c. f.	4	0	1	1	2	0	0
Manning, r. f.	4	0	1	2	1	0	1
Sutton, 3b.	3	0	1	1	1	4	0
Burdock, 2b.	3	0	0	1	1	7	2
Morrill, 1b.	3	0	1	0	15	1	0
Bond, p.	3	0	0	0	0	4	0
Snyder, c.	3	0	0	0	4	1	0
Totals	31	1	6	8	27	14	3

PROVIDENCE.

	AB.	R.	1B.	RB.	PO.	A.	E.
Higham, r. f.	4	0	1	1	1	0	0
York, l. f.	4	0	1	1	1	0	0
Murnan, 1b.	4	0	0	0	11	0	0
Hines, c. f.	3	0	0	0	1	0	0
Carey, s. s.	3	0	0	1	1	6	0
Brown, c.	3	0	0	1	3	3	3
Hague, 3b.	3	0	0	1	1	5	0
Corey, p.	3	0	0	0	1	4	0
Sweasy, 2b.	3	0	0	0	3	2	2
Totals	30	0	2	5	27	18	5

Innings	1	2	3	4	5	6	7	8	9	
Bostons	0	0	0	0	0	0	1	0	0	—1
Providence	0	0	0	0	0	0	0	0	0	—0

Umpire—Charles F. Daniels. Total bases—Bostons 17, Providence 9. First base on errors—Bostons 1, Providence 2. Left on bases—Burdock, Manning, Morrill, York, Hague, Corey. Passed balls—Brown 1. Struck out—Burdock, Snyder (2), Murnan, Hines. Two-base hit—Manning. Earned runs—0. Strikes called—Off Bond 16, off Corey 14. Balls called—On Bond 22, on Corey 14. Time of game—Two hours. Fouls struck—Bostons 22, Providence 11. Flies caught —Bostons 13, Providence 8.

THE LEAGUE MEETING.

Representatives of the League met in Providence, R. I., Aug. 9, and after considerable discussion agreed upon the following address to the public:

PROVIDENCE, R. I., Aug. 10, 1878.

The National League of Professional Baseball Clubs having met, as above stated, at a time when it is possible to accurately estimate the financial and other results of the season of 1878, offers the following as its conclusions for the present season and its recommendations for the future. The League believes its efforts to present the distinctively national game of the country as an exhibition in the best possible manner and under the most stringent regulations have been appreciated and approved, and that all lovers of pure and manly sport will concede that its efforts have been turned toward the elevation of the game. It is part of the experience of league clubs for the season of 1878 that business depression has so far affected the receipts that a loss is already assured. At the same time it is apparent that under the present system the loss must fall on the association from whom the players receive the money earned, and much more. The league declines to continue business on this principle, and takes this time to announce to players that in 1879 the aggregate salaries paid by each club must not exceed a sum which the experience of this year has shown can be earned. It has not, after discussion, seemed wise, at this time, to attempt to restrict any association as to what it shall pay any or all of the men in its employ. In the line of the reduction of expenses within the probable income, the League has, at the meeting above dated, entered into an agreement which binds its members to make the contract season of 1879 six months, and no longer, to wit: from April 1 to Sept. 30, both included. It is expected, by thus giving the player fully half the year for the pursuit of any trade or business which he may have, he will be enabled to devote the other half to play at less cost to the club than when (as in the past) he received his entire support from them. By the terms of agreement last-named, the club have bound themselves not to pay money advances during the Winter season, they believing that this practice has, in the past, encouraged idleness and discouraged some players from following such business or trade as they were fitted for.

A uniform style of contract has been approved. It has been announced to the league that certain clubs desired membership in it. It is therefore proper to say that the clubs now holding membership will expect, from applicants, compliance with the agreements above noted as a condition precedent to admission.

By order of the League. W. A. HULBERT, President.

Diamond Dust.

THE hard hitting was thoroughly enjoyed by all hands.

BURDOCK did not blow his bazoo, HARRY must have corked it.

FRANK FLINT's batting display was magnificent but "Silver" was in awful hard luck.

SUTTON plays third as he used to, and is by long odds the best man for that position in the country.

Shaffer will either play in Chicago or Cincinnati next year, with the chances of the latter club carrying off the blonde. President Neff was in Indianapolis on the 11th inst., and in close communication with Shaffer, but, as yet, the latter has signed no contract.

McCormick and Bradley will occupy the pitcher's square for the Indianapolis Club in the season of 1879.

There is strong and general opposition among the Indianapolis and other players to signing the present form of contract adopted by the league, and many assert their preference to playing in an international club rather than submit to the present arrangement. The main objections to the present contracts are the right reserved to lay players off if they fail to play a strong game, and also the right of the management of any club to deduct salary during the sickness of a player, or any wound or injury he may receive which would incapacitate him from duty.

The League Championship.

We publish below the final table, showing the position of the various clubs which have contended for the league pennant during the season just ended. As has been almost universally conceded from the outset, the prize goes, for the fifth time, to the Bostons. The remaining clubs stand in the following order: Cincinnatis, Providence, Chicagos, Indianapolis, Milwaukees:

CLUBS.	Bostons.	Cincinnatis.	Providence.	Chicagos.	Indianapolis.	Milwaukees.	Won.	Lost.	Per cent. won
Bostons		6	6	8	10	11	41	19	.68
Cincinnatis	6		9	10	4	8	37	23	.61
Providence	6	3		6	10	8	33	27	.55
Chicagos	4	2	6		8	10	30	30	.50
Indianapolis	2	8	2	4		8	24	36	.40
Milwaukees	1	4	4	2	4		15	45	.25

BASEBALL.

THE LEAGUE CLUB AVERAGES.

The following are the official averages of the sixty-seven players who took part in the League club championship matches during 1878, and who played in six or more games:

	Batting Rank.	Fielding Rank.	Per cent. in Batting	Per cent. in Fielding
1. Dalrymple, Milwaukee	1	33	.356	.833
2. Hines, Providence	2	32	.347	.836
3. Start, Chicago	3	2	.345	.967
4. Shaffer, Indianapolis	4	31	.344	.844
5. Anson, Chicago	5	36	.334	.818
6. Ferguson, Chicago	5	19	.334	.881
7. Pike, Cincinnati	6	37	.331	.816
8. Higham, Providence	7	39	.320	.810
9. Brown, Providence	8	17	.315	.810
10. Peters, Milwaukee	9	23	.311	.872
11. York, Providence	10	24	.310	.847
12. Dickerson, Cincinnati	11	20	.309	.877
13. J. White, Cincinnati	12	35	.308	.824
14. Gerhardt, Cincinnati	13	12	.303	.906
15. Harbidge, Chicago	14	21	.294	.876
16. Jones, Cincinnati	15	14	.287	.893
17. Clapp, Indianapolis	16	8	.286	.924

THE CHAMPIONSHIP TEAMS OF 1879.

THE LEAGUE TEAMS.

The following are the names and positions of the League club teams for 1879, the names being the same as contained in the League book, and the positions those assigned them by the local journals of each city. We give the clubs in alphabetical order.

BOSTON.
Snyder, c.
Bond, p.
Morrill, 1st b.
Burdock, 2d b.
Sutton, 3d b.
Houck, s. s.
Jones, l. f.
John O'Rourke, c. f.
C. Foley, r. f.

BUFFALO.
J. Clapp, c.
Galvin, p.
Hornung, 1st b.
Fulmer, 2d b.
Richardson, 3d b.
Force, s. s.
Crowley, l. f.
Eggler, c. f.
McGunnigle, r. f.

CINCINNATI.
J. White, c.
W. White, p.
McVey, 1st b.
Barnes, 2d b.
Gerhardt, 3d b.
Burke, s. s.
Dickinson, l. f.
Hotaling, c. f.
Kelly, r. f.

CHICAGO.
Flint, c.
Larkin, p.
Anson, 1st b.
Quest, 2d b.
Williamson, 3d b.
Peters, s. s.
Dalrymple, l. f.
Hankinson, c. f.
Schaffer, r. f.

CLEVELAND.
Kennedy, c.
J. McCormick, p.
Phillips, 1st b.
Strief, 2d b.
Glasscock, 3d b.
Carey, s. s.
W. Riley, l. f.
Warner, c. f.
Eden, r. f.

PROVIDENCE.
Brown, c.
Ward, p.
Start, 1st b.
McGeary, 2d b.
Hague, 3d b.
Geo. Wright, s. s.
York, l. f.
Hines, c. f.
Jas. O'Rourke, r. f.

SYRACUSE.
Dorgan, c.
McCormick, p.
Carpenter, 1st b.
Farrell, 2d b.
Allen, 3d b.
Richmond, s. s.
M. Mansell, l. f.
Purcell, c. f.
Macullar, r. f.

TROY.
C. Reilley, c.
Bradley, p.
A. Clapp, 1st b.
Hawkes, 2d b.
Doscher, 3d b.
Caskins, s. s.
Thos. Mansell, l. f.
A. Hall, c. f.
Evans, r. f.

BOSTON vs. BUFFALO.

The League championship season in Buffalo was opened May 1 by a game between the Bostons and Buffalos. The weather was far from being favorable for good fielding, and only about five hundred persons witnessed the game. The Bostons opened badly in the field, making three of their four errors in the first inning, Houck letting the first ball struck by the Buffalos go past him. Good hits by Jones and Burdock—the latter's being a rattling three-baser—gave the Bostons a run at the start; they made two more runs in the fifth inning on singles by Burdock, Houck and Morrill, and a fumble by Walker, and concluded run-getting in the eighth by scoring two more; O'Rourke and Morrill, after being missed on foul-flys by Clapp, making three-basers, and Burdock hitting safely for a single. Three times the Buffalos got a man on third base—twice by three-basers of Eggler and Fulmer—but they did not succeed in scoring a run, the nearest approach being in the eighth inning, after two men were out, when Galvin struck for two bases and went to third on Crowley's safe hit. Force, being given his base on called balls, filled the bases, and the excitement ran high; but Clapp struck an easy one to Burdock, and the side was out. The batting of Burdock and Morrill, the second-base play of Burdock and Fulmer, and a wonderful one-handed catch by Hornung were the chief features of this one-sided game.

BOSTON.	T.	R.	1B.	PO.	A.	E.	BUFFALO.	T.	R.	1B.	PO.	A.	E.
Jones, l. f.	5	1	2	0	0	0	Crowley, r. f.	4	0	1	0	1	1
O'Rou'ke, c. f.	5	1	2	0	0	0	Force, s. s.	4	0	0	0	0	0
Burdock, 2b.	4	2	3	4	3	0	Clapp, c.	4	0	0	8	2	5
Houck, s. s.	4	0	2	1	2	1	Richard'n, 3b	4	0	0	1	0	0
Hawes, r. f.	4	0	0	1	0	0	Eggler, c. f.	4	0	1	1	0	0
Morrill, 1st b	4	1	3	8	0	0	Walker, 1st b	4	0	1	6	2	1
Sutton, 3d b.	4	0	0	0	0	1	Fulmer, 2d b.	4	0	1	8	1	1
Bond, p.	4	0	1	1	8	1	Hornung, l. f.	3	0	0	3	0	0
Snyder, c.	4	0	0	12	0	1	Galvin, p.	3	0	2	0	6	2
Totals	38	5	13	27	13	4	Totals	34	0	6	27	12	10

Boston	1	0	0	0	2	0	0	2	0	—5
Buffalo	0	0	0	0	0	0	0	0	0	—0

Earned run—Boston, 1. Two-base hit—Galvin. Three-base hits—O'Rourke, Burdock, Morrill, Eggler, Fulmer. First base on balls—Force. First base on errors—Boston, 1; Buffalo, 1. Struck out—Boston, 6; Buffalo, 5. Balls called—on Bond, 96; on Galvin, 78. Strikes called—off Bond, 8; off Galvin, 16. Double-plays—Houck, Burdock and Morrill. Passed balls—Clapp, 1. Wild pitches—Galvin, 2. Umpire, T. Gillen of London. Time, 2h. 30m.

PROFESSIONAL FOLLY.

The Buffalo Commercial Advertiser of Dec. 8 says: "Oscar Walker, who is spending the Winter with other baseballists near New York, and practicing every pleasant day, says he is sorry he signed so early with the Buffalos, as he has had several flattering offers since." This is but one of the many instances of folly exhibited by professional players in not remaining with clubs in which they are sure of their pay and are well treated because some other club offers them one or two hundred dollars more salary for a season. The moment a player establishes himself in favor with the club and the public of a city where he has played, it becomes his pecuniary interest to remain with that club, no matter what apparently better offers in mere money he may have made him by other clubs. There are plenty of cases where a salary of a thousand dollars a season is worth more to a player in one club than the offer of double the amount would be in another. The first consideration with a professional should be to see that he is with good and true men in the directors of the club he engages with. This done, he is foolish if he does not remain with that club as long as he can. The rolling professional, like the stone, gathers no moss.

Providence, 15; Clevelands, 4.

CLEVELAND, O., May 1.—A clear, beautiful, but chilly day inaugurated the league game here. Both clubs were in good condition. The game was characterized by the strong batting of the Providence nine. The score:

PROVIDENCE.

	AB.	R.	1B.	TB.	PO.	A.	E.
O'Rourke, r. f.	6	3	2	3	1	0	0
Start, 1b.	5	3	3	4	13	2	0
Hines, c. f.	6	2	2	3	4	1	1
Brown, c.	6	1	1	2	5	3	0
McGeary, 2b.	6	1	2	2	0	2	2
Wright, s s.	5	2	3	3	1	3	0
Ward, p.	5	3	3	4	0	5	0
York, l f.	4	0	3	4	1	0	0
Hague, 3b.	5	0	1	1	2	4	1
Totals	48	15	20	26	27	20	4

CLEVELANDS.

	AB.	R.	1B.	TB.	PO.	A.	E.
Eden, r. f.	4	1	1	1	2	1	1
Philips, 1b.	4	0	0	0	11	0	1
Glasscock, 3b.	4	1	1	1	0	1	1
Kennedy, c.	4	0	0	0	6	2	0
Carey, s. s.	4	0	0	0	1	4	0
Warner, c. f.	4	0	1	1	3	0	0
Strief, 2b.	4	0	0	1	2	4	2
Riley, l. f.	3	1	1	1	1	0	0
McCormick, p.	3	1	2	2	1	3	0
Totals	34	4	6	7	27	15	5

Innings	1	2	3	4	5	6	7	8	9	
Providence	2	0	5	1	1	3	0	3	0	—15
Clevelands	0	0	3	1	0	0	0	0	0	— 4

First base by errors—Providence, 6; Clevelands, 1. Left on bases—Providence, 7; Clevelands, 3. Bases on called balls—Providence, 2. Passed balls—Brown, 1; Kennedy, 1. Wild pitches—Ward, 1; McCormick, 3. Out on strikes—Providence, 1; Clevelands, 5. Umpire—E. G. Fountain.

THE LEAGUE ARENA.
The Providence Club Wins the Championship.

	Providence	Boston	Chicago	Buffalo	Cincinnati	Cleveland	Troy	Syracuse	Games Won	Victories Counting	Defeats Counting
Providence	..	7	7	6	10	8	10	10	58	54	25
Boston	4		4	9	7	10	11	9	54	49	27
Chicago	5	8	..	6	3	8	8	8	46	44	30
Buffalo	6	3	5		7	8	11	5	45	43	32
Cincinnati	2	5	8	3	..	8	9	8	43	38	35
Cleveland	4	2	4	4	3	..	5	4	26	23	53
Troy	2	1	3	1	2	6	..	4	19	19	56
Syracuse	2	3	1	3	4	7	2	..	22	15	27
Games lost	25	29	32	32	35	55	56	48	313		

Oct. 28

DEATH OF A PROFESSIONAL PLAYER.

James Hallinan, at one time a prominent professional player, died on Oct. 28 at his residence in Chicago, Ill., of inflammation of the bowels. He made his first appearance on the ball-field in 1870, with the Aetna Club of Chicago, and short-stopped four season for them. They were called the Franklins in 1874 and were an amateur nine, nearly all of whom were employed in the press-room of *The Chicago Times*. His first professional engagement was a brief one with the Western Club of Keokuk, Ia., in 1875, and on its disbandment, in June of that year, he joined the Mutuals of this city, and remained with them until the close of the season of 1876. He played in a few games with the Cincinnatis in 1877, and then went to Chicago for the remainder of the season. His last professional engagement was also with the Chicagos. He participated in sixteen championship games with that organization in 1878, and was then compelled by illness to abandon the ball-field in June of that year. He generally played in the short-stop's position, although his last appearances were in the outfield. He was a left-handed, hard-hitting batsman, and, being remarkably fleet of foot, was often credited with home-runs. He was of a very genial disposition, and had a host of friends, who will hear with regret of his untimely demise.

THE LEAGUE AVERAGES.

The Boston Herald gives the following figures as a record of the work with bat and ball of the players who have taken part in ten or more League championship games:

		Games.	First B. B. Av'e	T. B. R. Aver'e.	Field'g Aver'e.	Field'g Posit'n.
1	Hines, Providence	84	.352	.492	.910	15
2	J. White, Cincinnati	78	.338	.427	.804	57
3	O'Rourke, Boston	72	.337	.512	.892	21
4	Kelly, Cincinnati	78	.336	.488	.790	62
5	Gross, Providence	30	.320	.446	.784	16
6	O'Rourke, Providence	80	.330	.446	.906	16
7	Anson, Chicago	50	.318	.424	.965	3
8	Dalrymple, Chicago	70	.317	.365	.720	73
9	Start, Providence	66	.300	.366	.977	1
10	Foley, Boston	35	.304	.324	.829	47
11	Cogswell, Boston	49	.300	.351	.966	2
12	Farrell, Syracuse, Providence	61	.300	.352	.883	26
13	Jones, Boston	83	.294	.473	.952	7
14	McGuinness, Syracuse	12	.294	.392	.935	6
15	York, Providence	80	.293	.495	.868	20
16	Dickerson, Cincinnati	81	.290	.354	.800	59
17	Shaffer, Chicago	72	.288	.329	.764	90
18	Richardson, Buffalo	79	.287	.398	.824	49
19	Brouthers, Troy	39	.284	.437	.920	9
20	McVey, Cincinnati	81	.284	.400	.940	5
21	Williamson, Chicago	79	.281	.420	.851	38
22	Phillips, Cleveland	82	.281	.350	.912	12
23	Walker, Buffalo	73	.279	.381	.950	4
24	Hotaling, Cincinnati	81	.278	.379	.800	59
25	Crowley, Buffalo	62	.277	.336	.847	39

THE NEW RULES.

We have not space to comment in full on the changes made in the playing-rules of the game by the League this week. Briefly, the changes are as follows: Section 1 of Rule III now reads:

"The pitcher's position shall be within a space of ground four feet wide by six feet in length, the front line of which shall be distant forty-five feet from the centre of the home-base, and the centre of the square shall be equidistant from the first and third bases. Each corner of the square shall be marked by a flat iron plate or stone, six inches square, fixed in the ground even with the surface."

Section 13 of Rule IV now reads thus: "The batsman shall be declared out by the umpire as follows:

If a fair or foul ball be caught before touching the ground or any object other than the player, provided it be not caught in the player's hat or cap.

If a fair ball be securely held by a fielder while touching first base with any part of his person, before the base runner touches said base.

If, after three strikes have been called, he fails to touch first base before the ball is legally held there.

If, after three strikes have been called, the ball be caught before touching the ground.

If he plainly attempts to hinder the catcher from catching the ball, evidently without effort to make a fair strike, or makes a "foul strike."

Section 15 of Rule V. reads thus:

Any player running the bases shall be declared out if, at any time, while the ball is in play, he be touched by the ball in the hand of a fielder, without some part of his person is touching a base. The ball must be held by the fielder after touching the runner.

If a ball be held by a fielder on the first-base before the base-runner, after hitting a fair ball, touches at base, he shall be declared out.

Any base-runner failing to touch the base he runs for shall be declared out if the ball be held by a fielder while touching said base, before the base-runner returns and touches it.

Any base-runner who shall in any way interfere with or obstruct a fielder while attempting to catch a fair fly-ball or a foul ball shall be declared out. If he willfully obstructs a fielder from fielding a ball he shall be declared out, and, if a batted fair ball strike him, no base nor run shall be scored on such ball, but each base-runner shall be allowed to return to the base he left when the ball was hit without being put out.

If a base-runner in running from home to first base shall run inside the foul line, or more than three feet outside of it, he shall be declared out.

Section 4 of Rule V was amended by striking out the last words, namely, "the visiting club shall select the umpire," and substituting a clause providing that instead, when the chosen umpire is not on hand, the captains of the opposing clubs shall toss for the choice of umpire. This will obviate the Dean business practiced by the Indianapolis Club on the Cincinnatis last year.

In Rule VII a clause was incorporated providing that when an umpire imposes a fine upon a player the fine cannot be revoked. This was done to remedy the evil of forgiveness, which swayed the umpires last year. Out of all fines imposed, only one was enforced during the year 1878.

By Harry Wright's suggestion, the rules on umpiring were changed so that the umpire must call every unfair ball delivered from one to nine, and the ninth one shall entitle the batter to his base. This is no radical change except that, instead of calling every third unfair ball, the umpire calls every one up to nine.

The rule abolishing all foul-bound catches, and also the bound catch from three strikes, was adopted by the votes of the Boston, Syracuse, Buffalo and Cleveland Clubs, the Chicago voting no and Cincinnati on neither side.

Section 3 of Rule III was amended by the addition of a clause, proposed by Mr. Johnson, that the umpire may fine the pitcher from $10 to $30, at his discretion, as a penalty for purposely hitting a batsman.

Chicagos, 5; Providence, 4.

[Special Dispatch to the Boston Herald.]

CHICAGO, Ill., July 8, 1880. The closing game here for some time was played today between Chicago and Providence. The game had few points of interest, and the umpiring of Libby was very unsatisfactory to Chicago. The game today makes the 22d straight league victory for Chicago. The club starts East tomorrow. The score:

CHICAGOS.

	AB.	R.	B.	TBR.	PO.	A.	E.
Dalrymple, l.f.	5	1	1	5	4	0	1
Gore, c.f.	5	0	3	6	5	0	0
Kelley, r.f.	4	1	1	7	1	0	1
Williamson, 3b.	4	1	1	4	2	1	0
Anson, 1b.	4	0	1	2	10	0	0
Burns, s.s.	4	0	0	0	0	3	0
Corcoran, p.	4	0	0	5	1	5	1
Flint, c.	4	1	2	5	2	0	2
Quest, 2b.	4	1	1	8	2	1	1
Totals	38	5	10	42	27	10	6

PROVIDENCE.

	AB.	R.	B.	TBR.	PO.	A.	E.
Dorgan, r.f.	5	0	0	0	0	0	0
Farrell, 2b.	5	1	2	6	1	6	0
Ward, p.	5	0	1	2	1	3	0
Peters, s.s.	4	0	0	1	0	2	2
Hines, c.f.	4	0	1	1	1	0	0
Start, 1b.	4	1	1	6	14	0	0
Gross, c.	4	1	1	7	3	1	0
York, l.f.	4	1	0	4	4	0	1
Bradley, 3b.	4	0	0	3	0	1	1
Totals	39	4	6	30	24	13	4

Innings	1	2	3	4	5	6	7	8	9	
Chicagos	2	0	0	0	0	3	0	0		—5
Providence	0	0	0	1	0	0	1	1	1	—4

Earned runs—Chicagos, 2. Two-base hits—Anson, Flint. First base on balls—Chicagos, 2; Providence, 3. First base on errors—Chicagos, 3; Providence, 3. Struck out—Chicagos, 1; Providence, 2. Balls called—Corcoran, 82; Ward, 88. Strikes called—Corcoran, 38; Ward, 24. Passed balls—Flint, 2. Wild pitches—Corcoran, 1. Time—2h. Umpire—Libby.

Worcesters, 1; Clevelands, 0.

[Special Dispatch to the Sunday Herald.]

WORCESTER, June 12, 1880. The most wonderful game on record, and one of the shortest, was played this afternoon between the Cleve-

without an error and, for nine straight innings, retired their opponents in one two three order, not a man getting a base hit or reaching first base. The Worcesters made one run in the fifth innings on Dunlap's double error, the only lapse from perfect play made by the Clevelands during the game. Irwin reached first on a clean hit, Bennett was given first on balls, advancing Irwin to second. Whitney struck to McCormick, who threw to Dunlap for a double play, but the latter muffed the ball, and, recovering it, threw it over Kennedy's head, letting Irwin in. Bennett reached third in the play, and Whitney second. Sullivan then struck out. Corey went out on a fly to right field, and Creamer fouled out to Kennedy. Rain interrupted the play for eight minutes in the eighth innings. There were 700 people present. The score:

WORCESTERS.

	AB.	R.	B.	TBR.	PO.	A.	E.
Wood, l.f.	4	0	0	0	0	0	0
Richmond, p.	3	0	1	1	0	6	0
Knight, r.f.	3	0	0	0	1	1	0
Irwin, s.s.	3	1	2	5	2	3	0
Bennett, c.	3	0	0	3	8	0	0
Whitney, 3b.	3	0	0	2	1	2	0
Sullivan, 1b.	3	0	0	0	14	0	0
Corey, c.f.	3	0	0	0	1	0	0
Creamer, 2b.	3	0	0	0	0	4	0
Totals	28	1	3	11	27	16	0

CLEVELANDS.

	AB.	R.	B.	TBR.	PO.	A.	E.
Dunlap, 2b.	3	0	0	0	4	2	2
Hankinson, 3b.	3	0	0	0	0	0	0
Kennedy, c.	3	0	0	0	9	1	0
Phillips, 1b.	3	0	0	0	7	0	0
Shaffer, r.f.	3	0	0	0	2	0	0
McCormick, p.	3	0	0	0	0	10	0
Gilligan, c.f.	3	0	0	0	1	0	0
Glasscock, s.s.	3	0	0	0	0	2	0
Hanlon, l.f.	3	0	0	0	1	0	0
Totals	27	0	0	0	24	15	2

Innings	1	2	3	4	5	6	7	8	9	
Worcesters	0	0	0	0	1	0	0	0		—1
Clevelands	0	0	0	0	0	0	0	0	0	—0

First base on balls—Bennett. Struck out—Richmond (2), Wood, Bennett, Sullivan, Corey (2), Shaffer, Hanlon, Dunlap, Glasscock, Phillips. Balls called—Richmond, 43; McCormick, 81. Strikes called—Richmond, 9; McCormick, 16. Double plays—Glasscock, Dunlap, Phillips. Time—1h. 27m. Umpire—Bradley.

BUNKER HILL.

SPECIAL DISPATCH TO THE ENQUIRER.

PROVIDENCE, R. I., June 17.—The Providence boys encountered the Buffalos at eleven this morning, being their second championship game, and administered a stunning defeat to the visitors. There were 1,800 persons present, who pronounced the fielding and batting exhibition of the home nine the best ever played here. The Buffalos were unable to secure a safe hit. Neither did the champions allow any player to get to the first bag. The Providence scored a run in the second inning on Farrell's two-bagger and a wild throw by Walker. In the fourth Farrell crossed the home-plate on a single, a wild pitch and a passed ball. In the seventh, eighth and ninth Bradley, Farrell and Start were the run-getters on two three-basers and three singles, a wild pitch and a wild throw of Crowley. Hines made a splendid fly catch in the second. Peters' playing at short was excellent. For the visitors Easterbrook and Hornung take the honors.

SCORE.

PROVIDENCE.	A.B.	R.	1B.	B.H.	P.O.	A.	E.
Hines, c. f.	5	0	3	3	2	0	0
Start, 1b.	5	1	1	3	14	0	0
Dorgan, r. f.	5	0	2	2	0	0	0
Gross, c.	5	0	0	0	5	1	0
Farrell, 2b.	4	2	3	3	0	2	0
Ward, p.	4	0	1	1	2	6	0
Peters, s.s.	4	0	1	3	0	6	0
York, l. f.	4	0	2	4	3	0	0
Bradley, 3b.	4	1	1	1	1	4	0
Total	40	5	13	20	27	19	0

BUFFALOS.	A.B.	R.	1B.	B.H.	P.O.	A.	E.
Crowley, r. f. and c.	3	0	0	0	3	0	0
Richardson, 3b.	3	0	0	0	0	1	0
Rowe, c. and r. f.	3	0	0	0	4	1	1
Walker, l. f.	3	0	0	0	3	0	1
Hornung, 2b.	3	0	0	0	2	3	0
Mack, s.s.	3	0	0	0	3	3	1
Easterbrook, 1b.	3	0	0	0	10	0	0
Poorman, c. f.	3	0	0	0	2	0	1
Galvin, p.	3	0	0	0	0	5	0
Total	27	0	0	0	27	13	4

Innings	1	2	3	4	5	6	7	8	9
Providence	0	1	0	1	0	0	1	1	1—5
Buffalo	0	0	0	0	0	0	0	0	0—0

Runs Earned—Providence, 2.
Two-Base Hit—Farrell.
Three-Base Hits—Start, York, Bradley.
Total Bases on Clean Hits—Providence, 7.
Struck Out—Hines, 1; Gross, 1; Crowley, 1; Richardson, 1; Rowe, 1; Mack, 1.
First Base on Error—Providence, 1.
Wild Throws—Walker, 1; Rowe, 1.
Passed Grounder—Poorman, 1.
Fumbled Grounder—Mack, 1.
Passed Ball—Crowley, 1.
Wild Pitches—Galvin, 2.
Balls Called—On Ward, 58; on Galvin, 62.
Strikes Called—Off Ward, 15; off Galvin, 10.
Time of Game—One hour and fifty minutes.
Umpire—Daniels.

The eleventh Boston-Chicago game was played at Chicago, Ill., on Aug. 19, when the visitors received their eighth defeat of the series. The contest was a remarkable one, as Corcoran not only shut the Bostons out without a run, but they did not get a safe hit off his pitching. Gore hit safely each time he went to the bat, including two double-baggers and two singles. Anson retired twenty-one of the Bostons, and would have been credited with three more men put out but for errors of infielders. Richmond's sprained ankle caused him to give way to John O'Rourke in the fourth inning. Trott received a damaged finger, and Flint in the last inning had his thumb split. After Bond had been pounded for eleven hits in six innings, Foley was put in to pitch, and was not hit at all.

BOSTON.	T.	R.	1B.	PO.	A.	E.
Jno R'ke, c.f.	2	0	0	1	1	0
Richm'd, s.s.	2	0	0	0	1	1
Jas. R'ke, s.s	4	0	0	1	3	1
Burdock, 2b.	4	0	0	2	4	1
Jones, l. f.	3	0	0	5	0	0
Morrill, 1b.	3	0	0	10	0	1
Foley, r.f., p.	3	0	0	2	1	0
Sutton, 3d b.	3	0	0	2	3	0
Bond, p., r. f.	3	0	0	0	2	0
Trott, c.	3	0	0	1	2	1
Totals	30	0	0	24	17	5

CHICAGO.	T.	R.	1B.	PO.	A.	E.
Dalr'mple, l.f.	4	2	0	0	0	0
Gore, c. f.	4	0	4	3	0	0
Wil'mson, 3b	4	0	1	0	6	1
Anson, 1st b.	4	0	1	21	0	0
Kelly, r. f.	4	0	0	0	0	0
Burns, s. s.	4	1	2	0	3	1
Corcoran, p.	4	1	1	1	3	0
Flint, c.	4	0	0	1	0	0
Quest, 2d b.	4	2	2	2	3	2
Totals	36	6	11	27	15	4

Boston	0	0	0	0	0	0	0	0	0—0
Chicago	1	0	2	0	0	3	0	0	—6

Earned runs—Chicago, 2. Two-base hits—Gore (2). First base on balls—Chicago, 1. First base on errors—Chicago, 4; Boston, 4. Struck out—Chicago, 1. Balls called—Corcoran, 88; Bond, 84; Foley, 23. Strikes called—Corcoran, 28; Bond, 25; Foley, 8. Double-plays—Quest and Anson. Passed ball—Trott, 1. Umpire, Doscher. Time, 2h. 30m.

Buffalos, 1; Worcesters, 0.

[Special Despatch to The Boston Globe.]

BUFFALO, N. Y., August 20.—Galvin accomplished a feat, this afternoon, which no pitcher except Ward, Richmond and Corcoran ever did, in playing a full game without having a base hit made off him. Not a Worcester saw third, and of the six who reached base on errors only two were left. Hornung's lucky run came off his single and Esterbrook's three-baser. The grounds were wet and muddy from recent rains, and the ball became soft and slippery as the game progressed. Moynahan made his debut. Score:

BUFFALOS.

	AB.	R.	1B.	TB.	PO.	A.	E.
Crowley, r. f.	4	0	0	0	1	0	0
Richardson, c.	4	0	0	0	4	2	1
Hornung, l. f.	4	1	1	1	4	0	0
Esterbrook, 1b.	4	0	1	1	11	0	1
Moynahan, s. s.	4	0	0	1	0	3	1
Force, 2b.	3	0	1	1	4	3	2
Galvin, p.	3	0	0	0	1	5	0
Driscoll, c. f.	3	0	1	3	1	0	0
Stearns, 3b.	3	0	0	0	1	2	2
Totals	31	1	4	7	27	15	7

WORCESTERS.

	AB.	R.	1B.	RB.	PO.	A.	E.
Stovey, 1b.	4	0	0	0	11	0	0
Irwin, s. s.	4	0	0	0	2	5	1
Dickerson, c. f.	3	0	0	0	2	0	0
Whitney, 3b.	3	0	0	1	2	3	0
Knight, r. f.	3	0	0	0	0	0	1
Bennett, c.	3	0	0	0	7	2	1
Wood, l. f.	3	0	0	1	1	0	0
Corey, p.	3	0	0	1	0	6	1
Creamer, 2b.	3	0	0	3	2	0	0
Totals	29	0	0	6	27	16	4

Innings	1	2	3	4	5	6	7	8	9
Buffalos	1	0	0	0	0	0	0	0	0—1
Worcesters	0	0	0	0	0	0	0	0	0—0

Earned runs—Buffalos, 1. First base by errors—Buffalos, 3; Worcesters, 6. Total left on bases—Buffalos, 4; Worcesters, 2. Bases on called balls—Buffalos, 1. Passed balls Richardson, 1; Bennet, 1. Three-base hit—Esterbrook. Out on strikes—Buffalos, 5; Worcesters, 2. Double plays—Force and Esterbrook; Galvin, Force and Esterbrook. Balls called—On Galvin, 64; on Corey, 77. Strikes called—Off Galvin, 21; off Corey, 20. Fumbles—Force (2), Irwin. Muffed thrown ball—Esterbrook. Muffed flies—Stearns, Knight. Wild throws—Stearns. Time—1 hour 40 minutes. Umpire—Bradley.

THE LEAGUE CHAMPIONSHIP.

The Close of the Season of 1880.

The contests for the League championship of 1880 ended Oct. 1, and below we give the several tables comprising the work done by the eight competing clubs. The season has not been a financial success, except to the Chicago Club, and this result is largely due to the enforcement of the half-dollar tariff for admissions. For the first time in the history of the League no club has disbanded before the League season ended, and neither has the season's play been disgraced by the retirement of any team from the field on account of alleged unfair decisions by the umpire. The full record of the games played shows Chicago in the van, with Providence occupying second place and Cleveland third. The struggle for fourth place was close, but Troy won it, and, though Boston tied Worcester for fifth place, the latter won by having fewer defeats and the best percentage of victories, leaving the Bostons occupants of sixth place for the first time in ten years. Buffalo stood seventh and Cincinnati last. The record is as follows:

	Chicago	Providence	Cleveland	Troy	Worcester	Boston	Buffalo	Cincinnati	Won	Played	Drawn	Per cent. of Victories	Victories in 1879	P'l Vict's in 1879
Chicago	..	9	8	10	10	9	11	10	67	84	2	.79	44	46
Providence	3	..	9	7	6	7	10	10	52	84	3	.61	55	59
Cleveland	4	3	..	9	6	7	9	9	47	84	1	.55	24	27
Troy	2	5	3	..	5	5	11	10	41	83	0	.49	19	19
Worcester	2	6	6	7	..	8	3	8	40	83	2	.48	..	..
Boston	3	5	5	7	4	..	9	7	40	84	2	.47	49	54
Buffalo	1	2	3	1	9	3	..	6	25	83	2	.30	44	46
Cincinnati	2	2	3	1	3	5	5	..	21	81	2	.25	38	43
Lost	17	32	37	42	43	44	58	60	333					

Seven drawn games were played, and the Cincinnati Club had three games unfinished, one each with Worcester, Troy and Buffalo. All the other clubs played their full schedule out.

The appended monthly record shows how each club progressed from first to last.

	May		June		July		August		Sept.		Total		Unf'shed Games
	W.	L.	W.	L.	W.	L.	W.	L.	W.	L.	W.	L.	
Chicago	14	2	16	1	11	6	11	3	15	5	67	17	0
Providence	8	7	11	6	9	[illegible]	11	3	13	8	52	32	0
Cleveland	9	6	9	8	10	5	6	10	13	8	47	37	0
Troy	7	9	5	9	10	7	11	4	8	13	41	42	1
Worcester	9	7	7	10	8	7	6	10	10	9	40	43	1
Boston	7	9	9	8	7	10	6	8	11	9	40	44	0
Buffalo	5	12	6	9	6	11	4	10	4	16	25	58	1
Cincinnati	4	11	2	13	5	12	4	11	6	13	21	60	3

BEGINNING THE SEASON IN APRIL.—In explaining the right of the League to change the schedule from May 2 to April 30 President Hulbert says: "In no case is the created greater than the creator. The League has a habit, long in use, of pledging itself to vote for an amendment to the constitution at the succeeding annual meeting that would cover any manifest exigency. For instance, when in 1880 the Troy Club left Providence with its series incomplete, in violation of a constitutional provision, and it was discovered, to the surprise of all, that no penalty attached, the League promptly convened and unanimously pledged itself in writing to vote at the next annual meeting for an amendment expelling any club that failed to finish a series when it was possible to do so, and for the remainder of the season the clubs pledged themselves not to play with any club that again left its series incomplete."

TRYING TO BRIBE A BALL-PLAYER.

CHICAGO, May 28.—The *Tribune* to-morrow will publish the exposure of an attempt to bribe James E. Clapp, Captain and catcher of the Cleveland base-ball nine, into false play, whereby the nine was to win or lose games. Approaches were first made to Clapp through letters from Chicago above a fictitious name, which being answered, the writer became confidential and disclosed his identity as James S. Woodruff, manager of a bankrupt store at No. 1,846 State-street, and arranged for a system of cipher dispatches from Clapp, whereby Woodruff was to be kept informed as to what pools to buy on games of the Cleveland nine. Clapp handed the letter to Mr. Evans, President of the Cleveland Club, and, with his counsel, wrote decoy letters, which to-day resulted in Woodruff's identification by Detective Pinkerton. The case will be laid before the Grand Jury, with the view of procuring an indictment against Woodruff for bribery and unlawful conspiracy.

The Chicagos outfielded the Providence nine June 25, when they met again at Chicago, and secured thereby the victory. Goldsmith and Mathews were substituted in the pitcher's position by their respective clubs, and were each hit hard. Gore's wonderful base-running was the chief feature, he making five runs, stealing second base five times and third twice.

PROVIDENCE.	T.	R.	1B.	PO.	A.	E.	CHICAGO.	T.	R.	1B.	PO.	A.	E.
Hines, 2d b.	5	1	3	1	1	2	Dalrymple, l. f.	5	3	1	0	0	0
Start, 1st b.	5	1	1	11	0	0	Gore, c. f.	5	5	3	2	0	1
Farrell, c. f.	5	1	1	2	2	Kelly, r. f.	5	1	2	0	0	0
York, r. f.	5	1	1	0	7	0	Anson, 1st b.	5	2	2	11	0	0
Ward, r. f.	5	1	1	3	1	Williamson, 3d b.	5	2	2	1	3	0
McClellan, s. s.	4	1	1	5	1	Burns, s. s.	5	0	1	1	2	0
Gross, c.	4	0	2	6	1	Goldsmith, p.	4	0	1	0	7	1
Mathews, p.	4	0	0	0	4	Flint, c.	4	0	2	7	0	2
Denny, 3d b.	4	1	3	0	2	2	Quest, 2d b.	4	0	1	3	5	0
Totals	41	8	13	24	18	10	Totals	42	12	15	27	17	4

Providence............0   0   0   3   0   2   0   0—8
Chicago...............3   2   0   3   0   2   2—12

Earned runs—Chicago, 3; Providence, 4. Two-base hits—Anson, Flint, Hines, Start, McClellan. Three-base hit—Williamson. First base on balls—Chicago, 3. First base on errors—Chicago, 5; Providence, 1. Struck out—Chicago, 1; Providence, 4. Balls called—Goldsmith, 8; Mathews, 87. Strikes called—Goldsmith, 32; Mathews, 25. Double-play—Gross, Mathews and Start. Passed balls—Gross, 3. Wild pitches—Mathews, 1; Goldsmith, 1. Umpire, Bradley, Time, 2h. 15m.

1ˢᵗ GRAND SLAM

TROY vs. WORCESTER.

The twelfth and last championship game between the Troys and Worcesters was played Sept. 10 in Albany, N. Y. The Troys fielded poorly; errors by Connor, Cassidy and Ewing giving five unearned runs to the Worcesters, who made two more by good batting in the sixth inning. Cassidy's two-bagger, Connor's single and Stovey's muff gave the Troys two runs in the first inning, and they added another run on Cassidy's three-bases and Bushong's error in the fifth. The Troys went to the bat in the last half of the ninth inning, wanting four runs in order to tie their opponents' score. Welch, Ewing and Hankinson filled the bases on safe hits, Evans was retired, Keefe was given his base on called balls, sending in Welch. Cassidy was the second man out, and Connor cleared the bases and made a clean home run, thus winning by the appended score:

WORCESTER.	T.	R.	1B.	PO.	A.	E.	TROY.	T.	R.	1B.	PO.	A.	E.
Dickerson, l. f.	5	1	2	4	1	0	Cassidy, s. s.	5	2	2	1	5	1
Stovey, 1st b.	5	0	0	5	0	1	Connor, 1st b.	5	2	2	5	0	4
Richmond, p.	5	0	1	0	4	0	Ferguson, 2d b.	4	0	0	4	1	3
Nelson, s. s.	5	1	1	1	6	0	Gillespie, l. f.	4	0	0	2	0	0
Hotaling, c. f.	5	2	1	2	1	0	Welch, p.	4	1	1	1	0	0
Corey, r. f.	5	1	2	1	0	1	Ewing, c.	4	1	3	7	2	1
Carpenter, 3d b.	5	1	2	1	3	0	Evans, r. f.	4	0	2	0	0	0
Creamer, 2d b.	5	0	0	3	2	0	Hankinson, 3d b.	4	1	3	3	2	1
Bushong, c.	4	1	2	9	2	1	Keefe, p.	4	1	0	2	0	1
Totals	44	7	11	26	16	4	Totals	38	8	11	27	16	11

Worcester.............0   1   0   0   0   5   0   0   1—7
Troy..................2   0   0   1   0   0   0   0   5—8

Runs earned—Troy, 2; Worcester, 2. Two-base hits—Cassidy, Ewing (2), Corey. Three-base hit—Cassidy. Home run—Connor. Bases on balls—Troy, 2. Bases on errors—Troy, 3; Worcester, 8. Struck out—Troy, 4; Worcester, 4. Left on bases—Troy, 4; Worcester, 10. Double plays—Cassidy and Connor, Dickerson and Bushong, Nelson, Creamer and Stovey. Passed balls—Ewing, 1. Balls called—Richmond, 80; Keefe, 84. Strikes called—Richmond, 25; Keefe, 35. Umpire, Mr. Higham. Time, 2h. 25m.

N. E. YOUNG.

The subject of our illustration and biographical sketch this week is N. E. Young, the well-known secretary of the League, and who has been for many years thoroughly identified with professional baseball. He was born about thirty-eight years ago in Amsterdam, N. Y., where his first experience in ball-playing was gained, and he attained a prominent position as a cricketer. During the late war, when the mimic conflicts of the ball-field were changed to the sanguinary contests of "grim-visaged war," he served gallantly in one of the New York regiments of the Third Army Corps, and spent his few spare hours in playing baseball. Shortly after the close of the war he took up his permanent residence in Washington, D. C., and was appointed to an important clerical position in the Second Auditor's office, Treasury Department, which he still continues to hold, thus amply evidencing the ability with which he has filled his onerous duties. He assisted in organizing the Olympic Club of Washington in 1867, and formed one of its nine for four successive seasons. He played right-field in a majority of games, and was noted for his safe and effective batting, having had the best average in that respect in the contests with professional clubs during 1870, the last season that he participated actively on the diamond. He represented Washington in the international cricket match Oct. 8, 10, 1868, in Philadelphia. Young managed the Olympics in 1871, and it was at his suggestion that a meeting of delegates from the various professional clubs throughout the country was held in this city on March 17 of that year, when the Professional Association was organized. Young was elected secretary at this meeting, and was re-elected unanimously to that responsible and honorable position at the conventions of the Professional Association held in Cleveland, Baltimore and Boston in 1872, 1873 and 1874, respectively. In 1872 he acted as manager of the Baltimore Club, and during the following two seasons he acted in the same capacity for the Washington and Chicago Clubs. He also officiated as umpire with rare impartiality in many of the championship games played in Philadelphia from 1871 to 1875, inclusive. At the organization of the League on Feb. 2, 1876, he was elected secretary, and has filled that position ever since, and the mention of the fact that the League club-delegates have annually paid him the flattering compliment of an unanimous re-election is sufficient proof of the competent manner in which he has performed his arduous duties. Each year he gives a carefully-compiled recapitulation of the work with bat and ball of the players taking part in League championship games, and we can safely say that more complete and accurate tables of baseball statistics have never been published. Modest and unassuming, he has secured great popularity, personally and officially, and has won hosts of friends. At the special meeting of the League held March 8, 1881, in Buffalo, the eight League clubs evidenced their regard for their secretary by the presentation of a costly fishing-rod, Nick being an ardent disciple of old Isaac Walton. Mayor Thompson of Detroit made the presentation-speech, giving well-merited praise to Mr. Young.

THE AMERICAN ASSOCIATION

is now ready for the coming campaign. It includes six clubs equally divided between the East and West, and forming a splendid circuit. The six cities represented, viz., Philadelphia, St. Louis, Baltimore, Cincinnati, Pittsburg and Louisville, contain over two million inhabitants, while the eight cities of the rival professional association foot up but little more than one-half that number. The six clubs are all in splendid financial condition, have good teams, and the season promises to be a brilliant success. At the recent meeting in Philadelphia the playing-rules of the League were adopted, the only modifications being the adoption of a more liberal policy. It was decided to return to original principles, and allow the manager on the field with the nine. The rule governing the composition of the ball was amended so as to make it the duty of the manufacturer to seal each and every one shipped. The League rules concerning the selection of umpires were eliminated, and the matter was left entirely to the home club, it to choose and pay the expenses of that official, it being the unanimous opinion that the scheme of umpires traveling with clubs should be discountenanced. The scoring-rules were amended to the effect that an "assist" should be recorded to the credit of the pitcher on every chance offered to the catcher for a "put out" on a foul ball. Several amendments were made to the constitution for the formation of an American Alliance, in which such clubs as are not included in the membership of the Association may enter and derive special benefits accruing from its protective features. This was done to afford the managers of such clubs protection from the violation of contracts by players. The American Association will hold its annual meeting Dec. 13 in Columbus, O,

BASEBALL UNDER DIFFICULTIES.

From the account published in *The New York Herald* of April 7 of the wreck and rescue of the crew of the bark Trinity, of New London, Ct., lost off Heard's Island, in the South Indian Ocean, where the men suffered much hardship for many months on a cold, bleak and rocky island, we clip the following, which shows how they relieved the tedium of weary hours, and, at the same time, engaged in healthy exercise: "Finally, to cap the climax, a baseball club was organized, and on one sunny day the first of a series of the national game was inaugurated. There was some little difficulty at first because one of the Portuguese was appointed referee and was not posted on the rules of the League, but it was finally arranged by putting the colored man in the field, and appointing the cook to the responsible judicial post, which he filled to the satisfaction of all, notwithstanding the dinner was somewhat late in consequence. It was a queer sight when the wooden ball prepared by the carpenter after a vast amount of consultation flew from the bat, and was chased by a number of bearded and hairy-coated fielders. The game was a success and was followed by others."

THE FUNERAL OF PRESIDENT HULBERT

took place from his residence in Chicago on April 14, and it was largely attended by the business friends of the deceased gentleman and the baseball fraternity. The remains, inclosed in a cloth-covered casket, were placed in the front parlor, surrounded by innumerable large and elaborate floral tributes. Most conspicuous of these were a floral baseball field of smilax, ferns and ivy, with bases marked by handsome squares of lilies and roses. "Our President" was wrought in purple and white flowers across the pitcher's point. The Providence Club sent a pillow of roses, across the face of which "Providence" was wrought in white and colored flowers. A lofty stand of bats, one emblematically broken, surmounted by a ball of flowers, represented the Boston Club. Besides these were stars and anchors, crosses, coronets and other tasteful studies of the floral art, contributed by personal friends. Rev. F. Williams, pastor of the South Congregational Church, conducted the funeral exercises, referring in his eulogy with feeling to the strict integrity of all Mr. Hulbert's dealings which he had been able to infuse into the sport with which his name is identified. The following gentlemen acted as pall-bearers: J. B. Lyon, T. E. Courtney, A. C. Anson, A. G. Spalding, W. J. Culver, and Charles T. Trego. The interment was in Graceland Cemetery.

BASE BALL.

The Worcesters Shut Out from Making a Hit or a Run.

[Special Dispatch to the Herald.]

CHICAGO, Ill., Sept. 20, 1882. In the last game here this season the Chicagos shut out the Worcesters from making a run or even a base hit. Corcoran's pitching was a stumbling block to the visitors. Mountain did better work than Richmond in the preceding games. The attendance numbered 1200. The score:

CHICAGOS.

	A.B.	R.	B.	T.B.	P.O.	A.	F.
Dalrymple, l.f.	4	0	1	2	0	0	0
Gore, c.f.	3	0	1	1	1	1	0
Williamson, 3b	3	2	0	0	3	4	0
Anson, 1b	4	0	2	2	10	0	1
Kelly, r.f.	4	1	2	3	3	1	0
Burns, s.s.	3	0	1	1	1	3	1
Corcoran, p.	3	1	1	1	0	3	0
Quest, 2b	3	1	1	1	2	3	0
Flint, c.	3	0	0	0	7	0	3
Totals	30	5	9	11	27	15	5

WORCESTERS.

	A.B.	R.	B.	T.B.	P.O.	A.	F.
Stovey, l.f.	4	0	0	0	1	0	1
Evans, r.f.	4	0	0	0	1	0	1
Corey, c.f.	2	0	0	0	3	0	0
Hayes, c.	3	0	0	0	2	2	4
Smith, 1b	3	0	0	0	11	1	0
Irwin, 3b	3	0	0	0	0	2	0
Mountain, p.	3	0	0	0	0	3	0
Creamer, 2b	3	0	0	0	3	4	1
McLaughlin, s.s.	3	0	0	0	3	1	0
Totals	27	0	0	0	24	13	7

Innings	1	2	3	4	5	6	7	8	9	
Chicagos	0	1	0	1	2	1	0	0	..	—5
Worcesters	0	0	0	0	0	0	0	0	0	—0

Earned runs—Chicagos, 1. Two-base hits—Dalrymple, Kelly. First base on balls—Chicagos, 4; Worcesters, 2. First base on errors—Chicagos, 1; Worcesters, 2. Struck out—Chicagos, 1; Worcesters, 3. Double plays—Gore and Williamson; Quest and Anson; Hayes and Smith. Passed balls—Flint, 1. Hayes, 1. Time—1h. 30m. Umpire—Kelley.

CHICAGOS, 35; CLEVELANDS, 4.

[Special Dispatch to the Herald.]

CHICAGO, Ill., July 24, 1882. The Chicagos again trounced the Clevelands today by the surprising score of 35 to 4. It was a terrific batting display by Chicago, and muffing by Cleveland. Rowe was pie for the Chicagos, there being three home runs, and doubles without ends. The covers were knocked off of two balls by the Chicagos. Two thousand people saw the circus. The score:

CHICAGOS.

	A.B.	R.	B.	T.B.	P.O.	A.	E.
Dalrymple, l.f.	8	4	4	4	1	0	0
Gore, c.f.	6	5	4	8	0	0	1
Kelly, s.s.	8	4	4	7	4	3	2
Anson, 1b	6	5	1	1	14	0	0
Williamson, 3b	6	5	4	6	1	3	0
Burns, 2b	6	5	4	7	4	4	0
Corcoran, p.	6	1	0	0	1	4	0
Flint, c., r.f.	7	3	4	11	2	1	1
Nicol, r.f., s.s.	6	3	4	6	0	2	3
Totals	59	35	29	50	27	17	7

CLEVELANDS.

	A.B.	R.	B.	T.B.	P.O.	A.	E.
Dunlap, 2b	5	1	1	2	6	12	1
Glasscock, s.s.	4	0	1	2	4	3	3
Phillips, 1b	4	0	0	0	12	0	3
Shaffer, r.f.	3	0	0	0	0	0	1
Estabrook, l.f.	4	0	0	0	2	1	3
Muldoon, 3b	4	1	0	0	0	2	1
Wilgrod, c.f	4	0	1	1	0	0	1
Rowe, p.	2	1	1	1	0	1	3
Briody, c.	4	1	1	1	3	3	6
Totals	34	4	5	7	27	22	22

Innings	1	2	3	4	5	6	7	8	9	
Chicagos	5	0	4	9	2	4	1	7	3	—35
Clevelands	0	0	3	0	0	0	0	0	1	—4

Earned runs—Chicagos, 15; Clevelands, 2. Two-base hits—Gore, Kelly, Williamson (2), Burns (3), Nicol (2), Dunlap, Glasscock. Three-base hits—Kelly. Home runs—Gore, Flint (2). First base on balls—Chicagos, 7; Clevelands, 3. First base on errors—Chicagos, 9; Clevelands, 4. Struck out—Clevelands, 1. Double plays—Chicagos, 1; Clevelands, 4. Passed balls—Flint, 1; Kelly, 2; Briody, 6. Wild pitches—Rowe, 3. Time—2h. 40m. Umpire—Pearce.

ATHLETIC vs. BALTIMORE.

The initial game between the above-named clubs for the championship of the American Association was played May 2 in Philadelphia, Pa., twenty-five hundred people being present. The Baltimore team, including seven Philadelphians, played much better than was expected, and led at the end of the sixth inning. The Athletics bunched seven safe hits in the seventh and eighth innings, when they scored seven runs, and thus secured the victory by the appended score:

BALTIMORE.	T.	R.	1B.	PO.	A.	E.	ATHLETIC.	T.	R.	1B.	PO.	A.	E.
Myers, s. s.	5	1	2	0	3	1	Dorgan, r. f.	5	2	3	0	0	1
Wise, c. f.	5	1	1	0	0	1	Say, s. s.	5	2	3	0	3	1
Shetzline, 2d b.	5	1	1	4	3	0	Latham, 1st b.	5	1	1	11	0	0
Whiting, c.	5	1	1	4	2	3	Birchall, l. f.	5	1	2	2	0	1
Householder, 1st b	4	1	1	11	0	0	Weaver, p.	5	0	2	2	10	0
Jacoby, 3d b.	4	1	1	1	3	1	O'Brien, c.	5	1	1	11	1	0
Nichols, p.	4	0	1	0	2	1	Blakiston, 3d b.	4	0	1	1	2	1
Waitt, r. f.	4	0	1	0	0	0	Stricker, 2d b.	4	2	0	0	2	0
Burt, l. f.	4	1	1	4	0	1	Landis, c. f.	4	1	1	0	0	2
Totals	40	7	10	24	13	8	Totals	42	10	13	27	17	6

Baltimore	0	2	0	0	3	0	0	2	0	—7
Athletic	1	1	0	1	0	0	3	4		—10

Runs earned—Athletic, 2; Baltimore, 1. Two-base hits—Dorgan, O'Brien, Wise, Shetzline, Burt. First base on errors—Athletic, 2; Baltimore, 5. Struck out—Baltimore, 6. Left on bases—Athletic, 6; Baltimore, 4. First base on called balls—Athletic, 4. Double-play—Shetzline and Householder. Umpire, Wm. McLean. Time, 1h. 50m.

CINCINNATI vs. ECLIPSE.

On Sept. 11 these clubs met in Cincinnati, on which occasion the home-team sustained defeat. On this occasion it was a signal victory for the visitors. White handled the ball with telling effect for the Cincinnatis, only three base-hits being scored off his pitching; but the Cincinnatis could not secure even a single hit off Mullane's delivery. Score:

CINCINNATI.	T.	R.	1B.	PO.	A.	E.	ECLIPSE.	T.	R.	1B.	PO.	A.	E.
Sommers, l. f.	4	0	0	1	0	0	Browning, s. s.	4	0	0	2	5	0
Wheeler, r. f.	4	0	0	1	1	1	Hecker, 1st b.	4	0	0	8	0	0
Carpenter, 3d b.	4	0	0	1	3	1	Sullivan, c.	3	0	0	6	1	1
Snyder, c.	4	0	0	6	1	0	Wolf, r. f.	3	0	0	0	0	0
Stearns, 1st b.	4	0	0	11	0	0	Mack, 2d b.	3	0	0	5	2	0
Fulmer, s. s.	3	0	0	0	2	1	Mullane, p.	3	0	1	0	6	0
McPhee, 2d b.	3	0	0	3	2	1	Schenck, 3d b.	3	1	0	2	3	2
Macullar, c. f.	3	0	0	1	0	0	Maskrey, l. f.	3	0	0	4	1	0
White, p.	3	0	0	0	5	0	Reccius, c. f.	3	1	2	0	0	2
Totals	32	0	0	24	14	4	Totals	29	2	3	27	18	5

Cincinnati	0	0	0	0	0	0	0	0	0	—0
Eclipse	0	0	0	0	0	0	0	2	0	—2

Three-base hit—Reccius. Left on bases—Cincinnati, 5; Eclipse, 3. Struck out—Eclipse, 2; Cincinnati, 2. Double-plays—Maskrey and Hecker, 1; Browning and Hecker, 1. Bases on called balls—Cincinnati, 3. Passed balls—Sullivan, 1; Snyder, 1. Umpire, M. Walsh. Time, 1h. 40m.

THE LATE LEAGUE MEETING.

It is now denied that the Troy and Worcester Clubs voluntarily resigned their membership in the League. Director Simester of the Worcesters says that a resolution was adopted declaring it the sense of the meeting that these clubs be not represented in the association next season. The vote stood 6 to 2, Troy and Worcester of course voting in the negative. The resolution was offered by Thompson of the Detroit Club, who had been the prime mover in the scheme to change the membership of the League, and who recently made a personal canvass of the six clubs voting in the affirmative, to work up and secure concerted action at the meeting. The reason given for kicking out Worcester and Troy was that the patronage in either of these cities is not large enough to give the visiting clubs a share of gate-money sufficient to pay their expenses, and that, as New York and Philadelphia were anxious to be admitted, it was simply a question of business whether two non-paying cities should be continued in the copartnership when two paying cities could be secured to take their places. The representatives of Troy and Worcester made a vigorous resistance to the carrying out of the plan of the other clubs, but were powerless against the majority. As the matter stands they can remain in the League during the present week, and then they are practically out of the association, although their membership does not cease until the annual meeting of the League, in December. The League transacted no other business than to adopt the resolution offered by Mr. Thompson, and to vote to allow the clubs to engage players for next season. A director of the Troy Club also denies that they have resigned, and says that a resolution was adopted expelling the club after Dec. 2, against the protest of its representatives. The directors of the Troy Club have been at great expense this year in laying out new grounds, and according to the constitution of the League no club can be expelled unless it has violated the League rules. At the meeting the representatives of all the other clubs admitted that they had violated no rule. The directors declare that if the League insists upon the expulsion a suit for heavy damages will be begun by the Troy Club. The Troy players express indignation at the way Troy has been used, and say that they will remain there next season in preference to going to any other city.

A THRILLING ESCAPE.

The Cincinnati Club Preciptated Three Stories Down on a Broken Elevator.

The Cincinnati team had a marvelous escape at the Beckel house, in Dayton, last Wednesday. About 2 o'clock the entire nine dressed in uniform in a room on the third floor of the hotel, and left in a body for the elevator. The boy in charge carelessly let too many of them crowd into the car. White, Reilly, McPhee, Fulmer, Sommer, Jones, Corkhill and Mr. Frank Wright, of the *News Journal*, got safely into the elevator. Carpenter hesitated, remarking that the "thing might break." One of the boys said, "Crowd in, Hick, you might as well die now as any other time," and Hick did step through.

In a moment after, before the boy in charge could get the door closed, the car shot down like a meteor and landed on the cellar floor almost before anyone realized the danger. The shock was terrific. Every particle of glass in the elevator was broken out. The utmost confusion prevailed a moment later. Carpenter and Fulmer made a dash at the door at the same time, and both stuck fast. They say Reilly yelled "Let me out at this floor," that Jones shouted, "Slide, slide;" that White muttered something about a "down shoot." Fulmer gasped "Reserved, by gosh," and McPhee called for "judgment." John Corkhill's six hairs stood straight on ends and, like *Banquo's* ghost, would not down. Joe Sommer called "time," and tried to crawl out at the top.

Seriously, though, it was a marvel to everybody that no one of the nine men in the elevator was seriously hurt. Carpenter was cut in the left index finger by some broken glass, which, with the exception of a general jolting up, was the extent of the injury done to the men. The worst sufferer was the elevator boy, who was considerably bruised and cut about the face. Powers came up in time to see the car shoot down, with his fellow-players inside, and he was the most scared of all. A whiter-faced set of men were never seen than the Champions as they crawled out of the hole into the cellar. In spite of all they went straight to the grounds and played a splendid game of ball, beating the Dayton club 15 to 0.

CARRIER PIGEONS IN BASE BALL.

How the Winged Messengers are Utilized to Carry the News.

"Here he comes; we'll know how it went in a minute," exclaimed one of the keepers out at the Philadelphia Zoological Garden Wednesday afternoon to another, as they lounged on the rail by one of seal tanks, and almost while he spoke a homing pigeon flashed across the Schuylkill and an instant later reached its coop on the top of the deer-house. The first speaker captured the bird, and took from one of its legs a little slip of paper. "All O. K.; 6 to 2; the Mets, got one in their last inning" read the message.

"The bird belongs to James Murray, the keeper in charge of the deer-house," said the man in answer to an inquiry from a bystander. "Murray has twenty of them, and sends some over to almost every match played on the Athletic or Philadelphia grounds, and, as it only takes about two minutes for the birds to come home, we keep posted right up to time and can know how an inning went before the men are out in the field for the next one. Murray has had the birds for about two years, but this is the first season they have been used to bring messages to the Zoo."

Pigeons are also sent from the base ball grounds to other places about the city, and on some days as many as half a dozen birds will be released at the end of an inning.

A BALL PLAYER'S FRENZY.

"Terry" Larkin Shoots his Wife and Cuts his Throat.

From the New York Herald, 25th.

A grocer ran breathless into the Fourth street police station in Williamsburg at four o'clock yesterday afternoon and said to the sergeant at the desk that Frank Larkin, of No. 230 North Fifth street, had threatened to shoot him and that the man was crazy from long continued debauches and would certainly kill some one if he was not speedily arrested. Policeman Timothy Phelan was sent to Larkin's house. As he neared it he heard the screams of a woman issuing from the second story, and a moment later the sound of a pistol shot rang out. Phelan rushed to the second floor and tried to enter the room where the noise had been heard, but he found the door locked. He shook the door in an effort to burst the lock. A bullet crashed through the pannel and skimmed over the policeman's cheek, leaving a deep raw furrow. The policeman then burst the door from its fastenings and, entering the room, saw a woman lying on the floor, her face covered with blood, while a man with a razor by his side on a table and a smoking pistol in his hand stood facing the doorway and threatening to blow out the brains of any one who dared to enter. The man was Frank Larkin, the ball player. He was bleeding at the throat. Policeman Phelan sprang upon him and felled him to the floor, where he held him till another policeman entered the house and helped to secure him. Then it was discovered that the woman on the floor—who was Mrs. Catharine Larkin, his wife—had been shot and seriously wounded.

Larkins had entered his apartments drunk. When his wife remonstrated with him he took a pistol from his hip pocket and shot her in the mouth, causing a compound fracture of the lower jaw. He then picked up a razor from the mantel and cut his own throat, and when he heard the policeman trying to force the door in he again picked up his pistol and fired through the panel. Larkin was arrested, but subsequently he was sent to St. Catharine's Hospital, where his wife had previously been taken. It was said last night that both husband and wife were in a dangerous condition.

Larkin is one of the best known ball players in America. He is often called Terry Larkin. At one time he pitched for the Chicago Club, but he was forced to retire as his arm gave out In 1881 he played with the Atlantic Club, of Brooklyn. Last season he played a fine game with the Metropolitan, of this city, and when Manager Barnie, of last year's Atlantic Club, took charge of the Baltimore Club for this season Larkin was the first man he engaged, but he has not yet played with the club. It is laid to his absence that the club has lost so many games this season. Larkin wrote Mr. Barnie recently that he would join the club in time to open the championship season, which will begin next week.

LARKIN AGAIN ATTEMPTS SUICIDE.

Frank Larkin, made an attempt on Wednesday afternoon to kill himself in St. Catharine's Hospital. In the morning a sister of his wife visited him. She said there were no hopes of her recovery. This information had a very depressing effect on him. He had appeared in a good frame of mind before that time, the Sisters and doctors having given him the impression that his wife would recover.

Soon after his sister's departure he arose from his bed, and asked Policeman Delaney, who was on watch over him, to be allowed to see his wife, who is in an adjoining ward. Delaney prevailed upon him to return to his bed. Half an hour afterward he suddenly sprang up in bed, and before Delaney could interpose he plunged headforemost against the steam register at the foot of his couch. When he was picked up he was bleeding from an ugly gash on his head. After being placed in the bed he was strapped down, and his hands were bound with a strap. He refused thereafter to accept anything from the Sisters or doctors. He said to the policeman when they were not present: "For God's sake hit me in the head and put an end to my suffering."

Editorial Chat on the National Game.

If the reserve rule stands it will practically help to kill the interest in base ball. Variety is the spice of life, and one of the means of keeping the base ball fever at a white heat, even during the winter, is the speculation indulged in concerning the composition of the nines for the ensuing season, and their relative merits and demerits are canvassed and discussed throughout the idle months, and this makes people impatient for the season to open, and when it does open they flock in crowds to the grounds. This gives managers a chance to reap a financial harvest early, giving them a nest egg for the latter part of the season, when, in the cities where the clubs are hopelessly in the rear, the interest begins to flag. Now, let the rule stand and keep the clubs just as they are now, and not one-half the interest will be created and shown by the public. Everybody knows about what the clubs are capable of, and their relative standing at the close of the season is almost irrevocably fixed before the championship season opens. For instance, should either the Athletic or Cincinnati clubs win the Association pennant, or the Cleveland or Providence that of the League, there would no doubt be a struggle between these clubs next season, but for the other clubs, which would merely act as pawns, there would be no show, and hence no drawing power in their cities. No theatre could live without a change of plays, no person without a change of diet, neither can base ball clubs go on, year after year, without a change of players except, perhaps, the team at the top of the heap. Constant change is the order of the universe. Motion is life; stagnation, death.

QUITE A SUCCESS.

Base Ball Played at Night by Aid of Electric Lights.

Correspondence SPORTING LIFE.

FORT WAYNE, Ind., June 5.—The game of base ball, between the Quincys, of Illinois, and a picked nine of Fort Wayne players, by electric light, took place last Saturday evening. The inclosure, which is four hundred by four hundred and fifty feet, was lighted by seventeen of the lamps of the Jenney Electric Light Company, of Fort Wayne. They were suspended as masts, except three that were attached to the front of the grand stand. One of the lights was behind the pitcher, which seemed to light up the diamond splendidly, while the light at the corner made it light enough to see the ball plainly in the center field. The atmosphere was heavy at times, which caused a very noticeable and favorable effect on throwing the light down on the field. All the lights had a powerful reflector behind them. The only thing to mar the exhibition was the light going entirely out twice, caused by defective brushes at the power-house. It was found necessary to change the ball quite often. When a ball became dirty, it could not be seen. With between twenty-five and thirty lights there is no question but what electric light ball playing is an assured success. Another exhibition game, with this number of lights, will be played in a short time. The game was unimportant, as far as the score was concerned and some trouble was experienced in catching the ball from the bat, particularly the high ones, but not the least difficulty was found at the bat. But seven innings were played, Quincy winning by 19 to 11. The playing was between the pitcher and catcher, who were enabled to work fairly. The out-fielding was unsatisfactory, owing to the insufficient number of lights used. The grounds were crowded with spectators, whose interest was centered more on the effect the lights had on the flying ball than on the game itself.

THE NEW UNION LEAGUE.

[*Special Dispatch to the Herald.*]

NEW YORK, Sept. 25, 1883. A meeting of delegates from professional base ball clubs not represented in the League or American Association was held in this city today to perfect a new organization, to be known as the Union League of Base Ball Clubs. The design of the organization is to form a league which shall embrace cities composing a good travelling circuit from Richmond, Va., to Boston, there being no club represented in any association in Boston (except the league club), which offers a good opening for a club which will join the new league. The following clubs will be included in the new association: The Boston club, the Virginias of Richmond, Nationals of Washington, Oriole club of Baltimore, Quicksteps of Wilmington, Keystone club of Philadelphia, the Trenton club, Hartford club, the Springfield club, and a new club from this city.

CHINESE PLAYERS.

Striking Successfully for Higher Wages Nine Times in Succession.

Manager Lang's Chinese Base Ball Club, composed of Messrs. One to Nine Lungs, inclusive, and a substitute whose name is Wash-Tub Tommy, are again giving that enterprising gentleman much trouble. They were originally engaged at $10 a week and expenses. After one day's practice they struck for $12 a week and expenses, which was granted. The nine practiced another day and struck again, demanding that three of their number should get $15 and the rest $12. This was granted. Demand number three was that six should get $15 and four receive $12, and to this also Mr. Lang gracefully acceded. The smiling Celestials slept peacefully on their third victory, and in the morning struck for the fourth time, their cry being for $15 each, with the exception of Wash-Tub Tommy, who was only to get $10. Again Mr. Lang "saw the raise." The club members now congratulated themselves on having struck a soft thing, and, after giving Mr. Lang time to catch his breath, they made their fifth demand for increased pay. The schedule presented to the unhappy manager on this occasion was that three should be paid $20, six $15 and one $10. Mr. Lang ground his teeth, swore that he would pan out no longer and then gave in. That night the Lungs, together with Tommy, the substitute, sat in secret session in Two Lung's laundry, but their chuckles of delight could be distinctly heard from the sidewalk. The following morning witnessed the usual strike—"nine to get $20 and one $10," and the nine to pay their own expenses. Lang refused point-blank, and the blue-eyed strikers returned to their tubs. The next day their demands were allowed, but with the distinct understanding that the final raise had been granted. Practice proceeded, and the prospect was becoming rose-colored, when the seventh strike occurred, to wit, for $20 per week, each and all their expenses to be paid by Lang. This was the straw that broke the camel's back, but the camel's back recovered, and for the seventh time the strikers had struck successfully. The Chinamen now swore by Confucius and a dozen of the lesser Celestial gods that they were at last fully satisfied, and Manager Lang proceeded with his arrangements for putting them in the field. Then came the eighth strike. It was more modest than its predecessors, and called for their wages in advance. With a sigh Manager Lang said "yes," but naturally wanted some security for their appearance during the week he was to pay for. The Lungs produced persons who offered to go security for their faithful appearance "for $50,000 if necessary." Mr. Lang said that that sum was quite unnecessary, and $500 in Government bonds deposited in any Trust Company's hands, to be forfeited should the Chinamen not come up to time, would satisfy him; but the backer refused this modest offer and said he would only go security for $190, the amount of one week's salary. At the same time the now permanent committee on strikes, consisting of Two, Five and Eight Lungs, appeared and struck on behalf of their brothers for the ninth time. They modestly demanded that an increased allowance be granted them to cover their wash bills. A Chinaman's washing not amounting to much, this was allowed, but not until each man had signed a paper to forfeit his precious pigtail in case of any further demands. The expense of getting the nine into shape has been considerable, and Mr. Lang hopes yet to arrange matters satisfactorily with the Chinamens' backer. In the meantime the Lungs and Tommy are arranging the details of the tenth strike.

SACRIFICE HITTING.

An Experiment in That Direction by Captain Anson.

Chicago *American Sports*, Sept. 8th.

In the course of a discussion last Wednesday morning at the club house a good deal was said on the subject of "sacrifice hits" and "placing the ball." Anson took the ground that he could bat a ball in any direction he chose. Corcoran held the contrary, and offered to bet a dollar on every ball hit, that Anson couldn't do it. The wager was not accepted, but Anson declared he would demonstrate his claim in the afternoon game. This is how he demonstrated it: Out of six times at bat he failed to make a safe hit—precisely what *American Sports* declared must be the result of attempting to "place the ball," with men on bases; the ball once went on the ground to short stop, once on a fly to right field, once on a fly to right field, once on a foul fly to first baseman, and once on the ground to pitcher; the other two hits were on the ground to short stop and second base, only one-half the hits were to right field, and two out of the six were easy fly balls; and all this time, according to previous announcement, Anson was trying to "place the ball." Admitting that Anson can probably come nearer to controlling the direction of a batted ball than any batsman in the League can do, it will be seen that he cannot do it more than half the time, and even then cannot regulate the hits as between fly balls, grounders or fouls. Like every other batsman who faces curve throwing, Anson will accomplish more for his side and improve his individual batting record by limiting his efforts to hitting the ball hard and strong than by attempting the folly of "sacrifice hitting."

SUPERSTITIOUS NOTIONS.

More Instances of Their Prevalence Among Ball-Tossers.

The Cleveland *Leader* says that John Clapp, manager of the New York, during the game last Friday, noticed a little man standing at the foot of the stairway leading up into the grand stand. "Why don't you go up and look at the game?" asked John. "Well, you see when the Clevelands are behind at the eighth inning, I always come and stand here, and they are sure to win." Clapp looked at the little fellow and smiled sarcastically, for the New Yorks were three to nothing, with the chances of their winning very favorable. In that inning, however, the Clevelands scored three runs and tied the game, which they won in the fourteenth inning. "What do you think of me now?" asked the superstitious individual, when some one called in that Cleveland had made three. "I think you'd better take a walk," gruffly replied John, as he went and looked at the game from one of the peep-holes in his side of the building.

After the 22–9 beating in New York Saturday, the Chicagoes concluded to change their uniforms "just for luck," and on Monday the nine appeared in white shirts and stockings and caps and red pantaloon. They won by 5 to 2.

Wanted--An Inventor.

On Saturday last McCormick, the fine pitcher of the Cleveland Club, while running the bases, caught his foot under one of the bags and sprained his ankle so severely that he was unable to play the rest of the week, to the serious loss of his club. Only recently Corey was laid up from the same cause, and Lang, of the Anthracite, is now getting a broken limb in shape, the accident being caused in the same manner. The season is long yet and there is no telling how many good men may be crippled. When we consider that upon such accidents may depend the results of important championship games, it seems as though some effort should be made to invent something more suitable for the purpose than the present base-bag. Where are our inventors?

Sullivan as a Pitcher.

At St. Louis, Nov. 4th, John L. Sullivan, pugilist, pitched for a picked nine against the St. Louis Club and the result was his dismal failure as a pitcher. For six innings he was batted all over the field, the Browns knocking the ball to the fence nearly every time. Sullivan played short the last three innings. Three balls were knocked to him; the first bounced out of his hands and rolled to the second baseman, and the base runner from first was forced out. The second ball knocked him off his feet, but the third one, a grounder, he stopped, and put a man out at first with it. At the bat he was also a failure, not being able to knock the ball out of the diamond. The game was a regular farce as far as ball playing was concerned. About five thousand people were present, half of them men who take no interest in base ball, and who went only to see the big slugger. Sullivan's share of the proceeds was sixty per cent., or nearly $1,400.

"BASE BALL WRECKERS."

That is What the Chicago Club's Organ Calls the Union Association

From the Chicago *American Sports*.

As foreshadowed last week, a movement toward the formation of a rival base ball association has taken shape at a meeting in Pittsburg last Wednesday, whereat was organized what is called "The Union Association of Base Ball Clubs." Officers were elected, and a constitution adopted which is said to be similar to that of the American Association, "with a few changes." What these changes were may be inferred from the adoption of a resolution that "while we recognize the validity of the League and American Association, we cannot recognize any agreement whereby any number of ball players may be reserved for any club for any time beyond the term of his contract with said club." The meaning of this is that the new Association proposes to adopt the club-wrecking policy and go into the "cut-throat" business helter skelter. If this programme were backed up by men of means, responsibility, and respectability, the League and Association clubs might well feel alarmed at an outlook so injurious to their own prospects and so detrimental to the interests of base ball generally. But we search the list of officers and directors in vain for the name of one person of means or responsibility, or whose business and social standing is such as to inspire confidence either among ball-players or ball-patrons. The organization savors of the wildcat species all through. Nevertheless a wildcat may scratch around and do considerable mischief when people are off their guard. Believing firmly that a wide-open competition for players will force salaries up to a point where financial failure and insolvency are a certainty, and that in this way an injury will be inflicted upon players and upon the game of base ball, *American Sports* favors the reserve system as wise and judicious, and condemns the policy of the new association as mischievous and censurable. Players will be foolish if they fall into any such trap as that set by the adventurers and speculators who made up the Pittsburg meeting. There is a vast difference between a big salary promised in May and a big salary not paid in July or August, and if players allow themselves to be tempted by a large offer by parties without capital or character they will have nobody but themselves to blame for the consequences.

He Has One Friend.

Chicago *American Sports*

The first removal among the National League staff of umpires occurred on Wednesday, when Mr. Odlin received a telegram from Secretary Young announcing that three clubs had joined in the complaint of incompetency preferred by Detroit, and his removal was therefore compulsory under the rule. While it is doubtless true that Mr. Odlin made some unfortunate mistakes in Detroit, it is difficult to perceive the necessity for the haste and harshness shown toward him by the Detroit Club, especially as he stood ready to resign provided his services did not prove acceptable in Chicago or Cleveland. He served with fair acceptability in the first two games of the Boston-Chicago series, and created the impression that he was rapidly acquiring the experience necessary to make him an excellent umpire.

Add to rule 65—No home run can be made on a ball hit over a fence less than 210 feet from the home base, and if the fence is not the required distance the base-runner is entitled to only two bases. This rule was so amended as to legislate the Chicago right-field fence iniquity out of existence. With a fence only 196 feet from the plate that team was enabled to make about 127 home runs this season to the manifest advantage of the club and individual averages.

METROPOLITAN PARK.

Opening of the New Grounds of the Metropolitan Club.

Metropolitan Park, the new ground of the Metropolitan Base Ball Club, was opened to the public May 13th. Over 4,000 persons were present, one quarter of whom were there by special invitation. The grounds are situated at One Hundred and Eighth street and Harlem River. The ground is filled in and the filling is of such a nature as to be decidedly unpleasant to the olfactory organs, but Mutrie is having that defect remedied. The grounds within the inclosure are well laid out, and the well-sodded diamond is one of the prettiest in the country. Jack Goulding, the well-known superintendent, says that he will have the entire grounds covered with grass before long. The grand stand is a "single decker," plain but substantial. The catcher's 90-foot run up behind the bat terminates at the stand, and allows a catcher but little freedom because of its construction. The space reserved for reporters is at the front of the stand just behind and on a line with the home plate, and a wire screen prevents passed balls or fouls from entering the stand. The home plate, however, is so near the limits of the grounds that foul balls always go outside. In the first game played in the grounds half a dozen balls were lost in this manner. However, the manager has worked hard to get the ground into good shape, and the result, on the whole, is gratifying to the club and public.

BUFFALO VS. DETROIT.

At Detroit, Aug. 4, the game was a strange and brilliant one for the visiting team, while Detroit met with the most disastrous defeat of the League season of 1884. Galvin and Meinke pitched, and while the gentle one was not hit safely during the entire game, Meinke was hit hard and consecutively for eleven earned runs. Buffalo fielded beautifully, while the visitors fell to pieces in two innings under the vigorous hitting. The score follows:

BUFFALO.	T.	R.	B.	P.	A.	E	DETROIT.	T.	R.	B.	P.	A.	E
Bro'thers,1b	6	1	2	12	0	1	Wood, lf	4	0	0	1	1	1
O'Rourke, lf	6	3	2	2	0	0	Farrell, 3b	3	0	0	2	2	0
Rowe, c	6	2	4	8	2	1	Hanlon, cf	3	0	0	1	0	1
Rich'ds'n,2b	6	2	2	1	5	0	Bennett, 2b	3	0	0	2	5	1
White, 3b	5	1	2	0	2	0	Scott, 1b	3	0	0	10	0	0
Lillie, rf	6	4	3	1	0	0	Weidman,rf	3	0	0	1	0	1
Force, ss	4	2	2	0	1	0	Meinke, p	3	0	0	0	8	2
Eggler, cf	5	1	3	3	0	0	Buker, ss	3	0	0	1	5	2
Galvin, p	5	2	2	0	9	0	Ziller, c	3	0	0	6	2	1
Total	49	18	22	27	19	2	Total	28	0	0	24	23	9

Buffalo .... 1 1 8 1 0 2 0 5 x—18
Detroit .... 0 0 0 0 0 0 0 0 0—0
Earned runs—Buffalo 11. Two base hit—O'Rourke. Three-base hit—Lillie. First on balls—Buffalo 2. First on errors—Buffalo 3. Detroit 2. Struck out—Buffalo 5. Detroit 7. Double plays—Buker, Bennett and Scott. Passed balls—Ziller 3. Wild pitches—Meinke 2. Time—1:45. Umpire—McLean.

BALL PLAYERS WHO WON'T PLAY.
REASONS WHICH MAY LEAD TO THE DISBANDMENT OF THE PROVIDENCE CLUB.

PROVIDENCE, R. I., July 22.—The truth has at last come out, and the mysterious trouble which seemed to be undermining the Providence Baseball Club and bringing it to ruin has been unveiled. Some time ago crookedness was suspected, and to-day the cold fact stares the management in the face that they have been "played for sailors." When the season of 1883 closed Radbourn threatened not to sign for this year. A combination was formed by him and Carroll not to sign, and only after prolonged persuasion could either be induced to put their names to contracts, Carroll only giving in when he was cornered and almost obliged to give up a hunting trip with Radbourn, the management threatening to hold him until Oct. 1 and make him come to this city before he would be paid off and released for the year. When this season opened Radbourn and Sweeney became jealous of each other. Sweeney had been kept in the background, and Radbourn billed as the star pitcher. Sweeney asked leave to occupy the "points." He did so, and proved such a success that he even pitched on days when Radbourn was to toss the sphere, and was paid extra for these games. When Sweeney became lame Radbourn had to do double duty, and "kicked" because he was not also paid extra for Sweeney's dates. About this time Radbourn began to show an ugly disposition, and finally, in games last week, he is charged with throwing a game because everything did not go to suit him. Since then Sweeney has been ow'sh, and to-day his disaffection, like Radbourn's, took a tangible shape. His first kick over the traces was yesterday, when the club went to Woonsocket to play an exhibition game. He appeared on the grounds with a woman whom he gave a seat on the grand stand, and after the game, when ordered to pack up and come home with the boys, he refused to do so, remaining until a late train. To-day he began to pitch a "stuffy" game; he was surly and owlish, and pitched without speed or any great effort to win. At the close of the seventh inning Providence had 6 to 2 runs and had the game won, as the Philadelphia Club was batting weakly and fielding badly. To ease up on Sweeney's lame arm, Manager Bancroft told the Californian to go into the field and let Miller pitch out the game. He became very angry and left the field, evincing jealousy of young Miller who is a promising ball-tosser. Philadelphia went to the bat in the inning, and it was found that Providence had but eight men in the field. Sweeney was missing. Bancroft went in search of him, and found him in the dressing room with his store clothes off. He requested him to go out and play, but was most villainously abused. Director Allen then threatened to lay Sweeney off without pay, but to this threat Sweeney sarcastically replied that he did not care, as he could make more money if he did not play here. Providence went on and finished the game with eight men. The eight innings was handsomely played, but in the ninth, fly balls were hit between the regular out-field positions, and the men being unable to cover so much ground, the hits became safe. Then Miller was pounded for five hits. Providence giving him bad support, as bad as could be looked for, and the Philadelphia Club won the game. Convinced from what Sweeney had said, and from his conduct and Radbourn's peculiar actions that the "Wreckers' Union" had been at work, the management to-night expelled Sweeney from the league and will cause his name to be put on the black list.

A meeting will probably be held to-morrow to consider whether the club shall be disbanded. There are no pitchers to be had, and, with the present feeling in the team, the pennant cannot possibly be won. If the association stops short to-day there will be a surplus of $17,000 on hand. The St. Louis Union Association are suspected of having approached the malcontents. There is still further trouble, based upon Catholicism and Protestantism.

FAT SALARIES

Paid to the Members of Von der Ahe's Pet Club.

The St. Louis team has been generally regarded as the highest salaried club in the American Association. Certainly the erratic president, Mr. Von der Ahe, has spared no expense in putting together the team which made the Athletics hustle for the championship last year and which stands an excellent chance of winning it this season. From contracts seen in Mr. Von der Ahe's office, and from the lips of the players, the exact amounts paid out by the St. Louis Club in salaries has been obtained, and the amounts are presented below. It will be noticed that it is not the hardest working player that is the best paid. For example, Quest draws nearly $100 a month more than Strief, while Comiskey, perhaps the most pains-taking player of all, is paid less than Deasley, the most reckless of the lot, and Dolan, who does the same work as Deasley, and does it about as well, is paid just a little over half as much as Deasley, or $900 less for the season. Davis, who has been pitching better than O'Neill, if anything, is paid $500 less than that player, while McGinnis, who is worth the two put together, only receives $75 more than O'Neill. But here are the figures, and in looking them over let it be remembered that the ball player's season commences April 1 and ends October 1, and that the salary is for these seven months:

PLAYER.	SEASON.	MONTH.	DAY.
Williams, manager	$2,500	$357	$12 00
Deasley, catcher	2,500	357	12 00
Comiskey, 1st baseman	2,100	300	10 00
Quest, 2d baseman	2,100	300	10 00
McGinnis, pitcher	1,975	282	9 50
O'Neill, pitcher	1,900	272	9 00
Gleason, short stop	1,800	257	8 50
Lewis, centre field	1,800	257	8 50
Latham, 3d baseman	1,800	257	8 50
Nicol, right field	1,600	230	7 50
Dolan, catcher	1,600	230	7 50
Strief, left field	1,400	200	7 00
Davis, pitcher	1,400	200	7 00
Goldsby, substitute	1,400	200	7 00

The above is believed to represent a considerable increase in salaries over last year.

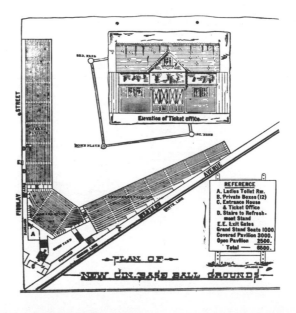

REFERENCE
A. Ladies Toilet Rm.
B. Private Boxes (12)
C. Entrance House & Ticket Office
D. Stairs to Refreshment Stand
E.E. Exit Gates
Grand Stand Seats 1000.
Covered Pavilion 3000.
Open Pavilion 2500.
Total 6500.

PLAN OF
NEW ORL. BASE BALL GROUNDS.

CHAMPIONS OF THE WORLD.

The League Leaders Down the American Champions.

The long-standing question of superiority between League and American Association clubs has been finally settled by a regular series of games between the champions of the respective organizations. The Providence and Metropolitan clubs contested in New York last week for the world's championship, a purse and gate receipts, and the result clearly proclaims the Providence Club "Champions of the World."

UNION ASSOCIATION.

The Record.

The Union Association finished the first championship season Oct. 19, St. Louis winning the pennant. Of the original eight clubs that started the season but five remained. The Altoona Club disbanded on May 31, and Kansas City took its place and struggled through the season. The Keystone, of Philadelphia, disbanded on August 7, and the Wilmington Club, seceding from the Eastern League, filled the vacancy until Sept. 15, when it, too, dropped out. The Chicago Club was transferred to Pittsburg on August 25, and lasted until September 19, when it also slipped out of sight. Clubs from Milwaukee and St. Paul were then taken in and assisted in completing the schedule. The following is a complete record of all the championship games played during the season, commencing on April 17 and ending on October 19:

CLUBS.	Altoona.	Baltimore.	Boston.	Pittsburg.	Cincinnati.	Keystone.	National.	St. Louis.	Kansas City.	Wilmington.	Milwaukee.	St. Paul.	Total won.
Altoona.........		1	1	0	0	1	3	0	0	0	0	0	6
Baltimore......	3		10	6	3	10	12	1	10	1	0	0	56
Boston.........	1	6		4	5	8	12	8	8	4	2	0	58
Pittsburg......	0	6	8		6	3	4	1	12	0	0	0	40
Cincinnati.....	3	11	11	8		8	10	2	10	2	0	3	68
Keystone.......	3	2	3	5	0		4	0	4	0	0	0	21
National.......	1	4	4	8	6	4		3	8	4	1	0	47
St. Louis......	8	13	8	11	14	8	13		10	4	0	2	91
Kansas City....	0	2	4	3	0	4	0	0		0	1	0	14
Wilmington.....	0	0	0	0	1	0	1	0	0		0	0	8
Milwaukee......	0	3	2	0	0	0	3	0	0	0		0	8
St. Paul.......	0	0	0	0	0	0	0	1	1	0	0		3
Total lost...	19	48	51	45	35	46	66	16	63	15	3	6	413

Percentage:—St. Louis .85, Milwaukee .72, Cincinnati .66, Baltimore .53, Boston .53, Chicago .47, National .41, Keystone .31, St. Paul .25, Altoona .24, Kansas City 17, Wilmington 11.

BATTING AVERAGES.

Rank.		Games.	Runs.	B.H.	Av.
1—Dunlap, St. Louis.........		81	134	153	.420
2—Glasscock, Cincinnati......		34	42	60	.388
3—Dickerson, St. Louis.......		41	48	72	.372
4—Taylor, St. Louis.........		38	36	60	.355
5 { Shafer, St. Louis.........		89	111	140	.354
{ Briody, Cincinnati.........		19	9	28	.354
6—Moore, National.........		107	72	154	.337
7—Powell, Cincinnati.........		35	48	52	.333
8—Gross, Chicago............		23	12	32	.326

No "Lushing" Next Year—New Men Selected.

Mr. Brunell writes in the Cleveland *Herald*:—The public can rely upon it that whatever may be the playing quality of the Cleveland team of 1885, there will be less "lushing" than at any time since "lushing" has been a fashionable trimming to a League club. Cleveland has now been in the League since 1880. Four or five drinkers have always been in the ranks. One season we played through with seven of them. In 1884 we started in with the usual five and finished with two. Murphy, McCormick and Briody dropped away. Next season we shall open with one, and he a very mild one. The theory of sober and mediocre players playing better ball than fuddled and superior players is to be tested. It will be found good in practice. To-day, were I making up a ball team, I would rather have a sober man with averages of .250 and .850 than a "lusher" with figures of .280 and .890. Sobriety's worth fifty per cent. on both averages, and some practical base ball men value it higher.

NATIONAL AGREEMENT PLANS.

The Reserve Rule to be Maintained and the Union Association to be Ignored.

An interview recently by a reporter with President Spalding, of the Chicago Club, resulted in his ascertaining two important facts as likely to govern the action of the League and American Association at their coming December convention. The one is the certain continuance in force of the reserve rule, perhaps with some modifications, as to the limit of the salary of a reserved player to not less than $1,000 a season for base players and fielders, and to not less than $1,200 for pitchers and catchers. The other is a full determination not to recognize the Union Association, nor to allow that organization to become part and parcel of the National Agreement. He says that the players who have of late jumped contracts in League and American clubs under the idea that the existing war with the Union Association will end with the present season will find out their mistake before the close of the present year. Mr. Spalding evidently voices the sentiment of the League clubs when he states that the Union Association will never be admitted to club intercourse with the League nor with any association connected with the National Agreement combination. It is the determination of the League to keep out every man who this season breaks his contract with a League organization.

TRICKY MULLANE.

This Slippery Customer Makes Another Dishonorable Jump.

TOLEDO, Nov. 4.—Tony Mullane has made a most dishonorable jump from the St. Louis to the Cincinnati Club. On Saturday, Oct. 25, the directors of the Toledo Club decided to accept the offer of Chris. Von der Ahe, of the St. Louis Club, to take five of the Toledo players, he to pay them for their release a stipulated sum. The Toledo Club, as is well known, closed the season in bad shape, being some $10,000 or $11,000 in the hole. The prospects for next season were considered to be little better than last and it was for this reason that the club was disbanded. The five who were to go to St. Louis were Mullane, Morton, Barkley, Welch and Poorman. All of them perfectly understood the terms upon which they were to go, and that their release by the Toledo Club was granted upon the express understanding that they should sign to play with St. Louis. Each of the five passed his word of honor to stand by the agreement. The ten days which must elapse before a released player can sign with another club expired last night. The boys were to sign at 1 o'clock this morning, at which time Morton, Barkley, Welch and Poorman affixed their signatures to the contracts. But Mullane failed to show up and brief inquiry revealed the fact that he had jumped his agreement, and at 12:15 A. M. had signed to play with the Cincinnati Club, at a salary of $5,000 for the season, with $2,000 advance money. Immediately after signing and securing his $2,000, he visited several saloons where he boastingly displayed his ill-gotten wealth. At 2 A. M. he boarded an east bound train for his home in Erie, Pa., wisely concluding that the atmosphere in Toledo would be too warm for him when his baseness should become generally known. By his action, the Toledo Club loses several hundred dollars. Few clubs would have treated Mullane as well as did the Toledo Club. Last fall he jumped his contract with the St. Louis Club and signed with the St Louis Unions. To prevent being blacklisted he jumped his contract with the Unions and came to Toledo. During the past season he was bitterly persecuted by Lucas, of the St. Louis Unions, and in defending him in the courts the Toledo Club paid out more than $1,000. When the directors, a few weeks ago, decided to disband the club, he suggested that arrangements might be made with Von der Ahe to take a part of the players and pay well for them. He agreed to everything, and upon his agreements he secured his release. His action last night has called forth the most severe condemnation of his warmest friends, and they predict ere long he will be sorry for adopting such a dishonorable course.

EXHIBITION GAMES.

"THE WORLD'S CHAMPIONS."

The St. Louis Club Wins the Series and the $1,000 Stake From the Chicagos.

When the St. Louis and Chicago clubs came upon the field at Cincinnati Saturday, Oct. 24, it was announced that the clubs had cancelled all future dates, and would make this the final game of their series. The first game at Chicago, Oct. 14, resulted in a tie of 5 to 5. In the second game at St. Louis Oct. 15 the score stood 6 to 5 in favor of Chicago when a row occurred; St. Louis left the field and the game was awarded to Chicago by 9 to 0. The third and fourth games were also played at St. Louis, Oct. 16 and 17, and both were won by the American team by scores of 7 to 4 and 3 to 2. The fifth and sixth games were played at Pittsburg and Cincinnati respectively and Chicago won both by scores of 9 to 2 each. This left the record in favor of Chicago by three victories to St. Louis' two. Before Saturday's game, however, it was mutually agreed to throw out the forfeited game, leaving the clubs even at two games each, and that Saturday's game decide the series. Under this agreement the game was played and the result was an easy victory for the American champions. Clarkson did not appear until late and McCormick was put in the box for Chicago. He was badly pounded and received wretched support. The Chicagos took a lead of two runs in the first inning on hits by Sunday and Kelly and an error of Barkley. In the third inning Welch made a three-bagger and crossed the plate through Dalrymple's poor fielding. Barkley and Comiskey made hits, and Barkley scored while Comiskey was forced out by Robinson. Robinson stole to second and scored on a passed ball. The St. Louis Club won in the fourth inning by hitting McCormick safely five times. The fielding of the League champions in this inning was the worst seen there for some time. Anson made two bad muffs, Williamson a wild throw, Dalrymple a wild throw and Flint had two passed balls. The result was six runs for the St. Louis team. In the fifth inning the Chicagos made two un-earned runs, but they had no chance to overcome the lead of their opponents and the game thereafter was devoid of interest. The attendance was 1,200. Score:

ST. LOUIS.	A.B.	R.	B.	P.	A.	E.	CHICAGO.	A.B.	R.	B.	P.	A.	E.
Gleason, ss..	4	2	2	3	3	1	Dalrymple, lf.	3	0	0	0	1	2
Welch, cf.....	5	3	2	2	0	0	Sunday, cf....	4	1	1	3	0	0
Barkley, 2b...	3	2	2	3	3	2	Kelly, rf......	4	2	2	2	0	1
Comiskey, 1b.	4	1	1	10	0	1	Anson, 1b.....	4	1	2	7	2	4
Robinson, rf..	4	3	1	1	0	1	Pfeffer, 2b....	4	0	2	4	3	0
O'Neil, lf.....	4	0	1	0	0	0	Will'mson, ss	3	0	0	2	6	2
Latham, 3b...	3	0	0	1	3	0	Burns, 3b.....	4	0	0	0	1	2
Foutz, p......	4	1	2	0	6	2	McCormick, p	4	0	1	0	5	3
Bushong, c...	4	1	1	4	1	3	Flint, c......	3	0	1	2	3	3
Total........	35	13	12	24	16	10	Total........	33	4	9	21	21	17

St. Louis............................ 0 0 4 6 2 1 0 x –13
Chicago............................. 2 0 0 0 2 0 0 0– 4

Earned runs—St. Louis 4. Two-base hits—Kelly 2. Three-base hits—Welch, Robinson. Passed balls—Flint 3, Bushong 2. First on balls—McCormick 3, Foutz 2. First on errors—St. Louis 6, Chicago 3. Struck out—McCormick 1, Foutz 4. Double play—Gleason and Comiskey. Umpire—Kelly.

The Chicago Club is much chagrined at the defeats inflicted by St. Louis, a club they underrated, and the loss of the "world's championship," a title which amounts to little, is yet irritating to the white-hosed lads. Per consequence, they would like another go at the Browns, and accordingly have expressed a willingness to put up $1,500, if the Browns will do the same, making a purse of $3,000, all of which will go to the club winning the game. Both clubs disbanded Saturday, but the teams may keep together and the game yet be arranged. If so, it will be played to-day or some time this week. The Browns will name the city in which the game is to be played, and if they conclude that St. Louis can stand another game they will select Sportsman's Park; if not, the two clubs may play in one of the Southern cities.

LADY ENTHUSIASTS.

How the Gentle Creatures Can be Carried Away by the Great Game.

The Southern ladies have taken to the game like a duck to water. In Nashville last Saturday 1,200, by actual count, of the fair sex were present. The Southern ladies enjoy the game keenly, enter fully into its spirit and have their likes and dislikes quite as strongly as the male portion of the audiences. All are bitter partisans and swear by the home club. An instance showing how they will, in exceptional cases, allow their feelings to master them is cited by the Atlanta *Constitution*, which says that recently two ladies of the highest social standing were coming from the ball grounds on a Peachtree street car. One of the ladies was from Augusta, while the other claims Atlanta as her home. Soon after the car started the Atlanta lady began abusing the umpire.

"Oh, he is awful mean," she said. "He just cheated us out of the game. My, but wouldn't I like to have him here!"

"I think you don't know what you are talking about," responded the Augusta lady. "That umpire was just as fair as he could be."

"He wasn't," retorted Atlanta, as her face grew red.

"He was, I say he was," replied the Augustinian, as she clinched her little fist.

"And I say you don't know what you are saying," answered Atlanta, as she rose to her feet.

"I guess I do," replied Augusta, as she arose, too.

For a brief second the two ladies looked at each other, and then Atlanta raised her parasol. At the same time Augusta reached out and, with gloved hand, grabbed her adversary by the shoulder. Just at this instant, when a battle seemed certain, an old gentleman stepped between the belligerent pair and said:

"Ladies, for you look like ladies, this won't do. Come, sit down."

For the first time the ladies appeared to realize what they had done. Instantly both dropped into their seats, out came two little lace handkerchiefs, and in a second both were crying.

The only parallel to this in the North that has fallen under our observation is here in Philadelphia. The greatest rivalry exists between the Young America and Riverton clubs, our leading purely amateur organizations, composed of the best class of young citizens. The female friends and relatives of the gentleman players attend the games between them in large numbers, and share in the rivalry to such an extent that the Riverton ladies will not exchange courtesies with the Young America ladies and vice versa. The Young America ladies have rather the best of it though, as their heroes win the most games.

SUNDAY PLAYING IN CLEVELAND.

Sommers, the Catcher, Convicted—The Case to be Strongly Contested.

The case of J. A. Sommers, catcher of the Cleveland Club, who was arrested for playing ball last Sunday at Cleveland, O., was heard before a jury in the police court May 28. The court refused to admit any testimony outside the act of ball playing, and as it was admitted by the defendant the court charged the jury so strongly that after an hour's deliberation the jury returned a verdict of guilty. A motion for a new trial was filed on the principal ground that the court erred in its charge to the jury in failing to charge as requested and also in not allowing certain testimony to be introduced by the defendant. The club was represented by J. L. Athey, Mr. V. P. Kline being engaged in the Common Pleas Court. The motion for a new trial will be argued next Tuesday at nine o'clock. The defence set up by Mr. Athey was that the defendant was engaged in his usual avocation of a professional base ball player, and that section 7,032 and its amendment, under which he was arrested, did not apply, as he was engaged in common labor, to which section 7,033 applied. It was also adduced that base ball had been played on the flats for the past five years without interference, and that other amusements were permitted. The claim was made that the law was unconstitutional, because it made no exception in favor of those who conscientiously kept some other day of the week as their Sabbath. Proper exceptions were taken by defendant so as to raise the entire question as to the constitutionality of the law.

LO! THE POOR PLAYER.

The Hard Lot of the Men Who Toss the Ball for a Living.

The Buffalo *Commercial* man thus wittily portrays the ways of life of the average ball player:

"The base ball season has closed and about 200 professional ball tossers became gentlemen of leisure for the next six months. The professional ballist has a hard time. He rises every morning at 10 o'clock, takes a snug breakfast in the cafe, reads the Metropolitan newspapers, strolls out in the corridors and smokes a Reina Victoria, takes a nap before dinner, dines at 2 o'clock and strolls out to the ball field about 3 o'clock, takes a little exercise for a couple of hours, returns for supper, smokes again, and goes to the theatre in the evening with his girl and, of course, draws his salary—oh, the ball tosser never forgets that.

"And is he paid handsomely for working himself to death in this way? Yes, altogether too handsomely. His income, compared with that of others in the same stratum of society, is simply princely. The small boy worships him, the young girls dote on him, and his friends and neighbors look upon him as immense, perfectly elegant, the howlingest kind of a swell.

"Yes, the professional ballist has a tough time. Two hours a day for twenty-four days in a month and five months in a year this elegant creature has to play ball—something everybody knows is a great deal harder than ploughing or shoveling coal. It is, really, very hard to stand up on a beautiful grass lawn about one hour and watch for flies, or sit down on a bench for the other half of the game and admire others watching for flies. That's pretty tough. It saps a man's vitality, too, to stand up to the home plate three times a day and swing a base ball bat in the air in the vain hope of hitting something. That's positively fatigueing, not only to the striker, but to the people in the grand stand. And after all this work is done comes the most tiresome thing of all, taking a bath in the dressing-room. That's almost cruel. It breaks up the average ball tosser quicker than anything else—he's so unaccustomed to water.

"All in all, the life of a ballist is not a happy one. He's criticised by the newspapers and hissed at by the spectators in the grand stand. He's sensitive, very sensitive—men of refined natures are apt to be—and these things grate on him harshly. But for the next six months he will have nothing to do but heal his wounded heart and nurse his battered hands. And when next spring the robins nest again he will come out from his winter quarters fat and sleek, wholly satisfied with himself, having new spheres to conquer and other hearts to win."

PRESTO, CHANGE!

The Cincinnati Club Under a New Owner.

Sold to One of the Richest Men in the City of Pork.

Special to SPORTING LIFE:

CINCINNATI, O., Feb. 27.—The Cincinnati Base Ball Club has changed hands. John Hauch, the wealthiest brewer of Cincinnati and president of the German National Bank, now owns the entire club. He has put the entire business management into the hands of O. P. Caylor, and the policy of the club will be to elevate the tone of it and cater especially to the best classes.

O. P. C.

AMERICAN ASSOCIATION GAMES.

The Athletic, St. Louis and Cincinnati Clubs Winners—An Eleven Inning Tie Game.

Barring Atkisson's execution with the ball and Bradley's grand stop in the fourth inning there was absolutely nothing deserving of special mention in the Athletic-Metropolitan contest in this city Saturday, May 1. It was a closely played game, it is true, but the fielders had an easy task before them, as the batting was very light, five hits being the total of the eighteen innings. Atkisson's feat of retiring the visitors without a solitary hit to their credit was quite a difficult one, and he has the honor of being the first pitcher to make this record in any of the championship games thus far played. Roseman scored the first run of the game upon a base on balls, a pass by O'Brien and Coleman's missed fly at right field. Bradley's bad error in the ninth inning sent Orr to second base, and upon the outs of Hankinson and Brady he succeeded in reaching home. A base on balls, Stovey's wicked hit past short and Foster's terribly bad throw to first base sent two of the Athletics across the home plate in the third inning. Another, and what proved to be the winning run, was scored by Stovey in the sixth inning. He hit for two bases, and came home on Behel's missed fly at left. Score:

ATHLETIC.	AB.	R.	B.	P.	A.	E	METS.	AB.	R.	B.	P.	A.	E
Stovey,1b..	4	2	2	13	0	0	Behel, lf....	3	0	0	1	0	1
Larkin, lf..	3	0	1	2	0	0	Roseman, cf.	3	1	0	1	0	0
Coleman, rf.	4	0	0	1	0	1	Orr, 1b......	4	1	0	11	1	0
Shaffer,cf..	4	0	1	1	0	0	Hank'son,3b	4	0	0	1	1	0
O'Brien,c..	4	0	0	6	1	0	Brady, rf...	3	0	0	2	0	0
Milligan,3b.	4	0	1	2	4	0	M'La'lion,ss	4	0	0	1	1	0
Bauer,2b...	3	0	0	0	2	1	Foster, 2b...	3	0	0	2	4	1
Bradley,ss..	3	0	0	1	2	1	Holbert, c...	3	0	0	8	5	2
Atkisson,p..	3	1	0	1	0	0	Cushman,p.	3	0	0	3	0	0
Total.......	36	3	5	*26	10	3	Total......	30	2	0	*26	16	4

*Orr out, hit by batted ball.

†Larkin out for not touching third base.

Athletic........ 0 0 2 0 0 1 0 0 0—3

Metropolitan.. 1 0 0 0 0 0 0 0 1—2

Earned runs—Athletic 1. Stolen bases—Shaffer and Bradley. Two-base hits—Stovey and Larkin. First on errors—Athletic 4, Metropolitan 3. Left on bases—Athletic 2, Metropolitan 4. Struck out—Shaffer 2, Milligan 3, Bauer, Bradley 2 and Atkisson 2. Passed balls—O'Brien 4. Time—1:50. Umpire—Curtin.

Baltimore 6—Pittsburg 0.

PITTSBURG, PA., October 6.—The pitching of Kilroy to-day was the finest exhibition of ball-twirling seen here this season. The home team were completely at his mercy, and he shut them out without a single hit. Only three men reached first base during the game, and not one got as far as second. The visitors made their runs by bunching their hits, and errors of Shomberg and Smith. The attendance was the smallest of the year, not over three hundred people passing through the turnstile.

PITTSBURG.	R	1B	PO	A	E	BALTIMORE.	R	1B	PO	A	E
Brown, r.f...	0	0	3	0	0	Manning, r.f..	0	0	0	0	0
Mann, c.f....	0	0	2	1	0	Purcell, l.f.....	1	1	0	0	0
Shomberg,1b.	0	0	10	0	1	Sommers, 2b...	1	1	2	2	0
Coleman, l.f..	0	0	0	0	0	Souders, c.f....	1	1	1	0	0
Carroll, c....	0	0	1	2	0	Davis, 3b......	1	1	1	4	3
Barkley, 2b...	0	0	0	4	0	Scott, 1b......	1	0	10	0	1
Whitney, 3b..	0	0	0	4	1	Macullar, s.s...	0	0	2	3	0
Smith, s.s....	0	0	3	1	1	Dolan, c.......	1	1	1	1	0
Morris, p.....	0	0	1	0	1	Kilroy, p......	0	2	0	2	0
Totals.......	0	0	24	12	3	Totals.........	6	7	27	12	4

Innings...	1.	2.	3.	4.	5.	6.	7.	8.	9.	
Pittsburg	0	0	0	0	0	0	0	0	0	0
Baltimore	4	0	0	1	0	0	1	0	—	6

THE FLAG WON.

Chicago Retains the Base Ball Pennant.

The Bostons Beaten with Ease.

A Large Crowd Much Disappointed.

Ferguson's Pitching Twice Defeats the Detroits.

The New York Giants Finish the Race a Sorry Third.

Chicago Jubilant Over the Triumph of Its Favorites.

Kansas City Comes in Ahead of Washington.

LARKIN AGAIN IN TROUBLE.

He Monkeys With Loaded Pistols and is Placed in Jail.

Frank Larkin, the well-known ball player, is again in trouble, his murderous propensities having once more landed him behind the bars of a jail. This time the charge against him is attempting to shoot his late employer, James T. McAnany, a Brooklyn saloon-keeper. Larkin was McAnany's bartender, but was discharged recently. On Monday last Larkin went to McAnany's saloon under the influence of liquor and insisted upon fighting a duel with McAnany. He produced two loaded pistols and insisted upon McAnany's taking one and fighting a duel then and there. McAnany tried to reason with Larkin, but the latter stubbornly refused to listen to anything else but about the duel. Finally, being afraid that Larkin would murder him, McAnany took one of the revolvers and started for a corner. When he reached a door he slid out, locking Larkin in. He hailed an officer who arrested Larkin. He was arraigned the next morning before Justice Naeher. To him Larkin said he only wanted a square fight. The other fellow did not run any more risk than he did. Larkin's examination was adjourned for a week, so that he could get the liquor out of him.

ST. LOUIS WINS.

The Browns Champions of the World.

The Chicago League Team Defeated by St. Louis by Four Games to Two.

CHICAGO.	AB.	R.	B.	P.	A.	E	ST. LOUIS.	AB	R	B.	P.	A.	E
Gore, cf......	5	0	2	0	0		Latham, 3b..	4	0	1	2	0	
Kelly, c......	5	0	0	9	2	0	Caruthers, p	4	0	0	2	0	0
Anson, 1b....	4	0	0	13	0	0	O'Neill, lf...	3	0	1	5	0	0
Pfeffer, 2b...	4	3	2	0	1	0	Gleason, ss..	4	0	0	3	0	
Williamson, ss	4	0	0	2	1		Comiskey,1b	4	0	1	7	0	1
Burns, 3b....	4	0	2	1	5	1	Welch, cf...	4	2	1	5	0	0
Ryan, rf.....	4	0	1	3	1	0	Foutz, rf...	4	1	0	3	0	1
Dalrymple, lf	4	0	1	0	0	0	Robinson, 2b	4	0	0	1	3	1
Clarkson, p..	3	0	0	0	2	0	Bushong, c..	2	1	0	6	0	0
Total.....	38	3	6	28	13	2	Total.....	33	4	4	30	3	3

Chicago.............. 0 1 0 1 0 1 0 0 0—3

St. Louis............ 0 0 0 0 0 0 0 3 1—4

Earned runs—Chicago 2, St. Louis 2. Two-base hit—Burns. Three-base hits—Latham, O'Neill. Home run—Pfeffer. First on balls—Off Clarkson 1, off Caruthers 2. Struck out—By Clarkson 9, by Caruthers 4. Passed ball—Bushong. Wild pitches—Clarkson 1, Caruthers 1. Time—2:15. Umpire—Grace Pierce.

PLAYING RULES.

But few changes were made in the playing rules.

The proposed rule of giving a batsman his base as a penalty when hit by the pitcher was vigorously discussed, but it was not carried through.

Rule 5 was amended to give the pitcher an extra foot of space in his box, which in the future will be 7 feet by 4 feet instead of 6 feet by 4 feet.

Rule 70 was amended so that in the future credit will be given in the summary for stolen bases, and battery errors will also appear in the summary instead of the tabulated account.

JAMES HALL, who died recently of consumption in Brooklyn, N. Y., was at one time the short stop of the Atlantics, having filled that position in 1871 and 1872. He was a younger brother of George Hall, well known from his connection with the Atlantic, Boston, Athletic and Louisville clubs.

IN TROUBLE.

Well-known Base Ball Players Charged with Theft.

RICHMOND, Ind., Dec. 30.—Some time last summer two pairs of pantaloons, belonging to John Hart, who is the cutter at Simon Fox's tailoring establishment, were stolen from his room at the Grand Hotel. Friday morning Officer Chrisman discovered George Rhue, the ball player, wearing a pair of the garments, which Rhue said he had bought from Harry Smith when they were both members of the Henleys. Smith's room was next to Hart's at the hotel, and Mr. Hart believes Smith nipped the property, as he is accused also of taking a pair of base ball shoes from Shorty Barnes' room and selling them to Mitchell, the pitcher of the Sandusky team, when it was here last summer. Rhue left the city Saturday for Columbus, O., where he intended to visit before going to Atlanta, Ga., where he plays next season. Saturday night Kate Rader, a member of the demi-monde, followed Rhue to Columbus and compelled him to give back a gold watch he took with him. Since this affair the officers believe now that Smith is innocent and that Rhue is the party who nipped the trousers, and will endeavor to have him brought back on a charge of larceny.

SOLVED AT LAST.

Play by Electric Light Possible.

The Scheme to be Again Tried at Staten Island—Difficulties Overcome.

The scheme of having electric lights on the St. George Grounds at Staten Island, to admit of playing ball at night, was supposed to have long since been abandoned. Such, however, appears not to be the case. Mr. Johnson, of New York, president of the Edison Electric Light Company, in a conversation last Wednesday, stated that the reason of failure so far to provide an artificial light capable of meeting all the requirements of ball playing was because all efforts in that direction had been based on the idea of placing the illuminants at a great height above the field and throwing the original rays directly on it, thus either blinding the players by the glare, or casting shadows, either of which make it impracticable. Mr. Johnson visited the Staten Island grounds with Mr. Wiman and his family and was struck with phenomena which induced him to conduct some experiments with the illuminated fountain, which he claims has solved the problem to his satisfaction, so much so that he is entirely confident of ultimate success and thoroughly believes that base ball by electric light will eventually be an accomplished fact at Staten Island. The lights illuminating the fountain are placed below or beneath the column of water. At Mr. Johnson's request the lights were turned on while the fountain was not in play, and procuring an old, soiled ball he had it thrown many times through the column of light. The effect was marvelous. The ball glistened "like a meteor" and was for that reason more distinct than is usual in the natural light. With the initial idea engrafted in his mind by this experiment, and elaborating and developing it by others, he at last unfolded his plans to Mr. Edison, who, after careful consideration, pronounced them feasible. The rough outline of the plan is this: Mr. Johnson proposes to line the *outside* of the diamond, foul lines and extremes of the outfields with electric lights placed *beneath the ground* and projecting, by means of powerful reflectors, the rays upward through covering-plates of corrugated glass. The lights themselves are to be so arranged that no direct rays will shine in the eyes of the players. From the success of additional experiments he expects a softer light to be deflected downward by atmospheric influences illuminating the surface of the diamond and field with the brilliancy of the noonday sun, minus the glare of the original direct rays of the artificial light, and also minus those optical illusions called in the player's vernacular "high sky," etc., etc. Before undertaking the work at Staten Island Mr. Johnson proposes to make a practical demonstration on a smaller scale by illuminating in the same manner the tennis ground at his country place.

Undoubtedly base ball people and others will be inclined to pronounce the accomplishment of this scheme impossible, but in the light of the annihilation of "impossibilities" in our century, and calling to memory those wonders of modern times—the phonograph, the telephone, the electric railway, which is in practical operation in Baltimore; the telegraph, etc., etc.—it would be no more than the part of wisdom to withhold the expression of a positive opinion at the present time.   T. T. T.

UNENVIABLE NOTORIETY.

A Couple of St. Louis Ball Tossers in Trouble About Women.

Several of the St. Louis Browns are in trouble with the fair sex. King's trouble was briefly alluded to in a special despatch in our last issue. It appears that a seduction suit has been brought against him by Emma Goldenlogen, a comely German girl. She stated that she became acquainted with him in 1883. After he had been calling on her a couple of years he seduced her, she alleges, under promise of marriage. A child was born, but he did not keep his promise to marry her, alleging that he was not in proper circumstances to do so, but would fulfill his pledge as soon as he could. Last year he told her he was in better financial circumstances and would marry her. Under this promise she accompanied him to St. Joe, where she lived with him as his wife while he was playing ball there. She is now about to become the mother of another child, and she says that he seems to have taken a fancy to another girl, and has no intention of keeping his pledge to her. In her statement she also said that King now receives $250 per month, and is fully capable of supporting her.

Latham is also in trouble. A year ago he obtained a divorce from his Massachusetts wife and married a handsome St. Louis girl. For a time all went well, but lately a coolness has existed between the couple which ended in separation. Last Saturday Mrs. Latham No. 2 swore out a warrant against him for assault and battery at St. Louis on May 28. The gallant third baseman ran away from the constable to East St. Louis, where he waited for the train which took the Browns East, and joined his team two hours after the chase. This helped him out of the scrape temporarily, but what will he do when he must return to the Mound City with his team?

THE COLORED LEAGUES.

Games Played to Date—One Club Already Financially Distressed.

The championship season of the Colored League is now in progress and quite a number of games have been played, results of which will be found below. It augurs ill for the success of the League that one club should already be in such serious financial trouble as to be unable to meet scheduled engagements. The Resolutes, of Boston, after playing one championship game were last week stranded at Louisville and unable to get to Pittsburg to play there May 10. The game was postponed and the club assigned to the city within easiest reach from Louisville—Baltimore—but it failed to connect there also for the game with the Lord Baltimores on the 11th.

THE LEAGUE UMPIRES.

Some Slight Modification in the System Probable Next Season.

A Washington correspondent quotes President Nick Young as saying that at the next meeting of the League a proposition will be made to improve the umpire system. At present the League staff are paid $1,000 and actual traveling expenses. The numerous changes in the personnel of the staff during the present season has occasioned much trouble and unnecessary expense. The only solution of this problem seems to be to increase the salaries of umpires to $1,500 per season with traveling expenses and appoint only men who can command the respect of players and public. A superior class of men can be secured at this increased figure, who will be retained throughout the season, regardless of protests from managers, unless it can be proven that they are totally incapacitated to remain on the staff. Five instead of four men will compose the staff, and while the odd man is laying off he will only be paid at the rate of $1,000. Whenever an umpire is injured or deserves a short vacation, the fifth man slips into harness at a full rate of compensation.

The Noted Alexander J. McKinnon Joins the Great Majority.

Alex. J. McKinnon, who was well-known as the first baseman of the Pittsburg Club, died of typhoid fever July 24, at Charleston, Mass. His last game was played in Philadelphia on the morning July 4. He complained of not feeling well that night, and on the next day he was reluctantly compelled to give up and start for home. He was there carefully nursed by his wife and his mother, and it was not thought the illness would prove serious; but he gradually sank until July 24, when he died. McKinnon was born Aug. 14, 1856, in Boston, Mass., and commenced his career on the diamond in 1875, when he was first baseman of the Stars, an amateur club of his native city, which also included in its ranks Morrill, now of the Bostons, Charley Foley, Lew Brown and John L. Sullivan, the champion knocker-out.

WHAT THEY WANT.

Members of the Brotherhood Ventilating Their Grievances.

Burdock, of the Boston Club, was interviewed last week, and he had this to say about what the Brotherhood intended to do:—"The players as yet are not sufficiently organized to fight the National League. It will take time to get them in a position in which they can insist upon their rights. But the day is near at hand when they will be in that position. We are satisfied with the reserve rule and the salaries paid, but we are not at all satisfied with the form of contract now in use by the managers. No player who is a member of the Brotherhood of Base Ball Players will ever again sign that contract. We must and will have a new form. The present contract won't stand law. It is too one-sided and gives the player no show. As soon as a man signs it he binds himself for life to a club and becomes a mere chattel so long as he depends upon base ball as a means of livelihood. The managers can do with him as they please. If they don't want him to play ball he can't, and must remain idle forever. The manifest injustice of this appears when it is understood that in such an event he does not receive a salary. The managers of a club can lay a player off without pay and even, under the present ironclad contracts, prevent him from signing with another club that might be glad to avail itself of his services. That means that they have it in their power to take the bread and butter out of our families' mouths."

Arthur Irwin, of the Philadelphia Club, in talking about the Brotherhood and its objects, said just before leaving for California:—"The League doesn't seem to want to give us any privileges whatever. We have proposed to join hands with the managers and help to elevate base ball, and what we ask in return is very reasonable. We ask that a man who has fulfilled his contract with a club for a term of years shall be at liberty to make another contract where and with whom he sees fit, and without restraint; that it shall not be in the power of any club to say to a man: We are going to release you to such and such a club, and you will play there or nowhere."

A WARNING.

A New Evil That Threatens Base Ball.

Illegality of the New Fashion of "Loaning" Ball Players.

It is surmised that one of the principal objects of the special meeting of the American Association was to take some action in regard to the new fashion creeping in of clubs loaning strong players, who cannot be conveniently used, to clubs of outside organizations, to the detriment of weaker fellow clubs. The Detroit League Club started the ball by loaning several players to Kansas City; the Cincinnati American Association Club followed suit by temporarily transferring Kappel to Memphis, and as we write we learn that Indianapolis has also joined by loaning Quinn to Duluth. The Athletic, Cleveland, Metropolitan and Brooklyn Association Clubs are bitterly opposed to this innovation and there is reason to believe that the League clubs also look with disfavor upon Detroit's action.

RESULTS.

The most important meeting, in its present and possible future effects, ever held by the National League, is now a matter of history. It was a stormy gathering and at one time a rupture between League and players seemed inevitable. But happily all the dangers were overcome and the meeting adjourned with its internal affairs in good shape, with a circuit undisturbed, a settlement of the financial question satisfactory to nearly all, and with a clear understanding with its players. Some wounds have doubtless been given and received, but time will probably heal them. The recognition of the Brotherhood was the event of the meeting. It added a new factor to League base ball, and the League is no longer supreme in direction, now that its employees have been given a voice in the disposition of affairs. But the new factor has begun its work wisely and well, and the reforms advocated and insisted upon by it are all in the line of the steady march of the national game to a higher plane. The officials of the players' organization have cleared away all the misapprehension concerning it, silenced misrepresentation, and have solved doubt as to its motives into admiration for its prudence and conservatism.

THE WORLD'S SERIES.

Detroit Wins the World's Championship From the St. Louis Club.

The Detroit Club enjoyed another week of almost uninterrupted successes over the holders of the world's championship, and on Friday gained the game that wrested the proud title from the St. Louis Browns. The series, however will be finished, weather permitting. The clubs will play at Detroit, Monday, Oct. 24; Chicago or Louisville, Tuesday, Oct. 25; and St. Louis, Oct. 26. This will wind up the scheduled series. Three more exhibition game will, however be played—two at Kansas City, Oct. 27 and 28, and one at St. Louis, Oct. 29. The great series has been a most pronounced success financially, and in a playing sense, and there is no room for dissatisfaction in any particular, the management having been excellent. The clubs have so far been singularly lucky as regards weather, but one postponement having occured. To this good fortune the financial success of the series may be largely attributed. The Detroits have outplayed the Browns at all points and are fairly entitled to all the credit of their achievements without quibble. They deserved to win, because they played the best ball. The record of the games is herewith continued:

INDIVIDUAL BATTING AVERAGES.

O'Neil, of St. Louis, is the premier batsman of the Association, with the highest average ever reached in the League or Association. It is worthy of note that neither Cincinnati, the second club, nor the tail-ender, Cleveland, have a representative in the first dozen of sluggers. Fennelly, who leads the Cincinnati batsmen, is fifteenth, and Cleveland's best man, Hotaling, is sixteenth.

Rank.		Games.	B.H.	S.B.	Ave.
1—O'Neill	St. Louis	123	277	30	.492
2—Browning	Louisville	134	281	121	.471
3—Lyons	Athletic	137	284	118	.469
4—Caruthers	St. Louis	98	195	59	.459
5—Robinson	St. Louis	124	220	81	.426
6—Mack	Louisville	128	227	28	.410
7—Radford	Metropolitan	128	232	85	.404
8—Orr	Metropolitan	85	147	19	.403
9—Stovey	Athletic	124	219	143	.402
10—Burns	Baltimore	140	245	57	.401
11—Burch	Brooklyn	48	86	20	.400
12—Foutz	St. Louis	103	176	21	.393
13—Hogan	Metropolitan	32	55	10	.377
14 { Larkin	Athletic	125	201	33	.374
{ Hecker	Louisville	91	153	49	.374
15 { Fennelly	Cincinnati	134	223	74	.368
{ Fulmer	Baltimore	56	85	38	.368
{ Griffin	Baltimore	136	214	98	.368

Trouble About Several Players.

A despatch from New Orleans on Wednesday stated that several members of the New York combination were very much intoxicated when they played the New Orleans team on Monday. Kelly, Ewing and Denny were particularized as the offending players and a number of friends of these three who attended the game were in the same condition. Their conduct was disgraceful, and Secretary Kaufman called upon a police officer to eject them from the grounds. When the officer attempted to arrest them Mike Kelly tried to prevent the arrest, but no attention was paid to him. Captain Ward took his wife from the grounds, and, placing her in a carriage, sent her to the St. Charles Hotel, because of the disgraceful exhibition of some of the spectators and players. It was also stated that the club would probably disband instead of going to 'Frisco.

CASEY AT THE BAT.

A Ballad of the Republic, Sung in the Year 1888.

The outlook wasn't brilliant for the Mudville nine that day:
The score stood four to two with but one inning more to play.
And then when Cooney died at first, and Barrows did the same,
A sickly silence fell upon the patrons of the game.

A straggling few got up to go in deep despair. The rest
Clung to that hope which springs eternal in the human breast;
They thought if only Casey could but get a whack at that—
We'd put up even money now with Casey at the bat.

But Flynn preceded Casey, as did also Jimmy Blake,
And the former was a lulu and the latter was a cake;
So upon that stricken multitude grim melancholy sat,
For there seemed but little chance of Casey's getting to the bat.

But Flynn let drive a single, to the wonderment of all,
And Blake, the much despis-ed, tore the cover off the ball;
And when the dust had lifted, and the men saw what had occurred,
There was Johnnie safe at second and Flynn a-hugging third.

Then from 5,000 throats and more there rose a lusty yell;
It rumbled through the valley, it rattled in the dell;
It knocked upon the mountain and recoiled upon the flat,
For Casey, mighty Casey, was advancing to the bat.

There was ease in Casey's manner as he stepped into his place;
There was pride in Casey's bearing and a smile on Casey's face.
And when, responding to the cheers, he lightly doffed his hat,
No stranger in the crowd could doubt 'twas Casey at the bat.

Ten thousand eyes were on him as he rubbed his hands with dirt;
Five thousand tongues applauded when he wiped them on his shirt.
Then while the writhing pitcher ground the ball into his hip,
Defiance gleamed in Casey's eye, a sneer curled Casey's lip.

And now the leather-covered sphere came hurtling through the air,
And Casey stood a-watching it in haughty grandeur there.
Close by the sturdy batsman the ball unheeded sped—
"That ain't my style," said Casey. "Strike one," the umpire said.

From the benches, black with people, there went up a muffled roar,
Like the beating of the storm-waves on a stern and distant shore.
"Kill him! Kill the umpire!" shouted some one on the stand;
And it's likely they'd have killed him had not Casey raised his hand.

With a smile of Christian charity great Casey's visage shone;
He stilled the rising tumult; he bade the game go on;
He signaled to the pitcher, and once more the spheroid flew;
But Casey still ignored it, and the umpire said, "Strike two."

"Fraud!" cried the maddened thousands, and echo answered fraud;
But one scornful look from Casey and the audience was awed.
They saw his face grow stern and cold, they saw his muscles strain,
And they knew that Casey wouldn't let that ball go by again.

The sneer is gone from Casey's lip, his teeth are clinched in hate;
He pounds with cruel violence his bat upon the plate.
And now the pitcher holds the ball, and now he lets it go,
And now the air is shattered by the force of Casey's blow.

Oh, somewhere in this favored land the sun is shining bright;
The band is playing somewhere, and somewhere hearts are light,
And somewhere men are laughing, and somewhere children shout;
But there is no joy in Mudville—mighty Casey has struck out.

—PHIN.

CHICAGO BEATS NEW-YORK

THE GIANTS COULD ONLY SCORE IN TWO INNINGS.

OVER TEN THOUSAND PERSONS WITNESS THE VICTORY OF CHICAGO—KEEFE'S FIRST DEFEAT IN 20 GAMES.

After pitching successfully in 19 straight games Keefe finally lost yesterday to the Chicago Club. In justice to Keefe, however, it is only fair to state that the defeat was not due to any poor work on his part. He pitched the ball with his accustomed skill, but the contest was lost by poor work in the field. Shortly before the game began Short Stop Ward said that he was sick and unable to play, and his place was taken by Hatfield. Of course the latter did not have the necessary practice and could not be expected to handle the ball as skillfully as the regular short stop. He made two errors at critical points of the game which gave the Chicago Club two runs and the game. Poor Hatfield was roundly hissed, the spectators forgetting, perhaps, that he has not had enough practice to fill the position as it ought to be filled.

There were 10,200 persons on the grounds, and the defeat was anything but pleasant to them. They looked at the efforts of the Giants to win, cheered and tried to urge them on, waited and hoped, but with no success, and left the grounds in an unhappy frame of mind. Col. McCaull, De Wolf Hopper, Mathilde Cottrelly, Marion Manola, and about 30 members of the McCaull Opera Company were eye witnesses of the defeat of the Giants. They came to the grounds in large tally-ho coaches, and kept cheering the New-Yorks from start to finish. De Wolf Hopper was exasperated. If comedians could weep he certainly would have done so. Miss Cottrelly thought it was too real mean, and Miss Manola regarded it as the height of impoliteness on the part of Mr. Anson and his men to take a game from the Giants, especially when the latter were at home and in the bosom of their families. Some blamed the defeat to the umpire, others to the poor batting of the Giants at opportune moments, but it was neither. The Chicago men outplayed the local club and fairly won the game. Their fielding when men were on bases was perfect. Krock's pitching was hit hard, but sharp work and good judgment, combined with a vigorous use of the legs, kept down the base-hit column and prevented several of the Giants from crossing the scoring goal.

For three innings both sides failed to score, although the New-Yorks by poor base running on the part of Richardson sacrificed a chance in the first inning. He foolishly allowed himself to be caught off third base. In the fourth inning the Chicago men went to the front. Anson started off with a safe hit to short centre. Then Pfeffer, usually a right field hitter, sent the ball along the left-field foul line for two bases, and the big Captain came home. A ground ball to Connor by Williamson advanced Pfeffer to third, and he came in on Burns's hit to right field for two bases. Flint struck out and Krock ended the inning by sending a bounder to Hatfield. New-York started to score in the fifth. After Slattery and Whitney had gone out Keefe hit over Van Haltren's head for two bases. He finished the circuit of the bases on Ewing's timely hit to left field. Ewing ran down to second, but remained there, as Richardson fouled out to Burns. Chicago increased the lead in the fifth inning. Ryan hit a bounder, which Whitney fumbled. Not to be outdone by his side partner, Hatfield allowed Van Haltren's ball to bound through his hands, whereas if he had stopped it a double play would have been the result. At that juncture Keefe took part in the error-making. In trying to catch Ryan napping at second base, he threw wide to Richardson, and the two runners each moved up a base. Duffy hit to Hatfield, who threw wildly to the plate. Ryan came in and Van Haltren ran down to third. He scored on Anson's difficult grounder to Richardson. Pfeffer flew out to Tiernan, Williamson struck out, and the score was 4 to 1 in Chicago's favor.

After Hatfield had fouled out in the sixth inning Tiernan sent a thrill of joy to the hearts of the spectators. He hit a ball with all his might; it sailed over the head of Duffy, and landed over the picket fence in right field. Before it could be recovered the fleet base runner had cleared the bases, and the score was 4 to 2. With the Giants' characteristic luck nobody was on base when this hit was made. Chicago tried hard to increase the lead in the seventh inning, but failed. Ryan made a two-base hit, and Van Haltren a single, but both were thrown out at the plate by Whitney. After putting out Van Haltren, Ewing threw to first base like a rifle shot. The ball got there ahead of the batter thus completing one of the prettiest double plays seen here this season. From this point both sides tried hard to score, but their efforts were useless. As a result the Chicago men won by two runs. Appended is the score:

NEW-YORK.	R.	1B.	PO.	A.	E.	CHICAGO.	R.	1B.	PO.	A.	E.
Ewing, c.	0	2	8	4	1	Ryan, c. f.	1	2	3	0	0
Rich'son, 2b.	0	1	0	2	0	V'nH'l'n, lf.	1	1	2	0	0
Hatfield, s.s.	0	0	0	3	2	Duffy, r. f.	0	0	1	1	0
Tiernan, r. f.	1	1	3	0	0	Anson, 1b.	1	1	13	1	0
Connor, 1b.	0	0	10	0	0	Pfeffer, 2b.	1	1	0	3	2
O'Rourke, lf.	0	1	1	0	0	Willms'n, s.s.	0	0	0	1	0
Slattery, c. f.	0	0	1	0	0	Burns, 3b.	0	1	2	4	1
Whitney, 3b.	0	0	0	2	1	Flint, c.	0	0	6	1	1
Keefe, p.	1	2	1	9	2	Krock, p.	0	1	0	3	0
Total	2	7	24	20	6	Total	4	7	27	14	4

RUNS SCORED EACH INNING.

New-York	0	0	0	0	1	1	0	0	0—2
Chicago	0	0	0	2	2	0	0	0	..—4

Earned runs—New York, 2; Chicago, 2. First base on errors—New York, 2; Chicago, 5. Left on bases—New York, 6; Chicago, 7. First base on balls—Connor, 1; Van Haltren, 1. Stolen bases—Tiernan, 1; Van Haltren, 1; Krock, 1. Struck out—Ryan, 1; Duffy, 2; Williamson, 2; Burns, 1; Flint, 2; O'Rourke, 1. Home run—Tiernan. Two-base hits—Richardson, 1; Keefe, 1; Pfeffer, 1; Burns, 1. Double plays—Duffy and Anson; Whitney, Ewing, and Connor. Passed balls—Ewing, 1. Umpire—Mr. Lynch. Time of game—Two hours and fifteen minutes.

A COMING ROW

Over "the $2,000 Salary Limit" Rule

Special to SPORTING LIFE.

CLEVELAND, April 21.—It can be announced that a war is brewing between the Brotherhood of Ball Players and the National League. The cause for action is the existence of the $2,000 limit clause. Until a few weeks ago, on assurances from the League that its members on the Board of Arbitration had honestly tried to secure its repeal, but had been blocked by the American Association members of the Board, the Brotherhood believed that the League had acted in good faith. It now suspects that the League did not *honestly* try to secure the repeal of the obnoxious clause, and it suspects aright. Consequently there is a collection of facts going on, and a row will follow the discovery that the diplomacy of the League was so deftly used to nullify the concessions to the Brotherhood.

F. H. BRUNELL.

THE WOLRD'S SERIES.

The Final Game—Averages of the Contestants—News Incidents and Gossip.

The tenth and last game of the series was played at St. Louis Oct. 27, and was really a farce. As the Giants had already settled the question of supremacy and many of the players gone home, they had an unique team in the field, as the score will show. There was no real significance in the game and the players showed it in their work. Titcomb pitched for four innings and then Hatfield finished the burlesque. A detailed account of the game would be wearisome and useless. The St. Louis Browns had everything their own way and won the game with the utmost ease, through the assistance of errors, as of the eighteen runs they scored only six were earned, while the New Yorks earned the seven they scored. Only about two hundred people witnessed the game. Score:

ST. LOUIS.	AB.	R.	B.	P.	A.	E.	NEW YORK.	AB.	R.	B.	P.	A.	E.
Latham, 3b, p.	6	3	4	0	2	0	Tiernan, rf.	4	1	2	2	0	1
Robinson, 2b	5	1	2	6	2	0	O'Rourke, ss	5	0	1	1	4	0
O'Neil, lf.	5	3	3	3	0	1	Gore, 3b.	2	2	2	1	1	2
Comiskey, 1b	5	1	1	10	1	0	George, 1b.	4	2	2	10	1	2
McCarthy, rf	6	3	2	2	0	0	Slatte'y, cf, 2b	4	0	1	4	3	1
Boyle, cf.	6	2	2	2	0	0	Whitney, lf.	4	0	2	1	0	0
White, ss.	4	1	2	1	4	2	Hatfield, 2b, p	3	1	1	2	4	1
Milligan, c.	3	2	1	3	3	0	Murphy, c.	4	0	0	4	1	1
Chamber'n, p	3	2	0	0	1	0	Titcomb, p, rf	4	1	2	1	5	0
Total	43	18	17	27	13	3	Total	34	7	13	*26	19	8

*Robinson declared out.

St. Louis	0	1	0	5	0	5	4	2	1—18
New York	3	1	0	0	0	0	0	2	1—7

Earned runs—St. Louis 10, New York 7. First on errors—St. Louis 4, New York 1. First on balls—Robinson, O'Neil, Milligan 2, Chamberlain 2; Tiernan, Gore 2, Hatfield. Stolen bases—Latham 2, Tiernan, Gore, Whitney. Struck out—Latham 2, Robinson, O'Neil, George. Home run—McCarty, O'Neil, George. Two-base hits—Gore, Titcomb. Double plays—Comiskey, Robinson; White, Robinson, Comiskey; Milligan, Comiskey. Hit by pitcher—Comiskey. Wild pitches—Titcomb 1, Hatfield 2, Chamberlain 1. Umpire—Gaffney. Time—2h.

THE GREAT TRIP.

Playing Base Ball on Historic Ground.

A Contest Under the Shadows of the Pyramids—The Palestine Trip Abandoned.

[COPYRIGHTED]

CAIRO, Egypt, Feb. 9.—The great American game was played to-day for the first time on the burning plains of Egypt, under the gaze of the same forty centuries which looked down upon Napoleon. The Spalding party arrived at Suez Thursday, debarked from the Salier and came directly to Cairo, where they arrived in the evening. It was impossible to arrange for a game yesterday, but this morning at 10 o'clock the whole party drew up in front of the Hotel d'Orient, the Chicagos mounted on donkeys, the Americus on camels and the ladies in carriages, and in this order started through the town led by Ward and Anson. The cavalcade proceeded directly over the Bridge Kasielnil and along the Nile to the village of Ghizeh, through a double line of shouting and wondering natives, who were quite unable to make the affair out.

A NEW HOME.

Special to SPORTING LIFE.

NEW YORK, April 27.—While the Giants are satisfied to rally around their pennant flags at St. George this summer, the players don't seem to like the idea of making St. George their permanent home. I don't think the team will stay there, in spite of Mr. Day's assertion that in case he likes the place that he "may conclude to make Staten Island the permanent home grounds of the Giants." I am informed on good authority that the future home grounds of the New York Club will be embraced in the territory bounded by One Hundred and Forty-fifth and One Hundred and Forty-seventh streets and Seventh and Lenox avenues. The grounds are now being filled in, and will be ready for next season's games, I think. Much of the place is marshy, and not only has to be filled in, but innumerable pile drivers will be kept at work for several weeks yet. Standing at the corner of One Hundred and Forty-seventh street and Seventh avenue yesterday, I noticed the work going on, and wondered what it was all about. The contractor approached, and I asked him. "Why, that is the future home ground of the Giants," said he. "The grand stand will be built in that corner where the men are sinking so many piles into the soft earth. They propose to put up a monster grand stand there, and they want a solid foundation for it. You don't believe it, do you? Well, I will bet you $100 to $25 that the Giants play right here next year." I did not take the bet. The man seemed to know what he was talking about. The contractor also told me the reason why the New York Club did not purchase the Lynch property at One Hundred and Fifty-seventh street and Eighth avenue. "That is low, marshy ground," said he, "and in case the company wanted to sell it for building purposes in a few years they would find they had a white elephant on their hands. That is the reason that a few weeks ago Mr. Day advertised for some persons to purchase that property, agreeing to pay $6000 a year rental for a five or ten years' lease." STACKHOUSE.

League Umpires No Longer to Stand Within the Diamond.

WASHINGTON, D. C., May 31.—Editor SPORTING LIFE:—Among the communications received at League headquarters during the past week was a vigorous protest from Col. John I. Rogers against umpires going behind the pitcher or standing elsewhere within the diamond to judge plays at the plate.

President Young says there is much wisdom in the above suggestions and he has accordingly instructed the various League umpires to render their decisions from behind the plate and move around in the vicinity of the bases when base plays are being made. R. M. LARNER.

ANOTHER PITTSBURG TALE.

A Story Which Bears Improbability Upon Its Face.

The Pittsburg Times last week gave space to the following pleasing little tale:—"The League officials will be startled to learn that a strike was thought of by the Brotherhood on July 4, and only failed because of a lack of unity among the members of the body named.

A CHANGE FOR THE BETTER.

There is batting galore under the new four-ball rule, and the public is, of course, duly pleased. The new rule also brings relief from that perennial nuisance, the countless pitching phenomenons which arrive each season and flourish for a brief time. Pitching wonders will be as few and far between this season as angel visits, and the regular, steady-going pitchers who lay no claim to extraordinary merits, but pitch with stout hearts, cool heads and steady arms will have the call. No pitcher, however great his merits, need expect to go through this season without an occasional lively pounding. The one regrettable drawback to the present pleasing state of affairs is the increase in the number of bases on balls, which would have been obviated had the pitching distance been increased. In the League, for instance, up to last Saturday, in the thirty-five games played 246 men were given their bases on balls and 685 base hits were made, while in the first thirty-five games of last season under the five-ball rule only 140 bases on balls were given and 602 base hits were made. This leaves 106 more bases on balls and eighty-three more base hits under the present four-ball rule than under the old five-ball rule. Still, even bases on balls are far preferable to the old pitchers' strike-out games, as they at least put men on bases, thus giving increased chances for runs or plays and adding vastly to the life and movement of the games.

League Standing.

The long, hard fight is over and New York retains the much-coveted bunting. The last week has been the most exciting of the season. Boston held the lead at one time, but lost it the day the captain saw fit to render himself unfit to lead his men at the most critical part of the season. Both leaders are deserving of credit for the way in which they contested every foot of ground. Chicago made a spurt at the last moment and beat the Phillies for third place. On the last day too, Pittsburg was true to the part she was playing in the struggle, and by beating Boston for but the third time this year, deprived the Hub nine of all show for the pennant and at the same time jumped ahead of Cleveland into fifth place. These were the only changes of the week.

CLUBS.	New York.	Boston.	Chicago.	Philadelphia.	Pittsburg.	Cleveland.	Indianapolis.	Washington.	Games won.	Per Cent. Won.
New York...	0	6	13	12	14	13	13	13	83	.650
Boston......	8	0	10	13	16	12	10	14	83	.648
Chicago......	5	7	0	9	10	11	13	12	67	.503
Philadelphia.	7	6	10	0	9	13	9	63		.496
Pittsburg...	7	3	9	9	0	13	10	10	61	.462
Cleveland...	4	8	9	10	7	9	14	61		.474
Indianapolis.	7	10	7	4	10	10	0	11	59	.440
Washington..	5	5	7	7	1	7	0	41		.329
Games lost...	43	45	65	64	71	72	75	83		....

CLUBS AND PITCHERS.	Boston.		N. Y.		Phila.		Chicago		Cleve.		Pittsb'g		Ind.		Wash.		Total.	
	Won.	Lost.	Won.	Lost.	Won.	Lost.	Won.	Lost.	Won.	Lost.	Won.	Lost.	Won.	Lost.	Won.	Lost.	Won.	Lost.
BOSTON:																		
Clarkson............	..	..	8	9	13	6	10	7	12	5	16	3	10	10	14	5	83	45
Radbourn...........	..	..	6	1	3	2	1	4	2	5	10	1	4	6	8	2	50	19
Madden.............	..	..	2	2	4	1	2	4	0	1	1	3	1	..	9	1	19	11
Daley..............	..	..	..	..	..	..	1	0	1	1	3	0	1	0	2	0	9	3
Sowders............	..	..	..	..	0	1	1	0	..	..	2	0	1	0	..	..	3	2

Baltimore Resigns From the Association and Leaves It Without a Quorum.

Special to SPORTING LIFE.

BALTIMORE, Nov. 30.—The withdrawal of the Syracuse Club from its proposed entrance to the American Association was supplemented to-day by the resignation of the Baltimore Club. The owners of the Baltimore and Washington clubs did not come to terms during the week after all, and at the hour of going to press the deal appeared to be entirely off. Mr. Hewitt wanted far more cash for his mere franchise than Mr. Vonderhorst considered it worth, in view of the fact that Hewitt could not guarantee to deliver any of the old players. The other proposition, a combining of the two franchises, also fell through, owing to disagreement over minor details. Whether the deal will be resumed is not known, but whether it is or not the Baltimore Club is done with the Association forever, and if nothing better presents itself and no deal with the Brotherhood can be made, it will enter the Atlantic Association.

EVENTS OF MOMENT

A Week of Surprising Moves and Changes.

A DEATH-BLOW TO THE ASSOCIATION.

Cincinnati and Brooklyn Jump to the League.

THE LEAGUE MADE A TEN-CLUB BODY.

LEAGUE POLICY.

No Quarter For Brotherhood Leaders If Their Movement Should Fail.

PITTSBURG, Dec. 11.—The plan of the National League clubs in dealing with players seems to be an assumption of indifference until the time for action arrives. With it all there is a growing feeling of hostility toward the Brotherhood leaders on the part of the magnates that bodes no good to the former in case the players are compelled to return to their old employers.

THE GRAND STAND OF THE BROOKLYN PLAYERS' LEAGUE CLUB.

W. R. HAMILTON,

Champion Base-Runner of the American Association in 1889.

The above is a splendid likeness of W. R. Hamilton, the champion base-runner of 1889. Mr. Hamilton was born in Newark, N. J., in 1866, and is therefore 24 years of age. His first engagement as a professional ball player was with the Waterbury Club, of Waterbury, Conn., in 1887. In 1888 he commenced the season with the Worcester, Mass., Club, and remained with it until August, when Kansas City purchased his release. He played in Kansas City the balance of 1888 and all of 1889. He has always played in the outfield. He is a hard left-hand hitter and a very quick fielder, being very fast on his feet. It is as a base-runner that he excels, having stolen 117 bases in 137 games last season, the highest record by any player in the profession. In addition to being a very fast runner he is a remarkably quick starter and a successful slider. He is a rather small man being about 5 feet 6 or 7 inches and heavily built. His present home is in Clifton, Mass. He is now playing with the Philadelphia League Club this season.

THE END OF SUITS.

JOHN M. WARD WINS ANOTHER LEGAL VICTORY.

The New York Club Abandons the Injunction Suit Against the Players' Leader.

Short Stop and Lawyer John M. Ward's victory over the League was made complete March 31. Judge Lawrence, in the special term of the Supreme Court, granted the motion made by ex-Judge Howland, the Brotherhood's counsel, to dismiss the complaint in the suit brought by the Metropolitan Exhibition Company to restrain Ward from playing with the Brotherhood Club of Brooklyn this season.

The Judge evidently thought that the opinions of Judge, Thayer, of Philadelphia, and Judge O'Brien, his associate upon the Bench of the Supreme Court, were conclusive, for he handed down only a short opinion as follows:—"As I am informed by counsel for the plaintiff that they do not intend to submit a brief in the case, and as I am of the opinion that the contract referred to in the complaint is one which a court of equity will not enforce, judgment will be granted dismissing the complaint with costs."

The counsel for the National League evidently concluded that the law was against him and practically abandoned the case.

EXIT BROOKLYN.

KENNEDY'S TEAM NO LONGER IN EXISTENCE.

The Association Tail-enders Play the Last Games and Drop Out---The Players Scattered, Etc.

The Brooklyn Association team played its final series of three games with the Syracuse Club at Syracuse, and on Aug. 25 disbanded. It was intended to play six games at Syracuse with Brooklyn, but Manager Frazer could not get consent to transfer the Brooklyn games to Syracuse.

Barnie didn't relish the transfer of the final series between Brooklyn and Syracuse to Syracuse even a little bit, and entered a protest against the transfers. This was quite proper, considering that the Baltimore is compelled to take Syracuse's record and percentage.

PLAYERS GRABBED UP.

At 9 o'clock Monday evening Kennedy and his players left for New York, with the exception of Peltz, who signed with Syracuse. The men felt rather blue, as salaries were four weeks in arrears, but consoled themselves with the fact that the Association is responsible and will pay up. Of the defunct team Peltz and Pitz have signed with Syracuse, O'Brien has gone to Denver, Murphy to the Albanys and Gerhardt to the St. Louis Browns. Barnie is said to be after Davis, and Ed Daily is at present the bone of contention among the St. Louis, Louisville and Athletic Association and the New York League clubs.

KENNEDY'S PARTING WORDS.

In reference to the disbandment of the team Manager Kennedy said: — "Nobody could have jumped in at the eleventh hour, as I did, and secured a team that would make any kind of a showing in the pennant race. Had I started to get players together last fall I would have had little trouble in landing a strong team. As it was, the Brooklyn Association team at the time of its disbandment would have been as strong as the other teams had it been supplied with good pitchers. The rumor is true that the players are owed about five weeks' salaries. The Association, however, is responsible for every cent, and, of course, the players will receive all that is coming to them, for the Association had the controlling interest in the team."

A DISGRACEFUL MOVE

INTRODUCING FEMALES INTO PROFESSIONALISM.

A Speculator's Proposal to Organize a League of Female Base Ball Clubs.

NEW YORK, Aug. 26.—There is a movement on foot to degrade base ball by organizing a number of base ball clubs with women players, and already one club is on the road. The organizer is W. S. Franklin, and yesterday his office, at No. 1162 Broadway, was besieged with females of all ages, who had come in answer to the following *World* advertisement, and offered themselves as candidates for base ball honors:

WANTED—50 girls to play base ball; $5 to $15 per week and all expenses; long engagement to travel to experienced player; ladies' league of 4 to 6 clubs now organizing for 1891; must be young, not over 20, good looking and good figure. Call Monday or Tuesday, 2 to 6 P. M., on Mr. Franklin, at Dramatic Agency, 1162 Broadway, or 8 to 10 P. M., at 158 West 50th street. Applicants outside of city must sent photo, which will be returned.

Besides the numerous applicants who appeared in person a big batch of letters was received in answer to the advertisement. Manager Franklin says that the exhibitions are free from any objectionable feature.

A SERIOUS CHARGE.

Catcher E. Harry Decker Reported to be in Another Scrape.

The New York *Herald* on Tuesday stated that it had received recent information from J. Palmer O'Neill, of Pittsburg, to the effect that catcher Decker, of the Pittsburg Club, had gotten himself into another scrape. Mr. O'Neil says that on Monday last he received a telegram from C. V. Havemyer, of the Bingham Hotel, Philadelphia, telling him he had cashed a check for Decker on the Second National bank of Pittsburg, signed by President O'Neill, but that it had been refused by the bank because no funds had been deposited there. Mr. O'Neill said he never had an account with the Second National Bank, but with the Fifth National Bank. He drew some money from this bank as far back as Oct. 6, but nothing since then. He says Decker received $60 advance money on next year's contract and that $40 more was due him in January. The check presented by Decker to Havemyer is, according to Mr. O'Neill, a forgery.

Three Games at Brooklyn.

BROOKLYN. Sept. 1 [SPECIAL].—The first game of the final series between the Brooklyn and Pittsburg teams was played at Washington Park this morning. The principal feature of the contest before the ninth inning was Clark's batting. Hard hitting gave the visitors nine runs in the last inning. The score came near being tied, as Miller was caught at the plate after a pretty hit on which three men had scored. The score:—

BROOKLYN (N. L.)	R.	H.	O.	A.	E.	PITTSBURG (N. L.)	R.	H.	O.	A.	E.
Collins, 2b	2	1	5	8	2	Burke, cf	1	1	1	0	0
Pinkney, 3b	0	1	1	1	0	Miller, 3b	1	1	2	3	1
O'Brien, lf	2	2	0	1	0	Berger, 2b	1	0	1	0	0
Foutz, 1b	1	0	15	0	0	Wilson, c	0	0	4	2	2
Terry, cf	1	1	3	0	0	Hecker, 1b	1	1	9	0	1
Burns, rf	2	1	0	0	0	Osborn, rf	1	0	1	0	0
Clarke, c	1	3	2	1	0	Sales, ss	1	0	2	4	0
Smith, ss	0	1	1	2	0	Jordan, lf	1	2	4	1	2
Carruthers, p	1	1	0	1	1	Baker, p	1	2	0	1	1
Totals	10	11	27	14	3	Totals	9	7	24	11	7

INNINGS.

Pittsburg .... 0 0 0 0 0 0 0 0 9—9
Brooklyn .... 4 0 2 1 0 1 2 0 x—10

Earned runs, Brooklyn 2. Two-base hits, Burke, Baker, O'Brien, Clarke. Three-base hits, Miller, Clarke. Sacrifice hits, Pinkney, Burns 2, Clarke. Bases stolen, Collins, O'Brien, Foutz, Terry 2, Burns. Double plays, Sales, Wilson, and Hecker; Collins (unassisted). Left on bases, Pittsburg 2, Brooklyn 5. Struck out, Foutz, Carruthers 2, Wilson. First base on called balls, by Baker 4, by Carruthers 2. Hit by pitched ball, Burke, Osborn, Burns. Wild pitch, Baker. Umpire, Strief.

THE SECOND GAME.

Probably the largest crowd of the season was on the Washington Park grounds when the Brooklyn and Pittsburg Clubs began the second game. It was a wild, rip-roaring crowd, and for once at least, this season, that part of Brooklyn has had a waking up. The score:—

PITTSBURG (N. L.)	R.	H.	O.	A.	E.	BROOKLYN (N. L.)	R.	H.	O.	A.	E.
Burke, cf	0	1	4	0	0	Collins, 2b	0	1	1	2	0
Miller, 3b	0	1	1	2	0	Pinkney, 3b	2	2	0	1	0
Berger, 2b	0	2	1	1	0	O'Brien, cf	0	1	5	0	0
Decker, c	0	0	4	0	0	Foutz, 1b	0	0	5	0	0
Hecker, 1b	0	1	7	0	0	Terry, lf	0	0	1	0	1
Osborne, rf	0	0	4	0	0	Burns, rf	1	1	0	0	0
Sales, ss	0	1	1	3	0	Daily, c	0	0	11	0	1
Jordan, lf	0	0	2	1	0	Smith, ss	0	0	3	3	0
Anderson, p	1	1	0	1	0	Lovett, p	0	0	2	1	0
Totals	2	7	24	8	0	Totals	3	5	27	7	3

INNINGS.

Pittsburg .... 0 0 1 0 0 0 0 0 1—2
Brooklyn .... 1 0 0 1 1 0 0 0 x—3

Earned runs, Brooklyn 2, Pittsburg 2. Two base hit, Berger. Three-base hits, Sales, Pinkney, Burns. Sacrifice hits, Miller, O'Brien, Daily 2. Bases stolen, Burke, Jordan, Collins, Pinkney. Double play, Collins, Smith and Foutz. Left on bases, Brooklyn 2, Pittsburg 7. Struck out, Daily, Burke, Decker, Hecker, Jordan, Anderson, O'Brien, Foutz, Terry. First base on called balls, off Anderson. Hit by pitched ball, Sales. Passed ball, Decker. Umpires, Strief and Pike.

THE THIRD GAME.

Day was to have pitched the third game for the Pittsburgs, but Manager Hecker, owing to Anderson's great work in the box, decided to pitch him again. But one game in a day is enough for any pitcher, and, notwithstanding that the Brooklyns hit him hard in the first two innings, he regained his cunning and the Brooklyn made but three hits in the final innings. The score:—

PITTSBURG (N. L.)	R.	H.	O.	A.	E.	BROOKLYN (N. L.)	R.	H.	O.	A.	E.
Burke, cf	0	1	4	0	0	Collins, 2b	2	1	4	5	0
Miller, 3b	1	1	2	4	0	Pinkney, 3b	0	0	1	4	0
Berger, 2b	1	1	4	2	1	O'Brien, cf	1	2	1	0	0
Decker, c	1	1	1	0	0	Foutz, 1b	1	2	10	0	1
Hecker, 1b	1	0	9	1	0	Terry, p	0	0	1	1	0
Osborn, lf	0	0	1	0	0	Burns, rf	1	1	2	0	0
Sales, ss	0	1	1	5	2	Daily, c	1	1	3	4	0
Jordan, rf	0	0	0	0	1	Smith, ss	1	1	3	4	0
Anderson, p	0	0	0	1	0	Carruthers, lf	1	1	1	0	0
Wilson, rf	0	0	2	0	0	Totals	8	9	27	14	1
Totals	4	5	24	14	4						

INNINGS.

Pittsburg .... 0 0 0 1 0 3 0 0 0—4
Brooklyn .... 3 4 0 0 0 0 1 0 x—8

Earned runs, Pittsburg 1, Brooklyn 4. Two-base hits, Collins, O'Brien. Home run, Burns. Sacrifice hit, Anderson. Base stolen, Hecker. Left on bases, Pittsburg 5, Brooklyn 7. Struck out, Decker, Anderson 2, Sales. First base on called balls, by Anderson 4, by Terry 2. Hit by pitched ball, Collins. Wild pitches, Anderson 1, Terry 1. Umpires, Strief and Pike.

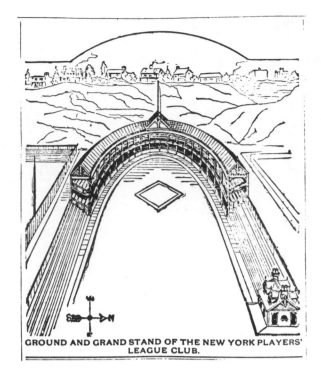

GROUND AND GRAND STAND OF THE NEW YORK PLAYERS' LEAGUE CLUB.

A PLAYER'S FATE.

FIRST BASEMAN LYNCH A VICTIM OF THE PISTOL.

The Ball Player Fatally Wounded During a Saloon Row in Cohoes.

TROY, Oct. 27.—Thomas Lynch, the well-known ball player, who had guarded first base at different times for the Athletic, Atlanta, Hartford, Hamilton, Birmingham, Syracuse and Wilmington clubs, returned to his home in Cohoes a few days ago. He is a muscular fellow and able to hold his own with most anybody. About three years ago he had a quarrel with Richard Doyle, who is his inferior in size and strength. Doyle is a jack-spinner in one of the Cohoes mills. Lynch, who had been out with friends and was considerably under the influence of liquor, met Doyle this morning in John Donovan's saloon on Columbia street. Several drinks were had and the story of the old quarrel was revived. Finally, Lynch struck Doyle in the face. Doyle did not return the blow, but said:

"Lynch, you are a good deal bigger man than me, but I am going home, and when I come back if you hit me again you'll get the worst of it."

Doyle returned in about an hour, meeting Lynch, Donovan, and others outside the place. When Lynch saw him, he said—"You want more, do you?" and again struck him. Doyle pulled a revolver and fired, the ball striking Lynch in the left breast just below the nipple. Doyle put the weapon in his pocket and walked away, while Lynch, who claimed that he was not badly hurt, was looked after by Donovan and others.

They took him to a house near lock 14 on the Erie Canal, where he became so weak that Dr. Parker was sent for. He pronounced the wound a dangerous one, and had Lynch taken to his home on Lancaster street. He is not expected to live forty-eight hours. Dr. Parker notified the police, who instituted an unsuccessful search for Doyle, but this afternoon he walked into the station house and surrendered, admitting that he was the man who shot Lynch.

IMPORTANT MOVE.

THE RESERVE RULE TO BE PARTIALLY SUSPENDED.

A Step Which Will Ultimately Result in Wiping Out the Obnoxious Rule.

CINCINNATI, Sept. 17.—The League is soon to take a flank movement on the Brotherhood. The Brotherhood leaders announced at the outset that they intended to drive the National League off the face of the earth before the Fourth of July. They did not flaunt it to the world in so many words that they would not ask or give any quarter, but their actions conveyed that meaning. The League is fighting the revolt on the same ground. There will be no compromise unless the League has the big end of the deal. If there is not a flag of truce raised in Brotherhood quarters the League will go on with the war of extermination. To more successfully conduct their campaign the League leaders will wipe out a rule that has hitherto proved a handicap. In short, it is the intention of the League clubs which lost some of their players by the revolt to waive their reserve claim to such players. In other words, any League player in Brotherhood company can be signed by any League club that wants him.

The League club with which he played before he joined the Brotherhood will allow him to be negotiated with by any other League club. To illustrate, take Mike Kelly for instance. He jumped the Boston League Club, and under the reserve rule Boston has the first right to his services should he return to the League. This right the Boston Club will waive, and the Cincinnati Club, the Chicago Club or any other club in the League will, under the new order of affairs, be privileged to sign him. The Cincinnati Club will not be asked to waive claim to anybody, for the simple reason that it did not lose any players by the revolt. This change will give the League a great advantage, and several League players now in the revolt who left their old League club because they did not like the management will be glad to get back into the League when they are given the choice of clubs.

END OF THE PLAYERS' LEAGUE.

The Organization Dissolved—Details of the Last Meeting—A Bit of History—Terms of Surrender, Etc.

When THE SPORTING LIFE went to press last Friday afternoon the settlement of the base ball situation hinged upon the action of the Players' League, whose meeting was set for that day at the St. James Hotel in New York City. Had the Players' League remnants decided to maintain their organization the situation would have become most complicated and different history would to-day be written. They decided otherwise, however, and when the shades of Friday night fell all that was left of the Players' League was the Cleveland Club, the property of staunch and loyal Al Johnson.

Up to Wednesday night, the 14th, all who were on the inside of the Players' League fully expected to see that organization maintained. This belief was the result of positive pledges to that effect by President Prince. Some time ago both Philadelphia and Boston became apprehensive that Messrs. Thurman and Spalding would not be able to carry out their plan of settlement, the determined opposition of the Boston triumvirs and the bold front of the Athletic-minority-stockholder-Russell combination lending color to the belief of the Boston-Philadelphia people, who felt decidedly panicky.

THE TEAM FOR 1891 OF THE BOSTON CLUB OF THE NATIONAL LEAGUE.

HEAVILY SAT UPON.

CHADWICK CRUSHED IN THE HOUSE OF HIS FRIENDS.

The Board of Control Eliminates His "Runs-Batted-In" Rule From the Playing Rules.

The "Father of Base Ball" has been humiliated and crushed in the National Agreement Temple, wherein he has for these many moons been posing as one of the high priests of the old base ball dispensation. The venerable defender of the trust system now has his reward. The following surprising despatch was put upon the wires last Monday night and flashed to the uttermost ends of the country:

"WASHINGTON, May 11.—The National Board of Professional Base Ball Associations has amended the national playing rules by striking out section 6 of rule 69. This change renders unnecessary the fourth column headed 'B. B.' in the official score blanks.

"N. E. YOUNG, Chairman."

Rule 69 refers to what shall be contained in the summary of scores. Sec. 6 says:—"The number of runs batted in by each batsman." According to the despatch, the summary of scores will no longer contain "runs batted in," and President Young must now issue a new notice to official scorers, because some of them are even now likely to get badly mixed over what is meant in the despatch.

YOUNG M'GILL'S LOSS.

The Father of the Boy Pitcher Dies From His Injuries.

Special to SPORTING LIFE.

INDIANAPOLIS, May 15.—Pitcher McGill, of the St. Louis team, left Baltimore last Monday for this city, where his father was lying at the point of death at St. Vincent's Hospital. The young pitcher arrived just in time to see his father expire on Tuesday. The boy is distracted with grief and is a prey to remorse, as he considers himself indirectly responsible for the loss of a fond father. It will be remembered that some time ago young McGill and Ned Crane got on a spree in Louisville while the Cincinnatis were playing there. When McGill senior, who fairly idolized his son, heard of the boy's escapade he left Chicago at once for Louisville, in order to straighten his son up. En route he was caught in a railroad wreck near this city, and received the injuries from which he died Tuesday.

Cincinnati Evacuated and Milwaukee Admitted---Details of the Deal---The Outlook For Peace, Etc.

The past week was marked by a great change in the base ball situation, and was withal an exciting one by reason of the mass of contradictory rumors and statements which were inflicted upon the public daily until order came out of chaos and the real purpose and action of the American Association, which was the storm centre, was made plain. The result briefly summed up is:—The American Association has evacuated Cincinnati for this season, thereby saving nearly $20,000 hard and needful cash, without committing itself to a permanent retirement from Porkopolis. It has admitted Milwaukee as a ninth club—Cincinnati being now merely an inactive member—thereby dealing the National League's strongest ally, the Western Association, a heavy blow and materially weakening the National Agreement alliance. And finally, it has opened the way for an honorable and equitable agreement with the National League, and placed itself in better position to maintain its independence and successfully continue the battle with the League if the latter shall prefer costly war to honorable peace and equitable agreement. Whatever shortsighted partisans and hot-headed heelers of either faction may say to the contrary, the Association is to-day apparently in better position and condition than at any time since the break-away.

HE'S A $10,000 BEAUTY.

Breitenstien Pitches a Remarkable Game.

Only One Man Reached First Base, and He Got There on Balls.

St. Louis and Louisville Close the Season with a Victory Each.

ST. LOUIS, Mo., Oct. 4.—The Browns and Louisvilles each closed the championship season here today by playing two games. Last Friday's game between these clubs was an exhibition contest.

The first game this afternoon was one of the most remarkable played on any diamond this year. Breitenstein, the young amateur, pitched his first nine innings for the Browns, and not a hit could the Louisvilles make off his delivery.

Only one Colonel reached first base during the whole contest, and that was Taylor, by a base on balls in the first inning. The score:

ST. LOUIS—A. A.

	A.B.	R.	B.H.	T.B.	S.H.	P.O.	A.	E.
Hoy, c. f	4	0	0	0	0	3	0	0
Fuller, s. s	4	1	1	1	0	2	2	0
McCarthy, r. f	4	2	2	2	1	0	0	0
O'Neil, l. f	4	0	1	3	1	0	1	0
Comiskey, 1b	5	0	0	0	1	9	1	0
Boyle, 3b	4	1	1	1	0	4	1	0
Eagan, 2b	4	1	1	1	0	4	4	0
Munyan, c	2	2	1	1	1	7	1	0
Breitenstein, p	3	0	0	0	1	0	0	0
Totals	34	8	7	8	5	27	9	0

LOUISVILLE—A. A.

	A.B.	R.	B.H.	T.B.	S.H.	P.O.	A.	E.
Cline, l. f	4	0	0	0	0	3	0	0
Weaver, c. f	3	0	0	0	0	1	1	0
Taylor, 1b	2	0	0	0	0	12	0	0
Jennings, s. s	3	0	0	0	0	2	6	1
Wolf, r. f	3	0	0	0	0	2	0	0
Kuehne, 3b	3	0	0	0	0	1	1	0
Shinnick, 2b	3	0	0	0	0	1	4	0
Cahill, c	0	0	0	0	0	0	0	0
Shilhasse, c	3	0	0	0	0	4	1	0
Meekin, p	3	0	0	0	0	0	2	0
Totals	27	0	0	0	0	27	15	2

Innings	1	2	3	4	5	6	7	8	9
St. Louis	2	1	0	0	0	1	2	2	0	—8

Earned runs—St. Louis, 2. Two-base hit—O'Neil. Stolen bases—Fuller, O'Neil, Boyle. First base on balls—Fuller, McCarty, O'Neil, Munyan (2), Breitenstein, Taylor. First base on errors—St. Louis, 1. Hit by pitched ball Hoy. Passed balls—Cahill 3, Shilhasse 1. Wild pitch—Meekin 3. Struck out—Fuller, McCarty, Egan, Breitenstein, Taylor, Wolf (2), Shinnick, Meekin. Umpire—Dolan. Time—2h.

A PLAYER DEAD.

Third Baseman Smalley Gone to His Rest.

Special to Sporting Life.

BAY CITY, Mich., Oct. 16.—Will Smalley, the well-known third baseman, died at the home of his uncle, D. C. Smalley, in this city, last Sunday, of cancer of the stomach. He was but 20 years of age. The remains were taken to his home in Haywards, Cal., for interment.

Smalley made a great reputation in the California League two years ago as a third baseman, and was secured by the Cleveland Club for 1890. He did not come up to expectations in the National League, and when Tebeau went back to the Cleveland Club after the collapse of the Players' League Smalley was released. He signed with Washington for this season, but was unable to do himself justice, as the malady which ended his earthly career had already begun its inroads upon his constitution. After a month's play he asked and obtained his release. He then joined the Syracuse team, but in a short time had to retire from active service. He then went to his uncle's home in Bay City, where he died as above stated.

Pfeffer Notified That He Will be Enjoined if He Signs With the New Chicago Club.

When Fred Pfeffer, the manager-captain of the new Chicago Club, on the 2d inst., went to draw his monthly salary from the Chicago League Club President James A. Hart, of the Chicago Club, notified him that as soon as he signed a contract with the American Association club of Chicago he will begin proceedings against him to enjoin him from playing with any but the Chicago League Club, which considers that it holds a five years' contract with him. Pfeffer declared that he did not consider the contract he signed last spring one for more than one year, and that when it lapsed he should certainly sign with the Chicago Association Club. He had, he said, taken legal advice, and was prepared to go on the way he had marked out.

Pfeffer and the Association people declare that they will make their fight on the inequitable ten days' release clause, and the Chicago League Club will rest its case on the option clause in the contract—provided, of course, that the twelve-club scheme, by which the new club would be wiped out, does not materialize.

Further details and general news from Chicago will be found in the appended letter from our special Chicago correspondents.

THE STAR LEAGUE PITCHER.

It is Hutchison. But Rusie, Ewing, Clarkson and Staley Are Nearly as Good.

The eight clubs in the National League tried sixty-two pitchers the past season, and of this number but few showed any extraordinary skill. The Philadelphias tried eleven pitchers, and the New York and Cleveland clubs ten each. The champion Boston Club had nine pitchers, while Anson thought seven were enough to win the championship with. The three tail-enders, Brooklyn, Cincinnati and Pittsburg, had the least number, each having tried six. But twelve of the sixty-two pitchers won more than half of their games. These were:—Clarkson, of Boston, Esper, Ewing, Gumbert, Hutchison, Lovett, Nichols, Rusie, Staley, Stein, Vickery and Young. Of this number Hutchison has a better percentage than any of the others.

When half of the season had been concluded it was a neck-and-neck race between Hutchison and Rusie, but Anson's man kept pegging away, with the result that he leads the National League twirlers. Rusie, Ewing, Clarkson and Staley are not far behind Hutchison. Hutchison, however, not only leads them in percentage, but he also pitched more games than any other pitcher.

The following will show the victories and defeats, and how many complete games and parts of games each pitcher took part in. The figures are:

	Won	Lost	Compl'd	Partial		Won	Lost	Compl'd	Partial
Baldwin, Pi.	22	30	48	4	Knauss, Cl.	0	3	1	2
Beatin, Cl.	1	4	3	2	Killen, Cl.	0	1	1	0
Berger, Pi.	0	1	0	1	Lovett, Br.	24	19	38	5
Bryan, Bo.	0	1	0	1	Lowe, Bo.	0	1	0	1
Barr, N. Y.	0	5	4	1	Luby, Ch.	11	17	19	9
Caruthers, Br.	19	20	28	11	Maul, Pi.	1	5	1	5
Clarkson, Bo.	2	3	1	4	Mullane, Ci.	24	26	41	9
Clarkson, N. Y.	36	19	47	8	Nichols, Bo.	32	17	44	5
Casian, Pi.	1	3	3	0	Nicol, Ci.	2	1	0	3
Coughlin, N. Y.	3	4	5	2	Radbourn, Ci.	13	13	23	2
Crane, Ci.	4	10	10	4	Rhines, Ci.	19	23	39	8
Dunning, N. Y.	0	1	0	1	Rusie, N. Y.	38	20	49	9
Davis, Cl.	0	1	0	1	Ryan, Ch.	1	2	0	3
Duryea, Ci.	1	8	8	1	Saylor, Ph.	0	1	0	1
Esper, Ph.	21	16	25	12	Seward, Cl.	2	1	1	2
Ewing, N. Y.	21	11	26	6	Shultz, Ph.	0	6	0	6
Foutz, Br.	3	2	4	1	Sharrott, N. Y.	6	5	7	4
Galvin, Pi.	15	16	24	7	Smith, Ph.	1	2	0	3
Gerzein, Bo., Cl.	4	8	8	4	Staley, Pi., Bo.	23	14	31	6
Gleason, Ph.	25	27	40	12	Stein, Ch.	8	6	9	5
Gruber, Cl.	12	22	27	7	Stratton, Pi.	0	2	2	0
Gormaly, Ph.	0	1	1	0	Sullivan, N. Y.	2	2	4	0
Gumbert, Ch.	23	14	30	7	Sb arow, Cl.	1	4	4	1
Hemming, Br.	9	1	18	9	Stephens, Cl.	0	1	1	0
Hutchison, Ch.	45	18	54	9	Terry, Br.	7	18	17	8
Inks, Br.	3	10	10	3	Thornton, L.	17	18	22	13
Keefe, N. Y., Ph.	6	11	12	5	Tucker, B.	0	1	0	1
Kling, Ph., Pi.	5	6	4	7	Vau, Cl.	17	4	32	9
Kelly, Bo.	0	1	1	0	Vickery, Ci.	7	5	7	6
Kilroy, Ph.	0	2	0	2	Welch, N. Y.	5	15	14	8
King, Pi.	15	31	49	6	Young, Cl.	28	22	41	9

There were eight tie games played during the season. New York, Cleveland and Pittsburg took part in three each; Chicago two; Cincinnati, Philadelphia and Boston one each. The pitchers who occupied the box in these games were: Rusie, three; Hutchison and Galvin, two; Rhines, Gruber, Kling, Keefe, Young, Vau, Staley, Gumbert, Vickery and Baldwin, one each.

THE REVOLUTION!

THE LEAGUE AND ASSOCIATION CONSOLIDATED INTO ONE GREAT TWELVE-CLUB LEAGUE.

Some of the Secret Preparatory Work Detailed---How the Basis For the Big League Was Laid.

PROFESSIONAL BASE BALL ON A NEW AND SUBSTANTIAL BASIS!

Old Lines Obliterated, Old Issues Swept Away and a New Start Made!

THE CONSUMMATION OF THE ONE-LEAGUE SCHEME REACHED AT INDIANAPOLIS AFTER A MONTH'S HARD WORK.

Details of the Joint Meeting of League and Association---Dissolution of the Latter---The Basis on Which the New Structure Stands, Etc.

Special to Sporting Life.

INDIANAPOLIS, Dec. 17.—That which everybody deemed impossible has been achieved, thanks to the honesty of purpose and the intelligent, systematic working out of a clearly-defined plan by Messrs. Byrne, Brush and Robison, of the National League, Messrs. Wagner, Elliott and Von der Ahe, of the Association, and the editor of THE SPORTING LIFE, who acted as intermediary, brushed aside all obstacles, smoothed the way, and finally brought the two apparently irreconcilable parties together. After one month of hard work, without fuss or feathers, without the least publicity, and with no more friction than would attend the working of a well-balanced machine, the two great warring organizations of the country were brought together in this city on Tuesday last.

The result is that as we go to press the month's hard labor of the two committees and the two days' travail of the League and Association has culminated in the consolidation of the National League and American Association into one grand league of twelve clubs, which big league has been laid upon such broad lines that it should be able to withstand all shocks, either from without or from within, for many, many years.

HERE WE ARE AGAIN.

THE OPENING OF THE MOMENTOUS SEASON OF 1892.

ANOTHER PLAYER GONE.

The Grim Reaper Gathers in Ex-Catcher Edward Rowan.

BRIDGEPORT, Ct., Feb. 23.— Edward Rowan, the noted ex-ball player, died early last night. He had been suffering from general debility and hemorrhages of the lungs. He was 38 years old.

TWO NOTED BALL PLAYERS JOIN THE GREAT MAJORITY.

Pitcher "Darby" O'Brien Dies of Pneumonia and Catcher Tip O'Neil Succumbs to Consumption.

AN INSANE PLAYER.

A Tip That Blighted McHale's Reason.

Very few ball players have suffered from the ravages of paresis. Horace Phillips is one of the exceptions. He has virtually dropped out of public sight and mind. Then there was outfielder Hall, whose leg was broken in a game out at the Cincinnati grounds one afternoon years ago. He afterward became insane. Tom Deasley is a harmless imbecile about Philadelphia, but drink brought him down. From California comes a story that places one more unfortunate on the list—Bob McHale, the Sacramento outfielder. He was jailed on the suspicion that he is crazy. For some time he has been acting strangely, constantly swinging an axe handle in a threatening manner. He went riding with a friend named Kasta some days ago and suddenly turned upon him and nearly beat him to death before his victim could escape. If McHale's mind is unbalanced his insanity was probably caused by an accident on the ball field. While playing behind the bat he was hit on the head by a foul tip and this blow may prove to be the cause of his present mental darkness.

LATER—M'HALE ADJUDGED INSANE.

Since the above was written, the news has been received that M'Hale has been taken to the Stockton Insane Asylum. It is said that his malady was brought on by witnessing a performance of "Dr. Jekyll and Mr. Hyde." The unfortunate youth imagined that he was enacting the role of "Mr. Hyde," and developed homicidal tendencies.

IMPORTANT DECISION

WHICH WILL LIGHTEN THE BURDEN OF CLUBS.

RR Railroads May Now Lawfully Give Reduced Rates to Traveling Ball Clubs.

The Supreme Court of the United States on Monday last rendered a decision to the effect that railroad companies may lawfully give reduced rates to traveling amusement companies. This will be good news to base ball clubs, to whom the decision applies equally as well as to theatrical combinations.

FAIR BALL TOSSERS.

BASE BALL PART OF A FEMALE COLLEGE COURSE.

How the Lady Students at Smith College Practice This Essentially Masculine Sport.

NORTHAMPTON, Mass., May 30.—For several years the girls of Smith College have been known to excel in tennis, riding, and other sport, but it was not till within the last two weeks that the national game of base ball was added to the athletic acquirements of Smith College. The game is not general with the girls yet, but is confined to the aristocratic and oligarchical few. Neither is it exactly the game that John Kelly or Tim Keefe plays. President Seeyle, of Smith, when the matron of the dormitories in which most of the fair base ballists live, approached him in high dudgeon about it, recognized this fact. The matron, highly wrought up, said:

"It's disgraceful, President Seeyle, outrageous, to think of these girls playing base ball just like men!"

President Seeyle, his eyes twinkling with suppressed merriment, responded:—"Really, I do not remember ever having seen men playing exactly like that!"

A BASE BALL STUDY.

A PREVALENT MISCONCEPTION AS TO PATRONAGE CORRECTED.

Evidence That the National Sport Appeals to the Better Classes as Well as to the Masses.

The Boston *Journal* has been able to make a test of the kind of people that are interested in base ball, and the result ought to be encouraging to those who are eager to see the game grow in popular favor. Like a good many other enterprising newspapers, it announced that it would send a base ball schedule to whomsoever would send his address to its office and enough stamps to pay the postage. It kept a record of these letters as a quest, out of a curiosity to learn whether it is true, as some critics claim, that "no one cares about base ball except boys and cranks." The first hundred letters received show that this criticism is unauthorized.

After closely examining them the *Journal* found that the letters asking for the base ball schedule were almost without exception well written and excellent in penmanship, spelling and punctuation; in short, "as creditable a series of letters as ever came into the *Journal* office on any subject." Forty-six of the 100 were written on letter-head paper, indicating that the occupations of the writers could be classed as follows:

General mercantile...... 16	Court......................... 1
Manufacturing compa's 13	Physician.................. 1
Railroad offices............ 5	Broker...................... 1
Educational institutions 3	Miscellaneous.............. 6
National banks............ 2	
Insurance company...... 1	Total...................... 46

This is a pretty conclusive reply to the generally held opinion that the better class of people are not interested in base ball. There is probably no other amusement nearly 50 per cent. of the devotees of which come from a higher class.

The *Journal* from these proofs arrives at two conclusions, which all fair-minded people will have to acquiesce in, and they are:— First, that the interest in base ball is general and wide-spread, and second, that this interest is not limited to boys and cranks. All this is encouraging to those who wish to see the game elevated and given that place in athletics that its merits deserve. The past few years have done much to dissipate the notion that base ball is too boisterous a game to be indulged in or enjoyed by the refined and cultured. A visit to the grounds of any first-class base ball club will show that the game is receiving an increased patronage each year from business and professional men, and that it has grown in popular favor in just the degree that it has been improved.

No people work like the Americans do. The constant strain of work and worry makes Americans old at the time they should be enjoying life with undiminished zest. The English business and professional man is through with his day's labor two hours before his American cousin. More rest for mind and body, more relaxation for brain and muscle is the great want in this country. The growth of base ball in popular favor is one indication that this fact is coming to be recognized.

WILBERT ROBINSON'S 7 FOR 7

June 10

BALTIMORE	AB	R	H	O	A	E	ST. LOUIS	AB	R	H	O	A	E
Shindle, 3b	7	2	2	1	2	1	Crooks, 2b	2	1	0	3	2	3
Van Haltren, rf	5	2	2	2	0	0	Carroll, lf	5	1	1	1	0	1
Halligan, 1b	5	3	3	13	0	2	Werden, 1b	4	1	1	10	1	1
Shoch, ss	4	3	3	0	4	0	Glasscock, ss	4	1	1	1	2	0
Welch, cf	6	4	2	3	0	0	Brodie, cf	4	0	2	2	1	0
Gunson, lf	5	4	2	2	0	2	Caruthers, rf	4	0	0	0	0	1
McGraw, 2b	6	3	3	4	7	1	Pinckney, 3b	4	0	1	3	1	1
Robinson, c	7	7	7	3	0	0	Buckley, c	1	0	0	2	2	0
McMahon, p	7	0	0	0	3	0	Getzein, p	2	0	0	0	0	0
							Young, p	2	0	0	0	0	0
Totals	54	25	25	27	16	6	Bird, c	2	0	0	0	0	0
							Breitenstein, p	1	0	0	0	2	0
							Stricker, 2b	2	0	1	2	2	0
							Totals	37	4	7	27	14	8

BALTIMORE 5   5   4   6   3   2   0   0   0—25
ST. LOUIS 1   0   0   0   0   1   0   0   2— 4

Earned runs—Baltimore 9. Two-base hits—Robinson, Glasscock, Shindle, Shoch. Three-base hit—Shindle. Stolen bases—Robinson, McGraw. Double play —Shindle, McGraw, Halligan. First on balls—Baltimore 6, St. Louis 1. Hit by pitcher—Welch, Gunson 2. Struck out—By McMahon 3, by Young 1, by Breitenstein 2. Passed ball—Robinson 1. Wild pitch—Young 1. Umpire—Hurst. Time —1:50.

COMISKEY'S SALARY.

How the Captain Managed to Get His Share of Base Ball Fat.

President Von der Ahe tells how Captain Comiskey got his Cincinnati contract at a sky-scraping salary. Comiskey offered his services to Von der Ahe for $6000. Von der Ahe said $5000, and no contract was signed. Then Comiskey negotiated with John T. Brush at Indianapolis. Comiskey said in his deliberate, convincing, don't-care-a-hang style that he was offered $6000 by Von der Ahe and would sign with New York or Cincinnati for $7000, $3500 of which was to be in advance. Brush swallowed the bait and got the hook as well. In Mr. Von der Ahe's opinion it's a fair gamble at about even money that Comiskey will not be at the helm in Cincinnati after his advance money is worked out.

Games Played Monday, June 20.

BOSTON VS. WASHINGTON AT BOSTON JUNE 20 (P. M. AND P. M.)—Boston won the first game by good play, although Emslie gave them the best of the deal. Gastright took Knell's place in the fifth, but the visitors could do little with Nichols. Dan Richardson fielded wonderfully, beating the short stop record by accepting 19 out of 20 chances. The score:

BOSTON.	AB.	R.	B.	P.	A.	E	WASHING'N.	AB.	R.	B.	P.	A.	E
McCarthy, rf	5	0	2	1	0	0	Radford, rf	3	0	0	0	0	0
Duffy, cf	4	1	1	3	0	0	Raymond, 3b	3	0	0	1	4	3
Long, ss	5	3	1	1	2	0	Hoy, cf	4	1	1	1	1	0
Kelly, c	4	2	3	9	1	1	Larkin, 1b	4	0	1	13	0	1
Tucker, 1b	2	1	0	3	1	0	Milligan, c	2	0	0	2	0	0
Nash, 3b	4	2	0	1	6	0	Donovan, lf	4	2	2	0	2	0
Stovey, lf	4	1	1	2	0	1	Richard'n, ss	4	0	1	6	12	1
Lowe, 2b	4	0	1	7	4	0	Knell, p	2	0	0	1	0	0
Nichols, p	5	0	0	1	1	0	Robinson, 2b	3	0	0	3	0	0
Total	37	9	11	27	10	2	McGuire, c	2	0	1	3	1	0
							Gastright, p	2	0	0	1	1	1
							Total	33	3	6	27	15	6

Boston.................2 0 0 3 1 0 2 0 1—9
Washington..............0 1 1 1 0 0 0 0 0—3

THE BUNT.

Hanlon Agrees With Anson That It is Overdone.

"Manager Hanlon and Captain Anson sat together in the Carrollton Hotel for a long time discussing the advisability of abolishing the bunt hit, so frequently used to the apparent disgust of the spectators. Both agreed that as far as the public was concerned it would be better to do away with bunting, notwithstanding the bunt is scientifically an advancement in the national game. To be a successful bunter a man must be a very fast runner to first base, and even then it is a matter of skill to successfully drop the speedy ball from the bat to the ground so that it will not roll too fast to the fielders. There are some players who can never learn this mode of hitting. Both Manager Hanlon and Captain Anson recognize this, and also that in a close game, where not much successful hitting is done, the bunt hit is most valuable in working base-runners around the bases. At the same time they recognize that what the public wants to see is hard hitting, which gives a chance for fine running catches and good base-running. The question is being discussed in all the League cities, and the managers and players are about equally divided on "bunt or not to bunt." Manager Hanlon and Captain Anson would vote with the other men to abolish bunting, to call a bunt hit a strike and to treat it the same as a dead ball when men are on bases. The subject will receive considerable attention at the meeting of the League in November, and it will be decided if this scientific feature of base ball is to be sacrificed to the popular demands of the spectators."
—Baltimore Sun.

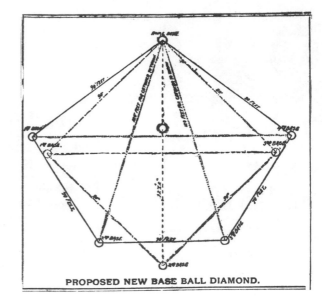

PROPOSED NEW BASE BALL DIAMOND.

CINCINNATI VS. PITTSBURG AT CINCINNATI OCT. 15.—The home team closed the season with a victory, due chiefly to the wonderful pitching of Bumpus Jones, the Southern League pitcher, who kept Pittsburg from making a single hit. This was Jones' first appearance in League company, and this makes his feat against the hard-hitting Pittsburgs at this season of the year the more remarkable. The score:

CINCINNATI.	AB.	R.	B.	P.	A.	E	PITTSBURG.	AB.	R.	B.	P.	A.	E
Holliday, cf	4	1	2	3	0	0	Donovan, rf	2	1	0	1	0	0
Latham, 3b	3	1	1	3	0	Farrell, 3b	3	0	0	0	1	0
McPhee, 2b	4	0	3	2	0	V'nHalt'n, cf	4	0	0	1	0	1
Brown'g, rf	4	1	1	1	0	0	Miller, ss	3	0	0	3	5	0
Vaughn, c	4	1	1	4	0	0	Beckley, 1b	3	0	0	9	1	0
Hoover, lf	4	1	0	1	0	E. Smith, lf	2	0	0	0	0	0
Comiskey, 1b	4	1	3	13	1	0	Mack, c	3	0	0	5	2	0
Smith, ss	3	1	2	1	8	0	Bierbau'r, 2b	3	0	0	3	5	0
Jones, p	2	0	0	0	0	1	Baldwin, p	3	0	0	2	0	1
Total	32	7	10	27	14	1	Total	26	1	0	24	14	2

Cincinnati.....................0 1 0 0 2 0 0 4 x—7
Pittsburg......................0 0 1 0 0 0 0 0 0—1

Earned runs—Cincinnati 5. Two-base hit—Comiskey. Home run—Smith. Stolen base—Donovan. Double plays—Miller, Bierbauer, Beckley 2; Latham, Comiskey, Vaughn; McPhee, Comiskey. First on balls—By Jones 4, by Baldwin 2. Hit by pitcher—By Baldwin. Struck out—By Jones 3, by Baldwin 5. Passed ball—Vaughn. Umpire—McQuaid. Time—1.18.

ABOLISH THE FLAT BAT.

For myself I am heartily sick of the "fungo" hitting batting of the old period, and I want to see it replaced by scientific batting, which is neither more nor less than making an effort to place a finely pitched ball, and the bunt hit is a sample of one class hits in placing a ball, and as such it is skilful batting, which slugging for home runs is not, and never has been, because it is something any novice at the bat can readily accomplish in a regular match between muffin players. It would not be a bad plan to do away with the flat bat because that would make the bunt hit more difficult of attainment than it now is; but don't place an obstacle in the way of the growth of scientific batting as is proposed by the absurd change advocated in the article I allude to.
Very truly yours,
HENRY CHADWICK.

BOSTON EASILY TRIUMPHS OVER THE TEAM FROM THE FOREST CITY.

The Lively Spiders Fail to Win a Game in the Series---The Bostons Superior at Every Point.

The series of games for the world's championship between Boston, champion of the first season, and Cleveland, champion of the second season, came to an end on Monday last. About 32,000 people witnessed these contests—20,000 in Cleveland and 12,000 in Boston. The series resulted in a walk-over for Boston, who won every game played—five in all. The Clevelands were outplayed in all departments. They were also outlucked and proved inferior to their Eastern opponents in the important matter of nerve.

In short, the series left no doubt as to the relative superiority of the Bostons in all departments of the game. Beginning with the desperate eleven-inning struggle at Cleveland, in which the local men were prevented from scoring by phenomenal work on the part of the Bostons, the latter beat the Western men by one run in each of the two following games, thus showing that they could beat their rivals on their own stamping grounds.

The Clevelands kept up their courage until the end of the first game in Boston, which they lost by 4 to 0, and then they went to pieces, losing the next game by 12 to 7 and the final game by 8 to 3. The series was to have been nine games, but the Bostons, by winning five in succession, a remarkable feat in world's championship contests, brought the proceedings to a close. It was also the second time in the history of a contest for the world's pennant that one team failed to win a game. The games were played under the supervision of President Young, who attended each game with his full staff of umpires, two of whom were selected to officiate each day just before the game began. The record of the games played since our last issue is appended:

Ryan Also Makes a Display.

Outfielder Jimmy Ryan, of the Chicago Club, at Chicago on the evening of July 1, after the game assaulted a reporter of the Evening News named Geo. Bechel. The latter had criticised Ryan and when he appeared in the club house after the game Ryan picked a quarrel with him. He then attacked him, using him up pretty badly.

THE GRAND STAND WHEN COMPLETED.

HE'S A WHITE MAN.

Treadway Says There's No Negro Blood in Him.

The Baltimore right fielder, Treadway, denies the insinuation that there is negro blood in him, and attributes the report to the spite of a fellow-player. Says the Baltimore *News* anent the matter:

"Treadway, Baltimore's right fielder, is exceeding wroth over the statement which originated with Sam McKee, of the Louisville *Courier-Journal*, and which was published in THE SPORTING LIFE last week, to the effect that he (Treadway) has negro blood in his veins. Speaking to a *News* man of the matter, he said:—'There is no more negro blood in me than there is in any white man that walks the face of God's green earth. The story is the result of a piece of spite work on the part of a former member of the Baltimore team, and, knowing the man as I do, I am not surprised that such a thing should emanate from him. Nobody but a cur and a cut-throat would say such a thing about a man, especially through the press. Why couldn't he have come to me and made the assertion to my face? I could tell a true story about this same friend (?) of mine that would kill him eternally, as far as the base ball profession is concerned, but I prefer not to act in that backhanded way. I will wait till I meet him, and then the world will know who is more worthy to associate with decent people—he or I.'

Mr. Vonderhorst and Manager Hanlon, before Treadway arrived in Baltimore last Spring, were informed that Treadway was a colored man, and both were annoyed by the rumor and at once decided to investigate it. Manager Hanlon felt satisfied that the report was without truth and Treadway was made a member of the team.

WASHINGTON VS. BALTIMORE AT WASHINGTON Aug. 16.—Hawke accomplished the feat of retiring the Washingtons without a single safe hit. Not a Senator reached second base, while only twenty-eight men for Washington faced the pitcher, and only twenty-six are credited with turns at the bat, two being given bases on balls. Stephens, lately of the Chattanooga Club, occupied the box for Washington, and did good work. The score:

WASHINGTON	AB.	R.	B.	P.	A.	BALTIMORE	AB.	R.	B.	P.	A.
Hoy, cf	3	0	0	1	0	McGraw, ss	4	0	0	4	2
Farrell, c	2	0	0	2	0	Kelley, cf	4	0	0	2	0
Wise, 3b	3	0	0	1	3	Shindle, 3b	4	1	2	0	3
O'Rour'e, lb	3	0	0	11	0	Taylor, 1b	3	1	0	8	1
Abbey, lf	3	0	0	4	0	Treadway, rf	4	1	1	3	0
Sullivan, ss	3	0	0	2	4	Long, lf	4	1	1	1	0
Radford, rf	3	0	0	1	0	Reitz, 2b	4	1	2	0	0
Stricker, 2b	3	0	0	2	1	Robinson, c	4	0	0	8	2
Stephens, p	3	0	0	0	2	Hawke, p	3	0	1	1	0
Total	26	0	0	24	13	Total	34	5	7	27	8

Washington ....0 0 0 0 0 0 0 0 0—0
Baltimore ....0 2 0 0 0 0 0 3 x—5

Earned runs—Baltimore 2. First on errors—Baltimore 3. Left on bases—Washington 1, Baltimore 6. First on balls—Off Stephens 2, off Hawke 2. Struck out—By Stephens 2, by Hawke 6. Three-base hit—Shindle. Two-base hit—Long. Sacrifice hits—Long, Hawke. Stolen bases—Robinson, Taylor, Farrell, Wild pitch—Stephens. Umpire—Emslie. Time—1.45.

A FORWARD STRIDE.

The Committee on Rules Agrees Upon a Report.

THE PITCHER TO GO INTO THE CENTRE OF THE DIAMOND!

THE LOANING OF KELLY.

A Bad and Dangerous System Creeping Into Use in the League.

"'King' Kelly is not yet 'in form,' and we apply the word in a double sense. His form in picking winners at Morris Park has been even worse than it has been at picking out base hits at the Polo Grounds. He has accordingly been laying off without pay at both places.

"'Kel' is a sort of Will-o'-the-wisp of the diamond, anyhow. It is now stated that he is only loaned by the Bostons to the New Yorks, and is to be returned as good as he was when received by the Giants next fall. This is a new idea in base ball. A New York magnate is liable any day to drop in on Messrs. Reach and Rogers and exclaim:—'Hello, boys, I've just run down here to borrow a pitcher for a few days,' and then R. & R. will say:—'Why, cert, old man! Just go out to the barn and help yourself; you'll find a few hanging up in the haymow.'

"Come to think of it why should it be any more peculiar to loan a base ball player than to sell him? He may be used for all sorts of base purposes. Next thing we hear some of the boys will be bound out as apprentices or rented by the day. But it costs something to borrow club jewels. The New York Club had to send Kelly $500 before he consented to be loaned. When you borrow a player it is not necessary to make a contract with him, you know. Just say:—'I borrowed you for a year, and all you've got to do is to go in and catch every day as long as you last. Salary? Why, yes! You get it as long as you remain borrowed. But if you get a little stiff I may let you lie off on your natural income.'"—New York *Herald*.

ONE EFFECT OF RULE CHANGES

The Batting Makes Much Harder Work For Umpires.

Gaffney considers it harder to umpire this year than ever before in the history of the game. He has been doing as good work as any umpire on the staff. "I wish I had six eyes," said he, "and then I might be quick enough to see everything and even look around corners. What makes our work harder this year is because, on account of the heavier batting, there are so many more men on bases than there were formerly, and a man has to be very quick to watch the men on bases and call balls and strikes. Maybe this would be the time for the double umpire system, but that has been done away."

SMALL GROUND FOR THE TALK OF A COMBINE.

The Story Due to the New League's Efforts to Prevent Ruinous Competition---The League Building on a Sound Basis.

From St. Louis, which now bears the title formerly held by Pittsburg, as the "champion fake town," comes a story to the effect that there is a combine in the Western League between Kansas City, Milwaukee and Minneapolis to hog the most desirable players available outside of the National League and Eastern League. The St. Louis name for this alleged combination is the "dreibund" which anglicized, means triple alliance.

SLENDER BASIS FOR COMPLAINT.

President Ban Johnson emphatically denies the existence of such a combination, indeed of any combination in the new league. The story is probably due to the fact that the clubs of the new league agreed, at the organization meeting, to name such players as they wanted, and whenever two clubs desired the same player players President Johnson was to act as arbitrator, and assign the player or players in dispute, just as President Young does in the big league, to prevent ruinous competition. Kansas City, Milwaukee and Minneapolis being the first to organize and secure capable managers, naturally got in their lists first. They also had the good sense to compare notes before filing claim, so as to not claim the same players. Hence, the howl of some of the slower clubs and managers, and the usual kick from parties who didn't get just whatever players they happened to want.

There has been some criticism because in the arrangement for allotting players it was stipulated that no publication of allotment should be made. In defense of this necessary rule, Manager Watkins says:

"The Western League opens up an entire new set of books, without a single player under reserve. If we were to announce the names of the players we wanted, we would simply be inviting the attention of Eastern and other minor league managers to men they might have overlooked. I really think that the National League could make our claims as officially good as a reserve list. It would certainly be in the line of keeping the game on a living basis."

Whatever outside, and ill-informed critics may say the Western League is proceeding on sound business-like lines, whose wisdom has been proven by practice in the big League. It should, therefore, proceed unmoved in the proper path marked out, and place the League on a sound and permanent basis.

BENNETT'S AWFUL FATE.

Both of the Great Catcher's Legs Cut Off by a Train.

Special to "Sporting Life."

Wellsville, Kan., Jan. 12.—Charles Bennett, the famous catcher of the Boston champion base ball club, will never appear on the diamond as a player again. His brilliant career came to an end Wednesday night in this city, when he was run over by a Santa Fe passenger train and had both his legs cut off.

Bennett was on the way from Kansas City to Williamsburg and got off at Wellsville to speak to a friend, and, getting on, slipped and fell under the wheels. His left leg was cut off at the ankle, and the other at the knee. He is in the Santa Fe Hospital there suffering intense agony.

CHARLEY BENNETT'S LETTER.

A Cheerful Note From the Badly Maimed Ball Player.

Boston, Feb. 22.—The following letter, written by Catcher Charlie Bennett to President Soden, will be read with interest:

Williamsburg, Feb. 10.—A. H. Soden, Esq.—Dear Sir:—Your very kind and welcome letter of sympathy came duly to hand, and I am very much obliged to you for your kindness.

It was a very sad accident, indeed; but when I think of how much worse it might have been, I have a great deal to be thankful for.

I am glad to know that my services while with you were satisfactory, and that I was thought enough of to be missed a very little the coming season.

Well, the future doesn't look very bright for one maimed and crippled as I am, but I look forward to the time when I can stumble around with artificial limbs. The doctors gave me lots of encouragement, as I have two good stumps, as good as they could possibly be. They could have saved both legs below the knee if it had not been that the bone was cracked on the right limb clear to the knee. I have had a great deal of pain through the knitting of tissues and muscles. The doctors told me I would suffer, as they never amputated a limb with as much hard muscle. They said there was not the least bit of fat to be seen anywhere. I suffered for three nights and days so much that I could not get any sleep at all, and it told on me a great deal.

I am very glad to hear that I have so many friends in Boston, and I am very thankful to them for their kind sympathy for me in my hours of pain and suffering. I cannot find words to express my appreciation to one and all for their kindness to me. I have a great many letters and telegrams of sympathy from friends all over the country; and it was with much pleasure I heard them read to me, and to know I had so many kind friends in all parts of the country.

Hoping the Boston Club will make as good a showing this season as it did last, and with kindest regards to all inquiring friends, I am, respectfully yours,
C. W. BENNETT.

A VETERAN GONE.

FAMOUS ED. WILLIAMSON GOES TO HIS LONG HOME.

The End Comes to Him Near Hot Springs While Seeking Restoration to Health---Brief Sketch of a Notable Career on the Diamond.

Chicago, March 7.—Edward Williamson, the famous base ball player, who was for many years short stop of the Chicago Club, died at Willow Springs, near Hot Springs, Ark., March 3. Williamson had been at Willow Springs for the past two months receiving treatment for a liver ailment. He was also suffering from heart trouble.

M'NABB'S CRIME.

AWFUL RESULTS OF ILLICIT CONNECTION WITH AN ACTRESS.

The Well-Known Base Ball Player Fatally Shoots the Woman and Commits Suicide---Details of the Shocking Tragedy.

Pittsburg, Feb. 28.—A probable murder and suicide occurred to-night at the Hotel Eiffel, on Smithfield street, when E. J. McNabb, a base ball player, shot Mrs. Louise Rockwell, an actress, and then killed himself. The two were lovers, and passing at the hotel as man and wife. What caused the crime is not known.

McNabb was a pitcher for the Baltimore Club last season, but had signed with the Grand Rapids, Mich., Club for this year. Mrs. Rockwell is a soubrette, and has been playing with the Alvin Joslyn Company of Charles L. Davis. Her stage name is Louise Kellogg.

McNabb and Mrs. Rockwell arrived in Pittsburg Tuesday night about 9 o'clock, coming here from New York. They went to the Eiffel Hotel, where they registered as E. J. McNabb and wife, of Columbus, Ohio.

Mrs. Rockwell went to-day to Braddock, where her father, P. J. Lewis, resides. She returned in the evening shortly after 8 o'clock. In the meantime McNabb spent the time about town. He met L. Gilliland, a friend, who was a former ball player, and they made an engagement to go to the theatre.

NO QUARREL APPARENT.

McNabb and Gilliland met at the hotel this evening. They were down stairs when Mrs. Rockwell returned and she and McNabb started up to their room together. Both were laughing and talking.

They had been in the room about five minutes, when screams and pistol shots were heard. Gilliland and several others ran up stairs and the former kicked open the door, which was locked. On the floor near the door lay Mrs. Rockwell in a pool of blood. A little distance from her lay McNabb, covered with blood and a revolver in his hand.

McNabb was unconscious. As soon as Mrs. Rockwell saw Gilliland she exclaimed:

"My God, Lou! He's killed me!"

McNabb in a few minutes breathed his last. The woman would not tell why McNabb had attempted her life, but asked anxiously if she was going to die.

HER CONDITION CRITICAL.

She said he struck her on the head with the revolver, and then shot at her three times. He then placed the muzzle of the revolver, a 32-calibre, in his mouth and fired.

Mrs. Rockwell was taken to the Homœopathic Hospital, and the body of McNabb removed to the morgue.

It was found that two bullets had struck the woman on the left side of the neck. One passed out at the back, while the other lodged in her spinal column. From the effects of it the lower part of her body was paralyzed, and her condition is critical.

Mrs. Rockwell is about 30 years old and a good-looking and shapely blonde. Her husband is R. E. Rockwell, an ice dealer of Seattle, Washington. He was also President of the Pacific and Northwest League of Ball Clubs.

McNabb was 27 years old, and his home was in Mount Vernon, Ohio. A bundle of letters in his satchel showed his relations with the woman had been intimate for some time.

Among the woman's effects the following telegram from Charles L. Davis was found, dated at New York to-day:

"Have made arrangements. Accept thanks for your kind offer. Best wishes."

Gilliland could assign no reason for McNabb's act. It might have been jealously, but he knew of no reason for that. It is believed, however, that the couple were penniless and McNabb used this means to end their troubles.

HANLON YIELDS.

In Deference to Public Sentiment the Baltimore Club's Manager Decides Not to Sign the Pugilistic Champion, Jim Corbett.

Champion pugilist Corbett will not play ball in Baltimore during the coming season. Manager Hanlon said that, owing to the opposition developed in many quarters, he had ceased negotiations with Corbett. Said he:

"I have given up the idea of securing Corbett, because I do not want to antagonize the League, and thereby injure base ball, especially in Baltimore. My chief interest is in the success of the Baltimore team, and base ball in general, and if any part of the base ball public objected to Corbett I would not have signed him."

That settles the whole matter, and Mr. Von der Ahe might as well pigeonhole the resolution which he intended introducing at the League meeting, and thus let the subject drop. In view of the expression of public opinion in this case, it is not likely that any manager will make a similar break in a hurry, hence the passage of a resolution on the subject by the League would be superfluous and only calculated to revive memories of a disagreeable incident whose redeeming feature, however, was that it once more accentuated the cleanliness of the national game.

A SCANDAL WAVE.

JACK SNEED DESERTS HIS WIFE FOR A YOUNG GIRL.

Columbus, O., March 6.—The wife of Jack Sneed, the well-known base ball player, who has been engaged in the ticket-scalping business in this city since leaving the diamond, is looking anxiously for her husband, who has mysteriously disappeared, taking with him her diamonds, valued at $2000, and a sum of money secured by selling some valuable pictures belonging to her. Miss Alice Shipley, a young girl whom Sneed has had in his employ for some time, and with whom he made a quiet trip to Louisville a year ago, causing a scandal, has also disappeared, and Mrs. Sneed thinks they have eloped.

Captain Tebeau Bled.

Cleveland, O., March 5.—Manager Patsy Tebeau was made the victim of a blackmailing scheme here Friday night to the extent of $250. On Thursday afternoon a friend of Tebeau's went out for a time, visited several abodes of the demi-monde, imbibed freely of wine, and became gloriously inebriated. Captain Tebeau was informed that his friend was at the notorious resort kept by a woman named Nettie Strong, on Lake street, and was in a helpless condition, and liable to be robbed. Pat at once hastened to the place. He found his friend there stretched upon a couch, the proprietress and an inmate seated beside him. Tebeau aroused the young man, and attempted to take him from the joint. The inmates interfered, and in a violent manner attempted to prevent Tebeau from taking the intoxicated man away. A row ensued, and Friday evening a special constable arrested the ball player, and brought him to the Lake street dive. The woman claimed that Tebeau had kicked her, and struck the other in the face with his fist. The outcome of the affair was that Tebeau, in order to avoid the unsavory notoriety of a lawsuit, permitted himself to be bled for the amount named. The warrant was then destroyed and the case dismissed at Tebeau's cost.

THE NEW CINCINNATI STEEL AMPHITHEATER.

May 30

Lowe Made a Record for Batters to Shy At.

BOSTONS TO THE FRONT TWICE.

Patrons Saw Great Batting and Fielding and the Cincinnatis Bite the Dust.

The Bostons won both games from the Cincinnatis yesterday, the morning game 13 to 10 after a great rally in the eighth inning, the score at that time standing 9 to 3 against them.

The champions then went in and made nine runs, winning the game, 13—10.

The atendance at the morning game was over 3000, and at the afternoon game 8500, a total of over 11,500 for the day. The Bostons won the afternoon contest 20 to 11.

Both games were great for a holiday, being full of hard hitting and brilliant fielding.

The morning ame was noteworthy for the way the Bostons pulled an apparent defeat out of the fire.

The afternoon game was noted for the tremendous hitting on both sides, and for Lowe's unprecedented streak of batting. After he had struck out in the first inning, he made four home runs in succession over the left field fence, and followed this with a single.

June 18

The morning game between the champions and the Baltimores yesterday was a record-breaker, from the fact that the champions made 16 runs and won the game in the first inning.

Twenty-two men came to the bat in the inning and made 11 hits, including a double and three home runs, while Pitcher Mullane gave seven bases on balls and hit one man.

Twice in this inning did Mullane send in a run by forcing a man when the bases were filled.

Three times did Lowe, Long and Duffy succeed in reaching first base in the first inning. Lowe and Long made two hits each in the inning, and Stivetts performed the unusual feat of making three hits in the first inning of a game.

The hitting was all hard and not at all scratchy.

The crowd got impatient on account of the numerous bases given on balls, and cried to have Mullane taken out, but Manager Hanlon kept him to his medicine, and it was not until he was pounded for five more runs in the sixth inning that he was taken out to make room for Inks. The Bostons also hit this pitcher well enough.

Innings	1	2	3	4	5	6	7	8	9	
Bostons	16	1	0	0	0	5	2	0	.	24
Baltimores	0	0	3	0	0	1	0	1	1	6

Earned runs Bostons 15, Baltimores 2. Two-base hits—Lowe, McCarthy, Nash, Tucker 2, Stivetts, Kelley, Clarke. Home runs—Duffy, Bannon, Stivetts. Stolen bases—McGraw, Jennings. First base on balls Long 2, Duffy 3, McCarthy, Tucker, Bannon 2, Stivetts. First base on errors Bostons 1, Baltimores 4. Struck out—Bannon, Clarke 3. Double plays—Long and Tucker, Long and Lowe. Wild ... Stivetts 1, Mullane, 1. Hit by pitched ball Lowe. Time 2h. Umpire Emslie.

Aug. 21

RESULTS IN A NUTSHELL.

	R.	B.H.	E.	Att'ce
Boston	18	17	0	4,464
Cincinnati	3	9	7	
Boston	25	21	1	
Cincinnati	8	12	3	
Baltimore	17	19	1	4,270
Pittsburg	11	18	3	
New York	13	10	5	2,500
Chicago	11	17	3	
Brooklyn	20	24	2	786
St. Louis	11	13	9	
Washington	15	17	6	1,608
Louisville	9	13	4	
Philadelphia	12	14	6	3,458
Cleveland	6	13	3	

Games played in city first named.

April 24

A DULL THUD IN BALTIMORE.

Extraordinary Experience of the League Champions.

The Home Club Scores 14 Runs in the Ninth Inning—Stivetts and the Umpire Battled by the Crowd—Stivetts Is Ordered Out of the Game—

BALTIMORES.

	A.B.	R.	B.	T.B.	P.O.	A.	E.
McGraw, 3b	5	2	3	3	0	2	1
Keeler, r.f	5	2	1	1	0	0	0
Brodie, c.f	5	1	1	3	1	0	0
Brouthers, 1b	5	1	1	1	13	0	0
Kelley, l.f	3	3	1	5	5	0	0
Reitz, 2b	2	2	1	1	0	4	0
Jennings, s.s	5	1	1	1	3	7	1
Robinson, c	5	2	3	4	4	2	0
McMahon, p	5	1	1	1	1	0	1
Totals	38	15	15	18	27	15	3

BOSTONS.

	A.B.	R.	B.	T.B.	P.O.	A.	E.
Lowe, 2b	5	0	3	6	3	4	0
Long, s.s	5	0	1	1	1	3	0
Duffy, c.f	3	0	0	0	3	1	1
McCarthy, l.f	4	0	1	2	2	0	0
Nash, 3b	3	0	0	0	1	1	0
Tucker, 1b	4	1	1	1	8	0	0
Bannon, r.f	4	1	1	1	2	0	0
Ganzel, c	3	0	0	0	3	1	0
Stivetts, p	3	1	1	2	1	0	0
Nichols, p	1	0	0	0	1	0	2
Totals	35	3	8	13	27	12	3

Innings	1	2	3	4	5	6	7	8	9	
Baltimores	0	0	1	0	0	0	0	0	14	15
Bostons	0	2	0	0	0	1	0	0	0	3

Earned runs—Baltimores 6, Bostons 1. Two-base hits—Robinson, Lowe 3, McCarthy, Stivetts. Three-base hit—Brodie. Home run—Ganzel. Stolen bases Keeler 2, Kelley 2. First base on balls—Duffy, Nash, McGraw, Kelley 2, Reitz 2, Robinson 2. First base on errors—Bostons 2, Baltimores 1. Left on bases—Bostons 7, Baltimores 6. Struck out Ganzel. Double plays—McCarthy, Nash and Lowe. Wild pitches—McMahon. Time—2h. 19m. Umpire—Hurst.

J. C. M.

BOSTON'S ILL LUCK.

FIRE WIPES OUT THE CLUB'S FINE GRAND STAND.

The Costly Structure Set on Fire by Boys During a Game and Completely Destroyed --- The Brotherhood Ground to be Used.

Boston, May 15.—Boys set fire to some rubbish under the seats at the Boston base ball grounds yesterday. The flames spread rapidly, and in less than three hours ran over 12 acres of territory. The base ball grand stand and bleachers, a large school house, an engine house and 164 wooden buildings were destroyed. One thousand families were rendered homeless. The loss is variously estimated at from $300,000 to $1,-000,000.

The fire was discovered just as the third inning of the game between Boston and Baltimore began. In the excitement which followed the game was called and the spectators hastened from the burning edifice, which was wholly destroyed. It was probably the finest base ball grand stand in the country, excepting that at Philadelphia, and cost the Boston Club $75,000. The club owns the ground, embracing a whole block, for which they were recently offered $200,000 by the Boston and Providence Railroad Company. When the game was called each club, Boston and Baltimore, had made three runs.

The Boston Club has made arrangements to play games on the Congress street grounds, which were built by the late Players' League Club of this city, with a $50,000 grand stand. The grounds are very handy to the business portion of the city and are in good shape.

The League Directors Throw Out a Chicago-Pittsburg Game.

Special to "Sporting Life."

Chicago, July 19.—Chicagos have one less game lost to their credit. The protested Chicago-Pittsburg game played in this city on May 23 has been declared off by the Board of Directors of the National League and the game has been stricken from the records. The League orders that the game shall be played over in Pittsburg on August 13. Umpire Emslie called the game in question at the close of the sixth inning to allow the Pittsburgs time to catch a train for Cleveland. Emslie went with the team and did not leave the city until about 8 o'clock. It was a trick on the part of the Pittsburg management to secure a game to which it had no right. When the game was called the score stood 10 to 9 in the visitors' favor. Had it been finished it is likely that the Colts would have won, as they were in fine batting form on that day. Chicagos have no open date with Pittsburg. The postponed New York game will also be played off in the East, local patrons thus missing two games in the regular home series.

Umpire Gaffney's Explanation.

Special to "Sporting Life."

Cincinnati, July 19.—Umpire Gaffney denies the story that he was out on a lark with the Brooklyn players in St. Louis. He says: "That is a nice way to use a man who is doing his best to do what is right. I have not touched a drop of intoxicating liquors since last Christmas, and did not see the row between Daily and Kinslow. I was with them early in the evening. Treadway, Corcoran, Daily, Kinslow and myself went out to the electric light races. I came from the races back to the hotel and went to bed. The next morning I heard that Kinslow and Daily had a fight. This is all I know of it; I did nothing to bring myself into trouble."

Ex-Pitcher Charlie Sweeney Charged With Murder.

Special to "Sporting Life."

San Francisco, Cal., July 19.—Charles B. Sweeney, formerly one of the best base ball players in the country, had a charge of murder placed against him yesterday. He shot Con. McManus during a saloon quarrel Sunday, and the victim died Monday.

The Temple Cup.

Above is an excellent likeness of the beautiful and valuable cup presented by ex-President Temple, of the Pittsburg Club, to the League, for contest among the clubs at the close of each championship season. The cup was designed and made by E. A. Thrall, 3 Malden Lane, New York city, and cost over $700.

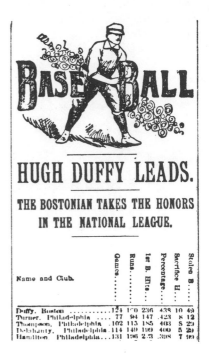

HUGH DUFFY LEADS.

THE BOSTONIAN TAKES THE HONORS IN THE NATIONAL LEAGUE.

Name and Club.	Games.	Runs.	1st B. Hits.	Percentage.	Sacrifice H.	Stolen B.
Duffy, Boston	124	160	236	438	10	49
Turner, Philadelphia	77	94	147	.423	8	12
Thompson, Philadelphia	102	113	185	.403	8	29
Delahanty, Philadelphia	114	149	189	.400	5	20
Hamilton, Philadelphia	131	196	223	.398	7	99

SCHRIVER'S FEAT.

A LONG STANDING TRADITION AT LAST EXPLODED.

The Chicago Player Catches a Base Ball Tossed From the Top of the Washington Monument, a Distance of 500 Feet.

Washington D. C., Aug. 26.—William Schriver, one of the catchers of the Chicago Base Ball Club, smashed to smithereens yesterday a tradition of long standing, that no base ball player could ever catch a regulation ball tossed to him from one of the windows in the top of the Washington Monument. It is 500 feet from the base of the monument, where visitors enter, to the landing where the elevator stops, and it was from this level that Schriver accomplished the feat which has hitherto caused so much speculation.

AN OLD TRADITION.

As regularly as the ball teams visited Washington there would be a controversy that no base ball player could catch a ball thrown from this height to the ground beneath, and attention has frequently been called to the failure of the great fielder, Paul Hines, to catch a regulation ball at this spot. It has been held that no man could hold fast to a ball dropped 500 feet in sheer space. First, because the height was too great for a man to see the ball, and, secondly, because the impetus it would receive would break every finger in the outstretched hand of the mortal who thus tempted fate.

THE FINAL GAME.

New York Makes It Four Straight With Ease.

The fourth and last game played at the Polo Grounds October 8 was won easily by the Giants. This game ended the series, according to agreement, as the New Yorks had now four straight, a majority of the series of seven games.

There were 12,000 people present, and there was the same enthusiasm which had marked each game. Van Haltren looked the picture of happiness in the second inning, when Digby Bell walked out to the home plate and in behalf of the centrefielder's hosts of friends presented him with a silver bat of regulation size. Van responded with a two-bagger. In the sixth inning Van met with an accident, which caused him to retire from the game. He collided with Jennings while trying to steal second base, and was knocked unconscious. When he recovered his nose appeared to be broken, but later it was found to be only an abrasion. Murphy took his place in centre field. Jennings was seriously cut on the forehead and retired in favor of Bonner.

Only five safe hits were made off Meekin, who pitched great ball. They bunched two in the second innings, but failed to score. In the last four innings they did not connect successfully with his curves even once. On account of darkness hostilities were stopped at the end of the eighth inning. There were many sensational plays—a stop by Davis being one of the finest ever seen on any ball field. Farrell, Van Haltren, Bonner and Brodie did phenomenal fielding. The score:

NEW YORK.	A.B.	R.	B.	P.	A.	E.
Burke, lf.	4	2	1	3	0	0
Tiernan, rf.	3	1	1	1	0	0
Davis, 3b.	3	2	1	1	2	0
Doyle, 1b.	5	2	4	7	1	1
Ward, 2b.	5	1	1	2	1	0
Van Hal'n, cf.	3	2	3	1	0	0
Murphy, cf.	1	0	0	0	0	0
Fuller, ss.	5	2	3	2	4	0
Farrell, c.	4	3	3	6	1	0
Meekin, p.	5	1	3	1	0	0
Total	38	16	20	24	8	4

BALTIMORE.	A.B.	R.	B.	P.	A.	E.
Kelly, lf.	3	1	2	0	1	0
Keeler, rf.	3	1	0	2	1	0
Brout's, 1b.	4	0	0	5	0	0
McGraw, 3b.	3	1	1	2	3	2
Brodie, cf.	3	0	0	4	2	0
Reitz, 2b.	4	0	1	4	3	0
Jennings, ss.	3	0	0	1	1	0
Bonner, ss.	1	0	2	0	0	0
Robinson, c.	4	0	2	4	3	0
Hawke, p.	2	0	0	0	0	1
Gleason, p.	1	0	0	0	0	0
Total	31	3	8	24	14	3

New York .... 1 0 1 3 5 1 5 0—16
Baltimore .... 2 0 1 0 0 0 0 0—3

Earned runs—New York 10. First on errors—Baltimore 3. Left on bases—New York 5, Baltimore 8. First on balls—Off Meekin 3, off Hawke 1, off Gleason 5. Struck out—By Meekin 4. Two-base hits—Davis, Doyle 2, Van Haltren. Stolen base—Burke 2, Doyle 2, Van Haltren, Fuller, Farrell 2, Reitz. Double plays—Ward, Doyle; Keeler, Reitz; Brodie, Brouthers. Hit by pitcher—McGraw. Wild pitches

KELLY DEAD.

Baseball King Passed Away Last Night.

Michael J. Kelly, who was the most widely known ball player in the land, died last evening at the Emergency Hospital from pneumonia, the end coming at 9:55 p. m.

The most popular of ball players is no more. The idol of the South End bleaching boards in '87, '88 and '89, and of the Congress street ground patrons in '90, has trod the diamond for the last time, and will never more go to bat.

This will be sorrowful news to a host of people, for Mr Kelly was beloved by thousands who had associated and mingled with him on and off the baseball diamond. He was confined to his bed only four days, although when he took passage on the Fall River line at New York for Boston Sunday evening he felt quite ill.

HOW THEY DIVIDED.

NEAT SUM REALIZED FROM THE TEMPLE CUP GAMES.

The Bulk of the Cash Was Contributed by the Cleveland Public—Over $500 For Each Cleveland Man and Over $300 For Each Baltimorean.

The receipts of the Temple Cup series were divided last week among the players of the Cleveland and Baltimore teams. Each Cleveland player received $528 and each Baltimore player $316. While this falls somewhat short of the amount realized last year, yet it is really more considering the distance between Cleveland and New York in the matter of population and base ball enthusiasm.

GOOD FOR CLEVELAND.

The Baltimore team regretted that they were obliged to play off with Cleveland, for they were sure the Spiders would have much the best of them in regard to receipts. They figured that Cleveland would contribute little to the fund, compared with what the generous rooters in Baltimore would throw into the pot. As a matter of fact, the receipts in Cleveland from the third game were greater than those in Baltimore for the two games. The total amount received in Cleveland was $10,656.50 and in Baltimore $4651.

THE STATEMENT.

Following is the statement of receipts and expenditures:

RECEIVED AT CLEVELAND.

Oct. 2	$2,547 50
Oct. 3	3,337 00
Oct. 5	4,772 00
	—$10,656 50

RECEIVED AT BALTIMORE.

Oct. 7	$3,043 00
Oct. 8	1,608 00
	—$4,651 00

Total receipts	$15,307 50

AT CLEVELAND.

Ground expenses	$82 75
Paid umpires	165 85

Total	$248 60

AT BALTIMORE.

Ground expenses	$70 30
Paid umpires	235 75

Total	$306 05
Total to be divided	$14,752 85

The Cleveland Club received 60 per cent. ... 8,851 71
Receipts from score card sales, etc... 538 87

Total Cleveland Club's receipts	$9,390 58

Less traveling, printing and other expenses ... 937 30

Total to be divided	$8,453 28
Each player's share	$528 33

The money was divided between the following players, and each received $528.33: O. Tebeau, Young, Cuppy, Knell, Wilson, Wallace, Zimmer, O'Connor, O'Meara, Childs, McGarr, McKean, Burkett, McAleer, Blake and George Tebeau.

REAL HARMONY.

The good feeling that prevails among the members of the team and the generous spirit that actuates the Clevelands are noted by the fact that they agreed to divide equally, although Knell, Wilson and O'Meara have been with the players but a portion of the year. Last year the Baltimores in dividing the purse gave the new comers but a share of the regular allotment received by the old members of the team. The matter was discussed by the Cleveland players and it was unanimously agreed that each member of the team should share alike. It is flattering to the men to be able to say that they reached such a conclusion when it was apparent they would have been perfectly justified in dividing the player's share between Wilson and O'Meara and giving Knell a slightly smaller proportion than was awarded to the older members.

Burkett Leads All the Sluggers, Hamilton Leads in Stolen Bases and Jennings in Sacrifice Hits—Five Phillies Among the First Seven Batsmen.

Washington, Oct. 13.—President Young has finished the batting averages of players of the National League who have participated in 15 or more games during the late base ball season. Some interesting facts and figures are developed as the result of the compilation, the principal feature being the high batting average of 70 players, the lowest of whom attained .301. Burkett, of Cleveland, leads the League with a percentage of .423, his nearest competitor being Delahanty, of the Philadelphia, with .400. In stolen bases Hamilton, of Philadelphia, is first, with 95, followed by Lange, of Chicago, with 79. The following are the averages:

	Games	A.B.	B.H.	Pct.	SH	SB
Burkett, Cleve	132	555	235	.423	7	47
Delahanty, Phila	116	481	192	.399	6	46
Keeler, Balt	131	560	221	.394	21	57
Thompson, Phila	118	533	210	.394	2	24
Hamilton, Phila	121	517	208	.393	9	95
Clements, Phila	84	324	126	.389	3	14
Turner, Phila	46	209	81	.388	3	14
Lange, Chi	122	479	188	.388	9	79
Jennings, Balt	131	528	204	.386	22	80
Stenzel, Pitts	131	520	200	.384	6	53
Holmes, Lou	39	157	60	.382	3	12
McGraw, Balt	96	385	144	.374	6	53
Kelley, Balt	131	510	189	.370	12	59
Brodie, Balt	130	523	193	.365	9	36
Everett, Chi	133	552	197	.352	9	51
Tiernan, N. Y	119	474	168	.354	4	94

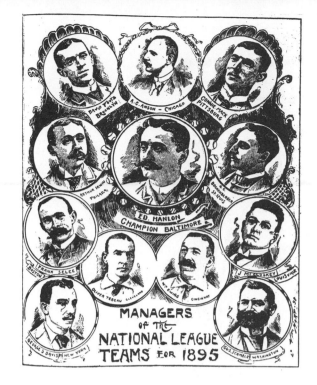

MANAGERS of THE NATIONAL LEAGUE TEAMS FOR 1895

A BASE BALL DRAMA.

THE FIRST PLAY STAGED FOUNDED ON OUR NATIONAL GAME.

Anson to be the Central Figure in the Drama From the Rise to the Fall of the Curtain—Synopsis of the Play.

New York, Nov. 12.—Captain Anson, the famous ball player, will make his debut as a dramatic star at Syracuse next Saturday night in "A Runaway Colt," a play written for him and around him by Charles A. Hoyt. As he is the base ball hero of America he becomes the consistent star of the only base ball play ever staged, and he has no minor part in the cast, but is on the stage in every game scene from the rise of the curtain until he makes the home run hit in the last act which "rings down" the proper climax.

The scene of the first act is laid in the home of Rev. Dr. Manners, near Racine, Wis. There Anson goes to visit the minister's son, Manly Manners, who is a famous young college pitcher, and whose services the Chicago captain wants to secure for his club. Manly's parents look upon Anson and all professional ball players as ruffians, and rather reluctantly consent to let Manly invite him to dinner on the day of his arrival. But Anson announces himself as Mr. Adrian, a friend of young Manners, and is received by the mother and by Mercy, the young collegian's sweetheart, who do not suspect that they are entertaining the awful, ruffianly Captain Anson. Both ladies do their best to entertain "Mr. Adrian," and the fun begins.

WRIGHT IS DEAD.

THE FATHER OF PROFESSIONAL BASE BALL CALLED OUT.

After a Painful Illness of Several Weeks the "Noblest Roman of Them All" Passes Away at Atlantic City

A PLAYER EXECUTED

"PACER" SMITH HANGED; HARRIS REPRIEVED.

The Ex-Player Repentant on the Scaffold —He Meets His Doom Bravely— His Crime the Murder of His Own Child and a Sister-in-Law.

Decatur, Ill., Nov. 29.—Charles N. Smith was executed at 12 M. to-day. He went to the scaffold without a tremor, attended by Fathers Mackin and Brady, of Decatur, and Huggens, of Taylorville.

His only statement was: "I am sorry." Deputy Sam Stabler adjusted the noose; Deputy M. Holmes fixed the straps and adjusted the black cap. As that was done Smith said: "Good-by."

Sheriff Jerry P. Nicholson pulled the trap at exactly 11.54. Smith kept his nerve to the last, though pale and with tears trickling down his face, but made no statement in regard to other crimes of which he has been accused. The jail was packed with spectators.

Frank Harris, the Freeport, Ill., murderer, who was to have been hanged to-day, but was reprieved by Governor Altgeld, is Smith's old catcher. Both played together as a battery for several seasons. "Pacer" wrote Harris a letter telling him to die game.

"PACER" SMITH,
As he appeared with the Memphis team in '87.

STORY OF THE CRIME.

Smith was 38 years of age and a noted ball player. He was familiarly called "Pacer." On September 28 Smith shot and killed his sister-in-law, Edna Bouchert, a girl of 17, and his daughter, Louise Smith, aged 5 years. He attempted to kill his wife at the same time, but she escaped. Details of the crime appeared in "Sporting Life" at the time it occurred.

The tragedy was the culmination of several years of domestic infelicity, coupled with a career of drunkenness and immorality on the part of Smith. He had frequently threatened to kill his wife and child, and he went to the Bouchert home on the day of the tragedy partly intoxicated and armed with a revolver. He fired four shots, two at his wife, whom he missed; one at his sister-in-law, fatally wounding her, and one at his little daughter, hitting her in the head.

SMITH'S BASE BALL CAREER.

Smith was born in Pendleton, Ind., on August 4, 1853. He was, after his eighteenth year, known as a skilful amateur base ball player, and in 1876 was offered and accepted a position with the Red Stockings of Cincinnati, O., with whom he played during the seasons of '76 and '77, from whence he went to the Baltimore Blues, of Baltimore, Md., with whom he also played two seasons, '78 and '79; during the season of '80, with the Nashvilles, of Nashville, Tenn.; of '81 with the base ball club of Terre Haute, Ind., which was a member of the Northwestern League, as was also the team of Indianapolis, with which he played the seasons of '82 and '83; during the season of '84 with the base ball club of Noblevive, Ind.; during the season of '85 he played alternately with the teams of Jacksonville, Fla., and Greencastle, Ind.; in '86, alternatively with the teams of Decatur, Ill., and Little Rock, Ark., going from the Decaturs to Little Rock; during '87, part of the season with the Memphis (Tenn.) Club, but for personal reasons he demanded and obtained his release, and finished the season alternately with the teams of Wichita, Kas., and Champaign, Ill. He started the season of '88 with the Decatur (Ill.) Club, but upon their again disbanding he finished the season with the Bloomington (Ill.) team. He played the season of '89 alternately with the teams of Elkhart, Ind., and Fort Madison, Ia., and Monmouth, Ill.; during the season of '90, at Ottawa, Ill.; '91, Shreveport, Ill.; in '92 with Panino, Ill., and Muncie, Ind., in '93. Since that time he had no regular employment, and became much addicted to drink.

KNOCK THEM ALL DOWN YOU GET A PENNANT!

Then, Boys, Don't Let Baltimore Knock Them All Down Again."

THE FIRST TO CURVE.

HOW ARTHUR CUMMINGS MADE THE DISCOVERY.

An Idea Born of Idly Throwing Clam Shells Nearly a Quarter of a Century Ago—Cummings' Modest Talk of His Art and Career.

According to Tim Murnane, the art of curve pitching was first conceived by its inventor, Arthur Cumming, through throwing clam shells. Regarding the matter, Sir Timothy says in the Boston "Globe:" The art of curving a base ball was discovered nearly 30 years ago by W. A. Cummings, a junior member of the Excelsior Club, of Brooklyn, N. Y., while pitching against the Harvard University team on Holmes' field, Cambridge, Mass.

Up to 1874 Cummings alone knew the secret of the out curve. Bobby Mathews, a Baltimore pitcher, had mastered the raise ball and was very effective against all the strong teams of that time. It was years later that Mathews understood the art of all the curves.

ARTHUR CUMMINGS, INVENTOR.

Many of the crack players of the early 70s are alive and can testify to the fact that Cummings was the originator of curve pitching. Among those are Geo. Wright, John C. Chapman, A. G. Spalding, A. J. Leonard, Doug Allison, N. E. Young, Richard Pierce, Richard Higham, A. C. Anson, Weston Fisler, Thomas Pratt and James White. The above names should be a guarantee that Mr. Cummings' claim is a just one, and should put forever the credit of first curving a ball where it belongs.

For years the scientific men laughed at the idea of a man making a ball curve in the air; but that prejudice has passed away, as many of the learned men of the day can go out on a field and fully illustrate the science of curve pitching themselves.

M'JAMES TO QUIT.

The Rising Pitcher Says He Prefers Medicine to Base Ball.

One of the finds of the past season was young pitcher McJames, of the Washington Club. As a pitcher he is acknowledged by all players to be a wonder. He sprang into prominence suddenly, and his brilliancy was all the more dazzling on that account. This young man of 25 years is a typical Southerner. His home is at Charleston, where his father is a medical practitioner of renown. Jimmy began his ball playing on the nine of the University of South Carolina, of which he is a graduate. In 1895 he was with the Petersburg team, of the Virginia League, from which he was drafted by the Washingtons in the fall. Young McJames speaks with the delightful drawling "r-less" dialect of the South. He is most intellectual and entertaining and popular with all who know him. He is an especial favorite of Washington young ladies. The young Southerner is ready at all times to discuss the free coinage of silver at 16 to 1, of which he is a strong advocate, and on which topic he can give arguments and figures by the yard. His hero politically is Senator Tillman, whom he knows personally and whom he never tires of praising and defending. He has entered the Charleston Medical College, and announces his intention of abandoning professional base ball.

"CHOPPING" THE BALL.

The Champions Credited With Practicing Something New in the Way of Batting.

From the Baltimore "News" we learn that the inventive genius of the Orioles has lately been given a new bent. Says our esteemed Baltimore contemporary:

"The Baltimore Club has already originated several distinctive plays which have made it famous and which have been copied with more or less success by others. Foremost among these are the "hit and run" tactics. Now a new style of hitting will be recorded in the base ball history of '96 and credited to the Orioles. It is "chopping" the ball, and a chopped ball generally goes for a hit. It requires great skill in placing to work this trick successfully, and it is done in this fashion: A middle-height ball is picked out and is attacked with a terrific swing on the upper side. The ball is made to strike the ground from five to ten feet away from the batsman, and, striking the ground with force bounds high over the head of the third or first baseman. In nearly every game lately has this little teaser been successfully employed, and yesterday two such hits were made.

SACRIFICE HITTING.

Manager Selee Thinks It Should be Abandoned.

"I may be an odd number, and there are many managers, captains and players in the League who are opposed to my idea, but I still insist that sacrifice hitting should be abandoned," says Manager Frank Selee, of the Boston team. "I would suggest that a sacrifice hit should figure as a time at the bat, and if this idea of mine will be made a law there wouldn't be much sacrificing. In making the rules of base ball the public, first of all, should be considered, and I believe that the average patron of the game is not in favor of sacrificing. They want to see the ball hit out hard and clean. It often occurs that the most scientific batsmen fail in their effort to sacrifice, and what is the result? They are sore, and if they slip up in their efforts to sacrifice in a game on the home grounds they are often jeered by the fans. Sacrifice hitting handicaps base running, and if it is abandoned you will see more hitting, and the public want hitting above all things, while there will be an improvement of base running."

BUCKSHOT FOR UMPIRE.

A Base Runner Gets His Gun, Shoots and Goes on With the Game.

Wheeling, W. Va., May 16.—At Vivan, on the Norfolk & Western Railroad to-day, a gang of colored miners, off for a half holiday, engaged in a game of base ball. A player named Jim Carrigan tried to make a home run, but was declared out at the home plate by Umpire Charley Hunt.

This so enraged Carrigan that he went home, got his shotgun and fired a load of buckshot into the umpire, inflicting wounds which will probably kill him. A new umpire was substituted and the game went on, Carrigan taking part in it.

X-RAYS ON A PLAYER.

A Splinter Removed From the Wrist of First Baseman Cassidy.

Louisville, Ky., April 8.—The first base ball player in the history of the national game to be mixed up with the now famous N rays is Peter Cassidy, the Colonels' first baseman. Late Monday afternoon Doctors Vance and Stucky took a photograph of Cassidy's wrist with cathode rays. It was a very successful trial. The young man had been suffering with his wrist for some time, and ordinary remedies did not seem to do him any good. Then the X-rays were thought of.

The photograph shows that in Cassidy's wrist there is a loose piece of bone, a splinter which moves about in the wrist. This was what caused all the trouble. Every time the wrist got a jar the little piece of bone moved to another part of the member, keeping the wrist sore all the time. The removal of the splinter was readily achieved by a surgical operation.

BIG BATTING FEATS

RECALLED BY DELEHANTY'S RECENT ACHIEVEMENT.

A Resume of the Most Notable Performances With the Bat Under the Modern Conditions of Pitching and Fielding.

The great record of four home runs and a single for five times at bat performed by Delehanty, of the Phillies, at Chicago, July 13, has created lots of talk as to batting records. Following is a resume of the best feats accomplished under modern conditions:

"The feat of Bottenus, of the Buffalos, who in 1895 made four home runs and a two-bagger five times at bat, stands unchallenged by batsmen of modern professional base ball. His nearest competitor is Lowe, of the Bostons, who, in one of the games of May 30, 1894, made four home runs and a single. This total was once equaled by Larry Twitchell, and has just been equaled by Delehanty. Lowe also made two home runs in one inning. In 1882 Charley Smith made eight successive hits. Frank Fennelly, once of Cincinnati, has a record of six successive hits, with a total of 18. Guy Hecker, when with Louisville, in 1886, made three home runs, a triple and a double. Jerry Denny is credited with seven successive hits, while Dave Orr and Larkin beat all records for successive and successful batting by 10 hits each in one game. George Rooks, of Oshkosh, once made three home runs in a game against Eau Claire, with which Bobby Lowe was playing. Crooks, of Washington, in 1889, made five safe hits, four of which were home runs. Fitzgerald, of Wilkesbarre, in 1889, made two home runs in one inning. Charley Jones, while playing with Buffalo, in 1880, made two homers in one inning. George Gore, of Chicago, in a game against Boston is credited with nine successive hits, five of which were doubles, and Elmer Smith once secured three home runs in a game. Roger Connor last season, out of six times at bat, made three singles, two doubles and a triple."

In the old days of underhand pitching and a much more lively ball we believe the late Harry Wright made seven or eight home runs in one game, but home runs in that style of playing were almost as frequent as two-base hits are now. If Delehanty had made his home runs on the Boston ground or on the Phillies' own ground much would have been taken from the honor of the performance, for in Boston the left and right field fences and in Philadelphia the right field fence are so near the diamond that many fly balls go over which count as home runs, but which with an unobstructed field would be easy outs. All of Delehanty's four-base hits were inside of the inclosed Chicago grounds. They were good long drives which could not be returned by the fielders till after the noted Philadelphia batsman had made the circuit of the bases. Another thing which adds to Delehanty's batting feat is the fact that it was not generally a heavy hitting game.

PLAYERS GO TO CHURCH.

The Cincinnati Team Listens to a Base Ball Sermon.

Last Sunday week the Association team in a body all went to church to hear Rev. Stephen A. Northrop, of the First Baptist Tabernacle, preach a base ball sermon. The announcements were printed in red and embodied the team's slogan "Cincinnati for Cincinnati."

"There is no room for the pugilistic element in base ball," said Dr. Northrop in the course of his sermon, and he cited the expulsion of Billy Merritt from the game at Pittsburg and praised Harry Vaughn for possessing self-control enough not to respond to the assault in kind. Every one of the Reds appreciated the talk.

"I believe that more ministers at the ball park would help the game," said he. "I've rubbed elbows with fans who have jabbed me in the side in moments of excitement, and once a rooter ripped out an oath. We got to discussing the game, and I handed him my card. He apologized for swearing. I am glad that the ministry of to-day is drawing closer to the people. I don't believe that the preacher should get into the pulpit and stay there aloof from his congregation. He should be a mixer, able to share in the joys and sorrows of those around him."

NED CRANE IS DEAD.

Rochester, Sept. 21.—Edward N. Crane, noted as a National League and an Eastern League pitcher, ended his life here Saturday night, Sept. 19, by accidentally taking an overdose of chloral. For the past two years Crane has been intimately identified with Rochester base ball. He came here in July, 1895, having been released by Toronto. He did good work for the Canadians, but Rochester wanted him, and was obliged to pay good money for him. He proved to be a failure, but played the season out. This year he started in with Providence, but his arm was in poor shape, and he received his release. Then he went to Springfield, but he did no better, and he wandered further West. He umpired several games for Rochester, but was not a success, and President Pat Powers released him.

GOOD AND BAD EYES.

HOW THE NATIONAL LEAGUE PLAYERS BATTED.

The Official Averages Make Burkett, of Cleveland, the Leader of Them All For the Second Consecutive Time— What the Others Accomplished.

President Young has promulgated the official batting averages of players of the National League who took part in 15 or more championship games of base ball during the season of 1896.

At the head of the list stands Burkett, of the Cleveland Club, with a percentage of .410, while Jennings, of Baltimore, is second, with .397. Delehanty, of Philadelphia, gets the third bracket with .394; Keeler and Kelly, of Baltimore, take fourth and fifth places, with .392 and .370, respectively; Stenzel, of Pittsburg, finishes sixth, with .366, and the lucky number, seven, falls to Hamilton, of Boston, with .363. There is a tie for eighth place between Dahlen, of Chicago, and Clements,

JESSE BURKETT.
The Little Man To Whom the Ball Looks Big As a Barn.

of Philadelphia, at .362, and Tiernan, of New York, slipped into the 10th hole with .361. E. E. Smith, of Pittsburg, stands 11th, with .358; McGraw, of Baltimore, 12th, with .356, while the unlucky number, 13, is awarded to Demontreville, of Washington, with .355. Robinson, of Baltimore, ranks 14th, with .354, while Stivetts, of Boston; Van Haltren, of New York, and Jones, of Brooklyn, fight for 15th honors, with .353.

JOHNSON IS JOLLY

OVER ANOTHER SUCCESSFUL WESTERN LEAGUE SEASON.

He Once More Asserts That All of the Clubs, With One Exception, Cleared a Profit and That the Outlook is All That Could be Desired.

Cincinnati, Oct. 5.—President Ban Johnson, of the Western League, takes issue with Business Manager Bancroft, of the local club, on the question of Western League success. Bancroft claims that Mr. Vonderbeck told him that the season of the Western League was not satisfactory, that only three clubs made money, all the rest, including the champion team, lost more or less heavily, and that there would be a smash-up unless a reduction of salaries all round could be effected. In his counter comment Mr. Johnson said:

A SUCCESSFUL SEASON.

"That is one of Bancroft's regular post-season games. The season of 1896 was 35 per cent. better than 1894. Kansas City did not do as well as last year, but about equaled 1894. Minneapolis made money in spite of any statements to the contrary. The salary list was high, but there was a cut and this saved considerable. Mr. Haines told me only a short time ago they would quit $5000 winner, and that is a great deal for a club with such a salary list. As for St. Paul losing that is absurd. Comiskey told me on July 7 that he had taken in enough to pay all running expenses, salaries, railroad fares and hotel bills until the end of the season, and all after that would be velvet. After making the statement he brought his team East on the most successful trip of the year, and his home attendance was good on the next home series. He made more money, if anything than last year, although he did not take in quite as much at the gates.

THE FUTURE.

Mr. Johnson sees no breakers in the way of the Western League, other than the excessive salaries being paid by some teams. The League will take united action on this and in cutting the salaries will make the playing strength of the clubs more equal. There is apt to be a radical change in the spring.

Mr. Johnson will also repeat his proposition to the National League to increase the pay of its drafted Western League players only when they demonstrate beyond doubt that they are fit to stay in National League company. Then the Western League will not be flooded with discarded National League players at National League salaries.

Mr. Johnson further said: "The annual meeting would be held in Chicago November 11, at the Victoria Hotel. I haven't any idea as to what will be done. Applications for franchises continue to pour in. I do not think that there is a possible chance for Omaha or Des Moines."

CHARLEY ZIMMER ROBBED.

The Big Catcher Rudely Awakened From Temple Cup Dreams.

Charley Zimmer, the big and popular catcher of the Cleveland Base Ball Club, had a unique experience on the night of September 24. He was sound asleep at his home, 43 Steinway street, Cleveland, dreaming about the Temple Cup money, when he was awakened by a sharp dig in the ribs by his wife. When the chief opened his eyes he found himself looking into a pair of revolvers. His wife was lying all a tremble beside him, too frightened almost to breathe. Back of the big pistols were two masked men. As soon as Zimmer came to a full realization of the situation one of the burglars remarked coolly:

"Do you know us, Chief?"

"No, I don't," replied the catcher of foul tips.

"Well, we know you, all right," returned the burglar.

"You know what we are here for, though, don't you?" he added.

"I guess so," said Zimmer. "There are my clothes. Help yourselves."

While one of the intruders took Zim's $60 gold watch and $20 the other covered the ball player and his wife with his revolvers. The rifling of the clothes ended the two burglars backed out of the house. As they reached the outside door the spokesman said: "So long, Charley."

"So long," responded Zimmer.

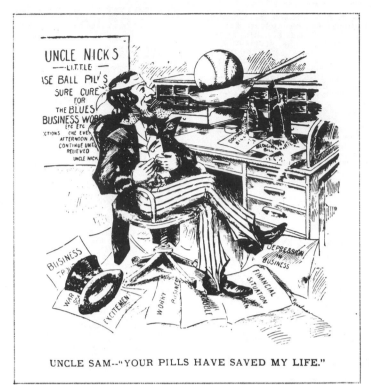

UNCLE SAM--"YOUR PILLS HAVE SAVED MY LIFE."

RADBOURNE'S RELIEF

DEATH ENDS THE SUFFERING OF A NOTED MAN.

The Former "King of Pitchers" Pays the Debt of Nature—The Brilliant Career of a Man Unequalled in His Special Line of Work.

Bloomington, Ill., Feb. 9.—Charles Radbourne, who was in his day the king of pitchers, died in this city on Friday, the 5th inst., at 1 P. M., from paresis. He had been in failing health for a long time and latterly he had been subject to convulsions. He had been in a comatose condition for several days before his demise. His brain had been more or less affected for a year or longer, and about a year ago he lost the sight of one eye by the accidental discharge of a gun. Radbourne invested his savings some years ago in a building in Bloomington and established a saloon, billiard room and sportsmen's resort. He was a famous member of a family all of whom are locally noted nimrods, and until prostrated by illness he spent much of his time in the fields.

CLEVELAND CLOSED

TO PROFESSIONAL BALL PLAYING ON THE SABBATH.

Sunday ball in Cleveland, for this season at least, is doomed. The jury in the case of John Powell, the member of the Cleveland Club, charged with playing base ball on Sunday, returned a verdict of guilty in both counts at noon June 10. The deliberation of the jury lasted from 7 o'clock the previous evening. On the 12th Powell was fined $5 and costs, the latter amounting to $153. Powell is given thirty days in which to make an appeal from judgment. Mr. Robison will now carry the case to the Supreme Court, but no decision is expected in time to avail the Cleveland Club this season. Mr. Robison says that in case the highest court decides against Sunday ball an effort will be made to repeal the "Sunday amusement" law at the next session of the Ohio Legislature.

ONE JOB IS ENOUGH.

Washington, D. C., August 9.—The president of the National Base Ball League, Nicholas E. Young, on Saturday resigned from the position he has occupied for 31 years in the service of the Government as a clerk in the office of the Auditor for the War Department. Mr. Young has been president for many years past of the National League. The duties of the place, at first light, have gradually become heavier until they demand so much attention at his hands that he felt that with due regard to his health he could not discharge them in connection with those attaching to the clerkship he has for so many years held in the Government service. The question arising as to a choice, Mr. Young, whose devotion to the national game is a household word, decided to tender his resignation to Secretary Gage. This was done Saturday, and at the request of Mr. Young the Secretary accepted the resignation at once, leaving him free to devote his entire attention to the manifold affairs of the National League.

THEY WOULD NOT BUNT.

The Secret of Baltimore's Loss of a Game to Pittsburg with Killen in the Box.

There was once a time when the Baltimore Champions used to get Killen, Pittsburg's big left hander, on the verge of insanity by bunting and all sorts of tricks with their sticks, and when they had sufficiently shattered his nervous system they would bat out a victory at their leisure.

But the Orioles have stopped bunting or sacrificing or batting with science. They have become such mighty sluggers that nothing less than doubles and three-baggers will suit them. They have left bunting and such work to teams that are struggling along in second place or lower, like Boston. It is true that the Orioles are great batters and have been winning in brilliant fashion, but sometimes their heavy hitting does not arrive on schedule time. Such an occasion was Saturday afternoon, when the Birds and the Pittsburgers played the last game of the Pittsburg's first Eastern trip.

Killen was in great form, and it was very clear early in the game that he was unhittable, more especially because the batters were seriously handicapped by a strong wind against them. It was an occasion which seemed to call urgently for bunting and bunting, but the Baltimores continued to try to drive the ball over the fence against a strong head wind, and the consequence was that the outfielders did considerable business and the Orioles very little scoring. In fact, they would have been shut out but for Doyle's base running. He got a base on balls in the second inning, stole second and third bases and scored on O'Brien's single.

Unlike the Orioles, however, the visitors bunted a number of times, and while their bunting was not as successful as it might have been, it kept the Orioles nervous, drew Bowerman up behind the bat a number of times and materially assisted in the run-getting of the visitors in the eighth and ninth innings. Elmer Smith's run in the eighth was assisted by a sacrifice, and it was that run which won the game.

The moment the visitors got one run ahead Hoffer, who had been pitching up to that time as well as Killen, weakened, and, assisted by Jennings' error, the visitors batted out five runs. It was the first game of the season in which Keeler did not make a hit. Both sides fielded brilliantly, Jennings and Ely being the stars.

The official score of Saturday's game follows:

BALTO.	R	B	H	O	A	E	PITTSBURG	R	B	H	O	A	E
McGraw, 3.	4	0	0	0	1	0	Smith, l..	2	2	1	7	0	0
Keeler, r..	4	0	0	2	0	0	Padden, 2.	1	1	0	4	1	0
Jennings,s	3	0	1	6	1	1	Davis, 3..	0	1	0	2	3	0
Doyle, 1..	3	1	0	15	0	0	Brodie, cf.	5	0	1	2	0	0
Reitz, 2..	4	0	2	0	3	0	Donovan, r	2	1	1	1	0	0
O'Brien, l.	4	0	1	3	0	0	Ely, s....	0	1	2	7	0	0
Quinn, cf.	3	0	0	3	0	0	Merritt, 1.	4	0	1	10	1	1
Bow'rm'n,c	3	0	3	0	0	0	Sugden, c.	3	1	1	1	1	1
Hoffer, p.	3	0	1	0	4	0	Killen, p..	4	1	0	0	4	0
Total.....	31	1	8	27	14	1	Total....	34	7	8	27	16	2

SCORE BY INNINGS.

Clubs.	1	2	3	4	5	6	7	8	9	Total.
Baltimore..............	0	1	0	0	0	0	0	0	0	1
Pittsburg..............	1	0	0	0	0	0	0	1	5	7

Earned run—Pittsburg, 1. Two-base hits—Jennings, Smith. Three-base hit—Davis. Sacrifice hits—Padden, Ely. Bases stolen—By Doyle, (1,) Quinn, Donovan, (2.) Bases on balls—By Hoffer, 4; Killen, 2. Bases on balls—To Jennings, Doyle, Smith, (3.) Struck out—By Hoffer, 2, (Davis, Killen;) by Killen, 1, (Bowerman.) Passed balls—Bowerman, 2. Left on bases—Baltimore, 5; Pittsburg, 6. First base on errors—Baltimore, 1; Pittsburg, 1. Time of game—Two hours. Umpire—Hurst.

CHICAGO VS. LOUISVILLE AT CHICAGO JUNE 29.—
This was a good batting matinee, the locals scoring
thirty-six runs on thirty-two hits for a total of fifty-
one bases. Frazer lasted two and a half innings,
then gave way to Jones, but to no advantage. Johnson had an eye badly cut by an ugly bounder and
Decker was painfully injured by a pitched ball, both
being forced to retire. The score:

CHICAGO.	AB.R.B. P. A	LOUISVILLE.	AB.R.B. P. A
Everett, 3b..	7 3 2 0 3	Clarke, lf..	4 0 3 2 1 0
McCork, ss	5 6 4 1 0	McCrea'y, rf	4 1 0 0 0 0
Lange, cf..	7 4 4 0 0	Pickering, cf	5 1 2 1 3 3
Anson, 1b..	4 4 1 10 1 0	Stafford, ss	5 1 0 3 8 3
Ryan, rf..	6 5 2 0 0	Werden, 1b	5 1 3 14 1 1
Decker, lf..	4 2 3 0 0	Dexter, 3b..	5 0 4 1 6 1
Connor, 2b..	6 4 4 2 3	Butler, c..	5 0 0 3 0 2
Callahan, p..	7 4 5 1 2	Johns'n, 2b	4 0 0 0 0 0
Donahue, c..	5 3 3 5 1 0	Frazer, p..	0 0 0 1 2 0
Thornton, lf	2 2 2 1 0	Jones, p..	3 2 1 0 0 0
Total..	57 36 32 27 11	Deleha'y, 2b	3 1 1 1 1 2
		Total..	39 7 14 26 23 9

*Connor out for cutting third base.

Chicago .... 3 5 7 1 2 1 2 7 8—36
Louisville .... 0 0 1 0 5 0 1 0 0—7

Earned runs—Chicago 19, Louisville 6. Left on
bases—Chicago 6, Louisville 7. Two-base hits—
Everett, Ryan, Decker, Callahan 2, Donahue, Wer-
den 2, Dexter 2, Jones, Delehanty. Three-base hits
—McCormick, Lange, Connor. Home runs—McCormick, Ryan. Sacrifice hits—Everett, McCreary.
Stolen bases—McCormick 2, Lange 2, Connor 2, Callahan, Donahue. Struck out—By Callahan 4. Passed
ball—Butler. First on balls—By Callahan 2, by Frazer 5, by Jones 5. Hit by pitcher—Ryan, Decker.
Umpire—Sheridan. Time—2.15.

FOR DOUBLE UMPIRES.

New York, Sept. 30.—The League will be asked
to adopt the double-umpire system at its annual
meeting. Andrew Freedman, of the New York
Club, is hot on the subject. He says: "I am
unqualifiedly in favor of two umpires. Suppose it does cost a little more money. It gives
satisfaction. We are running this League to
meet the tastes of the public, as I understand it.
If we're not we'd better get out of the business.
Situations arise on a ball field where one man
cannot see all the plays correctly. One man
misses a portion of the crowd, by reason of the
semi-circular arrangement of seats about the
field, does see, and then trouble begins. I
want to see that rectified. Why talk about
this umpire business, look at New York's record.
We have been asked whom we would like to have
serve on our grounds as umpire. Only once this
season has the New York Club made any request
to President Young, and then, in connection with
an official of another club, we did ask for the
services of Umpire Lynch in the recent Baltimore
series. The games were important. We thought
none but the best man should be behind the plate.
What was the result? Umpire Lynch telegraphed
that he would resign before he would umpire
a game in which the Baltimores took part. Now,
isn't that a fine situation?"

GREATEST OF ALL.

As a Consistent Batsman No One Ever Equalled Anson.

One of Anson's strong points ever since
his connection with professional base ball
began over twenty years ago has been
his handiness with the stick. That fact
alone has kept him in the game when his
fielding would have compelled him to retire
to a minor league if not altogether from
the game. Only twice during a service of
twenty-two years in the National League
has his batting average at the close of the
season been less than .300. That was in
'91 and '92. He is probably the most consistent sticker in the history of base ball,
as his appended record for twenty-two consecutive years will show:

Year. Rank.	Average.
1876—Fifth	342
1877—Fourth	335
1878—Fifth	336
1879—First	407
1881—First	399
1882—Second	348
1883—Second	413
1884—Fourth	337
1885—Sixth	310
1886—Second	371
1887—Second	421
1888—First	343
1889—Third	341
1890—Seventh	311
1891—Eleventh	294
1892—Forty-second ..	274
1893—Thirty-eighth	322
1894—Sixth	394
1895—Twenty-seventh	338
1896—Twentieth	335
1897—Sixty-eighth	302

The complete records show that Anson
participated in 2053 full championship
games with the Chicago team. In that time
he has been 9093 times at the bat, and out
of those times he has been credited with
3034 base hits. For 22 years his grand
average at the bat has been .322.

THE PITCHING GUN.

SOME FACTS ABOUT PROFESSOR HINTON'S INVENTION.

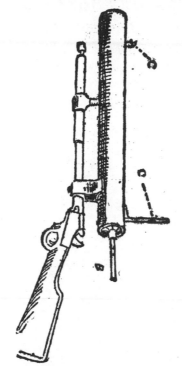

THE PERFECTED GUN.

I—Screw rod governing false breech. OO—
Wind sights. (Note—The method of shooting this
gun is to hold the stock of the rifle firmly under
the right arm. This will bring the sights on a
level with the eye. The fingers of this gun are
concealed within the muzzle.)

AN OPEN QUESTION

WHETHER PLAYING-MANAGERS EXCEL BENCH-MANAGERS.

The Best Results, However, in All Base
Ball Leagues Are Shown by the
Record to be Attributable to the
Non-Playing Managers.

There are eight manager-captains in the
League—Anson in Chicago, Tebeau in
Cleveland, Clarke in Louisville, Hallman
in St. Louis, Brown in Washington, Donovan in Pittsburg, Ewing in Cincinnati, and
Joyce in New York. But the two leading
teams of the National League have bench
managers.
It is also a strong point worth noting
by the advocates of the player-managers
that the leading teams in all of the leagues
have bench managers. Here is the list:
Selee and Hanlon, of Boston and Baltimore; Irwin, of Toronto in the Eastern
League; Watkins, of Indianapolis, in the
Western League; Mike Finn, of Newport,
in the New England League; Charles Stro-
bel, of Toledo, in the Interstate League;
Frank Palmer, of St. Joseph, in the Western Association, and Deacon Ellis, of Newark, and Frank Rinn, of Lancaster, in the
Atlantic League.
It would therefore seem that the advocates of the bench-manager have a great
deal the best of the argument, judging
from results—the only thing that counts
for anything in base ball or, for that matter, in anything else.

SHOES WON THE PENNANT!

Catcher Robinson Blames Billy Earle's Brogans as Hoodoes.

"If you were behind the bat last Thursday in
Baltimore and heard Robbie's theory of the loss
of the game to Mercer you would have agreed
with me that ball players are the most superstitious lot on earth, and this doesn't bar the
soubrettes with the 10-20-30-cent vaudeville
shows, who cheat on the complexion of the hair,
and who believe that spilling salt on the table
knocks them out of a salary," observed Tim
Hurst. "In that game on Thursday Robinson
was away off in throwing to the bases. He made
errors that cost three runs. I heard him holding
a conversation with himself as early as the
fourth inning. 'Well, I'm a stiff; I'm a Jonah;
I knew those shoes would turn the trick!' said
Robbie. Visions of John McCullough, Billy Scanlan and Bartley Campbell entered into my head,
and I began to place Robbie in the same class.
'What do you mean by shoes turning the trick,
Robbie?' said I. 'Tim,' he said, 'Billy Earle
came to town last week, and he was broke. He
touched me for $5, and I asked him what he
could give me for security. He produced a pair
of base ball shoes, and they fitted me like an
old slipper. I gave Billy the $5 and took the
shoes. This is the first day I have worn them,
and I have been catching a bum game, Tim.
Now, what's the cause of it? Nothing but the
shoes. Earle has Jonahed me. I always said he
was a Jonah ever since I heard he put guys to
sleep with that hypnotism racket he springs.'
After the game I heard Robbie telling his woes
to the Baltimore players, and they all agreed
with him that Billy Earle's shoes had put them
out of the race with the Boston push."

A SEASON'S RESULTS.

WHAT THE OFFICIAL LEAGUE AVERAGES FOR 1897 SHOW.

Batting Was About the Same as in
1896 While Base Running Declined,
Thus Indicating Retrogression Instead of Improvement.

According to the official batting averages of the National League for the season of 1897, compiled by Secretary Young,
and given in full below, little Willie
Keeler, of the Baltimore Club, is the
champion batsman of the National League,
and consequently the premier batsman of
the entire profession. He has the fine average of .432, or almost a hit for every
two times at bat. Keeler made the most
hits and also has the distinction of making
more runs than any other player in the
League, except Billy Hamilton, who is the
king pin in that respect, having in fewer
games, and with a much less number of
hits, scored 153 runs to Keeler's 147.

THE HAND OF PFEFFER

AS IT SHOWED UP UNDER THE WONDERFUL X-RAYS.

A Peculiar Bone Ailment Revealed, Thus Explaining the Cause of His Compulsory Retirement From the Game in Which He Was so Conspicuous.

Chicago, Feb. 5.—The former king of second basemen, Fred Pfeffer, has found what it was that ended his career on the base ball field. "Unser Fritz" has caught the popular craze. He has submitted his right hand, the one that was always lame during his last season on the diamond, to a careful examination with the aid of the X-ray. The result is a great relief to Pfeffer. His is not a pretty hand. No ball player's is.

A PECULIAR TROUBLE.

Perhaps Fred's is not so bad as some of them. But the marvelous light that went through the great right hand of the former king showed some remarkable things. It showed that the soreness in Pfeffer's throwing hand was caused by some kind of a peculiar boney growth on the middle knuckle. The enlargement is shown in the cut. Whenever Pfeffer caught two or three hard-hit or thrown balls the

fleshy cushion over this bone would puff up at once and make the handling of the hard ball a matter of considerable pain.

Pfeffer consulted the doctors and surgeons in vain to get relief. The swelling was easily reduced, but it returned at once when the ball first came his way.

GROSS OUTRAGE PERPETRATED UPON MR. VON DER AHE.

Kidnapped in St. Louis Through a Plot and Taken to Pittsburg at the Instigation of Nimick, Von Der Ahe's Bondsman in the Baldwin Suit.

St. Louis, Mo., Feb. 8.—Editor "Sporting Life."—Ex-President Von der Ahe, of the St. Louis Club, was abducted to-day and carried out of the State to Pittsburg by a Pittsburg detective named Bendel, and Al. Standrett, at the instigation of W. A. Nimick, formerly president of the Pittsburg Club, who went security for Mr. Von der Ahe in the Mark Baldwin damage suit in the sum of $2500. The St. Louis man fell into a trap laid by his former friend, and the latter succeeded in his unprecedented action. The whole city of St. Louis resents the outrage and a heavy damage suit against Mr. Nimick will result. As for Chris, he is again the hero of the hour in his home.

THE CAUSE OF THE TROUBLE.

It appears that when Baldwin secured his final judgment against Von der Ahe, he had an execution issued against Mr. Von der Ahe. The Sheriff made returns that the defendent could not be found in Allegheny County and then Von der Ahe's bondsman, Nimick, decided to have him brought to Pittsburg to forestal proceedings for recovery on the bond. Hence a trap was laid for Mr. Von der Ahe, and he was forcibly seized in the streets of this city and taken out of the State by force without legal warrant or requisition papers.

THE SCHEME WORKED OUT.

Detective Bendel, accompanied by two attorneys, arrived in this city yesterday. While he was arranging the capture of Von der Ahe and the spiriting of him out of town before he could appeal to the courts, the attorneys of Mr. Nimick held a conversation with the law firm of Jones & Jones, of this city. They were pitcher Baldwin's attorneys when he was imprisoned by Von der Ahe during the year in which the Brotherhood of ball players fought the National League. Neither member of the firm had ever heard of such a thing as taking Von der Ahe literally by force or kidnapping him as proposed by Nimick's attorneys. When the plan was laid before them they gave it as their opinion that it was entirely legal and offered any assistance in their power.

VON DER AHE TRAPPED.

In the meantime Detective Bendel had arranged everything for the capture of the German. A note from the St. Nichols Hotel was sent to Von der Ahe at the Sportsman's Club. The note bore the signature of Robert Smith, of New York. It requested Von der Ahe to honor Mr. Smith with his presence at a dinner given by the latter at the St. Nicholas Monday evening. Von der Ahe answered the note and said it would give him the greatest of pleasure to attend the function.

Meantime Detective Bendel had secured the services of a trusty "cabby." His instructions were to drive anywhere he wanted until the detective told him to go to the depot of the Ohio & Mississippi Railroad. It was not the intention to give Von der Ahe any opportunity to appeal to the courts. Detective Bendel's idea was to take him out of town as soon after his capture as possible.

OFF FOR PITTSBURG.

As soon as the two men were in the carriage the driver whipped up his team and at a furious clip drove off of the prominent thoroughfares. When "Der Boss Manager" found out where he was going he objected vigorously and long. He even threatened the detective with his life. He wanted to go and see his attorney, but Bendel would not have it that way, and slipped one end of a pair of handcuffs onto his prisoner's wrist. The other end was attached to his own wrist. In this rather badly handicapped condition Chris was driven into the relay station in East St. Louis, where Von der Ahe was forcibly taken aboard the train. The journey to Pittsburg was started.

OFFER TO ORIOLES

IN LIEU OF THE VANISHED TEMPLE CUP PRIZES.

A Fat Purse Hung up by the Baltimore Club For the Players to Share Under Certain Conditions Comparatively Easy of Fulfillment.

The day before the opening of the League championship season Manager Hanlon, of the Baltimore Club, called his Orioles and gave final instructions to them. He said:

"I will divide among you $4000 at the close of the season if you win the pennant, and if you come in second there will be $1800 to be distributed to those of you who are deserving. This money will not necessarily be equally divided. That depends solely upon yourselves. If each of you keeps before him but one thing—playing to win—and takes care of himself accordingly, well and good. Each will receive an equal share. But if I find that certain men play indifferently, perhaps are loose in habits or do not keep themselves in condition to give to the club the best services of which they are capable, just so surely will they receive a smaller proportion, or, if the case is aggravated, nothing at all. I want you to understand, however, that I have no thought at this time that any one of you will prove recreant to my trust in you. I believe you constitute the greatest team on earth, and I hope and believe you will win the larger sum of the amount I have just offered you."

Manager Hanlon preceded his remarks on the bonus question by reading the rules recently adopted by the League. He told them they might sign those receipt blanks if they wished, and in doing so fulfill the promise made at the meeting held at St. Louis. Not one of the men has yet signed.

NO HIT.

Not Even a Scratch.

Breit Pitched a Marvelous Game.

Ten-thousand-dollar Breitenstein performed a feat in the pitching line yesterday that will send his name down to baseball posterity as one of the shining lights of the national game.

His remarkable no hit victory over the Pittsburg Club is the "high water mark for pitchers, and is likely to stay such for years to come.

For nine innings the Pennsylvanians vainly endeavored to solve the mystery of his deceptive shoots and curves that came from the high-priced twirler's vigorous left hand. Try as they might his occult power remained potent to the last, and the close of the game found them the victims of one of the most complete coats of calcimining ever administered in baseball.

In nine innings the Pittsburgs had just 28 turns at the bat, or, in other words, just one more time than the amount required to retire the regulation three to an inning.

In seven out of the nine innings the Pittsburg batters fell in one-two-three order. In only two innings did the visitors have a man on base, and then only for a very short space of time.

THE SCORE.

CINCINNATI.	AB.	R.	1B.	SH.	SB.	PO.	A.	E.
Holliday, cf.	5	1	1	0	0	2	0	0
Smith, rf.	3	1	2	1	0	3	0	0
Beckley, 1b.	5	1	1	0	0	11	0	0
Miller, rf.	4	2	1	0	0	2	0	0
McPhee, 2b.	4	2	1	0	0	3	1	0
Corcoran, ss.	4	1	1	0	0	1	4	1
Steinfeldt, 3b.	5	2	2	0	0	0	1	0
Peitz, c.	3	0	0	0	0	5	2	0
Breitenstein, p.	3	1	1	0	0	0	1	0
Totals	36	11	10	1	0	27	11	1

PITTSBURG.	AB.	R.	1B.	SH.	SB.	PO.	A.	E.
Padden, 2b.	3	0	0	0	0	2	4	0
Donovan, rf.	3	0	0	0	0	0	0	0
Brodie, cf.	3	0	0	0	0	2	0	0
McCarthy, lf.	3	0	0	0	0	0	0	0
Davis, 1b.	3	0	0	0	0	9	1	0
Gray, 3b.	3	0	0	0	0	2	2	0
Ely, ss.	3	0	0	0	0	2	2	0
Schriever, c.	3	0	0	0	0	8	2	0
Hastings, p.	2	0	0	0	0	0	3	0
Gansel	1	0	0	0	0	0	0	0
Totals	27	0	0	0	0	27	16	0

Innings	1	2	3	4	5	6	7	8	9	
Cincinnati	0	0	1	1	3	0	5	0	1	—11
Pittsburg	0	0	0	0	0	0	0	0	0	—0

Pitchers	Innings Pitched	At Bat Opponents	Base Hits by Opponents	Runs Scored by Opponents	Hit by Pitched	Bases on Balls	Struck Out	Wild Pitches
Breitenstein	9	28	0	0	0	1	2	0
Hastings	8	34	10	11	0	4	2	0

First Base on Errors—Cincinnati, 4; Pittsburg, 1.
Double Play—Ely and Davis.
Left on Bases—Cincinnati, 7; Pittsburg, 1.
Condition of Weather—Fair.
Condition of Playing Field—Good.
Time of Game—1:56.
Names of Umpires—O'Day and McDonald.

HUGHES DID WELL.

Pitched the Game Without a Hit.

Baltimore, April 22.—Pitcher Hughes was a problem to-day which the Boston batters could not solve, and no runs and no hits was their portion. The Orioles at times played magnificent ball, but two of their errors were very yellow. The visitors fielded superbly, and Baltimore was compelled to bat out the victory, three of Lewis's passes to first resulting in runs by timely hitting.

Herman Long was injured three times, and finally retired in favor of Hughes, who threw hard to first and struck the runner on the head. Later he was in a collision with Jennings and McGann, and his foot and leg were injured by their spikes. Attendance, 1,800. Score:

BALTIMORE.	AB.	R.	1B.	PO.	A.	E.
McGraw, 3b.	5	1	1	4	1	0
O'Brien, rf.	4	0	2	0	0	0
Jennings, ss.	3	1	2	1	2	1
Keeley, lf.	5	2	3	1	0	0
Stenzel, cf.	5	3	3	1	0	0
Demont, 2b.	4	1	2	1	2	0
McGann, 1b.	2	1	0	9	0	0
Clarke, c.	4	2	1	9	2	0
Hughes, p.	4	0	1	1	4	0
Totals	36	12	27	11	0	

BOSTON.	AB.	R.	1B.	PO.	A.	E.
Hamilton, cf.	3	0	0	3	0	0
Tenney, 1b.	4	0	0	11	0	0
Long, ss.	3	0	0	1	0	0
Klester, ss.	1	0	0	1	0	0
Duffy, lf.	4	0	0	2	0	0
Collins, 3b.	3	0	0	2	0	0
Stahl, rf.	3	0	0	1	0	0
Lowe, 2b.	3	0	0	2	2	0
Bergen, c.	2	0	0	3	1	0
Lewis, p.	3	0	0	0	0	0
Totals	29	0	0	24	11	0

Innings	1	2	3	4	5	6	7	8	9	
Baltimore	3	0	0	0	2	0	1	3	x	—9
Boston	0	0	0	0	0	0	0	0	0	—0

Stolen Base—Stenzel. Two-Base Hit—Stenzel. Three-Base Hits—Stenzel, Keeley, 2, Jennings. Double Plays—Long, Lowe and Tenney; Jennings and McGann. First Base on Balls—Off Lewis, 5; off Hughes, 3. Hit by Pitcher—McGann. Struck Out—By Hughes, 3; by Lewis, 3. Left on Bases—Baltimore, 8; Boston, 4. Earned Runs—Baltimore, 5. Time—1:45. Umpires—Lynch and Connolly.

DIAGRAM OF THE NEW BROOKLYN GROUND.

EBBETTS' EXPERIENCE.

Will Have No More Bench Managers For Brooklyn.

Only two of the sextet of clubs which make up the first division of the League have playing managers. Out at Washington Park, in Brooklyn, the other day the question of managers was being discussed by Presidents Brush and Ebbets, and the latter said:

"I may be considered old-fashioned in my views, but I don't believe in a non-playing manager. I have nothing against Billy Barnie, but I believe that the team will, in time, make a better showing under Griffin than it did with Barnie on the bench. Anson and Comiskey were in their day two of the greatest the sport has seen, and I think that in the player we have the material for the best management. We have not won any more games than we did under Barnie, but the team is playing better ball, and you will notice that we have lost many a game by one run in the last two months. Mike Griffin has the confidence of all the players, and I don't think the Brooklyn Club will ever carry any more excess baggage in the shape of a bench manager, at least as long as I have anything to do with the team."

THE CURVE BALL.

THE FAMOUS CUMMINGS SETTLES THE CONTROVERSY.

The Inventor of the Curve Speaks in His Own Behalf—He Says He Originated the Delivery and Taught It to Professor Avery, of Yale.

Athol, Mass., Aug. 16.—Editor "Sporting Life:"—Enclosed you will find copy of a clipping of the Brooklyn "Union," July 9, 1870, which I think will answer Goldsmith's article on the curve ball in your issue of July 16. Will say I never played with the Atlantics of Brooklyn in '69, or any other year. Also I taught Ham Avery how to curve the ball and explained the theory to the entire satisfaction of Prof. Eaton, of Yale. Yours respectfully,

W. A. CUMMINGS.

BATTLE-SCARRED VETERAN.

James C. Nolan Back From the War With a Wound.

Special to "Sporting Life."

Philadelphia, Pa., Sept. 8.—James C. Nolan, the noted base ball man, who gave up the sporting editorship of the Louisville "Dispatch" and the official scorership of the Louisville Club, to go to the war is in the Hahnemann Hospital here with a wounded leg, which is healing nicely, but will even when healed leave him crippled for life. The wound was caused by a piece of shell that burst near him when the First Kentucky and Sixteenth Pennsylvania carried a block house at Coamo several days after the American troops landed on Porto Rico soil. Nolan was sent North on the hospital ship "Relief" from Ponce, Porto Rico, and sent at once to the hospital here. He expects to be able to leave for his mother's home in Galveston to-morrow, where he will seek to restore his shattered health. The hardship of the campaign told plainly upon him, he having fallen off from 230 pounds to about 150 pounds. In common with most of the volunteers he speaks harshly of the official neglect the soldiers were subjected to and declares that he has had enough of war.

BASE BALL AND THE WAR TAX

Exhibitions of Playing Come Under the Provisions of Paragraph 8.

Washington, D. C., Sept. 13.—The Commissioner of Internal Revenue has ruled as follows upon questions arising under the war tax law:

"Merchants or others who have a place of business where credits are opened by the deposit or collection of money or currency, subject to be paid or remitted upon draft, check or order, or where money is advanced or loaned, or promissory notes are received for sale are subject to the special tax as brokers.

"Exhibitions of speed of horses on race tracks and exhibitions of base ball playing (to which an admission fee is charged), are not subject to tax under paragraph 7, but are subject to tax under paragraph 8. Traveling base ball clubs are not subject to tax under paragraph 8 if the special tax under that paragraph has already been paid for the grounds on which the game is played.

"Agricultural societies at whose fairs horse races are exhibited are not required to pay special tax under paragraph 7. The special tax required of them is to be paid under paragraph 8. Exhibitions of the speed of horses on race tracks are not the feature of horsemanship contemplated by paragraph 7."

THE LONG SEASON

STEADILY GAINING IN THE MAGNATES' FAVOR.

Little Doubt Now That the 154-Game Schedule Will be Given Another Trial Next Season by the National League Magnates.

PITCHER WILSON SHOT.

The Cleveland Twirler Wounds and is Wounded.

Special to "Sporting Life."

Montgomery, Ala., Feb. 9.—In an encounter at a road house, near this place, on the 4th inst., Frank Wilson, pitcher for the Cleveland (Ohio) Base Ball team, was shot in the hip and seriously wounded. During the trouble Wilson cut several gashes in the side and face of Joseph Toole. It was about a woman.

JOHN J. M'GRAW,
The Brilliant Player and Capable Manager of Baltimore.

EXILES IN FACT.

CLEVELAND WILL SEE NO MORE LEAGUE BALL.

The Team to be Kept on the Road For the Rest of the Season Owing to Poor Attendance in Cleveland and Refusal of Other Clubs to Go There.

The long-expected has happened. The Cleveland team, owing to lack of support, will be withdrawn from the Forest City after July 1 and will play out the balance of the schedule on foreign ground, just as the Cleveland team of last season did. President Robison made this announcement on Monday last. The cause, he says, is the refusal of nearly every club that has played in Cleveland this season to return, owing to the poor attendance. This year the gate receipts at the grounds of the Cleveland Club have not averaged much over $25 per day. And so good-bye forever to Cleveland as a National League city.

PREACHER BOUNCED

From a Ball Park For Endeavoring to Enact the Contemptible Role of Sneak and Spy.

Fort Wayne, Ind., July 10.—Editor "Sporting Life:"—A preacher was escorted out of the base ball grounds yesterday by the police. The game was between the Fort Wayne and the New Castle teams. Owing to the agitation against Sunday ball which is being carried on by the Good Citizens' League the crowd was on the alert for any representative of that league. When the Rev. Sherman Powell, of the Trinity M. E. Church, was seen in the crowd copying the names of spectators for witnesses the cry went up to throw him out. Some one grabbed his pencil and another took his note book and score card and tore them up.

The management feared that trouble would ensue, as the crowd gathered around threatening Mr. Powell. The police were then called. His admission money was offered to Mr. Powell, and as he refused to accept it he was led from the park by the police. He went to police headquarters, where Superintendent Gorsline told him that he had been taken away from the grounds for fear that he would incite a riot and cause mob violence. Mr. Powell, when seen to-night, refused to make a statement other than to say that when the fight is over the Good Citizens' League will win and will stop all Sunday violations in the city.

DEATH'S DOING.

MANAGER M'GRAW, OF BALTIMORE, SADLY AFFLICTED.

His Young Wife Expires in His Arms From the Effects of a Surgical Operation For Appendicitis—The Disastrous Effect Upon His Team.

Death has laid its heavy hand upon the popular young manager of the Baltimore Club, John J. McGraw, and taken from him the lovely young woman who became his wife but little over two years ago. Mrs. Minnie R. McGraw submitted to an operation for a sudden attack of appendicitis on Aug. 27, from the effects of which she died on Aug. 31, in the arms of her devoted husband, who had been summoned from Louisville where his team was playing at the moment the surgeons in Baltimore were taking a desperate chance to save the life of the young wife. Mrs. McGraw was the daughter of Michael J. Doyle, for many years prominent in Baltimore Democratic politics. She was about 23 years old, and was married on Feb. 3, 1897. The funeral took place from the McGraw residence, 2738 St. Paul street, Baltimore, on the 3d inst., and was largely attended. We really doubt whether the able little player and manager ever before realized the extent of his popularity. Telegrams of sympathy poured in from every quarter of the land, and the McGraw residence was constantly besieged by sympathetic callers. The funeral was imposing and impressive. Nearly every club in the League sent floral pieces, and base ball men were numerous among the mourners. The Brooklyn Club was represented at the melancholy event by Treasurer Harry Vonderhorst, Manager Hanlon, Captain Kelley, Hugh Jennings and William Keeler, who acted as pallbearers.

CLEVELAND HAD LOST 24 IN A ROW

Washington vs. Cleveland at Washington Sept. 18—(P. M. and P. M.)—Cleveland won the first game in the tenth inning, when Dowd scored on a single by Hemphill, it being their first victory since Aug. 25. Harper, of Springfield, pitched finely. Score:

WASHING'N	A.B.	R.	B.	P.	A.	E	CLEVELA'D	A.B.	R.	B.	P.	A.	E
Slagle, cf	5	0	1	3	0	0	Dowd, cf	5	1	1	3	0	0
Mercer, 3b	5	0	1	1	0	0	Harley, lf	5	1	2	2	1	0
O'Brien, lf	5	1	1	0	0	0	Kruger, 2b	3	0	0	4	5	0
McGann, 1b	4	1	2	14	1	0	Hemphill, rf	5	0	2	1	0	1
Freeman, rf	5	1	6	3	0	0	Sullivan, 3b	4	1	0	1	3	1
Barry, ss	4	0	0	1	3	1	Duncan, 1b	4	1	1	8	1	0
Stafford, 2b	4	0	0	2	4	0	Lockhe'd, ss	3	0	2	5	1	0
Kittridge, c	4	0	2	4	2	0	Sugden, c	4	0	0	6	1	1
Magee, p	4	1	1	0	4	0	Harper, p	2	1	0	0	1	0
Total	40	4	12	28	14	2	Total	35	5	8	30	13	3

*One out when winning run was scored.

Washington .... 0 2 0 0 1 0 0 1 0 0—4
Cleveland .... 0 1 0 0 0 0 2 1 1—5

Earned runs—Washington 2, Cleveland 3. Two-base hits—Freeman, Dowd. Three-base hit—Hemphill. Home run—Duncan. Double play—Harley, Kruger. First on balls—Off Magee 3, Harper 1. Hit by pitcher—Lockhead, Kruger, Barry. Stolen bases—Slagle, O'Brien, McGann, Freeman, Harley. Struck out—By Magee 3, Harper 6. Left on bases—Washington 8, Cleveland 6. Umpire—Dwyer. Time—2.05.

THE BLACK TOURISTS

Will Parade and Even Play Ball in Dress Suits.

Findlay, O., Aug. 7.—Editor "Sporting Life:"—Dr. W. H. Drake and Bud Fowler, the organizer of the famous Page Fence Giants, will take a team to California in September, playing through Ohio, Indiana, Illinois, Missouri, Kansas, Colorado, Utah, California, returning by New Mexico. This will be the greatest colored ball club ever organized, and called the Colored All-American Black Tourists. It will be composed of the best colored players in the United States. They will travel in their own palace car. The great feature of this club will be their daily parades, which will be made in full dress suits, black pants, white vests, swallow-tail coats, opera hats, silk umbrellas and by request of different managers, will play the games in full-dress suits. All clubs wanting dates can get them by writing to Dr. Drake, secretary, or Bud Fowler, manager, Findlay, O.

IN SHEER MADNESS

THE AMERICAN LEAGUE WOULD WRECK ITSELF.

Fatal Consequences Absolutely Certain to Follow the Proposed Willful and Unsanctioned Invasion of Chicago by the Minor League.

According to all reports the American Gate Western) League has decided to place a club in Chicago with or without the consent of the Chicago Club, or of the National League. This amounts practically to a declaration of war, as it is not likely that the Chicago League Club will consent to share its territory with any other club, especially not in the face of a rebellious attitude and a hostile declaration; and even if the Chicago Club should, by any possibility be brought into line on this proposition, it is almost certain that the League would not consent

THAT NEW LEAGUE.

DATE FOR ITS FIRST MEETING HAS BEEN SET.

The Projectors to Meet in St. Louis on the 14th Inst. and to Settle Definitely Upon the Circuit—A Declaration by One of the Boomers.

St. Louis, Mo., Sept. 11, Editor "Sporting Life"—The first meeting of the new league will be held in this city on Thursday, September 14, three days after the close of the season in the Western League. The fact that the new league waited until the close of the Western League season before going into the actual business of its organization leads to the belief that some of the Western League magnates will attend the meeting—in fact, it is hinted by those who profess to know the inside workings of **THE PROPOSED LEAGUE.**

that Tom Loftus, Comiskey and the president of the Western League will attend the meeting. The circuit will be selected at this meeting and forfeits posted to show their good faith in the continuing of the new league. The projectors of the league still are reticent in regard to the circuit, and the prime movers, otherwise the financial men, in the league. However, they claim that when the names of the backers of the enterprise are published they will create a decided sensation.

A TALKER TALKS.

It is certain that Cincinnati never has been considered in connection with the new league. Said one of the new league boomers: "Cincinnati was not considered for several reasons. In the first place the city is not large enough to warrant the dividing of the patronage. Then, again, Mr. Brush is too tough a proposition for promoters of an infant enterprise to stack up against. In Chicago the patrons are sore on Mr. Hart, and here Tebeau and his crowd have failed to come up to expectations; so that we are certain of these cities, and that they will support us. And it is the same with several of the cities of the East."

A BIT SKEPTICAL.

Among the followers of the game here there is a decided difference of opinion as regards the prospect of the league, and its strongest supporters are laying great wagers that the new league will be a go. While the local promoters of the new organization refuse to say who will be the representatives and what cities they will represent, there seems no doubt that Western League magnates will be here in abundance and it would not be at all surprising if Ban Johnson, president of the Western League, would be elected president of the new organization.

GEORGE SCHAEFER,

the local promoter, is as confident as ever that the thing will be a go. Said he to-day: "In St. Louis our games will be played at Athletic Park. In the East we will be located at Philadelphia, New York, Baltimore and Washington. We have got good people interested at New York and Philadelphia, and at Baltimore Mc-Graw and Robinson will be in charge, while Mike Scanlan, the veteran, will be at the head in Washington. In the West we have St. Louis, Chicago, Kansas City, Detroit, Milwaukee and Minneapolis to choose from. 'Scrappy' Joyce will be in charge of the local club. Our infield is as good as signed, and will include Joyce on first, 'Kid' Gleason on second, Jimmy Collins on third and George Davis at short."

LIKE HANLON'S SYNDICATE

Big Pittsburg And Louisville Deal—Colonels' Best Players Gone.

PITTSBURG, Dec. 8.—The biggest baseball deal made in this city since 1885, when Pittsburg purchased the entire Columbus club, was consummated today, and the many rumors concerning the Pittsburg Club's future are set at rest. The story is as follows:

On October 31 Barney Dreyfus resigned as president of the Louisville Club and sold all his holdings. Mr. Dreyfus then closed a deal with the Pittsburg management and got a large block of stock and the assurance of his election as president at the club meeting next week, just after the National League meeting. Today Harry Pulliam, who succeeded Mr. Dreyfus as president of the Louisvilles, came to the city, conferred with Messrs. Kerr, Auten and Dreyfus, and announced that he had sold to Pittsburg 14 Louisville players, the consideration being $25,000 in cash and four members of the local club. They are Chesbro, O'Brien, Fox and Madison. The 14 players bought from Louisville are:

Clarke, who will be manager and captain of the new Pittsburg Club; Wagner, Ritchey, Leach, Kelly, Zimmer, Latimer, T. Messitt, Waddell, Cunningham, Philippe, Flaherty, Charles Doyle and Woods.

All interested in the deal declare that there is no syndicate ball in the move, but solely an endeavor to put a pennant winner in this, one of the best ball cities in the country. A radical change from the past policy of the Pittsburg Club will be the playing of Sunday games this season. The new acquisitions give Pittsburg 30 players, some of whom will doubtless be put on sale during the League meeting in New York.

President Hanlon Goes To New York

President Edward Hanlon, of the Baltimore Baseball Club, will leave early this morning for New York to attend the National League meeting next week and the annual meeting of the Brooklyn Club to-day.

The League will assemble on Tuesday. Mr. Hanlon is still of opinion that the 12 club league will continue in existence. If any change is made he believes that Cleveland and Louisville franchises may be dropped or transferred. He favors a good 12 club circuit, and does not believe the advocates of an eight-club circuit will succeed at this meeting.

Speaking of the Pittsburg Louisville deal, he said the pick of the two teams, if properly managed, should put in an argument for the championship. Dreyfus' election as president did not mean that Mr. Kerr had sold a controlling interest in the Pittsburgs.

AMERICAN LEAGUE

IS THE NEW TITLE OF THE OLD WESTERN LEAGUE.

A Clever Move to Take the Wind Out of the Rival New League's Sails and Pave the Way For a Legitimate Successor to the Association.

The change of title of the old Western League to the "American League" is a clever political move of the Western people, guided by Messrs. Hart, Brush and Robison, and emphatically gives the lie to the wild statements of the Chicago papers relative to a split in the all-powerful Western triumvirate. This shrewd and unexpected move is designed to deprive the proposed new rival American Association of the benefits of a traditional title, without infringing upon the League's rights in the matter; to remove the ex-Western League from its hampering sectional basis, and to place it in position to become nationally known; in short to make it the legitimate nucleus around which to build the National Agreement successor to the old American Association when the time comes for the reduction of the National League circuit to eight cities, and the restoration of the game to its old and popular basis of two major Leagues, working harmoniously under the indispensable National Agreement.

M'GRAW TO ABELL.

Will Not Permit Himself to be Transferred From Baltimore, the City of His Choice.

In last week's "Sporting Life" appeared an interview with Director Abell, of the Brooklyn Club, in which Mr. Abell describes how contemptuously Mr. Freedman turned down an offer to sell McGraw and Robinson to the New York Club. In com-

VALE, 1899 SEASON.

BROOKLYN THE NEW CHAMPION OF THE LEAGUE.

Complete Record of the Senior Organization For the Campaign of 1899—A Comparison With the Results of the Preceding Year.

The eighth campaign of the National League as a twelve-club organization came to an end Oct. 15, with Brooklyn as the champion club. This is the first time under the amalgamation that the championship has been wrested from the Boston-Baltimore circle, wherein it has been bandied back and forth ever since 1891, and even now Boston holds the place with Baltimore fourth. Philadelphia finished a close third. The first four places are thus monopolized by the East. The West holds the next five positions St. Louis finishing fifth, Cincinnati sixth, Pittsburg seventh, Chicago eighth, and Louisville ninth. The East has two rear-end teams in New York and Washington, the former finishing tenth and the latter eleventh. The West furnished the actual tail-ender in Cleveland, which made a most ignoble showing—the worst ever made by any League team.

FINAL RECORD, 1898.				FINAL RECORD, 1899.			
	Won.	Lost.	Pct.		Won.	Lost.	Pct.
Boston	102	47	.685	Brooklyn	101	47	.682
Baltimore	96	53	.644	Boston	95	57	.625
Cincinnati	92	60	.605	Philadelp'a	94	58	.618
Chicago	85	65	.567	Baltimore	86	62	.581
Cleveland	81	68	.544	St. Louis	84	67	.556
Philadelphia	78	71	.524	Cincinnati	83	67	.553
New York	77	73	.513	Pittsburg	76	73	.510
Pittsburg	72	76	.486	Chicago	75	73	.507
Louisville	70	81	.464	Louisville	75	77	.493
Brooklyn	54	91	.372	New York	60	90	.400
Washington	51	101	.396	Washington	54	98	.355
St. Louis	39	111	.260	Cleveland	20	134	.129

THE CLEVELAND TEAM

was destined from the start to become one of the poorest tail-end teams in the history of the League. It was hopelessly weak to begin with in all departments of the game, and the best that was expected of it was a fairly decent showing. When that appeared likely the team was further weakened by being despoiled of several of its best players to bolster up the St. Louis kite, and was deprived of a home through having nearly all of its home games transferred to foreign grounds. The transfers were by wholesale, surpassing even the Pittsburg 1890 record, the Clevelands playing no less than 130 of their scheduled 154 games abroad. Under such conditions it is small wonder that the Exiles broke all records with 134 defeats and the loss of every series by double figures. It is but just to the Cleveland team to state that it did the best it could in every game, always played to win and very often upset all calculations by winning when least expected; moreover, it was never a sure thing even for the strongest teams. More it could not achieve, considering its fatal weakness in pitching and batting. With proper strengthening in those two all-important points the team would surely have given a better account of itself and thereby added a little more interest to the dragging race of 1899.

SERIES WON AND LOST.

As a finale we give an interesting table for quick reference of the series won, lost and tied during the past season by the twelve League teams:

Clubs.	W.	L.	T.	Clubs.	W.	L.	T.
Brooklyn	11	0	0	Cincinnati	5	5	1
Boston	7	3	1	St. Louis	6	5	0
Philadelphia	7	3	1	Louisville	4	4	1
Baltimore	6	4	1	Washington	4	7	0
Chicago	6	5	0	New York	4	7	0
Pittsburg	6	4	1	Cleveland	0	11	0

And so endeth the eighth chapter of the interesting history of the twelve-club combination known as the National League. Now for the ninth and next to last chapter.

—EDITOR "SPORTING LIFE."

menting upon this matter Manager McGraw said the other day:

"Yes; I have read Mr. Abell's remarks. Now I cannot say whether the offer was made or not, but if it was Mr. Abell should have known that it amounted to nothing, because we would not have gone. We were begged to go to Brooklyn, and refused. Why should Mr. Abell suppose we would be willing to go to New York? They are all talking about how much they wish to sell out their interests in the Baltimore Club, but I notice Mr. Abell says that the value of the club, franchise and players has doubled since before the season began. Baltimore has proven this year that it is a better ball town than Brooklyn."

PRESIDENT EBBETS HOME.

Says Cleveland and Louisville Have Agreed to Leave the League.

Charles H. Ebbets, President of the Brooklyn Baseball Club and part owner of the Baltimore Club, returned yesterday from Cleveland, where he attended the meeting of the Circuit Committee of the National League. Mr. Ebbets said that the question of reducing the circuit to eight clubs this season was thoroughly discussed, but no definite action was taken.

As the question now stands the committee has decided to go along on a ten-club basis, the Cleveland and Louisville clubs having accepted the offer of the League to drop out. It is not known, however, whether the League will adopt a circuit of ten clubs. If it decides against a ten-club circuit two other cities will have to be added, and the twelve-club agreement carried out until its expiration in 1902.

Mr. Ebbets announced that the Baltimore Club would proceed to send contracts to the Baltimore players despite the reports that McGraw, Robinson, and others of the team will join the American Association. He did not believe the report that the new association had secured the lease of the grounds of the Baltimore Club, as the present lease covers the season of 1900.

JACK TAYLOR DEAD.

The Famous League Pitcher Succumbs to Kidney Disease.

Special to "Sporting Life."

New York, Feb. 7.—Pitcher John Taylor died to-day at New Brighton, Staten Island, of Bright's disease, aged 28 years. He pitched for the Philadelphia team for some years, and last season was with the Cincinnatis.

RIVAL ASSOCIATION FAILS.

Philadelphia Not Ready to Deposit Cash and McGraw Withdraws.

BALTIMORE, Feb. 15.—The new baseball association received a set back to-day that will probably delay its organization for a year, if it does not entirely blast its hopes. When the meeting of the association at Chicago adjourned, it was agreed between McGraw and Anson, that if Philadelphia did not post its money within a week, that the two leaders would drop out. McGraw was assigned to see Mr. Gilmore, proprietor of the Auditorium Theatre in Philadelphia, who was said to be willing to put up the cash.

As the City of Philadelphia owned the only available ball grounds in the city, and that they were to be improved, Mr. Gilmore stated that, in the absence of an option on suitable grounds, he preferred not to deposit the money. Mr. Gilmore asked that the association wait three weeks.

McGraw thereupon threw up his hands and telegraphed Anson that he would withdraw from the association. He said to-night that it was useless to try to do business with a six-club circuit, and that the loss of Philadelphia meant the failure of the association.

A meeting of the company which was organised to back the Baltimore Club will be held to-morrow night, and these matters will be explained to them.

AN AWFUL TRAGEDY.

A BALL PLAYER'S TRIPLE MURDER AND SUICIDE.

Martin Bergen, the Famous Boston Catcher, Kills His Wife and Two Children and Then Cuts His Own Throat in a Moment of Insanity.

North Brookfield, Mass., Jan. 20.—Editor "Sporting Life:" Martin Bergen, one of the best-known ball players in the country and one of the Boston Club's catchers last season, killed his wife and two children with an axe and then cut his own throat with a razor at his home in North Brookfield yesterday morning.

CIRCUIT REDUCTION.

The Four Clubs Go Out Upon Their Own Terms After All.

On Thursday the matter of circuit reduction came to a head. After fruitless negotiations the Circuit Committee had come to a satisfactory agreement with Louisville only, which club agreed to lay down for $16,000. Cleveland wanted $25,000. Washington wanted $46,500 and Baltimore stood by three propositions, running from $75,000 for everything down to $30,000 and privilege of disposing of its players. These demands were known to the League magnates before the Committee made its report, and, as there appeared no likelihood of a concession from any quarter, a majority of the clubs finally declared themselves in favor of settling on the above basis. Two clubs, however, said to be Boston and New York, held out against the Baltimore, Cleveland and Washington prices, and these three clubs accordingly formed a combine to block all progress.

THE BIG LEAGUE

ADDS A SHAMEFUL CHAPTER TO ITS HISTORY.

The Virtual Death of the Twelve-Club Organization Attended by Incidents That Have Lost the League What Little Public Confidence and Respect It Still Had Prior to This Meeting.

After weeks of weary waiting and idle speculation and after much harmful comment and many bitter controversies the ruling faction in the National League has achieved its set purpose of cutting down the circuit from twelve clubs to eight, and the National League is now to all intents and purposes a more compact, impregnable monopoly than ever before.

BASEBALL IN BALTIMORE.

McGraw is Trying to Get Old Players for the New Association.

Special to The New York Times.

BALTIMORE, Jan. 26.—Ned Hanlon's loss by his star players like McGraw and Robinson casting their fortunes with the new association will amount to $50,000. He vaued the releases of McGraw and Robinson alone at $20,000.

It is apparent here that there will be a big bolt of players from the League to the association. Robinson, McGraw, and "Bill" Clarke say the blacklisting threats of the National League are a joke. All declared that they welcomed an organization which would treat them like men, and not sell them around like slaves.

McGraw to-day sent letters to every member of the old Baltimore team asking them to sign with the new association. "Bill" Clarke says that he knows a number of good players now with league teams who will go with the association if the salary offered them is reasonable.

BALTIMORE OUT OF LEAGUE

Circuit Is Reduced To Eight Clubs—Unanimous Vote.

[Special Dispatch to the Baltimore Sun.]

NEW YORK, March 8.—The agony is over. Baltimore is out of the National League of Baseball Clubs, with Washington, Cleveland and Louisville.

Just before midnight the League by unanimous vote decided to reduce the circuit to eight clubs. The utmost harmony prevailed. Chairman John T. Brush, of the circuit committee, refused to give out the exact figures, but the plan of purchase is given below, as known earlier to-day. The members shook hands gleefully after the vote was taken, and adjourned filled with the belief that baseball would have the greatest year in its history.

At 11 o'clock to-night the League owners were still warmly debating the question of circuit reduction, with no prospect of an early adjournment. The Boston and New York clubs were averse to paying what was demanded by the four clubs that were wanted to retire.

The circuit reduction committee made its report as soon as the delegates assembled in the afternoon. It followed exactly the lines predicted in these dispatches. The League was informed that Cleveland and Louisville could be bought and that Baltimore wanted a stiff price. Then it was announced that the committee had not conferred with Washington's officials and a recess was asked. This was granted while Messrs. Brush, Soden, Hart and Rogers talked the matter over with the Wagners. They were willing to cut off $7,500 from their demand of $46,500, because Boston had paid that amount for three of the club's best players. This made their price $39,000.

The Baltimore people were brought in again. They shaded their former price a little, saying they would take $30,000 for the franchise alone if the League would agree to permit them to sell their players for what they could get. The circuit committee's plan was not of this nature. It was willing to pay each of the four clubs $10,000 outright for its franchise and would protect the club in selling its players and would stand good for certain sums that had been incurred in ground rental. Washington and Baltimore naturally wanted a heap more, and Cleveland and Louisville were not quite satisfied with $10,000, as it occurred to them that a franchise was worth at least $15,000 and, in addition to that, neither of them had any players to sell that were worth anything.

The delegates talked about the matter a little and then came to the conclusion that no agreement could be reached on empty stomachs and adjourned for dinner. J. Earl Wagner was the most aggressive chap in the lot. He said that he would not cut his price one penny if the League argued with him from now until doomsday. The Baltimore owners were more conciliatory. They wanted all they could get, but were willing to meet the League half way. Two little conferences were held among some of the members most interested and the circuit committee went off by its lonesome and consulted again.

Patrick Donovan, who was captain of the Pittsburgs last year, is likely to be made captain of the Chicagos this year. If Baltimore and Washington should go into the Eastern League William Barnie may manage in Baltimore and Thomas Burns in the national capital.

M'GRAW'S LATEST.

HE AND ROBINSON HAVE A BRAND NEW SCHEME.

In Order to Remain in Baltimore and Stand Off the Loss of the St. Louis Salary They Say They Will Start a Baltimore City League.

From Baltimore comes a story to the effect that McGraw and Robinson have decided definitely not to be sold to St. Louis, but to remain in Baltimore this season, no matter what happens. To emphasize the assertion, they are said to be arranging with James L. Kernan, a theatrical manager, to run a city league of six or eight clubs. Kernan is to build a base ball park at Riverview, a suburban resort, and it is expected to alternate games at Electric Park. McGraw is pretty sure that the enterprise will be a go; and that it will also improve the business interests of the firm of Robinson & McGraw. Notwithstanding this announcement Manager Hanlon is positive that the pair will go to St. Louis when the time comes. Outside of Baltimore the impression is that McGraw and Robison are simply holding out for a purpose not yet revealed by any of the parties interested.

CLEVELAND CHAFING

OVER A HITCH IN THE AMERICAN LEAGUE PLANS.

The Robisons' Terms For the Lease of Their Ball Park Said to be so Excessive That the American League May Abandon the Forest City.

President Ban Johnson, of the American League, has secured Cleveland capital for the location and maintainance of an American League club at Cleveland, and has everything now in shape for business, except that very necessary adjunct—a ball park: and here is where Mr. Johnson's people have struck a snag. President Robison, of the old League club, it is understood, has named a price for the lease on the present base ball park, which is considered excessive. As a result the American League people may seek another location. In speaking of the probable new Cleveland team Mr. Johnson said it would be made up largely of the best players to be dropped by the National League.

Outfielder John (Hannes) Wagner, of Pittsburg.

A TRANSFER?

President Young Admits That the Brooklyn Team May Yet be Transferred to Washington.

Special to the "Sporting Life:"

Washington, D. C., June 21.—President Young admitted to-day that there is something after all in the talk about transferring the Brooklyn Club to Washington. "If the Brooklyn Club should come to the Capital after completing its Western schedule," said he, "the capacity of the base ball park here would be tested to the limit. It has been a discouraging season financially for the Brooklyn management, particularly on their home grounds, and nobody can blame them for wanting to better such a condition of affairs.

NOT PAYING.

Mr. Young said, further: "Returns made to me of the receipts at the games thus far at Brooklyn show an average attendance of about 1000 at other than holiday games, even counting in the 25-cent patrons. Anyone who knows anything about the necessary expenses attendant upon maintaining a first-class base ball club knows that such attendance is not a paying one by any means. When the National League dropped the Washington Club from membership care was taken to preserve franchise and grounds in case of an emergency.

MAY BE A TRANSFER.

"This emergency seems to have arisen in the case of the Brooklyn Club and the remedy lies with the League Directors and the management of the Brooklyn Club. That they will see fit to apply the remedy speedily there is not the shadow of a doubt, particularly in view of the practical financial results which would follow the transfer of the Brooklyn team to this city. Consequently, it need be no surprise for the base ball patrons of Washington if they wake up some morning in the near future and find a first-class base ball club installed at Capitol Park. Everything is in readiness and the grounds have been cared for just as though they were in daily use."

BALL BELOW ZERO.

PLAYING OUR GAME NEAR THE NORTH POLE.

An American Crew Defeats an English Nine in a Base Ball Game With Eskimos as Spectators and the Players Clad in Furs.

MATHEWSON'S DEBUT

BROOKLYN vs. NEW YORK AT BROOKLYN JULY 17.—When Brooklyn tied the score in the fifth inning Captain Davis took Doheny out and substituted Matthews, late of the Norfolks. New York immediately went up in the air, and through errors and poor pitching Brooklyn won as it pleased. The score:

NEW YORK.	AB.	R.	B.	P.	A.	E.	BROOKLYN.	AB.	R.	B.	P.	A.	E.
VanHal'n, cf	5	2	3	6	0	0	Jones, cf	4	2	1	2	0	0
Selbach, lf	5	0	1	2	0	0	Sheckard, rf	3	0	2	0	1	0
Doyle, 1b	5	1	2	10	0	0	DeMon'e, 2b	3	2	2	1	2	1
Smith, rf	3	1	1	0	0	0	Kelley, lf	3	2	2	4	0	0
Davis, ss	3	1	0	1	6	2	Dahlen, ss	4	0	0	3	2	0
Grady, 2b	4	1	1	3	0	0	Cross, 3b	4	1	1	3	1	0
Hickman, 3b	4	1	0	0	5	2	Daly, 1b	4	1	0	6	1	0
Bowerm'n, c	4	0	2	2	1	1	Farrell, c	4	0	0	5	1	1
Doheny, p	2	0	0	0	0	0	McGinty, p	5	2	3	1	1	1
Matthews, p	2	0	0	0	2	0							
Total	37	7	11	24	14	5	Total	33	13	9	27	8	4

New York .... 2 0 0 3 0 1 0 0 1—7
Brooklyn .... 0 0 1 5 5 1 0 x—13

Earned runs—New York 3, Brooklyn 2. Two-base hits—VanHaltren, Doyle, Smith 2, DeMontreville. First on errors—New York 1, Brooklyn 2. Left on bases—New York 7, Brooklyn 8. Sacrifice hits—DeMontreville 2, Kelley, Cross. Stolen base—Selbach, Grady, Bowerman, DeMontreville, Kelley, Cross. Struck out—By Matthews 1, McGinty 4. First on balls—Off Doheny 4, Matthews 3, McGinty 2. Double play—Dahlen, Daly. Hit by pitcher—By Doheny 1, Matthews 3, McGinty 3. Wild pitch—Doheny. Passed balls—Bowerman 2. Umpire—Swartwood. Time—2.31.

THAT WAR AVERTED.

THE AMERICAN LEAGUE ACHIEVES ITS OBJECT.

The National League For the First Time Bows to a Minor League and Consents to Waive a Principle to Avoid a Conflict Just at This Time.

The threatened war between the National League and American League over the question of the latter's invasion of the sacred Chicago territory has been averted through the diplomacy of the National League, which, at the last moment, after bluffing to the limit, accepted "Sporting Life's" advice to "cut out all brag and bluster and try a little mild suasion." Through an intermediary, which the League always knows how and where to dig up, the contending factions were brought together in conferences from which a compromise was evolved, by which, under conditions, the American League is permitted to enter Chicago. Thus ends all probability of war, and with it we presume also ends all chance of the organization of that bluff "American Association."

The American League thus gains its main object, and with it secures also the credit of being the first minor league to compel the National League to recede from a position or yield a vital point. Whether the American League gave away more than it gained depends upon the conditions which the National League extracted for its unwilling compliance—the nature of which conditions has not yet been fully revealed. It would not be surprising, however, to learn, soon or late, that the crafty old League had, in some way, tied the American League up sufficiently to prevent future full development.

March 28

PLAYER-SIGNING.

The American League Meeting With Some Disheartening Experiences But Making Good Headway.

Ball players as a rule, claim to be in sympathy with the American League not only because it opens up a wider avenue of employment for players of major league calibre, but because it probably saved the stars from heavy salary cuts and the lesser players from relegation to minor leagues. The players, as a rule, are of opinion that but for the American League's split with the National League the latter would either have cut salaries heavily directly or achieved the same purpose indirectly by cutting the League's playing season from six months to five months.

MORE CONTRACT-JUMPING.

Under the circumstances it would be imagined that the majority of players would be grateful to the American League and that such of them as belonged to or would join that organization would be loyal to it under all circumstances. Such is not the universal rule, however, as several players, to their shame be it said, have played double with the American League. The cases of Crawford, Taylor and Rheckard have already been commented upon in our columns. To these must now be added in

THE CONTRACT-BREAKING COLUMN

the names of Outfielder Davis, of Minneapolis, who refuses to carry out his agreement with Connie Mack. Pitcher Dineen, of Boston, who has signed another contract with the Boston League Club, Outfielder Slagle, who breaks his pledge to Jimmy Manning and Heidrick and Wallace of St. Louis, who have broken their contracts with Comiskey and rejoined St. Louis. The conduct of the last named two players is particularly flagrant, as they long ago professed the utmost animosity to the St. Louis club officials and fairly begged for the privilege of signing with the American League. In view of the conduct of Heidrick and Wallace, and the avowed purpose of the National League clubs to reclaim the players—whom they regard as their personal property—at any cost, the American League has reason to be apprehensive of further treachery. At this writing it is said St. Louis hopes to make Cy Young stop back, and Brooklyn expects to induce Jones to return.

SOME COMPENSATION.

As a set off, however, to the losses sustained during the past week the American League has made some brilliant coups by capturing such good men as Lajoie, Mercer, Callahan, "Gaff" Gammons, Jimmy Williams and Micky Donlin. Following is a correct list of additional players signed during the past week:

Boston—Pitcher Cuppy, of Boston.
Baltimore—Third baseman Williams, of Pittsburg; outfielder Mike Donlin, of St. Louis.
Philadelphia—Pitcher Bernhard, of Philadelphia; infielder Lajoie, of Philadelphia; outfielder Fred Ketcham, of Syracuse; outfielder Flournoy, of Mansfield.
Washington—Third baseman Coughlin, of Kansas City; pitcher Wm Mercer, of New York.
Chicago—Pitcher Jimmy Callahan, of Chicago; outfielder Mertes, of Chicago.
Cleveland—Pitcher Hoffer, catcher Bob Wood, of Cincinnati.
Milwaukee—Catcher Tom Leahy, of Providence; catcher Joe Connor, of Boston.
Detroit—Pitcher Platt, of Philadelphia; pitcher Dunkle, of Providence.

To date the American League has captured forty-three players from the National League. Even should it lose some of these men, as seems quite likely, it will still hold enough men to bring its teams up to a plane approaching the National League standard. The threat of National League damage suits against players signing with the American League has brought a statement from President Johnson to the effect that the American League will defend all such players and will pay costs and damages, if the Courts so rule.

THE OPENING.

Only One of the Four Scheduled Was Played.

CHICAGO VS. CLEVELAND AT CHICAGO APRIL 24.—The American League season was formally opened at Chicago before 14,500 people, with decorations, music and the hoisting of the championship pennant. Hoffer was wild at the start, six gifts and four hits in the first two innings giving the champions their first game. Bradley, Shugart and both outfields did sensational fielding. Score:

CHICAGO.	A.B.	R.	B.	P.	A.		CLEVEL'D.	A.B.	R.	B.	P.	A.
Hoy, cf	5	0	1	3	0		Pickering, rf	4	0	1	0	0
Jones, lf	2	2	1	4	0		McCarthy, lf	3	0	0	2	0
Mertes, lf	3	2	1	4	0		Genins, cf	4	0	0	0	0
Shugart, ss	3	2	1	4	0		Lochs's, 2b	4	0	1	1	0
Isbel, 1b	3	1	1	8	0		Bradley, 3b	4	0	0	2	0
Hartm'n, 3b	4	0	1	0	5		Beck, 2b	3	1	2	2	4
Brain, 2b	4	0	1	3	0		Hallman, ss	3	0	1	3	1
Sullivan, c	4	1	2	2	0		Wood, c	4	0	1	3	0
Patterson, p	4	0	1	0	0		Hoffer, p	4	0	1	0	0
Total	31	8	7	27	13	1	Total	33	1	7	24	13	3

Chicago .... 0 0 3 0 0 0 1 3 x—8
Cleveland .... 0 0 0 1 0 0 0 0 x—1

Left on bases—Chicago 5, Cleveland 3. Two-base hit—Beck. Double plays—Brain, Shugart, Isbel; Hoffer, Hallman, Lochaero. Struck out—By Hoffer 1. First on balls—Off Patterson 2, Hoffer 6. Umpire—Connolly. Time—1.30.

NOTE.—Rain prevented the Philadelphia-Washington, Baltimore-Boston and Detroit-Milwaukee games.

CLUB STANDING APRIL 24.

	Won.	Lost.	Pct.		Won.	Lost.	Pct.
Chicago	1	0	1.000	Detroit	0	0	.000
Philad'a	0	0	.000	Milwaukee	0	0	.000
Baltimore	0	0	.000	Washington	0	0	.000
Boston	0	0	.000	Cleveland	0	1	.000

CLEVELAND VS. CHICAGO AT CLEVELAND MAY 9.—Earl Moore held the Chicagos down for nine innings without a hit and gave only one base on balls. In the meantime both teams had scored twice, Cleveland on hits and Chicago on an error by Moore. In the tenth inning two singles and a rank decision gave Chicago the game. The score:

CLEVELA'D.	A.B.	R.	B.	P.	A.		CHICAGO.	A.B.	R.	B.	P.	A.
Pickering, rf	4	1	2	0	0		Hoy, cf	3	0	0	2	0
McCarthy, lf	4	0	0	2	0		Jones, rf	4	1	0	3	0
Genins, cf	4	0	1	4	0		Mertes, 2b	3	1	1	2	0
Lochead, ss	4	0	1	1	5		Isbel, 1b	4	1	0	1	0
Bradley, 3b	4	0	0	1	1		Hartm'n, 3b	4	1	1	1	2
Beck, 2b	3	0	0	3	2		Shugart, ss	4	0	2	4	0
Rhea, ss	4	0	0	0	0		McFarl'd, lf	4	0	0	3	0
Wood, c	4	1	2	0	0		Sullivan, c	4	0	2	0	0
Moore, p	3	0	1	3	1		Katoll, p	3	0	0	0	0
*Yeager	1	0	0	0	0		Total	33	4	2	30	11	0
Total	34	2	6	30	13	2							

*Batted for Moore in tenth.

Cleveland .... 0 0 2 0 0 0 0 0 0 0—2
Chicago .... 0 0 0 2 0 0 0 0 0 2—4

LATE NEWS BY WIRE.

THE BOSTON LEAGUE CLUB FORCED TO CUT PRICES.

For the First Time in the History of Base Ball the Triumvirs Lower the Price of League Ball in Boston to 25 Cents, General Admission.

Special to Sporting Life.

Boston, June 19.—The Boston National League Club directors have reduced the price of admission to their grounds to 25 cents, and the extra fee to all parts of the grand stand will be the same. That means that henceforth National League ball will be served to Boston patrons at the rate of 50 cents for the best seat in the grounds, unless some few selected seats are excepted.

This is the first time in the history of the National League that this has been done in Boston, conceded to be one of the best base ball cities in the country, and generally known as a "fifty-cent town" in all sports. The last straw that broke the camel's back was the experience of Monday and Tuesday.

June 17, Bunker Hill day, is an ancient Boston holiday, and the National League grounds have always seen big crowds then; but yesterday their attendance was 1500, according to the official statement, against 10,210 for the American League. Tuesday the National attendance was scattering, while at the American grounds there were over 4000 people. From now on the National directors will fight the American with their own weapon—base ball at popular prices.

THE LAJOIE DECISION.

A HARD BLOW TO ORGANIZED BALL, YET A BLESSING.

The Law Takes No Account of Base Ball Contracts, Wherefore Magnates Must Get Together and Run the Business Under Laws of Their Own Creation.

By Francis C. Richter.

The Philadelphia Court has handed down its decision in the Lajoie case. The opinion is given in full below. The prayer for injunction is denied chiefly on the ground of non-mutuality of the contract—a result expected by almost everybody in base ball except the plaintiff. While the decision delivers the American League from a precarious position, it is, in its ultimate effect, a blow at organized base ball as it strikes at the very foundation of the professional sport as a business—thus affecting the American League as well as the National League and its allies. The only gainers are the players, and their advantage is but temporary and in the long run injurious to themselves.

Stripped of its verbiage the decision practically makes all base ball contracts, except straight contracts, illegal, and closes all avenues of redress for violation except via damage suits, which really is no remedy at all. The magnates are thus just where they were years ago before horse sense permitted itself to be elbowed out by legal "learning." As base ball can hardly be profitably, or even safely, conducted under straight contracts, it is obvious that the professional sport must be operated under its own special code of laws, self-administered.

It is equally obvious that, inasmuch as it is impossible to make base ball a law unto itself without concerted action and recognition of "community of interest," the men who have capital invested in base ball must get together for the protection of their investment and for the preservation of the sport as a business. That being the case the sooner a new protective deal is made the better, else magnates, business and sport will surely be consumed by the great body of the players, who, in matters of dollars and cents, are burdened with no more sentiment, and a great less consideration and foresight, than the magnates.

THE DECISION.

Lack of Mutuality in the Contract Causes a Refusal of the Application For Injunction.

Judge Ralston on May 17 on behalf of the Philadelphia Common Pleas Court No. 5, handed down his decision in the Lajoie injunction suit brought by the Philadelphia League club. The injunction was refused mainly because of the non-mutuality of the contract.

THE JENNINGS CASE

SETTLED TO THE INJURY OF THE AMERICAN LEAGUE.

The Star Player Lost to Both Mack and McGraw, While Two Important Clubs of the Opposition are Very Much Strengthened.

By Francis C. Richter.

The needless and foolish deadlock in the American League over Player Jennings resulted just as was to have been expected. While Baltimore and Philadelphia were quarrelling over the precious bone the National League slipped in and walked off with the prize; and, furthermore killed several birds with one stone. By securing Jennings the Philadelphia League club prevented its local rival from acquiring much needed strength, at the same time vastly strengthening itself, and furthermore, it made it possible for still another important League club to mend its fences, as will be the case if the Brooklyn club can induce Third Baseman Lauder to join its team as part of the Jennings' deal—a by no means improbable contingency. All this is bad enough and sad enough for the American League, but, apart from the immediate disastrous results of the asinine wrangle which enabled the National League for the first time to score a point over the American League, the worst effect is still to come, as the case has made wounds which will be a long time healing and which may in the future serve as the entering wedge of further discord and possible disruption. In all times, and in all leagues, such inter-club quarrels have led to bitter feeling, factional fights and all round disastrous effects upon organization.

SPEED TO FIRST.

INTERESTING EXPERIMENTS WITH FAST BALL PLAYERS.

Stop Watch Records of the Time Required by Various Players to Traverse the Ninety Feet Between the Home Plate and First Base.

By J. Ed Grillo.

Cincinnati, Aug. 10.—During the Cincinnati-Pittsburg game of Aug 4, in this city, the difference in the speed of ball players from the home plate to first base was definitely determined with the aid of a stop watch, says the Cincinnati "Commercial Gazette." It was made evident during these trials that the batsman's speed to first depends largely upon how the swing at the ball affects him. The time was taken every time the opportunity presented itself, and only the best performances are given below. Beckley, Crawford and Hahn could not be timed. Beckley did not have a chance to sprint, because he hit no grounders, and Crawford's only grounder was right at Bransfield. No time could be gotten on Davis, either, from home to first, but the watch showed that he circled the bags in the first inning, when he made his home run, in 13⅗ seconds. This, too, is very fast time, but Wagner beat it in the eighth, when he went from home to third in 10⅗ seconds on his single to left, which got away from Harley. Dobbs and Harley went to first in .03⅗. Fox was half a second slower, but he batted right handed. The record:

CINCINNATI TEAM.

Players.	Distance. Feet.	Time. Seconds.
Dobbs	90	3⅙
Harley	90	3⅙
Fox	90	3⅔
Bergen	90	[illegible]
Magoon	90	4
Bay	90	4
Peitz	90	5

PITTSBURG TEAM.

Players.	Distance. Feet.	Time. Seconds.
Beaumont	90	3
Ritchey	90	3⅕
Clarke	90	3⅔
Leach	90	3⅗
[illegible]	90	3⅘
Wagner	90	4
Wagner	270	10⅗
Davis	360	13⅗
Bransfield	90	4⅓

The time was taken from the moment the bat connected with the ball until the runner's foot hit first base.

BROOKLYN VS. CINCINNATI AT BROOKLYN JUNE 21.—Brooklyn won hands down by terrific batting. Kennedy was in good form and held the visitors well in hand. Keeler led the batting with a home run, a double and three singles in five times at the bat, and scored five runs. Sheckard's left field play was the feature. The score:

BROOKLYN.	AB.	R.	B.	P.	A.	E.	CINCINNATI.	AB.	R.	B.	P.	A.	E.
Keeler, rf...	5	5	5	0	0	0	Dobbs, cf....	4	0	1	1	0	0
Dolan, rf....	1	0	1	0	0	0	Harley, lf....	4	1	3	2	1	0
Sheckard, lf	5	3	3	9	0	0	Beckley, 1b	4	0	1	9	1	0
Daly, 2b.....	6	2	2	5	2	0	Crawford, rf	3	1	0	3	0	0
Dahlen, ss..	6	3	4	2	2	0	Magoon, ss..	4	0	1	2	4	3
McCreery, cf	6	0	1	2	0	0	Steinfeld, 2b	3	1	0	3	7	1
Farrell, 1b..	6	3	3	4	1	1	Irwin, 3b.....	4	0	1	0	1	0
Gatins, 2b...	5	1	1	0	0	0	Peitz, c......	3	0	0	3	1	0
McGuire, c..	4	2	3	4	0	1	Parker, p....	3	0	0	1	1	0
Kennedy, p..	5	2	3	1	2	0	Total.....	32	3	7	24	16	4
Total.....	49	21	26	27	7	2							

Cincinnati	0	1	2	0	0	0	0	0	0	—3
Brooklyn	1	1	4	1	7	1	6	0	x	—21

First on errors—Brooklyn 2. Left on bases—Brooklyn 7, Cincinnati 4. First on balls—Off Kennedy 2, Parker 2. Struck out—By Kennedy 3. Stolen bases—Keller, Sheckard, Daly, Farrell, McGuire, Crawford, Irwin. Home run—Keeler. Two-base hits—Keeler, Sheckard, Dahlen 2, Dobbs, McGuire. Double plays—Daly, Farrell; Parker, Steinfeld, Beckley; Steinfeld, Beckley. Wild pitch—Parker. Umpire—Dwyer. Attendance—2,500. Time—1.47.

SURE OF ST. LOUIS.

THE AMERICAN LEAGUE INVASION A POSITIVE FACT.

Ban Johnson Says Local Backing is Not Needed, and That All Arrangements Have Now Been Perfected For the Entrance of the American Into St. Louis.

Special to Sporting Life.

Jas. McAleer.

St. Louis, Mo., Nov. 20.—Editor "Sporting Life." It is now a settled fact that this city will have an American League club next season whether local backing be forthcoming or not. Ban Johnson and Charley Comiskey came to town last Friday for the purpose of selecting a site for a park. While here Mr. Johnson said everything had been arranged to his satisfaction. Said he: "It is thoroughly settled that we will enter St. Louis. We have not wanted any local backing, for the simple reason that we are following the plan used in Philadelphia and Boston last season. The American League has never depended upon outside capital in its expansion moves and will not do so this year. We shall establish the St. Louis club and later if local capitalists wish to invest they will be given an opportunity to do so. The St. Louis team is practically made up with McAleer slated as manager. Wallace, Heidrick, Burkett, Padden, Powell and Harper have affixed their signatures to contracts. The talk of their going back to the National League is entirely unfounded." Johnson also said the Milwaukee club would be dropped, St. Louis taking its place. When asked as to the truth of the report that the American League intended to place a club in New York also, Mr. Johnson said, "No. The winter is long, however, and we may change our views, but at present we have no such intention."

MILWAUKEE VS. BALTIMORE AT MILWAUKEE SEPT. 3.—(P. M. AND P. M.)—In the first game the Brewers could not hit the reinstated McGinity and were shut out.

BALTIMORE.	AB.	R.	B.	P.	A.	E.	MILWAUKEE.	AB.	R.	B.	P.	A.	E.
Donlin, 1b..	4	4	2	9	0	0	Hogriev'r, lf	4	0	0	5	0	0
Seymour, rf	3	3	2	3	0	0	Conroy, ss...	4	0	0	3	4	1
Williams, 2b	4	2	4	2	4	1	Anders'n, 1b	4	0	3	10	1	0
Keister, ss..	5	0	2	1	3	0	Gilbert, 2b...	4	0	0	3	4	1
Brodie, cf...	5	0	2	2	0	0	Hallman, rf	4	0	0	1	0	0
Dunn, 3b...	5	0	0	1	1	0	Friel, 3b.....	4	0	1	0	6	0
Howell, lf...	5	0	1	3	0	0	Bruyette, cf	3	0	0	2	0	0
Bresnah'n, c	3	1	0	5	0	0	Maloney, c..	3	0	0	3	1	2
McGinity, p	5	0	1	1	1	0	Sparks, p.....	3	0	2	0	0	1
Total......	39	10	14	27	9	1	Total.....	33	0	6	27	18	5

Baltimore	1	0	2	0	1	0	2	4	0	—10
Milwaukee	0	0	0	0	0	0	0	0	0	—0

Two-base hits—Williams, Friel, Seymour, Howell, Anderson. Three-base hits—Anderson, Donlin 2, Sparks, Williams. First on balls—Off Sparks 6. Stolen bases—Seymour, Brodie 2, Williams, Keister, Donlin. Wild pitch—Sparks. Struck out—By Sparks 2, McGinity 2. Double plays—Gilbert, Conroy, Anderson; Dunn, Williams, Donlin. Left on bases—Baltimore 9, Milwaukee 6. Umpire—Hart. Time—1.50.

McGinnity also pitched the second game finely, but lost as his team could not connect with Hustings. The score:

BALTIMORE.	AB.	R.	B.	P.	A.	E.	MILWAUKEE.	AB.	R.	B.	P.	A.	E.
Donlin, 1b...	4	0	1	11	0	0	Hogriev'r, lf	3	2	1	5	1	0
Seymour, rf	4	0	0	0	0	0	Conroy, ss..	4	2	1	3	3	2
Williams, 2b	2	0	0	1	2	0	Anders'n, 1b	3	0	1	8	0	1
Keister, ss..	4	0	2	0	3	0	Gi'bert, 2b...	3	1	1	0	4	0
Brodie, cf...	3	1	2	5	1	0	Hallman, rf	4	0	2	2	0	0
Dunn, 3b...	3	0	0	2	3	2	Friel, 3b.....	3	1	0	2	3	0
Howell, lf..	3	0	0	3	0	0	Bruyette, cf	4	0	0	1	0	1
Bresnah'n, c	3	0	0	2	2	0	Maloney, c..	4	0	2	4	4	0
McGinn'y, p	3	0	0	0	3	0	Hustings, p	4	0	1	2	0	0
Total.....	29	1	5	24	14	2	Total.....	32	6	9	27	15	4

Baltimore	0	1	0	0	0	0	0	0	0	—1
Milwaukee	2	0	1	0	1	0	0	2	x	—6

Two-base hits—Brodie, Gilbert. Three-base hits—Hogriever, Maloney. First on balls—Off Hustings 3, McGinnity 4. Hit by pitcher—Anderson. Stolen bases—Friel, Seymour. Struck out—By Hustings 4, McGinnity 2. Double play—Gilbert, Conroy, Anderson. Left on bases—Baltimore 6, Milwaukee 6. Umpire—Hart. Attendance—1,500. Time—1.40.

BALTIMORE VS. ATHLETIC AT BALTIMORE SEPT. 12.—(P. M. AND P. M.)—The first game looked like a victory for the Athletics until the ninth, when Plank, who had been pitching excellently, weakened and allowed four hits, including a three-bagger by Williams. The score:

BALTIMORE.	AB.	R.	B.	P.	A.	E.	ATHLETIC.	AB.	R.	B.	P.	A.	E.
Donlin, 1b...	4	0	1	4	0	0	Fultz, cf.....	5	1	3	4	0	0
Seymour, rf	4	0	0	2	0	1	Davis, 1b.....	5	1	1	12	0	0
Williams, 2b	4	1	2	3	2	1	Lajoie, 2b...	5	0	3	3	4	0
Keister, ss..	4	2	2	2	3	1	Seybold, rf..	4	0	0	1	0	0
Brodie, cf...	3	1	3	3	0	0	McIntyre, lf	5	0	0	0	0	0
Dunn, 3b....	4	0	0	1	0	1	Ely, ss.........	3	0	0	3	3	0
Jackson, lf..	3	0	1	5	0	0	Steelman, c	4	0	0	3	3	0
Robinson, c	4	0	1	6	0	0	Dolan, 3b...	3	1	0	0	4	0
McGinn'y, p	3	0	0	1	0	1	Plank, p......	4	0	0	0	2	0
Total.....	33	4	10	27	5	5	Total.....	38	3	7	*26	16	0

*Two out when winning run was scored.

Baltimore	0	0	0	0	2	0	0	0	2	—4
Athletic	2	1	0	0	0	0	0	0	0	—3

Sacrifice hit—Lajoie. Two-base hit—Jackson. Three-base hit—Williams. Stolen base—Dunn. Double play—Ely, Lajoie, Davis. First on balls—Off McGinnity 3, Plank 1. Hit by pitcher—By Plank 1. Struck out—By Plank 2, McGinnity 2. Left on bases—Baltimore 2, Athletic 11. Umpire—Sheridan. Time—1.55.

McGinnity also pitched the second game, and had the Athletics guessing until the last inning when the Athletics scored the winning run on a hit by Ely, an error by Keister, a force hit and a long fly. The score:

BALTIMORE.	AB.	R.	B.	P.	A.	E.	ATHLETIC.	AB.	R.	B.	P.	A.	E.
Donlin, 1b...	3	3	1	9	0	0	Fultz, cf.....	5	1	1	1	1	0
Seymour, rf	5	0	3	4	0	0	Davis, 1b...	4	1	3	10	3	0
Williams, 2b	3	0	2	3	3	0	Lajoie, 2b...	3	0	1	3	1	0
Keister, ss..	5	0	2	4	4	2	Seybold, rf..	4	0	1	0	1	0
Brodie, cf...	4	0	0	3	0	0	McIntyre, lf	4	0	1	2	0	0
Dunn, 3b...	4	1	1	4	2	0	Ely, ss......	4	1	1	1	5	1
Jackson, lf..	3	0	0	0	0	0	Powers, c...	4	0	0	5	1	0
Robinson, c	2	0	0	0	0	0	Dolan, 3b...	4	1	1	2	4	0
McGinn'y, p	4	0	1	0	6	0	Bernhard, p	4	1	2	3	1	0
Total.....	33	4	10	27	14	2	Total.....	35	5	10	27	18	1

Baltimore	1	0	0	0	1	0	1	1	0	—4
Athletic	0	0	0	1	3	0	0	0	1	—5

THE NEW CINCINNATI GRAND STAND.

Shows the Famous Fireproof "Palace of the Fans," Which is One of the Finest Base Ball Structures in the Country. Seats Have Been Placed Underneath the Stand For the Accommodation of the Rooters.

SHOT FOR STAHL.

A Young Woman With a Pistol Goes Gunning For the Handsome and Popular Boston Club Player.

Fort Wayne, Ind., Jan. 26.—This quiet little town had quite a sensation to-day. Miss Lulu Ortman, a pretty stenographer, aged 20 years, came near

"Chic" Stahl

putting an end to the career of fielder "Chic" Stahl, of the Boston American League team. Stahl formerly paid much attention to the young lady, but recently became interested elsewhere. To-day Miss Ortman armed herself with a revolver and started out. After two hours' searching she found him and attempted to shoot him. The superintendent of police, who happened by, probably saved Stahl's life. The young woman was locked up. She has nothing to say, only that Stahl has jilted her for another and that she intends to shoot him on sight. Stahl was seen to-night, but refused to talk, except to say that the girl had no reason to attempt his life.

BASE MULLANE.

The First to Jump, He is One of the First to Break his Contract.

A despatch from Toledo Jan. 30 stated that Tony Mullane, who was the first player to jump the reserve rule by signing with the St. Louis Unions, has now gone back on that contract and signed with the Toledo Club. Mullane was in Toledo for a few days last week in company with Manager Morton, of the Toledo Club, and on Wednesday agreed to sign a contract with the Toledo Club, if the proper release could be secured from St. Louis. As this had been previously arranged, the St. Louis Club was notified by telegraph. An answer came back that the release would be forwarded to Secretary Wikoff, of Columbus, O., at once. The terms are the same as paid by Lucas, $2,500, with $500 advance. The advance paid him by Lucas will be returned to that gentleman at once. Toledo is thus assured one of the best pitchers in the country, but his action is severely commented upon, even by those who expect to profit by his act. The Toledo nine will be composed of Mullane, Cushman and O'Day as pitchers; Walker, Bullas and Brown as catchers; Moffitt, first base; Barkley, second base; Morton, third base; Miller, short stop; Poorman, right field; Welch, left field; Gilman, centre field; Tilley and Lane substitutes.

President Lucas says he has received no official notice of Mullane's action, but promises to prosecute him if such is the case. He also says that if Mullane goes he will enter the camp of the opposition in his search for a pitcher and secure a first-class one at any cost.

GALVIN GONE.

The Veteran Ball Player, Once One of the Greatest of Pitchers, Passes into Eternity.

When our last issue went to press the famous ex-pitcher James Galvin was approaching dissolution, at his home in Allegheny, Pa. The end came on the evening of March 7. He had been unconscious for five days and did not regain consciousness. Catarrh of the stomach was the immediate cause. Galvin was born in St. Louis in 1855, and learned the game in the "Kerry Patch." His professional career was briefly summarized in our last issue. The funeral was held on March 9, and was largely attended by base ball men. He died in absolute poverty, leaving a wife, four sons and one daughter. Local friends have donated sufficient to tide the stricken family over for a short time, and the well-known James Mason has completed arrangements for a monster benefit for Jimmy Galvin at Old City Hall, Saturday, March 22.

DONLIN'S DESERTS.

THE PUNISHMENT METED OUT TO FIT HIS CRIME.

The Ex-Baltimore Player Will Spend Six Months in Jail For His Brutal Assault Upon a Young Woman and Her Voluntary Protector.

Baltimore, March 24.—Editor "Sporting Life:"—Michael Donlin, the ball player, when arraigned in Criminal Court March

Mike Donlin

19 on an indictment for striking Miss Minnie Fields, an actress, and Ernest Slayton, of Chicago, her escort on the night of March 12, pleaded guilty and said as he was drunk at the time he did not know what he was doing. Miss Fields told of the assault, showed her bruised and blackened face, and said the blow felled her to the ground and rendered her unconscious. Mr. Slayton's blackened eyes were also in evidence as to the weight of the ruffian's fist. Donlin's lawyers asked for mercy. They agreed he had been severely punished by his dismissal from the Baltimore Base Ball Club, in which he was paid $2800 a year, and that if he was sentenced to jail might never be able to get another position with any of the major league teams. Judge Ritchie, however, sentenced him to six months in jail and a fine of $250. He scored the prisoner, saying the assault was certainly a most aggravated one. It was probably true that he would not have committed it had he been sober, but nevertheless the people on the streets, and especially the women, must and shall be protected. "Giving full consideration to every extenuating circumstance brought out on behalf of this young man," concluded the judge, "I still must impose a penalty in some degree commensurate with the offense." An appeal will be made to the Governor for pardon. Donlin's daily task will now for six months be to daily polish brass and steel. Outside meals have been refused him. He is much depressed.

THE FOUL RULE.

Father Chadwick Explains the Rule as Regards Strikes on Foul Balls and Commends Some Umpires.

By Henry Chadwick.

Henry Chadwick

Brooklyn, N. Y., May 10.—Editor "Sporting Life:"—I have had so many questions sent me in regard to the rule of strikes on foul balls that I deem it timely to give enquirers a few remarks about the rule and its workings this season. It will be remembered that the Buffalo Convention adopted a compromise rule presented by Mr. Hart, which new rule was printed in the code they had printed. This compromise rule was rejected both by the American and National Leagues, and was last week rejected by the Eastern League. The National Association of Leagues left it at the pleasure of their clubs to adopt the compromise rule, but all have rejected it. As it stands now the American League rejected the strike rule entire, and the National League re-adopted the strike rule of 1901. The universities and colleges have rejected the strike rule entire, and the National League alone retains it.

I saw both Brown and O'Day umpire last week and I greatly admired the work they both did in their arduous position. The charges made of "rotten umpires" by the "kid" writers of the local press were alike untrue and grossly partisan. Better umpiring is bound to follow the timely advice of the National League Committee.

WADDELL'S WAYS.

The Erratic Pitcher Not so Hard to Handle When One Knows How to Take Him Right.

"So George Edward Waddell is to return to the game," mused Jess Tannehill. "He is certainly one of the greatest char-

G. Ed. Waddell

acters that ever played ball. Whenever he lost a game while with the Pirates he was apt to growl: 'How can a fellow be expected to win with a lot of left handers on the team.' Waddell doesn't like to be called 'Rube,' but if you address him as 'Eddy,' he will fight for you and swear to be your friend for life. 'Rube' and Barney Dreyfuss have had many heart-to-heart talks, and it is one of Barney's whispered boasts that 'Rube' is the only ball player he ever met who couldn't give him the worst of it. Drawing his salary in dribs is one of Waddell's strong points, and he used to tap Barney for small amounts, rarely asking for over $5 a throw. After an all-winter's run on Barney's bank, the story leaked out that 'Rube' had been drawing on a $128 balance of his own that he didn't know was coming to him. One of the most touching living pictures I've ever seen has been 'Rube' going to Harry Pulliam and asking for the loan of a dollar. Throwing his arm around his shoulder Pulliam would look the eccentric twirler in the eye and ask, in all seeming seriousness: 'Eddie, what did you do with that dollar I gave you day before yesterday?' and then the 'Rube' would compromise and take a quarter." Perhaps Frank Selee can control the southpaw.

STUNNING SURPRISE

DEALT THE ATHLETIC CLUB OF THE AMERICAN LEAGUE

BY THE SUPREME COURT DECISION IN THE LAJOIE CASE.

The High Court Reverses the Decision of the Lower Philadelphia Court Refusing the Philadelphia Club an Injunction Against Lajoie, Bernhard and Fraser.

Philadelphia, Pa., April 22.—The Supreme Court of Pennsylvania in an opinion handed down yesterday reversed the decision of Common Pleas Court No. 5 dismissing the bill of complaint of the Philadelphia Ball Club against Napoleon Lajoie. The matter came before the Court on an appeal by the Philadelphia Ball Club, and the Court says the specifications of error are sustained and the decree of the Court below dismissing the bill is reversed, and the bill is reinstated. The bill in equity referred to was filed to prevent Lajoie from playing with any other ball club than the Philadelphia Club, under an option clause in the contract.

Napoleon Lajoie

THE EFFECT.

This decision will prevent Lajoie from playing with any other club than the Philadelphia Club during the present year, for the Court says:

"Upon a careful consideration of the whole case, we are of opinion that the provisions of the contract are reasonable, and that the consideration is fully adequate. The evidence shows no indications of any attempt at overreaching or unfairness. Substantial justice between the parties requires that the Court should restrain the defendant from playing for any other club during the term of his contract with the plaintiff."

The effect of the Supreme Court's decision is that if Napoleon Lajoie is to play ball this season he will have to do so with the Philadelphia Club. The same is true of Charles C. Fraser and William Bernhard, who left the Phillies at the same time Lajoie did, and against whom similar suits were brought.

THE NEXT STEP.

All of the cases were brought in Common Pleas Court No. 5, and it was agreed that Lajoie's should be made the test case, and its decision will bind the other two. Colonel Rogers will immediately have the record in the Lajoie case certified back to Common Pleas Court No. 5, when it is likely injunctions against the three players will be asked for if they do not return and report for duty to the club. The issuance of the injunctions is a matter of course and will follow upon formal motion, as the decision of the Supreme Court is final and must be obeyed without argument, or delay. There were players other than Fraser, Lajoie and Bernhard who left the Phillies and against whom no suits were brought. These men will also be notified at once to report to the Philadelphia Club, and if they refuse suits will be brought against them. The Philadelphia Club last year reserved all of these players for the present season, and Lajoie, under his contract, is not only bound to play with the Philadelphia Club for this season, but can be reserved for the season of 1903.

John I. Rogers

EMINENT OPINION.

Philadelphia, Pa., April 29.—William Draper Lewis, the dean of the Law Department of the University of Pennsylvania, the other day discussed the decision of the Supreme Court of the State in the case of the Philadelphia National League Club against Lajoie, in a lecture before the graduating class of the University. Dr. Lewis is an expert upon this branch of equity jurisdiction, thoroughly drilled in his subject by constant class-room work and exhaustive private research. He has lately published a number of articles in the "American Law Register," the legal organ of the University, upon the defense of lack of mutuality, which the court bowled out in the Lajoie case.

DR. LEWIS' VIEW.

"The opinion," said the dean yesterday, "from the standpoint of the Supreme Court, is unquestionably the proper conclusion. The court decides that there is a peculiar value possessed by the services of the defendant, for the loss of which pecuniary damages are not adequate compensation. There is no question but that this is correct. It was not necessary to say that Lajoie was the best base ball player in the world, but it is evident that, in the condition of the base ball labor market, his services are not duplicable.

May 6

A BLOW TO BASE BALL.

What is good law and sound reason in staid old Pennsylvania is neither one or the other in wild and wooly Missouri. A St. Louis Court has passed upon the National League contract and has rendered a judgment directly opposite the sage conclusions reached by the Pennsylvania Supreme Court. In a sweeping decision a Missouri Solon declares the League contract inequitable, unconscionable and contrary to public policy. The St. Louis Judge even went further and stigmatized the contract as unconstitutional and the base ball business as illegal. This remarkable decision in full is given in another column and we entreat for it careful perusal.

This decision has been hailed as a victory for the American League, and the ball player. Only unthinking or short-sighted partisans can so regard it. Viewed from any angle for its effect upon the stability, the discipline and the investments of the game, Judge Talty's decision is a calamity—or would be such were it the final judgment of a superior Court, which could command general respect and wide acceptance. Fortunately, the St. Louis decision represents but the opinion of two inferior judges—instead of the united opinion of the highest Court of an American Commonwealth—and is therefore subject to appeal and reversal.

In conclusion, we feel constrained to warn the players that this St. Louis decision is not really a victory for them, either. Its immediate effect may be subversive of discipline—as witness the recrudescence of contract-jumping since that decision—but that can only be temporary. A system that would breed Sheckards and Wrights by the wholesale would either quickly kill the game or compel the warring magnates to get together in short order. In the latter event, the players' harvest would be over, and their last state become worse than the first. Under the Pennsylvania decision the Reserve Rule could in time be modified or abandoned. Under the St. Louis decision, which would make the national game an outcast, the Reserve Rule and other iron-clad measures would be absolutely essential for self-preservation, and, therefore justifiable.

SOMERS SUCCEEDS

IN CAPTURING THE ENJOINED PLAYERS, LAJOIE AND BERNHARD.

The Famous Stars Leave Philadelphia For Cleveland, Where They Will Sign Contracts Beyond the Jurisdiction of the Pennsylvania Courts.

Philadelphia, May 27.—It was reported on what seems good authority that Lajoie and Bernhard left for Cleveland at 11.05 last night to sign contracts with the American League Club of that city. This move is taken to avoid any possible complications by signing contracts in Philadelphia and to have the best possible defense in case of any legal controversy. Manager Armour, of the Cleveland team, said last night that even if the players sign contracts immediately, he does not expect them to join the club before the beginning of the Baltimore series. Lajoie's contract, it is said, is for four years at a salary of $35,000.

Napoleon Lajoie

COLONEL ROGERS INDIGNANT.

Colonel Rogers, when seen yesterday at his office, expressed himself as absolutely astounded at the turn of affairs, and said:

"I can hardly bring myself to believe that Lajoie and Bernhard would do such a foolhardy trick, but from what I read in all the papers I must confess that it looks very much as if the men had put their heads in the lion's mouth. I shall go into Court and ask for an attachment of contempt against the players at once, and shall also consult attorneys to see what action can be taken against those who are the instigators of this crime against the law."

The Colonel then sent the following telegram to Robert Young, son of Nick Young, at Washington:

"Go to game to-day, and if Lajoie or Bernhard take part in same swear to affidavit of fact and send it to me immediately."

This looks as if the Colonel intended to take up the battle at once, and warm times are expected.

CLEVELAND VS. BOSTON AT CLEVELAND JUNE 4.—Lajoie made his debut with Cleveland before an immense crowd. He received an ovation, got a hit and run, fielded grandly and was the pivot in two lightning double plays which shut off runs and saved the game. Hickman, late of Boston, also played with Cleveland. The score:

CLEVEL'D.	AB.	R.	B.	P.	A.	E	BOSTON.	AB.	R.	B.	P.	A.	E
Pickeri'g, cf	4	0	0	1	0	0	Doughe'y, lf	5	1	1	1	0	0
McCart'y, lf	4	2	2	1	0	0	Collins, 3b.	4	1	0	0	2	0
Flick, rf	3	0	0	4	0	0	Stahl, cf.	3	0	1	2	0	0
Lajoie, 2b.	3	1	1	2	3	0	Freeman, rf	3	0	2	0	0	0
Hickm'n, 1b	4	0	0	12	0	1	Parent, ss.	4	0	1	0	6	1
Bradley,3b.	3	0	2	0	3	2	Lachan'e,1b	3	1	1	8	0	0
Gochna'r,ss	3	0	1	7	2	0	Ferris, 2b.	4	0	0	2	5	1
Wood, c.	3	1	1	6	1	0	Warner, c.	4	0	2	1	0	0
Moore, p.	3	0	0	0	2	0	Prentiss, p.	3	0	0	0	2	0
Total	30	4	6	27	16	5	*Gleason	1	0	0	0	0	0
							Total	34	3	8	24	15	2

*Batted for Prentiss in the ninth.

Cleveland.................. 0 0 0 2 0 1 1 0 x—4
Boston.................... 2 0 0 1 0 0 0 0 0—3

Earned runs—Cleveland 2. Two-base hits—Bradley, McCarthy 2, Lajoie, Wood, Freeman, Lachance. Sacrifice hits—Stahl, Lajoie. Stolen bases—Pickering, Freeman. Double plays—Bradley, Lajoie, Hickman; Gochnaur, Lajoie, Hickman. First on balls—Off Moore 3, Prentiss 1. Left on bases—Cleveland 4, Boston 8. Struck out—By Moore 3, Prentiss 1. Umpire—Johnstone. Time—1.40. Attendance—9,827.

M'GRAW DESERTS.

THE BALTIMORE MANAGER GOES OVER TO NATIONAL LEAGUE.

Severs His Connection With the Baltimore Club and Signs With New York —Other Baltimore Players Will Follow McGraw, It is Believed.

Special to Sporting Life.

John J. McGraw

Baltimore Md., July 8.—John J. McGraw last night severed his connection with the Baltimore Base Ball Club as manager and left this city for New York to become the manager of the New York National League team. He will retain his stock in the Baltimore Club until he can dispose of it. At a meeting of the Baltimore owners and stockholders last night, at which John J. Mahon, the president, was present, it was decided to give McGraw his release. Joseph Kelley, son-in-law of President Mahon, together with Wilbert Robinson, the business partner of McGraw, will temporarily be joint managers of the Baltimore Club, although it is believed that in a short time McGraw will secure them, and probably other players of the Baltimore team, for the National League.

THE PLAYERS CHIP IN

WITH A CONTRIBUTION TO THE GAYETY OF THE NATION.

The Players' Protective Association Decides to Remain Alive, Elects Officers, and Votes Unanimously to Expel All Contract Jumpers This Year.

NEW YORK SELECTED; PITTSBURG REJECTED.

AN UNEQUIVOCAL DECLARATION AT LAST BY PRESIDENT BAN JOHNSON.

The American League Has a Ground in New York and Will Enter That City—Loyalty to Detroit Eliminates Pittsburg.

TRAITORS IN CAMP.

THE AMERICAN LEAGUE'S NARROW ESCAPE FROM SERIOUS DISASTER.

Baltimore Magnates, With the Aid of McGraw, Sell Out the Club to National League Agents and Disband the Team —Ban Johnson Saves the Day.

Baltimore, Md., July 21.—Editor "Sporting Life:"—John J. McGraw last week almost accomplished what he tried to do a year ago. Not satisfied with deserting Baltimore, which made him all he is in base ball, he cold bloodedly tried to wreck the club and to drive the city out of Major League base ball. Associated with McGraw in this selfish scheme were President Mahon and his son-in-law Joe Kelley. When McGraw resigned from the club he ostensibly disposed of his Baltimore club stock to President Mahon. Rob-

Harry Goldman

inson did likewise to secure enough money to buy out McGraw's interest in the saloon in North Howard street, heretofore jointly owned by them. The holdings of Father John G. Bowland were also purchased by Mr. Mahon. These holdings gave Mr. Mahon 201 shares of the 400 shares of the Baltimore Base Ball Club. It was supposed that all this was done to let McGraw and Robinson out as stockholders, and to have the club run by business men, but behind it all there was a deep laid and cunningly worked out plot to sell Baltimore out to the National League.

THE SELL-OUT.

Late at night on July 16 the bomb exploded. That day John T. Brush and John J. McGraw, acting as agents for Mr. Freedman, came to Baltimore secretly and at their instance the 201 shares held by President Mahon were transferred to Joseph C. France, a local lawyer, representing Mr. Freedman. The consideration could not be learned, but it was later given out that $50,000 was the price paid by Mr. Freedman. The scheme was for him to have first choice at the

W. Robinson

Baltimore players and John T. Brush the second choice, such other League clubs as wanted any of the players to pay for them pro rata. But the last part of the deal was blocked by the refusal of some of the players to consent to any transfer. Six of the players were at once released—four, McGinnity, Cronin, McGann and Bresnahan to New York, and two, Kelley and Seymour, to Cincinnati. Great pressure was brought to bear upon Selbach and Williams to have them sign with certain other National League clubs, but they refused all overtures, stating that they would hold the Baltimore club to its two year contract.

BADLY TREATED PEOPLE.

The deal was made without the knowledge of Robinson, who was in Hudson, Mass., attending the funeral of his mother. The minority stockholders, including Harry Goldman, Sidney Frank and Theodore Straus, who were to be thrown down in cold blood, of course were also in ignorance of the scheme until it was consummated. The treatment of these gentlemen by McGraw was doubly despicable, for the reason that when the club was organized they put up all the money for improvements and current expenses and made McGraw and

Sydney Frank

Robinson a present of 51 per cent. of stock—the very stock now used to give Mahon the majority necessary to consummate the sell out, which was nothing short of robbery of the minority stockholders.

JOHNSON SAVES THE SITUATION.

Fortunately President Ban Johnson was in Washington when the betrayal of Baltimore occurred, and he at once came over and in conjunction with the minority stockholders, assumed charge of affairs. Under the provisions of the American League constitution, the ground lease of the Baltimore club had been assigned to him. This gave him a powerful lever to start with. Another piece of good fortune was that enough players remained loyal to afford a nucleus for another team, at short notice. Besides overlooking the ground lease matter the conspirators also gave President Johnson another handle by not leaving or furnishing enough players to put some sort of a team in the field to protect their American League franchise. This serious blunder enabled President Johnson to get rid of the Baltimore club legally, to keep the city in the circuit and to protect the minority stockholders.

THE CLUB FORFEITS.

President Johnson on July 17, after consultation with Messrs Goldman, Frank and Straus, authorized the latter to frame up a new company. He then received the loyal players, Selbach, Williams, Howell, Gilbert, Shields and Oyler. After complimenting them upon the honorable stand and assuring them that the American League would take care of their base ball future, he appointed Selbach team captain. In the afternoon at the regular hour set for the scheduled game with St. Louis, before a large crowd the game was officially forfeited to the St. Louis club by Umpires Carruthers and Johnstone, the Baltimore club not presenting a team for the contest. President Johnson then addressed letters to President Mahon and Secretary Goldman, of the Baltimore club, citing them to appear before the Board of Directors and show cause why the club franchise should not be forfeited, according to the provisions of the constitution, for its failure to play its schedule. Mr. Johnson had previously called a special meeting of the League Directors for Baltimore July 18. He also wired the other clubs for extra players to fill out a new Baltimore team.

THE LEGAL EXPULSION.

On Friday, July 18, a quorum of the American League Board of Directors met at Rennert's Hotel and declared the franchise of the Baltimore Base Ball Club and Athletic company forfeited. A mail vote will be taken as a matter of form. There is not the slightest doubt about the action of the board being sanctioned by the club members. Wilbert Robinson appeared before the Board of Directors of the American League at the Hotel Rennert and explained his business relations with McGraw. As a result President Johnson and Messrs. Kilfoyle and Shibe exonerated Robinson from any connection with the jumpers and he was immediately elected manager of the Baltimore team. Harry Goldman was appointed business manager on behalf of the American League, pending the organization of a new club by the Goldman-Frank coterie. The experience of Frank, Brinkley and Strouse, in base ball has been unpleasant, and Johnson and his fellows of the American League are using their best efforts to induce them to try it again, and it is likely that they will succeed.

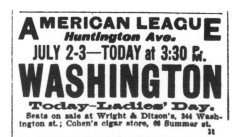

SETTLEMENT SECURED; PEACE PROCLAIMED!

THE POPULAR DOUBLE LEAGUE SYSTEM SCORES A SPLENDID TRIUMPH.

The Warring Major Leagues Reach an Agreement in Which Each League Fully Preserves Its Autonomy.

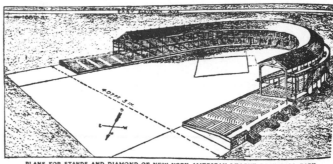

PLANS FOR STANDS AND DIAMOND OF NEW YORK AMERICAN LEAGUE BASE BALL PARK.

'BEWARE OF WOMEN' WAS MERCER'S WARNING

Letters written by Winnie Mercer, the suicide, show that his determination to die was brought about through unfortunate entanglements. To his mother, Mrs. Maggie Mercer, of East Liverpool, Ohio, he wrote as follows:

Dear, Darling Mother: I do not want to break your heart, but I am afraid I will by the act I am about to commit. I think I am doing the right thing, dear mother, so please forgive me.

Women have gotten the best of me, but I forgive them; and even though they are my downfall, God bless them.

Well, dear mother, I must say good-bye forever. Please forgive me, dear mother and brothers. I love you all, and am sorry to leave you.

Again I say good-bye to mother, Howard, Ross, Clifford, Hazel, Robert and all my dear uncles, aunts and cousins. From WINNIE.

WAIL OF REMORSE.

In a letter to Miss Martha C. Porter of Pennsylvania avenue, Washington, D. C., Mercer wrote:

Dearest Martha: With tears streaming from my eyes, I pen these few lines to you, the dearest and sweetest little girl in the whole world.

The act I am about to commit is simply terrible, but I cannot help it, dearie. I am to blame—nobody else—so I am going to face it as rigid as I have many other wrong acts.

Please forgive me, dear Martha. I love you till the last. Oh, if I could only kiss you once more, I would be satisfied to go.

Good-bye to your father, mother, Nellie, Itha, John and my dear pal, Harry.

I am sorry to leave you, but I think it best that I should. Your unfortunate WINNIE.

Another letter was written by Mercer to his old friend and associate, "Tip" O'Neill. In this the man about to die shows that in his extreme moment he had thought for the men who worked with him:

THOUGHT OF BUSINESS.

Dear Morris: Please pardon me for the act I am about to commit. God only knows that I am sorry to do it, but I think it best that I should.

A word to my friends: Beware of women and a game of chance. The following bills are to be collected from the boys and paid in the company:

Monte Cross	$251.00
Kahoe	101.40
Coughlin	15.25
Beckley	15.60
Hartsel	50.00
Bernhard	(ticket) 110.00

You will find tickets in my trunk, which is in No. 2 on the third. Search my clothes for trunk key.

Well, dear pal, with tears in my eyes I say good-bye forever. May every one connected with our trip forgive me. I wanted to do right. Forgive me, dear friends. WIN.

P. S.

Due O'Neill	$200.00
Due Tannehill	82.00
Due Joss	120.00

You will find two sacks of money in the safe, also $63 in my trousers pockets. WIN.

MERCER MURDERED?

HIS FRIENDS CONVINCED THAT THERE WAS FOUL PLAY.

The Gang That Recently Tried to Secure His Funds by the Forgery Trick Suspected of Having Resorted to Murder to Secure the Cash.

Win Mercer

The brief dispatch in "Sporting Life's" last issue to the effect that pitcher Win Mercer—who was to have managed the Detroit team next season—had committed suicide proved to be true. The famous player went to the Occidental Hotel, in San Francisco, on the evening of Jan. 12, registered as George Murray, and then committed suicide by inhaling illuminating gas. His identity was established by letters addressed to Tip O'Neill, his mother and a young woman at East Liverpool, O., to whom he was to have been married next spring. He was the chief support of his aged mother. He had always sent her a monthly check, purchased a comfortable home for her and provided her with a snug bank account. He left a statement of his accounts as treasurer of the California Tourists, which were found to be correct. In the letter addressed to O'Neill he warned his friends against women and gambling. Mercer's tragic end proved a great shock to the Tourists, to his personal friends, to the great body of players, with whom he was very popular, and to the thousands of patrons who admired him as a great ball player. Mercer's body was shipped to East Liverpool on Jan. 19 in charge of Harley and Joss.

PITTSBURG VS. PHILADELPHIA AT PITTSBURG JUNE 8.—The Pirates scored their sixth successive shut-out on luck. Sparks outpitched Leever, and but for a wonderful one-handed jumping catch by Wagner of Douglas' liner the score would have been tied in the ninth. Outfielder Titus, of Concord, made his debut with the Phillies and created a favorable impression. The score:

PITTSBURG	AB.	R.	B.	P.	A.	E.	PHILA.	AB.	R.	B.	P.	A.	E.
Beaum't, cf.	3	1	1	3	0	0	Thomas, cf.	4	0	2	3	0	0
Clark, lf.	4	0	1	3	0	0	Wolver'n, 3b	3	0	0	0	1	0
Sebring, rf.	4	0	2	0	0	0	Hallman, 3b	1	0	1	0	3	0
Wagner, ss.	3	1	2	3	0	Keister, rf.	4	0	1	0	0	0
Bran'sfi'd, 1b	3	0	0	12	0	0	Titus, lf.	4	0	0	2	0	0
Leach, 3b	3	0	0	2	1	1	Barry, 1b	4	0	1	12	0	1
Ritchey, 2b	3	0	1	3	4	0	Hulswitt, ss	4	0	0	1	3	0
Phelps, c	3	0	2	1	0	Gleason, 2b	4	0	1	1	2	0
Leever, p.	3	0	0	5	0	Roth, c.	4	0	1	3	2	1
Total	29	2	7	27	14	1	Sparks, p.	2	0	1	2	2	1
							*Douglas	1	0	0	0	0	0
							Total	35	0	8	24	13	3

*Batted for Sparks in ninth inning.

Pittsburg .... 1 0 0 1 0 0 0 0 x—2
Philadelphia ..... 0 0 0 0 0 0 0 0 0—0

Two-base hit—Sebring. Double play—Leach, Bransfield. First on balls—Off Leever 1, Sparks 1. Sacrifice hit—Wagner. Stolen base—Wagner. Struck out—By Leever 1, Sparks 1. Umpire—O'Day. Time—1.30. Attendance—3,150.

NEW YORK'S CLUB

FULFILLS ALL OF ITS PROMISES TO THE PUBLIC.

The New Ball Park in New York City Opened on the Scheduled Date With Imposing Ceremonies—The Crown to Six Weeks of Herculean Labor.

Joseph Gordon

The climax to the American League's long and hard battle to establish a club in New York city came April 30, when the new ball park on Washington Heights was opened by a championship game between Manager Griffith's Greater New York team and the Washingtons, before over 16,000 people, who found no trouble in reaching the grounds comfortably and in good time. The men who did most to bring all this about, Ban Johnson; Contractor McAvoy, who undertook the task of transforming a rock-ribbed hill into a ball ground; Contractor Foster, who supplied the spacious and comfortable stands, and President Gordon, who watched the progress of the work with untiring vigilance, were on hand to oversee and enjoy. Presidents Shibe, of Philadelphia, and Postal, of Washington, were also present. The want of finish to the grounds and stands, finish being something only age can impart, was relieved by gorgeous decorations. A myriad of flags of a myriad of colors snapped in the fine breeze which swept the hill and took off the discomfort of the heat. With a small American flag in the hand of every player the two teams paraded across the field, led by the Sixty-ninth Regiment Band. They were loudly cheered and saluted by the waving of the thousands of flags, one of which was presented to each spectator as he entered the ground. President Ban Johnson threw out the new ball and Umpire Connolly said the word that redeemed the promise of the Greater New York management to open their grounds as announced. Notwithstanding the absence of Dave Fultz and Herman Long, Griffith's men made a very favorable impression and won the game from the start, thereby putting a fine finishing touch to a memorable day in the base ball annals of New York city.

M'GRAW AS A KID.

A Reminder of the Time When John Started—Board, Shaving, Washing and One Cigar a Week His Ambition Then.

Below will be found a copy of the first contract ever signed by the now noted player and manager John J. McGraw. It was with the independent Ocala, Fla., club—McGraw's first professional engagement. Note the humble beginning:

Ocala, Fla., Feb. 14, 1891.—To the Directors of the Ocala Base Ball Association, Gentlemen: We, the undersigned base ball players, and members of the Ocala Giants, agree to play with the Ocala Club, until further notified, for board, shaving and washing expenses; also a cigar once a week.

(Signed)

JOHN J. M'GRAW,
C. F. THORP,
J. CONNER,
ED. MARS,
FRANK STRATTON.

NEW WAR CLOUDS DARKEN HORIZON.

THE MISERABLE DAVIS CASE LIKELY TO CAUSE A NEW CONFLICT.

President Pulliam Precipitates a Crisis by Authorizing the New York Club to Play Davis on a Technicality.

By Francis C. Richter.

The base ball politicians are again occupying the centre of the stage. Scarcely has the consolidation scare died out when another and more serious incident arises to disturb and disgust the base ball world. In giving the New York Club permission to employ George Davis, the player awarded to Chicago by the Peace treaty, on claim of a technical violation of that treaty by two American League Clubs, President Pulliam has caused a renewal of strained relations between the two major leagues and paved the way for a resumption of ruinous hostilities. Acting upon President Pulliam's advice the New York Club has committed the overt act, and it now remains for the National League to endorse or disapprove President Pulliam's course. Either decision will inevitably entail renewed discord within the recently tolerably harmonious organisation. Where there was but one dissatisfied club, there will henceforth be several disgruntled and distrustful clubs. Should the National League approve the seizure of Davis by New York it will remain for the good sense or patriotism of the American League to avert a war over one player of no great value, and decline to play into the hands of one club which would obviously have more to gain, in the way of strengthening itself, by war than by peace. So far as the American League is concerned the game would not be worth the candle.

International Bridge, Black Rock, Buffalo, N. Y., Where Edward Delehanty Lost His Life.

Buffalo, N. Y., November 2. Editor "Sporting Life:"—I take great pleasure in sending you a photograph of the place where the famous Edward Delehanty lost his life. It may be of interest to your readers.　　　Yours truly, GORDON COBURN. (Aged 15.)

GEORGE DAVIS' CASE.

THE MAJOR LEAGUE STAND NOT TO BE CHANGED.

Law or No Law the Recalcitrant Shortstop Will Not Be Permitted to Play Anywhere But on Charles Comiskey's Chicago American League Team.

"DEL." IN THE FOLD.

THE FAMOUS OUTFIELDER TO PLAY WITH WASHINGTON.

Special to Sporting Life.

Washington, D. C., April 13.—Edward J. Delahanty, the premier batsman of the American League last year, who is said to be responsible for the two big associations getting together along peace lines on account of his jumping a Washington contract, has made his peace with the local magnates, and will again play ball with the Senators this season. "Del" has been in Washington for the past two weeks and has grown very anxious over his future in the base ball world. Manager Loftus ignored his appeals for something definite until this afternoon, when the two got together and after an hour's conference all the details were patched up. Delahanty has agreed to return all advance money to the New York National League Club and will abide by his contract with the Washington Club. Manager Loftus and the big fellow were very happy over the peaceful solution of the trouble and the Washington patrons of the game will welcome "The Only Del" with open arms as his splendid stick work last season won many games for the Senators.

Ed Delehanty

DELEHANTY DEAD.

THE FAMOUS PLAYER FINDS HIS END IN NIAGARA RIVER.

Put Off a Train at Fort Erie For Violent Conduct, the Only "Del." Walks Through the Open Draw of a Bridge and is Swept Over Niagara Falls.

Delehanty, the mighty batsman and famed player, is no more. He was drowned July 2 in the Niagara River, into which he either fell or was thrown from the International bridge, at Fort Erie, Ont. He was put off a Michigan Central train that night for drunkenness, and was not turned over by Conductor Cole to a constable, as the Canadian authorities say should have been done. After the train had disappeared across the bridge Delehanty started to walk, which is against the rules. He met a night watchman, who attempted to stop him. The sturdy ball player pushed the man to one side and went on. The draw was open and Delehanty plunged into the river.

AN OFFICIAL STATEMENT.

Manager Loftus has received a letter from John K. Binnett, district superintendent, of Washington, which throws some light on the last hours of the famous base ball player. The letter in part follows:

"A passenger in one of our cars July 2 had some altercation with the Michigan Central train conductor and was ejected at Fort Erie, Ont. Later according to reports, a bridge tender found a man standing on the international bridge who had succeeded in evading the guard. On putting his lantern to the passenger's face the passenger was angered, and, I understand, they had some words, and the bridge tender states that when his attention was called in another direction he heard a splash and the man was gone. It is supposed the man jumped into the river, or fell in, and that he was the man ejected from the train. A dress suit case and black leather bag were found on our train afterward and are supposed to belong to this gentleman; and I find in the suit case a complimentary pass. No. 26, of your club.

In going over his record Secretary Walter Hewitt of the Washington Club found that Delehanty had a complimentary pass numbered 26.

INCIDENTS OF THE TRAGEDY.

Frank Delehanty, of the Syracuse team, and E. J. McGuire, a brother-in-law from Cleveland, went at once to Fort Erie to investigate the matter. They found that "Del" had been on a spree in Detroit before starting for the East. Conductor Cole made affidavit that in the sleeper on the Michigan Central train on the way down from Detroit Delehanty had five drinks of whisky, says Conductor Cole, and he became so obstreperous that he had to be put off the train at Bridgeburg, at the Canadian end of the bridge. Cole says Delehanty had an open razor and was terrifying others in the sleeper. Kingston, the night watchman of the bridge, also averred that Delehanty pushed him aside and walked through the open draw into the dark waters of the Niagara River.

THE BODY FOUND.

On July 9 the body of Delehanty was found in the Niagara River below the Falls, and was at once identified by M. A. Green, a stockholder in the Washington Club, who identified the body by the teeth, two crippled fingers and the clothing. Mr. Green had previously identified the luggage left by Delehanty on the train at the bridge, night of July 2, when he was put off. In it was a pass to the Washington grounds made out to Mrs. Delehanty. The effects were shipped to Mrs. Delehanty at Washington by the Pullman Company. The body was also shipped to Cleveland. It was much mangled, one leg and one arm being broken, presumably by the propeller of the "Maid of the Mist," near whose landing the body was found. Most of the clothing had been washed off the body, together with about $1500 in diamonds and $200 in money the deceased is known to have carried with him. The clothes had probably been torn off in the passage of the rapids and in going over the Horseshoe Falls. The body was much bloated.

Sept. 14

In the second game Ames, McGraw's new pitcher, made his debut. His beginning was very propitious, St. Louis not having a hit off him when the game was called at the end of the fifth inning on account of darkness. The score:

ST. LOUIS.	A.B.	R.	B.	P.	A.	E.	NEW YORK.	A.B.	R.	B.	P.	A.	E.
Dunle'y, rf	2	0	0	0	0	0	Browne, rf	3	1	1	0	0	0
Smoot, cf	1	0	0	3	0	0	Bresna'n, cf	3	1	1	0	0	0
Brain, ss	2	0	0	2	0	0	McGann, 1b	3	0	0	4	0	0
Burke, 3b	2	0	0	2	0	0	Mertes, lf	2	1	0	0	0	0
Barclay, lf	2	0	1	0	0	0	Babb, ss	1	1	0	3	2	0
Ryan, c	2	0	0	3	0	0	Lauder, 3b	2	0	1	0	0	0
Fremont, 2b	1	0	0	3	0	3	Gilbert, 2b	3	0	0	1	2	0
Murphy, 1b	0	0	0	0	0	1	Warner, c	3	1	1	7	0	0
Hackett, 1b	0	0	0	3	0	1	Ames, p	2	0	0	0	0	0
O'Neill, p	1	0	0	3	0	0	Total	22	5	4	15	4	0
Total	14	0	0	15	7	5							

St. Louis .... 0 0 0 0 0—0

New York .... 3 1 0 0 1—5

LUCKY THEY'RE ALIVE

STAR AMERICAN BALL PLAYERS IN A TRAIN WRECK.

The Cleveland and St. Louis Players Are Tossed in an Overturned Sleeper and Several Received Minor Injuries —How the Accident Happened.

The Cleveland and St. Louis American League teams had a very narrow escape from serious injury or death in a wreck on the night of August 29 on the Wabash Railroad near Napoleon, Ohio, while en route to St. Louis. At the crossing of the Wabash and Detroit Southern tracks the train was derailed. The engineer, Baker, evidently became confused and thought he saw a white light, indicating that he had the right of way, and pulled his train into the derail, running at the rate of about 40 miles

Napoleon Lajoie

an hour. As soon as he felt the forward trucks of the engine strike the ties he slapped on the emergency brake and by so doing probably saved the life of more than one ball player. He succeeded in reducing the headway of the train so that when the cars went into the ditch the sides were not crushed in. The Cleveland sleeper turned completely over on one side, and the boys on the upper side were thrown over on top of those who occupied berths on the opposite side of the car. The injured were: William Sudhoff, pitcher, of St. Louis, right wrist cut and sprained; Sidney Mercer, secretary of St. Louis team, rib fractured; Emmett Heidrick, centre fielder, St. Louis, face cut and leg bruised; Napoleon Lajoie, face cut and knee sprained. As soon as possible the train was made up at Peru, Ind., and hurried on to St. Louis to enable the two teams to play their scheduled game there last Saturday, which they succeeded in doing.

SOMERS' SHOCK.

Vice President Somers, of the Cleveland Club, was in the rear car next to Manager McAleer, of the St. Louis Club, at the time of the accident, and escaped with nothing worse than a good shaking up, as that car did not turn completely over as did the Cleveland sleeper. It was an anxious moment for Mr. Somers, however, when he reached the ground and stepped forward to see what had happened. There lay the car containing the Cleveland players on its side, with the lights all out, enveloped in steam from the engine, and not a sign of life anywhere. Most of the Napoleons were asleep at the time the car turned over and it took every one about five minutes to realize, in the darkness that pervaded the car, just where they were and what had happened. When they grasped the situation every one was cool, and then began asking one another if they were all right until every man was accounted for before any attempt was made to communicate with the outside world.

PITCHING RECORDS.

By Harry R. Beringer.

Following are the unofficial records of the National League pitchers for the season of 1903:

	W.	L.	Pct.		W.	L.	Pct.
Ames	2	0	1000	Sparks	11	15	.423
Leever	25	7	.781	Duggleby	13	18	.419
Thatcher	3	1	.750	Fraser	12	17	.413
Winham	3	1	.750	Brown	9	14	.391
Phillippi	25	9	.735	Willis	12	19	.387
Mathewson	30	13	.697	McFarland	10	16	.385
Wicker	20	9	.689	Rhoades	5	8	.385
Weimer	20	9	.689	Poole	8	13	.380
Kennedy	10	5	.666	Platt	9	15	.375
Thompson	2	1	.666	Carney	3	5	.315
Schmidt	22	12	.647	Murphy	4	8	.333
Hahn	22	12	.647	Miller	2	5	.285
Doheny	16	9	.640	Evans	3	8	.273
McGinnity	31	19	.620	Currie	5	15	.250
Taylor, Ch.	21	14	.600	O'Neill	4	13	.235
Cronin	6	4	.600	Hackett	1	4	.200
Jones	22	15	.595	Falkenburg	1	4	.200
Sutthoff	16	11	.592	Sanders	1	5	.166
Wilhelm	5	4	.555	McFetridge	1	11	.083
Phillips	7	6	.538	Doescher	0	1	.000
Ewing	14	13	.518	Graham	0	1	.000
Harper	7	7	.500	Scanlon	0	1	.000
Reidy	6	6	.500	Lovett	0	1	.000
Veil	4	4	.500	Wiggs	0	1	.000
Hardy	1	1	.500	Butts	0	1	.000
Lundgren	10	11	.476	Hines	0	1	.000
Menefee	8	9	.470	Moran	0	1	.000
Taylor, N.Y.	12	14	.461	Moren	0	1	.000
Williams	8	7	.461	Vickery	0	1	.000
Dunleavy	6	7	.461	Ragan	0	1	.000
Garvin	16	20	.459	McLaughlin	0	2	.000
Pittinger	18	22	.450	Thielman	0	3	.000
Mitchell	11	14	.440	Burchell	0	3	.000
Malarkey	11	15	.423	Washburn	0	4	.000

NEW YORK VS. PHILADELPHIA AT NEW YORK AUG. 31.—(P. M. AND P. M.)—McGinnity pitched both games and for the third time this season scored a double victory. In the first contest neither side made a misplay, and this was remarkable, considering the wretched condition of the field from the recent heavy rains.

A SHOCKING CALAMITY.

Many Killed and Hundreds Injured by the Sudden Collapse of a Part of a Bleacher at Philadelphia Ball Park—The Club Officials Entirely Blameless in the Matter.

On Saturday afternoon, precisely at 5.15 o'clock, there occurred at the famous and beautiful Philadelphia Ball Park the most

James Potter

shocking disaster in the history of the national game. The double-header between the Phillies and Bostons drew more than 10,000 people to the park, a great number of whom were seated on the left field bleachers, on the Fifteenth street side of the park. During the first half of the fourth inning of the second game, just as the fourth Boston batsman, Stanley, stepped to the plate, the most frightful accident on record in base ball occurred in a moment and without warning. An altercation in the street between two drunken men and some children, who were following and jeering them, caused others to leave their seats and join those near the rail. The gallery, or passageway, projects three feet beyond the brick wall and overhangs the sidewalk twenty feet below. Its main support was a series of 3-by-8-inch hemlock timbers nailed on the top of the sloping timbers of the bleacher seats and resting across the top of the brick wall.

DOWN TO RUIN AND DEATH.

One of the drunken men turned and struck a little girl in the group of children who were annoying him. This caused an outcry from the spectators in the gallery, and others rose from their seats and ran to the rail. Despite the efforts of Officer Muschert, of the Thirty-first District Police, to keep back the spectators they kept piling up on the footway, until at least 500 men and boys were crushing against the rail. The strain was too great for the rotten timbers. There was a sound of rending, splintering wood, a great cry of horror and alarm from the men and boys crowded along the rail, and they plunged headlong to the stone pavement below. The gallery for about 150 feet of its length had given way and the crowd of 500 people standing upon it had gone with it. They were piled up on the street in a mass of struggling, writhing, groaning humanity, with the broken planks and beams of the gallery pressing upon those underneath and adding to their misery.

AN AWFUL SCENE.

The scene on the street was horrible and simply indescribable, resembling nothing so much as a battle at close quarters or a massacre. Legs and arms were broken, skulls were fractured and many of the unfortunates were rendered unconscious. From the middle of the square almost to Lehigh avenue the ground was covered with writhing sufferers. Blood ran everywhere in streams. The great cry of the victims as they plunged from the wall and the heart-rending groans which followed gave the alarm to the people in the near-by stores and houses and they responded nobly. So did the people from inside the grounds. In a moment willing hands were at work dragging the victims from under the wreckage and turning them over to others to look after their injuries.

DOHENY DEMENTED.

The Pittsburg Pitcher Becomes Violent and is Restrained.

Special to "Sporting Life."

Andover, Mass., Oct. 14.—Edward Doheny, the famous Pittsburg pitcher, has been committed to an insane asylum. On

Ed R. Doheny

Sunday last Doheny assaulted his nurse, Oberlin Howarth, at his home, with a poker, and for more than an hour held a score of neighbors and several policemen at bay. Finally he was overpowered, and after an examination by two physicians was adjudged insane and committed to the asylum at Danvers. The nurse, Oberlin Howarth, is seriously hurt, but it is believed he will recover. Doheny first showed signs of insanity several weeks ago, when he suddenly deserted the Pittsburg Club. After a few weeks' rest at his home here, he rejoined the team, but did not regain his old form. When he returned home at the end of the season Doheny was a nervous wreck, and since that time has been constantly under the care of a physician. When the latter called Sunday Doheny ejected him from the house and warned him not to return. Later, while the nurse's attention was attracted in another direction, Doheny attacked and felled him with a poker and started to smash things right and left. His wife hurried to the neighbors for assistance, but Doheny defied them and threatened to kill the first man who attempted to take him. For more than an hour the madman held the crowd at bay, but finally Chief of Police Frye and Officer Mills caught him off his guard and overpowered him.

FAKING IMPOSSIBLE.

A LEAGUE PLAYER'S TESTIMONY TO THAT EFFECT.

Famous Joe Tinker, of the Chicago Cubs, in Explaining the Chicago Post-Season Series, Shows the Impossibility of "Fixing" or "Throwing" Ball Games.

Kansas City, Mo., November 17.—Editor "Sporting Life:"—Joe Tinker and Kling, of the Chicago League team, are at home here

Joseph Tinker

for the winter. In discussing the unsatisfactory series between the two Chicago teams Tinker made the assertion that it is absolutely impossible to "fix" a ball game. Said he: "Soreheads howl fake as a rule after post-season games, but if they would only stop to think they could see that it is out of the question. To fake in a base ball game everyone on both teams must be in on the deal. This makes it impossible to 'fix' matters. Some often say that the pitchers are bought. Now what does that amount to? Every team has at least four pitchers, and if one was really bought how long would he be allowed to stay in the box if the opposing team was bumping him? Three hits in succession generally mean the temporary retirement of a pitcher, so it can be seen that a slab artist cannot do much in the way of throwing games.

It is hereby agreed by and between Pittsburg Club of the National League and the Boston American League Club of the American League as follows:-

1,- That a post season series shall be played between said base ball clubs consisting of a series of 9 games, if it be necessary to play that number before either club should win 5 games, said series however to terminate when either club shall win 5 games.

2,- Said games to be played at the following times and places: At Boston, Mass., Oct. 1, 2, & 3 (Thursday, Friday and Saturday) At Pittsburg, Pa., " 5, 6, 7 & 8 (Monday, Thuesday, Wednesday and Thursday) At Boston, Mass., " 10 and 12 (Saturday and Monday); providing however, in the event of the weather being such as to prevent a game being played on either of said days, such game shall be postponed until the next succeeding day when the weather will permit such game to be played at the city where scheduled. And in that event there shall be a moving back of the aforesaid schedule for the day or days lost on account of said inclement weather.

3,- Each club shall bear the expense of the games played on their respective grounds, excepting the expense of umpire.

4,- Each club shall furnish and pay the expenses of one umpire to officiate during said series and it is agreed that the umpire so agreed upon to be furnished shall be O'Day from the National League and Connelly from the American League.

4½ No player to participate who was not a regular member of team Sep. 1, 1903.

5,- The minimum price of admission in each city shall be 50 cts. and the visiting club shall be settled with by being paid 25 cts. for every admission ticket sold.

6,- A statement to be furnished the visiting club after each game, final settlement to be at the close of the series.

The respective captains of each team shall meet with the umpires above designated before the beginning of the series to agree upon a uniform interpretation of the playing rules.

IN WITNESS WHEREOF the parties hereto have caused these presents to be signed by their respective Presidents this 16 day of September, A. D. 1903.

In Presence Of

PITTSBURGH ATHLETIC CO.
by *Barney Dreyfuss*
President.

BOSTON AMERICAN LEAGUE BALL CLUB
by *Henry J. Killilea*
President.

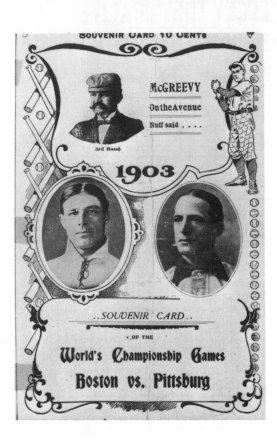

SOUVENIR CARD 10 CENTS

McGREEVY
On the Avenue
Nuff said....

3rd Base

1903

..SOUVENIR CARD..

OF THE

World's Championship Games

Boston vs. Pittsburg

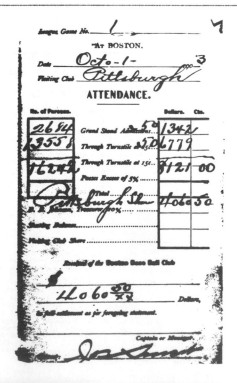

AT BOSTON.
Date Octo-1-1903
Visiting Club Pittsburgh
ATTENDANCE.

No. of Persons.		Dollars.	Cts.
2644	Grand Stand Admissions	1342	
3551	Through Turnstile at 25c.	6779	
8124	Through Turnstile at 15c.	1121	00
	Pass's Excess of 5%		
		10060 50	

11060 00/XX Dollars.

FIRST WON BY PIRATES

Boston Lost Opening World's Championship Game.

PHILLIPPE OUTPITCHED YOUNG

More Than 16,000 People Present to See Champions of Rival Leagues Battle for the Supremacy—Noisy Crowd Made Both Teams Nervous—Four Errors by Boston Helped Pittsburg to Score.

Boston, Oct. 1.—The masterly pitching of Phillippe brought about the downfall of the Boston Americans to-day in the first game of the world's championship series with Pittsburg, the National League pennant winners. The score was 7 to 3, and 16,000 people witnessed the battle. So completely were the American Leaguers under the spell of Phillippe that until the seventh inning only one Boston runner reached third, and then only on an error.

In the second inning the Pittsburg pitcher struck out the side. His control was faultless and his method perfect. Barring two errors, the Pittsburgs played ball that was clean cut and snappy, while their outfielding throughout was brilliant.

With a big and noisy crowd to excite them, both teams were nervous at the start, and the visitors going first to the bat, took advantage of an attack of stage fright on the part of Criger and Ferris. The crowd surrounded the field and hits beyond the ropes went for three bases. Leach got the first of these hits with two out in the first inning, and on hits by Wagner and Sebring, helped along by the errors of Criger and Ferris, Pittsburg piled up four runs.

They earned another run in the third on Bransfield's triple and Sebring's single. An error by Ferris gave the visitors another run in the fourth. Stahl quit on Sebring's hit in the seventh, and the ball stopped short of the crowd, Sebring coming home. Young was hit hard all the way, but Phillippe never let up until the lead looked safe.

In the seventh triples by Freeman and Parent brought in two runs, and from Wagner's error another resulted in Boston's final inning. For Pittsburg, Clarke, Beaumont, Ritchey, and Leach excelled in the field, while the batting of Clarke, Leach, and Sebring was terrific. Young passed Wagner, apparently with intention. For Boston, Collins, Parent, and La Chance fielded cleverly. Score:

PITTSBURG.	AB.	R.	1B.	PO.	A.	E.
Beaumont, cf.	5	1	0	3	0	0
Clarke, lf.	5	2	4	0	0	0
Leach, 3b.	5	1	4	0	1	1
Wagner, ss.	3	1	1	1	2	1
Bransfield, 1b.	5	2	1	7	0	0
Ritchey, 2b.	4	1	0	1	2	0
Sebring, rf.	5	1	3	1	0	0
Phelps, c.	4	0	1	10	0	0
Phillippe, p.	4	0	0	2	0	0
Totals	40	7	12	27	7	2
BOSTON.	AB.	R.	1B.	PO.	A.	E.
Dougherty, lf.	4	0	0	1	0	0
Collins, 3b.	4	0	2	3	0	0
Stahl, cf.	4	0	1	2	0	0
Freeman, rf.	4	2	2	2	0	0
Parent, ss.	4	1	2	4	4	0
La Chance, 1b.	4	0	0	4	0	0
Ferris, 2b.	3	0	1	6	1	2
Criger, c.	3	0	0	1	2	0
Young, p.	3	0	0	1	4	0
O'Brien*	1	0	0	0	0	0
Farrell†	1	0	0	0	0	0
Totals	35	3	6	27	14	4

*Batted for Criger in ninth. †Batted for Young in ninth.

Pittsburg .... 4 0 1 1 0 0 1 0 0—7
Boston .... 0 0 0 0 0 0 2 0 1—3

Earned runs—Boston, 2; Pittsburg, 3. Three-base hits—Freeman, Parent, Leach (2), Bransfield. Home run—Sebring. Stolen bases—Wagner, Bransfield, Ritchey. First base on balls—Off Young, 3. Struck out—By Young, 5; by Phillippe, 10. Passed ball—Criger. Umpires—Messrs. O'Day and Connolly. Time of game—1 hour and 35 minutes.

BOSTON vs. ATHLETIC AT BOSTON MAY 5.—Young broke all pitching records by shutting the Athletics out without a hit or run, and letting only 27 men face him, the side going out in order throughout the game. Young's pitching was wonderful. He struck out eight batsmen. Only six men went out on flies to the outfield, and only three on flies to the infield. There was not an error on the Boston side and Parent and Ferris had only seven grounders to look after. Young himself assisted on two grounders. There was not even a semblance of a hit. While the Champions batted Waddell hard, sharp fielding by the visitors kept down the runs. The score:

BOSTON.	AB.	R.	B.	P.	A.	E.		ATHLETIC.	AB.	R.	B.	P.	A.	E.
Dougherty, lf	4	0	1	1	0	0		Hartsel, lf	1	0	0	0	0	0
Collins, 3b	4	0	2	2	0	0		Hoffman, cf	3	0	0	1	0	0
Stahl, cf	4	1	1	3	0	0		Pickering, cf	3	0	0	1	0	0
Freeman, rf	4	0	1	2	0	0		Davis, 1b	3	0	0	5	0	1
Parent, ss	4	0	2	1	4	0		L. Cross, 3b	3	0	0	4	1	0
Lachance, 1b	3	0	1	9	0	0		Seybold, rf	3	0	0	2	0	0
Ferris, 2b	3	1	0	3	0	0		Murphy, 2b	3	0	0	1	2	0
Criger, c	3	1	1	9	0	0		M. Cross, ss	3	0	0	2	3	0
Young, p	3	0	0	2	0	0		Schreck, c	3	0	0	7	0	0
								Waddell, p	3	0	0	1	0	0
Total	32	3	10	27	0	0		Total	27	0	0	24	8	1

Boston .... 0 0 0 0 0 1 2 0 x—3
Athletic .... 0 0 0 0 0 0 0 0 0—0

Earned runs—Boston 2. Two-base hits—Collins, Criger. Three-base hits—Stahl, Freeman, Ferris. Sacrifice hit—Lachance. Double plays—Hoffman, Shreck, L. Cross, Davis. Struck out—By Young 8, Waddell 8. Umpire—Dwyer. Time—1.25. Attendance—10,000.

JOYLESS JONES.

THE NOTED CHICAGO OUTFIELDER IS IN WRONG.

The New York National League Club Has Relinquished All Claim to the Player Who Must Now Play With the Chicago White Sox or Remain Idle.

Chicago, April 16.—Editor "Sporting Life:"—President Johnson has given out some facts in the case of Fielder Jones, which shows the hopelessness of the Jones' case against the New York National League Club, with which team he wishes to play in preference to the White Sox. Jones has been notified by President Pulliam of the National League that New York relinquished all claims to him. He cannot collect from the Gotham Club the sum stipulated in the contract with New York, but only the difference between that sum and his salary when playing under Comiskey. The difference is very slight, and unless Jones gets onto the band wagon soon he will be a loser on the season. Since Jones has stated so emphatically that he would not play in Chicago, Detroit has approached Comiskey with an offer to trade its crack outfielder, Jimmy Barrett, for him. All offers are treated the same by Comiskey, who considers that it would be an outrage upon the base ball public of the city to let such a player get away from the White Sox.

Fielder Jones

Jennings Able to Attend His Classes.

Ithaca, N. Y., March 1.—Hugh Jennings, the base ball player and coach of the Cornell nine, who was injured by diving into the empty swimming pool at Cornell gymnasium last week, was able to attend his classes at the university to-day. Jennings, however, is still suffering from his injuries, and his right wrist will require treatment for several weeks before he will have the use of it.

NEW YORK vs. CHICAGO AT NEW YORK JUNE 11.—Another enormous crowd witnessed the game in which McGinnity sustained his first defeat of the season, after twelve victories. It was a twelve-inning game, and the visitors won out on a hit by Chance, two outs and a single by Evers. For the visitors Wicker pitched splendidly, and the locals were unable to make their only hit off him until the tenth inning. The score:

CHICAGO.	AB.	R.	B.	P.	A.	E.		NEW YORK.	AB.	R.	B.	P.	A.	E.
Slagle, lf	5	0	0	2	1	0		Bresnahan, cf	5	0	0	4	0	0
Casey, 3b	5	0	2	1	3	1		Browne, rf	5	0	0	1	0	0
Chance, 1b	5	1	3	15	3	0		Devlin, 3b	5	0	0	4	0	0
Kling, c	5	0	0	10	0	0		McGann, 1b	4	0	0	18	1	0
Jones, rf	5	0	2	2	0	0		Mertes, lf	4	0	1	4	0	0
Evers, 2b	3	0	2	3	7	0		Dahlen, ss	4	0	0	4	6	0
Tinker, ss	4	0	1	0	3	1		Gilbert, 2b	4	0	0	2	4	0
Williams, cf	4	0	1	0	0	0		Warner, c	3	0	0	3	4	0
Wicker, p	4	0	0	2	2	0		McGinnity, p	4	0	0	0	6	0
Total	40	1	10	36	19	2		Total	39	0	1	36	25	0

Chicago ...... 0 0 0 0 0 0 0 0 0 0 0 1—1
New York .... 0 0 0 0 0 0 0 0 0 0 0 0—0

Two-base hit—Evers. Sacrifice hits—Evers 2. Stolen bases—Browne, Devlin, Tinker. Double play—Gilbert, Dahlen, McGann. Left on bases—Chicago 5, New York 3. First on balls—Off Wicker 1. First on errors—New York 2. Struck out—By McGinnity 2, Wicker 10. Umpires—Emslie and O'Day. Time—2.15. Attendance—27,805.

BITTER BOSS BRUSH

STILL RETAINS EXTREME HATRED FOR RIVALS.

Authoritative Announcement There Will be No World's Championship Series if The Two New York Clubs Win Major League Championships.

SPECIAL TO SPORTING LIFE.

New York City, July 5.—The statement is made here on the highest authority that the New York Nationals will refuse to play the New York Americans for the world's championship if each wins the pennant in its respective league. President Brush, of the New York Nationals, has repeatedly asserted that under no circumstances would he allow his team to play the rival organization in this city. From one of Mr. Brush's closest friends it was learned to-day that Brush will go so far as to violate the agreement made by the both leagues at the beginning of the season to play a series of seven games for the world's championship. Mr. Brush will disregard the demands of the public for a series of championship games if both New York teams win pennants, and will be satisfied to let the Giants rest on their laurels.

John T. Brush

The Champion Batter of the National League Wants to See the Foul-Strike Rule Abolished and the Pitching Distance Increased.

The champion batsman and base runner of the National League, Hans Wagner, has declared himself an enemy of the pitcher-favoring foul-strike rule. He says he thinks it should be done away with, and also advocates moving the pitchers back and making them twirl a longer distance than at present. Wagner figures out that the batsmen are laboring under too many handicaps at present. Says he: "If I had my way I would eliminate the foul-strike rule. I do not think it would make the games much longer than they are

John Wagner

at present to do away with it. If this was done a rule could be inserted making it obligatory upon managers to hustle their teams out to the field when innings were over, and thus quicken the game. I would also say that some legislation should be made against the use of the 'spit ball,' but I do not see how this is possible. The delivery is not illegal and cannot be stopped. Under these circumstances I favor moving the pitcher back about three feet from his present position. The 'spit ball' wouldn't break so well then, and the batsman might have a little chance. If this were done, the pitcher would have a better chance to field his position, and the bunting game would then be the proper racket, for the batsman would have more of a chance to lay the ball down without being thrown out. Another plan that would help batting would be to decrease the number of balls allowable from four to three, making the number of balls and strikes equal."

NEW YORK vs. CINCINNATI AT NEW YORK SEPT. 22.—(P. M. AND P. M.)—In the first game the Giants scored the 100th victory and clinched the pennant beyond all doubt. The famous Jim O'Rourke of Bridgeport, a member of the first New York champion team in 1885, caught and showed that though past 50 he was still in the game. He was very nimble and caught McGinnity well. The score:

CINCIN'T.	AB.	R.	B.	P.	A.	E.		NEW YORK.	AB.	R.	B.	P.	A.	E.
Seymour, cf	5	1	2	3	0	0		Donlin, lf	5	1	3	1	0	0
Dolan, lf	5	0	1	7	0	1		Browne, rf	5	1	2	3	0	0
Seibring, rf	5	0	1	0	0	0		McGann, 1b	2	1	1	7	1	0
Odwell, lf	5	2	1	5	0	0		Bowerman, 1b	2	0	0	2	0	0
Steinfeldt, 3b	4	0	2	1	2	0		Mertes, cf	4	0	2	3	0	0
Hughes, 2b	4	1	2	2	3	0		Devlin, 3b	4	1	0	3	3	1
Pelz, ss	4	0	0	1	0	0		Gilbert, 2b	4	1	1	2	4	1
Schlei, c	3	0	0	2	0	0		O'Rourke, c	4	1	1	5	1	0
Corcoran, ss	4	1	1	0	1	0		McGinnity, p	4	0	0	1	0	0
Kellum, p	4	0	0	2	0	0								
Total	38	5	24					Total	37	7	11	27	14	4

Cincinnati .... 0 1 0 0 0 1 2 0—5
New York .... 0 3 0 4 0 0 0 x—7

Two-base hit—Dolan. Three-base hits—Donlin. Home runs—Seymour, Corcoran. Sacrifice hit—Steinfeldt. Stolen bases—McGann 2. Left on bases—New York 6, Cincinnati 5. First on balls—Off McGinnity 1, Kellum 2. First on errors—New York 2, Cincinnati 2. Hit by pitcher—By Kellum 1. Struck out—By McGinnity 2, Kellum 4. Umpires—Emslie and Carpenter. Time—1.40.

PLAYER HEROES.

BOSTON AMERICAN MEN PREVENT HOTEL FIRE.

Hotel Employees in Panic, But Dineen, Gibson, Parent and Ferris, Unaided, Succeed in Quenching the Flames, Preventing a Disaster.

BY JAY KNOX.

Cleveland, O., Aug. 8.—Editor "Sporting Life:" Four of the Boston champions are entitled to Carnegie medals for bravery. The four are Bill Dineen, pitcher; Norwood Gibson, shortstop Parent and second baseman "Hobe" Ferris. The team had just returned to the Hotel Euclid last Tuesday evening from League Park, where they had defeated the locals, and were feeling quite elated. The last to go to their rooms were the quartet in question. Their rooms are on the sixth floor, but when an elevator arrived at the fifth floor the players smelled smoke. They had the car stopped, and, stepping into the corridor, saw flames bursting from a room near by, while several of the hotel employes were running about, panic-stricken. The players took in the situation at a glance, and, grabbing several fire extinguishers and putting the fire hose into operation, soon extinguished the flames, which already had spread to an adjoining room. It was not necessary to call the fire department, and the loss was trifling, although it might have been heavy had it not been for the prompt action of the ball-tossers. Painters had been at work in the room, and the fact that several cans of paint were still about was the cause of the flames spreading with such rapidity. What caused the fire is unknown.

Wm. Dineen

1903 1904

WHEN THE PINCH IS UP TO BILL,
IS WILLIAM WITH US STILL ?
BETCHERLIFE

P. DOUGHERTY
9TH INNING STRIKE OUT

CHAMPIONSHIP IS LANDED BY BOSTON AGAIN

Collins Boys Keep Title by Beating New York in First Game.

DINEEN ALSO BIG FACTOR

Dougherty Could Have Saved Day, but Bill Struck "Pat" Out.

Williams' Damaging Error Enables Boston to Tie New York Score.

THE SCORES OF THE TWO GAMES.

First Game

Innings	1	2	3	4	5	6	7	8	9	
Boston	0	0	0	0	0	0	2	0	1	—3
New York ..	0	0	0	0	2	0	0	0	0	—2

Second Game

Innings	1	2	3	4	5	6	7	8	9	
Boston	0	0	0	0	0	0	0	0	0	—0
New York ..	0	0	0	0	0	0	0	0	1	—1

STANDING OF THE TWO TEAMS.

	Won	Lost	P.C. won
Boston	95	59	.617
New York	92	59	.609

[Special dispatch to The Boston Herald]
NEW YORK. Oct. 10, 1904. A wild pitch by Chesbro in the ninth inning of the first game today enabled Boston to renew its title to the championship of the American league. Up to that time the score stood 2 to 2, and the locals certainly had as good a chance as the champions for the pennant. The close of the game was exceedingly exciting, for New York had two men on bases, two hands out and "Pat" Dougherty at the bat.

One can imagine how anxious "Pat" was to land a hit. It meant a tie, perhaps the game and the championship. Two strikes were on him, then three balls, but he failed to turn the trick and went out on strikes, while the Boston rooters fairly hugged each other in the exuberance of their joy. Louie Criger tossed his cap in the air as he ran off with the ball.

SHOULDERS THE BLAME.

Manager McGraw Says That He and Not Mr. Brush or the Players is Responsible For Non-Playing of Series.

Special to "Sporting Life."

New York, Oct. 10.—In a statement issued by John J. McGraw, manager of the National League Base Ball Club, he says that he, and not John T. Brush, president of the club, is the one responsible for not playing a post-season series of games with the New York American League teams. He further says that he is supported in his stand by every man on the champion team. He says his team is not afraid to play any team in the world, which is true, for there was not a man on his team that was not anxious for this series of games.

John J. McGraw

John T. Brush Makes Official Statement to That Effect.

HIS REASONS FOR DECLINING THE GAGE OF BATTLE.

Sees No Necessity For a Post-Season Series, Holds the National League Pennant to be Supreme Glory and, by Implication, Classes the American League as a Minor League.

NOT IN THE SPRING

Will a World's Championship Series be Played.

THE WRONG TIME IS THE BOSTON OPINION.

The Brush Plan, However, Prepares the Way For Making the Series a Compulsory Annual Event Under Fixed Rules and Regulations.

FOR CONTROL OF THE WORLD'S CHAMPIONSHIP GAMES

Has Been Elaborated in Detail by Mr. Brush and Submitted For National Commission Adoption Through the Chairman, Mr. Herrmann.

SPECIAL TO SPORTING LIFE.

New York, Jan. 11.—President Brush, of the New York National League Club, has forwarded to President Herrmann, chairman of the National Com-

John T. Brush

mission, a series of conditions which he thinks should govern all world's championship games of the future. In the suggestions the double umpire system is provided for, one judge of play to be selected from the American League by the president of the National League and one handler of the indicator from the National League is to be selected from the old league by the president of the American League. A silver cup, suitably inscribed, is to be the trophy to be played for, and it is to be insured and will remain in the custody of the winning club only so long as it is the champion aggregation. President Brush suggests a division of receipts in line with the plan outlined in his recent letter to President Pulliam, of the National League. The contesting clubs are not to sacrifice any of their constitutional rights, and the same safeguards are to be thrown around the games as prevail during the championship series. If the plan of Mr. Brush is followed skeptical ones will have no chance to cry hippodrome. The National Commission is to have full charge of the series.

CANADA "JUSTICE"

KICKS THE BEAM WHEN WEIGHED AGAINST A RAILROAD.

The Canadian Court of Appeals Deprives the Widow and Child of the Late Edward Delehanty of the Damages Awarded by a Lower Court.

SPECIAL TO "SPORTING LIFE."

Buffalo, N. Y., July 10.—According to authentic reports which reached here from Toronto, the Canadian Court of Appeals has deprived the widow and daughter of Ed. Delehanty, the late base ball player, of damages they recently won in the lower Canadian court as a result of the death of the famous outfielder. Delehanty bought a ticket from Detroit to Buffalo just two years ago and boarded a Michigan Central train for this city. While near Bridgeport, in Canada, across the Niagara River

Ed Delehanty

from Buffalo, he became disorderly while intoxicated, it is alleged, and was ejected from the car. He got on the international bridge and was drowned in the Niagara River. Mrs. Delehanty and her daughter brought action against the Michigan Central, charging negligence, and the case was tried at Welland, Canada, some time ago. The jury brought in a verdict of $3000 for the widow and $2000 for the daughter. The Michigan Central then took the case to a higher court.

"MATTY," AUTHOR!

THE GREAT PITCHER THIRSTS FOR LITERARY FAME.

Discarding the Biblical Warning, He Will Write a Book—His Story, Soon to be Printed, to Deal With Life in College and on Diamond.

SPECIAL TO SPORTING LIFE.

New York, March 1.—Christy Mathewson, one of the twirlers of the champion Giants, hopes to make his mark in the literary world. It is a well-known

C. Matthewson

fact that the Bucknell College man wields a facile pen, and, according to Frank Bowerman, his battery partner, the great twirler contemplates writing a story under the title "A Modern Prince." In a letter to a friend in New York, Bowerman says that Christy has been collecting material for his story for some time, and a well-known Gotham firm of publishers has agreed to print the book. The story has to do with college and diamond life, with an interesting love story interwoven. For some time "Matty" has been contributing a number of interesting short stories to magazines and other publications. Other baseball men, like Anson, Ward and Sullivan, have written books, but the pitching idol of New York fans contemplates writing a story of a more pretentious nature than any that have been published from the pens of diamond warriors, and one that will be read after the fireside, in college dormitories and elsewhere. Mathewson is a voracious reader, and, aside from an occasional spin over the roads near Lewisburg, Pa., in the open air, has put in most of the past winter in his "den" at home. The news that "Matty" contemplates writing a book makes interesting news, and fans will await the product of his pen with much curiosity.

July 4

The afternoon game went twenty innings—a record for the American League, and major league record for that number of innings with result. After the tenth inning each side made just four hits. Many brilliant plays were made by the Boston infield and the Athletic outfield. Boston scored its runs in the first on Selbach's single, Parent's sacrifice and doubles by Burkett and Stahl. The Athletics tied on Lord's single and Davis' homer, and won in the twentieth, when Murphy was safe on Collins' fumble. Knight was hit by a pitched ball and Ferris fumbled Schreck's sacrifice, filling the bases. Waddell forced Monte Cross, who ran for Knight, Murphy scoring. A hit by Hoffman scored Schreck. Score:

BOSTON.	AB.	R.	B.	P.	A.	E.	ATHLETIC.	AB.	R.	B.	P.	A.	E.
Selbach, rf.	7	1	1	3	0	0	Lord, lf.	9	0	1	5	0	1
Parent, ss.	6	0	2	3	10	1	Hoffman, cf	9	1	1	6	0	0
Burkett, lf.	9	1	3	2	0	1	Davis, 1b.	9	1	3	21	1	0
Stahl, cf.	9	0	2	2	0	0	L. Cross, 3b	8	0	2	4	6	0
Unglaub,1b	9	0	2	31	1	0	Seybold, rf.	8	0	1	5	1	0
Collins, 3b.	8	0	2	3	4	2	Murphy, 2b	8	1	0	4	5	1
Ferris, 2b.	9	0	0	4	12	1	Knight, ss.	7	0	2	3	4	1
Criger, c.	8	0	3	12	2	0	Schreck, c.	8	1	3	11	1	0
Young, p.	9	0	0	4	0	0	Waddell, p.	8	0	0	0	5	1
Total.	73	2	15	60	33	5	M.Cross, ss	0	0	0	1	0	0
							Total.	74	4	13	60	23	4

Boston—

2 0 0 0 0 0 0 0 0 0 0 0 0 0 0 0 0 0 0 0—2

Athletic—

0 0 0 0 0 2 0 0 0 0 0 0 0 0 0 0 0 0 0 2—4

Two-base hits—Burkett, Stahl, L. Cross, Schreck 2, Unglaub. Three-base hit—Parent. Home run—Davis. Double plays—Davis, Knight; Parent, Ferris, Unglaub; Seybold, Knight; Collins, Unglaub, Criger. First on balls—Off Waddell 4. Hit by pitcher—By Young 1. Sacrifice hits—Parent 2. Stolen base—Parent. Struck out—By Young 9, Waddell 11. Passed ball—Schreck. Umpires—McCarthy and Kelley. Time —3.31. Attendance—12,000.

OFFICIALLY AWARDED TO THE NEW YORK AMERICANS.

The Young California Player Joins the Highlanders in the South, Receives His First Trial and is Pronounced the "Find of the Season."

SPECIAL TO "SPORTING LIFE."

New York City, April 4.—The much-sought Hal Chase is not only with the New York American team but is now

Clarke Griffith

legally the property of the New York Club, as the National Commission on March 29 rendered a decision that Chase, Newton, Frisk and Blankenship were properly drafted. The Commission held that the Pacific Coast League's claim to these players was due to a misunderstanding of the special extension of drafting time allotted that league at the peace settlement. Accordingly the Commission recommends that all parties to the National Agreement meet and amend the drafting section so as to embody the views of the Pacific Coast League. Chase joined the Highlanders at Jackson, Miss., on March 28 and at once created a favorable impression by his appearance and demeanor. He is a tall, handsome-looking chap, with light hair and complexion, and has the appearance of an athlete. He looks capable of upholding the big reputation he made on the Pacific coast. He bears himself confidently and like the well-bred college boy he is. Chase is about six feet tall and weighs 175 pounds. On the 29th he played his first game at the Highlanders' first base and at once made good. He was in every play, caught well, knew what to do with the ball always, was fast on his feet, and showed up strong in left-handed throwing, a la Tenney. At the bat and on bases he also handled himself well. He made a hit with everybody and the veteran Sam Crane wired his paper that Chase would prove the biggest "find" of the season. Manager Griffith thinks he has a jewel of a youngster, who, in addition to his other virtues, is a worker.

CHICAGO VS. NEW YORK AT CHICAGO JUNE 13.—The triumph of Mathewson's career came in this game, when he changed the tide of defeat which seemed to have set in against New York and shut Chicago out without the vestige of a base hit. Moreover, he did not give a base on balls and hit nobody. Only twenty-eight men batted for Chicago, two reaching first on infield fumbles, one of these being subsequently captured. Brown's pitching was also gilt-edged until the ninth, when he was hit for four consecutive singles. Score:

CHICAGO.	AB.	R.	B.	P.	A.	E.	NEW YORK.	AB.	R.	B.	P.	A.	E.
Slagle, cf.	4	0	0	3	0	0	Donlin, cf.	4	0	1	3	0	0
Schulte, lf.	3	0	0	1	0	0	Browne, rf.	4	0	1	1	1	0
Maloney, rf	3	0	0	5	0	0	McGann, 1b	4	1	1	14	0	0
Chance, 1b.	3	0	0	8	0	0	Mertes, lf.	4	0	1	3	0	0
Tinker, ss.	3	0	3	4	1	0	Dahlen, ss.	4	0	1	2	3	1
Evers, 2b.	3	0	2	2	0	0	Devlin, 3b.	1	0	0	1	0	0
Casey, 3b.	3	0	1	2	0	0	Gilbert, 2b.	3	0	1	5	1	
Kling, c.	3	0	0	4	2	1	Bowerm'n,c	3	0	0	3	0	0
Brown, p.	3	0	0	0	0	0	Mathew'n,p	3	0	0	4	0	
Total.	28	0	0	27	10	2	Total.	30	1	5	27	14	2

Chicago........ 0 0 0 0 0 0 0 0 0—0

New York........ 0 0 0 0 0 0 0 0 1—1

Left on bases—Chicago 1, New York 4. Stolen bases—Schulte, Dahlen. Double play—Brown, McGann. Struck out—By Brown 3, Mathewson 2. First on balls—Off Brown 2. Balk—Brown. Umpires—Bausewine and Emslie. Time—1.25. Attendance—9000.

Aug. 31

Cobb Makes Good on First Appearance

OUTFIELDER COBB.

The latest Tiger recruit played his first game with Detroit yesterday. He slammed out a two-bagger and fielded his position well.

Sept. 6

The second game put Smith in the no-hit class, as not a local player even came near landing on him safely. Wiggs had started to pitch for Detroit, but was no wild that, with the errors behind him, Chicago scored eight in the first inning. Disch, who relieved Wiggs, was hit hard and often. Score:

DETROIT.	AB.	R.	B.	P.	A.	E.		CHICAGO.	AB.	R.	B.	P.	A.	E.
McIntyre,lf	3	0	0	3	0	1		Green, rf	4	3	1	2	0	0
Lindsay,1b	4	0	0	10	2	1		Isbell, cf	5	2	2	4	0	0
Schaefer,2b	2	0	0	1	1	0		Davis, ss	5	0	0	1	0	0
Lowe, 2b	2	0	0	2	1	0		Callahan,lf	5	1	2	1	0	0
Crawfo'd, lf	2	0	0	1	0	0		Donohue,1b	4	1	1	9	1	0
Cobb, cf	2	0	0	0	0	0		McFarl'd, c	5	2	2	11	0	0
Cough'n,3b	3	0	0	1	4	0		Rohe, 3b	5	1	1	1	3	0
O'Leary, ss	3	0	0	4	4	2		Tannehill,2b	4	2	1	2	1	0
Warner, c.	0	0	0	2	0	0		Smith, p	4	3	2	1	0	0
Doran, c.	3	0	0	2	0	0		**Total**	41	15	12	27		
Wiggs, p.	0	0	0	0	1	0								
Disch, p.	3	0	0	1	2	0								
Total	27	0	0	27	14	5								

Detroit .... 0 0 0 0 0 0 0 0 0— 0
Chicago .... 8 1 0 1 0 5 0 0 x—15

Hits—Off Wiggs 1 in one inning. Disch 11 in eight innings. Two-base hits—McFarland, Smith, Green. Three-base hit—Callahan. Sacrifice hit—Davis. Stolen base—Isbell. First on balls—Off Wiggs 5, Disch 1, Smith 3. Hit by pitcher—By Disch 1. Left on bases—Detroit 3, Chicago 7. Struck out—By Wiggs 2, Disch 2, Smith 8. Earned runs—Chicago 5. Umpires—O'Loughlin and McCarthy. Time—1.43. Attendance—3500.

BALTIMORE HOPES

OF RE-ENTERING MAJOR LEAGUE COMPANY REVIVED.

Report That the Maryland City Will Take the Place of Brooklyn in the National League—Ban Johnson Quoted as Being of That Opinion.

BOSTON VS CHICAGO AT BOSTON SEPT. 26.—(P. M. AND P. M.)—The former "world's champions" continued their miserable work against Chicago. With a lead of four runs in the first game they lost out on poor pitching and wretched fielding. Walsh pitched both games after shelving White with none out in the first inning of the first contest. Because Walsh had not warmed up the home players scored five runs in this inning, but at no time thereafter were they dangerous. Score:

CHICAGO.	AB.	R.	B.	P.	A.	E.		BOSTON.	AB.	R.	B.	P.	A.	E.
Jones, cf	5	3	4	2	0	0		Parent, ss	5	1	2	1	3	0
Isbell, 2b	5	3	4	1	2	0		Stahl, cf	5	1	2	2	0	1
Davis, ss	5	3	2	2	4	1		Ungla'b, 3b	4	1	1	3	1	1
Callahan, lf	2	0	0	2	1	1		Burke,tt lf	5	0	0	1	0	1
Donohue,1b	4	0	2	14	1	0		Freeman,1b	4	1	1	8	0	2
Green, rf	5	0	1	0	0	0		Selbach, rf	1	1	0	5	1	1
Rohe, 3b	5	0	0	0	2	0		Ferris, 2b	4	0	2	4	3	0
Sullivan, c.	4	0	2	5	2	0		Armbru'r, c	4	0	1	2	3	0
White, p	0	0	0	0	0	0		Winters, p.	4	0	0	0	4	0
Walsh, p	4	1	1	0	4	0		**Total**	36	5	9	27	13	6
Total	39	10	16	27	16	2								

Chicago .... 1 0 3 0 4 0 0 0 2—10
Boston .... 5 0 0 0 0 0 0 0 0— 5

Two-base hit—Donohue. Three-base hit—Davis. Home run—Isbell. Sacrifice hits—Callahan 2. Stolen bases—Callahan 2. Double plays—Parent, Ferris, Freeman; Selbach, Winter, Freeman. Hits—Off White 1, Walsh 8 in nine innings. First on balls—Off Walsh 4, Winter 3. Struck out—By Walsh 5, Winter 2. Time—1.52. Umpire—Connor.

Chicago also won the second game, thus capturing five successive double-headers from the champion team of the American League. Darkness ended the game after the seventh inning just as Chicago had secured the winning runs. Score:

CHICAGO.	AB.	R.	B.	P.	A.	E.		BOSTON.	AB.	R.	B.	P.	A.	E.
Jones, cf	3	0	0	0	0	0		Parent, ss	3	0	1	1	2	0
Isbell, 2b	4	0	1	2	4	0		Stahl, cf	2	0	0	0	0	0
Davis, ss	3	3	1	4	3	0		Unglaub,3b	4	0	0	1	1	0
Callahan, lf	2	1	1	3	0	0		Burkett, lf	4	0	0	1	0	0
Donoh'e, 1b	3	0	1	7	1	0		Freeman,1b	4	0	1	3	0	0
Green, rf	4	0	1	1	0	1		Selbach, rf	3	0	1	2	0	0
Rohe, 3b	3	0	0	1	0	0		Ferris, 2b	3	0	0	3	4	0
Sullivan, c.	4	0	1	2	1	0		Criger, c.	3	1	1	3	1	0
Walsh, p	4	0	1	0	1	0		Harris, p	3	0	1	1	2	0
Total	30	4	7	24	10	1		**Total**	28	1	5	24	14	1

Chicago .... 1 0 0 0 0 0 3—3
Boston .... 0 0 0 1 0 0 0—1

Three-base hit—Parent. Sacrifice hit—Donohue. Stolen bases—Davis, Selbach, Criger. Double play—Davis, Donohue. First on balls—Off Harris 5, Walsh 1. Struck out—By Harris 1, Walsh 6. Passed ball—Criger. Wild pitches—Walsh 2, Harris 2. Time—1.40. Umpire—Sheridan. Attendance—3495.

IS NEW AND NOVEL.

MAKING A SPRING TRAINING TRIP A VOYAGE.

President Comiskey, of the Chicago American Club, Building a House Boat For the Use of His Men in the South Next Spring.

SPECIAL TO "SPORTING LIFE."

Chicago, Ill., September 27—News comes from Racine, Wis., to the effect that Charles Comisky, president and owner of the Chicago American League Club, last week gave a contract for a house boat, to be delivered on November 1 at Chicago. The price is $5000. When fitted out ready for service it will represent an investment of $6500. It will be 50 feet long with a beam 10 feet and 6 inches and draft of 1 foot and 4 inches when loaded. There will be sleeping accommodations for twenty guests besides the crew, dining-room, gallery and crew's quarters. It will be used in the spring, when the White Sox will be ordered South for practice work at different cities along the river. The team will practically live on board throughout the training season. This is a new idea in training trips, and was first suggested by Joe Cantillon.

Chas. Comiskey

NEW YORK WINS CHAMPIONSHIP OF THE WORLD

MATHEWSON'S PITCHING GIVES THE VICTORY

NEW YORK, Oct. 14.—STRUGGLING to hit the elusively mocking drop balls hurled by that magician of the pitchers' slab, Christy Mathewson, the Athletics went down to defeat for the fourth time and saw the world's pennant clutched by the eager hands of John McGraw and his cohorts. It was a remarkable exhibition of pitching by the blonde collegian and rounded up his marvelous performance in shutting out a champion team three times in one series.

Bender pitched as good a game as one could desire, but the giant slabman was irresistible and had the Quakers hypnotized from start to finish. As soon as a Philadelphian got on a base he was either forced at second on a grounder or left standing there on a pop fly or a strike out.

ATHLETICS.

	ab.	r.	bh.	th.	sh.	sb.	po.	a.	e.
Hartsel, lf	4	0	2	2	0	0	4	1	0
Lord, cf	4	0	0	0	0	0	3	0	0
Davis, 1b	4	0	1	1	0	0	10	0	0
L. Cross, 3b	4	0	0	0	0	0	1	2	0
Seybold, rf	3	0	1	1	0	0	1	0	0
Murphy, 2b	3	0	0	0	0	0	3	1	0
M Cross, ss	3	0	1	1	0	0	1	3	0
Powers, c.	3	0	1	2	0	0	5	1	0
Bender, p.	3	0	0	0	0	0	0	6	0
Totals	31	0	6	7	0	0	24	14	0

NEW YORK.

	ab.	r.	bh.	th.	sh.	sh.	po.	a.	e.
Bresnahan, c.	4	0	2	3	0	0	5	2	0
Browne, lf	4	0	1	1	0	0	1	0	0
Donlin, cf	4	0	0	0	0	0	1	0	0
McGann, 1b	3	0	0	0	0	0	12	1	0
Mertes, lf	3	1	1	1	0	0	4	1	0
Dahlen, ss	2	0	0	0	0	1	4	5	0
Devlin, 3b	2	0	0	0	1	0	1	4	0
Gilbert, 2b	2	0	1	1	0	0	2	3	0
Mathewson, p.	2	1	0	0	0	0	1	3	1
Totals	26	2	5	6	1	0	27	20	1

Athletics
Runs .... 0 0 0 0 0 0 0 0 0—0
Base hits .... 1 2 0 0 1 2 0 0 0—6
New York—
Runs .... 0 0 0 0 1 0 0 1 x—2
Base hits .... 0 1 1 0 0 2 0 1 x—5

Two-base hits—Powers, Bresnahan. Left on bases—Athletics 4; New York. Struck out—Lord, L. Cross, Seybold, Bender, Dahlen, Donlin. Double plays—Dahlen, Gilbert and McGann. First base on errors—Athletics, 1. First base on balls—Mertes, Dahlen, Mathewson. Missed grounder—Mathewson. Umpires—Sheridan and O'Day. Time—1.35. Attendance—30,000.

Record of Series

FIRST GAME.
Played at Philadelphia.

Giants 3
Athletics 0

PITCHERS.
Mathewson for Giants.
Plank for Athletics.

SECOND GAME.
Played at Polo Grounds.

Giants 0
Athletics 3

PITCHERS.
McGinnity and Ames for Giants.
Bender for Athletics.

THIRD GAME.
Played at Philadelphia.

Giants 9
Athletics 0

PITCHERS.
Coakley for Athletics.
Mathewson for Giants.

FOURTH GAME.
Played at Polo Grounds.

Giants 1
Athletics 0

PITCHERS.
McGinnity for Giants.
Plank for Athletics.

FIFTH GAME.
Played at Polo Grounds.

Giants 2
Athletics 0

PITCHERS.
Mathewson for Giants.
Bender for Athletics.

A NEW BALL RULE

HAS BEEN INAUGURATED IN THE AMERICAN LEAGUE.

By Order of President Johnson, Hereafter the Umpires Will Have Sole Charge of All Balls Used in a Game, Starting With a Dozen Balls.

Washington, D. C., April 29.—Editor "Sporting Life." — More weight has been added to the umpire's burden in the American League by the introduction of a new rule which was first tried out in last Tuesday's game in Philadelphia. Hereafter the arbitrator is custodian of the ammunition of the game. He carries a package of new base balls and whenever there is occasion for the introduction of a new ball in the game he throws it out instead of the manager of the home team, and thus all chances of any "doctored" or "mushy" ball getting into play is eliminated.

Ban Johnson

BOSTON VS. CHICAGO AT BOSTON MAY 25.—After twenty consecutive defeats—nineteen of them at home—the Bostons broke their streak by beating Chicago. Tannehill pitched a two-hit game and shut out the visitors, while Boston scored three runs aided by Chicago's misplays. The score:

BOSTON.	AB.	R.	B.	P.	A.	E.	CHICAGO.	AB.	R.	B.	P.	A.	E.
Parent, ss	4	0	0	1	1	0	O'Neil, rf	3	0	1	0	0	0
Stahl, cf	4	0	0	1	1	0	Jones, cf	4	0	0	2	0	0
Grims'w, 1b	4	1	1	10	0	0	Isbell, 2b	4	0	1	1	3	0
Selbach, lf	3	0	0	1	0	0	Donohue, 1b	4	0	0	10	1	0
Godwin, 3b	3	1	0	2	2	0	Hahn, lf	3	0	0	2	1	0
Freem'n, rf	2	1	1	1	0	0	Sullivan, c	3	0	0	3	0	0
Ferris, 2b	2	0	0	1	5	1	Rohe, 3b	3	0	0	1	1	0
Peterson, c	3	0	2	10	0	1	L. Tann'l, ss	3	0	0	2	7	1
J. Tann'l, p	3	0	0	0	1	1	White, p	3	0	0	2	1	1
Total	28	3	4	27	10	3	Total	30	0	2	*23	14	2

Boston	0	1	0	2	0	0	0	0	x	—3
Chicago	0	0	0	0	0	0	0	0	0	—0

*Godwin out, hit by batted ball.

First on errors—Boston 1, Chicago 2. Left on bases—Boston 3, Chicago 4. First on balls—Off Tannehill 1, White 1. Struck out—By Tannehill 6, White 2. Three-base hit—O'Neill. Sacrifice hits—Godwin, Freeman. Umpire—O'Loughlin. Time—1.19. Attendance—3003.

NEW YORK VS. CHICAGO AT NEW YORK JUNE 7.—The Chicagos simply overwhelmed the Giants, beating them 19 to 0, scoring 11 runs in the first inning and scoring in every inning but three thereafter. In the first inning fifteen men came to bat, there were three singles, two doubles and one triple. Also there were three bases on balls, a fumble by Gilbert and a bad mix up in running down a base runner, in which McGinnity and Dahlen made errors, and Slagle, Sheckard and Schulte each scored twice. Matthewson retired after the first three men had hit safely and McGinnity finished that inning. Ferguson went in in the second inning and finished the game. After the third inning Chicago hardly tried to score and Reulbach after the seventh inning was given some practice. New York's hits were so widely scattered that they could not score. The score:

CHICAGO.	AB.	R.	B.	P.	A.	E.	NEW YORK.	AB.	R.	B.	P.	A.	E.
Slagle, cf	5	2	4	0	0	0	Bresna'n, cf	1	0	0	2	0	0
Sheckard, lf	3	2	2	3	0	0	Browne, rf	4	0	0	1	1	0
Schulte, rf	5	3	1	0	0	0	McGann, 1b	4	0	0	13	2	0
Chance, 1b	5	2	2	9	1	0	Mertes, lf	4	0	0	2	0	0
Steinfe't, 3b	6	2	4	3	2	0	Dahlen, ss	2	0	1	1	7	1
Tinker, ss	6	1	1	2	7	0	Devlin, 3b	3	0	1	1	4	1
Evers, 2b	6	2	2	4	0	0	Gilbert, 2b	3	0	1	4	2	2
Hoffm'n, 2b	2	0	1	0	1	0	Bower'n, c	4	0	1	3	2	0
Moran, c	6	3	3	5	3	0	Math'n, p	0	0	0	0	0	0
Pfeister, p	3	2	2	1	1	0	McGin'y, p	0	0	0	0	1	1
Reulbach, p	1	0	0	0	0	0	Ferguson, p	3	0	0	0	4	0
Total	48	19	22	27	15	0	Total	28	0	4	27	23	5

Chicago	11	3	2	1	1	0	0	1	0	—19
New York	0	0	0	0	0	0	0	0	0	—0

First on errors—Chicago 2. Left on bases—New York 8, Chicago 12. First on balls—Off Mathewson 1, McGinnity 2, Ferguson 5, Pfeister 6, Reulbach 1. Struck out—By McGinnity 1, Ferguson 2, Pfeister 2. Home run—Schulte. Three-base hit—Steinfeldt. Two-base hits—Slagle, Tinker. Sacrifice hits—Sheckard, Pfeister. Stolen bases—Dahlen, Devlin 2, Evers. Passed ball—Bowerman. Hits—Off Mathewson 3 in one third inning, McGinnity 5 in one and one-third innings, Ferguson 14 in seven and one-third innings, Pfeister 3 in seven innings, Reulbach 1 in two innings. Umpires—Emslie and O'Day. Time—2.10. Attendance—6000.

BROOKLYN VS. PITTSBURG AT BROOKLYN AUG. 1.—This was a thirteen-inning pitchers' battle. Not a hit was made off McIntyre in ten innings, while Liefield kept his hits well scattered. Pittsburg won in the thirteenth when Ganley's single, Wagner's double and Nealon's single yielded the only run. Score:

Pittsburg.	AB.	B.	P.	A.	E.	Brooklyn.	AB.	B.	P.	A.	E.
Leach, lf	5	0	1	0	0	Maloney, cf	5	0	1	0	0
Beaum't, cf	5	0	2	0	0	Casey, 3b	5	1	1	2	0
Ganley, rf	5	1	1	0	0	Lumley, rf	5	1	2	0	0
Wagner, ss	5	1	6	8	0	Jordan, 1b	5	1	14	0	0
Nealon, 1b	4	1	17	2	0	Alper'n, 2b	5	2	2	3	1
Sheehan, 3b	5	0	1	4	0	McCarthy, lf	4	2	1	0	0
Ritchey, 2b	4	1	5	7	0	Lewis, ss	4	1	5	5	0
Phelps, c	4	0	6	1	0	Bergen, c	4	0	13	1	0
Liefield, p	4	0	0	4	0	M'Intyre, p	5	1	0	4	0
Totals	41	4	39	26	0	Totals	42	9	39	15	1

Pittsburg	0	0	0	0	0	0	0	0	0	0	0	0	1	—1
Brooklyn	0	0	0	0	0	0	0	0	0	0	0	0	0	—0

Run—Ganley. Two-base hits—Wagner, Lumley. Sacrifice hits—Maloney, McCarthy, Bergen. Stolen bases—Casey, Lewis. Double plays—McIntyre, Lewis, Jordan; Alperman, Lewis, Jordan; Wagner, Ritchey, Nealon. Left on bases—Pittsburg 2, Brooklyn 9. First on balls—Off McIntyre 1, Liefield 2. First on errors—Pittsburg 1. Hit by pitcher—By Liefield 1. Struck out—By McIntyre 8, Liefield 5. Umpire—Johnstone. Time—2.12. Attendance—2000.

Games Played Thursday, August 23.

WASHINGTON VS. CHICAGO AT WASHINGTON AUGUST 23.—Chicago won its nineteenth straight victory, defeating Washington. Patterson outpitched Falkenberg, allowing the locals to get more than one hit in but one inning, when two hits scored their solitary run. The score:

Washin'n.	AB.	B.	P.	A.	E.	Chicago.	AB.	B.	P.	A.	E.
Nill, 2b	4	0	2	1	0	Hahn, rf	5	1	0	0	0
C. Jones, cf	4	0	0	0	0	F. Jones, cf	2	0	6	0	0
Altizer, ss	4	1	4	3	0	Isbell, 2b	4	3	0	5	0
Cross, 3b	4	1	1	3	1	Davis, ss	3	1	2	3	0
Anderson, lf	3	0	2	0	0	Donohue, 1b	4	0	10	2	0
Hickman, rf	4	3	2	0	0	Dougher'y, lf	3	1	2	0	0
Stahl, 1b	4	1	13	1	0	Sullivan, c	4	1	4	0	0
Warner, c	3	0	3	6	0	Tannehill, 3b	4	1	1	2	0
Falkenb'g, p	3	1	0	2	0	Patterson, p	3	0	2	0	0
*Wakefield	1	0	0	0	0						
Totals	34	7	27	16	1	Totals	32	8	27	12	0

*Batted for Warner in ninth.

Washington	0	0	0	1	0	0	0	0	0	—1
Chicago	0	0	0	1	2	0	1	0	0	—4

Runs—Hahn, Jones, Isbell, Donohue, Hickman. Earned runs—Washington 1, Chicago 1. Two-base hits—Tannehill, Falkenberg, Hickman. Three-base hit—Stahl. Sacrifice hit—Dougherty. Stolen base—Isbell. Left on bases—Washington 7, Chicago 6. First on balls—Off Falkenberg 4. First on error—Chicago. Hit by pitcher—By Patterson 1. Struck out—By Falkenberg 5, Patterson 4. Passed ball—Warner. Umpire—O'Loughlin. Time—1.40. Attendance—4200.

Games Played Saturday, September 1.

BOSTON VS. ATHLETIC AT BOSTON SEPTEMBER 1.—This game resulted in a record-breaking event, it being the longest major league game ever played. Twenty-four well-played innings were necessary to decide the contest in which both teams made many brilliant plays at critical stages. Two games were to have been played but, of course, the second one had to be called off. Coombs and Harris, two youngsters, the first just out, had the honor of pitching this record game and the Athletic man on the whole outpitched the local twirler. Time after time Boston got men on second and third bases with no one out, but the heady work of Coombs, aided by coaching from Powers, prevented the necessary run from coming across the plate. Both infields did wonderful work. Parent made three successive hits while Knight made the splendid record of five successive clean hits, two of them for three bases, but oddly enough not one of the hits figured in the scoring. Coombs struck out 18 men and Harris 14. The Athletics scored a man in the third on Coombs' single and steal, Hartsel's out and Lord's single. Boston tied in the sixth on Parent's triple and Stahl's single. Freeman batted for Carrigan in the fifteenth inning and then Criger caught balance of game. Davis retired in the eleventh because of illness and Schreck, who took his place, later batted in the winning run. The Athletics landed the game in the twenty-fourth, when Hartsel singled to center, stole second and, with two out on strikes, Schreck singled, sending him home. Seybold and Murphy followed with triples, sending two more runs in. Boston was easily retired in its half of the final inning. The score:

Boston.	AB.	B.	P.	A.	E.	Athletic.	AB.	B.	P.	A.	E.
Hayden, rf	9	2	7	0	0	Hartsel, lf	10	2	2	1	0
Parent, ss	10	4	6	9	0	Lord, cf	9	1	6	0	0
Stahl, cf	7	2	5	0	0	Davis, 1b	4	0	12	1	0
Ferris, 2b	9	1	5	9	0	Schreck, 1b	6	2	16	0	0
Hoey	10	3	4	0	0	Seybold, rf	10	1	4	0	0
Grim'w, 1b	8	2	25	2	0	Murphy, 2b	9	3	3	7	1
Morgan, 3b	6	0	2	3	0	Cross, ss	9	1	9	8	1
Carrigan, c	5	0	6	2	2	Knight, 3b	7	5	1	4	0
Criger, c	4	0	11	1	0	Powers, c	9	1	16	7	0
Harris, p	8	1	1	6	0	Coombs, p	9	1	1	10	0
*Freeman	1	0	0	0	0						
Totals	77	14	72	38	2	Totals	82	16	72	38	2

*Batted for Carrigan in fifteenth inning.

Boston
0 0 0 0 0 1 0 0 0 0 0 0 0 0 0 0 0 0 0 0 0 0 0 0—1
Athletic
0 0 1 0 0 0 0 0 0 0 0 0 0 0 0 0 0 0 0 0 0 0 0 3—4

Runs—Parent; Hartsel, Schreck, Seybold, Coombs. First on errors—Boston 2. Left on bases—Boston 16, Athletic 10. First on balls—Off Harris 2, Coombs 6. Struck out—By Harris 14, Coombs 18. Three-base hits—Knight 2, Schreck, Seybold, Parent. Two-base hits—Parent, Ferris. Sacrifice hits—Morgan 2, Ferris, Knight, Lord, Hoey. Stolen bases—Cross, Coombs 2, Lord, Stahl, Knight, Hartsel. Double plays—Ferris, Parent, Grimshaw; Cross, Murphy, Davis. Hit by pitcher—By Harris 1, Coombs 1. Umpire—Hurst. Time—4.47. Attendance—18,047.

THE COMPLETE 1906 RECORD.

BY FRANCIS C. RICHTER.

The thirty-first annual campaign of the National League, which began April 12, ended October 7 with Chicago as the pennant-winner for the second time in twenty years. The Chicagos won the flag this year with 116 victories—a feat never before equalled in major league history. Prior to this year six National League teams won more than 100 games in a race: Boston 102 in 1892, Boston 102 in 1898, Brooklyn 101 in 1899, Pittsburg 103 in 1902, New York 106 in 1904, New York 105 in 1905. The Chicago campaign was also remarkable for the fact that it was never attended by any slump. The New Yorks, champions of the world this year, got a poor start, met with accidents to valuable players and early lost so much ground that after mid-season the team had to give up pennant hopes and make a battle with Pittsburg for second place, which was finally clinched in the last month of the campaign. Pittsburg started with high pennant hopes, but variable pitching forced the team to the rear and ultimately made impossible anything better than third place. These three teams were in a class by themselves, as the fourth place team, Philadelphia, never got within hailing distance of any of the trio and won fourth place with less than .500. Cincinnati finished this season in sixth place, one peg lower than last year, thus showing marked decline. Brooklyn advanced from the tail end last year to fifth place this season, showing greater relative improvement than any of the second division teams. St. Louis, after a most experimental season, finished in seventh place—one peg lower than last year. Boston traveled at about last year's gait, but finished last instead of seventh, owing to the advance of Brooklyn. Following is the complete 1906 record:

American League Clubs' Standing.

	W.	L.	Pct.		W.	L.	Pct.
Chicago	91	58	.611	St. Louis	76	73	.510
New York	90	61	.596	Detroit	71	78	.477
Cleveland	89	64	.582	Washington	55	95	.367
Philadelp'ia	78	66	.542	Boston	49	104	.320

National League Clubs' Standing.

	W.	L.	Pct.		W.	L.	Pct.
Chicago	116	36	.763	Brooklyn	66	86	.434
New York	96	56	.632	Cincinnati	64	87	.424
Pittsburg	93	60	.608	St. Louis	52	98	.347
Philadelp'ia	71	82	.464	Boston	48	103	.318

List of Goose Egg Games.

Aug. 2—Chicago, 3; Boston, 0 [White].
Aug. 3—Chicago, 4; Boston, 0 [Walsh].
Aug. 3—Washington, 1; St. Louis, 0 [Hughes].
Aug. 4—Chicago, 1; Boston, 0 [Patterson].
Aug. 4—Washington, 2; St. Louis, 0 [Patten].
Aug. 6—Cleveland, 4; Boston, 0 [Joss].
Aug. 7—Chicago, 4; Philadelphia, 0 [Walsh].
Aug. 8—Chicago, 1; Philadelphia, 0, ten innings [Patterson].
Aug. 8—Boston, 1; Cleveland, 0 [Harris].
Aug. 8—Washington, 6; Detroit, 0 [Patten].
Aug. 10—St. Louis, 1; Philadelphia, 0 [Powell].
Aug. 12—Chicago, 3; New York, 0 [Walsh].
Aug. 13—Chicago, 0; New York, 0 [White-Chesbro].
Aug. 13—Philadelphia, 8; St. Louis, 0 [Waddell].
Aug. 15—Chicago, 6; Boston, 0 [Walsh].
Aug. 17—Detroit, 6; New York, 0 [Donahue].
Aug. 18—Chicago, 10; New York, 0 [Walsh].
Aug. 21—Cleveland, 2; Washington, 0 [Rhoades].
Aug. 22—Washington, 4; Cleveland, 0 [Smith].
Aug. 25—New York, 2; Cleveland, 0 [Doyle].
Aug. 25—New York, 2; Cleveland, 0 [Chesbro].
Aug. 27—Chicago, 1; Philadelphia, 0 [Walsh].
Aug. 30—New York, 3; Washington, 0 [Doyle].

Oct. 7

DOPE MAKES BROWN STAR.

SPUD TWIRLER THE PITCHING SENSATION OF YEAR.

Outshines Even the Great Mathewson at His Best, Winning Twenty-seven Out of Thirty-three Games He Is In—Eight Shutouts to His Credit—Reulbach Next in Point of Effectiveness Among Chance's Box Men—Other Records.

In addition to two major league pennants and a world's championship Chicago has produced this year a pitching wonder, greater than the great Mathewson, even at Christy's best. Mordecai Brown of the new National league champions, with only three working fingers, is the man who has beaten Mathewson's record of last season.

Chance's star twirler this year easily has surpassed Mathewson's work, but the New Yorker has been palpably out of form and his admirers would resent any comparison between the two pitchers based on the present year alone.

Brown has won twenty-seven and lost only six games this year, giving him the lofty percentage of .818. Mathewson's 1905 record was thirty-one victories and nine defeats, a percentage of .775. While Mathewson won four more games last year than Brown has this season he also lost three more, and it is not on the cards that Brown would have lost three out of seven games at the rate he was going when the Spuds cinched their pennant and enabled Mordecai to lay off to rest a lame shoulder in preparation for the world's series. Mathewson's record this year to date is twenty-two games won and twelve lost, leaving him a percentage of only .647.

Remarkable Work by Brown.

The work of the great Chicago slabman has been remarkable otherwise than in the victories he has contributed toward winning the pennant. Brown has pitched two games in which his opponents made only one hit, one game in which he allowed only two hits and five games in which only three hits were made off him. Eight of the twenty-seven victories to his credit have been shutouts. No pitcher in his league has approached that record of effectiveness on the slab against all comers, although Young of Tenney's staff has pitched three games in which only one hit was made off his delivery. In general, however, Young's effectiveness has been in streaks, while Brown's has been almost continuous.

Twice Brown has held Pittsburg down to a single hit in nine innings, and one of the occasions was the freak battle of July 4, in which Spuds and Pirates made one hit apiece and Chance's men scored the only run in the ninth, Leifield being the loser.

Reprinted with courtesy of
The Chicago Tribune

Oct. 15

WHITE SOX'S FLAG; BEAT CUBS 8 TO 3.

American League Champions Take Sixth and Deciding Game of World's Series by Great Batting.

DRIVE BROWN FROM SLAB

Three Runs in the First and Four in the Second Settle Result; Dr. White Effective Throughout.

FINAL RESULT.

	Won.	Lost.
White Sox	4	2
Cubs	2	4

HITE SOX, World's Champions of 1906, to be emblazoned on pennant and blankets next season, was spelled out in actual play at the south side grounds yesterday before thousands of frenzied fans when Jones and his erstwhile hitless wonders, by an irresistible batting bee, enacted the final scene in the taming of Chance and the Cubs by a score of 8 to 3.

With the premier pitcher of the National league, three fingered Mordecai Brown, who had worked in two previous games, pitted against the premier pitcher of the American league, Southpaw Harry White, partisans of the west siders saw their idol driven to the bench in the second inning under an avalanche of eight safe hits. These yielded five runs and paved the way for two more before big Overall, called to the rescue as on the day previous, settled to his task. Except in the initial period, White, with the big lead in favor of the Sox, never was in serious danger, holding Chance's sluggers well in hand all the way.

Reprinted with courtesy of
The Chicago Tribune

UMP. O'DAY'S IDEA

REGARDING A TECHNICAL CHANGE IN THE RULES.

The National League Umpire Believes That Matters Would be Improved If the Batsman's Lines Were Defined by Rubber Instead of Chalk.

SPECIAL TO "SPORTING LIFE."

H. O'Day.

Chicago, Ill., Dec. 26.—Veteran "Hank" O'Day, the umpire, today told President Murphy, of the Chicago Nationals, that the Rules Committee would have to make an important change in marking out the batsman's box before one of the radical evils of the game would be corrected. "Umpires cannot see the box lines three minutes after play begins," said O'Day. "The batters rub out the chalk lines with their feet. How is an umpire standing behind the pitcher, say, to tell whether a batter is stepping out of his box when the lines are gone? The rules should specify that white rubber should be provided. Then a batter who seeks to get an unfair advantage may be detected and punished." With the Schedule Committee meetings still a considerable time off, alarmists are affecting to believe that there will be an irreconcilable clash between the National and the American League on the schedule. "I look for no clash," said Mr. Murphy today. "The National League will plan to open its 154 games schedule on April 11. If the American League wants to open later, why it has the right."

Stahl Accepts the Appointment.

Ft. Wayne, Ind., Dec. 11.—Charles Sylvester Stahl, the Boston outfielder, today suplemented the announcement of his appointment to the Boston team management with this official statement:

"I have accepted terms to manage the Boston Club in 1907 and I feel confident of being able to satisfy the Boston public. I know that the club finished last this year, but it will do better next year or I lose my guess. We had all kinds of hard luck. For 1907 we have thirty-six men under reservation. Mr. Taylor has several trades in view by which the club will be strengthened, and if possible the trades will be pushed through at the League meeting next week. I am perfectly satisfied. I feel also that I will get the club on a sound basis, if I didn't I wouldn't have agreed to manage the club, for yours truly doesn't intend to manage any lemon-champions."

CHAMPION MANAGER'S RULES FOR CHAMPIONS.

John J. McGraw, manager of the New York team, champions of the National League, lays down these rules for a championship nine, at the beginning of the practice season:

Alertness at all times.
Quick movement in going after the ball.
Desire to take advantage of other fellows' mistakes.
Display of interest in every second of the game.
Backing up other fielders on every play.
Jollying other members of the team to exert themselves.
Being wide awake on the bases all the time.

STAHL, SUICIDE.

INEXPLICABLE ACT OF A FAMOUS BALL PLAYER.

John I. Taylor

West Baden, Ind., March 30.—Charles Sylvester Stahl, captain and star outfielder of the Boston American Club, committed suicide here at the West Baden Springs Hotel on March 28 by swallowing carbolic acid. The act is ascribed to melancholia due to nervous breakdown. The cares of the team management weighed upon him so heavily that his appetite failed and he could not sleep. At Louisville on the 25th inst. he resigned the team management, but under persuasion by President John I. Taylor agreed to retain the team captaincy. That he committed suicide and that the act was contemplated for several days before its commission are now admitted facts among his closer friends on the team, as they recall certain peculiarities of action which they commented upon at the time, but they rejected the suspicion then, and for that reason took no steps to prevent the deed.

HOW IT HAPPENED.

Stahl was up early on the morning of March 28 and spoke to Jimmie Collins, his roommate, about the outlook for a good day for practice. He seemed to be in fine spirits and dressed himself with more than his wonted care and went down to break fast and ate a hearty meal. An hour later he returned to his room while the members of the team were dressing for practice and complained to Collins that he was not feeling well. He was apparently in a tremor, as though from chill, and Collins asked what was the matter. Stahl made a half intelligible reply that he was racked with pain or something to that effect and staggered to the bed and fell upon it. Collins called several of the players into the room and they gathered around the bed, each asking Stahl what ailed him, but he made

NO COHERENT REPLY.

Stahl's condition was now alarming, and though evidently trying to suppress expressions of pain he was turning about on the bed, breathing heavily and muttering inaudibly to himself. The remaining players rushed into the room and for a moment the dying man seemed to steady himself with a mighty effort and said: "Boys, I couldn't help it. It drove me to it." These were the last words that he uttered, and a moment later he was dead. On a stand nearby was an empty four ounce bottle marked poison and the strong odor of carbolic acid told the method that the noted ball player had chosen to end his life. The members of the team were shocked by the sudden ending of the career of their captain. They notified the hotel management and sent telegrams to Mrs. Stahl and other relatives at Fort Wayne and to parties in Boston.

CAUSE A MYSTERY.

Stahl's statement "It drove me to it" was wholly unintelligible to his friends, for no one knew what he referred to when he spoke of being driven to suicide. So far as his relations with the team as a whole or of its members as individuals were concerned there was no cause whatever for the act. All of the members of the team liked and many of them openly admired him. But though a cause for the act cannot be found, it is admitted among Stahl's friends that he had not been himself for several days. Stahl in October last married Miss Julia Marie Harmon, of Roxbury, Mass., and his domestic relations are said to have been exceptionally happy. According to a Boston despatch Mrs. Stahl received a letter from her husband on March 27 in which he expressed relief at being able to give up the management of the team. Previously he had written that he could not sleep. The Coroner's inquest was held yesterday afternoon and afterwards the body was shipped to Ft. Wayne, Ind., for burial.

Stahl's Last Word to Wife.

Boston, Mass., March 29.—"Cheer up little girl and be happy. I am all right now and able to play the game of my life." This was the message received by Mrs. Charles Stahl only on Wednesday from her husband. This morning the bride he wedded here last November was told of his suicide. Last evening, though hardly able to travel because of grief and the shock, she left for Fort Wayne. "I knew 'Chick' had been worrying over his troubles as manager," Mrs. Stahl said tonight, "but his last letter was cheerful and gave no hint of this terrible tragedy." Local fans are shocked at Stahl's suicide. Because of his geniality as well as his fine playing he was a general favorite. Stahl had been playing in Boston for the past ten years with National and American League clubs, and was one of the most popular ball players ever connected with a Boston team. Stahl was married last October to Miss Julia Marie Harmon, of Roxbury.

DOLAN'S DEATH.

Within twenty-four hours after the suicide of Charles Stahl, of the Boston American League Club, came tidings of the untimely death of Harry Dolan, of the Boston National League Club, from typhoid fever—that peculiar disease so dreaded by, and fatal to, athletes of every kind, but particularly base ball players. The deceased, while not a star, was a ball player of great ability and of such calibre that he was considered one of the best men in the Boston team. He will be greatly missed by his club as well as mourned in the profession. It is rather a peculiar coincidence that the two Boston clubs should be robbed by death within one day and that each victim should be the star outfielder of his team.

SINGULAR FATALITY.

A Base Ball Player Choked to Death by a Gumdrop.

Montezuma, Ia., April 21.—Choked to death by a piece of candy was the fate of Orrie McWilliams to-day, while he was playing ball. An exciting game was in progress, and McWilliams was catching. He had a gumdrop in his mouth. The ball was thrown to him to shut out a run home by a man on third. McWilliams caught the ball, but fell to the ground in a violent fit of strangulation. A doctor was summoned, but the boy was dead before he arrived. The gumdrop was found lodged in his windpipe.

BURNED BRAINS

IS THE CAUSE OF SUMMER OUTBREAKS BY PLAYERS.

President Pulliam, of the National League, Ascribes Increase of Scrappiness in Mid-Summer to Hot Weather Effect On Players.

SPECIAL TO "SPORTING LIFE."

New York, April 27.—"There is no doubt in my mind now that hot weather produces a sort of brain storm among ball-players that makes them misbehave slightly on the field, a condition that does not exist during the cooler months," said President Harry Pulliam of the National League. "Early in the season I attributed the lack of trouble between umpires and players to the cool weather that prevailed an extraordinary length of time after the season had opened. People laughed at me and my ideas of base ball.

BRAIN STORMS.

Then came the hot weather of July and August, and with it spats between umpires and players that became so serious that several suspensions have taken place; and I don't doubt that there will be still more to follow. At the same time, I believe that there will be less punishment inflicted upon players this season than during any previous season in the history of the game. The list of suspensions to date is

EXTREMELY SMALL.

including only Dave Brain, of Boston; Manager McGraw, of New York; Phil. Lewis, of Brooklyn; Billl Galeson and Mike Doolin, of Philadelphia; Manager Chance and Johnny Kling, of Chicago, and Manager McCloskey, of St. Louis. Neither Cincinnati nor Pittsburg has had a man suspended this year, although both have had players benched. That looks pretty good for the increase in good behavior in the National League, and the gradual dwindling away of demerits."

MISHAP MARRED

A CONTEMPLATED RAISING OF THE WORLD'S FLAG,

Through the Breaking of the Flag-Pole. This Depressing Accident, Topped by a Storm, Also Prevented the Game for Two Days.

SPECIAL TO "SPORTING LIFE."

Chicago, Ill., May 21.—The "hoodoo" got in his deadly work on world's championship flag-raising day and now there is gloom among the White Sox's followers, all of whom regard the event of last Tuesday as ominous of future ill fortune for Comiskey's men.

Chas. Comiskey

A series of mishaps, commencing with the breaking of the flagpole and ending with a furious wind and rain storm, marred the demonstration at the raising of the world's championship base ball pennant at the American League Park on May 14. Forty ball players and officials laid hold of the halyards to haul the great 35-foot pennant to the top of the staff. Their combined effort was too much for the slender staff, which snapped at the cross-trees. Mayor Busse, August Herrmann, chairman of the National Base Ball Commission, and President Johnson, of the American League, delivered their speeches, however, and the pennant was declared "officially" raised. Preceding the exercises at the park the Chicago and Washington teams were escorted from the City Hall to the park in automobiles by all the uniformed teams of Chicago and vicinity. Some four hundred ball players were in this parade, which consisted of fourscore automobiles, horsemen from the stockyards, three brass bands, mounted police and one hundred Indians from a wild west show. Lowering clouds caused Umpire O'Loughlin to start the game ten minutes ahead of schedule time, but despite this precaution only half an inning was played before the storm broke. Washington failed to score in its first time at bat. The following day the game was again prevented by rain.

A SOLID FACT.

Is the Invention of Pneumatic Batter's Head Protecting Device.

While Roger Bresnahan, of the New Yorks, was laid up from the effects of being hit on the head by a pitched ball it was announced that hereafter he would wear a headgear, supplementary to his famous shinguards. Those who regarded this as a joke or as impracticable will be undeceived by a glance at the advertisement of the A. J. Reach Company in our advertising columns. In this advertisement is announced the fact that this responsible and enterprising house has put upon the market the Reach Pneumatic Batters' Head Protector, a device Bresnahan is now using.

It was stated in the public prints that Bresnahan had invented this headgear. This was untrue. The headgear was invented and patented by the Reach Company and was put upon the market some years ago. Immediately upon hearing of Bresnahan's accident the Reach Company sent him a headgear. He acknowledged receipt of it and said he would wear it upon his reappearance with the New York team. We suppose that is how the report of his "invention" arose.

In the Reach Company's advertisement in this issue an illustration of the device in use is given, together with description of its points and merits. All players—those who have been hit with pitched balls especially—should take a few moments to look the advertisement over and to give the matter earnest consideration.

DOVES BITE DUST TWICE IN ST. LOUIS

KARGER, IN SECOND, IS MOST INHOSPITABLE

Would Not Give Visitors a Chance to Hit the Ball— Only Seven Innings.

ST. LOUIS. Mo., Aug. 11, 1907. Today's double-header between the Boston and local National league clubs ended most disastrously for the visitors, who lost each game, the second of which terminated by agreement at the conclusion of the seventh inning in order to permit the two clubs to take a train for Boston, where they will continue their present series Tuesday afternoon.

In the second game the visitors found Karger invincible for the seven innings that he was in the box. Not a hit was made off his delivery by Capt. Tenney's men, and Karger was in a fair way to pitch a full no-hit game when play ended with the termination of the seventh inning. The St. Louis club has recently taken a most decided brace, and the men started for the East with far more confidence than has marked their departure for either of the preceding tours of the eastern country.

The scores follow:

SECOND GAME.

ST. LOUIS.	ab.	r.	bh.	tb.	po.	a.	e.
Bryne, 3b	2	0	1	1	0	2	0
Barry, r.f	2	0	1	1	1	0	0
Konetchy, 1b	2	1	1	1	13	0	0
Burnett, c.f	2	1	1	1	1	0	0
Holly, s.s	1	0	1	2	2	3	0
Murray, l.f	3	0	1	2	0	4	0
Hostetter, 2b	3	0	0	0	2	0	0
Marshall, c	3	1	0	0	2	2	0
Karger, p	2	1	0	0	1	0	0
Totals	20	4	6	7	21	11	0

BOSTON.							
Bridwell, s.s	3	0	0	0	3	0	0
Tenney, 1b	3	0	0	0	10	0	0
Sweeney, 3b	3	0	0	0	1	5	0
Beaumont, c.f	2	0	0	0	2	0	0
Flaherty, r.f	2	0	0	0	2	1	0
Randall, l.f	2	0	0	0	1	2	0
Ritchey, 2b	2	0	0	0	3	0	0
Needham, c	2	0	0	0	2	1	0
Dorner, p	1	0	0	0	0	1	0
Boultes, p	1	0	0	0	0	1	0
Totals	21	0	0	0	13	13	0

Innings.	1	2	3	4	5	6	7	
St. Louis	0	0	0	1	1	2	.	—4

Two-base hit—Murray. Base hits—Off Dorner, 1 in 3 1-3 innings; off Boultes, 5 in 2 2-3 innings. Sacrifice hits—Barry, Holly. Stolen bases—Konetchy. Left on bases. St. Louis 4. First base on balls—Off Dorner 2, off Boultes 1. Struck out—By Karger 2, by Boultes 2, by Dorner 1. Wild pitch—Boultes. Time—1h. 20m. Umpires—Beebe and Young.

COMISKEY, INVESTOR.

The White Sox Chief Purchases Residential Land in Chicago.

Special to "Sporting Life."

Chicago, Ill., September 3.—Charles A. Comiskey, president of the American League Chicago club, is to build a handsome residence on the north side, it is said. He has just bought the land from John G. Neumeister, 100x180 feet, at the northeast corner of Sheridan road and Ardmore avenue, running back to Lake Michigan, for $12,500, with an incumbrance of $4000 assumed.

MUTES FOR UMPIRES.

A Texas Mute Printer Reported as Working on Scheme of Employment for Deaf and Dumb People.

A deaf mute umpire for a base ball game would be an oddity, as the arbitrator is supposed to do considerable during the progress of the game in calling balls and strikes and making his decisions. Rayden T. Cole, a deaf mute printer of Dallas, formerly of the deaf mute college team, of which he was the star twirler, is just completing a system of his own which will make the task of umpiring an easy stunt for a man who can neither hear nor speak. He proposes to ''call'' strikes with his right hand, indicating the number with his fingers, and the left hand will be used in calling balls. Cole says he wil shortly patent a pneumatic base with a whistle attachment which will prevent any room for doubt of a base runner cutting a base. When the base runner's foot strikes the base the pneumatic whistle will so announce his arrival. It is also proposed by Cole to patent a similar device in the way of a pneumatic whistle to be placed in the player's uniform, so that when he is tagged the whistle will sound.—Dallas ''Dispatch.''

ATHLETIC VS. DETROIT AT PHILADELPHIA SEPT. 30.—(P. M. and P. M.)—Only one game of the two arranged could be played as the first game was prolonged until darkness ended it after 17 innings play with the score a tie. There were more than 24,000 paid persons inside the grounds—the biggest crowd in the history of the game except for a world's series contest—and many more thousands on surrounding roofs. Several hundred climbed the fence and thousands were turned away. The Detroits were far behind at one stage, but by a long and splendid brace tied the score in the ninth inning. Each team tallied once in the eleventh, which ended the scoring. Donovan was hit hard in the early stages, but pulled himself together in fine style and only six hits were made off his delivery in the last ten innings. Dygert, of spit ball fame, lasted a little over one inning. Waddell succeeded him and was invincible for a while. But the Tigers finally diagnosed his twisters and drove him to cover. Plank finished the game out and did well. There was a squally time in the fourteenth inning. Davis sent a fly to center field, and Crawford, going after the ball, was interfered with by a policeman in the crowd. The Athletics claimed that Crawford had muffed the ball before he was near enough to the crowd to be interfered with. While the matter was being argued Rossman and Monte Cross came together in a scrap and exchanged punches. Rossman was put out of the game, the crowd meanwhile surging over the field in no good humor and requiring some lively work by the police before the field was cleared. Umpire O'Loughlin declared Davis out for the interference in center field. This decision cost the Athletics the game, and perhaps the championship, as Murphy's single which followed and was wasted would have scored Davis with the winning run. The Athletics having bumped Donovan severely, it looked all over but the shouting when the seventh inning rolled around. Right here, however, the Detroits took up the cudgels in earnest. A muff by Oldring, a base on balls and a fumble by Nichols filled the bases. Crawford doubled and before the side had been retired four runs were in. After Crawford's single in the ninth Cobb tied the score with a home run over the right field fence. Each side made a run in the eleventh, the Detroits on hits by Cobb and Rossman, and the Athletics on a hit by Nichols, a wild pitch and an outfield fly. Score:

Detroit.	AB.	R.	B.	P.	A.	E.	Athletic.	AB.	R.	B.	P.	A.	E.
Jones, lf	7	1	1	5	0	0	Hartsel, lf	9	1	4	3	0	0
Schaefer, 2b	9	1	3	2	6	0	Nichols, ss	6	1	2	4	9	1
Craw'd, cf	8	2	2	7	0	0	Seybold, rf	8	2	1	1	0	0
Cobb, rf	8	1	3	1	0	0	Davis, 1b	8	3	3	19	1	0
Rossm'n, 1b	7	1	2	13	0	0	Murphy, 2b	7	1	2	2	6	0
Killian, 1b	0	0	0	1	0	0	J. Collins, 3b	8	1	1	3	5	0
Mullin, lb	1	0	0	0	0	0	Oldring, cf	7	0	3	3	0	1
Downs, cf	1	0	0	2	0	0	E. Collins, ss	1	0	1	0	0	0
Cough'n, 3b	6	0	1	3	3	0	Schreck, c	3	0	0	9	1	1
Schmidt, c	8	0	3	3	1	1	Powers, c	4	0	0	4	0	1
Payne, c	0	0	1	0	1	0	Dygert, p	0	0	0	0	2	0
O'Leary, ss	8	1	2	1	6	0	Waddell, p	2	1	0	0	1	0
Donovan, p	7	1	1	2	7	0	Plank, p	4	0	1	2	1	0
Totals	70	9	15	51	21	1	Totals	67	9	20	51	21	6

*Batted for Oldring in seventeenth inning.

| Detroit | 0 | 0 | 0 | 0 | 0 | 4 | 3 | 0 | 1 | 0 | 1 | 0 | 0 | 0 | 0 | 0 | 0 | —9 |
| Athletic | 3 | 0 | 2 | 0 | 2 | 1 | 0 | 0 | 0 | 0 | 1 | 0 | 0 | 0 | 0 | 0 | 0 | —9 |

Left on bases—Athletic 13, Detroit 17. First on balls—Off Dygert 1, Waddell 1, Plank 3, Donovan 2. Struck out—By Waddell 7, Plank 3, Donovan 11. Home runs—Davis, Cobb. Two-base hits—Hartsel 3, Nichols, Davis, Oldring 2, J. Collins, Crawford, Cobb, O'Leary. Sacrifice hits—Nichols 2, Powers, J. Collins, Crawford, Donovan. Stolen bases—Hartsel, Cobb, Coughlin, O'Leary. Wild pitch—Donovan. Hit by pitcher—By Plank 1. Hits—Off Dygert 1 in one and one-third innings, Waddell 7 in seven and two-third innings, Plank 7 in eight innings. Umpires—O'Loughlin and Connolly. Time—3.50. Attendance—24,127.

CY YOUNG'S RECORD.

A Wonderful Percentage Made In His Long Career.

Cy Young, of the Boston Americans, holds the long distance pitching record of the world. Since 1890 he has won 457 games and lost 271 for a percentage of .628. His best year came in 1892 with Cleveland, when he won thirty-six out of forty-six for a percentage of .700. Again in 1895 he won thirty-five out of forty-five for Cleveland, and his mark was .777. Following is his record of victories since 1890:

	Won	Lost	Pct.
1890—Cleveland	10	7	.588
1891—Cleveland	27	22	.551
1892—Cleveland	36	10	.780
1893—Cleveland	34	17	.667
1894—Cleveland	25	22	.532
1895—Cleveland	35	10	.777
1896—Cleveland	20	16	.644
1897—Cleveland	21	18	.558
1898—Cleveland	24	14	.631
1899—St. Louis	26	15	.634
1900—St. Louis	20	18	.526
1901—Boston	31	10	.756
1902—Boston	32	12	.727
1903—Boston	28	9	.757
1904—Boston	26	16	.619
1905—Boston	18	19	.486
1906—Boston	13	21	.382
1907—Boston	22	15	.595
Totals	457	271	.628

START WITH DRAW.

Twelve Innings Played in First Game Without Result.

CHICAGO VS. DETROIT AT CHICAGO, TUESDAY, OCT. 8.—The opening game of the world's championship series between the Chicago National champions and the Detroit American champions was played before 24,377 people—one of the largest crowds to ever witness a world's championship game. Singularly, the very first game following the National Commission's decision that a tie game shall entitle the players to participation in the receipts of an extra game resulted in a draw after twelve desperately-contested innings.

Orval Overall

PROPOSED EIGHTEEN MEN RULE CALLED A JOKE.

BY W. A. PHELON.

Chicago, Dec. 9.—Editor ''Sporting Life.'' Both Charlie Murphy and Charles Comiskey are having many quiet smiles over the declarations recently made by brother Dovey of Boston—that clubs should be restricted to eighteen men and that only five additions should be made to any team during a season. The local magnates can't help laughing. Where would either the Sox or Cubs have been if restricted to eighteen performers the past two years? Doubtless a cut-down to eighteen would be a life-saver for Boston in two ways—financially and in the percentage column. But that is about all.

W. A. Phelon

'08 BASEBALL SEASON

REPUBLICAN PRESIDENTIAL CONVENTION CHICAGO
DEMOCRATIC PRESIDENTIAL CONVENTION DENVER

PUBLIC INTEREST

"THEY'LL HAVE TO HUMP IT."

HENRY CHADWICK

Veteran Journalist and "Father of Base Ball."

Born, October 5, 1824.
Died, April 20, 1908.

THAT NEW RULE

CREDITING A RUN-SCORING FLY AS A SACRIFICE.

Is Objected to Seriously By Manager Fielder Jones of the Chicago White Sox as Rather Detrimental to Team Work.

SPECIAL TO "SPORTING LIFE."

Chicago, Ill., April 13.—Manager Fielder Jones, of the White Sox, the other day furnished justification for Comiskey's claim that more players are needed on the Rules Committee to inject practical ideas into the playing rules. This is apropos to the new rule giving a batsman a sacrifice hit for scoring a runner from third base on a long fly. "That rule is the direct opposite of what is needed in base ball today," said the Sox manager. "Team work is the goal of every club that wants to become a winner and individual records of players are a handicap in the modern game, although they used to be the whole works years ago. Rules should be formed to encourage team work and discourage individuals playing for records. The new sacrifice fly rule will not make more team players."

Fielder Jones

TWO UMPIRES

WOULD BE THE PROPER MAJOR LEAGUE CAPER.

President Kilfoyl, of Cleveland, an Enthusiastic Convert to the Double-Umpire System, Which He Wants Put Into Effect at Once

SPECIAL TO "SPORTING LIFE."

Cleveland, O., July 14.—"There isn't any doubt according to my way of thinking as to the advisability of having two umpires instead of one in every game," said President Kilfoyl of the Cleveland Club to-day. "Good umpires, however, are scarce; scarcer, probably, than good ball players, and goodness knows they are hard enough to find. Every American and National League club is represented by a scout all season and the 16 of them do not find a handful of new players from April to October. Probably Ban Johnson figures that eight poor umpires would be worse than six 'tolerable' ones, but it ought to be possible to find four more men in the O'Loughlin-Sheridan-Evans-Hurst-Connelly-Egan class. They are good men and I am sure each one of them has done his level best in every game played. I think the trouble with most umpires is that they give their decisions too quickly. If they would all take a second or two to see the finish of a play there would be far less fault found with their decisions. The double umpire plan would probably mean the appointment of four new arbitrators, making ten in all—or two extra men for emergencies. There are six umpires now, giving two cities in the league the benefit of the double umpire system every day. Even if only eight umpires were on the staff it would be a change for the better. In rare instances where one of the arbitrators failed to appear the arrangement would be no worse than it is now."

J. M. Kilfoyl

MERKLE'S DANGER.

He May Lose a Foot Through Serious Blood Poisoning.

Special to "Sporting Life."

Cincinnati, July 13.—Reports from the Good Samaritan Hospital, where infielder Fred Merkle, of the New York Giants, underwent two operations on his foot for blood-poisoning, are to the effect that serious complications have arisen. Unless they are checked it is likely that the foot will have to be amputated. Merkle had planned to go to Pittsburg with the Giants last Thursday night, and from the Smoky City go to his home in Toledo, but the hospital physicians stated yesterday that it would be some time before the ball player would be able to leave the institution. Merkle realises that he is in pretty bad shape, but is trying to keep the public in ignorance of his condition in order to alleviate the fears of his family in Toledo. The foot is about the size of a big pumpkin, and even the lower leg up to the knee is affected. The breaking of the skin between the great toe and the next one is primarily responsible for Merkle's condition.

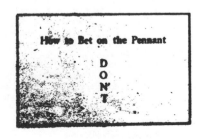

How to Bet on the Pennant

D O N T

BOSTON AT NEW YORK JUNE 30.—Boston shut out New York and Cy Young not only pitched a no-hit game for the third time in his long career, but batted in four of the eight runs made by the visitors. Only one of the local men—Niles—succeeded in reaching first base. Young gave but one base on balls, and this man was caught trying to steal second. Score:

Boston.	AB.	R.	B.	P.	A.	E	New York.	AB.	R.	B.	P.	A.	E
Thoney, lf.	5	0	0	0	0	0	Niles, 2b.	2	0	0	3	6	0
Cravath, lf	5	0	1	4	0	0	Keeler, rf.	3	0	0	2	1	1
Sullivan, cf	5	1	1	0	0	0	Moriar'y, 1b	3	0	0	10	1	1
McCon'l, 2b	3	2	2	2	4	0	Hemphill, cf	3	0	0	0	0	0
Gessler, rf.	3	0	1	2	0	0	Ball, ss	3	0	0	3	3	0
Laporte, 3b	4	0	2	2	2	0	Stahl, lf	3	0	0	2	1	0
Unglaub, 1b	4	2	2	13	0	0	Conroy, 3b	3	0	0	0	1	0
Wagner, ss	4	2	1	0	3	0	Blair, c.	3	0	0	7	2	0
Criger, c.	3	0	0	3	2	0	Manning, p	0	0	0	0	2	0
Young, p.	5	1	3	0	1	0	Newton, p.	1	0	0	0	1	1
							Lake, p.	2	0	0	0	0	0
Totals..	35	8	13	27	12	0	Totals..	26	0	0	27	18	3

Boston .... 1 1 2 1 0 1 0 0 2—8
New York .... 0 0 0 0 0 0 0 0 0—0

Hits—Off Manning 3 in 1 2-3 innings. Newton 3 in 2-3 inning. Lake 7 in 5 2-3 innings. Sacrifice hits—McConnell 2. Criger 2. Stolen base—McConnell. Double play—Stahl, Blair. Left on bases—Boston 11. First on balls—Off Manning 3. Newton 1. Lake 1. Young 1. First on errors—Boston 2. Hit by pitcher—By Manning 1. Newton 1. Struck out—By Manning 1. Newton 1. Lake 4. Young 2. Time—2h. Umpire—O'Loughlin. Attendance—1500.

CUBS WILL FILE PROTEST

Chicagoans Get Short End of 1-0 Verdict in Pittsburg.

MIXUP COMES IN THE TENTH.

Gill Fails to Touch Second and Umpire Does Not See Play.

BY I. E. SANBORN.

Pittsburg, Pa., Sept. 4.—[Special.]—In a magnificently pitched and stubbornly fought battle here today the Cubs received the short end of 1 to 0 verdict in ten innings, thereby dropping nearly three games behind the leaders and a game and a half behind the Pirates.

But there is some chance—just an outside chance—that the defeat may be wiped out and the Cubs and Pirates ordered to do it all over again on the strength of a protest which the Cub management intends to file with President Pulliam.

This protest, which, if sustained, would wipe out Pittsburg's run in the tenth inning, grows out of Jack Evers' ability to think faster than one bush league player and one veteran major league umpire, to wit: Pirate Gill and Hank O'Day. The success or failure of Chicago's protest rests on whether the veteran umpire will admit the facts in the case, which would make his decision a direct violation of the playing rules, or will wise up sufficiently to assert his ignorance of the exact facts, which would exempt him from the charge of ignoring the rules and make it necessary for the league to uphold the umpire's verdict. The whole question depends on whether O'Day says First Baseman Gill touched second base in that woozy tenth inning today or admits that the player failed so to do.

Reprinted with courtesy of
The Chicago Tribune

GAME ENDS IN TIE MAY GO TO CUBS.

"Bush League" Baserunner Costs Giants a 2 to 1 Victory in the Ninth.

DISPUTE UP TO PULLIAM.

Chicago Claims Forfeit on Account of Interference; O'Day Says "No Contest."

Standing of the Clubs.

	W.	L.	Pct		W.	L.	Pct.
New York	87	50	.635	Cincinnati	68	73	.482
CHICAGO	90	53	.629	Boston	60	82	.423
Pittsburg	89	54	.622	Brooklyn	48	92	.343
Philadelphia	74	64	.536	St. Louis	47	95	.331

BY CHARLES DRYDEN.

New York, Sept. 23.—[Special.]—Minor league brains lost the Giants today's game after they had it cleanly and fairly won by a score of 2 to 1. In the ninth round Merkle did a bone-head base running stunt identical with the recent exhibition which Mr. Gill, also a minor leaguer, gave at Pittsburg three weeks ago. But this time "Hank" O'Day had his eagle eye peeled and the winning run which the Giants compiled in the ninth inning was tossed into the discard.

O'Day ruled "no contest," and, as the field could not be cleared, the game may be forfeited to the Cubs.

It must chagrin the Giants aplenty to think how they kiboshed themselves. In a swell combat worth going miles to see Mathewson had the better of Pfiester, and the game looked as safe as the Bank of England when Bridwell tore off what should have been a hit in the ninth.

Tinker's home run in the fifth was all the Cubs had in the way of visible assets. Steinfeldt's bum heave and a couple of singles knotted the count in the sixth after a most gallant defense. Then came the bone-head finish, which left the bugs puzzled and wondering. And they won't know what happened until they see the public prints—i. e., newspapers—in the morning.

Pulliam to Award Game.

President Pulliam would not make a statement tonight, but he intimated the game would not be played over. That means either that the contest goes to the Cubs by forfeit because of the crowd on the field or that Pulliam will overrule O'Day's decision that the run in the ninth did not count. This would give the game to New York.

Round 9 for the Giants opened with the out of Seymour. Then Devlin singled and McCormick forced him. Merkle's safety to right put McCormick on third. On the first ball pitched Bridwell pasted a neat but not gaudy single to center. McCormick crossed the plate, but Merkle, who was at first base, ran halfway down to second, then turned, and hotfooted for the clubhouse.

Unless the said Merkle planted a hoof on second base, Bridwell could not be credited with a hit, and McCormick could not score. The Cubs and Hank O'Day were primed for the situation, having been through it once before, in Pittsburg. With one voice the Cubs set up a yelp like a cage of hungry hyenas, and O'Day, working behind the plate, ran to the pitching slab to see what came off at second base. Capt. Donlin realized the danger about to overtake the Giants, so he set off after the fat headed Merkle while McGinnity, who was coaching at third base, butted into the fracas coming off at the middle cushion.

Facts Gleaned from Survivors.

The facts in the case gleaned from active participants and survivors are these: Hofman fielded Bridwell's knock and threw to Evers for a force play on the absent Merkle. But McGinnity, who was not in the game, cut in ahead and grabbed the ball before it reached the eager Trojan. Three Cubs landed on the iron man from as many directions at the same time and jolted the ball from his cruel grasp. It rolled among the spectators, who had swarmed upon the diamond like an army of starving potato bugs.

At this thrilling juncture "Kid" Kroh, the demon southpaw, swarmed upon the human potato bugs and knocked six of them galley-west. The triumphant Kroh passed the ball to Steinfeldt after cleaning up the gang that had it. Tinker wedged in, and the ball was conveyed to Evers for the force out of Merkle, while Capt. Donlin was still some distance off towing that brilliant young gent by the neck.

Some say Merkle eventually touched second base; but not until he had been forced out by Hofman, to McGinnity, to six potato bugs, to "Kid" Kroh, to some more Cubs, and the shrieking, triumphant Mr. Evers, the well known Troy shoe dealer. There have been some complicated plays in baseball, but we do not recall one just like this in a career of years of monkeying with the national pastime.

"Cops" Balk Peerless Leader.

Meanwhile a more turbulent scene was being enacted elsewhere. Peerless Leader Chance ran at O'Day to find out what Hank had to say, but the sparrow cops, specials, 200 cops and Pinks—slang for Pinkertons—thought Chance was going to bite Hank on the ankle. Half a hundred men in uniform surrounded the P. L., and thousands of bugs surrounded them. Bill Marshall, who is an expert on bacteria, and Del Howard rushed in to help the Peerless Leader. Another squad of cops had O'Day in tow some yards away.

Hank didn't know Chance wanted to converse with him, and they couldn't get together anyhow. Finally the cops got O'Day into a coop under the stand and tried to slam the door in the face of the Peerless Leader. He jammed his robust frame in the opening and defied the sparrow chasers. Chance later got to O'Day, who said Emslie, working on the bases, did not see the second base play because of the crowd, but Hank informed Chance that McCormick's run didn't count.

Still later Hank submitted gracefully to an interview by war scribes. He said Merkle was forced at second base and the game ended in a tie, at 1 to 1. None of the Giants remained to make public statements. Part of the crowd lifted a player in white to their shoulders and bore him to the clubhouse. The Giant thus honored was not Mr. Merkle. He left long before the trouble started, and his departure caused it. Some base runners should have a groove cut in them so they couldn't go wrong.

SCORE OF THE CUBS-GIANTS GAME.

CHICAGO.	AB	R	BH	TB	BB	SH	SB	P	A	E
Hayden, rf	4	0	0	0	0	0	0	1	0	1
Evers, 2b	4	0	1	1	0	0	0	4	7	0
Schulte, lf	4	0	0	0	0	0	0	1	0	0
Chance, 1b	5	0	1	1	0	1	0	11	1	0
Steinfeldt, 3b	3	0	0	0	0	1	0	1	1	1
Hofman, cf	3	0	1	1	0	0	0	1	0	0
Tinker, ss	3	1	1	4	0	0	0	3	7	2
Kling, c	3	0	1	1	0	0	0	5	1	0
Pfiester, p	3	0	0	0	0	0	0	0	1	0
Totals	32	1	5	8	0	3	0	27	18	4

NEW YORK.	AB	R	BH	TB	BB	SH	SB	P	A	E
Herzog, 2b	3	1	1	1	1	0	1	1	1	0
Bresnahan, c	3	0	0	0	1	0	1	11	1	0
Donlin, rf	4	0	1	1	0	0	0	2	0	0
Seymour, cf	4	0	1	1	0	0	0	1	0	0
Devlin, 3b	4	0	2	2	0	0	0	0	2	0
McCormick, lf	3	0	0	0	0	1	0	1	0	0
Merkle, 1b	3	0	1	1	0	0	0	9	1	0
Bridwell, ss	4	0	1	1	0	0	0	2	3	0
Mathewson, p	3	0	0	0	0	0	0	2	2	0
Totals	31	1	6	6	3	1	3	27	9	0

CHICAGO	0	0	0	0	1	0	0	0	0—1
NEW YORK	0	0	0	0	0	1	0	0	0—1

Home run—Tinker. Struck out—By Mathewson, 9. Bases on balls—Off Pfiester, 2. Double plays—Tinker-Chance (2); Evers-Chance; Mathewson-Bridwell-Merkle. Hit by pitcher—McCormick. Time—1:30. Umpires—O'Day and Emslie.

Reprinted with courtesy of
The Chicago Tribune

CHICAGO AT BROOKLYN SEPTEMBER 26 (P. M. and P. M.)

CHICAGO AT BROOKLYN SEPTEMBER 26 (P. M. and P. M.)—Reulbach pitched both games for Chicago and scored two shut outs. In the first game he yielded five hits, which he kept well scattered, while Chicago bunched hits on Wilhelm in the last three innings. Score:

Chicago.	AB.R.B. P.A.E	Brooklyn.	AB.R.B. P.A.E
Hayden, rf	4 0 0 2 0 0	Catterson, lf	4 0 0 4 0 0
Evers, 2b	4 1 1 2 3 0	Lumley, rf	4 0 0 2 0 0
Schulte, lf	4 1 0 1 0 0	Hummel, 2b	4 0 1 3 1 1
Chance, 1b	4 0 0 8 0 0	Jordan, 1b	3 0 0 9 2 0
Steinf't, 3b	4 0 3 1 1 0	Burch, cf	4 0 0 2 0 0
Hofman, cf	4 0 0 2 0 0	McMillan, ss	3 0 1 1 1 0
Tinker, ss	4 1 0 1 3 0	Sheehan, 3b	3 0 1 0 2 0
Kling, c	4 2 3 9 1 0	Dunn, c	3 0 2 5 1 0
Reulbach, p	2 0 0 1 0	Wilhelm, p	3 0 0 0 5 0
Totals..	34 5 9 27 9 0	Totals..	31 0 5 27 11 2

Chicago .... 0 0 0 0 1 0 1 2 1—5
Brooklyn .... 0 0 0 0 0 0 0 0 0—0

First on errors—Chicago 2. Left on bases—Chicago 7, Brooklyn 4. First on balls—Off Reulbach 1, Wilhelm 1. Struck out—By Reulbach 6, Wilhelm 5. Two-base hits—Evers, Kling. Sacrifice hits—Evers, Hayden, Schulte, Reulbach. Stolen bases—Steinfeldt, Kling 2. Passed ball—Dunn. Umpires—Owens and Emslie. Time—1.40.

The second game was really as one-sided as the first, though the Cubs made fewer runs, because Reulbach was even more effective in this game than in the first. They couldn't do a great deal with Pastorius' pitching, but there were Brooklyn errors to help them. Errors figured in both of their scoring seasons. Score:

Chicago.	AB.R.B. P.A.E	Brooklyn.	AB.R.B. P.A.E
Hayden, rf	4 1 1 2 0 0	Catterson, lf	4 0 1 5 0 0
Evers, 2b	4 1 2 1 2 1	Lumley, rf	4 0 2 2 0 0
Schulte, lf	2 0 1 3 0 0	Hummel, 2b	4 0 0 4 1 0
Chance, 1b	4 0 0 10 0 0	Jordan, 1b	3 0 0 6 0 0
Steinf'L, 3b	4 0 0 1 1 0	Burch, cf	3 0 0 2 0 0
Hofman, cf	3 0 0 1 0 0	McMillan, ss	3 0 0 2 2 1
Tinker, ss	3 0 0 5 1 1	Sheehan, 3b	3 0 0 1 2 1
Kling, c	3 0 1 2 1 0	Dunn, c	3 0 2 5 1 0
Reulbach, p	1 1 0 1 2 1	Pastorius, p	2 0 0 1 3 0
		*Pattee	1 0 0 0 0 0
Totals..	28 3 4 27 10 2	Totals..	28 0 3 27 11 4

*Batted for Pastorius in ninth inning.

Chicago .... 0 0 1 0 0 0 2 0—3
Brooklyn .... 0 0 0 0 0 0 0 0 0—0

First on errors—Chicago 2, Brooklyn 1. Left on bases—Chicago 2, Brooklyn 3. First on balls—Off Reulbach 4, Pastorius 2. Struck out—By Reulbach 2, Reulbach 4. Sacrifice hit—Reulbach. Stolen base—Schulte. Double plays—Reulbach, Tinker, Chance; Hummel, Jordan. Wild pitches—Reulbach, Pastorius. Umpires—Emslie and Owens. Time—1.15. Attendance—10,000.

"CASEY AT THE BAT."

D'vys, A Boston Literary Man, Claims He, and Not Ernest L. Thayer, Was the Author of the Famed Poem.

According to the Cambridge, Mass., "Times," the authorship of one of the best known American poems, long in dispute, and claimed by many, including Earnest Thayer, is now definitely cleared up. The poem is "Casey at the Bat," and is now credited to George Whitefield D'vys, of Cambridge, Mass. D'vys has written numerous sea stories and poetry, but not any have been more widely read than his base ball poems. His "Dolan's Five Base Hit" and "At the Pipe" vie with "Casey" in charm and merit. The latter was first published in "Sporting Life" in 1906. The grand ballad, now a classic, saw light in 1886, being written on Sunday, May 8, while D'vys was lying on the grass in Franklin Park, Boston. Casey was founded on the famous Mike Kelly, who a few days previously in Boston had fanned at an inopportune time. The poem was sent out anonymously for the reason that the author's father, a master mariner, was opposed to literature and poetry and would have no "literary fellow" about his craft. It was accepted by O. P. Caylor, editor of the New York "Sporting Times," who, despite hundreds of requests for the name of the author, steadfastly refused to reveal his identity.

Sept. 30

E. WALSH DEFEATS RED SOX TWICE.

White Sox "Man of the Hour" Is Successful in Double Slab Duty.

SCORES 5 TO 1 AND 2 TO 0.

Jones Again Put Out of Game for Quarreling with Umpire Over a Decision at the Plate.

Standing of the Clubs.

	W.	L.	Pct.		W.	L.	Pct.
Detroit	86	61	.585	Boston	70	76	.479
Cleveland	86	62	.581	Philadelphia	65	79	.451
CHICAGO	85	62	.578	Washington	61	81	.430
St. Louis	82	65	.558	New York	48	97	.331

BY I. E. SANBORN.

Eddie Walsh, the man of steel, added a double laurel wreath to his already overloaded brow yesterday by pitching both games of the double header with Boston, and not only winning both but missing a double whitewash performance by the narrowest possible margin. The scores were 5 to 1 and 2 to 0.

The single run scored off Walsh came early in the first game, and was made on a hot smash so near to first base that all the White Sox asserted it was a foul ball. That decision, and one on which he was called out at the plate in the fifth inning of the first game, so roiled Manager Jones that he protested himself out of the field of battle for the rest of the afternoon. But for that lucky rap by McConnell, Walsh would have blanked the visitors for eighteen straight rounds yesterday, giving him three straight shutouts against the Red Sox this trip.

Only seven safe hits were made off Big Eddie, three in the first game and four in the second. All three of those ripped off in the first encounter came together in the third inning, while the four in the other scrap were scattered through different innings. Fifteen batsmen were set down on strikes by Walsh during the day, ten of them in the first game and five in the second.

Reprinted with courtesy of
The Chicago Tribune

GANZEL'S ANKLE.

A Novel Surgical Appliance Is Brought Into Use.

Cincinnati, O., July 20.—Two years ago Capt. John Ganzel, of the Cincinnati team, splintered an ankle bone stepping off a street car in Grand Rapids, Mich. The split in the bone stands open like a crack in an oak tree. Next Monday, a local surgeon will place iron bands and bolts on the ankle like fastenings around a smokestack, and the Spartan athlete will continue to play. This is a new wrinkle in base ball surgery.

COBB MARRIED.

The Famous Outfielder of the Detroit Team Weds a Georgia Heiress—Honors for the Happy Bridegroom.

Augusta, Ga., August 6.—Tyrus Raymond Cobb, the great batsman of the American League, and Miss Charlie Lombard were married to-day at The Oaks, the home of the bride's father. The wedding was followed by a banquet at the Gevesta Hotel, at which covers were laid for fifty. The presents came in wagon loads, six loads being taken to the Lombard home yesterday and to-day. Cobb and bride left this afternoon for Detroit where he will resume his hitting. Miss Lombard is an heiress, her father being worth about $300,000.

Tyrus Cobb

The couple will visit Japan after the base ball season closes. Cobb had a hard time finding a preacher to perform the ceremony, owing to so many Augusta pastors being out of town on vacations, and he was very nervous lest something should keep the Rev. Mr. Walker away. All Georgia was interested in the wedding and Cobb received telegrams from Gov. Hoke Smith and other prominent men. The Detroit and Athletic players sent congratulations to Cobb. He will not tarry on his honeymoon. He left Augusta to-night and wired Manager Jennings that he would appear in Detroit Saturday in time to play against Washington. The honeymoon will be spent on the next Eastern trip, the Detroit Club paying all expenses as a wedding gift to the star and his wife. Members of the Detroit team bought a cutglass outfit for him. Mr. and Mrs. Cobb will spend a few days visiting several Georgia towns, after which he will rejoin the Detroit team, his wife traveling with him. At the end of the season it is the intention of the couple to visit Europe.

RACES ARE NOT FIXED!

President Comiskey of Chicago Declares That in Over 30 Years of His Connection

With Base Ball He Has Never Had Cause to Doubt the Honesty of the Great Sport.

NO HIT CONTEST DEFEAT FOR SOX.

Joss Equals Record and Cleveland Wins Sensational Game, 1 to 0.

BATTLE OF THE PITCHERS

Walsh "Fans" 15 Men—Passed Ball and Isbell's Wild Peg Are Costly—Schreck Hurt.

Standing of the Clubs.

	W.	L.	Pct.		W.	L.	Pct.
Detroit	88	61	.591	Boston	71	77	.480
Cleveland	88	62	.587	Philadelphia	66	81	.449
CHICAGO	85	63	.574	Washington	62	83	.428
St. Louis	82	66	.554	New York	49	98	.333

BY I. E. SANBORN.

Cleveland, O., Oct. 2.—[Special.]—Chicago's White Sox went down to defeat today in what undoubtedly was the greatest and most sensational battle of pitchers in modern baseball. Between them Addie Joss and Eddie Walsh tied one world's record and broke one season's record and one catcher's finger. Cleveland's star hurler won out, 1 to 0, while Chicago's king of pitchers lost on a cross between a passed ball and a wild pitch which will become almost as famous in history as Chesbro's 1904 wild pitch.

Joss of Juneau won the right to write his chop suey name on the same line of the same page with that of the veteran "Cy" Young by duplicating against Jones' men today the Ohio farmer's feat performed against Philadelphia a couple or three years ago. That feat was the pitching of an absolutely perfect game, without run, without hit, and without letting an opponent reach first base by hook or crook, on hit, walk, or error, in nine innings.

Walsh Strikes Out Fifteen.

Walsh, although beaten, pitched an even better and more remarkable game, for he struck out fifteen of the Clevelands' heavy hitters and did it in eight innings, thereby wiping into the discard "Rube" Waddell's trick of fanning seventeen men in ten innings. But in performing this feat Walsh broke a finger on Schreck's throwing hand near the finish of the battle and this heavy handicap, added to that of the loss of the game, makes the White Sox's chances to cut up the receipts of the next world's series thinner than the watery mustard which is served with the jumbo pretzels at Philadelphia Athletic park. And that, a distinguished co-worker can testify, is some thin.

Walsh, according to the testimony of his enemy, never showed such terrific speed nor such startling and crazy shoots as he possessed today. Ossie Schreck, who for years has been handling freak curves, was fooled twice by Eddie's phenomenal spit ball. The first time it cost the White Sox the game and the second time it cost Chicago a catcher and Schreck the use of his throwing hand until the ruptured tendons of his forefinger are welded together again. Schreck himself said he never in his life saw anything break the way Walsh's spit ball did. Considering the fact that it broke one of Ossie's fingers off so cleanly that only the skin kept it from falling off, that spit ball certainly did some record breaking.

SCORE OF SOX-NAPS GAME.

CHICAGO.	AB	R	BH	TB	BB	SH	SB	PO	A	E
Hahn, rf	3	0	0	0	0	0	1	0	0	
Jones, cf	3	0	0	0	0	0	0	0	0	
Isbell, 1b	3	0	0	0	0	0	0	1	1	
Dougherty, lf	3	0	0	0	0	0	0	0	0	
Davis, 2b	3	0	0	0	0	0	0	0	0	
Parent, ss	3	0	0	0	0	0	1	3	0	
Schreck, c	2	0	0	0	0	0	13	0	0	
Shaw, c	0	0	0	0	0	0	3	0	0	
*White	1	0	0	0	0	0	0	0	0	
Tannehill, 3b	2	0	0	0	0	0	0	0	0	
**Donohue	1	0	0	0	0	0	0	0	0	
Walsh, p	2	0	0	0	0	0	1	3	0	
***Anderson	1	0	0	0	0	0	0	0	0	
Totals	27	0	0	0	0	0	24	7	1	

CLEVELAND.	AB	R	BH	TB	BB	SH	SB	PO	A	E
Goode, rf	4	0	0	0	0	0	1	0	0	
Bradley, 3b	4	0	0	0	0	0	0	0	0	
Hinchman, lf	3	0	0	0	0	0	3	0	0	
Lajoie, 2b	3	0	1	1	0	0	1	3	0	
Stovall, 1b	3	0	0	0	0	0	16	0	0	
Clarke, c	3	0	0	0	0	0	4	1	0	
Birmingham, cf	3	1	2	2	0	0	2	0	0	
Perring, ss	3	0	1	1	1	0	0	1	1	0
Joss, p	3	0	0	0	0	0	0	5	0	
Totals	28	1	4	4	1	0	1	27	16	0

*Batted for Shaw in ninth. **Batted for Tannehill in ninth. ***Batted for Walsh in ninth.

CHICAGO	0	0	0	0	0	0	0	0	0	0—0
CLEVELAND	0	0	1	0	0	0	0	0	*	—1

Struck out—By Walsh, Goode (4), Lajoie (2), Clarke (2), Joss (3), Bradley, Hinchman, Birmingham; by Joss, Dougherty, Jones, Donohue. Passed balls—Schreck (2). Time of game—1:32. Umpires—Connolly and O'Loughlin.

MAGNATES AT 'TRIBUNE' GAME A SIDE LIGHT ON THE SHOW.

Johnson and Comiskey at the Electrical Display of Ball Playing in Orchestra Hall.

BY HARVEY T. WOODRUFF.

While the exultant Cub admirers were cheering the efforts of the champions as they viewed THE TRIBUNE scoreboard reproduction of the Cincinnati game at Orchestra hall yesterday afternoon; while the Sox partisans, massed in the south section of the building, were applauding the brilliant work of Walsh, there was one box near the center of the house in which scarcely a dozen sentences were spoken during the entire hour and one-half of that 1 to 0 victory for the Naps at Cleveland.

In the shadows of that box, where no admirers could detect him and demand a speech, sat "Old Roman" Comiskey, President Ban Johnson, and half a dozen friends. In adjoining boxes the board of trade contingent was pulling and cheering for the two local teams. In the Comiskey party all eyes were intent on the little lights of the scoreboard, which showed in perfect detail every move in the great pitchers' duel at Naptown. There was no conversation; it was silent, tense excitement.

Now and then "Commy" himself ventured a remark, more to himself than to his friends. As the strikeout total of Walsh was mounting rapidly in the sixth inning he said: "Walsh is pitching a great game. Bu' we can't get a man to first. We can hardly hit out of the infield."

After the eighth inning, when the announcement was made that Shreck had broken his finger, Billy Sullivan, his own split thumb not yet well, sought out his chief and said: "Shall I go to Cleveland tonight?"

"Wait," Comiskey said. "We're not beaten yet; we've three more men to get put out." And again in the ninth, when Jones put in White as the first of the three substitute batsmen in a desperate attempt to turn the tide, Commy mused: "Just the proper man in that pinch."

Then Donohue struck out, and Anderson, batting for Walsh, was retired at first, and the game was over.

Not a word of sympathy from any one in the party was offered Comiskey, who sat a full minute in abstracted silence. The disappointment was too deep. Then Comiskey roused himself. "That game must have broken Walsh's heart. If I were a betting man, I'd have bet anything he would win."

"PHONY" FINISH TO GAME

Mixup at Detroit in a Game with the St. Louis Team.

TIGERS GET BETTER OF IT.

In Losing the Decision Browns Lose Combat by Score of 7-6.

Detroit, Mich., Oct. 2.—[Special.]—There was a "phony" finish to today's game with St. Louis. After Bush had scored on his hit and Crawford's double, Rossman hit down third base foul line so close that the spectators did not even cheer. But the umpire said "Fair," and Cobb and Rossman kept running. Stone got his hands on the ball but it was deflected into the crowd. Cobb turned third and started for home, but stopped, while the players of both teams swarmed around Sheridan. Jennings almost carried Cobb to the plate and set his feet upon it.

Finally the umpires sustained Detroit's contention that as ground rules covered only the right field crowd, which was roped off, left field being clear and the runners being entitled to take as many bases as they could, a ball hit fair in that territory and deflected into the crowd in foul territory was a hit for as many bases as the runner could take before the fielder retrieved it. It goes for a three bagger, as Cobb's tally from third finished the game with no necessity for Rossman going further. Score:

Detroit.	R	H	P	A	E	St. Louis.	R	H	P	A	E
McIntyre, lf	1	2	3	0	0	Stone, lf	1	1	1	0	1
Bush, ss	2	1	0	3	0	T. Jones, 1b	0	3	10	2	0
Crawf'rd, cf	1	2	3	0	1	Hartzell, rf	0	1	1	0	0
Cobb, rf	2	1	3	0	0	Hoffman, cf	1	1	4	1	0
Rossman, 1b	0	2	11	0	0	Ferriss, 3b	1	1	2	3	0
Schaefer, 3b	0	1	1	1	0	Will'ms, 2b	1	3	2	1	0
Schmidt, c	0	1	4	0	0	Wallace, ss	1	4	1	5	0
Downs, 2b	0	0	2	4	3	Smith, c	0	0	1	0	2
Summers, p	0	0	0	3	0	Spencer, c	1	1	1	2	1
Mullin, p	0	0	0	1	0	Waddell, p	0	0	0	1	0
*D. Jones	1	0	0	0	0	Howell, p	0	0	2	2	1
Totals	7	10	27	12	4	Totals	6	15	25	17	5

*Batted for Summers in seventh.

Detroit	3	0	0	0	0	2	0	2		—7
St. Louis	0	0	0	0	3	1	1	0		—6

Two base hits—Crawford [2], Cobb, Rossman. Hits—Off Summers, 12 in 7 innings; off Waddell, 2 in 1 inning. Sacrifice hits—Crawford, Downs, T. Jones, Smith. Double plays—Bush-Downs-Rossman; Hoffman-Smith-Ferriss. Stolen bases—McIntyre [3], Cobb [3], Rossman, Schaefer, T. Jones. Bases on balls—Off Summers, 2; off Howell, 2. Hit by pitcher—By Howell, 3. Struck out—By Summers, 2; by Mullin, 1; by Howell, 2. Passed ball—Spencer. Time—2:00. Umpires—Sheridan and Egan.

SENATORS GET NINETEEN HITS.

New York Pitchers Are Hammered All Over the Lot and Washington Wins the Game, 12 to 2.

TIGERS WIN FLAG BY CRUSHING SOX

Greatest of American League Pennant Races Ends with 7 to 0 Score.

THREE BLOWS ARE FATAL

Single, Double, and Triple in the First Spell Wreck of Local Hopes.

Standing of the Clubs.

	W.	L.	Pct.		W.	L.	Pct.
Detroit	90	63	.588	Boston	74	78	.487
Cleveland	90	64	.584	Philadelphia	67	84	.444
CHICAGO	88	64	.579	Washington	64	85	.429
St. Louis	83	69	.547	New York	51	100	.338

BY I. E. SANBORN.

No more pitiable, heart rending spectacle ever was, or can be, imagined than that presented by Chicago's White Stockings yesterday, when on the last day of the greatest American league pennant race, with the championship almost in their grasp, Comiskey's men went down in quick defeat before the greatest week day crowd in the south side park's history, surrendering by the crushing score of 7 to 0 the crucial game and the pennant to Detroit.

Three fierce, resounding, death dealing blows from the bats of the Tigers wrenched from the grip of the White Sox the flag for which they had fought so gamely, coming back time and again after they had been counted down and out, and made the pride of Michigan (but not of the American league) two times champions. Those three blows landed on as many curves from the south hand of Doc White in the first inning, and in the short space of five minutes turned an occasion of joyous anticipation to one of blankest, deepest disappointment.

Reprinted with courtesy of
The Chicago Tribune

BASE BALL BABY.

Born at Chicago Park During the Deciding Game With Pittsburg.

Chicago, Ill., October 10.—Just as pitcher Mordecai Brown swatted the ball bringing Joe Tinker in in the last half of the sixth inning, killing the immediate possibility of a tie game between Chicago and Pittsburg at Chicago Sunday, and as the host in the grand stand rose to cheer, a baby was born far up on the stand, in the midst of the dense crowd. There is considerable mystery attached to the birth of the "base ball baby." The mother fell forward in her seat and the crowd, thinking she had fainted, fell back to give her air. To a woman who raised her head she told of the happening and immediately mother and child were carried to the clubhouse, where medical attention was summoned. Then an ambulance was summoned and both were taken away. The woman refused to give her name, and the West Side hospitals denied that any such case had been brought to their attention.

NATIONAL LEAGUE.

Manager Chance and the Cubs will leave on a fast train this afternoon for New York, there to play off at the Polo grounds tomorrow the tie game of Sept. 23 as ordered by the National league board of directors.

The winner of Thursday's game will become champions of the National league providing the Giants again beat Boston today.

Should rain prevent today's New York-Boston game, the winner of Thursday's game still will be National league champions.

Should New York lose today and win on Thursday Chicago, New York, and Pittsburg would be tied for first place.

Should New York lose today and Thursday Chicago would be undisputed champions.

CUBS CHAMPIONS; BEAT GIANTS IN FINAL GAME, 4-2

Third Successive Pennant Is Wrested from Confident Enemy Before Openly Hostile Crowd.

BROWN SAVES THE GAME.

Three Fingered Hero Called to Pfiester's Rescue in First Inning; Chance Assaulted by Rowdy Fan.

BY I. E. SANBORN.

New York, Oct. 8.—[Special.]—No more glorious victory ever was won on a baseball diamond than that which Chicago's world's champions achieved on the Polo grounds today when they made themselves three times champions of the National league and put themselves in line for another world's pennant by defeating New York's Giants 4 to 2 under the heaviest handicaps ever imposed on a championship contender.

It was the second time within the week that Chance's warriors have been compelled by the exigencies of a sensational season to stake their all on the issue of a single game. Twice within the space of five days they were called upon to fight in their last trenches for their third pennant. Yet the size of the stakes and the desperate situation in which they found themselves only nerved them to greater effort.

Reprinted with courtesy of
The Chicago Tribune

THUG'S VICTIM?

TRAGIC FATE OF "CHICK" STAHL'S WIDOW.

The Woman Found Dead Under Most Mysterious Circumstances and With Her Costly Jewelry Missing—The Coroner's Verdict

SPECIAL TO "SPORTING LIFE."

Charles Stahl

Boston, Mass., November 16.—Mrs. Julia Stahl, the widow of "Chick" Stahl, the famous Boston ball player, who committed suicide in Indiana while on a training trip in the spring of 1907, was found dead in the doorway of a tenement house at 7 Ellery Terrace, South Boston, early to-day. Mrs. Stahl was fully and richly dressed. It is believed she was murdered for her jewelry. The neighborhood of Ellery Terrace is one of the poorest in town, and Mrs. Stahl, with her expensive clothes, attracted a great deal of attention when she appeared there last evening. It is said that when Mrs. Stahl left her home last evening she wore jewelry valued at $2,000, all of which, with the exception of a gold-mounted comb and a wedding ring, was missing from the body when found. In seeking to account for the loss of Mrs. Stahl's jewelry and her presence in the neighborhood in which her body was found the police sought a man who was seen to cross Andrews Square, South Boston, with Mrs. Stahl just before she entered the hall in which she died. This man is believed to have helped her into the doorway, but was not seen to leave the house. Up to the time that relatives of Mrs. Stahl noticed the absence of jewelry to-day, the police had believed the case to be one of heart disease, but with the advent of robbery as a possible motive the case appeared to be one of murder. Marks were found on the woman's throat, but it is not thought these had to do with her death. The body was identified by her father, Mr. Harmon. After completing an autopsy, Medical Examiner McGrath announced that death was due to natural causes, "probably exhaustion brought on by the use of drugs and alcohol." The police stated that they were convinced that Mrs. Stahl lately had worn very little jewelry besides the wedding ring which was found on her finger.

The Present and Future Players of World's Championship Teams Are to Be Given Gold Diamond-Studded Medals Size of a Nickel.

SPECIAL TO "SPORTING LIFE."

Frank Chance

Cincinnati, November 23.—The design for the emblems to reward the Chicago Cubs for their victory over the recent World's Championship Series has been received by the National Commission, and two of the members of this body—Garry Herrmann and Harry Pulliam—like it and have recommended its adoption. The new emblem, which replaces the ornate and bizarre scarf-pins the Chicagoans would have received if Johnson and Pulliam had not entered strenuous objections, is in the form of a solid gold piece and is about the size of a nickel.

THE HALF MILLION DOLLAR BALL PARK OF THE ATHLETICS
(PHILADELPHIA AMERICAN LEAGUE CLUB)

Opened Monday. April 12, for the Season of 1909. Seating capacity, 23,000—with standing room 40,000 can witness the game. Size 455 x 520 feet, making a total of 252,200 square feet—a greater area than contained in any other ball park in the country.

THE GREATEST BASE BALL GROUNDS IN THE WORLD

ANSON'S ATTITUDE.

The "Grand Old Man" Will Not Accept Charity, Though Broke.

Special to "Sporting Life."

Chicago, Ill., February 1.—Adrian C. Anson, who was manager and first baseman of the old Chicago White Stockings in the '80s, when that team created as much terror in National League ranks as the Cubs do to-day, has declined to be the recipient of a public benefit. The dignity of Anson's refusal is more weighty when the fact that "Anse" is "busted," according to his own statement, made in the debtor's court recently. But the old-timer does not expect always to be in such an annoying predicament, and he adheres to the refusal made by him over ten years ago, when he declined a similar proposition at the time he retired from the management of the West Side club.

GETS HIS LICENSE.

Infielder Abbaticchio, of the Pirates, Is Happy Once More.

Latrobe. Pa., April 3.—The Westmoreland County Court, in handing down the annual license list, granted a license to Edward Abbattichio, second baseman of the Pittsburg base ball team, to sell liquor at the Latrobe House. Arcangelo Abbaticchio, father of the ball player, runs the hotel in the son's absence. The high license law in Pennsylvania, as interpreted by the courts in the Western end of the State, puts many restrictions on saloonkeepers, and they must make applications each year for a license, and the court has full power to grant or refuse an applicant.

"FORBES FIELD"

The Title Selected by Dreyfuss for His New Park in Pittsburg.

Special to "Sporting Life."

Pittsburg, Pa., April 20.—"Forbes Field" is the name of the new million-dollar ball park being created by Barney Dreyfuss in the centre of Pittsburg and which will be ready for occupancy about July 1. The name has just been announced by Mr. Dreyfuss, who was fairly swamped by suggestions, getting 100,000 in all and by mail. Some time ago Dreyfuss promised that he would permit the people of Pittsburg to select the name for the new park. The time limit was last night and it was very late when the owner of the Pittsburg Ball Club finally announced Forbes Field as his choice. It is so named in honor of the famous English General, John Forbes, who had a big part in the founding of Pittsburg.

BROOKLYN AT NEW YORK APRIL 15.—A crowd estimated at 30,000 witnessed the opening game and watched the home team go down to defeat by a score of 3 to 0 after 13 innings of marvelous ball. Ames did not allow a hit in the first nine innings, only 27 men facing him in this time. In the extra periods the Brooklyns got to him strongly, making four hits in the last round. Manager Lumley started his team on the road to victory in the thirteenth inning by tripling. Jordan was purposely passed in the hope that a double play could be pulled off on Lennox, who, however, singled, scoring Lumley. Two more runs were tallied on hits by Bergen and Burch and Sohlei's error. A great throw to the plate by Sebring in the eighth inning prevented New York from winning in that round. Wilhelm held the New Yorks to three singles, the first of which was made in the eighth inning. Second baseman Doyle, of New York, was not allowed to play by Manager McGraw as he had not yet signed his contract. Richard Croker, in the absence of Mayor McClellan, threw out the ball from an upper box in the grand stand when Umpire Johnstone called play. Score:

Brooklyn	AB.R.B. P.A.E	New York	AB.R.B. P.A.E
Burch, lf	6 0 1 5 0 0	Herzog, 3b	5 0 0 1 3 0
Alperman, 2b	6 0 1 3 1 0	Fletcher, 2b	5 0 0 1 0 1
Hummel, cf	6 0 1 2 0 0	McCormick, lf	5 0 0 1 0 0
Sebring, rf	5 0 0 1 1 0	Murray, rf	5 0 0 2 0 0
Lumley, rf	5 1 1 1 0 0	Tenney, 1b	5 0 0 24 1 1
Jordan, 1b	4 1 1 19 0 0	O'Hara, cf	3 0 0 0 0 0
Lennox, 3b	4 1 1 1 2 1	Devlin, 3b	3 0 0 3 2 0
Bergen, c	5 0 1 12 2 0	Bridwell, ss	4 0 0 3 6 0
Wilhelm, p	5 0 0 4 6 0	Schlei, c	4 0 1 10 1 1
		Ames, p	4 0 0 1 1 0
Totals	45 3 7 29 22 1	†J. Myers	1 0 0 0 0 0
		Totals	40 0 3 30 20 3

*Batted for Fletcher in thirteenth inning.
†Batted for Ames in thirteenth inning.

Brooklyn .... 0 0 0 0 0 0 0 0 0 0 0 0 3—3
New York .... 0 0 0 0 0 0 0 0 0 0 0 0 0—0

Two-base hits—Alperman 2, Jordan. Three-base hit—Lumley. Stolen bases—O'Hara, Burch. Left on bases—Brooklyn 5, New York 9. First on errors—Brooklyn 1, New York 1. Double play—Fletcher, Bridwell, Tenney. Struck out—By Ames 10, Wilhelm 4. First on balls—Off Wilhelm 7, Ames 3. Time—1.30. Umpires—Johnstone and Cusack. Attendance—30,000.

CAN'T LOSE BROWNS.

A Priest Loves Them So Much That He Refuses Transfer.

St. Louis, May 20.—Transferred by Archbishop Glennon to the Catholic Church at Byrnesville, Mo., a hamlet of 150 souls, 12 miles from a railroad station, the Rev. Father John A. Tracey, aged 58 years, pastor of the Church of Our Lady of Good Counsel, an enthusiastic base ball fan, defiantly announced to-day that he will remain in St. Louis and continue to root for the Browns. Said he: "They said I am a base ball fan. Well, I guess I am. I narrowly escaped being a professional base ball player myself. In 1869, '70 and '71 I played ball on the team of St. Vincent's College, of Wheeling, W. Va., and might have gone with the Cincinnati Reds. Harry Wright wanted me to sign to play left field. If this means retirement for me, I have a beautiful home waiting for me in Clarksburg, W. Va."

CHASE RETURNS

THE HIGHLANDERS' STAR RE-JOINS HIS TEAM.

The Great First Baseman in Good Condition After His Distressing Experience and Long Confinement in a Southern Pest House.

SPECIAL TO "SPORTING LIFE."

Augusta, Ga., April 26.—Hal Chase, who has been in the pesthouse here suffering from smallpox, is well and left the hospital Saturday, starting immediately for New York. Before leaving he said that he would get back into the game as soon as he could. Chase declared that he was in the finest trim, that he never felt better, and that he would be fit in a very short time after he gets back with the New York team. Chase suffered no ill effects from his illness except that a number of red splotches are showing themselves on his body. He declared that he had been royally treated in the hospital and that, all things considered, he survived his trouble most luckily. His wife, who has been in Augusta since he was put in the hospital, went to New York with him. During his detention in the hospital Chase amused himself daily in watching the ball games of the South Atlantic League clubs. The park is not far from the hospital and the play can be seen from the roof of the building. At night he entertained himself by getting the base ball scores from the newspaper offices.

Harold Chase

HANDCUFF GAMBLERS.

That's How Bettors at Boston Will Be Treated Hereafter.

Special to "Sporting Life."

Boston, Mass., May 17.—The local police department, backed by President George Dovey, of the Doves, and the entire National League, has commenced a crusade against betting at the base ball games, which gives promise of ending this menace to the National sport. President Dovey said recently: "Base ball has always been the cleanest of professional sports and we are going to keep it so. Since the organization of the National League the breath of scandal touched the game but once, and it is well known that that did not affect the integrity of the players or the management of the clubs. In every city there are a lot of gamblers, and I regret to say that since the ban has been put on open betting on the horse races, this element has turned its attention to base ball. It is not a pleasant sight to see a man with nippers on his wrists being led out of the bleachers or grand stand during a game, but this appears to be the only way to stop gambling, and that is what we propose to do."

BOSTON AT CLEVELAND JULY 19 (P. M. and P. M.)—Cleveland won the first game easily. Ball's playing was a decided feature. He made an unassisted triple play in the second inning, and when he came to bat in the same inning he hit for a home run to deep centre. In the second game both Boston started a hit-and-run play. Ball caught McConnell's liner, touched second, putting Wagner out, and then touched out Stahl, who was running toward him and had no chance to return to first base.

Cleveland	AB.R.B. P.A.E	Boston	AB.R.B. P.A.E
Flick, rf	3 1 1 0 0 0	Niles, lf	4 0 0 1 0 0
Stovall, 1b	4 1 1 11 1 0	Lord, 3b	4 0 1 1 2 0
Easterly, c	4 1 1 4 1 0	Speaker, cf	4 0 0 2 0 0
Hinch'n, lf	3 1 2 3 0 0	Gessler, rf	4 0 0 2 0 0
Perring, 3b	3 0 0 1 3 0	Wagner, ss	4 0 1 2 2 0
Birmi'm, cf	3 0 1 2 0 0	Stahl, 1b	4 0 1 9 0 0
Bradley, 3b	4 1 1 1 2 0	McConnell, 2b	4 1 1 4 2 0
Ball, ss	4 1 3 2 4 0	Donahue, c	3 0 0 4 2 0
Young, p	3 0 0 0 2 0	Check, p	2 0 0 0 1 0
		Collins, p	1 0 0 0 0 0
		*Wolter	1 0 0 0 0 0
Totals	32 6 10 27 13 0	†Gardner	1 0 0 0 0 0
		Totals	32 1 5 24 10 2

*Batted for Donahue in ninth inning.
†Batted for Collins in ninth inning.

Cleveland .... 1 1 2 0 0 0 2 0 x—6
Boston .... 0 0 0 0 1 0 0 0 0—1

BULLET WOUND FATAL TO PULLIAM

National League President Dies From Effects of Pistol Shot Through His Head

Worried Over Base Ball Matters and Continued Ill Health—Was Head of League Since 1902

NEW YORK, July 29.—Harry Clay Pulliam, president of the National League of Baseball Clubs, died shortly before 8 o'clock this morning from the wound of a bullet which he fired through his head with suicidal intent last night in his room at the New York Athletic Club. Broken in health from overwork in his long flight to maintain a high standard of baseball, Pulliam, in a moment of mental aberration, his friends say, shot himself.

Pulliam went to his room early last night, and lying on a sofa, fired a bullet into his head. The ball entered the right temple, fracturing the frontal bone, tore out the right eye and passed out at the left temple. He was found lying near the telephone by a club servant who was sent to find out who was trying a telephone connection.

"I think he struggled on the floor for two hours," said Dr. T. Hamilton Burch, "and that he was so overcome with the intense pain that he tried to get to the telephone to send for me. He probably got the receiver off the hook and then lost his strength entirely."

Reprinted from
The Philadelphia Inquirer

HIT-AND-RUN

Is the Play That Has Lowered the Individual Batting.

The Washington "Post's" able critic, J. Ed Grillo, is herewith quoted on batting decline. Says he: "How many times during a season do you see the hit-and-run play successfully pulled off, though there is not a game that it is not tried anywhere from five to twenty times? More poor base ball results from this feature of the game than all the misplays that can be crowded into a season's campaign. Good hitters are forced to hit at wild pitches and made to look foolish or base runners are thrown out ten feet by the catcher because the base runner on the hit usually does not take the lead he would if it were a straight steal. Much of the deterioration in batting can be directly attributed to the inauguration of the hit-and-run feature. So long as one or two teams were playing it and the opposing batteries were not trying to outguess the batter and base runner it gave these teams an advantage, but now that every team plays it more or less, it is really a detriment to the game, for it not only cuts down the batting, but it has virtually robbed the game of one of its most attractive features, base running."

PISTOLS BARRED.

Chicago Judge Refuses to Sanction Umpire's Act Against Fans.

Chicago, August 9.—A base ball umpire has no legal right to draw a revolver for protection, even if he sees forty or more infuriated fans rolling up their sleeves and rushing towards him. This, in effect, was the decision of Municipal Judge Goodnow at the Englewood Court when he fined R. L. O'Keefe, 19 years old, an umpire of the Chicago Amateur League, the costs of Court on a charge of disorderly conduct.

WORLD'S CHAMPION IS PITTSBURG TEAM; DETROIT SHUT OUT

Adams Allows Tigers Only Six Hits in Seventh Game of Series.

LION'S SHARE OF CREDIT IS DUE TO HIS PITCHING

By Score of 8 to 0 Pirates Take Deciding Contest.

TOTAL RECEIPTS, $188,302.50

Third Successive Defeat of American League and Detroit for Pennant.

Reprinted from
The Washington Evening Star

DETROIT, Mich., October 16.—Pittsburg has won the world's base ball championship, defeating Detroit today by the overwhelming score of 8 to 0 in the seventh and decisive game of one of the greatest battles ever fought for the world's title.

This gives the National League champions the victory by the count of four games to three.

This is the third successive defeat of the American League champions in the world's series, and consequently the third straight victory for the National League. The Chicago team defeated Detroit in 1907 and 1908.

Credit Largely Due Adams.

To Charles Adams, the phenomenal young pitcher from the Louisville American Association team, belongs the lion's share of credit. His wonderful pitching has crowded Wagner, Leach, Clarke and the other Pittsburg stars into the background.

Today's victory was his third of the series. He held Detroit safely throughout the entire game.

He allowed but six hits. In only one inning—the fourth—did Detroit get more than one safety.

Adams allowed only one base on balls. In four innings he retired the hard-hitting American Leaguers in one, two, three order.

The crowd today was a distinct disappointment. There were only 17,562 paid admissions.

WASHINGTON AT CHICAGO AUGUST 29 (F. M. and P. M.).—In the first game Gray performed the peculiar feat of holding the White Sox to one hit, but allowed them to score six runs without an error by his support. In the second inning he gave eight bases on balls, and seven of these came in succession, forcing in five runs. The only hit was a high bounder over Unglaub's head, with which Dougherty opened the second. Score:

Chicago.	AB.	R.	B.	P.	A.	E.	Washing'n.	AB.	R.	B.	P.	A.	E.
Altizer, rf.	2	1	0	2	0	0	Browne, rf.	5	0	1	1	0	0
Parent, ss.	3	0	1	2	3	0	Schaefer, 2b	5	0	2	0	3	0
Cole, cf.	3	0	0	2	0	0	Unglaub, 1b	4	0	0	15	0	0
Dougherty, lf	3	1	1	1	0	0	Lelivelt, cf.	3	1	3	4	0	0
Isbell, 1b.	3	0	0	13	0	1	Milan, lf.	3	1	0	0	0	0
Tannehill, 3b	3	1	0	2	4	0	Killifer, 3b.	3	0	0	1	2	0
Atz, 2b.	3	1	2	5	6	0	McBride, ss	4	1	1	1	3	0
Owens, c.	3	1	0	4	0	0	Street, c.	4	1	1	1	1	0
Scott, p.	1	1	0	0	2	0	Gray, p.	2	0	0	0	2	0
							*Slattery	1	0	0	0	0	0
Totals	23	6	1	27	15	2	Totals	35	4	9	24	14	0

*Batted for Gray in the ninth inning.

Chicago	0	0	0	6	0	0	0	0	0	—6
Washington	0	2	0	0	0	0	0	0	2	—4

LAJOIE IS DONE

WITH MANAGING CLEVELAND'S LUCKLESS TEAM.

After Five Years of Vain Efforts to Land the American League Pennant the Great Star Gives Up the Thankless Job.

THE PIRATES CLEARED THE DECK.

The Head of the Nation, President W. H. Taft, Tossed Out the Ball That Started the Initial Game, the First Instance of the Kind.

SPECIAL TO "SPORTING LIFE."

Washington, D. C., April 18.—On Thursday, April 14, opening day of the American League championship race, the season was formally inaugurated under the auspices of the Administration. President Taft, Vice-President Sherman and everybody else in Administration and Congressional circles who possibly could get to the ball grounds was there, including Charley Bennett, Secretary of the Senate, who will remember it for a long time because of the terrific crack which a foul tip gave his head. Just before play was started, Umpire "Billy" Evans made his way to the Taft box, in the right wing of the grandstand, and presented the President with a new ball. The President took the sphere in his gloved hand as though he were at a loss what to do with it until Evans told him he was expected to

Thos. C. Noyes

THROW IT OVER THE PLATE

when he gave the signal. He handed the ball to Mrs. Taft, who weighed it carefully in her hand, while the President was doffing his bright, new kid gloves in preparation for his debut as a base ball pitcher. President Taft then formally opened the game and the season, by throwing out the ball. He made a good throw of it, too, and Walter Johnson, the Washington Club's star pitcher, caught it. Then Johnson tossed the ball to Charles Street, the catcher, and Street promptly stowed it away among

THE SACRED RELICS.

Washington has never seen such a base ball crowd as greeted the President when he entered the grounds. With the President were Mrs. Taft, her sister, Mrs. More, and Mrs. Eckstein, of Cincinnati, who is a guest at the White House. The immense crowd, numbering well over 12,000, jumped to their feet as they made out the President, and gave him a thundering round of cheers. Soon after the President and his party were seated, Mr. Noyes, president of the Washington Club, took McAleer and Mack, the managers of the two teams, up to the presidential box and introduced them to Mr. Taft. The President is a good "rooter" and cheered the home team whenever it made a good play. He saw the last man put out in the ninth inning before he made a move to leave his box.

A VALUED AUTOGRAPH.

On Friday pitcher Johnson sent the ball tossed out to him by the President at the start of the opening game of the season to the White House with a plea that the President place his autograph upon it. The President wrote:

For Walter Johnson, with the hope that he may continue to be as formidable as in yesterday's game.
WILLIAM H. TAFT.

After succeeding, with difficulty, in penning these lines on the ball the President dispatched a White House messenger to the base ball park, where Johnson proudly displayed his treasure to his fellow-players and the members of the visiting Athletic team.

DETROIT AT CLEVELAND APRIL 21.—Cleveland's new park was dedicated in the presence of an enormous crowd. Prior to the start of the game the Cleveland and Detroit players, the owners of the Cleveland Club, August Herrmann, chairman of the National Commission, and Ban B. Johnson, president of the American League, paraded to centre field, where the club flag was raised. Johnson then pitched the first ball, it being muffed by Herrmann. Presidents of the Detroit, Washington and Philadelphia Clubs were present. The dedication was not auspicious for Cleveland from a base ball standpoint, as Detroit won, 5 to 0. Cleveland could do but little with Willett, while Detroit bunched hits off Young in the third and seventh innings. Score:

Detroit.	AB.	R.	B.	P.	A.	E.	Cleveland.	AB.	R.	B.	P.	A.	E.
McIntyre, lf	4	0	1	4	0	0	Krueger, lf.	3	0	0	2	0	0
Bush, ss..	4	0	0	0	6	0	Bradley, 3b	4	0	1	2	1	0
Cobb, rf...	4	0	0	3	0	0	Turner, 2b.	4	0	0	2	3	1
Crawford,cf	4	1	2	0	0	0	Lajoie, 1b..	4	0	1	9	0	0
Deleha'y,2b	4	1	1	2	1	0	Lord, rf...	4	0	0	1	0	0
Moriarty,3b	3	1	0	1	4	0	Clarke, c...	3	0	2	6	1	0
T. Jones, 1b	4	0	2	17	0	0	Birmi'm, cf	3	0	0	5	0	0
Stanage, c.	3	1	1	1	2	0	Ball, ss....	3	0	0	1	1	0
Willett, p..	3	1	1	0	4	0	Young, p...	3	0	1	1	5	0
Totals..	33	5	8	27	17	0	Totals..	31	0	5	27	11	1

Detroit	0	0	2	0	0	0	3	0	0	—5
Cleveland	0	0	0	0	0	0	0	0	0	—0

Two-base hits—Stanage, McIntyre, Clarke, Young. Sacrifice hit—Stanage. Stolen base—Crawford. First on balls—Off Young 2, Willett 2. Hit by pitcher—By Willett 1. Struck out—By Young 6. Wild pitch—Young. First on error—Detroit. Left on bases—Cleveland 7, Detroit 4. Time—1.31. Umpires—Sheridan and Kerin. Attendance—18,832.

ST. LOUIS AT CHICAGO JULY 1.—This was the opening game at the new White Sox Park. An enormous crowd saw the game. Many base ball celebrities helped open the park with appropriate ceremonies. Pelty pitched an effective game, while Walsh was not as effective. Sullivan caught his first game of the season for Chicago. He had been out of the game with an injured foot since the training trip. Score:

St. Louis.	AB.	R.	B.	P.	A.	E.	Chicago.	AB.	R.	B.	P.	A.	E.
Stone, lf..	4	1	3	0	0	0	Zeider, 3b.	1	0	0	0	1	0
Hartzell, 3b	3	0	0	2	3	0	French, 2b.	3	0	0	1	0	0
Wallace, ss	4	0	1	2	2	0	Browne, cf.	4	0	1	3	0	0
Newnam, 1b	3	0	1	11	0	1	Collins, rf.	2	0	0	2	1	0
Schweit'r, cf	3	0	1	0	0	0	Block, c...	1	0	0	1	1	0
Hoffman,rf	3	0	0	1	0	0	Dougher'y, lf	4	0	1	1	0	0
Truesd'e,2b	3	1	1	5	3	0	Gandil, 1b.	4	0	0	5	1	0
Killifer, c.	3	0	0	6	4	1	Purtell, 3b	4	0	0	2	1	0
Pelty, p...	3	0	0	0	5	0	Blackb'n, ss	3	0	2	2	2	0
							Sullivan, c.	4	0	0	8	3	1
Totals..	30	2	7	27	17	2	Payne, rf..	1	0	0	0	0	0
							Walsh, p..	3	0	1	2	4	0
							Totals...	31	0	5	27	14	1

St. Louis	0	0	2	0	0	0	0	0	0	—2
Chicago	0	0	0	0	0	0	0	0	0	—0

Two-base hit—Stone. Three-base hits—Dougherty, Stone. Sacrifice hit—Hartzell. Stolen bases—Collins, Truesdale, Stone 2, Hartzell, French. Double play—Zeider, Sullivan, Purtell, Blackburn. Left on bases—Chicago 6, St. Louis 1. First on balls—Off Walsh 1, Pelty 2. Struck out—By Walsh 6, Pelty 4. Time—1.36. Umpires—Connolly and Dinneen. Attendance—30,000.

WASHINGTON AT CHICAGO SEPTEMBER 28.—Walter Johnson, Washington's crack pitcher, made a new world's strike-out record for a season and helped the Senators defeat the White Sox. Johnson struck out 10 men, making his total 307 for the year. The former record was 301, made by "Rube" Waddell in 1903. Score:

Chicago.	AB.	R.	B.	P.	A.	E.	Washin'n.	AB.	R.	B.	P.	A.	E.
McCon'l, 2b	3	0	0	1	1	0	Milan, cf..	5	2	1	0	0	1
Lord, 3b..	3	0	0	2	5	0	Elberfeld,3b	5	1	2	0	0	0
Meloan, rf	4	0	0	2	0	0	Cunnin'm,2b	5	1	3	0	6	0
Doughe'y,lf	3	0	0	1	0	0	Somerlot, 1b	5	0	1	15	0	0
Chouin'd,cf	4	0	0	1	1	0	Schaefer, rf	4	0	4	0	0	0
Blackb'e,ss	4	0	0	2	0	0	McBride, ss	4	0	0	3	5	1
Mullen, 1b.	3	0	1	11	1	0	Ralston, lf.	4	0	0	0	0	0
Payne, c..	3	0	1	5	1	0	Ainsmith, c	4	0	1	9	1	0
White, p..	3	1	1	2	8	0	Johnson, p.	4	1	2	0	3	1
Totals..	30	1	3	27	12	0	Totals...	40	5	14	27	15	3

Chicago	0	0	1	0	0	0	0	0	0	—1
Washington	0	0	0	0	0	1	0	1	3	—5

Two-base hits—Schaefer, Somerlot, Cunningham, Johnson. Three-base hit—White. Stolen bases—Lord, Schaefer, Dougherty. Left on bases—Chicago 7, Washington 8. First on balls—Off Johnson 3. First on error—Chicago. Struck out—By Johnson 10, White 4. Time—1.38. Umpires—O'Loughlin and Sheridan. Attendance—5000.

JUNIOR LEAGUE

PERPETUATES ITSELF FOR TWENTY MORE YEARS

And Incidentally Rewards Ban Johnson's Great Services With a 20-Year Term at $25,000 Per Annum—A 154-Game Schedule.

Aug. 30

In the second game Hughes, New York's pitcher, twirled hitless ball for nine innings. He retired the first man who faced him in the tenth, but two hits were then made off him. In the eleventh Hughes weakened and on five hits and a pass the visitors got five runs. Kaler allowed only three safeties. Scores:

Cleveland.	AB.	R.	B.	P.	A.	E.	New York.	AB.	R.	B.	P.	A.	E.
Turner, 3b.	4	1	0	0	3	0	Daniels, lf.	5	0	1	3	0	0
Thomas'n,rf	5	1	1	2	0	0	Wolter, rf.	4	0	0	2	0	0
Niles, lf...	5	1	2	2	0	0	Chase, 1b..	4	0	0	13	1	0
Lajoie, 2b..	5	1	2	3	2	0	Knight, ss.	3	0	1	1	8	0
Stovall, 1b	5	0	1	13	1	0	Laporte, 2b	3	0	0	1	2	0
Birmin'm,cf	4	0	0	4	0	0	Cree, cf...	4	0	1	3	0	0
Ball, ss...	4	0	0	2	0	0	Austin, 3b..	2	0	0	2	4	1
Land, c...	4	0	0	6	3	0	Criger, c...	4	0	0	8	0	0
Kaler, p..	4	1	1	1	5	0	Hughes, p..	3	0	0	0	2	0
							*Roach	1	0	0	0	0	0
Totals..	40	5	7	33	13	0	Totals...	33	0	3	33	17	1

*Batted for Hughes in eleventh inning.

Cleveland	0	0	0	0	0	0	0	0	0	0	5—5
New York	0	0	0	0	0	0	0	0	0	0	0—0

Sacrifice hits—Austin, Laporte. Stolen base—Lajoie. Left on bases—Cleveland 3, New York 4. First on error—Cleveland. First on balls—Off Kaler 2, Hughes 1. Struck out—By Kaler 6, Hughes 7. Umpires—Egan and O'Loughlin. Time—1.58. Attendance—12,000.

BALL AT NIGHT

ONCE MORE PROVEN ABSOLUTELY FEASIBLE.

With the Proper Plant at the New White Sox Park, Inventor Cahill Convincingly Demonstrates His Lighting Theory as Practical.

SPECIAL TO "SPORTING LIFE."

Chicago, Ill., August 28.—Base ball by night is one of the certainties of the near future. The scheme has at last been given a full and fair trial under the electric-light system evolved and patented by Mr. George Y. Cahill, of Holyoke, Mass., at Comiskey's grand new ball park, and has been found to be entirely practicable. For some time the work of installing the electric-light plant and the Cahill lamp towers has been in progress at White Sox Park. By Tuesday last the installation work was practically completed, and on the night of Wednesday, August 24, night was turned in to day at the White Sox Park, when the system received its initial test. Electricians fairly swarmed around the park, and ten powerful lights, representing almost 2,000,000 candle power, were turned on, with the result that night became as day under their powerful glare, and that, too, despite the fact that the full force of the lighting plant was not turned on, only half of the twenty lamps being in service. The lamps were operated in pairs. Ten of them were on the roof of the park, while a like number were operated from the ground.

Chas. Comiskey

A SUCCESSFUL TEST.

The lighting system received its first real try-out night of Thursday, August 25, when the Illinois Athletic Club and Calumet la crosse teams battled for over two hours in a fast match in the glare of over one million candle power of light, which constitutes a portion of the light plant that will give Chicago night base ball in the future. The plant proved itself equal to the occasion, for the test held up to what was expected. The Illinois A. C. won the game, 11 to 10, but this fact was lost to view in the interest resulting from the pronounced success of the light plant. At that the ground lights were curtailed, and only half the power was in use. At no time during the eighty minutes of play did the players find it hard to follow the ball, but the game proved as fast and as interesting as if it had been played in broad daylight. No complaint was heard from the players, and, with the roof lights uncovered, the contestants were in no way bothered by the force of these lamps.

NIGHT BASE BALL.

Night base ball, played in Chicago last night for the first time, proved a great success. Over 20,000 fans gathered at the new White Sox Park and watched the Logan Square and the Roger Park teams go through nine innings of excellent ball under the glare of twenty 137,000 candle-power arc lights which made the diamond bright as day.

CHAMPS

OFFICIAL SCORE

Second Game

Cy Young's 500th Victory

Of A Baseball Game for the Championship of the AMERICAN LEAGUE of P. B. B. C.

Played in the City of WASHINGTON on JULY 19 1910, Between

WASHINGTON B. B. C. and the CLEVELAND B. B. C.

	VISITING CLUB PLAYERS	Pos.	A.B.	Runs	Hits	T.B.	1B.	2B.	3B.	H.R.	Sac. Hits	Stolen Bases	Bases on Balls	Hit by Pitcher	Struck Out	P.O.	A.	E.	D.P.
1	NILES,	RF	4	1	0											0	0	0	
2	GRANEY	LF	2	2	2	2										4	0	0	
3	TURNER	SS	4	2	2							1				2	4	1	
4	LAJOIE	2B	5	0	2	2		1								2	4	0	
5	EASTERLY	C	3	0	0							1				5	3	0	
6	STOVALL	1B	4	0	0	2		1								16	0	0	
7	BIRMINGHAM	CF	3	0	0				1							3	0	0	
8	PERRING	3B	5	0	0											1	2	0	
9	YOUNG	P	4	0	0											0	6	1	
	TOTALS		34	5	8	8		4	1			1				33	19	2	

Passed Balls: (Name Runner & Battery Catcher)
No. Left on Bases 6
Number Out When Winning Run Scored:

a. Batted for   in   inning.   1. Batted for   in   inning.   a. Batted for   in   inning.

a. Batted for   in   inning.   1. Ran for   in   inning.   2. Ran for   in   inning.

Double Plays (Names)

Grounded Into Forced Double Plays (Names)

	HOME CLUB PLAYERS	Pos.	A.B.	Runs	Hits	T.B.	1B.	2B.	3B.	H.R.	Sac. Hits	Stolen Bases	Bases on Balls	Hit by Pitcher	Struck Out	P.O.	A.	E.	D.P.
1	MILAN	CF	3	2	1	1										3	0	0	
2	LELIVELT	LF	5	0	1	1										2	0	0	
3	CONROY	3B	5	0	1	1										1	1	0	
4	GESSLER	RF	4	0	0											3	1	0	
5	M'BRIDE	SS	4	0	0											4	2	0	
6	KILLIFER	2B	4	0	0											2	6	0	1
7	HENRY	1B	3	0	0											10	2	0	
8	UNGLAUB	1B	0	0	0											1	1	1	
9	STREET	C	1	0	0											1	1	1	
10	REISLING	P	1	0	0											0	3	1	
11	GROOM	P	1	0	0											0	2	0	
12	SCHAEFER (5)		1	0	0											0	0	0	
13	ELBERFELD (7)		1	0	0														
	TOTALS		36	2	4			1								33	19	2	1

Passed Balls: (Name Runner & Battery Catcher)
No. Left on Bases 5
Number Out When Winning Run Scored:

a. Batted for REISLING in 9th inning.   1. Batted for HENRY in 10 inning.   a. Batted for   in   inning.

a. Batted for   in   inning.   1. Ran for   in   inning.   2. Ran for   in   inning.

Double Plays (Names)

Grounded Into Forced Double Plays (Names)

Score by innings	1	2	3	4	5	6	7	8	9	10	11	12	13	14	15	16	17	18	19	Totals
Visiting Club CLEVELAND	0	0	0	0	0	0	0	0	2	0	3									5
Home Club WASHINGTON	1	0	0	0	0	0	0	1	0	0	0									

PITCHERS' SUMMARY

WON	PITCHER	CLUB	Innings Pitched	OPPONENTS									Started	Finished
				At Bat	Runs	Hits	Sacrifice Hits	Bases on Balls	Struck Out	Hit Batsmen	Wild Pitches	Balks		
✓	YOUNG	CLEVELAND	11	36	2	4		1	3			3		✓
	REISLING	WASHINGTON	9		5			2	1	3			✓	
	GROOM	WASHINGTON	2		3			2						✓

ALWAYS FILL IN COMPLETELY

NAME ALL RELIEVING PITCHERS   When Relieved   Number of Men on Base   NAME FIRST BATTER TO FACE RELIEVER   NAME ALL RELIEVING PITCHERS   When Relieved   Number of Men on Base   NAME FIRST BATTER TO FACE RELIEVER

Weather Conditions: Ground Conditions: Time   Official Scorer

Umpires: McKEANE

NOTE:

IT'S ALL OVER. MACKMEN WIN FINAL GAME 7-2

No Flaw to Title Taken by Athletics in Four Victories Over Chicago

AMERICANS WIN FAIR AND SQUARE

Reprinted from
The Philadelphia Inquirer

The Chicago Offer of $30,000 for Mathewson Elicits a Counter Offer of 30 Cents for the Entire Chicago Team, Including Cole.

BY E. J. LANIGAN.

New York, November 4.— Mr. John T. Brush, owner of the Giants, was much amused yesterday when he read that Mr. C. Webb Murphy, owner of the World's Losers, stands ready to pay $30,000 for Christy Mathewson. Big Bill Gray, the demon secretary of the Giants, and Eddie, the office boy, almost went into fits when they heard of Mr. Murphy's offer. Brush summoned McGraw, and owner and manager had a long consultation about the matter. Finally Mr. Brush decided that he didn't need Mr. Murphy's 30,000 simoleons, as he had a few bones left in his inside pocket.

John T. Brush

GAMES PLAYED SUNDAY, SEPTEMBER 25

ATHLETICS AT CHICAGO, SEPTEMBER 25 (P M and P M.) The Athletics won the first game in 14 innings, thus stopping Chicago's winning streak at nine straight victories. Coombs relieved Plank in the ninth inning and won out, this making 29 victories for him. A wild throw by Sullivan enabled the Athletics to tie in the ninth and a wild pitch yielded them the winning run in the final inning. Score:

Chicago	AB	R	B	P	A	E	Athletics	AB	R	R	P	A	E
McCon'l, 2b	6	0	1	1	3	0	Hartsel, lf	5	1	2	3	0	0
H. Lord, 3b	6	0	1	1	1	0	B. Lord, cf	5	0	1	0	0	0
Melean, rf	5	0	1	0	1	0	Collins, 2b	6	0	1	3	4	0
Doughe'y, lf	5	0	1	4	0	0	Baker, 3b	6	0	1	3	0	0
Chouin'd, cf	3	0	6	5	0	0	Murphy, rf	4	0	1	2	0	0
Zeider, ss	4	0	0	5	0	17	Davis, 1b	5	0	0	17	1	0
Mullen, 1b	5	0	0	17	1	0	Barry, ss	5	1	2	3	3	0
Sullivan, c	5	0	2	7	0	1	Livingstone, c	3	5	5	1	0
*Messenger	1	0	0	0	0	0	Houser	2	1	1	0	0	0
							Plank, p	1	0	0	0	1	0
							†McInnes	1	0	0	0	0	0
							‡Lapp, c	1	0	0	1	0	0
							Coombs, p	1	0	1	1	0	0
Totals	44	1	5	42	24	5	Totals	45	3	9	42	18	0

*Batted for Walsh in fourteenth inning.
†Batted for Livingstone in ninth inning.
‡Batted for Plank in ninth inning

Chicago .... 0 0 0 0 0 0 0 0 1 0 0 0 0 0—1
Athletics ...... 0 0 0 0 0 1 0 0 0 1 0 0 0 2—3

Hits—Off Plank 5 in 8 innings, Coombs 2 in 6 innings. Sacrifice hits—Melean 2, Chouinard, B. Lord. Stolen bases—Chouinard. Double plays—Zeider, McConnell, Mullen, B. Lord, Livingstone, Baker. Left on bases—Chicago 8, Athletics 7. First on balls—Off Walsh 3, Coombs 4. Struck out—By Walsh 8, Plank 1, Coombs 4. Wild pitch—Walsh. Time—2.40. Umpires—O'Loughlin and Sheridan.

Coombs started the second game, but was knocked out in the third inning. This ended his run of consecutive runless innings pitched at 53—an American League record. Lange allowed but two hits in five innings, when darkness ended the game. Score:

Chicago	AB	R	B	P	A	E	Athletics	AB	R	R	P	A	E
McCon'l, 2b	3	0	1	1	3	0	Hartsel, lf	2	1	1	0	0
H. Lord, 3b	3	1	1	0	3	0	McInnes, lf	1	0	0	0	0
Melean, rf	3	0	2	1	0	0	B. Lord, cf	2	1	1	1	0
Doughe'y, lf	2	1	1	0	0	0	Collins, 2b	1	0	0	1	3	0
Chouin'd, cf	3	0	0	0	0	0	Baker, 3b	0	0	0	0	0
Zeider, ss	3	0	1	1	0	0	Davis, 1b	2	0	0	8	1
Mullen, 1b	2	1	1	6	0	0	Murphy, rf	2	0	0	0	0
Payne, c	1	0	0	0	0	0	Barry, ss	1	0	1	0	1
Lange, p	2	0	1	1	0	0	Lapp, c	1	0	0	5	2	0
							Coombs, p	1	0	0	0	1	0
							Atkins, p	0	0	0	0	0	0
Totals	22	5	9	15	6	0	Totals	13	2	3	15	8	5

Game called on account of darkness.

Chicago .... 0 3 1 1 0—5
Athletics ...... 0 1 0 1 0—2

Two-base hits—Lange, B. Lord. Three-base hit—McConnell. Hits—Off Coombs 5 in 3 innings, Atkins 1 in 2 inning. Sacrifice hit—Payne. Stolen base—Chouinard. First on balls—Off Lange 2, Coombs 4, Athletics 2. First on errors—Chicago 4. Struck out—By Lange 4, Coombs 3, Atkins 2. Wild pitch—Lange. Time—1.10. Umpires—O'Loughlin and Sheridan. Attendance—20,000.

SORRY RESULT

OF CONTEST FOR BATTING HONOR AND PRIZE.

A Finish of the Struggle Between Lajoie and Cobb, for an Automobile, That Gives Opportunity to Attack the Game's Integrity.

SPECIAL TO "SPORTING LIFE."

St. Louis, Mo., October 11.—Each of the five St. Louis sporting writers, in commenting on Sunday's American League base ball games between the Cleveland and St. Louis teams, charged yesterday that certain members of the St. Louis team allowed Napoleon Lajoie, of Cleveland, to obtain hits. The object of this, it is charged, was to enable Lajoie to score a larger batting average during the season than was credited to Tyrus Cobb, of Detroit. Lajoie is credited by the official scorer as being at the bat four times in each game of the double-header.

Napoleon Lajoie

Each time he obtained a hit. In the summary he is also credited with a sacrifice hit. The first time at bat Lajoie hit a liner, and made three bases on it. The ball went over the center fielder's head. Six other times he bunted down the third-base line, and either beat third baseman Corriden's throw to first base or else Corriden did not attempt to throw. Another time Lajoie grounded to Wallace, who threw wild to first base. Once Lajoie bunted to Corriden, who fielded the ball, but threw wide to first. This was the play that gave Lajoie the sacrifice hit. When Lajoie was at bat Corriden played far back of third base, the writers say. He ran up each time that Lajoie hit toward him. Malloy and Nelson were the St. Louis pitchers. In the only other game that Malloy pitched against Cleveland Lajoie got one hit in three times at bat. Nelson never pitched to Lajoie before. President Hedges, of the St. Louis team, refused to discuss the team's playing. "Lajoie outguessed us," said Manager O'Connor, of the Browns. "We figured he did not have the nerve to bunt every time. He beat us at our own game. I will not send in any of my players to play up close to Lajoie when he tries to bunt."

The Official Scorer's Statement.

St. Louis, Mo., October 13.—E. V. Parish, who officially scored Sunday's double-header between the St. Louis and Cleveland American League teams, Wednesday night made the following statement of the Lajoie case:

"The first game, in which I gave Lajoie four hits for as many attempts, was without incident, save that there was a continual procession to the press box for information regarding the scoring, which was given. Sometimes the scoring pleased the fans, at other times it did not. The game was scored as I saw it, and had I to score it again, I would credit Lajoie with four hits for his efforts. In the second game Lajoie bunted his first time up. It was a clean hit. His second time up, which was in the third inning, he bunted again. Corriden, third baseman of the St. Louis team, fumbled the ball and Lajoie was safe at first. A runner was on first with none out. He advanced to second. In my opinion, Corriden could have gotten Lajoie at first easily by clean handling of the ball. There was but one way to score the play, a sacrifice hit and an error for Corriden. As to the scoring of the hits, I have this to say: That, in my opinion, there is no question of their legitimacy. They were clean scoring hits and had they been recorded otherwise it would have been an injustice to Lajoie."

Parish claims that during the second game a messenger boy handed him the following unsigned note: "Mr. Parish: If you can see where Lajoie gets a B. H. instead of a sacrifice, I will give you an order for a forty-dollar suit of clothes—sure. Answer by boy. In behalf of——, I ask it of you."

Corriden's Satisfactory Explanation.

Chicago, Ill., October 14.—In obedience to a summons from President Johnson, third baseman Corriden, of the Browns, appeared at the American League offices here yesterday. After the grilling to which he subjected Corriden, President Johnson said:

"I found that Corriden had a perfectly logical and, as I believe, an absolutely truthful explanation of the reason why Lajoie made so many hits. There has been some misrepresentation over the character of the hits. One that was represented as a bunt was a low, rifle drive, which it would have been dangerous to field. Others were cleverly placed bunts that a veteran fielder would have difficulty in getting, and a player new in major league company might be excused for missing them. Anyone familiar with Lajoie's skill as a batter can understand how it would be quite possible for him to make hits against a recruit when he can turn the trick against the most experienced veterans of the game time and again. I give Corriden a clean bill, and do not think that any suspicion of blame should attach to him. I am very glad to find the facts as they are."

According to a Cleveland dispatch, when Lajoie was informed of Corriden's vindication he said: "I'm too busy with my farm to bother about that automobile. Corriden's story couldn't have been other than straight."

Official Figures Make Cobb Lead Lajoie by Fraction of a Point—Each Man Secures an Automobile, But O'Connor Loses Job.

SPECIAL TO "SPORTING LIFE."

Chicago, Ill., October 15.—Tyrus Cobb, by official verdict of President Johnson, was the leading batsman of the American League during the last season, with a winning percentage over Lajoie, of Cleveland, of .000860.

Tyrus Cobb

As the National Leaguers dropped out of the batting contest some time ago, President Johnson's announcement means that Cobb is the champion hitter of the country. The automobile, over which trophy there has been so much excitement and not a little criticism, goes to the Detroiter, but the Cleveland captain, by permission of President Johnson, will be allowed to accept a duplicate car from the same manufacturer. The batting record of Lajoie and Cobb, as turned in by the official scorers, and approved and promulgated by President Johnson, is as follows:

Player.	At Bat.	Base Hits.	Pct.
Cobb	509	196	.384944
Lajoie	591	227	.384084

Third baseman Corriden, of St. Louis, is vindicated in the statement, and Umpire Evans is quoted as saying that not only were Lajoie's eight hits all legitimate, but that he really should have been credited with nine hits. Johnson stated that he has requested President Hedges, of the St. Louis Club, to probe further the charge that some one connected with his club attempted to influence the official scorer. In conclusion President Johnson said: "Neither Cobb nor Lajoie asked for or received favors from pitchers or players from opposing teams, and each attained his average in merit, but each has been criticised more or less, Lajoie on the St. Louis incident and Cobb for leaving the team before the close of the race. An automobile similar to the one which Cobb gets as champion will be presented to Lajoie."

The Rival Batsmen Satisfied.

Cleveland, O., October 15.—Napoleon Lajoie, in an interview to-night, stated that he did not wish to question the figures given out by President Ban Johnson, but that he still believed that he should have been credited with nine hits in the much-discussed St. Louis games. "I am quite satisfied," he said, "that I was treated fairly in every way by President Johnson, but I think that the scorer at St. Louis made an error in not crediting me with nine hits. However, I am glad that the controversy is over. I have the greatest respect for Cobb as a batter and am glad of his success."

COBB'S TROUBLE.

The Oculist Treating Him Defines His Eye Affliction as "Cyclitis."

Special to "Sporting Life."

Detroit, Mich., September 12.—Dr. R. W. Gilliam, the oculist to whom Ty Cobb, the ball player, submitted his inflamed eye for examination, has issued an official statement, in which he says:

"Tyrus Cobb is being treated by me for cyclitis of the right eye. This condition is serious, as it is an inflammation of one of the most important structures of the eye. The binocular vision is seriously affected. The treatment demanded in his case necessitates the relaxation of the focusing apparatus of the eye. I have advised him to remain out of the game for several days at least. I feel sure that no permanent injury to his sight will result from this inflammation, provided that he now 'takes a stitch in time' by way of complete rest."

Manager O'Connor Loses Out.

St. Louis, Mo., October 15.—Manager O'Connor, of the Browns, went to Chicago yesterday and was examined by President Johnson as to the batting incident. After the interview it was intimated that the manager had corroborated statements of others interested in the Lajoie incident, and that O'Connor had proved blameless in the matter. To the general surprise President Hedges, of the St. Louis Club, to-day threw a bombshell by announcing the discharge of both Manager O'Connor and Scout Harry Howell.

PLAYER PRIZES

TO BE DISCOURAGED BY THE MAJOR LEAGUES.

Indirect Discouragement the Only Way in Which Leagues Can Abate or Prevent What Has Come to Be a Nuisance in Base Ball.

BY I. E. SANBORN.

Thos. J. Lynch

Chicago, Ill., January 1, 1911.—Editor "Sporting Life."—If official displeasure can discourage makers of automobiles, shoes, cigars and clothing, the increasing practice of offering prizes for ball-playing feats will decrease in future. The National League at its recent meeting had the matter brought to its attention officially by President Lynch, and it was the sense of the meeting that the practice should be discouraged. The American League had its troubles last Fall with the Cobb-Lajoie contest, which resulted in all three members of the National Commission announcing that no prizes would be hung up again with their official sanction. The annual report of President Lynch touched upon the matter, according to President Murphy, of the Cubs. In it

WERE MENTIONED INSTANCES

that had come to his knowledge in which charges of unfairness had been made and in which scorers had been accused of giving batters undeserved home runs because it meant shoes or suits of clothes for them. The question was discussed by the club owners, Mr. Murphy said, and the conclusion reached that they should do their best to discourage it. "Discouragement" is almost the only weapon that can be employed. There is no reasonable way by which major or minor leagues or the National Commission can prevent the offering of prizes for ball players by any person or firm that wants and is willing to pay for the advertising it brings. If the

ADVERTISEMENTS OFFERING PRIZES

are kept out of ball parks they can be put up outside the parks or hung in the air from kites. If the leagues decline to sanction prizes or to take charge of awarding them the advertisers can leave the award to a group of fans, to reporters or to the judges of the Supreme Court of the United States and get a lot more advertising out of doing something that is quasi-forbidden. It is possible only to frown on the practice and to prevent the presentation of such prizes at ball games or other public events under the control of organized base ball. The awarding of such prizes could be made more difficult and less satisfactory by concealing the identity of the official scorers of a league, but that would be not only difficult, but unsatisfactory inside the league to every one except the official scorers. The National League went as far as it could at its last meeting and if a general policy of denying official sanction to the practice of offering and awarding prizes is adopted it will have its effect.

A MILITANT UMPIRE

Uses a Gun On a Crowd of Players and Hits a Reporter.

Special to "Sporting Life."

Los Angeles, Cal., March 14.—In a shooting fray at Murietta Hot Springs, on the 12th inst., William Tozier, a pitcher of the Los Angeles Pacific Coast Base Ball Club, was wounded in the left arm and right shoulder, and Lou Guernsey, a newspaper reporter, received a bullet in the foot. The shooting was done by "Flo" Israel, a race-track follower, who is said to have fired six or seven shots into a crowd of base ball players. The ball team is training in Murietta Springs, and in a game played yesterday Israel acted as umpire. It is understood that Israel took exception to adverse comments upon his umpiring. Neither Tozier nor Guernsey is seriously wounded.

BOSTON AT WASHINGTON, WEDNESDAY, APRIL 12.—For the second time during his term of Chief Executive, President Taft this day officially opened the American League base ball season. From his box in the new grand stand at the local grounds he tossed the first ball to Pitcher Dolly Gray, of the Washington team. A crowd estimated at 16,000, breaking all Washington records, cheered the President first and then forgot all about him, when in the sixth inning the home team, overcoming a lead of four runs piled up by the visitors in the third and fourth sessions, batted Wood out of the box and scored six runs. Gray, who started in to pitch for Washington, gave way to Walker in the sixth, having been removed to make a place for a sub-batter. The Boston team's fielding was decidedly off color. It was due more to bad support than poor pitching that Wood was taken out for the visitors. Uncle Nick Young, former president of the National League, was one of the distinguished spectators. Score:

Washin'n.	AB	R	B	P	A	E	Boston.	AB	R	B	P	A	E
Milan, cf	5	1	2	1	0	0	Gardner, 2b	5	0	1	1	0	1
Lelivelt, lf	3	0	0	0	0	Hooper, rf	4	1	1	1	0	0
Schaefer, lf	2	1	1	2	0	0	Speaker, cf	4	0	1	3	0	0
Elberfd, 3b	5	1	2	0	4	4	Lewis, lf	4	0	2	0	0	0
Cunn'm, 2b	4	0	0	1	2	0	Wagner, ss	3	1	0	0	0	0
Gesler, rf	4	0	1	2	1	0	Williams, 1b	2	0	0	7	0	0
Henry, 1b	4	1	2	0	0	0	Engle, 3b	4	1	0	3	3	1
McBride, ss	4	1	0	2	5	0	Kleinow, c	4	0	0	4	0	0
Street, c	3	2	1	9	0	0	Madden, c	4	1	2	5	0	0
Gray, p	2	0	0	0	2	0	Wood, p	1	1	1	5	0	0
Walker, p	1	0	0	0	0	0	Karger, p	1	0	1	0	0	0
*Miller	1	1	0	0	0	0	Yerkes	0	0	0	0	0	0

Totals: 38 9 10 27 11 2   Totals: 42 5 7 24 5 3

*Batted for Gray in 6th inning.
†Batted for Karger in ninth inning.

Washington .... 0 0 0 0 0 6 ...
Boston ....

PRESIDENT LYNCH ACTS.

Umpires Ordered to Stop Catchers Abusing the Batsmen.

Special to "Sporting Life."

New York, N. Y., April 24.—President Lynch, of the National League, has instructed umpires to stop the attacks made on batters by Roger Bresnahan and possibly other catchers in the league. Mr. Lynch has sent a letter to his judges of play, ordering them to prevent the use of Billingsgate and bad language to the man at the bat. This is another move in the President's policy of keeping the game clean and decent. One thing that Mr. Lynch will not stand for is the constant use of profane and indecent language on the field, whether it is addressed to the umpire or to the players of the opposing team.

TY COBB'S ADVENTURE.

Captures Youth Who Ran Off With His Automobile After Sensational Sprint.

Detroit, Mich., May 23.—Tyrus Cobb, centre fielder of the Detroit American League Base Ball Club, after a sensational sprint across Cadillac Square last night, succeeded in recovering his automobile and capturing 19-year-old John Miles, who borrowed it without permission. Miles was locked up. Cobb's automobile, which was presented to him last Fall for his batting prowess, was standing empty in front of a hotel, but the owner was in another car near-by when Miles cranked up. A few moments later the chase was on and after a sprint of over 100 yards, Cobb, disregarding consequences, leaped into the front seat and hurled the youth into the street. Cobb did not desire in court this morning to prosecute John Miles for driving off his world's championship automobile last night. Miles is only 19 years old and had been married only eight months. The bride of the young man talked to Cobb this morning and then Cobb decided that he did not want to prosecute. "They have been married only a little while and things have not been breaking well with them," he said in court. "I'm in favor of letting him go." Justice Stein found that Miles had been mixed up in a similar scrape. Because of this, a warrant charging unlawfully driving away an automobile was sworn to by Cobb and Miles was arraigned and released on his personal recognizance.

BLOW TO BRUSH

FIRE SWEEPS THE HISTORIC POLO GROUNDS.

The Great Grand Stand and the Left Field Bleachers Destroyed in a Fierce Blaze Which Causes a Loss of About $100,000.

SPECIAL TO "SPORTING LIFE."

John T. Brush

New York, April 17.—The historic Polo Grounds, home of the New York National League team, famous as the Giants, was visited by fire early on the morning of Friday, April 14, and the great horseshoe grand stand and left-field bleachers were completely destroyed. Only the right field bleachers, a portion of the seats in centre field and the club house are left standing. It was after midnight when a watchman in the elevated road's towers, which lie just outside the grounds, saw tiny tongues of flame shoot into the darkened sky from the grand stand inside of the grounds. Immediately there was a roar, as the unchecked flames wrapped themselves about the grand stand, and soon that portion of the structure was a mass of flames. The watchman gave the alarm, but by the time the first piece of apparatus had arrived, the big double-decked stand had been reduced to a pile of smoking ruins, with the steel uprights alone remaining like gloomy sentinels over the heap of debris. By this time the fire had swept around the grounds, attacking the left field bleachers and a portion of the seats standing in centre field. The left field seats were soon engulfed in flames, and the efforts of the firemen were devoted toward saving the right field seats and a part of the centre field stands. After a tough and exciting battle the Fire Department conquered, and ten thousand bleacher seats were saved. The club house was untouched by the fire, and the players' property was uninjured. Men are hard at work removing the debris. With the 10,000 seats as a nucleus, an attempt will be made to hold the rest of the home games there, and by the time the team returns from the trip around the circuit it hopes to have the stands temporarily rebuilt. Ultimately a concrete, fireproof stand must replace the burned structure. Temporary stands will be erected as speedily as possible. The loss is estimated at $100,000. The elevated company suffered a like loss by the destruction of its storage yards, just outside the grounds. The cause of the fire is unknown. Rudolph Miller, the superintendent of the Bureau of Buildings, said Saturday that he would not approve the plans for the new grand stand at the Polo Grounds unless the roof, supports and flooring were of fireproof construction. He thought that the chairs might be of wooden construction. It was also suggested that a brick wall be built between the grand stand and the bleachers. These were not touched by the fire and are considered to be safe.

JOSS IS AT REST

THE GREAT PLAYER HIGHLY HONORED IN DEATH.

Impressive Services at the Joss Funeral in Toledo, at Which Evangelist Billy Sunday, the Ex-Player, Preached the Sermon.

April 16

Red Sox Hammer $7000 Beauty

TENNEYS LAND IN 10TH INNING

Takes Them That Long to Get Combination on Alexander's Offerings.

LEAK IN SYSTEM SLOWS PLAY

Curtis Starts Pitching, but Gives Way to Pfeffer in Second Round.

By R. E. McMILLIN.

Grover Cleveland Alexander, the youngster who a few days ago was sighing for more world's champions to conquer, just having trimmed the Macks in Philadelphia civil war, succumbed yesterday to the local Heps, 5 to 4, in 10 rounds. He should have succumbed in nine had the locals played airtight baseball, but beating such a name in one extra inning is something not to be sneezed at. Jeff Pfeffer did the Heps's pitching after Curtis had worked one inning, discovering therein that his arm was a bit kinky, although he escaped without damage as far as hostile runs were concerned. Pfeffer suffered from a couple of cases of wobbly support. Alexander's trouble was liberality in the pinches.

Reprinted from the **Boston Herald**, courtesy the **Boston Herald American**

TO EXPEDITE GAME.

President Johnson Orders Pitchers to Omit the Five-Ball Practice.

Special to "Sporting Life."

Chicago, May 23.—Long-drawn-out ball games and tardy dinners will be a thing of memory before long. The coming of the "more lively" ball and the resultant long games has caused consternation, and with it took form on Saturday in an announcement from B. B. Johnson, president of the American League, who ordered that hereafter there shall be no more delay occasioned by pitchers in their practice of warming up to the extent of five balls at the beginning of each inning, and, in most cases after each put-out. It is figured that this alone will knock 20 minutes off the length of the game, and if this does not suffice there will follow a shift in the starting time of matinee affairs in the American League. The managers have also come in for their share of instructions. It is claimed that many of the team bosses at different times make every possible effort to delay play, but this will also die a natural death if the umpires fill the demands of their chief.

One Hundred and Ninety-One Miles From Columbus to Pittsburg Made in 3.35—Narrow Escape of the Club From Deadly Gases.

SPECIAL TO "SPORTING LIFE."

Pittsburg, Pa., June 3.—No team ever took a wilder ride or more desperate chances to keep a date than the Cubs took to play off a postponed game here May 29. The Pennsylvania railroad had to break its own record between Columbus and Pittsburg to get Chance's men here in time, lowering the fastest previous running time by five minutes. This speed was necessary by the fact the regular train by which the Cubs were traveling was an hour and a half late into Columbus. A special had been arranged for, anyway, to land the Cubs

Frank Chance

here in time for dinner and a little practice before the game. On account of the delay the original schedule laid out for the special would not get the team here in time to play at all. Consequently a new one was made out by the railroad men. A dining car was shanghaied and was tacked on behind the two Cub sleepers and, with a heavy baggage car for ballast, away they went with Casey Jones at the throttle and a clear track all the way to Smoketown, stopping half way to change engines and let Casey Jones' brother climb into the cab.

SPEED RECORD LOWERED.

The run of 191 miles was covered in 218 minutes. The best it had ever been done in before was 220 minutes, or 3:40:00 in athletic formula. That necessitated doing better than a mile a minute a lot of the way, and considering the curves in the right of way, that listened like 90 miles an hour, on a straightaway track. It was like walking the quarterdeck of a lake steamer in a cyclone to go the length of a car, and once the dining car tilted so far that Doc Semmens, who was trying to inhale some cold roast beef, was thrown out of his chair into the aisle, with a bunch of crockery on top of him. That was the only accident that marred the wild ride, but before it ended the merriest of the carefree players was sobered by the thought of what a misplaced or a split switch meant at that gait, and every switchyard looked like straightaway going to Casey Jones and his brother. An accident meant more to the Chicago National League ball team than to any player, however. The players had only their lives at stake, while the club owners were risking assets worth $100,000 at least. That is the commercial way of looking at it.

NARROW ESCAPE FROM DEATH.

The Cubs had a narrow escape just after leaving the St. Louis Station Sunday night. The porter in one of their sleepers was new to the run and was not aware the train was going through the tunnel full of deadly gases leading to the Eads bridge. Consequently, the sleeper was wide open everywhere when it went into the tunnel. The quick thinking that has won so many pennants was illustrated right there. The instant the Cubs got a whiff of that gas they knew somebody had blundered. Working frantically, the men in the car closed every window and ventilator in a few seconds, but not until the car was so full of suffocating gas and smoke that breathing was painful.

MERCY TO MAGEE

PRESIDENT LYNCH REINSTATES HIM ON PROBATION.

The Phillies' Star Outfielder Will Be Eligible to Rejoin His Team on August 16 and Remain Eligible Only During Good Conduct.

SPECIAL TO "SPORTING LIFE."

New York, N. Y., August 12.—Sherwood Nottingham Magee, star outfielder of the crippled Philadelphia Nationals, will again be eligible to play when the Phillies return to their home grounds, Wednesday, August 16. Magee was suspended for the remainder of the present season some weeks ago for an inexcuseable assault upon umpire Finneran. Through the influence of President Horace Fogel, of the Phillies, Magee was able to secure a rehearing of President Lynch's ruling by appeal to the Board of Directors of the National League. This board upheld the verdict of President Lynch in every particular. But after

Sherwood Magee

he was exonerated by the league directors the President's heart began to soften toward the Phillies in their afflictions. Manager Dooin, one of the finest catchers in the circuit, was crippled for the season with a broken leg. Communications to Mr. Lynch, imploring him in the fair name of sport to make an exception to rigid discipline in the case of a team so badly shattered and reinstate Magee, poured in from every quarter. Finally the executive decided to reinstate the player on probation. Magee will be permitted to finish the year for his club, provided he keeps the peace.

COBB'S NATIVE STATE.

The Distinguished Ball Player Is Claimed By North Carolina.

Special to "Sporting Life."

Asheville, N. C., Aug. 14.—North Carolina, which disputes with South Carolina the honor of being the birthplace of Andrew Jackson, is seeking further laurels in the line of the parentage of noted men by challenging the claim that Tyrus Cobb is a Georgia product. H. Taylor Cobb, an uncle of the Detroit fielder, who visited the city Thursday, stated that Ty Cobb was born on Mocassin Creek, in Cherokee county, North Carolina, and that he did not move to Georgia with his father until he was 10 years old. He attended the village school at Belleville, the uncle said, for several years before going to the Cracker State.

BOSTON AT CHICAGO, AUGUST 27.—Ed. Walsh pitched the first no-hit game of his career. Only one of the visitors reached first base, Engle getting a base on balls. The locals fielded well behind Walsh, who struck out eight batsmen. The locals bunched hits off Collins, and, with the assistance of an error and a wild pitch, scored five runs. Early in the game, Henriksen and Speaker collided when running for Tannehill's long fly. Speaker retired from the game, and Henriksen was taken to a hospital suffering severe pains in the shoulders, side and legs. Score:

Chicago	AB.	R.	B.	P.	A.	E.	Boston	AB.	R.	B.	P.	A.	E.
McIntyre, lf.	5	1	1	3	0	0	Henriksen, cf.	1	0	0	0	0	0
Lord, 3b.	3	0	1	0	3	0	Riggert, rf.	3	0	0	1	0	0
Callahan, rf.	4	1	1	0	0	0	Speaker, cf.	1	0	0	0	0	0
Bodie, cf.	4	1	2	1	0	0	Williams, 1b	2	0	0	6	0	1
McConnell, 2b	4	0	1	0	5	0	Engle, cf.	2	0	0	4	2	1
Tannehill, ss	4	1	2	0	3	0	Lewis, lf.	3	0	0	3	0	0
Mullen, 1b	3	0	0	10	0	0	Gardner, 3b.	3	0	0	1	5	0
Block, c.	4	0	2	6	2	0	Carrigan, c.	3	0	0	4	0	0
Walsh, p.	4	1	1	0	2	0	Wagner, 2b.	3	0	0	1	0	0
							Yerkes, ss.	3	0	0	4	3	0
							Collins, p.	2	0	0	0	1	0
							*Nunamaker	1	0	0	0	0	0
Totals..	35	5	11	27	15	0	Totals..	27	0	0	24	10	3

*Batted for Collins in ninth inning.

Chicago .... 3 0 0 0 0 0 1 1 x—5
Boston .... 0 0 0 0 0 0 0 0 0—0

Two-base hits—McConnell, Lord, Tannehill. Three-base hits—McIntyre, Tannehill. Sacrifice hits—Lord, Mullen. Left on bases—Chicago 8, Boston 1. First on balls—Off Walsh 1. Struck out—By Walsh 8, Collins 1. Wild pitch—Collins. Time—1.50. Umpires—Evans and Mullen.

ST. LOUIS AT NEW YORK, SEPTEMBER 29.—
New York won a farcical game. The visiting pitchers
issued 13 passes, and the New Yorkers stole 13
bases on Stevens and Clarke, six of them being in a
single inning—the second. Score:

New York.	AB	R	B	P	A	E		St. Louis.	AB	R	B	P	A	E
Daniels, rf	3	2	2	2	0	0		Moulton, 2b	4	2	1	0	2	1
Dolan, 3b	3	3	2	0	0	0		Shotten, cf	1	1	2	3	0	0
Chase, cf	4	3	2	3	0	0		Hogan, lf	4	2	0	0	0	0
Cree, lf	3	1	2	1	0	0		Laporte, 3b	5	1	2	1	0	0
Knight, 1b	3	1	1	10	1	1		Compton, rf	5	1	2	3	0	1
Martsell, ss	4	2	1	3	5	0		Kutina, 1b	5	1	2	8	0	0
Curry, 2b	4	2	1	1	1	0		Hallinan, ss	3	0	0	6	5	1
Williams, c	5	3	1	3	3	0		Wallace, ss	1	0	0	1	0	0
Warhop, p	1	0	0	0	0	0		Stephens, c	1	0	0	0	1	1
Quinn, p	3	0	1	0	2	0		Clarke, c	1	0	0	1	0	0
								Hamilton, p	2	0	0	0	1	0
Totals	33	18	13	27	13	6		Brown, p	2	1	1	0	0	0
								Nelson, p	2	1	0	0	2	0
								Totals	60	13	13	24	20	6

New York . . . . 8 1 3 1 1 2 2—18
St. Louis . . . . 0 1 3 0 1 1 5—13
First on errors—New York 3. St. Louis 3. Two-
base hits—Kutina, Nelson. Three-base hit—Williams.
Sacrifice by—Quinn. Stolen bases—Chase 4, Daniels
3, Dolan 3, Cree 4, Martsell. Left on bases—New York 5,
St. Louis 9. First on balls—Off Warhop 6, Quinn 1.
Hamilton 3, E. Brown 5, Nelson 5. Struck out—By
Warhop 1, Quinn 3, Nelson 3. Hit by pitcher—By
Warhop 1. Wild pitches—Nelson 3. Passed balls—
Stephens, Clarke, Williams. Hits—Off Hamilton 6
in 2 innings, E. Brown 1 in 2 innings, Nelson 6 in
4 innings, Warhop 2 in 3½ innings, Quinn 9 in 6½
innings. Umpires—O'Loughlin and Egan. Time—
2.16.

THE INDIVIDUAL BATTING.

In individual batting the American League's 1911 season furnished the most striking illustration of the great increase in batting, no less than 35 men batting .300 or better in 1911 as against 13 such batsmen in 1910, nine in 1909, seven in 1908, and nine in 1907; and two men, Cobb and Jackson, batted over .400 in 1911. Ty Cobb, of Detroit, who was last year the actual leader with .385 in 140 games, is again the leader in 1911 with the magnificent average of .420 in 146 games—which is only two points short of Lajoie's American League record of .422, made in 1902, when he was a member of the Athletic team. Cobb is thus the actual leader of the American League for the fifth successive season, during which time his record was as follows: 1907, .350; 1908, .324; 1909, .377; 1910, .385, and 1911, .420. Second to Cobb in batting this year is Joe Jackson, Cleveland's phenomenal youngster, who was the titular leader last year with .387 in 20 games, and this year has a clear title to second place with .408 in 147 games. Cobb's high batting average made him again king of the profession, as the National League leader once more fell considerably below Cobb's remarkable record.

PLAYERS TURNED DOWN BY THE NATIONAL COMMISSION

Moving Picture Proceeds Will Not Be Divided Among Ball Tossers—"Books Are Open," Moguls Say.

SPECIAL TO THE PITTSBURGH POST

NEW YORK, Oct. 22.—The members of the National baseball commission, Ban Johnson, August Herrmann and Tom Lynch, were amused to-day when they learned that the players taking part in the world's series had decided to make a firm demand for a share of the moving picture privileges. It appears that when the Athletics and Giants received formal notice from the commission on Friday that they must pose for the camera men several ringleaders announced that there would be a strike.

"We will not obey the order," they were quoted as saying, "because we don't see where the commission comes in to pocket a big rakeoff for this privilege. If we don't get 60 per cent of this coin there will be trouble."

A. J. Flanner, representing the commission, at the Waldorf-Astoria to-day said that the price paid for the moving picture privilege this year was $3,500, as against $500 in 1910. He showed that by the time this sum was divided up on the regular percentage basis—60 per cent to

the players and 30 per cent to the club owners and 10 per cent to the commission each player wouldn't have a great deal to show for his protest. Mr. Flanner said that while it was the policy of Messrs. Herrmann, Lynch and Johnson to ignore irresponsible cries calculated to stir up trouble, they wanted the public to understand that they had nothing to conceal, that their accounts were open for inspection at any time and that receipts and expenditures were itemized in black and white.

Mr. Flanner said:

"The commission acts as trustee and transacts a large amount of business in a comparatively short time. Last year, for instance, the commission handled $194,460 in connection with the world's series, including each club's $10,000 forfeit, which later was returned. When all the players had been paid the club owners had received their share and current expenses of the commission had been met, there was a balance of $8,816.06, which was banked to the commission's account.

Reprinted from
The Pittsburgh Post

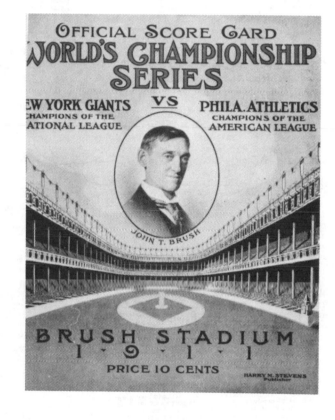

FRANK BAKER CHAMPION BATSMAN OF 1911 WORLD'S SERIES BATTLES

Athletics' Third Baseman Hit for .375 in Six Games—Barry Second at .368—Doyle and Meyers Lead New York Players At Bat.

CHICAGO AT CINCINNATI, Thursday, April 11.—Before by far the largest crowd that ever saw a ball game in Cincinnati, the Reds defeated Chicago in the opening game of the National League season. The game marked the formal opening of the new grand stand and park. Both Cole and Frank Smith were forced to retire early in the game under an avalanche of hits. Charley Smith, who relieved Cole, did little better and was relieved in the final inning by Richie. Humphries, who relieved Frank Smith for Cincinnati, had the Cubs at his mercy with the exception of the seventh inning, when a single and a triple accounted for a run. The score:

Chicago	AB	R	B	P	A	E	Cincinnati	AB	R	B	P	A	E
Evers, 2b.	5	1	1	4	3	0	Bescher, lf.	5	3	2	4	0	0
Sheckard, lf	5	1	3	1	0	0	Bates, cf.	4	1	3	3	0	0
Schulte, rf	4	1	2	0	0	0	Hoblitzel, 1b	3	1	1	5	2	0
Chance, 1b	2	1	0	9	0	0	Marsans, rf	4	1	1	1	0	0
Lennox, 3b	5	1	1	2	0	0	Egan, 2b.	4	2	3	3	3	1
Hofman, cf	3	1	1	1	0	0	Phelan, 3b.	4	1	2	1	0	0
Tinker, ss.	4	0	1	3	6	1	Esmond, ss	4	1	1	1	3	0
Archer, c.	4	0	1	5	0	0	McLean, c.	4	1	1	5	0	0
Cole, p.	2	0	1	0	0	0	F. Smith, p	3	0	0	0	0	0
C. Smith, p	1	0	0	0	0	0	Humphries, p	0	0	0	0	0	0
Richie, p.	0	0	0	0	0	0	†McDonald	1	0	0	0	0	0
*W. Miller	1	0	0	0	0	0							
Totals..	36	6	10	24	13	1	Totals..	36	10	14	27	10	1

*Batted for C. Smith in eighth inning.
†Batted for F. Smith in third inning.

Chicago	0	0	5	0	0	1	0	0	0	— 6
Cincinnati	1	0	0	5	0	0	3	1	x	—10

NEW YORK AT BOSTON, APRIL 20.—New York made a strong effort to figure in the "games won" column, but lost the sixth straight game in an 11-inning battle. Boston's new grounds were opened before a big crowd. "Buck" O'Brien, pitching for Boston, allowed New York five runs in the first three innings and was taken out after the fourth inning, following a lucky scrape with three men on bases. Hall, who succeeded him, pitched masterly ball. Boston used up three Highland singers. Caldwell was driven from the box in the fourth inning after he had allowed Boston to get in position to score three runs. Quinn, who succeeded him, was hammered for six hits and Boston twice tied the score during his occupancy of the box. Boston put two men on bases in the ninth and tenth innings, but was unable to score on Vaughn until Speaker sent Yerkes home on a single. After Yerkes had got a base through Dolan's error, Yerkes hit safely the first five times at bat, twice for doubles, but fielded poorly. Wolter injured his ankle and was forced to retire. Score:

Boston	AB	R	B	P	A	E	New York	AB	R	B	P	A	E
Hooper, rf							Zinn, lf	5	1	1			
Yerkes, 2b.	7	3	5	6	2	3	Wolter, cf.	4	1	1			
Speaker, cf	6	0	2	2	0	0	Kauff, rf.	4	1	1			
Stahl, 1b.	6	1	3	11	1	0	Chase, 1b.	6	0	2			
Gardner, 3b	6	1	2	1	2	0	Hartzell, ss	6	1	2			
Lewis, lf.	6	0	1	3	0	0	Daniels, cf	2	1	1			
Wagner, ss.	6	1	1	3	5	0	Dolan, 2b.	4	0	0			
Nunamaker, c	5	1	1	6	2	0	E. Gardner, 3b	5	0	1			
Carrigan, c	1	0	0	2	0	0	Street, c.	4	0	1			
O'Brien, p.	1	0	0	0	0	0	Caldwell, p	1	0	1			
Hall, p.	3	0	1	0	0	0	Quinn, p.	3	0	0			
*Henriksen	1	0	0	0	0	0	Vaughn, p.	3	1	1			
†Engle	1	0	0	0	0	0							
Totals..	48	7	16	33	14	7	Totals..	48	6	8	30	18	3

*Batted for O'Brien in the fourth inning.
†Batted for Nunamaker in the tenth inning.
‡Two out when winning run was scored.

Boston	2	0	1	2	1	0	0	0	0	0	1	—7
New York	2	0	3	0	0	0	0	1	0	0	0	—6

A POSSIBLE MENACE

Public Betting on Base Ball Becoming So General and So Heavy As to Cause Concern to the Magnates.

BY JOE VILA.

New York, April 18.—While the governors of the national game are doing their best to suppress betting inside the ball parks it will be impossible to check speculation on the games elsewhere. In this city with no horse racing to command attention, base ball has become a medium for wagers large and small. Sporting men who never cared for the national game when the race tracks were open, now make their bets before going to the ball parks. Presidents Brush and Farrell have

ENGAGED PRIVATE DETECTIVES

who will patrol the grand stands and bleachers in search of private bettors, and if such persons are caught in the act they will be ejected and also turned over to the police.

Giants Wallop Yanks

NEW YORK, April 21.—A large crowd of spectators saw the New York Nationals easily defeat the local American League team in a game played for the benefit of the survivors of the Titanic today. The Giants outplayed the Highlanders in every department and won the game in the first inning on five hits, two bases on balls, three stolen bases and a muff of a thrown ball by Chase.

	r.	h.	e.
N.Y. Nationals.5	0	0	5	0	0	0	0	1—11	12	1
N. Y. Amer.	1	1	0	0	0	0	0	0—2	10	5

Batteries—Maxwell, Fullenwider and Wilson; McConnell and Fisher.

Reprinted from
The Philadelphia Inquirer

A WONDERFUL RUN

Konetchy, of St. Louis, Accepts 592 Chances Without an Error.

Special to "Sporting Life."

St. Louis, Mo., July 18.—With a record of 592 perfect chances in the field, Ed. Konetchy, the Cardinals' first baseman, had his mark shattered in the fifth inning of yesterday's game with Brooklyn. Moran, of the visitors, hit one against the right field wall which was only good for a single, due to Evans' fast fielding. Konetchy raced out into the pasture to get Evans' relay and would have nipped Moran easily, who was trying to stretch his hit into a double, but his throw was wide of the mark. Konetchy's last error was on May 10, and since that time he played 54 successive games and accepted 592 chances without a break.

DETROIT'S DAY

WAS THE ONE DEDICATING THE NEW PARK

A Red-Letter Event in the History of the National Game in the Old Town—Spirit, Ceremonies, and the Game Result All in Keeping.

BY PAUL HALE BRUSKE.

Detroit, Mich., April 21.—Editor "Sporting Life."—Detroit and its Tigers have just celebrated the most momentous

Paul H. Bruske

occasion in the history of Michigan base ball. The opening of the new Navin Park can be adequately described in no other way. For the first time in history, Detroit has a ball yard worthy of its rank among the cities—a worthy setting for the wonderfully successful club which has represented the city in the American League, and a monument to William H. Yawkey, Frank J. Navin and Hugh A. Jennings, whose money and executive ability have made it possible. Saturday, April 20, 1912, should be a red-letter date in the diary of the Detroit sportsman.

THE DRINK EVIL!

TO BE TAKEN IN HAND BY THE CLUBS

President Dreyfuss, of Pittsburgh, Leading a Timely Movement for the Insertion of a Total Abstinence Clause In Player-Contracts

---

COBB'S SPEED

IS CONVINCINGLY DEMONSTRATED BY THE CAMERA

By Quick Thinking and Fast Running the Detroit Club's Star Outfielder Gets Into the Same Group Picture Twice.

Tyrus Cobb

Detroit, Mich., April 30.—Getting into the same photograph of the Tigers' team in two different places without blurring or spoiling the picture, is the remarkable feat of Ty Cobb's lightning thinking and speed have enabled him to accomplish. It is not a fake picture, either. It was the sort of a stunt that makes Ty the greatest of all ball players. The Tigers were lined up in the new ball yard Sunday, April 21, for a group photo. Standing side by side, they made a line too long for an ordinary camera. So a panorama camera was used. Cobb was fourth from the left end of the line. The camera exposes only a small portion of the film at a time, the lens traveling in an arc from one end of the line to the other. When Cobb noticed the rate at which it was going, the idea popped into his head that he could beat it. So the instant the lens passed him, he dashed out around to the rear of the machine and dug for the other end of the line, like he goes when stealing home. He arrived in time to take up a position at the side of Manager Jennings and in the photo appears there smiling and as composed as he appears in the fourth place from the right.

TAFT'S REMEDY

ALLUDING TO A PLAYER AND NOT TO POLITICS

The President of the Nation Directs An Army Surgeon to Find a Way of Fixing Outfielder Moeller's Easily-Dislocated Shoulder Blade

SPECIAL TO "SPORTING LIFE."

Washington, D. C., August 24.—One of the great drawbacks to the pennant aspirations of the Washington Nationals' team this season has been the fact that the shoulder of "Daredevil" Dan Moeller, the star right fielder, is easily dislocated upon the slightest provocation or awkward movement. However, President Taft, who is an ardent fan, has a remedy in hand. At one of the recent games attended by the President, Moeller threw his "collapsible" shoulder out. President Taft then inquired of Major T. L. Rhoades, his military aid and surgeon in the army, if an operation would

William H. Taft

not fix the ball player's shoulder to prevent such frequent dislocations. Major Rhoades, after an examination of Moeller's shoulder, said he thought it would. The result of the incident is that Major Rhoades and Clark Griffith, manager of the Senators, will hold a conference to decide about the operation. It is believed that the ligaments of Moeller's shoulder can be tightened in such a manner as to eradicate the defect.

SHORT-LIVED REVOLT

N EW YORK, N. Y., May 16.— Tyrus Raymond Cobb, of the Detroit Americans, hails from Georgia, and is conceded to be the greatest ball player of all time, appeared in a new role on the Hilltop yesterday, while the Highlanders were losing the final game of the series to the visitors by a score of 8 to 4. Just as the Detroits were preparing to go to bat in the fourth inning Cobb leaped into the grand stand and chastised a fan who had called him names. Tyrus was followed by the entire Detroit squad, but no one interfered until Cobb had handed the fan a good thrashing. Some of President Farrell's private graycoats finally broke up the scrap. The beaten fan requested the park police to arrest Cobb, but they refused, and he was led out of the stand by Thomas Davis, secretary of the New York Club. When Cobb returned to the bench his face was distorted with anger. He was immediately put out of the game by Umpire O'Loughlin. After the incident Hugh Jennings, the Detroit manager, went over to the press stand and explained that the fan had called Ty Cobb "a half-nigger." Jennings said no Southerner would stand such an insult. "I heard the remark," said Jennings, "but I knew it would be useless to restrain Ty, as he would have got his tormenter sooner or later. When Ty's Southern blood is aroused he is a bad man to handle." According to the "American," the man whom Cobb assaulted, is Claude Lueker, secretary for Tom Foley, formerly sheriff. He is a pressman by trade, but lost one hand and most of the other a little more than a year ago while working on a morning newspaper. Lueker is quoted by the "American" as saying that he did not know why Cobb singled him out for attack, and that after Cobb knocked him down he (Cobb) kicked Lueker and spiked him in the side.

TY COBB

May 19

TIGERS QUIT FIELD WHEN TOLD COBB'S SUSPENSION STOOD

Johnson and Navin Hasten Here to Confer on Strike

President of League Stands Pat---Players May Be Suspended for Season

Realizing that they were inviting the severest punishment by defying the stringent regulations governing the conduct of the players of the American League, the entire Detroit team went on a strike yesterday with the declaration that not a man composing it would play again under the colors of their club until Ty Cobb was reinstated.

As they had announced on Friday, every one of the players, including such well-known ball tossers as Sam Crawford, Jim Delehanty, George Mullin and Ownie Bush, refused to meet the Athletics at Shibe Park during the afternoon, when they learned that President Ban Johnson, of the American League, had not revoked his suspension of Cobb for striking a spectator at the New York Highlanders' grounds on last Wednesday.

All of the nineteen or twenty men of the Tigers' team left Shibe Park and returned to the Aldine Hotel, where they are stopping, just as the scheduled conflict between Detroit and the Athletics was due to begin and Hughey Jennings, their manager, had to substitute several college boys, "park sparrows," two or three old timers and himself in order to prevent the Detroit club from being fined $5000 for not turning out a team.

Reprinted from
The Philadelphia Inquirer

STRIKEBREAKERS RUDELY TREATED

Macks Slaughter Jennings' First-to-the-Aid Job Fillers Under 24 to 2 Score

Game Was Howling Farce, But Mackmen Profited Greatly Their Individual Averages

BY JIM NASIUM

In the absence of the regular employes of the Detroit baseball machine, who have revolted against the mailed fist of plutocracy by laying down their tools and walking out of the shop just before the whistle blew, our Athletics yesterday met the Detroit "strikezreakers" inside the stockade of the works and wallowed them around in the mire of defeat to the merry tune of 24 to 2, while outside the mob howled and across the moor a little bird sang to its mate "cuckoo! cuckoo!"

The strikers themselves sat in the upper pavilion and piped off the guys who were trying to nab their jobs, but no attempt was made to picket the works and there was no rioting or use of violence in order to prevent the strike breakers from going to work. There wasn't a brick thrown by the strikers during the whole afternoon. There wasn't anything shown by the strikebreakers that necessitated such severe measures by the men who had walked out, but the fact that the spectators restrained themselves only goes to show what a long suffering assemblage it was.

It would be a libel on the national frolic to dip into the details of the course of events and attempt to give any idea of how the runs scattered over the pan, and the show was such a travesty on the popular pastime that fully one-third of the fifteen thousand persons who had gathered at Shibe Park just to see what would come off started for the gate to get their money back before four innings had been floundered through. When they failed in this they returned, however, and took the whole thing as a huge joke. Now it's up to somebody to show us who the joke is on.

* * *

ATHLETICS

	ab.	r.	bh.	tb.	sh.	sb.	po.	a.	e.
Maggert, lf	4	2	3	6	0	0	0	0	0
Strunk, cf	6	3	4	7	0	0	0	0	0
Collins, 2b	6	4	5	7	0	0	1	0	0
Baker, 3b	5	3	2	4	0	5	1	0	0
Murphy, rf	3	4	2	4	0	2	2	1	0
McInnis, 1b	6	2	4	6	0	1	7	1	1
Barry, ss	4	2	2	3	1	0	2	1	0
Lapp, c	4	1	1	1	0	0	16	1	0
Coombs, p	1	0	0	0	0	0	0	0	0
Brown, p	3	2	2	4	0	0	0	2	0
Pennock, p	1	1	1	2	0	0	0	1	0
Totals	43	24	26	42	2	10	27	8	1

DETROIT

	ab.	r.	bh.	tb.	sh.	sb.	po.	a.	e.
McGarr, 2b	4	0	0	0	0	0	3	3	1
Maharg, 3b	1	0	0	0	0	0	0	2	1
Irwin, 3b	3	0	2	6	0	0	0	1	0
Travers, p	3	0	0	0	0	0	1	7	0
McGarvey, lf	3	0	0	0	0	0	1	1	1
Leinhauser, cf	4	0	0	0	0	0	1	0	0
Sugden, 1b	4	1	1	1	0	0	13	3	0
McGuire, c	2	1	1	1	0	0	3	3	1
Coffee, 3b	0	0	0	0	0	0	2	0	0
Meany, ss	2	0	0	0	0	0	3	2	0
Ward, rf	2	0	0	0	0	0	2	0	0
zJennings	1	0	0	0	0	0	0	0	0
Totals	29	2	4	8	0	1	24	24	7

zBatted for Travers in ninth.

Athletics—
Runs .... 3 0 3 0 8 4 4 2 x—24
Base hits ...... 3 1 3 2 7 4 3 x—26

Detroit—
Runs .... 0 0 0 0 2 0 0 0 0—2
Base hits ...... 0 0 0 1 2 0 0 0 1—4

Hits—Off Coombs, 0 in 3 innings, 8 at bat; hits off Brown, 3 in 3 innings, 12 at bat; hits off Pennock, 1 in 3 innings, 9 at bat. Runs Earned—Athletics, 14. Two-base hits—Strunk, Maggert, Pennock, Barry. Three-base hits—McInnis, Murphy, Brown, Strunk, Maggert, Baker, Irwin, 2. Left on bases—Athletics, 4; Detroit, 4. Struck out—By Coombs, 3; Brown, 5; Pennock, 7; Travers, 1. Double plays—Meany to Coffee. First base on errors—Athletics, 2. First base on called balls—Off Coombs, 1; Pennock, 1; Travers, 7. Hit by pitched ball—By Brown, 1; (Meany); by Pennock, 1 (Coffee). Missed grounders and fumbles—McGarvey, Sugden. Wild throws—Lapp, 1; McGuire, 2; Irwin, 1. Dropped thrown balls—McGarr, Meany. Umpires—Dineen and Perrine. Time, 1.45.

Reprinted from
The Philadelphia Inquirer

STRIKING TIGERS FINED
$100 EACH---JOHNSON DOES
NOT REINSTATE TY COBB

May 21

DETROIT PLAYERS' STRIKE OFF: COBB STILL SUSPENDED

Navin May Pay Fines Imposed, Games Will Be Resumed at Washington Today

The strike of the Detroit team was declared off yesterday.

It was Ty Cobb who acted as a peacemaker when the players, who declared on Saturday that they would not don a Detroit uniform again until his suspension was lifted, were approached by Frank J. Navin, the president of the Detroit club, after the latter's conference with President Ban Johnson, of the American League.

Cobb told his team mates that he had appreciated what they had done for him in running the risk of being expelled from the American League and thereby being practically blacklisted, but that he did not want them to jeopardize their future as ball players by continuing to refuse to play until he had been reinstated.

Every one of the recalcitrant players finally agreed, after being assured by President Navin that the Detroit club would meet any penalties in the way of fines that might be heaped upon them for their unprecedented action, to return to the game. It was explained to them by Cobb himself that he was still under suspension, but that he was prepared, rather than that they should suffer, to abide by the decision of President Johnson in putting him out of the game following the former's attack upon a man who had hurled opprobrious epithets at him during last Wednesday's game between Detroit and New York.

Reprinted from
The Philadelphia Inquirer

DETROIT AT CHICAGO, MAY 26.—Detroit celebrated Ty Cobb's return to the game by defeating Chicago. Mullin pitched splendid ball, holding Chicago safely for eight innings. In the ninth the locals got to him for five hits and were only able to score one run. Callahan and Bodie were put out of the park in the ninth inning for protesting when Bodie was called out at the plate. Score:

Chicago	AB.	R.	B.	P.	A.	E.	Detroit	AB.	R.	B.	P.	A.	E.
Rath, 2b..	3	0	1	2	4	0	Bush, ss..	4	0	1	3	2	1
Lord, 3b..	3	0	1	2	0	Jones, lf..	5	0	2	1	0	0
Callahan, lf.	4	0	1	1	0	0	Cobb, cf..	4	1	5	1	0
Bodie, cf..	4	0	1	0	0	Crawford, rf	5	1	2	1	0	0
Collins, rf..	3	2	2	0	0	Delaha'y, rf	3	1	2	3	0
Zeider, 1b..	4	2	12	1	2	Gainor, 1b.	5	2	7	0	0
Weaver, ss	4	0	4	5	1	Moriarty, 3b	5	1	1	1	0
Sullivan, c	2	0	5	1	0	Stanage, c	4	0	1	0	0
Kuhn, c...	2	0	1	1	0	Mullin, p.	5	1	2	0	0
Bens, p...	2	0	1	5	0							
Peters, p..	0	0	0	0	0	Totals...	42	6	12	27	11	1
*McIntyre..	1	0	0	0	0							
†Fournier..	1	0	0	0	0							
‡Lange...	1	0	0	0	0							
§Mattick..	1	0	1	0	0							
Totals..	32	2	11	27	18	4							

*Batted for Sullivan in seventh inning.
†Batted for Bens in seventh inning.
‡Batted for Kuhn in ninth inning.
§Batted for Peters in ninth inning.
Chicago .... 0 0 0 0 0 1 0 1—2
Detroit .... 0 0 1 1 0 0 3 0—6
Two-base hits—Crawford, Delahanty. Three-base hit—Delahanty. Hits—Off Bens 8 in 7 innings. Peters 3 in 2 innings. Sacrifice hits—Lord, Rath. Stolen bases—Jones 2, Zeider. Gainor 3, Rath. Double plays—Weaver. Zeider. Delahanty, Bush. Left on bases—Chicago 7. Detroit 13. First on balls—Off Bens 3. Mullin 2. Peters 3. Struck out—By Bens 5. Mullin 4. Time—2:05. Umpires—O'Loughlin and Westervelt.

MODEST PITCHER HERO

The Sensational Marquard, Who Was Stopped By the Cubs After 19 Consecutive Victories, and Thereby Deprived of the Opportunity to Establish a New Record, Has No Censure for Poor Support.

BROOKLYN AT NEW YORK, JULY 3 (P. M. and P. M.)—New York stretched its winning streak to 16 consecutive victories by taking a double-header from Brooklyn. In the first game, Marquard tied Tim Keefe's major league record by winning his nineteenth straight game of the season. He was outpitched by Rucker, but proved strong in the pinches. In the first three innings, eight Brooklyn men were left on the bases. Score:

Brooklyn.	AB.	R.	B.	P.	A.	E.	New York.	AB.	R.	B.	P.	A.	E.
Moran, cf..	5	0	1	2	1	0	Snodgr's, lf	4	0	0	6	0	0
Northen, rf	5	0	2	1	0	0	Doyle, 2b..	3	0	2	2	1	0
*Cutshaw..	0	0	0	0	0	0	Merkle, 1b..	3	0	1	6	0	0
Smith, 3b..	4	1	1	1	1	1	Murray, rf.	3	2	1	3	0	0
Daubert, 1b	4	0	1	4	0	0	Becker, cf..	2	0	1	3	0	1
Wheat, lf..	4	0	1	3	0	0	Herzog, 3b..	3	0	0	3	1	1
Hummel, 2b	4	0	0	5	5	0	Myers, c...	2	0	0	4	0	0
Tooley, ss..	2	0	1	1	0	1	Fletcher, ss	3	0	1	0	1	1
Miller, c..	4	0	1	7	2	0	Marquard, p	3	0	0	0	1	0
Rucker, p..	4	0	1	0	0	0							
Totals..	36	1	9	24	6	2	Totals...	26	2	4	27	4	3

*Ran for Northen in ninth inning.
New York .... 0 0 0 1 0 0 1 0 x—2
Brooklyn .... 0 0 1 0 0 0 0 0 0—1
First on errors—New York 2, Brooklyn 2. Two-base hit—Murray. Stolen bases—Murray. Wheat. Sacrifice flies—Tooley, Myers. Left on bases—New York 2, Brooklyn 14. Double plays—Moran, Hummel; Herzog. Doyle, Merkle; Myers, Herzog. First on balls—Off Marquard 3. Rucker 5. Struck out—By Marquard 5. Rucker 3. Time—1.56. Umpires—Brennan and Emslie.

R. MARQUARD, NEW YORK, N. L., 1912.	
60 Feet, 5 inches; 24-inch Slab; One Step.	
Date.	Opposing Club.
April 11—Marquard 18, Brooklyn 3.	
April 16—Marquard 5, Boston 2.	
April 24—Marquard 11, Philadelphia 4.	
May 1—Marquard 11, Philadelphia 4.	
May 7—Marquard 6, St. Louis 2.	
May 11—Marquard 10, Chicago 3.	
May 16—Marquard 4, Pittsburgh 1.	
May 20—Marquard 3, Cincinnati 2.	
May 24—Marquard 6, Brooklyn 3.	
May 30—Marquard 7, Philadelphia 1.	
June 2—Marquard 8, St. Louis 3.	
June 8—Marquard 6, Cincinnati 2.	
June 12—Marquard 3, Chicago 2.	
June 17—Marquard 9, Pittsburgh 2.	
June 19—Marquard 6, Boston 3.	
June 21—Marquard 3, Boston 2.	
June 25—Marquard 2, Philadelphia 1.	
June 29—Marquard 8, Boston 6.	
July 3—Marquard 2, Brooklyn 1.	

PITCHER MARQUARD

By William F. Kirk.

Who "put it over" nineteen straight?
    Marquard.
Who seems the base ball pet of Fate?
    Marquard.
Who walks along Manhattan's streets
With cheers from every man he meets?
Who drove the knockers from their seats?
    Marquard.

Who'll lose a game some day, perhaps?
    Marquard.
Who reached a throne in spite of raps?
    Marquard.
Who, when the scroll is rolled up tight,
When players nevermore shall fight,
Will get the praise that is his right?
    McGRAW.

DETROIT AT WASHINGTON, AUGUST 23 (P. M. and P. M.)—Johnson pitched the opener and negotiated his sixteenth straight victory. The Nationals knocked Dubuc out of the box in the third inning, when Foster and Moeller followed each other with home run drives. Score:

Washin's.	AB.	R.	B.	P.	A.	E.	Detroit.	AB.	R.	B.	P.	A.	E.
Milan, cf..	3	1	0	3	0	0	Jones, lf...	4	0	1	1	0	0
Foster, 3b..	4	1	3	1	1	0	Bush, ss..	3	1	1	0	5	0
Moeller, rf..	4	1	1	0	0	0	Cobb, cf..	4	0	1	0	0	0
Gandil, 1b..	4	2	1	9	1	0	Crawford, rf	4	0	0	3	0	0
Morgan, 2b	2	1	0	3	0	Corriden, 2b	4	0	2	4	0
Shanks, lf..	3	2	1	1	0	0	Onslow, 1b..	4	0	1	13	0	1
McBride, ss	3	0	0	3	6	0	Deal, 3b..	4	0	1	3	0	2
Ainsmith, c	4	0	3	7	2	0	Stanage, c..	4	0	6	2	0
Johnson, p..	4	0	1	3	0	Dubuc, p...	1	0	0	2	0
							Works, p...	3	0	0	3	0
Totals..	31	8	7	27	14	1							
							Totals...	33	1	7	24	16	4

Washington .... 0 1 3 0 0 3 0 1 x—8
Detroit .... 0 0 0 0 0 0 0 1 0—1
Two-base hits—Gandil, Crawford, Foster. Three-base hit—Shanks. Home runs—Foster, Moeller. Hits—Off Dubuc 3 in 3 innings. Works 4 in 5 innings. Sacrifice hits—Morgan. Stolen bases—Bush, Crawford 2, Onslow, McBride 2, Ainsmith, Shanks 2. Double plays—Bush, Corriden, Onslow; McBride, Morgan, Gandil. Left on bases—Detroit 7, Washington 4. First on balls—Off Dubuc 2, Johnson 2. First on errors—Washington 2. Struck out—By Dubuc 1. Works 3, Johnson 8. Wild pitch—Works. Time—1.45. Umpires—Egan and Evans.

ST. LOUIS AT WASHINGTON, AUGUST 29.—The Browns made it three out of four in the series. Walter Johnson allowed only four hits, but he was wild and his support was poor. The defeat ended any possible controversy as to whether he could beat the record of Marquard of 19 straight victories. Powell was effective in the pinches. Score:

St. Louis.	AB.	R.	B.	P.	A.	E.	Washin's.	AB.	R.	B.	P.	A.	E.
Shotten, cf..	3	0	1	2	0	0	Moeller, rf..	4	1	1	1	0
Compton, lf	4	0	2	3	0	0	Foster, 3b..	4	0	1	3	0
Williams, rf	3	0	0	1	0	0	Milan, cf..	4	0	2	1	0
Pratt, 2b..	4	0	0	2	0	0	Gandil, 1b..	4	0	1	7	1	0
Kutina, 1b..	4	0	0	10	0	0	Morgan, 2b..	4	1	0	2	0
Austin, 3b..	3	0	0	1	2	0	Kenwor'y, lf	4	0	1	1	0
Wallace, ss	4	0	1	5	8	1	McBride, ss	4	0	0	1	2	0
Krichell, c..	3	2	0	3	1	0	Ainsmith, c	3	0	1	13	3	0
Powell, p..	2	1	0	0	0	0	Johnson, p..	3	0	0	0	3	0
Totals .	30	3	4	27	13	2	Totals..	34	2	7	27	13	2

St. Louis .... 0 0 2 0 0 0 1 0 0—3
Washington .... 0 1 1 0 0 0 0 0 0—2
Two-base hits—Foster, Moeller, Wallace, Ainsmith. Double play—Johnson, Ainsmith, Gandil. Left on bases—St. Louis 5, Washington 5. First on balls—Off Johnson 4. First on errors—St. Louis 3, Washington 2. Hit by pitcher—By Johnson 1. Struck out—By Powell 3, Johnson 12. Passed balls—Ainsmith 2. Wild pitch Johnson. Time—1.45. Umpires—Evans and Egan.

A POSSIBLE SNAG

THAT FULTZ'S NEW FRATERNITY MAY ENCOUNTER

Yearly Dues to Support the Proposed Players' Organization and Its Non-Playing Officials Already the Subject of Hostile Criticism.

SPECIAL TO "SPORTING LIFE."

New York, N. Y., September 10.—How long will the Base Ball Players' Fraternity, engineered by David L. Fultz, last? The big club owners and persons iden-

Dave Fultz

tified with the organized leagues have been quietly making an investigation with the result that they have come to regard the players' movement as entirely harmless. Careful probing has developed the fact—so the magnates declare—that the players under contract to American League clubs have no grievances of any kind and that only two National League club owners are charged with unfair treatment. The most serious obstacle in the path of the fraternity, however, appears to be the question of dues. Each player has been asked, according to good authority, to pay $18 a year into the treasury. As 286 players have enrolled this would mean

A YEARLY REVENUE OF $5148,

with more to come when the minor league players are asked to join the organization. It is understood that Fultz, who is slated for the presidency, will draw a salary and that other officials will receive compensation. Many of the big league players, it is said, cannot make themselves believe that such a large revenue is necessary and some of them are inclined to refuse to dig up their share. This was the trouble with the Players' Protective Association formed on similar lines a dozen years ago. There was much enthusiasm until the players were asked to peel greenbacks from their salaries. Then the association

WENT UP IN SMOKE.

The Players' Brotherhood, started in 1889 to abolish "slavery," gathered a big bankroll with which to conduct a revolt against the magnates. The Players' League was formed and in a disastrous war with organized base ball several millions of dollars were lost. The players were forced to surrender and they came back to the fold at greatly reduced salaries. If the new fraternity lives it is predicted that it will not be long before the players, encouraged by moneyed backers, will attempt to break loose from their present employers. But will it live?　　JOE VILA.

PITTSBURGH AT BROOKLYN, SEPTEMBER 17.—After 12 consecutive victories the Pirates went down to defeat. The visitors used four pitchers. Home runs by Daubert and Wheat in the fifth inning were features. Wheat, Fisher and Wagner did great fielding. Charley Stengel, a Brooklyn optional purchase from the Southern League, made four singles, walked and stole a base. It was his first appearance. Score:

ATHLETICS AT DETROIT, SEPTEMBER 11.—Collins featured in all departments of the game. With five trips to the plate he got four hits and stole six sacks. The Tigers rallied in the ninth, when they succeeded in clubbing home four runs. An excited fan heaved a pop bottle at Umpire Connolly and his aim was true, the bottle striking the umpire in the mouth. The cause of the assault was brought about by Cobb being ruled off the ball. Connolly declaring the batter stepped out of the box. Score:

BOSTON AT DETROIT, SEPTEMBER 20.—After winning 16 straight games Joe Wood lost his opportunity of setting a new American League record when Boston lost to Detroit. Wood paved the way for his defeat by walking four Tigers in succession in the third inning after two men were out. Covington was chased in the fifth for objecting to O'Loughlin's decisions. Lake, who replaced him, held the Champions helpless. Score:

ATHLETICS AT ST. LOUIS, SEPTEMBER 23 (P. M. and P. M.)—In the opening contest Collins made four singles, stole six bases and scored three runs. McInnis stole three bases. Plank easily held the Browns safe. Score:

WASHINGTON AT CHICAGO, SEPTEMBER 22 (P. M. and P. M.)—The Senators beat the White Sox in both games and Clyde Milan exceeded the base stealing record of the American League. Milan stole three bases in the two games and brought his total to 84. Cobb with 82, held the record. This was established in 1911 and smashed the one of 82 made by Eddie Collins in the opening contest and also profited by Scott's wildness in the first and second innings. Ellis Johnson, a Chicago recruit, relieved Scott in the third and pitched good ball. Score:

WASHINGTON AT PHILADELPHIA, SEPTEMBER 27.—Two games were to have been played, but the second game could not even be started, as the first game went 19 innings—a major league record for the 1912 season. The visitors scored four runs in the first two innings on five hits, two battery and fielding errors and a fielder's choice. After that Plank held them to no runs and si xhits for 16 successive innings. In the nineteenth Williams received a base on balls and Johnson beat out a bunt. Williams was forced at third on Moeller's grounder. Foster forced Moeller at second, Barry to Collins. In trying for a double play Collins threw wild and Johnson scored the winning run. Groom pitched the first nine innings for Washington. Twice with the bases filled scoring was prevented by double plays, and in the seventh, with the bases filled and one out, the home team scored on an out. Four hits and an error in the ninth enabled the Athletics to tie the score. Johnson, who took Groom's place in the tenth inning, was also hit harder than Plank, but brilliant fielding, especially by Foster and McBride, prevented scoring. Plank, a veteran of 12 seasons, out-twirled both of his younger opponents, the majority of Washington's runs being due to battery and fielding misplays. Score:

Oct. 16

7th Game

COBB CENSURES ROYAL ROOTERS

Puts Blame for Wood's Defeat on Delay in Starting Game

ROOTERS WRATHY

Though there was much dissatisfaction in Boston fandom regarding the distribution of the sale of tickets for yesterday's game, perhaps the wrath of the "Royal Rooters" was the fiercest. The rooters, over 800 in number, made the trip over to New York on Sunday afternoon and on Monday demonstrated to the Gothamites just what Boston fandom was capable of doing in the rooting line.

After the game a telegram was sent Treasurer McRoy, asking that the usual seats in left field be reserved for the rooters who were due to reach town before the game.

Seats Were Sold

However, when the rooters arrived at the field they found that their usual seats had been sold. This was not to their liking. Most of the rooters managed to find their way into the park, but they were widely scattered and were a very much dissatisfied lot. Many of them were unable to get into the park.

The rooters gathered together after the game and after parading around the field stopped in front of the New York bench and in loud terms expressed their dissatisfaction with the Boston management and then gave a cheer for the New York management. They then paraded around onto Jersey street and in front of the local club office again expressed themselves.

Treasurer McRoy stated that the reason why the seats were not reserved was because they were not called for until 1:30 p. m. Timothy Mooney, who looked after the rooters' tickets, claims that he applied for the tickets at the American league office, at exactly 1:30 p. m.

Reprinted from **The Boston Post,** with permission of **The Boston Globe**

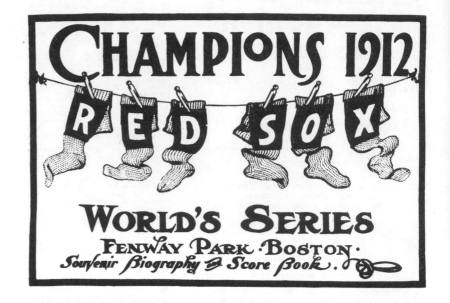

DEATH OF BRUSH

THE FAMOUS NATIONAL LEAGUE MAGNATE NO MORE

He Expires in His Private Car While on the Way From New York to California as a Last Desperate Resort to Prolong Life

St. Louis, Mo., November 26.—John T. Brush, the famous President of the New York National League Club, died last night in his private car attached to a train for California. He expired between Louisiana and St. Louis, Mo. His car was at once detached from the train and started back to this city where it arrived at 6.59 this morning. The deceased started from New York for Los Angeles, Cal. Mr. Brush was carried from the Hotel Imperial in New York to an automobile and was placed in the Pullman sleeper while in a semi-conscious condition. It is said that his physicians advised the long trip to sunny California as a last resort, for the owner of the Giants has been at death's door recently. Mr. Brush has been a sufferer from locomotor ataxia for many years.

J. T. Brush

DESPERATE FINISH WINS SERIES FOR RED SOX IN TENTH, 3 TO 2

Mathewson Weakens After Snodgrass Drops Engle's Easy Fly—Speaker's Single and Gardner's Sacrifice Fly Give Boston Two Runs and the Final Game—Errors Lost for New York

Hooper's Wonderful Catch Robs Doyle of Home Run—Wood Pitches Last Three Innings

How the Red Sox Won Game in Tenth Inning

This is the story of how the Red Sox won the game and the championship of the world in the 10th inning of the deciding game of the most sensational series for the big title ever waged. The Giants had managed to take a one-run lead in their half of the inning, so that the Red Sox faced the loss of the game, the title and the big end of the players' share of the receipts unless they scored at least one run. They made two.

In the emergency Engle was called to bat in place of Wood. He sent a fly to left centre which Snodgrass muffed, Engle taking second on the error. Hooper sent another fly to Snodgrass, but this time the New York centre fielder made no mistake and Hooper was out. Mathewson walked Yerkes. Speaker, coming up amidst an ovation from the now frenzied spectators, swung hard at the first ball pitched, but a groan went up when it was seen that he had raised a puny foul near the coacher's box at first. Merkle and Meyers both started for it, became mixed up and let the ball drop between them. Then Speaker singled to right, scoring Engle with the run that again tied up the game. Yerkes took third and Speaker second on Devore's throw to catch Engle at the plate. Lewis was purposely passed, the Giants planning on a double play with the bases filled. But Gardner sent a long fly to right. Devore caught it and threw to the plate, but not in time to catch Yerkes, who came across with the winning run.

Reprinted from **The Boston Post,** with permission of **The Boston Globe**

Charley Comiskey Visits His Old Employer and Friend, Chris von der Ahe, Who Is Lying Incurably Ill at His Home in St. Louis

C. Von Der Ahe

St. Louis, Mo., February 22.—Charles A. Comiskey, owner of the Chicago White Sox, on the night of Monday, February 17, gladdened the heart of his old employer, Chris von der Ahe, who has a secure niche in base ball history as President of the famous St. Louis Browns, four-time pennant winners in the old American Association. Comiskey came from Chicago to visit Von der Ahe. He was met by Chas. C. Spink, who tried to inveigle him to a banquet. "I came down to see Chris von der Ahe," said Commy, "take me to him." Spink whisked Comiskey to Von der Ahe's home. "That's the same house in which Chris lived when he first signed me to play ball at $75 in 1882," said Comiskey, as the car drew up in front of a stone house Chris built in his palmy days. "This is the proudest moment of my life," said Von der Ahe, who physicians say is stricken with an incurable malady. "It certainly makes me feel good to think that you came here just to spend three hours with your old boss." "How are you fixed," asked Comiskey. "I've got a lot and a nice monument already built for me in Bellefontaine cemetery," replied Chris as the tears began to fall. Comiskey brushed away a tear too, and into the hand of his old "boss" the magnate slipped a check. Von der Ahe wept like a child and a physician signified that the visit must end. Comiskey will plan a benefit for Von der Ahe if the old boss is spared until the White Sox return from California.

THE SPECIAL OPENING

The Ebbets Field Formally Dedicated on Wednesday, April 9.

PHILADELPHIA AT BROOKLYN, APRIL 9.—Philadelphia beat Brooklyn in the special opening game of the National League season, which marked the formal occupation of Ebbets Field. The cold, raw wind kept the attendance down to about 12,000, but did not affect the players, who put up a remarkable battle. Both Seaton and Rucker pitched brilliant ball, the former just shading the noted southpaw in a 1-to-0 shut-out. The opening ceremonies were impressive, the two teams parading across the field headed by a band, and Borough President Alfred E. Steers threw out the first ball. Benny Meyer, the heavy-hitting recruit from Toronto, lost the game for Rucker in the first inning. With one out Knabe doubled to right. Meyer muffed Lobert's foul in the sun field, but Stengel overcame this error by making a sensational catch of a long fly from the same batter. Then Meyer muffed Magee's fly, letting Knabe in with the only run of the contest. Score:

Philad'a.	AB.	R.	B.	P.	A.	E.	Brooklyn.	AB.	R.	B.	P.	A.	E.
Paskert, cf	4	0	1	1	0	0	Stengel, cf	4	0	0	1	1	0
Knabe, 2b	3	1	2	2	0	0	Cutshaw, 2b	4	0	0	1	1	0
Lobert, 3b	3	0	1	2	1	0	Meyer, rf	2	0	0	0	0	2
Magee, rf	3	0	0	2	0	0	Erwin	1	0	0	0	0	0
Dolan, lf	4	0	1	0	0	0	Wheat, lf	4	0	2	1	1	0
Luderus, 1b	4	0	0	12	0	0	Daubert, 1b	3	0	1	12	1	0
Doolan, ss	3	0	1	5	0	0	Smith, 3b	3	0	0	1	2	0
Dooin, c	3	0	1	3	6	0	Fisher, ss	3	0	1	3	1	0
Seaton, p	3	0	1	1	2	0	Miller, c	4	0	1	6	2	0
							Rucker, p	2	0	0	1	3	0
							†Callahan	1	0	0	0	0	0
							Ragan, p	0	0	0	0	0	0
Totals	30	1	8	27	13	0	Totals	30	0	6	27	16	3

*Batted for Meyer in ninth inning.
†Batted for Rucker in eighth inning.

Philadelphia .... 1 0 0 0 0 0 0 0 0—1
Brooklyn .... 0 0 0 0 0 0 0 0 0—0

First on errors—Philadelphia 3. Two-base hits—Knabe. Sacrifice hits—Magee, Lobert. Stolen base—Daubert. Left on bases—Philadelphia 5, Brooklyn 4. First on balls—Off Rucker 1, Seaton 1. Struck out—By Rucker 3, Ragan 1, Seaton 7. Wild pitch—Seaton. Hits—Off Rucker 8 in 8 innings, Ragan 0 in 1 inning. Umpires—Klem and Orth. Time—1.55.

THE FEDERAL LEAGUE

That's the Title of the New League John T. Powers Is Promoting—Cincinnati to Be Invaded via Covington, Ky.

Special to "Sporting Life."

Indianapolis, Ind., March 10.—John T. Powers, of Chicago, was elected president of the Federal League of Base Ball Clubs here late Saturday afternoon. The organization was incorporated under the laws of Indiana earlier in the day. Other officers are: M. R. Bramley, Cleveland, vice-president; James A. Ross, Indianapolis, secretary, and John A. George, Indianapolis, treasurer. The board of managers is composed of William T. McCullough, Pittsburgh; Michael Kenney, St. Louis; Charles X. Zimmerman, Cleveland; John A. Spinney, Cincinnati; Jas. A. Ross, John A. George and John S. Powell, Indianapolis, and Charles L. Sherlock, Chicago. Each club will be required to post a forfeit of $5000 before the opening of the season, which is scheduled to take place between May 10 and May 15. It was announced that the Indianapolis Club would be incorporated Tuesday with a capital of $100,000. The circuit, it is understood, will include St. Louis, Detroit, Pittsburgh, Chicago, Cleveland and Indianapolis. Cincinnati also seeks a berth in the new organization and may get the one now offered to Pittsburgh. If Cincinnati is successful, the park probably will be located in Covington, Ky., with grounds that can be reached from downtown Cincinnati 10 minutes easier than the National League park can be reached. In Chicago the new league has secured the use of the Riverview Park grounds, but its designs upon a site closer to the city and much more accessible. Little has been given out as to the actual backers of the Indianapolis club, but it was stated today that local business men were behind the venture and that capital to the amount of $100,000 had been raised. The Riverside Bathing Beach is the site most favored. As to the guaranty of good faith each applicant for a franchise was plainly required to lay down proof that the club he represents controls playing grounds and on top of that each was required to deposit a check to insure that his club will carry out the schedule through the playing season. The big money behind the league, it appears, comes from a company which now owns nine motordromes and amusement parks in the Central West.

THE FEDERAL LEAGUE

Does Not Propose to Interfere With Major League or Minor League Players Under Contract, or to Buck Organized Ball More Than Can Be Helped.

STEALING THIRD

Why That Is a Harder Feat Than the Pilfering of Second.

The question of "why is it harder to steal third base than to steal second?" has been raised numerous times during the past few weeks. When in Detroit recently Manager Hugh Jennings answered it. He said: "It is popularly supposed that the runner on second gets a better lead than the runner on first, but this is not true. When a man is on second he is not only further away from the coacher, but he has to watch more men than when on first. He must be ready to go either way at an instant's notice, and naturally, then, he does not get the set start given a man leading off first. The runner on second has to watch the shortstop, second baseman, pitcher and catcher, whereas the runner on first only watches the pitcher. The coacher at first watches the other fielders and advises the runner. When a man is on second he has to look out for himself. That is why he doesn't get the lead."

COOMBS ILL, SENT HOME BY MACK

Attack of Grippe Will Keep Iron Man of Hurling Staff Out of Game for Some Time

Special to The Inquirer.

WASHINGTON, April 15. That supposedly impregnable defense of the Philadelphia Athletics was rocked, jarred and deprived of one of its most potent parts today when "Jack" Coombs was sent back to the home town suffering from a severe attack of grippe. Connie Mack thought that the clever twirler was in excellent shape and would be able to perform regularly until it was possible to decide whether any of the young slabmen who have been picked up would do. However, about noon today Coombs developed a case of grippe that suddenly grew so bad that the athlete was shipped home at 4 o'clock.

According to the manager, Coombs will be able to resume work in about a week, but others say that the absence of the player may be more extended. If Coombs is held out it will be an awful blow to the Mackmen, as his work at this period was thought to be essential to the improvement of the chances of the team that is now considered as the chief rivals of the Nationals for premier honors in the American League.

Reprinted from
The Philadelphia Inquirer

CLEVELAND AT NEW YORK, JUNE 4.—The Naps won on hard hitting. The New Yorks also hit Blanding hard, but he was strong with men on bases, and 12 of the locals were left on base. In the second inning Jackson made one of the longest hits ever seen in New York when he hit a ball over the right field wing of the grand stand. This is the first time this feat has been accomplished since the Brush stadium was constructed in 1911. Score:

Cleveland.	AB.	R.	B.	P.	A.	E.	New York.	AB.	R.	B.	P.	A.	E.
Johnston, 1b	5	0	0	7	0	1	Hartzell, rf	3	4	3	2	0	0
Chapman, ss	5	1	1	4	3	0	Wolter, cf	5	1	1	4	1	1
Olson, 3b	5	1	2	2	2	0	Borton, 1b	5	1	2	13	0	0
Turner, 2b	5	1	1	4	0	0	Cree, lf	4	1	3	0	1	0
Jackson, rf	4	3	3	1	0	0	Sweeney, c	4	1	2	5	0	0
Ryan, cf	5	2	2	4	0	0	Zeider, 2b	4	1	0	6	3	2
Graney, lf	3	2	2	3	0	0	Midkiff, 3b	5	0	0	2	3	0
O'Neill, c	5	1	3	3	1	0	Peckin'h, ss	4	0	1	2	4	0
Blanding, p	4	1	2	0	2	0	Ford, p	2	0	0	1	2	0
							*Daniels	1	0	0	0	0	0
							McConn'l, p	0	0	0	0	0	0
							†Caldwell	1	1	1	0	0	0
							Clark, p	0	0	0	0	0	0
Totals	39	9	15	27	12	1	Totals	39	5	13	27	14	3

*Batted for Ford in sixth inning.
†Batted for McConnell in eighth inning.

Cleveland .... 0 1 1 0 0 2 1 0 2 3—9
New York .... 0 0 0 1 0 0 1 2 1 5—5

First on errors—New York 1, Cleveland 2. Two-base hits—Cree, Wolter. Home runs—Jackson, Sweeney. Graney. Stolen bases—Hartzell, Cree. Sacrifice hits—Sweeney, Turner, Blanding. Left on bases—New York 12, Cleveland 9. Struck out—By Ford 1, Blanding 3. First on balls—Off Ford 2, Warhop 1, Clark 1, Blanding 4. Double play—Zeider, Borton. Hits—Off Ford 8 in 6 innings, Warhop 3 in 1 inning (none out in eighth). McConnell 0 in 1 inning. Time—2.15. Umpires—Evans and Egan.

Johnson's New Pitching Record

PITCHER WALTER JOHNSON, of the Washington Club, of the American League, has set a new major league record for shut-out innings pitched. From April 10 to May 10, inclusive, Johnson pitched 56 innings without a run being made off his delivery. On April 10 he yielded a run in the first inning of the Washington-New York game of that date, and, thereafter, he pitched invincibly against New York twice, Boston four times, Athletics once, Chicago once, and against St. Louis on May 14 for 3 and one-third innings, when the string was cut and the second run of the 1913 season was scored on him. Here is a summary of Johnson's record and the two next best major league records:

JOHNSON'S RECORD IN 1913.

April 10—New York	1	0	0	0	0	0	0	0	0—0
April 19—New York	0	0	0	0	0	0	0	0	0—0
April 23—Boston ..	0	0	0	0	0	0	0	0	0—0
April 25—Boston ..	.	.	.	.	.	.	.	.	0—1
April 29—Athletics.	0	0	0	0	0	0	0	0	0—0
*May 3—Boston ...	.	.	.	.	.	.	.	0	0—2⅔
†May 5—Boston ...	.	.	.	.	0	0	0	0	0—5
May 10—Chicago ..	0	0	0	0	0	0	0	0	0—0
May 11—St. Louis..	0	0	0	1	.	.	.	.	.—3⅓

Total—56 innings.

*Relieved Engel in the seventh inning with one out, consequently he pitched ⅔ inning and finished the game, making 2⅔ innings of the game without a run.

†Relieved Engel at the end of the seventh inning and pitched the last five innings of a 12-inning game.

It was generally supposed that the major league record up to the present year was held by pitcher "Doc" White, of the Chicago White Sox. He was credited with having pitched 56 consecutive shut-out innings. An investigation made by George L. Moreland, the noted Pittsburgh statistician, showed that Jack Coombs, of the Athletics—and not "Doc" White—was the holder of the record up to 1913. Here is what Mr. Moreland discovered:

COOMBS' RECORD IN 1910.

September 5—New York....	1 0 0 0 0 0 0 0 0—8
September 9—Boston	0 0 0 0 0 0 0 0 0—9
September 12—Washington .	0 0 0 0 0 0 0 0 0—9
September 16—Detroit	0 0 0 0 0 0 0 0 0—3
September 21—Cleveland	0 0 0 0 0 0 0 0 0 0 0-11
*September 25—Chicago	. . . 0 0 0 0 0 0—6
†September 25—Chicago	. . . . 0 3—1

Total—53 innings.

*Pitched last six innings, first game.

†Pitched two innings, second game.

According to Mr. Moreland's books, White's record in 1904 was only 45 innings, starting September 12 with Cleveland, followed by full games with Cleveland, St. Louis, Detroit, Athletics, New York. His streak was ended in the first inning of the first game of the Chicago-New York double-header of October 2, making his record as follows:

WHITE'S RECORD IN 1904.

September 12—Cleveland ...	0 0 0 0 0 0 0 0 0—9
September 16—St. Louis ...	0 0 0 0 0 0 0 0 0—9
September 19—Detroit	0 0 0 0 0 0 0 0 0—9
September 25—Athletics	0 0 0 0 0 0 0 0 0—9
September 30—New York ...	0 0 0 0 0 0 0 0 0—9
October 2—New York	1 . . . .—0

Total—45 innings.

The world's record for consecutive shut-outs in professional base ball is 78 innings, made by pitcher Faulkner, of the Wilmington, Del., Club, in 1903. The next best minor league record was made by pitcher Alexander (now with the Philadelphia Nationals) in 1910, when, pitching for the Syracuse Club, of the New York State League, he shut-out his opponents seven straight games, he pitching 52 innings without a run, during which time he yielded only 22 hits.

WASHINGTON AT ST. LOUIS, MAY 14.—Walter Johnson started the game for the visitors and held St. Louis scoreless for three and one-third innings, making 56 consecutive scoreless innings he has pitched against opposing teams. Today's victory was Johnson's ninth straight win. Counting today's score made by St. Louis in the fourth inning, only two runs have been made off him this season. Washington had no trouble piling up a big score on St. Louis, as Leverenz was unsteady and Allison was hit hard by the visitors. Boehling relieved Johnson in the sixth and was hit hard. St. Louis scored four runs in the eighth on a base on balls, four hits and an error. Score:

Washin'n.	AB.	R.	B.	P.	A.	E.
Moeller, lf.	3	3	2	1	0	0
Milan, cf..	3	1	1	2	0	0
Morgan, 2b	0	0	0	0	0	0
Gedeon, 2b	3	0	1	0	2	0
Gandil, 1b	2	0	0	4	0	0
A.Will's, 1b	3	0	1	5	0	0
Laporte, 3b	5	0	0	1	2	0
Ainsmith, c	4	1	0	9	1	0
Shanks, lf.	4	1	2	3	0	0
McBride, ss	4	2	3	2	2	1
Johnson, p.	3	3	2	0	0	0
Boehling, p	0	0	0	0	1	0
Totals..	33	10	12	27	8	1

St. Louis.	AB.	R.	B.	P.	A.	E.
Compton, cf	4	1	0	2	0	0
Johnson, lf.	3	0	0	0	0	0
Maisel, lf..	3	1	2	1	0	0
C.Will's, rf	5	2	2	0	0	0
Pratt, 2b..	4	1	2	2	3	0
Brief, 1b..	4	0	1	12	0	1
Austin, 3b.	2	0	0	1	4	1
Graff, 3b...	1	0	1	0	0	0
Walsh, ss..	4	0	1	4	4	0
McAllister.c	0	0	0	0	0	1
Alexander, c	3	0	0	4	1	0
Leverenz, p.	0	0	0	0	1	0
Allison, p..	3	0	0	0	3	0
*Wallace ..	1	0	0	0	0	0
†Agnew ...	0	0	0	0	0	0
Totals .	36	3	10	27	17	3

*Batted for Alexander in ninth inning.

†Batted for Allison in ninth inning.

Washington	1	5	0	0	0	3	0	1	0—10
St. Louis	0	0	0	1	0	0	0	4	0— 3

Two-base hits—McBride 2, Johnson, Maisel, Graff. Three-base hits McBride, Johnston, Moeller. Hits—Off Leverenz 1 in 1 inning, Allison 11 in 8 innings, Johnson 3 in 6 innings, Boehling 7 in 3 innings. Sacrifice fly—Milan. Double plays Walsh, Pratt, Brief; Walsh, Brief; Austin, Brief; Williams unassisted. Left on bases Washington 6, St. Louis 7. First on balls—Off Leverenz 3, Allison 2, Boehling 3. Hit by pitcher By Allison 1. Struck out—By Johnson 7, Boehling 1, Allison 4. Time 2.00. Umpires—Ferguson and O'Loughlin.

A Question of Income Tax

New York, N. Y., May 29.—If a base ball player receives as much as $4000 or more for his season's work, would he be exempt from the income tax now being entertained by Congress in case he pleaded that the amount was received for six months' work, and that he did not earn that much as a year's salary? To the fans who tackle statistics, figures, and all sport dope, this will prove rather an interesting query. According to the income tax bill now being given consideration, one must pay one per cent. on a year's salary of $4000, the tax increasing in ratio with the increase in yearly wage. At present there are quite a number of big league players who receive $4000 for their year's services on the diamond, and there are quite a few who receive much more than that amount. Now the question is, will these ball players admit that such is a yearly wage or a half yearly one, should the tax be passed? Should they declare that the amount implies a full year's wages, then they would not be exempt, but should they explain they receive that amount for but six months, and that they do not receive an annual salary, would legal complications, as to what construction must be placed on the law, follow?

ATHLETICS AT WASHINGTON, SEPTEMBER 29.—Walter Johnson added the thirty-sixth victory to his season's string by defeating the Athletics, 1 to 0. This was "McBride Day," having been set aside in honor of George McBride, Washington's captain and shortstop. He was presented a handsome diamond watch fob and a huge basket of flowers by the fans of Washington. Vice-President Marshall made the presentation speech. The lone run of the game came in the seventh inning. The locals could do little with Wyckoff, who pitched a sterling game. His support, however, was wobbly. Gandil opened with a single and stole second. Morgan beat out an infield tap, Gandil going to third. Williams then forced Morgan at second, Gandil coming home with the winning run. Score:

Washin'n.	AB.	R.	B.	P.	A.	E.
Moeller, rf	4	0	0	1	0	0
Milan, cf..	3	0	0	0	0	0
Foster, 3b.	3	0	0	1	0	0
Gandil, 1b	3	1	1	15	1	0
Morgan, 2b	3	0	1	1	4	0
Williams, c	3	0	0	8	0	0
Acosta, lf..	2	0	0	0	0	0
McBride, ss	2	0	1	0	6	0
Johnson, p.	3	0	0	1	2	0
Totals..	26	1	3	27	13	0

Athletics.	AB.	R.	B.	P.	A.	E.
Daley, cf..	4	0	2	2	0	0
Walsh, lf..	4	0	1	0	0	1
Fritz, 3b..	4	0	0	2	1	1
Carrou's, 2b	4	0	0	3	1	1
Brickley, rf.	3	0	1	0	0	0
Pfeffer, ss.	3	0	0	1	4	1
Orr, 1b....	3	0	1	15	1	1
McAvoy, c..	3	0	0	1	1	0
Wyckoff, p.	3	0	0	0	6	0
*Strunk ...	1	0	0	0	0	0
Totals...	32	0	5	24	14	5

*Batted for Brickley in ninth inning.

Washington	0	0	0	0	0	0	1	0	x—1
Athletics	0	0	0	0	0	0	0	0	0—0

Three-base hit—Brickley. Sacrifice hit—McBride. Stolen base—Gandil. Double play—McBride, Morgan, Gandil. Left on bases—Athletics 7, Washington 3. First on balls—Off Wyckoff 3, Johnson 1. First on errors—Washington 3. Hit by pitcher—By Johnson 1. Struck out—By Wyckoff 1, Johnson 9. Passed ball—Williams. Time—1.25. Umpires—Dineen and Connolly.

BOSTON AT WASHINGTON, OCTOBER 4.—Washington won the final game of the season from Boston in a weird exhibition. Clark Griffith, the famous old-timer, twirled the eighth inning and did not allow a run. Five Washington players took turns at pitching in the ninth, Boston scoring six runs. Walter Johnson played centre field for the Senators and Duffy Lewis held down third base for Boston. Score:

Boston.	AB.	R.	B.	P.	A.	E.
Rehg, lf...	4	0	2	0	0	0
Mundy, 1b	5	0	0	13	1	1
Hooper, cf.	4	1	0	2	2	0
Lewis, 3b .	4	1	3	2	1	0
C. Engle, rf	4	2	4	1	0	0
Hall, 2b ..	2	0	0	0	3	0
Yerkes, 2b	2	1	1	0	4	0
Janvrin, ss	3	2	2	2	4	0
Snell, c....	4	1	1	4	2	0
Anderson, p	3	0	0	0	3	0
*Thomas..	1	1	1	0	0	0
Totals..	36	9	15	24	20	1

Washin'n.	AB.	R.	B.	P.	A.	E.
Acosta, lf .	4	2	1	1	1	0
Moeller, rf.	2	2	2	0	0	0
Sch'r, rf,cf,p	3	0	2	3	2	0
Gedeon,3b,p	2	0	0	0	0	0
Foster, 3b..	3	1	2	0	1	0
Johnson,cf,p	3	2	2	2	1	0
Gandil, 1b ..	2	0	2	3	1	1
Willia's,1b,c	0	1	0	3	1	0
Ains'h, 2b,p	2	0	0	2	1	0
Morgan, 2b	2	0	0	3	0	0
Henry, c, 1b	3	1	2	4	4	0
Griffith, p,rf	1	0	1	0	0	0
Shanks, ss..	2	0	1	1	2	1
McBride, ss	2	0	2	3	3	0
Ryan, c....	1	0	0	1	1	0
R.Willia's,p	2	1	1	1	2	0
Bentley, p.	1	0	0	0	0	0
Engel, p...	0	0	0	0	1	0
Totals...	35	10	18	27	21	2

*Batted for Anderson in ninth inning.

Boston	0	2	0	1	0	0	0	0	6— 9
Washington	3	0	3	3	1	0	1	0	x—10

First on error—Washington. Left on bases—Washington 5, Boston 3. First on balls—Off R. Williams 2, Engel 1, Anderson 3. Innings pitched—By R. Williams 4, Bentley 2, Engel 1, Griffith 1, Schaefer ⅓, Ainsmith ⅓. Hits—Off R. Williams 4, Bentley 1, Engel 1, Griffith 1, Johnson 3, Ainsmith 2, Schaefer 2. Struck out—By R. Williams 1, Bentley 2, Anderson 3. Home runs—Janvrin 2. Three-base hits—Acosta, Rehg 2, Thomas, Foster, Henry 2. Two-base hits—Johnson, Gandil, Griffith, Yerkes. Sacrifice hit—A. Williams. Stolen bases—Acosta, Moeller, Johnson 2, Gandil, A. Williams, R. Williams, Rehg, C. Engel 2, Snell. Double play—Lewis, Mundy, Snell. Passed balls—Snell 2. Umpires—Connolly and Dineen. Time—1.45.

ATHLETICS DEFEAT GIANTS, 3-1, FOR BASE BALL TITLE

Plank Outpitches Mathewson in Fifth Game of World's Championship Series.

PHILADELPHIA SOUTHPAW ALLOWS ONLY TWO HITS

Holds New York Safe Throughout Game Before 36,682 Fans At Polo Grounds.

VICTORS WIN THROUGH MERIT.

American League Standard Bearers Show Superior Playing Strength in Every Department—McGraw Congratulates Mack.

Reprinted from
The Washington Evening Star

THE OFFICIAL SCORE.

PHILA.	AB.	R.	H.	PO.	A.	E.
E. MURPHY, rf	3	1	2	3	0	0
OLDRING, lf	4	2	0	3	0	0
COLLINS, 2b	4	0	1	2	3	0
BAKER, 3b	3	0	2	2	2	0
McINNIS, 1b	2	0	0	14	0	0
STRUNK, cf	4	0	0	2	0	0
BARRY, ss	4	0	0	2	7	0
SCHANG, c	4	0	1	1	1	0
PLANK, p	3	0	0	0	1	0
Totals	30	3	6	27	13	1

NEW YORK	AB.	R.	H.	PO.	A.	E.
HERZOG, 3b	4	0	0	1	0	0
DOYLE, 2b	4	0	0	1	7	1
FLETCHER, ss	3	0	0	2	3	0
BURNS, lf	3	0	2	3	0	1
SHAFER, cf	2	1	0	2	0	0
MURRAY, rf	3	0	0	2	0	0
McLEAN, c	3	0	0	3	1	0
MERKLE, 1b	3	0	0	14	0	0
MATHEWSON, p	2	0	0	0	2	0
CRANDALL*	1	0	0	0	0	0
Totals	28	1	2	27	15	2

*Batted for Mathewson in ninth inning.

Philadelphia .... 1 0 2 0 0 0 0 0 0—3
New York ...... 0 0 0 0 1 0 0 0 0—1

Sacrifice hits—Collins, McInnis. Sacrifice flies—Baker, McInnis. Double plays—Collins, Barry, McInnis; Barry, Collins, McInnis. Left on bases—Philadelphia, 5; New York, 4. First base on balls—Off Plank, 1; off Mathewson, 1. First base on errors—Philadelphia, 1; New York, 1. Struck out—By Plank, 1; by Mathewson, 2. Time of game—1 hour 39 minutes. Umpires—At the plate, Klem; on the bases, Egan; left field, Rigler; right field, Connolly.

BY J. ED GRILLO.

NEW YORK, October 11.—The Philadelphia Athletics are champions of the base ball world for 1913, winning the title at the Polo Grounds this afternoon by defeating the New York Giants 3 to 1, in the fifth and deciding game of the series.

It was a battle fought on its merits, the better team winning the day and the series. The result today was never in doubt. It was perhaps an easier victory than any of the previous three, though the score was small. Superior playing in every department gave the stronger team the advantage. All the scoring of the victors was done in the first three innings. After that they rested on their laurels and busied themselves keeping their lead from being threatened.

Mathewson and Plank, who last Wednesday fought a ten-inning affair at Philadelphia which the former won, met again today, but the result was reversed. This time Plank came out the winner, though it must be said that had Mathewson received the support he was entitled to he would have had a chance to win or at least forced the play into extra innings. But Mathewson did not pitch as good ball as did his rival. Plank allowed but two hits and one run, and that was virtually a gift resulting from a blunder which was inexcusable.

Plank Never in Danger.

There really never was a time when Plank was in danger. He went through the nine innings without once faltering and displayed even better form than in his previous contest with the master of them all, Mathewson. Inning after inning he mowed down the Giants, and it was not until the fifth that he allowed one of his opponents to reach the bases. It was in this inning that the Giants scored their lone tally and they really never threatened thereafter. In fact, but one more man reached first and he died a moment later in a lightning double play, which ended all possible chance the Giants may have had of again becoming troublesome.

With Mathewson it was different. He was not effective in the early innings and when his support wavered at critical stages he yielded enough runs to give the Athletics a lead from which they were never shaken. He gave a beautiful exhibition after the third inning, but the damage had been done and the game was lost.

CHAMPIONS 1913
WORLD'S SERIES
SHIBE PARK, PHILADELPHIA.
SOUVENIR SCORE BOOK.

WADDELL IN SORRY PLIGHT

ST. LOUIS, November 18.—"Rube" Waddell, formerly one of the greatest pitchers in base ball, was picked up wandering about the streets yesterday, exhausted and suffering from consumption. He could not speak above a whisper. Friends took him in charge and provided him with enough money to go to San Antonio, Tex.

Federal League to Respect Contracts

CHICAGO, Ills., January 14.—There is no chance of any players who are under signed contracts with any club in organized ball whatsoever being signed by the Federal League as long as James Gilmore remains as president of the organization. Mr. Gilmore said yesterday: "My statement that no contracted players will be signed by the Federal League stands. I have no objections to my managers going after players who are merely held by the reserve clause, but as to signing a contracted player, that is a different matter. All managers of the Federal League must look to me for orders and I must pass upon any contract they sign, and if I learn they have signed a player who is under contract I shall immediately refuse to accept such a contract. As soon as any manager learns that a player is under contract he must drop all negotiations with him." A dispatch yesterday from Pittsburgh, Pa., states that John B. Barbour, president of the Pittsburgh (Federal League) Club, explained his offer to Jake Daubert in the face of President Gilmore's injunction to let players who had signed up alone. Mr. Barbour is quoted as saying: "We did not know Daubert was signed, and accordingly our offer to him was withdrawn as soon as we learned it. We are not after players who have signed contracts; this is contrary to the policy of our league. When I made the offer I acted on the supposition that ball players signed from year to year." Incidentally Mr. Barbour said that the figures mentioned in the Daubert story were "rot and tommyrot." "We made no such offer," he said.

LATEST REPORT AS TO NUMBER OF SIGNED PLAYERS

Almost Enough Players Now Under Contract to Equip Eight Teams, Over Four-Score of the Men Being Major Leaguers.

CHICAGO, Ills., January 26.—Magnates of the Federal League, after two secret committee sessions, on Saturday issued two optimistic reports—one that 127 players, including eight managers, had been signed, 83 of whom were major leaguers, and the other, that the construction of all the stands would be under way this week. Among the 83 big leaguers are Rollie Zeider, of the New York Americans, who, it was announced, signed a contract last Friday night to play

J. A. Gilmore

with Tinker's Chicagoans; William Bradley, of the Toronto International League team, who signed to manage the Toronto Federals; and pitcher Claude Hendrix, of Pittsburgh, signed with the Chicago Federals. Zeider accepted the Federal terms after Arthur Irwin, the New Yorks' representative, had declined to promise him a $5000 salary and a chance at playing third base. Bradley gained fame as an infielder with Cleveland. The committee which heard reports on players consisted of Walter Mullin, Buffalo; E. H. Hanlon, Baltimore, and Chas. Weeghman, Chicago. The committee on stands, to which was referred reports on contracts and plans, consisted of Edward Steininger, St. Louis; President J. A. Gilmore, and Edward E. Gates, Indianapolis. Everybody concerned denied a widely-circulated report that the St. Paul American Association team, to be purchased by Weeghman, would be transferred to Chicago and would play on the North Side grounds leased for the Federals. Weeghman said he would stand by the Federal League, and President Chivington declared there would be no change in the Association.

NEW YORK'S PRIOR RIGHTS ESTABLISHED

Cole Charges That His Federal Contract Was Made Subsequent to His Acceptance of New York's Terms, But Was Ante-Dated.

NEW YORK, February 8.—The Cole case was settled during the past week, developments having shown that the New York American Club alone had legal claim upon him and that it was within its rights in taking him away again from the Federal League. It also developed that not only had the New York Club the legal right to Cole's services, but that the Chicago Federal League Club in signing Cole did not live entirely up to the announced policy of the Federal League to deal only with players on whom there was no legal claim; as the reclaimed player, pitcher Cole, in a published letter charged the Chicago Federal people with deception.

F. J. Farrell

Great Hurler, Eccentric to Last, Dies in Sanitarium.

SAN ANTONIO, Tex., April 1.—George Edward Waddell, the famous "Rube," as he was known wherever baseball is played, died at a sanitarium here late today, a victim of tuberculosis, after a long fight for life. Waddell, once one of the greatest of baseball pitchers, came to west Texas four months ago already weakened by pulmonary trouble, but buoyant and hopeful that a few months would see him restored to health and "back in the game." He located on a ranch near Boerne, but instead of improving, his strength grew weaker from day to day, until his condition became so serious last month that he was brought to a sanitarium here.

Reprinted from
The Cleveland Plain Dealer

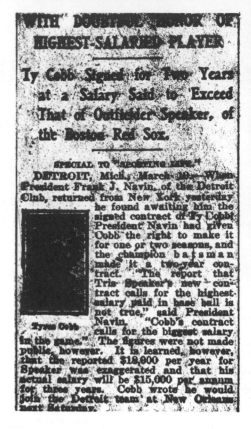

WITH DOUBTFUL HONOR OF HIGHEST-SALARIED PLAYER

Ty Cobb Signed for Two Years at a Salary Said to Exceed That of Outfielder Speaker, of the Boston Red Sox.

SPECIAL TO "SPORTING LIFE."

DETROIT, Mich., March 10.—When President Frank J. Navin, of the Detroit Club, returned from New York yesterday he found awaiting him the signed contract of Ty Cobb. President Navin had given Cobb the right to make it for one or two seasons, and the champion batsman made it a two-year contract. "The report that Tris Speaker's new contract calls for the highest salary paid in base ball is not true," said President Navin. "Cobb's contract calls for the biggest salary in the game." The figures were not made public, however. It is learned, however, that the reported $18,000 per year for Speaker was exaggerated and that his actual salary will be $15,000 per annum for three years. Cobb wrote he would join the Detroit team at New Orleans next Saturday.

Tyrus Cobb

WORLD'S CHAMPIONS SUBJECT TO INCOME TAX

Athletic Players Make Their Statement Upon Return From the South—The Local Championship Series Under Way.

PHILADELPHIA, Pa., April 6.—"Hullo there, Home Run Baker," shouted a base ball fan as J. Franklin, on his toes, brushed aside several letter carriers and rushed into the Internal Revenue Office at the Federal Building last Thursday. "Why, it's the whole Athletic team," volunteered a second fan. "No, I tell you now, it's only Baker, Jack Barry, Eddie Murphy, Rube Oldring, Jack Lapp and Bob Shawkey," pointed out a third rooter for the World's Champions who said he knew them for he hadn't missed a game at Shibe Park all last season. True, there were only six members of the World's Champions. A bargain sale in home run bats? Mercy, No! More serious expressions were on the faces of the Mackmen. In the mad rush to get into condition for the 1914 American League pennant race, the half dozen employes of C. Mack & Company had lost all track of the fact there was such a thing as the income tax. Various replies were made to the clerks in the office concerning the lateness of the Mackmen making their returns. They were informed that the $3200 they received as their share in the World's Series spoils was a part of their income and had to be declared as such. According to the regulations, the six Mackmen who only yesterday sent in their income tax returns are subject to a fine. The ball tossers related their reasons for the delinquency and asked for leniency in view of the fact they were not aware of the conditions surrounding the new regulation. Other members of the Athletics team, for all who shared in the World's Series spoils of 1913, are subject to the income tax, had previously filed their returns before going on the Southern trip to Jacksonville, Fla., last month.

Frank Baker

THE THIRD LEAGUE STARTS

The Initial Championship Contest of the New Major League Played Under Brilliant Auspices Before a Record-Breaking Baltimore Crowd.

BUFFALO AT BALTIMORE, APRIL 13. The first championship game of the Federal League as a major organization was played this day between Baltimore and Buffalo. When Mayor Preston, of Baltimore, with Mayor Fluhrmann, of Buffalo, standing beside him, this day tossed out the ball for the opening game of the Federal League series between Baltimore and Buffalo and President Gilmore gave the signal for the raising of "Old Glory" on the tall pole in centre field, 27,692 persons who had paid, and enough who had gotten in on passes to make the total 30,000, filled every place except the diamond in Terrapin Park. It was the biggest crowd that ever gathered at a Baltimore ball game and it was also the most enthusiastic. There was scarcely standing room in the Federal Park, but just across the way in Oriole Park, the diamond of which could be seen from the Terrapin Park grand stand, John McGraw's famous New York Giants and Jack Dunn's International League Orioles, who had been pitted as a strong counter attraction to the Federal opening, played before some 1500, even the bleachers being only one-third filled. The tremendous ovation given the Federals was Baltimore's approval of the change in local base ball conditions. Hundreds of lovers of the game have not seen a game played in Baltimore since the National League team was transferred to Brooklyn, but they all were on hand this day. So intense was the interest that at six o'clock in the morning a line had formed at the gates in wait to buy tickets. A procession from the heart of the city preceded the game. In the carriages were Federal magnates including President Gilmore, President Robertson, of the Buffaloes, and George S. Ward, of Brooklyn. At the park, just before the game started, John E. Madden, on behalf of Manager Knabe's Philadelphia friends, presented him with a silver loving cup. Manager Knabe decided to use Jack Quinn on the mound, while the Buffalo Federals sent Earl Moore to the firing line. Louden made the first error in the Federal League by booting Jacklitsch's grounder in the second inning. It fell to the fate of Manager Knabe to make the first error for the locals. Quinn's two bagger, followed by a slashing double to left by Swacina, broke the ice in the fourth inning and before the smoke had cleared away Baltimore tallied three runs. A pass and a steal by Doolan was followed by Jacklitsch's two-bagger into the crowd, scoring Swacina and Doolan. The Buffaloes made a game rally in the fifth inning, but could not tie and failed to score thereafter. Score:

Otto Knabe

Baltimore.	AB.	R.	B.	P.	A.	E.	Buffalo.	AB.	R.	B.	P.	A.	E.
Meyer, rf..	4	0	1	2	0	0	Hanford, cf.	5	0	2	2	0	0
Knabe, 2b	4	0	1	0	4	1	Downey, 2b.	3	0	0	2	2	0
Zinn, cf..	2	1	1	1	0	0	Louden, ss..	4	0	0	1	1	1
Simmons, lf	4	0	0	0	0	1	Bonnin, rf..	4	0	0	2	0	0
Swacina, 1b	4	1	2	11	0	1	Delahanty, lf	3	0	1	1	0	0
Walsh, 3b.	3	0	0	1	3	0	Smith, 3b..	3	0	0	1	0	1
Doolan, ss.	2	1	0	4	1	0	Agler, 1b..	3	0	1	3	0	1
Jacklitsch, c	4	0	1	8	3	1	Blair, c...	3	1	1	10	2	0
Quinn, p..	4	0	0	0	2	1	Moore, p..	2	0	0	0	0	0
							Krapp, p..	1	0	0	0	2	0
Totals..	31	3	6	27	13	5	*Young	0	1	0	0	0	0
							Totals...	30	2	5	24	7	3

*Batted for Moore in fifth inning.

Baltimore	0	0	0	3	0	0	0	0	x	—3
Buffalo	0	0	0	0	2	0	0	0	0	—2

Two-base hits—Knabe, Jacklitsch, Swacina, Hanford, Zinn, Meyer. Sacrifice hits—Smith, Walsh. Stolen bases—Bonnin, Doolan. Double plays—Krapp, Blair, Alger. First on balls—Off Quinn 1, Moore 1, Krapp 1. Hit by pitcher—By Krapp 2. Struck out—By Quinn 8, Moore 3, Krapp 5. Wild pitch—Moore. Left on bases—Baltimore 4, Buffalo 4. First on errors—Baltimore 2, Buffalo 3. Time—3.30. Umpires—Busch and Mannassau.

CHICAGO AT WASHINGTON, MAY 14.—Washington beat Chicago in the tenth inning of a magnificent pitching duel between Ayers and Scott. In the last of the tenth Gandil, first up, singled and scored the winning run on Shanks' double. For nine innings Scott held the locals hitless. Score:

Chicago.	AB.	R.	B.	P.	A.	E.	Washin'n.	AB.	R.	B.	P.	A.	E.
Demmitt, rf	4	0	1	1	0	0	Moeller, rf.	4	0	0	6	0	0
Berger, ss.	4	0	0	2	1	0	Foster, 3b..	4	0	0	0	1	1
Chase, 1b..	4	0	1	17	1	0	Milan, cf..	4	0	0	3	1	0
Collins, lf.	4	0	0	1	0	0	Gandil, 1b	4	1	1	14	2	0
Bodie, cf..	4	0	1	2	0	0	Shanks, lf.	4	0	1	0	0	0
Alcock, 3b	3	0	0	0	0	0	Morgan, 2b.	3	0	0	0	7	1
Blackb'n, 2b	4	0	0	2	8	2	McBride, ss	2	0	0	2	5	0
Schalk, c.	3	0	0	2	1	1	Henry, c...	2	0	0	3	0	0
Scott, p..	3	0	0	0	5	0	Ayers, p...	3	0	0	2	0	0
Totals..	33	0	3	*27	16	2	Totals...	30	1	2	30	16	2

*None out when winning run was scored.

Chicago	0	0	0	0	0	0	0	0	0	0	—0
Washington	0	0	0	0	0	0	0	0	0	1	—1

Two-base hit—Shanks. Three-base hit—Chase. Stolen bases—Collins, McBride. Double play—Morgan, McBride, Gandil. Left on bases—Chicago 4, Washington 4. First on balls—Off Scott 3, Ayers 1. First on errors—Chicago 2, Washington 2. Struck out—By Scott 2, Ayers 1. Time—2.00. Umpires—Dineen and Connolly.

PHILANTHROPY HAS NO PLACE IN BASE BALL

Wherefore the Profit-Sharing Scheme of President R. B. Ward, of the Brooklyn Federal League Club, Will Not Work Out.

BY JOE VILA

NEW YORK, N. Y., June 8.—President Robert B. Ward, of the Brooklyn Federals, makes the interesting announcement that his players will receive shares of the club's common stock, so that they may cut in on the profits at the end of the coming season. When President Ward disclosed this profit-sharing plan at the Baltimore meeting, Edward Hanlon, veteran manager and one of the promoters of the Feds in that city, probably recalled the days of the Brotherhood, when players were stockholders and directors of the various clubs embraced by that ill-starred circuit. Hanlon was the manager of

R. B. Ward

THE PITTSBURGH BROTHERHOOD CLUB

just twenty-five years ago. The chief backers were P. L. Auten of Chicago and Captain W. W. Kerr. The board of directors included several star players who had received shares of stock, gratis, and they soon asserted their authority when Hanlon attempted to tighten the reins of discipline. The crisis came when, after the player-directors had failed to appear at a hotel in this city until long after 12 o'clock one night, Hanlon tried to suspend and fine them. "You have no authority!" the player-directors rudely informed the manager. "Mind your own business or the board of directors will release you at once."

THE SAME CONDITIONS

prevailed in other Brotherhood clubs. The player-directors and stockholders defied the managers, and also bulldozed the umpires on the ball field. Discipline amounted to nothing, and the men who put up their money to free the players from "slavery" were glad to make terms of peace with the National League. Oddly enough, many of the players who had served as directors were among the first to desert the Brotherhood cause when they seemed convinced that the venture was a sure failure. If the players had remained loyal to their backers it is a fact that the National League would have gone to the wall.

PITTSBURGH AT PHILADELPHIA, JUNE 9.—After Conzelman fanned Reed and Becker in the sixth inning Philadelphia scored enough runs to win on Lobert's single, a pass to Magee, Cravath's single and Luderus' double. Wagner, the veteran shortstop of the Pittsburgh National League team, made his three thousandth hit in 18 years of major league base ball. It was a two-bagger off pitcher Mayer, with no one on base, in the ninth inning. He subsequently scored Pittsburgh's only run of the game on two outs. Score:

Philad'a.	AB.	R.	B.	P.	A.	E.	Pittsburgh.	AB.	R.	B.	P.	A.	E.
Reed, 2b..	4	0	0	0	[illegible]	0	Kelly, cf.	4	0	0	1	0	0
Becker, lf.	4	0	1	4	0	0	Carey, lf.	4	0	0	2	0	0
Lobert, 3b.	2	1	1	2	2	0	Mowrey, 3b	4	0	2	0	0	0
Magee, ss.	3	1	2	4	2	2	Wagner, ss.	3	1	1	3	1	0
Cravath, rf	3	1	2	1	0	1	Konet'y, 1b	3	0	0	7	1	0
Luderus, 1b	3	0	1	7	0	0	Viox, 2b...	4	0	1	3	0	0
Paskert, cf.	3	0	1	2	0	0	Mitchell, rf	4	0	0	1	1	0
Killifer, c.	3	0	0	7	1	0	Gibson, c..	3	0	0	6	1	0
Mayer, p..	3	0	1	0	2	0	Conzelman, p	3	0	1	1	2	0
Totals..	28	3	9	27	10	3	Totals...	32	1	5	24	6	0

Philadelphia	0	0	0	0	0	3	0	0	x—3
Pittsburgh	0	0	0	0	0	0	0	0	1—1

Two-base hits—Mowrey, Wagner, Magee, Luderus. Sacrifice hit—Lobert. Stolen bases—Mowrey, Lobert. Left on bases—Pittsburgh 6, Philadelphia 4. First on balls—Off Conzelman 2, Mayer 2. First on errors—Pittsburgh 2. Struck out—By Conzelman 4, Mayer 4. Time—1.26. Umpires—Orth and Byron.

PITTSBURGH AT ST. LOUIS, JULY 1.—Casey Hageman pitched his first full game for St. Louis and won from Pittsburgh. Until the ninth inning only two men reached second base. In the seventh inning, with St. Louis at bat, the reserve players on the Pittsburgh bench hooted Umpire Klem. Klem warned them, and when they continued their demonstration he fined each of them—nine in all—$10 each. This angered Manager Clarke and he abused Klem in violent language. The umpire then ordered Clarke and his utility players from the field. Score:

St. Louis.	AB.	R.	B.	P.	A.	E.	Pittsburgh.	AB.	A.	B.	P.	A.	E.
Huggins, 2b	3	2	1	2	5	0	Viox, 2b..	4	0	0	1	5	0
Magee, cf..	1	0	0	1	0	0	Carey, lf..	3	0	0	3	0	0
Dolan, lf..	3	0	1	2	0	0	Mowrey, 3b	4	0	1	1	1	0
J. Miller, 1b	3	0	1	13	0	0	Mitchell, rf	4	1	0	3	0	0
Wilson, rf.	3	2	1	2	0	0	Wagner, ss.	4	0	2	3	1	2
Butler, ss..	2	1	1	3	3	0	Konet'y, 1b	4	0	1	8	0	0
Wingo, c..	3	0	1	4	1	0	Coleman, c.	1	0	0	2	1	0
Beck, 3b..	3	0	0	0	2	1	Jo Kelly, cf	2	0	1	2	0	0
Hageman, p	3	0	1	0	3	0	Hyatt, c...	2	0	0	1	0	0
							Conzel'n, p	1	0	0	0	2	0
Totals..	24	5	7	27	14	1	McQuillan, p	1	0	0	0	1	0
							*Leonard ..	0	0	0	0	0	0
							Mamaux, p.	0	0	0	0	0	0
							†Mensor ...	1	0	0	0	0	0
							Totals...	31	1	5	24	11	2

*Batted for McQuillan in eighth inning.
†Batted for Mamaux in ninth inning.

St. Louis	0	1	1	1	1	0	0	1	x—5
Pittsburgh	0	0	0	0	0	0	0	0	1—1

Home run—Wilson. Hits—Off Conzelman 2 in 3 innings, McQuillan 5 in 4 innings, Mamaux 0 in 1 inning. Sacrifice hits—Butler, Magee 2. Sacrifice flies—Beck, J. Miller, Wingo, Joseph Kelly. Stolen base—Butler. Double plays—Hageman, Huggins, J. Miller; Mowrey, Viox, Konetchy. Left on bases—Pittsburgh 8, St. Louis 6. First on balls—Off Conzelman 3, McQuillan 1, Hageman 3, Mamaux 1. Hit by pitcher—By Hageman 1. Struck out—By Conzelman 2, Hageman 4, Mamaux 1. Passed ball—Hyatt. Time—2.00. Umpires—Klem and Emslie.

Note. The New York-Brooklyn game was postponed on account of rain.

CLUB STANDING WEDNESDAY, JULY 1

	W.	L.	Pct.		W.	L.	Pct.
New York ..	37	23	.617	Philadelphia..	30	31	.492
Chicago	36	31	.537	Pittsburgh ...	30	32	.484
St. Louis	35	34	.507	Brooklyn	27	33	.450
Cincinnati ..	33	33	.500	Boston	26	37	.413

New Charge in Marsans Case

ST. LOUIS, Mo., July 27.—Armando Marsans, Cuban player, in an answer filed afternoon of July 23, to the petition of the Cincinnati National League Club, asking for a permanent injunction restraining Marsans from playing with the St. Louis Club, of the Federal League, charged the Cincinnati Club with violation of the federal alien labor contract law. Marsans says last January, while he was in Havana, Cuba, the Cincinnati Club sent a representative to him to sign a contract, which is in violation of the federal law that prohibits the importation of aliens for contract labor. The answer also charges Organized Ball is violating the Sherman anti-trust law by controlling and setting salary limits for ball players. Marsans also attacks the ten-day clause, which gives the club magnates the right to abrogate a contract with a player after ten days' notice, while the player is denied the same privilege.

PIRATES LOSE IN 21 INNINGS

Meet Defeat When Doyle Drives Out Home Run in Record Breaking Game.

Babe Adams and Rube Marquard Heroes of Long Contest.

PITTSBURG, July 17.— Beacher's single and a home run by Doyle gave New York a 3 to 1 victory in a twenty-one-inning pitchers' duel between Marquard and Adams today. It was the longest game ever played in the National league. From the close of the third inning until the opening of the twenty-first inning neither team was able to score, so effective was the pitching. Sharp fielding characterized the work of both sides. The work of Burns, Fletcher, Kelly and Mowrey was brilliant.

N. York.	A	R	H	O	A	Pittsburg	A	R	H	O	A
Beacher,cf.	9	2	3	7	1	Mensor,lf.	7	1	1	8	0
Doyle,2..	9	1	2	8	6	Mowrey,3.	7	0	1	2	9
Burns,lf..	8	0	2	11	0	Wagner,s..	9	0	3	5	6
Rob'tson,rf	8	0	0	3	0	Viox,2..	7	0	2	5	7
Fletcher,s.	8	0	2	2	11	Konetchy,1	8	0	2	23	0
Merkle,1..	8	0	0	25	0	Mitchell,rf	9	0	1	3	0
Meyers,c..	6	0	2	3	1	Kelly,c..	9	0	2	10	0
*Murray..	0	0	0	0	0	Gibson,c..	4	0	1	9	0
McLean,c..	2	0	0	1	1	‡Carey..	0	0	0	0	0
Stock,3..	5	0	0	2	4	Coleman,s.	4	0	1	1	2
†Snodgrass	1	0	0	0	0	Adams,p.	7	0	1	0	3
Grant,3..	1	0	0	2							
Marquard,p	8	0	1	0	5	Totals..	71	1	15	63	27

Totals.. 73 3 12 63 31

*Ran for Meyers in fifteenth
†Batted for Stock in eighteenth
‡Ran for Gibson in tenth

N. Y.. 0 0 1 0 0 0 0 0 0 0 0 0 0 0 0 0 0 0 0 0 2 3
Pitts. 1 0 0 0 0 0 0 0 0 0 0 0 0 0 0 0 0 0 0 0 0 1

Errors—Robertson, Fletcher, Wagner 2, Viox.

Three-base hits—Burns, Wagner. Home run—Doyle. Stolen bases—Burns 2, Fletcher, Beacher 2. Double plays Viox to Wagner to Konetchy; Fletcher to Doyle to Merkle (2). First base on balls off Marquard 2. Hit with pitched ball By Marquard (Mensor). First base on errors New York 2, Pittsburg 2. Sacrifice hits Mowrey 2. Adams, Viox, Mensor, Stock. Sacrifice by Burns. Left on bases New York 10, Pittsburg 15. Struck out By Marquard 2 By Adams 6. Time—3.42. Umpires—Byron and Johnson.

Reprinted from
The Cleveland Plain Dealer

Federal League Misfortune

KANSAS CITY, Mo., September 7.—Two hundred families were driven from their homes, houses were swept away and there were many narrow escapes from death, when Turkey Creek, a local drainage stream ran out of its banks and inundated Rosedale, Kan., a suburb. The creek extended its bounds to the Federal League Base Ball Park, where fences were washed away, the clubhouse was demolished, and all the uniforms, bats, and other equipment of the ball club was lost. Manager Stovall, of the club, said the team would leave tonight for its final road trip without any equipment.

ATTENDANCE RECORD

To the Pittsburgh National League Club Falls the "Honor" of the Smallest Paid Attendance at Any Game of Record.

BY JAMES J. LONG

PITTSBURGH, Pa., July 17.—The figures published in the "Sun" on Monday, showing that Baltimore's claim to a world's record for light base ball attendance on the strength of only 26 persons having paid to see an International League game there on Saturday, July 11, was knocked out by the Pittsburgh National League Club's mark of 17 admissions in 1890, were read with much interest by A. G. Pratt, the veteran local base ball man. Mr. Pratt now comes to the front with information that puts Pittsburgh's figures so low as to establish a record beyond question. "For the sake of having the record established beyond dispute, I am going to divulge an ancient office secret," said Mr. Pratt, who acted as business manager for the Pittsburgh Nationals during the disastrous season of 1890. The 'Sun's' count of 17 spectators at that record-breaking game is absolutely correct, but I have some information that makes the attendance that day even more of a record. The paid admissions totaled only six. There were 17 persons at the game. J. Palmer O'Neil, Willis Orth and I were the only spectators in the boxes, there were six in the grandstand and eight in other parts of the park. Only the six in the grandstand paid to see the game, and I believe they were not Pittsburghers at that, but traveling men."

The Giants won the afternoon game by hard hitting. After Snodgrass was hit by a pitched ball in the sixth inning of the afternoon contest, the crowd booed when he went to centre field. His contemptuous motion in response to this reception was followed by a volley of bottles from the bleachers in his direction. The game was held up five or ten minutes and during the demonstration Mayor Curley went to the field and demanded of a police lieutenant that Snodgrass be removed from the park. Neither the officer nor the umpires would comply. Score:

New York.	A.	B.	R.	B.	P.	A.	E.	Boston.	A.	B.	R.	B.	P.	A.	E.
Snodgrass, cf	4	0	2	2	0	0	Moran, rf.	3	0	0	2	0	0
Beacher, cf.	0	0	0	0	0	0	Evers, 2b.	4	0	0	3	1
Doyle, 2b.	5	0	1	3	4	1	Connolly, lf	4	1	1	2	0	0
Burns, lf.	4	1	0	1	0	Mann, cf.	4	0	0	0	0
Fletcher, ss	4	1	1	3	0	Deveore, cf.	1	0	0	0	0
Murray, rf.	4	1	1	0	0	Schmidt, 1b.	3	0	1	13	0
Grant, 3b.	3	3	0	1	0	Smith, 3b.	4	0	0	2	0
Merkle, 1b.	4	1	1	7	1	Maran'e, ss	3	0	1	4	0
McLean, c.	3	5	3	10	1	Gowdy, c.	3	0	0	3	3
Tesreau, p.	4	1	2	1	0	Tyler, p.	3	0	0	1	1
							Crutcher, p.	1	0	0	1	
Totals..	36	10	14	27	10		Totals..	29	1	4	27	10	4

New York .... 0 0 1 0 4 4 1—10
Boston .... 0 0 0 0 0 0 1— 1

Two-base hits—Murray, Snodgrass, Connolly, Maranville, McLean, Smith. Sacrifice fly—Merkle. Stolen bases—Burns 2. Double plays—Merkle, Tesreau; Maranville, Evers, Schmidt; Doyle, Fletcher, Merkle. Hits—Off Tyler 12 in 7 innings, none out in eighth; Crutcher 2 in 2 innings. First on errors—Boston 1, New York 1. Left on bases—Boston 5, New York 7. First on balls—Off Tyler 4, Tesreau 4. Struck out—By Tyler 2, Tesreau 10. Hit by pitcher—By Tyler 1. Wild pitch—Tyler. Time—2.00. Umpires—Klem and Emslie.

THE INJUNCTION DISSOLVED IN BUFFALO COURT

The Organized Ball Contract Held to Be Inequitable and the System Declared to Be a Complete Monopoly Under Common Law.

Organized Ball Loses Chase Case

BUFFALO, N. Y., July 21.—The Federal League won another big victory here this morning, when Supreme Court Justice Herman P. Bissell dissolved the injunction of the Chicago American League Base Ball Club, restraining Hal Chase, the first baseman, from playing with the Buffalo Federal League team. Justice Bissell's opinion covers 25 pages of typewritten copy. The lack of mutual obligation in the so-called ten day clause of the contract under which Chase was playing with the Chicago team, whereby the club could terminate the contract on ten days' notice while the player was bound under several provisions of the National Agreement, formed the basis of the decision vacating the injunction. Chase was served with injunction papers on June 23, while he was playing with the Buffalo team at Federal Park. He has been on the bench since. In his affidavit upon which the motion to vacate the injunction was based, Chase alleged that he gave the Chicago Club ten days' notice of his intention to leave, at the expiration of which time he signed the Buffalo contract.

Harold Chase

WITH FELLOW SUFFERERS FROM THE HORRID WAR

The National League to Donate Portion of Gate Receipts to the Red Cross Society Whose Resources Will Be Taxed to Limit.

NEW YORK, N. Y., August 24.—The National League of Professional Base Ball Clubs last week departed from a precedent of many years' standing by arranging to set aside one day of its championship playing schedule and designating it as "Red Cross Day," when a percentage of the gate receipts throughout the circuit will be turned over to the Red Cross for the relief work in the European war. According to Secretary John A. Heydler's announcement, it is expected all leagues in organized base ball will take a similar action. The date of Red Cross Day is yet to be selected.

J. A. Heydler

Secretary John A. Heydler's circular letter on this subject is herewith given in full:

"NEW YORK, N. Y., August 20.—The National Base Ball League has come forward promptly in response to the appeal of the American Red Cross in aid of the society's war relief fund. The senior league will shortly designate a day of its regular championship schedule, the same to be known as Red Cross Day. On this day a percentage of the gate receipts will be set aside for the urgent needs of the Red Cross in the European war. In reserving a day of its schedule for a special purpose, the National League has departed from a precedent of many years' standing. It is expected that all leagues in organized base ball will take similar action. In a letter addressed to President Tener in furtherance of the Red Cross appeal, Miss Boardman, president of the American society, asks the co-operation of the base ball leagues of the country."

BOSTON BRAVES ARE WORLD'S CHAMPS

Taking Fourth Straight Game From Famous White Elephants, Stallings' Band Put Beans on the Map

Reprinted from
The Philadelphia Inquirer

From a Staff Correspondent.

BOSTON: Mass., Oct. 13.—That one timely sting to centre by Johnny Evers, in the fifth inning, scoring the two runs, and which gave the Braves the world's championship and sixty per cent. of the players' receipts, marred a great game Bob Shawkey had pitched and really sent him into retirement. Up to that inning the Braves had made one hit off Bob, that coming in the fourth inning, and being an infield tap at that. They would not have scored in this fourth round had not Eddie Collins booted Connolly's grounder long enough to prevent the possibility of a double play. That slight break enabled the Braves to tie up the Macks and they won out in the next frame when Evers singled in the two runs, after two men were out.

Evers has figured prominently in all four games and around him really centres the entire defensive and initiative work of the Braves. In the four games, he hit safely seven times, from sixteen trips to the plate, for a .438 per cent., even outhitting the dangerous Gowdy, who whacked out six safeties, they being made in the first and third games. It has been Mack luck all through this series, to have the man who is hitting among the Bostons to come up at a crucial moment, and it was Evers, who, stepping into the breach today in that fateful fifth, who decided this world's championship. Shawkey had a 3-2 count and had to groove the next ball or else let Johnny walk. He choose the groove and lost the final chance the Athletics had to carry the series an extra game, by so doing.

BOSTON AT PHILADELPHIA, SEPTEMBER 3
(P. M. and P. M.)—The Braves won both games and went into the lead for the first time this season. The Braves won the first game on inferior fielding and base running by the Phillies. Score:

Boston	AB.	R.	B.	P.	A.E	Philad'a	AB.	R.	B.	P.	A.E
Moran, rf.	5	1	1	0	1 0	Lobert, 3b.	5	1	1	2	1 2
Whitted, 2b	4	1	2	1	5 0	Becker, lf.	5	0	1	2	0 0
Cather, lf.	1	0	0	1	5 0	Magee, 1b.	5	0	1	1	0 0
Connolly, lf	3	1	1	0	0 0	Cravath, rf.	4	1	1	1	0 0
Mann, cf.	2	0	1	0	1 0	Byrne, 2b..	4	0	0	2	1 0
Gilbert, rf.	3	0	1	0	1 0	Irelan, 2b..	3	1	2	1	0 1
Schmidt, 1b	4	2	2	7	1 0	Paskert, cf.	4	0	2	2	1 0
Smith, 3b..	4	1	2	2	3 0	Martin, ss.	4	0	2	3	4 0
Maranv'e,ss	4	1	2	6	4 0	Killifer, c.	4	0	1	7	2 0
Gowdy, c..	2	0	0	8	4 0	Rixey, p...	1	0	0	0	1 0
Rudolph, p.	4	0	0	0	0 0	Marshall, p	1	0	0	0	1 0
						Baumgart'r,p	0	0	0	0	1 0
						*Reed ...	1	0	0	0	0 0
						†Burns ...	1	0	0	0	0 0
Totals..	36	7	11	27	16 0	Totals...	37	5	13	27	10 2

*Batted for Marshall in fifth inning.
†Batted for Baumgartner in ninth inning.

Boston	0	3	0	0	2	0	0	1	1—7
Philadelphia	0	0	0	1	1	1	0	2	0—5

Two-base hits—Schmidt, Moran, Paskert 2, Irelan. Three-base hit—Whitted. Home runs—Magee, Cravath. Hits—Off Rixey 4 in 2⅔ innings. Marshall 3 in 2½ innings. Baumgartner 4 in 4 innings. Sacrifice hits—Cather, Whitted. Stolen base—Lobert. Double play—Mann, Maranville. Left on bases—Boston 7, Philadelphia 7. First on balls—Off Rixey 2, Marshall 1, Rudolph 2. First on errors—Boston 2. Struck out—By Rixey 1, Baumgartner 2, Rudolph 3. Time—2.10. Umpires—Klem and Emslie.

In the second game Boston hammered Tincup off the rubber in the first inning, and Oeschger was taken out after the first four men to face him in the second session had singled. Rixey filled out the inning. Mattison yielded three runs in the third, after which he settled down. Evers was unable to play, owing to stomach trouble, and his substitute, Dugey, split his finger in practice, Whitted going to second base. Score:

NEW YORK AT CLEVELAND, SEPTEMBER 27
(P. M. and P. M.)—Cleveland and New York divided the double-header. Lajoie, of Cleveland, made his three thousandth big league hit in the first game, it being a two-base hit, the ball being taken out of play and presented to Lajoie as soon as he reached second. Score:

Cleveland	AB.	R.	B.	P.	A.E	New York	AB.	R.	B.	P.	A.E
Smith, cf..	4	1	2	2	0 0	Maisel, 3b.	3	1	1	0	0 0
Chapman, ss	2	0	0	3	2 1	Hartzell, lf.	4	0	1	5	0 0
Johnston, 1b	4	0	0	1	0 0	Cook, rf..	4	0	2	0	0 0
Leibold, rf.	4	0	0	0	0 0	Cree, cf...	4	0	1	1	0 0
Lajoie, 2b..	3	2	2	1	5 0	Mullen, 2b.	4	0	1	3	2 0
Graney, lf..	2	1	1	3	0 1	Peckin'h, ss	4	1	0	1	2 0
Barbare, 3b	3	0	1	1	1 2	Sweeney, c.	4	1	1	3	3 0
Egan, c....	3	0	1	5	2 0	Boone, 2b..	4	1	2	3	3 0
Morton, p..	2	0	0	0	0 0	McHale, p..	1	0	0	1	2 0
						Brown, p...	0	0	0	0	0 0
						*Daley ...	1	0	0	0	0 0
						†Truesdale	1	0	0	0	0 0
Totals..	27	5	7	27	11 2	Totals..	33	3	7	24	19 0

*Batted for McHale in seventh inning.
†Batted for Brown in ninth inning.

Cleveland	1	0	0	0	3	1	0	0	x—5
New York	1	0	1	0	0	0	1	0	0—3

Two-base hits—Smith, Lajoie 2. Sacrifice hits—Morton, Chapman. Sacrifice fly—Chapman. Double play—Egan. Hits—Off McHale 7 in 6 innings, Brown 0 in 2 innings. First on balls—Off Morton 2, McHale 1. Hit by pitcher—By Morton 1. Struck out—By Morton 5, McHale 4, Brown 1. Passed ball—Sweeney. First on error—New York. Left on bases—Cleveland 2, New York 6. Time—1.48. Umpires—Dineen and Egan.

Eddie Collins Sold to Chicago White Sox

PHILADELPHIA, Pa., December 8.—One of the most surprising announcements in the history of base ball was made here today, when Manager Connie Mack, of the Athletics, gave out the statement that he had just sold Eddie Collins, his great second baseman, and one of the best all-around ball players in the game, to President Comiskey, of the Chicago American League Club, for a sum of $50,000. Manager Mack said that the entire matter was a cash transaction, but reports from New York credited President Ban Johnson, of the American League, with the announcement that players were involved in the deal. This is one more of the sweeping changes inaugurated by Manager Mack, of the champion local club, following the cutting loose of Bender, Plank and Coombs, his three great veteran pitchers. It is regarded as a war move, destined to strengthen the Chicago White Sox, which have opposition both from the National and Federal League Clubs. Collins signed a five-year contract in New York today.

OFFICIAL SCORE

BOSTON

	ab.	r.	bh.	tb.	sh.	sb.	po.	a.	e.
Moran, rf	4	1	1	2	—	—	—	—	—
Evers, 2b	3	1	1	1	—	—	3	6	—
Connolly, lf	2	—	—	—	—	—	1	—	1
Mann, lf	2	—	—	—	—	—	1	—	—
Whitted, cf	3	—	2	2	—	1	1	—	—
Schmidt, 1b	4	—	1	1	—	—	12	—	—
Gowdy, c	2	—	—	—	—	—	8	2	—
Maranville, ss	3	—	—	—	—	—	1	3	—
Deal, 3b	3	—	—	—	—	—	1	4	—
Rudolph, p	2	1	1	1	—	—	—	1	—
Totals	28	3	6	7	—	1	27	16	—

ATHLETICS

	ab.	r.	bh.	tb.	sh.	sb.	po.	a.	e.
Murphy, rf	4	—	—	—	—	—	—	—	—
Oldring, lf	4	—	1	1	—	—	3	—	—
Collins, 2b	4	—	1	1	—	—	1	4	—
Baker, 3b	4	—	1	1	—	—	1	3	—
McInnis, 1b	4	—	1	1	—	—	15	1	—
Walsh, cf	2	—	1	2	—	—	1	—	—
Barry, ss	3	1	1	1	—	—	—	5	—
Schang, c	3	—	—	—	—	—	3	—	—
Shawkey, p	2	—	1	2	—	—	—	3	—
Fennock, p	1	—	—	—	—	—	—	1	—
Totals	31	1	7	9	—	—	24	18	—

Athletics	0	0	0	0	1	0	0	0	0—1
Boston	0	0	0	1	2	0	0	0	x—3

Two-base hits—Walsh, Shawkey, Moran. Hits—Off Shawkey, 4 in 5 innings; off Pennock, 2 in 3 innings. Double play—Gowdy and Evers. Left on bases—Athletics, 4; Boston, 5. First base on balls—Shawkey, 2; Pennock, 2; Rudolph, 1. Struck out—By Pennock, 3; by Rudolph, 7. Passed ball—Schang. Wild pitch—Rudolph. Time—1.49. Umpires—Plate, Byron; bases, Hildebrand; left field, Klem; right field, Dineen.

The Great Issue Reached!

Chicago, Ills. January 5.—Charging the National Commission, its laws and the National Agreement under which its members work, are in violation of the common law and the Anti-Trust Law, the Federal League today filed suit in the United States District Court of Chicago, asking that the National Commission be declarel illegal and its members enjoined from further commission of illegal acts. The suit is to come up before Judge Kenesaw Mountain Landis, who, several years ago fined the Standard Oil Company $29,000,000, on January 20. One of the causes charged is that the contracts are null and void. The Federal League especially asked that the National Commission be enjoined from trying to get the players who have gone to the Federal League back, to prevent them referring to the players as "contract-jumpers," and to the League as an "Outlaw League." The suit was filed against the National League and its eight clubs, the American League and its eight clubs, and against Presidents Tener, of the National League; Johnson, of the American League; and Chairman August Herrmann.

Lajoie Sold to Athletics

Philadelphia, Pa., January 5.—Manager Mack, of the Philadelphia Athletics, announced this afternoon that he had purchased the famous Napoleon Lajoie, second baseman of the Cleveland Club, and will play him at second base this season in place of Eddie Collins, who was sold to Chicago. The deal was a straight cash transaction, Manager Mack paying out a goodly slice of the money he received for Collins to the Cleveland Club and assuming Lajoie's contract. Manager Mack believes that Lajoie has much good base ball left in him and will get it out of him with Jack Barry and Stuffy McInnis playing on his flanks. Lajoie returns here after an absence of twelve years and will be a great popular idol.

THE BABE'S FIRST

BOSTON AT NEW YORK, MAY 6.—In the most exciting game played this season, the New Yorks scored a 13-inning victory over Boston. Ruth pitched well, errors by Wagner and McNally and the inability of the Boston catchers to stop base runners preventing him from winning in nine innings. Warhop was hit fairly hard, but Pieh, who pitched the last five innings, was invincible. Boone's double drove home the tying run with two out in the ninth inning, and the winning run was scored in the thirteenth on High's single and steal, and Cook's single. Score:

Boston.	AB.	R.	B.	P.	A.	E.	New York.	AB.	R.	B.	P.	A.	E.
Hooper, rf..	5	0	0	1	1	0	Maisel, 3b..	5	1	2	3	1	1
Wagner, 2b	5	0	3	4	2	1	Hartzell, lf.	4	0	0	0	0	0
Speaker, cf.	4	0	0	2	0	0	High, cf....	6	1	3	4	2	0
Lewis, lf...	5	1	3	2	0	0	Pipp, 1b....	6	0	1	14	0	0
Hoblitzel,1b	5	0	0	20	0	0	Cook, rf....	5	2	2	2	0	0
Scott, ss...	5	0	1	0	6	0	Peckin'h, ss	5	0	0	3	6	0
McNally, 3b	6	0	0	2	5	1	Boone, 2b..	4	0	2	4	3	0
Carrigan, c.	4	1	1	3	1	1	Nunam'r, c	5	0	0	10	2	0
*Henriksen.	1	0	1	0	0	0	Warhop, p..	2	0	0	0	1	0
Thomas, c..	0	0	0	2	0	0	†Mullen ...	1	0	0	0	0	0
Ruth, p....	5	1	3	1	5	1	Pieh, p....	2	0	0	0	2	1
Totals..	46	3	12	‡37	20	4	Totals..	45	4	10	39	17	2

*Batted for Carrigan in eleventh inning.
†Batted for Warhop in eighth inning.
‡One out when winning run was scored.

Boston	0	0	1	0	0	0	1	1	0	0	0	0	0	—3
New York	0	0	0	0	1	0	0	1	1	0	0	0	1	—4

Two-base hits—Carrigan, Lewis, Scott, Boone. Home run—Ruth. Stolen bases—Cook 2, Maisel, Hooper, Hartzell, High. Earned runs—New York 3, Boston 3. Sacrifice hits—Speaker, Hartzell, Hoblitzel. Double play—Peckinpaugh, Pipp. Left on bases—New York 9, Boston 10. First on errors—New York 2, Boston 2. First on balls—Off Warhop 4, Ruth 3. Hits—Off Warhop 10 in 8 innings, Pieh 2 in 5 innings. Hit by pitcher—By Ruth 1. Struck out—By Warhop 1, Pieh 6, Ruth 3. Wild pitch—Ruth. Time—2.35. Umpires—Evans and Mullaney.

ATHLETIC AFFAIRS

Third Baseman Baker Speaks in Self-Defence—His Hold-Out Not Due to Greed—Improving Work of Athletic Team.

By Chandler D. Richter

PHILADELPHIA, Pa., May 10.—Frank Baker, home-run king and the lone hope of the Mackmen, has taken the bull by the horns. Baker has become indignant at the roasting he has received in local papers for his alleged "hold-up" of the management of the Athletics and on Saturday night the climax was reached when Baker went to North Philadelphia Station to meet Mack before the team departed for Cleveland. Baker, it is said, accused Mack of misrepresenting his case to the fans and declared that he had never tried to hold up the club for money and defied Connie to prove that he had. Baker ended up by telling Connie he was ready to join the team at once at the salary he signed for providing Connie would tear up his contract which calls for his services for 1916 also. Baker says he is perfectly

SATISFIED WITH THE TERMS.

but that he really wanted to retire and announced the same to the entire team after the final game of the World's Series in Boston last Fall. The sale of Collins to Chicago and the poor start of the Athletics have caused the fans to shift the blame to Baker, which the Trappe farmer says is an injustice. He say he does not need the money or want to play, but he will play the game of his life if Connie will give him a one-year contract and let him retire at the end of the 1915 season. Baker told several newspaper men that Connie did not even treat his proposition in the right spirit and told him to live up to his contract for two more years. This Baker refuses to do and the general impression is that Mack is carrying his

PRINCIPLES TOO FAR

if he refuses to grant Baker's request. If Baker decides to continue in the game after 1915 it is almost a certainty that the differences can be ironed out in the meantime and Baker be retained by the Athletics. The fans argue that Connie should let 1916 take care of itself and grasp this opportunity to make 1915 a success instead of a failure, as seems certain to result, judging by the form shown to date. With Baker the Athletics have as good a chance for the pennant as any other club in the league, but without him several teams look much better.

ANOTHER COURT CASE

Benny Kauff to Sue the New York National League Club for the $5000 Bonus Promised Him for Signing a Contract.

By W. S. Farnsworth

NEW YORK, N. Y., June 9.—Benny Kauff, the hard-hitting outfielder of the Brooklyn Federal League Club, who jumped to the Giants one fine May afternoon, only to find that he had to return to the campus over on the other side of the East River, is looking for a $5000 bonus he alleges Manager McGraw and President Harry N. Hempstead promised him the day he signed the New York contract. The Ty Cobb of the independents has secured Attorney John M. Ward, a diamond wizard in the days of Anson, Sam Crane and others around and over the Osler limit, to get him the $5000. Yesterday Mr. Ward wrote Mr. Hempstead a letter asking the Giants' chief what he had to say about the matter. Mr. Hempstead, however, is in the West, traveling with his team. Mr. Ward will take the case to court should Mr. Hempstead refuse

TO SETTLE WITH BENNY.

Kauff is so sure of winning the case that, it is said, he would not sell out his claim for $4999.99. It seems that the morning Benny agreed to jump to the Giants he was promised a bonus of $5000. At least that is what Benny claims. And he declares that he has it in black and white, too. "We will give you $5000 if you will sign this contract," Hempstead and McGraw are alleged to have told Benny. So Benny affixed his John Hancock. Then he asked for $5000. Did he get it? He did—not.

KAUFF'S SIDE OF CASE

As a personal friend of Kauff's told me last night the story of the deal follows: "Kauff signed a contract for the seasons of 1915-16-17 at a salary of $8000 per. The second he signed this contract he was to receive a bonus of $5000. Before the ink had dried Kauff asked for the bonus. Then started the big stall. Benny was told that they wanted to play him in the game that afternoon; that he would get the bonus right away, but that they didn't have time to bother with that trivial matter at the time. So they rushed Benny to the Polo Grounds, threw him into a uniform and rushed him onto the field. Boston refused to play with Kauff in the game. Then came the big squabble. Kauff finally was forced to return to the Tip Tops. Since that day he has been asking for his $5000. But asking hasn't brought it, so yesterday Attorney Ward stepped into the limelight."

M'GRAW AS WITNESS

Incidentally, I have learned that Kauff promises some very excellent reading matter in case he is forced to go into the courts to get his bonus. It's a cinch that he will call McGraw as a witness against his own club. Also, we will then be able to learn just who quit McGraw when he made his "steal" of the Federal star. It's just possible that the New York Club will settle with Benny rather than let the inside facts of this case get before the public. It's a cinch that the case, if tried, will force Organized Base Ball to show part of its hand in the warfare being waged on the Federal League. And it doesn't seem improbable, either, that the Federal League is urging Kauff on in the matter. There is undoubtedly a "nigger in the woodpile" here.

BROOKLYN AT CHICAGO, JUNE 17.—Battling neck and neck in a great exhibition of pitching, Zabel, of Chicago, and Pfeffer, of Brooklyn, fought a 19-inning game to a finish which was heart-breaking from the standpoint of the visiting pitcher, for the Cubs won, 4 to 3, despite his brilliant work. Twice the score was tied when the game seemed over. With two out in the eighth, and Chicago leading, 2 to 1, Fisher fumbled O'Mara's grounder and Myers scored him with a double. In the fifteenth Cutshaw singled, took third because nobody covered second when Phelan threw there on Wheat's hit, and scored on Miller's drive. Then Saier tied the count again by hitting to the scoreboard for a home run. Fisher's single in the nineteenth and Schulte's long fly placed the former on second, whence he scored on Cutshaw's fumble. McCarty was injured by a collision with Getz and forced out of the play. Score:

Brooklyn.	AB.	R.	B.	P.	A.	E.	Chicago.	AB.	R.	B.	P.	A.	E.
O'Mara, ss.	8	1	1	7	2	0	Goode, rf...	9	1	1	1	0	0
Meyers, cf..	8	0	2	3	0	1	Fisher, ss..	8	1	3	4	8	1
Daubert, 1b	3	1	0	18	1	0	Schulte, lf..	8	1	3	7	0	0
Cutshaw, 2b	8	1	3	6	10	1	McLarry, 2b	7	0	0	0	6	2
Wheat, lf..	8	0	3	5	0	0	Saier, 1b...	6	1	1	30	1	0
Stengel, rf.	6	0	1	4	1	1	Williams, cf	9	0	2	4	1	0
McCarty, c	4	0	1	4	1	0	Bresnahan,c	8	0	1	8	4	0
Miller, c...	3	0	1	6	1	0	Phelan, 3b.	5	0	3	6	7	1
Getz, 3b...	6	0	0	2	3	0	Humph's, p	0	0	0	0	0	0
Pfeffer, p..	7	0	0	1	4	0	Zabel, p...	7	0	1	1	7	0
Totals..	63	3	11	*56	23	3	Totals..	67	4	15	57	34	4

*One out when winning run was scored.

Brooklyn ..	100	000	010	000	001	000	0	—3
Chicago ...	200	000	000	000	001	000	1	—4

Two-base hits—Phelan, Bresnahan, Schulte, Meyers, O'Mara. Home run—Saier. Stolen bases—Getz, Williams. Earned runs—Chicago 2. Sacrifice hits—Zabel, Fisher, Schulte, Getz. Double play—Getz, Cutshaw, Daubert. Left on bases—Brooklyn 8, Chicago 18. First on errors—Brooklyn 4, Chicago 3. First on balls—Off Zabel 1, Pfeffer 8. Hits—Off Humphries 2 in ⅔ inning, Zabel 9 in 18⅓ innings. Struck out—By Zabel 6, Pfeffer 6. Time—2.15. Umpires—Rigler and Hart.

ST. LOUIS AT CHICAGO, JUNE 28.—Felch's triple, with the bases filled, gave Chicago a lead which St. Louis could not overtake and the locals won. George Sisler, a former University of Michigan twirler, reported to Manager Rickey and made his debut in the sixth inning, when he batted for Perryman. He then went on the slab and pitched a creditable game. Score:

Chicago.	AB.	R.	B.	P.	A.	E.	St. Louis.	AB.	A.	B.	P.	A.	E.
Felch, cf.	4	1	1	1	0	0	Shotton, lf.	4	1	1	1	0	0
Weaver, ss.	4	0	1	3	2	1	Austin, 3b.	3	0	1	2	3	0
E. Collins, 2b	4	0	2	4	2	0	Pratt, 2b.	4	0	1	2	2	1
Fournier, 1b	4	0	1	7	1	0	C. Walker, cf	3	0	0	4	0	0
J. Collins, rf	4	0	1	0	0	0	E. Walker, rf	3	0	1	0	0	0
Roth, lf.	3	0	1	3	0	0	Leary, 1b.	3	1	1	6	1	0
Schalk, c.	3	1	2	8	3	0	Lavan, ss.	3	0	1	2	2	0
Blackb'n, 3b	1	1	0	0	1	0	Agnew, c.	3	0	0	5	2	0
Scott, p.	2	1	0	0	5	0	Lauder'k, p	0	0	0	0	1	0
							Perryman, p	2	0	0	0	1	0
Totals	29	4	8	27	14	1	Sisler, p.	2	0	0	0	1	0
							Totals	26	2	6	24	13	1

Chicago .... 0 0 4 0 0 0 0 0 x—4
St. Louis .... 1 0 0 0 0 0 0 1 0—2

Two-base hits—Shotton, Leary, Lavan, E. Collins. Three-base hits—Fournier, Schalk, Felch. Stolen base—E. Collins. Earned runs—Chicago 4, St. Louis 2. Sacrifice hit—Austin. Double play—Lavan, Pratt, Leary. Left on bases—Chicago 4, St. Louis 1. First on errors—Chicago 1, St. Louis 1. First on balls—Off Scott 1, Laudermilk 2, Sisler 1. Hits—Off Laudermilk 4 in 2 innings, none out in third; Perryman 3 in 3 innings, Sisler 2 in 3 innings. Struck out—By Scott 7, Laudermilk 1, Sisler 2. Time—1.53. Umpires—Evans and Chill.

Boston Red Sox Secure Barry

BOSTON, Mass., July 4.—Jack Barry, the famous shortstop of the Athletic Club, is now a member of the Boston Red Sox, his outright release having been purchased by the Boston Club on Friday last, no players being involved in the deal. Although Connie Mack, of the Athletics, and President Lannin, of the Red Sox, positively refused to name the price paid for Jack Barry, the Athletics' shortstop, who was sold to the Boston Red Sox, it is said on good authority that Lannin paid Mack $8000 for Barry and assumed the player's contract. Barry is reported to be receiving $5000 a year and has a contract which has two years more to run. Barry will play second base instead of shortstop for Carrigan's team. Boston needs a second baseman badly, for Heinie Wagner's arm has been bothering him all season and his throwing has been very bad. Barry has not played second base since he left Holy Cross College, in 1908, but he is a natural infielder, and Manager Carrigan believes he will prove just as great a star at second as at short.

WASHINGTON AT CLEVELAND, JULY 19.—Washington made it five straight from Cleveland. Washington is believed to have broken a league record when it stole eight bases in the first inning. The victory assured. Altrock, Washington coach, pitched the final three innings, allowing four runs. Score:

Washin's.	AB.	R.	B.	P.	A.	E.	Cleveland.	AB.	R.	B.	P.	A.	E.
Moeller, rf	4	2	2	1	0	0	Southw'h, cf	5	1	3	3	0	1
Foster, rf.	3	0	1	4	1	1	Chapman, ss	5	1	2	2	2	0
Milan, cf	3	3	2	3	0	0	Graney, lf.	3	1	1	4	0	1
Shanks, lf.	3	1	0	3	0	0	Kirke, 1b.	3	1	0	7	0	1
Gandil, 1b	5	2	4	9	0	0	Smith, rf.	4	0	2	3	0	0
Connolly, 2b	3	0	0	1	2	0	Barbare, 3b	3	2	1	0	2	1
Neff, 3b.	4	0	1	0	0	0	Wambs's, 2b	4	0	2	0	0	0
Ainsmith, c	5	1	3	8	0	0	O'Neill, c.	4	0	2	4	2	1
McBride, ss	4	1	2	7	0	0	Hagen, p.	2	0	0	0	3	0
Johnson, p.	3	1	1	0	0	0	Jones, p.	0	0	0	0	4	0
Altrock, p.	1	0	0	0	0	0	Coumbe, p.	0	0	0	0	1	0
*Williams	1	0	0	0	0	0	†Hoffman	1	0	1	0	0	0
							‡Enches	1	0	1	0	0	0
Totals	35	11	14	27	10	1	Totals	36	4	9	27	12	4

*Batted for Connolly in ninth inning.
†Batted for Jones in seventh inning.
‡Batted for Coumbe in ninth inning.

Washington .... 0 0 0 1 0 2 3 3 2—11
Cleveland .... 0 0 0 0 1 0 0 3 0—4

Earned runs—Cleveland 3, Washington 4. Two-base hits—Chapman 2, Moeller, Gandil. Three-base hits—Moeller, Gandil 2. Sacrifice fly—Foster 2, Connolly, Graney. Stolen bases—Moeller 3, Milan 2, Ainsmith 2, McBride. Hits—Off Hagerman 1 in ½ inning, Jones 8 in 6⅔ innings, Coumbe 2 in 2 innings, Johnson 2 in 6 innings, Altrock 7 in 3 innings. Balk—Hagerman. First on balls—Off Hagerman 3, Jones 2, Coumbe 1, Altrock 1. Struck out—By Jones 2, Altrock 2. Passed ball—O'Neill. First on error—Cleveland. Left on bases—Cleveland 7, Washington 6. Time—1.33. Umpires—Chill and Evans.

Federals Win Marsans Case

Decision in Favor of the St. Louis Federal Club on Only One of Three Points, Namely, That the Option Clause in the 1914 Contract Was Nullified and of No Effect for 1915 and 1916.

ST. LOUIS, Mo., August 21.—The injunction restraining Armando Marsans playing with the St. Louis Federals was dissolved by Judge Dyer, in the Federal District Court, here on Thursday, August 19, and Marsans was set at liberty to play ball with the St. Louis team. Judge Dyer, in deciding the case considered only one of the three points raised by the attorneys for Marsans in their petition for a modification or dissolution of the injunction. This was that Marsans' contract with Cincinnati was not binding after October 14, 1914. The two points not considered by the court were the charge that the Cincinnati Club did not comply with its contract with Marsans and that the contract was not binding because it lacked in mutuality. Technically, the decision of Judge Dyer is a modification and not a dissolution of the injunction against Marsans. The court did not decide the entire question raised in the Marsans injunction suit, but set aside that part of the injunction that restrained Marsans playing with any other team in 1915 or 1916.

BOUND ONLY FOR ONE YEAR

The decision reserves for final determination the question of the mutuality of Marsans' contract with Cincinnati—that is the ten days' clause—but sets forth that Clause 8 of the contract applies only to the season of 1914. This clause fixes Marsans' salary at $4400. The court held that this clause did not bind Marsans to play for Cincinnati during the 1915 and 1916 seasons, and sets forth that the three-year claim of Cincinnati to the Cuban player cannot be grounded on this clause. The court decision says in part:

"If the defendant (Marsans) is bound for three years, the contract easily could have been made so to state. Clause one of the contract relates only to a plain obligation, and though it may have bound the plaintiff (the Cincinnati Club) to employ the defendant (Marsans) in the seasons of 1915 and 1916, yet it does not follow that the defendant bound himself to play for the club and for no other party during those years. Considering clause eight, it is manifest the defendant (Marsans) agreed to play for the plaintiff (Cincinnati) and for no other party during 1914, and did not so agree for 1915 and 1916."

Judge Dyer's decision, in effect, sets aside the reserve clause, for Marsans was to receive $1100 from Cincinnati as an "option" on his services for 1915 and 1916. This $1100 was included in the $4400 salary, but the contract read that the "total compensation for the season herein contracted for" was $4400. Under Judge Dyer's ruling the "season contracted for" terminated October 14, 1914.

MODIFICATION APPEAL DENIED

Immediately after the decision was handed down the counsel for the Cincinnati Club filed a motion to set aside the Federal Court's decree modifying the injunction. This was heard yesterday by Judge Dyer and denied. But Judge Dyer granted an appeal to the Circuit Court of Appeals, pending which Marsans will play with St. Louis. Phil Ball, principal owner of the St. Louis Federals, said that if the case is definitely settled in favor of St. Louis the local club will file suit against Cincinnati to recover money advanced to Marsans. Marsans left here yesterday to join the team at Brooklyn.

A. Marsans

GAMES PLAYED WEDNESDAY, AUGUST 18

ST. LOUIS AT BOSTON, AUGUST 18.—The Braves' new park was opened for the first time and the largest crowd that ever attended a game was present, the attendance being estimated at 46,000. The game between the Braves and Cards was an interesting one, in which Boston gained an early lead by timely batting, with the assistance of one pass. Rudolph pitched well until the ninth inning, when the visitors made three hits, but scored only once, notwithstanding an error by Compton. Score:

St. Louis.	AB.R.B. P.A.E	Boston.	AB.R.B. P.A.E
Huggins, 2b	4 0 1 2 2 0	Moran, rf	4 2 2 0 0 0
Butler, ss	4 0 1 1 4 0	Evers, 2b	3 0 1 2 2 0
Beacher, cf	4 1 2 2 0 0	Compton, cf	1 0 0 2 0 1
Miller, 1b	4 0 0 12 0 0	Magee, lf	3 1 1 3 0 0
Long, rf	4 0 2 2 0 0	Schmidt, 1b	2 0 1 8 1 0
Wilson, cf	4 0 2 3 0 0	Smith, 3b	3 1 1 0 4 0
Snyder, c	4 0 1 5 1 0	Maranville, ss	4 1 2 2 4 0
Betzel, 3b	3 0 0 1 0 0	Gowdy, c	4 0 1 7 1 0
Sallee, p	2 0 0 0 1 0	Rudolph, p	3 0 0 0 3 0
*Hyatt	1 0 0 0 0 0		
Meadows, p	0 0 0 0 0 0	Totals	29 5 7 27 15 1
Totals	35 1 8 24 11 1		

*Batted for Sallee in eighth inning.

St. Louis .... 0 0 0 0 0 0 0 0 1—1
Boston .... 0 1 2 0 2 0 0 0 x—5

Two-base hits—Long, Gowdy. Stolen base—Smith. Sacrifice hit—Schmidt. Double plays—Huggins, Butler, Miller; Maranville, Evers, Schmidt. Left on bases—St. Louis 6, Boston 9. First on balls—Off Rudolph 1, Sallee 3, Meadows 2. Hits—Off Sallee 5 in 7 innings; Meadows 2 in 1 inning. Struck out—By Rudolph 6, Sallee 3, Meadows 1. Umpires—Klem and Emslie. Time—2:05.

CHICAGO AT ST. LOUIS, SEPTEMBER 7 (P. M. and P. M.)—Davenport, who jumped to the Feds from the Cincinnati Club, of the National League, pitched a no-hit, no-run game and enabled St. Louis to shut out Chicago in the first game of a double-header. Davenport's no-hit game was the fourth pitched in the Federal League this season. The other members of the 1915 no-hit chapter are Frank Allen, of Pittsburgh; Claude Hendrix, of Chicago, and Miles Main, of Kansas City. Only two Chicago men reached first base in Davenport's game, both on bases on balls, and each was retired on a double play. Four of Davenport's offerings were hit to the outfield, but all fell into the local fielders' hands before reaching the ground. Three of these were caught by Ward Miller. Score:

Chicago.	AB.R.B. P.A.E	St. Louis.	AB.R.B. P.A.E
Zeider, 2b	4 0 0 1 1 0	Tobin, rf	4 1 1 1 0 0
Flack, lf	3 0 0 1 0 0	Vaughn, 2b	4 0 1 0 2 0
Zwilling, cf	3 0 0 1 0 0	Miller, 1b	4 0 0 6 3 0
Wilson, c	3 0 0 2 0 0	Marsans, cf	4 0 0 0 0 0
Hauser, 3b	0 0 0 0 0 0	Borton, 1b	3 1 2 10 0 0
Westersil, 3b	3 0 0 1 2 0	Walsh, 3b	3 1 2 1 4 0
Mann, lf	3 0 0 2 0 0	Hartley, c	3 0 1 3 0 1
Beck, 1b	3 0 0 12 0 0	E. Johnson, ss	3 0 0 2 2 0
Doolan, ss	3 0 0 2 4 0	Davenport, p	3 0 0 0 2 0
Brennan, p	2 0 0 0 4 0		
*Hanford	0 0 0 0 0 0	Totals	31 3 8 27 8 1
†Fischer	1 0 0 0 0 0		
Totals	28 0 0 24 13 0		

*Ran for Westersil in eighth inning.
†Batted for Brennan in ninth inning.

Chicago .... 0 0 0 0 0 0 0 0 0—0
St. Louis .... 0 0 0 2 0 0 0 1 x—3

Two-base hit—Walsh. Three-base hit—Vaughn. Stolen base—Vaughn. Double plays—Johnson, Borton 2. Left on bases—St. Louis 4, Chicago 2. First on balls—Off Davenport 2. Struck out—By Davenport 3, Brennan 5. Wild pitch—Brennan. Umpires—O'Brien and McCormick. Time—1:14.

BROOKLYN AT PHILADELPHIA, OCTOBER 6 (P. M. and P. M.)—Demaree, Mayer and Alexander worked in the order named in the first contest. Demaree was hit hard in one inning. Mayer yielded only a safety in four, and Alexander, taking an inning workout was found for two singles. Cravath made his twenty-fourth home-run drive of the season, but did not play in the second contest. Score:

Philad'a.	AB.R.B. P.A.E	Brooklyn.	AB.R.B. P.A.E
Stock, 3b	4 0 0 1 7 0	O'Mara, ss	4 1 1 1 1 0
Bancroft, ss	4 2 2 0 4 0	Olson, ss	1 0 0 1 0 0
Paskert, cf	4 2 2 1 0 0	Daubert, 1b	4 1 1 9 0 0
Cravath, rf	3 1 1 3 0 1	Stengel, rf	4 1 1 3 0 0
Luderus, 1b	4 1 1 14 0 0	Z. Wheat, lf	3 0 0 3 0 0
Whitted, lf	3 1 1 4 0 1	Cutshaw, 2b	3 1 1 2 4 0
Niehoff, 2b	4 1 1 2 0 0	Myers, cf	4 1 2 1 0 0
Burns, c	4 0 2 3 0 0	Getz, 3b	4 1 2 0 2 1
Demaree, p	1 0 0 0 0 0	M. Wheat, c	4 0 0 4 0 0
Mayer, p	2 1 1 0 1 0	Marquard, p	2 0 0 0 1 0
Alexander, p	0 0 0 0 0 0	Mails, p	1 0 0 0 0 1
*Dugey	0 0 0 0 0 0	†Smith	1 0 0 0 0 0
Totals	34 9 11 27 14 2	Totals	35 6 8 24 8 2

*Batted for Mayer in eighth inning.
†Batted for Mails in ninth inning.

Philadelphia .... 0 0 0 3 1 3 2 0 x—9
Brooklyn .... 4 0 0 0 0 0 0 0 2—6

Two-base hits—Daubert, Stengel, Cutshaw, Whitted. Home runs—Cravath, Mayer. Earned runs—Brooklyn 5, Philadelphia 3. Double play—Cutshaw, Daubert. Left on bases—Brooklyn 4, Philadelphia 5. First on balls—Off Mails 4, Mayer 1. Hits—Off Marquard 7 in 5 innings, Mails 4 in 3 innings, Demaree 5 in 1 inning, Mayer 1 in 4 innings, Alexander 2 in 1 inning. Hit by pitcher—By Mayer 1. Struck out—By Marquard 2, Mails 2, Mayer 1. Wild pitches—Marquard, Mails. Passed ball—Burns. Umpires—Rigler and O'Day. Time—1:50.

New York Wins Benton Case

The National League Directors Award the Pitcher Claimed By Pittsburgh to the Giants, and Throw Out the Victory Benton Won for the Pirates When He Was Pitched in Defiance of President Tener.

AT a meeting held in New York City on August 24, the National League Directors decided that Rube Benton, formerly of the Cincinnati Club, is legally the property of the New York Club. Cincinnati, it was decided, must pay back to Pittsburgh the money paid by Pittsburgh to Benton. In announcing its decision, the Directors exonerate from all blame the Pittsburgh Club, which, they say, acted in good faith in holding the pitcher. The Directors also announced that the game between Chicago and Pittsburgh teams, played on August 17, and which was won by the latter, has been thrown out and will be replayed on September 3 or 4, when the two teams play again. This was the game in which Benton pitched for Pittsburgh. After the announcement of the decision, John McGraw said Benton would probably participate in one of the games of August 25, against the Pirates—which he did, Benton being hit quite hard. Following is the official finding:

FEDS GIVE CHICAGO ONE FLAG WINNER AS WHALES REWARD

Tinker's Team Noses St. Louis Out of Title by One Point.

Battle That Decides Pennant Ends With Cushion Fight.

CHICAGO, Oct. 3.—In the tightest league race ever staged the Chicago Federals narrowly won the flag by winning the second game of a double header from Pittsburg after having dropped the first game.

Darkness held off just long enough to permit the Chicago team to take the title and put Pittsburg in third place. Three runs in the sixth inning of the second game, however, settled the ownership of the emblem.

The scores were, Pittsburg 5-4, Chicago 4-3. The first game went to eleven innings, while the second was called after the visitors' half of the seventh inning.

The league race was in doubt until the final game was played today, as for weeks past there had been a constant shifting of positions on the part of Pittsburg, Chicago and St. Louis, the Missouri city not being eliminated until yesterday when a defeat by Kansas City put it out of the running.

Clubs.	W.	L.	Pct.
Chicago	86	66	.5658
St. Louis	87	67	.5649
Pittsburg	86	67	.5621

Reprinted from
The Cleveland Plain Dealer

COBB'S 96TH STEAL

Oct. 5

DETROIT.					CLEVELAND.				
	AB	H	O	A		AB	H	O	A
Bush, s	5	2	2	2	Wille, l	4	2	2	0
Vitt, 3	4	1	2	1	Chapman, s	4	1	3	5
Cobb, m	4	2	1	0	Roth, m	5	1	1	0
Veach, l	3	0	0	0	Smith, r	5	1	3	0
Crawford, r	4	0	1	0	Kirke, 1	5	2	14	0
Burns, 1	4	2	12	0	Barbare, 3	4	1	0	2
Young, 2	4	1	2	5	Turner, 2	4	1	0	2
McKee, c	4	1	7	2	O'Neill, c	3	2	2	1
James, p	0	0	0	2	Jones, p	0	0	0	1
*Moriarty	1	0	0	0	†Wambsg'ss	1	0	0	0
Dubuc, p	0	0	0	0					
Totals	36	12	27	17	Totals	38	12	24	17

*Batted for Coveleskie in sixth inning.
†Batted for Klepfer in eighth inning.

	1	2	3	4	5	6	7	8	9	R
Detroit	1	3	1	0	0	0	0	1	*	—6
Cleveland	0	0	1	2	1	0	1	0	—	5

Errors—Bush, Smith, Kirke, O'Neill. Pitching summary—11 hits off Coveleskie in 6 innings; 2 hits off James in 2 innings; no hits off Dubuc in one inning; 11 hits off Klepfer in 7 innings; 1 hit off Jones in 1 inning. Three-base hit—Smith. Struck out—By Coveleskie 4; by James 1; by Dubuc 1; by Barbare 2. Bases on balls—Off Coveleskie, 3; off Klepfer, 1. Stolen bases—Bush, Cobb. Sacrifice fly—Dubuc. Double plays—Turner, Chapman and Kirke; Cobb, Young and McKee. First base on errors—Detroit 2. Left on bases—Detroit 7, Cleveland 9. Time—1:50. Umpires—Wallace and Evans. Attendance—5,429.

Reprinted from
The Detroit News

Where Federal League Players Will Play

WITH the opening of the major league base ball season accomplished, it is a matter of general interest among the fans to know just how many Federal Leaguers have landed with the National and American Leagues, and the three Class AA organizations. In all, we have a record of 137 former members of the Gilmore circuit having signed to play in Organized Ball this year. There are a few more not listed, who have signed under assumed names in minor leagues which have understandings barring jumpers and other Federals.

Fifty-seven Federals have joined major league clubs, 36 being in the National and 21 in the American. The Chicago Nationals and St. Louis Americans, which were combined with the Federal League clubs in those cities, naturally have the greatest number of Feds on their rosters. New York City has the biggest representation, with ten Feds. The Giants have four, and the New Yorks and the Superbas three each. The Giants have Fred Anderson, the Buffalo pitcher; Benny Kauff, of Brooklyn, and Ed Rousch and Bill Rariden, of Newark. The New Yorks have Lee Magee, Brooklyn; Nick Cullop, Kansas City lefthander, and Joe Gedeon, who signed, but did not play, with Newark. Brooklyn's Federals are Jimmy Johnston, Newark; Mike Mowrey, Pittsburgh, and Dave Hickman, Baltimore.

The latest Federal to join the majors is Hal Chase, signed by Cincinnati several days ago. Chase will play alongside Bill Louden, another Buffalo Fed, while Al Schulz, another Buffalo man, will pitch for Herzog's club. The complete list of Feds signed in Organized Ball is as follows:

NATIONAL LEAGUE

Chicago—Tinker, Bailey, Prendergast, Zwilling, Mann, Flack, Doolan, Yerkes, Fischer, Hendrix, Seaton, Zelder, McConnell, Brown and Packard.

New York—Kauff, Rousch, Anderson and Rariden.

Boston—Allen, Knetzer, Konetchy and Reulbach.

Brooklyn—Johnston, Mowrey and Hickman.

Cincinnati—Mosely, Esmond, Schultz, Louden, Huhn and Chase.

Philadelphia—Bender, Cooper.

Pittsburgh—Art Wilson, J. Smith and Moran.

AMERICAN LEAGUE

New York—Magee, Cullop, Gedeon and Schaefer.

St. Louis—Tobin, Ward Miller, McKechnie, Deal, Crandall, Hartley, Chapman, Plank, Davenport, Groom, Borton, Ernest Johnson, Campbell, Marsans and Clemons.

Detroit—Erickson.

Philadelphia—Pick.

INTERNATIONAL LEAGUE

Providence—Comstock, Billiard.

Toronto—Mills, Hearne.

Richmond—Suggs.

AMERICAN ASSOCIATION

St. Paul—Fred Smith, Nash, Land, Finneran, Upham, Halt, Berghammer, Brennan, Gilmore.

Toledo—Stovall, Rawlings, Evans, Bedient.

Kalserling, Main.

Columbus—Pratt, Bradley.

Kansas City—Hanford, Beck, Berry.

Indianapolis—Wickland, Rogge.

Louisville—Roach, Whiteman, Luque, McCarthy.

Minneapolis—Menosky, Dickson, Burke, Owens.

OTHER MINOR CLUBS

Denver—Oakes.

Lowell—Lord.

Memphis—Burger, Walsh, Willett, Drake and Chadbourne.

Vernon—Quinn and George Johnson (claimed by Cincinnati).

Atlanta—Lennox, Lafitte, McDonald.

Scranton—Schlafly and Zinn.

Nashville—Bridwell, Herbert, Kores.

Chattanooga—Krapp.

Little Rock—Swacina, Kirby.

Topeka—Agler.

Omaha—George Anderson.

Syracuse—Fritz.

Albany—Wiltse, Tesch.

Portland, Ore.—Vaughn.

Sioux City—Watson.

Peoria—W. Jackson.

Bloomington—Bluejacket, Simon.

New London—Russell, Gilbert, Whitehouse.

Rome, Ga.—Troutman.

San Francisco—R. Myers.

Binghamton—Reed.

Troy—Reed.

Wilkes-Barre—Kane.

Portland—Honck.

Vernon—Griggs.

Fort Worth—A. R. Johnson.

Tacoma—Roberts, Koch.

St. Joseph—Sommers.

DETROIT AT PHILADELPHIA, MAY 10.—Detroit won another weird game from the Athletics. All three pitchers used were wild, but Boehler managed to hold down the Mackmen when men were on the bases, which was just the opposite to Sheehan and Nabors. Eighteen passes were issued, making 48 in two games and breaking all records for inaccuracy. Score:

Detroit.	AB.	R.	B.	P.	A.	Athletics.	AB.	R.	B.	P.	A.
Bush, ss..	5	0	0	1	1	Witt, ss..	4	1	0	2	2
Vitt, 3b.	3	2	1	1	4	Walsh, rf.	3	1	1	1	0
Cobb, cf.	3	2	2	3	0	Strunk, cf	4	1	3	1	1
Crawf'd. rf	3	1	2	0	0	Oldring, lf.	4	0	0	1	0
Heilman. lf	4	1	0	0	0	Lajoie, 2b.	3	0	1	4	7
Burns, 1b.	4	1	2	11	0	McInnis, 1b	2	0	0	12	0
Young, 2b	4	0	2	5	4	Pick, 3b..	3	0	0	2	3
Stanage, c	5	1	2	6	3	Schang, c.	3	0	0	3	5
Boehler, p	3	1	0	0	2	Sheehan, p	1	0	0	1	3
						Nabors, p..	0	0	0	0	1
Totals.	34	9	11	27	14	*Thompson	0	0	0	0	0
						†Stellbauer	1	0	0	0	0
						Totals .	28	3	5	27	22

*Batted for Sheehan in seventh inning.
†Batted for Nabors in ninth inning.

Detroit .... 0 2 3 0 1 0 0 3 0—9
Athletics .... 1 0 0 1 0 1 0 0 0—3

Errors—Bush, Burns, Witt 2, Pick, Schang, Sheehan.

Two-base hit—Strunk. Three-base hits—Strunk 2. Stolen bases—Cobb, Young 2, Burns, Schang. Sacrifice hit—McInnis. Sacrifice fly—Burns. Double plays—Burns, unassisted; Pick, Lajoie, McInnis. Left on bases—Detroit 10, Athletics 7. First on errors—Detroit 3, Athletics 1. First on balls—Off Boehler 7, Sheehan 7, Nabors 4. Hits and earned runs—Off Boehler, 5 hits, 2 runs in 9 innings; Sheehan, 7 hits, 1 run in 7 innings; Nabors, 4 hits, 3 runs in 2 innings. Hit by pitcher—By Boehler 1. Struck out—By Boehler 7, Sheehan 1, Nabors 1. Wild pitch—Boehler. Umpires—Chill and O'Loughlin. Time—1.45.

No Fraternity Strike at All

NEW YORK, N. Y., February 28.—There is no intention on the part of the Base Ball Players' Fraternity to call a strike of its members following the opening of the major league season, on April 12. This official announcement comes from David L. Fultz, president of the Fraternity. Fultz not only denied yesterday that there was any such action contemplated, but declared that he never knew the matter had been discussed by the players. Just why the ball players should contemplate a strike against the magnates of Organized Ball is a mystery. Base ball has just gone through two years of strife through the invasion of the Federal League and survived in healthy condition. President Fultz has been quoted as declaring that the reserve clause and the option clause contracts are not equitable, but recognized that it would practically be impossible to operate base ball without some such conditions, and therefore the Players' Fraternity would make no fight against contracts. This is taking a sensible view of it.

MATTY TO MANAGE REDS' TEAM TODAY

Deal Whereby Herzog Becomes a Giant Finally Finish at Cincinnati

CINCINNATI, Ohio, July 20.—After an absence of sixteen years, during which time as a member of the New York Giants, he made a reputation as being the premier pitcher of professional baseball, Christy Mathewson returns here tomorrow to manage the Reds, the team that allowed him to slip through its fingers without a trial.

With Mathewson comes two of his team mates, Outfielder Rousch and Infielder McKechnie, while New York obtains the services of Charles Herzog, manager of the local team for the last two years, and who, incidentally was a member of the Giants previous to his coming to Cincinnati, and Outfielder Wade Killifer.

Some years ago, Manager McGraw, of the Giants, established a rule that provided that he would never ask Mathewson to retire from a game in which he was pitching. In principle, this rule was adhered to to the last, as a statement issued by President Hempstead, of the New Yorks, today, revealed the fact that it was not until "Matty" had asked for permission to negotiate for a managerial berth that the idea of trading him entered their minds.

Reprinted from
The Philadelphia Inquirer

MACKS SHARE LOSS RECORD WITH SOX

Tie Up American League Mark by Dropping Twenty Consecutive Games

Tigers Just Toy With Often-Riddled Athletics, Cobb Getting Closer to Speaker's Batting Average

Special to The Inquirer.

DETROIT, Mich., Aug. 8.—Although the Tigers won today's ball game by a score of 9 to 0 and did it without even getting up a perspiration, the real honors of the occasion went to the Athletics, whose defeat enabled them to tie the American League record for consecutive defeats, which is just plain 20 in a row. Anybody can win a battle now and then, but it takes genius to lose as consistently as the Macks have been losing lately. For ten years, tail-end clubs have been shooting at the mark established by the Red Sox in 1906 and this is the first time that anybody has been able to equal it. Now that Connie's subterranean denizens have succeeded in equaling it, they may go out and hang up a new one to stand for all time.

Reprinted from
The Philadelphia Inquirer

COBB TO SPEAKER

Said Tristam Speaker to Tyrus Cobb,
"Smoke up, kid, or I'll cop your job."
"October will find you a darnsite meeker,"
Said Tyrus Cobb to Tristam Speaker.

GIANTS TAKE DOUBLE HEADER FROM PHILS

With Perritt Pitching Both Games Champions Never Had Chance to Win. Record Crowd Witnessed Downfall of Moranmen

Reprinted from
The Philadelphia Inquirer

From a Staff Correspondent.

NEW YORK, Sept. 9.—"Poll" Perritt, who has been a rank in and outer all season, rose to the dizziest height of his career here today, when he outpitched, outgamed and outdistanced a pair of Phil flingers and pitched the Giants into a double victory over the champions by scores of 3 to 1 and 3 to 0. The double jolt, which delighted over 35,000 fans, dropped the Phillies back to second place in the race and elevated the Dodgers to their old leading perch in the scramble for the National gonfalon. The Robins helped boost themselves by reason of their triumph over the demoralized Braves.

Sept. 29

TAINTED FIELDING LOST NABORS GAME

Elongated Jack Would Have Beaten Senators Had His Support Been Pure

Elongated Jack Nabors tried hard enough to stave off defeat No. 115 for the Athletics yesterday, but pop-eyed support by Witt and Grover enabled two Washingtonians to travel the 360 feet of pathway around the diamond and these runs were sufficient enough to give the Senators their second victory over the much-abused Mackmen. The final verdict was 4 to 1, the other two markers being compiled in the ninth, when Rube Bressler, who succeeded Nabors in this round, gave a weird exhibition of pitching.

Had Jack been flawlessly supported the Senators would not have reached the counting station. Grover's fumble of Menesky's roller in the sixth, when two were down and a man on second, set the stage for Smith to single in the first counter for the Capital brigade. In the very next inning "Whitey" Witt, who showed up poorly all day, erred on Shank's bouncer and that bull blossomed into the second tally scored on Nabors.

Nabors pitched equally as good ball as did Gallia, who has developed into one of Griffith's winning pitchers. Seven hits the outfit from the District of Columbia negotiated off Lanky Jack, two being infield safeties. It was one of Nabors' best exhibitions, for he forgot to pass a man, eliminated wild pitches from his repertoire and in general behaved with all the skill and cunning a regular moundman uses in his daily labors.

Reprinted from
The Philadelphia Inquirer

Sept. 24

ALEX JUST ABOUT HANGS UP RECORDS

Grover Not Only Bumps Reds 7-3 and 4-0, But Smashes All Former Pitching Marks for Big League Twirlers

BY JIM NASIUM

Thoroughly aroused by the rapidly growing custom prevalent among the lesser lights of the pitching fraternity to horn in on some of the spotlight by heaving and winning two ball games in the short space of one autumnal afternoon, Grover Cleveland Alexander, the "Nebraska Cyclone," Monarch of the Pitching Peak, shed his duster yesterday and showed 'em how the job ought to be done.

Facing a crucial series with Old Christy Mathewson's rejuvenated Cincinnati ball club that had just finished mopping up the Back Bay district of Massachusetts with the Boston Braves, a series that meant much to his ball club, this Lanky Nebraskan poised himself nonchalantly on the pitching peak and in the short space of two hours and thirty-six minutes pitched the Phils into two triumphs over the fast-traveling Reds by scores of 7 to 3 and 4 to 0 respectively.

He not only did this, b'gosh, but he shattered about all the pitching records that had been left lying around loose in the shattering zone. He added another notch to the shutout record with his fifteenth no-score engagement of the season, in the second encounter, he tied his last season's record of victories by amassing his thirtieth and thirty-first victories of the season, while in the second battle he shaved Matty's record for the fewest number of balls pitched mighty close and established a season's record, and what we believe to be a big league record, for short games in a crucial series by completing the pastime in the short time of one hour and seven minutes.

Reprinted from
The Philadelphia Inquirer

1st PINCH HIT GRAND SLAM EVER!

FREAK HOMER WAS LEONARD'S UNDOING

Pinch Hitter Kavanagh's Drive Rolls Under Screen and Four Indian Runs Result

CLEVELAND, O., Sept. 24.—With the bases filled and one out in the fifth inning, Kavanaugh, pinch hitting for Boehling, drove a sizzling grounder over third base, which rolled under the screen in far left field. The drive went for a home run and Cleveland checked the Championship advance of the Boston, the score being 5 to 3.

Reprinted from
The Philadelphia Inquirer

New York Wins 26 Straight

NEW YORK, September 30.—After Rube Benton shut out Boston in the first game of a double-header, 4 to 0, for New York's twenty-sixth victory, the great winning streak of the home team was broken in the second game, which Boston won, 8 to 3. A pair of home runs stopped New York in the seventh inning of the second game. George Tyler, who stopped the Giants in their winning streak, pitched a strong game and did not permit an earned run. In pitching New York to its twenty-sixth victory in the first game, Rube Benton allowed only one hit and only 28 men faced him. Of the three to get to first base two of them were retired on double plays. The record:

Date.	Team.	Score.	Pitcher.	Date.	Team.	Score.	Pitcher.
Sept. 7	Brooklyn	4-1	Schupp.	Sept. 19	Pittsburgh	5-1	Tesreau.
Sept. 8	Philadelphia	9-3	Tesreau.	Sept. 20	Chicago	4-2	Schupp.
Sept. 9	Philadelphia	3-1	Perritt.	Sept. 21	Chicago	4-0	Perritt.
Sept. 9	Philadelphia	3-0	Perritt.	Sept. 22	Chicago	5-0	Sallee.
Sept. 10	Philadelphia	9-4	Tesreau.	Sept. 23	St. Louis	6-1	Tesreau.
Sept. 12	Cincinnati	3-2	Benton.	Sept. 23	St. Louis	5-0	Benton.
Sept. 13	Cincinnati	3-0	Schupp.	Sept. 25	St. Louis	3-2	Schupp.
Sept. 13	Cincinnati	6-4	Perritt.	Sept. 25	St. Louis	1-0	Perritt.
Sept. 14	Cincinnati	3-1	Tesreau.	Sept. 26	St. Louis	6-1	Sallee.
Sept. 16	Pittsburgh	8-2	Benton.	Sept. 27	St. Louis	5-2	Anderson.
Sept. 16	Pittsburgh	4-3	Anderson.	Sept. 28	Boston	2-0	Tesreau.
Sept. 18	Pittsburgh	2-0	Schupp.	Sept. 28	Boston	6-0	Schupp.
Sept. 18	Pittsburgh	1-1	Perritt.†	Sept. 30	Boston	4-0	Benton.
Sept. 19	Pittsburgh	0-2	Anderson.‡				

*Smith, Ritter, Tesreau. †Benton, G. Smith, Ritter. ‡Benton.

BROOKLYN WINS CHAMPIONSHIP OVER PHILLIES

New York Giants Play Listless Ball and Mc-Graw Leaves Field

Becomes Disgusted With Exhibition and Charges Men Disregarded His Orders

Special to The Inquirer.

NEW YORK, Oct. 3.—The failure of the Giants to win from Brooklyn today and the inability of the Phillies to win either of the two games from Boston, at Philadelphia, gave Brooklyn the National League pennant for 1916.

The Brooklyn Dodgers, therefore became contenders with the Boston Red Sox, winners of the American League race in the World's Series, which by prearrangement will begin at Boston on Saturday.

After hanging up a record of twenty-six victories the Giants, after losing a game to Boston, were twice running by Brooklyn on the days that the Phillies were engaged in doubleheaders with the Boston team. The game today, which was won by Brooklyn by the score of nine to six was played very listlessly by the Giants; so much so, in fact, that Manager McGraw refused to remain on the bench to see the finish. He retired to the clubhouse in the fifth inning.

Reprinted from
The Philadelphia Inquirer

SPEAKER AND CHASE THE BATTING KINGS

Tris and Hal Lead American and National Leagues With .383 and .335 Respectively—Cravath Tops the Phils

These averages are compiled expressly for The Inquirer and include all games played in both leagues for season of 1916

HAL CHASE, of the Cincinnati Reds, one of the few real comebacks of baseball, is the virtual batting leader of the National League for the season of 1916, his first as a player in that organization. Although headed by McCarty and young Hoelke, of the Giants, the leadership honors go to the famous Hal, since his lesser contemporaries have not made their appearance in the official box scores often enough to gain recognition. Chase ended the season with a mark of .335 over a stretch of 142 games, during which he scored 67 runs and drove out 181 safe hits to secluded parts of eight National League parks. Next in line is Jake Daubert, of the Brooklyn champions, with a .322 average, with Hinchman, Wheat, Robertson and Hornsby in the offing.

Cravath and Luderus led the Phil offensive for the year, but neither was able to squeeze into the exclusive society of .300 hitters. Gabby finished up the season at .288, which bettered Ludy's efforts by just two points. Stock, Whitted and Paskert were close up.

Little or no comment is necessary on the American League race for the batting supremacy. Tris Speaker, of the Cleveland Indians, went out during the palmy days of April and intrenched himself behind a 30 point lead, which was large enough to successfully ward off all efforts to dislodge him. Tris ended the campaign at .383, with Ty Cobb, inhaling the dust of a conqueror for the first time in nine long years, trailing along at .366.

Reprinted from
The Philadelphia Inquirer

The American League Pitching Records

BABE RUTH, a pitcher whom Connie Mack could have bought two years ago had he cared to pay the price asked by Jack Dunn, manager of the then Baltimore Internationals, won the honor of topping the list of American League pitchers, arranged in the order of their effectiveness in repressing the earned-run activities of the opposing teams. Eddie Cicotte, of the White Sox, crowds Babe with a record of 1.78. Walter Johnson is not far behind Cicotte.

Will Washington Be Moved?

A Boston Report That Toronto May Get the Capital City Club—Conditions in Washington Very Grave According to Report.

BOSTON, Mass., October 8.—An international flavor may be added to the American League before the beginning of another season, it was learned today on what seemed the most reliable authority. Toronto, Ont., is likely to replace Washington as a member of the Ban Johnson circuit. "The matter has been seriously discussed for more than a year," admitted a club owner of the American League today. "Whether any action is likely to be taken at our annual meeting I am not prepared to say."

GAINER'S BASE BLOW BRINGS HOME BACON

Boston Pinch Hitter Raps Out Single In Fourteenth With One On

"Babe" Ruth and Smith in Battle Royal, With the Former Having Just a Shade

BY JIM NASIUM

BOSTON, Mass., Oct. 9.—The second battle for the supremacy of the great, throbbing world of baseball, staged on the mammoth Braves' field here this afternoon, was productive of considerably better baseball than the initial encounter, and was well worthy of the name of baseball classic. In the number of innings necessary to arrive at a decisive result, if no other way, today's brawl on the Fenways of Boston established a record for World's Series contests, the Red Sox and Dodgers being all snarled up in a complete deadlock and fighting into the fourteenth period of play before Del Gainer, in the role of pinch hitter, cuffed a clean base hit through the gathering gloom and chased the youthful Mr. McNally, pinch runner, over the plate with a run that gave the Red Sox the long end of a 2 to 1 score and their second consecutive triumph over the Dodgers.

TWIRLING RECORD FOR BIG SOUTHPAWS

Ruth and Smith Go Fourteen Innings Like Iron Men in Greatest Baseball Classic Ever Staged for World's Honors

From a Staff Correspondent.

BOSTON, Mass., Oct. 9.—Probably no two pitchers covered themselves with such a mantle of World's Series glory as did big Babe Ruth and Sherrod Smith today in this greatest and longest postseason tiff ever held. For two pitchers to hurl through fourteen nerve-racking innings in one of the biggest monied series ever staged was indeed enough glory for the two flingers to achieve, but when taken into consideration that these two practically one-year regulars are left-handers their feat of going the entire distance without showing any visible signs of cracking under the spell proved conclusively enough that a southpaw can be depended upon in such a series just as much as any tried and true right-hander.

Even Rube Waddell in the hey-day of his fame never pitched any better ball than did Ruth and Smith today. Their control was excellent, considering everything, and their refusal to rattle and wobble at the many critical stages was most commending.

Reprinted from
The Philadelphia Inquirer

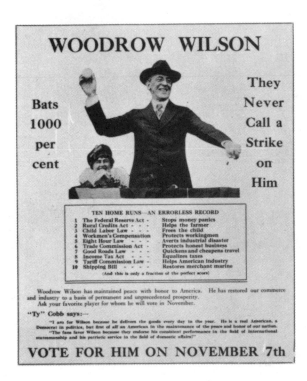

The Official Score

BOSTON

	ab.	r.	bh.	tb.	sh.	sb.	po.	a.	e.
Hooper, rf.	6	—	1	1	—	—	2	1	—
Janvrin, 2b.	6	—	1	2	—	—	4	5	—
Walker, cf.	3	—	—	—	—	—	2	1	—
Walsh, cf.	3	—	—	—	—	—	1	—	—
Hoblitzell, 1b.	2	—	—	—	—	—	21	1	—
McNally, zz	—	1	—	—	—	—	—	—	—
Lewis, lf.	3	—	1	1	2	—	1	—	—
Gardner, 3b.	5	—	—	—	—	—	3	7	1
Gainer, z	1	—	1	1	—	—	—	—	—
Scott, ss.	4	1	2	4	—	—	1	8	—
Thomas, c.	4	—	1	3	1	—	5	4	—
Ruth, p.	5	—	—	—	—	—	2	4	—
Totals	42	2	7	12	3	—	42	31	1

BROOKLYN

	ab.	r.	bh.	tb.	sh.	sb.	po.	a.	e.
Johnston, rf.	5	—	1	1	—	—	1	—	—
Daubert, 1b.	5	—	—	—	—	—	18	1	—
Myers, cf.	6	1	1	4	—	—	4	1	—
Wheat, lf.	5	—	—	—	—	—	2	—	—
Cutshaw, 2b.	5	—	—	—	—	—	5	6	1
Mowrey, 3b.	5	—	1	1	—	—	3	5	1
Olson, ss.	2	—	1	1	2	—	2	4	—
Miller, c.	5	—	1	1	—	—	4	1	—
Smith, p.	5	—	1	2	—	—	1	7	—
Totals	43	1	6	10	2	—	x40	25	2

x—One out when winning run was scored.
z—Batted for Gardner in fourteenth.
zz—McNally ran for Hoblitzell in fourteenth.

Brooklyn	1	0	0	0	0	0	0	0	0	0	0	0	0	0—1
Boston	0	0	1	0	0	0	0	0	0	0	0	0	0	1—2

Two-base hits—Smith, Janvrin. Three-base hits—Scott, Thomas. Home run—Myers. Double plays—Scott, Janvrin and Hoblitzell; Mowrey, Cutshaw and Daubert; Myers and Miller. Left on bases—Brooklyn, 5; Boston, 9. First base on errors—Brooklyn, 1; Boston, 1. Bases on balls—Off Smith, 6; Ruth, 3. Hits and earned runs—Off Smith, 7 hits, 2 runs in 13⅓ innings; off Ruth, 6 hits, 1 run in 14 innings. Struck out—By Smith, 2; Ruth, 4. Umpires—At plate, Dineen; on bases, Quigley; left field, O'Day; right field, Connolly. Time—2.32.

Latest News of the Philadelphia Club—Alexander a Sure-Enough Hold-Out With a Demand of $15,000 Per Annum for Three Years.

BY THOMAS D. RICHTER

HILADELPHIA, Pa., January 30.—A dispatch from Lincoln, Neb., brings the news that Grover Alexander, pitching premier of the National League, has demanded a $15,000 salary and three-year contract from the Philadelphia Club. Unless his demands are met by President Baker, of the Phillies, Alexander announced today at his home in St. Paul, Neb., that he would retire from professional base ball and join the semi-pros.

WHAT ALEXANDER SAYS

"This is no strike on my part," said Alexander, "and the Fraternity row has nothing to do with the affair. I feel simply that I am not being compensated in proportion with my ability and worth to the Philadelphia Club; if Ty Cobb is worth $15,000 to Detroit, I believe I am worth that much to the Phillies. I want a three-year contract because I believe I can go on pitching at my best for at least that term of years. I drew $6000 in salary last year and received a bonus of $1000 for winning 25 games. The record will show I won nearly 35 games, so I guess I earned the money. President Baker knows my terms and he must meet them or I will not play with the Phillies this year."

Braves Defeat Dodgers Twice

Take First 6 to 5 and Second 7 to 3—Gowdy Leaves to Join National Guard

BY ED M'GRATH

BROOKLYN, June 26.— Hank Gowdy, master backstop of the Braves, played his final game as a member of the club this afternoon, an afternoon wherein the much defeated men of Stallings came out of a long slumber to slug out two wins over the Dodgers in a double bill. Two batting rallies did the business, a ninth-inning uprising hauling the first game out of the last column, 6 to 5, while the second resulted 7 to 3.

Groom Holds Whitesox Hitless for 11 Innings

Old Bob Pitches Last Two Innings of First Game of Doubleheader and Then Goes Route in Second Contest Without Being Touched for Bingle—Browns Win Both.

ST. LOUIS, Mo., May 7.—Old Bob Groom did not allow Chicago a hit for 11 innings here today and St. Louis took both games of the double-header, the first 8 to 4 and the second 3 to 0.

In the fourth inning of the first game, St. Louis drove Russell from the mound, making five runs. The Browns added three more in the eighth on two singles, a double, a sacrifice and E. Collins' error.

Plank retired for a pinch hitter in the seventh and Groom relieved him on the mound. From then on to the end of the second game, Chicago could not get a hit.

Only 28 men faced Groom in the second game. Four men reached first base—one hit a sacrifice, three got a base on balls and one was hit—and only one, Risberg, in the sixth, got beyond first base.

St. Louis made a run in the first inning, when Sisler singled and Jacobson doubled. In the second, Johnson doubled and scored on Lavan's single.

BOB GROOM.

In the eighth, Austin singled and took third when Sisler singled. Sisler stole second and went to third when Austin was thrown out at the plate on Marsans' fielder's choice. He scored when Marsans was caught in a run-down between first and second.

Carmen Hill, pitcher, who for the past two years has shared with Lee Meadows, of St. Louis, the distinction of being the only pitchers in major league base ball wearing glasses, on January 6 was released by the Pittsburgh Nationals to the Birmingham Club, of the Southern League.

Charley Deal, who has burned up as much railway mileage riding back and forth between major and minor league berths as any man in the country, is due for another chance to do big time next season. Fred Mitchell plans to give him a thorough tryout at third with the Cubs.

The young members of the Giants and the newspaper writers will leave New York on February 23. McGraw will probably stay in New York until the regulars report. It is said that the Little Napoleon hopes to land a first-class pitcher in a few weeks from one of the Western clubs.

Toney and Vaughn Set World's Record; Former Permits No Hits in 10 Innings; Latter None in First Nine; Reds Win, 1-0

CHICAGO, May 2.—A world's record was established here today in a 10-inning game between Cincinnati and Chicago, when, after the game had gone nine innings neither club had registered a hit or run. Cincinnati won 1 to 0.

For the nine innings, Vaughn, assisted by remarkable defense by the Chicago infield, did not permit a Cincinnati player to reach second base, and in this only slightly surpassed his pitching opponent, Toney, who allowed but one Chicago runner to reach second.

Vaughn struck out 10 Cincinnati batsmen, while only three were fanned by Toney.

The game was won when, in the the tenth inning, after one was out, Kopf singled, advanced to third when Williams dropped Chase's fly and scored when Thorpe hit a slow bounder to Vaughn.

The Cincinnati outfielders several times saved the game for Toney, Cueto on one occasion backing into the left field fence for Merkle's fly. The score:

CINCINNATI	AB.	R.	B.	P.	A.	E.
Groh, 3b	3	0	0	2	1	0
Getz, 3b	1	0	0	0	1	0
Kopf, ss	4	1	1	1	5	0
Neale, mf	4	0	0	1	0	0
Chase, 1b	4	0	0	13	0	0
Thorpe, rf	4	0	1	2	0	0
Shean, 2b	3	0	0	3	2	0
Cueto, lf	3	0	0	5	0	0
Huhn, c	3	0	0	3	1	0
Toney, p	3	0	0	0	0	0
Totals	30	1	2	30	10	0

CHICAGO	AB.	R.	B.	P.	A.	E.
Zeider, ss	4	0	0	2	3	0
Wolter, rf	4	0	0	5	4	0
Doyle, 2b	4	0	0	1	1	0
Merkle, 1b	4	0	0	7	1	0
Williams, mf	3	0	0	2	0	1
Mann, lf	3	0	0	0	0	0
Wilson, c	3	0	0	14	1	0
Deal, 3b	3	0	0	1	0	0
Vaughn, p	3	0	0	0	3	0
Totals	30	0	0	30	9	2

*Batted for Groh in seventh.
Cincinnati .... 000 000 000 1—1
Chicago .... 000 000 000 0—0
Stolen base—Chase.
Double plays—Doyle to Merkle to Zeider; Vaughn to Doyle to Merkle.
Left on bases—Chicago 2, Cincinnati 1.
First base on errors—Cincinnati 2.
Base on balls—Off Toney 2, off Vaughn 2.
Struck out—Vaughn 10, Toney 3.
Umpires—Orth and Rigler.
Time—1:50.

Big No-Hit Hero

FRED TONEY

Fred Toney Fourth Twirler to Travel Ten Hitless Heats

Big Fred Toney of the Reds, who twirled 10 hitless innings at Chicago yesterday, is the fourth major league boxman to accomplish this rare feat. The others were Kimber of Brooklyn, McIntyre also of Brooklyn and Wiltse of New York.

Kimber's performance took place on October 4, 1884, when the Brooklyn club belonged to the American Association. He was pitching against Toledo and the game was called in the early portion of the eleventh inning on account of darkness. Neither side had crossed the plate. Not a hit had been made off Kimber in the 10 chapters.

Harry McIntyre of the Dodgers held the Pirates hitless for 10 innings, on August 1, 1906, but the game continued until the thirteenth frame when Pittsburgh won by a score of 1 to 0, Lefty Leifield being credited with the victory.

George Wiltse of the Giants held the Phillies hitless and runless, on July 4, 1908, New York winning, 1 to 0.

Yesterdays' affair was the third of the season in the big show in which the no-hit stunt has been pulled. Eddie Cicotte of the Chicago Americans held the Browns without a single recently. George Mogridge of the New York Americans did the same feat at the expense of the world's champion Redsox.

He Nearly Made It

JAMES VAUGHN

SHORE PITCHES RECORD GAME AFTER RUTH IS CANNED FOR HITTING UMPIRE

If Shore won a no-hit victory over the Senators, Babe Ruth, one of the greatest assets in the Red Sox pitching corps, likewise accomplished a no hit performance over Brick Owens, for, at the very start of the double matinee, he committed an assault upon that official which is likely to cost himself and the Boston club pretty dearly. No matter how much the umpire may have been wrong in his judgment, there can be little justification for Ruth's act, a demonstration which has never before been made by a Red Sox player in this city.

This act, committed at the beginning of the first game, and before half of the big crowd of 16,000 odd had entered the park, was the consequence of the umpire's judgment in sending Morgan to first base on balls. Morgan was the first of the Washington men to bat, and after he had been awarded first base Ruth lost his temper and asked Owens to keep his eyes open.

Umpire Warns Ruth

"You get back there and pitch or I'll run you out of the ball park," the arbiter threatened.

"If you run me out of the ball park I'll take a punch at you on my way," the angry player retorted.

"You're out now," yelled Owens, waving his arm in a gesture of banishment.

Ruth lost his head completely and rushed for the umpire. Catcher Thomas sprang in front of the big pitcher and as Ruth swung at the umpire's head, Thomas apparently deflected the blow. Before Babe could reach the umpire again not only Thomas but Barry himself had gotten in the way and the result was that Babe was exiled without any further collision between himself and the umps. The Boston club will wait anxiously to see what punishment Ban Johnson may mete out.

According to the umpire, Ruth did succeed in hitting him although he admits it was a light, glancing blow on the cheek, but Manager Barry, Heinie Wagner and others of the Boston team insist that Thomas warded off the blow and on that account they are hoping that Babe will be mercifully dealt with.

Boston Team Handicapped

The real explanation of it seems to be that the Boston team has been handicapped all season by bad umpiring and some of the players have just about reached the conclusion that the arbiters have decided to give all the breaks against them. Ruth, who is normally one of the best tempered fellows in the world, has done a lot of kicking about the way that the umpires behind the plate have been judging them lately.

On the length of the sentence imposed will depend to a great measure Boston's chances in the pennant fight, and it may also determine whether the powers that be are as anxious to see some other team than Boston win.

Owens showed good judgment in making no effort to return the blow. His coolness probably prevented further trouble, although the police were promptly on the spot.

It is rather unfortunate that this incident in a way dimmed the magnificent performance of Shore. Taking Ruth's place with a brief warming up and handicapped by having a man on first base Shore proceeded to go through with a feat that will have the whole baseball world sitting up and taking notice.

Agnew in Great Form

Agnew, who caught a marvelous game and batted terrifically, caught Morgan when he tried to steal. Then Shore retired the next 26 men just as fast as they came to bat, three brilliant plays, one by Scott and two by Duffy Lewis, making the achievement possible.

Lewis' spectacular catch off Henry in the ninth and Barry's clever running catch of an attempted bunt by a pinch hitter finally clinched Shore's claim to take his place with the pitching immortals.

First Game

Enraged at Umpire Owens' judgment, which gave Morgan, the first man up, a base on balls, Ruth said something to the arbitrator with the result that he was ordered from the game. He then committed the assault, which is liable to exact a heavy fine from his salary and hurt the team's chances. This forced Thomas out automatically. Shore and Agnew succeeding. Agnew's nice throw foiled Morgan's attempt to steal and sharp playing got the next two men up.

Gardner began the second with a clean hit to right, and as Lewis' intended sacrifice got away from Judge Duffy got the credit for a scratch hit. Walker sacrificed. After Scott popped up Gardner scored on a hit by Agnew. That was the net result of three hits.

Agnew led off in the fifth with his second safe one, and Shore sacrificed nicely. Fine plays by Morgan and Foster cheated Hooper and Barry out of hits and prevented a score. The first ball that the Senators could knock out of the infield was a weak fly that Henry lifted to Walker with one out in the sixth.

Walker doubled to the score board in the seventh. He was first man up. Scott sacrificed. Then Agnew, who had driven in one run, made his third safe hit, a double to the left field and brought Tillie in. Shore hit to Ayers, who held the ball too long and then threw to third where Agnew would have been a dead bird had not Foster muffed the throw. This let Shore get to second, and Leonard replaced Foster, who had hurt his hand. Hooper hit safely, scoring Agnew and Shore. Barry's hit dropped safely in right, but as Rice made a bad throw to second, where he could have forced Hooper at second, he is credited with an error and Barry loses a base hit. A fast double play on Hoblitzell's liner prevented more runs.

As the game waned and it became apparent that Shore was on his way to a no-hit game the tension grew greater. In the eighth the fast fielding of Shore himself saved a hit, and in the ninth a wonderful catch by Lewis and a pretty play by Barry gave Ernie the credit of pitching the greatest battle ever twirled at Fenway Park.

FIRST GAME.

BOSTON.	AB.	BH.	PO.	A.	WASHINGTON	AB.	BH.	PO.	A.
Hooper, rf	4	1	0	0	Morgan, 2b	2	0	4	2
Barry, 2b	4	0	2	1	Foster, 3b	3	0	1	3
Hoblitzell, 1b	4	0	12	0	Leonard, 3b	0	0	0	0
Gardner, 3b	4	1	2	1	Milan, cf	3	0	1	0
Lewis, lf	4	2	2	0	Rice, rf	3	0	3	0
Walker, cf	3	1	4	0	Judge, 1b	3	0	11	1
Scott, ss	3	0	1	5	Jamieson, lf	3	0	0	0
Thomas, c	0	0	0	0	Shanks, ss	3	0	1	2
Agnew, c	3	3	3	1	Henry, c	3	0	1	0
Ruth, p	0	0	0	0	Ayers, p	2	0	1	2
Shore, p	2	0	2	0	*Menosky	1	0	1	0
Totals	31	9	27	12	Totals	29	0	24	10

*Hit for Ayers in 9th.

Boston .... 0 1 0 0 0 3 0 .— 4

Runs—Gardner, Walker, Agnew, Shore. Errors—Foster 2, Rice. Two-base hits—Walker, Agnew. Sacrifice hits—Walker, Shore, Scott. Base on balls—Off Ruth 1. Struck out—By Shore 2. Double plays—Ayers to Foster to Judge, Ayers to Judge. Time—1h. 45m. Umpires—McCormick and Owens.

ALEX PITCHES HIS THIRTIETH WIN FOR YEAR

Giants Beat Phils 5-2 in 12 Innings, But Fall Before the Quaker Star, 8-2, in Second Contest.

PHILADELPHIA, Oct. 1.—Philadelphia and New York broke even here today. New York winning the first game in 12 innings, 5 to 2, and the home team getting the second, 8 to 2.

A muffed fly ball by Fletcher with two men out in the ninth inning of the opening game prevented Perritt from getting a shutout and caused the score to be tied. New York won this game in the twelfth inning on three hits and two errors.

The second game marked Alexander's thirtieth victory of the season. It was the third successive year that he reached this mark. In 1915 he won 31 games, while in 1916 he won 33.

NO HITS OFF LEONARD

Only Tiger to Reach First Base Is Given Free Transportation.

DETROIT, Mich., June 4.—Holding Detroit hitless, Leonard pitched Boston to a 5-to-0 victory yesterday afternoon. Only one Detroiter reached first base, the result of the only base on balls Leonard issued.

Boston batted Dauss freely, bunching the blows with bases on balls and errors.

Ruth, sent to center field to replace Strunk, duplicated his home run of yesterday by placing the ball in the right field bleachers. Score:

```
Boston.........  1 0 0 1 1 2 0 0 0—5
Detroit.........  0 0 0 0 0 0 0 0 0—0
```

Two-base hit—Whiteman. Three-base hit—Hooper. Home run—Ruth. Stolen bases—Whiteman, Hooper, McInnis. Sacrifice hit—Thomas. Double play—Yelle and Vitt. Left on bases—Boston, 7; Detroit, 1. First base on errors—Boston, 2. Bases on balls—Off Leonard, 1; off Dauss, 2; off Cunningham, 1. Hits—Off Dauss, 8 in six innings; off Cunningham, none in three innings. Struck out—By Dauss, 5; by Cunningham, 2; by Leonard, 4. Wild pitch—Dauss. Losing pitcher—Dauss.

RUTH HAS SUDDEN DEATH HOMER

ANOTHER GAME FOR RUTH.

Boston Player Beats Cleveland with Triple Into Bleachers.

BOSTON, July 8.—Boston and Cleveland divided honors today. Ruth's triple into the right-field bleachers in the last of the tenth scored Strunk, who had singled, with the only run of the first game. Morton held Boston to three hits, two of them scratchy, in the second game, Cleveland winning, 4 to 3.

The scores:

FIRST GAME.

BOSTON. (A.)	Ab	R	H	Po	A		CLEVELAND. (A.)	Ab	R	H	Po	A
Hooper,rf	5	0	1	2	0		Johnston,1b	4	0	0	12	0
Shean,2b	4	0	1	2	2		Chapman,ss	4	0	0	1	3
Strunk,cf	4	1	1	3	0		Speaker,cf	3	0	0	4	0
Ruth,lf	4	0	2	3	0		Roth,rf	4	0	0	0	0
McInnis,1b	3	0	0	12	2		Wambsganss,2b	4	0	1	3	4
Scott,ss	3	0	2	2	4		Wood,lf	4	0	1	2	1
Barbare,3b	3	0	0	3	2		Evans,3b	4	0	2	1	4
Stansbury,3b	0	0	0	0	0		O'Neill,c	3	0	0	5	1
Agnew,c	3	0	0	3	0		Coveleskie,p	3	0	0	0	4
Jones,p	2	0	1	3	2							
aSchang	1	0	0	0	0		Total	33	0	4	29	17
Total	31	1	8	30	12							

aBatted for Barbare in ninth.
*One out in tenth when winning run scored.

```
Boston .............  0 0 0 0 0 0 0 0 1 1—1
Cleveland ..........  0 0 0  0 0 0  0 0 0—0
```

Three-base hits—Ruth, Scott. Sacrifice hits—Shean, Barbare, McInnis. Double play—Scott and McInnis. Left on bases—Cleveland, 4; Boston, 11. Base on balls—Off Coveleskie, 6; Jones, 1. Struck out—By Coveleskie, 4; Jones, 2.

BRAVES ARE RESTRAINED

Connie Mack Resorts To Courts To Hold Scott Perry.

MAJOR AGREEMENT IN DANGER

Cleveland Judge Allows Athletics Full Use Of Pitcher Pending Final Hearing Of Suit.

Cleveland, June 17.—The national baseball agreement between the American and National Leagues is in danger of being abrogated as a result of a suit filed in Common Pleas Court today by Manager Connie Mack, of the Philadelphia Americans, asking for an injunction restraining the Boston Nationals from interfering with his playing Pitcher Scott Perry, awarded to the Boston Nationals by a majority vote of the National Commission.

Perry was purchased by Boston from the Atlanta club last year, partial payment being made. After 17 days of "bench duty" Perry left the Boston club. He was not on the Boston reserve list last winter and Manager Mack signed him as a free agent and pitched three full games and part of another this season before the Boston club put in a claim for him, according to Manager Mack.

Recently Chairman August Herrmann, of the National Commission, with President John K. Tener, of the National League, concurring, and President B. B. Johnson, of the American League, dissenting, awarded Perry to the Boston Nationals.

Manager Mack refused to abide by the decision and says he will fight to hold Perry.

Common Pleas Judge Morgan granted the restraining order, allowing the Philadelphia Americans full and uninterrupted use of Perry pending final hearing of the suit.

Boston Will Fight, Says Secretary.

Boston, June 17.—"Connie Mack's unusual procedure in resorting to a court of law to nullify a decision of the National Commission will not deter the Boston National League club one iota in seeking to gain possession of Pitcher Scott Perry," Walter E. Hapgood, business manager of the club, announced today.

"Perry has been declared the property of the Boston club by organized baseball's court of last resort," Hapgood said in a statement, "and every club in each major league is pledged to support and abide by decisions of this nature. It is impossible to believe that a majority of the American League club owners will uphold the position the Philadelphia club has taken in this case. It is a very radical move on the part of the Athletics and is likely to lead to interesting developments."

National Leaguers Silent.

New York, June 17.—In the absence of President John K. Tener, of the National League, other officials of the organization refused to comment upon the action of Manager Mack, of the Philadelphia Americans, in securing an injunction preventing the Boston Nationals from making use of the services of Pitcher Scott Perry. President Tener was reported to be out of the city and the date of his return was unknown to other members of the National League staff.

"Within Right," Says Ban.

Chicago, June 17.—President Ban Johnson of the American League tonight declared that Manager Connie Mack of the Philadelphia Americans was entirely within his rights in going to court to attempt to nullify the award by the National Commission of Perry to the Boston Nationals. Johnson added that "the American League will claim Perry until the final decision."

"The decision of the National Commission in awarding Perry to Boston was, in my opinion, unfair," said President Johnson. "Perry was signed by Philadelphia after he had been declared a free agent. The National League made no effort to get him until after Mack had spent time and money in developing him."

ROBINS' PARK FOR WARE-HOUSE TILL WAR IS OVER.

New York, Aug. 8.—Ebbets Field, home of the Brooklyn National League Baseball Club will be closed for the duration of the war, after the game with Philadelphia next Wednesday, and converted into a storage warehouse. This action was decided upon at a meeting of the board of directors of the club today.

Immediately after the final home game of the curtailed season on August 14, special structures will be erected upon certain portions of the field and these in conjunction with space in and under the grandstands utilized for storage purposes. The former Federal League Baseball Park in Brooklyn, is being used for similar purposes.

The action of the Brooklyn Club directors is taken to indicate that the officers of the organization do not contemplate a continuation of big league baseball in 1919.

RUTH ALWAYS VALUABLE

When Not Busy With Bat He Is Pitching Fine Ball.

TIGERS EAT OUT OF HIS HAND

Red Sox Bunch Two Doubles Behind Two Passes, Winning Game In Opening Inning.

Detroit, Aug. 8.—Although Babe Ruth is not making homers these days, or even getting his usual share of safeties, he is pitching great ball for the Red Sox, proving he always can turn his hand to something to aid his team. He pitched splendid ball today against Detroit and Boston won, 4 to 1.

Two passes followed by two doubles gave the Red Sox three runs in the opening session. Score:

BOSTON.	Ab	R	H	O	A	E		DETROIT.	Ab	R	H	O	A	E
Hooper,rf	4	2	1	2	0	0		Bush,ss	5	0	0	1	2	1
Shean,2b	4	0	3	3	0		R.Jones,3b	4	1	1	0	1	0
Strunk,cf	2	1	1	3	0	0		Cobb,cf	3	0	2	3	0	0
Ruth,p	4	0	1	0	1	0		Veach,lf	3	0	1	2	0	
McInnis,1b	4	1	1	12	0	0		Griggs,1b	3	0	0	10	0	0
Miller,lf	4	0	2	1	0	0		Harper,rf	3	0	2	4	0	1
Scott,ss	4	0	1	6	0		Young,2b	4	0	1	1	4	0
Mayer,c	4	0	1	6	0	0		Spencer,c	4	0	0	5	0	0
Cochran,3b	4	0	1	0	1	0		Boland,p	2	0	0	1	3	0
								Kallio,p	0	0	0	0	1	0
								aKavanagh	1	0	0	0	0	0
								bWalker	0	0	0	0	0	0
Totals	34	4	8	27	13	0		Totals	32	1	7	27	11	2

aBatted for Boland in seventh.
bBatted for Kallio in ninth.

```
Boston....................  3 0 0 0 0 0 1 0 0—4
Detroit...................  0 0 0 0 1 0 0 0 0—1
```

Two-base hits—McInnis, Miller, Mayer, Strunk. Three-base hit—R. Jones. Stolen bases—Cobb, Veach. Sacrifice hit—Shean. Sacrifice fly—Cobb. Double plays—Cochran, Shean and McInnis; Bush, Young and Griggs. Left on bases—Boston, 7; Detroit, 9. Bases on balls—Off Boland, 3; off Ruth, 4. Hits—Off Boland, 7 in 7 innings; off Kallio, 1 in 2 innings. Struck out—By Boland, 4; by Ruth, 3. Wild pitch—Ruth. Losing pitcher—Boland.

CONTINUATION OF BASE BALL IS UP TO LEAGUE DIRECTORS

Magnates of American and National Circuits to Meet Within Few Days to Decide Whether Game Shall Go On.

BY DENMAN THOMPSON.

Base ball received a knockout wallop yesterday when Secretary Baker ruled it to be a non-essential occupation and decided the players in the draft age must obtain employment calculated to aid in the successful prosecution of the war or shoulder guns and fight. But although shaken from stem to stern and hanging on the ropes the sport has not yet taken the count and it is possible the magnates may take some action to continue the game even if it is but a shadow of its former self.

President Johnson of the American League, who estimates that between 85 and 90 per cent of the players in his circuit will be affected by the order, has issued a statement in which he says that whether his organization will continue, with players above and below the draft age, will be left to the administration. President Tener of the National League already has called a special meeting of the directors of his circuit to be held in New York next Tuesday, when the order of Secretary Baker will be fully discussed and a decision reached as to what course the league shall pursue.

President Minor of the Washington club had no comment to make on Secretary Baker's decision, and Manager Griffith, in discussing the order, confined himself to saying: "If it is the desire of the President that there be no more base ball I will gladly abide by his wishes."

The sport did not die overnight. It is badly stunned, but still alive, as visitors to American League Park this afternoon will discover when they see the Nationals and White Sox clash in the second game of their series. Furthermore, it is assured the contests set for Sunday and Monday also will be played, but beyond that developments must be awaited.

Some of the owners undoubtedly feel that it is the patriotic duty of every base ball owner to close his park until the war ends, but all leaders of the sport will not hold this view. For instance, John Heydler, secretary of the National League, and one of the most prominent men connected with the game, thinks the game should and will go on.

"Despite the fact that most of our players will be affected by Secretary Baker's construction of the work or fight order, it is my impression that the major leagues will make every effort to complete the season," says Heydler. "The clubs will try to recruit their teams from men who are above the draft age.

"We believe the base ball public, understanding the predicament in which the sport is placed, and retaining its fondness for this great outdoor recreation, will be willing to patronize the new clubs which we will endeavor to put in the field."

Wants World Series in August.

President Harry H. Frazee of the Boston club, which has obtained a big lead in the American League race, says he will not consider the possibility of continuing the season with the array of inferior players it would be necessary to call upon to fill up the rosters of the various clubs. Of his team only Shean, Wagner, Whiteman and Truesdale would be left.

Frazee has embodied in a telegram to the national commission a suggestion to end the major league base ball season at the completion of 100 games of the schedule, which calls for 154 contests, with a world championship series between the winning clubs in the American and National Leagues early next month. The Red Sox have played eighty-six of their scheduled games. Under Frazee's plan the season would end with two-thirds of the schedule completed. Regardless of Frazee's views he will have to abide by the majority opinion of the league directors. He will have no choice but to complete the full schedule should the league as a body decide to do this.

Will Let President Decide Whether Parks Shall Close

CHICAGO, July 20.—President B. B. Johnson of the American League expected to issue a call today for a special meeting of the organization for the purpose of taking action on Secretary Baker's ruling that base ball players within the draft age must seek other employment. Mr. Johnson said he believed the club owners of the league may ask President Wilson to decide whether they shall close their ball parks for the duration of the war or continue with men outside the draft age. In any event, he said it was the desire of the American League to be wholly responsive to the wishes of President Wilson, and the ultimate decision whether the American public needs base ball as a recreation probably will be left to the President.

"Secretary Baker's ruling means the loss of 80 or 90 per cent of our players," said President Johnson. "I do not know if the game could be continued with men outside the draft age, and surely we do not want to continue it if that is not the will of the administration."

Reprinted from
The Washington Evening Star

PLAYERS MUST WORK OR FIGHT

Secretary Of War Makes Ruling On Baseball In Ainsmith Case.

TO SERVE AS GUIDE FOR DRAFT BOARDS

Baker Says Times Are Not Normal And All Must Make Sacrifices.

PLANS GAMES FOR PARIS

Evers Says McGraw Is Ready To Take Team Of Major Leaguers To France.

New York, July 19.—John J. McGraw, manager of the New York Giants, has promised to take a team of big league players to Paris for a series of games with former professional players now in the army and navy, according to an announcement here today by Johnny Evers, former Chicago Cub manager, now of the Knights of Columbus athletic department, overseas.

"American soldiers are scheduled to witness some 'big timber' games in France," said Evers. "McGraw assured me it would not cost the Knights of Columbus a cent. I have in mind some of the players now fighting the Huns, who will play McGraw's bunch. The nucleus of my team is Alexander, pitcher; Gowdy, catcher; Miller, of Cleveland and Philadelphia, first base, and Evans, of Cleveland, third base. The others I shall select as soon as I arrive in France."

Evers said he had packed in his trunk for his trip to Paris his old Cub uniform, including gloves and shoes.

KNABE AMONG FOUR LEFT.

Chicago, July 19.—All but four of the Chicago National League players would be affected by Secretary Baker's ruling that baseball is a nonessential occupation it became know today. The four are Manager Fred Mitchell, Coach Otto Knabe, Dode Paskert and Rollie Zeider, the latter two being active players. Several of the Cubs are in Class 1 of the draft.

GRIFF READY TO PROCEED.

Washington, July 19.—Clark Griffith, manager of the Washington team, said tonight he had no complaint to make and was ready to abandon baseball for the war or undertake to carry the game on with men above or below the draft age, as the league might determine. He expects President Johnson to call a meeting of the league directors at once to decide what shall be done.

SEVEN MEN FOR TWO CLUBS.

St. Louis, July 19.—The St. Louis Americans have three players—Lowdermilk, Leifield and Demmitt—and the St. Louis Nationals have four—Ames, Wallace, Heathcote and Gonzales—who will not be affected by Secretary Baker's ruling that professional baseball is a non-essential occupation, and that players of draft age must work or fight.

FIVE WHITE SOX ESCAPE.

Chicago, July 19.—Five members of the Chicago Americans, world's champions, will not be affected by Secretary of War Baker's ruling, if it holds to mean only those players who are in the draft age. The players who are not in the draft are Pitchers Shellenback, Cicotte and Benz, Outfielder John Collins and Manager Rowland.

Reprinted from
The Baltimore Sun papers

CARL MAYS TWICE PITCHES TO VICTORY

Mackmen So Easy in First Game Boston Hurler Continues on Mound

Misplays Give Perry Bad Start and Athletics Are Defeated in Afterpiece 4-1

Special to The Inquirer.

BOSTON, Aug. 30.—Connie Mack's Athletics proved no obstacle in the path of the Red Sox in a double-header this afternoon before one of the largest crowds of the season at Fenway Park, but although they trounced the Macks; 12-0 in one game and 4-1 in the other, the Sox are still outside the championship because of Cleveland's ability to take both ends of a bargain set with Detroit.

The Bostons behind Carl Mays in both games broke loose with some fine hitting, rolling up an 8 to 0 lead against Johnson and Jamieson and later, mainly because of an inexcusable error by Dykes at second base, got a three-run edge on Scott Perry, who was going along in fine style and who would have been a hard man for the leaders to beat had he had good support.

Reprinted from
The Baltimore Sun papers

WOUNDED SOLDIERS SEE RED SOX WIN.

Boston, Sept. 9. Forty wounded American soldiers, who came back from France last Saturday, enjoyed today's world's series game from grandstand seats. The soldiers stormed hospital physicians for permission to see the game and the Boston chapter of the Red Cross furnished automobiles to transport them to the field.

Reprinted from
The Baltimore Sun papers

RUTH SETS PITCHING RECORD— 29 2/3 W. S. SHUTOUT INNINGS

SCORE OF FOURTH GAME OF THE WORLD'S SERIES.

Boston.

	AB.	R.	H.	O.	A.	E.
Hooper, rf	3	0	0	1	0	0
Shean, 2b	3	0	1	4	4	0
Strunk, cf	4	0	0	0	0	0
Whiteman, lf	3	1	0	1	0	0
Bush, p	0	0	0	0	0	0
McInnis, 1b	3	1	1	16	1	0
Ruth, p, lf	2	0	1	0	4	0
Scott, ss	3	0	0	3	8	0
Thomas, 3b	3	0	0	2	3	0
Agnew, c	2	0	0	0	1	0
Schang, c	1	1	1	0	0	0
	27	3	4	27	21	0

Chicago.

	AB.	R.	H.	O.	A.	E.
Flack, rf	4	0	1	3	0	0
Hollocher, ss	4	0	0	2	0	0
Mann, lf	4	0	1	2	0	0
Paskert, cf	4	0	0	3	0	0
Merkle, 1b	3	0	1	9	1	0
Pick, 2b	2	0	2	0	2	0
Zeider, 3b	0	0	0	1	2	0
Deal, 3b	2	0	1	1	3	0
Wortman, 2b	1	0	0	1	0	0
Killefer, c	2	1	0	1	0	0
Tyler, p	0	0	0	1	4	0
Douglas, p	0	0	0	0	0	1
a O'Farrell	1	0	0	0	0	0
b Hendrix	1	0	1	0	0	0
c McCabe	0	1	0	0	0	0
d Barber	1	0	0	0	0	0
	29	2	7	24	12	1

a Batted for Deal in seventh.
b Batted for Tyler in eighth.
c Ran for Hendrix in eighth.
d Batted for Killefer in ninth.

Boston ...0 0 0 2 0 0 0 1 x—3
Chicago ..0 0 0 0 0 0 2 0—2

Two-base hit—Shean. Three-base hit—Ruth. Stolen base—Shean. Sacrifice hits—Ruth, Hooper. Double plays—Ruth, Scott, and McInnis: Scott, Shean and McInnis (2). Left on bases—Boston 4, Chicago 6. Base on error—Boston 1. Base on balls—off Tyler, 2; Ruth, 6. Hits—off Tyler, 3 in 7 innings; off Douglas, - in 1 inning; off Ruth, 7 in 8 innings: off Bush, none in 1 inning. Struck out by Tyler, 1. Wild pitch, Ruth, 1. Passed balls—Killefer, (2). Winning pitcher Ruth, losing pitcher Douglas.

RUTH'S BIG BAT DEFEATS CUBS

Baltimore Boy Hits For Three Sacks With Two Pals On Base.

RED SOX NOW LOOK LIKE REAL WINNERS

More Than 20,000 Fans See World's Series Contest In Boston.

Reprinted from
The Baltimore Sun papers

GIANTS

Pass On To New Owners

New York Broker and McGraw Are Chief Stockholders.

"Little Nap" Is Vice President and Manager of Club.

Hempstead Retains a Portion of His Holdings—History of Team Which Made Baseball History.

SPECIAL DISPATCH TO THE ENQUIRER.

New York, January 14.—The New York National League Baseball Club passed from the control of Harry Hempstead and N. Ashley Lloyd, of Norwood, Ohio, to-day to Charles A. Stoneham, John J. McGraw and Judge Francis X. McQuade. Hempstead and Lloyd as co-executors under the will of John T. Brush had guided that club since the death of the former owner a few years ago.

Harry Hempstead, the former President, declared that he still retained a portion of his stock, but that the men named above had the controlling interest.

Reprinted from
The Cincinnati Enquirer

YANKEES GET MAYS

In Exchange For Several Players When Deal Is Made With Boston.

New York, July 30.—At a conference here to-day attended by Harry Frazee, President of the Boston Americans, and Jacob Ruppert and T. L. Huston, owners of the New-Americans, the local ers of the New York Americans, the local Boston in exchange for Pitchers Hobert McGraw and Allan Russell, a third player to be selected later and a cash sum said to be about $25,000. The New York club was obliged to bid against the Chicago Americans, which submitted a straight cash proposition.

William Gleason, manager of the Chicago American baseball club, announced here to-day that he had signed the veteran pitcher Patrick Ragan, who yesterday was released by the New York Nationals.

Mays left the club July 13, when it was in Chicago on its recent Western tour. He is expected to report to New York to-morrow. He joined the Boston club in 1914 and until this season was one of the club's most reliable pitchers.

Reprinted from
The Cincinnati Enquirer

QUAKERS

Beaten Twice By Giants

Double Victory Puts Back in First Place—Second Game Goes Ten Innings.

Philadelphia, July 7.—New York had to go 10 innings to win its fifth straight victory over Philadelphia to-day, 7 to 2, after winning the first game of a double header, 10 to 5, and going back into first place. In the second game Hogg held the Giants to five hits until the tenth, when he struck out Burns, passed Young and then yielded five hits and a sacrifice fly, the entire visiting team going to bat. The first game was a runaway slugging match. Of the 12 stolen bases eight of them came in the ninth inning to Philadelphia's credit, the Giants making no effort to stop them. Scores:

First Game.

NEW YORK.	AB.	H.	PO.	A.	PHILADELPHIA.	AB.	H.	PO.	A.
Burns,lf	6	1	0	0	Callahan,rf	5	2	3	0
Young,rf	5	1	1	0	Pearce,2b	4	0	4	3
Fletcher,ss	4	1	1	3	Baird,3b	3	1	0	5
A.Baird,ss	1	0	0	2	Cavana'h,3b	1	0	0	0
Doyle,2b	4	2	2	4	Meusel,cf	4	0	2	0
Kauff,cf	4	2	2	0	Luderus,1b	3	2	11	1
Zimme'n,3b	5	3	1	0	Whitted,lf	4	0	2	0
Chase,1b	5	3	14	0	Bancroft,ss	2	0	1	4
Gonzales,c	5	2	6	0	Sicking,ss	2	1	0	1
Barnes,p	4	1	0	0	Cady,c	4	1	4	0
*King	1	0	0	0	Packard,p	0	0	0	0
Perritt,p	0	0	0	1	Woodwa'd,p	4	0	0	1
					†Murray,p	2	0	0	1
Totals	44	16	27	10	†Cravath	1	1	0	0
					Totals	36	8	27	16

*Batted for Barnes in ninth. †Batted for Murray in ninth.

Innings	1	2	3	4	5	6	7	8	9	
New York	0	2	3	0	2	2	0	0	1	—10
Philadelphia	0	1	0	0	0	1	0	3	—	5

Errors—Zimmerman, Chase, Pearce 2. Bancroft. Two-Base Hits—Gonzales, Callahan. Stolen Bases—Fletcher, Gonzales, Young, Burns, Luderus 2, Sicking 2, Cady 2, Cravath 2. Double Plays—Doyle and Chase, Bancroft and Luderus. Left on Bases—New York, 11; Philadelphia, 5. Bases on Balls—Off Perritt, 1; off Woodward, 1; off Murray, 2. Hits—Off Barnes, 5 in 8 innings; off Perritt, 3 in 1 inning; off Packard, 5 in 2 1-3 innings; off Woodward, 5 in 3 2-3 innings; off Murray, 6 in 4 innings. Hit by Pitcher By Packard (Fletcher). Struck Out—By Barnes, 5; by Murray, 3. Winning Pitcher—Barnes. Losing Pitcher—Packard.

Reprinted from
The Cincinnati Enquirer

RECORD FOR BREVITY

Is Established in First Game Between Giants and Phillies.

New York, September 28.—A season record for brevity was set in the first game of to-day's double-header between New York and Philadelphia, when in 51 minutes the Giants scored a victory, 6 to 1. New York won the second contest also, 7 to 1. In the first game Barnes won his twenty-fifth victory, the only National League pitcher to touch that mark.

The nearest approach to to-day's record was the time of 55 minutes, made by Cincinnati and Brooklyn a week ago. A few years ago the Giants played an exhibition game with Philadelphia in 32 minutes, while preparing for the world's series with Boston.

First Game.

PHILADELPHIA.	AB.	H.	PO.	A.	NEW YORK.	AB.	H.	PO.	A.
Lebour'u,lf	4	0	2	2	Burns,lf	2	1	1	0
Black'ne,3b	4	1	2	2	Young,rf	3	1	0	0
Williams,cf	4	0	4	0	Kauff,cf	4	1	1	0
Meusel,rf	4	0	0	0	Doyle,2b	4	2	3	8
Luderus,1b	4	2	10	1	Fletcher,ss	4	2	3	7
Bancroft,ss	3	1	1	4	Frisch,3b	4	1	2	3
Paulette,2b	3	0	2	3	Kelly,1b	4	3	16	0
Adams,c	3	0	2	1	Smith,c	3	1	1	0
Meadows,p	3	1	1	2	J.Barnes,p	4	1	0	1
Totals	33	5	24	15	Totals	32	13	27	19

Innings	1	2	3	4	5	6	7	8	9	
Philadelphia	1	0	0	0	0	0	0	0	0	— 1
New York	0	1	3	0	0	2	0	0	x	— 6

Error—Fletcher. Two-Base Hits—Blackburne, Burns, Young, Fletcher, Kelly, J. Barnes. Stolen Base—Burns. Sacrifice Hit—J. Barnes. Sacrifice Fly—Burns. Double Plays—Bancroft and Blackburne; Bancroft, Luderus and Paulette. Left on Bases—Philadelphia, 6; New York, 7. Bases on Balls—Off Meadows, 3. Struck Out—By J. Barnes, 2; by Meadows, 1.

Reprinted from
The Cincinnati Enquirer

Cincinnati Clinches Pennant

BUNTING

Copped By the Reds.

Moran's Men Grab Flag By Defeating Giants.

Cannot Lose Now, No Matter What Happens.

Exciting Game Winds Up the Crucial Struggle.

Ruether Is Hit Hard, But Receives Perfect Support — Fred Toney Is Driven From Mound.

WHITE SOX CLINCH FLAG

Joe Jackson's Single In Ninth Decides Uphill Battle.

CICOTTE UNABLE TO FINISH

Veteran Hurler Is Unsteady And Yields To Kerr, Who Starts The Winning Rally.

Chicago, Sept. 24.—Chicago won the American League pennant today by defeating St. Louis, 6 to 5. Joe Jackson's single in the ninth inning was the blow which made Chicago the club which will meet Cincinnati, winner of the National League pennant, on October 1 for the championship of the world.

Chicago played an uphill game, and it rested with little Dick Kerr to pull the local club through. Kerr started the ninth inning rally with a single to left; Liebold followed with a single in the same direction and McMullin walked, filling the bases. Weaver flied to Jacobson and Kerr scored after the catch, tying the score. Jackson then delivered his hit to right-center and sent Liebold home with a run which gave Chicago the championship of the American League.

RUTH BOOSTS TOTAL TO 28

New York, Sept. 24.—The Boston Red Sox shut out the Yankees, 4 to 0, in the first game of a double-header here today, and then lost a 13-inning battle by 2 to 1. The winning run was scored on a three-bagger by Pipp and a sacrifice fly by Pratt.

Ruth broke the home-run record of 27 by Ed. Williamson in 1884 by driving the ball over the roof of the right-field grandstand in the ninth inning of the second game. This tied the score and resulted in a 13-inning game.

ROBINS JUMP ON PHILS

Come From Behind In First Game, But Land Second Easily.

ENDURANCE RECORD IS BROKEN

Luderus Is Honored By Club And League Presidents For Consecutive Playing Feat.

Philadelphia, Sept. 24. — Brooklyn came from behind in the closing innings and won the first game of today's double-header, 4 to 1. The second was easy for the visitors, 14 to 7. It was "Luderus Day," and between games the local first baseman was presented with a diamond stickpin by John A. Heydler, president of the National League, and with a gold watch by William F. Baker, president of the local club.

The second game was the five hundred and twenty-fifth successive contest Luderus has played. The presents were given to commemorate his breaking of the major league endurance record.

CICOTTE CRABS OWN ACT

Veteran Too Anxious, And Makes Boots That Give Reds Game.

GANDIL FAILS IN A PINCH

Ring's Wildness Keeps Him In Hot Water, But Brilliant Fielding Saves The Day.

By C. Starr Matthews.

Chicago, Oct. 4.—When Eddie Cicotte, old as he is in baseball, learns that there are eight other men on the field he may be able to beat the Cincinnati Reds. His meddling today brought about his second defeat, while his desire to put so much stuff on the ball as to be invincible lost the first game of the world's series for the White Sox.

Having learned that he must depend somewhat upon his fielders, Cicotte twirled well enough today to win any ball game, for in eight of the nine innings only three men faced him. But, it was first a wild throw, after he had interfered with a bouncer that Risberg would have handled with ease, and then it was his unsafe manner of intercepting a throw from the outfield that finally crabbed the game and gave the Reds two runs in the fifth inning, all that the Patmorans needed to win with such pitching as Jimmy Ring served up.

Sharing the unfortunate position in the limelight with Cicotte was Chick Gandil. Once again the first baseman failed miserably when only a decent fly ball was needed. Upon three occasions in this series Gandil has had the opportunity to give the Sox a lift and a run, but was unable to get the ball out of the infield. Twice he has come through with punches which resulted in runs.

Cicotte Better Than Ring.

While the Reds outhit the Sox, Cicotte looked much the stronger pitcher at all times, for Ring was wild. He not only passed two batters, one purposely, but hit two others and yielded three hits. He was constantly in hot water on the batters, but always managed to worm his way out or was saved by the brilliant fielding of his teammates. On the other hand, Cicotte never was in bad on the pitching end of his work. He was steady throughout, and instead of straining, as he did in the opening contest of the diamond classic, he was as cool, collected and as much at home as Dick Kerr was yesterday.

But, when everything is said, the Reds played better baseball, brainy baseball. They played as a team, a well-oiled machine, while the Sox played as stars. The tide has turned against the Sox and it probably now will run with the Reds, for it will be hard for Kid Gleason's men to win four games before the Pat Morans can annex two. It will be extremely difficult, inasmuch as the teams will roam back to Cincinnati after tomorrow's contest and the Rhinelanders will have the edge.

Where Sox Look Weak.

If the Sox lose Kid Gleason may blame it upon two things. First, there is too much individualism, not enough team work on his club. It is a collection of clever ballplayers, and it is being beaten by a team of plain ballplayers. Then, it must be admitted that the White Sox have shown no particular brilliancy on the offensive. The Reds have outplayed them there, taking advantages of every break, and have mixed up their attack.

For the most part the Sox have played the Grand Army game, which does not seem at all like Kid Gleason. The style of play strikes one as coming from the Connie Mack school. Surely it is not the old Oriole style. No risks have been taken, nothing has been changed to meet a situation when desperate methods might bring results. Nothing new has been tried and the squeeze play, with Ray Schalk at bat, is the only scientific or unexpected effort that has been uncovered.

The widely-heralded brains of the White Sox have been kept under cover, except upon a couple of rare occasions. Moreover, Liebold, who has been leading off against the righthanded pitchers, has reached first just once in nine attempts and Eddie Collins has been checked. Weaver has done fairly well with the willow and Jackson always has been in the limelight, but it can be seen that the Red pitchers have had the Indian sign on most of the men who constitute the punch of the Chicago crew.

SCORE OF FOURTH WORLD'S SERIES GAME

CINCINNATI (NATIONALS.)	AB.	R.	H.	O.	A.	E.	CHICAGO (AMERICANS.)	AB.	R.	H.	O.	A.	E.
Rath,2b	4	0	1	5	1	1	Liebold,rf	5	0	0	0	0	0
Daubert,1b	4	0	0	9	1	0	E. Collins,2b	3	0	0	3	5	0
Groh,3b	4	0	2	3	1	Weaver,3b	4	0	0	0	3	0
Roush,cf	3	0	0	2	0	0	Jackson,lf	4	0	1	3	0	0
Duncan,lf	3	1	0	1	0	0	Felsch,cf	3	0	1	0	0	0
Kopf,ss	3	1	1	1	1	0	Gandil,1b	4	0	1	14	0	0
Neale,rf	3	0	1	4	0	0	Risberg,ss	3	0	0	3	4	0
Wingo,c	3	0	2	2	0	0	Schalk,c	1	0	0	4	3	0
Ring,p	3	0	0	1	2	0	Cicotte,p	3	0	0	2	2	
							*Murphy	1	0	0	0	0	0
	30	2	5	27	6	2		31	0	3	27	17	2

*Batted for Cicotte in ninth inning.

Cincinnati Nationals	0 0 0 0 2 0 0 0 0—2
Chicago Americans	0 0 0 0 0 0 0 0 0—0

Two-base Hits—Jackson, Neale. Stolen Base—Risberg. Sacrifice Hit—Felsch. Double Plays—E. Collins to Risberg to Gandil; Cicotte to Risberg to Gandil. Left on Bases—Cincinnati Nationals, 1; Chicago Americans, 10. Bases on Balls—Off Ring, 3 (Risberg, Schalk, 2). Hit by Pitcher—By Ring, 2 (E. Collins, Schalk). Struck Out—By Cicotte, 2 (Kopf, Ring); by Ring, 2 (Jackson, Gandil). Umpires—Nallin, behind plate; Quigley, at third; Evans, at second; Rigler, at first. Time, 1.37.

BETWEEN $125,000 AND $150,000 PAID FOR BOSTON STAR

Frazee Gives Reasons for Sale—Johnson Not Consulted, Ruppert Says.

NEW YORK, January 6.—George Herman (Babe) Ruth, who established a major league record for home runs last season with twenty-nine to his credit, yesterday was purchased by the New York Yankees from the Boston Red Sox for a price in excess of $100,000.

Needless to say, this is the highest price ever paid for a base ball player in the history of the sport.

When the Yankees bought Carl Mays last summer for a cash consideration and two players it was estimated that the pitcher, who has been the subject of so much litigation since, cost the New York club more than $50,000.

"Big" Marquard Deal Recalled.

Followers of the national pastime recalled that it was not so many years ago the base ball world was staggered at the news that the New York Giants had purchased Rube Marquard for $11,000. Since then the sale of diamond stars has mounted even faster than the high cost of living. Until the sale of Ruth yesterday the record price was $50,000 and two players, paid by Cleveland for Tris Speaker, and $50,000 by the Chicago Americans for Eddie Collins.

The most popular indoor sport in New York today was guessing how much the Yankees paid for Ruth, the home-run monarch. The nearest approach to anything of an official nature was the smiling admission of Col. Jacob Ruppert, the Yankees' president, that he understood an offer of $100,000 for Ruth was refused last summer by Harry Frazee of the Boston club. Sporting writers estimate the price paid from $425,000 to $150,000.

Col. Ruppert's Comment.

In talking of the purchase Col. Ruppert said:

"This is our answer to those who would like to drive us out of base ball. We entered into negotiations for the famous player in pursuance of a definite policy to give the club's loyal following in New York an aggressive, strong, well balanced team, which will be in all respects worthy of the league's greatest city and one which New York fans can be proud of."

Col. Ruppert also said that the sale of Ruth did not indicate that Frazee had any intentions of selling the club and retiring from base ball. On the contrary, he plans to use the money to strengthen his club further. When questioned as to what Ban Johnson would think of the deal, Col. Ruppert said:

Not Afraid of Johnson.

"We are no longer afraid of Johnson or care what he thinks. Ruth will be with the Yankees when the season opens. That fact is settled.

"We have taken over Ruth's contract from Boston, which has two more seasons to run, at $10,000 a year, but, in all probability, we will make a new contract which will satisfy the player in every particular.

"As a matter of fact, Miller Huggins, manager of our team, is now in Los Angeles, Cal., with authority to sign Ruth to a contract just as soon as he hears from us that the deal is completed. We have now advised him by wire."

LOSS OF INDIANS' STAR MAY COST TEAM FLAG

Shortstop Fails to Survive Operation Following Blow on Head by Carl Mays in Game With Yankees.

NEW YORK, August 17—Raymond Chapman, shortstop on the Cleveland American base ball team, who was hit on the head by a ball thrown by Pitcher Carl Mays in yesterday's game with the New York Americans, died in the St. Lawrence Hospital at 4:50 o'clock this morning. He never regained consciousness after an operation, which was hurriedly decided on shortly after midnight, when a portion of his fractured skull was removed by surgeons, who hoped against hope that he might recover.

Shortly before it was decided to operate Manager Tris Speaker, already deeply apprehensive of his condition, telephoned news of the accident to Chapman's wife in Cleveland, who immediately started for New York.

News of his death cast gloom over the members of both teams, and the base ball world in general. Carl Mays was overcome with grief when the news was told to him.

As a result of Chapman's death, today's game between Cleveland and New York has been postponed.

The accident occurred at the outset of the fifth inning. Chapman was the first batter up and was hit by the first ball pitched. So terrific was the blow that the report of the impact caused spectators to think the ball had struck his bat. Mays, who pitched the ball, acting under this impression, fielded the ball, that rebounded half way to the pitchers' box, and threw it to first base, in order to retire Chapman.

Collapses at Plate.

Then it was noticed that Chapman had collapsed at the home plate. He was lifted to his feet by other players, then he stood dazed for a moment, staggered and crumpled up at their feet. Physicians were immediately called from the grandstand and they administered first aid, still not knowing that he had suffered a fractured skull. Two players, with Chapman's arms about their shoulders, started to walk him off the field. He appeared to walk at first almost unaided, but a few moments later his legs became limp and he had to be carried bodily to an ambulance.

VERDICT IN FAVOR OF CHICAGO CLUB

Lee Magee Loses Suit and Will Appeal

CINCINNATI, June 9—The jury in the trial of Lee Magee, Cincinnati baseball player, in his suit against the Chicago National league club for $9500, returned a verdict for the defendant in the United States district court here late today. The jury deliberated about an hour before it reached a decision. Robert Alcorn, attorney for Magee, announced after the verdict had been rendered that the case would be appealed.

Magee, who formerly played with the Cincinnati, Brooklyn, Chicago Nationals and other major league clubs, charged that he was released by the Chicago Nationals without just cause last February, thereby being deprived of earning a living as a professional baseball player.

He admitted on the witness stand that he had made a bet on the first game of a double-header played in Boston on July 25, 1918, and was under the impression that the bet was placed on the Cincinnati team, on which club he was then playing. He testified that the bet was made by Hal Chase, the Cincinnati first baseman, and that he was not aware that it was made against his team until Chase, after the game, informed him that the bet had been lost.

Jimmy Costello, a Boston pool-room proprietor, testified that Magee proposed to him to "toss" the game, and President Heydler of the National league and President William Veeck of the Chicago Nationals, testified that Magee had made a "midnight confession" to them in which he said he desired to make a clean breast of the entire matter.

26-INNING GAME ENDS IN TIE, 1-1

Braves and Brooklyn Struggle Nearly Four Hours to No Decision—Game Finally Called by Darkness—Set New Record for Organized Baseball—Great Pitcher's Duel

Oeschger and Cadore Both Go the Entire Distance in Spectacular Fashion

No Run Scored in the Last 20 Innings—Both Pitchers Have Great Support

From 3 o'clock until nearly 7 in the evening, and until the fast gathering gloom made further play impossible, George Stallings' men, with big Joe Oeschger pitching the grandest battle of his career, held in check the powerful sluggers from the City of Churches and it was not until the end of the 26th inning, when the lights were appearing in the windows across the Charles, that Umpire McCormick called the game with both sides boasting a single run.

Plate Kept Clean

For more than 20 innings Oeschger kept his opponents from crossing the rubber and Cadore had held the plate unsmirched for the last 20 rounds of the contest. It was a pitchers' duel pure and simple, with members of the rival teams expecting that at any time one of the great pair would crack under the strain. Oeschger, with a team that wobbled slightly at the start, was master on all occasions after the fifth, the single inning where he allowed his opponents to hang up a tally. This big run, due to no fault of his support, but directly attributable to his own slipup in fielding, only served to strengthen the forces behind him. From this time onward the fielding of the Braves was something to marvel at.

Cadore, on the other hand, was hit freely in the one inning where the Braves got their solitary man across the plate, and he can thank Providence for his narrow escape in the sixth. Here the locals secured only one run from a triple, a single and a double and it was the magnificent support accorded him by his outfield that made it possible for him to enter upon such a long overtime battle.

Back Up Pitchers

As the game went beyond the allotted session both teams rallied strongly to their pitcher's support and the work of the fielders was inspiring. Only the stone wall defence of the Boston infield and a wonderful play by Hank Gowdy saved the situation in the 18th. This was the only round after the fifth where Oeschger was in any danger of being scored upon.

The Braves cast away countless opportunities through the weakness of certain of their batters in the pinches. Pick had chances galore to send the winning run across, but he was all at sea when it came to delivering the punch against Cadore. Time and again a clean drive by Boeckel, Holke or Maranville would seem to afford a promising opening, yet the usually reliable sticker always fell down.

BOX SCORE OF THE RECORD-BREAKING GAME

BOSTON.	AB.	R.	BH.	TB.	PO.	A.	E.
Powell, c f	7	0	1	1	6	0	0
Pick, 2b	11	0	0	0	7	8	2
Mann, l f	10	0	2	2	6	1	0
Cruise, r f	9	0	1	3	4	0	0
Holke, 1b	10	0	2	2	43	1	0
Boeckel, 3b	11	0	3	3	1	7	0
Maranville, ss	10	0	3	4	1	9	0
O'Neill, c	2	0	0	0	4	3	0
Gowdy, c	6	0	1	1	6	1	0
Oeschger, p	9	0	1	2	0	11	0
*Christenbury	1	0	1	1	0	0	0
Totals	86	1	15	19	78	41	2
BROOKLYN.	AB.	R.	BH.	TB.	PO.	A.	E.
Olson, 2b	10	0	1	1	5	9	1
Neis, r f	10	0	1	1	9	0	0
Johnston, 3b	10	0	2	2	3	1	0
Wheat, l f	9	0	2	2	3	0	0
Myers, c f	2	0	1	1	2	0	0
Hood, c f	6	0	1	1	8	0	0
Konetchy, 1b	9	0	2	1	32	1	0
Ward, ss	10	0	0	0	4	3	1
Krueger, c	2	1	0	0	4	3	0
Elliott, c	7	0	0	0	7	3	0
Cadore, p	10	0	0	0	1	12	0
Totals	85	1	9	9	78	33	2

*Hit for O'Neill in ninth.

Boston ..0 0 0 0 0 1 0 0 0 0 0 0 0 0 0 0 0 0 0 0 0 0 0 0 0 0—1
Brooklyn 0 0 0 0 0 1 0 0 0 0 0 0 0 0 0 0 0 0 0 0 0 0 0 0 0 0—1

Two-base hits—Oeschger, Maranville. Three-base hit—Cruise. Sacrifice hits—Powell, O'Neill, Cruise, Oeschger, Holke. Stolen bases—Myers, Hood. Bases on balls—Off Oeschger 4, off Cadore 5. Struck out—By Oeschger 7, by Cadore 7. Double plays—Olson to Konetchy, Oeschger to Gowdy to Holke to Gowdy. Wild pitch—Oeschger. Time—3h. 50m. Umpires—McCormick and Hart.

RUTH MAKES ONE MORE HOME RUN

Runs Total to 54; Yanks Twice Beat Athletics

PHILADELPHIA, Sept. 29—Six home runs featured New York's double victory over Philadelphia today, 7 to 3 and 9 to 4. The second game went 11 innings. Hasty weakening after shutting out New York for nine innings. He relieved Naylor after Lewis's home run into the left field bleachers came with two on bases in the first inning. C. Walker had one home run in each game. Ruth's 54th homer of the season came in the ninth inning of the first game with Ward on base. It was a drive over the right field wall.

Reprinted from the **Boston Herald Traveler,** courtesy the **Boston Herald American**

Dec. 15

They're For Spitball Pitchers.

The league voted to recommend to the new advisory council created under the new agreement that spitball pitchers now playing in the league be permitted to use that delivery until the end of their careers in the league. This action was taken as a result of a communication from Pitcher Bill Doak, of the St. Louis Club, and affects besides himself his teammate, Goodwin; Fillingim and Rudolph, of Boston; Douglas, of New York; Grimes and Mitchell, of Brooklyn; Fisher, of Cincinnati, and Hendrix, of Chicago. Doak in his communication declared that if the spitball was barred it would deprive those pitchers of their earning power as players.

Reprinted from **The Baltimore Sun papers**

Smith Makes Home Run With Bases Full And Wambsganss An Unassisted Triple Play

Cleveland, Oct. 10.—In a baseball game erupting sensational, unique and thrilling plays far beyond the wildest dreams of imaginative fiction or scenario writer, the Cleveland Americans defeated the Brooklyn Nationals, 8 to 1, in the fifth contest of the world's series here this afternoon.

An unassisted triple play by William Wambsganss, a native son of Cleveland, and home runs by Elmer Smith and Jim Bagby were a trio of individual feats which formed flashlight photographs on the brains of the fans which no future diamond battle can erase.

The victory broke the tie existing between the pennant winners of the two major leagues, and tonight Cleveland is confident that the first American League pennant ever won by this city will be overshadowed by the great glory of the world's series banner to be flung to the breeze next spring.

Today the stage setting was much the same. Both Kilduff and Miller had singled to center in turn at the beginning of the fifth inning and were perched on second and first, respectively, when Pitcher Mitchell came to bat.

The Brooklyn hurler, who had previously relieved Grimes in the box, drove a hot liner high and to the left of second base. Wambsganss leaped into the air and came down with the ball clutched in the gloved hand. For the fraction of a second he appeared to hesitate, and it looked as though the play would take the usual course of a force out.

GRASPS GOLDEN CHANCE.

Then Wamby realized the golden fielding opportunity that confronted him, and before the startled spectators could grasp the play he had sprinted to second and, stepping on the canvas bag, eliminated Kilduff, who was well on his way to third. Miller was tearing down to the midway sack, under the belief that the hit was an absolutely safe one, and it was a comparatively easy matter for Wambsganss to run up the base line and, touching the oncoming runner, complete the first triple ever made by one player in the long history of the world's series.

Cleveland's offensive opened with another play which would have, under any other circumstances, stood out as a feature supreme. With the bases loaded with Indians who had singled in succession off the slants of Burleigh Grimes, right fielder Elmer Smith, of Milan, Ohio, stepped to the plate and, catching one of the Brooklyn twirler's fast, sharp-breaking spitballs on the very end of his bat, lifted the sphere up and over the towering screen which tops the right field fence, clearing the bases and breaking the hearts of the opposing players with a four-run lead, which the Robins never even threatened to overcome.

HITS HOUSE ACROSS STREET.

The ball was so hard hit that it not only cleared the screen, but continued on its way until it crashed into the front of a house across the street from the ball park, the roof of which was crowded with spectators.

Score Of Fifth World's Series Game

CLEVELAND.	Ab.	R.	H.	O.	A.	E.
Jamieson, lf..	4	1	2	2	1	0
Graney, lf....	1	0	0	0	0	0
Wamb'g'ss, 2b	5	1	1	7	2	0
Speaker, cf...	3	2	1	1	0	0
E. Smith, rf..	4	1	3	0	0	0
Gardner, 3b..	4	0	1	2	2	1
W. Johnston,1b	3	1	2	9	1	0
Sewell, ss....	3	0	0	2	4	0
O'Neill, c....	2	1	0	3	1	1
Thomas, c....	0	0	0	1	0	0
Bagby, p.....	4	1	2	0	2	0
Totals	33	8	12	27	13	2

BROOKLYN.	Ab.	R.	H.	O.	A.	E.
Olson, ss....	4	0	2	3	5	0
Sheehan, 3b..	3	0	1	1	1	1
Griffith, rf...	4	0	1	1	0	0
Wheat, lf....	4	1	2	3	0	0
Myers, cf....	4	0	2	0	0	0
Konetchy, 1b.	4	0	2	9	2	0
Kilduff, 2b...	4	0	1	5	6	0
Miller, c.....	2	0	2	0	1	0
Krueger, c....	2	0	1	2	1	0
Grimes, p....	1	0	0	0	1	0
Mitchell, p...	2	0	0	1	0	0
Totals	34	1	13	24	17	1

Brooklyn .... 0 0 0 0 0 0 0 0 1—1
Cleveland .... 4 0 0 3 1 0 0 0 x—8

Three-base hits—Konetchy, E. Smith. Home runs—E. Smith, Bagby. Sacrifices—Sheehan, W. Johnston. Double-plays—Olson to Kilduff to Konetchy; Jamieson to O'Neill; Gardner to Wambsganss to Johnston; Johnston to Sewell to Johnston. Triple play—Wambsganss (unassisted). Left on bases—Brooklyn, 7; Cleveland, 6. Base on balls—Off Grimes, 1; Mitchell, 3. Hits—Off Grimes, 9 in 3 1-3 innings; Mitchell, 3 in 4 2-3 innings. Struck out—By Bagby, 3; Mitchell, 1. Wild pitch—Bagby. Passed ball—Miller. Losing pitcher—Grimes. Umpires—Klem (at the plate); Connolly (at first); O'Day (at second); Dineen (at third). Time—One hour and 49 minutes.

Reprinted from **The Baltimore Sun papers**

INDIVIDUAL BATTING.
(Fifteen or More Games.)

	Bats	G.	AB.	R.	H.	TB.	2B.	3B.	HR.	SH.	SB.	BB.	BBP.	CS.	SO.	HB.	Pct.
R. J. Nieuhaus, Cleveland........	L	19	9	0	4	0	0	0	0	2	1	0		3	0		.444
George H. Sisler, St. Louis........	L	154	631	137	257	399	49	18	19	13	42	46	122	17	19	2	.407
T. E. Speaker, Cleveland........	L	150	552	137	214	310	50	11	8	20	10	97	107	13	13	5	.388
Joe Jackson, Chicago........	L	146	570	105	218	336	42	20	12	16	9	56	121	12	14	7	.382
Geo. H. Ruth, New York........	L	142	458	158	172	388	36	9	54	5	14	148	137	14	80	3	.376
Edward T. Collins, Chicago........	L	153	601	115	222	294	37	13	3	34	19	69	75	8	19	2	.369
William Jacobson, St. Louis........	R	154	609	97	216	305	34	14	9	16	11	46	122	7	37	2	.355
J. P. Evans, Cleveland........	R	56	172	32	60	87	9	9	0	1	6	15	23	2	3	1	.340
George E. Uhle, Cleveland........	R	27	32	4	11	11	0	0	0	1	2	2	2	2	2	0	.344
John Tobin, St. Louis........	L	147	593	94	202	268	34	10	4	18	21	39	62	13	23	2	.340

TWO CHICAGO PLAYERS CONFESS SELLING GAMES; EIGHT ARE INDICTED

"EDDIE" CICOTTE
Star Pitcher of the White Sox Who Confessed to Throwing World Series Games

"JOE" JACKSON
Chicago Outfielder Who Admitted He Took Bribe to Lose World Series Games

Cicotte in Tears Tells of Getting $10,000 Under His Pillow from Gamblers

COMISKEY SUSPENDS ALL MEN IMPLICATED

Jackson Admits His Part in Losing World Series—Set His Price at $20,000, Was Buncoed $15,000

OFFERS YANKEE TEAM

Comiskey, However, Declares He Cannot Accept Proposal

NEW YORK, Sept. 28—A telegram offering to place the entire New York American baseball team at the disposal of Charles A. Comiskey, who today suspended seven of his players indicted in connection with alleged fixing of games, was sent tonight to the White Sox club owner by Jacob Ruppert and T. L. Huston, owners of the Yankee club. The message follows:

"Your action in suspending players under suspicion, although it wrecks your entire organization and perhaps your cherished lifework, not only challenges our admiration but excites our sympathy and demands our practical assistance. You are making a terrible sacrifice to preserve the integrity of the game. So grave and unforeseen an emergency requires unusual remedies.

"Therefore, in order that you may play out your schedule and if necessary the world series, our entire club is placed at your disposal. We are confident that Cleveland sportsmanship will not permit you to lose by default and will welcome the arrangement. We are equally certain that any technicalities in carrying it out can be readily overcome by action of the national commission."

Reprinted from the **Boston Herald**, courtesy the **Boston Herald American**

CHICAGO, Sept. 28 (By the Associated Press)—Indictments were returned against eight baseball stars today and confessions obtained from two of them, when the "Old Roman," Charles A. Comiskey, owner of the oft-time champion Chicago White Sox, smashed his pennant chasing machine to clean up baseball. The confessions told how the Sox threw last year's world's championship to Cincinnati for money paid by gamblers.

Seven Sox regulars and one former player comprise the players against whom true bills were voted by the Cook county grand jury, and the seven were immediately suspended by Mr. Comiskey. With his team only one game behind the league-leading Cleveland Indians, the White Sox owner served notice on his seven stars that, if they were found guilty, he would drive them out of organized baseball for the rest of their lives.

The exact nature of the information Mr. Comiskey put before the grand jury was not disclosed. The men whom the jury involved as a result of testimony uncovered by their owner were:

Eddie Cicotte, star pitcher, who waived immunity and confessed, according to court attaches, that he took a $10,000 bribe.

Arnold Gandil, former first baseman.

"Shoeless Joe" Jackson, heavy hitting left fielder.

Oscar ("Hap") Felsch, centre fielder.

Charles ("Swede") Risberg, shortstop.

Claude Williams, pitcher.

George ("Buck") Weaver, third baseman.

Fred McMullin, utility player.

(continued on facing page)

(continued from facing page)

Officials of Chief Justice Charles Mc-Donald's court, desirous of giving the national game the benefit of publicity in its purging, lifted the curtain on the grand jury proceedings sufficiently to show a great hitter, Joe Jackson, declaring that he deliberately just tapped the ball; a picture of one of the world's most famous pitchers, Cicotte, in tears, and glimpses of alleged bribes of $5000 or $10,000 discovered under pillows, or on beds, by famous athletes about to retire.

Around the court room at one time or another were some of baseball's greatest leaders, among them John J. Mc-Graw, manager of the New York Giants, awaiting a call to testify tomorrow, and John A. Heydler, president of the National league, who went before the grand jurors this afternoon.

While the grand jurors voted their true bills, the Old Roman, seated in the midst of his crumbling empire out at White Sox Park, issued the telegram suspending those involved, paid off Weaver, Cicotte and Jackson on the spot, and announced that checks for pay due the others would be sent them at once. With his voice trembling, Mr. Comiskey, who has owned the White Sox since the inception of the American league, said this was the first time scandal had ever touched his "family," and that it distressed him too much to talk about it.

Cicotte Weeps as He Confesses

The rush of players to bare their part in the affair started today when Cicotte appeared at the criminal court building and asked permission to testify. Cicotte wept, court attaches said, and exclaimed in anguish his sorrow for his two small children as he told how he did his utmost to lose rather than win the 1919 world series after he had "found" $10,000 beneath his pillow, where it had been placed by professional gamblers.

He said he lobbed the ball to the plate so slowly "you could read the trademark on it" in the first game at Cincinnati, when he was taken out of the box after ??? innings had been played.

Both Cicotte and Jackson were closeted with the grand jury for a considerable time today and later court officials reported that they told their stories in substantial detail. As they left the room they were taken into custody by detectives of the state attorney's office. Their detention was not in the nature of an arrest and it was announced that they would be released later.

Double-Crossed by Gamblers

Cicotte, who earlier in the day had vehemently denied any part in the alleged plot, as described by Maharg at Philadelphia, admitted on the stand, officials of the court said, that the Philadelphian's story was substantially correct.

The court officials also quoted Cicotte as saying that the players had believed that "Chick" Gandil, who, he said, was interested in the dealings with the gamblers, had "double-crossed" them and that Maharg's story was the first intimation they had had that Attell had "held out" on the $100,000 which had been promised.

Jackson, it was said, testified he was promised $20,000 by "Chick" Gandil, but received only $5000. Claude Williams, according to the witnesses, got $10,000.

"Buck" Weaver, after learning of his indictment and suspension, denied that he had agreed to throw any world series games and that he had received any of the money.

"I batted .333 and made only four errors in 30 chances in the world series," he said. "That should be a good enough alibi."

Three More Men Indicted in World's Series "Frame"

CHICAGO, Oct. 22.—Indictments against 13 persons believed to have been implicated in the throwing of games in the 1919 world series by Chicago American league players were returned today by a special Cook county grand jury which has been investigating the baseball scandal for more than a month. The indictments charged conspiracy to commit an illegal act. Further indictments are expected when the jury reconvenes next week, the state's attorney's office said.

Indictments against 10 of the men named today previously had been voted, but were revoted to overcome legal technicalities. The other three, Abe Attell, Hal Chase and William Burns, had only been unofficially mentioned in connection with the investigation.

Chase and Burns, former major league players, and Attell, once the featherweight boxing champion of the world, have been accused by witnesses of being three of the clique which "framed" the world series and arranged to bribe the White Sox players for sums ranging from $2000 to $10,000 to try to lose games in the contests for the world's baseball championship.

According to testimony presented, "at least several hundred thousand dollars" was bet and won on the world's series. Chase was the first man to suggest throwing the series, it was said, and called in the others to help him. Harry Long, a Chicagoan, told the jury he alone placed $27,000 in bets on Cincinnati for "Sport" Sullivan of Boston. Testimony has been received concerning many other large bets.

Besides Chase, Attell and Burns, today's indictments covered two alleged gamblers, Sullivan and a man known to the jury only as "Brown" and the eight players owned by the Chicago American league club against whom true bills previously had been voted. They are: Joe Jackson and Oscar Felsch, outfielders; Eddie Cicotte and Claude Williams, pitchers; "Swede" Risberg, shortstop; "Chick" Gandil, first baseman in 1919, but who was not in the big leagues this year; Fred McMullin, utility infielder, and "Buck" Weaver, third baseman.

Williams, Jackson and Cicotte previously had made sworn confessions before the jury. Cicotte said he received $10,000, while Williams said he received $10,000, which he split with Jackson, who confirmed the statements of the two pitchers. Weaver, McMullin and Risberg have announced that they will fight the case and contest the suspension placed on all eight players by Owner Charles A. Comiskey.

Officials of the state's attorney's office today said testimony had been given that Chase, who was expelled from the major leagues and barred from league parks in the West for alleged gambling, was one of the chief instigators of the game selling.

The jury was said to have received more testimony concerning Chase than any of the others. President Heydler of the National league, Garry Herrmann, owner of the Cincinnati Reds, Manager John McGraw, President Stoneham, Fred Toney and Benny Kauff of the New York Giants and others testified concerning the man who, during his major league career, was known as the "prince of first basemen."

This testimony was said to show that Chase approached Abe Attell before the 1919 world's series and asked him if he could raise $100,000 with which to bribe the Chicago players and if he then could place large sums in bets. Attell was said to have gone to a New York gambler who has been mentioned in connection with the jury investigation and also to have approached "Sport" Sullivan on the proposition.

Chase, according the testimony, also was said to have approached Sullivan, telephoning him from the room in New York occupied by Jean Dubuc, former Detroit pitcher. Through the activities of Chase and Attell, officials said the testimony which "threw" the world's series and wrecked the Chicago championship club, was arranged.

Burns, a former pitcher for the Chicago Americans, Cincinnati Reds and Philadelphia Nationals, was brought into the deal by Chase, it was said, his work, according to state officials, being primarily to superintend the placing of bets. Dubuc testified some time ago that Chase telegraphed him the series had been fixed and Rube Benton, New York National pitcher, testified he was present when the telegram was received. Working with these men, the testimony was said to show, were "Chick" Gandil and another player who were said to have represented some of the Sox players in the deal.

ROTHSTEIN TO TELL ALL THAT HE KNOWS

NEW YORK, Oct. 22.—Arnold Rothstein, whose name has been frequently mentioned in the Chicago grand jury inquiry of alleged irregularities in the conduct of the 1919 world's series, said tonight he would leave this city Monday for Chicago and would tell the jury all he knows about the baseball scandal.

Rothstein said he had notified the Chicago authorities to this effect; had waived immunity and had made but one request, that after his testimony "he is to be publicly given a clean bill of health and freed from further connection with the affair."

He said his testimony would show him innocent of complicity in debauchery of the Chicago American league team of 1919.

Owners Break Bread and Bury Baseball Hatchet; Talk Turkey, Says Landis

CHICAGO, Jan. 12—Organized baseball today swept the last vestige of disagreement from its ranks in a series of conferences which brought signed peace agreements, not only between the major and minor leagues, but between individual club owners who have vigorously opposed each other in affairs of administration and policy.

Frazee Will Sign

The two major leagues signed the new national agreement, making Judge Kenesaw M. Landis baseball commissioner with supreme powers, and the major leagues also signed an agreement with Judge Landis as their ruler, but it differed in one empowering word from that signed by the majors. This difference, it developed, was due to a misunderstanding in the joint meeting of drafting committees yesterday when the agreement was drawn up, and it was announced that the minors later would sign an agreement identical with the one approved by the major organizations.

Besides signing the national agreement, the individual major league club owners affixed their signatures to a contract in which they agreed not to criticise publicly each other or talk about one another and to accept any decision made by Judge Landis, regardless of their personal opinion of it.

Included in the signatories to this agreement were President B. B. Johnson of the American league and two of the three club owners who have fought his administration—Charles A. Comiskey of Chicago and Jacob Ruppert of New York. Harry Frazee of Boston, the third club owner who opposed Johnson in recent American league disagreements, announced that he would sign the contract. He was not present when it was drawn up.

No Fooling the Judge

The signing of the new national agreement brought a sharp statement from Judge Landis concerning the powers he must have and led to erroneous reports that he had issued an ultimatum giving the club owners 15 minutes in which to make changes he demanded. The judge did not set a time limit, but did tell the club owners that his powers must be supreme.

When the copy of the new national agreement was brought before the league representatives, it contained a section saying that the commissioner, after investigating any affair he considered detrimental to baseball, could "recommend such action as he deemed advisable."

Judge Landis interrupted the reading of the document to say that this must be made to read "to take such action."

"You have told the world that my powers are to be supreme," he said. "To give me the power merely to 'recommend' takes all power out of my hands. I will retire from the room, gentlemen, and you can discuss this matter. But I want you to know that either I must have power to take such action as I wish, or else you had better seek a new commissioner. I wouldn't take this job for all the gold in the world unless I knew my hands were to be free."

Draft Restored

On motion of President Johnson, the major leaguers voted to substitute the word "take" for "recommend," but it was found that the minors were not in official session and the matter would have to go through their drafting committee again.

Aug. 3

Sox and Jury Have a Party

Chicago—In a little Italian restaurant on Chicago's West side, the former White Sox players indicted in the baseball scandal, early Wednesday accidentally met the 12 jurors who Tuesday night found them not guilty of the charges brought by the state and the 12 judges of fact in the case joined with the men whose fate had been in their hands for five weeks in a celebration which did not end until sunrise.

The jurors went to the restaurant for a farewell dinner before returning to their homes. The players and their attorneys went for the same purpose. After several hours the two parties discovered each other in adjoining rooms. The doors were thrown open and the party became one.

The jurors and the recent defendants left the restaurant together, singing Hail, Hail, the Gang's All Here.

Oct. 31

TYRUS COBB HEADS LEAGUE IN HITTING FOR THIRTEENTH TIME

BY FRANCIS J. POWERS.

For the thirteenth time since his sensational entry into the major leagues, the American league batting crown rests on the fast thinning locks of Tyrus Cobb. The unofficial figures give Cobb an average of .390 to .387 for Harry Heilmann, also of the Detroit team, who has waged a neck-and-neck battle with the indomitable Georgian since midseason.

On Thursday, Heilmann was leading his manager by one point. Friday Detroit did not play and Cobb was suspended by Ban Johnson for a run in with an umpire. On Saturday, Heilmann went hitless in five times at the bat and yesterday, in the finale of the season, made one in four times up.

Calculation shows that Cobb made 197 hits in 505 times at bat while Heilmann made 222 blows in 603 trips to the rubber. The batting race was the tightest since 1910 when Ty Cobb and Nap Lajoie went into the final game of the year with the batting leadership undecided. That was the season in which a St. Louis third baseman allowed several bunts to go safe when Lajoie was at the bat.

WEAVER TO SUE CHICAGO FOR SUSPENDED SALARY

Others Of Discredited Players May Seek Payment Of Bonus For 1919 Series.

BAN ON ACQUITTED PLAYERS

Comiskey And Judge Landis Bar "Black Sox" From Playing In Organized Baseball.

Chicago, Aug. 3 (Special).—Interest in aftermath developments of the trial that resulted in acquittal of the "Black Sox" centered tonight in the announcement that "Buck" Weaver probably will bring suit against the Chicago American League Club to recover salary which was stopped when he was suspended.

That others of the discredited players may bring action to force payment of the bonus to which they were "entitled" when the White Sox won second place in the 1919 world's series also was suggested.

When those who rule the destinies of Organized Baseball promptly rejected the not guilty verdict last night as reason why the freed players should be reinstated, rumors indicated suits based on "injuries to reputations" were contemplated. Attorneys for the defense, however, did not confirm such reports.

"My clients, as far as I have been informed, will not seek any redress," said Benedict Short, who defended Eddie Cicotte, Claude Williams and Joe Jackson. "The jury has cleared them, and I believe they will let it go at that."

Thomas D. Nash and Michael J. Ahern, attorneys for Weaver, Oscar Felsch and Charles Risberg, also seemed inclined to the "let well enough alone" policy—so far as damage suits are concerned. But Mr. Ahern said Weaver has a legitimate claim in connection with the contract.

"Weaver's contract," he said, "was to have run through the season of 1922. He probably will ask us to bring action to recover what is due him for 1921, less what he has earned this year. He was receiving about $7,500 a season."

Charles A. Comiskey, owner of the White Sox, was undisturbed by reports concerning civil action.

Earlier in the day Mr. Comiskey, Judge Landis, dictator of professional baseball, and Ban Johnson, president of the American League, had issued separate statements, each of which seemed to contribute its bit toward destroying any hopes the Black Sox may have cherished for reinstatement.

"Cicotte confessed to me that he had been 'crooked,'" said the White Sox chief, "and implicated seven other players. Until they all are able to explain this to my satisfaction none of them will play with the Sox."

Judge Landis' statement read, in part:

"Regardless of the verdict of juries, no player that throws a ball game; no player that undertakes or promises to throw a ball game; no player that sits in a conference with a bunch of crooked players and gamblers where the ways and means of throwing games are planned and discussed, and does not promptly tell his club about it, will ever play professional baseball."

Ruth Has Hit 162 Out of Lot in Seven Years

NEW YORK, Oct 2. Babe Ruth's fifty-ninth home run of the season today brought his grand total in league games in the last seven seasons to 162, of which 113 were made in 1920 and 1921.

The greatest interest attaches to the possibilities of Ruth's batting in the coming world series, which will be the third for the home run king. In the two previous series in 1916 and 1918 as a member of the Boston Red Sox Ruth performed as a pitcher and was not expected to do any great feats with the bat. His only world series' hit, a triple, won a game for the Red Sox in 1918.

Reprinted from
The Cleveland Plain Dealer

BABE HITS 59TH HOMER; YANKS PULL OUT IN 9TH

Peckinpaugh Doubles With Two Men On in Final Against Red Sox.

NEW YORK, Oct 2. The New York Americans again defeated Boston, 7 to 6, in the final game of the league season.

A two run rally in the ninth gave the Yankees the victory. Peckinpaugh's double scoring Devormer and Miller.

Bost.	A	R	H	O	A	New York.	A	R	H	O	A
						Miller,cf	5	2	1	1	0
						Peckinpaugh,s	4	1	2	2	0
						Ruth,lf	4	1	2	1	0
						Meusel,rf	4	0	0	0	0
						Pipp,1	4	0	0	8	0
						Ward,2	2	1	1	3	3
						Fewster,3	1	0	0	1	3
						McNally,3	4	1	2	0	0
						Devormer,c	4	1	2	3	0
						Shawkey,p	1	0	0	0	1
						W.Collins,p	1	0	0	0	0
						Piercy,p	1	0	0	0	1
						*Baker	0	0	0	0	0
						†Haas	0	0	0	0	0
Totals							35	7	10	27	16

*Batted for Piercy in ninth.
†Ran for Baker in ninth.

Two out when winning run was scored.

Boston .... 0 0 0 2 3 0 0 1 0—6
New York .... 0 2 3 0 0 0 0 0 2—7

Errors—Ruth, Pipp, Ward. Two base hits—McNally 2, Devormer 2, McInnis, Peckinpaugh. Three base hits—Pratt, Ruth. Home run—Ruth. Stolen bases—Ruth, Pittenger. Double plays—Peckinpaugh to Ward to Pipp, Peckinpaugh to Ward. Left on bases—New York 6, Boston 10. Bases on balls—Off Shawkey 3, off W. Collins 2, off Piercy 3, off Fullerton 2. Hits—Off Shawkey, 2 in 3 innings; off W. Collins, 5 in 113 innings; off Piercy, 2 in 123 innings. Struck out—By Shawkey 1, by W. Collins 1 by Fullerton 4. Winning pitcher—Piercy. Losing pitcher—Fullerton. Umpires—Wilson, Chill and Connolly. Time—1.42.

Reprinted from
The Cleveland Plain Dealer

LANDIS BARS RUTH FROM BASEBALL UNTIL MAY 20

MEUSEL, PIERCY ALSO BANISHED FOR ONE MONTH

BY LARRY WOLTZ.

Babe Ruth knows his sentence. And it is a severe one. For having participated in a barnstorming tour following last Fall's world's series the famous home run king of the New York American League club will not be permitted to appear in the lineup of his club until May 20, 1922. In addition he forfeits his share of the '21 world's series, amounting to $3,362.26. The same punishment was handed outfielder Bob Meusel and pitcher Bill Piercy, who were members of Ruth's team. The sentence was announced yesterday by Judge K. M. Landis, commissioner of baseball.

Hear Ye, Culprits.

The order promulgated by the baseball ruler follows:

"In re Players Meusel, Piercy and Ruth. These players were members of the New York American League team, a contestant for the world's championship in 1921. Immediately after this series willfully and defiantly they ignored the rule forbidding their participation in exhibition games during the year in which that world's series was decided.

"This rule was enacted in 1911, only after repeated acts of insubordinance by world's series participants made its adoption imperative for the protection of the good name of the game. The rule was known to all players, and particularly to these men, upon one of whom a fine was imposed in 1917 for its violation.

Baseball Looks Bigger.

"This situation involves not merely rule violation, but rather a mutinous defiance intended by the players to present the question:

© 1921, Chicago Tribune Company, used with permission.

Which is the bigger, baseball, or any individual in baseball?

"There will be an order forfeiting their shares of the world's series funds and suspending them until May 20, 1922, on which date and within ten days thereafter they will be eligible to apply for reinstatement."

The sentence handed Ruth and his mates did not cause much surprise along the baseball Rialto. It was a foregone conclusion that he would draw a slight suspension, but it was not expected that he would be asked to forfeit the entire amount of his share of the last world's series.

Longer Term Before Footlights.

The big hitter now is in vaudeville. He probably will take a couple of weeks' extra "time," as it will not be necessary for him to accompany the Yankees on the southern training trip. As he will not be permitted to appear in league games until May 20 he will be able to start getting in shape after the opening of the regular season.

The Yankees will be severely crippled by the loss of Ruth and Meusel. Piercy, a left-handed pitcher, was of little value to Huggins last season, but when two-thirds of the outfield and the main hitting strength of the club is taken away for the early part of the pennant grind the club is likely to get into a rut and remain there.

It will be necessary for Manager Huggins to dig up two good outfielders to sub for Ruth and Meusel. He probably will use Bob Roth and Chick Fewster. Roth now is in a local hospital as the result of an operation on his knee and it is not known whether or not he will be fit for duty next Spring.

Rule to Stand.

There will be no getting away from the Landis ruling. Once issued by the baseball commissioner the rule will stand. And it was formally issued yesterday.

As has been asserted in these columns several times, Judge Landis did not make the baseball laws. But he is paid a handsome salary to see that they are observed. Club owners dare not appeal.

At the major league meetings in New York next week a new ruling, no doubt, will be made governing the playing of post season games. Baseball men have indicated as much.

How Robertson Became the Third Pitcher to Twirl No-Run, No-Hit, No-Man-Reach-First Game

First Inning	Second Inning	Third Inning	Fourth Inning	Fifth Inning
Blue fanned.	Veach flied to Mostil.	Rigney flied to Hooper.	Blue fanned.	Veach flied to Hooper.
Cutshaw popped to Collins.	Heilmann flied to Hooper.	Manion fouled to Schalk.	Cutshaw flied to Collins.	Robertson threw out Heilmann.
Cobb grounded to McClellan.	Jones flied to Hooper.	Pillette grounded to Mulligan.	Cobb flied to Mostil.	Jones lifted to McClellan.

Sixth Inning	Seventh Inning	Eighth Inning	Ninth Inning
Rigney fouled to Sheely.	Collins threw out Blue.	Veach struck out.	Clark struck out.
Manion grounded to Collins.	Cutshaw grounded to McClellan.	Heilmann fouled to Sheely.	Manion flied to Collins.
Pillette struck out.	Cobb struck out.	Jones grounded to Collins.	Bassler lined to Mostil.

Once to Every Generation

DETROIT.

	AB	R	H	O	A	E
Blue, 1b	3	0	0	10	3	1
Cutshaw, 2b	3	0	0	3	2	0
Cobb, cf	3	0	0	1	0	0
Veach, lf	3	0	0	0	0	0
Heilmann, rf	3	0	0	1	0	0
Jones, 3b	3	0	0	2	5	0
Rigney, ss	2	0	0	2	1	0
Manion, c	3	0	0	6	1	0
Pillette, p	2	0	0	0	3	0
*Clark	1	0	0	0	0	0
†Bassler	1	0	0	0	0	0
Totals	27	0	0	27	15	1

CHICAGO.

	AB	R	H	O	A	E
Mulligan, ss	4	0	1	0	0	0
McClellan, 3b	3	0	1	1	3	0
Collins, 2b	3	0	1	4	3	0
Hooper, rf	3	1	0	3	0	0
Mostil, lf	4	1	1	3	0	0
Strunk, cf	3	0	0	0	0	0
Sheely, 1b	4	0	2	9	0	0
Schalk, c	4	0	1	7	0	0
Robertson, p	4	0	0	0	1	0
Totals	32	3	7	27	7	0

*Batted for Rigney in ninth.
†Batted for Pillette in ninth.

Detroit	0	0	0	0	0	0	0	0	0	0
Chicago	0	2	0	0	0	0	0	0	x	3

Two-base hits—Sheely, Mulligan. Struck out—By Pillette 5, Robertson 6. Sacrifice hits—Strunk, McClellan, Collins. Bases on balls—Off Pillette 2. Time—1:46. Umpires—Nallin and Evans.

36,000 WATCH RUTH IN DEBUT

Neither He Nor Williams Get Homers; Browns Win in Ninth Inning.

NEW YORK, May 20.—A capacity crowd, some 40,000, came out to see George H. "Babe" Ruth and Bob Meusel, American league sluggers, in action for the first time in 1922 and stayed to see the New York Americans lose one of the freakiest games in years.

The Yankees led by a score of 2 to 1 going into the ninth inning, and Jones retired the first two men up, but before New York could put over the last put out St. Louis had scored seven runs and won the game 8 to 2.

CUBS HAND CARDS A JOLT

Chicago, May 30.—Chicago bunched its hits this afternoon and made it two straight from St. Louis, 3 to 1. The Cubs won the morning game, 4 to 1. The afternoon contest was a pitching duel between Doak and Aldridge, the former suffering a bad inning.

Heathcote and Flack, outfielders, who were traded each for the other by the clubs after the morning game, played this afternoon with their new teammates. Score:

CHICAGO.	AB	R	H	O	A	E	ST. LOUIS.	AB	R	H	O	A	E
Statz, cf	4	1	2	5	0	0	Flack, rf	4	0	1	2	1	0
Hollocher, ss	4	0	1	1	0	0	Toporcer, ss	4	0	1	2	4	1
Krug, 3b	4	1	1	1	5	0	Smith, cf	3	0	0	1	0	0
Grimes, 1b	2	1	0	9	0	0	Hornsby, 2b	3	0	2	2	0	0
Heathcote, rf	4	0	2	2	0	0	Fournier, 1b	4	0	1	9	1	0
Barber, lf	3	0	2	4	1	0	McHenry, lf	3	1	2	1	0	0
Terry, 2b	3	0	1	2	3	0	Stock, 3b	4	0	2	1	1	0
O'Farrell, c	3	0	5	2	0	0	Clemons, c	3	0	6	2	0	0
Aldridge, p	3	0	0	1	0	0	Doak, p	3	0	0	0	3	0
Totals	30	3	9	27	12	0	Totals	31	1	7	24	14	1

Chicago	1	0	0	0	0	0	2	x	—3
St. Louis	0	1	0	0	0	0	0	0	—1

Sacrifice hits—Barber, Terry. Double play—Krug to Grimes. Left on bases—St. Louis, 6; Chicago, 4. Bases on balls—Off Doak, 3; off Doak, 2. Struck out—By Doak, 6; by Aldridge, 3. Umpires—McCormick and Sentelle. Time of game—1:45.

CHICAGO.	AB	R	H	O	A	E	ST. LOUIS.	AB	R	H	O	A	E
Statz, cf	4	0	1	3	0	0	Smith, rf	4	0	0	2	0	1
Hollocher, ss	4	1	3	1	2	0	Toporcer, ss	4	0	0	3	4	0
Krug, 3b	3	1	2	4	3	0	Stock, 3b	3	0	0	4	0	0
Grimes, 1b	3	1	1	8	1	0	Hornsby, 2b	3	0	2	2	2	0
Flack, rf	4	0	0	0	0	0	Fournier, 1b	3	0	3	5	0	0
Terry, 2b	4	0	2	3	1	0	McHenry, lf	4	1	1	2	0	0
O'Farrell, c	2	0	0	4	2	0	Heathcote, cf	4	0	1	3	0	0
Steuland, p	4	0	1	1	1	0	Ainsmith, c	3	0	1	6	1	0
							Sherdel, p	4	0	0	0	0	0
							Walker, p	1	0	0	0	0	0
							Bailey, p	0	0	0	0	0	0
							*Schultz	1	0	0	0	0	0
Totals	32	3	11	27	19	0	Totals	29	1	4	24	9	2

*Batted for Walker in eighth inning.

Chicago	0	0	0	0	0	0	0	0	x	—3
St. Louis	0	1	0	0	0	0	0	0	0	—1

Two-base hits—Hornsby, Krug, Grimes, Stock. Sacrifice—Krug, Grimes. Double plays—Hollocher to Terry to Grimes; O'Farrell to Krug; Hornsby to Toporcer to Fournier. Left on bases—St. Louis, 5; Chicago, 8. Bases on balls—Off Steuland, 4; off Sherdel, 2. Struck out—By Sherdel, 2; by Steuland, 4; by Walker, 3; by Bailey, 1. Hits—Off Sherdel, 6 in 3 2-3 innings; off Walker, 5 in 3 1-3 innings. Time 1:44. Umpires—Sentelle and McCormick.

Court Decision For Base Ball

NEW YORK, May 31.—The Supreme Court's decision in holding that the Sherman Anti-Trust Law does not apply to organized base ball was hailed as "a great stimulus to the future development of base ball" in a statement made public today by President John A. Heydler of the National League.

"After years of litigation, we finally have the clear cut ruling that base ball is a sport, and not a trade." Mr. Heydler said, adding that it was "a tribute to the foresight and wisdom of the men who laid the foundations of the sport."

He declared that its result would be to stabilize the whole structure of American base ball and insure protection for the owners and players as well as benefit the public.

LANDIS BARS MAJOR LEAGUE CLUBS FROM MONTREAL; THEN LOOK WHAT PIRATES SAY

Montreal, July 7.—Moist Montreal has seen its last American big league baseball team in action, it was learned today when officials of the local club began negotiations with the religious sect of the House of David to send its long-haired team here for an exhibition game. Chinese and Japanese nines are also being sought.

The new move followed receipt of word that Commissioner Landis had quietly passed the word that henceforth the big leaguers should play only on their own side of the international fence. The order followed a recent visit to Montreal of a National League club.

Sam Watters, secretary of the Pirates, expressed surprise yesterday when informed that big league teams of the United States would not show in the "moist" city of Montreal again. "The Pirates made the most recent trip to Montreal," Mr. Watters said. "I accompanied the team. We were to play an exhibition. The players went to the ball park, but were unable to take the field because of rain. They returned to their hotel immediately and played cards until train time. The behavior of the players, with one exception, was of the best. This exception was not at all bad. So far as I know, Commissioner Landis has passed no word for big league teams to stay on their own side of the international fence."

Reprinted from
The Pittsburgh Post

July 8

SIX BLOWS EACH REGISTERED BY MAX CAREY AND JOHN GOOCH

By EDWARD F. BALINGER, Baseball Editor, Pittsburgh Post.

More than 4,000 fans sat for four hours and 19 minutes at Forbes Field yesterday and watched the Pirates give the New York Giants the toughest battle of the season. The world's champions were triumphant, 9 to 8, but the twilight shadows were settling down upon Panther Hollow when George Kelly delivered a four-sacker that scored Ross Young ahead of him and decided the struggle in the eighteenth inning. This was the big first baseman's second home run smash of the afternoon.

Captain Max Carey of the Corsairs set a shining example, playing one of the most sensational games of his entire career. He made nine visits to the plate with his bat over his left shoulder and never failed to reach the paths. He worked the various New York moundsmen for three bases on balls. On his six other efforts he delivered safe swats, thereby making his batting average perfect for the day.

Reprinted from
The Pittsburgh Post

Nov. 15

Man Who Made First Triple Play, Arrested

Washington.—Paul A. Hines, "midfielder" for the Providence Baseball club of the old National league in the seventies and for the Washington club in the early eighties, was arrested Tuesday night on a pickpocket charge. He is said to be the first major league player to make a triple play unassisted—on May 8, 1878, when with the Providence club. He was released under bond of $1,000. Hines, who is 69, when confronted with the charge broke down and said: "I have played my last game and lost." In recent years Hines has been employed in the post-office division of the department of agriculture.

Reprinted from
The Milwaukee Journal

Two World's Records Smashed, Two Others Equalled, Big Slugfest

Chicago, Aug. 25.—Two world's records were smashed and two other marks were equalled in a hectic slugging match which Chicago won from Philadelphia today, 26 to 23.

Biggest Score of All Time.
The total runs scored by both clubs—forty-nine is the biggest score in a game of all time, according to records available here. On July 12, 1890, Brooklyn and Buffalo (P. L.) scored forty-four runs. The previous world's mark, made since 1876 was forty-three runs made in the game between Chicago and Louisville on June 29, 1897, when Chicago collected thirty-six and Louisville seven. The greatest score since 1900 was made in the Boston-Philadelphia game of May 30, 1901, when a total of thirty-five runs was scored.

Most Hits Since 1900.
The record for the most hits by both teams since 1900 in one game was also shattered, a total of fifty-one hits being made. New York and Cincinnati in the National League scored forty-nine hits during a contest June 9, 1901. St. Louis and Cleveland while in the American Association, made fifty-three hits on April 16, 1897. Bases on balls at that time, however, were counted as hits. Philadelphia outhit Chicago today, 26 to 25.

Callaghan Equals Record.
Outfielder Callaghan of the Chicago club equalled the world's record for the number of times to face a pitcher in one inning. He came up three times during the fourth inning batting rally of the Cubs and smashed out two hits and struck out once. This record is shared by T. Burns, Fred Pfeffer, F. Goldsmith and Billy Sunday, who faced the pitcher three times each in the seventh inning of a game between Chicago and Detroit on September 6, 1883. This record was tied on June 18, 1894 by T. McCarthy in the Baltimore-Boston game in the National League and again by R. L. Murphy in the Washington-Baltimore (American Association) game on June 17, 1891.

By scoring fourteen runs in one inning the Cubs tied the modern major league record made by the New York Americans against Washington on July 6, 1920. The world's mark is eighteen, made in the Detroit-Chicago game of September 4, 1883.

It required three hours and one minute to play the game.

Score:

PHILADELPHIA

	AB	R	BH	PO	A	E
Wrightstone, 3b	7	3	4	0	4	0
Parkinson, 2b	5	1	4	0	6	0
Williams, cf	6	2	4	4	0	0
Lebourveau, cf	1	0	0	0	0	0
Walker, rf	5	4	3	1	0	0
Mokan, lf	5	3	3	2	0	0
Fletcher, ss	4	2	1	0	2	0
J. Smith, ss	1	0	0	0	1	0
Leslie, 1b	4	1	1	5	0	0
Lee, 1b	2	1	2	6	0	0
Henline, c	5	2	3	5	1	0
Withrow, c	1	0	0	1	0	0
Ring, p	2	0	0	1	0	0
Weinert, p	2	1	1	0	0	0
Rapp, x	1	0	0	0	0	0
Totals	**53**	**23**	**26**	**24**	**14**	**0**

CHICAGO

	AB	R	BH	PO	A	E
Heathcote, cf	4	2	3	4	0	1
Hollocher, ss	5	3	3	0	1	0
Kelleher, ss	1	0	0	1	1	0
Terry, 2b	5	2	3	2	4	0
Friberg, 2b	1	1	1	0	0	0
Grimes, 1b	6	3	5	7	1	0
Callaghan, rf	7	3	2	0	0	0
Miller, lf	5	4	3	0	0	0
Krug, 3b	5	3	1	1	1	0
O'Farrell, c	3	3	2	5	1	0
Hartnett, c	2	0	0	1	0	1
Kaufmann, p	2	0	0	0	1	0
Barber, z	1	0	0	0	0	0
Stueland, p	1	0	0	0	0	0
Maisel, zz	1	0	0	0	0	0
Eubanks, p	0	0	0	0	0	0
Morris, p	1	0	0	0	0	0
Osborne, p	0	0	0	0	0	0
Totals	**45**	**26**	**25**	**27**	**9**	**3**

x—Batted for Weinert in 9th.
z—Batted for Kaufmann in 4th.
zz—Batted for Stueland in 7th.

Phila.	0	3	2	1	3	6	0	4	4	—23
Chicago	1	10	0	14	0	1	0	0	x	—26

Two-base hits, Terry, Krug 2, Mokan, Hollocher, Heathcote 2, Grimes, Withrow, Friberg, Parkinson, Walker; three-base hits Walker, Wrightstone; home runs Miller (2) O'Farrell; stolen bases Hollocher, Weinert; sacrifices Leslie, O'Farrell, Hollocher, Walker; double plays J. Smith to Parkinson to Lee (2); Wrightstone to Parkinson to Lee; left on bases Philadelphia 16; Chicago 9; bases on balls, off Kaufmann 3; Ring 5, Weinert 5, Stueland 2; Eubanks 3, Morris 1; Osborne 2; struck out by King 3; Weinert 3; Stueland 1; Morris 1; Osborne 2; hits off Kaufmann 9 in 4 innings; off Stueland 7 in 3, off Eubanks 3 in 2-3 innings; off Morris 4 in 1-3; off Osborne 3 in 1; off Ring 12 in 2 1-3; off Weinert 13 in 4 2-3; hit by pitcher by Weinert (Grimes); wild pitch, Stueland; winning pitcher, Kaufmann; losing pitcher Ring; umpires Hart and Rigler; time 3.01.

Reprinted from
The Hartford Courant

Douglas's Scheme Uncovered; Pitcher Banned From Game

Pittsburgh, Aug. 16.—"Shuffling Phil" Douglas, premier pitcher of the New York Giants, was placed on its permanent ineligible list by the club today. Douglas is charged with writing a letter to a competing team offering to desert the Giants if it "would make it worth his while."

Statement By Club.

Douglas has been put on the permanent ineligible list by the New York National League baseball club for writing a letter to a member of a competing team offering to desert his club if it would make it worth his while," said a statement by the club. "Douglas does not deny he wrote the letter. We went through with this at the solicitation of Mr. Heydler, president of the national league."

Will Not Disclose Names

President John A. Heydler of the National League and Manager John J. McGraw of the New York National League baseball club declined tonight to go into details regarding the summary dismissal today of "Shuffling Phil" Douglas—one of the pitching mainstays of the New York Giants. Heydler and McGraw declared that the names of players involved would not be disclosed.

"We have issued a statement charging that Douglas wrote a letter to members of a competing team, offering to 'lay low' if financial inducements were 'worth while,'" said McGraw. "We also announced that Douglas admitted his guilt. So far as I am concerned, the affair is a closed incident."

Kenesaw M. Landis of Chicago, supreme arbiter of baseball, witnessed the game between New York and Pittsburgh here today. During the contest he declined to discuss the affair "until after the game" and later, when approached by newspapermen, he said sharply: "My only statement is that I'm going back to Chicago tonight."

Rumors Untrue.

President Dreyfuss, of the Pittsburgh Club, told the Associated Press tonight that local rumors that Douglas made the offer to friends on the local club were untrue.

"I am positive that no one on the Pittsburgh roster knew anything regarding Douglas's scheme," said Dreyfuss.

Late this afternoon, President Heydler told a sport writer that he was confident that the offer was not made to anyone on the Chicago National League team.

Reprinted from
The Hartford Courant

Dec. 4

American League Batting Title Is Won by Sisler; Cobb Second

Johnson Overrules Official Scorer Here to Give Detroit Manager His Third Mark of .400 or Better—St. Louis Takes First Honors in Club Averages.

The leading batter of the year in the American League, according to the official records released for publication today, was George H. Sisler, star first baseman of the St. Louis Browns, who hung up the remarkable average of .419, the second successive year in which this player has reached the .400 mark.

However, the greatest surprise in the records was contained in the average credited to Ty Cobb of Detroit, whose mark has been changed by Ban Johnson from its original .398 to .401, thereby entitling the veteran to join Jesse Burkett in the very select circle which can boast of three .400 marks or better in its big-league career. The records reveal for the first time that President Johnson officially overrode the decision of the scorer in New York on one play and changed an official error into an official hit.

In the game with the Yanks here on May 15 Cobb hit a grounder to Scott, who fumbled and was credited with an error by the official scorer. The unofficial box score gave Cobb a single, and it was this one play which made the difference between .398 and .401. At the end of the season, while reviewing the records to see if Cobb had been unjustly deprived of a .400 average, Johnson came upon this discrepancy, and now he has ruled in favor of the Detroit manager.

TRIPLE CROWN WINNER

HORNSBY BATS SELF INTO HALL OF FAME

Rogers Lands Among The Select .400 Hitters In Big Leagues.

MARK FOR YEAR IS .401

Is First Man In National Circuit To Accomplish Feat Since 1899.

Chicago, Oct. 1.—Rogers Hornsby, of the St. Louis Cardinals, today batted himself into the hall of fame among the select .400 hitters, the first man in the National League to accomplish the feat since 1899, when Ed Delehanty, of the Philadelphia club, won the batting honors with an average of .408. Hornsby's mark for the season is .401. This is the third consecutive season the St. Louis star has won the batting championship of the senior major league circuit.

Reprinted from
The Baltimore Sun papers

RUTH, FLIVVERER, MUST RE-ESTABLISH HIMSELF

BY JOHN B. FOSTER.

NEW YORK, October 9.—The vital point in the world series of 1922, which ended with the Giants the winners in four straight games, as the tie is exempt, is that a team which won the championship of the American League after such a brilliant race should so completely flunk, as the Yankees did, with their bats.

The Giants did not do such great things with the bat, but they were playing against a team that did nothing with the flail, and in three of the games the pitchers of the Yankees were unquestionably careless at moments when it was fatal not only to their records but to the success of their team.

Ruth No Longer King.

The Yankee sluggers suffered the most astounding collapse ever seen in a world's series. And chief of the punctured tires was Babe Ruth. Ruth was of as little use to his team as though he had come from the bushes the day before the series started. True, the so-called king of swat, did drive in two runs with his bat during the series. But Ruth, it must be remembered, was supposed to be the Yankee proverbial tower of strength. As a ball player Ruth is ancient history until he can re-establish his reputation. The champion home run hitter of the world, a man who should never think of batting under .300 with the good, natural skill which the Lord gave him, he did not bat better than .125, or as well as some one armed pitcher. In five games and seventeen times at bat Ruth, the erstwhile slamming bambino, got two hits. But no there wasn't a time value to his team in the series was X minus Y, the remainder to be subtracted from zero.

Had Ruth, with his ability to do things with his bat crossed the pitchers of the Giants instead of devoting himself each time he faced them to attempting to land the ball in the next door yard he might have appeared to be a boost instead of a bust. But no, there wasn't a time Ruth went to bat that he didn't have home run filling his mind.

Reprinted from
The Washington Evening Star

"JUSTICE AND FAIR PLAY VIOLATED," SAYS COMMISSIONER

Former Giant Southpaw Awarded to Reds; Charges Should Have Been Made Two Years Ago, Not Now, Is Czar's Opinion; "If Not Clean Enough for Majors, He Is Not Clean Enough for Minors."

CANNOT DEPRIVE PLAYER OF LIVELIHOOD ON DEFERRED CHARGES

CHICAGO, March 8.—Branding current charges against Pitcher Rube Benton by major league baseball magnates as violating "every conception of justice and fair play," Baseball Commissioner Kenesaw Mountain Landis handed down a decision tonight declaring Benton eligible to organized baseball.

Evidently resentful at the recent action of the magnates in passing him the buck and whatever blame might be attached to his action one way or the other, Landis takes the stand that the time to investigate the charges of shady transactions by Benton was at the time they became known, and not two years later.

"It has never been asserted," Landis points out, "that Benton has been guilty of dishonest playing."

Ordered to Reds.

Under Landis decision Benton will play this season with the Cincinnati Reds, following a season with the St. Paul club of the American Association in which he won 22 games and lost 11.

Landis also upholds the position of some baseball authorities that if Benton was not "clean" enough for the majors, which whisked him from the New York Giants to the minors by the waiver process, he should not be allowed to play with the minors. The standards of integrity of these two classes of leagues, he declares, are identical.

The commissioner, by taking the stand that there is no case against Benton, has failed in convicting Charlie Herzog, who was accused by Benton, by inference. Herzog not only goes unmentioned but Landis' decision is such as to make no definite decision whether Benton was all right or all wrong in the first place.

Landis recognizes two charges against Benton, which were recently discussed at a meeting of the National League following the Rube's purchase from St. Paul by Garry Herrman, but were referred to the commissioner in an evident attempt to pass the buck: first, that he failed to sustain charges made against Herzog, and that he received a tip on the day of the first game of the celebrated 1919 world's series and failed to communicate his information promptly to any responsible baseball authority.

All this was fought out verbally in the press and elsewhere by Benton, Herzog

and others, and as Landis points out, the details were set forth in full.

Landis Cites Reason.

"All evidence was then at hand," says Landis. "But no disciplinary action was taken against Benton, or apparently even considered, by the authorities charged with baseball administrative responsibility at that time, and (so far as the commissioner has ascertained) no charges against Benton's eligibility were presented to them, nor were any objections to his continued major league service made by any major league club.

"Without objection, or any intimation from any source that he was objectionable, Benton played the remainder of the 1920 season, and until August 1, 1921, with the New York Nationals and the succeeding year and a half with St. Paul.

"After more than two years of unquestioned eligibility, during which time his conduct apparently has been unimpeachable, these old matters are now brought forward for the first time in the form of charges, notwithstanding no new facts respecting them have been submitted or developed by a thorough investigation by the commissioner.

"This is at war with every conception of justice and fair play. Certainly the time to present and to act upon charges which seek to permanently deprive a man of his chief means of livelihood is at the time the matters alleged became known, not at the objectors' discretion upwards of two years later.

"Player Benton is declared eligible and his transfer from St. Paul to Cincinnati is approved."

Reprinted from
The Pittsburgh Post

Sisler to Undergo Operation For Eye Trouble This Week

ST. LOUIS, April 10 (Associated Press).—George Sisler, adjudged the best all-around player in the American League, will undergo an operation for infected sinus condition, probably Friday, it was learned today. The sinus condition has affected in some degree the star's vision, but the exact nature of the eye trouble has never been disclosed. Sisler's eyes is the principal topic of conversation among local fans. The uncertainty of his appearance on the field was emphasized today when an eye specialist treating Sisler, said he could not fix the date Sisler's recovery could be expected, adding that the star's vision was "normal in each eye." He emphasized the word "each." The oculist refused to amplify the later assertion. There has been an unverified report that Sisler is "cross-eyed." Sisler's trouble is the result of an attack of influenza last February, which left in its wake a sinus affection.

BABE RUTH STINGS BALL FOR A HOMER

Witt And Dugan Are On The Sacks When Bambino Connects.

SHAWKEY IS BRILLIANT

Red Sox Are Able To Garner But Three Hits Off The Slants Of Pitcher.

New York, April 18.—Before a record throng officially announced as 74,200, the New York Yankees, American League champions, opened their new stadium and the 1923 season today with a 4-to-1 triumph over the Boston Red Sox.

The Yankees did all of their scoring in the third inning, Babe Ruth getting off to a lusty start in his 1923 home-run campaign by driving into the right-field bleachers for the circuit, scoring Witt and Dugan ahead of him.

Bob Shawkey, veteran Yankee hurling star, pitched brilliantly, holding the Red Sox to three hits, one of which, a triple by McMillan, scored the only Boston run in the seventh. Ehmke was effective except in the third inning.

NEW YORK.							BOSTON.					
	AB	R	H	O	A	E		AB	R	H	O	A E
Witt.cf	3	1	1	2	0	0	Fewster,ss	5	0	0	2	6 0
Dugan,3b	4	1	1	1	0	0	Collins,rf	4	0	0	2	1 0
Ruth,rf	4	1	1	2	0	1	Skinner,cf	4	0	0	4	0 0
Pipp,1b	3	0	0	12	0	0	Harris,lf	4	0	0	2	0 0
Meusel,lf	4	0	1	0	0	0	Burns,1b	4	1	1	9	2 1
Schang,c	4	0	0	4	2	0	McMillan,cf	3	0	1	2	0 0
Ward,2b	3	0	1	4	4	0	Shanks,3b	3	0	0	3	0 0
Scott,ss	4	1	1	4	6	0	Devormer,c	3	0	0	6	2 0
Shawkey,p	3	1	1	0	0	0	Ehmke,p	3	0	0	1	4 0
							[Menosky	1	0	0	0	0 0
							Fullerton,p	0	0	0	0	0 0
Totals	28	4	7	27	12	1	Totals	29	1	3	24	15 1

1Batted for Ehmke in eighth inning.

New York	0	0	4	0	0	0	0	0	x—4
Boston	0	0	0	0	0	0	1	0	0—1

Two-base hits—Meusel, Scott. Three-base hit—McMillan. Home run—Ruth. Sacrifice hit—Scott. Double play—Scott, Ward and Pipp. Left on bases—New York, 5; Boston, 4. Bases on balls—Off Shawkey, 2; off Ehmke, 5; off Fullerton, 1. Struck out—By Shawkey, 5; by Ehmke, 4; by Fullerton, 1. Hits—Off Ehmke, 7 in 7 innings; off Fullerton, none in 1 inning. Hit by pitcher—By Shawkey (Fewster). Losing pitcher—Ehmke. Umpires—Connolly, Evans and Holmes. Time of game—2.05.

Reprinted from
The Baltimore Sun papers

JOHNSON AND SCOTT BOTH MAKE RECORDS

Yankee Shortstop Center of Attention—Few Aware of Twirler's Mark.

Washington, May 2.—Walter Johnson, Washington's veteran. in shutting out the New York Yankees today. 3 to 0, pitched his 100th scoreless game as a major leaguer—and he did it on the day Everett Scott, Yankee shortstop, was playing his 1000th consecutive major league game.

Johnson Game's Hero.

Scott was the center of atten n; Johnson was the hero of the game. All of the 5,000 fans who flocked to American League Park to join Ban Johnson, president of the American League, and Secretary Denby in honoring Scott knew he had already participated in 999 straight games. Few of them realised, however, that their pitching idol had scored 99 shutouts since joining the Washington team in 1907.

Scott Gets Medal.

Ceremonies had been planned in honor of Scott. Before the game, the two teams lined up at the home plate while Scott, escorted by President Johnson and accompanied by the Marine Band, marched between the line of players to Secretary Denby who pinned a gold medal on the New York player in honor of his record. Later a delegation of admirers from Scott's home town, Bluffton, Ind., presented him with a horseshoe floral wreath.

Sept. 15

Burns of Red Sox Makes Triple Play

Boston — George Burns, first baseman of the Red Sox, Friday broke into the permanent record of odd and interesting achievements in baseball when he made a triple play, unassisted, retiring the Indians almost in a single gesture.

It was in the second inning. Stephenson was on second and Lutzke on first, with none out. Burns was playing off first base, towards second.

Brower drove a liner into this groove. Burns reached out; caught the ball, tagged Lutzke on the path and then leaped to second, extinguishing Stephenson before he could haul up and return to the sack.

The last unassisted triple putout was made by Bill Wamby of the Indians in a world series game with the Dodgers three years ago.

One Safe Blow Secured by Champs is Infield Scratch That Gets Away From Shanks.

(Plain Dealer-Times Wire)

NEW YORK, Sept. 11.—Howard Ehmke, the Boston right-hander, who pitched a no-hit, no-run game against the Athletics last Friday, Sept. 7, held the Yanks to one scratch single at the stadium today and thereby gave future generation twirlers something to shoot at. One hit in eighteen innings is not merely miraculous pitching; it constitutes the greatest exhibition of box work in the history of baseball.

The Red Sox trimmed the Yankees by a count of 3 to 0. To open the game, Whitey Witt bounced a sharp grounder at Howard Shanks, the Boston third baseman. The ball bounded perfectly at Shanks, but hit him in the chest and rolled toward second base. Before Shanks could retrieve the ball Witt, a fast man, had beat the throw to first base.

The play was correctly scored as a single and the official scorer also correctly refused to reverse his decision later on when it seemed that Ehmke might pitch another no-hit game. Joe Tinker, the old Cub shortstop, who was sitting in a field box near third, called the play an error, but. on the other hand, Frank Chance, manager of the Red Sox, admitted that it could have been called either a hit or an error. If the play had occurred in the eighth or ninth innings, it would have been scored as an error, but under the conditions it was an infield single, and a single it remained.

This slim margin kept Ehmke from a pitching record that probably would have defied duplication throughout all baseball history. Pitchers who twirl no-hit, no-run games are rare enough and those who have pitched two no-hit games can be counted easily on the fingers of one hand. There never has been any who pitched two consecutive hitless contests, and, for that matter, there never have been any who allowed only one hit in eighteen successive innings.

Ehmke let only six Yankees get to first base and in seven innings pitched to only three batters. After Witt had singled to open the game, Dugan hit to the pitcher. who threw wildly to second trying to stop Witt. Whitey chased to third. but was cut down by Reichle's throw to Shanks. Ruth then forced Dugan, becoming the third Yankee to get to first during the inning.

In the next eight rounds only three Hugmen reached the initial station. Schang walked with two out in the second and was forced by Scott. In the eighth, Ward was hit by a pitched ball. Thus, of the six Yanks who dug their spikes into first base three got there on force plays.

Boston	A	R	H	O	A			A	R	H	O	A
Mitchell,s.	3	0	0	1	1	Witt,cf	4	0	1	4	0
Picinich,c.	4	1	1	7	0	Dugan,3	4	0	0	2	2
Reichle,rf	2	0	1	5	0	Ruth,rf	3	0	0	1	0
Flagstead,rf	3	0	2	0		Pipp,1	3	0	0	15	0
Harris,1	4	0	0	7	2	Meusel,lf	3	0	0	0	0
Shanks,3	4	0	0	1	1	Ward,2	2	0	0	0	2
Menosky,lf	4	0	1	0		Schang,c	2	0	0	3	1
McMillan,2	3	1	1	1	3	Scott,s	3	0	0	1	3
Ehmke,p.	4	1	2	2		Pipgras,p	2	0	0	0	2
						Hendrick	1	0	0	0	0
Totals	31	3	6	27	9	Totals	27	0	1	27	13

*Batted for Pipgras in ninth.

Boston . . . . . 0 0 0 2 0 0 0 0 1 — 3
Boston . . . . . 0 0 0 0 0 0 0 0 0 — 0

Errors Ehmke, Schang. Home run Picinich. Stolen base McMillan. Sacrifice Flagstead. Double plays Pipp unassisted; Ehmke and Harris. Left on bases New York 5, Boston 6. Bases on balls. Off Pipgras 6, off Ehmke 1. Struck out By Pipgras 5, by Ehmke 5. Hit by pitcher by Ehmke Ward. Umpires Holmes, Connolly and Dineen. Time 1.

JONES NEARLY HAS ANOTHER NO-HITTER

Gives Two Bingles to Red Sox, Making 16 2-3 Hitless Innings in Row.

NEW YORK, Sept 10.—The New York Yankees made it three straight from Boston. winning easily, 8 to 1, today. Sam Jones, who pitched a no-hit game against Philadelphia last week, nearly duplicated that feat today. He did not yield a hit until Burns singled with one out in the seventh Mitchell made the only other Boston hit, a triple in the ninth. Including a game on Aug. 31 with Washington, Jones went sixteen and two-thirds innings without yielding a hit, which is believed to be a record.

Ruth again tied Williams for the season's home run honors, when he hit his thirty-fifth home run.

Boston	A	R	H	O	A		New York	A	R	H	O	A
Mitchell,s	4	0	1	4	4	Witt,cf	5	0	1	0	0
Picinich,c	3	0	0	5	1	Dugan,3	4	0	0	1	1
Reichle,cf	2	0	0	1	0	Ruth,rf	3	2	1	2	1
Burns,1	3	1	1	10	1	Pipp,1	4	2	2	13	0
Harris,lf	3	0	0	1	0	Meusel,lf	3	1	2	5	0
Shanks,3	3	0	0	0	1	Ward,2	4	2	3	3	2
Flagstead,rf	3	0	0	0	1	Schang,c	3	0	3	3	1
McMillan,2	3	0	0	2	4	Scott,s	4	1	1	1	4
Quinn,p	2	0	0	0	2	Jones,p	3	0	0	0	3
*Menosky	0	0	0	0	0						
Odoul,p	1	0	0	0	0						
Totals	27	1	2	24	13	Totals	34	8	13	27	12

*Batted for Quinn in eighth.

Boston . . . . . 0 1 0 0 0 0 0 0 0 — 1
New York . . . . 0 1 0 2 0 0 1 4 x — 8

Errors Ward. Schang. Three-base hit Mitchell Home run Ruth. Stolen bases Meusel, Ward Sacrifice Meusel Double plays McMillan, Mitchell and Burns; Ruth and Pipp; Scott. Ward and Pipp. Left on bases New York 6, Boston 3 Bases on balls off Jones 4, off Quinn 1. off Odoul 2. Struck out By Jones 2, by Quinn 4. Hits Off Quinn, 9 in 7 innings, off Odoul. 4 in 1 inning. Losing pitcher Quinn. Umpires Dineen, Holmes and Connolly Time 1.35.

YANKEES WIN WORLD SERIES WITH BIG RALLY

[*By the Associated Press.*]

New York, Oct. 15.—Beaten, crushed after one of the most spectacular World Series fights in history, the New York Giants today surrendered to the Yankees the world championship banner they have flown for the last two years. And tonight, with this record-shattering $1,000,000 title battle at an end, the emblem of supremacy flutters atop the Yankee Stadium, greatest and costliest monument of the diamond.

The Yankees won the sixth and final game this afternoon at the Polo Grounds, lair of the Giants, by coming from behind and scoring five runs in a dramatic, pulse-gripping eighth-inning rally just when it seemed that the Mc-Grawmen, fighting desperately with their backs to the wall, would tie the series and force a seventh contest to decide the struggle. The final score was 6-4.

More Than 300,000 At Six Games.

Thus the American League champions swept to their third successive triumph, completed the rout of the once proud and mighty Giant machine and, by the decisive margin of four games to two, gained their first world title in more than two decades of embattled history.

Thus, too, was written into the annals of the national game a struggle for the highest stakes it has ever known, a gigantic spectacle eclipsing all previous records, that was witnessed by more than 300,000 fans who paid more than $1,063,000 in gate receipts.

Ruth Fans With Bases Full.

The story of that eighth inning today, coming when it appeared that the deadly southpaw arm of Arthur Nehf and the inspired play of Frank Frisch had checked the headlong rush of the Yankees, will go down as one of the most startling, decisive championship turns of all time.

That brief thrilling yet tragic span witnessed with amazing suddenness the ascendency of the Yankees to the pinnacle of their career, and, simultaneously, the utter collapse of the Giants, the crushed hopes of John McGraw for three successive world titles—a debacle so stunning that tonight it seems to have marked the passing for all time from championship heights of the Giant machine as it emerged, broken, from the test. It witnessed, too, the failure of the game's idol of idols to answer a call to fame that would have raised him to heights greater than any he has ever touched. For Babe Ruth, star of stars, the mightiest hitter ever, while he had started the Yankees off in the first inning with his third home run of the series, fell down miserably in the eighth inning pinch, striking out with the bases full and the Yankees yet one run behind.

TRIPLE PLAY PULLED BY ROOK SHORTSTOP

Ernest Padgett of Braves Makes Three-Ply Killing, Unassisted, in Tilt With Phils.

BOSTON, Oct. 6.—Boston closed its season today by defeating Philadelphia twice, winning the first game, 5 to 4, in fourteen innings and the second, 4 to 1, in four and one-half innings. Ernest Padgett, recruit Boston shortstop, made a triple play unassisted in the fourth inning of the second game. Tierney and Lee had singled and were on second and first bases respectively. Holke lined to Padgett who caught the ball. He ran to second forcing Tierney, and then caught and touched Lee before he could get back to first base.

Reprinted from
The Cleveland Plain Dealer

INDIVIDUAL BATTING.
(Fifteen or more games.)

Player and Club.	Bats.	G.	AB.	R.	H.	TB.	2B.	3B.	HR.	RH.	SB.	CH.	Pct.
H. F. Heilmann, Detroit	R	144	524	121	211	331	44	11	18	23	8	7	.403
M. Archdeacon, Chicago	L	23	85		35	42	5	1	0	1	3		.402
G. H. Ruth, New York	L	152	522	151	205	399	45	13	41	5	17	21	.393
Tris Speaker, Cleveland	L	150	574	133	218	350	59	11	17	22	10	9	.380
G. E. Uhle, Cleveland	R	53	144	25	52	68	10	3	0	5	2	1	.361
E. T. Collins, Chicago	L	145	505	89	182	229	22	5	5	39	49	20	.360
K. R. Williams, St. Louis	L	147	555	106	198	360	37	12	29	10	18	17	.357
Joe Sewell, Cleveland	L	153	553	98	195	263	41	10	3	24	9	6	.353
C. P. Jamieson, Cleveland	L	152	644	130	222	284	26	12	2	12	19	12	.345
J. R. Cobb, Detroit	L	145	556	103	189	261	40	7	6	22	9	10	.340
Joe Harris, Boston	R	142	485	82	152	224	28	11	13	13	7	5	.335
H. Manush, Detroit	L	100	308	59	103	145	20	5	4	13	3	5	.334
George Burns, Boston	R	146	523	91	181	250	47	5	7	12	9	7	.328
H. W. Summa, Cleveland	L	157	575	78	180	229	20	6	3	25	9	13	.322
B. H. Veach, Detroit	L	114	296	52	119	135	13	3	2	14	10	4	.321
J. R. Stephenson, Cleveland	R	91	300	45	104	143	20	6	3	8	6	5	.319
J. T. Tobin, St. Louis	L	151	617	95	202	303	32	15	13	13	8	7	.317
G. Walberg, Philadelphia	L	28	41	1	13	17	1	0	0	3	0	0	.317
E. C. Rice, Washington	L	148	585	117	188	268	35	18	3	13	20	8	.316
Harold Ruel, Washington	R	136	449	63	142	172	24	3	0	21	4	6	.316
Hollis Thurston, St. Louis-Chicago	R	47	79	10	25	32	5	1	0	1	0	0	.316
E. E. Rigney, Detroit	R	129	470	63	148	197	24	11	1	33	7	5	.315
R. R. Fothergill, Detroit	R	101	241	34	76	101	18	2	1	11	4	4	.315
A. A. Strunk, Chicago	L	54	54	7	17	17	0	0	0	3	1	0	.315
L. W. Witt, New York	L	146	596	113	187	243	18	10	6	19	2	7	.314
J. I. Judge, Washington	L	113	407	76	127	189	24	6	2	18	11	7	.314
R. Meusel, New York	R	132	460	70	144	220	29	10	9	10	13	15	.313

WALTER JOHNSON HURLS NO-HITTER

Holds Browns Helpless for Seven Innings, Nats Winning, 2 to 0.

WASHINGTON, Aug. 25.—Holding St. Louis hitless, Johnson today pitched Washington to a 2 to 0 victory in the first game of a scheduled double header which was halted by rain after seven innings.

The second game was called off on account of wet grounds. It was Johnson's sixth scoreless game of the season and the 107th shutout victory of his career.

Davis forced in the first local run by issuing a base on balls with the bases filled in the third. The other tally was due to McNeely's single and a triple by Goslin in the seventh.

BANISHED GIANTS CALL ON LANDIS

Verdict is Unchanged, Says Commissioner.

(By Associated Press)

POLO GROUNDS, New York, Oct. 7.—The case against Jimmy O'Connell and Cozy Dolan, members of the New York Giants, banished from baseball for their part in an attempted bribery deal, remained "unchanged" today, Commissioner Landis announced, after he had received a visit from the two players, and told them both he had no reason now to change the verdict which expelled them from the game.

According to the commissioner, Dolan's principal object in visiting him was to explain that when he told Landis he "didn't remember" the circumstances related in O'Connell's confession, he, Dolan, meant he knew nothing about the whole affair. Dolan has steadily denied implication in the affair, as charged by O'Connell.

O'Connell, Landis said, had not received official notice of the action against him, and desired to clarify his position. He made no change in his confession, in which he implicated other Giants besides Dolan, according to the commissioner.

Cards Run Wild.

BROOKLYN, Sept. 16.—The St. Louis Cardinals pounded five Brooklyn pitchers for eighteen hits and a total of thirty-four bases today and won, 17 to 3.

Bottomley made six hits in six times up, including two homers in succession and a double for a total of thirteen bases.

He drove in twelve runs, which is believed to be an all time major league record.

Sherdell held the Dodgers safely for eight innings and then was retired to give Rehm a work out.

Ehrhardt was charged with the defeat, breaking his string of five straight victories.

TWO NEW RECORDS MADE BY HORNSBY

St. Louis Star Leads League in Batting Fifth Year in Row With Mark of .42351.

ST. LOUIS, Sept. 29.—Rogers Hornsby, Cardinal second baseman, today took a place beside the greatest hitters in baseball history. In the season just closed Hornsby established two new records, one in batting average and the other in leading his league for the fifth consecutive season.

Hornsby finished with 227 hits in 142 games, making a season average of .42351, 4 points above George Sisler's mark of two years ago. Sisler had an approximate .420 average which tied Tyrus Cobb's record set in 1911, the high mark of modern baseball.

The previous consecutive year batting record was held by Honus Wagner, who led his league four successive years.

Hornsby failed in his effort to lead the league in runs scored. He tallied only once in the double-header yesterday and thus raised his total to 121, which ties Frankie Frisch of the New York Giants.

Between games yesterday the Cardinal slugger was presented with a silver bat and ball, known as the Dick Richards trophy, for leading his team in batting.

GIANTS ARE FIRST TO WIN 4 IN ROW

Bentley Finds Phils Easy Picking in 5 to 1 Tilt that Tells Story.

NEW YORK, Sept. 27.—The New York Giants today broke a precedent of forty-one years and won the National League championship for the fourth time in succession by defeating Philadelphia here today, 6 to 1, while Brooklyn was losing to Boston.

No other National or American league club ever has won four successive pennants. Manager McGraw of New York was thwarted in his ambition for four straight pennant winners, when the Boston club beat out his Giants in a September finish ten years ago.

The championship is McGraw's tenth, twice as many as were won by any other National league managers.

Bentley found the Philadelphians easy picking and held the visitors to four hits. A muff by Jackson gave Philadelphia its only run in the first inning.

CAPITAL CITY IS IN UPROAR OVER VICTORY

Nothing is Quiet Along the Potomac When Wires Tell of Nats' Triumph Over Boston.

WHITE HOUSE SHARES IN GENERAL REJOICING

Coolidge to Attend Celebration for Champions Tomorrow.

BY JAMES L. WRIGHT.
Plain Dealer Bureau,
611 Albee Bldg.,
WASHINGTON, Sept. 29.

Wasington, wet and bedraggled, went home hilariously happy tonight.

Thousands who stood in the streets, unmindful of a steady downpour of rain, to watch electric scoreboards record the progress of the game in Boston that brought Washington its first major league pennant in all baseball history, threw their hats in the air and yelled at the top of their voices when the ninth inning ended with a double play, leaving Washington winner, 4 to 2.

Bedlam broke loose all over the District of Columbia.

Reprinted from
The Cleveland Plain Dealer

JOHNSON BATTLES TO HIS GOAL AT END OF EIGHTEEN-YEAR TRAIL

Crack of M'Neely's Bat in Twelfth Inning Kindles Conflagration of Wild Enthusiasm, in Which President Participates.

(By Associated Press)

WASHINGTON, Oct. 10.—The miracle of baseball, the dream of forty years, came true this afternoon when Washington won the baseball championship of the world from the New York Giants in the most thrilling, dramatic climax that any diamond series has seen.

Out of the depths of two crushing defeats, Walter Johnson, one of the greatest pitchers the game has ever known and idolised, came back to the heights and reached his goal, the end of the eighteen-year trail, by leading the Senators to victory by a score of 4 to 3 in twelve innings of spectacular, pulse-gripping baseball.

And when Earl McNeely, young outfielder from the Pacific coast, drove in Muddy Ruel with the winning run, after the mighty bat of Bucky Harris had kept the Senators in their greatest fight, the rookie also drove a vast crowd of more than 30,000 that included President and Mrs. Coolidge into an outburst of victory-inspired frenzy unprecedented in the history of the national game.

DAUBERT BURIAL PLANS ARRANGED

Body Will be Shipped to Jake's Old Home in Pennsy.

CINCINNATI, Oct. 9—The body of Jacob Ellsworth Daubert, veteran captain and beloved member of the Cincinnati National league baseball club who died in a hospital here early today, will be taken to his old home at Schuylkill Haven, Pa., for burial.

The body will lie in state at a funeral chapel here after 5 p. m. Friday. Funeral services probably will be held tomorrow evening by the Masonic and Elk orders, of which Daubert was a member.

Dr. Harry Hines, who operated on Daubert Oct. 1 for the removal of his appendix and to drain his gall bladder, said exhaustion resulting from indigestion was the immediate cause of death.

* * * *

Jacob Ellsworth Daubert was born April 17, 1885, in the mining town of Shamokin, Pa. He started his baseball career in 1906, playing his first professional engagement with the Kane (Pa.) semi-professional club. In 1907 he joined the Marion (O.) club, in the old Ohio-Pennsylvania league, and made his major league debut with Cleveland the following year, but was released under option to Nashville of the Southern league.

Recalled by Cleveland in 1909 Daubert was sold to Toledo in the American association and finished out the year with the Northern league. The next year Daubert went to Brooklyn where he became a regular first baseman, which position he held for nine seasons before coming to Cincinnati.

Reprinted from
The Cleveland Plain Dealer

STRICKEN SLUGGER IS RESTING WELL

Doctor Denies Early Reports Famous Hitter Has Concussion of Brain.

COLLAPSES AS TRAIN REACHES NEW YORK

New York, April 9.—(By The Associated Press.)—George Herman Ruth—baseball's mighty "Babe"—was resting comfortably in St. Vincent's Hospital tonight, suffering from influenza, acute indigestion and minor injuries suffered when he fainted and fell to the washroom of his private car, as the train was entering Pennsylvania station shortly after 1 o'clock this afternoon.

No Concussion of Brain.

Early reports from attending physicians said Ruth had a slight concussion of the brain and a possible fracture of the skull, but these were later denied at the hospital by Dr. Edward King, the New York American League doctor, who gave the home run slugger a thorough examination upon his arrival.

"Ruth is resting as comfortably as can be expected and is in no danger," said Dr. King immediately after the examination.

"He has a fever and a temperature of 10¹, but there is no concussion of the brain or evidence of a fracture of the skull."

The accident, which rendered Ruth unconscious for nearly two hours, happened as he was washing up preparatory to departing from the train. In company with Paul Kritchell, the New York American League scout, and a party of newspapermen, Ruth was returning from Asheville, N. C., where Tuesday he had suffered a slight attack of acute indigestion with a touch of influenza.

Just as the train was entering the Pennsylvania tube between Manhattan transfer, N. J., and the Pennsylvania station, Ruth entered the washroom. He asked Kritchell to get him a comb and prepared to wash his hands and face. While Kritchell was gone Ruth fainted and fell to the floor, striking his head against the washbasin, rendering him unconscious. He was picked up by Kritchell and newspapermen aboard the train and carried to his compartment.

Fans In Gloom.

Ruth's illness, coupled with the unverified report of his death which gained widespread publicity before it was officially denied, shrouded New York fandom in gloom and the Pennsylvania station was crowded with anxious baseball fans when the train arrived at the terminal.

The collapse of the mighty slugger was the culmination of a hectic morning for the fans. The report of his death, circulated late last night, had not been entirely cleared up until nearly noon. Newspapers were swamped with inquiries and everywhere in baseball circles there was an unsettled feeling.

RUTH PLAYS FOR FIRST TIME THIS SEASON— FAILS TO HIT

New York, June 1.—(Associated Press.)—"Babe" Ruth made his first major league appearance of the season today and failed to get a hit.

Features in Field.

In the clean-up position of the Yankees' batting order again after almost two months' confinement to a hospital with influenza and indigestion, Ruth's opening successes were limited to fielding features.

Both of the opportunities were presented the champion hitter of the American League in the fifth inning of the New York-Washington game, when he speared a high fly off the bat of Ruel and then made a spectacular running catch of Judge's drive, rolling over on the ground as he speared the ball.

Three times Ruth went to the plate to sample the pitching of the veteran Capital hero, Walter Johnson. Once he reached first base on a pass. On two other attempts, he grounded out to Johnson and to Harris.

Gets Rousing Ovation.

Ruth's return to the game was the signal for a rousing outburst by 18,000 fans and the frantic clicking of cameras. He was the first batter up in the second inning, and Johnson's initial pitch looked good to him. He lunged at it with a full swing, but the ball rolled weakly to the Washington pitcher.

In the fourth with Combs on first as the result of a single, Babe drew a pass. Meusel's double scored Combs, and "Babe" tried desperately to count also, but failed to post his first run of the season after a headlong slide to the plate as the ball arrived ahead of him by seconds.

After grounding out to Harris in the sixth, Ruth gave way to Veach, Manager Huggins considering it inadvisable to permit him to overexert himself in his first game of the year.

WRIGHT, PIRATES, HAS TRIPLE PLAY

Joins Unassisted Heroes as Cardinals Win, 10 to 9, on Six-Run Rally.

PITTSBURGH, May 7.—St. Louis came from behind today and, scoring six runs in the eighth, defeated Pittsburgh, 10 to 9. The feature of the game was a triple play, unassisted, by Glenn Wright, Pittsburgh shortstop, in the ninth inning. With Cooney and Hornsby on base, Bottomley hit a liner into Wright's hands. He touched second, retiring Cooney, who had started to third, and then touched out Hornsby, who had dashed for second.

'MISCONDUCT OFF FIELD' IS RESPONSIBLE

Star to be Out of Game Indefinitely; Assessment of $5,000 is Largest on Record.

HUGGINS SILENT ON WHEN LAYOFF WILL TERMINATE

Refuses to Give Specific Cause; Season Bad for Bambino.

ST. LOUIS, Aug. 29.—(AP)—Babe Ruth, baseball's premier slugger, today was fined $5,000 and suspended indefinitely by Manager Miller Huggins of the Yankees for "misconduct off the field."

Ruth made no comment when Huggins told him to pack up and leave St. Louis for New York.

At an early hour tonight Ruth could not be reached for a statement. He was said to have appeared at a residence in the West End, but left a few minutes before newspaper men arrived, saying that he intended catching a 5 o'clock train for New York.

Ruth was not on the train, however, and had not appeared at the station when it departed.

First news that there had been trouble came this afternoon when the Yankees took the field for the game against the Browns, and Ruth was absent from the line-up. Inquirers were informed that Ruth had deserted the club and gone to New York, but when Huggins was confronted with the report he admitted the fine and suspension, and that he had ordered the slugger to New York.

Huggins said that neither Col. Ruppert, owner of the Yankees, nor Business Manager Ed Barrows knew of his decision to suspend Ruth, nor had been consulted about it.

YANKS WIND UP BY BEATING ATHLETICS

Ruth and Meusel Crash Homers—Simmons Gets 251 Bingles.

New York, Oct. 3.—(Associated Press.) The New York Yankees ended their season today with a 9 to 5 victory over the Athletics giving the latter the edge on the year, thirteen triumphs and nine defeats.

Babe Ruth hit his twenty-fifth and Bob Meusel his thirty-third homer in the fifth while Earl Combs scored the winning tally with two out in the ninth. Meusel is the home run champion of the American League with Ruth now tied with Ken Williams for the runner up honors.

Al Simmons of the Athletics ran his season's hits to 251, seven short of Sisler's 1922 mark which stands as a baseball record.

HEILMANN TAKES BATTING HONORS

Detroit Slugger Overtakes Tris Speaker On Last Day Of Season.

Chicago, Oct. 4 (AP). Harry Heilmann, star slugger of the Detroit Tigers, is the new champion hitter of the American League. He overtook Tris Speaker, Cleveland manager, today, when he collected six hits in nine times at bat in the double-header against the St. Louis Browns.

Heilmann's unofficial average is .393 plus and Speaker's .390 plus. This is the second year Heilmann has won the batting honors. In 1921 he finished with .394. Speaker has not been playing regularly of late, his only appearance being as a pinch-hitter.

Heilmann's average is a result of 225 hits in 572 times at bat, while the Cleveland pilot's mark was attained on 167 hits in 428 times at bat.

1925 Home-Run Crown Captured By Hornsby

Chicago, Oct. 4 (AP).—Rogers Hornsby, manager of the St. Louis Cardinals, and champion hitter of the National League, is the 1925 home-run champion of the major leagues.

The St. Louis star hit thirty-nine in the season ended today, while his nearest rival, Bob Meusel, of the Yankees, came through with thirty-two. Babe Ruth, who holds the record for home runs in the Majors, with fifty-nine smashed out in 1921, got a late start this year and did not play regularly, but he cashed in with twenty-five, tying Ken Williams, of the St. Louis Browns, for third place among four-base clouters. In 1922 Hornsby had forty-two homers, a record for the National League.

Players with twenty or more circuit blows this season follow:

American League: Bob Meusel, New York, 33; Williams, St. Louis, 25; Ruth, New York, 25; Simmons Philadelphia 24; Gehrig New York, 20 National League: Hornsby, St. Louis, 39; Hartnett, Chicago, 24; Fournier, Brooklyn 22; Emil Meusel New York, 21; Kelly, New York, 20.

Oct. 5

'ROG' HORNSBY EQUALS MODERN RECORD BY HITTING .400 AGAIN

Rogers Hornsby has joined the immortal batsmen of baseball. As the National League curtain rang down yesterday the affable leader of the St. Louis Cards once more was out in front, making the sixth consecutive time "Rog" had done that trick, which is two seasons more than the great Wagner was able to do it. He is still shy a few years on the mark established, and which will likely never be equalled, by Ty Cobb, who led his league for 12 years, nine of these seasons consecutively. And by amassing an average of .403 this season, after having for a time dropped out of that select circle, Hornsby steps up on an even plane with Cobb and Jess Burkett, both of whom did this stunt three times.

Hornsby blossomed into a .300 hitter in 1916. Since that time he has only once fallen below that mark, and that was in 1918 the war year. Since 1920 Hornsby has not had a rival, and every season since that time he has been leading the pace.

His hitting mark since he began as a major leaguer is as follows:

1915	.246	1921	.397
1916	.313	1922	.401
1917	.327	1923	.384
1918	.281	1924	.424
1919	.318	1925	.403
1920	.370		

Wagner led his league eight times and in four of these years, 1906-7-8-9 grabbed off the honor which Hornsby took away from him last year. Cobb, with 12 titles hanging to his belt, for nine years showed the way, being the premier from 1907-18.

Not only has Hornsby been a leading hitter, but he has jumped to the front as a home-run hitter, having 39 this year, the best figure in either league. Last year he walloped 25 of these circuit blows while in 1922 he had 42, the high mark of National League slugging.

All of which puts Rog in the same breath with Anson, Brouthers, Kelly, Burkett, Duffy, Lajoie, Delehanty, Speaker and Sisler.

Reprinted from
The Pittsburgh Post

MATHEWSON, IDOL OF BALL FANS, DIES

Old Master Of Pitching Mound Victim Of Tuberculous Pneumonia.

END WAS UNEXPECTED

Health Began To Decline Five Years Ago Following Gasing In World War.

Saranac Lake, N. Y., Oct. 7 (AP). Christy Mathewson, baseball's "Big Six," lost his fight against tuberculosis at 11 o'clock tonight just as the game's great climax, the World Series, in which he played an all-important part in 1905, had got under way at Pittsburgh.

More than five years ago the great pitcher, loved and honored wherever the game is played, began what was to be a losing struggle. Gassed in the World War in France, where he served with distinction as a captain in the Chemical Warfare arm of the A. E. F., Mathewson returned from overseas to coach with the Giants, the club with which he won his fame, but the illness which was finally to take his life forced him to retire in 1920.

October 10, 1925

Honorable Kenesaw M. Landis,
Commissioner of Baseball,
Willard Hotel,
Washington, D.C.

My dear Judge Landis:

I called this evening to see you but did not find you in. I merely came to give you information which I think you should have and which you probably already have, in regard to the alleged home run of Catcher Smith of the Pirates.

When I returned to my hotel after the game I learned from a number of people who sat very near where the ball fell into the bleachers, that Rice did not catch the ball. It touched his glove and fell into the stand where it was retrieved by a colored man who handed it to Rice. Hundreds of people know that this ball was not caught. I don't know what you can do about the matter nor whether you are disposed to do anything. Mr. Erb, who is secretary for Honorable Stephen G. Porter, chairman of Foreign Relations Committee of the House, was one of the men who told me that Rice positively did not catch the ball. An ex-ballplayer who resides in Baltimore and who gave me his name and address, was within twenty feet of where the ball fell, and he tells me that the ball was not caught. I have the names of a number of other persons who say without the slightest qualification that Rice did not catch the ball. There seems to be an army of people from that section of the bleachers, largely Washington "fans", who know that a colored man handed the ball to Rice. Unfortunately the blunder in this case is Rigler's.

The situation is unfortunate and can do Baseball no good. No matter what else may be said about the situation Rigler's blunder uncorrected leaves Pittsburgh robbed of a run which in the interests of all fairness the team is entitled to.

If you care to have the personal statements of the man I refer to they can be had. I have furnished Mr. Fred Clark of the Pittsburgh team a memorandum of the evidence offered by a number of spectators.

For my identification I enclose my professional card. You may recall having received a letter from me last fall as a member of the Barney Dreyfuss Silver Anniversary celebration held at Pittsburgh. I wrote you at that time urging you to attend the banquet. My object in writing you is merely to acquaint you with what has happened and to impress upon your mind the fact that no doubt thousands of "fans" know that Smith is entitled to a home run and that in a spirit of fair play and honesty he should not be cheated out of it.

Very truly yours,

A. C. Thresher

Temporary address: Lee House
Washington, D.C.
Permanent Address: 541 Union Trust
Bldg. Pittsburgh, Pa.

Oct. 11

PROTEST OF RICE'S CATCH ABANDONED BY PIRATES

By the Associated Press.

CONTEMPLATED protest by Pittsburgh of today's Washington victory in the third world series game on the ground that Sam Rice failed to make a fair catch of Earl Smith's eight-inning drive to the centerfield bleachers was abandoned by Bill McKechnie, Pirate manager, after a conference with Commissioner Landis.

McKechnie, taking up the issue with Landis, was told that since a question of fact was involved, no protest could be considered, since the umpire's judgment—in this case that of Charles Rigler—could not be reversed off the field.

Oct. 11

FEAT OF RICE UNRIVALED IN ANNALS OF BASE BALL

Nerve of Marberry in Ninth Approaches Best Ever Shown in Pastime — Puzzling Bunt by Goose Helped Much in Victory.

BY JOHN B. KELLER.

FANS of ancient vintage and usually blase veteran players who saw the 1924 world series pronounced it the most thrilling and dramatic they had ever witnessed in the more than 20 years the champions of the two big leagues had struggled for base ball's supreme laurels. Now these same critics claim that the present fight between Nationals and Pirates will excel that between Nationals and Giants for dramatic intensity and brilliancy of individual effort.

In the first game, the sparkling Walter Johnson made world series history when he pitched one of the greatest games of his illustrious career. In the second game, Victor Aldridge bested Stanley Coveleskie in one of the keenest pitching duels ever staged in the annual classics. In yesterday's contest Sam Rice and Fred Marberry did much to make that third clash of the series the most colorful ever recorded in the annals of the yearly championship fight.

Rice's Catch Unrivaled.

Without question that catch by Rice in the eighth inning that kept a tying home run from Earl Smith was the most wonderful fielding feat ever accomplished in or out of a world series. And without question Marberry's steadiness while pitching in that tense ninth inning excelled by far the performance that won fame for Aldridge in the fifth and ninth innings of the game in Pittsburgh on Thursday.

Old base ball men, players and writers, searched their memories for a catch that could rival Rice's, but found none. Clark Griffith, president of the Nationals, who played base ball when the game was in short trousers and since has followed the sport in administrative capacities, declared he had never seen any catch approaching it. "It was a catch you are lucky to witness in a lifetime," Griffith said. "I have seen many fine catches by famous outfielders, but Rice's was far ahead of any of them."

Nick Altrock, coach of the Nationals, who has been in and around base ball almost as long as Griffith, was rendered almost speechless by Rice's stunt.

Speaker's 700th Double

Chisox 7, Indians 2

Cleveland, Aug. 11—(Associated Press)—After pitching brilliantly for twelve innings, Shaute weakened after two were out in the 13th inning and Chicago scored five runs, winning 7 to 2. Lyons started the winning rally with a single. Mostil doubled. Hunnefield singled, scoring two runs. Sheely doubled, scoring another while Falk's home run scored two more. Falk made five hits in six times up.

An error of judgment by Shaute allowed Chicago to score its first run and prevented him winning in nine innings. With a runner on third, he elected to throw to first for the put out and allowed the runner to score.

Edwards pitched effectively for seven innings but retired because of lame knee.

Burns hit his fifty-third double of the season in the thirteenth. Score:

CHICAGO.

	A.B.	R.	H.	P.O.	A.	E.
Mostil, cf	6	1	2	2	0	0
Hunnefield, 2b	6	1	2	5	8	0
Sheely, 1b	6	1	2	2	0	0
Falk, lf	6	3	5	1	0	0
Barrett, rf	6	0	1	3	0	0
Kamm, 3b	5	0	1	1	3	0
Schalk, c	6	0	0	3	1	0
Berg, ss	5	0	0	3	4	0
Edwards, p	3	0	0	0	1	0
Lyons, p	2	1	1	0	0	0
Totals	50	7	13	39	18	0

CLEVELAND.

	A.B.	R.	H.	P.O.	A.	E.
Jamieson, lf	6	1	1	4	0	0
Spurgeon, 2b	5	0	1	3	5	0
Speaker, cf	6	0	2	5	0	0
Burns, 1b	5	0	1	19	0	0
J. Sewell, ss	5	0	1	4	6	0
Summa, rf	5	0	1	1	1	0
L. Sewell, c	4	0	0	0	0	0
Myatt, c	0	0	1	0	4	0
Lutzke, 3b	5	0	0	0	3	0
Shaute, p	5	0	0	0	0	0
McNulty, z	1	0	0	0	0	0
Totals	46	2	10	39	19	0

Score by innings:

Chicago ...... 010 100 000 000—7
Cleveland .... 100 000 100 000—2

Two base hits, Falk, Mostil, Sheely, Speaker, L. Sewell, Lutzke, Burns; home run, Falk; sacrifice, J. Sewell; double plays, Berg to Hunnefield to Sheely, Hunnefield to Sheely; left on base, Chicago 6, Cleveland 1; base on balls, off Edwards 1, Lyons 3; struck out, by Edwards 1; hits, off Edwards 7 in 7, Lyons 3 in 6; winning pitcher, Lyons; umpires, Moriarity, Ormsby and Hildebrand; time, 3.27.

z—McNulty batted for Summa in 13th.

Sept. 27

Second Place for Cleveland

Cleveland—(AP)—Cleveland won second place in the American league Monday by defeating Philadelphia, 5 to 4. It was Uhle's twenty-seventh victory of the season. George Burns, who made his sixty-fourth 2-base hit of the year, drove in all of Cleveland's runs.

PHILADELPHIA					CLEVELAND				
	AB	R	H	E		AB	R	H	E
Dykes,2b	5	1	2	1	Jamieson,lf	4	2	1	0
French,rf	2	0	0	0	Spurgeon,2b	4	1	1	0
Grove,p	2	0	0	0	Speaker,cf	3	1	1	0
Jenkins,cf	4	0	0	0	Burns,1b	4	0	3	0
Hale,3b	3	1	1	0	J.Sewell,ss	4	0	0	0
Simmons,cf	4	1	2	0	Summa,rf	4	0	1	0
Poole,1b	3	0	0	0	L.Sewell,c	3	0	1	0
Cochrane,c	3	0	1	0	Lutzke,3b	4	1	1	0
Galloway,ss	4	0	2	1	Uhle,p	3	0	0	0
Grove,p	0	0	0	0					
Quinn,p	0	0	0	0	Totals	33	5	10	0
Welch,rf	2	0	0	0					
Metzler,cf	1	0	0	0					
Lamar	1	0	1	0					
Wamby	0	1	0	0					
Totals	34	4	9	3					

Metzler batted for Grove in second. Lamar batted for French in fifth. Wamby ran for Lamar in fifth.

Philadelphia .. 0 1 0 0 3 0 0 0 0—4
Cleveland ..... 2 0 1 0 1 0 0 0 1—5

Two base hits—Lamar, Summa, Burns, L. Sewell; Three-base hit—Simmons; Stolen base—Spurgeon; Sacrifices—Poole, Welch, Speaker, L. Sewell; Left on base—Philadelphia 7, Cleveland 10; Bases on balls—Off Grove 1, Quinn 1, Uhle 3; Struck out—By Gray 3, Uhle 6; Hits—Off Grove 2 in 1 inning; Gray 6 in 4 1/3, Quinn 2 in 3; Losing pitcher—Gray.

Big Train Wins His 400th Game for A. L. Champs

Washington—In defeating the St. Louis Browns Wednesday afternoon, 7 to 4, Walter Johnson won the four hundredth game of his major league career. It was the Big Train's sixth victory in seven starts this season.

Walter Johnson

This is the veteran's twentieth year in the American league. Old Barney, who has spent his entire career as a member of the Capitol team, broke into the American league in 1907. He is 38 years old. His victory Wednesday marked game No. 655 he has been either credited with winning or charged with losing. His record by years:

	Games won		Games won
1907	5	1917	23
1908	14	1918	23
1909	13	1919	20
1910	25	1920	8
1911	25	1921	17
1912	32	1922	15
1913	36	1923	17
1914	28	1924	23
1915	27	1925	20
1916	25	1926	6

Johnson's average for the 20 years is .611.

Johnson Chalks Up Sixth Win This Year

Washington—Tom Zachary had nothing with which to fool his former mates Wednesday and Washington made it two straight over St. Louis, winning, 7 to 4. It was Johnson's sixth victory and fifth in a row.

ST. LOUIS					WASHINGTON				
	AB	R	H	E		AB	R	H	E
H. Rice,2b	5	0	1	1	McNeely,cf	4	2	1	0
Durst,rf	4	1	2	0	S. Harris,2b	3	2	2	0
Sisler,1b	4	0	1	0	S. Rice,rf	4	0	2	0
Williams,lf	4	1	1	0	Goslin,lf	4	0	2	0
McManus,3b	4	1	2	0	Judge,1b	3	0	1	0
Jacobson,cf	4	0	2	0	Bluege,3b	4	0	1	1
Lamotte,ss	4	0	1	0	Peck,ss	3	1	0	0
Dixon,c	3	0	0	0	Ruel,c	4	1	2	0
Zachary,p	3	1	1	0	Johnson,p	3	1	1	0
Davis,p	0	0	0	0					
Schang	1	0	0	0	Totals	34	7	14	1
Hargrave	1	0	0	0					
Totals	35	4	9	2					

Schang batted for Dixon in ninth.
Hargrave batted for Davis in ninth.

St. Louis .... 0 0 0 3 0 0 1 0 0—4
Washington ..... 2 1 0 1 2 0 1 x—7

Two-base hits—Zachary, S. Harris, Goslin, Jacobson. Three-base hits—McNeely, McManus, S. Rice. Stolen bases—Ruel, S. Harris. Sacrifices—S. Rice, Judge 2, Lamotte, Johnson 2. Double play—Bluege to Judge. Left on bases—St. Louis 7, Washington 8. Bases on balls—Off Johnson 1, Davis 1. Struck out—By Davis 1, Johnson 4. Hits—Off Zachary 12 in 7 innings; 2 more out in eighth; Davis 2 in 1. Balk Zachary. Losing pitcher Zachary.

Reprinted from
The Milwaukee Journal

RULING ON PIRATES UPHELD BY HEYDLER

But National League Head Says Ousted Trio Acted From "Mistaken Zeal."

PITTSBURGH, August 17—(AP)—The attempt of three veteran Pittsburgh National league players to oust Fred Clarke, assistant manager, from the bench, was termed "mistaken zeal" to further what they honestly believed to be for the best interests of the club, John Heydler, president of the league, said tonight after holding extended hearings into the controversy.

The league executive added that should the players, Max Carey, Carson Bigbee and Babe Adams leave the team, "they will do so with a good name."

Summing up his findings, the league executive, whose only action was to clear the names of the players, said:

Clears Their Good Names.

"I cannot go back of the right of the officials of a league club to release, suspend, or ask waivers on any of its players, nor would I wish to do so if I had the right; but it is my opinion after a most complete and thorough hearing of this case that none of the three players—Carey, Bigbee and Adams—has been guilty of wilful insubordination of malicious intent to disrupt or injure the club.

Heydler came to Pittsburgh to inquire into the affair when he was appealed to by Carey, who contended that he and his two team-mates had not been given a fair hearing before their dismisal, which Dreyfuss, treasurer, and Bill McKechnie, manager.

The league head held a number of secret hearings, the first being attended by club officials and the players. Later he met with Carey alone and prior to issuing his statement tonight, he conferred again with Dreyfuss and Clarke.

Heydler said he felt that the three players, by reason of their long and honorable baseball career, "were entitled to a full hearing of any grievance they may have in their passing or threatened passing from the Pittsburgh club." They have been charged with stirring up dissension among Pirate players, he said, and with being ringleaders in an attempt to drive Clarke from the bench.

COVETED ST. LOUIS STAR OVER STRETCH OF YEARS

Trades Frisch and Ring for Cardinal Manager in Biggest Deal in Pastime's History—Worth of Players Involved Put at $350,000.

By the Associated Press.

NEW YORK, December 21.—The biggest deal in modern base ball history, involving players whose diamond worth is estimated at more than half a million dollars, brings Rogers Hornsby of the world champion Cardinals to share the metropolitan spotlight with Babe Ruth.

The transaction was completed last night over the telephone after Hornsby and President Sam Breadon of the St. Louis team had failed to bridge a gap resulting from Rogers' demand for a three-year contract.

Although rumblings of negotiations for Hornsby's services by Manager John McGraw had reached base ball row, many observers believed that Breadon would be unwilling to part with his brilliant second baseman, the first manager to bring St. Louis a pennant in 38 years.

Believe Money Involved.

Base ball men today insisted that Hornsby was worth more to the Giants than the two players McGraw gave in exchange—Infielder Frankie Frisch and Pitcher Jimmy Ring. They maintained that a cash payment of at least $100,000 in addition to Frisch and Ring would be required to satisfy the Cardinals. Presidents Breadon and Charles A. Stoneham of the Giants denied, however, that any money payment had been involved. Hornsby's value is estimated at $350,000.

According to President Stoneham, Breadon broached the trade to him, suggesting Frisch and Ring in payment. Denying that the trade had been arranged prior to his telephone conversation with the Cardinal owner, Stoneham asserted that he "was as much surprised as anybody."

"We had talked with Breadon about Hornsby in an offhand way," admitted the Giant owner, "but the negotiations did not get very far. We were not very hopeful."

For several years McGraw has cast longing eyes on Hornsby, six-time National League batting champion. A few years ago the Giant manager offered $250,000 and several players for the great Cardinal second sacker.

ALEXANDER CUTS YANKS' GORDIAN KNOT, 3 TO 2, IN LAST TWO STANZAS

Old-Time Hurler Puts Out Lazzeri and Allows Ruth to Take Base on Balls After Haines Had Passed Him; Koenig and Meusel Are Left Handed "Heroes" Through Fumbles; St. Louis Gets All Runs in Fourth Inning.

BY HENRY P. EDWARDS.

YANKEE STADIUM, Oct. 10.—Alexander the Great again came to the rescue today and the St. Louis Cardinals carried off the deciding battle of the world series 3 to 2.

It was in the seventh inning of the seventh game that he made his third appearance of the classic. The Cardinals led by a single run, but the bases were filled with American leaguers.

An American league crowd was yelling frenziedly as Tony Lazzeri, the Italian boy from Telegraph Hill, San Francisco, went to bat.

Jess Haines, stalwart right-hander, was on the rubber. Something was wrong with him. He had allowed a hit and had walked two of his adversaries. But, there were two out.

Lazzeri strode to the plate, determination in his eye, Rogers Hornsby, St. Louis manager and his fellow infielders clustered about their pitcher.

"Go on with the game! Make him pitch," yelled the crowd.

Umpire Hildebrand ran down to the pitcher's box.

Up went Hornsby's hand. He was signaling to the bullpen hidden behind the left field bleachers. But no one came in answer to the summons.

Yank Fans Start Roar.

"Make him pitch," yelled the Yankee fans again.

Again Hornsby signalled without result. Then Left Fielder Hafey turned in his tracks and ran back to relay the summons.

A red-sweatered form appeared around the corner.

"Who is it?" was the cry that rippled through the stands.

"Alexander!" was the answer that was roared back.

Yes, it was Alexander, Grover Cleveland Alexander, who sauntered nonchalantly in from that far off corner of baseball's greatest amphitheater. And the original Alexander, the Great, never received a greater reception than did this thirty-nine-year-old pitcher, who was discarded by the Chicago Cubs, but a few short months ago.

Never was greater homage bestowed on that famous monarch of the days of long ago than on this sorrel-topped, freckled-faced, weather-beaten hurler, hero of fifteen campaigns in the major leagues as he slowly trudged across the turf to where his colleagues awaited him.

Nonchalantly, he tossed his sweater to one of his mates.

"Who's up?" he asked.

"Lazzeri."

"How many out?"

"Two."

"Don't worry. Keep your shirts on."

Reprinted from
The Cleveland Plain Dealer

Ty Cobb and Speaker Deny 'Throwing' Ball Game

Dutch Leonard Lies, Is Answer of Tris

CHICAGO—(AP)—The attention of the baseball world centered Wednesday on a 7-year-old game, that between the Detroit and Cleveland American league teams on Sept. 25, 1919, around which charges of fixing, involving two of the greatest players known to the game, have been made.

The long smoldering bombshell, the subject of many recent rumors, broke Tuesday and sent fragments into many places, but Wednesday those named as conspirators came back quickly with denials of wrongdoing.

Ty Cobb and Tris Speaker, idols of thousands of baseball fans, and holders of many baseball records, declared they were innocent of assertions that they were involved in a conspiracy to "throw" the ball game and to benefit by betting on the outcome of the contest, made by Hubert (Dutch) Leonard, one time pitcher for Detroit, and made public by Baseball Commissioner Landis.

In addition they declared they had attempted to get Leonard, now living on a ranch in California, to face them, and Commissioner Landis, in giving out Leonard's testimony, mentioned that the former ball player repeatedly had refused to present the charges at a hearing at which Cobb and Speaker could be present. Finally the commissioner called upon Leonard in his California home.

Never Bet, Says Ty

Cobb, who recently resigned as manager of the Tigers, said in Chicago that he had "never bet a cent on an American league baseball game," and denied that he knew of any plan to "throw" the game, while Speaker, who likewise resigned his managerial berth with Cleveland after the close of the season, asserted in Cleveland that he was "innocent of any wrongdoing," charging that "Leonard deliberately falsified any statement he has made that implicates me."

Commissioner Landis, in making public 100 pages of testimony in the case, made no ruling because Cobb, Speaker, Leonard and Joe Wood, the Cleveland pitcher mentioned in the case, all were out of baseball, but said that a decision as to the attitude of organized baseball would be forthcoming if required by changed conditions.

Leonard's testimony was that Cobb, Speaker, Wood and himself met under the grandstand of Navin field, Detroit, on Sept. 24, 1919, and agreed that Detroit should win its game with Cleveland the following day, giving the Tigers a chance to finish third in the American league pennant race. In addition, Leonard said, the four planned to benefit on the outcome, with each putting up a sum of money, but that only he and Wood won $130 apiece when Detroit won, as Cobb and Speaker did not put up their share of the money. The charges were supported by two letters, one from Wood and another from Cobb, both containing allusions to betting.

Ty Acknowledges Letter

Cobb acknowledged he had sent a letter to Leonard, but called the bet to which it referred as wholly legitimate and one of the sort frequently entered into by baseball players. The Georgia Peach said that, while he refused to bet on games in his own league, it was a frequent custom among players to make such bets. "I have been in baseball 22 years," he said. "I have played the game as hard and square and clean as any man ever did. All I thought of was to win, every year, every month, every day, every hour. My conscience is clear. I will rest my case with the American fans."

The Fatal Game

Cleveland—	AB	R	H	PO	A	E
Graney, lf	4	1	2	1	0	1
Lunte, ss	4	1	2	1	5	1
Speaker, cf	3	2	3	0	0	0
Harris, 1b	5	0	1	11	1	1
Gardner, 3b	5	0	0	2	6	0
Wambsganss, 2b	3	0	1	3	4	0
Smith, rf	4	0	1	2	0	0
O'Neil, c	4	1	1	4	2	0
Myers, p	4	0	1	0	3	0
Totals	36	5	12	24	21	3
Detroit—	AB	R	H	PO	A	E
Bush, ss	4	2	2	2	1	0
Young, 2b	4	0	0	4	1	0
Cobb, cf	5	2	3	1	1	0
Veach, lf	4	1	2	4	0	0
Heilmann, 1b	4	0	2	9	2	0
Shorten, rf	4	1	3	1	0	0
Jones, 3b	4	0	1	1	2	0
Ainsmith, c	3	2	2	1	1	0
Roland, p	2	1	1	2	2	0
Totals	35	9	16	27	14	0

Cleveland .... 0 0 2 0 1 1 1 0 0—5
Detroit .... 2 2 0 0 2 1 0 2 *—9

Two-base hits — Harris, Heilmann, Graney. Three-base hits—Speaker, 2; Roland. Struck out—By Myers, 1. Sacrifice hits—Young, Ainsmith, Lunte, Roland, Gardner. Stolen bases—Bush, Cobb 2. Bases on balls—Off Roland, 2. Double play—Bush, Young and Heilmann. Left on bases—Detroit, 5; Cleveland, 5. Wild pitch—Roland. Time—1:06. Umpires — Nallin and Owens.

Always Played to Win—Cobb

Chicago—(AP)—Here are some statements made in connection with the new baseball disclosure concerning the Detroit-Cleveland game of Sept. 25, 1919:

Ty Cobb—I have played the game as hard and square and clean as any man ever did. All I thought of was to win. There are two fellows absolutely clean. I know I am and I think the same of Speaker.

Tris Speaker—I know nothing of any wagers being made in this contest or of any fixing. The only thing they have against me is the word of a man who is behind this flareup, Leonard.

Hubert (Dutch) Leonard, Former Detroit Pitcher—I will not deny or affirm the commissioner's statement. I wish to be noncommittal at present.

E. S. Barnard, President of the Cleveland Club— While both Speaker and Cobb from the inception of the charge have denied their personal participation in the matter, there is conclusive evidence to prove that there was something wrong with the game in question.

Frank J. Navin, President of the Detroit Club—Commissioner Landis has the entire matter in charge. Whatever statement he makes at this time will be sufficient.

Ban Johnson, President of the American League—Both Cobb and Speaker saw the handwriting on the wall and decided to pull out.

Elmer Myers, Who Pitched for Cleveland—I was sent out to win and that's what I tried to accomplish. I know nothing of any betting.

Dick Nallin, Who Umpired—One of the requirements of our job was to make reports of unusual conditions and I saw none.

Feb. 9

Ty Cobb Signs

Peach to Receive Salary of $60,000

PHILADELPHIA — (AP) — Tyrus Raymond Cobb will wear the uniform of the Philadelphia Athletics this year.

The veteran of 22 American league pennant campaigns has accepted the terms of Manager Connie Mack and probably will close his baseball career as a member of Mack's team. The contract is for the season of 1927 and Cobb has announced that he will retire from the game at the close of the season.

The Georgia Peach announced at the Philadelphia sports writers' dinner, where he was a guest Monday night, that he had accepted Mack's offer, the terms of which he said would have to be disclosed by the manager of the Athletics if they were to be made public. Mack declined to discuss the financial details.

Persons close to both Cobb and Mack said the contract called for $60,000 — $25,000 for signing, $25,000 salary and a $10,000 bonus. Others placed the amount at $75,000. Either figure would be the highest salary ever paid a baseball player.

NEUN'S TRIPLE PLAY FEATURES TIGER VICTORY

DETROIT, May 31 (A. P.)—Johnny Neun, substitute first baseman, made a triple play unassisted as the Tigers shutout Cleveland, 1 to 0, here today. In the ninth inning, with Myatt on second and Jamieson on first, Summa lined to Neun. Neun caught the ball without moving out of his tracks, ran over and tagged Jamieson. He then raced to second and reached it before Myatt could return. The score:

DETROIT	ab	bh	po	a	CLEVELAND	ab	bh	po	a
Warner,3.					Jamieson.lf				
Gehringer,2					Summa.r.				
Manush,cf					Fonseca,2				
Fothergill,lf					Burns,1.			10	
Heilman,r.					J. Sewell,s				
Neun,1.			18		L Sewell,c.				
Tavener,s					Nels.cf				
Woodall,c.					Hodapp,3.				
Collins,p.					Buckeye,p				
					*Myatt				
Totals...	36	6	27	17	Totals ..	27	4	24	15

*Batted for Buckeye in ninth.

Innings	1	2	3	4	5	6	7	8	9	
Detroit	1	0	0	0	0	0	0	0	—	1

Run, Warner. Error, L. Sewell. Three-base hit, L. Sewell. Double plays, Hodapp, Fonseca and Burns; J. Sewell, Fonseca and Burns; Buckeye, Fonseca and Burns; Collins, Gehringer and Neun. Triple play, Neun (unassisted). Left on bases, Cleveland 2, Detroit 5. Base on balls, off Buckeye 1, off Collins 1. Struck out by Collins. Time, 1h 54m. Umpires, Evans, Hildebrand and McGowen.

May 30

Bucs' Winning Streak Halted

Pittsburgh—(P)—Jimmy Cooney, Chicago National's shortstop, executed an unassisted triple play in the fourth inning of the morning game Monday. With L. Waner on second and Barnhart on first, Cooney took P. Waner's liner, stepped on second and tagged Barnhart.

After seeing their 11-game winning streak shattered by the Cubs in the morning, 7 to 6, the Pirates came back in the afternoon to win, 6 to 5.

July 18

TY COBB MAKES 4000TH SAFE DRIVE AS A MAJOR LEAGUER

Double at Detroit Puts Famous Georgian on Mark Never Approached by Any Other Hitter in Long History of Diamond Game

By A. C. GIBSON

By hitting safely yesterday, Tyrus Raymond Cobb, famous son of Georgia, established a record which has never been approached by any of the great batsmen who have flashed across the baseball stage, gathered their base hits for their allotted spell and then passed from the diamond picture.

For yesterday Ty Cobb sent his 4000th safe drive—a double—sizzling out of the reach of hostile fielders and set a mark which probably will go down through the ages to come as the only feat of its kind in the history of the diamond game. It was appropriate that he reached that wonderful mark in Detroit, the city where he played so long.

Four thousand hits—think of it! Hans Wagner, "Cap" Anson, Dan Brouthers, Larry Lajoie, all the mighty club swingers of all the years major league baseball

Reaches 4000-Hit Goal

When the 1927 campaign opened the greatest manufacturer of hits the world has ever seen was far out in front of the pack, having amassed 3902. Now he has placed to his credit the 98 he needed to reach the 4000 goal and by a huge margin leads the big parade of swatsmiths.

Not only in number of hits, but in average and in almost every other branch of offensive play, the mighty Georgian stands out. Nine times he has made 200 or more safe drives in a single season, 212 in 1907, 216 in 1909, 248 in 1911, 227 in 1912, 208 in 1915, 201 in 1916, 225 in 1917, 211 in 1922 and the same number in 1924.

Thrice Cobb has had an average of better than .400, and never since the year he broke in, 1905, in which he played only 41 games, has he fallen below the .300 mark.

Reprinted from
The Detroit News

YANKEES SHOW CLASS BEATING THE WHITE SOX

CHICAGO, Aug 16 (A. P.)—Paced by Babe Ruth, who drove his 37th homer of the season over the double-decked stands in right field in the fifth inning, the Yankees walloped Chicago, 8 to 1, today. Ruth's clout, placing him one behind his team mate, Lou Gehrig, was one of the longest of the Babe's career. No one was on base at the time.

The Yankee assault drove Al Thomas from the mound at the end of five innings. Bert Cole finished the game. Bob Meusel, who has been in a batting slump, pulled out today with four hits and a sacrifice in five trips to the plate. The score:

NEW YORK	ab	bh	po	a	CHICAGO	ab	bh	po	a
Combs,cf	5	2	2	0	Flaska'per,s	3	1	3	4
Koenig,s	5	1	2	0	Kamm,3	4	1	2	2
Ruth,lf	3	2	3	1	Metzler,c	3	0	1	0
Gehrig,1	4	1	10	0	Barrett,r	3	0	3	0
Meusel,r	4	4	1	0	Falk,lf	2	0	4	0
Lazzeri,2	4	0	5	1	Cole,p	2	0	0	1
Dugan,3	4	1	1	5	Ward,2	4	3	2	4
Collins,c	4	2	3	1	Clancy,1	4	1	11	0
Pennock,p	2	0	0	4	Berg,c	2	0	0	0
					Thomas,p	1	0	0	2
Totals	35	13	27	14	Nels,lf	3	1	0	0
					Totals	33	9	27	11

Innings	1	2	3	4	5	6	7	8	9	
New York	2	0	2	0	1	0	0	3	0	—8
Chicago	0	0	0	0	0	0	1	0	0	—1

Runs, Combs 2, Koenig 2, Ruth 2, Gehrig, Collins, Ward. Error, Berg. Two-base hits, Meusel, Gehrig, Berg 2, Ward, Combs, Ruth. Three-base hit, Combs. Home run, Ruth. Stolen base, Meusel. Sacrifices, Pennock 2, Meusel, Lazzeri, Metzler. Double plays, Ruth and Collins; Dugan, Lazzeri and Gehrig; Flaskamper, Ward and Clancy 2. Left on bases, New York 8, Chicago 3. Base on balls, by Thomas 3, by Pennock 1, by Cole. Struck out, by Pennock 2, by Thomas. Hits, off Thomas, 7 in 5 innings; off Cole, 6 in 4 innings. Hit by pitcher, by Pennock, Flaskamper. Losing pitcher, Thomas. Time, 2h 4m. Umpires, Geisel, Rowland and Connolly.

GEHRIG TIES RUTH IN HOME RUN MARATHON

NEW YORK, Sept 5 (A. P.)—Lou Gehrig caught up with Babe Ruth again in the home run race by banging No. 44 off Ruffing in the first clash with the Red Sox today. Cy Williams of the Phils increased his National League home run mark to 26 by connecting for two four-baggers at Brooklyn. The Ruth-Gehrig standing:

	Yankees' Games	Homers
Ruth, 1921	131	55
Ruth, 1927	131	44
Gehrig, 1927	131	44

RUTH HITS NO. 55 AS YANKEES LOSE

NEW YORK, Sept 21 (A. P.)—The Yankees gave their worst fielding exhibition of the season today and lost the opener of a series to Detroit, 6 to 1, running the Bengal winning streak to seven. Sam Gibson pitched a strong game for the Tigers and had the New Yorkers shutout until Babe Ruth hit his 55th home run of the year in the ninth. Not only were the Hugmen guilty of six errors, but all sorts of mental lapses cropped out, with throws to wrong bases and failures to throw the ball. The score:

DETROIT	ab	bh	po	a	NEW YORK	ab	bh	po	a
Blue,1	3	1	11	1	Combs,cf	5	1	3	0
Gehringer,2	4	2	1	2	Koenig,s	5	0	4	2
Manush,cf	4	1	1	0	Ruth,r	5	3	4	1
Heilmann,r	5	3	1	0	Gehrig,1	4	2	9	0
Foth'gill,lf	4	1	4	0	Meusel,lf	3	0	1	0
McManus,3	3	0	4	1	Lazzeri,2	4	0	2	4
Tavener,s	5	2	0	4	Dugan,3	4	0	1	4
Woodall,c	4	1	5	0	P Collins,c	4	1	3	0
Gibson,p	4	0	0	2	Ruether,p	3	0	0	3
Totals	36	11	27	10	Totals	37	7	27	13

Innings	1	2	3	4	5	6	7	8	9	
Detroit	0	1	0	3	0	1	0	1	0	—6
New York	0	0	0	0	0	0	0	0	1	—1

Runs, Blue 2, Gehringer, Manush, Heilmann, McManus, Ruth. Errors, Blue, Gehringer, Tavener, Gibson, Combs, Koenig 3, Gehrig, Lazzeri. Two base hit, Gehrig. Home run, Ruth. Stolen bases, Blue, Gehringer. Sacrifices, Fothergill, McManus. Double plays, Dugan, Lazzeri and Gehrig; Ruth and Koenig; Gehringer and Blue. Left on bases, New York 14, Detroit 10. Base on balls, by Ruether 5, by Gibson 5. Struck out, by Ruether, by Gibson 4. Time, 1h 45m. Umpires, Nallin and Ormsby.

BAMBINO HAS 12 MORE HOMERS TO GO FOR RECORD OF 59

NEW YORK, Sept 6 (A. P.)—The close National League race was obliged to share the spotlight with one Babe Ruth today, the Yanks' big gun crashing out three homers during a double session at Boston to tie his last season's total of 47. Two of them were made in the first game. At this corresponding period in 1921, Ruth's gala year, the Babe had accumulated 54 homers. With 21 contests left on the New York schedule, the Bambino will have to knock out 12 more home runs to catch up with his record. Gehrig connected for his 45th circuit belt in the first game. The standing:

	Yankees' Games Played	Homers
Ruth, 1921	133	54
Ruth, 1927	133	47
Gehrig, 1927	133	45

Ban Retires as A. L. Head

Chicago—(AP)—The resignation of Byron Bancroft Johnson, founder and president of the American league for 27 years, was accepted Monday by the league's board of directors.

Frank Navin, vice president of the league and head of the Detroit club, said he would take charge of the league's affairs until a meeting could be called and Johnson's successor elected.

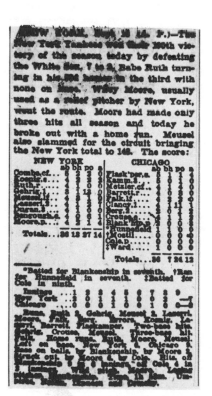

NEW YORK, Sept 29 (A. P.)—The New York Yankees won their 109th victory of the season today by defeating the White Sox, 7 to 2, Babe Ruth turning in his 59th homer in the third with none on base. Wiley Moore, usually used as a relief pitcher by New York, went the route. Moore had made only three hits all season and today he broke out with a home run. Meusel also slammed for the circuit bringing the New York total to 148. The score:

NEW YORK	ab	bh	po	a	CHICAGO	ab	bh	po	a
Combs,cf					Flask'per,s				
Koenig,s					Kamm,3				
Ruth,r					Metzler,cf				
Gehrig,1					Barrett,r				
Meusel,lf					Falk,lf				
Lazzeri,2					Clancy,1				
Dugan,3					Berg,c				
Bengough,c					Blankenship,p				
Moore,p					Connally,p				
					Cissell				
Totals	36	13	27	14	Ward				
					Totals	36	7	24	12

*Batted for Blankenship in seventh. †Ran for Barnfield in seventh. ‡Batted for Cole in ninth.

RUTH WITH 60th HOMER MAKES 1927 BANNER YEAR

By the Associated Press.

NEW YORK, October 1.—The base ball season has ended successfully for Babe Ruth. In the next to the last game of the Yanks in the American League season Babe produced No. 60 yesterday, establishing a new record for home runs in a single season.

While some 8,000 fans got a thrill, Ruth crashed the ball into the bleachers to erase his old mark of 59, first achieved by himself in 1921, which he tied on Thursday.

Babe has been pulling for the new mark for six years. The veteran pitcher, Tom Zachary, had the distinction of hurling the ball which made the dream come true. It happened in the eighth inning, with one strike and one ball on the Babe.

Col. Ruppert paid more than $1,000 for each home run, as the idol of the base ball fans rates $70,000 per year.

Since 1915, when he started bludgeoning with the Boston Red Sox, Ruth has made 416 of his mammoth wallops. Figure demons have doped out that if the distances of Ruth's 416 big drives were pieced together they would stretch for 50 miles. Delving further, it has been found that the Babe has traveled approximately 30 miles on the base paths in scoring on all circuit belts.

Not until 1919 did Ruth start corraling four-baggers to any noticeable extent. He made 29 in that season, with the Red Hose. With that same team he had connected for 4 runs in 1915, 3 in 1916, 2 in 1917 and 11 in 1918.

This is what he has done with the Yanks:

1920, 54 homers; 1921, 59; 1922, 35; 1923, 41; 1924, 46; 1925, 25; 1926, 47; to date in 1927, 60.

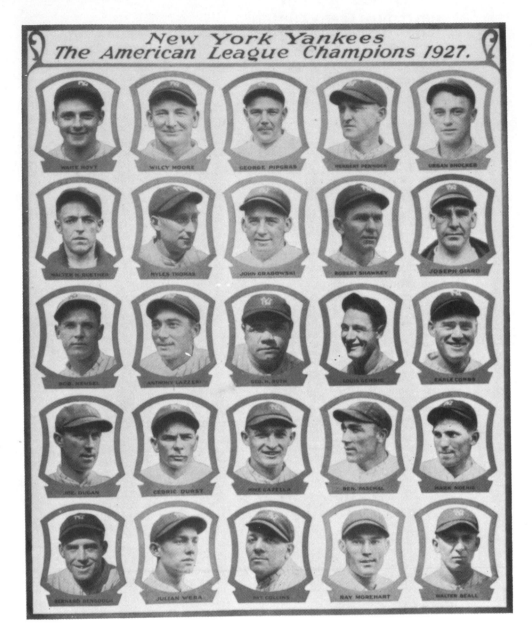

New York Yankees
The American League Champions 1927.

Oct. 8

Ruth's Homer in Fifth Puts Mates Ahead

Hill Opens on Slab Against Wilcy Moore; Miljus Sent in to Finish Battle

Yankee Stadium, New York—The Yankees defeated the Pirates 4-3 in the fourth game of the world series here Saturday afternoon and won the championship of the universe without giving the enemy a single victory.

Wilcy Moore, the "sinker ball" expert of the Yanks was on the hill for the winners. He pitched great ball in the pinches, forcing the Pirates to hit into double plays with men on bases. Carmen Hill, the bespectacled hurler of the Pirates, also hurled fairly good ball, but he was clouted for a homer by the mighty Babe Ruth in the fifth inning. Miljus finished for the Pirates and was the losing pitcher, as the Yanks scored the winning run in the ninth on a wild pitch

Reprinted from
The Milwaukee Journal

Big Train Accepts Higher Offer Than Two Major League Clubs Made; Expects to Pitch a Few Games of 1928 Campaign.

WASHINGTON, Oct. 26.--Walter Johnson, for years the premier pitcher of the American League, today agreed to manage the Newark Club of the International League.

Paul Block, millionaire newspaper publisher and new owner of the Newark Club, conferred with the hurling ace here this afternoon and they came to an agreement that Johnson would manage and perhaps pitch a few contests for the Bears during the coming seasons.

A signed contract, however, was postponed by the fact that the American League clubs have not yet waived on the speedball twirler and until Nov. 1 he will not be entirely free to hook up with any minor league outfit. Until waivers are received by President Clark Griffith of the Washington Club, Johnson will remain the technical property of the Senators. It is certain, however, that the American League owners will not stand in his way.

May 3

COBB'S 700TH DOUBLE

Mackmen Get but Four Hits

Boston, Mass.—(AP)—The Athletics winning streak of seven straight was shattered Thursday when Big Ed Morris, recruit right hander from Mobile, pitched the Red Sox to a 3-1 decision in the last game of the series. He held the Mackmen to four hits, the first of which was Ty Cobb's double in the seventh. Cobb subsequently scored the visitors' only run.

Sensational support was given Morris by Flagstead, who also contributed two runs to the Boston total. In the first his walk off Orwoll was worked into a run and in the sixth his triple to right started a two-run rally.

PHILADELPHIA	AB	R	H	E		BOSTON	AB	R	H	E
Bishop,3b	4	0	1	0		Flagst'd,cf	3	2	2	0
Cobb,rf	4	1	1	0		Todt,1b	3	0	1	0
Speaker,cf	4	0	1	0		Myer,3b	4	0	1	0
Hauser,1b	3	0	0	0		K Will'ms,lf	3	0	1	0
Cochrane,c	3	0	0	2		Regan,2b	3	0	1	0
Miller,lf	4	0	0	0		Taitt,rf	3	0	0	1
Hale,3b	3	0	0	0		Gerber,ss	3	0	0	0
Boley,ss	3	0	0	0		Heving,c	3	0	0	0
Haas	1	0	0	0		Morris,p	3	0	0	0
Dykes,p	0	0	0	0						
Orwoll,p	3	0	1	0		Totals	28	3	6	1

Totals 31 1 4 2

Haas batted for Boley in eighth.

Philadelphia . 0 0 0 0 0 0 1 0 0—1
Boston . . . . 1 0 0 0 0 2 0 0 x—3

Runs batted in—Hauser, Williams, Myer. Two base hits—Cobb, Williams, Heving. Three base hit—Flagstead. Stolen bases—Taitt, Flagstead. Sacrifices—Hauser, Todt. Double play—Speaker to Bishop to Boley. Left on bases—Philadelphia 5, Boston 3. Bases on balls—Off Orwoll 1, Norris 1. Struck out—By Orwoll 4, Morris 3.

Urban Shocker Dies in Denver Hospital

DENVER, Sept. 9.—Urban Shocker, former pitching ace of the New York Yankees, died here this morning.

The news of his death cast a pall of gloom over hundreds of baseball parks throughout the country, where thousands of fans received the announcement in the midst of demonstrations of the sport to which Shocker had devoted his life.

Shocker, who was recognized from 1921 to 1924 as one of the best pitchers in the baseball world, made his major league debut in 1916 with the Yankees.

His health began to fail last fall. This was generally regarded as the reason for his failure to go south to train last spring. Although he agreed, later in the year, to join the Yankees, Shocker only appeared in two or three games before he drew his release.

Soon after leaving the Yankees, Shocker came here for his health.

COBB'S 3000TH GAME

RUTH'S TWO HOME RUNS HELP YANKS ROUT MACKS, 10-4

Meusel Also Hits One as New York Lead Mounts to Twelve Games; Browns Win, 5-3.

PHILADELPHIA, June 28.—(AP)—Babe Ruth hit two home runs to run his season's total to 30 here today as the Yankees won their second straight over the Athletics, 10 to 4. The victory sent the Hugmen into a lead of twelve games over the second-place As and gave them a record of nine out of ten at Shibe Park this season, with one decision yet to be reached tomorrow.

Bob Meusel added a home run of his own to Ruth's first drive in the opening inning with Rube Walberg in the box. Another New York assault for two runs in the second sent Walberg to the bench and brought George Earnshaw into action. The Yankees totaled fifteen hits for 22 bases. Ruth's second homer was off Earnshaw in the eighth.

N. York.	A	H	O	A		Philadel.	A	H	O	A
Combs,cf	6	0	4	0		Dykes,2	4	3	1	0
Koenig,s	6	2	2	2		Cobb,rf	5	1	3	1
Ruth,lf	5	3	1	0		Hauser,1	4	1	5	0
Gehrig,1	4	2	6	1		Simmons,lf	4	1	5	0
Meusel,rf	4	3	3	0		Haas,lf	0	0	0	0
Lazzeri,2	3	3	3	2		Foxx,x	3	0	0	0
R'bertson,3	5	3	1	2		Hale,3	4	1	1	1
G'bowski,c	3	0	4	0		Miller,cf	4	0	1	0
P.Collins,c	0	0	1	0		Boley,s	1	0	0	1
Pipgras,p	4	1	0	2		Hassler,s	1	1	1	0
*Durst	1	0	0	0		Walberg,p	0	0	0	1
						Earnsh'w,p	3	2	0	1
Totals	41	15	27	9		‡E.Collins	1	1	0	0
						†Orwoll	1	0	0	0

Totals . . 35 10 27 6

*Batted for Grabowski in sixth.
†Batted for Boley in fourth.
‡Batted for Earnshaw in ninth.

New York . . . . . 320 002 030—10
Philadelphia . . . 002 011 000— 4

Runs—Koenig 2, Ruth 3, Gehrig 2, Meusel, Lazzeri, Pipgras, Dykes 2, Hassler, Earnshaw. Error—Hale. Runs batted in—Ruth 3, Meusel 2, Gehrig, Lazzeri, Robertson 2, Dykes 3, Cobb. Two-base hits—Simmons, Gehrig. Home runs—Ruth 2, Meusel, Dykes. Stolen bases—Lazzeri. Sacrifice—Gehrig. Double play—Lazzeri, Koenig and Gehrig. Left on bases—New York 12, Philadelphia 7. Bases on balls—Off Pipgras 3, off Walberg 1, off Earnshaw 6. Struck out—By Pipgras 2, by Earnshaw 10. Hits—Off Walberg, 8 in 2 innings; off Earnshaw, 7 in 7 innings. Wild pitch—Earnshaw. Passed balls—Grabowski, Foxx. Losing pitcher—Walberg. Umpires—McGowan, Connolly and Barry. Time—2:24.

Sept. 18

TY COBB TO QUIT GAME THIS YEAR

Famous Peach Would Stick With Athletics Until End of Season.

Tyrus Raymond Cobb, the greatest and most colorful player the national pastime has ever known, has finally decided to hang up the spiked

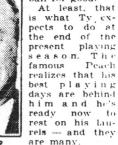

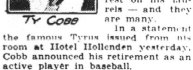

TY COBB

shoes and the old glove and turn his back on baseball for good.

At least, that is what Ty expects to do at the end of the present playing season. The famous Peach realizes that his best playing days are behind him and he's ready now to rest on his laurels — and they are many.

In a statement the famous Tyrus issued from his room at Hotel Hollenden yesterday, Cobb announced his retirement as an active player in baseball.

Invalid Ruth Ties Own Circuit Mark

By Westbrook Pegler.

ST. LOUIS, Oct. 9.—That pale and trembling invalid, Mr. Babe Ruth, achieved something startling in the way of a convalescence out in the open air and summery sun-glow this afternoon.

Three times he laid his crutch in the way and knocked the baseball out of the St. Louis baseball park and finally, in the last half of the ninth inning, shook his groaning chassis into a wild, loose-legged run to the rail of the temporary seats in left field, where he leaned over and plucked a foul ball out from the feathers on a lady customer's millinery for the final putout of the world series of 1928.

The Yankees won this last game, 7 to 3, and though the citizens of St. Louis seem somewhat depressed and disgusted, the members of the Cardinal team gave an impression that the loss of four games in succession to such noted opponents was approximately their idea of a distinguished honor.

Reprinted from
The Cleveland Plain Dealer

Dec. 13

TEN MEN TEAM SUGGESTION

BASE-BALL

DOES IT MEAN TEN ---

..AND OUT—THE THRILL OF A PITCHER WINNING HIS OWN GAME?

Reprinted from
The Brooklyn Eagle

Heydler's Ten-Men Idea Likely to Be Spurned, But May Come to Pass

By ED HUGHES.

JOHN HEYDLER'S interesting suggestion calling for 10 men to a baseball team will probably be blocked by the American League moguls in Chicago today, but the idea is bound to churn up comment for many months. Heydler's idea of an official pinch hitter operating throughout a game for the pitcher has many advocates as well as scoffers. A good many baseball players seem to think well of the proposed innovation, too. At any rate it wasn't considered ridiculous all around, which means the thing may some day come to pass.

Personally the writer doesn't favor the idea for several reasons. In the first place baseball, since it has become a perfected instrument of sport, has endured with less tampering with rules than any other game on earth. Changes aplenty were necessary in the pioneer days and they were made as the need cropped up. Today, after 83 years of growth, about all that remains of the original scheme of the game is the distance between base paths. This is still 90 feet, and probably will remain so until eternity.

ED HUGHES.

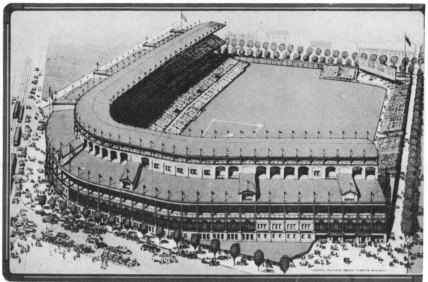

WRIGLEY FIELD, HOME OF "THE CUBS"

Pirates Victims in 11-0 Whitewashing

First Southpaw to Enter Hall of Fame Since 1918;
Only Five Bucs Reach First; Tension Unnerves
N. Y. Defense; Ott Clouts Two Homers.

NEW YORK, May 8.—(AP)—Carl Hubbell, star left-hander of the Giant staff, entered the hall of baseball fame at the Polo Grounds today by pitching a no-hit, no-run game against the Pirates. The Giants pounded Jess Petty, Fred Fussell and Remy Kremer for twelve hits and 29 bases, including two home runs by Melvin Ott and one each by Chuck Fullis and Andy Cohen, to win eased up behind Hubbell's fine effort, 11 to 0.

Hubbell's performance was the first no-hit game in the majors since Aug. 1, 1926, when Ted Lyons of the White Sox let down the Red Sox without a safety. It was the first hitless effort by a southpaw since June 3, 1925, when Hub Leonard whitewashed the Tigers.

OLD ALEX BREAKS MATTY'S RECORD

Flings 373d N. L. Victory as Cards Break Even With Phillies.

PHILADELPHIA, Aug. 10.—(AP) —Grover Cleveland Alexander broke the lifetime National League winning record of the late Christy Mathewson by defeating the Phillies in the second game of a double-header, 11 to 9, here today. It was old Pete's 373d triumph as a Philly, a Cub and a Cardinal.

Alex entered the game with the Cardinals trailing late in the game, but the champions tied the score with one in the ninth, and won out with two more in the eleventh.

SECOND GAME.							
St. Louis.	A	H	O	Phila.	A	H	O
Douthit,cf..	3	1	4	0	Thomp'n,2	6	1	2
High,3..	6	1	3	2	Friberg,lf..	5	3	2
Frisch,2..	6	3	3	O'Doul,rf..	5	2	3	0
Bot'mley,1	6	2	10	Klein,cf..	6	3	2	1
Hafey,lf..	4	3	0	Whitney,3.	3	4	1
Roettger,rf	6	1	0	Hurst,1..	4	2	13
Gelbert,s..	6	3	1	7	Trev'now,s	6	1	5
Wilson,c..	6	3	5	0	Lerian,c..	4	1	3	1
Haines,p..	1	0	0	Sweetl'nd,p	3	2	0
Hald,p..	1	0	0	2	McGraw,p	1	0	1
*Holm..	1	0	0	2	‡Williams.	1	0	0
Sherdel,p..	1	0	0	Collins,p..	0	0	0	1
†Orsatti..	1	0	0				
Alex'nder,p	1	0	2	Totals.47	16	33	16

Totals.47 19 33 18

*Batted for Hald in ninth.
†Batted for Sherdel in eighth.
‡Batted for McGraw in ninth.

St. Louis .... 000 003 411 02—11
Phila. ...... 510 021 000 00— 9

Runs—Douthit, High 2, Frisch 3, Bottomley 2, Hafey, Roettger, Wilson, Thompson, Friberg 2, O'Doul, Klein, Whitney, Hurst 2, Thevenow. Errors—Gelbert, Hald, Thompson.
Runs batted in—O'Doul 2, Whitney, Hurst 2, Sweetland 2, Klein, Hafey 5, Bottomley 2, Roettger 2, High, Gelbert. Two-base hits—Douthit, Lerian, Friberg 2, Frisch, Bottomley, Klein. Three-base hit—Friberg. Home runs—Hurst, Hafey, Roettger. Sacrifices—Hurst 2, Douthit, Hafey, Roettger. Double plays—Thevenow, Thompson and Hurst, Gelbert, Frisch and Bottomley, Whitney and Hurst, Klein, Thevenow and Whitney. Bases on balls —Off Haines 1, off Hald 1, off Alexander 2, off Sweetland 2, off Collins 2. Struck out—By Sweetland 2, by Collins 1, by Sherdel 1, by Alexander 2. Hits—Off Haines, 8 in 3 innings, off Hald 3 in 4 innings, off Sherdel 3 in 2 innings, off Alexander, 2 in 4 innings, off Sweetland, 13 in 6⅔ innings, off McGraw, 3 in 2⅓ innings, off Collins, 3 in 2 innings. Left on bases, St. Louis 8, Philadelphia 11. Winning pitcher, Alexander. Losing pitcher, Collins. Umpires, McLaughlin, Moran and Quigley. Time—2:28.

Babe's 30th for 1929 Is No. 500

BABE'S HOME RUN RECORD	
Year	No.of Runs
1915	4
1916	3
1917	2
1918	11
1919	29
1920	54
1921	59
1922	35
1923	41
1924	46
1925	25
1926	47
1927	60
1928	54
1929	30
	500

CLEVELAND.	AB.	R.	H.	O.	A.	E.
Morgan, rf	5	1	1	1	0	0
J. Sewell, 3b	5	0	1	1	2	0
Averill, cf	5	1	2	3	0	0
Fonseca, 1b	4	0	1	14	1	0
Falk, lf	4	1	1	1	0	0
Hodapp, 2b	4	1	3	4	8	0
Gardner, ss	4	1	1	1	3	1
L. Sewell, c	4	1	2	3	0	0
Hudlin, p	4	0	1	3	2	0
Totals	37	6	13	27	19	1

NEW YORK.	AB.	R.	H.	O.	A.	E.
Combs, cf	4	0	0	3	1	0
Robertson, 3b	5	0	0	1	1	0
Gehrig, 1b	3	2	1	9	0	1
Ruth, rf	3	1	2	2	0	0
Lazzeri, 2b	3	0	1	2	2	0
Meusel, lf	4	0	1	3	0	0
Dickey, c	3	0	2	1	0	0
*Lary	0	0	0	0	0	0
Koenig, ss	4	1	1	2	3	0
Wells, p	3	0	0	1	1	0
Sherid, p	1	0	0	0	0	0
†Durst	1	0	0	0	0	0
Totals	34	5	8	24	9	4

*Ran for Dickey in ninth.
†Batted for Sherid in ninth.

Cleveland .... 000 312 00*—6
New York .... 010 112 000—5

Runs batted in—Hodapp 2, J. Sewell, Averill, Falk, L. Sewell, Ruth, Gehrig, Meusel 2. Two-base hits—Meusel, Averill. Home runs—Ruth, Gehrig. Sacrifice —Falk. Double play—Combs and Dickey. Left on bases—New York 6, Cleveland 9. Bases on balls—Off Wells 1, off Hudlin 4. Struck out—By Wells 1, by Hudlin 2. Hits—Off Wells, 12 in 5⅔ innings; off Sherid, 1 in 2⅓ innings. Losing pitcher —Wells. Umpires—Nallin, Dinneen and McGowan. Time—2:00.

Reprinted from
The Cleveland Plain Dealer

YANKEES WIN AS PILOT SUCCUMBS

Outslug Red Sox in Eleven Innings, 11-10; Browns Edge Tigers, 3-2.

BOSTON, Sept. 25.—(AP)—Playing for five innings without knowledge of the death of their manager, Miller Huggins, in a New York hospital, the Yankees defeated the Red Sox, 11 to 10, in eleven innings here today, cleaning up two straight in their short stay in the Hub.

Just before the sixth inning started players of both teams lined up at the plate and the spectators stood in one minute of silent prayer for Miller Huggins.

New York.	A	H	O	A		Boston.	A	H	O	A
Combs.cf..	6	2	0	6		Reeves.3..	6	2	1	4
Lary.3..	6	2	0	3		Barrett.rf..	2	1	4	0
Ruth.lf..	5	1	2	0		Narlesky.s.	5	0	2	3
Lazzeri.2..	6	4	4	6		M.Gaston.p	1	0	0	1
Durocher.2.	0	0	1	0		Scarritt.lf.	6	2	1	0
Gehrig.1..	4	3	11	2		Regan.2..	6	3	2	6
Paschal.rf.	3	1	2	0		Todt.1..	5	1	15	2
Durst.rf..	2	0	2	0		Cicero.cf..	6	1	3	0
Koenig.s..	6	1	4	1		Heving.c..	6	1	2	1
Benzough.c	3	0	0	0		A.Gaston.c.	1	0	1	0
Dickey.c..	1	1	7	0		Dobens.p..	2	2	2	0
Nekola.p..	3	2	0	2		Durham.p..	0	0	0	1
Sherid.p..	0	0	0	0		†Ruffing..	1	0	0	0
Heimach.p.	0	0	0	0		Carroll.p..	0	0	0	0
Moore.p..	0	0	0	0		Rhyne.s..	3	1	0	0
*Jorgens..	1	0	0	0		‡Bigelow..	1	0	0	0
Pipgras.p..	1	0	0	2		§Gerber..	0	0	0	0
Totals.	47	17	33	16		Totals.	46	13	33	16

*Batted for Moore in eighth.
†Batted for Durham in sixth.
‡Batted for Heving in ninth.
§Ran for Regan in eleventh.

New York.. 2 0 3   0 0 2   0 3 0   0 1—11
Boston.... 2 0 0   0 1 1   7 0 0   0 0—10

Records Fall as Phils Win.

PHILADELPHIA, Oct. 5.—(AP)—The once-lowly Phillies ended their 1929 campaign here today in what to them was a blaze of glory. They divided two games with the Giants to slip into fifth place ahead of Brooklyn, which dropped two contests to Boston, and saw Frank O'Doul and Charlie Klein break two National League records as O'Doul clinched the batting championship. The Phils won the opener, 5 to 4, but the clan McGraw snatched the nightcap, 12 to 3.

O'Doul, one-time Yankee pitcher, got six hits, including his 32d home run, in eight times at bat to run his total for the season to 254 and his batting average to an even .400. The Philly outfielder's total of safe blows is four ahead of the league record set by Rogers Hornsby in 1922 and three short of George Sisler's major league mark of 257 made in 1920. O'Doul is the first .400 batter in the National League since 1925, when Hornsby led with .403.

FIRST GAME.

Phil.	A	H	O	A		New York.	A	H	O	A
T'mpson.2.	3	0	3	4		Fullis.lf..	4	1	1	0
O'Doul.lf..	4	4	3	0		Roush.cf..	2	0	1	0
Klein.rf..	4	1	1	1		Landst'm.3	4	1	0	1
Whitney.3.	4	1	2	1		Terry.1..	4	0	13	0
Hurst.1..	4	0	12	3		Ott.rf..	3	1	2	0
Friberg.cf.	4	0	1	0		Jackson.s.	3	1	3	1
Thevenow.s	3	0	2	3		Hogan.c..	3	0	4	0
Lerian.c..	3	1	2	1		Marshall.2	3	0	1	5
Sw'tland.p.	3	1	1	4		Fitzs'ns.p.	2	1	0	4
Koupal.p..	0	0	0	0		*Veltman.	0	0	0	0
Totals..	32	8	27	17		†Leach..	1	0	0	0
						‡Cohen..	1	0	0	0
						Totals..	28	4	24	12

*Batted for Hubbell in eighth.
†Batted for Hogan in ninth.
‡Batted for Marshall in ninth.

Philadelphia .... 0 0 3 0 2 0 0 0 *— 5
New York .... 0 0 0 2 0 0 0 2 0— 4

Runs—Thompson, O'Doul 2, Klein, Sweetland, Fullis, Ott, Jackson, Veltman. Error—O'Doul.
Runs batted in—Klein 2, Whitney 2, Jackson, Roush, O'Doul, Lindstrom. Home runs—O'Doul, Klein. Sacrifice—Roush. Double play—Thevenow, Thompson and Hurst. Left on bases—New York 4, Philadelphia 5. Bases on balls—Off Sweetland 6, off Hubbell 1. Struck out—By Sweetland 1, by Hubbell 2. Hits—Off Hubbell, 8 in 7 innings; off Fitzsimmons, none in 1 inning; off Sweetland, 4 in 7 innings (none out in eighth); off Koupal, 1 in 2 innings. Winning pitcher—Sweetland. Losing pitcher—Hubbell. Passed ball—Lerian. Umpires—Jorda, Klem and McWughlin. Time—1:30.

SECOND GAME.

New York	A	H	O	A		Phila.	A	H	O	A
Fullis.lf-cf	6	0	2	0		Thom'son.2	5	3	3	3
Roush.cf..	2	1	0	0		O'Doul.lf..	5	2	3	0
Leach.lf..	2	0	2	0		Klein.rf..	5	1	3	0
Lindst'm.3	4	1	1	0		Whitney.3.	5	1	3	0
Crawf'rd.1	5	3	9	0		Hurst.1..	4	3	6	1
Ott.rf..	1	1	1	0		Friberg.cf.2	4	1	1	3
Jackson.s.	3	2	4	3		Thevenow.s	4	1	1	2
Hogan.c..	5	3	4	1		Davis.c..	4	3	3	3
Marshall.2	4	2	2	2		Smythe.p..	0	0	1	1
Walker.p..	4	2	0	2		Dailey.p..	1	0	0	0
Farrell.3..	2	1	2	1		Collins.p..	3	1	1	0
						Sikman.cf.	0	0	0	0
Totals..	38	16	27	9		Totals..	40	14	26	11

*Crawford out, hit by batted ball.

New York ..... 0 3 3 3 0 0 0 1 2—12
Philadelphia .... 0 0 1 1 0 1 0 0 0— 3

Runs—Roush, Crawford 2, Ott 3, Jackson 2, Hogan 2, Marshall 2, Walker, Hurst, Davis 2. Errors—None.
Runs batted in—Hogan 4, Marshall 2, Roush, Hurst, Walker, Davis, Thompson, Jackson, Farrell. Two-base hits—Hurst, Hogan, Thompson. Three-base hit—Friberg. Home runs—Davis, Hurst. Sacrifices—Walker, Marshall. Hits—Off Smythe, 8 in 2⅓ innings; off Dailey, 3 in 1 inning; off Collins, 5 in 6 innings. Struck out—By Dailey 1, by Walker 1, by Collins 2. Bases on balls—Off Smythe 2, off Dailey 3, off Collins 5. Double play—Thevenow, Thompson and Hurst. Left on bases—New York 11, Philadelphia 11. Losing pitcher—Smythe. Balk—Dailey. Umpires—Klem, McLaughlin and Jorda. Time—1:50.

Oct. 14

Great Uphill Battle Brings Final Victory

Mule Haas Hits Homer With 1 On to Tie Score; Miller Drives in Winning Tally

BY MANNING VAUGHAN

PHILADELPHIA, Pa.—Echoes of that mighty 10 run rally in the seventh inning of Saturday's game here had hardly died down when the Macks rose in all their terrible might again Monday and defeated the Cubs in the fifth and deciding game of the world series, 3 to 2.

Held to two hits by Pat Malone for eight innings and trailing 2 to 0 at the time the Macks let loose all the TNT in their bats in the ninth and chased home all their runs. It was a finish that left the crowd limp and weak.

Bing Miller, our own Al Simmons, Mule Haas and Bishop were the batting heroes of the battle.

Bishop Singles

Bishop started the sensational uprising with a single over third after one out in the ninth and Haas tied the score with a screeching home run over the right field fence. Cochrane was thrown out by Hornsby but Simmons started the rally all over by lining a double to center and after Foxx had been purposely passed, Bing Miller drilled a single to center that sent Simmons home with the winning run. Miller was given credit for a double by the official scorer after the game.

The crowd let out a whoop after Miller's hit that must have echoed in the canyons of Chicago's loop. The first excitement passed, however, fans actually got limp from the intenseness of the game. President Hoover occupied a box.

Consecutive Game Mark Ends at 1102

JOE SEWELL

Joey Sewell's hopes of shattering Everett Scott's consecutive game record of 1 307 were blasted in Boston yesterday when the Indian thirdsacker was unable to appear in the line-up for the first time since the end of the 1922 campaign.

Little Joe who has been battling a siege of flu for the last few days, had a temperature of 102 and spent the day in bed. Sewell had run in straight game record to 1,102 or 205 short of Scott's sensational figure.

Reprinted from
The Cleveland Plain Dealer

May 3

NIGHT BASE BALL PROVES FEASIBLE

Success in Western League Tilt From Lighting and Money Standpoint.

By the Associated Press.

DES MOINES, Iowa, May 3.— Apparently only the turnstile approval of base ball fans now is needed to make night base ball under artificial lighting a success.

The Des Moines and Wichita, Kans., clubs of the Western League last night demonstrated before nearly 12,000 spectators that mechanically the game may be played as well under powerful lights as in the sunlight—and probably better than on gray days.

Des Moines defeated the league-leading Wichita club, 13 to 6, by a wild first inning, which netted 11 runs, but there was no indication that the unusual conditions were responsible. The pitching was as good as in the daytime, and the players handled ground balls and throws without hesitation. Wichita played errorless base ball, while Des Moines was charged with four misplays. Of the errors made by Des Moines, all were in the infield, outfielders having no difficulty with towering flies.

Both of the team managers, Claude Davenport of Des Moines and Art Griggs of Wichita, were enthusiastic over the prospect of regular night attractions. Griggs believed a little more light would improve the game, while Davenport agreed with the opinion of E. Lee Keyser, president of the Des Moines club, that night contests would be the salvation of minor league base ball.

So enthusiastic was Keyser, who has planned and experimented for seven years with lighting systems suitable for night base ball, that he decided today's contest would be called at 8 p.m., instead of in the afternoon as scheduled.

BENTON ALLOWS
6 HOME RUNS
IN GAME

May 13

Bruins Equal an Old Record

Chicago — (P) — Baseball records of years standing trembled Monday as the New York Giants slugged out a 14-12 victory over the Chicago Cubs.

The Cubs equaled the record made by Pittsburgh in 1894, when they clubbed out four home runs in the seventh inning. Heathcote, Beck, Wilson and Grimm hit for circuit drives during the wild inning, the first two getting their second homers of the game.

The nine home runs collected by the two teams fell one short of the record set by the Cardinals and Phillies in 1923. The Cubs also lacked one home run of equaling the record made by one team in a game, when they clubbed out their six circuit drives.

NEW YORK	AB	R	H	E.	CHICAGO	AB	R	H	E
Leach.lf	6	1	1	0	English.ss	6	1	2	1
Lindstrom.3b	4	2	3	0	Heathcote.rf	4	2	2	0
Terry.1b	4	1	1	0	Cuyler.lf	5	0	1	0
Ott.rf	4	2	2	0	Wilson.cf	2	2	1	0
Crawford.2b	5	1	0	0	Grimm.1b	5	1	1	0
Jackson.ss	6	1	0	0	Bell.3b	5	1	1	0
Reese.cf	6	2	2	0	Hartnett.c	4	3	1	0
Hogan.c	5	2	3	2	Beck.3b	5	2	3	1
Benton.p	4	2	3	0	Blake.p	1	0	1	0
Heving.p	0	0	0	0	McAfee.p	0	0	0	0
Genewich.p	0	0	0	0	Teachout.p	3	0	1	0
					Stephenson	1	0	1	0
Totals	46	14	15	2	Totals	41	12	15	4

Stephenson batted for Teachout in ninth.

New York	0	4	7	0	1	0	0	0	2— 14
Chicago	0	0	0	0	1	3	5	1	2— 12

Runs batted in Leach 3, Ott 3, Jackson, Reese, Hogan, Benton 3, Heathcote 2, Beck 5, Wilson, Grimm, Cuyler, Stephenson, English. Two-base hits Reese, Lindstrom 2, English, Hartnett. Home runs Leach, Ott, Benton, Beck 2, Heathcote 2, Wilson, Grimm. Stolen base Heathcote. Double plays Jackson to Crawford to Terry, Crawford to Jackson to Terry. Left on bases New York 12, Chicago 8. Bases on balls Off Blake 3, Heving 1, Benton 5, Teachout 2. Struck out By Benton 5, Teachout 5. Hits Off Blake, six in two and two-thirds innings, McAfee, three in none, Teachout, six in six and one third, Benton, nine in six and two-thirds, Heving six in one and two-thirds, Genewich, none in two thirds. Winning pitcher Benton. Losing pitcher Blake.

BABE RUTH AND GEHRIG SMASH THREE APIECE

Sixth in Two Days Brings Bambino's Total to 12; Nats Bounce Red Sox Twice; Tigers Win.

PHILADELPHIA, May 22.—(AP)—The New York Yankees turned the tables on the Athletics today and won both games of their second successive double header in a pair of amazing slugging matches. The scores were 10 to 1 and 20 to 13.

One record was broken and two were tied in the second game. Babe Ruth set a mark of his own by hitting two home runs in the first game and one in the second to make it six in two days and twelve for the season. His total put him in a tie with Hack Wilson for major league leadership.

Lou Gehrig hit three homers in the second game and equaled the American League record by batting in eight runs. Ten home runs in this contest, divided by the two teams, tied the record for the major league. The former American League mark was eight.

'OLD PETE' PASSES FROM BIG LEAGUES

Alexander Made Free Agent by Phillies; Seeks Coast League Job.

PHILADELPHIA, June 3.—(AP)—Father Time has beckoned another former star out of the major leagues. Grover Cleveland Alexander, veteran pitcher of the Phillies who holds the National League record for victories,

GROVER ALEXANDER

was given his unconditional release today.

What Old Pete expects to do in a baseball way he says he does not know, but he would like to continue to play the game with a minor league club, preferably on the Pacific Coast. He was 43 year old last February.

"I think I would like to play in the west," he said. "You know, I was raised in the west and I guess I'm sort of used to it out there. I've been around the east for a long time, now, and I think I'm ready to try it in the other direction.

"I'd like the coast," the former star added, "I've only seen it on spring exhibition trips, but it looked good to me.

"I'm afraid I'm through as a big league pitcher, it's like the one horse shay, you know, it doesn't last forever."

Alexander came to the Phillies as a rookie in 1911 from the Syracuse (N. Y.) club, and was traded to the Chicago Cubs in the winter of 1917. He was released by the Cubs on waivers to the St. Louis Cards in June, 1926, and came back to the Phils last winter.

July 26

SIMMONS GETS 24TH HOMER IN ONSLAUGHT

Wildness and Errors Send Indians to Defeat; A's Engineer Pair of Triple Steals.

By Sam Otis.
Plain Dealer Sports Editor.

When a club intends to rid itself of a lot of bad baseball—and they all do every so often it is a better than fair hunch to do the unloading on the same afternoon Janky Bob Grove is delivering one of his frequent top-notch pitching performance. That is what the Indians did yesterday—combined the two almost certain causes of defeat, so that instead of dropping a pair of games, they lost only one to the Athletics, 14 to 1.

Such a fall from grace should have been expected, perhaps, after the great showing the tribe had been making lately, but the lop-sided lacing was none the more pleasant to take, nevertheless. For half the afternoon the Indians looked really bad. Grove's foes for most of the time, but it would not have been so exasperating if inability to hit the Mackian ace had been the only redskin failing. Grove yielded just six hits.

A dozen blows the world's champions got, including Al Simmons' 24th homer of the season and round trippers by Max Bishop and Bing Miller but it was not the heavy hitting that did the real damage. To illustrate the Athletics scored their first ten runs on five safeties. Weak fielding pathetic pitching and general all-around let-down staked the visitors to such a lead that it was not a contest at any time.

Triple Steal Twice.

Pete Jablonowski and Pinkey Shoffner turned in some of the bushiest of sandlot hurling passing a total of ten men in five and a third innings and both falling sound asleep while the Athletics engineered a pair of neat triple steals. Two triple thefts in one game! Need more be said of how bad the Indians looked?

Reprinted from
The Cleveland Plain Dealer

Bill Terry Equals N. L. Mark for Hits

NEW YORK Sept. 28 — Bill Terry, Giants' first baseman, who easily won the 1930 National League batting championship with a mark of .401, equaled Frank O'Doul's National League mark for number of hits in one season with 254. This is three behind George Sisler's all time record.

Lou Gehrig of New York's Yankees staged a final hitting splurge and by making three hits in five times at bat placed himself a point ahead of Al Simmons of Philadelphia in the unofficial figures.

The standing of the five leaders in each league follows:

AMERICAN LEAGUE.
1930

Player—Club.	G.	AB.	R.	H.	Pc.	Pc.
Gehrig, N. Y	154	576	143	220	382	377
Simmons, Phil	138	554	153	211	381	381
Cochrane, Phil	130	484	110	175	362	356
Reynolds, Chi	138	561	103	202	360	306
Ruth, N. Y	145	518	131	186	350	319

NATIONAL LEAGUE.
1930

Player—Club.	G.	AB.	R.	H.	Pc.	Pc.
Terry, N. Y	154	633	138	254	401	380
Herman, Bkln	153	614	143	241	393	365
Klein, Phil	156	648	158	250	386	331
O'Doul, Phil	140	528	122	202	383	317
Lindst'm, N. Y	148	666	127	232	383	345

Hack Wilson Wins Home Run Honors

NEW YORK, Sept. 28 — (AP)—Hack Wilson, stocky Cub outfielder, set one National League record and one big league mark in the season that ended today.

His 56 home runs set a National record, led the Cubs to a major league record of 171 and beat Babe Ruth by seven.

His 190 runs driven in beat Lou Gehrig's big league mark of 175.

Other high lights of the season:

The champion Cardinals are credited with .314 in team batting, seven points higher than any other pennant winner, and 366 doubles, 22 more than Cleveland Indians made in 1921.

The Athletics went to bat 5,496 times, eclipsing Detroit's 1929 major league record of 5,529.

St. Louis won the National pennant with 92 wins, 62 defeats, two games worse than second place Washington in the American. The A's won 102, lost 52.

Klein Sets Three Records.

The Yankees set a pair of team marks by scoring 1,060 runs and having 960 runs batted in.

Chuck Klein, Philly outfielder blasted three records by making 59 doubles, five ahead of the old record; 445 bases on his hits and 158 runs.

Final home run standing:

HOME RUNS YESTERDAY—Gehrin Browns, 2; Foxx, Athletics, Off Giants Alexander Tigers, Chabman Yankees, Shoffner, Indians, Thurston, Robins.

THE LEADERS—Wilson, Cubs 56; Ruth, Yankees 49 Gehrig Yankees 41; Klein, Phillies 40; Berger Braves, 34; Hartnett, Cubs, 37; Goslin Browns, 37; Foxx, Athletics, 37; Simmons, Athletics, 36; Herman Robins, 35.

LEAGUE TOTALS—National, 892; American 673. Grand total, 1,565.

Six Teams Bat Over .300

CLUB BATTING.

Club.	G.	AB.	R.	Opp. Runs.	H.	TB.	2B.	3B.	HR.	SH.	SB.	PC.
New York	154	5553	959	814	1769	2628	264	83	143	165	59	.319
Philadelphia	156	5667	944	1199	1783	2594	345	44	126	148	34	.315
St. Louis	154	5512	1004	784	1732	2595	373	89	104	185	72	.314
Chicago	156	5581	998	870	1722	2684	305	72	171	148	70	.309
Brooklyn	154	5433	871	738	1654	2469	308	73	122	147	53	.304
Pittsburgh	154	5346	891	928	1622	2403	285	119	86	196	76	.303
Cincinnati	154	5245	665	857	1475	2096	265	67	74	174	48	.2812
Boston	154	5356	693	835	1503	2103	246	78	66	154	69	.2806
League Total		43695	7025	7025	13260	19572	2386	625	892	1317	481	.303

BABE AND LOU STAGE ACT AS YANKEES WIN

Hit Successive Clouts in 3d; Bambino Pays $10 to Get Ball Back as Souvenir.

ST. LOUIS, Aug. 21.—(AP)—Babe Ruth started things off again today when he walloped his 35th home run of the season and the 600th of his major league career in the third inning against the Browns. The homer, followed immediately by Lou Gehrig's 34th of the year, put the Yanks on the road to an 11 to 7 victory over St. Louis.

Ruth and little Tony Gallico engaged in a business transaction after the game, much to the satisfaction of each.

The Babe was anxious to get his home run ball, which hit a motor car outside the park.

"I'd give a $10 bill and a new ball to get that one back," the Sultan of Swat announced.

Tony Collects.

Tony arrived before long with the old ball, collected the $10 and the new ball from the Babe and then paid a brief visit to the press box.

The Babe left the game in the seventh inning by order of Umpire Van Grafian when he protested long and loudly that Ralph Kress' homer had hit the bleacher wall instead of going into the stands.

Goose Goslin also hit a homer for the Browns, his drive coming with one on in the ninth and ending Henry Johnson's stay on the mound.

New York.	A	H	O	A		St. Louis.	A	H	O	A
Combs.cf..	5	4	2	0		Schulte.cf..	4	3	0	0
Sewell.3..	5	2	0	3		Melillo.2..	4	0	4	6
Ruth.lf..	4	3	0	0		Goslin.lf..	4	2	1	0
Byrd.lf..	1	0	0	0		Kress.rf..	4	2	0	0
Gehrig.1..	5	2	11	2		Ferrell.c..	4	1	4	1
Chapman.rf	4	0	0	0		Storti.3..	5	1	2	2
Lary.s..	5	0	4	1		Burns.1..	4	2	10	0
Dickey.c..	4	2	5	0		Levey.s..	4	1	1	1
Lazzeri.2..	4	1	4	5		Bl'holder.p.	0	0	0	0
Johnson.p..	5	2	1	0		Stiles.p..	2	0	0	1
Ruffing.p..	0	0	0	0		*Grimes..	1	0	0	0
						Kimsey.p..	0	0	0	1
Totals..42		16	27	11		Totals..36		10	27	12

*Batted for Stiles in seventh.

New York ...... 1 0 5 1 0 0 1 3 0—11
St. Louis ...... 0 0 1 0 0 0 3 1 2— 7

Runs—Combs 4, Sewell 2, Ruth, Gehrig 2, Chapman, Johnson, Schulte 2, Goslin 2, Kress, Storti. Errors—Lary, Melillo 2, Kimsey. Runs batted in—Ruth 3, Sewell 2, Gehrig, Lary, Goslin 3, Kress 3, Burns. Two-base hits—Goslin, Storti. Three-base hits—Combs 2. Home runs—Ruth, Gehrig, Kress, Goslin. Sacrifice—Sewell. Stolen bases—Chapman, Lazzeri. Double plays—Melillo and Burns; Storti, Melillo and Burns; Lazzeri and Gehrig. Wild pitches—Stiles, Kimsey. Hit by pitcher—By Blaeholder (Lazzeri). Left on bases—New York 8, St. Louis 8. Bases on balls—Off Johnson 6, off Blaeholder 1, off Kimsey 2. Struck out—By Stiles 2, by Kimsey 1, by Johnson 4. Hits—Off Blaeholder, 6 in 2 innings (none out in third); off Stiles, 7 in 5 innings; off Kimsey, 3 in 2 innings; off Johnson, 10 in 8 innings (none out in ninth); off Ruffing, none in 1 inning. Winning pitcher—Johnson. Losing pitcher—Blaeholder. Umpires—Guthrie, Dinneen and Van Graflan. Time—2:23.

Few Major League Records Fell During '31 Season

Gehrig Sets Mark by Driving In 182 Runs; Webb Hit Most Two-Baggers

New York, N. Y.—(AP)—In contrast to the record breaking spree staged in the major leagues last year, only a few marks of any importance fell during the 1931 campaign. And to make the contrast more sharp, all of the three big individual records which were broken were smashed by American league players, while the National leaguers, who sent one mark after another tumbling in 1930, failed to connect with the less lively ball this year for a single new record.

In the batting end Lou Gehrig of the New York Yankees and Earl Webb of the Boston Red Sox were the leading record smashers. Gehrig, according to the final unofficial records, batted in 182 runs during the season which closed Sunday, seven more than his 1927 total, which set an American league mark. Webb broke the major league record for two-base hits set by George Burns in 1926, when he clouted 67 doubles. Burns' record was 64.

31 for Grove

Bob Grove, ace of the Philadelphia Athletics, had no difficulty finishing the season with the highest percentage in games won and lost made by a major league pitcher since 1909. Although the Athletics' southpaw lost his last game of the year to the New York Yankees Sunday, he finished the season with 31 victories and four defeats for an average of .886. The former record was .872, set in 1912 when Smoky Joe Wood won 34 games and lost five for the Boston Red Sox.

The close battle for the National league batting championship wound up in something like a triple tie, according to the unofficial averages, and the winner probably will not be known until the official figures are released next winter. As they appear now. Chick Hafey of the St. Louis Cardinals has a fractional margin over Bill Terry of the New York Giants with Jim Bottomley of the Cardinals. Al Simmons scored a clean cut victory in the American league batting race with an unofficial average of .390, 17 points ahead of Babe Ruth.

Share Homer Title

Ruth regained a half share in the role of home run king tying with Lou Gehrig with a total of 46 for the year when Gehrig clouted one in the last game yesterday. It was the tenth season in which the Babe has hit 40 or more homers.

The final standing of the major league leaders follows:

NATIONAL LEAGUE

Batting Hafey Cardinals .3479
Terry Giants .3478. Bottomley Cardinals .3477
Runs: Terry, Giants; Klein Phillies, 121
Runs Batted In Klein Phillies 122 Terry Giants, 114
Hits: L. Waner Pirates 214. Terry Giants 213
Doubles Adams. Cardinals. 46 Berger Braves 44
Triples Terry. Giants. 20. Herman Robins 16
Home Runs: Klein Phillies 31. Ott Giants 29
Stolen Bases: Frisch Cardinals 28 Martin Cardinals, Herman Robins 17
Pitching Haines, Cardinals, won 11 lost three. Derringer, Cardinals won 18 lost eight.

AMERICAN LEAGUE

Batting Simons. Athletics .390 Ruth Yankees .373
Runs Gehrig Yankees, 163 Ruth Yankees, 149
Runs Batted In Gehrig. Yankees. 182. Ruth. Yankees. 160
Hits: Gehrig Yankees, 211. Averill Indians, 209
Doubles Webb, Red Sox. 67. Alexander Tigers 46
Triples John-on. Tigers. 19. Blue White Sox. Gehrig. Yankees. 15
Home Runs Ruth and Gehrig Yankees 46.
Stolen Bases Chapman. Yankees 61 Johnson Tigers, 33
Pitching Grove. Athletics won 31 lost four. Marberry, Senators won 16 lost four.

Melillo, Coffman End Grove's Winning Streak

Oscar's Double Drives In Only Run of Game to Beat Southpaw by 1 to 0

St. Louis, Mo.—(P)—Lefty Grove will have to be content with being a joint holder of the American league record for consecutive pitching victories for the present at least, instead of owning the record outright.

Already a joint holder of the record of 16 straight games, established in 1912 by Smoky Joe Wood of the Boston Red Sox and equaled the same year by Walter Johnson of the Washington Senators. Grove attempted to better it Sunday at the expense of the St. Louis Browns but ran up against a three hit pitching performance by Dick Coffman, who shut out the A's, 1 to 0, in the first game of a double header. The Athletics won the nightcap, 10 to 0, behind Waite Hoyt's airtight hurling.

Grove, as usual, was good Sunday but Coffman was a little better. The Browns touched the southpaw fire ball artist for seven hits, compared to three allowed by Coffman. Grove fanned six, two more than Coffman. The only base on ball was issued by Coffman. Grove made a wild pitch.

The Browns put over the only run in the third inning on a single by Schulte and a double, which Moore misjudged, by Melillo, after two were out.

Coffman, in blanking the A's, became the first American league pitcher of the year to accomplish the feat.

FIRST GAME

PHILADELPHIA	AB	R	H		ST. LOUIS	AB	R	H
Bishop.2b	4	0	0		Schulte.cf	4	1	3
Cramer.cf	4	0	1		Melillo.2b	4	0	2
Cochrane.c	4	0	0		Goslin.lf	4	0	0
Moore.lf	3	0	1		Kress.3b	4	0	0
Foxx.1b	4	0	1		Bettomer rf	3	0	1
Miller.rf	2	0	0		Burns.1b	3	0	0
McNair.ss	3	0	0		Bengough.c	3	0	0
Williams.ss	3	0	0		Levey.ss	3	0	1
Grove.p	3	0	0		Coffman.p	2	0	0
Totals	30	0	3		Totals	30	1	7

Philadelphia . . 0 0 0 0 0 0 0 0 0
St. Louis . . . 0 0 1 0 0 0 0 0 0

Runs batted in Melillo. Two base hit Melillo. Sacrifices Moore. Coffman. Left on bases—Philadelphia 5, St. Louis 6. Bases on balls—Off Coffman 1. Struck out—By Grove 6, Coffman 4. Wild pitch Grove.

A'S RELY ON BIG RIGHT-HANDER IN LAST-DITCH STAND IN SERIES; ADMIRING CROWD MOBS MARTIN

"Can Hit Any Pitcher That Ever Lived," Says Hero.

Street Retains Faith in Mound Rookie Who Lost Opener.

Today's game between the Athletics and Cardinals will be reproduced on The Post's magnetic scoreboard, beginning at 2:30 o'clock.

By EDWARD J. NEIL.

ST. LOUIS, Oct. 8 (A.P.). — Another "we" — "Pepper" Martin and the St. Louis Cardinals—came today to a heroic welcome as the "Spirit of St. Louis" once more rode along the banks of the Mississippi.

At least 2,000 of the most rabid faithful stormed the railroad terminal, shouting, mauling, surging in to get their hands on the simple youngster who almost single-handed has routed the world champion Philadelphia Athletics to give the Cardinals a 3 to 2 lead in games and lift a National League champion to within one game of the first world series conquest for that circuit in five years.

They will see him tomorrow, these riotous rooters, eagerly taking his cut against the sweeping slants of "Big Jarge" Earnshaw in the sixth game at Sportsman's Park, opening of the final act of one of the most thrilling baseball dramas of all times. But they could not wait to express their delight at the feats of the youthful hitting and base running dynamo, a demoralizing .667 hitter in his first world series.

The moment the special train of the Cardinals drew into the station here at 12:45 p. m. (C.S.T.), after a swift run from Philadelphia, Martin's particularly brilliant playground, the faithful burst through the guarding lines and swarmed over the platform.

Meek and mild for the first time since the series opened, grinning sheepishly, "Pepper" stepped down into the throng that yelled his name, patted his shoulders until his big gray sombrero kept slipping down over his eyes, and made an effort to get him up on their shoulders for a parade of triumph.

Hangs to Arm Of Wife.

Then it was that "Pepper" quailed, perhaps for the first time in his life,

and he grabbed the arm of Mrs. "Pepper" Martin and hung on. The leaders seemed to debate for a moment the possibility of hoisting them both into the air, but discretion prevailed, and the greatest baseball hero since Babe Ruth was in his prime was allowed to escort his wife through cheering lines to a taxicab.

Gabby Street, the old sergeant of the Cards, sat in a taxicab at the station exit and grinned while he puffed his briar pipe and watched the rest of his stars, including left-handed Wild Bill Hallahan and the pugnacious spitballer, Burleigh Grimes, march through the lane that kept crying:

"There's Martin? Lemme see Martin. Which one's Martin? He's the guy we want to see."

Latest About Martin: Bags Rabbits on Foot

Dallas, Tex., Oct. 8 (A.P.).—The Texas League has its own legends about the amazing speed of Pepper Martin, hero of the world series, and one of the best is told by Roy Moore, teammate of Pepper on the 1929 Houston Club.

"Old Pepper goes out on the prairie and scares up a bunch of rabbits," Moore explained, in recounting Martin's prowess as a hunter.

"He runs along with these rabbits. He reaches down and feels the sides of these rabbits.

"If the rabbit is a bit thin, he lets him go, and takes out after another one, but if the rabbit is nice and fat, old Pepper picks him up and puts him in his bag."

SIX RECORDS MAY GO TO MARTIN

Macks Have Played Errorless Ball for Five Games.

ST. LOUIS, Oct. 8 (A.P.).—Pepper Martin has a good chance of cracking six world series records.

The rollicking rookie of the Cardinals already has equaled two all-time series marks by running his total of hits up to twelve and driving in four runs, in the fifth game.

Buck Herzog, Joe Jackson and Sam Rice shared the total-hit record previously. Those who have driven in four runs in a single game included Elmer Smith, who did it with the bases full for Cleveland in 1920; also Goose Goslin, Babe Ruth, Lester Bell and Al Simmons.

Martin also is within gunshot of four other series records as a result of accumulating four stolen bases, four doubles, five extra-base hits altogether and totaling nineteen bases for all his safe blows.

The base-stealing record of six was set in 1907 by Jim Slagle, of the Chicago Cubs. Chick Hafey, of the Cardinals, hit five doubles in 1930 for a new mark. Babe Ruth, in 1926, hit six extra-base blows and totaled 22 bases for records.

The Cardinal captain, Frankie Frisch, has another chance this series to tie Babe Ruth's achievement of hitting .300 or better in five world championships. Frisch was at or above this mark four years in a row when he played with the Giants of 1921-22-23-24. Twice before with the Cardinals his batting fell off. He hit only .231 in 1928 and .208 last year. His mark for the present series now is exactly .300.

The Athletics have broken defensive records anyway, by playing errorless ball for five successive games. The best previous mark was four straight without an error, by the 1918 Red Sox.

The A's total also equals the mark of the Giants, who had five errorless games altogether in the 1921 series with the Yankees. Together, the A's and Cards, with eight errorless contests, have tied the combined best defensive efforts of the Yankees and Giants in 1921.

March 3

Morris, Sox Hurler, Dies From Wounds

Century, Fla. – (AP) – Wounds of a knife plunged into big Ed Morris' chest during a fight at a fish fry given in his honor Monday night caused the death of the veteran pitcher for the Boston Red Sox Thursday.

Soon after he died Joe White, a gasoline station operator at Brewton, Ala., was arrested and charged with murder.

Witnesses said he and the pitcher engaged in an argument at the party that was intended as a farewell to Morris on the eve of his departure for the Red Sox training camp at Savannah, Ga.

Morris was considered one of the major league baseball's best right handed pitchers a few years ago, but a sore arm had impaired his usefulness to the Boston Red Sox during the 1930 and 1931 seasons.

June 3

GEHRIG'S 4 HOMERS TIES AGED RECORD

By the Associated Press.

LOU GEHRIG, long accustomed to play second fiddle to the one and only Babe Ruth, today had carved himself a place in baseball's permanent record, the result of a home-run spree never equaled by his illustrious teammate or by any other big league batsman in the last 38 years.

The Yankee first baseman yesterday crashed four consecutive homers over the right-field fence at Shibe Park as his team beat the Philadelphia Athletics, 20 to 13.

Only once before had the feat been equaled. Robert Lowe of the Boston Nationals of 1894 did it. Ed Delehanty of Philadelphia hit four in one game in 1896, but only three were consecutive.

TERRY GIVEN FULL POWER BY M'GRAW

Will Rescind Strict Rules, but Reign as Czar—Job Comes as Surprise.

By the Associated Press.

NEW YORK, June 4. — The New York Giants now have the youngest manager in the National League, but there is little danger any of them will attempt to take advantage of Bill Terry.

The big fellow from Memphis is only 33, but he has a mind of his own, and he doesn't hesitate to speak it. He will be manager of the Giants right up to the hilt.

The first thing he attended to after he was notified that he had succeeded John J. McGraw was to post a notice to that effect in the club house. Then he called in the players, many of them his teammates for years, and had a through understanding.

"I told them that from here on they take orders from me and from nobody else. I told them I was going to ease up on some of the strict rules we've had and give them a chance to play ball for me and get out of the basement. If they can do that there will be some change."

July 4

It Was a Costly Punch; Dickey Pays $1,000 Fine

Chicago, Ill. – (AP) – Catcher Bill Dickey of the New York Yankees must park himself on the bench until Aug. 4 and pay a fine of $1,000 for landing that jaw breaker on Carl Reynolds, Washington outfielder.

Bill Dickey

The penalty, one of the heaviest ever assessed on a major league player for fighting, was announced Saturday by President Will Harridge of the American league, after several days' study of the assault. The suspension went into effect after the battle.

Dickey, one of the big cogs in the Yankee machine, was infuriated when Reynolds scored standing up on a squeeze play. He struck him on the jaw. The lower jaw was broken in two places. Reynolds has been unable to eat solid food since. He will be out of the game for at least another month.

Whether Reynolds or the Washington club will receive all or part of the heavy fine Dickey must pay has not been determined. The question undoubtedly will come up before the American league club owners at their annual summer meeting in Cleveland Monday. The Washington club has incurred heavy doctor and hospital bills in the case and probably will be given the $1,000.

Saturday's fine was the fifth handed out this season by President Harridge. Manager Lew Fonseca and three White Sox players – Charlie Berry, Milton Gaston and Frank Grube – were fined for engaging in a fight with Umpire George Moriarty at Cleveland Memorial day. Gaston was suspended for 10 days and fined $500; Fonseca was fined $500, Berry $250 and Grube $100. Saturday's fine, while heavy, was dwarfed in comparison to the one handed Babe Ruth for barnstorming after the 1922 world series. The Babe was suspended for 40 days at the start of the 1923 season and his world series check of $3,362 denied him by Kenesaw M. Landis, baseball commissioner.

President Harridge, caught in the penalizing mood Saturday, also ordered all American league umpires to stop the practise of throwing the "bean ball." He ordered the umpires to eject any pitcher caught in the act of attempting to intimidate batters by "dusting them off."

Carl Reynolds

Records Flop As Athletics Take Indians

CLEVELAND, July 10 (AP).— Cleveland and Philadelphia battled wildly and stubbornly today for eighteen innings—two full regulation games—before Jimmy Foxx crossed the plate with the run that gave the Athletics a hard-earned 18-to-17 victory.

Fifty-eight base-hits rattled off the offerings of five pitchers in today's baseball marathon, three of them home runs by Foxx and one a home run by Earl Averill.

Three New Records.

Two new all-time records and one modern record were established during the course of the long affair. Between 'em, the two clubs made a total of fifty-eight hits, as compared with an all-time record of fifty-one made by the Phillies (26) and the Cubs (25) on Aug. 25, 1922. Today the Athletics made twenty-five hits and the Indians thirty-three.

Nine of the Indians' hits were made by Shortstop Johnny Burnett in eleven times at bat. The previous record was seven hits in seven times at bat made by Wilbert Robinson, former Dodger manager, while playing for Baltimore against St. Louis, June 10, 1892.

Cleveland's thirty-three hits established a new modern record for hits by one club in one game, surpassing the thirty-one made by the Giants against Cincinnati, June 9, 1901. The all-time record is thirty-six, made by the Philadelphia Nationals against Louisville, Aug. 17, 1894.

A Giddy Thing.

In the ninth inning, Ed Morgan, Cleveland first sacker, allowed Dykes' easy roller to go between his legs. The error snatched victory from the Tribe, which was leading, 14 to 13, with two men out. As it was, Simmons walked and the irrepressible Foxx then singled to score both runners and keep the A's in the running.

Foxx hit homers Nos. 31, 32 and 33, batting in eight runs, scored the winning run and played hobb generally with the Indians.

PHILADELPHIA						CLEVELAND					
	ab	r	h	o	e		ab	r	h	o	e
Haas,rf	9	3	2	8	0	Porter,rf	10	3	3	3	0
Cramer,cf	8	2	3	5	0	Burn't,ss	11	4	9	11	1
Dye,3b	10	2	3	7	0	Aver'l,cf	9	3	5	5	0
Sim'ns,lf	9	4	5	2	0	Vosm'k,lf	10	2	2	9	0
Foxx,1b	9	4	6	21	0	Mor'n,1b	11	1	3	16	1
M'N'r,ss	10	0	2	9	0	Myatt,c	7	2	1	1	0
Heving,c	4	0	0	1	0	Ciss'l,2b	7	1	4	1	2
Madk'c	5	0	0	10	0	Kamm,3b	7	0	3	1	1
Wil's,2b	8	1	2	14	0	Brown,p	4	0	2	4	1
Krause,p	1	0	0	1	0	Hudlin,p	0	0	0	0	0
Rom'l,p	7	2	3	7	1	Ferrell,p	5	0	0	0	0
Totals	80	18	25	85	1	Totals	88	17	33	81	5

Phila . . .201 201 702 000 000 201—18
Cleveland .303 011 601 000 000 200—17

Runs batted in—Porter 2, Burnett 2, Averill 4, Vosmik, Morgan 4, Cissell 3, Cramer, Dykes 4, Simmons 3, Foxx 8, Rommel, McNair, Two base hits—Burnett 2, Myatt, Cissell, Vosmik, Morgan 2, Haas, Dykes, Kamm, Porter, McNair, Foxx. Home runs—Foxx 3, Averill. Stolen base—Cissell. Sacrifices—Kamm, Ferrell. Double plays—Williams-McNair-Foxx, Burnett-Cissell-Morgan, Kamm-Cissell-Morgan, Williams-Madjeski-Foxx. Bases on balls—Off Krause 1, Brown 1, Hudlin 2, Ferrell 4, Rommel 9. Struck out—By Brown 3, Ferrell, Rommel 7. Hits—Off Krause 4 in 1. Rommel 29 in 17, Brown, 13 in 6 2-3, Ferrell 12 in 11 1-3. Wild pitches—Rommel 2. Winning pitcher—Rommel. Losing pitcher—Ferrell. Umpires—Hildebrand and Owens. Time—4.05.

80,284 WATCH A'S BLANK TRIBE

Record Crowd Sees First Game in New Muny Stadium.

CLEVELAND, Ohio, July 31 (A.P.). What is claimed to be the largest crowd ever to witness a major league baseball game turned out today for the Cleveland Indians' debut in the Municipal Stadium and saw the Tribe lose a thrilling 1-to-0 battle to Philadelphia.

The official attendance was announced as 80,284, of which 76,979 were cash customers—a scant handful more than the previous mark recorded by the American League. Semiofficial record books, however, credit the Yanks and the A's with a crowd of 85,265.

Grove Wins 16th Of Year.

Robert Moses Grove, the Athletics' ace southpaw, was in rare form and held the Indians to four scattered hits to win his sixteenth game of the season. Mel Harder, the Indians' young right-hander, was almost equally stingy with hits and kept the A's harmless except in the eighth inning.

Bishop drew one of Harder's two passes to start the eighth, went to second on Haas' sacrifice, and scored the lone run of the game on Cochrane's single.

The Indians threatened only once, in the seventh, when Averill and Vosmik got infield singles in succession. Grove then set the Tribe down in order.

The game was the Indians' first in the Municipal Stadium after a 41-year stand at League Park.

Phila.	AB	H	O	A	Cleveland.	AB	H	O	A
Bishop,2b	3	1	1	3	Porter,rf	4	0	3	0
Haas,cf	3	1	3	0	Burnett,ss	4	1	1	1
Cochrane,c	3	1	5	1	Averill,cf	4	1	3	0
Sim'ons,lf	4	1	2	0	Vosmik,lf	4	1	1	0
Foxx,1b	4	1	12	2	Morgan,1b	4	0	8	0
McNair,ss	3	0	0	2	Sewell,c	4	0	5	1
Miller,rf	4	0	3	0	Cissell,2b	2	1	3	1
Dykes,3b	4	0	1	0	Kamm,3b	4	0	0	1
Grove,p	3	1	0	4	Harder,p	2	0	0	2
					*Ferrell	1	0	0	0
Totals	31	6	27	14	Hil'brand,p	0	0	0	0
					Totals	33	4	27	7

*Batted for Harder in eighth.
Philadelphia . . . . . . .000 000 010—1
Cleveland . . . . .000 000 000—0

Run—Bishop. Error—Morgan. Run batted in—Cochrane. Two-base hit—Foxx. Sacrifices—Kamm, Haas, McNair. Double play—Burnett to Cissell to Morgan. Left on bases—Philadelphia, 7; Cleveland, 5. First base on balls—Off Grove, 2; off Harder, 2. Struck out—By Grove, 6; by Harder, 3. Hits—Off Harder, 5 in 8 innings; off Hildebrand, 1 in 1 inning. Losing pitcher—Harder. Umpires—Guthrie, Ormsby, Geisel and Connolly. Time of game—One hour 50 minutes.

Nov. 22

Gelbert of Cards Has Shattered Leg

Philadelphia, Pa.—(AP)—His left leg shattered, the result of a hunting accident, Charlie Gelbert, shortstop of the St. Louis Cardinals, Monday was raced 150 miles from Chambersburg, Pa., to a Philadelphia hospital, where he will undergo an operation.

Doctors said Gelbert's future baseball career depends on the success of the treatment.

Gelbert's condition is more serious than believed at first, attendants explained afterward, and he cannot be operated upon for three or four days.

Explanations Indefinite as Rajah Loses Third Post. Grimm Successor.

BY WILLIAM WEEKES,
Associated Press Sports Writer.

CHICAGO, August 3.—Baseball's most famous Nomad, Rogers Hornsby, was on his way again today—deposed as manager of the Chicago Cubs.

The announcement of Hornsby's dismissal came last night, with a suddenness so startling as to leave the base ball world agog —as much agog as when John McGraw, without warning, quit as manager of the New York Giants last June.

In making his announcement, William L. Veeck, president of the club, said, without elaboration:

"It was to the best interests of the club that Hornsby retire at this time."

Not only is the Rajah, probably the stormiest figure in modern National League history, all done as manager of the club—the third to be placed in his charge—but he is no longer a member of the club, having also been released as a player.

FOXX HITS NO. 58, BUT MACKMEN BOW

Senators Win, 2-1, Despite His Perfect Day at Bat—Take Season's Series, 12-10.

CROWDER EXCELS ON MOUND

Scores 26th Triumph and 15th in Row to Lead League in Pitching Victories.

WASHINGTON, Sept. 25 (AP). Jimmy Foxx blasted his fifty-eighth home run of the season in a perfect day at bat, but the Senators defeated the Athletics by 2 to 1 today in closing their 1932 rivalry.

Foxx made a homer and two singles in three times at bat.

General Alvin Crowder of the Senators took the league lead in games won, chalking up his twenty-sixth of the year and fifteenth straight. Except for Foxx, only two Athletics got as far as second and none to third off his delivery.

The victory gave the third-place Washington team a lead of two games over the Mackmen for the season, the Senators winning 12 and losing 10 to their second-place opponents.

Cain, the Philadelphia pitcher, got into trouble right off the start, but a double play, McNair to Foxx, saved him and resulted in the Senators being held to one run on four singles in the first inning.

The box score:

PHILADELPHIA (A.)					WASHINGTON (A.)				
	ab	r	h	po	a		ab	r	h	po	a
Williams,2b	5	0	1	1	1	0	Rice,lf	3	1	1	3	0
Haas,cf	4	0	2	4	0	Kerr,2b	2	1	1	3	0
Madj'k,c	4	0	0	5	1	Reynolds,rf	4	1	1	1	0
Sim'ons,lf	5	0	1	1	0	Cronin,ss	4	0	2	4	1
Foxx,1b	3	1	3	12	0	Kuhel,1b	3	0	1	11	0
McNair,ss	4	0	2	2	1	West,cf	4	0	1	4	0
Miller,rf	4	0	1	0	0	Bluege,3b	3	0	0	1	0
Dykes,3b	3	0	0	1	0	Spencer,c	4	0	1	2	0
Cain,p	3	0	1	0	1	Crowder,p	3	0	0	1	0
Total	35	1	6	24	4	1	Total	29	2	7	27	12

Philadelphia . . . . . . .100 000 000—1
Washington . . . . .100 000 001—2

Runs batted in—Kuhel, Cronin, Foxx. Two base hits—Cronin. Home run—Foxx. Sacrifices—Kerr, Rice and Kuhel. Double plays—McNair to Foxx, Cronin, Kerr and Kuhel; Madjeski and Williams. Left on bases—Philadelphia 6, Washington 6. Base on balls—Off Cain 2, Crowder 1. Struck out—By Cain 4, Crowder 1. Umpires—McGowan, Van Graflan and Nallin. Time of game—1:17.

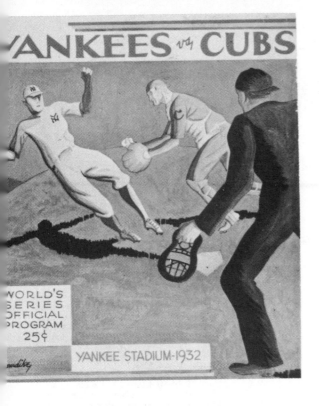

YANKEES vs CUBS

WORLD'S
SERIES
OFFICIAL
PROGRAM
25¢

YANKEE STADIUM-1932

Official Box Score

NEW YORK (A. L.)

	Ab.	R.	H.	O.	A.	E.
Combs, c.f.	4	4	3	2	0	0
Sewell, 3b.	6	1	3	0	2	1
Ruth, l.f.	5	0	1	2	0	0
Byrd, l.f.	0	0	0	0	0	0
Gehrig, 1b.	4	2	2	12	0	1
Lazzeri, 2b.	5	2	3	1	4	0
Dickey, c.	6	2	3	4	0	0
Chapman, r.f.	5	0	2	4	0	0
Crosetti, s.s.	6	1	1	2	5	2
Allen, p.	0	0	0	0	0	0
W. Moore, p	3	0	1	0	1	0
1Ruffing	0	0	0	0	0	0
2Hoag	0	1	0	0	0	0
Pennock, p.	1	0	0	0	0	0
Totals	45	13	19	27	12	4

1Batted for W. Moore in seventh.
2Ran for Ruffing in seventh.

CHICAGO (N. L.)

	Ab.	R.	H.	O.	A.	E.
Herman, 2b.	5	1	1	2	2	0
English, 3b.	5	1	1	1	0	0
Cuyler, r.f.	5	0	1	2	0	0
Stephenson, l.f.	5	1	2	1	0	0
Demaree, c.f.	3	1	1	3	0	1
Grimm, 1b.	4	2	2	4	2	0
Hartnett, c.	4	0	1	8	0	0
3Hack	0	0	0	0	0	0
Jurges, s.s.	4	0	1	5	2	0
Bush, p.	0	0	0	0	0	0
Warneke, p.	1	0	0	1	0	0
May, p.	2	0	0	1	0	0
Tinning, p.	0	0	0	0	1	0
Hemsley, c.	1	0	0	0	0	0
Grimes, p.	0	0	0	0	0	0
Totals	39	6	9	27	7	1

3Ran for Hartnett in eighth.

New York........ 1 0 2 0 0 2 4 0 4—13
Chicago......... 4 0 0 0 0 1 0 0 1— 6

Runs batted in—Gehrig, 3; Demaree, 3; Jurges, Lazzeri, Combs, 2; Sewell, 2; Ruth, Chapman, English. Two-base hits—Gehrig, Grimm, Sewell, Crosetti, Chapman, Lazzeri, 2; Combs. Double play—Herman, Jurges and Grimm. Left on base—New York, 13; Chicago, 7. Base on balls—Off Bush, 1 (Lazzeri); off Warneke, 1 (Combs); off May, 3 (Chapman, Combs and Ruffing); off Pennock, 1 (Demaree); off Grimes, 1 (Gehrig). Struck out—By Warneke, 1 (W. Moore); by May, 3 (Ruth 2, W. Moore); by Tinning, 2 (Dickey, Crosetti); by W. Moore, 1 (Jurges); by Pennock, 3 (Herman, Hemsley, Cuyler). Hits and runs—Off Bush, 2 hits, 1 run in 1⅓ inning; off Warneke, 5 hits, 2 runs in 2⅔ innings (none out in fourth); off Allen, 5 hits, 4 runs in 2⅔ inning; off Grimes, 4 hits, 4 runs in 1 inning; off W. Moore, 2 hits, 1 run in 5⅓ innings; off May, 8 hits, 6 runs in 3⅓ innings; off Pennock, 2 hits, 1 run in 3 innings; off Tinning, no hits, no runs in 1⅔ innings. Hit by pitcher—By Bush (Ruth); by May (Gehrig). Winning pitcher—Moore. Losing pitcher—May. Umpires—Magerkurth (N. L.), plate; Dinneen (A. L.), first; Klem (N. L.), second; Van Graflan (A. L.), third. Time—2.27.

RUTH ENJOYS RAZZING CUBS

Raises His Fingers To Show Strike Count, Then Hits Homer

HERMAN HOLDS PACE

Has Got On Base First Time At Plate In Every Game

[By the Associated Press]

Chicago, Oct. 1—Babe Ruth stole the third show of the World Series today and had the time of his life doing it.

As he belted ball after ball into the bleacher seats during batting practice he kept up a rapid-fire conversation with the awe-stricken Cubs.

"You've had your last look at the stadium (meaning Yankee Stadium)," he shouted to Pat Malone. "You good-hearted guys, why I've got more money than all of you."

Ruth's sally on wealth was one of many. The big fellow has been razzing the Cubs ever since the big show started for leaving Rogers Hornsby out of their World Series split and giving Mark Koenig only a half slice of the melon.

When he came to the plate in the fifth inning, the Cub bench sitters shouted derisively as he missed the first pitch. The Babe held up one finger and finally two on each hand with the count two and two. Then wham! He caught Root's next pitch and they never got the ball back. It arched ten feet over the center-field fence to the right of the scoreboard. It was probably the longest home run in Wrigley Field's history. As he trotted around the bags he held up four fingers, signifying a home run.

In banging out two homers today, Gehrig may win the World Series long-distance clouting championship from Ruth for the first time. He has three to Babe's two so far. Lou failed to collect one in his first two World Series. He got four in 1928 against St. Louis.

YANKEES SWEEP WORLD SERIES

Win Final Game, 13 To 6, For Third One-Sided Triumph

LAZZERI'S BAT BUSY

Connects For 2 Homers. Final Contest Smashes Records

Ruth Contributes To 13 Of 17 Series Marks Set

Chicago, Oct. 2 (AP)—The 1932 World Series, concluded today, was featured by 17 outstanding additions to the list of championship records. Altogether in four games, 15 records were broken and two others equaled.

Babe Ruth figured in exactly 13 record feats. The list follows:

1. Most consecutive victories total series, 12 by Yankees.
2. Most home runs, two clubs, one game, six in third game.
3. Most home runs, one inning, one club, two in succession, third game, by Ruth and Gehrig, equaling former mark.
4. Most home runs, total series, 15 by Ruth.
5. Most total bases, total series, 96 by Ruth.
6. Most long hits, total series, 22 by Ruth.
7. Most extra bases, total hits, 54 by Ruth.
8. Most bases on balls, total series, 33 by Ruth.
9. Most strikeouts, total series, 30 by Ruth.
10. Most strikeouts, one game, 5 by George Pipgras, of Yankees, third game.
11. Largest score, both clubs, one game, 19 runs, fourth game.
12. Most series played, 10 by Ruth.
13. Most runs, total series, 37 by Ruth.
14. Most runs batted in, total series, 33 by Ruth.
15. Most runs batted in, one game, 4 by Ruth, third game, and 4 by Lazzeri, fourth game, equaling record formerly held by Ruth and five others.
16. Most time played on world championship club, 7 by Ruth.
17. Most time batted .300 or over, total series, 6 by Ruth.

YAWKEY, COLLINS BUY THE RED SOX

Wealthy New Yorker Becomes Club President and Athletics' Ex-Star His Assistant.

PLEDGE WORK TO REBUILD

New Owners Determined to Put Boston at Top Again— Price Put at $1,000,000.

By The Associated Press.

BOSTON, Feb. 25. After apologizing to the Boston baseball public for his failure to achieve his ambitions for the Boston Red Sox, Bob Quinn today sold the club to Thomas A. Yawkey, 30-year-old New York millionaire and a son of a former owner of the Detroit Tigers.

Yawkey will succeed Quinn as president of the last-place American League club and will be assisted by Edward Trowbridge (Eddie) Collins, famous star of the old Athletics, who will act as vice president and general manager. Collins, according to Yawkey, took over a substantial stock interest when the club passed out of Quinn's hands.

BABE'S SPECIALTY GETS NEEDED RUNS

49,000 Pay $52,000 to See All-Star Game. Won 4-2. Crowder, Cronin Help.

BY WILLIAM WEEKES,
Associated Press Sports Writer.

CHICAGO, July 7.—Baseball's dream game has been played and the story thereof is largely another tale about the man who made the home run famous—George Herman Ruth.

Thirteen hand-picked stars from American League teams defeated 17 selected National Leaguers, 4 to 2, yesterday at Comiskey Field, before a capacity attendance of 49,000 fans. And it was one of old Mr. Ruth's copyrighted blasts that accounted for the two big runs.

The typical Ruthian gesture came in the third inning, with Charlie Gehringer of the Detroit Tigers on first base. Wild Bill Hallahan of the St. Louis Cardinals, who was Wild Bill at his wildest while he was in there, was the victim. With the count one ball and a strike, Hallahan served the next one up about knee-high and outside. A mighty swing by the 39-year-old Ruth and the ball sailed on a line into the lower deck of the right field stands.

---

18 Scoreless Innings for Hubbell

Sets Big League Record for Year as Giants Beat Cards, 1-0.

NEW YORK, July 2 (A.P.).— In what was probably the greatest exhibition of hurling seen here in a good many years, the Giants took a pair of 1-to-0 decisions from the St. Louis Cardinals today to go 5½ games ahead of the second place club.

With 45,000 fans cheering him on, Carl Hubbell blanked the Cards for 18 innings of the opener, which was the longest game played in the major leagues so far this season. Leroy (Bud) Parmelee followed by allowing only four blows in the regulation nine innings and fanning 13.

Hubbell gave up only six hits in his double duel and didn't issue a pass. Tex Carleton opposed him for 16 frames on even terms before he was lifted for a pinch hitter.

Crit's Hit Decisive.

Jess Haines followed. In the eighteenth he started by walking Joe Moore. Gus Mancuso sacrificed Moore to second. Travis Jackson, pinch-hitting for Blondy Ryan, was purposely passed, and when Hubbell forced him at second, Moore reached third. Hughie Critz, with the count three and two on him, smashed a single through the box to bring home Moore with the winning run.

Aug. 21

New York.	AB	H	O	A	Chicago.	AB	H	O	A
Combs,cf..	8	1	3	0	Swanson,rf	6	2	4	0
Sewell,3b.	7	0	3	9	Haas,cf..	7	1	3	0
Walker,lf.	8	2	5	0	Dykes,3b.	9	1	0	6
Gehrig,1b.	6	1	23	1	Simmons,lf	8	3	6	0
Chap'n,rf.	7	2	1	0	Appling,ss.	5	1	4	7
Lazzeri,2b.	7	2	8	10	Kress,1b..	5	1	24	3
Dickey,c..	7	1	6	5	Hayes,2b..	7	2	4	6
Crosetti,ss	6	1	3	4	Berry,c....	2	0	4	0
Devens,p..	3	0	0	2	*Lyons....	1	0	0	0
Pennock,p.	2	1	2	1	Grube,c...	2	0	3	1
					Gaston,p..	3	0	1	4
Totals..	59	11	54	32	†Fonseca..	1	0	0	0
					‡Jones....	0	0	0	0
					Faber,p..	3	0	1	3
					Totals..	57	11	54	30

*Batted for Berry in eleventh inning.
†Batted for Gaston in eleventh inning.
‡Ran for Fonseca in eleventh inning.

New York...... 000 000 001 020 000 000—3
Chicago...... 000 000 001 020 000 000—3
(Called on account of darkness.)

Runs—Combs, Walker, Gehrig, Simmons, Kress, Hayes. Runs batted in—Gehrig, Chapman, Lazzeri, Swanson (2), Kress. Stolen bases—Combs, Crosetti. Sacrifices—Sewell, Pennock (2), Haas, Appling, Kress, Lyons. Double plays—Sewell to Lazzeri to Gehrig, Gehrig to Dickey to Gehrig, Appling to Hayes to Kress, Kress to Appling, Faber to Appling to Kress. Left on bases—New York, 10; Chicago, 19. First base on balls—Off Devens, 7; off Pennock, 8; off Gaston, 3; off Faber, 2. Struck out—By Devens, 3; by Pennock, 2; by Gaston, 4; by Faber, 2. Hits—Off Devens, 3 in 8 innings (none out in ninth); off Pennock, 8 in 10 innings; off Gaston, 9 in 11 innings; off Faber, 2 in 7 innings. Wild pitch—Devens. Umpires—Geisel, Kolls and Moriarty. Time of game—Four hours 11 minutes.

St. Louis.	AB	H	O	A	New York.	AB	H	O	A
Martin,3b.	7	0	3	6	Critz,2b..	9	3	4	12
Frisch,2b.	7	0	7	5	O'Doul,lf..	4	1	0	0
Orsatti,cf.	7	1	0	0	James....	0	0	0	0
Collins,1b.	7	2	15	5	Davis,cf..	2	0	2	0
Medwick,lf	7	1	7	0	Terry,1b..	6	2	26	1
Allen,rf...	6	0	4	0	Ott,rf....	8	2	3	0
Wilson,c..	6	2	11	0	Verges,3b.	7	0	3	6
Dur'her,ss	3	0	3	4	Moore,cf,lf	7	0	3	0
*Hornsby.	1	0	0	0	Mancuso,c.	7	1	13	1
Slade,ss..	1	0	1	2	†Ryan,ss..	6	2	0	5
Carleton,p	4	0	3	3	‡Jackson..	0	0	0	0
†O'Farrell.	1	0	0	0	Hubbell,p.	7	1	1	7
Haines,p..	0	0	0	2					
Totals .57		6	53	29	Totals .50	10	54	27	

*Batted for Durocher in eleventh.
†Batted for Carleton in seventeenth.
‡Two out when winning run was scored.
§Ran for O'Doul in eleventh.
¶Batted for Ryan in eighteenth.

St. L....00000000000000000000—0
N. Y....00000000000000000001—1

Babe Hurls, and Downs Red Sox

Pitches Entire Game, Hit Hard at Times, But Steers Yanks to 6 to 5 Victory

BY PAUL H. SHANNON

NEW YORK, Oct. 1 — Enacting for the second time in 13 years a role that he abandoned long before joining the Yankees in 1920, big Babe Ruth, still the idol of fandom, went to the mound against the Red Sox this afternoon, pitched the entire game, and though hit hard at times, and seemingly very tired toward the end, was able to steer his hard-hitting teammates to a 6 to 5 win in the season's final contest.

EXIT BABE, SMILING

N. Y. (A)	AB	R	BH	TB	PO	A
Combs, lf						
Walker, rf						
Ferrell, 2b	5	1	0	0	0	0
Ruth, p	3	2	2	1		
Gehrig, 1b						
Chapman, rf, lf	4	1	2			
Lary, 3b	2	1	0	0		
Glenn, c	4	0	1	1		
Crosetti, ss	4	0	1	1		
Byrd, cf	4	0	0	0		
Totals	34	6	10	15	27	

BOSTON (A)	AB	R	BH	TB	PO	A
Werber, ss						
Almada, lf	3	0	1	1		
Jolley, rf						
Ferrell, c		1	1			
Judge, 1b						
Welch, p	1	0	0	0		
aWarstler	1	0	0	0		
Stumpf, cf	3	1	2	3		
Walters, 3b	4	2	2	2		
Muller, 2b	2	0	0	0		
Kline, p						
McManus, 1b						
Totals	39	5	12	13	24	12

New York	3	0	0	0	0		6
Boston	0	0	0	0	0	4	5

KLEIN TRIPLE CROWN

KLEIN KING OF SWAT IN OLD LEAGUE

Phillies' Ace Leads National in Five Departments

NEW YORK, Oct. 7—Dominating the slugging of the National league as few players have in late years, Chuck Klein finished first in five departments of play in the senior circuit and also won the major league batting crown.

.368 AVERAGE

The Phillies' hard hitting outfielder won the batting title with an average of .368, was first in total hits with 223, showed the way in two-base blows with 44, led on home runs with 28 and sent 120 runs across the plate to top the list in runs batted in, according to the final unofficial averages.

Only in runs scored, stolen bases and triples was Klein forced to yield to another. Pepper Martin, the Cardinals' World's Series hero of 1931, led in total runs with 122 and stole the most bases—26, while Floyd Vaughan cracked out 19 three-baggers.

Only Klein's failure to hit in the closing days of the campaign kept him from beating Lefty O'Doul's mark of 1932. As it was Klein tied his former teammate's figures and finished 20 points above his average for last year.

Hubbell Wins Pitching Duel; Series Is 3-1

Blondie Ryan Drives in Winning Counter With Single in Eleventh Inning: Weaver Loses

Washington, D. C. Carl Hubbell, slim southpaw of the New York Giants, pitched his second victory and the third for his team by defeating Washington, American league champions, in the fourth game of the series here Friday afternoon, 2 to 1 The game went 11 innings.

Monte Weaver, who started for the Nationals, was relieved by Jack Russell after the eleventh inning after the Giants had scored the deciding run on three hits.

Ryan Bats in Run

Blondie Ryan, spark plug of the Giant infield, swung the big bat that drove in the winning tally Travis Jackson led off by beating out a drag down the third base line, moved ahead on Mancuso's sacrifice and finished his tour of the runways on Ryan's single to left. Hubbell followed with a hit in the same spot, putting Ryan on second At this stage Russell replaced Weaver and struck out Moore and retired Critz on a fly to Schulte

The Senators made a big threat to win the game in their half of the eleventh, combing Hubbell for two hits and loading the bases on an intentional pass, but a rapid fire double play via Ryan-Critz-Terry ended the overtime battle.

Schulte opened the Nationals' eleventh with a single to left. Kuhel bunted down the first base line and beat it out, putting Schulte on second. Both runners advanced on Bluege's sacrifice, Jackson to Critz An intentional pass to Sewell gave the Nationals a full house. Bolton, hitting for Russell, then rolled to Ryan, who started the double play that ended the game.

Official Score

NEW YORK	AB	R	H	PO	A
Moore, lf	5	0	1	3	0
Critz, 2b		0	0	6	5
Terry, 1b	5	1	1	12	0
Ott, rf		0	0	0	0
Davis, cf		0	1	0	0
Jackson, 3b	5	1	2	0	0
Mancuso, c		0	1	6	0
Ryan, ss	5	0	2	1	5
Hubbell, p	4	0	1	1	3
Totals	40	2	11	33	15

WASHINGTON	AB	R	H	PO	A
Myer, 2b					
Goslin, rf-lf		1	0	0	0
Manush, lf	1	0	0	0	0
Harris, rf		0	0	0	0
Cronin, ss		0	0	0	0
Schulte, cf	5	0	1	0	0
Kuhel, 1b		0	1	14	0
Bluege, 3b		0	1	1	0
Sewell, c		0	0	0	0
Weaver, p		0	0	0	0
Russell, p		0	0	0	0
Bolton		0	0	0	0
Totals	38	1	8	33	17

Bolton batted for Russell in eleventh.

New York	0	0	1	0	0	0	0	0	0	0	1—2
Washington	0	0	0	0	0	0	1	0	0	0	0—1

Runs batted in—Terry, Sewell, Ryan Two base hit—Moore. Home run—Terry. Sacrifices—Davis, Goslin, Bluege 2, Hubbell, Mancuso Double plays Myer to Kuhel, Ryan to Critz to Terry. Left on bases—New York 12, Washington 11 Bases on balls—Off Weaver 4 Moore Ott, Mancuso 2; Hubbell 4 Manush, Myer, Harris, Sewell Struck out—By Weaver Jackson, Ryan, Davis; Russell 1 Moore; Hubbell 5 Kuhel Weaver 2, Cronin Hits—Off Weaver 11 in ten and one third innings; Russell none in two thirds Losing pitcher Weaver. Umpires Plate, Ormsby (A L); first base, Moran (N L); second base Moriarty (A L); third base Hildenbrand (N L) Time 2:09

MACK SELLS GROVE AND 4 OTHER STARS

Athletics' Pilot Breaks Up Club in Startling Deals, Receiving $300,000.

RED SOX GET HURLING ACE

Acquire Bishop and Walberg Also—Cochrane to Tigers, Earnshaw to White Sox.

By The Associated Press.

CHICAGO, Dec. 12.—Connie Mack, veteran leader of the Philadelphia Athletics, who startled baseball way back in 1914 by breaking up his famous "$100,000 infield," tonight went even further in player transactions.

He sold pitchers Lefty Grove and Rube Walberg and Infielder Max Bishop to the Boston Red Sox, Mickey Cochrane to the Detroit Tigers and pitcher George Earnshaw to the Chicago White Sox.

Financial pressure, forced by Philadelphia bankers, was assigned as the reason for the sales, some of the most important in the history of baseball. The deals all but complete a break-up of the famous Athletics who won the world's championship in 1929 and 1930.

Babe Ruth's Home Run No. 700 Gives Yankees 4 To 2 Edge

Detroit, July 13 -- (AP.) —Babe Ruth rose to another important occasion today and clouted a home run that led the Yankees back into first place in the American League with a 4 to 2 victory over the Tigers in the second game of their "crucial" series.

After Lou Gehrig had been put out of action in the second inning as the result of a severe cold in his back, the Babe took it upon himself to win the game and provided the impetus for the Yankee victory. Ruth's homer was his seven hundredth since he came up to the American League with the Red Sox something over 20 years ago and his 14th of the current season.

The blow coming with Earl Combs on base, started the scoring in the mound duel between Red Ruffing and Tommy Bridges. The other Yankee runs came in the eighth when Bill Dickey rapped a double with Ruth and Ben Chapman on the base through passes.

Both pitchers hurled expertly but Ruffing had the edge most of the way as he granted only six hits. Detroit scored a run in the third on a walk to Joyner White, Goose Goslin's double and Charley Gehringer's fly. Their second tally again followed a Yankee pair as Gehringer singled in the eighth. Bill Rogell forced him and Hank Greenberg brought Rogell home with a triple. Bridges yielded nine hits but saved himself a lot of trouble by fanning eight.

Score

NEW YORK

	AB	R	H	PO	A	E
Combs, cf	5	1	1	4	0	0
Saltzgaver, 3b, 1b	4	0	1	7	1	0
Ruth, lf	3	2	1	1	0	0
Byrd, lf	0	0	0	0	0	0
Gehrig, 1b	1	0	1	1	0	0
Rolfe, ss	2	0	1	1	2	0
Chapman, rf	3	1	1	0	0	0
Dickey, c	4	0	2	5	0	0
Crosetti, ss, 3b	3	0	1	2	3	0
Heffner, 2b	4	0	1	6	0	0
Ruffing, p	4	0	0	0	0	0
Totals	33	4	9	27	6	0

DETROIT

	AB	R	H	PO	A	E
Fox, rf	5	0	0	4	0	0
White, cf	2	1	0	2	0	0
Goslin, lf	4	0	1	1	0	0
Gehringer, 2b	4	0	1	1	1	0
Rogell, ss	4	1	1	2	4	0
Greenberg, 1b	4	0	2	8	0	0
Cochrane, c	3	0	1	8	2	0
Owen, 3b	3	0	0	1	0	0
Bridges, p	3	0	0	0	3	0
Walker, z	1	0	0	0	0	0
Totals	33	2	6	27	10	0

Score by innings
New York .... 002 000 020—4
Detroit .... 001 000 010—2

Runs batted in Ruth 2, Gehringer, Dickey 2, Greenberg, two base hits, Greenberg, Goslin, Dickey, three base hit, Greenberg, home run Ruth, stolen bases White, Chapman, Cochrane, double play Fox to Gehringer, left on bases Detroit 8, New York 6, base on balls off Bridges 4, off Ruffing 4, struck out by Bridges 8, Ruffing 3, wild pitches Bridges 2, umpires, Donnelly, McGowan, Owens, time, 2:12

z Walker batted for Bridges in 9th.

2,000 Passes Give Babe Ruth 34 Miles of Free Traveling

New York, N. Y. (P) Thirty-four miles of free transportation to first base through the wildness or caution of American league pitchers that's Babe Ruth's record to date.

The Babe received his two thousandth base on balls in Tuesday's game with the Cleveland Indians and thus reached another milestone in perhaps the most remarkable career in baseball history.

Eleven times Ruth has led the American league in total walks. Twelve times he has been given more than 100 free tickets in a season, setting up an all-time record of 170 in 1923.

Senators Bow to Young Star by 4-2 Score

Tigers Rally in Ninth to Save Game; Homer by Greenberg Starts Team to Victory

Washington, D. C. (P) Schoolboy Rowe, Detroit Tiger pitching ace, Saturday won his bid for his sixteenth consecutive victory and baseball's hall of fame by driving in the winning run for the Tigers' 4 to 2 victory over Washington in the ninth inning.

The victory for the 22-year-old right hander makes him the joint holder of the American league's record for consecutive games with Walter Johnson, Joe Wood and Lefty Grove.

Detroit also advanced further toward the flag, extending its margin over New York to five full games.

Greenberg Hits Homer

Until the ninth it looked as if all the Schoolboy's pitching and hitting were futile. Washington, playing a sparkling defensive game behind Monte Weaver, led 2 to 1, but Hank Greenberg, first up in the ninth inning, hit a home run over the right field wall. Owen singled and Weaver was replaced by Russell. Fox followed with a single to center. The Washington infield drew in and up walked Rowe. He blasted a single to left center. That was enough to win, but an error let another run in.

Rowe had struck out only one until the ninth, but with a rain threatening to stop proceedings and cause a Washington victory, he bore down. Schulte, first up, was safe on Rogell's bad throw. Susko forced Schulte and in quick succession Rowe fanned two pinch hitters, Harris and the last one, Travis, on three pitched balls.

The crowd roared and his team mates surrounded Rowe to beat their congratulations into his shoulders.

Tigers Tie in Sixth

Washington scored in the third inning on Stone's single and Manush's double. Detroit tied it in the sixth on Rogell's triple and a grounder by Greenberg.

The Senators, however, went ahead again in the seventh on Susko's single, a sacrifice and Myer's single. They stayed there until the ninth.

Rowe allowed nine hits but he did not walk a man and he got a double and a single in addition to his game-winning single in the ninth.

A heavy rain began to fall only a few minutes after the last man was out.

DETROIT	AB	R	H		WASHINGTON	AB	R	H
White, cf	4	0	0		Myer, 2b	5	0	0
Cochrane, c	5	0	0		Stone, rf	4	0	1
Gehringer, 2b	4	0	0		Manush, lf	4	0	1
Goslin, lf	5	0	0		Cronin, ss	4	0	0
Rogell, ss	4	1	2		Powell, cf	4	0	0
Greenberg, 1b	4	1	3		Kuhel, 1b	4	0	0
Owen, 3b	4	1	2		Bolton, c	4	0	0
Fox, rf	4	1	1		Susko, 1b	4	1	1
Rowe, p	4	0	3		Bluege, 3b	3	0	1
					Weaver, p			
					Russell, p	1	0	0
					Harris	1	0	0
					Travis	1	0	0
Totals	33	4	12		Totals	36	2	1

Harris batted for Bluege in ninth inning.
Travis batted for Russell in ninth.
Detroit .... 0 0 0 0 0 1 0 0 3—4
Washington .... 0 0 1 0 0 0 1 0 0—2

Runs batted in Manush, Greenberg 2, Myer, Rowe, Two base hits—Manush, Rowe, Three-base hit, Rogell, Home run—Greenberg, Sacrifice, Bluege, Double plays—Myer to Susko, Left on bases—Detroit 6, Washington 7, Bases on balls—Off Russell 1, Struck out—By Rowe 3, Weaver 1, Hits —Off Weaver, 10 in eight (none out in ninth), Russell 2 in one, Losing pitcher—Weaver

---

Dizzy Dean Blanks Reds, 9 to 0, For 30th Victory as Season Ends

Cardinals' Ace, With Bases Filled in Ninth, Fans Two and Gets Another on Foul to Score 7th Shutout—Delancey and Collins Drive Homers as 35,274 Look On.

By The Associated Press.

ST. LOUIS, Sept. 30.—Baseball's most amazing pennant rush since the campaign of George Stallings and his "miracle men" of Boston ended in glorious triumph today as the St. Louis Cardinals nailed the National League flag to their masthead with a rousing 9-0 victory over the Cincinnati Reds in the season's final game.

The stirring drive, started on Sept. 7, when the Cardinals trailed the then formidable-looking New York Giants by seven full games, had a double-barreled finish. The Brooklyn Dodgers had already beaten the Giants, 8 to 5, when Dizzy Dean was in the ninth inning of his great hurling performance against the lowly but bristling Reds.

Given his wide lead, Dizzy was pitching his heart out at the start of the ninth for his seventh shutout of the year. As Pool singled, Schulmerich doubled and Comorosky walked, to fill the bases with none out, his dream of becoming the shut-out king of the major leagues faded.

Rises to the Heights.

Then came the final flash from the Brooklyn-Giant game. The Dodgers had won; the pennant belonged to the Cardinals for sure. Grinning in that cocksure way of his, Dizzy rose to the heights then. He struck out Clyde Manion and Ted Petoskey, a pinch-hitter for Frey, and then pumped a fast one down the middle to little Sparky Adams, who fouled out to Bill Delancey.

RED SOX WIN ON ONE HIT.

Fail to Connect for Nine Innings but Top Newsom in 10th, 2-1.

ST. LOUIS, Sept. 18 (P).—For nine innings today Buck Newsom held the Red Sox hitless, but he weakened in the tenth, gave two passes and a single and the Browns were defeated, 2 to 1. The winning run was scored by Bishop, who, with Werber, had been passed before R. Johnson singled.

Boston's first tally, in the second, came on two walks, an error by Melillo and a fielder's choice. In this inning Wes Ferrell objected strenuously to a third called strike, and when Brother Rick joined his protest the Ferrells were put out of the game by Umpire Kolls.

The box score:

BOSTON (A)						ST. LOUIS (A)					
Bishop, 2b	3	1	0	1	4	0	Melillo, 2b	4	0	2	4	0
Werber, 3b	3	0	0	2	1	0	Garms, lf	3	0	2	4	0
Almada, cf	5	0	0	3	0	0	Burns, 1b	4	0	1	7	0
R. Johnson, lf	4	1	2	0	0	0	Pepper, cf	3	0	1	1	0
Cooke, rf	4	0	0	1	0	0	Campbell, rf	4	0	1	1	0
R. Ferrell, c	4	0	0	5	0	0	Grace, 1b	4	0	1	0	0
Reddig, ss	4	0	0	2	0	0	Hemsley, c	3	0	1	2	0
Morgan, 1b	3	0	0	15	0	0	Strange, ss	3	0	1	1	0
W. Ferrell, p	1	0	0	0	2	0	Newsom, p	3	0	1	3	0
Walberg, p	3	0	0	0	1	0						
Total	35	2	1	30	9	3						

Batted for Campbell in tenth.
Boston .... 0 1 0 0 0 0 0 0 0 1—2
St. Louis .... 0 0 0 0 0 1 0 0 0 0—1

Runs batted in Garms, Strange, R. Johnson. Two base hit, Grace, Burns, Stolen bases—Cliff, Burns, Sacrifice, Garms, Left on bases—Boston 9, St. Louis 7, Bases on balls off W. Ferrell 1, Walberg 1, Newsom 7, Struck out by W. Ferrell 3, Walberg 2, Newsom 9, Hits—Off W. Ferrell 1 in five innings, Walberg 0 in five, Winning pitcher, Walberg. Umpire, Kolls and Geisel. Time of game 2:22.

July 11

American League Stars Defeat Nationals, 9 to 7

Al Simmons Gets Three Hits in Five Trips to the Plate; Lefty Hubbell Fans Five Batters in Row; Frisch and Medwick Each Connect for Home Runs; Averill Hero at Plate

BY PAT GANNON
STAFF CORRESPONDENT OF THE JOURNAL

New York, N. Y.—Blasts and pitchers fading like autumn leaves. Siege guns banging and runs thundering home on the winds of doubles, triples and homers. Pitching at times as fantastic in its greatness as the wildest fiction. Babe Ruth hitless. Fabulous fielding intermixed with unaccountable lapses. Pitchers coming and going in battalions and base hits rattling down in clusters.

Such were the ingredients of the all-star contest at the Polo Grounds Tuesday, with about 50,000 fortunate onlookers shouting themselves hoarse while 15,000 others milled about the gates unable to buy even a rafter seat. For $53,000 the fans received a capsule world series and they rode every pitch on a league game fare. In the end the drab totals counted the day won by the American league, 9 to 7, but, scored as an all-star encounter, the honors were about even.

It was a bedlam of baseball for almost three hours in which eight pitchers—five National and three American—marched up the hill and then marched down again unable to stop the bludgeoning. Only two of the cream of the leagues suppressed the sluggers in a mad afternoon, with a fifth inning slugfest that saw 19 men at bat for a total of nine runs.

In the center of things loomed the slim figure of Carl Hubbell, Giants' master pitcher whose performance outshone the efforts of two score stars. Behind him came the trim Mel Harder of Cleveland, who stopped the national clouters in the fifth and held them helpless thereafter.

Averill Pounds Ball

In the slugging departments Earl Averill of Cleveland, who with a triple belted the longest hit of the afternoon, distancing even two homers, contributed the chief scoring punch for the American league. Ranged with him was Al Simmons, who twice served as detonator for the younger loop's rallies and figured with a hit in the third scoring punch. In addition, Simmons contributed a sparkling catch, an effort perhaps outclassed only by Arky Vaughan, who tore far into left field to snare a hit over his shoulder.

It was a dizzy day with umpires on the grid most of the time. Five and six major league managers were on the field simultaneously at times, with three more on the benches, a total of nine brain trusters. To cap it all two of them, Joe Cronin and Mickey Cochrane, both were run down between bases in one inning to make four outs.

Oddly, too, with all the master minds about, Billy Herman of the Cubs got into the game as a pinch hitter in the third and then came back as a relief man for Frisch in the seventh without a visible protest. With two murdered rows master minds went for a dime a dozen and pitchers were merely obstacles to base hits.

Hubbell Fans Three

In the first inning the master of the screw ball struck out three of the greatest hitters in baseball with two on. The king and the two princes of swat—Ruth, Gehrig and Foxx—all came up and whiffed. The elegant Gehringer was then chafing impatiently on third as the result of a hit, a walk by Manush and a stolen base. Hubbell went on to breeze them by the mighty Simmons and Joe Cronin in the next round and added Gomez for his sixth strikeout after Dickey got on by a single. Looking at a line-up of .350 hitters from top to bottom—enough T N T to blast four other pitchers virtually into obscurity—Hubbell doled out just two hits in three rounds and whiffed six men, **five in a row and as mighty a row perhaps as baseball has ever assembled. The stands rocked in roaring ovations three times as Hubbell left the mound.**

Reprinted from
The Milwaukee Journal

GEHRIG WINS TRIPLE CROWN; RUTH'S LAST YANKEE GAME

Nats 5, Yanks 3

Washington, Sept. 30. (AP). The triumphal last appearance of Babe Ruth as a Yankee regular and Lou Gehrig's 49th home run of the season weren't enough to keep the Senators from winning their final game of the 1934 season today as they slammed out a 5 to 3 decision over the Yankees in one big inning.

Two runs behind going into the fifth, the Senators belted Charley Ruffing for three straight hits following an error by Red Rolfe to make up their rally. After the misplay and singles by Sewell and Kerr had accounted for one run, Johnny Stone slammed a triple over Ruth's head with the bases loaded and scored the final tally on Sington's fly.

Gehrig hit three times in four attempts to clinch the league batting crown.

WASHINGTON

	AB	R	H	PO	A	E
Powell, cf	4	0	0	4	0	0
Myer, 2b	4	1	0	2	3	0
Stone, rf	4	0	3	2	0	0
Sington, lf	4	0	1	1	0	0
Susko, 1b	4	0	0	10	1	0
Bluege, 3b	4	0	1	3	0	0
Sewell, c	3	1	1	4	1	0
Kerr, ss	2	2	2	1	4	0
Armbrust, p	4	0	0	1	4	0
Thomas, p	0	0	0	0	0	0
Totals		5	6	27	16	0

NEW YORK

	AB	R	H	PO	A	E
Crosetti, ss	4	0	0	2	3	0
Saltzgaver, 2b	4	0	0	2	3	1
Rolfe, 3b	4	0	1	2	1	1
Ruth, lf	4	1	1	1	0	0
Hoag, cf	4	0	0	2	0	0
Gehrig, 1b	4	2	3	6	2	0
Selkirk, rf	4	0	1	3	0	0
Lazzeri, 2b	4	0	0	0	0	0
Heffner, 2b	2	0	0	1	2	0
Chapman, cf	4	0	1	0	0	0
Jorgens, c	4	0	0	4	1	0
Ruffing, p	2	0	1	2	1	0
Totals	44	3	8	24	8	1

Score by innings:
Washington . . . . 000 050 00x—5
New York . . . . . 010 101 000—3

Runs batted in—Gehrig, Selkirk, Kerr, Stone 3, Sington, Heffner, two base hits—Gehrig, Sington, Selkirk, three base hit—Stone, home run—Gehrig, double play—Bluege to Myer to Susko, left on bases—New York 5, Washington 4, base on balls—off Armbrust 1, Ruffing 2, struck out—by Ruffing 5, Armbrust 2, Thomas 1, hits—off Armbrust 7 in 7 (none out in 8th), Thomas 1 in 2, passed ball—Sewell, winning pitcher—Armbrust, umpires—Owen and Geisel, time—2:00.

ST. LOUIS WINS WORLD SERIES; RIOT OCCURS

Cardinals Triumph By 11-0 Score To Break All-Time Record

DIZZY DEAN HOLDS DETROIT TO 6 HITS

Medwick Removed From Game After Bleacher Fans Bombard Him

By ALAN GOULD
Associated Press Sports Editor.

Detroit, Oct. 9—Completing the spectacular saga of the Deans with a history-making climax, the great Jerome Herman (Dizzy) Dean pitched St. Louis to the baseball championship of the world today with a record shutout triumph, 11 to 0, as the Cardinal clouting crew hammered and routed the pitching staff of the Detroit Tigers in as wild and riotous a finish as any World Series ever has witnessed.

The National League champions blasted the last defense of Mickey Cochrane's battered Bengals with a smashing seven-run attack in the third. They bombarded six pitchers all told for a total of seventeen hits, while Dizzy Dean, turning in the fourth victory for his team and family, emerged from the seventh and final game with the most lopsided shutout margin in series history. The previous record was set by the New York Giants when Christy Mathewson blanked the Athletics, 9 to 0, in 1905.

Outburst Delays Game 17 Minutes

Before the clouting Cardinals dashed off the field with the final decision, four games to three, and their third world championship in nine years, they survived a riotous outburst by the left-field bleacher fans, who let loose a barrage of missiles, aimed at Joe (Ducky Wucky) Medwick, interrupted the game for seventeen minutes and subsided only after the St. Louis left fielder and clean-up clouter was removed from the game, mainly for safety's sake, by Kenesaw Mountain Landis, baseball commissioner.

The demonstration, one of the worst in series history, was prompted by a run-in at third base in the Cardinal half of the sixth inning, when Medwick slid into the bag after a booming triple to right and exchanged kicks with Marvin Owen, Tiger infielder. The two players almost came to blows before they were separated by players and umpires, but Medwick's return to his position at the end of the inning was the signal for a wild outbreak by the thousands packed in the temporary open stands off leftfield.

Three Volleys By Bleacherites

Medwick was the target for fruit, hot dogs and a few dozen pop bottles, all of which he dodged before beating a retreat to the infield, where his teammates clustered around him. Yelling and hooting, the members of the crowd quickly littered up most of deep left field with food or anything else they could get their hands on.

Players, umpires and finally Manager Cochrane went out to plead for order, but on each of three times that Medwick tentatively started back to his position, after workmen had cleared the field, the bleacherites broke loose with another terrific volley.

Landis Calls Conference

Finally Commissioner Landis called the two players involved in the mix-up, as well as the managers and umpires into a conference, and ordered Medwick to the bench after a short parley. From the stands it appeared Owen was to blame for the incident, as he kicked Medwick first, after which the Cardinal slugger showed both feet sharply into the third baseman's legs, but Landis decided that the only way to continue the game was to remove Medwick and avoid the possibility of the outfielder being "beaned" by a pop bottle or otherwise attacked by the rampant fans.

A detail of six policemen escorted Medwick to the clubhouse as he left the field, after giving way to Chick Fullis in left, and a cordon of sixty uniformed policemen surrounded Medwick and the rest of the St. Louis players as they boarded a bus and returned to their hotel. Dizzy Dean led the Cardinal exit and helped keep the crowd in good humor with his antics, with the result that except for another noisy outburst outside the park there was no further disorder.

FOR THE CHAMPIONSHIP of the WORLD

DETROIT TIGERS vs. ST. LOUIS CARDINALS

WORLD'S SERIES OFFICIAL PROGRAM

PRICE 25 CENTS

1934 NAVIN FIELD DETROIT 1934

Cards' Pool Has 25.

TWENTY-FIVE members of the Cardinals, including 21 players, were voted full shares of the team's world series pool. Besides the active players, Coaches Mike Gonzales and Clyde Wares, Traveling Secretary Clarence Lloyd and Trainer Doc Weaver will get full shares.

Charley Gelbert, who has been out of action for two years as a result of gunshot wounds in the leg, will receive $1,000. Several others connected with the club in non-playing roles will receive sums ranging from $100 to $500.

The "line" at the bleacher gate for Friday's world series game formed early today while St. Louis was still celebrating the Cardinals' victory. The "line" was George Harle, who said he expected to be the first person admitted to the park.

Oct. 26

Yawkey Spends Record Amount for Young Star

Report Washington Receives $150,000 for Its Shortstop; Lyn Lary Goes to Nats in Exchange

Washington, D. C. (AP)—In the biggest baseball deal of recent years, Joe Cronin, young Washington playing manager, Friday was sold to the Boston Red Sox of the American league for a reported price of $150,000, said to be the highest ever paid for a player.

The Washington shortstop was given a five-year contract as player-manager of the Red Sox and will replace Stanley (Bucky) Harris. Owner Tom Yawkey and General Manager Eddie Collins paid President Clark Griffith of the Senators what the latter said was "the largest price ever paid for a baseball player," and threw in Shortstop Lynford Lary in the trade.

RUTH BEGINS NEW CAREER IN BLAZE OF GLORY

Responsible For All Of Braves' Counters In 4-2 Victory Over Giants

[By the Associated Press]

Major league baseball launched new pennant campaigns yesterday and overcame the handicap of widespread cold weather with a series of spectacular developments that found George Herman Ruth and Jerome (Dizzy) Dean and other veterans of the game taking full possession of the spotlight.

Rising once more to the occasion, Ruth, fat and 40, celebrated his entry into the National League after twenty-one brilliant years in the American by taking full charge of the Boston Braves' 4-to-2 victory over Bill Terry's New York Giants. Swinging against Carl Hubbell's southpaw slants, the mighty Bambino whacked out a first-inning single and a fifth-inning home run—the seven hundred and twenty-fourth of his major league career—to personally account for all four Braves' runs.

Ruth Hits 3 Homers but Braves Lose, 11-7; Gets an Ovation From Fans in Pittsburgh

By The Associated Press

PITTSBURGH, May 25. Rising to the glorious heights of his hey-day, Babe Ruth, the sultan of swat, crashed out three home runs against the Pittsburgh Pirates today but they were not enough and the Boston Braves took a 11-to-7 defeat before a crowd of 10,000 at Forbes Field.

The stands rocked with cheers for the mighty Babe as he enjoyed a field day at the expense of Pitchers Red Lucas and Guy Bush, getting a single besides the three circuit blows in four times at bat and driving in altogether six runs.

Ruth left the game amid an ovation at the end of the Braves' half of the seventh inning and after his third home run—a prodigious clout that carried clear over the right-field grandstand, bounded into the street and rolled into Schenley Park. Baseball men said it was the longest drive ever made at Forbes Field.

In his first appearance at the plate the Bambino drove the ball into the stands, scoring Urbanski ahead of him. Lucas was the victim. Again in the third, while Guy Bush was pitching, the Babe found his eye and smashed one that landed on top of the stands. Mallon was on base at the time.

In the seventh Ruth lined out a single to score Mallon again. His last home run drove Bush out of the box and Waite Hoyt finished the game.

NEW YORK _____ 19__ **No. 714**

THE CHASE NATIONAL BANK
OF THE CITY OF NEW YORK
SEVENTY-THIRD ST. BRANCH, BROADWAY AT 73RD ST.   1-74/210   16

PAY TO THE ORDER OF _____ $ _____

_____ DOLLARS

BABE RUTH

REDS' NIGHT GAME DRAWS 25,000 FANS

Many Notables See Contest, First Under Lights in History of Major Leagues.

CINCINNATI BEATS PHILS

Wins, 2-1, Behind Derringer—Sparkling Plays Are Seen in Errorless Battle.

By The Associated Press

CINCINNATI, May 24.—Night baseball came up from the minors for its first big league tryout tonight, and 25,000 fans and the Cincinnati Reds liked the innovation. Some of the affection of the Reds for the nocturnal pastime was because they defeated the faltering Phillies, 2 to 1.

The official paid attendance was announced at 20,422, the third largest crowd of the season.

The flood light inaugural, with President Roosevelt switching on the lights from Washington, was staged before a host of baseball notables, including Ford Frick, president of the National League, and Prexy Will Harridge of the American.

The contest was errorless, despite the fact it was the first under lights for practically all the players. The hurlers, Paul Derringer for the Reds and Bowman for the Phils, performed in great style, the former allowing six hits and the visitor only four.

Wilson Gives Approval.

Manager Jimmy Wilson of the Phils said the lights had nothing to do with the low hit total.

"Both pitchers just had all their stuff working, that's all. You can see that ball coming up to the plate just as well under those lights as you can in daytime."

Jimmy, however, let it be known that he "thinks night baseball is all right, if the fans want it, but I'd rather play in the daytime."

Picture plays were prevalent throughout the game. Myers went far back into left field for Todd's fly in the seventh, Byrd crashed into the centre field wall in the sixth but held on to Camilli's drive, while Camilli snatched several throws out of the dirt from the Phil infield at first.

Myers Comes Home.

Two long flies were dropped by Philadelphia outfielders, but both were scored as hits. The first led to the Red score in the opening frame. Myers pulling up at second as Watkins let the ball get away when he fell against the left-field wall. Myers came home as Riggs and Goodman grounded out.

Singles by Sullivan and Pool, and Campbell's infield out produced the winning Red marker in the fourth. The Phils got their lone tally in the fifth when Todd singled, took third on Haslin's drive to centre, and counted on Bowman's roller to Myers.

PHILADELPHIA (N).	ab.r.h.po.a.e.	CINCINNATI (N).	ab.r.h.po.a.e.
Chiozza, 2b	5 0 1 1 4 0	Myers, ss	4 1 1 1 2 0
Allen, cf	4 0 1 3 0 0	Riggs, 3b	4 0 0 1 3 0
Moore, lf	4 0 1 0 0 0	Goodman, rf	3 0 0 3 0 0
Camilli, 1b	3 0 1 13 0 0	Sullivan, 1b	3 1 2 8 2 0
Todd, c	4 1 1 5 1 0	Pool, lf	4 0 1 1 0 0
Watkins, rf	3 0 0 0 0 0	Campbell, cf	4 0 0 5 0 0
Haslin, ss	3 0 1 1 3 0	Goodman, cf	3 0 0 4 0 0
Bowman, p	3 0 0 0 3 0	Kampouris, 2b	3 0 0 4 3 0
aWilson	1 0 0 0 0 0	Derringer, p	3 0 0 1 2 0
Bivin, p	0 0 0 0 0 0	Total	28 2 4 27 12 0
Total	33 1 6 24 14 0		

aBatted for Bowman in eighth.

Philadelphia .... 000 010 000—1
Cincinnati .... 100 100 00.—2

Runs batted in—Bowman, Goodman, Campbell. Two-base hits—Myers. Stolen bases—Vergez, Bowman, Myers. Double play—Riggs, Kampouris and Sullivan. Left on bases—Philadelphia 4, Cincinnati 3. Bases on balls—Off Bowman 1. Struck out—By Bowman 1, Bivin 1, Derringer 3. Hits—Off Bowman 4 in 7 innings, Bivin 0 in 1. Losing pitcher—Bowman. Umpires—Klem, Sears and Pinelli. Time of game—1:55.

Koenecke, Ball Player, Is Killed In Plane as He Attacks the Crew

Dodger Outfielder, Sent Home by Team, Is Hit Over Head by Pilot With Fire Extinguisher After 15-Minute Mid-Air Battle With Ship Out of Control Over Toronto.

By The Associated Press.

TORONTO, Tuesday, Sept. 17.— Len Koenecke, outfielder for the Brooklyn Dodgers, was killed in mid-air over Long Branch race track early today after a fight with the two-man crew of an airplane.

Koenecke had chartered the plane at the city airport at Detroit last night. The ship was damaged when the pilot managed to land it.

Pilot William Joseph Mulqueeney of Detroit and his helper, Irwin Davis, were held by the police.

Police said that Koenecke was struck over the head with a small fire extinguisher after a wild battle.

Police said that they were told that Koenecke started a fight when the ship was about half way between Detroit and Buffalo, its destination.

The pilot and his helper told officers that Koenecke appeared to be under great stress of some kind when they started the flight.

Mulqueeney told the police that Koenecke had been drinking and was quiet for the first few minutes of the trip. The ball player sat up front with the pilot.

Then, said Mulqueeney, Koenecke for no particular reason began to nudge him with his shoulder.

"I told him to cut it out, that I had no time to play," the pilot said. "But when he kept up the horseplay I told him to get into the back seat with Davis."

Koenecke sat quietly for a moment or so and then began to poke Mulqueeney in the shoulder again, the pilot said.

Davis, sitting beside Koenecke, then took a hand. He tried to force the ball player to be quiet and then the real battle began, Mulqueeney related.

Koenecke bit Davis in the shoulder and the two went to their knees of the floor of the plane locked in a desperate grip.

Mulqueeney said the ship was rocking dangerously and he lost all sense of direction as the struggle went on for 10 or 15 minutes. He said he had all he could do to keep the ship on an even keel without trying to aid Davis.

"Then," said Mulqueeney, telling his story to Constable Whithered of the police of New Toronto, suburb of Toronto, "I had to come to a decision. It was either a case of the three of us crashing or doing something to Koenecke.

"I watched my chance, grabbed the fire extinguisher and walloped him over the head.

"With the passenger quiet, I took a look around, saw the open field with possibilities of fair landing and came down."

We don't know what MR. COCHRANE smokes and he is not endorsing our cigarette *but he is an outstanding man in the baseball world and has won his place on merit*

In the cigarette world, Chesterfields are thought of as outstanding... — *they have won their place strictly on merit*

MICKEY COCHRANE — of the Detroit Tigers, American League Champions; player-manager, one of baseball's greatest catchers.

Outstanding

.. for mildness
.. for better taste

© 1935, LIGGETT & MYERS TOBACCO CO.

LEE SUBDUES CARDS AS CUBS TAKE FLAG

Overcomes 2-Run Deficit in First When Mates Batter Dizzy Dean to Win, 6-2.

LINDSTROM GETS 4 BLOWS

Hack Hits Homer in the Eighth —Rally in 9th of Nightcap Brings 21st in Row, 5-3.

By The Associated Press.

ST. LOUIS, Sept. 27.—Hang up the warning signs in the Detroit jungleland. The rampaging Cubs are on their way with leveled sights that seem as if they can't miss.

Rising to the crest of baseball greatness and crushing even the mighty Dizzy Dean with a devastating fifteen-hit barrage, the sensational men of Grimm capped their almost unbelievable drive today by battering the Cardinals, 6 to 2, for their twentieth straight victory and the National League pennant.

With this triumph they clinched the flag no one dreamed they would win last July 6, when they started their spectacular comeback from fourth place—ten and one-half games behind the then pace-setting Giants.

Sept. 30

Braves Split in Welcome Finale

End Disastrous Season by Dropping First to Giants, 5-3, and Taking Nightcap, 3-0

BY PAUL H. SHANNON

With gridiron activities fast chasing the baseball season into the background, the Braves and Giants staged the closing session of the year at the Wigwam, yesterday afternoon, with hardly 3500 fans in at the death, and the Tribesmen broke even with those one time prospective pennant winners. Both engagements were closely contested, the Terrymen, minus the services of their peppery leader, winning the opener by the score of 5 to 3, and then being forced to accept a disagreeable coat of whitewash when Dapper Danny MacFayden applied the brush that blanked them to the tune of 3 to 0.

NATIONAL LEAGUE STANDING

Club	Won	Lost	Pct	Pos 1934
Chicago	100	54	.649	3
St. Louis	96	58	.623	1
New York	91	62	.595	2
Pittsburg	86	67	.562	5
Brooklyn	70	83	.458	6
Cincinnati	68	85	.445	8
Philadelphia	64	89	.418	7
Boston	38	115	.248	4

Facts And Rumors From Meeting Of Big Leagues At Chicago

[By the Associated Press]

Chicago, Dec. 10—Facts and rumors from the major league baseball meetings:

Facts:

Boston Red Sox purchase First Baseman Jimmy Foxx and Pitcher Johnny Marcum from Athletics for approximately $150,000 in cash and Pitcher Gordon Rhodes and Catcher George Savino, who hit .265 for Syracuse, of the International League, last season.

o—o

Detroit Tigers counter Red Sox deal by purchasing Outfielder Al Simmons from Chicago White Sox for $75,000 in a straight cash deal.

o—o

National League approves financial reorganization plans of the Boston Braves, whereby Bob Quinn, former general manager of the Brooklyn Dodgers, will serve as president and general manager, answerable to Braves stockholders.

o—o

Baseball men figure Owner Tom Yawkey of the Red Sox has spent more than $3,500,000 since he entered baseball by buying the Boston club.

o—o

Wally Schang, former Athletic catcher and manager of the Muskogee (Okla.) Western Association club last season, signed as coach of the Cleveland Indians.

o—o

Pitcher Allyn Stout and Second Baseman Al Cuccinello, who went to the St. Louis Cardinals from the New York Giants in the Roy Parmelee-Burgess Whitehead deal, were sent to the Card farm of Columbus in the American Association.

o—o

Rumors:

The Red Sox already have purchased Infielder Eric McNair and Outfielder Roger Cramer from the Athletics for cash and players, to be announced some time in January.

o—o

Red Sox will peddle Outfielder Roy Johnson. They are hot after Pitcher Monte Pearson, of Cleveland. Yankees have offered Pitcher Johnny Allen to Indians in a hoped-for deal for Pearson.

o—o

Washington has the veteran Outfielder Heinie Manush on the trading block.

o—o

Pitcher Curt Davis, of the Phillies, will be traded to the Chicago Cubs for Outfielder Chuck Klein, former home-run idol of Baker Bowl.

BEDLAM REIGNS IN TIGERS' CITY

500,000 Screaming Fans Pack Downtown Detroit In Record Celebration

TRAFFIC IS HALTED

[By the Associated Press]

Detroit, Oct. 7—The Tiger let loose a roar of victory tonight—a roar that started way down deep in the Navin Field bleachers as the winning run crossed the plate for a world championship and shuddered its way across town and back again, gathering volume all the way.

As though by signal, no sooner had that last run been scored than a surge for the downtown area began. Within two hours police reserves rushed into the celebration sector estimated at least 500,000 screaming, jubilant fans were parading the streets, on foot and in automobiles, in a celebration that for exuberance was an armistice, a Mardi Gras and an American Legion convention all rolled into one.

Goslin Center Of Throng

Goose Goslin, who cracked out the hit that put the Bengals over the hill in the ninth inning, never got to his hotel. As he was driven up by a white-faced taxi driver a swarming avalanche of fans pinned the car to the curb and the Goose couldn't even get the door open. Giving up, Goslin eventually got out of the crush and departed for seclusion.

Loud-speaker trucks, sound apparatus pitched to maximum, paraded the streets blaring triumphant parody of "Hold That Tiger."

Meanwhile, traffic packed itself into a jam that outdid the wildest nightmare ever dreamed by the oldest traffic cop on the force. It wasn't just snarled. It didn't move.

Official Box Score

CHICAGO (N. L.)

	Ab.	R.	H.	O.	A.	E.
Galan, lf	5	0	1	2	0	0
Herman, 2b	4	1	3	3	4	0
Klein, rf	4	0	0	0	0	0
Hartnett, c	4	0	2	9	1	0
Demaree, cf	4	0	2	2	0	0
Cavarretta, 1b	4	0	1	8	0	0
Hack, 3b	4	0	2	0	4	0
Jurges, ss	4	1	1	3	2	0
French, p	4	1	1	1	2	0
Totals	37	3	12	*26	13	0

*Two out when winning run scored.

DETROIT (A. L.)

	Ab.	R.	H.	O.	A.	E.
Clifton, 3b	5	0	0	2	0	0
Cochrane, c	5	2	3	7	0	0
Gehringer, 2b	5	0	2	0	4	0
Goslin, lf	5	0	1	2	0	0
Fox, rf	4	0	2	2	1	1
Walker, cf	2	1	1	0	0	0
Rogell, ss	4	1	2	2	3	0
Owen, 1b	3	0	1	11	0	0
Bridges, p	4	0	0	0	3	0
Totals	37	4	12	27	11	1

Chicago.... 0 0 1 0 2 0 0 0 0—3
Detroit..... 1 0 0 1 0 1 0 0 1—4

Runs batted in—Herman (3), Fox, Bridges, Owen, Goslin. Earned runs—Chicago, 3; Detroit, 4. Two-base hits—Fox, Gehringer, Hack, Rogell. Three-base hit—Hack. Home run—Herman. Sacrifice—Walker. Double play—Gehringer to Rogell to Owen. Left on bases—Chicago, 7; Detroit, 10. Base on balls—Off French, 2 (Walker, Owen). Strikeouts—French, 7 (Owen, Clifton (2), Cochrane, Bridges (2), Rogell); Bridges, 7 (Hartnett, French (2), Demaree, Galan, Cavarretta, Jurges). Umpires—Quigley (N. L.) at plate; McGowan (A. L.) at first; Stark (N. L.) at second; Moriarty (A. L.) at third. Time, 1:57.

Ty Cobb Achieves Highest Niche In Modern Baseball Hall of Fame

Georgian Gets 222 Votes, 4 Short of Perfect Score and 7 More Than Ruth and Wagner—Mathewson and Johnson Only Others With Enough Ballots to Be Named in Nation-Wide Poll.

By The Associated Press.

CHICAGO, Feb. 2.—Tyrus Raymond Cobb, fiery genius of the diamond for twenty-four years, will be the No. 1 immortal in baseball's permanent hall of fame.

The famous Georgian, who shattered virtually all records known to baseball during his glorious era, won the distinction as the immortal of immortals today by outscoring even such diamond greats as Babe Ruth, Honus Wagner and Christy Mathewson in the nation-wide poll to determine which ten players of the modern age should be represented in the game's memorial hall at Cooperstown, N. Y.

Margin of Seven Ballots

Only Cobb, Ruth, Wagner, Mathewson and Walter Johnson, probably the speed ball king of them all, received the required majority to win places in the hall of fame, but Cobb had a margin of seven votes over his closest rivals, Ruth and Wagner.

Of 226 ballots cast by players and writers, the Georgia Peach received 222, or four less than a unanimous vote. Ruth and Wagner received 215 each. Mathewson was fourth with 205 and Johnson fifth with 189. Seventy-five per cent of the total votes, or 169, were needed.

Napoleon Lajoie, Tris Speaker, Cy Young, Rogers Hornsby and Mickey Cochrane ran in that order for the other five positions left for the moderns, players who starred from 1900 and on, but as none received 75 per cent of the total vote their cases will be submitted to the Cooperstown committee in charge of the memorial to be erected in time for baseball's centennial in 1939. Their names will be submitted in another poll next year with five or seven places open.

May 4

Yankees Outslug St. Louis, 14 to 5

New York, N. Y.—Led by Gehrig and Chapman with four hits apiece the Yanks prolonged St. Louis' losing streak with a 14-5 victory here Sunday. The Yanks combed four Brown pitchers for 17 hits.

Joe Dimaggio, sensational rookie outfielder who was making his big league debut, appeared in the Yankee line-up and came through with three hits.

ST. LOUIS	AB	R	H	O		NEW YORK	AB	R	H	O
Lary,ss						Crosetti,ss				
Pepper,cf						Rolfe,3b				
Solters,lf						Dimaggio,lf				
Bottomley,1b						Gehrig,1b				
Bell,rf						Dickey,c				
Clift,3b						Chapman,cf				
Hemsley,c						Selkirk,rf				
Giuliani,c						Lazzeri,2b				
Carey,2b						Murphy,p				
Knott,p										
Caldwell,p										
Coleman										
Hogsett,p										
West										
Van Atta,p										

Reprinted from
The Milwaukee Journal

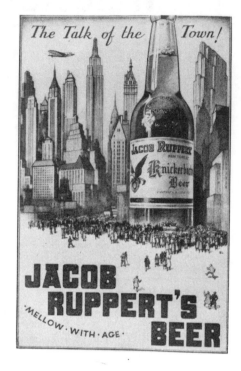

The Talk of the Town!

JACOB RUPPERT'S BEER

·MELLOW·WITH·AGE·

May 25

Tony Drives In Eleven Runs

League Records Fall Right and Left as Joe McCarthy's Men Enjoy Wild Hitting Spree

BY LEASED WIRE TO THE JOURNAL

Philadelphia, Pa.—Tony (Poosh 'Em Up) Lazzeri hammered his way to baseball fame Sunday with an exhibition of batting unparalleled in American league history as he set the pace in the Yankees' crushing 25-2 victory over the Athletics at Shibe park.

The 32-year-old veteran of the New York infield blasted three home runs, two of them with the bases loaded, two of them in successive times at bat. He missed a fourth by a matter of inches and had to be content with a triple. With his three-bagger in the eighth with two on, Lazzeri erased the American league record for runs batted in by a player in a single game. His homers with the bases filled came in the second and fifth. His third started the seventh.

Drives In 11 Runs

Tony's hitting gave him the distinction of driving in 11 runs. The best previous mark was that of Jimmy Foxx, who drove home nine in Cleveland with a double, a triple and a home run in 1933. The National league record is 12, set by Jim Bottomley in 1924.

Lazzeri's two homers with the bases filled in a single game created a new major league record. Babe Ruth comes closest to this distinction. He hit homers with the bases loaded in two consecutive games, accomplishing the feat twice, once in 1927 and again in 1929.

Lazzeri also set another major league mark with seven homers in four consecutive games. He walloped three in Saturday's double header and three Sunday and had one in the last previous game in Detroit. The previous mark of six was held by Babe Ruth, Ken Williams, Chuck Klein, Jim Bottomley and Bill Terry. He also beat the

mark of five home runs in three consecutive games. Babe Ruth and eight others hit five. Tony blasted six.

The McCarthymen collected 19 hits for 46 bases, on six homers, three triples, as many doubles and seven singles. Their total of runs scored was three short of the modern record made by the Cardinals in 1929.

By scoring 25 runs Sunday, the Yankees came within three of the modern record. The Cardinals tallied 28 in 1929. In 1897, Chicago of the National league scored 36.

Yanks Get 46 Bases

The Yankees, with a total of 46 bases on their 19 hits, were two behind their own modern record, made in 1932. Cincinnati made 55 in 1893. Sixteen passes were issued to the Yankees. In 1916 Detroit drew 18, the record.

Ben Chapman's five bases on balls have been exceeded only once. Walter Wilmot of the Chicago Nationals was walked six times in 1891.

The New Yorkers established a new major league standard for most homers by one club in two consecutive games. They hit five in Saturday's nightcap and six Sunday for a total of 11. The Pirates set the old record of 10 in 1925. The pre-

vious American league mark of nine was made by the Yankees in 1930.

New York	AB	R	H	O		PHILADELPHIA	AB	R	H	O
Crosetti,ss	6	2	2	3		Finney,1b	3	1	2	5
Rolfe,3b	4	2	0	3		Dean,1b	1	0	1	0
DiMaggio,lf	7	3	3	3		Warstler,2b	2	1	1	1
Gehrig,1b	5	3	2	7		Peters,ss	4	0	0	4
Dickey,c	5	3	3	3		Moses,cf	4	0	1	4
Chapman,cf	3	4	2	2		Puccinelli,rf	3	0	1	1
Selkirk,rf	4	4	2	2		Higgins,3b	3	0	1	1
Lazzeri,2b	5	2	3	1		Johnson,lf	4	0	0	1
Pearson,p	2	2	1	0		Mailho,lf	2	0	0	0
Jorgens,c	1	0	0	3		Newsome,ss	4	0	0	5
Saltzgaver,1b	1	0	0	3		Berry,c	3	0	1	5
						Turbeville,p				
						Dietrich,p				
						Niemiec				
						Bullock,p				
						Fink,p				
						Upchurch,p				
						Hayes				
Totals	48	25	19	30		Totals	33	2	7	35

Niemiec batted for Dietrich in fourth; Hayes batted for Upchurch in ninth.

New York... 0 5 0 5 4 1 1 2 0—25
Philadelphia.. 1 0 0 0 1 0 0 0 0—2

Errors—Jorgens, Dickey. Runs batted in—Higgins, Lazzeri 11, DiMaggio 3, Gehrig, Dickey 3, Selkirk 2, Pearson 3, Crosetti 2. Two-base hits—DiMaggio, Chapman 2, Dean. Three-base hits—Dickey 2, Lazzeri. Home runs—Lazzeri 3, DiMaggio, Crosetti 3. Double plays—Newsome to Warstler to Finney; Crosetti to Gehrig. Left on bases—New York 9, Philadelphia 7. Bases on balls—Turbeville 5, Pearson 3, Dietrich 3, Bullock 4, Upchurch 2, Fink 3, Pearson 3, Upchurch 2. Hits—Off Turbeville 1 in one and one-third innings; Dietrich 5 in two and two-thirds; Bullock 1 in one-third; Fink 3 in two-thirds; Upchurch 5 in four. Wild pitches—Pearson, Bullock 2. Losing pitcher—Turbeville.

Reprinted from
The Milwaukee Journal

PRICES
of
Commodities Sold Within the Grounds

SCORE CARDS	.05	Canada Dry Ginger Ale (pts.)	.25
PENCILS	.05	Apollinaris (pts.)	.30
PEANUTS	.10	White Rock (pts.)	.30
Assorted Candies (Schrafft's)	.05	MILK (bottle)	.10
GUM (Beech-Nut)	.05	SANDWICHES	.15
ICE CREAM (Neapolitan)	.10	CAKE (Ward's per cut)	.10
SOFT DRINKS (Hi-Brow—8 oz. bottle)	.10	HOT FRANKFURTERS	.10
Coca Cola (bottle)	.10	CIGARETTES	.20
BEER Sold at Bars only		J. A. CIGARS, 13c...2 for	.25
		(Draught) .10 (Bottle)	.20

Klein's 4 Homers Set Record, Win for Phils

Pirates Lose, 9-6, in 10 Innings, Chuck Accounting for Six Runs

PITTSBURGH, July 10 (AP).—Chuck Klein, slugging Philadelphia outfielder, batted the Phillies to a 10-inning 9-6 victory over the Pirates today by smashing out four home runs to set a new modern National League record for circuit blows in one game.

By pounding the ball into the right-field stands in the first, fifth, seventh and tenth innings, Klein equaled the major league record and became the fourth player to do the trick. Lou Gehrig, of the New York Yankees, hit four homers on June 3, 1932. Bob Lowe, of the Boston Nationals, and Ed Delehanty, of the Phillies, both turned in the feat; but neither performance is listed in modern records.

CHUCK KLEIN

Philadelphia ......400010 1003—9
Pittsburgh ....000103 0020—6

a—Batted for Weaver in 8th.
b—Batted for Brown in 9th.
c—Ran for Schulte in 9th.

Time of game, 2.15.

WHITE SOX CRUSH ATHLETICS, 17 TO 2

Tie Modern Record for Hits Off Single Pitcher With 26 at Lisenbee's Expense.

THREE MAKE FIVE APIECE

Bonura, Appling and Kreevich Lead in the Attack—Stratton Limits Rivals to 6 Blows.

CHICAGO, Sept. 11 (AP).—Tying the modern major league record for hits off a single pitcher, the second-place White Sox today pounded a total of twenty-six safeties off Horace Lisenbee to overwhelm the Athletics, 17-2, in the first of a two-game series.

A ladies' day crowd of 14,000 saw Monte Stratton hold the Mackmen to six hits and easily win his second game within two weeks after being out since last May, when he was operated on for appendicitis. The White Sox now have won seven of their last eight games.

Leading the Chicago attack were Zeke Bonura, Luke Appling and Mike Kreevich, each of whom made five hits. Minter Hayes and Stratton contributed home runs.

INDIANS' ROOKIE FANS 15 TO SCORE

Feller, 17, is One Short of Modern League Record in Subduing Browns, 4-1.

TROSKY SMASHES 4 HITS

He Leads in Attack Producing 3 Runs in Sixth Inning and Another in Seventh.

CLEVELAND, Aug. 23 (AP).—Seventeen-year-old Bob Feller, making his first start for Cleveland, fanned fifteen batters in pitching the Indians to a 4-to-1 victory over the Browns today.

Feller's strike-out was one short of the modern American League record, set by Rube Waddell of Philadelphia in 1908, and two short of Dizzy Dean's National League record set in 1933.

The Adella, Iowa, rookie, who vaulted into the headlines when he struck out eight Cardinals in three innings during an exhibition game on July 6, restricted the Gashouse Gang's fellow townsmen to six hits. He held St. Louis scoreless except in the sixth inning, when Lyn Lary doubled and Roy (Beau) Bell followed suit.

Hal Trosky led the Indian attack with four hits. Cleveland reached three pitchers for nine hits and put over three runs in the sixth and one in the seventh inning.

Feller Whiffs 17, Ties Major Mark

Cleveland Rookie Allows 2 Hits As Mates Win Two

CLEVELAND, Sept. 13 (AP).—Bob Feller, husky high school rookie from Adel, Iowa, wound up under a dark sky at League Park today and blazed his fast one past the Philadelphia Athletics to strike out seventeen batters and allow only two hits, as the Cleveland Indians won both games of a double-header.

That was one more strikeout than Rube Waddell achieved 28 years ago when he set the American League record which stood until today. It also put Feller's name beside that of Dizzy Dean as co-holder of the major league record.

Feller's two-hit pitching gave the Indians the first game, 5 to 2, and they came back in the second game to win, 5 to 4.

The farm boy from Iowa who learned how to throw by pegging at a makeshift backstop in a cow pasture, walked the first man to face him and then struck out the next three batters. He struck out at least two batters in every inning but the fourth and ninth. In the first and sixth, he fanned three.

He struck out every man on the Philadelphia team but Moss, a pinch-hitter, who walked. He walked nine altogether, hit one man and made a wild pitch.

Galehouse and Pink each allowed seven hits in the second game, but a four-run rally in the seventh inning put the game away for Cleveland.

PHILADELPHIA	ab.	r.	h.	o.	a.	e.	CLEVELAND	ab.	r.	h.	o.	a.	e.
Finney c	1	1	0	1	0	0	Hughes 2b	3	2	1	0	1	0
Puccinelli lf	2	0	0	1	0	0	Knickerbocker ss	2	2	1	0	1	0
Moses rf-cf	1	1	5	0	0	0	Averill cf	2	1	1	1	0	0
Dean 1b	3	0	1	7	0	0	Trosky 1b	4	0	2	5	0	0
Johnson lf	4	0	0	4	0	0	Weatherly rf	4	0	0	2	0	0
Higgins 3b	2	0	0	0	1	0	Hale 3b	4	0	0	0	0	0
Peters ss	4	0	0	0	3	1	George c	4	0	1	17	0	0
Marcum p	4	0	0	3	1	0	Feller p	4	0	0	0	0	0
Gumpert p	3	0	0	0	0	0							
a-Moss	0	0	0	0	0	0							
Totals	29	2	2	24	8	1	Totals	30	5	7	27	3	0

a-Batted for Gumpert in 9th.

Philadelphia . . . . . 0 0 2 0 0 0 0 0 0—2
Cleveland . . . . 2 0 3 0 0 0 0 0 x—5

Error—Peters. Runs batted in—Averill 2, Weatherly, Dean. Two-base hits—Hughes, Averill. Stolen base—Finney 2, Higgins 2, Dean. Moses, Sacrifices—Knickerbocker. Double play—Luby, Peters and Dean. Left on bases—Philadelphia 10; Cleveland 7. Bases on balls—Off Gumpert, 3; Feller, 9. Strikeouts—Gumpert, 2; Feller, 17. Hit by pitcher—By Feller (Moss). Wild pitch—Feller. Balk—Gumpert. Umpires—Kolls, Johnston and Owens. Time—2.03.

REDS, BEHIND DAVIS, STOP CARDINALS, 3-2

Tally All Runs in Second Inning and Prevent Rivals From Clinching Second Place.

ST. LOUIS, Sept. 25 (AP).—The Cincinnati Reds—troublesome all season—kept the Cardinals from clinching second place in the National League today by winning their only victory of the present series, 3 to 2.

A 3-run attack in the second brought the victory. The Cards threatened in the ninth, however, when Pinch-hitter Rip Collins, first up, doubled. But Ray (Peaches) Davis bore down and retired the next three batters on two infield blows and a foul fly.

In the second Scarsella led off with a single and went to second on an infield out. Riggs walked. Gelbert tossed out Thevenow but Kampouris was purposely passed, loading the bases. Then Bill McGee, who had a good year with Columbus of the American Association before he returned to the Cardinal fold, uncorked a wild pitch which allowed Scarsella to tally. Pitcher Davis singled to center, scoring Riggs and Kampouris. That was all, but it was enough. McGee was charged with the defeat.

Joe Medwick of the Cards, who set a new National League record for doubles when he hit his sixty-third yesterday, added his sixty-fourth in the third frame today but was stranded when Mize flied out.

The box score:

CINCINNATI (N.)	ab.	r.	h.	po.	a.	e.	ST. LOUIS (N.)	ab.	r.	h.	po.	a.	e.
Walker, cf.	4	0	0	3	0	0	T. Moore, cf.	4	0	1	0	1	0
Goodman, rf.	4	0	0	1	0	0	Garibaldi, 2b	4	0	0	2	7	0
Cuyler, lf.	3	0	2	0	0	0	J. Martin, rf.	5	0	2	1	0	0
Scarsella, 1b.	3	1	1	11	1	0	Medwick, lf.	4	0	2	2	0	0
Campbell, c.	2	0	2	8	0	0	Mize, 1b.	4	0	1	11	0	0
Riggs, 3b.	3	1	0	1	1	0	Gelbert, ss.	4	0	0	4	3	0
Thevenow, ss.	4	0	2	1	7	0	Gut'ridge, 3b	4	2	2	2	1	0
Kamp'ris, 2b	3	1	0	5	3	0	Ogr'd'ski, c.	4	0	1	3	2	0
Ray Davis, p.	4	0	2	1	1	0	McGee, p.	0	0	0	0	0	0
							Heusser, p.	0	0	0	0	0	0
Total	30	3	7	13	0		Earnshaw, p.	0	0	0	0	0	0
							Parmelee, p.	0	0	0	0	0	0
							aKing	0	0	0	0	0	0
							bCollins	1	0	1	0	0	0
							cV. Davis	1	0	0	0	0	0
							d'ollins	1	0	1	0	0	0
							eS. Martin	1	0	0	0	0	0
							Total	37	2	11	27	14	0

aBatted for McGee in second.
bBatted for Heusser in fourth.
cBatted for Earnshaw in sixth.
dBatted for Parmelee in ninth.
eBatted for Garibaldi in ninth.

Cincinnati . . . . 0 3 0 0 0 0 0 0 0—3
St. Louis . . . . 0 0 0 1 0 1 0 0 0—2

Runs batted in—Ray Davis 2, T. Moore, V. Davis.
Two-base hits—Medwick, Collins, Gutteridge. Stolen base—Scarsella. Double plays—Thevenow, Kampouris and Scarsella; Gutteridge and Mize; Gelbert and Mize. Left on bases—Cincinnati 6, St. Louis 10. Bases on balls—Ray Davis 2, McGee 2, Heusser 2, Parmelee 2. Struck out—Ray Davis 1, McGee 5, Earnshaw 1. Hits—Off McGee 3 in 2 innings, Heusser 1 in 2, Earnshaw 2 in 2, Parmelee 1 in 3. Wild pitch—McGee. Losing pitcher—McGee. Umpires—Barr, Moran and Pinelli. Time of game—2:07.

CUBS DOWN CARDS, TYING FOR SECOND

Warneke Defeats Dizzy Dean, 6-3, Although Mates Are Outhit by 12-7.

THREE MEN ARE BANISHED

Sears Puts Grimm, Wares and Mize Off Field—Loss Costs Redbirds $10,000.

ST. LOUIS, Sept. 27 (AP).—In a rain-soaked battle filled with bitter disputes over ball and strike decisions, the Cubs beat the Cardinals, 6 to 3, today and closed the National League race tied with St. Louis for second place.

It was the thirteenth defeat for the Cardinals' ace hurler, Dizzy Dean, who gained twenty-four victories. Lon Warneke, who pitched for Chicago, gave twelve hits, while the Cubs were getting only seven off Dean, but he was brilliant in the pinches. It was his sixteenth victory, against thirteen defeats.

The defeat cost the Cardinals about $10,000, for they must now split second and third world series money with the Cubs, whereas if they had won they would have taken second place undisputed. Manager Charley Grimm and Coach Clyde Wares of the Cubs and First Sacker Johnny Mize of the Cards were banished from the field in wordy battles with Umpire Ziggy Sears.

The box score:

CHICAGO (N.)	ab.	r.	h.	po.	a.	e.	ST. LOUIS (N.)	ab.	r.	h.	po.	a.	e.
Galan, cf.	4	2	2	2	0	0	T. Moore, cf.	5	1	1	1	1	0
Cavaretta, 1b.	5	1	0	7	0	0	Garibaldi, 2b	3	0	0	1	2	0
Herman, 2b.	3	1	1	2	5	0	S. Martin, 2b	2	0	0	0	0	0
Demaree, lf.	4	1	1	3	0	0	J. Martin, rf.	5	0	3	1	0	0
Hack, 3b.	4	0	1	1	0	0	Medwick, lf.	5	0	2	0	0	0
Hartnett, c.	4	0	1	10	0	0	Mize, 1b.	3	0	2	4	1	0
Gill, lf.	4	0	1	1	0	0	Al'ton, 1b.	1	0	0	1	0	0
Jurges, ss.	4	0	0	2	4	0	Gelbert, ss.	4	0	1	0	4	0
Warneke, p.	4	0	0	0	1	0	Gut'ridge, 3b	4	0	2	3	3	0
							Ryba, c.	4	0	0	3	0	0
Total	36	6	7	27	14	0	aJ. Dean, p.	3	1	1	0	1	0
							Parmelee, p.	0	0	0	0	0	0
							aCollins	0	0	0	0	0	0
							bFrisch	1	0	0	0	0	0
							cKing	0	1	0	0	0	0
							Total	39	3	12	27	13	1

aBatted for Garibaldi in fifth.
bBatted for Mize in seventh.
cBatted for Parmelee in ninth.

Chicago . . . . 0 0 0 1 0 0 2 0 0—6
St. Louis . . . . 0 0 0 0 0 0 1 0 2—3

Runs batted in—Demaree 2, Mack 2, Gill, Hartnett, J. Martin 2, S. Martin.
Two-base hits—J. Martin, J. Dean 2, Herman. Stolen base—Hack. Sacrifices—Cavaretta 2, Herman. Double play—Moore and Gutteridge. Left on bases—Chicago 3, St. Louis 11. Bases on balls—By Warneke 2. Struck out—By Warneke 7, J. Dean 7. Hits—Off J. Dean 7 in 8 innings, Parmelee 0 in 1. Losing pitcher—J. Dean. Umpires—Sears, Ballanfant and Quigley. Time of game—2:13.

WORLD SERIES Giants vs Yankees 1936 Official Program

Yanks Turn Back Giants By 18 To 4

Records Broken on All Sides As American Leaguers Even Series by Powerful Batting

43,542 See Game, Roosevelt There

Lazzeri Hits Homer With Bases Loaded; Five Pitchers Sent to Mound by Bill Terry

BY ALBERT W. KEANE.
Sports Editor.

Polo Grounds, New York, Oct. 2.— The New York Yankees put on the greatest hit-making and run-producing show in the history of World Series baseball to smother completely the New York Giants, 1. to 4, this afternoon. The victory brought the American Leaguers on even terms with the Giants in the present series, each having won one triumph.

President Franklin D. Roosevelt and 43,542 other fans sat in amazement as the dynamite in the bats of the Yankees exploded into base hits and the safe drives developed into flocks of runs. Most of the attack was concentrated into two innings with the Ruppertmen getting seven runs in the third to break up the game and adding a half-dozen more in the ninth to break all World Series records for run and hit-making.

Records Fall on All Sides.

When the smoke of battle cleared away and the scorers were through checking their results, they found enough records broken or equalled to delight the heart of even a lukewarm statistician. Four records were bumped off the books and as many equalled.

Four new records go into the books. Tony Lazzeri and Bill Dickey each drove in five runs. The best previous record was four and it was shared by nine players. The game produced the most runs, the two teams scoring 22 to crack the mark of 19 made on October 2, four years ago today, by the Cubs and Yanks. The score that afternoon was New York 13, Chicago 6. The Yanks broke the most-runs-in-a-game mark of 13 which was held jointly by themselves, the Giants and the Athletics and the fourth mark established today was the most runs in the ninth inning. The Cubs, scoring five October 10, 1908, held that record for 28 years.

Four World Series records were equalled. Crosetti batted twice in the same inning and he also scored four runs to tie the marks of Earl Combs in 1932 and Babe Ruth in 1936. Lazzeri's homer tied him with Elmer Smith for driving in the most runs in an inning and also for the most home runs (one) with the bases filled. Smith hit his record-making homer on October 10, 1920.

Yanks In Hitting Mood.

From the top of the list to the bottom of it, the American Leaguers' heavy artillery blasted base hits in all directions. Frank Crosetti and Joe DiMaggio, two of San Francisco's Italian boys with the Yankees, each collected three hits. Tony Lazzeri, the third 'Frisco Italian, hit safely only once but his blow was the most damaging of all to Na-

tional League hopes of a second victory because it was a home run with the bases loaded in the third inning. and put the victory on the Yankee side of the records. And it also tied a record set 16 years ago by Elmer Smith of Cleveland, who slammed out a homer with the bases loaded in the series between the Indians and Brooklyn Dodgers.

Buster Lou Gehrig and Bill Dickey, two of the members of the Murderers' Row of the Yanks, each garnered a brace of hits. And one of Dickey's was a home run into the stands with two of his mates aboard the bases in the big ninth inning rally. Powell also put in a pair of safe drives while Selkirk hit safely once and even Lefty Gomez, listed as one of the world's worst batters, pushed a hit through in the ninth inning rally.

Terry Uses Five Pitchers.

Manager Bill Terry of the Giants, in his effort to stop the murderous attack by the American League artillerymen, used five moundsmen. Hal Schumacher started. After being nicked for a pair of singles and walking one in the first to help the winners to their first two runs, he bowed out in the third with the bases full and no one out. A hit by Crosetti, a base on balls to Rolfe and an error had loaded the bases. With the left-handed Gehrig and the equally left-handed Dickey coming up, Terry called in Southpaw Al Smith to pitch. Al's southpaw slants had no deception for his brother left handed hitters and Dickey and Gehrig singled. Selkirk flied out and Powell was passed. Up came Lazzeri, who is rated as sure-fire poison to left-handed pitching.

So Terry yanked Smith and called in Coffman. If Lazzeri is poison to left-handers he surely proved fatal poison to Coffman. Lazzeri sliced a drive into the lower right field stands for a home run and romped around behind Gehrig, Dickey and Powell in his record-making jaunt.

Davis Pinch Hits.

Coffman hurled the next frame without any damage and then gave way for George Davis to pinch hit for him. Gabler came in as the fifth opened and he struggled through until the ninth without being badly dented by the hot blasts from Yankee bats.

He gave one run in the sixth and two in the seventh. He escaped in the eighth when he was taken out for a pinch hitter. Gumbert was on the mound in the ninth when the storm broke in the ninth when a base on balls, four singles and Bill Dickey's home run furnished a fitting climax for a record-breaking afternoon of slugging and run-making.

Gomez Is Uncertain.

Meanwhile Vernon (Goofy) Gomez, American League southpaw star, was pitching a decidedly inconsistent brand of ball. His control was lacking in spots and during the first four innings it was an even bet that Gomez would not last the nine innings. Lazzeri's home run gave him a big lead. Confidence and his control came back and the final five frames found him furnishing a splendid exhibition of hurling against a most discouraged crowd of National League hitters.

In the first four innings, Gomez gave six bases on balls, wild pitched in the first run of the National Leaguers and was found for four hits. The net result of this inconsistent hurling was four tallies. In the next five frames Gomez passed but one batter and allowed but two hits. He struck out eight, passed seven, made one wild pitch and allowed six safe hits.

Weather Is Best.

Ideal weather conditions prevailed for the game. The temperature was like that of a late summer day, the sun shone brightly and there was little wind. Yet the anticipated overflow of baseball fans did not appear, in fact the stands were not filled. Official figures show that 43,-543 paid to see the game and as the seating capacity of the Polo Grounds is more than 51,000, there must have been about 7500 vacant seats.

Czar's Decision Sets Precedent In Baseball Law

Youngster Might Have Got $100,000 for Signing If He Had Been Made Free Agent

Bases Verdict On Recent Rule

New Agreement Between Major and Minor Leagues Helps Commissioner Decide Case

New York, Dec. 10 —(AP.)—Baseball Commissioner Kenesaw Mountain Landis ruled 18-years-old Bob Feller the property of the Cleveland Indians today in a long-deferred decision which cost Feller perhaps $100,000 and set a new precedent in baseball law.

Simultaneously, Landis directed Cleveland to pay $7500 to the Des Moines club of the Western League. Des Moines protested last July 7 that its efforts to obtain Feller had been frustrated by Cleveland's signing him in violation of the major-minor league agreement.

Landis based his decision on the recent relaxation of this agreement by both major and minor league officials. Backed by Landis' precedent in this case, the restrictions which hitherto have hampered major league officials in dealing for outstanding sandlot players seemed definitely to have been removed tonight.

In fact, several major league owners were predicting that what remains of the major-minor league agreement will be scrapped entirely sooner or later.

Slapnicka Violates Rule.

Landis ruled that when Cyril Slapnicka, an official of the Cleveland club, signed Feller to a contract of the Fargo-Moorhead club of the Northern League he did so in violation of a baseball law which forbade major league clubs to sign sandlot players.

Since then however both minor and major leagues have amended this law to permit major league officials to "recommend" a sandlot player to a minor league club. In effect, the minor league club becomes a mere stop-over for the player enroute to the major league club that "recommended" him.

Landis sought both the minor league meetings in Montreal and the major league meetings here to have passed a rule which would require major league officials to report all such "recommendations" to him, and to the presidents of the leagues involved. This suggestion was voted down at both places.

"This legislation must be regarded as construing the covenant of the majors not to sign sandlotters as fulfilled if the player first signs a minor league contract notwithstanding he was in fact signed by or for a major league club." Landis explained in a 1500-word statement. He continued:

"When Cleveland officially acquired Feller on July 13 1936, he had previously contracted with a minor club (Fargo-Moorhead), consequently the commissioner is precluded from entering an order invalidating the Cleveland-Feller contract."

Indians Must Pay.

In explanation of his order that Cleveland should recompense Des Moines in cash Landis pointed out that one of the objects of the agreement between the major and minor leagues was to protect the minor leagues source of revenue in selling players to the majors.

Cochrane's Skull Fractured By One of Hadley's Pitches

Wide World Photo

MICKEY COCHRANE,
manager and catcher of the Detroit Tigers, caught by the cameraman as he fell to the ground yesterday after being hit by a pitched ball.

Detroit Manager Felled in Fifth Inning of Game With Yanks by Former Washington Hurler; Condition Grave at New York Hospital.

By the Associated Press.

New York, May 25.—Gordon (Mickey) Cochrane, manager and catcher of the Detroit Tigers, suffered a fractured skull when he was hit by a pitched ball during today's game at the Yankee Stadium. Dr. Robert E. Walsh, Yankees' physician, said X-rays showed a skull fracture and that Cochrane was in a serious condition.

Mrs. Cochrane boarded a plane in Detroit to go to her husband's bedside.

Dr. Walsh said other details of the injury would not be known for several hours. Cochrane is in St. Elizabeth's Hospital, where he was reported resting quietly tonight.

He was hit by one of Irving (Bump) Hadley's pitches in the fifth inning of the Tigers' game with the Yanks, after hitting a home run his last time at bat in the third inning.

Hadley, a former Nat, threw high and inside, and Cochrane tried to duck. He droped to the ground as the ball hit him, but thousands in the stands thought he had been hit on the wrist.

May 27

Hubbell Wins in Relief Role

Ott's Ninth Inning Homer Sends New York Hurler to 24th Straight Victory

Cincinnati, Ohio (P). The New York Giants whipped the Cincinnati Reds, 3-2, Thursday on Mel Ott's homer in the ninth inning, after calling on Carl Hubbell to stop the Reds in a two-inning relief trick.

Hubbell was given credit for the victory, his twenty-fourth straight in the all-time run he started last July.

NEW YORK	AB	R	H	C	CINCINNATI	AB	R	H	C
Bartell,ss	4	0	2	7	Walker,rf	4	1	1	1
Chiozza,3b	3	0	0	0	Cuyler,cf	4	1	1	3
Danning	1	0	0	0	Goodman,rf	4	0	1	2
Hubbell,p	0	0	0	1	Jordan,1b	4	0	1	11
J.Moore,lf	4	0	1	2	V.Davis,c	4	0	0	8
Ripple,cf	4	0	1	1	Riggs,3b	3	0	1	2
G.Davis,cf	0	0	0	1	Myers,ss	3	0	1	5
Ott,rf	3	1	1	4	Kamp'ris,2b	3	0	1	6
Mancuso,c	4	0	1	6	Grissom,p	3	0	0	1
McCar'y,1b	3	0	0	10					
Whiteh'd,2b	4	2	2	4					
Schuma'r,p	2	0	0	0					
Haslin,3b	1	0	0	2					
Totals	33	3	9	38	**Totals**	32	2	7	42

Danning batted for Chiozza in eighth.

New York .... 0 0 1 0 0 0 0 1 1—3
Cincinnati .. 0 0 0 0 0 2 0 0 0—2

Errors None. Runs batted in Bartell 2, Ott, Goodman, Jordan. Two base hits - Bartell 2, Whitehead, Riggs, Kampouris. Three-base hit Ott. Home run Ott. Sacrifices McCarthy, Haslin. Double play Bartell to Whitehead to McCarthy. Left on bases New York 6, Cincinnati 3. Bases on balls Off Grissom 1. Struck out By Schumacher 4, Grissom 5. Hits Off Schumacher 6 in five and two-thirds innings. Coffman, 1 in one and one-third; Hubbell, none in two. Winning pitcher Hubbell.

Fifth Annual
ALL-STAR GAME

AMERICAN LEAGUE
vs
NATIONAL LEAGUE

GRIFFITH STADIUM   WASHINGTON

JULY · 7 · 1937

Dean Crippled By Averill's Hit In All-Star Game

St. Louis, July 9.—(AP.)—Dizzy Dean, ace of the Cardinals pitching staff, has more troubles—a sore big toe will keep him from taking his regular turn on the hill against the Reds Sunday.

Dean was injured while pitching to Earl Averill, the last man to face him in Wednesday's All-Star game at Washington. Averill's hit bounded against Dizzy's left foot, bruising the big toe.

YORK, TIGERS, SETS HOME-RUN RECORD

Clips Ruth Mark With Nos. 17 and 18 in a Month in 12-3 Conquest of Senators

RUDY HITS IN SEVEN RUNS

He and Gehringer Have Perfect Day at Bat—Lawson Hurls 17th Triumph

DETROIT, Aug. 21 (AP.)—Rookie Rudy York, hitting his twenty-ninth and thirtieth home runs of the season, topped one of Babe Ruth's records today as he led the Tigers in a 12-to-3 victory over Washington.

Ruth hit seventeen homers in a single month in September, 1927. York's two circuit smashes over the scoreboard at Navin Field were his seventeenth and eighteenth during August.

In addition, York collected two singles for a perfect day at bat, and drove in seven runs. Two mates, were on base when York hit each homer, one in the first and another in the sixth. Pete Fox, Detroit right fielder, hit one over the left field fence with the bases empty in the sixth.

WADE'S 1-HIT GAME STOPS ALLEN AT 15

Tigers Win, 1-0, Balking Try by Indian Ace to Tie League Record of 16 Straight

GREENBERG DRIVES IN FOX

Single Decides, Making Hank's Total Runs Batted In 181— Trosky Gets Tribe Blow

DETROIT, Oct. 3 (AP.)—Whistling Jake Wade let the Indians have only one hit today while the Tigers gained a 1-to-0 victory over Johnny Allen, who was trying to equal the American League record of sixteen straight victories. Allen allowed five hits.

Hal Trosky, whose two home runs had helped Cleveland beat Detroit yesterday, got the only hit from Wade, a single.

In the first inning Pete Fox smashed a double and came in on Hank Greenberg's single, making Greenberg's unofficial total of runs batted in 181 for the season.

The defeat was hard for Allen to swallow. A picture of woe, the loser in the dramatic finale fretted in the clubhouse after a battle so tense that 22,000 fans were gasping at the finish.

Words of sympathy couldn't soothe him as he berated his ill luck. The temperamental star allowed himself only a few tender words—to a small bulldog that played at his feet.

For Wade, rookie lefthander who has been good one day and bad the next, it was tough, too. He had a no-hit game until Trosky singled over second with two out in the seventh.

"I do everything backward," Wade said. "That's the way I should have been pitching in April, not October."

The teams, locked in one of the year's hottest fights after Detroit's single score in the first, saved some sharp thrills down to the last inning.

With two out and Lyn Lary on second from a walk and sacrifice, Trosky came up again—Cleveland's last chance for victory. While all the Indians—all save Allen—rose from the bench to watch, Wade calmly struck out Trosky.

The box score:

CLEVELAND (A.)	ab.	r.	h.	po.	a.	e.		DETROIT (A.)	ab.	r.	h.	po.	a.	e.
Lary, ss	2	0	0	4	4	0		White, cf	4	0	0	4	0	0
Kroner, 2b	3	0	0	2	3	0		Fox, rf	3	1	2	2	0	0
Averill, cf	4	0	0	2	0	0		Gehr'ger, 2b	4	0	1	2	9	0
Trosky, 1b	4	0	1	7	1	0		Gr'nberg, 1b	3	0	1	9	0	0
Solters, lf	3	0	0	1	0	0		York, c	3	0	1	7	1	0
Campbell, rf	3	0	0	1	0	0		Walker, lf	3	0	1	1	0	0
Hale, 3b	3	0	0	2	1	0		Owen, 3b	3	0	0	0	0	0
Pytlak, c	3	0	0	5	0	0		Rogell, ss	1	0	0	2	1	0
Allen, p	3	0	0	0	0	0		Wade, p	3	0	0	0	5	0
Total	35	0	1	24	9	0		Total	37	1	5	27	9	0

Cleveland .... 0 0 0 0 0 0 0 0 0—0
Detroit .... 1 0 0 0 0 0 0 0 *—1

Run batted in—Greenberg.
Two-base hits—Fox 2. Sacrifice—Kroner. Double plays—Lary, Kroner and Trosky; Trosky and Lary. Left on bases—Cleveland 4, Detroit 6. Bases on balls—Off Allen 4, Wade 4. Struck out—By Allen 4, Wade 7. Hit by pitcher—By Wade (Solters). Umpires—Hubbard, Ormsby and Johnston. Time of game—1:35.

Oct. 7

Majors Crown Bat Champs

Charley Gehringer, Detroit, Oldest Player Ever to Lead American League

New York, N. Y. (AP.)—The American and National leagues closed their seasons Sunday with Charley Gehringer, Detroit, and Joe Medwick, St. Louis, enthroned as the batting champions. Gehringer at 34 is the oldest player ever to lead the American league. He has been in the league 14 years. He hit .389. Medwick hit .374, to lead the league in his fifth year as a National leaguer.

Gehringer, 34, is the oldest player ever to lead the American league. He's been in the league 14 years.

Medwick slugged his way to the title in his fifth year in the league.

Carl Hubbell again won the National league pitching laurels with 22 victories and eight defeats. Johnny Allen, Cleveland, led the American leaguers with 15 victories and one defeat. Allen won 15 straight but lost his last game of the season Sunday when Jake Wade, Tigers' southpaw, came up with a one-hit performance to beat him, 1-0.

Other individual leaders follow:

Hits—(N) Medwick, 237; (A) Bell, Browns, 218.
Runs—(N) Medwick, 111; (A) DiMaggio, Yankees, 150.
Runs Batted In—(N) Medwick, 154 (A) Greenberg, Tigers, 181.
Doubles—(N) Medwick, 58; (A) Bell, 52.
Triples—(N) Vaughan, Pirates, 17; (A) DiMaggio, Stone (Senators) and Kreevich (White Sox) 15 each.
Home Runs—(N) Medwick and Ott (Giants), 31 each; (A) DiMaggio, 46.
Stolen Bases—(N) Galan, Cubs, 23; (A) Chapman, Red Sox, 33.

Dizzy Dean Is Traded by Cardinals for Three Chicago Cub Players

SURPRISING MOVE SHAKES ST. LOUIS

Mates Downcast and Pilot Frisch Sour—Pitcher Is Glad of Change.

By the Associated Press.

ST. LOUIS, April 16.—President Sam Breadon of the St. Louis Cardinals announced late today Dizzy Dean, star pitcher, had been traded to the Chicago Cubs for Pitchers Curt Davis, Clyde Shoun and Outfielder George Stainback.

Breadon made the announcement at the Cardinal offices. In a written statement he said further:

"To friends and supporters of the Cardinals in St. Louis and throughout the country:

"This deal has been thoroughly discussed by Mr. Rickey, Frankie Frisch and myself and we have agreed it was for the best interest of the Cardinal club."

Further details of the transaction were not disclosed by Breadon. This was taken as an indication that cash also was involved in the transaction.

Dean's entire professional base ball career has been under the Cardinal banner, most of the first two years being spent at farm clubs. He became a Cardinal regular in 1932.

Davis is a right-handed pitcher who won 10 and lost 5 with the Cubs last season. Shoun is a left-hander. Stainback is a right-handed outfielder.

Trade Makes Cards Unhappy.

The Cardinals were an unhappy gang of ball players when they were told of the trade after today's exhibition victory over the St. Louis Browns.

Dean said he was "glad to leave to go to Chicago, but I hate to leave the fellows."

"I'll bet they do all right by me there, though," he said, his face brightening. "I'll bet they give me $10,000 more than I'm making here."

Another ball player chimed in: "Yeah, and they'll probably give you a yacht, too, to ride around in on the lake."

Another said, "and lots of chewing gum."

Pepper Martin, sitting on a bench with a sad look on his face, was pessimistic.

"There goes our pennant and world series money."

Terry Moore declared "Yeah, we'd have been a cinch with Diz."

All the players asked over and over again who the Cardinals got for Dean.

They apparently were surprised that the Cardinals got only two pitchers and an outfielder for the "great one."

One suggested that the Cardinals must have gotten "a lot of cash" in the deal, and Martin commented, "You can't play cash on the baseball field."

June 22

Higgins Gets '12 for 12' as Boston, Tigers Split

Red Sox Infielder Sets New Record for Hits in a Row; Rudy York Slams Out Two Home Runs

Detroit, Mich. (P) Frank (Pinky) Higgins, veteran Boston Red Sox third baseman enjoying a sensational hitting streak, marched into baseball's hall of fame Tuesday by cracking out his twelfth consecutive safe hit while the Sox and Detroit Tigers split a double header.

Even two home runs with which Rudy York, Tiger slugger, entered a tie with Jimmy Foxx of Boston for the American league leadership at 19 each, fell into the background as Higgins, collecting eight hits, broke Tris Speaker's 18 year old major league record. The Sox won the first game, 8 to 3 and Detroit the second, 5 to 4.

Before a tense crowd of 26,400, Higgins made the big hit, his seventh single of the day in the eighth inning of the second game. It gave him a perfect day at bat.

The Sox third sacker made three singles and a double in the first game and four singles in the second, tying Speaker's record of 11 straight hits made in 1920 with a sixth inning single in the nightcap. Higgins began his streak with a double, three singles and a walk in a double header at Chicago Sunday. The Sox were idle Monday. Higgins walked once in the first game Tuesday.

The split pushed Boston into second place in the American league ahead of the New York Yankees, who were beaten by Cleveland.

FIRST GAME

Boston	AB	R	H	C	Detroit	AB	R	H	C
Cramer cf	4	0	3	6	Rogell ss	4	1	1	5
Vosmik lf	4	0	1	3	Walker lf	5	0	1	2
Chapman rf	5	0	0	1	Gehringer 2b	3	1	0	1
Foxx 1b	4	0	0	7	York c	4	1	2	6
Cronin ss	5	2	1	7	Fox rf	4	0	1	3
Higgins 3b	4	2	3	3	Greenberg 1b	4	0	0	11
Doerr 1b	4	2	1	3	Laabs cf	3	0	0	1
Desautels c	5	1	1	5	Ross 3b	3	0	1	3
Wilson p	0	0	0	0	Bridges p	3	0	1	0
Osterm'r p	5	1	2	0	Piet	0	0	0	0
Totals	40	8	12	35	Totals	33	3	7	35

Piet batted for Bridges in ninth.

| Boston | 0 | 0 | 1 | 0 | 0 | 3 | 0 | 0 | 3 | — | 8 |
| Detroit | 0 | 0 | 0 | 0 | 0 | 2 | 0 | 0 | 1 | — | 3 |

Errors Higgins, Bridges, Greenberg Runs batted in—Vosmik, Doerr 2, Desautels 2, Os-

termueller 2, Gehringer, York Two base hits—Ostermueller, Higgins, Rogell, Desautels Three base hit Doerr Double play Cronin to Foxx Left on bases Boston 10, Detroit 9 Bases on balls Off Wilson 3, Ostermueller 3, Bridges 4 Struck out By Ostermueller 4, Bridges 6 Hits Off Wilson 2 in 1 inning (none out in second) Ostermueller 5 in 8 Winning pitcher Ostermueller.

SECOND GAME

Boston	AB	R	H	C	Detroit	AB	R	H	C
Cramer cf	3	0	0	1	Rogell ss	3	1	0	3
Vosmik lf	4	1	0	1	Walker lf	4	2	1	3
Chapman rf	5	0	3	1	Gehringer 2b	4	0	1	5
Foxx 1b	4	1	0	13	York c	3	2	1	7
Cronin ss	4	1	2	7	Fox rf	4	0	0	2
Higgins 3b	4	1	4	5	Greenberg 1b	3	0	0	8
Doerr 2b	2	0	1	4	Laabs cf	4	0	3	8
Peacock c	4	0	0	2	Ross 3b	3	0	1	1
Wagner p	1	0	0	2	Lawson p	3	0	0	2
McKain p	1	0	0	0	Poffenberger p	1	0	0	0
Nonkamp	1	0	0	0					
Dickman p	0	0	0	0					
Gaffke	1	0	0	0					
Bagby p	0	0	0	0					
Totals	33	4	10	36	Totals	30	5	7	42

Nonkamp batted for McKain in seventh. Gaffke batted for Dickman in eighth.

| Boston | 0 | 0 | 0 | 0 | 0 | 0 | 1 | 3 | 0 | — | 4 |
| Detroit | 2 | 0 | 0 | 3 | 0 | 0 | 0 | 0 | x | — | 5 |

Error Laabs Runs batted in Foxx, Higgins, Peacock, Gaffke, York 2, Fox, Laabs 2 Two base hits Laabs, Walker, Chapman Home run York Stolen base Fox Double plays Fox to York Rogell to Greenberg, Gehringer to Rogell to Greenberg, Higgins to Doerr to Foxx Left on bases Boston 9 Detroit 7 Bases on balls Off Wagner 3, McKain 3, Lawson 7 Struck out By McKain 1, Bagby 1, Lawson 3 Poffenberger 1 Hits Off Wagner 2 in 2 innings (none out in third) McKain 2 in 4 Dickman 1 in 1 Bagby 2 in 1 Lawson 10 in 7 (none out in eighth) Winning pitcher Lawson Losing pitcher Wagner.

Vander Meer Twirls Second No-Hit Game

Cincy Hurler Triumphs, 6-0

No-Hit Game Against Boston Bees Last Saturday Is Duplicated Against Dodgers in Night Contest

From The Journal's N. Y. Bureau

New York, N. Y. The first night game of baseball in Brooklyn started in a circus atmosphere Wednesday night and resulted in Johnny Vander Meer's second no-hit game in a week as the Cincinnati Reds won 6-0. He had three men on in the ninth on walks but pulled through.

Vander Meer pitched a 3-0 no-hitter against the Boston Bees Saturday. His repetition Wednesday gives him a record of two consecutive no-hit performances, which never has been duplicated. In his last three starts, he has pitched 26 scoreless innings. To make it a better story Vander Meer performed his feat in Brooklyn, whose farm system property he once was. He was lost through careless paper work.

First Doubly in One Year

The records reveal only nine pitchers, before Vander Meer, credited with more than one no-hit game. Two of them, Cy Young and L. J. Corcoran, pitched three. No pitcher until Vander Meer, however, ever achieved two no-hitters in one season.

More drama was crowded into the final inning Wednesday night than a baseball crowd has felt in many a moon. Until that frame, only one Dodger had got as far as second base. Lavagetto got there when Vander Meer issued passes to him and Dolf Camilli in the seventh.

Vandy pitched out of that easily enough and the vast crowd, to a man, was pulling for him to come through. He mowed down Woody English (batting for Luke Hamlin), Kiki Cuyler and Johnny Hudson in the eighth, fanning the first and third men. Vito Tamulis, the fourth Brooklyn hurler, treated the Reds likewise in the ninth and Vandy came out for the crucial inning. Dodgers, pinch hitters twice. He issued eight passes. Added to his speed was a sharp breaking curve which seldom failed to break over the plate and at which the Dodger batsmen swung as vainly as at his fireball.

On the offense, well nigh forgotten as the spectacle of Vander Meer's no-hitter unfolded, the Reds made victory certain as early as the third frame when they scored four times and drove Max Butcher away.

Goodman's third single bounced off Tot Pressnell's right kneecap in the seventh, knocking the knuckle-baller out. He was carried off on a stretcher. Examination revealed no fracture.

Crowd Boos Grimes

He started easily, taking Buddy Hassett's bounder and tagging him out. Then his terrific speed got out of control and while the fans sat forward tense and almost silent, he walked Phelps, Lavagetto and Camilli to fill the bases. To show the mood of the fans, when Burleigh Grimes stopped the game to send Goody Rosen in as a runner for Phelps, the Dodger pilot was booed unmercifully.

All nerves were taut as Vandy pitched to Ernie Koy. With the count 1 and 1, Ernie sent a bounder to Lew Riggs, who was so careful in making the throw to Lombardi that a double play wasn't possible.

Leo Durocher, a tough hitter in the pinches, came up—the last hurdle for Vander Meer. The crowd groaned as he swung viciously, but it was a foul high into the right field stands. A moment later he swung again. The ball arched lazily toward short center field and Harry Craft camped under it for the putout which brought unique distinction to the young hurler.

Saved From the Crowd

A horde of admiring fans swarmed on the field. Vandy's teammates hugged and slapped Johnny on the back and then protected him from the mob as he struggled toward the Red dugout. Jim Weaver, giant pitcher, constituted himself an advance guard and a flying wedge in front of Vandy.

The crowd couldn't get Johnny but a few moments later it got his father and mother, who had accompanied a group of 500 citizens from Vandy's home town of Midland Park, N. J. The elder Vander Meers were surrounded and it required nearly 15 minutes before they could escape.

In the clubhouse, the blond young Giant had no comment except to reveal that Thursday he was going fishing in New Jersey. Vander Meer senior said that he hoped "Johnny would keep on being a good boy, because sometimes success like that turned a boy's head."

Cincinnati	AB	R	H	C	Brooklyn	AB	R	H	C
Frey,2b	5	0	1	4	Cuyler,rf	2	0	0	1
Berger,lf	5	1	3	1	Coscarart,2b	2	0	0	1
Goodman,rf	3	2	3	1	Brack	1	0	0	0
McCormick,1b	5	1	1	10	Hudson,2b	2	0	0	1
Lombardi,c	3	1	0	9	Hassett,lf	4	0	0	1
Craft,cf	5	0	3	1	Phelps,c	2	0	0	2
Riggs,3b	4	0	1	3	Rosen	0	0	0	0
Myers,ss	4	0	0	1	Lavagetto,3b	2	0	0	2
Van Meer,p	4	1	1	0	Camilli,1b	1	0	0	7
					Koy,cf	4	0	0	4
					Durocher,ss	4	0	0	3
					Butcher,p	0	0	0	1
					Pressnell,p	2	0	0	0
					Hamlin,p	0	0	0	1
					English	1	0	0	0
					Tamulis,p	0	0	0	0
Totals	38	6	11	30	Totals	27	0	0	30

Brack batted for Coscarart in sixth. English batted for Hamlin in eighth. Rosen ran for Phelps in ninth.

Cincinnati....	0	0	4	0	0	1	1	0	0—6
Brooklyn....	0	0	0	0	0	0	0	0	0—0

Errors—Lavagetto 2. Runs batted in—McCormick 3, Riggs, Craft, Berger. Two base hit Berger. Three base hit Berger. Home run McCormick. Stolen base—Goodman. Left on bases—Cincinnati 9, Brooklyn 8. Bases on balls—Off Butcher 3, Vander Meer 8, Hamlin 1. Struck out—By Butcher 1, Pressnell 3, Vander Meer 7, Hamlin 3. Hits—Off Butcher, 5 in 2⅓; Hamlin, 2 in 1⅔; Pressnell, 4 in 3⅓. Losing pitcher—Butcher.

The Hall of Fame

New York, N. Y. P When Johnny Vander Meer pitched his second no-hit, no-run game Wednesday night, he became the first hurler since Hub Leonard of the Boston Red Sox to chalk up a pair of the classics. Leonard pitched his no-hitters in 1916 and 1918. Vander Meer did his in four days.

Before Leonard, nine other pitchers had turned in two nine-inning no-hitters during their careers.

Two of them Cy Young and L. J. Corcoran each had three. The list follows:

Pitcher	Club and League	Dates
Johnny Vander Meer	Cincinnati, N. L.	June 11 and 15, 1938
Hub Leonard	Boston, A. L.	Aug. 30, 1916; June 3, 1918
Tom Hughes	*New York, A. L.	Aug. 30, 1910
	Boston, N. L.	June 16, 1916
Adrian Joss	Cleveland, A. L.	Oct. 2, 1908; Apr. 20, 1910
Frank Smith	Chicago, A. L.	Sept. 6, 1905; Sept. 20, 1908
Cy Young	Cleveland, N. L.	Sept. 18, 1897
	Boston, A. L.	May 5, 1904; June 30, 1908
Christy Mathewson	New York, N. L.	July 15, 1901; June 13, 1905
T. Breitenstein	St. Louis, A. A.	Oct. 4, 1891
	Cincinnati, N. L.	Apr. 22, 1898
William Terry	Brooklyn, A. A.	July 24, 1886; May 27, 1888
L. J. Corcoran	Chicago, N. L.	Aug. 19, 1880; Sept. 20, 1882; June 27, 1884
Jim Galvin	Buffalo, N. L.	Aug. 20, 1880; Aug. 4, 1884

*Lost game in tenth inning.

RECORDS FEATURE RED SOX TRIUMPH

Foxx Walks Six Times to Set Modern Mark in 12-8 Game With Browns

---

ALSO EQUALS STANDARD

No Time at Bat in Six Trips to Plate—Series Swept by Boston Team

---

ST. LOUIS, June 16 (AP).—A new modern Major League record was established and another tied today in a torrid game which gave the Red Sox a sweep of their series with the Browns. The score was 12 to 8.

Jimmy Foxx, Boston first baseman, drew six straight walks, the new Major League mark. The previous record was five, held by Mel Ott of the Giants and Max Bishop of the Athletics. The pre-1900 record was six, set by Walter Wilmot of the Cubs in 1891.

GREENBERG DRIVES HOMERS 57 AND 58

Detroit Star Needs Three in Five Remaining Games to Eclipse Ruth's Record

---

TIGERS WIN DOUBLE BILL!

Turn Back Browns by 5 to 4 and 10 to 2—Hank Collects Both Blows in Nightcap

---

By The Associated Press

DETROIT, Sept. 27.—Hank Greenberg, distance-slouting first baseman of the Tigers, poled two tremendous drives to center for his fifty-seventh and fifty-eighth home runs of the season today as Detroit swept a double-header with the Browns, 5 to 4 and 10 to 2.

With five games left to play, Greenberg is within striking distance of Babe Ruth's 1927 major league record of sixty homers in a single season.

Aug. 2

'Stitched Lemon' Makes Bow in Brooklyn Game

From The Journal's N. Y. Bureau

New York, N. Y.—Larry Mac-Phail of the Brooklyn Dodgers Tuesday backed another pioneering stunt at Ebbets field, using the yellow ball in the first game of a double header between the Cards and Dodgers.

The "stitched lemon" for which greater visibility, hence greater safety, is claimed, was used for the first time in a major league game.

Should the players report favorably, there is a possibility the canary colored ball eventually will become as much a part of the game as shinguards.

Though the rules do not specify a baseball must be white, there are clauses that it must not be intentionally discolored and must have the league president's signature. Consequently, Ford Frick ordered a special batch of balls, signed them and sent them to MacPhail with his blessings.

Reprinted from
The Milwaukee Journal

Sept. 29

Hartnett's Home Run Puts Cubs in Lead

Bruins Gain Slender Lead Over Pirates

Lee and Bauers Pitch Series Final; Chicago Uses Six Hurlers to Score 6-5 Victory; Brown Is Loser

---

By SAM LEVY
Of The Journal Staff

Chicago, Ill.—Gabby Hartnett was just as important front page news in this daffy baseball metropolis today as is the tense international situation. The smiling, aggressive manager of the Chicago Cubs squeezed the last ounce of power out of his pennant machine at twilight Wednesday and elevated the bruins to the top of the National league heap.

Gabby's home run with two out and two strikes on him in the ninth inning was lost in the shadows as it dropped over the left field wall. The disheartened Pittsburgh Pirates started to disappear while the ball was still on the way, but the 34,465 frenzied Cub rooters remained to witness the final rites of the buccaneers, occupants of first place since mid-July.

Reprinted from
The Milwaukee Journal

Automatic 'Pitcher' Invented by Banker

St. Louis, Mo. P. The wildness of a batting practice pitcher at a Yale-Harvard baseball game he witnessed last year provoked a St. Louis banker into inventing an elaborate contraption he hopes will revolutionize this part of the game.

"I'm going to make a baseball machine on the order of a bean-shooter or slingshot," said Byron Moser, the banker, to his Harvard student son, "something that will get the ball over the plate nine times out of ten and give batters a chance."

Since then Moser and A. F. Howe, St. Louis inventor, have been working on the machine. And the result of their effort is attracting much attention in its initial "workouts" at a local park.

The mechanical pitcher—a large boxlike affair resembling an overgrown turkish bath compartment — is set up on the pitcher's mound.

Directly in the center in front is a slot from which baseballs pour at the rate of four a minute. They cut the plate every time. The balls can be regulated to any speed, and can be raised or lowered.

Inside the box is a complicated machine, manned by a two horse-power motor. The balls drop down from a hopper at the top. A huge rubber band, a foot in diameter, provides the punch that forces the hammerlike vise forward and shoots the ball to the plate. A bell rings just before the delivery.

The machine can be turned around to spray grounders to the infielders or pump fly balls to the outfield. It cannot throw a curve.

Yanks Debate Whether to Sell Games to Radio

New York, N. Y. — P — Baseball's last Major league holdout against radio, the New York Yankees, debated Saturday whether to sell the rights for its games next season.

While other clubs one by one yielded to the lure of sponsors' offers, the three Metropolitan clubs stood firm under a three power pact until the Brooklyn Dodgers broke the ranks two weeks ago and the New York Giants followed suit Friday night.

Sources close to the Dodgers have intimated they expect to receive about $77,000 for rights to their games both at home and away next summer. President Horace Stoneham of the Giants said that he thought the privilege of airing his games would bring $150,000. Whether road contests as well as the New York games would be broadcast will be largely up to the sponsor, he said.

Reports of Stoneham's action brought word from Ed Barrow, secretary of the Yankees, that he would confer with owner Jacob Ruppert Saturday on the broadcasting question and probably would have an announcement soon.

FELLER SETS MARK BY STRIKING OUT 18

But Indians Bow to Tigers, 4-1, 10-8—Greenberg Finishes With Homer Total 58

CLEVELAND, Oct. 2 (P). Bob Feller, young Cleveland marvel, enhanced his fame today, but the Indians bowed twice to the Tigers, 4 to 1 and 10 to 8.

Feller fanned eighteen batters in the opener to topple the major league record for strike-outs in one game, but couldn't pull the game out of the fire.

In 1937 Feller fanned seventeen Athletics to set an American League record and tie Dizzy Dean, who was then with te Cardinals.

Feller's eighteenth victim today was Chet Laabs, who struck out for the fifth time in the ninth. He fanned Pete Fox twice, McCoy twice, Hank Greenberg twice, Tony Piet once, Mark Christman three times and his mound rival, Harry Eisenstat, three times.

Bob allowed seven hits, walked seven men and hit Piet. Detroit scored twice in the seventh on Greenberg's double, Roy Cullenbine's single and George Tebbetts's double. Two walks, a sacrifice and Christman's single gained the other two Detroit runs. There were two men on base when Feller fanned Laabs for strikeout No. 18. He disregarded the runners and pitched with a full wind-up.

Today's feat raised Feller's strikeout total for the season to 240 which leads both major leagues in that department, and gave him a margin of fifteen over Buck Newsom of the Browns, who fanned ten today for a total of 225.

Eisenstat held the Indians scoreless until the ninth of the opener, allowing only four hits.

Greenberg failed to hit a homer and finished the season with fifty-eight, two under Babe Ruth's mark.

★ ★ ★ ★ ★

NEARLY *Every* MEMBER OF *Both*
ALL-STAR TEAMS
GOES FOR THIS
"Breakfast of Champions"
A BIG BOWLFUL OF WHEATIES WITH MILK OR CREAM AND FRUIT

Trust these champions of baseball to pick the breakfast dish that clicks with all-star appetites! Joe Di Maggio, Carl Hubbell, Charlie Gehringer, Joe Medwick—they and *hundreds* more of the game's greatest players agree that Wheaties, milk and fruit breakfast is tops for solid nourishment and flavor that leads the leagues!

The runs-batted-in leader of the American League stokes up with a "Breakfast of Champions" often.

Wheaties and advertising claims for them are accepted by the Council on Foods of the American Medical Association.

"Breakfast of Champions"
WHEATIES WITH MILK OR CREAM AND FRUIT

Wheaties and "Breakfast of Champions" are registered trade marks of General Mills, Inc.

★ ★ ★ ★ ★

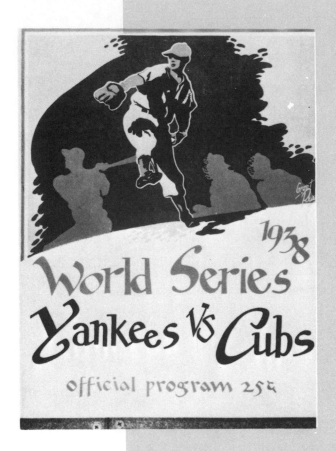

1938
World Series
Yankees vs Cubs

official program 25¢

Second Game Runs Gamut Of Emotions

All the Elements of Thrilling Three-Ring Circus in Yanks' Second Victory

Chicago, Oct. 6.—(AP.) — From homers and heartaches to comedy and tragedy, baseball's biggest show had everything today...

For seven and two-thirds innings, Dizzy Dean shackled the vaunted New York Yankee power. Then the Yankee bats boomed and old Diz walked slowly from the field, taking one fleeting glance at the distant left field wall. And in the Yankee dressing room, Joe McCarthy pointed to his heart and said: "The guy," he said slowly, "has it there."

There were all the elements of a thrilling three-ring circus in today's spectacle, in sharp contrast to the Yank's matter-of-fact victory Wednesday. Lou Gehrig stepped out of the box four times on one occasion, drawing a bellow from Dean; Infielders Hack and Jurges did a second inning tumbling act on Joe Gordon's slow roller that drew groans from Cub partisans. The sun suddenly beamed down brilliantly, taking some edge off the chill winds. The throng of 42,108 saw a real show, even though thousands of fans carried away a tragic picture of a great hearted athlete bowing in defeat.

Frank Crosetti is on his way toward honors as the greatest "money" player in the series. When the chips were down yesterday he came through spectacularly afield; when he and his mates trailed today, his home run sent the Yanks further toward a third straight world's championship. And Frankie received a riotous reception in the Yank dugout when he raced in after spearing a liner for the final out.

The game had its elements of suspense almost before it was well under way. In the second inning Umpire Sears held up his hand, started toward the boxes along first base line and the spectators craned their necks, probably expecting to see at least a fight. All "Ziggy" did was close a field gate that had been left open. Seconds later Joe Marty called for time, raced in toward the Cub dugout—and obtained sun glasses.

Some series pickups from field and stands: Stan Hack, in his first seven times at bat in the two games, had five singles and hit into two double plays . . . On his eighth trip, he fanned . . . The crowd had a laugh in the fourth . . . Lefty Gomez grounded to Herman, who relayed to Collins for the out . . . In a single motion, Collins caught the ball and relayed it to Lefty, who made a nice one-handed stab and kept right on trotting to his place on the hill . . .

The blankets, in which scores of bleacherites had sat huddled before game time, came off when the sun peaked through the clouds early in the contest . . . It was a cosmopolitan crowd in the huge open stands in center field . . . Priests, mailmen, laborers sat side by side, taking food from carriers ranging from one spacious valise to an old fashioned dinner pail . . .

Lefty Gomez, after being asked repeatedly to pose for cameramen with his wife, June O'Dea, growled repeatedly: "What is this, a personal appearance" . . . Roger Peckinpaugh, former Cleveland manager, chatting with Lou Fonseca and Jimmie Dykes . . . "Red" Ruffing stating he wished he could pitch to the Cubs often "because they haven't the power of the St. Louis Browns" . . .

The muttered comment of one woman as she walked toward the exit, "Gee, if Dizzy could have done it."

Nov. 29

Stratton's Right Leg Amputated at Knee

Operation Performed to Check Gangrene, Which Threatened Life of Sox Hurler

Dallas, Tex. - (AP) - The brilliant baseball career of Monty Stratton, young pitching star of the Chicago White Sox, was at an end Tuesday, cut short by the amputation of his right leg at the knee.

The operation to check spread of gangrene which threatened Stratton's life was performed here Monday after he had accidentally shot himself while hunting rabbits on his mother's farm at Greenville, Tex.

Bad luck has dogged Stratton's footsteps since he rejoined the White Sox two years ago. In 1937 an emergency operation followed by an ailing arm hampered his first season's performance. Even so he wound up with a season's record of 15 victories and 5 defeats. A recurrence of an arm injury put him on the sidelines for the first month of the 1938 campaign and an injured ankle added several days more but he gained credit as the Sox' leading hurler with 15 victories and 9 defeats.

Stratton, discovered with Galveston of the Texas league, probably could have been sold for $150,000 if Owner Comiskey had cared to place him on the baseball market. He began his baseball career with the Texas Red River league and first attracted the attention of the Sox scouts in 1934 while pitching for Galveston. Billy Webb, now a White Sox coach but then managing Galveston, urged Comiskey to purchase him.

TED WILLIAMS' DEBUT

April 20

```
NEW YORK              BOSTON
        AB H O A            AB H O A
Cr'setti ss  4 0 0 0   Cr'mer cf  4 1 2 0
Rolfe 3b     4 0 0 2   Vosmik lf  4 2 3 0
Powell lf    4 3 4 0   Foxx 1b    4 0 5 0
DiM'gio cf   2 1 3 0   Cronin ss  4 0 2 1
Gehrig 1b    4 0 6 0   Tabor 3b   4 0 1 1
Dickey c     3 2 7 0   Wil'ms rf  4 1 3 0
G'ber rf     3 0 3 0   Doerr 2b   4 1 4 3
G'rdon 2b    3 1 4 3   Des'tels c 3 0 3 1
Ruffing p    3 0 0 3   N'kamp x   1 0 0 0
                       Grove p    2 1 0 1
                       Peacock y  1 0 0 0

Totals     30 7 27 8   Totals    35 7 24 7
New York .............010 010 00x—2
Runs, Rolfe, Dickey; errors, Cronin,
Foxx, Gehrig; runs batted in, Dickey,
Powell; two base hits, Williams, Dickey,
Tabor, Vosmik; three base hit, Powell;
home runs, Dickey; double plays,
Doerr to Cronin to Foxx, Doerr to Foxx;
left on bases, New York 6, Boston 9;
bases on balls, off Grove 2, Ruffing 1;
strikeouts, by Grove 5, Ruffing 5; um-
pires, Ormsby Summers, Basil and Pip-
gras; time, 1:47; attendance, 30,278.
x—Nonnenkamp batted for Desautels
in 9th.
y—Peacock batted for Grove in 9th.
```

April 30

Gehrig on Bench After 2,130 Games

Detroit, Mich. — (P) — Manager Joe McCarthy of the New York Yankees announced Tuesday that Lou Gehrig, who has played in 2,130 consecutive games, would be benched at his own request in Tuesday's game with the Detroit Tigers.

McCarthy said Gehrig had asked to be put on the bench "because the way he was playing he thought it might help the club."

The Yankee manager said that Dahlgren, formerly of the Boston Red Sox, would take Gehrig's place at first base.

Giants Tie Own Home Run Mark Hitting Seven

Duplicate Early Season Feat in Opening Game Against Phillies

New York, Aug. 13.—(AP.)—Recovering from the embarrassment of defeats by the last place Phillies on two consecutive days, the Giants swept a doubleheader from Philadelphia today 1 to 2 and 6 to 2, tying the National League record for home runs in the first game.

Seven home runs, three of them coming in succession in the fourth inning, made it easy for Bill Lohrman to annex his tenth victory in the opener. Frank Demaree hit two of the homers, one in the first and another in the third, with one on. In the fourth, Zeke Bonura hit one and shortly afterward Alex Kampouris, Lohrman and Joe Moore bunched three in a row. Bob Seeds got the other in the eighth.

May 1

Dean, Chased in Benefit Game, Shows Arm Is Still Not in Shape

Dizzy Admits His High Priced Flipper Pains Him but Lays Blame on Cold Weather

Chicago, Ill. — (P) — The famed $155,000 right arm of Dizzy Dean is apparently no better than it was when he "throwed himself out" against the New York Yankees in the world series last October.

That was the impression prevailing Tuesday after Dean's first pitching assignment of the year. He faced the Chicago White Sox Monday in a benefit game which netted between $25,000 and $30,000 for Monty Stratton, onetime Sox pitching ace. The Sox whacked him for seven hits in four innings to win, 4 to 1, and unanimously asserted he didn't have a thing.

Shoulder Is Sore

Dean may be lost to the Cubs until at least midsummer. The colorful pitcher, after working four innings, admitted that his arm was sore and that it was weak and tired.

"There's no use kidding myself," Dean moaned. "It really hurts. It's sore as the deuce up here," pointing to a muscle over his shoulder. But he hastened to add, "it isn't sore where it was last year, under the shoulder blade. I'll just have to take things easy, I guess. I think it is just

Sox Take Early Lead Against Cubs in Game for Monte Stratton and Win in a Canter, 4-1

weakness. It looks as though I'll have to strengthen my arm, that's all."

Dean complained that he couldn't get warmed up because of the frigid temperature. His pitching cunning failed, partly because his control wasn't very good. There was none of the free arm fireballing that made him famous. There was more body than arm motion in his pitches.

Not only was Dean disheartened, so was Manager Gabby Hartnett. Hartnett indicated he would probably nurse the "great one" along until the hot weather sets in before giving him another pitching chance.

Doctors Find Lou Gehrig Has Infantile Paralysis

New York, N. Y. (AP)—Ed Barrow, president of the New York Yankees, announced Wednesday that Lou Gehrig is suffering from chronic infantile paralysis and will never play baseball again.

Barrow's statement came after Gehrig had turned over to him the formal report made by Mayo clinic experts. Gehrig had spent several days in the clinic in order to have a thorough check of his physical condition.

The onetime great first baseman had been worried about his condition all year. After making a bad showing in the field and at bat during the early part of the season, Gehrig voluntarily benched himself on May 2, ending his consecutive games streak at 2,130 games.

Fails to Regain Strength

He sat on the bench for several weeks but could not regain his strength. Finally he decided to put himself in the hands of experts to determine just why he had lost his baseball form so suddenly. His trip to the clinic followed.

Barrow said Gehrig apparently had been suffering from the ailment for two years and that only his remarkable physique had enabled him to play.

The veteran will be continued on the Yankee pay roll for the rest of the season at least and will remain as nonplaying team captain. After his conference with Barrow, Gehrig left for the clubhouse to don his uniform.

Barrow said he understood from the physicians' reports that the disease could be checked and that in any event it probably would not get worse.

Barrow Broken Up

The Yankee leader obviously was broken up as he made the announcement. Gehrig long has been one of his favorite players.

Gehrig was 36 years old on Monday.

Use of the phrase "chronic infantile paralysis" was taken from the official Mayo clinic report, which read as follows:

"To whom it may concern:

"This is to certify that Mr. Lou Gehrig has been under examination at the Mayo clinic from June 13 to June 19, 1939, inclusive.

"After a careful and complete examination, it was found that he is suffering from amyotrophic lateral sclerosis. This type of illness involves the motor pathways and cells of the central nervous system and in lay terms is known as a form of chronic poliomyelitis (infantile paralysis).

"The nature of this trouble makes it such that Mr. Gehrig will be unable to continue his active participation as a baseball player, inasmuch as it is advisable that he conserve his muscular energy. He could, however, continue in some executive capacity.

"(Signed)
"Harold C. Habein, M. D."

July 2

Mack Is 'Seriously Ill'; Resigns as Stars' Pilot

Boston, Mass. — (AP) — Described by his physician as being "very seriously ill," Connie Mack, 76 year old manager of the Philadelphia Athletics, was taken aboard a train Saturday night bound for his home in Philadelphia.

Mack, who was stricken last Thursday by what physicians described as an acute attack of indigestion, was accompanied by his wife, and his daughter, Mary. He was carried on a stretcher down the service elevator of the hotel, where he has been confined for three days, transported in an ambulance to South station, and placed aboard a train.

The whole maneuver was carried out in secrecy, and railroad police kept away the curious.

Dr. Eddie O'Brien, club physician of the Boston Red Sox, who has been treating Mack, described him as being "seriously ill."

"I am unable to discuss the case further," he said, "except to say that he went back to Philadelphia at his own request."

Dr. O'Brien declined to divulge the nature of the manager's illness.

Earlier the manager had wired to President Will Harridge of the American league his resignation as manager of his circuit's team in the all-star game at Yankee stadium July 11. Giving as his reason his present indisposition, Mack asked to be relieved of his duties, and Joe McCarthy, manager of the New York Yankees, was assigned to the job.

June 7

Five Giant Homers in Inning Set Mark

New York Pounds Reds, 17-3, in Vicious Attack; Tie Record With Seven Circuits in Game

New York, N. Y. — (AP) — The New York Giants, booed heartily Monday, reached baseball heights Tuesday by setting one major league home run record and equaling another, as they smashed the first place Cincinnati Reds, 17-3, in their most vicious attack of the year.

The new record was hung up in the fourth inning when five Giants

Harry Danning, Frank Demaree, Burgess Whitehead, Manuel Salvo and Joe Moore hit for the circuit. Previously the major league mark for homers was four in one inning, set by the Pittsburgh Pirates in 1894 and not equaled until the Chicago Cubs came through with a similar performance in 1930.

An Old Record

The record for seven homers in one game before that big fourth inning Joe Moore and Mel Ott had connected for four base blows—tied a record held jointly by the Detroit (National league) club of 1886, the Philadelphia Athletics of 1921 and the Pittsburgh Pirates of 1894.

GAME LEADERS HOLD BIRTHDAY

Baseball Celebrates 100th Anniversary At Cooperstown Field

Eleven Members Of Hall Of Fame Take Part In Festivities

[By the Associated Press]

Cooperstown, N. Y., June 12—The first 100 years are always the hardest and old man Baseball took off on his second century today after being hailed and feted at the biggest birthday party tossed him during his 100-year rule as the No. 1 figure in American sport.

There were parades, dedications, speakings, a Babe Ruth "comeback," clam bakes, ball games and what not for more than 11,000 people who poured into this pretty village where Abner Doubleday sat down on a hot day and invented the national pastime more than 100 years ago.

Commissioner K. M. Landis, high priest of baseball, was there to lead the cheering. He received plenty of lusty rooting assists from a score of men whose names are found in almost every baseball blue book ever published.

Museum Dedicated

The baseball museum and Hall of Fame with its relics of glorious bygone days, was dedicated; so was Doubleday Field, built on the actual spot where Doubleday's pioneers first trotted into action one hundred years ago. Eleven living members of the Hall of Fame renewed feuds and friendships and baseball as it was displayed in 1839, in the 1850's and in 1939—was reeled off by teams of schoolboys, soldiers and picked major leaguers, wearing the uniforms of the periods they represented

Men who have helped make baseball history—Babe Ruth, Connie Mack, Hans Wagner, old Nap Lajoi and Walter Johnson, to name just a few—sat on the platform as Landis dedicated the Hall of Fame "to all America."

It was accepted by Ford C. Frick and William C. Harridge, presidents of the National and American leagues, and William C. Bramham, president of the National Association of Professional Baseball Clubs, representing the minors. John A. Heydler, former National League president, who conceived the idea of the baseball party, was a guest of honor and introduced Commissioner Landis.

Receive Engraved Bats

Ten of the eleven living members of the Hall of Fame were presented with engraved bats, and a ruffle of drums and the sounding of taps answered the calling of the names of the fourteen deceased members.

Ty Cobb, the old Georgia Peach, of the Detroit Tigers, was delayed en route by illness and didn't arrive until after the ceremonies. But the other ten were there from Connie Mack, the 76-year-old dean, down to Babe Ruth, the freshman of the lot.

COOPERSTOWN BOX

COLLINSES

	Ab.	R.	H.	O.	A.
L. Waner (Pirates), cf	3	0	0	0	0
Thompson (Browns), cf	1	0	0	0	0
Herman (Cubs), 2b	4	0	0	0	0
Ott (Giants), lf	4	0	1	0	0
Greenberg (Tigers), 1b	2	0	1	9	0
Selkirk (Yankees), rf	3	0	0	0	0
T. Wright (Senators), rf	1	1	1	1	0
Jorgens (Yankees), c	3	0	0	2	0
Hack (Cubs), 3b	3	0	0	2	3
Travis (Senators), ss	1	0	0	1	1
Miller (Reds), ss	2	0	1	1	2
Dean (Cubs), p	1	0	0	1	2
VanderMeer (Reds), p	0	0	0	0	0
S. Johnson (Phillies), p	0	0	0	0	0
*Shilling (Indians)	1	0	1	0	0
Totals	27	2	6	18	9

1Batted for S. Johnson in seventh.

WAGNERS

	Ab.	R.	H.	O.	A.
Moses (Athletics), rf	1	0	0	1	0
T. Moore (Cardinals), rf	1	0	0	0	0
Vaughan (Pirates), ss	2	1	1	3	3
Gehringer (Tigers), 2b	2	0	0	1	3
Medwick (Cardinals), lf	3	0	0	2	0
Berg (Red Sox), c	1	0	0	0	0
F. Hayes (Athletics), c	2	1	1	2	0
Ruel (Washington), c	0	0	0	0	0
Arnorich (Phillies), cf	3	0	1	2	0
J. Wilson (Reds), 1b	1	1	1	5	0
Lavagetto (Dodgers), 1b	1	0	0	2	1
Owen (White Sox), 3b	1	1	1	1	1
Jurges (Giants), 3b	1	0	0	0	0
Grove (Red Sox), p	1	0	1	0	0
MacFayden (Reds), p	1	0	0	0	0
2Ruth	1	0	0	0	0
Allen (Cleveland), p	0	0	0	0	0
Totals	21	4	6	21	5

2Batted for MacFayden in fifth.

Collinses .... 0 0 0 0 2 0—2
Wagners .... 0 0 2 0 0 2 x—4

Errors—Vaughan, VanderMeer. Runs batted in—Hayes, Arnorich, MacFayden, Owen, Jorgens, Hack. Two-base hits—Owen, MacFayden, Vaughan, Hayes, Miller. Double plays—Vaughan to Gehringer to Lavagetto; VanderMeer to Jorgens to Greenberg to Jorgens. Left on bases—Collinses, 5; Wagners, 3. Base on balls—Vander Meer, 2; Johnson, 1; Allen, 1. Strikeouts—Dean, 2; MacFayden, 1; Allen, 2. Hits—Grove, 1 in 2 innings; MacFayden, 1 in 2; Allen, 4 in 3; VanderMeer, 3 in 1; Dean, 0 in 2; Johnson, 3 in 3. Umpires—Klem (N. L.), plate; Rommel (A. L.), bases. Time—1:40.

June 29

Yanks Hit 13 Homers in Winning Double Bill

Eight in First Sets a Record

Old Mark of Seven in Single Game Made by Detroit Back in 1886; Pearson, Gomez Hurl Victories

Philadelphia, Pa. (P)—Breaking the major league records for home runs in a single game and in consecutive games, the New York Yankees Wednesday battered the Philadelphia Athletics, 23 to 2 and 10 to 0, in a double header. The champions got eight homers in the first game and five in the second. Lefty Gomez gave three hits in the nightcap after Monte Pearson won the opener.

The old mark of seven in a game set by Detroit in the original National league back in 1886, had been tied five times—the most recent being June 6 when the New York Giants hit seven against the Cincinnati Reds.

The Yankees, equaled the old mark in the first six innings and broke it in the seventh on Babe Dahlgren's second homer of the game, with two mates aboard. Dahlgren's round tripper in the third also came with one on.

How They Got 'Em

Philadelphia, Pa. Here is the "count" on the New York Yankees' home run streak of 13 Wednesday:

Joe DiMaggio 3 (two in first game, one in second).

Babe Dahlgren 3 (two in first game, one in second).

Joe Gordon 3 (one in first game, two in second).

Bill Dickey 1 (first game).

George Selkirk 1 (first game).

Tommy Henrich 1 (first game).

Frank Crosetti 1 (second game).

DERRINGER TAKES DECIDING GAME, 5-3

His 25th Triumph Achieved Despite 14 Hits by Cards While Reds Make Eight

SIRENS HAIL FLAG VICTORY

Rivals' Poor Base-Running Saves Day for Cincinnati —Mates Lionize Hurler

By The Associated Press.

CINCINNATI, Sept. 28—There was joy on Vine Street tonight, for the Reds finally staggered to a 5-to-3 victory over the tenacious Cardinals at Crosley Field today and won for this city its first National League pennant in twenty long years.

In qualifying to tackle the Yankees in the world series starting next Wednesday at New York, Deacon Bill McKechnie's boys increased their margin over St. Louis to three and one-half games, with only three contests remaining for them at Pittsburgh, starting tomorrow.

JOE M'CARTHY PRAISES STAR

Manager And Players Congratulate Hurler On Marvelous Feat

McKechnie Refuses To Be Disheartened; To Pitch Thompson Next

By CHARLES DUNKLEY
Associated Press Staff Writer

New York, Oct. 5—Monte Pearson was a tremendously popular hero with the Yankees as they burst into song in the dressing room after conquering the Reds for the second straight time today.

Joseph Vincent McCarthy, leader of the Yanks, shouldered his way through the crowded room to be the first to congratulate Pearson on his marvelous two-hit pitching feat.

"Nice going, kid," the fatherly McCarthy beamed, clasping Pearson by the hand. Then one by one the Yanks came over to slap Pearson on the back in congratulation.

Pearson Supremely Happy

The 30-year-old Pearson was supremely happy. He said he had no thought of pitching a no-hitter and felt no relief after Beezer Lombardi, the Reds' big catcher, whacked a single off him in the eighth inning for the first hit the Reds got.

The Box Score

CINCINNATI (N. L.)

	Ab.	R.	H.	O.	A.
Werber, 3b.	3	0	1	0	1
Frey, 2b.	4	0	0	2	2
Goodman, rf.	3	0	0	1	0
McCormick, 1b.	3	0	0	7	0
Lombardi, c.	3	0	1	5	1
1Bordagaray	0	0	0	0	0
Hershberger, c.	0	0	0	0	0
Craft, cf.	3	0	0	3	1
Berger, lf.	3	0	0	1	0
Myers, ss.	3	0	0	5	3
Walters, p.	2	0	0	0	3
2Gamble	1	0	0	0	0
Totals	28	0	2	24	11

1Ran for Lombardi in eighth.
2Batted for Walters in ninth.

NEW YORK (A. L.)

	Ab.	R.	H.	O.	A.
Crosetti, ss.	4	0	1	1	2
Rolfe, 3b.	4	1	1	1	1
Keller, rf.	4	1	2	1	0
DiMaggio, cf.	4	0	1	4	0
Dickey, c.	3	0	1	8	1
Selkirk, lf.	3	0	1	3	0
Gordon, 2b.	3	0	0	2	0
Dahlgren, 1b.	3	2	2	8	0
Pearson, p.	2	0	0	0	5
Totals	30	4	9	27	9

Cincinnati (N. L.) . 0 0 0 0 0 0 0 0 0—0
New York (A. L.) . 0 0 3 1 0 0 0 0 x—4
Runs batted in—Crosetti, Keller, Dickey, Dahlgren. Two base hits—Dahlgren, Keller. Home run—Dahlgren. Sacrifice—Pearson. Double plays—Dickey to Crosetti; Walters to Myers to McCormick. Left on bases—New York, 3; Cincinnati, 2. Earned runs—New York, 4. Base on balls—Pearson 1 (Werber). Strikeouts—Pearson, 8 (Craft 3, Myers, Frey, Goodman, McCormick, Gamble), Walters, 5 (Dickey, Pearson, Selkirk, Gordon, Dahlgren). Umpires—Reardon (N. L.), plate; Summers (A. L.), first base; Pinelli (N. L.), second base; McGowan (A. L.), third base. Time—1.27.

Baseball Talent Worth $500,000 Lost to Detroit by Landis Edict

Pitcher Trout Considered Most Valuable of Players Cut Adrift in Biggest Ruling of Its Kind in Major Leagues

By The Associated Press.

DETROIT, Jan. 14—High officials of the Tigers, although they had expected some ruling by Commissioner Landis on their minor league baseball operations, were shaken today by the weight of the blow.

Official statements were withheld pending a conference tomorrow among Vice President Walter O. Briggs Jr., General Manager Jack Zeller and others. Zeller, who is in charge of the Tiger farm system, was en route from his home in Fort Worth, Texas. President Walter O. Briggs is vacationing in Miami Beach, Fla.

Baseball men were generally agreed, however, that the Landis ruling had cut adrift Tiger talent valued in excess of $500,000. It was considered the biggest free agency ruling of its kind in major league history. Two years ago Commissioner Landis freed more than 100 St. Louis Cardinal farmhands, but the Tiger players involved are in higher league classifications.

A. J. (Wish) Egan, scout, signed many of the players. He said tonight it would take the Tigers many years to rebuild their farm system.

Box-Office Attractions

Of the five first-line players freed, four were from Michigan and considered valuable at the box office as well as on the playing field. Benny McCoy is a 22-year-old infielder who was used as trading bait to get Outfielder Wally Moses from the Athletics. The deal now is canceled.

Roy Cullenbine was with the Tigers one full season, coming up from Toledo of the American Association. Lloyd Dietz, 26, entered the Tiger organization from Western State Teachers College, Kalamazoo. He was sold to St. Paul of the American Association last Fall but that deal also is annulled.

Steve Rachunok was a 20-game winner with Henderson of the East Texas League last year and was ranked as one of the game's best mound prospects.

The hardest blow of all to the Tigers was the freeing of Pitcher Paul (Dizzy) Trout, 24, the most valuable player in the Texas League in 1938, winning twenty-two games and losing six for Beaumont. Last season with the Tigers he showed promise of becoming one of the Tiger mainstays.

Hero of the Rose Bowl

Among the eighty-seven minor leaguers freed were Millard (Dixie) Howell, Alabama's hero in the 1935 Rose Bowl football game; Martin (Rube) Zachar, husky right-handed pitcher from Michigan Normal College; Pitcher Stanley Corbett, who went to two Tiger Spring camps; and several other Detroiters.

Others, while playing in obscure leagues, were vital members of Detroit's farm system. The Tigers employ a staff of nine full-time scouts, said to be the largest in the major leagues.

Of the players who were awarded monetary consideration in the ruling, Irving (Jack) Burns played first base for the Tigers in 1937 after Hank Greenberg had fractured his wrist.

First Baseman George Archie went to Seattle in the deal for Pitcher Freddie Hutchinson a year ago, and Outfielder Chester Morgan was traded to Boston in the deal for Third Baseman Frank (Pinky) Higgins.

Trout Is Delighted

TERRE HAUTE, Ind., Jan. 14 (AP)—Pitcher Paul (Dizzy) Trout told his sister, Mrs. Cora Crone, in a telephone conversation tonight he was "tickled pink" to receive his freedom.

Trout, who lives in Detroit during the Winter months, told Mrs. Crone he had received telephone calls from the Washington Senators and the St. Louis Cardinals indicating they would be interested in his services.

The ruling would "mean a lot of money to me," the young right-hander predicted.

INDIANS' ACE BEATS WHITE SOX BY 1-0

Feller Is Only One in Modern Major League History to Hurl Opening No-Hitter

FANS EIGHT, WALKS FIVE

Losers Fill Bases in Second—Single by Heath and Hemsley's Triple Win

By The Associated Press.

CHICAGO, April 16—Bob Feller of the Indians carved a niche for himself in baseball's hall of fame as the American League season opened today, pitching an amazing no-hit game to defeat the White Sox, 1 to 0, before 14,000 roaring fans.

It was the first opening day no-hit contest in modern major league history. It ended after 2 hours and 24 minutes of play as Ray Mack, Cleveland second sacker, made a great knockdown of Taft Wright's grounder and tossed him out at first by a step.

Floyd Giebell Handcuffs Indians, 2-0; Riotous Crowd Showers Winners With Fruit, Eggs

BY JUDSON BAILEY.

Cleveland, Sept 27—(AP)—Rudy York, the pale-faced Indian, nullified the courageous three-hit hurling of Bobby Feller today with one lofty home run that clinched the American League pennant for the Detroit Tigers.

The homer came with one on in the fourth inning and beat the Cleveland Indians 2 to 0 while a riotous crowd of 45,553, a third of them women, demonstrated its hostility to the Tigers with frequent showers of fruit, vegetables and eggs.

One fan dropped a basket of green tomatoes out of the upper deck of the grandstand and hit Catcher Birdie Tebbetts on the head, knocking him out but not injuring him seriously. This incident came after chief umpire Bill Summers stopped the game to warn the crowd that every Cleveland player who hit a fly ball would be out if Detroit fielders were interfered with by the fruit throwing.

Coscarart's Single Gives Team Victory In Last Inning, 2-1

Error By Cleveland's Hal Trosky at First Base Paves Way For Winning Run

Bob Feller Is Losing Pitcher

American Sluggers Are Held to Only Five Scattered Hits By Five Hurlers

Tampa, March 17.—(AP.)—The National League finally bristled up and licked the American League, 2 to 1, in a corking good all-star game at Plant Field today before an exultant crowd of over 13,000. The contest realized more than $20,000 for the Finnish Relief Fund.

Deadlocked 1 to 1 going into the last of the ninth inning after a sparkling sustained exhibition of pitching, the Nationals shoved across the deciding run before a man was retired on two sharp single and an error by Hal Trosky, Cleveland Indian first-baseman.

Al Lopez, Boston Bees' catcher and Tampa's only representative in the big leagues, crossed the rubber with the big run as his neighbors in the packed stands cheered. He had to battle his way through them to reach the dressing room.

Jimmy Foxx Hits 500th Homer As Boston Wins Two

Ted Williams, Foxx and Joe Cronin Slam Successive 4-Baggers in First

Philadelphia, Sept. 24 (AP) Jimmy Foxx hit his 500th homer of his career today as the Boston Red Sox clouted three round-trippers in succession to tie a major league record in beating the Athletics in both ends of a twin bill, 16 to 8 and 4 to 3.

The three homers in a row came in the sixth of the opener against George Caster. Ted Williams, Foxx and Joe Cronin slammed the ball out of the lot. Bobby Doerr then poked a mighty triple and was stopped at third although observers thought he could have got inside homer. Jim Tabor followed with the fourth round-tripper of the inning, one less than the major league mark set by the New York Giants June 6, 1939.

Altogether the Sox got six homers, three triples, five two-baggers and nine singles in the opener.

BOSTON	AB	H	O	A		PHILADELPHIA	AB	H	O	A
DiMag cf	6	2	0	1		Miles cf	5	3	2	0
Cramr rf	6	2	1	0		Valo lf	5	3	4	0
Willms lf	6	3	1	0		Moses rf	5	3	1	0
Foxx 1b	5	2	13	2		Wagner c	4	3	7	0
Lupien 1b	1	1	2	1		Siebrt 1b	5	1	6	1
Cronin ss	5	4	0	2		McCoy 2b	4	0	2	1
Carey ss	1	0	0	1		Gntbn 3b	4	1	0	1
Doerr 2b	6	4	0	4		Wlsea ss	4	1	3	4
Tabor 3b	4	2	2	2		Heusser p	0	0	1	0
Gibrt 3b	0	0	0	0		Caster p	1	0	1	0
Peacck c	5	1	6	0		McCbb p	2	0	0	1
Heving p	5	2	3	1		Eiland p	1	0	0	0
Totals	48					Totals	41	15	27	8

Boston 023 217 001 16
Philadelphia 003 000 050 8

Lombardi Is Laid Up For 10 Days, Report

Brooklyn, Sept. 16 (AP)—Ernie Lombardi, Cincinnati's heavy hitting first-string catcher, will be unable to play for about 10 days, Manager Bill McKechnie said today.

Lombardi suffered a sprained right ankle in the first game of yesterday's double-header with the Dodgers. He is now on crutches with his injured foot badly swollen.

Cleveland Players Demand Dismissal Of Oscar Vitt

Charge Manager With Insincerity and Ridiculing of Own Men in Mass Protest; Say Pilot's Actions Make Him Laughing Stock of League

Cleveland, June 13.—(AP.)—Veteran members of the Cleveland Indians today personally laid before President Alva Bradley a demand that Manager Oscar Vitt be fired.

The mass protest, believed unprecedented in major league baseball history, came as a majority of the players confronted Bradley in their return from a disastrous Eastern trip where they lost eight of 13 games.

The players told Bradley they could not play the kind of baseball of which they are capable as long as Vitt remained at the helm. Their charges, according to the Plain Dealer, included insincerity, ridiculing of players and caustic criticism.

Although the meeting was kept secret, Bradley later admitted that "a few of the boys wanted certain things corrected."

"Naturally I am going to look into the matter," Bradley said, "but until I have investigated thoroughly I can't say what action will be taken."

Few Are Absent.

It was learned that a few Indians were not at the meeting, absentees including Beau Bell and Al Smith, acquired this season, and Rookies Lou Boudreau, Ray Mack, Clarence Campbell and Mike Naymick.

"They (the absentees) didn't want any part of the protest," a spokesman for the group declared, "and we were glad they didn't. We felt Bradley would be more impressed by the testimony of the fellows who have been around long enough to know what they're talking about."

Bradley refused to divulge the nature of the charges. However, the Plain Dealer said the protesters made these accusations:

That Vitt had ridiculed his players in conversations with newspaper writers, fans and opposing players and managers;

That he had undermined the confidence and spirit of the individuals by sarcastic comments on their failures;

That he had proved himself insincere in his dealings with the players;

That he is a "wild man" on the bench, storming up and down, voicing caustic comments on his players' actions and communicating his "jitters" to the players;

Becomes Laughing Stock.

That his antics have made him a laughing stock among other teams and that the Indians have lost dignity and pride thereby;

That he has persisted in comparing the Indians unfavorably with minor league teams he has managed, notably the Newark Bears of 1937 who won the International League pennant by 25½ games.

Undercurrent rumblings against Vitt nearly reached the surface last season, but Bradley stepped in and signed him to a new contract. The Indians then finished strong and took third place.

"We made up our minds then we might as well make the best of a bad situation," a veteran player said recently. "When we went to spring training camp this year we were determined to wipe the slate clean and start over again. But before the season was two weeks old he had driven most of us half crazy. We are a good ball club and we've got a chance to win the pennant, but if he manages the team all year we'll be lucky to finish fourth."

Several incidents on the recent eastern trip were reported to have brought the protest to a head.

Criticizes Feller.

On Tuesday Bob Feller, ranked by many the best pitcher in baseball, was being hit hard by the Boston Red Sox. The Plain Dealer quotes players as describing Vitt's verbal reaction thus:

"Look at him! He's supposed to be my ace! I'm supposed to win a pennant with that kind of pitching."

Feller was reported to have heard the comment as he stood on the pitching mound.

Vitt became manager of the team in the spring of 1938 after the dismissal of Steve O'Neill, now pilot of Buffalo's International League club. The team finished third that year.

Vitt clashed frequently with his players during the 1939 unrest, his troubles with Julius Solters (now with Chicago), Jeff Heath and Roy Weatherly becoming known publicly. According to players much of the friction was caused by Vitt's open criticism of the three to writers, fans and other players.

Vice president C. C. Slapnicka, club directors and other Indian officials refused comment on the protest move and Vitt was not immediately available.

Cincinnati Relief Catcher Kills Self In Boston Hotel

Willard Hershberger, 29, of Reds, Reported Depressed On Friday, Found Dead After Failing to Appear at Field

Boston, Aug. 3.—(AP.)—Willard Hershberger, 29, catcher for the Cincinnati Reds baseball club, committed suicide in his hotel room today by cutting his throat with a razor blade, Medical Examiner Timothy Leary announced tonight.

Dr. Leary said Hershberger, who had been in professional baseball for a decade and was in the midst of his third year with the Reds, was found lying over the bathtub in his room, his coat and shirt off. There were no notes.

Police said they found several uncashed paychecks in his pocket.

Gabriel Paul, traveling secretary for the Cincinnati club, said in a statement that Manager Bill McKechnie had noticed Hershberger's "depressed mental condition following Friday's doubleheader," both games of which the Reds lost.

McKechnie, Paul said, talked to the catcher for some time and afterward Hershberger "was in much better spirits and sat around the lobby with some of the players."

Hershberger was in "good spirits" this morning, the club secretary said, but when asked by his roommate, Bill Baker, if he was going to the park, replied he would go out a bit later.

When Hershberger failed to appear, Paul said they called him on the telephone at 1:10 p. m. (EDT) and that he answered:

"I'm sick and can't play, but I'll come out right away anyway."

Paul said that Sam Cohen, a Cincinnati businessman and close friend of Hershberger's, went to the hotel to get him, but found the door locked.

He was admitted by a maid, Paul said, and they found the body in the bathroom.

Hershberger's "jugular vein was cut," the club secretary said.

Hershberger was a native of Lemon Cove, Calif., and made his home at Three Rivers, Calif.

He was serving his third year with Cincinnati, having been acquired from Newark of the International League in December, 1937, where he was the Bears' mainstay backstop.

CINCY EDGES BROOKLYN, 4-3

Magerkurth Floored By Flatbush Fan On 10th-Inning Ruling

Other Fights Flare Up When Coscarart's Muff Is Disputed

Standing Of The Clubs

	W.	L.	P.C.		W.	L.	P.C.
Cincinnati	91	47	.659	Chicago	68	73	.482
Brooklyn	83	59	.585	New York	66	73	.475
St. Louis	73	65	.529	Boston	59	82	.418
Pittsburgh	73	66	.525	Philadel'a	46	94	.329

[By the Associated Press]

Brooklyn, Sept. 16—The Cincinnati Reds came close to clinching their second successive National League pennant today by downing the Brooklyn Dodgers, 4 to 3, in 10 innings with the help of a disputed play that caused an attack on Umpire George Magerkurth after the game.

After the Reds rallied to tie the score in the ninth with one run, they loaded the bases with one out in the tenth on Mike McCormick's double, a walk to Ival Goodman and an error by Pete Coscarart, which caused all the trouble.

Coscarart Errs

Frank McCormick grounded to shortstop, and Johnny Hudson threw to Coscarart, who dropped the ball while pivoting to throw to first in a double-play attempt. Umpire Bill Stewart called Goodman, out, but appealed to Magerkurth near third base when Manager Bill McKechnie and the Reds protested vociferously.

Magerkurth ruled Goodman was safe, filling the bases, and his decision stood in spite of a vocal storm from the Dodgers, which ended only with the banishment of Manager Leo Durocher from the field.

On the next play Catcher Bill Baker drove a liner to left and Mike McCormick scored the deciding run.

Fan Socks Ump

After the game hundreds of the 6,782 fans swarmed onto the field. One of them shook Magerkurth's hand, but another rushed up and started a fist fight. The towering umpire, at least 6 feet 3 inches tall and weighing probably 225 pounds, was knocked to the ground and pounded by his smaller foe until the other umpires and uniformed ushers rushed to his aid.

Other fans became involved in numerous scattered arguments and light fighting with ushers and other spectators, but order was restored after police arrested Magerkurth's assailant.

1940 WORLD SERIES
REDS — NATIONAL LEAGUE CHAMPIONS
DETROIT TIGERS — AMERICAN LEAGUE CHAMPIONS
AT CROSLEY FIELD ★ CINCINNATI, OHIO
Souvenir OFFICIAL SCORE BOOK
PRICE 25 CENTS

GREENBERG TO ARMY DUTY

Detroit, May 6. — (AP.) — Big Hank Greenberg closed out a baseball season and perhaps a career by belting two home runs, his first of the year, as the Detroit Tigers today defeated the New York Yankees, 7 to 4, for a sweep of the three-game series.

Greenberg, one of the game's great power hitters, exploded with the precision of a time bomb at his farewell party and before he checked in his uniform to Manager Del Baker the Tigers were lodged in second place in the American League standing four games behind the Cleveland Indians.

Notified in the dressing room that his local draft board had authorized his appearance at the American League pennant raising ceremonies tomorrow, Greenberg said he would report on schedule at 6:30 a. m. tomorrow for induction into the Army.

"I've asked no favors and I'll accept none now," Hankus Pankus said flatly. "I'll do the best I can to become a good soldier."

The American League's most valuable player will be a buck private at Fort Custer, Mich., by nightfall tomorrow, draft officials said. He automatically goes off the Detroit payroll at a reported $50,000 a year and starts his Army life at $21 a month.

DiMaggio Keeps Streak Going As Yanks Beat Red Sox Twice

Joe Ties Keeler's Old Record, But Winners' Home-Run String Is Snapped At 25 Tilts

[By the Associated Press]

New York, July 1—Base hits continued to blaze off Joe DiMaggio's bat today as the Yankee hero ran his consecutive hitting streak to 44 games, tying the all-time big league record set by Willie Keeler in 1897 and helping the Yanks administer two pastings to the Boston Red Sox, 7 to 2 and 9 to 2.

While the slugging outfielder was keeping his streak intact, though, another batting string of which the Yankees were almost equally proud was snapped when they failed to hit a home run in the first game.

Up to today they had clouted at least one round-tripper in 25 consecutive games, breaking the previous record of 17 straight games set by the Detroit Tigers last year.

Lou Gehrig, Famous First Baseman Of Yankees 14 Years, Dies Aged 37

One of Baseball's Greatest Stars Had Been Ill Two Years of Rare Disease; Served On New York Parole Commission

New York, June 2.—(AP.)—Lou Gehrig, great first baseman of the New York Yankees for 14 years, died tonight after two years illness of a rare disease that everyone except he himself believed incurable.

The "Iron Horse" of baseball, who would have been 38 years old June 19, passed away at his home in the presence of his wife after a critical span of only three weeks. He did not lose consciousness until just before death at 9:10 p. m. (EST).

The disease which erased Gehrig from the lineup of the mighty Yankees on May 2, 1939, was diagnosed as "amyotrophic lateral soclerosis," a hardening of the spinal cord which caused muscles to shrivel.

He wasted away sharply in the final weeks and was reported 25 pounds underweight and barely able to speak shortly before he died.

He had served for a year and a half as a member of the New York City parole commission and visited his office regularly until about a month ago, when he decided to remain at home to conserve his energy.

LOU GEHRIG.

Grounds Out Three Times Walks Once

Hits Into Double Play in Last Chance; Yanks, However, Win Game, 4 to 3

Cleveland, Ohio, July 17.—(AP)— Joe DiMaggio's 56-game hitting streak was snapped here tonight as his New York Yankees beat Cleveland 4 to 3. The slugger's string began May 15 against Cleveland bettered George Sisler's modern record of 41, established in 1922, and Willie Keeler's 1897 mark of 44.

Going to bat in the eighth inning with his team leading, 4 to 1, and the bases filled, DiMaggio hit into a double play to end the rally. In three previous appearances he grounded twice to Third Baseman Ken Keltner and walked once.

Al Smith faced the Yankee slugger the three times while Jim Bagby induced him to bounce into the double play, Lou Boudreau to Ray Mack to Oscar Grimes.

A throng of 67,468, the largest night baseball crowd in history, watched the two top teams of the American League battle.

Lefty Gomez stopped the Indians with four hits and one run for eight innings, but the slim southpaw was routed by the determined Redskins in a ninth-inning rally. Fireman Johnny Murphy pitched a triple to Larry Rosenthal, batting for Ray Mack, to allow two runs but bore down to retire Pinch-Hitters Clarence Campbell and Hal Trosky and Roy Weatherly to end the game.

DiMaggio's streak, started May 15 against Chicago, might have been extended but for some sharp fielding by Ken Keltner, Cleveland third baseman. In the first and seventh innings he made sensational stops of hot smashes and threw out the rangy Yankee outfielder. The other time Smith pitched to DiMaggio he walked him on a three and two pitch.

Joe had his last chance in the eighth, coming to bat against Bagby with the bases filled and one out. However, he bounded to Lou Boudreau for a fast double play.

After the game DiMaggio said: "I can't say that I'm glad it's over. Of course I wanted to go on as long as I could.

"Now that the streak is over, I just want to get out there and keep helping to win ball games."

The largest crowd in night baseball history saw two home runs. Gerry Walker getting his fourth of the season for Cleveland's first run in the fourth and Joe Gordon putting the Yanks in the lead in the seventh with his 15th.

The Yanks picked up eight hits, Smith being shelled out in the eighth inning rally that produced the two deciding runs. Charley Keller started the fireworks with a drive to center field which Weatherly misjudged and allowed to get by him for a triple. Singles by Gomes and Johnny Sturm and Red Rolfe's double did the rest of the damage.

NEW YORK	AB	R	H	O	A		CLEVELAND	AB	R	H	O	A
Sturm 1b	4	1	1	10	2		Weatherly cf	3	1	1	4	0
Rolfe 3b	4	2	2	2	3		Keltner 3b	3	1	1	1	4
Henrich rf	3	1	1	4	0		Boudreau ss	3	0	0	2	3
DiMag cf	3	0	2	1	0		Heath rf	4	0	1	4	0
Gordon 2b	4	1	2	1	1		Walker lf	3	1	1	4	0
Rosar c	4	0	0	5	1		Grimes 1b	3	0	1	12	0
Keller lf	3	1	1	3	0		Mack 2b	3	0	0	4	7
Rizzuto ss	3	0	0	2	1		Rosenthal z	1	0	1	0	0
Gomes p	4	1	2	1			Hemsley c	3	0	1	3	0
Murphy p	0	0	0	0	1		Trosky y	1	0	0	0	0
							Smith p	3	0	1	0	0
							Bagby p	1	0	0	0	0
							Campbell x	1	0	0	0	0
Totals	33	8	27	10			Totals	32	7	27	14	

New York .... 100 000 120—4
Cleveland .... 000 100 002—3

Runs, Rolfe, Gordon, Keller, Gomes, Walker 2, Grimes; runs batted in, Henrich, Walker, Gomes, Gordon, Rolfe, Rosenthal 2; two base hits, Henrich, Rolfe; three base hits, Keller, Rosenthal; home runs, Walker, Gordon; sacrifice, Boudreau; double play, Boudreau, Mack and Grimes; left on bases, New York 5, Cleveland 7; base on balls, off Smith 3, off Bagby 1, off Smith 2 in 7 1-3 innings, off Bagby 1 in 1 2-3; off Gomes 6 in 8 (none out in 9th); off Murphy 1 in 1; passed ball, Hemsley; winning pitcher, Gomes; losing pitcher, Smith; umpires, Summers, Rue and Stewart; time, 1:58; attendance (actual), 67,468.

z—Rosenthal batted for Mack in 9th.
y—Trosky batted for Hemsley in 9th.
x—Campbell batted for Bagby in 9th.

Two On, Two Down When Bostonian Hits Ball Far Into Stands

Story Book Finish

AMERICAN.

	AB	R	H	O	A	E
Doerr, Boston, 2b	3	0	0	0	0	0
Gordon, New York, 2b	2	1	1	2	0	0
Travis, Wash., 3b	2	1	1	1	2	0
J. DiMaggio, N. Y., cf	4	3	1	1	0	0
Williams, Boston, lf	4	1	2	3	0	0
Heath, Cleveland, rf	2	0	1	0	0	0
D. DiMaggio, Bost., rf	1	0	1	1	0	0
Cronin, Boston, ss	2	0	0	3	0	0
Boudreau, Cleve., ss	2	0	2	0	1	0
York, Detroit, 1b	3	0	1	6	2	0
Foxx, Boston, 1b	3	0	0	2	2	0
Dickey, New York, c	3	0	0	4	2	0
Hayes, Philadelphia, c	0	0	0	2	0	0
Feller, Cleveland, p	0	0	0	0	1	0
Cullenbine, St. Louis, z	1	0	0	0	0	0
Lee, Chicago, p	0	0	0	0	1	0
Hudson, Washington, p	0	0	0	0	0	0
Keller, New York, b	1	0	0	0	0	0
Smith, Chicago, p	0	0	0	1	0	1
Keltner, Cleveland, k	1	1	1	0	0	0
Totals	36	7	11	27	11	3

NATIONAL.

	AB	R	H	O	A	E
Hack, Chicago, 3b	2	0	1	3	0	0
Lavagetto, Brooklyn, 3b	1	0	0	0	0	0
Moore, St. Louis, lf	5	0	0	0	0	0
Reiser, Brooklyn, cf	4	0	0	6	0	2
Mize, St. Louis, 1b	4	1	1	5	0	0
McCormick, Cinci., 1b	0	0	0	0	0	0
Nicholson, Chicago, rf	1	0	0	1	0	0
Elliott, Pittsburgh, rf	1	0	0	0	0	0
Slaughter, St. Louis, rf	2	1	1	0	0	0
Vaughan, Pittsburgh, ss	4	2	3	1	2	0
Miller, Boston, ss	0	0	0	1	1	0
Frey, Cincinnati, 2b	1	0	1	1	3	0
Herman, Brooklyn, 2b	3	0	2	3	0	0
Owen, Brooklyn, c	1	0	0	0	0	0
Lopez, Pittsburgh, c	1	0	0	3	0	0
Danning, New York, c	1	0	0	3	0	0
Wyatt, Brooklyn, p	0	0	0	0	0	0
Ott, New York, x	1	0	0	0	0	0
Derringer, Cinci., p	0	0	0	0	1	0
Walters, Cincinnati, p	1	1	1	0	0	0
Medwick, Brooklyn, a	1	0	0	0	0	0
Passeau, Chicago, p	1	0	0	0	0	0
Totals	35	5	10	26	7	2

American .... 000 101 014—7
National .... 000 001 220—5

Runs batted in: Williams 4, Moore, Boudreau, Vaughan 4, D. DiMaggio, J. DiMaggio. earned runs, Nationals 7; Americans 7; two base hits: Travis, Williams, Walters, Herman, Mize, J. DiMaggio; home runs: Vaughan 2, Williams; sacrifice hits, Hack, Lopez; double plays, Frey to Vaughan to Mize, York to Cronin; left on bases, Nationals 6, Americans 6; base on balls. Wyatt (Williams), Walters 2 (DiMaggio, Heath), Hudson (Hack), Passeau (Travis); struck out by Feller 4 (Hack, Reiser, Nicholson, Ott), Derringer 1 (Heath), Walters 2 (Cronin, Doerr), Hudson 1 (Moore), Smith 2 (Reiser, Slaughter), Passeau 3 (Keller, Williams, Foxx); hits, off Feller 1 in 3 innings. Lee 4 in 3. Hudson 3 in 1. Smith 2 in 2. Wyatt 0 in 2. Derringer 2 in 2. Walters 3 in 2. Passeau 6 in 2 2-3; winning pitcher, Smith; losing pitcher, Passeau; umpires. Summers (AL) Jorda (NL). Grieve (AL) and Pinelli (NL); time, 2:23; attendance (paid) 54,674.

z—Cullenbine batted for Feller in 3d.
b—Keller batted for Hudson in 7th.
k—Keltner batted for Smith in 9th.
y—Two out when winning runs were scored.
x—Ott batted for Wyatt in 3d.
a—Medwick batted for Walters in 7th.

Thunderous Climax Before 56,674 Fans at Detroit Gives American League Sixth Victory

Vaughan Tilt's Previous Hero

Pirates' Shortstop Pounds Two Circuit Drives, Each With Man on Base, Earlier in Game

BY JUDSON BAILEY.

Briggs Stadium, Detroit, July 8.—(AP.)—In the most thunderous climax in the history of baseball's big all-star spectacle, willowy Ted Williams smashed a 3-run homer 90 feet high against the top of the right field stands in the ninth inning today to lift the American League to a 7 to 5 triumph over the National League.

The crowd of 56,674, third largest in the 9-year life of the fans' "dream game," had been dazzled earlier by brilliant pitching and by two booming home runs by Arky Vaughan which brought the National League up to the final frame with an apparently impregnable 5 to 3 advantage.

Then two singles and a walk loaded the bases with one out and there was a shrill, spontaneous outburst from the fans as Joe DiMaggio stalked to the plate. He forced a runner at second, one run scoring, and there was an obvious dramatic tenseness as Williams, slender Boston Red Sox slugger with a batting average of .405, took his place in the box and worked the count to two balls and one strike.

Grove's 300th Victory Scored Over Indians

Red Sox Rally Twice to Tie, Then Win in Eighth on Foxx's 2-Run Triple, 10-6

BOSTON, July 25 (AP).—After staggering momentarily, Robert Moses Grove recovered today and trudged sturdily into the company of baseball's immortals, achieving the 300th victory of his fabulous major league career as the Boston Red Sox surged from behind to defeat Cleveland's Indians, 10 to 5.

Twice the Sox had rallied from four-run and two-run handicaps to tie, but it remained for Jimmy Foxx, who jumped to fame with Grove as a member of the Philadelphia Athletics, to provide the pay-off clout in the eighth inning, a triple with two on.

From then on Old Mose just breezed to his well-earned triumph, which he had been twice denied in two previous attempts to gain the select circle last reached by Grover Cleveland Alexander.

The score:

CLEVELAND (A. L.)	ab	r	h	po	a		BOSTON (A. L.)	ab	r	h	po	a
Boudr'u, ss	5	2	3	2	3		DiMag'o, cf	4	1	0	4	0
R'nthal, cf	4	1	1	2	0		Finney, rf	4	1	1	0	0
Walker, lf	4	1	2	2	1		Cronin, ss	4	2	0	2	1
Heath, rf	4	2	2	1	0		L. N'oune, ss	0	0	0	0	0
Keltner, 3b	4	0	2	4	0		Williams, lf	3	2	2	4	1
Trosky, 1b	2	0	1	4	0		Spence, lf	0	0	0	1	0
Mack, 2b	1	0	0	0	0		Foxx, 1b	3	1	1	6	0
Grimes, 2b, 1b	4	0	0	1	3		Tabor, 3b	4	2	3	1	4
Des'tels, c	3	0	1	8	0		Doerr, 2b	5	0	0	1	1
Hemsley, c	1	0	0	0	0		Peacock, c	3	0	2	8	1
Kraka'as, p	2	0	0	0	1		Grove, p	4	0	1	0	1
Harder, p	1	0	0	0	0							
Milnar, p	0	0	0	0	1							
Bell	1	0	0	0	0							
Totals	36	6	12	24	9		Totals	34	10	10	27	10

*Batted for Desautels in ninth inning.
†Batted for Milnar in ninth inning.

Cleveland .... 013 000 200—6
Boston .... 000 220 24x—10

Errors—Trosky, Mack, Grimes, Williams. Runs batted in—Boudreau, Walker, Heath, Keltner, Grimes, Tabor (4), Williams (2), Foxx (2), Peacock. Two-base hits—Keltner (2), Boudreau, Grove. Three-base hits—Walker, Foxx. Home runs—Boudreau, Tabor (2), Williams. Stolen bases—Boudreau, Heath. Sacrifice—Finney. Left on bases—Cleveland, 4; Boston, 9. Bases on balls—Off Krakauskas 4; off Harder, 2; off Milnar, 2; off Grove, 1. Struck out—By Krakauskas, 3; by Harder, 1; by Milnar, 1; by Grove, 6. Hits—Off Krakauskas, 1 in 3 innings (none out in fourth); off Harder, 6 in 3 2-3; off Milnar, 3 in 1 1-3. Losing pitcher—Milnar. Umpires—McGowan, Quinn, Grieve. Time—2:27. Attendance (estimated)—10,000 paid; 5,000 ladies.

STAR GETS 6 HITS AS RED SOX SPLIT

Williams Becomes First Big Leaguer in 11 Years to Bat .400 or Better

WALLOPS 37TH HOME RUN

Adds Three Singles in 12-11 Victory Over Athletics, Who Take Nightcap, 7-1

PHILADELPHIA, Sept. 28 (AP)—Ted Williams of the Red Sox today became the first American Leaguer to hit .400 or higher for a season since 1923, when Harry Heilmann batted .403 for Detroit. Bill Terry was the last National League player to turn the trick. He batted .401 for the Giants in 1930.

Making six hits in eight times at bat while Boston and the Athletics split a double-header, Williams finished with a mark of .4057. He started the twin bill with an average of .39955. Williams played in 143 games this season, getting 185 hits in 456 times at bat.

Boston won the first game, 12 to 11, and the second was called on account of darkness after eight innings, with Philadelphia on top, 7 to 1.

Williams made his thirty-seventh home run and three singles in five chances in the opener, and a double and single in three attempts in the second encounter.

For the season he batted in 120 runs, scored 135 and walked 151 times. He struck out twenty-six times. Williams is the sixth American Leaguer to bat .400. Nap Lajoie, Ty Cobb, George Sisler, Joe Jackson and Heilmann were the others. Jackson hit .408 for Cleveland in 1911, but lost the batting title to Cobb, who finished with .420.

Yanks Are Jubilant In Clubhouse

Tommy Henrich Sorry For Owen But Rest of Mates Whoop It Up After Pulling Out Victory

Ebbets Field, Brooklyn, Oct. 5 (AP) The dramatic and explosive ninth inning victory the Yankees scored over the Dodgers today started another explosion even louder when Manager Joe McCarthy led the American League champs into the dressing room.

The mighty Bronx Bombers trailed the vanquished Dodgers coming up the long passage way and each had a smile a mile wide. They were happy and they wanted the world to know it.

Coach Art Fletcher, gray-haired and past middle age, who tried in vain to raise some excitement after victory in the first battle, finally succeeded. He let out the first war whoop and the gang joined in without another invitation.

Johnny Sturm, the black-haired Yankee rookie first baseman, pulled off his shoes, and perched himself on top of a trunk and began to rib Fletcher, now going through his twelfth World Series.

"Don't tell me you ever saw a World Series game like that," Sturm yelled. "There'll never be another game like that played."

McCarthy smiled with boyish enthusiasm.

Breaks Of Game.

"What the hell," he said, "that's the breaks of baseball. We had a lot of men on bases and were bound to get those base hits sooner or later. You can say for me that Joe DiMaggio did a great piece of base running."

McCarthy said that Ernie Bonham, winner of nine games in 15 starts this season, would oppose the Dodgers in the fifth of the series tomorrow.

Tommy Henrich felt a bit sorry for Mickey Owen, Dodger catcher who dropped the third strike that started all the fireworks.

"That was a tough break for poor Mickey to get," said Tommy. "I bet he feels like a nickel's worth of dog meat."

The dressing room was stifling hot but this didn't dampen the enthusiasm of the victorious Yanks.

The Dodgers marched back stoop-shouldered and disappointed, but still insistent that the Yankees "have got all the breaks so far, and we should start getting them soon."

"The Lord must be on their side," mourned slim Dixie Walker.

Mickey Owen was nearly in tears from the dropped third strike which opened the doors to Yankee victory.

"Sure, it was my fault, he admitted. "The ball was a low curve that broke down. It hit the edge of my glove and glanced off, but I should have had him out anyway.

"But who ever said those Yanks were such great sluggers? They're the real bums in this series, with that great reputation of theirs."

Relief pitcher Hugh Casey wiped the perspiration off in the steaming dressing room and shrugged off the tough breaks.

"I guess I've lost 'em just about every way now," he related. "Everything happens to me. I've lost one when a balk was called against me, and just about every funny way you can think of. But I never lost one by striking out a guy.

"I had Henrich 3-2 on the count, so I figured I'd r'ar back and give him the curve. It broke too much. Then when Keller came up I gave him the same pitch and he caught hold of it for two bases."

One To Go

NEW YORK

	AB	R	H	O	A	E
Sturm, 1b	5	0	0	9	1	0
Rolfe, 3b	5	1	0	0	2	0
Henrich, rf	4	1	0	0	0	0
DiMaggio, cf	4	1	2	3	0	0
Keller, lf	5	1	1	1	0	0
Dickey, c	2	1	0	6	1	0
Gordon, 2b	5	1	2	3	3	0
Rizzuto, ss	4	0	0	2	3	0
Donald, p	2	0	0	0	1	0
Breuer, p	1	0	0	0	1	0
Selkirk, x	1	0	0	0	0	0
Murphy, p	1	0	0	1	0	0
Totals	39	7	12	27	11	0

BROOKLYN

	AB	R	H	O	A	E
Reese, ss	5	0	2	1	4	0
Walker, rf	5	1	2	3	0	0
Reiser, cf	5	1	2	1	0	0
Camilli, 1b	4	0	0	10	1	0
Riggs, 3b	3	0	0	0	3	0
Medwick, lf	2	0	0	1	0	0
Allen, p	0	0	0	0	0	0
Casey, p	2	0	1	0	3	0
Owen, c	2	1	0	2	1	1
Coscarart, 2b	3	0	1	4	2	0
Higbe, p	1	0	0	0	0	0
Wasdell, lf	3	0	1	2	0	0
French, p	0	0	0	0	0	0
Totals	35	4	9	27	14	1

New York ..... 100 200 004—7
Brooklyn ..... 000 220 000—4

Error, Owen; runs batted in, Keller 3, Sturm 2, Wasdell 2, Reiser 2, Gordon 2, two base hits, Camilli, Keller 2, Wasdell, Walker, Gordon, home run, Reiser; double plays, Gordon, Rizzuto and Sturm; earned runs, New York 3, Brooklyn 4, left on bases, New York 11, Brooklyn 8, bases on balls, off Higbe 2 (DiMaggio, Dickey), off Casey 2 (Dickey, Rizzuto), off Donald 3 (Owen 2, Coscarart), off Breuer 1 (Riggs), off Allen 1 (Dickey), struck out, by Donald 2 (Reiser, Coscarart), by Higbe 1 (Donald), by Breuer 2 (Riggs, Casey), by Casey 1 (Henrich) by Murphy 1 (Coscarart), pitching summary, off Higbe 4 hits and 3 runs in 3 2-3 innings, off French no hits and no runs in 1-3 inning, off Allen 1 hit and no runs in 2-3 innings, off Casey 5 hits and 4 runs in 4 1-3 innings, off Donald 6 hits and 4 runs in 4 innings (none out in 5th), off Breuer 3 hits and no runs in 3 innings, off Murphy no hits and no runs in 2 innings; hit by pitcher, by Allen (Henrich); winning pitcher, Murphy, losing pitcher, Casey, umpires, Goetz (NL) plate, McGowan (AL) 1b, Pinelli (NL) 2b, Grieve (AL) 3b, time 2:54; attendance 33,813.

x—Selkirk batted for Breuer in 8th

Cubs Get Costly 5 To 4 Triumph Over Cardinals

St. Louis, April 14. (AP) — Lacing Mort Cooper for three singles and a double for three runs in the sixth inning Jimmy Wilson's Chicago Cubs nosed out the pennant-minded St. Louis Cardinals 5 to 4, in the season opener before a crowd of 13,821 cash customers and 1000 soldiers here today.

It was a rather costly first game victory, however, as two players were retired with injuries and manager Wilson was banished from the field by Umpire Al Barlick in the fourth inning following an argument over a base line collision between Enos Slaughter and Lou Stringer.

Dominic Dallessandro crashed into the left field wall while after a fly ball and Charley Gilbert twisted an angle. Neither injury was believed serious.

Ken O'Dea's homer with one man on base put the Cards ahead momentarily in the fourth.

Stan Musial and Ray Sanders, the Cards' two prize rookies, made a brilliant start. Musial getting a single and a triple and Sanders a single.

CHICAGO					ST LOUIS				
	AB	H	O	A		AB	H	O	A
Hack 3b	4	1	0	2	Crespi 2b	5	0	2	3
Gilbert cf	4	0	2	0	Musial lf	5	2	1	0
Dhlgrn 1b	1	0	1	0	Moore cf	3	1	1	0
Nehlan rf	5	1	1	0	Slghtr rf	4	1	0	0
Disndro lf	2	1	1	0	Sandrs 1b	4	1	5	1
Lwry lfcf	1	0	1	0	Hopp 1b	0	0	2	0
Cvrta 1blf	3	3	9	0	Brown 3b	4	2	0	1
McClgh c	4	0	7	0	O'Dea c	2	1	11	0
Stringr 2b	4	1	4	4	WCoopr c	1	0	3	0
Sturgn ss	3	1	1	5	Marion ss	3	0	1	3
Passeau p	3	0	0	1	Dusak z	1	0	0	0
Schmtz p	1	0	0	1	MCoopr p	2	0	0	0
					Beasley p	1	0	1	1
					Krwski x	0	0	0	0
Totals	35	8	27	13	Totals	34	8	27	9

Chicago .... 200 003 000—5
St Louis .... 000 301 000—4

Runs, Hack, Nicholson, Dallessandro, Cavarretta, McCullough, Moore, Sanders, Brown, O'Dea; errors, Sturgeon, Brown; runs batted in Cavarretta 2, Brown, O'Dea 2, Stringer, Slaughter; two base hits, Brown 2, Sturgeon, T. Moore, Cavarretta; three base hit, Musial; home run, O'Dea; stolen base, McCullough; sacrifice, Kurowski; double plays, Marion to Sanders, Hack to Stringer to Cavarretta; left on bases, Chicago 7, St Louis 7; bases on balls, off Passeau 1, Schmitz 2, M. Cooper 3; struck out, by Passeau 2, Schmitz 5, M. Cooper 6, Beasley 5; hits, off Passeau 5 in 5 innings (none out in 6th), Schmitz 3 in 4, Cooper 7 in 5 1-3, Beasley 1 in 3 2-3; hit by pitcher, by Beasley (Sturgeon); wild pitches, Passeau; winning pitcher, Passeau; losing pitcher, M. Cooper; umpires, Pinelli, Ballanfant and Barlick; time, 2:40; attendance (paid) 13,821.

z—Dusak batted for Marion in 9th.
x—Kurowski batted for Beasley in 9th.

Paul Waner Makes 3,000th Hit As Pirates Defeat Braves, 7 to 6

Elliott's Two Homers Help Pittsburgh to Set Back Rivals in Eleven Innings

BOSTON, June 19 (AP). — Pittsburgh and Boston picked on the day Paul Waner made his 3,000th major league hit to stage an eleven-inning thriller that went to the Pirates, 7 to 6, today on the strength of big Bob Elliott's second home run of the game.

Handing the Braves their sixteenth defeat in seventeen games, the Pirates banged out four homers —the last by Elliott in the eleventh with two on, enough to offset a two-run four-bagger by Nanny Fernandez in Boston's half of the finale.

But the big blow of the day was the thirty-nine-year-old Waner's fifth-inning single off Truett Sewell, Pittsburgh right-hander, who went the distance.

The safety lifted the veteran Boston outfielder, who has led the National League in hitting three times, into a select circle occupied only by Ty Cobb, Tris Speaker, Honus Wagner, Napoleon Lajoie, Eddie Collins and Adrian Cap Anson. After Waner's hit the plate umpire, Tom Dunn, halted the game to present "Big Poison" with the 3,000-hit ball. But before he could reach first base Pittsburgh players crowded around to congratulate the little veteran who spent fifteen of his seventeen big-league seasons with the Pirates.

First out of the dugout to shake Waner's hand was Frankie Frisch, Pittsburgh manager and a long-time playing rival.

The score:

PITTSBURGH (N. L.)						BOSTON (N. L.)					
	ab	r	h	p	o	a		ab	r	h	po	a
And'son, ss	6	2	3	4	2		Holmes, cf	5	3	3	3	0
Barrett, lf	4	0	2	5	1		Waner, rf	5	0	1	3	1
Fletch'r, 1b	4	2	2	12	0		Fern'ez, 3b	6	1	3	1	0
Elliott, 3b	5	2	2	0			West, 1b	4	1	2	10	0
V Ross, lf	6	0	0	1			Demaree, lf	6	0	2	3	0
DiMag'o, cf	4	0	0	4			Kluttz, c	5	0	1	7	0
Coscit, 2b	4	0	1	3			Miller, ss	4	0	1	1	3
Rikard	1	0	0	0			Sisti, 2b	5	1	2	3	0
Martin, 2b	0	0	0	0			Tost, p	1	0	0	0	0
Lopez, c	4	1	1	4			Earley, p	0	0	0	0	0
Phelps, c	0	0	0	1			Gremp	1	0	0	0	0
Sewell, p	4	0	1	1			Wallace, p	0	0	0	0	1
Wasdell	1	0	0	0			Lombardi	1	0	0	0	0
Dietz, p	0	0	0	0			Errick'n, p	0	0	0	0	0
							Ross	1	0	0	0	0
							Hutch'gs	0	0	0	0	0
							Sain, p	1	0	0	0	1
Totals	47	7	12	33	17		Totals	45	6	15	33	13

*Batted for Coscarart in tenth inning.
*Batted for Sewell in tenth inning.
*Batted for Zarles in fifth inning.
*Batted for Wallace in sixth inning.
*Batted for Errickson in eighth inning.

Pittsburgh ...... 000 220 000 03—7
Boston ...... 000 021 001 02—6

Veteran Righthander Clouts Three Homers To Win Game, 6 To 5

Blow in Eighth With Mate Aboard Proves Clincher; Lombardi, Miller Also Homer

Boston, May 13.—(AP.)—Jim Tobin, the veteran right hander, set a new major league home run slugging record for pitchers today by blasting out three consecutive circuit drives for a total of four runs while hurling the Boston Braves to a 6-5 victory over the Chicago Cubs.

Tobin, who lost three of his seven previous starts because his mates were unable to hit behind him, won his own game in the eighth by homering after Paul Waner had singled. He opened the fifth and seventh frames for the Braves by clearing the left field fence.

Ernie Lombardi gave the Braves their first round by clubbing a four-bagger in the fourth inning and Eddie Miller cleared the center field wall with two out and none on in the seventh.

While duplicating a feat that, as far as the record books reveal, was performed only by Pitcher Guy Hecker for the Louisville American Association club back in 1886, Tobin hit four homers in his last five turns at bat.

He poled out his second of the season as a pinch hitter against the Cubs yesterday.

As a result of today's prodigious clubbing, Jim, rated as Casey Stengel's ace moundsman, became that manager's top hitter with an average of .407 for his 27 turns at the plate.

While so doing, Tobin also took particular pains with his pitching chores. He limited the Cubs to five hits and three passes and two earned runs. A single, two errors and another safe hit gave the Cubs a pair of runs in the third inning. In the sixth, Bill Nicholson put the Cubs into a 4-2 lead by homering after Stan Hack had opened that frame with a single. The Cubs collected their fifth run in the ninth, when Pinch-Hitter Glen Russell drove in Phil Cavarretta with a double.

BOSTON					CHICAGO				
	AB	H	O	A		AB	H	O	A
Cooney 1b	5	1	11	0	Gilbert cf	4	0	3	0
Holmes cf	3	1	2	1	Merullo ss	4	0	3	3
Miller ss	4	1	3	3	Hack 3b	4	1	1	2
Fernaz 3b	3	0	3	2	Niclson rf	4	2	3	0
Lobardi c	2	1	1	0	Novikof lf	4	0	2	0
Masi c	2	0	1	0	Stringr 2b	3	0	1	3
West lf	3	1	0	0	Caveta 3b	3	0	9	0
Waner rf	3	1	3	0	McCullo c	4	1	2	1
Sisti 2b	4	0	3	2	Mooty p	3	0	0	1
Tobin p	4	3	0	5	Bithorn p	0	0	0	1
					Russell x	1	1	0	0
Totals	33	9	27	13	Totals	34	5	24	11

Boston .... 000 110 22x—6
Chicago .... 002 002 001—5

Bob Feller Routed In The Second

Trio of American League Hurlers Pitch Six-Hits Ball; Great Military Show Presented

Municipal Stadium, Cleveland, July 7. — (AP.) — The American Leagues mighty All-Stars refused to be awed even by the Army and Navy tonight and smothered the baseball stars of the two services 5 to 0 before a crowd of 62,094.

While this big assemblage was gatherin, hundreds of soldiers, sailors and marines provided a military show probably without precedent. It lasted for more than an hour as the bands played and the men marched and rode around the field in trucks and big tanks.

It was impressive, but the Army and Navy baseball team directed by Lieutenant Gordon (Mickey) Cochrane was not so potent as the mechanized battalions that preceded it on the field. Cochrane's outfit absorbed a thrashing more thorough than the American Leaguers gave the National League Monday night in the annual major league All-Star contest at New York.

Rickey Named Head of Brooklyn Dodgers

Former St. Louis Cardinal Manager Signs Contract for 5 Years; Salary Not Disclosed

New York, N. Y.-(AP)- Branch Rickey Thursday was named president and general manager of the Brooklyn Dodgers.

Rickey was signed to a five year contract, effective Nov. 1. He succeeds Larry MacPhail, who resigned the position to take a commission in the armed services.

The board of directors declined to name the salary terms, but as vice-president and general manager of the St. Louis Cards, Rickey's salary and commissions were believed to have run as high as $75,000 annually.

Created Farm System

Rickey comes to the Dodgers after a quarter century with the Cards as president, field manager and then vice-president and general manager of St. Louis' farm system, which he inaugurated around 1920.

He is referred to as the "father" of baseball's farm system, which yielded the Cards four world championships and six National league pennants starting in 1926. He closed out his career at St. Louis with a world series victory over the New York Yankees this fall.

Yanks Take Series Opener 7-4; Halt Belated Card Rally

Ruffing Stalls National Leaguers for Eight Innings; Wilts Under Hit Barrage

Redbirds Steal Show In Ninth

Game Ends With St. Louis Loading Bases in Final Frame; Errors Help Defeat

Sportsman's Park St Louis Sept 30.—(AP)—In a wild and turbulent beginning to a World Series that had been expected to be one of the tightest in history, the powerful New York Yankees stalled the St Louis Cardinals for eight innings today and won 7 to 4 after smothering an almost incredible ninth-inning outburst by the Redbards

Charles (Red) Ruffing thrilled a capacity crowd of 34,385 with one of the finest pitching performances in his long and lustrous career, establishing two World Series records while shutting out the indomitable Cardinals till the game was within one out of being over

Mort Cooper bearing all the hopes of the National League on his broad shoulders had been steadily shelled and finally removed from the scene and thousands of fans were on their way out of the park

Cardinals Come to Life.

Then the Cardinals suddenly showed the spirit and spark that had earned them a place in this year's baseball classic. They hammered Ruffing out of the box and continued their assault on Spurgeon (Fred) Chandler until the great crowd was near hysteria and they had four runs across, the bases loaded and one of their finest hitters, Rookie Stan Musial standing at the plate with what represented the winning run if they could get it across

But the pink-cheeked freshman missed a chance for fame by grounding out and the Yankees thankfully vacated the field with their victory

Ten Major League Clubs To Start Training Today

First Time Since First World War That Teams Have Trained in North; All Clubs Have Been Hard Hit By Calls to Military Service

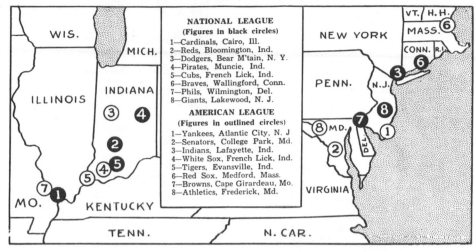

NATIONAL LEAGUE
(Figures in black circles)
1—Cardinals, Cairo, Ill.
2—Reds, Bloomington, Ind.
3—Dodgers, Bear M'tain, N. Y.
4—Pirates, Muncie, Ind.
5—Cubs, French Lick, Ind.
6—Braves, Wallingford, Conn.
7—Phils, Wilmington, Del.
8—Giants, Lakewood, N. J.

AMERICAN LEAGUE
(Figures in outlined circles)
1—Yankees, Atlantic City, N. J
2—Senators, College Park, Md.
3—Indians, Lafayette, Ind.
4—White Sox, French Lick, Ind.
5—Tigers, Evansville, Ind.
6—Red Sox, Medford, Mass.
7—Browns, Cape Girardeau, Mo.
8—Athletics, Frederick, Md.

Army Guards Any Trouble At Detroit

350 Armed Troops in Attendance as Tigers Split Double Header With Cleveland

Detroit, June 23 —(AP)—Under the careful scrutiny of 350 armed troops, the Detroit Tigers and Cleveland Indians divided a double-header today at Brigs Stadium, the Tigers taking the opener, 3 to 1, on Hal Newhouser's five-hitter adn the Indians winning the night-cap, 9 to 6, on Jeff Heath's 11th inning homer.

The rifle-bearing soldiers, members of the Michigan State troops, were stationed in small groups throughout the vast stadium as a precaution against further manifestations of Detroit's racial strife. Club officials expressed the opinion that the presence of troops was unprecedented in baseball

The Tiger front office announced that tomorrow's final game of the series would be played at 6 p. m. with approval of military authorities. A twilight game scheduled for Tuesday had been called off. The curfew under military rule is 10 p. m.

Throughout the five-hour program, there wasn't a spot of trouble. Later some of the troops clustered behind the Cleveland right-field bullpen, chatting with the players and collecting autographs

Batting Champion Receives 13 Of 24 First-Place Votes

New York, Nov. 2.—(AP.)—Stan Musial, right fielder whose stick-work brought him the National League batting championship and was a major factor in the drive of the St. Louis Cardinals to their second straight pennant, has been named the league's most valuable player for 1943.

The selection was made by a committee of the Baseball Writers' Association, and the personable young star polled a total of 267 points out of a possible 336, receiving 13 of 24 first-place votes

Chicago, Aug 24.—(AP)—The Philadelphia Athletics tied the all-time American League record of 20 consecutive defeats tonight when Luman Harris "blew" a ninth inning lead to lose a twilight game to the Chicago White Sox, 6 to 5, but they came back with an eight-run third inning to end the string in the night half of a double header, 8 to 1.

(First Game)

CHICAGO					PHILADELPHIA				
	AB	H	O	A		AB	H	O	A
Moses cf	5	2	2	0	Heffnr 2b	5	2	5	1
Hodgn rf	5	3	5	0	White cf	5	1	0	0
Crtrght lf	2	1	1	0	Ripple rf	5	3	2	0
Appig ss	4	2	2	2	Estlla lf	4	1	2	0
Cuello 3b	4	1	2	3	Siebert 1b	4	1	7	0
Kuhel 1b	4	0	1	0	Hall ss	5	2	5	3
Culler ss	4	1	2	4	Mayo 3b	5	0	2	1
Castino c	3	0	3	0	RSwift c	3	0	4	1
Tucker x	1	1	0	0	Harris p	3	0	0	1
Ross p	2	0	1	0					
Webb a	1	0	0	0					
Tresh b	1	0	0	0					

Totals 36 11 27 10   Totals 39 11x26 8

Chicago 103 000 002 6
Philadelphia . 102 020 000 5

Runs, Hodgin 2, Curtright 2, Appling, Tresh, Heffner, White, Ripple, Estalella, Siebert: errors, Heffner, Appling; runs batted in, Ripple, Siebert 2, Hall Hodgin, Curtright, Appling, Cuccinello, Culler; two base hits, Ripple, Siebert, Hall, Appling, Hodgin, stolen bases, Siebert, Hall, Moses, Cuccinello, sacrifice, Estalella; double play Hall to Siebert; left on bases, Philadelphia 11 Chicago 7; base on balls off Harris 3 Ross 3; strikeouts, Harris 3, Ross 3 umpires, Hubbard and Rommel; time 2:00; attendance 5000 estimated
x Tucker batted for Castino in 9th
a Webb batted for Ross in 9th
b Tresh ran for Webb in 9th
x—Two out when winning run scored

(Second Game)

PHILADELPHIA					CHICAGO				
	AB	H	O	A		AB	H	O	A
Heffner 2b	5	1	1	0	Moses cf	5	0	1	0
White cf	4	1	4	0	Hodgin rf	4	2	2	0
Ripple rf	5	1	1	0	Crtrgt lf	3	2	0	0
Estalla lf	4	2	2	0	Appling ss	4	0	1	5
Siebrt 1b	5	2	9	0	Cuenlo 3b	4	0	0	1
Wagner c	4	0	7	1	Kuhel 1b	4	0	20	0
Hall ss	4	2	2	1	Culler 2b	3	2	1	10
Mayo 3b	4	1	1	2	Tresh c	4	1	2	0
Wolff p	4	1	0	0	Dietrch p	0	0	0	1
					Solters x	1	0	0	0
					Haynes p	2	1	0	2
					Tucker y	1	0	0	0

Totals 39 9 27 10   Totals 35 8 27 19

Philadelphia . 008 000 000—8
Chicago ..... 000 000 010—1

Runs, Heffner, White, Ripple, Estalella, Hall, Mayo, Wolff, Haynes; errors, Siebert, Appling, Culler, Cuccinello, Kuhel; runs batted in, White, Ripple 3, Hall, Mayo, Wolff; two base hits, Ripple, Curtright, Culler; stolen base, Siebert; double play, Appling, Culler and Kuhel; left on bases, Philadelphia 6, Chicago 9; bases on balls, off Wolff 2, Haynes 2; strikeouts, Wolff 5; Dietrich 3; hits, off Dietrich 8 in 3 innings, Haynes 1 in 6; losing pitcher, Dietrich; umpires, Rommel and Hubbard; time, 1:54; attendance, 5503

144 American League Players in Service, But Clubs Will Have Big Squads Available

By The Associated Press.

CHICAGO, March 17 — The American League disclosed today that its number of baseball players in the armed forces now had reached 144, a figure that exactly equaled the league's service roll during all of World War I.

In addition nineteen players are remaining out of baseball this season to work in war plants or on farms.

However, team rosters show that each club will have from twenty-seven to thirty-four men available to start the season April 21.

League figures disclose that the St. Louis Browns, surprise team and third-place finisher in last year's race, currently hold the edge in manpower with a total of thirty-four athletes. Then come Detroit and Washington with 30 each; Cleveland and Chicago 28, and Boston, New York and Philadelphia, 27.

Leading the league with men in the armed forces were Detroit and Chicago, each with 23. These two clubs also have the most men remaining on jobs in essential industry—Chicago, 5, and Detroit, 4.

The number of men in service from the other clubs were: Philadelphia, 21; Cleveland, 17; Washington, 16; Boston and St. Louis, 15, and New York, 14.

A breakdown of the total number of men in service showed that pitchers led the way with 54, followed by infielders with 46, outfielders 28 and catchers 16.

Compared with the first World War, when 93 American League ball players went into the Army and 51 into the Navy, this war currently finds 79 in the Army, 55 in the Navy, 7 in the Coast Guard and 1 in the Marines and 2 in the Royal Canadian Air Force.

The one gold star on the league's service flag represents Gene Stack, former White Sox player and the first American Leaguer to be drafted. He died in service.

GIANTS DRUB DODGERS, 26-8

Brooklyn Takes Finale, 5-4, Before Crowd Of 58,068

New York. April 30 (AP)—The New York Giants and Brooklyn Dodgers divided a double-header today before the season's record crowd of 58,068, of which 52,037 were paid admissions.

Hal Gregg won his first major league game as the Dodgers won the final, 5-4, which was shortened to seven innings by darkness. The Giants won the opener, 26-8, to fall two runs shy of the modern major league scoring mark.

Cards Hold Record

The St. Louis Cardinals scored 28 runs against the Philadelphia Phillies July 6, 1929. The American League mark is 27, made by the Cleveland Indians July 7, 1923.

Phil Weintraub, Giants' first baseman, batted in 11 runs with a homer, triple and two doubles to just miss tieing the major league record of 12, set by Jim Bottomley, of the St. Louis Cardinals, on September 16, 1924. Ernie Lombardi, Giant catcher, drove in seven runs.

Ott Gets Five Walks

Mel Ott added two records to his all-time marks when he received five walks for the fourth time of his career, and scored six runs, a feat he has accomplished once before.

The Giants tied the league record for receiving the most bases on balls in a game, 17, from five Brooklyn pitchers. The Dodgers also received 17 bases on balls August 27, 1903.

BROOKLYN						NEW YORK					
	Ab.	R.	H.	O.	A.		Ab.	R.	H.	O.	A.
Bor'ay.rf.lf	5	2	1	2	0	Rucker.cf	7	3	2	3	0
Walker.lf	4	1	2	3	0	Haus'n.2b	5	2	1	1	3
P.W'ner.rf	1	0	1	1	0	Ott.rf	2	6	2	2	0
Olmo.2b	5	0	1	3	2	Medwick.lf	4	5	2	2	0
Galan.cf	4	0	1	2	0	Weint'b.1b	5	5	4	11	1
L.Waner.cf	1	0	0	0	0	Lombardi.c	6	1	3	5	0
Schultz.1b	4	2	3	6	0	Luby.3b	4	0	1	0	0
Hart.ss	3	1	1	3	0	Kerr.ss	5	2	1	5	3
Bragan.3b	5	1	1	0	3	C.Melton.p	2	0	0	0	2
Owen.c	2	1	2	3	1	Feldman.p	3	2	2	0	1
Jarvis.c	1	0	0	1	0						
F.Melton.p	0	0	0	0	0						
1Wyatt	1	0	0	0	0						
Webber.p	0	0	0	0	0						
Zachary.p	0	0	0	0	0						
Oster'ller.p	0	0	0	0	0						
2Smyres	1	0	0	0	0						
Warren.p	1	0	0	0	0						
Totals	39	8	12	24	6	T'als	43	26	18	27	10

1Batted for F. Melton in second.
2Batted for Ostermueller in fourth.

Brooklyn .... 2 0 0 5 0 0 1 0 0—8
New York .... 3 4 4 5 0 2 0 8 x—26

Errors—C. Melton, Kerr, Olmo, Walker. Runs batted in—Galan. Weintraub. 11; Luby. 2; Medwick. Lombardi. 7; Schultz. 2; Owen; Bordagaray; Olmo. 2; Kerr; Feldman. 2; Ott. Two-base hits—Weintraub 2. Owen, Rucker, Lombardi 2. P. Waner. Feldman, Hausmann, Medwick. Three-base hits—Rucker, Weintraub. Home runs—Schultz 2, Kerr, Weintraub. Stolen bases—Schultz, Hart, Ott. Sacrifices—Hausmann Double plays—Feldman, Kerr, Weintraub; Hausmann, Kerr, Weintraub. Left on bases—New York, 10; Brooklyn, 8. Bases on balls—F. Melton, 3; Webber, 4; Zachary, 2; Ostermueller, 2; Warren, 6; Feldman, 4. Strikeouts—C. Melton, 2; F. Melton, 1; Webber, 1; Ostermueller, 1; Feldman, 3; Warren, 2. Hits off —F. Melton, 2 in 1 inning; Webber, 1 in 1⅓ innings; Zachary, none in 0 (pitched to 2 batters); Ostermueller, 2 in 2⅔; Warren, 13 in 4; C. Melton, 11 in 3⅓; Feldman, 5 in 5⅔. Wild pitches—C. Melton, F. Melton, Warren. Winning pitcher—Feldman. Losing pitcher—F. Melton. Umpires—Reardon, Dunn and Goetz. Time—2.58.

REDS BLASTED BY CARDS, 18-0

Pound 5 Cincinnati Hurlers For 21 Hits In Shutout

Cincinnati, June 10 (AP)—The St. Louis Cardinals gave the Cincinnati Reds their lumps today by pounding out the most one-sided shutout victory in the National League in 38 years. When the firing was done the Cards won, 18 to 0.

In addition to coming close to the 38-year-old record set when Chicago defeated New York 19 to 0 in 1906, the Cards tied a major league mark by leaving 18 men on bases. The St. Louis Browns and New York Giants also left 18 last year.

Another mark went into the record books when Reds' Manager Bill McKechnie inserted 15-year-old Joe Nuxhall, Hamilton (Ohio) high school pitcher into the game. Nuxhall, the youngest pitcher ever to work in the majors, pitched two thirds of the ninth, giving up five runs on five passes, two singles and a wild pitch.

Lohrman Starts Game

Bill Lohrman started the game for Cincinnati but he was blasted in the second inning.

Six runs came in during the second, with the Cards more than batting around and chasing Ed Heusser as well as Lohrman. Buck Faussett, versatile minor leaguer whom the Reds brought up as a third baseman this year, finally got the last two outs.

Oddly enough, not an extra base hit was registered in the inning and even though Eddie Miller set up the first score by throwing the ball to an unoccupied base, all the runs were earned. Seven singles in all could be counted.

Spaced Hits Carefully

While Mort Cooper was slapping the Reds down systematically and spacing their hits skillfully, the Cards went on to fatten their batting averages in the latter innings.

ST. LOUIS						CINCINNATI					
	Ab.	R.	H.	O.	A.		Ab.	R.	H.	O.	A.
Hopp.cf	4	1	2	3	0	Will'ms.2b	3	0	2	2	3
Bergm'o.cf	3	2	1	0	0	Marsh'll.rf	4	0	0	5	0
Garms.3b	4	2	1	1	1	Walker.cf	3	0	0	1	0
Musial.rf	4	3	1	1	0	Clay.cf	1	0	0	0	0
Sanders.1b	5	2	3	5	0	Tipton.lf	3	0	0	2	0
W.Co'per.c	6	1	2	7	0	Criscola.lf	1	0	0	0	0
Litwhi'r.lf	5	2	1	4	0	McCo'k.1b	4	0	0	8	0
Marion.ss	6	2	4	3	3	Mueller.c	4	0	0	3	0
Verban.2b	1	0	1	0	0	Just.c	3	0	1	0	0
Fa'n.2b.ss	4	1	2	3	1	Mesner.3b	3	0	1	0	0
M.Co'per.p	6	2	2	0	0	Miller.ss	3	0	1	4	3
						Lohrm'n.p	0	0	0	0	0
						Heusser.p	0	0	0	0	0
						Fausett.p	3	0	1	0	0
						Nuxhall.p	0	0	0	0	0
						Eisenh't.p	0	0	0	0	0
Totals	48	18	21	27	8	Totals	31	0	5	27	8

St. Louis ...... 1 6 0 1 1 1 1 2 5—18
Cincinnati ..... 0 0 0 0 0 0 0 0 0—0

Errors—Miller, Fausett. Runs batted in—Hopp, Garms, Musial (3), Sanders (2), W. Cooper (3), Litwhiler (3), Verban (2), Fallon, M. Cooper. Two-base hits—Hopp, Fallon. Stolen bases—W. Cooper, Litwhiler. Sacrifice—Garms. Double plays—Marion, Sanders. Left on bases—St. Louis, 18; Cincinnati, 6. Base on balls—M. Cooper, 2; Lohrman, 2; Fausett, 6; Nuxhall, 5. Eisenhardt, 1. Strikeouts—M. Cooper, 2; Fausett, 2. Hits—Lohrman, 5 in 1 1-3 innings; Heusser, 4 in none (pitched to 4 batters); Fausett, 10 in 6 2-3; Nuxhall, 2 in 2-3; Eisenhardt, 0 in 1-3. Wild pitches—Fausett, Nuxhall. Losing pitcher—Lohrman. Umpires—Goetz, Jorda, Reardon. Time—2.23. Attendance—3,510.

Homer in 15th Wins for Phils As Braves Split

Northey's Blast Triumphs, 1-0, Then Tobin Pitches 5-Inning No-Hitter, 7-0

BOSTON, June 22 (AP).—Jim Tobin, of the Boston Braves, turned in his second no-hitter of the season, a 7-to-0 affair halted by darkness at the end of the fifth inning today, after his forces had dropped a fifteen-inning opener to the Phillies by a 1-to-0 margin.

The first half of the afternoon-twilight twin bill, which was delayed forty-five minutes by rain, was settled when Ron Northey blasted a homer off Al Javery, who went the full distance for the Braves. Charley Schanz, after relieving Bill Lee, the starter, in the seventh, limited the Braves to two hits during the last nine frames.

Tobin, given a three-run send-off in the first inning of the abbreviated nightcap, due to homers by Tommy Holmes and Butch Nieman, allowed only two Phils to reach base. Tony Lupien drew a pass in the first and Ray Hamrick was walked in the third, both with two out.

Tobin turned back the Brooklyn Dodgers without a hit over the nine-inning route early in the season. Today's success gave him an 8-and-7 record for the campaign.

SECOND GAME											
PHILADELPHIA (N.L.)						BOSTON (N.L.)					
	ab	r	h	po	a		ab	r	h	po	a
Hamrick, ss	1	0	0	2	2	Holmes, cf	3	3	2	3	0
Adams, cf	3	0	0	0	0	Ryan, 2b	3	1	1	1	1
Lupien, 1b	1	0	0	8	0	Workman, rf	3	1	2	0	0
Wasdell, lf	2	0	0	0	0	Nieman, lf	3	1	2	0	0
Northey, rf	2	0	0	0	0	Etchison, 1b	3	0	2	6	0
Cieslak, 3b	2	0	0	1	1	Masi, c	2	0	1	0	0
Finley, c	2	0	0	3	0	Wietelma'n,ss	2	0	0	1	1
Mullen, 2b	2	0	0	1	1	Phillips, 3b	2	0	0	1	1
Barrett, p	1	0	0	0	0	Tobin, p	1	1	1	0	3
Mussill, p	0	0	0	0	0						
Totals	15	0	0	15	6	Totals	21	7	9	15	6

Philadelphia .... 0 0 0 0 0—0
Boston .... 3 0 1 0 3—7

Error—Cieslak. Runs batted in—Holmes (2), Nieman (3), Ryan, Etchison. Two-base hits—Tobin, Holmes. Home runs—Holmes, Nieman. Sacrifices—Ryan, Masi. Left on bases —Philadelphia, 2; Boston, 2. Bases on balls—Off Tobin, 2. Struck out—By Barrett, 2; by Tobin, 2. Hits—Off Barrett, 6 in 4 innings; off Mussill, 3 in 1. Losing pitcher—Barrett. Umpires—Sears, Conlan and Barr. Time—1.02. Attendance—2,556 paid.

Aug. 9

BROWNS WIN PENNANT AS TIGERS LOSE

St. Louis Beats Yankees, 5-2, In Last Game To Take Its First Flag

St. Louis, Oct. 1 (AP)— The St. Louis Browns won the American League championship today—their first in 43 years of league history.

The Browns clinched the flag by defeating the New York Yankees, fading world's champions, for the fourth straight time, 5 to 2, while the last place Washington Senators scored a 4-to-1 upset over the Detroit Tigers to break the St. Louis-Detroit tie that existed on and off for five days.

The Brownies now will engage their St. Louis rivals, the Cardinals, champions of the National League, in a World Series starting Wednesday. St. Louis will become the third city in baseball history to have two rival teams in the same series. The Chicago White Sox and Cubs first played for the game's highest honors in 1906. Then the two New York teams, the Giants and Yankees, battled in 1921, '22 and '23 and again in 1936 and '37.

The Browns climaxed their greatest season before a record-smashing crowd of 37,815 and behind the six-hit pitching of tomato-faced Jack Jakucki, 32-year-old veteran of the minors.

Jakucki Hurls Six Hitter

Jakucki, recruited from a Houston (Texas) shipyard team this spring, pitched great ball in halting the Yanks and with better fielding behind him might have scored a shutout for his 13th victory of the year.

To offset the three costly errors his mates made in their burning ambition to triumph, the rugged, six-foot ex-soldier depended upon his courage when the going was tough and pitched out of danger.

NEW YORK					ST. LOUIS				
	Ab	R	H	O	A		Ab	R	H	O	A
Stirn's,2b	4	0	0	3	2	Gut'dge,2b	4	0	1	2	4
M'heny,cf	4	0	1	2	0	Kr'vich,cf	4	1	2	4	0
M'brn,rf	4	0	0	1	0	Laabs,lf	4	2	2	0	0
Lindell,lf	4	0	2	0	0	Steph's,ss	3	1	1	3	2
Etten,1b	4	0	2	9	1	Moore,rf	3	0	0	3	0
Crosetti,ss	3	0	0	2	2	McQu'n,1b	3	0	0	8	0
Grimes,3b	3	0	0	0	2	Christ'n,3b	3	1	0	0	1
Garbark,c	3	0	0	0	0	Hayw'th,c	4	0	1	5	1
Queen,p	2	0	0	1	0	Jakucki,p	3	0	0	2	2
Borowy,p	1	0	0	0	0						
Totals	32	2	6	24	6	Totals	29	5	6	27	10

New York ..... 1 0 1 0 0 0 0 0 0—2
St. Louis ..... 0 0 2 2 0 0 1 x—5
Errors—Stephens, Christman, Hayworth. Runs batted in—H. Martin, Laabs (4), Stephens, Lindell. Two-base hit—H. Martin. Three-base hit—H. Martin. Home runs —Laabs (2), Stephens. Stolen bases—Stirnweiss. Sacrifices—Crosetti, Moore. Double plays—Stephens. Outteridge, McQuinn. Left on bases—New York, 5; St. Louis, 5. Bases on balls—Jakucki, 1; Queen, 3. 2; Borowy, 4. Hits—Queen, 4 in 2-3 innings; Borowy, 2 in 3 1-3. Passed ball—Hayworth. Losing pitcher—Queen. Umpires —Summers, Rue, Rommel, Boyer. Time— 1.38. Attendance—35,518 (paid).

DETROIT LOSES PENNANT RACE

Leonard Hurls Senators To 4-1 Win In Payoff Game

Detroit, Oct. 1 (AP) — Emil (Dutch) Leonard, giving but four hits while facing only 30 batters, wrecked Detroit's pennant hopes before a dazed crowd of 45,565 fans today as the last place Washington Senators thumped Paul (Dizzy) Trout and the Tigers, 4 to 1, while the St. Louis Browns were whipping New York to grab the flag on the last day of the American League season.

Leonard, who hadn't beaten the Tigers in his last seven starts against them since 1941, was in command throughout and had a two-hit shutout through eight innings. Only one Detroit baserunner reached second before the ninth, when two hits and an outfield fly accounted for the only run off the 34-year-old veteran knuckleballer.

Trout Touched For 8 Hits

While Leonard had the Bengals in the palm of his able right hand, the Senators tagged Paul (Dizzy) Trout for eight hits, chasing across three runs in the fourth inning as Stan Spence hit his 18th home run, third in three days here and scored behind Joe Kuhel, who had singled.

Fred Vaughn and Jake Powell singled following Spence's blow. Vaughn scoring from third after Rick Ferrell's fly.

Washington made it 4-0 in the eighth when Gil Torres singled with one away, went to third on Spence's third hit, a single to right, and scored after Vaughn lifted to Dick Wakefield in left.

Tigers Score In 9th

Chuck Hostetler, pinchhitting for Joe Hoover in the Tiger ninth, led off with a single to left. Don Ross, batting for Trout, singled to center, sending Hostetler to third, from where he scored on Roger Cramer's fly to center. Leonard then cut down Eddie Mayo and Pinky Higgins to clinch the Washington victory.

The Nats' triumph, fifth this year in 22 games with the Tigers, sent Trout to his 14th defeat against 27 wins. Dizzy, making his third start in six days, was effective in every inning but Washington's big fourth. The Tigers kicked in with three errors under the pennant pressure.

WASHINGTON						DETROIT					
	Ab	R	H	O	A		Ab	R	H	O	A
Case,lf	5	0	0	2	0	Cramer,cf	4	0	0	4	0
Kuhel,1b	4	1	1	11	1	Mayo,2b	4	0	0	2	2
Torres,3b	4	1	1	3	5	Higgins,3b	4	0	0	2	2
Spence,cf	4	1	3	1	0	York,1b	3	0	0	10	0
Vaughn,2b	3	1	1	3	2	Wakefield,lf	3	0	1	2	0
Powell,rf	4	0	1	2	0	Outlaw,rf	3	0	0	2	0
Ferrell,c	4	0	0	3	0	Richards,c	3	0	1	0	0
Sullivan,ss	4	0	1	3	4	Hoover,ss	3	0	0	1	4
Leonard,p	4	0	0	2	2	Trout,p	2	0	0	1	0
						1Hostetler	1	1	1	0	0
						2Ross	1	0	1	0	0
						3Borom	0	0	0	0	0
Totals	36	4	9	27	12	Totals	29	1	4	27	12

1Batted for Hoover in ninth.
2Batted for Trout in ninth.
3Ran for Ross in ninth.
Washington ... 0 0 0 3 0 0 0 1 0—4
Detroit .... 0 0 0 0 0 0 0 0 1—1
Errors—Hoover, Mayo, Trout. Runs batted in—Spence (2), Ferrell, Vaughn. Cramer. Home run—Spence. Stolen base— Case. Sacrifices—Vaughn, Hoover. Double plays—Vaughn, Sullivan, Kuhel; Trout, Hoover, York. Left on bases—Washington, 6; Detroit, 2. Strikeouts—Leonard, 2. Umpires—Hubbard, Grieve, Weafer, Berry. Time—1.39. Attendance—45,565.

Oct. 6

Cardinals Win, 3-1; End World Series

Clock Strikes Twelve and Cinderella Boys of St. Louis Browns Return to Rags

By SAM LEVY
Of The Journal Staff

St. Louis, Mo. The clock struck 12 for baseball's Cinderella team, the St. Louis Browns, Monday afternoon when the rags to riches boys lost the sixth and deciding game of the world series to the Cardinals, 3-1. Nelson Potter, the Browns' ace, failed the American league champions for the second time in the role of Prince Charming. He had ordered the golden carriage to take his mates for a victory ride but they were waylaid en route by two pitching bandits, Max Lanier and Ted Wilks. The Cardinals won the series, four games to two.

Browns' Owner Cries With Joy

St. Louis, Oct. 1 (AP) — Tears trickled down the cheeks of Don Barnes, owner of the Browns, as his players hilariously swarmed into their dressing room today with the first American League championship ever won by a St. Louis team.

The pudgy-gray haired Barnes joined in the jubilation, accepting congratulations from every one who wanted to pump his hand while he laughed, shouted and mopped the increasing flow of tears as the celebration heightened. Stoical Luke Sewell, Browns' manager, calmly greeted well wishes as though he had been winning pennants for years.

Laabs Cheered

Chet Laabs, who pumped the two home runs into the left field bleachers, and Sigmund Jakucki, who pitched superbly in the pennant-winning game, were beneficiaries of most of the back-pounding by the players.

Joe McCarthy, Yankee manager, came in after allowing a few minutes for the celebration to level off. He quickly gripped Sewell's hand, said "good luck in the series" and departed as photographers vainly pleaded with him to remain for pictures.

"We're in good shape for the series," was all that Sewell would say in answer to queries about whether the neck-and-neck final drive had taken anything out of the players.

"We've been down but never out," Sewell said. "We've been in there fighting all the time. We didn't come up off the floor, we've never been on the floor."

Nov. 25

Judge Landis, Baseball Czar, Is Dead at 78

Chicago, Ill. Judge Kenesaw Mountain Landis, commissioner of baseball since 1921, died at St. Luke's hospital Saturday morning at 5.35. He was 78 years old.

Landis, who observed his last birthday Monday, entered the hospital Oct. 2 for a "rest cure." At that time his physician said he was suffering from fatigue and a severe cold. He suffered a heart attack several days ago.

Noted for his hardiness and general good health, Landis was not considered in serious condition until early this week, when he suffered a relapse and his physician described him as a "pretty sick man."

He rallied later in the week, however, but suffered another relapse Friday, when his physician described his condition as critical.

Landis was baseball's first and only high commissioner. Last week he was recommended for reappointment for another term by the joint National and American league committee.

Landis, a gruff speaking old man with shaggy white hair, battered hat and keen wit, became a legend in his lifetime. He was noted for his fairness and as a man who always gave the underdog a break.

Baseball was severely shaken by the "Black Sox" scandal in 1920 and needed someone to guide it through its darkest hour. Club owners turned to Landis, a 54 year old federal judge in Illinois who had gained nation-wide fame in 1907 when he fined the Standard Oil Co. $29,240,000 for accepting rebates on railroad shipments of oil.

April 18

Sewell Highly Satisfied With Pete Gray's Debut

St. Louis, Mo. (AP)—Pete Gray, one armed rookie outfielder with the St. Louis Browns, summed up his major league debut Tuesday with this observation: "It wasn't too good, but it was better than my first game for Memphis in the Southern association." Gray made one hit in four times at bat Tuesday and was robbed of a double by a sensational catch. In the field he slipped and fell on his only chance.

Pete Gray

The Browns won, 7-1. "In that first game for Memphis I hit the ball all five times up," Gray recalled, "but all five times it went right straight to the pitcher."

Gray faced Hal Newhouser three times. He grounded out to Shortstop Jimmy Webb, was called out on strikes, then sent a long line drive to right center. Roger Cramer dived for the drive, making a spectacular one handed catch. Gray had already rounded first when Cramer speared the ball. It would have been good for at least a double had the veteran center fielder missed.

"That left hander was really tough," Gray said of Newhouser. "He threw me every pitch in the book. When I was called out on strikes he used a fast curve that was almost passed me before I figured out where it was headed."

Gray made his hit, a sharp infield single, off Les Mueller, the second of three Detroit pitchers in the game.

Only two balls came in Pete's direction in left field. One was Paul Richards' home run into the left field bleachers. The other was a drive by Eddie Mayo. Gray slipped and fell as he approached the bouncing ball. He recovered and held Mayo to a double.

Manager Luke Sewell said he was satisfied with Gray's opening day performance. "He's okay for my money. I like his work."

SENATOR CHANDLER GETS BASEBALL POST

'Immediately Available.' New Commissioner Accepts for Seven Years at $50,000

NAMED ON FIRST BALLOT

M'Phail, Stoneham Lead Fight for Choice of 46-Year-Old Successor to Landis

CLEVELAND, April 24 (AP)—Baseball's five-month quest for a commissioner ended today with election of Senator Albert B. (Happy) Chandler of Kentucky to fill the position vacated by the death of Kenesaw Mountain Landis.

By unanimous vote of the sixteen major league club owners or their representatives, and on the first ballot, the 46-year-old junior Senator from the Bluegrass State was named for a seven-year term at an annual salary of $50,000.

Majors Lineup for War Fund

NEW YORK, July 7.—(AP)—The major league All-Star game, dropped this year as a travel conservation measure, will be replaced Monday and Tuesday of next week by seven games pitting National League teams against American League teams with war relief getting the receipts.

An eighth game, involving Pittsburgh and Detroit, was deleted at the request of the ODT because of the traveling it involved.

The program:
MONDAY NIGHT—Chicago Cubs at Chicago White Sox; New York Yankees at New York Giants; Cincinnati Reds at Cleveland Indians.
TUESDAY AFTERNOON — Boston Braves at Boston Red Sox.
TUESDAY NIGHT — St. Louis Browns vs. St. Louis Cards at Sportsmans Park; Brooklyn Dodgers at Washington Senators; Philadelphia Phils at Philadelphia Athletics.

July 1

Sore Arm Won't Stop Hank

Hank Greenberg has a lame arm, but it won't keep him from returning to the Detroit lineup today after a 30-month absence.

"I guess Hank has been throwing too much, trying to get the range in left field," explained Manager Steve O'Neill, who gave Greenberg the day off Saturday. "But he'll be all right." Greenberg has been working out for 10 days since going on the Army inactive list.

Greenberg will start the first game in left field and will bat fourth, with Rudy York dropping to sixth place behind Roger Cramer. Jimmy Outlaw will play left field in the second game.

Incidentally, there has been considerable fan reaction to the withdrawal from the lineup of Outlaw, the club's top hitter.

"I've had several hundred letters and phone calls on the subject," said O'Neill, "but there isn't much we can do about it."

Reprinted from
The Detroit News

(JULY 21, 1945—TIES AMERICAN LEAGUE RECORD)

DETROIT	AB	R	H	O	A	E
Webb,ss	10	0	2	8	10	1
Mayo,2b	9	0	0	6	12	1
Cullenbine,rf	7	1	2	5	0	0
York,1b	9	0	3	26	6	1
Cramer,cf	10	0	1	2	0	0
Outlaw,lf	8	0	1	2	1	0
*Greenberg	0	0	0	0	0	0
Hostetler,lf	0	0	0	0	2	0
Maier,3b	10	0	1	3	5	0
Swift,c	9	0	0	12	0	0
Mueller,p	7	0	1	2	3	0
Trout,p	2	0	0	1	1	0
Totals	81	1	11	72	34	3

PHILADELPHIA	AB	R	H	O	A	E
Hall,1b	11	0	2	6	3	0
Peck,rf	8	0	2	1	0	0
Siebert,1b	9	1	1	31	2	0
Estalella,cf	10	0	5	5	0	0
Rosar,c	9	0	2	13	2	0
McGhee,lf	8	0	2	9	0	0
Kell,3b	10	0	0	2	7	0
Busch,ss	10	0	1	3	11	1
Christopher,p	5	0	0	1	2	0
Berry,p	3	0	0	1	2	0
‡Burns	0	0	0	0	0	0
§Metro	1	0	1	0	0	0
Totals	84	1	16	72	34	1

*Batted for Outlaw in 22nd.
‡Batted for Berry in 24th.
§Batted for Burns in 24th.

Detroit .... 0 0 0 0 0 0 1 0 0 0 0 0 0 0 0 0 0 0 0 0 0 0 0 0—1
Philadelphia .... 0 0 1 0 0 0 0 0 0 0 0 0 0 0 0 0 0 0 0 0 0 0 0 0—1

Runs batted in—Rosar, Cramer. Two-base hits—Estalella, Cullenbine. Sacrifices—Siebert, Rosar. Double plays—Maier to York; Maier, Mayo to York; York, Webb to York; Webb, Mayo to York; Busch, Hall to Siebert. Left on bases—Detroit 15, Philadelphia 18. Bases on balls—Off Mueller 5; Christopher 2; Berry 2. Strike outs—By Christopher 8; Mueller 6, Berry 2; Trout 2. Hits—Off Mueller 13 in 19 2-3 innings; Trout 3 in 4 1-3 innings; Christopher 5 in 13 innings; Berry 6 in 11 innings. Umpires—Summers, Rue and Boyer. Time—4:48. Attendance—4,935.

Jackie Robinson Given Bonus And Assigned to Montreal Farm

MONTREAL, Oct. 24.—(AP)—Speaking for the Brooklyn ball club, Branch Rickey, Jr., said today the Dodgers may have the alligator by the tail in signing the first Negro player ever admitted to organized base ball, but if trouble's ahead "we won't avoid it."

Hiring Jackie Robinson, ex-UCLA foot ball ace and U. S. Army lieutenant, to do his 1946 infielding for the Dodgers' International League farm—the Montreal Royals—the son of the Brooklyn president predicted it "even may cost the Brooklyn organization a number of ball players."

"But even if some players quit," the Dodger farm system director added as he reviewed the possible reactions of players and fans at the surprise signing here last night, "they'll be back after a year or two in a cotton mill."

Earlier—before coming out flatly with the statement that his father and Royals' president, Hector Racine, "aren't inviting trouble, but won't avoid it"—young Rickey went over with Robinson all that the Negro's shortstop's entry into organized base ball might imply. He explained that there might be difficulties for the quiet six-foot, 190-pounder from both players and fans alike in some quarters. He reviewed prejudices that exist in certain sections.

HE'S AWARE OF IT

"I realize what I'm going into," Robinson said sincerely. "I also realize how much it means to me, to my race and to base ball. I'm very happy over this chance, and I can only say I'll do my very best to come through in every manner."

Brought up from the Kansas City Negro Monarchs, which he joined after leaving the Army last spring, Robinson represents a $25,000, three-year hunt by Branch Rickey, Sr., for Negro talent good enough to bring into the Brooklyn system, particularly as high as Double-A ball.

GREENBERG HAILED BY JOYOUS TIGERS

Hank Acclaimed at Home Plate After Winning Hit and in Clubhouse Celebration

ST. LOUIS, Sept. 30 (AP)— The bedraggled Tigers filed into their locker room today out of the rain and fog with their seventh American League championship, hailed Hank Greenberg for his pennant-winning grand-slam home run, whooped it up for a few minutes for news photographers and then settled down as though they had been accustomed to winning pennants all their lives.

It was the second burst of applause for Greenberg by his teammates, who poured out of the dugout to meet him at the home plate as he trotted in behind three other base-runners. Utility Infielder Eddie Borom leaped around Greenberg's neck and planted a kiss on his cheek at home plate.

Giants Win As Ott Hits 500th Homer

New York, Aug. 1 (AP)—Mel Ott slammed the five hundredth home-run of his major league career tonight to lead the New York Giants to a 9-2 victory over the Boston Braves. A crowd of 19,318 saw the Giant manager reach the milestone in the third inning with a drive into the upper right-field stand off Johnny Hutchings.

Only Babe Ruth, with 714 and Jimmy Foxx who has hit 531, are ahead of Ott.

The Giants clinched the game in the first inning with three runs on four straight singles off Nate Andrews before a man had been retired. Carroll Lockman hit his second homer in the fourth.

BOSTON	Ab	R	H	O	A	NEW YORK	Ab	R	H	O	A
Culler,ss	4	1	2	2	4	Lock'an,cf	5	3	2	4	0
Masi,c	3	0	1	5	0	Hausn,2b	5	1	2	3	5
Holmes,rf	4	0	1	4	0	Ott,rf	4	2	2	1	0
Medw'k,1b	4	0	1	11	0	Gardella,lf	4	0	1	1	0
Nieman,lf	3	0	1	1	0	Weint'b,1b	5	0	1	9	1
Gill'w,cf	4	1	2	0	0	Lomb'rdi,c	5	1	1	3	0
Work'n,3b	4	0	1	1	1	Kerr,ss	5	1	3	5	3
Wiete,ss	4	0	1	0	2	Jurges,3b	4	0	2	0	2
Andrews,p	0	0	0	0	0	Mungo,p	1	0	0	0	0
Hutch'gs,p	2	0	0	0	2	Emmer'h,p	3	1	1	0	1
Wright,p	0	0	0	0	0						
1Tobin	1	0	0	0	0						
Hend'k'n,p	0	0	0	0	0						
Totals	33	2	9	24	10	Totals	39	9	14	27	13

1Batted for Wright in seventh.

Boston .... 0 1 1 0 0 0 0 0 0—2
New York .... 3 0 1 1 2 2 0 0 x—9

Errors — Hausmann, Workman, Kerr. Runs batted in—Ott (2), Gardella, Weintraub, Workman, Holmes, Lockman, Hausmann, Jurges (2), Kerr. Two-base hits—Kerr, Hausmann, Jurges. Home runs—Ott, Lockman. Stolen base—Gardella. Sacrifice—Masi. Double plays—Kerr, Hausmann, Weintraub, Hausmann, Kerr, Weintraub. Left on bases—Boston, 6; New York, 11. Base on balls—Emmerich, 5; Hutchings, 2; Hendrickson, 1. Strikeouts—Mungo, 2; Hutchings, 3; Wright, 1; Emmerich, 1. Hits—Andrews, 4 in no inning (none out in first); Hutchings, 7 in 4 2-3; Wright, 3 in 1 1-3; Hendrickson, none in 2; Mungo, 5 in 2 1-3; Emmerich, 3 in 6 2-3. Hit by pitcher—Hutchings (Ott, Lockman). Passed ball—Lombardi. Winning pitcher—Emmerich. Losing pitcher—Andrews. Umpires—Bogess, Pinelli, Conlan. Time—2:15. Attendance—19,318 paid.

First Two-Timer Since Jimmy Foxx

Hal Newhouser, 24-year-old left hand pitcher of the World Champion Detroit Tigers, was voted the American League's most valuable player for 1945 for the second season in succession, it was announced today by the Base Ball Writers' Association of America. He will receive the second annual Kenesaw Mountain Landis Memorial Plaque as base ball's official designation.

The first player to win this honor twice in succession since Jimmy Foxx was elected in 1932 and 1933, Newhouser received 236 points, exactly the same number he polled last year. He was named first on nine of the 24 ballots and received nine seconds, two thirds, four fourths and two for fifth. Unlike last year when he beat out his teammate Dizzy Trout by one point, Newhouser this time was a decisive choice, 72 points ahead of his nearest rival. But for the second successive year, a Detroit teammate was runner-up. Second baseman Eddie Mayo was the second choice this year with 164 points, including seven votes for first honors.

Mexicans Get 2 More Players In Raid On National League

New York, Feb. 18 (AP)—The Mexican Professional Baseball League staged a double-barreled raid on National League talent today and obtained two out-fielders, raising to seven the number of major leaguers signed within the past few days.

Luis Olmo

Luis Olmo, a .313 slugger with the Brooklyn Dodgers last year, where he played in both the outfield and at third base, signed to play with the Vera Cruz club for three years at a salary reported to be $10,000 annually in addition to living and traveling expenses for himself and his wife.

Dan Gardella, an outfielder-first baseman with the New York Giants last year but in disfavor this spring, announced at Miami that he had agreed to a five-year contract. He did not mention the salary.

Robert Jamis, who represented the Mexican League in the negotiations, offered Dick Bartell. Giant utility infielder, $7,500 a year but the veteran rejected it.

Bernardo and Mario Pasquel, wealthy Mexican baseball addicts, have been doing most of the signing of the players.

Others who have inked contracts are Nap Reyes, New York Giant third baseman; Rene Monteagudo, Philadelphia Phil outfielder; Roberto Estallela, Philadelphia Athletics handyman; Fermin Guerra, Washington catcher, and Adrian Zebala, Giant pitcher.

Luque To Manage Team

Adolf Luque, former Giant coach, has agreed to manage one of the Mexican teams and Pasquel brothers also have put Infielder Roland Gladu, formerly of Boston in the National League and last year at Montreal, and Pitcher Jean Pierre Roy, also of Montreal, under contract.

They also have made offers to Pitcher Alex Carrasquel, of the Chicago White Sox; Infielder Gilberto Torres, Washington third baseman, and to Dick Sisler, son of George Sisler, who is the property of the St. Louis Cardinals.

Bob Feller's No-Hit, No-Run Pitching And Home Run By Hayes Beat Yankees, 1-0

Cleveland Speedballer Strikes Out 11 For Second Win of Year

New York, April 30—(AP.)— Rapid Robert Feller, Cleveland's fire-balling righthander from Van Meter, Iowa, convinced 37,144 Yankee Stadium fans and the New York Yankees today that he isn't slipping by throwing a no-hit, no-run game against the Bronx Bombers for a 1-0 decision on Frankie Hayes' ninth inning homer.

The 27-years-old speedster walked five men and struck out 11, allowing only one Yankee to reach third base, as he duplicated his opening day no-hit feat of 1940 when he blanked Chicago by the same 1-0 score.

Chandler Bars Door To Return Of Owen; Suspension Upheld

Cincinnati, Aug. 14.—(AP.)— Baseball Commissioner, A. B. Chandler refused today to open the door of American baseball to Mickey Owen, who jumped a Brooklyn contract to play ball in Mexico, and then asked to be taken into the fold again.

The commissioner declared his stand in a statement issued through his office here. He recalled he had announced earlier this year that any player who ducked his baseball obligations would be suspended for five years. He said he saw "no good reason" why he should change his mind.

The statement referred specifically to Owen's plea for reinstatement. But its wording plainly indicated that the door to reinstatement was barred as well to every other player who succumbed to the lure of fancy contracts in Mexican baseball.

The doughty little catcher went to the Mexican League this spring after his release from service instead of returning to the Brooklyn team. On May 9 the commissioner suspended him for five years and two weeks ago Owen returned to this country.

Cincinnati, Ohio, Aug. 14 — (UP.) — The office of baseball commissioner Chandler revealed today that Outfielder Luis Olmo had followed the lead of another ex-Dodger, Mickey Owen, and was seeking reinstatement into organized baseball after jumping to the Mexican League. A spokesman declared that the 27-years-old Puerto Rican had applied for reinstatement in an "indirect manner."

Reprinted from
The Detroit News

All-Star Facts

Result—American League 12, National League 0.

Standings—American League won nine, National League four.

Winning pitcher—Bobby Feller, Cleveland Indians.

Losing pitcher—Claude Passeau, Chicago Cubs.

Receipts—$111,338 (gross).

Attendance—34,906 paid.

* * *

N.L.	☹	☹	☹	☹	☹	☹	☹	😢	😢	☹
A.L.	2	😊	😊	1	3	😃	2	4	X	12

* * *

19 Scoreless Innings Set New Record

Dodgers, Reds Stage Endurance Contest Called by Darkness

Brooklyn, Sept. 11. (AP.) The Brooklyn Dodgers, with a chance to cut the St. Louis Cardinals National League lead to one full game, played 19 innings to a scoreless tie today with the Cincinnati Reds, the longest scoreless tie ever played in the major leagues.

The draw, coupled with the Cardinals defeat at the hands of the Philadelphia Phillies, reduced St. Louis' lead to one and a half games, all on the winning side of the ledger. Both teams are even in the losing side.

Johnny Vander Meer, of double no-hit fame, emerged the pitching hero. He went the first 15 innings for the Reds and gave up seven hits and fanned 14. He walked only two. Harry Gumbert finished, holding the Dodgers to one hit in four innings.

The Dodgers used four pitchers. Hal Gregg, the starter, went 10 innings, and he was followed by Hugh Casey, five; Art Herring, three; and Hank Behrman, one.

Twice the Reds missed scoring by a split second when Dodger outfielders Pete Reiser and Dixie Walker, cut them down at the plate. Walker's game-saving throw came in the 19th. With Dain Clay on second and Lonnie Frey on first as a result of walks, and one out, Bert Haas singled sharply to right. Walker fired a perfect throw to Catcher Bruce Edwards on one bounce, and the swift-footed Clay was caught.

Big Leagues Will Limit Pay Slashes

Cuts in Salary Set at 25 Per Cent; Owners Grant Concessions

New York, Sept. 16.—(AP.)—Major league magnates today approved practically all the players' demands for contract reforms including a surprising request to limit the reduction of a player's salary to 25 per cent of the wage paid the previous year.

Set $5000 Minimum.

As expected, the owners had been authorized to make whatever changes in contracts they deemed necessary, agreed in their joint meeting upon the $5000 minimum salary per year, an allowance of $25 per week to a player for training expenses other than transportation, board and lodging and the elimination of the 10-day release clause. They also agreed on a 30-day severance pay to unconditionally released players; extension of the barnstorming period from 10 to 30 days after the World Series; traveling expenses home at the end of the season and in case of trades, and salaries and hospitalization and medical fees guaranteed in event of injury.

However, the salary reduction limitation clause came as a complete surprise since it had never before been brought to light. It is expected to affect such high salaried stars and former stars as Hank Greenberg, Joe DiMaggio, Charlie Keller, Joe Gordon, Dick Wakefield, George Stirnweiss, Mort and Walker Cooper. All are in the top money bracket who have not done as well as expected of them this year. The new ruling means, for instance, that Greenberg, who reportedly earned $60,000 for this year's work, cannot be compelled to accept less than $45,000 in 1947. The only alternative the club owner has is to grant the player his unconditional release.

Other Concessions.

Other important concessions granted included:

(1) A player shall be guaranteed for the full season the salary specified in his contract regardless of assignment to another major league club or a minor league club.

(2) No player is to be given his unconditional release until waivers for that purpose are obtained. In such instances the waiver price shall be $1 and the waiver request may not be withdrawn. The player involved will be granted five days in which to decide whether he will report to the claiming club or accept his free agency.

(3) Cause for release of any player must be given.

(4) All contracts must be mailed to the player on or before February 1.

(5) Spring training is not to begin before February 15, in 1947 and not earlier than March 1 for 1948 and subsequent years.

CARDS BEAT DODGERS, 8-4, FOR PENNANT

Halt Brooklyn's Ninth-Inning Rally With Bases Full To Win Playoff

Brooklyn, Oct. 3 (AP.)—A hair-raising, ninth-inning rally by Brooklyn's battling Dodgers fell short today and the St. Louis Cardinals wrapped up their fourth National League pennant in five years by taking the second and deciding game of their unprecedented playoff series, 8 to 4, before a throng of 31,875 at Ebbets Field.

Held to two hits by Murry Dickson, a trim right-hander, for the first eight frames, Leo Durocher's scrappers slugged the pride of Tracy, Mo., from the hill with their final gasp in the last inning and rushed three runs across before Harry (The Cat) Brecheen finally stunned them into submission with two season-ending strikeouts.

The bases still were filled with Dodgers when Howie Schultz, tall Dodger pinch hitter, who had clouted a home run in the opening game of the playoff at St. Louis, swung from his heels at a third strike—and missed.

Fans Are Disappointed

So bitter was the disappointment of Brooklyn's fandom that a minute after the final out Enos (Country) Slaughter was wrapped in a fist-swinging session with a Dodger rooter near home plate. The cops finally pried them apart after several hundred fans had closed in on the combatants.

BOB'S TOTAL OF 348 ECLIPSES OLD MARK

Feller's Strike-Outs 5 More Than Waddell but 1 Short of Unofficial Record

INDIANS' ACE VICTOR, 4-1

Defeats Newhouser of Tigers for 26th Triumph of Year—47,876 Watch Contest

DETROIT, Sept. 20 (AP)—Bob Feller of the Cleveland Indians laid claim to one of the oldest major league records in the books today by fanning five Detroit Tigers to run his season total to 348, five more than officially credited to Rube Waddell of the Philadelphia Athletics in 1904.

Beating Detroit's ace, Hal Newhouser, 4 to 1, on a six-hit pitching job, Feller still fell one strike-out short of equaling an unofficial mark of 349 credited to Waddell through recent research.

Fans Newhouser in Fifth

The Tigers batted around twice before Feller got Newhouser on three pitches in the fifth inning for the strike-out that put him ahead of Waddell's 343 total, officially recognized by the American League.

Before the inning was over he fanned Hank Greenberg and got Dick Wakefield on a called third strike that drew a vigorous objection from the Tiger outfielder. The other two whiffings both came in the eighth when Bob struck out Greenberg for the second time and then fooled Jimmy Bloodworth.

Newhouser fanned seven—two more than Feller—but yielded nine hits, of which five came in succession in the fourth inning for three Cleveland runs, enough to hand him his ninth defeat to go with twenty-six victories.

Beats Tigers First Time

Feller, who lost fifteen, bagged his twenty-sixth victory by stopping the Tigers for the first time in five tries this season.

Despite overcast skies and temperatures that dipped to 58 degrees a crowd of 47,876 turned out to see Feller avenge a 3-to-0 loss to Newhouser a week ago in Cleveland.

The crowd hiked Detroit's home attendance for the season to a record count of 1,722,590.

The box score:

CLEVELAND (A.)	ab.	r.	h.	po.	a.	e.
Moss, 3b	4	0	0	0	2	0
Conway, ss	4	1	1	0	4	0
Robinson, 1b	3	0	0	12	0	0
Edwards, rf	2	1	1	3	0	0
M'k'wicz, rf	2	0	0	1	0	0
Mitchell, cf	4	1	[illegible]	1	0	0
Seerey, lf	4	1	1	[illegible]	0	0
Mack, 2b	3	0	1	[illegible]	4	0
Hegan, c	4	0	[illegible]	5	0	0
Feller, p	3	0	0	0	1	0
Total	33	4	9	27	11	0

DETROIT (A.)	ab.	r.	h.	po.	a.	e.
Lake, ss	1	1	0	0	0	1
Lipon, ss	2	0	1	1	5	0
Kell, 3b	5	0	[illegible]	0	4	0
Cramer, cf	3	0	1	0	0	0
[illegible]	[illegible]	[illegible]	[illegible]	[illegible]	[illegible]	[illegible]
[illegible]	[illegible]	[illegible]	[illegible]	[illegible]	[illegible]	[illegible]
[illegible]	[illegible]	[illegible]	[illegible]	[illegible]	[illegible]	[illegible]
[illegible]	[illegible]	[illegible]	[illegible]	[illegible]	[illegible]	[illegible]
[illegible]	[illegible]	[illegible]	[illegible]	[illegible]	[illegible]	[illegible]
[illegible]	[illegible]	[illegible]	[illegible]	[illegible]	[illegible]	[illegible]
[illegible]	[illegible]	[illegible]	[illegible]	[illegible]	[illegible]	[illegible]
[illegible]	[illegible]	[illegible]	[illegible]	[illegible]	[illegible]	[illegible]
[illegible]	[illegible]	[illegible]	[illegible]	[illegible]	[illegible]	[illegible]
Total	[illegible]	[illegible]	[illegible]	27	[illegible]	[illegible]

aBatted for Swift in [illegible].
bBatted for Newhouser in ninth.

Cleveland .... [illegible]
Detroit .... [illegible]

Runs batted in—Mitchell 2, Mack, Hegan, Cramer. Sacrifice—Robinson. Double plays—[illegible], Mack and Robinson; Lipon, Bloodworth and [illegible]. Left on bases—Cleveland [illegible], Detroit [illegible]. [illegible] Feller [illegible], Newhouser [illegible]. [illegible] Feller 5, Newhouser [illegible]. Wild pitch—[illegible]. Umpires—[illegible]. Time of game—1:[illegible]. Attendance—47,876.

WALTER JOHNSON DIES; 'BIG TRAIN' PITCHED WAY TO SPORTS IMMORTALITY

Washington Hurler's Terrific Speed Was Legendary

Washington, Dec. 10 (P)—Walter Johnson, 59, former strikeout king of the American League and a member of baseball's official Hall of Fame, died late tonight of a brain tumor.

The "Big Train," who retired to a farm near Germantown, Md., when his baseball days were over, suffered a stroke last April and had been under treatment at Georgetown University Hospital ever since.

Cards Take Top Honors Of Baseball

Score With Two Down In Eighth Inning to Whip Red Sox, 4-3

Harry Brecheen Pitching Hero

Joins Select Group Of Hurlers Who Have Won Three Games

BY BILL LEE,
Sports Editor.

St. Louis, Oct. 15. The Red Birds of St. Louis rule the roost of baseball today.

They won top honors for 1946 by beating the Boston Red Sox, 4 to 3, in the seventh game of one of the hardest fought World Series since the first one was played in 1903.

The Cardinals notched the winning run with two out in the eighth inning of a tense, exciting ball game played before a jam-packed crowd of 36,143 at Sportsman's Park when Enos Slaughter, running like a frightened doe, romped all the way from first base on Harry Walker's double to centerfield.

Slaughter had opened the inning with a single and had been anchored to first base while Whitey Kurowski bunted a pop foul fly into relief pitched Bob Klinger's hands in an abortive attempt to sacrifice.

The Cards put on the hit and run sign after Del Rice flied out. Slaughter was away with the pitch to Walker and went flying past second base as "Little Dixie" jammed his hit into centerfield.

Slaughter Keeps Going.

One of the fleetest of the flying Red Birds, Slaughter didn't slow down as he neared third base. Leon Culberson, who had replaced the injured Dom DiMaggio in centerfield for Boston, made the throw from the outfield. Shortstop Johnny Pesky took two steps toward the outfield to take the throw and relay it to the plate.

For some inexplicable reason, Pesky held the ball a split second, then saw to his dismay that Slaughter had kept right on going for the plate. Pesky threw to Roy Partee, Red Sox catcher, but Slaughter slid under him to score the winning run and nail down the sixth championship the Cardinals have won in World Series play.

Reprinted from
The Hartford Courant

Leo Durocher Draws Suspension For Year As Brooklyn Manager

Cincinnati, April 9. (AP.) Leo (The Lip) Durocher, one of baseball's most explosive characters since he became manager of the Brooklyn Dodgers eight years ago, today was suspended for the 1947 season by Commissioner A. B. Chandler.

"Durocher has not measured up to the standards expected or required of managers of our baseball teams," Chandler said.

The suspension of the belligerent Leo, who left a shortstop's job to become baseball's highest paid manager, an estimated $70,000 a year, was the "result of the accumulation of unpleasant incidents in which he has been involved," Chandler said.

Clyde Sukeforth, Brooklyn coach, tonight was named to manage the Dodgers in their exhibition game with the Montreal Royals at Ebbets Field tomorrow. For this game only, Sukeforth, a former big league catcher, scout and minor league pilot, will fill in the spot left open by the suspension of Durocher.

The announcement of Sukeforth's appointment for the day was made by Arthur Mann, assistant to club president Branch Rickey.

Whether the 44-years-old Sukeforth will be handed the reins of the colorful Dodgers for the regular season which opens Tuesday only Rickey and his brain trust knows.

Shortly after he was informed of Commissioner Chandler's suspension of Durocher, Rickey was asked who would manage the Dodgers.

"I have an idea who it will be but I can't tell you now," Rickey replied.

Besides Sukeforth those believed to be in the contention for the job include Coach Ray Blades and Scout John (Pepper) Martin, the one-time wild horse of the Osage in the days of the St. Louis Cardinals' Gas House Gang.

Although the name of Dixie Walker often has been mentioned in connection with the Brooklyn managerial post, Rickey quickly eliminated the popular, hard-hitting outfielder from consideration. "Walker never has been considered in a managerial capacity."

He said they "have been hitherto warned" against such association.

Chandler exonerated Larry MacPhail, president of the New York Yankees, from any association with know gamblers, and also said he was convinced that Branch Rickey, head of the Brooklyn club, had not made any statements which might be construed as detrimental to MacPhail's character and integrity.

But, "because their officials engaged in a public controversy damaging to baseball, the New York American League club and the Brooklyn Club are hereby fined $2000 each," he added.

The commissioner also suspended Chuck Dressen, former Dodger coach, for 30 days beginning April 15 because he allegedly broke a verbal contract with Brooklyn to join the Yankees this year.

Harold Parrott traveling secretary for the Brooklyn team, was fined $500 for "writing a deliberately derogatory" newspaper article about people in baseball. Parrott was "ghost" writer for Durocher in the Brooklyn Daily Eagle.

Chandler said both Rickey and Durocher had admitted making some statements regarding Mac-Phail's guests at the Havana game.

It was those statements, along with others made in a newspaper column under Durocher's name that led to hearings in Florida recently and to Chandler's decision today. MacPhail brought the case to a head by filing charges of defamation against MacPhail and Rickey.

Criticized MacPhail.

Durocher in the newspaper column criticized MacPhail as trying "to knock me" after, he said, he declined to become manager of the Yankees.

Chandler said today he was convinced MacPhail never had offered the job to Durocher.

But, "because their officials engaged in a public controversy damaging to baseball, the New York American League club and the Brooklyn club are hereby fined $2000 each," he added.

The words with which Chandler set down Durocher for a year and purportedly planning to fly west with his movie actress wife, Larraine Day, tonight were:

"Durocher has not measured up to the standards expected or required of managers of our baseball teams.

"As a result of the accumulated unpleasant incidents in which he has been involved Manager Durocher is hereby suspended from participating in professional baseball for the 1947 season."

And in conclusion, Chandler said:

"All parties to this controversy are silenced from the time this order is issued."

Walter Mulbry, secretary and spokesman for Chandler, said that meant that the persons involved in today's action were not to discuss it "or the situation from which it arose."

One-Time Associates.

The three main characters in today's stunning action are one-time associates.

Durocher starred at shortstop for the St. Louis Cards years ago. MacPhail and Rickey were with the same organization. Then Mac-Phail took a down-at-the-heels Brooklyn club, installed Durocher as manager and between them they whipped together one team that went into the World's Series.

Then Rickey took over the Brooklyn leadership when MacPhail left to join the Army, and last year the club tied St. Louis for the National League pennant. The Cards won in a playoff.

Pete Reiser's Hit Brings In Robinson For 5-3 Dodger Win

Reds 5, Phils 4

Cincinnati, July 25.—(AP.)—Although battered for 13 hits, Ewell Blackwell survived a ninth inning Philadelphia rally tonight to notch his sixteenth consecutive victory as the Cincinnati Reds trimmed the Phillies 5-4 before a crowd of 24,530.

Trailing 5-3, the Phillies, who lost to Blackwell by an identical score on July 15, loaded the bases in the final round after one was out but could count only one run.

The six-foot five-inch Cincinnati right-hander, although in trouble most of the way, fanned nine and walked none to equal a march of 16 straight set by Carl Hubbell of the New York Giants in 1936.

CINCINNATI (N)	ab	r	h	o	a	e	rbi
Baumholtz rf	2	1	0	1	0	0	0
Zientara ss	5	1	1	4	0	0	0
Hatton 3b	3	2	2	0	1	0	0
Haas c	2	1	2	2	0	0	0
Vollmer cf	0	0	0	2	0	0	0
Young 1b	4	0	0	10	0	0	0
Galan lf	3	0	2	0	0	0	2
Lamanno c	3	0	1	3	0	0	1
Miller ss	3	0	0	2	2	0	0
Blackwell p	4	0	1	3	1	0	
Totals	37	5	9	27	10	1	3
PHILA. (N)	ab	r	h	o	a	e	rbi
Albright ss	5	1	2	1	4	0	0
Wyrostek cf	5	0	1	2	1	0	0
Walker rf	5	0	1	2	0	0	1
Tabor 3b	5	0	1	1	0	0	1
Ennis lf	4	1	2	2	0	0	0
Padgett c	4	0	2	7	2	0	0
Schultz 1b	4	0	2	7	2	0	0
Verban 2b	4	1	1	5	1	0	1
Heintzelman p	1	0	0	0	0	0	0
Jurisich p	1	0	0	0	1	0	0
aGilbert	1	0	0	0	0	0	0
Schanz p	0	0	0	0	1	0	0
bJudd	1	0	1	0	0	0	0
cHundley	0	1	0	0	0	0	0
Totals	40	4	13	24	10	0	3

Cincinnati ... 104 000 00x—5
Philadelphia ... 001 100 011—4

Doby Strikes Out In League Debut, Cleveland Loses

Chicago, July 5.— (AP.)—The Cleveland Indians dropped a 6 to 5 decision to the Chicago White Sox today and Larry Doby, 22-years-old Negro athlete, struck out as a pinch batter for the Indians in his major league debut.

Luke Appling contributed three doubles and a single to the White Sox attack, one of the two base hits scoring the winning run.

Doby, purchased from the Newark, N. J., Eagles of the Negro National League, struck out with two Cleveland men on the bases and one out in the seventh inning.

The slim Easterner was the first Negro player to appear in the American League in the circuit's 47-years history.

Pittsburgh Sets Home Run Record

Pittsburgh, Aug. 17. — Home runs by Hank Greenberg and Frank Gustine for the Pittsburgh Pirates today in the first game of a twin bill with the St. Louis Cardinals set a new National League record of 16 round trippers in five games. The old mark was 15 homers, set by the New York Giants in 1924.

Brooklyn, April 15. (AP.) — Pete Reiser, key to Brooklyn's flag chances, blazed a seventh-inning double off the screen a foot inside the right-field foul line at Ebbets Field today to drive across the tying and winning runs as the pilotless Dodgers opened their 1947 campaign with a 5 to 3 victory over the Boston Braves.

Although he did not get a hit in three official times at bat, Jackie Robinson, first Negro to play in modern big league baseball, made his official debut as a Dodger by sprinting home with the deciding run on Reiser's smash and playing perfect ball at first base.

Reiser's hit, his second off of Johnny Sain, was only the sixth produced by the Dodgers, and it was their last as Mort Cooper and Anton Karl combined the rest of the way to hold them in check. Boston made eight blows off Lefty Joe Hatten and Hal Gregg, who relieved after Hatten had been lifted for a pinch hitter in the sixth.

With Brooklyn trailing, 3-2, to open the seventh, Eddie Stanky led off with a walk, bringing up Robinson. The Negro in three previous attempts had done no better than hit into a double play, roll to shortstop and loft an easy fly to left.

This time he laid down a perfect bunt midway to the pitcher's box and tore for first. Earl Torgeson grabbed the sphere and made a hard, hurried peg to first that hit Robinson on the leg and rocketed on into right field.

Robinson had no difficulty reaching second and Stanky pulled up at third. Reiser then weighed in with his double, a terrific clout. Reiser soon scooted home with the fifth and unneeded run on Gene Hermanski's fly to deep center.

A disappointing crowd of only 25,623 paid to see the Dodgers get away in front of one of their main rivals for the National League flag.

BROOKLYN (N)	ab	r	h	o	a	e	rbi
Stanky 2b	3	1	0	0	3	0	0
Robinson 1b	3	1	0	11	0	0	0
Schultz 1b	0	0	0	1	0	0	0
Reiser cf	2	1	2	2	0	0	2
Walker rf	3	0	1	0	0	0	0
Tatum rf	0	0	0	0	0	0	0
Vaughan lf	0	0	0	0	0	0	0
Furillo rf	4	0	1	3	0	0	1
Hermanski lf	2	0	0	2	0	1	1
Edwards c	0	0	0	0	0	0	0
bRackley	1	0	0	3	0	0	0
Bragan c	3	0	0	4	0	1	0
Jorgenson 3b	3	0	0	1	0	1	0
Reese ss	3	1	1	3	2	0	0
Hatten p	2	0	1	1	1	0	0
aStevens	1	0	0	0	0	0	0
Gregg p	1	0	0	0	1	0	0
Casey p	0	0	0	0	0	0	0
Totals	29	5	6	27	10	1	5
BOSTON (N)	ab	r	h	o	a	e	rbi
Culler ss	3	0	0	2	0	0	0
eHolmes	1	0	0	0	0	0	0
Sisti ss	0	0	0	0	0	0	0
Hopp cf	5	0	1	2	0	0	1
McCormick rf	4	0	3	2	0	0	0
R. Elliott 3b	2	0	1	0	2	0	0
Litwhiler lf	3	1	0	1	0	0	0
Rowell lf	1	0	0	0	0	0	0
Torgeson 1b	4	1	0	10	1	1	0
Masi c	4	1	3	4	0	0	2
Ryan 2b	3	0	1	3	4	7	0
Sain p	1	0	0	0	1	0	0
Cooper p	0	0	0	1	0	0	0
dNeill	0	0	0	0	0	0	0
Lanfranconi p	0	0	0	0	0	0	0
Totals	31	3	8	24	13	1	3

Brooklyn ... 000 101 30x—5
Boston ... 000 012 000—3

Winning Streak—1906 And 1947

New York, July 18.—(AP.)—Here are the comparison between the American League record winning streaks of the Chicago White Sox of 1906 and the New York Yankees of 1947.

NEW YORK.						CHICAGO.				
Date	r	h	e	opponents	opp. runs	Date	r	h	e	opponents	opp. runs
6/29	3	6	0	Washington	1	8/2	3	5	0	Boston	0
30	3	6	0	Boston	1	3	4	7	1	Boston	0
7/2	8	11	1	Washington	1	4	1	5	0	Boston	0
4	7	10	0	Washington	3	5	10	11	2	Philadelphia	2
4	4	9	0	Washington	2	6	7	8	0	Philadelphia	0
5	5	10	0	Philadelphia	1	7	4	6	0	Philadelphia	0
6	8	14	1	Philadelphia	2	8	1	2	0	Philadelphia	0
6	9	13	1	Philadelphia	2	9	3	9	0	Philadelphia	2
10	4	9	3	St. Louis	3	10	2	5	1	New York	1
11	3	3	1	St. Louis	1	11	8	8	2	New York	1
12	12	17	2	St. Louis	2	12	3	7	0	New York	0
12	8	11	2	St. Louis	5	13	0	6	0	New York (tie)	0
13	10	16	0	Chicago	3	15	6	6	0	Boston	0
13	6	10	0	Chicago	4	16	9	14	3	Boston	4
15	9	10	0	Cleveland	4	17	4	7	2	Boston	0
15	2	9	0	Cleveland	1	18	10	12	2	New York	1
16	8	14	0	Cleveland	2	20	4	5	1	New York	1
17	3	5	0	Cleveland	1	22	6	7	0	New York	1
17	7	10	0	Cleveland	2	22	11	13	6	New York	6
						23	4	8	0	Washington	1

Compilation—New York runs 119, opponents 41; Chicago runs 100, opponents 25; complete games by pitchers New York 11, Chicago 17 (not including tie game); won by shutouts—New York none, Chicago 5 (not including 0-0 tie); home runs—New York 17, Chicago one; winning pitchers—New York Reynolds 4, Shea 2, Page 2, Winsloff 2, Newsom 2, Raschi 2, Gumpert 1, Johnson 1, Chandler 1, Drews 1, Bevens 1; Chicago Walsh 7, White 5, Patterson 3, Owen 3, Altrock 1.

Freddie Hutchinson Squelches Yankees With Two Hits, 8-0

Detroit, July 18. — (AP.) —

Detroit, July 18. (AP.) -Freddie Hutchinson, serious Detroit New York Yankees' bid for their 20th straight victory - an american league record--with a near-perfect two-hit pitching performance today in which he yielded just two singles, one a bunt, as the Tigers halted the rampaging Yanks at 19 in a row by the shut-out count of 8 to 0.

Hutchinson, who faced only 28 men one more than the minimum - hadn't started a game in a month because of an ailing shoulder but had everything he needed today, and then some.

He struck out eight men and walked none as the Yanks hit only five balls out of the infield in their futile twilight bid for the record

Hutchinson himself, with two doubles and a single, got more hits than he gave the Yanks, and the Tigers put together their wildest hitting day of the season to register 18 safeties off the combined pitching of Randy Gumpert and Karl Drews.

Joe DiMaggio's sharp single to left in the second inning, when he was promptly erased in a double play, was New York's only hit until George (Snuffy) Stirnweiss beat out a bunt to the right of the mound leading off the seventh. Stirnweiss never got past first and he was the only runner the Yanks left on base.

Mize Smashes 51st Four Bagger To Tie Kiner In Home Run Race

Boston, Sept. 23. — (AP.) — Johnny Mize tied Ralph Kiner of Pittsburgh for the major league home run lead today when he belted his 51st four-bagger of the year to lead the New York Giants to a 3-1 victory over the Boston Braves.

Mize also smashed two singles and scored two runs to help rookie righthander Larry Jansen register his 21st victory against five defeats. Jansen doled out only seven hits and lost his shut-out in the ninth when the Braves scored their lone run on his own error. It was his sixth win over the Braves who have yet to beat him.

Johnny Sain was the starter and loser for the Braves, giving up six hits in eight innings. Sain was seeking his 21st victory too, but suffered his 12th defeat. Mize's homer came off Si Johnson in the ninth.

Ralph Kiner Clouts Two More Homers

Pittsburgh Slugger Passes Mize in 4-3 Win Over Braves

Pittsburgh, Sept. 12. (AP.)—Ralph Kiner, husky Pittsburgh Pirate outfielder, carried his team to a 4-3 victory over the Boston Braves tonight at Forbes Field by lashing out two home runs, his 48th and 49th of the season. In addition to taking over the major league home run leadership, he set a major league record of eight home runs in four consecutive games.

The old mark of seven in four games was established by the late Tony Lazzeri of the New York Yankees in 1936.

Kiner, who hit four homers in a twin bill yesterday, went hitless in his first two appearance tonight. His first circuit blow, which enabled him to pass Johnny Mize in their race for the major league leadership, came in the fifth inning with one man aboard and sent the Pirates into a 3-2 lead. No one was on base when he clouted his second in the seventh to make it 4-2.

JOE DIMAGGIO NAMED MVP

New York, Nov. 27. — (AP.) — Joe DiMaggio, star centerfielder of the world champion New York Yankees, has been voted the American League's 'Most Valuable' player award for 1947, by the narrowest possible margin, one slim vote, over Ted Williams, the circuit's batting king.

DiMaggio, who previously had earned the most valuable honors in 1939 and 1941, compiled a total of 202 votes to 201 for the Red Sox slugging outfielder in the vote of the 24-man committee of the Baseball Writers' Association of America for the Kenesaw Mountain Landis memorial award.

TED'S 2ND TRIPLE CROWN

WILLIAMS WINS BATTING TITLE

.343 Average Earns Outfielder Third Crown In 6 Years

Chicago, Dec. 20 (P)—Ted Williams's third American League batting title in six years today officially was awarded to the lanky Boston Red Sox outfielder, who did some "goat-getting" of his own this year with a championship average of .343 and three other attack titles.

Now the league's fourth three-time batting champion, Williams also led in home runs with 32; runs scored with 125, and total bases with 335, according to official league statistics.

Immortal Ty Cobb copped the junior circuit crown 12 times but after him the honor is harrowed to Harry Heilmann with four titles and Napoleon Lajoie and Williams with three each.

Three Years In Service

The Williams's batting saga is remarkable considering that after winning the title in 1941 with .406 and in 1942 with .356, the Boston big boy spent three seasons in military service and last year returned for a runner-up .342.

Dodgers' Only Hit Wins, 3-2, And Evens Series

Lavagetto's Pinch Double Drives In 2 Runs To Spoil Bevens's Mound Effort For Yankees

Rice describes roles of "outsiders" in Dodgers' victory *Page 11*

G. M. Gibbs discusses strategic tactics of game *Page 11*

By JESSE A. LINTHICUM

[Sports Editor of The Sun]

Brooklyn, N.Y., Oct. 3—Brooklyn evened the World Series with the New York Yankees this afternoon at two games each by winning in the ninth inning the most dramatic contest in the history of the annual baseball classic. The score was 3 to 2.

Floyd Bevens had only one Dodger to retire to become the first pitcher ever to turn in a World Series no-hit game, but his final offering to Cookie Lavagetto, a pinch hitter, was slammed against the right-field wall for a double, driving in the tieing and winning runs.

Constantly In Trouble

Although holding the National League champions hitless through 8 2-3 innings, Bevens constantly was in trouble because of wildness. He issued ten bases on balls, a series record, and two of the passes were given in the fateful ninth inning.

The game, by far the best of the four played to date, was tense from start to finish. It abounded in great fielding plays. the three Yankee outfielders turning in sensational catches to turn back the Dodger threats.

Bevens, obviously nervous as he went to the pitcher's box in the ninth, watched Lindell back up against the left-field wall to catch Edwards's long fly.

Furillo And Reiser Walk

Furillo walked. Jorgensen popped to McQuinn, and many fans made for the exits. Gionfriddo, who ran for Furillo, stole second, a pitch before Reiser, batting for Casey, received a pass. Miksis then was sent in to run for Reiser.

Lavagetto had the game placed squarely up to him as he went to bat for Stanky. He swung mightily at the first pitch, and missed. The next was a ball.

The third pitch was hit high

Reprinted from
The Baltimore Sun papers

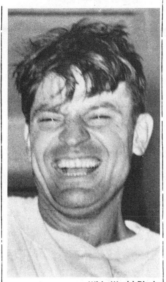

Wide World Photo

COOKIE LAVAGETTO

For Deputy Mayor

New York Oct 3 (P) - Brooklyn today nominated Cookie Lavagetto for Deputy Mayor of New York city.

Mayor William O'Dwyer, among those who saw the pinch-hitting Lavagetto slam the ninth-inning double which won today's World Series tilt for the Dodgers, hardly had returned to his office when the telephone began to ring.

It was Brooklyn calling Citizen by citizen insisted that very little, if anything, was too good for Lavagetto. Make him "deputy mayor," they said: or at least a "commissioner"

Replied the Mayor: "He deserves anything he wants."

But, his honor added quickly. "I am still neutral."

against the right-field wall, and Gionfriddo and Miksis raced around the bases as Lavagetto trotted to second base.

Brooklyn players and fans rushed on the field to greet Lavagetto. He was almost mobbed before he could reach the Dodger dugout.

Phil Rizzuto Has Job Proving He's Ballplayer

Brooklyn, N.Y., Oct. 3 (AP)—Little Phil Rizzuto, Yankee shortstop, arrived late at the ball park today.

He had a hard time convincing one of the cordon of police, which surrounded Ebbets Field, that he was a player.

"Go on, beat it," one officer said. "Don't give me that stuff. You can't even play first for a midget team."

NEW YORK (AMERICAN LEAGUE)	Ab	R	H	O	A
Stirnweiss, 2b	4	1	2	2	1
Henrich, rf	5	0	1	2	0
Berra, c	4	0	0	6	1
DiMaggio, cf	2	0	0	2	0
McQuinn, 1b	4	0	1	7	0
Johnson, 3b	4	1	1	3	2
Lindell, lf	3	0	2	3	0
Rizzuto, ss	4	0	1	1	2
Bevens, p	3	0	0	0	1
Totals	33	2	8	26	7

BROOKLYN (NATIONAL LEAGUE)	Ab	R	H	O	A
Stanky, 2b	1	0	0	2	3
5Lavagetto	1	0	1	0	0
Reese, ss	4	0	0	3	4
Robinson, 1b	4	0	0	11	1
Walker, rf	2	0	0	1	0
Hermanski, lf	4	0	0	2	0
Edwards, c	4	0	0	7	1
Furillo, cf	3	0	0	2	0
2Gionfriddo	0	1	0	0	0
Jorgensen, 3b	2	1	0	0	1
Taylor, p	0	0	0	0	0
Gregg, p	1	0	0	0	1
1Vaughan	1	0	0	0	0
Behrman, p	0	0	0	0	1
Casey, p	0	0	0	0	0
3Reiser	0	0	0	0	0
4Miksis	0	1	0	0	0
Totals	26	3	1	27	11

1Walked for Gregg in seventh.
2Ran for Furillo in ninth.
3Walked for Casey in ninth.
4Ran for Reiser in ninth.
5Doubled for Stanky in ninth.

New York (AL)   1 0 0 1 0 0 0 0 0—2
Brooklyn (NL)   0 0 0 0 1 0 0 0 2—3

Errors- Reese, Edwards, Berra, Jorgensen. Runs batted in- DiMaggio, Lindell, Reese, Lavagetto (2). Two-base hits - Lindell, Lavagetto. Three-base hit- Johnson. Stolen bases- Rizzuto, Reese. Gionfriddo. Sacrifices- Stanky, Bevens. Double plays- Reese, Stanky, Robinson; Gregg, Reese, Robinson; Casey, Edwards, Robinson. Earned runs- New York (AL), 1; Brooklyn (NL), 3. Left on bases- New York (AL), 9; Brooklyn (NL), 8. Bases on balls- Taylor, 1 (DiMaggio); Gregg, 3 (DiMaggio, Lindell Stirnweiss); Bevens, 10 (Stanky, 2, Walker, 2, Jorgensen, 2; Gregg, Vaughan, Furillo, Reiser). Strikeouts- Gregg, 5 (Stirnweiss, 2; Henrich, McQuinn, Bevens); Bevens, 5 (Edwards, 3, Gregg, Robinson. Pitching summary - Taylor, 1 run, 2 hits in 0 innings (none out in first); Gregg, 1 run, 4 hits in 7 innings; Behrman, 0 runs, 2 hits, in 1 1-3 innings; Casey, 0 runs, 0 hits, in 2-3 innings. Wild pitch—Bevens. Winning pitcher- Casey. Attendance- 33,443 paid. Time of game—2.20. Umpires—Goetz (NL) plate; McGowan (AL) first base; Pinelli (NL) second base; Rommel (AL) third base; Boyer (AL) left field; Magerkurth (NL) right field.

Returns To Dodger Managerial Position

Brooklyn, Dec 6 (P) — Leo Durocher returned to baseball today as manager of the Brooklyn Dodgers "without prejudice" from Commissioner A. B. Chandler, who had suspended him for the entire 1947 season.

Gracefully yielding to the inevitable, Burt Shotton, who won a pennant as the interim skipper last season, retired from active management to accept a vague but lucrative position that he termed "a nice, old man's job." The 63-year-old fatherly gentleman from Bartow, Fla., will oversee the work of the managers in the Dodgers' 26-club farm system.

Branch Rickey, Jr., acting in the absence of his father who is president of the Brooklyn club, made the brief one-sentence announcement that read:

No Terms Announced

"The 1947 contract of Leo Durocher has been renewed for 1948 by the Brooklyn baseball club."

No salary terms were announced but it was believed the figures will match the $50,000 reportedly called for last season. Actually, the contract has not been signed and may not be until spring training but that is a mere formality. It will be for one year.

While his son was breaking the not-too-well-kept news at a press conference in the Dodgers' plush offices, Rickey, Sr., was en route from a Philadelphia hospital where he had visited his daughter. Durocher, who has said "I want to stay in Brooklyn until the day I die," was driving to the airport to catch a plane for Los Angeles.

Pennock Funeral Services Today

KENNETT SQUARE, Pa., Feb. 2 (AP)—Funeral services will be held at 2 p.m. today for Herb Pennock, general manager of the Phillies who died suddenly in New York Friday.

The services will be private with only members of the immediate family attending. Interment will be in Union Hill Cemetery.

Several thousand friends and neighbors last night paid tribute to the former great pitcher who became one of baseball's foremost executives. Floral wreaths, a great many from teams in organized baseball, lined the walls of the American Legion Hall here.

JOE TINKER IS DEAD; A BASEBALL GREAT

End Comes to Cubs' Shortstop in Famous Double-Play Trio on His 68th Birthday

ORLANDO, Fla., July 27 (AP)—Joe Tinker, one of baseball's greats, died today on his sixty-eighth birthday. He was cheerful to the last hour of his life, although he died in an oxygen tent where he had been placed because of a respiratory ailment which no one considered serious.

Ten days ago the last surviving member of the Chicago Cubs' Tinker-to-Evers-to-Chance double play combination was taken to Orange Memorial Hospital for treatment for his indisposition and to have his diet straightened out.

Indians Toy With Idea Of Ball Park Nursery

By The Associated Press.

CLEVELAND, April 9 — Attention, all mother baseball fans:

Bill Veeck, president of the Indians, is toying with the idea of having a nursery installed at Municipal Stadium so women can park their youngsters and watch the ball game in comfort.

It would have gadgets for children, aged 2 to 6. That's for afternoon games only. At night he thinks children should be left home.

News Stuns Giants But Not Dodgers

"I Love Playing for Shotton," Robinson's Reaction to Change

Cincinnati, July 16. — (AP.)—Brooklyn Dodger players took a change of managers in stride today and indicated they would work equally hard for either Leo Durocher or Burt Shotton.

Burt Shotton, who managed the Dodgers to a pennant last season, was greeted warmly as he returned to the post vacated by Durocher. Durocher left to become manager of the New York Giants.

Comments by players included:

Outfielder Gene Hermanski: "It doesn't make much difference to me. Who's pitching against us? That's more important."

Pitcher Ralph Branca: "It makes no difference. You play as hard for one as you do for the other. You play to win for either manager."

Infielder Jackie Robinson: "I love playing for Shotton, but they're both great managers."

Shortstop Pee Wee Reese: "I've always been a Durocher man. He's a good manager. Shotton's good, too."

Third baseman Bruce Edwards: "I like both of them."

Commissioner Happy Chandler's comment was: "I'm glad to have Shotton back. He's a wonderful man."

WHITE SOX IN SPLIT AS SEEREY EXCELS

Pat Blasts 4 Homers in 12-11 Victory Over Athletics— McCahan Wins 2d, 6--1

PHILADELPHIA, July 18 (AP)—The White Sox split a pair of games with the Athletics today, winning by 12—11 in eleven innings and then losing, 6—1, in the five-inning nightcap cut short by Pennsylvania's Sunday curfew law.

Pat Seerey, the stocky left fielder of the White Sox, blasted four home runs in the first game to equal a long-standing major league record.

Not since Chuck Klein of the Phillies turned the trick in a ten-inning game in 1936 has a batter hit four homers in one game. Only four other players have driven four out of the park in a single contest.

The first game, one of the wildest contests of the year, took 3 hours and 44 minutes to complete and saw ten pitchers parade to the mound.

Philadelphia reeled off five quick runs, but lost the lead in the middle of the game when Seerey hit homers in three straight innings—the fourth, fifth and sixth—and Chicago gained an 11-7 lead.

But the Athletics surged back as Eddie Joost cracked for the circuit with two on and the score was tied, 11-11, at the end of the regulation nine innings.

The score stood until Seerey unlimbered his fourth circuit smash in the eleventh with no one on base. That swat earned Howie Judson the victory and gave Lou Brissie the defeat.

The Mackmen loaded the bases in the last of the eleventh, but Mario Pieretti came in and retired Ferris Fain for the final out.

Satchel Paige, Ace Negro Pitcher, Signed by Indians for Relief Role

Veteran, Who Admits to 39, Has Faced Many Big Leaguers in Exhibitions—Once Beat Dizzy Dean, 1-0, in 13 Innings

CLEVELAND, July 7 (AP)—The pennant-chasing Indians today signed that old veteran, Leroy (Satchel) Paige, as a relief pitcher.

The tall, lean hurler who has had a fabulous career in the Negro leagues and the exhibition circuit, put on a major league uniform for the first time today. But he isn't scared. He summed it all up:

"I'm starting my major league career with one thing in my favor, anyway. I won't be afraid of anybody I see in that batter's box. I've been around too long for that."

Paige has fogged his "hurry up" ball and "bat dodger" past major leaguers in many an exhibition game for years.

Just how long he has "been around" or how many games he has won isn't very clear.

Various Estimates on Age

"Born in Mobile," he said. "Sept. 18, 1908." His age has been estimated variously in the 40's and even 50's, but he says he was eligible for the draft all through the second World War.

But whatever age he admits to, President Bill Veeck signed him in the hope his right-hand relief pitching could bolster the Tribe's drive for a pennant. Veeck bought Paige's contract from the Kansas City Monarchs of the Negro American League. How much Satchel will be paid wasn't told, but his recent earnings have been estimated at upward of $30,000 annually.

In the past two decades Paige has made most of the major leaguers admit he is one of the all-time great hurlers. Babe Ruth and Ted Williams are about the only sluggers who haven't faced him on the exhibition circuit.

And how does he size them up? Of the present crop, Joe DiMaggio is the toughest.

High Praise for Gehringer

"Before DiMaggio, Charley Gehringer of the Detroit Tigers gave me more trouble than anyone else. He must have had the finest pair of eyes in baseball," he said. "He'd stand up there and take a pitch a quarter-inch off the place as calmly as if it had been two feet wide."

Last fall Paige faced Bob Feller's all-star assortment in Los Angeles to win an 8-0 decision in which he struck out sixteen.

Back in 1934 he faced Dizzy Dean at his peak and scored a 1-0 victory in thirteen innings, a game which Veeck calls "the best I've ever seen."

That was a big year for Satchel. He was pitching for Bismarck, N. D., a team which won 104 of the 105 games it played.

"And I pitched in every game, I guess. I know there was one month when I started twenty-nine games," he went on.

The Monarchs bought Paige an airplane in 1946 for keeping engagements. That was his best recent season. He helped the Monarchs win the league pennant, allowing only two runs in ninety-three innings and running a string of scoreless innings to sixty-four. Most of the time he threw only a few innings, but he pitched a full game to clinch the pennant.

His strike-out record for a single game is the same as Feller's—eighteen. That was in 1932, for the Monarchs and against the Baltimore Black Sox in Yankee Stadiums.

Says They Don't Count

He has pitched a "hatful" of no-hitters, but some of them were against feeble opposition and he says those don't count. He doesn't recall how many games he has won, nor his strike-out total. He got into baseball in 1925 with the Chattanooga Lookouts and in 1928 joined the Birmingham Barons. He has been with the Baltimore Black Sox, Chicago American Giants, the Pittsburgh Crawfords and the House of David.

Veeck and Manager Lou Boudreau had him down at the Municipal Stadium yesterday for a "secret tryout." It was the first time Boudreau had seen him in action. He threw fifty pitches "and only three or four of them were wide of the plate," said Veeck. Boudreau managed a few line drives, but said "Now I can believe some of the tall stories they tell about his pitching."

Three other Negroes now are in the major leagues—Larry Doby of the Indians, and Jackie Robinson and Roy Campanella of the Dodgers.

The newest Indian stands 6 feet 3½ inches and weighs 180. He is unmarried.

Ruth Dies in His Sleep In New York Hospital After Two-Year Illness

Home Run King Dies at 53

HOME RUN KING CANCER VICTIM, DOCTOR REVEALS

Lapsed into Unconsciousness After Saying Prayers, Priest Says

FAMILY AT HOSPITAL

Death of Baseball's Most Glamorous Figure Brings Flood of Tributes

NEW YORK, Aug. 16 — (AP) Babe Ruth, 53, who rose from the obscurity of an orphanage to become one of baseball's immortals, died tonight of cancer.

The once-mighty Yankee slugger, his frame and strength weakened by a long and painful illness, lapsed into unconsciousness shortly before death came to him—peacefully.

"The Babe," said a Catholic priest at the bedside of the long-time home run king, "died a beautiful death."

Dies In His Sleep

"He said his prayers," the priest added, "and lapsed into a sleep—and he died in his sleep.

Death came to one of baseball's brightest stars at 7:01 p.m. (EST) in New York City's Memorial Hospital Center for cancer and allied diseases.

At the end of Ruth's prayers, the priest, the Rev. Thomas H. Kaufman of the St. Catherine of Siena Parish, administered the last rites of the Catholic Church.

Scribe Clocks Boston Win Over Indians

Chronological Replay Reveals Concentrated Drama Before 40,135

BY WHITNEY MARTIN.

Boston, Oct. 6.—(AP).—One hour and 42 minutes of drama, or a chronological history of the Braves 1-0 victory in the series' opener:

1 p. m.—Johnny Sain throws first pitch to Dale Mitchell, a ball.

1:05—Tommy Holmes first up for Braves, and the band, with theme song for each Boston player, plays "Has Anybody Here seen Kelly?"

1:11—Earl Torgeson watches third strike go by for Bob Feller's first strikeout.

1:13—Joe Gordon watches third strike for Sain's first strikeout.

1:14—Ken Keltner singles over third for first hit of game.

1:18—Keltner dies on base.

1:24—Bob Elliott muffs Jim Hegan's bounder for first error.

1:27—Mitchell pops out and band plays "Pop Goes the Weasel."

1:27—Hegan steals second.

1:35—Lou Boudreau, hero of playoff, fans for Sain's third strikeout.

1:36—Joe Gordon gets second Cleveland hit, to left center.

1:39—Keltner fans as Gordon beats ball to second on hit and run.

1:43—Torgeson draws a walk from Feller and is first Brave on base.

1:48—Torgeson steals second.

1:51—Hegan gets third Cleveland hit.

1:52—Hegan sacrificed to second by Feller.

1:54—Umpires consult with Feller about habit of putting fingers to lips.

1:56—Marv Rickert gets clean single to right in fifth for first hit off Feller.

1:57—Salkeld sacrifices Rickert to second.

2:00—Larry Doby gets broken-bat single over second.

2:04—Rickert grabs Keltner's hard drive to quell Indian uprising.

2:15—Brief flurry of excitement when Feller appeared to have been injured covering first on Torgeson's grounder to Robinson.

2:25—Coach Bill McKechnie squawks to the plate umpire about Salkeld's foot being out of batter's box.

2:26—Salkeld walks to start last of eighth and be third Boston player on base. Phil Masi goes in to run for him.

2:28—Mike McCormick sacrifices Masi to second.

2:29—Eddie Stanky gets intentional pass and Sibby Sisti runs for him.

2:31—Masi nearly nipped off second, and Boudreau squawks at decision.

2:33—Tommy Holmes slices hit down third-base line to score Masi, sending Sisti to third and taking second himself on throw-in.

2:41—Elliott overthrows first base on what should have been an easy out, ending the game, Keltner taking second on the error.

2:42—Walt Judnich called out on strikes for third out and Braves swarm around Sain in noisy acclaim. Feller, who came so close to a pitching masterpiece, and lost, disappears down dugout steps with his thoughtful and morose teammates.

GENE BEARDEN PRAISED BY MANAGER BOUDREAU

Cleveland Pilot Modest About His Part In Playoff Victory Over Red Sox

Boston, Oct. 4 (AP)—While the screaming victory celebration in the visitors' dressing room at Fenway Park was at its height today, Lou Boudreau called a meeting of the Cleveland Indians squad.

That's an indication of how the Indians took their 8-to-3 victory over the Red Sox in the first pennant playoff in American League history.

They celebrated, joyously and noisily. That was only natural for a team that brought the pennant to Cleveland for the first time since 1920 and did it the hard way after almost blowing their big chance. But through the noise and handshaking and fond embraces there always was a note of solemnity. It was obvious that they believed their job wasn't finished. They still have to face a World Series with the Boston Braves day after tomorrow.

Playoff Box Score

CLEVELAND	Ab	R	H	O	A		BOSTON	Ab	R	H	O	A
Mitchell,lf	5	0	1	0	0		DiMaggio,cf	4	0	0	3	0
Clark,1b	2	0	0	5	0		Pesky,3b	4	1	1	3	4
Robinson,1b	2	1	1	9	0		Williams,lf	4	1	1	1	0
Boudreau,ss	4	3	4	3	5		Stephens,ss	4	0	1	2	4
Gordon,2b	4	1	1	2	3		Doerr,2b	4	1	1	2	3
Keltner,3b	5	1	3	0	6		Spence,rf	1	0	0	1	0
Doby,cf	5	1	2	1	0		Hitchcock	0	0	0	0	0
Kennedy,rf	2	0	0	0	0		Wright	0	0	0	0	0
Hegan,c	3	1	0	6	1		Goodman,1b	3	0	0	7	1
Bearden,p	3	0	1	0	2		Tebbetts,c	4	0	1	5	1
							Galehouse,p	0	0	0	0	0
							Kinder,p	2	0	0	0	1
Totals	35	8	13	27	17		Totals	30	3	5	27	14

1Walked for Spence in ninth.
2Ran for Hitchcock in ninth.

Cleveland	1	0	0	4	1	0	0	1	1—8
Boston	1	0	0	0	0	2	0	0	0—3

Errors—Gordon, Williams. Runs batted in—Boudreau (2), Keltner (3), Hegan, Stephens, Doerr (2). Two base hits—Doby (2), Keltner, Pesky. Home runs—Boudreau (2), Keltner, Doerr. Sacrifices—Kennedy (2), Robinson. Double plays—Hegan-Boudreau, Gordon, Boudreau, Robinson, Bearden, Gordon, Robinson, Stephens-Doerr-Goodman, Stephens, Doerr, Goodman. Left on bases—Cleveland, 7, Boston, 5. Base on balls—Bearden, 5 (Spence (2), Galehouse, Goodman, Hitchcock), Galehouse, 1 (Bearden) Kinder, 3 (Bearden, Hegan, Gordon). Strikeouts—Bearden, 6 (Goodman (2), Doerr, Stephens, Spence, Pesky), Galehouse, 1 (Hegan), Kinder, 2 (Hegan, Doby). Hits—Galehouse, 5 in 3 innings (none out in fourth), Kinder, 8 in 6. Wild pitch—Kinder. Winning pitcher—Bearden. Losing pitcher—Galehouse. Umpires—McGowan (plate), Summers (first base), Rommel (second base), Berry (third base). Time—2:24. Attendance—33,957.

BLACK WILL GET $40,380

Indians' Ailing Pitcher Benefits From Red Sox Game

CLEVELAND, Sept. 22 (P)—Paid attendance of 76,772 at tonight's game assured Don Black, injured Cleveland pitcher, of approximately $40,380 from the gate receipts. President Bill Veeck of the Indians had promised that Black would receive net receipts over the 25,000 advance sale, minus the share of the visiting Red Sox.

Black, still in serious condition at Charity Hospital from a cerebral hemorrhage suffered when he was at bat against the Browns Sept. 13, did not know of his good fortune.

Indians Capture World Series Beating Braves 4-3 In Vital Game

Gene Bearden Does Brilliant Relief Job To Protect Victory

BY BILL LEE
Courant Sports Editor.

Boston, Oct. 11. - The Cleveland Indians won the championship of baseball today with a 4 to 3 decision over the Boston Braves.

The Braves came from three runs behind to make a heart-stopping rally in the eighth and they had the tying run on first with nobody out in the ninth, but the breaks went against them in critical situations.

Cleveland used its two best pitchers, with Bob Lemon going as far as the eighth and Gene Bearden coming in to help him nail down the sixth game victory in a finish that had every man, woman and child in the crowd of 40,103 holding their breath. The result gave Cleveland the World Series, four games to two.

Try Behind Voiselle.

The Braves, trailing two games to three, tried to win the tying contest behind Bill Voiselle, one of their uncertain secondary pitchers, but the righthander from Ninety Six, S. C., needed more nearly perfect support to get by.

The Indians scored one in the third, two in the sixth and another in the eighth. But two of these runs would not have scored with just a little better than ordinary fielding by Tommy Holmes and Earl Torgeson.

Sixth Game Boxscore

CLEVELAND (A)	ab	r	h	o	a	e	rbi
Mitchell, lf	4	1	1	3	0	0	0
Kennedy, lf	1	0	0	1	0	0	0
Doby, rf	4	0	2	1	0	0	0
Boudreau, ss	3	0	1	2	2	0	1
Gordon, 2b	4	1	1	3	0	0	0
Keltner, 3b	4	1	1	0	3	0	0
Tucker, cf	3	1	1	3	0	0	0
Robinson, 1b	4	0	2	13	0	0	1
Hegan, c	4	0	1	2	2	0	1
Lemon, p	3	0	0	3	0	0	0
Bearden, p	1	0	0	1	0	0	0
Totals	35	4	10	27	15	0	4
BOSTON (N)	ab	r	h	o	a	e	rbi
Holmes, rf	5	1	2	1	0	0	0
Dark, ss	4	0	1	0	1	0	0
Torgeson, 1b	4	1	1	5	1	0	0
Elliott, 3b	3	1	3	4	3	0	0
Rickert, lf	3	0	0	5	0	0	0
Conatser, cf	1	0	0	0	0	0	1
Salkeld, c	2	0	0	4	1	0	0
Masi, c	1	0	1	3	0	0	1
M. McCormick, cf	4	0	1	2	0	0	1
Stanky, 2b	1	0	0	3	2	0	0
Voiselle, p	1	0	0	0	0	0	0
Spahn, p	0	0	0	0	1	0	0
a-F. McCormick	1	0	0	0	0	0	0
b-Sisti	1	0	0	0	0	0	0
z-Ryan	0	0	0	0	0	0	0
Totals	31	3	9	27	9	0	3

Cleveland .... 001 002 010—4
Boston .... 000 100 020—3

Two base hits, Mitchell, Boudreau, Torgeson, Masi; home run, Gordon; sacrifice, Voiselle; left on bases, Cleveland 7, Boston 7; bases on balls, off Lemon 4, Voiselle 2, Bearden 1; struck out, by Voiselle 2, Lemon 1, Spahn 4; hits, off Voiselle 7 in 7, Lemon 8 in 7 1-3, Spahn 3 in 2, Bearden 1 in 1 2-3; hit by pitcher, Boudreau (by Voiselle); balk, Lemon; double plays, Tucker to Robinson, Lemon to Boudreau to Robinson, Gordon to Boudreau to Robinson, Elliott to Stanky to Torgeson, Hegan to Robinson; winning pitcher, Lemon; losing pitcher, Voiselle; umpires.- Summers (A) plate; Stewart (N) 1b; Grieve (A) 2b, Barr (N) 3b; foul lines Paparella (A), Pinelli (N); time, 2:16; attendance, 40,103. a-F. McCormick grounded out for Voiselle in 7th; b-Sisti popped out for Spahn in 9th; z-Ryan ran for Stanky in 9th.

Casey Stengel Named Manager Of Yanks To Succeed Bucky Harris

New York, Oct. 12.—(AP.)—Casey Stengel, one of baseball's most colorful characters, today returned to the majors as manager of the New York Yankees for the next two years.

Fresh from a pennant and play-off victory with Oakland of the Pacific Coast League, Stengel flew in for a conference with Yankee officials last night that won for him one of the most coveted jobs in the game.

No salary terms were announced by President Dan Topping but it was understood that Casey will be paid about $25,000 a year under a two-year contract.

Stengel, freed by President Clarence (Brick) Laws of the Oakland Club to negotiate with the Yanks, said he had not made a decision on his coaches George Kelly, who worked under Johnny Neun and Bucky Walters at Cincinnati, and Neun were believed to be in line.

"The owners have promised to back me up," said Stengel in a press conference shortly after President Dan Topping of the club had announced his new manager. "I'll see what I need but I plan to go slow. You can tear a club down a lot faster than you can build it up."

Stan Musial Is Most Valuable In National League

New York, Dec. 2.   (AP.) - Stan Musial, the pitchers' nightmare, was the most valuable player in the National League in 1948.

The voting of the baseball writers wasn't close as the lean St. Louis Cardinal outfielder piled up an impressive margin.

If the pitchers voted, instead of the writers, it probably would have been unanimous, for Musial was a terror at the plate all season. He won as many races as Citation, leading with a .376 average, 135 runs, 230 hits, 131 runs-batted-in, 46 doubles and 18 triples.

Ralph Kiner of Pittsburgh and Johnny Mize of New York tied for home run laurels with 40, but Musial was right behind with 39.

Nov. 24

Hack Wilson, Former Star In Big League, Dies At 48

Hack Wilson, once a rebellious baseball star who last week advised youngsters to heed the advice of their elders and save their money, died yesterday in the City Hospitals. He was 48.

During the last year the former National League home-run champion had worked as a laborer with the City Parks Department and as manager of a swimming pool in Druid Hill Park.

His advice to the youth of the nation was given during an appearance on the "We, The People" radio program in New York.

Funeral Rites Incomplete

Funeral arrangements had not been completed last night. Friends were attempting to locate his second wife, Hazel, who was understood to be somewhere in Pennsylvania, and two sisters, who were reported to be residents of Philadelphia.

His last illness was diagnosed as internal hemorrhages complicated by a condition similar to pneumonia. He was brought to the hospital by a friend at 4.30 P.M. Monday.

Sometimes called one of baseball's "bad boys," Wilson had his best season in 1930 with the Chicago Cubs.

Hit 56 Homers

That year he hit 56 home runs, a record never equaled in the National League and only four less than Babe Ruth's high.

Waitkus's Doctor Expects First Sacker To Recover

Chicago, June 15. (AP.) - Eddie Waitkus, star Philadelphia Phillies first baseman, was shot and seriously wounded early today by a bobby sox baseball fan who had a secret crush on him. Waitkus, 28, was shot near the heart with a .22 caliber rifle bullet. The girl had lured him to her room in the fashionable Edgewater Beach Hotel. Illinois Masonic Hospital described his condition as "fair to poor."

Waitkus's physician said his condition was "serious" but that the bleeding was under control and he was getting along "as well as can be expected." He said he expected Waitkus to recover unless there were unusual complications.

A priest who visits Catholic patients at the hospital visited Waitkus's room several times, but hospital attendants said this was not unusual and did not indicate his condition was growing worse.

Later tonight, a lung specialist called in on the case said Waitkus's condition was "much improved but still guarded." He said the crisis might come any time during the night. The ballplayer was getting oxygen through a tube.

Ruth Steinhagen, 19, six foot, dark haired typist, gave a lengthy statement in which she related an urge to kill Waitkus "kept occurring to me all the time" for about two years. Friends said she had a crush on Waitkus, although the girl admitted she never had met him. The only times she saw him before was on the baseball field.

She told police she wanted to "do something exciting in my life."

Miss Steinhagen gave a statement relating details of the shooting to assistant state's attorney and Police Captain John T Warren. Later, as it was read back to Miss Steinhagen, State's Attorney John S. Boyle commented to her:

"Young lady, I hope you realize this is a serious offense."

"Oh," she replied, "it's just a simple shooting."

Ruth's mother, Mrs. Edith Steinhagen, said the girl had visited two psychiatrists who told her "nothing was wrong with her except that she should forget about Waitkus." She said the family would "stand by" the girl.

She said that when Waitkus was traded from the Cubs to the Phillies last winter, Ruth threatened to move to Philadelphia to be near him. She said Ruth was "so crazy" about Waitkus that she tried to learn to speak Lithuanian when she learned he was of Lithuanian extraction.

Waitkus, a leading National League first baseman and a war veteran who saw combat service in the Pacific theater, was lured to the girl's room in response to a note she sent him that she had something "important" to tell him. She also had pleaded with him on the telephone to come to her room.

Police Captain John T. Warren said the girl told him she was "a fit case for a psychiatrist" and that she had undergone treatment for a nervous disorder. She said she had an "urge to kill somebody" which had been building up for about two years.

Confirmed Bachelor.

Girl friends from her North Side rooming house said Ruth "had a real crush on Eddie," who played with the Chicago Cubs for three years before he was traded to the Phillies last winter.

"She wrote him lots of letters," said Joyce Stingley, 20, who roomed across the hall. "She phoned him whenever he was in town."

Her letters and phone calls went unanswered, Waitkus' sister, Mrs. Paul Kasperwicz, said in Boston today that Eddie was "a confirmed bachelor" who had no real romantic interest as far she knew.

Waitkus was extremely popular with Chicago Cubs fans. The Phillies, who stay at the Edgewater Beach Hotel, began a series with the Cubs here yesterday.

Ruth packed a suitcase, a .22 rifle and a pairing knife with a three and a half inch blade and checked into the hotel Monday afternoon. She gave a bellboy $5 to deliver a note to Waitkus' room. The note said:

"Mr. Waitkus It's extremely important that I see you as soon as possible.

"We're not acquainted, but I have something of importance to speak to you about. I think it would be to your advantage to let me explain it to you.

"As I'm leaving the hotel the day after tomorrow, I'd appreciate it greatly if you could see me as soon as possible.

"My name is Ruth Anne Burns, and I'm in Room 1297-A.

"I realize that this is a little out of the ordinary, but as I said, it's rather important.

"Please, come soon. I won't take up much of your time, I promise."

Re-Enacts Shooting.

Waitkus, returning to his room late last night, found the note and telephoned Miss Steinhagen, but she said she insisted that he see her in person.

She later re-enacted the shooting for police and gave this version:

Waitkus knocked on her door. She put the paring knife in the pocket of her skirt and opened the door, intending to stab Waitkus as he entered. But he hurried past her, sat in a chair and asked her what she wanted.

She said, "I have a surprise for you," reached into the closet and grabbed the rifle.

"For heaven's sake, what's going on here?" Waitkus asked as he jumped from the chair.

"For two years you've bothered me. Now you're going to die," she answered. She shot him at close range. She said she started to reload the rifle to shoot herself, but then she "blacked out."

She notified hotel authorities that "I just shot a man," she surrendered to hotel detective Edward Purdy.

Waitkus regained consciousness about two hours later at the hospital. Police said Miss Steinhagen did not answer when Waitkus asked her, "Why did you do it?"

The girl was taken to the women's lockup at downtown police headquarters and was held without charge. Dr. Edward J. Kelleher, director of the municipal court psychiatric institute, said she "apparently is either schizophrenic or deep in the influence of a major hysteria." (A schizophrenic is a person with a split personality.)

Ruth said she became a baseball and Waitkus fan in particular after watching him play in the first baseball game she ever saw July 7, 1946. Waitkus then was with the Cubs.

"He reminds me of everybody, especially my father," she said.

June 6

Trio Continues Damage Suits

Baseball Commissioner Tells 'Outlaws' to Apply to League Heads

Washington, D. C. (AP)—Baseball Commissioner A. B. Chandler extended an offer late Sunday to major and minor league players who jumped to Jorge Pasquel's outlawed Mexican league three years ago to reinstate them in organized baseball if they apply.

The jumpers were suspended by the commissioner in 1946 for five years after accepting large bonuses and salaries to play below the border. Many of them now are playing on Canadian teams, since Pasquel stopped offering his huge inducements.

Chandler said that the players need only apply to the presidents of their respective leagues. Ford Frick of the National league and Will Harridge of the American league.

June 6

Baseball's Jumpers

New York, N. Y. (AP)— The following players jumped organized baseball contracts to play in the Mexican league:

New York Giants — Pitchers Adrian Zabala, Sal Maglie, Harry Feldman and Ace Adams. Infielders Roy Zimmerman, Nap Reyes and George Hausmann, and outfielder Danny Gardella.

St. Louis Cardinals — Pitchers Max Lanier and Fred Martin and infielder Lou Klein.

Brooklyn Dodgers—Catcher Mickey Owen, outfielders Luis Olmo and Roland Gladu.

Philadelphia Athletics — Outfielder Roberto Estalella.

Washington Senators— Outfielder Roberto Ortiz and infielder Chile Gomez.

Chicago White Sox—Pitcher Alex Carrasquel.

Detroit Tigers—Infielder Murry Franklin.

Philadelphia Phillies—Outfielder Rene Monteagudo.

Chicago Cubs—Catcher Chico Hernandez.

Stricken Ernie (Tiny) Bonham Aware End Near Said, 'I Can't Get 'Em Out'

Pittsburgh, Sept 15 (AP)— Big Ernie Bonham knew what was coming.

He told it in the only language he knew, baseball.

"They're hitting me all over the field and I can't get them out."

He murmured this from a hospital cot to Pittsburgh Pirate Manager Billy Meyer.

Ernie died today just 16 hours later.

Complications from a recent appendicitis operation ended the diamond career of the 36-year-old veteran Pirate hurler.

Dr. Norman C. Ochsenhirt said Ernie's heart collapsed.

Ernie's wife, Ruth, who flew here from their Sacramento, Calif. home, was at his bedside.

Meyer and Pirate Coach Goldie Holt rushed to the hospital when they learned Bonham was sinking. They arrived seconds too late.

Bonham, jokingly dubbed "Tiny" because of his massive 210 pound, six foot frame, was believed to be recovering. He took a turn for the worse early today and was placed in an oxygen tent.

Stunned teammates had difficulty believing the news.

"I can't believe it." said Ralph Kiner. "Rip Sewell and I went to see him after yesterday's game and while he didn't look too good he assured us he would be up and about soon.

"As we left, he said. " 'So long Rip, I'm going to make it.' "

The big righthander was an ace of the New York Yankee pitching corps until the Pirates acquired him in an inter-league deal in 1946. He had won seven and lost four this year.

Sept. 22

Pirates Beat Don Black in Exhibition Game, 1-0

Indian Hurler Takes Mound for First Time Since Suffering Brain Injury Last Year

Don Black

Cleveland, Ohio (AP) Pitcher Don Black attempted to show the Cleveland Indians Wednesday night that he still belongs in the major leagues but he dropped a 1-0 decision to the Pittsburgh Pirates. Hurling his first regular game since he was felled by a strange brain injury last September during a game with St. Louis. Black worked in the first two innings of the exhibition contest. A crowd of 33,470 watched him walk four men and allow two doubles and a single. Stan Rojek scored the one Pittsburgh run on Pete Castiglione's single in the second. Double plays saved further worry in both innings.

Veeck Drives a Hearse As Indians Bury Pennant

By The Associated Press

CLEVELAND, Sept. 25. The Indians buried their pennant tonight in a grave behind the stadium's center-field fence and topped it with a tombstone.

Gagster to the end, Tribe President Bill Veeck, top hat and all, drove a horse-drawn hearse at the head of a pre-game funeral procession. Manager Lou Boudreau and his coaches were pallbearers.

Veeck added to the realism by wiping his eyes as he circled the field. The 35,000 fans howled.

On the cardboard tombstone was the simple inscription: "1948 Champs."

KINER'S 54TH HELPS PIRATES WHIP REDS

Pittsburgh Wins Night Game by 3-2 as Chesnes Holds Cincinnati to 4 Hits

PITTSBURGH, Sept. 30 (AP)— Ralph Kiner walloped his 54th home run of the season tonight and set a few more records as the Pittsburgh Pirates beat the Cincinnati Reds, 3—2, before 9,416 fans. Bob Chesnes allowed only four hits, two of them in the ninth when the Reds scored both their runs.

Kiner's long drive, which cleared the scoreboard clock in left field, set a new National League record for the most home runs hit by a player in a month. The old mark of fifteen was set by Fred (Cy) Williams of Philadelphia in May, 1923. The American League mark of eighteen belongs to Rudy York of Detroit. He turned the trick in August, 1937.

Oct. 6

Preacher Roe Gives Six Hits

Hodges' Single Scores Robinson in Second With Only Run

By SAM LEVY
Of The Journal Staff

New York, N. Y. The Brooklyn Dodgers pushed across their first run of the 46th world series in the second inning here Thursday, and that was all they needed to square matters with the New York Yankees before 70,053 fans at Yankee stadium. Elwin (Preacher) Roe, spindly 31 year old southpaw from Hardy, Ark., hurled six hit ball to nose out Vic Raschi in the second straight 1-0 game of the series.

This was the first time in world series history in which two such masterpieces had been pitched, let alone in succession.

Brooklyn scored when Jackie Robinson doubled to the left field corner, took third when Jerry Coleman fell after catching Gene Hermanski's foul and scored on Gil Hodges single to left.

Oct. 2

Win Pennants on Final Day

New Yorkers Edge Out Red Sox, 5-3; Brooklyn Beats Phils, 9-7

By the Associated Press

The New York Yankees and the Brooklyn Dodgers will open the 1949 world series in the Yankee stadium Wednesday following the tightest major league pennant races in 41 years.

Both world series foes clinched their pennants Sunday the final day of the season. The Yankees gained American league honors by dusting off the Boston Red Sox, 5-3, before 68,055 fans at the Yankee stadium. The victory enabled the Yanks to break a first place stalemate with the Red Sox and win by one game.

Brooklyn nailed down the National's flag by outslugging the Philadelphia Phillies, 9-7, in 10 innings at Philadelphia to finish one game in front of the St. Louis Cardinals. The Cardinals beat the Cubs, 13-5, in Chicago to no avail.

The Finish at a Glance

AMERICAN LEAGUE

	W	L	Pct.	GB
New York	97	57	.630	..
Boston	96	58	.623	1

NATIONAL LEAGUE

	W	L	Pct.	GB
Brooklyn	97	57	.630	..
St. Louis	96	58	.623	1

GB—Games behind.

For the Yanks, it will be their 16th appearance in baseball's blue ribbon classic. The Dodgers will be making their fifth bid to win baseball's highest honor. They have yet to win a series. The Yanks have 11 series scalps dangling from their belts.

There have been close races in either the National or American league before but the last day decisions in both leagues this year was unmatched since 1908.

Oct. 5

One Bad Pitch Beats Dodgers

Round Tripper Decides Duel Between Reynolds and Newcombe

By SAM LEVY
Of The Journal Staff

New York, N. Y.—You can't fool an old pro, especially one like Tom Henrich, who as a member of the Milwaukee Brewers in 1937 parleyed a 3c stamp into fame and fortune with the New York Yankees. Don Newcombe, Brooklyn pitcher, made only one bad pitch, just one, in the ninth inning of the 1949 baseball world series opener at Yankee stadium Wednesday afternoon and the old pro rifled it into the right field pavilion for a home run and a 1-0 Yankee triumph over Brooklyn's National league Dodgers.

One bad pitch, that's all it took to send 66,224 daffy fans on their way talking about the old pro. They will remember this one for a long, long time. There have been many thrill packed games in the stadium over the years, but none like the one Henrich broke up with his tremendous drive off Newcombe.

Homer Did It!

Brooklyn (N)	AB	R	H	C
Reese, ss	4	0	1	4
Jorgensen, 3b	3	0	1	2
Snider, cf	4	0	0	3
Robinson, 2b	4	0	0	4
Hermanski, lf	3	0	0	0
Furillo, rf	3	0	0	0
Hodges, 1b	2	0	0	4
Campanella, c	2	0	0	11
Newcombe, p	3	0	0	0
Totals	28	0	2	*28

*None out when winning run was scored.

New York (A)	AB	R	H	C
Rizzuto, ss	4	0	0	3
Henrich, 1b	4	1	1	9
Berra, c	3	0	0	3
DiMaggio, cf	3	0	0	2
Lindell, lf	3	0	1	0
Johnson, 3b	3	0	0	5
Mapes, rf	3	0	0	4
Coleman, 2b	3	0	1	1
Reynolds, p	3	0	2	1
Totals	29	1	5	28

Brooklyn (N) . 0 0 0 0 0 0 0 0 0—0
New York (A) . 0 0 0 0 0 0 0 0 1—1

Pirates Grab Bonus Hurler For $100,000

Bucs Take Contract Off Hands of Movie Producer Stephanie

Los Angeles, Jan. 31.—(AP.)—The Pittsburgh Pirates paid a record $100,000 today for an 18-years-old southpaw pitcher fresh out of high school.

He is Paul Pettit, a strapping, six-feet-two, 205-pounder, who stopped chewing gum long enough to sign a contract that will bring him a small fortune, win or lose.

The $100,000, of which Pettit gets the most, is believed to be the highest price ever paid a rookie untried in professional baseball.

The deal, an odd one with a bizarre Hollywood twist, was consumated in a movie agent's swank office on the Sunset Strip, with General Manager Roy Hamey of the Pittsburgh Pirates giving informal agreement that it was a hundred grand transaction.

Hamey said the $100,000 figure was "a good guess" and added that Pettit, who just last Friday got his diploma from tiny Marbonne High School at nearby Lomita, will play for the Pirate-owned New Orleans club of the double-A Southern Association.

The signing ended a scramble by several major league clubs known to be deeply interested in getting the fast-ball tossing athlete.

Dissatisfied Outfielder To Join Oakland

Wakefield Convinced By Chandler During Phone Conversation

Detroit, May 26. (UP.)—Dick Wakefield, baseball's riotous rebel, meekly agreed to report to a minor league team at Oakland, Calif., today on the "advice" of Commissioner A. B. Chandler.

The dulcet southern tones of the commissioner's voice caused a complete turn-about in Wakefield's position in less than an hour. Vowing heated protests, he telephoned the commissioner to protest his sale to Oakland by the New York Yankees. He had even threatened to challenge baseball rules in the courts if he did not get satisfaction.

But after he talked to Chandler and was told that his sale to Oakland was perfectly legal Wakefield suddenly pulled his turnabout. He said he will report to Oakland within 48 hours and "hit .400 to show George Weiss of the Yankees what a poor judge of baseball players he is."

Wakefield's decision apparently ended, for the moment at least, a bitter battle with the Yankees—a battle which began almost as soon as the one-time bonus sensation was traded by Detroit during the winter.

He first was a holdout, then refused to report to the Chicago White Sox when he was sold by the Yankees, and finally protested his sale to Oakland after the White Sox deal was cancelled by the baseball commissioner.

Red Sox Rout Browns 20-4 With 23 Hits

Dropo Wallops Homer, Stephens and Vollmer Hammer Two Apiece

Boston, June 7.—(AP)—Boston's Red Sox scattered 23 hits over and out of Fenway Park today in running out their largest score of the season, a 20-4 victory over the oft-beaten St. Louis Browns.

Boston, June 8.—(AP)—Offensive baseball records were shot to bits today as Boston's Red Sox slashed four St. Louis pitchers for 28 hits and a humiliating 29-4 victory over the last place Browns.

As a small crowd of 5105 yelled for more, the batting crazed Sox using friendly Fenway Park as a private hitting ground established these new marks:

The most runs in one game in modern baseball—formerly 27 by Cleveland in the American League and 28 by St. Louis in the National.

The most total bases in one game, 60, formerly 55 by Cincinnati in the National League and 53 by New York in the American.

Most runs in two games, 49. The old record of 40 was held by both New York and these same Red Sox.

Most hits in two games, 51, formerly 46 by Philadelphia and Boston American League clubs.

The Sox also set records of their own, equalled some others and approached still other marks.

By whacking four doubles, Boston's Al Zarilla equalled a mark held by several players for one game.

The Sox also came within one of the major league record of eight homers in one game.

Bobby Doerr hit three and now has six for the season.

Ted Williams and Walt Dropo each hit two, making their totals 16 and 14.

In this current home stand, which ends Sunday with a double-header against Detroit, the Sox have scored 104 runs to their opponents' 37 in seven games. They have won six of the seven.

Other oddities in today's dilly of a batfest included pitcher Chuck Stobbs' four consecutive bases on balls. Stobbs won his fourth game.

BOSTON	ab	r	h	o	a	e	rbi
Vollmer, cf	7	1	1	3	0	0	2
Pesky, 3b	7	3	5	0	1	0	2
Williams, lf	5	3	2	4	0	0	5
Stephens, ss	6	4	3	5	3	0	3
Dropo, 1b	6	5	4	5	1	0	7
Zarilla, rf	7	4	5	0	0	0	0
Doerr, 2b	6	4	4	2	1	0	8
Batts, c	6	2	2	6	0	0	2
Stobbs, p	3	3	2	0	0	0	0
Totals	53	29	28	27	6	0	29
ST. LOUIS	ab	r	h	o	a	e	rbi
Lenhardt, lf	4	2	2	4	0	0	0
Kokos, rf	4	1	2	2	0	1	1
Lollar, c	3	0	1	0	0	0	0
Moss, c	1	0	0	2	0	0	0
Sievers, cf	4	0	1	3	0	0	2
Arft, 1b	3	0	1	5	0	0	1
Friend, 2b	4	0	1	5	0	0	0
Upton, ss	3	0	0	1	5	0	0
Thomas, 3b	3	1	0	2	3	0	0
Fannin, p	0	0	0	0	0	0	0
a-Garver	1	0	0	0	0	0	0
Marshall, p	1	0	0	0	0	0	0
Schacht, p	2	0	0	0	0	0	0
Ferrick, p	0	0	0	0	0	0	0
Totals	33	4	8	24	8	1	4

Boston .... 085 720 25x—29
St. Louis ...... 003 000 001— 4

2b, Zarilla 4, Batts, Arft, Stephens, Vollmer, Pesky 2; 3b, Stephens; hr, Williams 2, Dropo 2, Doerr 3; dp, Dropo (unassisted), Doerr to Stephens to Dropo; left, St. Louis 10, Boston 11; bb, off Fannin 4, Marshall 5, Schacht 2, Stobbs 7; so, by Schacht 2, Stobbs 5; ho, Fannin 7 in 2 innings, Marshall 7 in 1 2-3, Schacht 13 in 3 2-3, Ferrick 1 in 2-3; hbp, Stobbs (Arft); winner, Stobbs (4-1); loser, Fannin (1-3); u, Hubbard, Rommel and Paparella; t, 2:42; a, 5105. a—Garver fanned for Fannin in 3d.

Tigers Beat Yankees On Evers' Homer

Overtake Bombers In Game Marked by 11 Home Runs

Detroit, June 23. (AP) Hoot Evers of the Detroit Tigers smashed a two-run homer in the last of the ninth to turn back the New York Yankees, 10 to 9, tonight in a wild-hitting game marked by a record-breaking 11 home runs.

All 19 runs came across the plate via homers as the Yankees pounded out six while detroit got five in stretching its American League lead to two full games over New York.

The barrage of four-baggers eclipsed the former major league record of 10 home runs in a game. In addition, the teams by collecting five home runs between them in the fourth, tied the major league record for a single inning.

The Tiger's four homers in that frame tied the American League record by one team in a single inning, but was short of the National League mark.

Simmons To Hurl Today For Phils

Philadelphia, Sept. 8. (AP) Pfc Curt Simmons, of the United States Army, gets another chance to pitch for the pennant-driving Philadelphia Phillies tomorrow against the Boston Braves.

Simmons, one of the main reasons the Phils are leading the National League today, has won 17 and lost eight this year. He'll be trying for win No 18 with only two days' rest.

The 21-year-old left-hander from Egypt, Pa., leaves for Camp Atterbury, Ind., Sunday with the 28th Infantry Division, Pennsylvania National Guard, just called to Federal service.

The chances are unlikely that he'll pitch again except maybe for Uncle Sam. Officers of Curt's artillery unit have announced there will be liberal passes for the men in the hours before they leave for camp.

Ailing McCarthy Announces Retirement From Baseball

Williams May Be Out for Season, Awaits Surgery on Broken Elbow

Doctor Hopes Operation Today Will Enable Red Sox Slugger to Return This Year—

Gil Hodges Clouts Four Homers Against Braves

Brooklyn First Baseman Ties Major League Record As Brooklyn Club Romps to One-Sided 19-3 Triumph Over Boston Rivals

Brooklyn, Aug. 31. (AP) First baseman Gil Hodges blasted out four home runs to tie a major league record tonight as the Brooklyn Dodgers trounced the Boston Braves, 19-3.

Hodges connected in the second, third, sixth and eighth innings off Warren Spahn, Norm Roy, Bob Hall and Johnny Antonelli. He drove in nine runs on his circuit drives. He was at bat six times.

Only other players to hit four home runs in one major league game are Bobby Lowe of the 1894 Boston Nationals, Ed Delahanty of the 1896 Philadelphia Nationals, Lou Gehrig of the 1932 New York Yankees, Chuck Klein of the 1936 Philadelphia Phils and Pat Seerey of the 1948 Chicago White Sox.

Hodges also tied a major league record for his total bases in a single game, 17. Lowe set the mark in 1894 when he added a single to his four homers and Delahanty tied it two years later with four homers and a single.

In his other two times at bat, Hodges singled and grounded out.

Klein and Seerey performed their feats in extra inning games. Klein hit his fourth in the tenth inning and Seerey his fourth in the 11th. Only Lowe and Gehrig hit their's in succession.

The 26-years-old slugger hit them all into the left field bleachers, the last sailing into the upper deck. Hodges now has tied his 1949 season total of 23 home runs.

BOSTON, July 12 (AP)—The Red Sox' pennant chances, already shackled with an eight-game deficit, suffered a bruising jolt today as X-rays disclosed Ted Williams had a fracture in the left elbow.

The jinx of exhibition contests sneaked up on the slugger yesterday in the first inning of the All-Star game in Comiskey Park, Chicago. Ted crashed into the left field wall hauling down a drive off the bat of Ralph Kiner, National League home-run king.

Surgeons will operate tomorrow to remove a bone fragment. The pessimistic pronouncement of the club physician, Dr. Ralph McCarthy, was that he hoped Ted would be back in the line-up before the season's end.

Arm Injured in First

Ted played eight innings yesterday, although he hurt his arm in the first frame. He knocked in a run to put the American eLaguers in a temporary lead and grabbed another Kiner slam in the third inning.

After he had been removed by American League manager Casey Stengel, Ted Went to the locker room and told Packy Schwartz, White Sox trainer, his elbow was paining. Schwartz worked on him for 30 minutes and then said: "He'll be O. K."

Gillette Inks New TV Pact With Baseball

Razor Company Buys Series Rights Through 1956 for Six Million

Cincinnati, Dec. 26. (AP) Baseball Commissioner A. B Chandler announced tonight that television rights for the World Series and major league all-star games through 1956 have been sold to the Gillette Safety Razor Co., for $6,000,000.

Chandler said that while the television hookup which will be used has not yet been determined "it is understood it will include the Mutual television stations in New York, Chicago and Boston."

The baseball commissioner said the money "will be applied in a large part to the baseball players' annuity and insurance plan."

Fluke Homer Ruins Mark For Maglie

Gus Bell's Hit Ends Scoreless Streak As Giants Win, 3-1

New York, Sept. 13—(AP)—One of the shortest, flukiest, wettest home runs ever hit in any ball park deprived Sal Maglie of a large helping of pitching immortality today.

The Giants righthander was only five putouts from shattering Carl Hubbell's National League record of 46⅓ consecutive scoreless innings. Then Gus Bell, Pittsburgh outfielder, plunked the sodden pellet against the screen bordering the right field foul line at the Polo Grounds, 257 feet from home plate. It was the only Pirate run, as New York won the game, called on account of rain after seven innings, 3-1.

Had the ball hit two feet to the right, it would have been a foul ball. A foot lower and it would have struck the wall and been held to a harmless single. But it hit the narrow screen which is place there to assist the umpires in telling foul balls from fair and fell back at the feet of Don Mueller, the Giants rightfielder.

Mueller picked up the ball and hurled it disgustedly back onto the soaked turf as Bell, who had hit only six previous homers this season, web-footed around the bases. Several thousand Giants fans huddled under the stands gave the offending Pirates a royal booing.

Dick Sisler Clouts Homer With Two Aboard In Tenth To Carry Phils Into Series

Brooklyn, Oct. 1.—(AP)—Dick Sisler, son of a Hall of Fame great, clinched the National League pennant for the Philadelphia Whiz Kids today, 4-1, with a 10-inning three-run homer to back up Robin Roberts' superb pitching job against the onrushing Brooklyn Dodgers in the last game of the season.

Young Roberts, celebrating his 24th birthday a day late, throttled a bases-loaded Dodger threat in the ninth to become the Phils' first 20-game winner since 1917 in the golden days of Grover Cleveland Alexander.

The handsome $25,000 bonus baby from the Michigan State campus, turned back the Dodgers with five hits in a throbbing contest watched by a turnaway crowd of 35,073.

One Ball and Two Strikes

Pulling the Phils out of a five-game losing tailspin that threatened to cost them their first flag since 1915, Roberts came through in real championship fashion.

Thus the Dodgers, who planned to sell tickets for a post-season tie playoff, ended their dramatic "miracle finish" two games out of first place. They missed their chance for a tie on the on the wings of Sisler's 13th homer of the year, a curling liner over Cal Abrams' head into the lower left field seats in the 10th.

Sisler, moved to the outfield last spring when Eddie Waitkus won back his first base job, took the count to one ball and two strikes before he ripped into Don Newcombe's next pitch for the homer that meant a World Series cut for every delirious Phil.

PHILADELPHIA	ab	r	h	o	a	e
Waitkus 1b	5	1	1	18	1	0
Ashburn cf	5	1	2	4	1	0
Sisler lf	5	1	1	4	0	0
Mayo lf	0	0	0	1	0	0
Ennis rf	4	0	2	2	0	0
Jones 3b	4	0	1	0	3	0
Hamner ss	4	0	1	2	4	0
Seminick c	3	0	1	1	0	0
a-Caballero	0	0	0	0	0	0
Lopata c	0	0	0	1	0	0
Goliat 2b	3	0	1	1	5	0
Roberts p	4	0	1	1	1	0
Totals	38	4	11	30	18	0
BROOKLYN	ab	r	h	o	a	e
Abrams lf	2	0	1	1	0	0
Reese ss	5	1	3	3	3	0
Snider cf	5	0	3	0	0	0
Robinson 2b	3	0	0	3	5	0
Furillo rf	4	0	0	2	0	0
Hodges 1b	4	0	0	9	0	0
Campanella c	3	0	1	3	0	0
Cox 3b	3	0	2	0	3	0
b-Russell	1	0	0	0	0	0
Newcombe p	3	0	3	2	0	0
c-Brown	1	0	0	0	0	0
Totals	33	1	5	30	17	0

Philadelphia 000 001 003 3—4
Brooklyn   000 001 000 0—1

2b, Reese; hr, Reese, Sisler; s, Roberts; dp, Reese, Robinson and Hodges, Roberts and Waitkus; left, Philadelphia 7, Brooklyn 5; bb, off Roberts 3, Newcombe 2; so, by Roberts 2, Newcombe 3; winner, Roberts (20-12); loser, Newcombe (19-11); u, Goetz, Dascoli, Jorda and Donatelli; t, 2:35; a, 35,073; A—Caballero ran for Seminick 9th; b—Russell struck out for Cox 10th; c—Brown fouled out for Newcombe 10th.

Jimmy Dykes Named Pilot Of Athletics After Mack Announces His Retirement

Ehlers Given Promotion In Front Office

Head of Farm System Handed New Position Of General Manager

Philadelphia, Oct. 18.—(AP)— Connie Mack, baseball's "Grand Old Man," resigned today after 50 years as manager of the Philadelphia Athletics.

And into his shoes as manager stepped Jimmy Dykes, 54, star third baseman of the Athletics when Connie Mack's team dominated the baseball picture two decades ago.

At the same time, Art Ehlers, 52, director of the American League club's farm system, was elevated to the position of general manager.

Although the lanky 87-years-old leader of the Athletics had been under fire for some time by sports fans as having outlived his usefulness, his resignation came as a surprise. The announcement was made at a press conference.

RICKEY SELLS ALL INTERESTS IN DODGER CLUB

2 Partners Buy Control Of Baseball Team For Reported $1,050,000

Brooklyn, Oct. 24 (AP)—Branch Rickey's two partners decided today to buy up his 25 per cent interest in the Brooklyn Dodgers for a reported $1,050,000 to gain control of the club.

Walter O'Malley, Dodger vice president, said he and Mrs. John L. Smith intend to "exercise prior rights" on Rickey's stock "well in advance" of the late January deadline. O'Malley and Mrs. Smith each own 25 per cent of the stock. The other 25 per cent is owned by Mrs. James Mulvey, daughter of the late Steve McKeever.

Yankees Rejoice, All But Woodling; He Cries

Yankee Stadium, N.Y., Oct. 7 (AP). The Yankees rejoiced over their thirteenth World Baseball Championship today, but Gene Woodling cried.

As the players romped into the dressing room after the 5-to-2 victory, the New York Leftfielder was a disconsolate figure.

With two out in the ninth, he had dropped Andy Seminick's long fly denying Young Ed Ford a pitching shutout.

Tears in his eyes, he brushed off his teammates and reporters sharply and went to his locker.

"Leave me alone awhile," he said.

Then later he said:

"It got in the sun, that's all. A guy can't catch what he can't see. But I wish, for Ford's sake, I'd got it."

Ford Was Happy

Across the room, 21-year-old Ford, one of the youngest men ever to win a World Series game, harbored no ill feeling either for Woodling or Manager Casey Stengel, who removed him in the last inning.

"Gee, that was a tough ball to catch," Ford said. "Gene was catching it going away and the sun was in his eyes when he looked back.

"I doubt if anybody could have caught it."

Ford, the Long Island rookie whose pitching in the late stages of the pennant race did much to bring the Yankees the flag, said he didn't blame Stengel for removing him.

The packed stands booed loudly when Stengel brought in Allie Reynolds to face Stan Lopata.

The Box Score

Philadelphia (N.)	Ab.	R.	H.	O.	A.
Waitkus, 1b	3	0	1	9	1
Ashburn, cf	4	0	1	3	0
Jones, 3b	4	0	2	0	4
Ennis, rf	3	0	1	1	0
Sisler, lf	4	0	0	2	0
2K. Johnson	0	1	0	0	0
Hamner, ss	4	0	1	2	2
Seminick, c	4	0	0	3	1
3Mayo	0	0	0	0	0
Goliat, 2b	4	0	1	4	4
Miller, p	0	0	0	0	0
Konstanty, p	2	0	1	0	1
1Caballero	1	0	0	0	0
Roberts, p	0	0	0	0	0
4Lopata	1	0	0	0	0
Totals	34	2	7	24	13

1Struck out for Konstanty in eighth.
2Ran for Sisler in ninth.
3Ran for Seminick in ninth.
4Struck out for Roberts in ninth.

New York (A.)	Ab.	R.	H.	O.	A.
Woodling, lf	4	1	2	4	0
Rizzuto, ss	4	0	0	2	4
Berra, c	4	2	2	10	0
DiMaggio, cf	3	1	2	1	0
Mize, 1b	3	0	1	5	1
Hopp, 1b	1	0	0	1	1
Brown, 3b	3	1	1	0	1
W. Johnson, 3b	1	0	0	0	0
Bauer, rf	3	0	0	1	0
Coleman, 2b	3	0	0	2	3
Ford, p	3	0	0	1	0
Reynolds, p	0	0	0	0	0
Totals	32	5	8	27	10

Philadelphia (N.) . . 0 0 0 0 0 0 0 2—2
New York (A.) . . . . 2 0 0 0 3 0 0 x—5

Errors — Goliat, Brown, Woodling. Runs batted in—Berra (2), DiMaggio, Brown, Bauer. Two-base hits—Jones, DiMaggio. Three-base hit—Brown. Home run—Berra. Double plays—Mize, Berra, Coleman, Rizzuto, Mize. Left on base—Philadelphia (N.), 7; New York (A.), 4. Base on balls—Ford, 1 (Waitkus). Strikeouts—Ford, 7 (Sisler, Ashburn, Goliat, Jones, Hamner, 2, Caballero). Konstanty, 3 (Ford, 2, DiMaggio); Reynolds, 1 (Lopata) Hits—Miller, 2 in 1-3 innings; Konstanty, 5 in 6 2-3; Roberts, 1 in 1. Ford, 7 in 8 2-3; Reynolds, 0 in 1-3. Hit by pitcher—Konstanty (DiMaggio), Ford (Ennis). Winning pitcher Ford. Losing pitcher—Miller. Umpires—Charlie Berry (A.), plate, Jocko Conlan (N.), first base, Bill McGowan (A.), second base, Dusty Boggess (N.), third base, Bill McKinley (A.), left-field foul line, Al Barlick (N.), right-field foul line. Attendance—68,098. Time—2:05.

Grover Alexander Dies After Lingering Illness

Death Comes to Baseball Immortal at 63; Won 373 Games During National League Career and Holds Record for Shutout Games With 90

St. Paul, Nebr., Nov. 4. (AP)—Grover Cleveland Alexander, a fabulous major league pitcher in his day, died tonight of a heart ailment.

Death came to the 63-years-old baseball immortal in the one rented room he occupied in a private home here. He had been living of late on $150 a month baseball pension.

Alexander had been in ill health in recent years he lost an ear to cancer but friends who saw him yesterday said he mentioned nothing about feeling ill.

Alexander got his last big baseball tribute in 1938 when he was voted into baseball's Hall of Fame at Cooperstown, N. Y.

Baseball Paper Claims Group Seeking To Buy Browns For Switch To Houston

St. Louis, Nov. 10. (AP). The Sporting News reported today William Zeckendorf of New York is negotiating for purchase of the St. Louis Browns with the idea of moving the American League club to Houston, Texas.

The Sporting News, national baseball weekly, said in a copyrighted article by its publisher, J. G. Taylor Spink, that Zeckendorf "already has interested a number of Texas multi-millionaires in the projected move."

Bill and Charlie DeWitt, owners of the Browns, were on a quail hunting trip and were not available for comment.

Others here denied knowledge of such negotiations.

Zeckendorf, head of the New York real estate firm of Webb and Knapp, recently tried to buy a 25 per cent interest in the Brooklyn Dodgers from Branch Rickey. He could not be reached immediately in New York

Later the St. Louis Star-Times said it was told by Zeckendorf in a long-distance telephone conversation:

"At present I have done nothing more than accept the invitation to join the group. So far, I haven't heard what progress has been made. At this time, I'd prefer not to name the Houston people involved. Let's just refer to them as 'a group of my close personal Texas friends.'"

MAYS' DEBUT

Giants, 8; Phils, 5

Philadelphia, May 25 (AP)—The New York Giants, who played sloppy ball in the field to give the Philadelphia Phillis a two-run edge in the seventh inning, exploded for five runs in the eighth and an 8-to-5 victory over the National League champions tonight.

NEW YORK						PHILADELPHIA					
	Ab.	R.	H.	O.	A.		Ab.	R.	H.	O.	A.
Stanky,2b	4	1	3	0	2	Waitkus,1b	5	1	4	8	0
L'kman,1b	5	0	2	11	0	Ashburn,cf	4	0	0	0	0
Mays,cf	5	0	0	4	0	Sisler,lf	5	0	1	3	0
Th'pson,3b	5	2	0	4	3	Ennis,rf	3	0	0	2	1
Westrum,c	2	1	2	4	1	W. Jo'es,3b	3	0	0	2	2
Irvin,rf	5	1	0	7	0	Hamner,ss	4	2	1	3	3
Dark,ss	5	1	1	3	3	Seminick,c	4	0	0	5	0
Th'ms'n,lf	4	2	1	0	0	Goliat,2b	4	1	4	4	2
Hearn,p	1	0	0	0	0	Church,p	3	0	1	1	0
1Mueller	1	0	0	0	0	Miller,p	0	0	0	0	0
Spencer,p	0	0	0	0	0	Konst'ty,p	0	0	0	1	2
2Jor'sen	1	0	0	0	0	3Whitman	1	0	0	0	0
8. Jones,p	0	0	0	0	0						
Totals	37	9	12	27	11	Totals	36	5	8	27	10

1Fouled out for Hearn in seventh.
2Flied out for Spencer in eighth.
3Flied out for Konstanty in ninth.

New York .... 0 1 0 1 0 2 1 5 0—8
Philadelphia .... 1 2 0 0 2 0 0 0—5

Errors—Lockman (2), Stanky, Dark. Ennis. Hamner. Runs batted in—Sisler. Hamner, Goliat, Waitkus. Dark (2). Westrum. Lockman (3). Thomson. Two-base hits—Stanky, Lockman, Waitkus. Three-base hit—Sisler. Home runs—Hamner, Goliat. Westrum. Sacrifice—Ashburn. Double plays—Goliat, Hamner, Waitkus; Ennis, Church. Left on base—New York, 8; Philadelphia, 7. Base on balls—Church, 4; Konstanty, 2; Hearn, 2. Strikeouts—Church, 5; Hearn, 1; Jones, 1. Hits—Hearn, 7 in 6 innings; Spencer, none in 1; Jones, 1 in 2; Church, 9 in 7. Miller, 2 in 1-3; Konstanty, 1 in 1 2-3. Winning pitcher—Spencer. Losing pitcher—Miller. Umpires—Goetz, Jorda, Dascoli. Time—2.52. Attendance—21,093.

Aug. 12

National				
Brooklyn	70	36	.660	—
New York	59	51	.536	13
Philadelphia	57	52	.523	14½
St. Louis	51	52	.495	17½
Boston	50	55	.476	19½
Cincinnati	49	58	.458	21½
Chicago	46	58	.442	23
Pittsburgh	44	64	.407	27

Yankees Recall Mantle, Again in Batting Form

By the Associated Press

DETROIT, Aug. 21.—The last time the Yankees were in town they shipped Mickey Mantle, boy wonder of the springtime, off to Kansas City for more seasoning.

The Yankees returned here yesterday, and during a twi-night doubleheader announced they were bringing Mickey back from their American Association farm club because he apparently had regained his batting eye. Through Sunday, Mickey had hit .364 in 40 games for Kansas City.

Bob Feller Hurls No-Hitter, Third Of Career As Indians Down Detroit Tigers Twice

Cleveland, July 1.—(AP)—Bob Feller today became the first pitcher in modern major league baseball history to hurl three no-hit games. He and the Cleveland Indians defeated the Detroit Tigers in the first game of a doubleheader 2-1.

Tribesmen also won the second, 2-0, to maintain their record of beating Detroit in every game they have played this season. The victory record is now 10.

Feller pitched his first no-hitter against the Chicago White Sox on opening day, April 17, 1940. His second masterpiece was achieved against the Yankees in New York, April 30, 1946. The 32-year-old righthander also has pitched 10 one-hitters, a major league record.

The famous Cy Young and Larry Corcoran were the others to notch three no-hitters. Young pitched his first in 1897 for Cleveland in the National League. He hurled his second for Boston in the American in 1904 and his third for the same Red Sox in 1907. Corcoran pitched all his no-hitters for the Chicago Nationals in 1880, 1882 and 1884.

Faced 31 Batters

Feller pitched to 31 batters. He struck out five including the last batter, Vic Wertz, who only about a month ago ruined a no-hit bid by Bob Lemon, another Indian righthander. Feller walked three.

The Tigers got their run in the fourth when Johnny Lipon reached first on shortstop Ray Boone's error, stole second, went to third when Feller threw wild on an attempted pickoff, and scored on George Kell's long fly.

Bob Cain was the Tiger loser. The Indians snapped a 1-1 tie in the eighth when Sam Chapman tripled with one out and scored on a single by Luke Easter.

Easter also batted in Cleveland's first run in the opening inning. Dale Mitchell led off with a single, raced to third on another one bagger by Bob Avila and crossed the plate on Easter's infield out. It was Cleveland's ninth straight victory over Detroit.

10 One-Hitters

He also has pitched 10 one-hitters, which is tops for the majors. The best in the National League was five, by Pete Alexander. Before Feller, the American League's best was seven, by Cleveland Addie Joss.

The pressure was building up against the 31-year-old hurler by the second as the Tigers came to bat in the ninth. Charley Keller went in as a pinch-hitter for Gerry Priddy and flied out to right. George Kell went out on a long fly to Bob Kennedy in right.

Then Vic Wertz, who ruined a perfect game for Tribesman Bob Lemon by smashing a homer in the eighth on May 29, came to bat. He fouled the first, missed the second and the next three were balls. Wertz watched the next slip by the outside corner for a strike and the game was over.

In the second contest Bob Chakales, 23-year-old rookie right hander, allowed the Tigers only four infield singles in pitching his first major league shutout. It was his third victory against two defeats.

Hurling Duel

He engaged Ted Gray in a hurling duel until the sixth, when the Tribe pushed over two runs. Bob Avila walked, Sam Chapman singled and Avila then scored on a single by Luke Easter. A double by Bob Kennedy brought in Easter.

In all, Gray, the loser, gave up six hits. Virgil Trucks relieved him at the start of the eighth.

(First Game) CLEVELAND	ab	r	h	o	a	e	rbi
Mitchell lf	3	1	1	3	0	0	0
Avila 2b	4	1	1	3	0	0	0
Chapman cf	4	0	1	1	0	0	0
c-Nielsen	0	0	0	0	0	0	0
Doby cf	4	0	0	0	0	0	0
Easter, 1b	3	0	1	13	0	0	2
Simpson 1b	0	0	0	0	0	0	0
Rosen 3b	4	0	0	4	0	0	0
Kennedy rf	4	0	0	3	0	0	0
Boone ss	3	0	1	2	5	1	0
Hegan c	3	0	1	3	0	0	0
Feller p	2	0	0	0	2	0	0
Totals	28	2	6	24	8	2	2
DETROIT	ab	r	h	o	a	e	rbi
Lipon ss	3	1	0	1	3	0	0
a-Hutchinson	1	0	0	0	0	0	0
Berry ss	0	0	0	0	2	0	0
Priddy 2b	3	0	0	2	1	0	0
b-Keller	1	0	0	0	0	0	0
Kell 3b	4	0	0	1	0	0	1
Wertz rf	3	0	0	1	0	0	0
Evers lf	3	0	0	5	0	0	0
Kryhoski 1b	3	0	0	8	1	0	0
Ginsberg c	3	0	0	3	1	0	0
Groth cf	3	0	0	1	0	0	0
Cain p	2	0	0	1	1	0	0
Totals	28	1	0	24	8	0	0

Cleveland .... 100 000 01x—2
Detroit ...... 000 100 000—1

3b, Chapman; sb, Lipon; left, Detroit 3, Cleveland 7; bb, Cain 3, Feller 3; so, Cain 3, Feller 5; Winner, Feller (11-2); loser, Cain (6-6); u, Berry, Napp, Hurley, Lassarella; t, 2:05. a—Hutchinson flied out for Lipon in 8th; b—Keller flied out for Priddy in 9th; c—Nielsen ran for Chapman in 8th.

SMALL MAN IN BIG LEAGUES: A VEECK STUNT

Ed Gaedel, a midget, batting for Frank Saucier of the Browns yesterday. Bob Swift is the Tigers' catcher and the umpire is Ed Hurley.

Wide World Photo

By The Associated Press

ST. LOUIS, Aug. 19 — Bob Cain, Detroit Tiger pitcher, walked the first St. Louis Brownie to face him today—he didn't know what else to do with him. He was a midget.

The Browns used Ed Gaedel, 26-year-old Chicago stunt man, as a pinchhitter for Outfielder Frank Saucier to start off their half of the first inning in the second game of a double-header.

Umpire Ed Hurley questioned Gaedel's eligibility, so the 3-foot, 7-inch man trotted back to the dugout and brought forth his signed contract with Bill Veeck, the new owner of the Browns, for proof.

Cain paused and tried to figure out how to pitch to Gaedel. The walk was the easiest way out.

Jim Delsing ran for Gaedel and the game returned to normal.

New Yorkers Defeated 2-0 After Taking 16 Straight

Pittsburgh's Howie Pollet Masters Sheldon Jones In Mound Duel by Turning in Six-Hitter; Stanky's Error Shatters Scoreless Tie

New York, Aug 28 (AP)—Howie Pollet shut out the tumbling New York Giants today on six hits as the Pittsburgh Pirates ended the longest winning streak in the National League since 1935, 16 games in a row, by winning 2-0.

A brilliant pitching duel between Pollet, the veteran left-hander, and the right-handed Sheldon Jones of the Giants collapsed with a loud bang in the eighth inning on errors by Eddie Stanky and Don Mueller.

PITTSBURGH	ab	r	h	o	a	e	rbi
Castiglione 3b	5	0	0	1	0	0	0
Metkovich 1b	3	0	1	11	0	0	0
Saffel rf	0	0	1	0	0	0	0
Thomas cf	5	1	2	1	0	0	0
Kiner lf	1	0	0	0	0	0	0
Bell rf	3	0	0	1	0	0	0
Phillips 1b	1	0	0	4	0	0	0
Garagiola c	1	0	0	2	1	0	0
McCullough c	1	1	1	1	0	0	0
Strickland ss	2	0	1	0	0	0	0
Cole 2b	3	0	2	2	0	0	0
Pollet p	3	0	0	0	0	0	0
Totals	29	2	3	27	12	0	0

NEW YORK	ab	r	h	o	a	e	rbi
Stanky 2b	4	0	1	3	3	1	0
Williams 2b	0	0	0	0	0	0	0
Dark ss	4	0	1	2	0	0	0
Mays cf	4	0	1	3	0	0	0
Irvin lf	4	0	1	0	0	0	0
Thomson 3b	4	0	3	2	2	0	0
Lockman 1b	3	0	0	11	1	0	0
Yvars c	3	0	0	4	1	0	0
Mueller rf	3	0	0	1	0	1	0
Jones p	2	0	0	1	2	1	0
Koslo p	0	0	0	0	0	0	0
a—Rigney	1	0	1	0	0	0	0
Kennedy p	0	0	0	0	0	0	0
Totals	33	0	6	27	11	3	2

Pittsburgh 000 000 020—2

2b. Garagiola, Kiner; s. Strickland, dp. Dark, Stanky and Lockman; Thomson, Stanky and Lockman; left, Pittsburgh 10, New York 6; bb. Jones 7, Koslo 1; so. Pollet 4; hr. Jones 3 in 7 innings (none out in 8th), Koslo 0 in 1, Kennedy 0 in 1; hbp. Jones (Garagiola); wp. Jones; winner. Pollet (5-10); loser. Jones (4-10); u. Dascoli, Stewart, Conlan and Gore; t. 2:35. a. 6,000. a—Rigney singled for Koslo in 8th.

N. Y. DEFEATS RED SOX TWICE; REYNOLDS HURLS NO-HIT, NO-RUN CONTEST

Yankees

New York, Sept 28 (AP)—The New York Yankees swamped the Boston Red Sox twice today to clinch their eighteenth American League pennant in 30 years, but the feat almost escaped notice as Allie Reynolds, the fire-baller from Oklahoma, spun his second no-hit game of the season in the opener.

Never before in the American League and only once before in the history of the major leagues had a hurler paralyzed enemy batsmen twice in a single campaign.

The wild scene in the Bombers' dressing room after the big Indian whomped the Hose, 8 to 0, even eclipsed the tumult of the "victory celebration" which followed Vic Raschi's 11-to-3 triumph in the decider.

Issues Four Walks

The triumphs boosted the Yanks' lead to 3½ games over second-place Cleveland and eliminated the Indians from the race. The Yanks have three games to play and the Indians two. The victories also clinched second place for Cleveland.

A crowd of 39,038 which had paid its way in to watch the champions sew up their third straight flag got double its money's worth as Reynolds, scoring his seventeenth decision of the year, permitted only four Bostons to reach first base on passes and choked them off right there. He gave the hemmed-in Sox nothing remotely resembling a safety.

Dodgers Beat Phils, 9-8, In 14th; Giants Triumph Over Braves, 3-2

The Box Score

Dodgers

BROOKLYN	Ab	R	H	O	A		PHILADELPHIA	Ab	R	H	O	A
Furillo.rf	7	1	2	2	0		Pellas'i.2b	6	1	2	5	6
Reese.ss	6	0	3	3	3		Ashburn.cf	8	0	4	2	0
Snider.cf	7	1	3	3	0		Jones.3b	4	0	1	3	3
Robi'n.2b	6	2	2	6	5		Ennis.lf	4	0	1	2	0
Camp'la.c	7	1	2	8	0		Brown.1b	2	1	1	1	1
Pafko.lf	7	0	1	7	2		Waitkus.1b	6	0	0	10	1
Hodges.1b	5	2	10	5			Clark.rf	1	0	1	0	0
Cox.3b	6	1	1	2	3		Nichol'n.rf	6	2	2	2	0
Roe.p	0	0	0	0	0		Hamner.ss	5	3	2	2	6
Branca.p	0	1	0	0	0		Semini'k.c	2	1	0	7	1
1Russell	1	0	0	0	0		Church.p	2	0	1	1	0
King.p	0	0	0	0	0		Drews.p	2	0	1	0	1
Labine.p	0	0	0	0	0		Roberts.p	1	0	0	0	1
2Belardi	1	0	0	0	0							
Erskine.p	0	0	0	0	0							
3Walker	1	0	1	0	0							
4Thom'on	0	1	0	0	0							
Newc'be.p	2	0	1	0	0							
Podbe'an	0	0	0	0	0							
Totals	56	9	17	42	18		Totals	53	8	15	42	21

1Fanned for Branca in fourth.
2Fanned for Labine in sixth.
3Doubled for Erskine in eighth.
4Ran for Walker in eighth.

Brooklyn 0 0 1 1 3 0 0 3 0 0 0 0 0 1—9
Phila'hia 0 4 2 0 2 0 0 0 0 0 0 0 0 0—8

Errors—Jones, Robinson. Runs batted in—Brown, Pellagrini (2), Ashburn (2), Church (2), Hamner, Reese, Pafko (2), Snider, Robinson (2), Walker (2), Furillo. Two-base hits—Jones, Hamner, Pellagrini, Snider, Walker, Campanella. Three-base hits—Reese, Campanella, Robinson, Hamner. Home runs—Brown, Robinson. Sacrifices—Jones (2), Robinson, Pellagrini. Double plays—Hamner, Pellagrini, Brown; Ennis, Pellagrini, Waitkus; Semini'k, Hamner, Pellagrini. Left on bases—Brooklyn, 9; Philadelphia, 18. Base on balls—Church, 3; Roe, 1; Branca, 2; Labine, 1; Newcombe, 6. Strikeouts—Church, 3; Drews, 2; Robert', 1; Roe, 1; Branca, 1; Labine, 2; Newcombe, 3. Hits—Roe, 5 in 1 2-3; Branca, 2 in 1 1-3; King, 3 in 1 (none out in fifth); Labine, 1 in 1; Church, 6 in 4 1-3; Drews, 5 in 3; Roberts, 6 in 6 2-3; Erskine, 2 in 2; Newcombe, 1 in 5 2-3; Podbellan, 1 in 1 1-3. Hit by pitchers; King (Jones), Newcombe (Pellagrini). Wild pitch—Branca. Winning pitcher—Podbellan. Losing pitcher—Roberts. Umpires—Jorda, Gore, Warneke, Goetz. Time—4.30. Attendance—31,755.

Giants

NEW YORK	Ab	R	H	O	A		BOSTON	Ab	R	H	O	A
Stanky.2b	5	0	1	3	1		Addis.lf	4	2	2	4	0
Dark.ss	4	0	1	2	5		Jethroe.cf	3	0	1	1	0
Mueller.rf	4	0	1	1	0		Torre'n.1b	4	0	0	8	0
Irvin.lf	4	0	1	1	0		Gordon.3b	4	0	1	2	1
Lock'an.1b	3	0	2	7	0		Cooper.c	4	0	0	4	0
Thom'n.3b	3	1	2	0	1		4Marsh'll.rf	4	0	0	4	0
Mays.cf	4	0	0	5	0		Kerr.ss	2	0	0	1	4
Westrum.c	3	2	0	7	0		Stall.2b.ss	3	0	0	1	4
Jansen.p	4	1	1	0	0		2Holmes	1	0	0	0	0
							1Bickford.p	1	0	0	0	0
							Wilson.p	0	0	0	0	0
							1Logan	1	0	0	0	0
							Burkont.p	0	0	0	0	0
							3Elliott	1	0	0	0	0
							Harts'd.2b	0	0	0	0	0
Totals	35	3	9	27	7		Totals	32	2	5	27	11

1Struck out for Wilson in sixth.
2Struck out for Kerr in eighth.
3Struck out for Surkont in eighth.
4Ran for Cooper in ninth.

New York 0 1 1 0 1 0 0 0 0—3
Boston 1 0 0 0 0 0 0 1 0—2

Runs batted in—Gordon, Torgeson, Thomson, Mueller, Irvin. Two-base hits—Addis (2), Dark. Home run—Thomson. Stolen base—Dark. Double play—Cooper, Stall. Left on bases—New York, 7; Boston, 4. Base on balls—Wilson, 3; Burkont, 1. Strikeouts—Wilson, 1; Burkont, 1; Jansen, 1. Hits—Wilson, 8 in 6 innings; Burkont, 1 in 2; Bickford, none in 1. Winning pitcher—Jansen. Losing pitcher—Wilson. Umpires—Conlan, Donatelli, Dascoli, Stewart. Time—2.01. Attendance—13,209.

Jackie Robinson Belts Game-Winning Homer For Brooklyn

Philadelphia, Sept. 30 (AP)—Jackie Robinson saved a game and the pennant for the Brooklyn Dodgers today when he blasted a home run in the fourteenth inning to give Brooklyn a 9-to-8 triumph over the Phillies.

As a result of Jackie's blow and his game-saving catch two innings earlier, the Dodgers finished the regular season in a tie with the New York Giants. They will meet in a three-game playoff, starting in Brooklyn tomorrow.

This marks the second time in National League history that a best-of-three playoff has been needed to decide the championship. In 1946, the Dodgers and St. Louis Cardinals ended in a deadlock and the Cardinals won the playoff in two games.

Playoff Needed In 1908

The only other time a postseason decision was needed in the National League was in 1908, the playoff of a regular season game after the celebrated Fred Merkle incident.

It was a dramatic climax to a game which saw the Dodgers come from far behind to tie the count at 8 to 8 in the eighth inning—after the Giants already had beaten Boston to clinch a tie for the flag.

It was played, too, in a World Series atmosphere. A crowd of 31,755, the largest to see a single game in Shibe Park this season, jammed the park and a big delegation of Dodger fans paraded noisily around the floodlighted field after the final out was made in the deepening dusk.

Dressen Names Branca

Manager Chuck Dressen named Ralph Branca, who pitched an inning and one third in relief today, as his starting pitcher for tomorrow's first playoff game.

Two were out in the fourteenth and it looked as if the Sunday curfew might halt the game without a decision when Robinson caught hold of one of Robin Roberts' pitches and drove it deep into the upper tier of the stands behind left field.

FRICK IS NAMED BASEBALL CZAR

National League Chief Picked To Succeed A. B. Chandler

Chicago, Sept. 20 (AP)—Ford Frick, president of the National League, was named commissioner of baseball tonight to succeed A. B. Chandler.

The new commissioner was chosen for the $65,000-a-year post at a closed session of the sixteen major league club owners at the Palmer House.

Frick, who was prominently mentioned as a successor to Judge K. M. Landis in 1945, has long been identified with baseball, first as a newspaperman in the West and in New York city, and since 1934 as president of the National League. He is 56 years old.

Thus ended a search that began last December 11 when the club owners refused to vote Chandler a new contract.

Game-Winning Homer In 9th Saves Bobby Thomson From Role Of Goat

Wide World Photo

THERE IT GOES!—Andy Pafko, Dodger outfielder, stands hopelessly against wall as Bobby Thomson's drive (arrow) sails into stands. The ninth-inning homer, with two runners on, enabled Giants to down Dodgers, 5 to 4, for National League pennant.

The Box Score

New York, Oct. 3 (AP)—Official box score of the third and final playoff game between Brooklyn and New York for the National League pennant.

BROOKLYN

	Ab.	R.	H.	O.	A.
Furillo, rf	5	0	0	0	0
Reese, ss	4	2	1	2	5
Snider, cf	3	1	2	1	0
Robinson, 2b	2	1	1	2	2
Pafko, lf	4	0	1	4	1
Hodges, 1b	4	0	0	11	1
Cox, 3b	4	0	2	1	3
Walker, c	4	0	1	2	0
Newcombe, p	4	0	0	0	0
Branca, p	0	0	0	0	0
Totals	34	4	8	*25	13

NEW YORK

	Ab.	R.	H.	O.	A.
Stanky, 2b	4	0	0	0	4
Dark, ss	4	1	1	2	2
Mueller, rf	4	0	1	0	0
3Hartung	0	1	0	0	0
Irvin, lf	4	1	1	1	0
Lockman, 1b	3	1	2	11	0
Thomson, 3b	4	1	3	0	1
Mays, cf	3	0	0	1	0
Westrum, c	0	0	0	7	1
1Rigney	1	0	0	0	0
Noble, c	0	0	0	0	0
Maglie, p	2	0	0	1	2
2Thompson	1	0	0	0	0
Jansen, p	0	0	0	0	0
Totals	30	5	8	27	11

*One out when winning run scored.
1Struck out for Westrum in eighth.
2Grounded out for Maglie in eighth.
3Ran for Mueller in ninth.

Brooklyn....1 0 0 0 0 0 0 3 0—4
New York....0 0 0 0 0 0 1 0 4—5

Errors—None. Runs batted in—Robinson, Thomson (4), Pafko, Cox, Lockman. Two-base hits—Thomson, Irvin, Lockman. Home run—Thomson. Sacrifice—Lockman. Double play—Cox, Robinson, Hodges; Reese, Robinson, Hodges. Left on bases—Brooklyn, 7; New York, 3. Base on balls—Maglie, 4 (Reese, Snider, Robinson, 2); Newcombe, 2 (Westrum, 2). Strikeouts—Maglie, 6 (Furillo, Walker, 2, Snider, Pafko, Reese); Newcombe, 2 (Mays, Rigney). Hits—Maglie, 8 in 8 innings; Jansen, none in 1; Newcombe, 7 in 8 1-3; Branca, 1 in 0 (pitched to one batter in ninth). Wild pitch—Maglie. Winning pitcher—Jansen. Losing pitcher—Branca. Umpires—Lou Jorda (plate), Jocko Conlan (first base), Bill Stewart (second base), Larry Goetz (third base). Time—2.28. Attendance—34,320 (paid).

This is the end of the rainbow, and only one of the two deadlocked National League clubs will find the pot of gold.

☆— ☆ —☆

Rah-Boo

IF THE Dodgers are a tired outfit—and they should be—there was no sign of it before game time.

The Giants were the first to make their appearance, and mingled cheers and boos greeted the white-uniformed athletes with the bright red letters "Giants" on their shirt front.

A brisk batting drill was held before a Dodger walked down the steps in center field leading to their dressing room.

A wag remarked that Chuck Dressen was giving his players a pep talk, a la football fashion.

"Dressen is telling his Dodgers he was only kidding in early August when he remarked the Giants had been knocked out of the pennant race by his Dodgers," the fan declared.

Chuck will never live down those words.

Sunlight -On- SPORTS

By
JESSE A. LINTHICUM
Sports Editor

NEW YORK, OCT. 3
IT IS 11.30 A.M. and the start of the third playoff game between the Giants and Dodgers is two hours distant. The unreserved grand-stand seats are filling, but only a handful of fans occupy the back-less benches in the center-field bleacher.

There is a heavy mist hanging over the Polo Grounds, and a threat of rain reminds one of the Stadium at home. The bleachers have no roof, and the fans still are mindful of the drenching they received yesterday.

But this is not an indication blasé New York is not baseball wild. Arguments spring up all over the baseball arena in which Giant and Dodger rooters are gathered for this all important baseball battle.

Reprinted from
The Baltimore Sun papers

MISPLAY HAD HALTED RALLY

Infielder Caught In Rundown In Second Inning

New York, Oct. 3 (AP)—Bobby Thomson's dramatic ninth-inning homer, besides giving the Giants the National League pennant, also saved him from the role of goat.

Thomson had singled in the second inning, sending Whitey Lockman to second, but was caught when he ran head down toward second. It broke the back of a possible Giant rally.

All this was forgotten, however, when the Staten Island Scot won the game in the ninth.

"I knew I hit the ball hard," he said afterward, "but it started sinking fast and I didn't think it would get in the stands."

Incidentally, Thomson won the first game of the playoffs with a two-run homer off Ralph Branca, the same pitcher he hit his homer off of today.

o——o

The pennant assured the Giants of a permanent place in the record books for it was their sixteenth, tying the Chicago Cubs for the National League high.

They won two in the 1890's to go with 14 since 1900. But they've been in only 12 previous World Series. In 1904 the Giants refused to play the upstarts from the American League.

Against the Yanks they're 2-3. The first all-New York series in 1921 and 1922 went to the Giants. In 1923 the Yanks discovered the secret. They walloped the Giants and did it again in 1936 and 1937.

With Don Mueller out of action because of a sprained ankle, Leo Durocher will break up his winning combination for tomorrow's series opener. Against Right-hander Allie Reynolds, he will play Hank Thompson in right field.

Thompson started the year at third base for the Giants but gave way to Bobby Thomson when Durocher decided to move him in from the outfield in late July.

o——o

The weatherman must be in cahoots with the Giants. The sun shone brightly at Ebbets Field Monday when New York won, 3-1. Yesterday's sunshine turned to showers as Brooklyn piled up a 10-0 margin. It threatened all morning but the sun finally peaked.

o——o

A gent in a box seat who kept tugging on a bottle of Scotch and yowling for the Dodgers, was so stunned by Thomson's homer he left 2 inches of Scotch in the bottle and wobbled toward Flatbush.

o——o

"We want Leo, we want Leo," chanted a throng of Giant fans who crowded around the door to the Giant dressing room in center field after the game. When Durocher appeared at the door, the fans let out a great cheer.

Durocher waved and smiled happily, then took off his cap and tossed it to the fans.

Virtually all the Giant team then appeared at the door, everyone getting a big hand.

o——o

Hans Lobert, former Giant star, was one of the first in the Giant through just before Thomson hit the jackpot. Giant fans basked in a cozy sunless warmth the rest of the night.

o——o

The ground crew will be from now until Saturday picking up the debris scattered by the delirious mob that swirled over the field after Thomson's pennant winning home run. It's a good thing the first two games are at the Yankee Stadium.

clubhouse. What a storybook finish, he enthused.

o——o

The score of reporters who had gathered in the Brooklyn clubhouse in the top of the ninth, expecting to greet the triumphant Dodgers, broke all speed records getting to the Giant dressing room when Thomson broke up the game.

The result was an emotional letdown for Brooklyn fans, especially the feminine contingent. Seated in the right-field stands after the game were half a dozen girls attired in Brooklyn-decorated jackets, crying their hearts out.

After Thomson's base-running homer in the second inning, virtually everyone in the press box laughed when it was announced "Thomson now has hit in 15 straight games."

But Bobby bounced back. Next time up in the fifth he belted a double to left. Then in the seventh, he flied deep to center, to bring home Monty Irvin with the run that temporarily tied the score at 1 to 1. What happened in the ninth is now baseball history.

o——o

The Giants now have won 39 of their last 47 games.

'WASN'T BAD PITCH'—BRANCA

Dodger Hurler Threw Thomson High Curve For Homer

New York, Oct. 3 (AP)—Ralph Branca sat on the steps, eyes wet, his head buried in his arms. Manager Charley Dressen paced the floor like a nervous lion. Big Don Newcombe moved around, silently and aimlessly, as if trying to figure out a reason for it all.

The others sat on the short, three-legged stools in their dressing room, eyes boring holes through the floor. None spoke. The room had a funereal quiet about it.

These were the men of Brooklyn, wondering what they had done against destiny to make destiny treat them so.

"We are three runs ahead going into the ninth inning," said Jackie Robinson, the Dodgers' brilliant second baseman. "We see ourselves in the World Series. And then—boom—five minutes later we are sitting in the clubhouse.

"Didn't Hit It Too Well"

Once before, these Dodgers had started counting World Series money—amounting to $5,000, may-

be $6,500. That was when they were 13½ games ahead on August 11. Then the great Giants' surge collared them and they fought back twice from the brink of elimination to today's final game.

Then it was all wiped out with one tremendous blow in the ninth inning by New York's Bobby Thomson, giving the Giants an unbelievable 5 to 4 victory.

"It wasn't a bad pitch," said Branca in a low, smothered breath. "It was a high curve ball. I didn't think he hit it too well. It was sinking when it went into the stands."

Branca Disconsolate

The big righthander was disconsolate because he was charged with both of the defeats in this best-of-three playoff for the National League pennant. He lost to the Giants, 1 to 3, Monday at Ebbets Field.

Branca relieved Newcombe, who had pitched magnificently for eight innings to carry his mates just a breath away from the champion ship.

One run was in and two men were on base as the result of rattling singles by Alvin Dark and Don Mueller and a double by Whitey Lockman. One was out and New York's Bobby Thomson at bat when Branca was called in to relieve a tiring Newcombe.

Branca threw one strike, and then dealt Thomson the high pitch that won the game.

"Had Stuff In Bullpen"

Asked if he had wanted to stay in the game, Newcombe said:

"The manager is paid to think. He can think better than I can. He makes the decisions. I'll stand by them."

Dressen said Newcombe was tired.

"They told me also that Branca had a lot of stuff in the bullpen. That's why I called him in."

Carl Erskine and Clem Labine, the rookie winner of yesterday's second game, were warming up at the same time.

Dressen Congratulates Durocher

Dressen was asked if he had ever considered walking Thomson, who is having a great year, to get to Willie Mays, who has been in a tremendous slump.

"We might have under certain circumstances—that is, if the count got up to three balls—but we wouldn't want to walk the potential winning run," the Brooklyn manager said.

The Brooklyn dressing room was closed to the press for about 15 minutes and, while the newsmen were still warming their heels in the corridor, Dressen was escorted across the hall to congratulate the Giants' Leo Durocher.

National Leaguers Triumph On Five-Run Rally In Fifth

Yankee Defense Falls Apart in Big Inning Before Crowd of 52,035 at Polo Grounds; Jones Finishes After Hearn Falters in Eighth

BY BILL LEE
Courant Sports Editor

New York, Oct. 6—At the end of the home half of the fifth inning at the Polo Grounds this balmy fall afternoon, a press box voice intoned an announcement for the working newspapermen.

"All five of the Giant runs are unearned," the stentorian voice said.

Maybe so, but the fact remains that these five unearned runs gave the New York Giants a 6 to 2 margin over the New York Yankees in the third game of the 1951 World Series and send the dime novel National League champions ahead two games to one in a series decided in favor of the first team to win four.

Unearned the runs may have been by the stodgy measurements of official scoring, but they may have gone a long way toward earning each member of the New York Giants the winning share of the World Series money, and the difference between each winning and losing share could be as much as $4,000.

Trailing by the whopping margin of 10 games on the losing side in their own National League struggle with the Brooklyn Dodgers, the incredible Giants have come storming from behind to beat the Dodgers in a dramatic playoff and now lead the defending champions 2 to 1 after three games.

Five Unearned Runs

Today the Giants were working on a squeeky one run margin behind Jim Hearn, the hero of one playoff victory in Brooklyn and they were trying to protect that slim margin against the rival pitching of Vic Raschi, powerful right-handed, top drawer pitcher o fthe American League champions.

Then, with startling and convincing suddenness, the charges of Lippy Leo Durocher broke the ball game wide open in the fifth, scored the previously mentioned five unearned runs and drove Raschi into the center field clubhouse amidst a wild fluttering of scorecards and handkerchiefs in the waving hands of the happily derisive Giant supporters in the adjoining bleachers.

These runs were more than enough to notch the ball game on the Giants' side of the World Series ledger. Hearn, the scorned former Cardinal pitcher the Giants picked up for the dirt cheap waiver price, calmly subdued the haughty Yankees, three times world champions, shut them out until the eighth and achieved the circle of World Series winners the first time he attempted the job in this rich post-season competition. Hearn himself opened the fateful inning by striking out with the customary ineptness of a pitcher with a bat in his hands. Eddie Stanky the next batter, worked on Vic Raschi the same way he operates on second rate stuff in his own league. He worked Raschi for a base on balls that may yet cost Yankee wives a mink coat or Yankee husbands a new Cadillac convertible.

Hit and Run Play

With Stanky aboard and one down, Leo Durocher's brain cooked up a hit and run play, with Alvin Dark, a righthanded batter trying to hit behind Stanky into the right field. The Yankees, however, anticipated the strategy; although by this time they probably wish they hadn't.

In any event, Stanky went down on the hit and run and Alvin Dark swung manfully at a wide pitchout that Vic Raschi and his catcher, Yogi Berra, fondly hoped would nail Stanky going into second base.

The Yankee defensive strategy worked perfectly. Berra took the pitch-out and winged a perfect throw down to Phil Rizzuto, covering the bag. The Scooter held the ball and waited for Stanky to slide into the tag. But Stanky had one desperate chance left. The massive crowd of 52,035, biggest in history at a World Series game in a National League park, saw the ball pop suddenly into center field and watched Stanky pick himself up and scoot safely to third.

Casey Stengel beefed vehemently that Stanky had left the base line to do Rizzuto dirt, but American League Umpire Bill Summers waved Stengel back to the dugout, and the Giants went on to break the Yankees' hearts.

Now, instead of working with two out and no one aboard, the fighting Giants had Stanky on third and only one down. The situation necessitated the Yankees drawing their infield in close to cut off a run at the plate if they could. This, a necessary stratagem, also backfired. Alvin Dark bounced sharply over second base and the ball went through for a hit that might have been within Rizzuto's scope had the Yankees infield been playing back. Stanky, the man who made all this possible, scored the first of five unearned runs.

Yogi Drops Ball

Hank Thompson followed his boss's order and singled beautifully behind the runner into right field, the precise hit needed to put Dark on third base. Now it was men on first and third, still only one out and dangerous Monte Irvin batting. Raschi worked hard on Irvin and got him to bounce sharply to Bobby Brown at third base. Brown fielded the ball neatly and threw to Berra. Yogi put the tag on the sliding Dark and Umpire Joe Passerella waved Dark out. Then, to the horror of all Yankee supporters in the vast crowd, Berra dropped the ball, forcing the umpire to reverse himself and spread his arms in the gesture that meant Dark was safe.

It used to be said of the great Yankee teams that you could not give them four outs and expect to live. The same may be said, in spades for the Giants. The Yankees tried to give them four outs today and got crushed in the explosion that followed.

With two runs in and two mates still aboard, Whitey Lockman decided that the Giants had fooled around with Yankee gratuities long enough. He slugged one of Raschi's pitches into the short right field seats barely inside the foul pole for three more runs, five in all and a whopping six-run lead that was all Jim Hearn needed to wrap it up.

The crushing home run detached Raschi from the contest and he had to make the long, long hike back across the ranch-like stretches of the Polo Grounds center field to receive the yowls of pitiless Giant rooters as he made his way up the steps to the clubhouse.

Six Runs Ample

The Giants didn't score on Bob Hogue or Joe Ostrowski, who finished Raschi's chore, but they didn't need to. Their six runs were ample. Their first run by the way, had come happily enough when Willie Mays broke out of his slump in the second to drive home Bobby Thomson, who had doubled.

Raschi and his successors accomplished one thing no Yankee hurler could do in the first two games—they blanked Monte Irvin, the big Giant leftfielder who was threatening World Series records with seven hits in nine times at bat before today. Monte was held to a walk in four trips to the plate. In his other turns he flied to center field, was safe on a fielder's choice and grounded out to Phil Rizzuto.

Two for Giants

NEW YORK (N)	ab	r	h	o	a	e
Stanky 2b	2	1	1	1	2	0
Dark ss	3	1	1	3	4	0
Thompson rf	3	1	1	2	0	0
Irvin lf	4	0	0	2	0	0
Lockman 1b	4	1	1	8	1	0
Thomson 3b	4	1	1	1	1	0
Mays cf	4	0	1	3	0	0
Westrum c	3	0	0	7	1	0
Hearn p	3	0	0	0	3	0
Jones p	1	0	0	0	0	0
Totals	31	6	7	27	15	0
NEW YORK (A)	ab	r	h	o	a	e
Woodling lf	4	1	1	3	0	0
Rizzuto ss	4	1	1	3	4	1
McDougald 2b	4	0	1	2	2	0
DiMaggio cf	3	0	1	1	0	0
Berra c	4	0	1	4	1	1
Brown 3b	4	0	1	0	2	0
Collins 1b	4	0	0	8	0	0
Bauer rf	4	0	0	0	0	0
Raschi p	2	0	0	0	2	0
Hogue p	0	0	0	0	0	0
a-Hopp	1	0	0	0	0	0
Ostrowski p	0	0	0	0	0	0
b-Mize	1	0	0	0	0	0
Totals	39	2	5	24	8	2

New York (N) ....
New York (A) ....

Earned runs, Yankee 2, Giants 1, 2b, Thomson; hr, Lockman, Woodling, Stanky, Dark and Lockman; 2b, Dark, Lockman and Dark; Rizzuto, McDougald and Collins. Left, New York (A) 10, New York (N) 5; bb, Raschi (Irvin, Thompson, Stanky); Hearn (Woodling, McDougald 2; Raschi, 2); rs, Hopp, Brown, Collins; so, Raschi 3 (Thompson, Stanky, Hearn); Ostrowski 1 (Lockman); Hearn 2 (DiMaggio, hr, Raschi 5 in 4 1-3 innings, Hearn 4 in 1 2-3, Ostrowski 1 in 2, Hearn 4 in 7 2-3, Jones 1 in 1 1-3; hbp, Raschi (Stanky), Hearn 1 (Rizzuto); winner, Hearn; loser, Raschi; u, Passerella (AL) plate; Al Barlick (NL) first base; Bill Summers (AL) second base; John Ballanfant (NL) third base; John Stevens (AL) left field foul line; Art Gore (NL) right field foul line.

Yankee Star May Take Job As Television Broadcaster

New York, Dec. 11 (AP)—Joe DiMaggio, who ranks beside Ty Cobb and Babe Ruth as one of the greatest of all ballplayers announced his retirement from baseball today.

While it was not a complete surprise, the announcement came as a shock to the nation's fans, who long had thrilled to the batting and fielding exploits of the New York Yankee outfielder.

DiMaggio, at a news conference in the Yankee offices before newsreel and television cameras, said he never would don a baseball uniform again. He said he never had entertained managerial or coaching ambitions and probably would accept a job with the Yankee organization as a television broadcaster.

Injuries Behind Decision

It is expected that DiMaggio, who collected, $704,769.71 during thirteen years playing with the club, would take the post of TV commentator of the Yankees' home baseball games. That post, left vacant when Dizzy Dean transferred to St. Louis to broadcast the Browns' games, reportedly will bring $50,000 a season.

DiMaggio, 37 years old last November 25, said a series of injuries and mishaps which hampered him throughout his major league career, all of it with the Yankees, prompted his decision to quit.

"I knew I was beginning to slip as far back as three years ago." he said. "The old timing was beginning to leave me and my reflexes were beginning to slow up."

CAIN, FELLER YIELD ONLY 1 BLOW EACH

Browns Score by 1-0 to Take First Place From Indians and Drop Tribe to Third

NEW LEAGUE RECORD SET

Young's Triple in 1st Helps Win as Two One-Hitters Establish a Low Total

ST. LOUIS, April 23 (AP)—Bobby Cain outpitched Bob Feller tonight in a unique duel in which the Browns defeated the Indians, 1 to 0, and took over first place in the American League.

Feller, like Cain, allowed only one hit, but the safety off the Cleveland veteran was a first-inning triple by Bobby Young, good for a run, whereas the only hit off Cain's delivery was a harmless single by Luke Easter in the fifth.

Young's triple opened the Brown's first inning and when the third baseman, Al Rosen, fumbled Marty Marion's grounder, Young scored the only run of the game.

It was Feller's eleventh one-hit game and the only one-hitter he ever lost. The game was played in 50 degree cold, before 7,110 shivering and delighted fans.

Second Victory for Cain

Cain, who came to the Browns last Valentine's Day in a seven-player deal with the Tigers, hasn't known a winning season as a major leaguer since breaking in with the White Sox in 1949. With tonight's excellent performance he now has a 2-0 record, one of three Browns as yet undefeated.

In two games the Browns have toppled the Indians out of a one-and-a-half game lead, breaking the Tribe's seven-game winning streak and reducing Cleveland to third place.

Ironically, Cain was Feller's victim when Bob pitched his third no-hitter last year. On July 1 the Cleveland right-hander defeated Cain and Detroit, 2—1, holding the Tigers hitless. Cain allowed six hits.

Tonight's game marked the sec-

ond time in modern baseball history that each pitcher allowed the opposition only one hit. On July 4, 1906, Mordecai (Three-Fingered) Brown of Chicago and Lefty Leifield of Pittsburgh permitted only one hit each as the Cubs defeated the Pirates, 1—0.

On May 2, 1917, Jim Vaughn of Chicago and Fred Toney of Cincinnati hurled a no-hitter each through nine innings. The Reds, however, nicked Vaughn for two hits and a run in the tenth to win, 1—0, as Toney hurled a ten-inning no-hitter.

The 33-year-old Feller and Cain, 25, battled on even terms all the way through the duel which goes into the record books as the lowest-hit game in the fifty-one-year history of the American League.

1913 Record Is Erased

The former American League record for the least amount of hits by both teams in one game was three, set by Washington, with one safety, and Detroit, with two, on June 10, 1913, and equaled by Washington (2) and Cleveland (1) July 27, 1915.

Cain, a southpaw, fanned seven and walked three. Feller struck out five and gave up two passes. The big strikeout for Cain came when he fanned Harry Simpson to end the game.

Only four Browns reached base. The Tribe put men on base the same number of times.

It was a stunning defeat for Cleveland, still staggered by Tuesday night's 8-3 Brownie victory.

There was much debate about whether Young's all-important triple could have been caught. Most writers believed it could have been.

Perhaps figuring that the wind would stall the ball in flight, Rookie Jim Fridley moved to his left in left field and stood hopeless as the ball sailed over his head.

The lone run was ruled an earned tally by the official scorekeeper despite the fact Rosen muffed Marion's grounder to allow Young to cross the plate. According to the official scorer, Young would have been able to score with or without Rosen's assistance.

The box score:

CLEVELAND (A.)	ab.	r.	h.	po.	a.
Simpson, rf.	4	0	0	1	0
Berardino, 2b.	3	0	0	1	5
Reiser, cf.	3	0	0	3	0
Easter, 1b.	3	0	1	10	0
Rosen, 3b.	3	0	0	0	0
Fridley, lf.	3	0	0	4	0
Boone, ss.	2	0	0	0	2
Tebbetts, c.	3	0	0	5	0
Feller, p.	2	0	0	1	1
aAvila	1	0	0	0	0
Total	25	0	1	24	8

ST. LOUIS (A.)	ab.	r.	h.	po.	a.
Young, 2b.	4	1	1	2	4
Marion, ss.	2	0	0	2	3
Rivera, cf.	2	0	0	4	0
Wright, lf.	3	0	0	1	0
Papp, rf.	3	0	0	1	0
Delsing, rf.	0	0	0	0	0
Goldsb'ry, 1b.	3	0	0	9	0
Thomas, 3b.	3	0	0	1	3
Courtney, c.	3	0	0	8	1
Cain, p.	3	0	0	0	0
Total	26	1	1	27	11

aFlied out for Feller in ninth.

Cleveland ....000 000 000—0
St. Louis ....100 000 00.—1

Error—Rosen.

Run batted in—Marion. Three-base hit—Young. Double plays—Courtney and Young; Young, Marion and Goldsberry; Marion, Young and Goldsberry. Left on bases—Cleveland 1, St. Louis 3. Bases on balls—Off Cain 3, Feller 2. Struck out—By Cain 7, Feller 5. Runs and earned runs—Feller 1 and 1. Winning pitcher—Cain (2-0). Losing pitcher—Feller (1-1). Umpires—Honochick, Rommel and Berry. Time of game—1:36. Attendance—7,110.

Briggs, 74, Tigers' Owner, Dies At Miami Beach Home

MIAMI BEACH, Fla., Jan. 17 (AP)—Walter Owen Briggs, Sr., 74, a giant in the automobile industry and sole owner of the Detroit Tigers of the American Baseball League, died today.

He was founder of the Briggs Manufacturing Company, a maker of automobile bodies which now has 15 plants, 9 of them in the Detroit area and 3 in England.

With the wealth earned in the automotive field, he became sole owner of the Tigers. He was a familiar figure at Tiger games which he watched from a wheelchair in the family box.

Briggs had not been a well man for years, but the kidney ailment which ended his life struck Sunday. He improved Monday and went for an automobile ride, but became worse Tuesday. He declined steadily thereafter until his death at 7.15 A.M. today.

He died in the big Mediterranean-style oceanfront mansion he built twenty years ago at 5151 Collins avenue, Miami Beach. With him at the end were Mrs. Briggs: their son, Walter O. Briggs, Jr., and the Most Rev. Allan J. Babcock, auxiliary bishop of the Catholic Archdiocese of Detroit who was a house guest at the time.

Briggs and Frank Navin were life-long friends. Navin was owner of the Tigers and sold a half interest in the club to Briggs and John Kelsey. Later Briggs took over Kelsey's share, and when Navin died he became sole owner.

Briggs saw his Tigers become world champions in 1935, 1940 and 1945.

His body will be flown in a special plane tomorrow to Detroit for funeral services at 11 A.M. Monday in the Cathedral of the Blessed Sacrament.

Flock Gets 15 Runs In First Frame

BROOKLYN, May 21 (AP)—Brooklyn set a new modern major league record with 15 runs in the first inning tonight on the way to a staggering 19-1 win over the Cincinnati Reds. Twenty-one Dodgers went to bat in the big inning as 19 men in succession reached first base. Twelve runs were scored after two were out in the rout of four pitchers.

Chris Van Cuyk lashed out four straight hits, two in the big inning, as he coasted to his third victory by scattering five Cincy hits.

Duke Snider hit the only homer of the record-breaking inning attack that included 10 hits, seven walks and two hit batsmen. Bobby Morgan later hit two homers, each with a man on base.

Willie Mays Thinks Induction Today Will Keep Him Too Busy To Play Ball

BROOKLYN, May 28 (AP)—Willie Mays, sensational young outfielder of the New York Giants, played his farewell game today before joining the Armed Forces tomorrow.

Mays has no idea whether he will be inducted into the Army, Navy or Marines. He doesn't even care. What he is most concerned about is where he will be sent and whether he will be permitted to play ball "right away."

"I expect I'll be too busy tomorrow to play ball anywhere," the 21-year-old "Say-Hey" Willie remarked innocently "but I sure would like to play somewhere Saturday. I hope they send me to a camp that has a ball club."

For the first time since he joined the Giants in May of 1951, Willie showed resentment toward the press.

Annoyed by Press

"Why don't you fellows leave me alone," he said in an annoyed tone, as he was besieged for pictures and interviews during practice before the game with the Dodgers.

"I want to get as much in as possible, my last day with the club."

The likeable lad had tears in his eyes as he described his thrilling one-year experience in the major leagues.

"Every day has been a thrill for me," said the Fairfield, Ala., Negro, "but my biggest one came when I made my first big league hit. It was a home run in the Polo Grounds off Warren Spahn of the Braves. I had gone 13 for 0 until then."

NEAR-PERFECT GAME SPOILED BY WALK IN 3D

Brooklyn Pitcher Registers Sixth Triumph Against One Loss

Brooklyn, N.Y., June 19 (AP)—(AP) — Carl Erskine, 25-year-old Carl Erskine, 25-year-old Brooklyn right-hander, pitched a near-perfect game today, turning in a no-hit no-run game as the Dodgers defeated the Chicago Cubs for the third straight time, 5 to 0.

Erskine allowed only one Chicago batter to reach base as he became the first National Leaguer to turn the trick this year. Virgil Trucks, of the Detroit Tigers, against the Washington Senators on May 15, is the only American Leaguer to turn in a no-hitter this season.

Ramsdell Draws Walk

Of all people, Williard Ramsdell, Chicago's second pitcher, was the Cub batter to reach base. He walked on four straight pitches in the third inning to ruin Erskine's bid for the first perfect game since Charley Robertson, of the Chicago White Sox, retired 27 Tigers in succession on April 30, 1922.

Erskine Gets $500 Check

Brooklyn President Walter F. O'Malley, happy beyond words, presented Erskine with a $500 check immediately after the game and ordered a case of champagne to be sent down to the clubhouse where the Dodgers celebrated as if they had just won the pennant.

"My control did it," beamed Erskine in the clubhouse as he was being besieged by photographers from all sides.

"I threw a lot of curves and some fast balls. I had them hitting the pitch I wanted them to. My control was so good I didn't have to resort to my change of pace, which is my best pitch."

Fine Defensive Help

Although only five balls were hit to the outfield, Erskine needed and received some fine defensive help from his mates. Twice Third Baseman Bobby Morgan made swell stops and throws to take away hits from the Cub batters. Shortstop Peewee Reese and Second Baseman Jackie Robinson also shone on defense. Erskine also chipped in with fine fielding plays. He figured in six of the putouts.

In the fifth inning Carl Furillo backed up against the right-field fence to gather in Ransom Jackson's deep fly. Furillo had to do the same thing to haul in Hank Sauer's deep smash in the seventh.

CHICAGO					BROOKLYN				
	Ab	R	H	O	A		Ab	R	H	O	A
Miksis,ss	4	0	0	4	6	Morgan,3b	4	0	0	0	4
Addis,lf	3	0	0	1	0	Reese,ss	4	2	2	2	3
Her'nski,rf	3	0	0	2	0	Rob'son,2b	3	0	0	0	5
Sauer,lf	3	0	0	2	0	Cam'ella,s	4	1	2	2	0
Atwell,c	3	0	0	2	1	Furillo,rf	4	1	1	3	0
Fondy,1b	3	0	0	12	1	Snider,cf	3	0	0	1	0
Jackson,3b	3	0	0	1	3	Hodges,1b	3	0	0	16	2
Rama'ti,2b	3	0	0	0	0	Patko,lf	3	1	2	1	0
Hacker,p	0	0	0	0	0	Erskine,p	3	0	0	2	4
Ramsdell,p	1	0	0	0	0						
1Cavar'tta	1	0	0	0	0						
Totals	27	0	0	24	11	Totals	31	5	7	27	18

1Cavarretta flied out for Ramsdell in ninth.

Chicago . . . . 0 0 0 0 0 0 0 0 0—0
Brooklyn . . . 2 1 0 0 0 0 0 1 x—5

Error—Atwell. Runs batted in—Campanella (3), Furillo, Patko. Home runs—Campanella, Furillo, Patko. Stolen bases—Reese. Left on bases—Chicago 1, Brooklyn 3. Base on balls—Ramsdell 1, Erskine 1. Strikeouts—Hacker 1, Ramsdell 3, Erskine 1. Hits—Hacker 4 in 1 1-3 innings, Ramsdell 3 in 6 2-3. Winning pitcher—Erskine. Losing pitcher—Hacker. Umpires—Conlan, Stewart, Guglielmo, Gore. Time—1:48. Attendance—7,732.

Piersall to Take Rest On Advice of Physicians

By The Associated Press.

BOSTON, July 19—Joe Cronin, general manager of the Red Sox, today announced Jim Piersall, rookie outfielder, would take an indefinite rest on advice of physicians.

Piersall has been in Boston while serving a three-day suspension from thte Birmingham (Ala.) Barons of the Southern Association.

"After consultation and advice of doctors," Cronin told newsmen, "Jimmy Piersall is going to take a rest."

"The ball club (Red Sox) is interested in Piersall himself, not in where he plays or what position he plays. I'm sorry I cannot elaborate on the subject."

At Piersall's home in suburban Newton, a woman identifying herself as a baby-sitter said he had gone to the beach.

Earlier Piersall had said he didn't know whether he was supposed to return to the Southern Association club tomorrow.

Piersall was suspended following an argument with a Southern Association umpire in a game with Atlanta. It was the fourth time he's been disciplined since the Red Sox sent him down on June 28 because his antics bothered Manager Lou Boudreau and his team-mates.

DROPO'S 12 CONSECUTIVE HITS

July 14-15

Triple, Double and 10 Singles

JULY 14—AT NEW YORK

FIRST INNING—Singled to short right off Jim McDonald, filling the bases.

THIRD INNING—Singled to center, advancing Johnny Groth to second.

FIFTH INNING—Singled to left, putting Vic Wertz on second.

SEVENTH INNING—Singled to left again with two men out.

EIGHTH INNING—Singled to left off Bob Hogue with the bases loaded, scoring Fred Hatfield and Groth.

JULY 15—AT WASHINGTON (FIRST GAME)

SECOND INNING—Singled to left off Walt Masterson, nobody on.

FOURTH INNING—Singled to left, sending Werts to second.

FIFTH INNING—Singled to center, scoring Pesky from third and sending Hatfield to second.

EIGHTH INNING—Singled off Masterson's glove while leading off.

JULY 15—AT WASHINGTON (SECOND GAME)

FIRST INNING—Tripled to center off Bob Porterfield, with bases filled.

THIRD INNING—Singled through shortstop, nobody on.

FIFTH INNING—Doubled off leftfield fence off Lou Sleater.

* * *　* * *　* * *

Tigers' Most Famous Pitcher (Today) May Even Be Off Trading Block

(SPECIAL TO THE DETROIT NEWS)

NEW YORK. Aug. 26.—It is no secret that from time to time the Detroit Tigers have considered trading Virgil Trucks. who pitched his second no-hit game of the season Monday when he shutout the Yankees, 1 to 0.

Trucks figured in speculation preceding both the nine-player deal with the Boston Red Sox in June and the eight-player swap with the St. Louis Browns this month. He has been mentioned authoritatively in reports of offers from Cleveland and the Chicago White Sox.

The Detroit front-office. facing a rebuilding job. doubtless pondered Trucks' value on the winter bargain counter before he fashioned his second masterpiece.

Now a fresh question presents itself to the Briggs Stadium executives: Shall they take Trucks off the list of "expendables" or merely raise the price?

* * *

Aug. 25

DETROIT

	AB	R	H	O	A	E
Groth, cf	4	0	0	2	0	0
Pesky, ss	4	0	0	3	1	1
Hatfield, 3b	3	0	1	2	0	0
Dropo, 1b	4	1	2	4	3	0
Souchock, rf	4	0	1	3	0	0
Delsing, lf	4	0	0	2	0	0
Batts, c	2	0	1	6	1	1
Federoff, 2b	3	0	0	1	1	0
Trucks, p	2	0	0	4	2	0
Totals	30	1	5	27	8	2

NEW YORK

	AB	R	H	O	A	E
Mantle, cf	3	0	0	3	0	0
Collins, 1b	4	0	0	10	1	0
Bauer, rf	4	0	0	0	1	0
Berra, c	3	0	0	7	0	0
Woodling, lf	3	0	0	3	0	0
Babe, 3b	3	0	0	3	2	0
Martin, 2b	3	0	0	1	4	0
Rizzuto, ss	2	0	0	0	5	0
*Mize	1	0	0	0	0	0
B'dewieser, ss	0	0	0	0	0	0
Miller, p	1	0	0	0	1	0
†Noren	1	0	0	0	0	0
Sc'borough, p	0	0	0	0	0	0
Totals	28	0	0	27	14	0

*Popped out for Rizzuto in eighth.

†Flied out for Miller in eighth.

DETROIT . . 000 000 100—1

New York . . 000 000 000—0

'We Can Always Win On Road,' Shouts Casey As Hilarious Yankees Celebrate

BROOKLYN. Oct. 7 (/P) — "We can always win on the road," shouted Casey Stengel and a roar of cheers and laughter swept through the jam-packed. hilarious Yankee dressing room this afternoon.

The American League champions had just won their fourth straight World Series championship in seven games that for drama. thrills. and fine plays must go down as one of the best.

"That boy hadn't been pitching hardly any all season. but he really went in there and threw hard."

Casey referred to Bob Kuzava, whose superb relief pitching from the seventh inning on saved the day against the Brooklyn Dodgers.

"That boy really hit," Casey shouted.

This time he meant Mickey Mantle, who homered for the third Yankee run and singled for the fourth in the 4-2 victory.

"This change your mind about retiring." someone yelled in Casey's ear.

Saigh Sells Holdings For $3,750,000

ST. LOUIS, Feb. 20 (P)—Anheuser-Busch, Inc., one of the nation's largest breweries, bought the St. Louis Cardinals today to make sure the National League club stayed in St. Louis.

The $3,750,000 sale was announced jointly by the brewery and Fred M. Saigh, whose departure from baseball was prompted by a 15-month prison sentence for income tax evasion.

Anheuser - Busch stepped into the negotiations after it appeared likely the club might be sold to an unidentified Milwaukee group, which made a strong bid for the Cardinal holdings.

August A. Busch Jr., president of the brewery, becomes president of the Cardinals and William Walsingham Jr., will remain as vice-president and operating head.

SURPRISE MOVE TURNS DOWN VEECK'S PLEA

Shift to Baltimore Is Defeated

Tampa, Fla., March 16 (AP)—The American league in a surprising move today turned down the proposal of Bill Veeck to move his St. Louis Browns to Baltimore.

It was not deemed advisable to transfer the club for the 1953 season because of the short period of time, the officials of the league said after a meeting lasting over five hours.

First Major League Switch Since 1903 Is Given Full Approval

ST. PETERSBURG, Fla., March 18 (AP)—The Boston Braves, a charter member of the National League, shifted to Milwaukee today in the first change in the major league lineup in a half century. The transfer, requested by Owner Louis Perini after several losing seasons in Boston, was approved unanimously by the owners of the seven other National League clubs.

The American Association, whose territory was invaded by the major league, also gave its assent to the move by a 7-1 vote. The Milwaukee franchise, owned by the Braves and operated by them for the past several years as a farm club, was transferred to Toledo, now "open" territory.

The changes will become effective with the opening of the seasons of the two leagues next month.

Take Bucs' Schedule

The Milwaukee club, to be known as the Milwaukee Braves, will become one of the Western clubs of the National League, taking over the schedule previously drawn up for the Pittsburgh Pirates. Pittsburgh will move into the Eastern division, assuming Boston's schedule.

The 1953 All-Star game, previously scheduled to be played at Braves Field July 14, was awarded to Cincinnati.

Cards' Deal for Browns' Park Paves Way for Improvement

By the Associated Press

ST. LOUIS, April 10.—Sportsman's Park has a new owner and a new name today.

St. Louis' two ball clubs—the Cardinals and Browns—reversed their tenant-landlord roles in an $800,000 deal. The Northside park now is Busch Stadium.

The park first was named Budweiser Stadium, but subsequently the new owners changed their minds.

Officials of Anheuser-Busch, Inc., owner of the Cardinals, and the Browns gave two reasons for the ownership change:

The Cardinals wanted to make expensive improvements, but not while some one else owned the park, and the Browns could use the money to help pay operating costs this year.

Rudie Schaffer, general manager of the Browns, speaking in the absence of President Bill Veeck last night, said the sale had no connection with the club's attempt to move to Baltimore last month.

Cards Paid $35,000 a Year.

The Cardinals had been renting the park for $35,000 a year under a lease running through 1960. They also footed half the maintenance costs, which last year added an estimated $105,000 to their bill.

The Browns now will rent from the Cards at $175,000 annually, but will have no maintenance expenses. They have taken a five-year lease which means they will return the sale price plus $75,000 in that time.

August A. Busch, president of the Cards, in announcing the purchase yesterday, said "the park was not maintained on a scale we regard as meeting major league standards."

Busch said a $400,000 face-lifting program will be carried out during 1953.

He said the Browns had told him they were heavily in debt.

Schaffer said the sale of the park would "materially help the Browns' immediate operations and enable the club to clear debts incurred in recent years."

Browns to Pay Mortgage.

Among those debts is a mortgage on the stadium of an undisclosed amount which the Browns will pay.

"The sale was prompted entirely by our inability to make necessary repairs and improvements and we are most appreciative of the fine co-operation we have received from all Anheuser-Busch officials," Schaffer added.

In 1885 Chris Von Der Ahe's old St. Louis Browns were playing ball in Sportsman's Park at Grand and Dodier streets. Robert Lee Hedges revived the Browns in the early part of this century and rebuilt stands on the same site in 1909.

The park was purchased by the Browns in 1946 from the estate of Phil Ball, former Browns' owner. It was modernized at that time.

The Cardinals, who previously played in another stadium a few blocks northwest of Sportsman's Park, became tenants in 1920.

MILWAUKEE'S DEBUT A SUCCESS

MILWAUKEE, April 14 (P)—Bill Bruton, 23-year-old Negro rookie, smashed a 10th inning home run for a 3-2 Milwaukee Braves' victory over the St. Louis Cardinals today in a dramatic return of major league baseball to Milwaukee after a 52-year absence.

Bruton's decisive blast, after he had tripled and scored for a 2-1 Milwaukee lead in the eighth, sent a capacity crowd of 34,357 paid at the $5,000,000 Milwaukee County Stadium into hysterics.

The payoff blow glanced off the upstretched gloved hand of Right Fielder Enos Slaughter and caromed over the squat, four-foot wire barrier.

At first Umpire Lon Warneke called the blow a ground-rule double, but after Charley Grimm, the Braves' manager stormed up to him in protest, Warneke waved Bruton across home plate with the winning run.

The game marked the first regular major league game in Milwaukee since the city belonged to the American League for one season in 1901.

MILWAUKEE	ab	r	h	o	a	e	rbi
Bruton, cf	4	2	3	6	0	0	1
Logan, ss	3	0	0	3	1	0	0
Mathews, 3b	3	0	0	2	7	0	0
Gordon, lf	4	0	1	4	1	0	1
Pafko, rf	4	0	1	0	0	0	0
Adcock, 1b	3	1	1	7	0	0	0
Crandall, c	4	0	1	2	1	0	1
Dittmer, 2b	4	0	0	1	2	1	0
Spahn, p	4	0	0	3	0	1	0
Totals	33	3	6	30	13	3	3
ST. LOUIS	ab	r	h	o	a	e	rbi
Hemus, ss	3	0	0	1	2	0	0
Schoendienst, 2b	5	0	0	1	2	0	0
Musial, lf-cf	5	0	1	0	0	0	0
c-Lowrey, rf	1	0	1	0	0	0	1
Bilko, 1b	4	0	0	14	0	0	0
Slaughter, rf	2	1	0	2	0	0	1
Jablonski, 3b	4	0	2	0	4	1	1
b-Haddix	0	1	0	0	0	0	0
Jorman, 3b	0	0	0	0	0	0	0
Repulski, cf	3	0	1	2	0	0	0
P. Rice, c	3	0	1	1	0	0	0
a-Benson	1	0	1	0	0	0	0
Fusselman, c	0	0	0	0	0	0	0
Staley, p	4	0	0	0	1	1	0
Totals	35	2	6×26	13	1	2	

Milwaukee .... 010 000 010 1—3
St. Louis .... 000 010 001 0—2

2b, Rice, Lowrey; 3b, Bruton; hr, Bruton; left, St. Louis 7, Milwaukee 6; bb, Staley 2, Spahn 3; so, Staley 6, Spahn 3; winner, Spahn; loser, Staley; hbp, Logan (Staley); u, Conlan, Warneke, Donatelli, Gorman; t, 2:29; a, 34,357. \—One out when winning run scored; a—Benson doubled for Rice in 8th; b—Haddix ran for Jablonski in 9th; c—Lowrey doubled for Repulski in 9th.

LOVE THAT BALL: Mickey Mantle of the New York Yankees holds the ball he socked for 565-feet Friday, the longest home run ever hit in Griffith Stadium. Mickey points to the dent in the ball where it hit a house (AP Wirephoto).

Rookie Baffles Athletics, 6 to 0, In His Debut as St. Louis Starter

Six Batters Reach First, Five on Walks and One on Error by Holloman in No-Hitter

ST. LOUIS, May 6 (AP)—Alva (Bobo) Holloman pitched his way into the record books tonight by hurling a no-hitter for the Browns in his first major league start to beat the Athletics, 6—0.

The 27-year-old Holloman is the second pitcher in baseball history to hurl a hitless game in his debut. Charley Jones did the trick for Cincinnati in 1892.

Holloman faced thirty-one batters, striking out three. Only six A's reached base, five via walks and one on the hurler's error in the fifth. He drove in three of the Browns' six runs with a pair of singles.

Three Athletics Walk in Ninth

In the ninth Holloman walked the first two men to face him, but forced Dave Philley to hit into a double play. Loren Babe then followed with another walk. Eddie Robinson lifted a fly to Vic Wertz in right field to end the game.

Holloman, a right-hander, won sixteen games and lost seven for Syracuse in the International League last year.

Brilliantly supported, particularly by Shortstop Bill Hunter, the 6-foot 2-inch rookie mowed down the Athletics until the ninth inning.

Holloman, who specializes in a fast ball and a sinker pitch, struck out Babe, Tom Hamilton, a pinch-hitter, and Philley.

It was the first nine-inning no-hitter by a Browns' pitcher since Bob Groom turned the trick thirty-six years ago, also on May 6.

The Browns built up an early lead for Holloman by picking up single runs in the second, third and fifth innings off Morris Martin's southpaw slants. Carl Scheib finished and allowed three more runs as the Browns fashioned thirteen hits.

"I realized that I was going

that I was charged with an error on that hopper of Zernial's," said Holloman after the game.

"But I wouldn't have had it but for that play by Billy Hunter in the eighth. That was the greatest play I have ever seen." Hunter made a diving stop, far to his left, of Joe Astroth's sharp grounder.

The Box Score

PHILADELPHIA (A.)	ab	r	h	o	a		ST. LOUIS (A.)	ab	r	h	o	a
Joost, ss	3	0	0	2	3		Groth, cf	5	0	1	4	0
Philley, cf	3	0	0	1	0		Hunter, ss	4	1	1	1	1
Babe, 3b	3	0	0	1	2		Dyck, lf	5	1	1	1	0
Robinson, 1b	3	0	0	9	0		Elliott, lf	4	0	1	1	0
Zernial, lf	4	0	0	1	0		Wertz, rf	5	1	2	1	0
Michaels, 2b	3	0	0	5	1		Young, 2b	3	0	0	2	4
Astroth, c	3	0	0	0	0		Courtney, c	4	1	1	7	0
Suder, 2b	1	0	0	0	1		Michaels, 2b	4	0	1	3	1
Hamilton	1	0	0	0	0		Holloman, p	3	0	2	1	1
Martin, p	0	0	0	0	1							
Scheib, p	0	0	0	1	1		Total	35	4	13	27	12
Valo	0	0	0	0	0							
DeMaestri	0	0	0	0	0							
Total	28	0	0	24	13							

aSingled out for Martin in sixth.
bWalked for Scheib in ninth.
cRan for Valo in ninth.

Philadelphia ...... 000 000 000—0
St. Louis .... 011 011 20x—6

Error—Michaels, Holloman. Runs batted in—Holloman 3, Dyck, Wertz, Groth. Two-base hits—Dyck 2, Hunter, Wertz, Elliott. Sacrifice—Holloman. Double play—Young and Stevens; Babe, Michaels and Robinson; Michaels, Young and Robinson. Left on bases—Philadelphia 4, St. Louis 12. Bases on balls—Off Martin 4, Holloman 5, Scheib 3. Struck out—By Martin 2, Holloman 3, Scheib 1. Hits—Off Martin 7 in 5 innings, Scheib 6 in 3. Runs and earned runs—Off Martin 3 and 2, Scheib 3 and 3. Hit by pitcher—By Scheib (Young). Winning pitcher—Holloman (1-1). Losing pitcher—Martin (1-1). Umpires—Duffy, Grieve, Passarella and Napp. Time of game—2:00. Attendance—2,473.

Dom DiMaggio of Red Sox Retires Rather Than Become 'Hanger-On'

BOSTON, May 12 (AP)—Dom DiMaggio, Red Sox center fielder and the last of the three DiMaggio brothers in major league baseball, announced his retirement tonight.

Shortly before the Red Sox-White Sox game got under way DiMaggio said:

"As of this date, May 12, 1953, I have voluntarily retired from baseball.

"I want it perfectly understood there is nothing wrong with my right eye, which recently underwent treatment.

"My vision is better than 20-20 in both eyes with glasses. I believe I could have played at least one more year of good baseball, but under the circumstances I prefer to turn my interests elsewhere rather than be a hanger-on."

KINER TRADED TO CUBS

By The Associated Press

PITTSBURGH, June 4—The Chicago Cubs happily obtained Ralph Kiner, the home run king, from the Pittsburgh Pirates today in a spectacular baseball deal involving ten players. Branch Rickey, the Pirates' general manager, gave up Kiner and three others for six players and a bundle of cash. He would not reveal the amount of money but it is reported to be about $100,000.

This is one of the few transactions in which a big league club has traded its star player while he was at the peak of his career. The most recent involved Hank Borowy, whom the Yankees turned loose in 1945 to the Cubs. But Rickey has a long record of trading players he thinks are past their prime. He ushered Dizzy Dean to the Cubs and Dixie Walker to the Pirates while operating other teams.

74,708 WATCH AS CHAMPIONS SWEEP SERIES

Berra Is Hitting Star In Both Games; Raschi Has 3-Hitter In 2d

Cleveland, June 14 (AP)—The rampaging New York Yankees ran their winning streak to 18 straight today, third highest in American League history, as they crushed the Cleveland Indians in both ends of a double-header, 6 to 2 and 3 to 0, before 74,708 chagrined fans, for a sweep of the four-game series.

Yogi Berra, Yankee catcher, paced the Bronx Bombers to both victories. He hammered a home run off Bob Lemon with two mates aboard in the eighth inning to win the opener, and tripled with two on off Mike Garcia in the fourth of the second game to feature a three-run outburst.

THUMP BY THUMP IN TIGERS' DEMISE

BOSTON, June 19.—Here is how Boston scored its 17 runs in the seventh inning yesterday against Detroit:

White singled to short right. Stephens singled to right, White taking third. Stephens stole second. Umphlett singled to left, scoring White and Stephens (1-2).

Lipon struck out. Kell doubled off the left field wall, Umphlett taking third. Goodman walked to fill the bases. Piersall singled to right, scoring Umphlett and Kell (3-4).

Gernert hit his 12th homer into the left field screen scoring Goodman and Piersall ahead of him (5-6-7).

Kinder singled to right. White walked. Weik replaced Gromek on the mound for Detroit. Kinder and White advanced on Weik's wild pitch.

Stephens doubled to short right, scoring Kinder and White (8-9). Umphlett walked. Lipon singled to left, scoring Stephens (10). Kell lined to Lund. Goodman singled to center, scoring Umphlett (11). Lepcio ran for Goodman.

Harrist replaced Weik. Zarilla batted for Piersall and walked. Gernert walked, forcing in Lipon (12). Kinder singled to center, scoring Lepcio and Zarilla (13-14). White singled to center, scoring Gernert (15).

Stephens singled to right, scoring Kinder (16). Umphlett singled to center, scoring White (17). Lipon walked, filling the bases. Kell flied to Lund.

17 runs, 14 hits, six bases on balls, no errors, three left.

Reprinted from
The Detroit News

SAY 6 AMERICAN LEAGUE CLUB OWNERS WILL VOTE TO TRANSFER TEAM HERE

Associated Press Writer In New York Quotes Baseball Official As Saying Franchise Will Go To Toronto Or Montreal

New York, Sept. 22 (AP)—The New York Yankees are keeping an open mind on the proposed shift of the St. Louis Browns and have joined no plot, President Dan Topping said tonight.

Commenting on an Associated Press story quoting a baseball official that the Browns would be moved to either Toronto or Montreal instead of Baltimore, Topping said:

"We want the Browns to shift to the city which would be best for the American League. At this time, Baltimore is as much in the picture as Toronto or Montreal."

CIVILIAN WILLIAMS HEADS FOR BOSTON

Marines Deactivate Slugger, 'Order' Him Back to Red Sox and Baseball Wars

WASHINGTON, July 28 (AP)—The Marine Corps "ordered" Capt. Ted Williams back to Fenway Park today and baseball's most celebrated citizen set out for Boston to resume his twice-interrupted career.

"I'm anxious to get back in the line-up," Williams said. "I can already hear those guys with the bazoos in left field—and that's all right with me."

The 34-year-old Red Sox outfielder, who flew thirty-eight combat missions over Korea, appeared to be in peak condition as he received his deactivation orders from Col. Kenneth B. Chapell. Williams said he was rusty and that he did not know when he would return to the line-up.

Williams said he would confer tomorrow with Joe Cronin, general manager of the Red Sox. "After all," he said, "I don't even know if they want me."

He praised the Marine Corps and the "wonderful bunch" of fellows he met in Korea. Then Chapell made a little speech praising Williams as an "inspiration to thousands and thousands of young men."

Then, with a wink, Chapell said: "These papers order you back to your home in Fenway Park."

Williams grinned. "That's where I'm going," he said.

Bill Veeck Eliminated From Organization By Sale Of His Holdings

BALTIMORE, Sept. 29 (AP)—Baltimore, the spawning ground of Babe Ruth, was awarded the St. Louis American League franchise today and the mayor of the Maryland city immediately predicted a pennant for next year.

By a unanimous vote of 8-0 at a meeting of the league owners, the third in three days, the Browns were moved to Baltimore which bowed out of the American League just 30 years ago in 1903.

Bill Veeck, the colorful owner of the Browns who has been trying to get out of St. Louis for more than a year, sold his 79 per cent controlling interest to a group headed by Attorney Clarence Miles for $2,475,000, including all minor league properties.

As a result of the transfer, the way also was paved for the league to expand to 10 clubs, including the two Pacific Coast cities of Los Angeles and San Francisco.

Expansion Promise

Del Webb, co-owner of the New York Yankees, who led the fight to award the Brownie franchise to Los Angeles, admitted that he voted for Baltimore "because I did not want any dissension in the league." In fact, he said, he made the Baltimore motion.

But, he added:

"I made this motion with the provision that the American League expand into a 10-club league to include the two Pacific Coast cities — Los Angeles and San Francisco."

Honus Will Be Missing From Wagner's Statue

PITTSBURGH, Aug. 17 (AP)—The Pirates' one-time great shortstop, Honus Wagner, is going to be John Peter Wagner on his statue despite a fiery protest from Councilman Bennett Rodgers.

"I never knew John Peter Wagner," Rodgers told the Council today, "but as a little boy, I knew Honus well, with that name, he endeared himself to three or four generations of Pittsburghers."

Other Councilmen explained that all the legal contracts for the statue, to be erected in Schenley Park near Forbes Field, have been drawn with 79-year-old Wagner's full name and that it is too late to change.

Outvoted but unconvinced, Rodgers withdrew from the field.

Outfielder Injured In Fist Fight

NEW YORK, Sept. 6 (AP)—Carl Furillo, Brooklyn rightfielder, suffered a broken bone in his left hand today in a fight with New York Manager Leo Durocher during the second inning of the Dodgers' 6-3 victory over the Giants. Preacher Roe scored his tenth consecutive victory.

The veteran outfielder, currently leading the National League in batting with a mark of .345, has his hand in a cast and will be out of action for about 10 days, according to club physician Dr. Eugene Zorn.

The injury resulted when Furillo's hand was stepped on while he and Durocher were grappling on the ground and players from both clubs were trying to separate them.

Intercepted

The trouble began when Giant pitcher Ruben Gomez hit Furillo on the right wrist with a pitched ball. The Dodger outfielder charged out to the mound but was intercepted by the umpires before any blows could be struck.

After about five minutes calm was restored and Furillo went to first base.

While Billy Cox, the next Dodger, was at bat Furillo and players in the Giant dugout carried on a heated exchange of words. Suddenly, with a 2-0 count on Cox, Carl made a beeline for the Giant bench. Just as he closed in, Durocher dashed out to meet him in front of the dugout steps. They immediately wrestled each other to the ground.

Players of both teams were quickly around them, trying to separate them. When order was finally restored both Furillo and Durocher were banished from the game by Umpire Dusty Boggess.

Furillo And Vernon Capture Batting Honors On Last Day

New York, Sept. 27 (P)—The battle for batting honors in both major leagues went right down to the wire today with Carl Furillo, of the Brooklyn Dodgers, winning the National by two percentage points, and Mickey Vernon, of the Washington Senators, capturing the American by one.

Furillo, sidelined since September 6 by a broken finger, saw his .344 stand up against the late-season drive of Red Schoendienst and Stan Musial, of the St. Louis Cardinals. Schoendienst, who had two for five against the Chicago Cubs in today's final game, ended the campaign with .342. Musial, the defending champion and six times leader in the National League, wound up third with .337.

Vernon needed his two hits in four times at bat in the season's finale against Philadelphia to win the crown for the second time with a .337. He led the league in 1946 with a .353.

Al Rosen, of the Cleveland Indians, seeking an American League triple crown, connected with three hits in five trips to the plate today for a season's average of .336. The Indians' third baseman ended the season with a 20-game hitting streak.

Rosen, however, paced the American circuit in home runs with 43 and runs batted in with 145. Ed Mathews. Milwaukee

third baseman, topped the National in homers with 47 and the runs batted in honors went to Brooklyn's slugging catcher, Ray Campanella, with 142.

Rosen's foot missed the first base bag on the last play of the season today to keep him from winning the three-way batting crown of the American.

Vernon ended the season with .33717.

It was the bottom of the ninth, two were out, and it was Rosen's last chance. He had singled in the first, doubled in the third, hit into a force-out in the fifth, and beat out a bunt in the seventh.

Al Aber, a former Cleveland pitcher, served three straight balls. Then Rosen fouled off four straight.

On the final pitch, he bounced a rather slow grounder to Jerry Priddy, who was playing deep at third base. Priddy moved a few feet to his left and fielded the ball.

It looked as though Rosen had beaten the throw to first, but when his foot missed the bag he made the last out of the season.

Manager Quits Berth But May Change Mind If Wife Reconsiders

BROOKLYN, Oct. 14 (P)—Manager Charlie Dressen, who directed the Brooklyn Dodgers to two successive pennants only to lose in the World Series, quit in a huff today when his demand for a three-year contract was rejected.

Walter O'Malley, president of the National League champions, told a startled press audience that Dressen had been offered a one-year contract "at a substantial increase in salary," but had turned it down.

The 55-year-old Dressen acknowledged he had asked for a three-year pact but said he would be willing to settle for two. He said definitely he would not consider a one-year contract.

"That's right," Dressen told newsmen in the early part of the conference. "I won't manage the team next year."

Shrugs Shoulders

Later, when asked the same question, he merely shrugged his shoulders and refused to give a direct answer. He said he planned to talk it over with his wife, who is in a hospital with a stomach disorder.

When asked whether he thought Dressen would reconsider, O'Malley said:

"I hope so, but I don't think so."

Baseball Held Exempt From Anti-Trust Suit

Washington, Nov. 9 (P)—Baseball won a major victory today when the Supreme Court ruled for the second time that, in the eyes of Federal law, the game is a sport and not an interstate business.

This means that baseball cannot be challenged in the courts as an illegal monopoly and that the game's controversial reserve clause will stay on the books unless Congress does something about it.

Representative Keating (R., N.Y.), chairman of the monopoly subcommittee of the House Judiciary Committee, said he knows of no legislation in the works to put baseball under the anti-trust laws or to exempt it specifically.

Studied Previously

He said, however, it was possible the Supreme Court decision

might lead to the introduction of a bill that would clarify how Congress stands on the issue.

The monopoly subcommittee studied the question extensively two years ago, but took no action.

Chief Justice Warren read today's brief opinion, to which two justices dissented. It was a "per curiam" decision, that is, one issued by the court rather than over the signature of an individual justice. Apparently, the court split 7 to 2 on the question.

Justice Burton got out a vigorous dissent, in which Justice Reed concurred.

The majority decision held that there is no reason to overturn the Supreme Court ruling of 1922, written by the late Justice Holmes, in which it was decided unanimously that baseball is not subject to the nation's anti-trust laws.

Alston Takes Job Of Managing Brooklyn After Long Experience As School Teacher

OXFORD, Ohio, Nov. 24 (P)—Walter Alston, named today as manager of the Brooklyn Dodgers, generally is recognized as one of nearby Darrtown's "solid citizens."

That was the expression used today when word came that he had picked off one of baseball's managerial jobs. Darrtown is where he lives in his new home.

Only a few days ago Alston, who has had long experience as a school teacher, gave this philosophy of managing a professional baseball team:

"Teaching students is very much like managing baseball players. You've got to encourage some. You've got to drive others if you are going to get the best out of every individual."

Until a year ago Alston spent the off-seasons from baseball as

a teacher and a coach. For six years he taught biology, industrial arts and coached basketball and the now non-existent New Madison High School in Darke County.

For the next 10 years he taught industrial arts and coached basketball at the high school in Lewiston, near Bellefontaine.

As a student at Miami, Alston was a pitcher and it was from his hurling achievements that he got the nickname "Smokey."

As a baseball manager, Alston has had a hand in developing some of the Dodgers' finest players—among them Roy Campanella, Don Newcombe, Junior Gilliam and Rocky Bridges who now is a member of the Cincinnati Reds.

Braves Get Bobby Thomson Of Giants

Calderone In Trade As Antonelli, Liddle Join New York Club

MILWAUKEE, Feb. 1 (AP)—The Milwaukee Braves today traded four players and tossed in an undisclosed amount of cash for outfielder Bobby Thomson and second-string catcher Sam Calderone of the New York Giants.

General Manager John Quinn said the Braves gave lefthanded pitchers Johnny Antonelli and Don Liddle, Ebba St. Claire, a utility catcher, and Billy Klaus, a rookie from Toledo, for Thomson and Calderone.

The trade, completed in New York, was the second in which the Braves have been involved this winter. They traded veteran Sid Gordon and pitcher Max Surkont to Pittsburgh late in December for infielder Danny O'Connell

"We hated to give up both Antonelli and Liddle," Quinn said, "but we had to have a hard-hitting outfielder and were desperate for a catcher to back up Del Crandall."

AARON'S 1ST HOMER

Braves Beat Cards

St. Louis, April 23 (AP)—Solly Hemus kicked a double-play grounder in the fourteenth inning tonight, setting up a situation in which Jim Pendleton delivered a pinch two-run single that enabled the Milwaukee Braves to beat the St. Louis Cardinals 7 to 5.

MILWAUKEE	AB R H O		ST LOUIS	AB R H O
Dittmer 2b	8 0 1 1		Repulski lf	6 0 0 3
O'Connell ss	1 4 5		Moon rf	7 2 5 8
Ma Sam cf	5 0 1 2		Schoe'st 2b	5 1 0 4
Aaron 1b	4 0 0 13		Musial rf	4 1 1 1
Pafko cf	4 1 2 4		Jablonski 3b	8 1 1 0
Asten p	2 2 3		Alston 1b	5 0 1 14
Toal rf	1 1 2		Yvars c	3 0 0 4
Crandall c	4 0 1 0		Frazier	1 0 0 0
Cally p	6 1 0 0		D Rice c	2 0 1 4
Pendleton 1b	0 0 0 0		Haddix	1 0 0 0
Crone p	0 0 0 0		Gramm's ss	1 0 0 0
Conley p	2 0 1 1		Hemus ss	1 0 0 0
Metkovich	0 0 0 0		Raschi p	3 0 0 2
Johnson p	0 0 0 0		Burgess	1 0 0 0
JC White	4 1 1 3		Brazle p	1 0 0 0
			Bilko	1 0 0 0
			Deal p	0 0 0 0
			Presko p	0 0 0 0
			Lint p	0 0 0 0
			Schofield	1 0 0 0
Totals	58 7 16 42		**Totals**	44 5 9 42

1Flied out for Conley in seventh
2Ran for Crandall in ninth
3Struck out for E Johnson in ninth
4Foiled out for Yvars in ninth
5Intentionally walked for Gramms
in ninth
6Struck out for Raschi in ninth.
7Flied out for Brazle in twelfth
8Singled for Jolly in fourteenth.
9Ran for D Rice in fourteenth
10Called out on strikes for Lint in
fourteenth

Milwaukee .... 1 0 0 1 0 1 0 0 1 0 0 6 1 2—7
St Louis .... 0 2 0 0 0 0 0 0 0 0 0 1 0—5

Errors—Aaron Hemus (2) Runs batted in—Aaron (2) Logan Dittmer C White Pendleton 2, Musial Jablonski (2) Schoendienst. Two-base hit—Crandall. Home run—Moon Home run—Jablonski. Logan Aaron. C White Stolen bases—Moon, Aaron. Sacrifices—Adcock. Sacrifice fly—Schoendienst. Double plays—Adcock and Logan. Con... Logan and Adcock. O'Connell Dittmer and Adcock Left on bases—Milwaukee 13, St Louis 8 Base on balls off Jolly 2 Crone 1 Raschi 1 Raschi 3 Stevens Conley 3 Jolly 1 Crone 1 Raschi 4. Brazle 2 Lint 1 Hits off Conley 4 in 5 innings. Jackson 1 in 2 Jolly 1 in 6 Crone 1 in 1 Raschi 10 in 9 Brazle 1 in 3 Deal 4 in 1-3 Presko 1 in 0 (faced 3 batters in 14th Lint 0 in 2-3 Runs and earned runs—Conley 4-3 E Johnson 1-1 Jolly 1 1 Crone 0-0 Raschi 4-4. Brazle 0-0 Deal 3-3 Presko 0-0 Lint 0-0 Winning pitcher—Jolly (1-0) Losing pitcher—Deal (0-1) Umpires—Barlick Warneke Donatelli Ballanfant Time—4 02 Attendance—14,577

Hits Five Off Giants Pitching With Three Coming In First Game

ST. LOUIS, May 2 (AP)—Stan Musial today broke one major league record and tied another by blasting five home runs in a doubleheader divided by the St. Louis Cardinals and the New York Giants. The Cards won the opener, 10-6, and the Giants the nightcap, 9-7. There were 12 homers in the two games.

Musial, six-time National League batting champion, smashed the major league mark for most homers hit in a twin-bill—4—and became the sixth man in history to hammer five in two consecutive games, a feat last accomplished by Don Mueller of the Giants on Sept. 1-2, 1951.

Musial whacked three of his home runs in the first game, including a three-run eighth-inning drive off Jim Hearn that broke a 6-6 tie. It was the first time in his brilliant major league career that the St. Louis slugger had hit three home runs in one game.

Continues Barrage

In the nightcap Stan drove in three runs with his two homers to give him nine runs batted in for the day while raising his batting average to .400. He walked twice, flied deep to center field and popped out in addition to his five homers which gave him a total of eight, tying Hank Sauer of the Chicago Cubs for the major league leadership.

Musial merely set the pace for slugging in the rain-delayed doubleheader watched by 26,662, for the Cardinals finished with eight homers and New York four.

In the opener Whitey Lockman and Wes Westrum hit back-to-back fifth-inning homers off starter Gerry Staley and Monte Irvin whacked one off reliever and winner Al Brazle.

The second game saw Tom Alston give the Cards a running start with a three-run first-inning double off Don Liddle, but the Giants won with eight runs in the fourth inning during which they routed Joe Presko and Royce Lint, collecting eight hits and two walks.

The big blow and the one that put them ahead to stay was a three-run pinch homer off loser Lint by Bobby Hofman.

However, when Musial tagged bullpen ace Hoyt Wilhelm for two homers, Larry Jansen came in to halt an uprising in the seventh and become the winner of a contest in which Don Mueller smashed out five straight hits—including a double and triple—for New York.

PENSION RAISE AGREED UPON

New Plan Must Be Ratified By Players And Owners

New York, Feb. 16 (AP)—A joint committee of major league owners and players agreed today to recommend changes in the players' pension plan which would increase the plan's funds from $450,000 to approximately $2,000,000 a year.

The group, in a five-hour session, also suggested that jurisdiction over these funds be placed in the hands of a committee of two owners and two player representatives who would have "full and complete control."

At the present moment the pension is operated by a four-man committee of owners and players and Ford Frick, the commissioner of baseball. Any final decisions must go before baseball's executive council, consisting entirely of owners.

Must Be Ratified

Under the proposed new plan, the commissioner would have no say in the pension plan and the entire operation would be in the hands of the owner-player committee, selected by their respective groups.

Today's recommendations must go before the owners and players for ratification.

Under the proposed plan, 60 per cent of the gross gate receipts and 60 per cent of the television and radio monies from the All-Star Game would go into the pension fund. Also 60 per cent of the TV and radio monies from the World Series.

Gave Them Everything

The plan would be put into effect at the end of the 1956 season, if adopted.

Under the present arrangement, these monies are placed into a general fund from which pension funds are taken.

"We gave them everything they wanted," said Hank Greenberg, general manager of the Cleveland Indians, a member of the owners' committee. "We want to get the entire matter cleaned up before the All-Star game in July."

"There wasn't a single argument—everything went smoothly," said J. Norman Lewis, attorney representing the players.

Willie Mays Enroute

FT. EUSTIS, Va., March 1 (AP)—Willie Mays, New York Giants outfielder voted 1951 "rookie of the year," was discharged from the Army here today after 21 months service.

Mays, who spent his entire Army hitch here, said he would catch a plane tonight for the Giants' spring training camp at Phoenix, Ariz.

The peppery outfielder was instrumental in sending the Giants into the 1951 World Series with the New York Yankees. When Mays left the New York team in 1952, the Giants were leading in the National League. However, they wound up the season in second place behind the Brooklyn Dodgers.

Mays twice before attempted to gain a discharge from the Army on grounds of dependency but was turned down. Base officials today said his release was granted three months before the regular 24-month tour of duty for enlisted personnel was up because he was able to show a "cyclic employment contract."

While stationed at Eustis, Mays played two seasons of service ball and kept in shape in the winter by playing basketball. Playing centerfield for the base's teams he led the local team in most departments batting .420 in 1952 and .389 in 1953.

First Game ST. LOUIS	ab r h o a rbi
Moon, rf	3 2 2 2 0 0
Schoendienst 2b	4 3 1 3 2 0
Musial, lf	4 1 1 2 0 0
Jablonski 3b	4 0 1 2 0 0
Repulski lf	3 0 0 0 0 0
Alston, 1b	4 1 0 5 2 0
Grammas ss	4 1 1 1 5 2
a-Hemus ss	1 0 0 1 0 0
Rice c	4 0 1 3 0 0
Staley p	1 0 0 0 0 0
b-Lint rf	1 0 0 0 0 0
Brazle p	1 0 0 0 0 0
Totals	33 10 27 10 4 10

NEW YORK	ab r h o a rbi
Williams 2b	4 1 1 4 2 0
Dark ss	4 1 1 1 1 0
Thompson 3b	4 1 1 1 4 1
Irvin lf	3 2 2 3 0 0
Mueller rf	4 0 1 3 0 0
Mays cf	3 0 0 2 0 0
Lockman 1b	4 1 1 9 1 1
Westrum c	4 1 2 7 0 1
Antonelli p	2 0 0 1 3 0
Hearn p	0 0 0 0 0 0
Pickone p	0 0 0 0 0 0
c-Hofman	1 0 0 0 0 0
Totals	33 6 9 24 11 3

St. Louis .... 201 120 04x—10
New York .... 000 321 000—6

Second Game NEW YORK	ab r h o a rbi
Lockman 1b	5 1 2 5 1 0
Dark ss	3 1 1 1 2 0
Thompson 3b	4 1 1 2 3 0
Irvin lf	5 1 1 0 0 0
Mueller rf	4 1 3 4 0 2
Mays cf	4 0 1 1 0 0
St. Claire c	3 1 2 1 0 0
b-Amarillozan	1 0 1 0 0 1
Westrum c	1 0 0 0 0 0
Samford 2b	1 0 0 1 0 0
a-Rhodes	1 1 1 0 0 0
Wilhelm p	0 0 0 0 0 0
Jansen p	1 0 0 0 1 0
Liddle p	2 0 1 0 2 0
b-Baxter	1 0 0 0 0 0
c-Hofman 2b	1 1 1 3 3 3
Totals	38 9 13 27 12 9

ST LOUIS	ab r h o a rbi
Moon, rf	5 1 2 3 0 0
Schoendienst 2b	4 2 2 2 2 2
Musial lf	3 2 2 1 0 2
Jablonski 3b	3 0 0 0 2 0
Repulski lf	4 0 1 4 0 0
Alston 1b	4 0 1 8 0 0
Grammas ss	4 0 1 2 5 0
Poholsky p	2 0 0 0 0 0
g-Lowrey	1 0 0 0 0 0
Deal p	0 0 0 0 0 0
Saini p	0 0 0 0 0 0
a-Hemus	1 0 0 0 0 0
Presko p	0 0 0 0 0 0
Lint p	0 0 0 0 0 0
Wright p	0 0 0 0 0 0
e-Schofield	1 0 0 0 0 0
f-Miller	0 0 0 0 0 0
Rice c	4 0 1 0 0 0
Totals	35 7 10 27 9 7

New York .... 000 800 001—9
St. Louis .... 300 030 100—7

Lanky First Baseman Ties Record As Club Cops Ninth Straight

BROOKLYN, July 31 (AP)—Joe Adcock, Milwaukee Braves' first baseman, slugged four home runs against the Brooklyn Dodgers today, tieing the major league record for most roundtrippers in a game and leading the red-hot Braves to their ninth straight victory in a 15-7 romp.

The four homers and the double also gave him a new major league record of 18 total bases in a nine-inning game. The previous record was 17 by Bobby Lowe of the Boston Braves in 1894, Ed Delehanty of the Philadelphia Phillies in 1896 and Gil Hodges of the Dodgers in 1950 in the same park. All three hit four homers and a single.

Fifth in Nine Innings

Adcock is only the fifth batter in major league history to hit four out of the park in nine innings. In addition to Lowe, Delehanty and Hodges, Lou Gehrig of the New York Yankees hit four in 1932.

Chuck Klein of the Philadelphia Phillies hit four in 10 innings in 1936 and Pat Seerey of the Chicago White Sox hit four in 1948 in 11 innings.

Adcock's blow enabled the clubs to tie the National League record of 10 home runs by both clubs in a game. Eddie Mathews hit two and Andy Pafko one for Milwaukee, while Brooklyn got home runs from Don Hoak, Hodges and Al Walker. The record was set in 1923 by Philadelphia and St. Louis and tied in 1947 by Pittsburgh and St. Louis.

Braves Triumph 14-6 Against Dodgers For 10 Straight Victories

BROOKLYN, Aug. 1 (AP)—Joe Adcock, Milwaukee's new slugging sensation, was beaned but evidently not seriously injured today as the Braves shellacked the Brooklyn Dodgers for the third straight time, 14-6, to stretch their winning streak to 10 games.

Adcock, who tied the major home run record with four against the Brooks yesterday, was hit near the left temple by Clem Labine and carried from the field. Never unconscious, Adcock recovered quickly except for a bump and headache and returned to his hotel.

Although there was quite a row on the field immediately following the "beaning" in the fourth inning, the umpires separating Jackie Robinson and Ed Mathews, no serious charges were made. Earlier in the game Adcock had been knocked down by Russ Meyer, the Dodger starter.

Manager Charlie Grimm said Adcock would be able to play in tomorrow's series final at Brooklyn. No X-rays were taken. The Milwaukee manager said he did not think his player was hit intentionally.

Conley Floors Robinson

Robinson was knocked down by Conley's first pitch in the sixth and Duke Snider also was hit by a pitched ball in the seventh.

The verbal rumpus between Robinson and Mathews broke out as they converged on home plate after Adcock slumped to the ground. Mathews came running in from second base where he was a base-runner. Players from both clubs milled around the field, but the umpires broke it up.

Labine visited Adcock in the Milwaukee clubhouse, telling him how sorry he was and insisting that he didn't try to hit him intentionally. Robinson also extended his sympathy. Adcock merely pointed to the imprint of the ball on the metal protector inside his cap, explaining that it hit him on the back of the head.

No X-Rays were taken.

Adcock had one double today for eight extra base hits in the series.

Baseball's Top Crowd Sees Cleveland Down Yanks In Both Games

CLEVELAND, Sept. 12 (AP)—Before the largest crowd ever to watch a major league baseball game—86,563 with 84,587 paid—the Cleveland Indians whipped the New York Yankees 4-1 and 3-2 today to take an 8½-game American League lead with only 10 more games to play.

Whitey Ford, who started for the Yanks, held the Tribe to two hits until the fifth inning, when Jim Hegan singled to center, took second on Lemon's sacrifice and scored on Avila's single.

New York's lone run came in the sixth, when Mickey Mantle doubled to right, made third on Berra's single, and scored when Irv Noren flied to Doby.

Reynolds Victim

In Cleveland's seventh, there were two out when Rosen slammed a double to center, scoring Al Smith, who had beat out a bunt, and Avila, who had walked.

Ford gave up a total of five hits in six innings, and Reynolds, pitching the last two, yielded three hits. Reynolds was the victim, suffering his fourth defeat in 15 decisions.

Smith reached first base in the eighth when Willie Miranda muffed his grounder, made third on Avila's single, and went all the way when the ball went through Enos Slaughter.

Early Wynn struck out 12 Yankees in winning the second game with a three-hitter, his 21st victory against 11 losses. He fanned Enos Slaughter, Mickey Mantle and Yogi Berra for a 1-2-3 ninth inning. Berra's mighty homer into the upper right field deck after Andy Carey's double put Wynn behind 2-0 in the first inning, but Wally Westlake's two-run double put Cleveland back in front in the fifth.

Hank Bauer's sixth-inning single was the only other hit off Wynn, who hurled a two-hitter in beating the Yanks in New York 6-1 Aug. 31.

Lemon's 22nd Win

Al Rosen's two-run double broke a 1-1 tie in the seventh of the opener which Bob Lemon won on six-hit pitching for his 22nd against six losses.

It was the fourth conquest of the Yanks this season for both Lemon and Wynn and ended the Indians-Yanks series in standoff of 11 games each for the second straight year.

The crowd surpassed the 86,288 who watched an Oct. 10 World Series game here in 1948, and the 82,781 who set the regular season record here June 20, 1948 for a doubleheader between Cleveland and Philadelphia. Thousands stood jamming the aisles and the space behind the outfield fence.

With the pair of victories, the Indians need only three more games to clinch the American League pennant, regardless of what the Yanks do.

A's Transfer To Kansas City Approved

Arnold Johnson Given American Loop's Okay For Purchase Of Club

NEW YORK, Nov. 8 (AP) — The Philadelphia Athletics were transferred to Kansas City today in the third major league shift in 20 months when the American League approved sale of the club to Arnold Johnson and three other Chicago industrialists for about $3,500,000.

As part of the deal, Johnson agreed to sell his interest in Yankee Stadium, home of the New York Yankees, within 90 days.

Clark Griffith, the "Old Fox" who owns the Washington Senators and Hank Greenberg, Cleveland general manager, reportedly voted against the move to Kansas City but the league approved 6-2 for the required three-fourth vote.

The league gave Johnson a unanimous 8-0 vote as the new owner who came up with the cash to buy the debt-ridden A's who have been owned by Connie Mack and his family since the league was organized at the turn of the century.

LOPEZ NOTES MAYS'S CATCH

Says 'Longest Out, Shortest Home Run Beat Us'

New York, Sept. 29 (AP)—"The longest out and the shortest home run of the season beat us, that's all.'"

That's how, Señor Al Lopez, Cleveland's smiling-in-defeat manager, summed up today's opening World Series victory by the New York Giants over his American League champions.

Mays's Catch Vital

He referred to the sensational catch by Giant Centerfielder Willie Mays of a screaming 450-foot drive off the bat of Vic Wertz, and the climactic 270-foot homer with which pinch-hitter Dusty Rhodes ended the game in the tenth.

The Indians had two aboard, the score was tied at 2-2, and Wertz had three straight hits when he came up in the eighth. He blasted a 2-1 pitch deep into center field, but Mays turned his back to the plate, made the catch near the wall, threw on the fly to second base to keep everyone away from the plate, and then fell to the ground.

Wind Catches Ball

Of Rhodes's home run, Lopez said:

"I thought it was just a routine out when it left the bat. Dave Pope said he thought he had the ball all the way, but the wind caught it. But it was a home run, and there's no defense against home runs."

Bob Lemon, who pitched all the way, had little to say about the homer.

"That's the way it goes," he said, "but I'll have to admit it's tough to lose on a hit like that one. I thought it was just another out, and all at once the game's over. Dusty hit under a curve ball and knocked it a mile high, but it got into the stands."

Ball Is 5 Feet Fair

The ball bounded back into the playing field, as fans failed to hold it after it dropped on top of the 11-foot right-field wall—about 5 feet fair—in front of the grand stand seats.

ORIOLES GET 2 INFIELDERS AND PITCHER

Segrist, Leppert, Miller Officially Received From New York

By LOU HATTER
[Sun Staff Correspondent]

Houston, Dec. 1—Contracts of nine players were exchanged today between the Orioles and Yankees as the second installment of baseball's biggest deal—an 18-player swap engineered a fortnight ago when New York sent six athletes to Baltimore for Pitchers Bob Turley and Don Larsen and Shortstop Billy Hunter.

Confirming an earlier rumor, the Birds this afternoon officially received Third Baseman Kal Segrist, Second Baseman Don Leppert and Southpaw Pitcher Bill Miller from New York and sent six players to the Yankee organization, one of them still unidentified.

Wide World Photo

DILLY BY WILLIE—Sequence camera catches Willie Mays, Giants, as he grabs Vic Wertz's 460-foot smash to center. Mays (top left) grabs ball, permits it to settle in his glove, whirls (bottom left) and fires ball back to infield to check runners.

World Series Box Score

New York, Sept. 29 (AP)—The official box score of the first game of the 1954 World Series:

CLEVELAND (A)	Ab	R	H	O	A	E	NEW YORK (N)	Ab	R	H	O	A	E
Smith, lf	4	1	1	1	0	0	Lockman, 1b	5	1	1	9	0	0
Avila, 2b	5	1	1	2	3	0	Dark, ss	4	0	2	3	2	0
Doby, cf	3	0	1	3	0	0	Mueller, rf	5	1	2	2	0	2
Rosen, 3b	5	0	1	1	3	0	Mays, cf	3	1	0	2	0	0
Wertz, 1b	5	0	4	11	1	0	7Thompson, 3b	3	1	1	3	3	0
4Regalado	0	0	0	0	0	0	Irvin, lf	3	0	0	5	0	1
Grasso, c	0	0	0	1	0	0	6Rhodes	1	1	1	0	0	0
Philley, rf	3	0	0	0	0	0	Williams, 2b	4	0	0	1	1	0
1Majeski	0	0	0	0	0	0	Westrum, c	4	0	2	5	0	0
2Mitchell	0	0	0	0	0	0	Maglie, p	3	0	0	2	0	0
Dente, ss	0	0	0	0	0	0	Liddle, p	0	0	0	0	0	0
Strickland, ss	3	0	0	2	3	0	Grissom, p	1	0	0	0	0	0
3Pope, rf	1	0	0	0	0	0							
Hegan, c	4	0	0	6	1	0							
5Glynn, 1b	1	0	0	0	0	0							
Lemon, p	4	0	1	1	0								
Totals	38	2	8	*28	12	0	Totals	38	5	9	30	8	3

*One out when winning run scored
1Announced as batter for Philley in eighth.
2Walked for Majeski in eighth.
3Called out on strikes for Strickland in eighth.
4Ran for Wertz in tenth.
5Struck out for Hegan in tenth.
6Hit home run for Irvin in tenth.

Cleveland (A)	2	0	0	0	0	0	0	0	0	0—2
New York (N)	0	0	2	0	0	0	0	0	0	3—5

Runs batted in—Wertz (2), Mueller, Thompson, Rhodes (3). Two-base hit—Wertz. Three-base hit—Wertz. Home run—Rhodes. Stolen base—Mays. Sacrifices—Irvin, Dente. Left on bases—Cleveland (A), 12, New York (N), 9. Bases on balls—Lemon, 5 (Dark, Mays 2, Thompson 2), Maglie, 2 (Lemon, Doby), Grissom, 3 (Mitchell, Doby, Pope). Strikeouts—Maglie, 2 (Strickland, Smith), Grissom, 2 (Pope, Glynn), Lemon, 6 (Maglie 2, Irvin, Thompson, Grissom, Mueller). Hits—Maglie, 7 in 7 (none out in eighth inning), Liddle, 0 in 1/3, Grissom, 1 in 2 2/3. Runs and earned runs—Maglie, 2-2, Liddle, 0-0, Grissom, 0-0, Lemon 5-5. Hit by pitcher—Maglie (Smith). Wild pitch—Lemon. Winning pitcher—Grissom. Losing pitcher—Lemon. Umpires—Al Barlick (NL), plate; Charlie Berry (AL), first base; Jocko Conlan (N), second base; John Stevens (AL), third base; Lon Warneke (NL), left field; Larry Napp (AL), right field. Time—3:11. Attendance—52,751 (paid). Receipts—$316,957.25 (net).

SENIOR LOOP GIVES UP IDEA OF 10 CLUBS

National League Baseball Action Announced By President Giles

New York, Jan. 29 (AP)—The National League today abandoned the idea of expanding to a ten-club league. President Warren Giles said "It is my conclusion there is no sentiment for any ten-club league now."

Giles said no "formal or informal" vote was taken at today's league meeting, but the expansion idea was discussed for an hour and a half.

Other Reasons Cited

Giles said the general sentiment of the club owners seemed to be that expansion to ten clubs might dilute the other eight teams already in the league. Other reasons cited, he said, were that there would be too many second division clubs in a ten-club league and that there weren't enough ball players of major league caliber to go around.

A'S TROUNCE TIGERS BY 6-2

Truman Tosses First Ball At Debut Of Kansas City

Kansas City, April 12 (AP)—The Kansas City Athletics made their American League debut in a resounding 6-to-2 victory over the Detroit Tigers today in colorful Municipal Stadium as ex-President Truman and 32,843 other fans cheered wildly.

The Athletics boomed nine hits off starter Ned Garver and Vanoide Fletcher who succeeded him in the seventh inning. One was a home run by Bill Wilson, lined over the left-field wall at the 370-foot mark in the eighth inning.

DETROIT					KANSAS CITY				
	Ab.	H.	O.	A.		Ab.	H.	O.	A.
Kuenn.ss	4	1	2	1	Power.1b	3	0	6	1
4Tuttel.1b	4	1	2	1	4Bollweg.1b	1	1	3	0
Kaline.rf	4	2	3	1	Suder.2b	5	0	4	4
Boone.2b	2	0	1	5	Finigan.3b	4	1	0	3
Porter.1b	4	1	7	0	Zernial.lf	4	1	2	0
Tuttle.cf	3	0	1	0	Renna.rf	4	1	2	0
J.Phillips.lf	3	0	2	0	W.Wilson.cf	3	3	3	0
1D'ls'g.lf	0	0	0	0	Dem'stri.ss	4	2	2	1
R.Wilson.c	4	3	4	1	Astroth.c	1	0	4	0
Garver.p	2	0	0	0	Kellner.p	2	0	0	4
2Pain	0	0	0	0	5Valo	0	0	0	0
3M'imb's	0	0	0	0	Bl'kwell.p	0	0	0	0
Fl'ch'r.p	0	0	1	0					
Totals	30	8	24	9	Totals	31	9	27	13

1Walked for Phillips in ninth.
2Walked for Garver in seventh.
3Ran for Pain in seventh.
4Singled for Power in sixth.
5Walked for Kellner in sixth.

Detroit . . . . . . 0 0 0 1 1 0 0 0 0—2
Kansas City . . . . 0 1 1 0 0 3 0 1 x—6

Harry Agganis of Boston Red Sox Dies; Ex-Football Star From Bay State Was 25

CAMBRIDGE, Mass., June 27 (AP) Harry Agganis, the Boston Red Sox first baseman and former Boston University football star, died today. His age was 25.

Mr. Agganis succumbed at Sancta Maria Hospital while apparently recovering from a chest ailment which had sidelined him six weeks ago.

Physicians said in a statement they believed death was caused by "a massive pulmonary embolism."

Mr. Agganis after a brilliant sports career at Boston University, passed up professional football to sign with the Red Sox following his graduation in 1953. He was sent to Louisville in the American Association where he hit twenty-three homers, drove in 108 runs and batted .281 in his first season.

Promoted to the Red Sox last year, Mr. Agganis hit only .251, but had eleven homers, eight triples, thirteen doubles and drove in fifty-seven runs. He lost his starting job at first base to a rookie, Norm Zauchin, at the beginning of this season, but won it back after a short time. He was hitting over .300 when he complained of chest pains and was hospitalized May 16.

LEAGUE HEAD SEES CINCINNATI TUSSLE

Giles in Stands as Fight of Tebbetts, Cards' Walker Starts Free-for-All

CINCINNATI, July 5 (AP)—Manager Birdie Tebbetts of the Cincinnati Redlegs and Harry (The Hat) Walker of the St. Louis Cardinals battled with their fists tonight in the ninth inning as the Redlegs rallied with four hits and two runs to beat the Cards 5—4.

Players from both squads mixed it up on the field after the Tebbetts-Walker battle. Both pilots were ejected from the game along with Bill Sarni, the St. Louis catcher.

The fight was preceded by an argument between Tebbetts and Umpire John B. (Jocko) Conlan. The umpire had been talking to Sarni and Paul LaPalme at the mound. Conlan returned to the plate and Walker joined the conversation.

Tebbetts Starts Swinging

Tebbetts stepped around Conlan and started swinging. Walker wrestled Tebbetts to the ground and the players poured from the dugouts and the fielders ran in to join the fray.

[The United Press reported that Ted Kluszewski, Cincinnati's 230-pound first baseman, grabbed the 160-pound Solly Hemus with one hand and held off two other St. Louis players with his other hand.]

Park policemen rushed out and restored order.

Tebbetts was bleeding from the mouth.

The Cincinnati manager was angered over what he considered the stalling tactics of the Cardinals with the score tied and two out in the ninth.

POLIO STRIKES VIC WERTZ

Hospitalized Ex-Bird Is Lost To Indians For Season

Cleveland, Aug 26 (AP)—Vic Wertz, hitting hero of the Cleveland Indians' 1954 World Series and a key man in the Tribe's uphill battle to retain the pennant, was stricken with polio today.

The husky 30-year-old first baseman became ill before last night's game with the New York Yankees. He complained of a headache, fever and sore throat.

Today at Lakeside Hospital, Dr. Don Kelly, the baseball club's physician, diagnosed the illness as infantile paralysis.

Plans No Team Inoculation

"It's safe to assume," Kelly said, "that Wertz will be out for the remainder of the season."

Kelly said there was no sign of paralysis and that Wertz's condition was "good." He said he planned no mass inoculation of the team and no quarantine, even for pitcher Art Houtteman, Wertz's room mate for road trips. The Indians have been at home a week.

Wertz and his wife Lucille, who make their home in Detroit, have no children.

GIANTS SPLIT 2 WITH PHILS

Mays Hits 51st Home Run; Triple Play Pulled

New York, Sept. 25 (AP)—Willie Mays hit his fifty-first home run of the season to tie the club record today as the New York Giants and Philadelphia Phillies split a double-header.

The Giants won the first game, 5-2, aided by Mays' homer, but dropped the second 3-1 marking the end of Leo Durocher's reign as manager of the Giants.

It was an inglorious finish, for the Phils got the final three outs in the ninth inning on a triple play after the New Yorkers had put two runners on with none out.

SCORE SETS STRIKEOUT MARK

Washington, Sept. 14 (AP)—The pesky Washington Senators halted Cleveland's rush toward the American League pennant tonight with a come-from-behind 3-to-2 victory that gave Ray Narleski his first defeat of the season.

The defeat narrowed Cleveland's lead over the second-place New York Yankees, winners today over Detroit, to one game, but the clubs are all even in the vital loss column. The Yankees have two more games to play than Cleveland.

The run that shattered Narleski's nine-game winning streak came across in the eighth inning on a single by Pete Runnels, a sacrifice and a sharply hit double to left by rookie Jose Valdivielso.

Ramos Pitching Winner

Lost in the Indian gloom was a new strike-out record set by starter Herb Score and a magnificent clutch relief job by Narleski an inning before the Runnels-Valdivielso combination wrecked him.

The winning pitcher was rookie Pedro Ramos, who delighted the crowd of 7,928 by stopping the Indians with one hit in the final two innings after he had scored the tying run as a pinch runner for starter Mickey McDermott.

Score struck out nine, raising his season's total to 235. Thus he broke the record of 227 strikeouts by a major league rookie set back in 1911 by Grover Cleveland Alexander, of the Philadelphia Phillies.

Washington, which has been the Indians' Achilles heel all season, wound up its season's series with Cleveland ahead, 13-9. No other club won a season series from the league leaders.

CLEVELAND	Ab	H	O	A	WASHINGTON	Ab	H	O	A
Smith,3b	4	2	0	1	Yost,3b	5	2	0	1
Woodl'g,rf	5	0	2	0	Oravetz,rf	4	1	4	0
Avila,2b	4	1	2	0	Vernon,1b	2	1	10	1
Rosen,1b	3	0	5	2	Sievers,lf	4	0	3	0
Evers,lf	3	1	1	0	Paula,rf	4	0	1	1
Doby,cf	4	1	1	0	Ump'ett,cf	0	0	1	0
Hegan,c	4	1	12	1	Runnels,2b	3	2	1	3
Str'k'd,ss	3	2	0	2	Fitzg'ald,c	2	0	2	0
Score,p	1	0	1	0	1Korchek,c	1	0	1	0
Narl'ski,p	0	0	0	0	Vald'so,ss	3	1	4	5
3Fain	0	0	0	0	McDerm't,p	3	2	0	1
4Harrell	0	0	0	0	2Ramos,p	1	0	0	0
5Mitch'l	1	0	0	0					
Totals	32	8	24	6	Totals	32	9	27	12

1Took third strike for Fitzgerald in fourth.
2Ran for McDermott in seventh.
3Walked for Strickland in ninth.
4Ran for Fain in ninth.
5Popped up for Narleski in ninth.

Cleveland	0	0	0	1	0	0	0	1	0	0—2
Washington	0	0	1	0	0	0	0	1	1	x—3

DODGERS WIN PENNANT IN RECORD TIME

Clinch Earliest Flag In League History, 10-2, At Braves' Expense

Milwaukee, Sept. 8 (AP)—Brooklyn's frolicking Dodgers bombarded their way past Milwaukee's Braves 10 to 2 today and clinched the National League pennant on the earliest date in the senior circuit's 79-year history.

It was the eighth straight victory for the Dodgers, who last won the flag in 1953. They took it like champions, beating five pitchers for an assortment of 11 hits while Rookie Roger Craig and Karl Spooner combined to hold Milwaukee to six hits, cramming the Braves into the runner-up spot—17 games behind.

Fans Rice To End Game

Spooner gave it a whirlwind finish, snapping off his curve and firing his fast ball past the Braves in 5 2-3 innings of no-hit relief work. The 24-year-old southpaw, a sensation at the season's close in '54, retired 13 Braves in order before he allowed a base runner with a walk in the eighth inning.

He struck out nine men—humming a third strike past Pinch-Hitter Del Rice to end it all for his seventh triumph of the season.

The Dodgers, who set the previous league mark for an early clinching when they won the '53 flag on Sept. 12, also here in Milwaukee's County Stadium, wasted little time getting the big one.

They rumbled across four runs in the first inning when Bob Buhl, the league's earned-run leader, walked three men and struck Roy Campanella with a pitch after two were out. Gil Hodges then lined a two-run single and Buhl was gone. Phil Paine came on and gave up a run-scoring single by Don Zimmer before getting the side out.

KALINE WINS
BATTING CROWN
AT AGE 20 —

BANKS SETS MARK IN 6-5 CUB DEFEAT

Hits 5th Grand-Slam Homer of Season—Cards Win on Four-Bagger in 12th

ST. LOUIS, Sept. 19 (AP)—Ernie Banks of the Cubs set a record tonight with his fifth grand slam homer of the season, but the St. Louis Cardinals scored a 6-5 victory on Rip Repulski's home run with two out in the twelfth inning.

Banks' forty-fourth homer broke a record of four bases-loaded drives in one season held by ten other players, including Babe Ruth. The 24-year-old Banks already had beaten the major league record for homers by a shortstop in one season when he hit No. 40. Vernon Stephens hit thirty-nine for the Boston Red Sox in 1949.

In contrast, the Cardinals tied the score in the eighth on a three-run homer by Harry Elliott, his first of the season. The blow capped a Cardinal comeback from a deficit of 3—0.

Lyndall McDaniel, the Cardinals' $40,000 bonus rookie, did a creditable job in his first start in organized baseball until Banks hit his homer. The 19-year-old Oklahoman had allowed one run and six hits in six innings.

Dee Fondy, Gene Baker and Glen Wade hit successive singles in the seventh, loading the bases, then Banks hit a drive into the left-field bleachers. The Redbirds scored two in the bottom of the seventh. Singles by Alex Grammas and Ken Boyer drove the runs across.

CHICAGO (N.)	ab.r.h.po.a	ST. LOUIS (N)	ab.r.h.po.a
Fondy, 1b	5 2 1 15 1	Boyer, 3b	6 0 1 1 3
Baker, 2b	5 1 2 4 5	Sch'ndnst.2b	4 0 0 6 8
Wade, cf	6 1 2 3 0	Musial, 1b	4 0 0 6 1
Banks, ss	5 1 3 1 6	dMackinson	0 0 0 0 0
Speake, lf	4 0 2 1 0	Wright, p	1 0 0 1 0
Ba'mholtz, rf	4 0 0 6 0	Repulski, lf	5 1 2 1 0
Miksis, 3b	5 0 0 0 4	Elliott, rf	5 1 2 1 1
Cooper, c	5 0 2 4 0	Whise'ant.cf.3	1 1 1 1
Minner, p	3 0 1 0 1	bVirdon cf	2 0 0 2 0
Tremel, p	0 0 0 0 0	Burbrink, c	5 0 1 8 0
Davis, p	1 0 0 1 1	Grammas,ss	5 1 2 3 1
		McDaniel, p	3 0 1 3 2
Total	45 5 13 36 18	aSarni	1 0 1 0 0
		Smith, p	0 0 0 0 0
		cMoon, 1b	2 0 0 4 1
		Total	46 6 13 36 21

*Two out when winning run was scored.
aSingled for McDaniel in seventh.
bFlied out for Whisenant in eighth.
cGrounded out for Smith in ninth.
dRan for Musial in ninth.

Chicago ......100 000 410 00—5
St. Louis .....000 000 410 00—6
Error—Burbrink.
Runs batted in—Baker Banks 4. Grammas, Boyer, Elliott 3. Repulski. Two-base hit—Cooper. Home runs—Banks, Elliott, Repulski. Sacrifice—Baumholtz. Double plays—Grammas and Schoendienst; Miksis, Baker and Fondy; Boyer, Schoendienst and Musial. Left on bases—Chicago 11. St. Louis 8. Bases on balls—Off Minner 1. Tremel 1. Davis 1 McDaniel 1. Smith 1. Struck out—By Minner 3. McDaniel 3. Smith 2. Wright 2. Hits—Off Minner 10 in 7 innings (faced three batters in eighth). Tremel 1 in 1 2-3. Davis 1 in 3. McDaniel 10 in 7. Smith 3 in 2. Wright 0 in 3. Runs and earned runs—Off Minner 5 and 5. Davis 1 and 1. McDaniel 5 and 5. Passed ball—Burbrink. Winning pitcher—Wright (2—3). Losing pitcher—Davis (6—11). Umpires—Warneke, Ballanfant, Barlick and Pinelli. Time of game—2:54. Attendance—4,953.

TIGERS WHIP INDIANS, 6-2

Boone Bats In Two Runs; Kaline Has Sore Wrist

Detroit, Sept. 25 (AP)—Ray Boone knocked in two runs with a single and double to push his r.b.i total to 116 and lead the Detroit Tigers to a 6-to-2 victory over a sub-dotted Cleveland Indian team today before a closing-day crowd of 17,888 in Briggs Stadium.

Bob Miller allowed seven hits in going the distance to beat the Indians for the second time in eight days. He chilled, and practically killed the Indian pennant hopes last Sunday.

Al Kaline, Detroit's brilliant right fielder, left the game after two innings because of a sore wrist and, although he was held hitless in this final 1955 time at bat, closed out the season with a .340 batting average to lead the league.

Kaline, becoming Detroit's nineteenth batting champion and first since George Kell in 1949, finished with an even 200 hits in 588 times at bat. Harvey Kuenn chipped in with his eighth home run as the Tigers spoiled Bud Daley's big league start.

Wide World Photo

CATCH THAT 'KILLED' YANKS: Sandy Amoros, Dodgers' left fielder, makes a spectacular gloved hand catch of bid for extra base hit by Yanks' Yogi Berra in sixth inning of yesterday's game. There were two Yankee runners on at time and both might have scored. Instead, Gil McDougald, who was on first base, was doubled to 'kill' the Yankee hopes of a bid inning

Game 7	October 4 at New York						
BKN	000	101	000			2	5 0
NY	000	000	000			0	8 1
Podres	Byrne, Grim (6), Turley (8)						

LEO DUROCHER GETS NBC JOB

Ex-Giant Pilot To Get $52,000 In Executive Position

New York, Sept. 27 (AP)—Leo Durocher bade farewell to baseball today after 30 years. He took an executive job with the National Broadcasting Company at a reported $52,000 a year.

Durocher resigned Saturday as manager of the New York Giants, a job that paid him an undisclosed salary, reportedly in the neighborhood of $60,000 a year.

NBC unveiled the fiery ex-manager at a news conference as the new "quiet, conservative" network executive. He will negotiate with talent and help in properly programming it. He also will fill in from time to time in the role of expert sports commentator, but will not be a regular broadcaster. His contract is for one year.

Sandy Amoros Gives Simple Explanation

NEW YORK, Oct. 4 (AP)—The key catch of the 1955 World Series was made in the sixth inning when Sandy Amoros, fleet Brooklyn outfielder, raced into the far left corner of Yankee Stadium to catch Yogi Berra's tricky high fly — and then doubled Gil McDougald at first, with Pee Wee Reese relaying the ball.

Two men were on and nobody out when the sensational catch and double play were made.

Amoros, a Cuban who talks little English, was asked afterwards if he thought he could catch the ball.

"I dunno," he said. "I just run like hell."

Clark Griffith, Washington Baseball Club Owner, Dies

Washington, Oct. 27 (P)—Clark Griffith, baseball's "Old Fox" of 85, died peacefully in his sleep tonight after a six-day bout with complications that developed unexpectedly from neuritis.

Griffith was "called out" at 8.40 P.M. (E.S.T.) by his physician, Dr. George A. Resta. The president of the Washington Baseball Club succumbed to stomach hemorrhages and lung congestion. He died at Georgetown University Hospital, which he entered October 19 expecting to remain a week. He was placed on the critical list October 22.

One of the game's best-known personalities, Griffith helped organize the American League in 1901 and was electetd to baseball's Hall of Fame in 1946.

CY YOUNG IS DEAD; FAMED PITCHER, 88

His Record of 511 Victories Has Never Been Surpassed —Hurled 3 No-Hit Games

NEWCOMERSTOWN, Ohio. Nov. 4 (P)—Denton True (Cy) Young, one of baseball's great pitchers died today at the age of 88.

A member of baseball's Hall of Fame, Mr. Young was stricken while sitting in a chair in the home of Mr. and Mrs. John Benedum, with whom he made his home near here.

Baseball Mourns Death Of Wagner

PITTSBURGH, Dec. 6 (P)—Time ran out for Honus Wagner today, and the baseball world mourned one of its all-time great stars.

The bandy-legged, broad-shouldered Honus died quietly in his sleep at the modest home in suburban Carnegie where he had been comfined for months by the illnesses of old age. He was 81.

Funeral services will be at 2:30 p.m. Friday from the Beinhauer Funeral Home, 2630 West Liberty Ave.

DUKE SNIDER TOPPED BY FIVE POINTS

Catcher Second In National League To Win Award 3 Times

New York. Dec. 8 (P)—Catcher Roy Campanella, who made a tremendous comeback to lead the Brooklyn Dodgers to another pennant and their first World Series victory, today was named the National League's most valuable player for 1955 after a close battle with teammate Duke Snider.

By the narrow margin of five points, the stocky, 34-year-old receiver nosed out the Duke, 226 to 221, to become the second player in league history to win the prized award three times.

Won in 1951 And '53

Stan Musial, the great St. Louis Cardinal outfielder, received the honor in 1943, 1946 and 1949.

Campanella won it previously in 1951 and 1953.

Only two other stars of the league ever won this distinction more than once. They were Rogers Hornsby in 1925 and 1929 and Carl Hubbell in 1933 and 1936.

Thus Campy joins another outstanding current catcher. Yogi Berra, of the New York Yankees. among the ultra elite of the game.

Just five days ago Berra was picked as the American League's most valuable for 1955 and that was the third time, too, for the hard-hitting Yankee catcher. Two others—Joe DiMaggio and Jimmy Foxx—also won the A.L.'s award three times.

CONNIE MACK DIES AT 93

Philadelphia, Feb. 8 (AP)—Connie Mack, who helped pioneer baseball from the sandlots to the number one sport in the nation, died today at the age of 93.

Known around the world as the Grand Old Man of Baseball and one of the most beloved men in the history of the game, Mack—born in East Brookfield, Mass., December 23, 1862—died quietly with his wife, four daughters and one of three sons at his bedside.

He had been failing steadily since falling out of bed and breaking his hip last October 1. He made two visits to the hospital in an effort to regain the full use of his legs.

No Walking Since Accident

The end for the man who changed his name from Cornelius McGillicuddy to Connie Mack to fit a baseball box score, came at 3.20 P.M. at the home of one of his daughters, Mrs. Frank Cunningham, in the Germantown section of Philadelphia.

Mack had been unable to walk since his accident and only last week a son, Roy, announced that for the first time since 1888 his father would not make his annual winter pilgrimage to the South.

Dodgers Edge Phils In 10th Inning, 5-4

Jersey City, N.J., April 19 (AP). Pinch-hitter Rube Walker's sacrifice fly scored pinch-runner Don Zimmer in the 10th inning to give Brooklyn a 5-to-4 victory over Philadelphia today in the first of seven "home on the road" games for the Brooklyn Dodgers at Roosevelt Stadium.

Trailing 4-3 in the last of the 10th, the Dodgers knocked out Murray Dickson and tied the score on Duke Snider's single and Roy Campanella's double, his 1,000th major league hit.

Erskine's No-Hit Job Blanks Giants, 3 To 0

Brooklyn, May 12 (AP)—Carl Erskine, of the Brooklyn Dodgers, hurled the second no-hit, no-run game of his career today, turning back the New York Giants, 3 to 0, in a game in which the losers' strongest threat was a blow that sailed over the fence foul by inches.

He did it before against the Chicago Cubs on June 19, 1952, and won that game by 5-0.

The foul "home run" was struck by Whitey Lockman in the ninth inning. The only hard fielding chances came off the bats of Ray Katt and Willie Mays. In the fifth inning Carl Furillo raced to the scoreboard in right-center field to make a gaudy catch off Katt.

Robinson Snares Ball

An inning earlier Jackie Robinson, still an agile athlete, made a diving catch at third base of a bullet hit by Mays. Al Dark had walked immediately before Mays batted.

Immediately after Dark slapped back to Erskine for the final out, the Dodgers mobbed the slender 29-year-old pitcher. Walter O'Malley, president of the Dodgers, promised Erskine a check for $500 even before he had reached the dressing room.

While the Dodger fans were watching the no-hitter being unfurled before them, many of them were listening on their portable radios to another. However, Don Ferrarese, of Baltimore, lost his chance to get into the record books with Erskine when Andy Carey, of the Yankees, sent a high bounder toward second that went for a hit to start the ninth. The rookie Baltimore pitcher won his game, however, 1-0.

Feat Before TV Cameras

The handsome Hoosier became the eighth pitcher since 1900 to register two no-hitters in his career, but his was the first to be televised nationally. The game was seen, coast to coast, on the usual Saturday Game of the Week TV show.

Bob Feller and Cy Young, of the Cleveland Indians, lead all the rest with three no-hitters, but one of Young's was pitched before 1900.

Erskine, who walked two and fanned three, now has won two games this season while losing the same number. His previous victory was against the Giants on April 25.

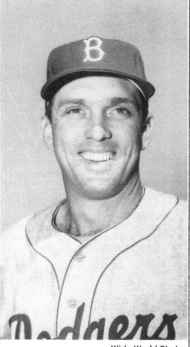

Wide World Photo

CARL ERSKINE
Pitches no-hitter for Dodgers

Hitless Till 10th, Braves Win in 11th

By The Associated Press.

MILWAUKEE, May 26—The Milwaukee Braves, who came within one out of winning a zany game in which they were held hitless by three Cincinnati hurlers for nine and two-thirds innings, pulled out a 2-1 decision in the bottom of the eleventh today to cling to the National League lead.

Frank Torre batted in both Milwaukee runs, and both were scored by Hank Aaron before 22,936 at County Stadium. Joe Black was the losing pitcher and Ray Crone, who shut out the Redlegs for eight and two-thirds innings, the winner.

The Box Score

CINCINNATI (N.)	ab.	r.	h.	po.	a.	MILWAUKEE (N.)	ab.	r.	h.	po.	a.
Temple, 2b	2	0	0	2	1	O'Conn'l. 2b.	3	0	0	1	2
dBailey	1	0	0	0	0	bCovington	1	0	0	0	0
Bridges, 2b	1	0	0	0	0	Dittmer, 2b.	1	0	1	1	1
Robinson, lf.	2	0	1	3	0	Logan, ss.	4	0	0	2	3
aCrowe	1	0	0	0	0	Mathews, 3b.	5	0	0	0	0
Palys, lf	0	0	2	0	0	Aaron, rf.	4	2	1	0	0
eThurman	1	0	0	0	0	Thomson, lf.	2	0	0	4	0
Black, p	2	0	0	0	0	gTanner	0	0	0	0	0
Bell, cf	5	0	1	3	0	Bruton, cf.	2	0	0	6	0
Klus'ski. lf.	4	1	1	5	1	Torre, 1b.	4	0	1	14	1
bDyck, 1b.	1	0	1	4	0	Crandall. c.	2	0	0	5	1
Post, rf	3	0	1	3	0	Crone, p.	2	0	0	0	2
Jab'nski, 3b.	5	0	0	1	2						
Burgess, c.	4	0	2	5	0	Total	30	2	3	33	10
McMill'n, ss.	2	0	0	3	1						
Klippst'n, p.	2	0	0	0	1						
Freeman, p.	0	0	0	0	0						
cFrazier, lf.	2	0	0	0	0						
Total	38	1	7	31	6						

*One out when winning run scored.
aFlied out for Robinson in third.
bStruck out for O'Connell in seventh.
cGrounded out for Klippstein in eighth.
dGrounded out for Temple in eighth.
eGrounded out for Freeman in ninth.
bRan for Kluszewski in ninth.
gWalked for Thomson in eleventh.

| Cincinnati | 000 000 001 00—1 |
| Milwaukee | 010 000 000 01—2 |

Error—Torre.
Runs batted in—Torre 2, Post.
Two base hits—Bell, Post, Dittmer. Three base hit—Aaron. Sacrifice—Crone, Bruton. McMillan. Sacrifice fly—Torre. Double play —O'Connell and Torre; Kluszewski and McMillan; O'Connell, Logan and Torre. Left on base—Cincinnati 9, Milwaukee 10. Bases on balls—Off Klippstein 7, Crone 4, Black 2. Struck out—By Klippstein 4, Crone 3. Hits—Off Klippstein 0 in 7 innings, Freeman 0 in 1, Black 3 in 3. Runs and earned runs—Off Klippstein 1 and 1, Black 1 and 1, Crone 1 and 1. Hit by pitcher—By Klippstein (Aaron). Winning pitcher—Crone (3-1). Losing pitcher—Black (2-2). Umpires —Secory, Landes, Goetz and Dascoli. Time of game—2:39. Attendance—22,936.

Dale Long's 8th Straight Homer Paces Bucs Win

PITTSBURGH, May 28 (P)— First baseman Dale Long of the Pittsburgh Pirates continued his almost incredible home run hitting tonight by blasting his eighth homer in as many games to set a major league record as the third-place Pirates beat the Brooklyn Dodgers 3-2.

Bobby Friend, the Pirates' ace right hander, gave up only two hits in winning his eighth game against two defeats—the best record of any major league hurler.

Standing Ovation

The crowd stood and cheered several minutes after Long's circuit clout and the big fellow finally stepped from the dugout to doff his cap. Earlier in the day he got a tangible reward for his tremendous slugging—a new contract which he said increased his salary by $2,500 to $16,000.

A tremendous crowd of 32,221 gave Long a standing ovation after his leadoff homer into the right field stands in the fourth inning off starter Carl Erskine, who hasn't won a game since pitching a no-hitter May 12 against the New York Giants. He now has a 2-4 record.

Long struck out on his last two appearances and grounded out in his first trip in the first inning. The Dodger infield put a deep shift to the right side of the infield for the southpaw swinging Long—the first time a team has done that all season. Long went into the contest hitting at a .419 clip.

Ted Williams Spits at Crowd, Fined $5,000

BOSTON, Aug. 7 (P)—Boston Red Sox General Manager Joe Cronin tonight fined Ted Williams $5,000 for his spitting gestures in today's game against the New York Yankees.

Cronin took the severe action an hour and a half after Williams' latest outburst, imposing the fine for what he termed "conduct on the field."

Williams said he was sorry it happened.

"Sorry"

"I was sorry the instant I did it," Williams said. Previously Ted was silent and sullen in the dressing room and had said nothing to the press immediately following the contest.

Williams had spit several times earlier this season—once in the presence of Major League Commissioner Ford Frick.

In addition to the spitting today, Williams threw his bat some 40 feet in the air after drawing a bases-loaded walk in the 11th inning as the Red Sox edged New York 1-0.

Cronin told writers he assessed the fine against Williams himself after conferring with Manager Mike Higgins and talking by telephone with owner Tom Yawkey in New York.

Gomez Gets Suspension And Fine

MILWAUKEE, July 19 (P)— One of the wildest melees of the current National League season resulted today in a $250 fine for pitcher Ruben Gomez of the New York Giants a $100 fine for first baseman Joe Adcock of the Milwaukee Braves and a three-day suspension for Gomez.

In addition, Gomez drew a severe reprimand from Warren C. Giles, league president, who stipulated that the fine be paid personally by the Giants' pitcher, not his team. Adcock was not suspended.

Mad Fracas

The Puerto Rican righthander touched off a mad fracas involving players of both teams in the second inning of last night's game at County Stadium when he twice hit Adcock — once with a pitched ball and once with a deliberately thrown ball. Adcock, with most of his teammates in pursuit, charged after Gomez who ran to the dugout and disappeared up the ramp leading to the clubhouse. Order was restored by the umpires and half a dozen police officers. The Giant eventually won in 11 innings, 8-6.

Giles told Gomez in a telegram:

"Your conduct in the game at Milwaukee last night was the most unsportsmanlike nature and could have had extremely serious results. For that conduct you are fined the sum of $250, payable at the league office before game time July 23. This fine is to be paid by you personally and the New York club is not to reimburse you in whole or in part."

The telegram to Adcock contained no comment other than to notify him that he had been fined $100.

Both Banished

Both players were banished from the game after the incident which had 33,230 spectators in an uproar.

The suspension means that Gomez won't face the Braves in the remaining two games of the series here, tonight and tomorrow. But Manager Bill Rigney of the Giants said he planned to pitch him against Milwaukee "the first chance I get. That's the only way we can straighten this out. I can't hide him from them. It certainly will be no later than next week when we play them in New York."

The Braves, front running, will play the Giants at the Polo Grounds July 24, 25 and 26.

Gomez had no comment today but Rigney said he had talked with him and that the pitcher regretted the incident.

The Braves had taken a one-run lead off Gomez in the first inning when the trouble started. Adcock, who has hit 17 home runs this year, seven in the last nine games, was the first man to bat in the second. Gomez threw a close pitch that hit the 220-pound Braves' slugger on the right wrist. Umpire Bill Jackowski motioned Adcock to first base.

Police Escort

As Adcock jogged along the baseline, rubbing his wrist, he yelled something and Gomez answered. Adcock suddenly charged toward the mound. Gomez froze for a second, then threw the ball at Adcock. It struck Joe on the thigh. Then the chase was on, with Gomez heading for the dugout and Adcock in close pursuit. Gomez didn't stop until he got to the safety of his own clubhouse under the Stadium. Later he was given a police escort out of the park.

"I run," Gomez commented. "I don't want him to break my ribs."

Said Adcock: "It's a good thing I didn't catch him; I was never so mad in my life. I got to make a living with my bat and I'm not going to stand up there and let 'em beat me to death with the ball."

Maglie Hurls No-Hitter, Keeps Dodgers In Race

BROOKLYN, N.Y., Sept. 25 —Sal Maglie, a picture of pitching magnificence, attained the finest hour of his checkered eight-year career in the majors tonight when he hurled a no-hit, no-run game against the Philadelphia Phillies to lead the Brooklyn Dodgers to a 5-0 victory and within a half game of the National League lead.

The 39-year old Maglie, red-hot in chilly 69-degree weather, walked only two batters and faced only 29 in becoming the oldest pitcher to toss a no-hitter since Cy Young did it as a 41-year-old for the Red Sox against the Yankees in 1908.

Like Money In Bank

Maglie, known as a "money pitcher," looked like a million dollars tonight as he permitted only four balls to be hit out of the infield and became the third major league pitcher this year, to toss a no-hitter.

Maglie used only 110 pitches in manufacturing this masterpiece. The partisan Dodger crowd was all with him in the ninth as he opened the frame by getting Roy Smalley on a foul pop. Dodger catcher Roy Campanella made a fine catch of the ball as he tumbled in the Brooklyn dugout.

Maglie then struck out pinch-hitter Harvey Haddix and hit Richie Ashburn with a pitch. But Marv Blaylock rolled to second-baseman Jim Gilliam for the final out.

WERTZ BELTS FOUR DOUBLES

Feat Ties Record; Vic Adds Single For 4 R.B.I.'s

Cleveland, Sept. 26 (AP)—Vic Wertz hit a single and four consecutive doubles and Herb Score won his twentieth game as the Cleveland Indians clinched a tie for second place with an 8-to-4 victory over the Kansas City Athletics tonight.

Score, a 23-year-old southpaw who has lost only nine games, fanned 12 to run his league-leading total to 263.

He became the Indians' third 20 game winner and fifth in the league. Bob Lemon and Early Wynn have won 20 for Cleveland. Chicago's Billy Pierce and Detroit's Frank Lary are the others.

Wertz, whose four doubles tied a major league record held by 26 others, collected five of the Indians' eight hits off loser Art Ditmar and three other Kansas City pitchers.

He singled in the first inning, and doubled in the third, fourth, fifth and seventh. He drove in the Indians' last four runs.

Boston Takes Final Game By 7 To 4 In 10 Innings

NEW YORK, Sept. 30 (AP)—Mickey Mantle became the first major league player since 1947 to win the triple crown today when he wrapped up the American League batting home run and runs-batted-in titles while his New York Yankees were losing their final game of the season to the Boston Red Sox, 7-4, in 10 innings.

Mantle appeared only as a punch hitter in the ninth inning and drove in a run with a grounder. That gave him a batting average of .327, 52 home runs and 130 RBI's

Ted Williams of the Boston Red Sox, the last player to turn the trick back in 1947 finished with a .345 batting average He retired from the game after walking in the first.

Reds 4, Cubs 2

CHICAGO, Sept. 30 (AP)—Herschel Freeman, making his 63rd relief appearance of the season, came to Hal Jeffcoat's rescue in the ninth inning today and stopped a last-ditch Chicago Cub rally to preserve a 4 to 2 victory for Cincinnati.

The Redlegs failed in their attempts to break the major league records for home runs in one season by a club. They tied the record of 221, set by the New York Giants, when Burgess homered yesterday.

Dodgers Win Flag By Beating Pirates

Home Runs Decisive In Close Game

World Series On Wednesday

BROOKLYN, Sept. 30 (AP)—The Brooklyn Dodgers climaxed one of the most exciting races in baseball history today, capturing their second consecutive National League pennant, on the final day of the season, by defeating the Pittsburgh Pirates 8-6.

The victory, Brooklyn's third straight over the Pirates, assured Manager Walter Alston's world champions of meeting the New York Yankees in the World Series next Wednesday. The Milwaukee Braves clinched second place by defeating St. Louis, 4-2. Brooklyn burst into a one-game lead yesterday with a doubleheader sweep over Pittsburgh while the Cardinals were turning back the Braves.

A sun-packed Ebbets Field crowd, numbering 31,983 paid spectators, came in for the kill and were treated to a flash of old time Dodger power. Determined to nail down their 10th flag, their fourth in the last five years, the Dodgers, led by Duke Snider, reached five Pittsburgh pitchers for 12 hits, five of them home runs, accounting for all but one of their runs.

2 Homers For Snider

Snider the league's new home run champion, blasted two home runs, driving in four runs, to increase his season's homer output to 43, a new club record. Sandy Amoros also had a pair, his 15th and 16th, and Jackie Robinson contributed his 10th of the season.

The Dodgers' mightiest home run demonstration of the season made it possible for Don Newcombe, Brooklyn's biggest winner in 32 years, to record his 27th triumph. The big righthander, however, was far from his best, and needed assistance from Don Bessent in the eighth inning, after the Pirates had clubbed him for 11 of their 13 hits and all their runs.

'Newk' Wins Young Award

NEW YORK, Nov. 28 (AP).—Don Newcombe, Brooklyn's 27-game winner, today was voted the first Cy Young Memorial Award by the Baseball Writers Association.

The award honors the right-hander who won 511 games pitching for Cleveland, the Cardinals and Red Sox.

Newcombe received 10 of the 16 votes of a special committee of writers. Sal Maglie, Newcombe's 39-year-old teammate, polled four votes, while Warren Spahn, Milwaukee southpaw, and Whitey Ford, Yankee lefthander, received one each.

Feller And No. 19 Quit Baseball

Cleveland, Dec. 28 (AP)—Bob Feller, who came out of Iowa as a kid with a bashful grin and blinding fastball 20 years ago to become one of baseball's greatest pitchers, hung up "No. 19" today.

The former right-hand speed-ball artist announced at a news conference that he was retiring as an active player to devote more time to his insurance business here and other interests. He had a 266-162 won and lost record with the Indians.

"I could have gone with a couple of other ball clubs, but anything I might have done with them would have taken the edge off the success I have had with the Cleveland club the last 20 years," Feller said.

In addition to his insurance business, Feller said he would become associated with a nationally known firm, which would take 50 days a year of his time in the interest of youth baseball. He said he was not at liberty to name the firm.

Feller will have to abandon his role as a player representative in the American League, but will continue to serve as president of the recently organized Major League Players Association and will remain as a member of the Major League Pension Committee.

LARSEN PITCHES PERFECT GAME, 2-0

N.Y. Hurler Retires 27 Dodger Hitters In Row

World Series Box

New York, Oct. 8 (*AP*)—The official box score of the fifth game of the 1956 World Series:

BROOKLYN (N.)	Ab.	R.	H.	O.	A.	E.	NEW YORK (A.)	Ab.	R.	H.	O.	A.	E.
Gilliam, 2b.	3	0	0	2	0	0	Bauer, rf.	4	0	1	4	0	0
Reese, ss.	3	0	0	4	2	0	Collins, 1b.	4	0	1	7	0	0
Snider, cf.	3	0	0	1	0	0	Mantle, cf.	3	1	1	4	0	0
Robinson, 3b.	3	0	0	2	4	0	Berra, c.	3	0	0	7	0	0
Hodges, 1b.	3	0	0	5	1	0	Slaughter, lf.	2	0	0	1	0	0
Amoros, lf.	3	0	0	3	0	0	Martin, 2b.	3	0	1	3	4	0
Furillo, rf.	3	0	0	0	0	0	McDougald, ss.	2	0	0	0	2	0
Campanella, c.	3	0	0	7	2	0	Carey, 3b.	3	1	1	1	1	0
Maglie, p.	2	0	0	0	1	0	Larsen, p.	2	0	0	0	1	0
1Mitchell	1	0	0	0	0								
Totals	27	0	0	24	10	0	Totals	26	2	5	27	8	0

1Called out on strikes for Maglie in ninth.

Brooklyn (N)	0	0	0	0	0	0	0	0	0—0
New York (A)	0	0	0	1	0	1	0	0	x—2

Runs batted in—Mantle, Bauer. Home run—Mantle. Sacrifice—Larsen. Double plays—Reese and Hodges; Hodges, Campanella, Robinson, Campanella and Robinson. Left on bases—Brooklyn (N), 0; New York (A), 3. Bases on balls—Maglie, 2 (Slaughter, McDougald). Strikeouts—Larsen, 7 (Gilliam, Reese, Hodges, Campanella, Snider, Maglie, Mitchell); Maglie, 5 (Martin, Collins 2, Larsen, Bauer). Runs and earned runs—Larsen (0-0), Maglie (2-2). Winning pitcher—Larsen. Losing pitcher—Maglie. Umpires—Pinelli (N) plate, Soar (A) first base, Boggess (N) second base, Napp (A) third base, Gorman (N) left field, Runge (A) right field. Time—2.06. Attendance—64,519.

Ex-Oriole Beats Maglie, Gives New York 3-2 Series Lead

By LOU HATTER
[Sun Staff Correspondent]

New York, Oct. 8—Don Larsen created everlasting baseball history here today by pitching a perfect no-hit game, the first in 53 years of World Series competition, as New York defeated Brooklyn, 2 to 0 before 64,519 Yankee Stadium spectators.

The feat by the 6-foot, 4-inch right-hander, during which Larsen retired in order all 27 Dodger batsmen to oppose him, boosted the Yankees into a 3-to-2 lead in the 1956 series which shifts tomorrow to Brooklyn's Ebbets Field.

Fans Seven Dodgers

Never before had a no-hitter of any description been achieved in the annual post-season championship.

Larsen, a cool, deliberate workman who two years ago was a chronic loser for the Baltimore Orioles, made the first one an unsurpassable masterpiece.

The 27-year-old native of San Diego struck out seven Dodgers and issued not a single base on balls while the Yanks were posting their third straight victory over the National Leaguers on the strength of Mickey Mantle's fourth-inning homer off Sal Maglie and a run-scoring single by Hank Bauer in the sixth.

Had 3 Balls On Reese

Only once did Larsen come close to giving up a walk. This occurred in the opening frame, when he issued three balls to Pewee Reese before retiring the Brooklyn shortstop on a called third strike.

Otherwise, backed up superbly by the infield defensive skill of Gil McDougald, Billy Martin and Andy Carey and by Mantle in the New York outfield, Larsen was in command from start to finish.

When Larsen, his teammates on the tips of their toes and the huge throng in a state of breathless anticipation, sneaked a third-strike fast ball past pinch-swinger Dale Mitchell for the final out, bedlam broke loose in this vast baseball arena.

Jackie Robinson Quitting Baseball
Never Intended To Play For Giants

NEW YORK, Jan. 5 (P)—Jackie Robinson, writing in a first-person, copyrighted story to appear in next Tuesday's issue of Look magazine, says he is "quiting baseball for good" because "I have to think of the future and the security of my family.

Robinson, who broke baseball's color line and became one of the game's greatest stars with the Brooklyn Dodgers, said he reached his decision before being traded to the New York Giants by the Brooks last Dec. 13.

In the Look article, titled "Why I'm Quitting Baseball," Jackie said 'I couldn't tell Mr. (Horace) Stoneham (owner of the Giants) I was through with baseball forever because I had agreed long ago to write this story—when the time came—exclusively for Look. And as a matter of fact, I was working on the story when Mr. Stoneham called" to tell him of the trade.

Worried About Future

"I'm quitting baseball for good," Robinson writes, "and there shouldn't be any mystery about my reasons. I'm 38 years old with a family to support. I've got to think of the future and our security."

Robinson, who broke into baseball with the Dodgers' minor league farm club at Montreal in 1946, added:

"At my age a man doesn't have much future in baseball and very little security.

"I've been thinking since I was 34 that I should be thinking of my future. After you've reached your peak there's no sentiment in baseball. You start slipping and pretty soon they're moving you around like a used car. You have no control control over what happens to you. I don't want that."

Jackie added, however, that he had signed a contract to become an executive with a New York restaurant chain before his trade to the Giants. He will become a vice president in charge of personnel relations this March.

Apologizes For Secrecy

Robinson, the National League's rookie of the year in 1947 and listed No. 3 among the league's active life-time hitters with a .311 average at the end of the 1956 season, kept his decision well hidden.

While many of his close friends among sportwriters suspected something was afoot, he did not officially disclose his decision until writing the Look article. And he apologized in the article for the secrecy.

"I'm through with baseball . . . I want to explain just how it happened because some people may now feel I haven't been honest with them these past few weeks when they have asked me about my plans.

"I've always played fair with my newspaper friends and I think they'll understand why this was one time I couldn't give them the whole story as soon as I knew it."

Robinson, who was not immediately available for comment (he was reported, en route to New York from California by a Look spokesman), apparently has junked any idea of becoming baseball's first Negro manager—for the present, anyway.

Brooklyn Fan

Jackie, insisting in the article that "I'll just be another fan—a Brooklyn fan, "wrote that his wife, Rae, didn't try to influence his decision. The Robinsons have three young children and live in Stamford, Conn.

The long-time star, who played in six All-Star games with a .333 batting average and appeared in six World Series with

the Brooks with a .234 batting mark, got his chance in baseball under Branch Rickey, then president of the Dodgers after an earlier try out with the Boston Red Sox.

It was speed and daring on the bases, his fierce competitive spirit and his penchant for being involved in the dramatic play, that carried him to the top. It was Jackie, for example, who delivered the winning hit in the sixth game of last fall's World Series against the New York Yankees, breaking up a splendid 10-inning pitching duel between Yankee Bob Turley and Dodger Clem Labine.

After that hit, Robinson felt "like a kid again" and announced he thought "I've got at least one more good year in these old legs of mine. I want to play one more year. I'm sure I can help win another pennant."

Yet Robbie, the loop's most valuable player in 1949, knew he was slowing up—"A step and a half,"—that same day as he talked to newsmen in the Dodger dressing room.

Forgotten Words

The greying but still sturdy infielder— who had to battle to keep his starting job with the Dodgers last season—said after that sixth series game:

"Money is not a factor. I think my wife would like for me to manage and slow down some. But, to me, I'd be like a fire horse put out to pasture."

In his major league career, following a brilliant college football career at UCLA and an equally successful single season at Montreal in the International, Robinson went on to take the NL batting championship in 1949 with a .342 average. Three times he led second basemen in fielding percentages (1948, '50, '51, setting a record (.992 in 1951) and twice as tops in stolen bases (29 in 1947, 37 in 1949).

Southpaw Hit In Eye
By Liner; Lemon Is
Relief Winner, 2-1

CLEVELAND, May 7 (P) — The Cleveland Indians beat the New York Yankees 2-1 tonight on two unearned runs and lost for an indefinite period the services of their prize southpaw, Herb Score, who was struck in the right eye by a hard - hit liner.

Score was taken to a hospital, and it will be "several days" before full extent of the damage to his badly cut eye can be ascertained.

Bob Lemon took over when Score was carried off the field with two out in the first inning and held the Yanks to six hits.

Tom Sturdivant, the loser, walked Rocky Colavito in the eighth inning with the bases filled to force home the winning run.

Former Yankee Gene Woodling singled with one out to start the Tribe to victory in its first 1957 meeting with the pennant winners before a crowd of 18,386. Woodling went to third when Al Smith looped a fly to right field which dropped in front of Hank Bauer and on which Bauer threw wild to second. A walk to Vic Wertz filled the bases, Roger Maris fanned, then came Colavito's costly pass.

Gil McDougald, second man up for the Yankees, slashed the liner which struck Score squarely in the right eye, cutting it badly. Bleeding freely from nose and mouth, as well as from the cut, Score was taken off the field on a stretcher.

The 23-year-old southpaw star never lost consciousness and was in good spirits at Lakeside Hospital where an eye specialist, Dr. Charles Thomas was called in. Dr. Don Kelly, club physician, said it would be "several days" before he would know whether Score's eye was damaged permanently.

A 20-game winner last season, Score had a 2-1 record going into tonight's game. In his third year with the Tribe he is considered one of the most valuable — if not the most valuable — player in baseball today.

Minoso's Great All-Star Game

ST. LOUIS, July 9 (P)—A jubilant Minnie Minoso, who thought he would have 'a vacation" today but produced the winning run and a game-saving throw for the American League, may be the good luck charm Casey Stengel needs for All-Star games.

This was the first All-Star game for the 34-year-old Chicago White Sox outfielder since 1954, the last time the American League had won before today's 6-5 triumph.

'When the seventh inning she come I theenk I going have vacation today," Minoso said. 'It sure feels good for the American League to win again."

The speedy Cuban doubled home what proved to be the winning run in the American's three-run ninth.

Then with the National staging a ninth inning rally, Minoso's perfect throw nipped Cincinnati's Gus Bell at third for the second out.

Except for Minoso, though, the American Leaguers weren't in a celebrating mood, they were still feeling the effects of that ninth inning scare.

Bauer Denies Smashing Night Club Patron's Nose

NEW YORK, May 16 (AP).— Yankee Outfielder Hank Bauer was accused in a report to police of striking and injuring a man early today in the basement of the Copacabana restaurant, but Bauer denied it.

There were no arrests but the district attorney's office ordered police to question all Yankee ball players who were at the restaurant with Bauer.

The injured man was reported by police to be Edwin Jones, 42, of Manhattan. He was treated at Roosevelt Hospital for a fractured nose and a possible fracture of the jaw, police said.

Bauer was named as the assailant by Jones' brother Leonard, police reported.

Reached by telephone at his hotel, Bauer told a newsman: "I definitely didn't hit any one."

Police made this report:

Leonard Jones told police that the assault took place in the basement of the night club just outside a lavatory. He said he, his brother and about 19 other men who are members of a bowling group had gone to the Copacabana after eating dinner in another restaurant.

Leonard Jones said they sat about two tables away from Bauer and several other Yankee players and their wives. He said his brother, a Yankee fan, went to the ballplayers' table, put his arm around Billy Martin's shoulder and congratulated him on his playing.

Leonard Jones said the players appeared to resent his brother's presence, there were words and Edwin Jones left the table. The assault took place later, Leonard said.

At the night club table, in addition to Bauer and Martin, were Mickey Mantle, Whitey Ford, Johnny Kucks and Yogi Berra. They were celebrating Martin's birthday.

'IT'S ALL OVER,' SAYS STONEHAM AFTER SHIFT IS FORMALIZED, 8 TO 1

Owner Joyful Following 2½-Hour Meeting That Sends Charter Member Of National League To San Francisco

New York, Aug. 19 (AP)—The New York Giants officially decided today to become the San Francisco Giants. The Brooklyn Dodgers may follow the Giants to California next week.

The historic decision to move westward was made during a 2½-hour meeting when the Giants' board of directors voted, 8 to 1, to shift the National League baseball franchise to San Francisco. The lone dissenter was M. Donald Grant, a minority stockholder.

The Dodgers, who have been given the green light by the league to move to Los Angeles, were expected to formalize their shift at a board meeting next week.

"It's All Over, Fellows"

"It's all over, fellows," the perspiring and obviously relieved club president, Horace Stoneham, told a gathering of reporters and photographers in the Giants' offices as he emerged from the closed meeting.

"We've just voted to transfer the club to San Francisco. That means we'll be playing on the West Coast next year. That is providing the mayor of San Francisco fulfills all the conditions promised and he agrees to the name of the Giants being retained."

Beat Cards In 11th To End Chase

MILWAUKEE, Wisc., Sept. 23 (AP)—The Milwaukee Braves won the National League pennant tonight as Hank Aaron hit a two-run homer in the 11th inning to defeat the runner-up St. Louis Cardinals, 4-2.

Aaron's 43rd homer of the season climaxed a bitter battle before 40,926 partisan fans and gave the Braves a six-game lead over the Cards with five games left to play.

Aaron's dramatic blow, producing Milwaukee's first championship since the club moved here from Boston in 1953, followed a single by Johnny Logan off the third St. Louis pitcher Billy Muffett.

The score had been tied from the seventh inning of a tense contest in which starter Lew Burdette and Card reliever Larry Jackson had hooked up in a bristling mound duel.

The winner of this historic game was elongated Gene Conley, who entered the game at the start of the 11th after Burdette had been lifted for a pinch-hitter.

Aaron smashed Muffett's first pitch to him in the 11th over the center field fence. The blow touched off a wild impromptu celebration in the County Stadium stands.

RED SOX EDGE SENATORS, 2-1

Williams Homers, On-Base Streak Ends At 16

Washington, Sept. 24 (AP) — Ted Williams smashed his thirty-eighth home run tonight as Boston defeated Washington, 2 to 1, behind the five-hit pitching of Frank Sullivan, who won his fourteenth decision.

Williams, who had his streak of reaching base safely 16 straight times broken by Hal Griggs in the first inning when he grounded out, slammed his home run in the fourth inning. It proved the decisive blow of the game. He later struck out and walked.

DODGERS TOP PIRATES, 2-0

McDevitt Hurls 5-Hitter In Last Ebbets Field Game

Brooklyn, Sept. 24 (P)—Young Danny McDevitt tossed a five-hit shutout tonight as the Brooklyn Dodgers, playing what in all probability was their final game in Ebbets Field, defeated the Pittsburgh Pirates, 2 to 0.

There was no "wait 'til next year!" wail from the meager crowd of 6,702 at the end of this one. Not with the Dodgers apparently headed for Los Angeles for the 1958 season.

McDevett Fans Nine

The "new" Dodgers, wherever they land, certainly have plans for McDevitt. The kid southpaw gained a 7-4 record with his second shutout after losing three in a row. The 24-year-old rookie fanned nine, walked only one and three of the Pirate hits were infield singles.

The Brooks backed him up with a run in the first on a walk, error and Elmer Valo's double, then added another in the third on Gino Cimoli's infield single, an infield out and Gil Hodges's single.

Daniels Makes First Start

Both runs were off Rookie Bennie Daniels, making his first major league appearance.

The 23-year-old right-hander, who had a 17-8 record at Hollywood this season, gave up all five Dodger hits, walked three and struck out two before giving way to a pinch hitter in the eighth.

McDevitt, who hadn't won since August 14, didn't give up a hit after Dick Groat singled to center with two out in the sixth. He fanned Bob Skinner for the final out of the frame—and then whiffed the side in the seventh for four straight strikeouts.

PITTSBURGH					BROOKLYN				
	Ab	H	O	A		Ab	H	O	A
Baker,3b	4	0	0	0	Gilliam,2b	3	0	3	4
Mejias,rf	4	0	0	0	Cimoli,cf	4	1	0	0
Groat,ss	3	1	2	4	Valo,rf	4	1	2	0
Skinner,lf	4	1	2	0	H'ges,3b,1b	4	1	5	1
Fondy,1b	4	0	13	1	Amoros,lf	3	0	3	0
Maz'ski,2b	3	1	0	3	Gentile,1b	2	0	4	0
Clemte,cf	3	1	0	0	Reese,3b	1	0	0	1
Peterson,c	3	1	5	0	Camp'lla,c	2	0	2	0
Daniels,p	2	0	1	3	Furillo,no	1	0	7	0
1Rivera	1	0	0	0	Zimmer,ss	2	1	4	4
Face,p	0	0	1	0	McDevitt,p	1	0	0	0
Totals	31	5	24	11	Totals	27	5	27	10

1Safe on error for Daniels in eighth.

Pittsburgh   0 0 0 0 0 0 0 0 0—0
Brooklyn   1 0 1 0 0 0 0 0 x—2

Runs—Gilliam, Cimoli. Errors—Daniels, Reese. Runs batted in—Valo, Hodges. Two-base hits—Valo, Zimmer. Sacrifice—McDevitt. Double plays—Hodges, Gilliam and Gentile; Mazeroski, Groat and Fondy; Zimmer and Hodges. Left on bases—Pittsburgh, 5; Brooklyn, 5. Base on balls—Daniels, 1; McDevitt, 1. Strikeouts—Daniels, 2; McDevitt, 9.

PIRATES WHIP GIANTS, 9 TO 1

New Yorkers Bid Farewell To Polo Grounds

New York, Sept. 29 (P)—The New York Giants and 11,606 pall bearers bade farewell forever to the historic Polo Grounds today as the San Francisco-bound Giants lost to Pittsburgh 9 to 1.

As many of the "old" Giants as possible were fielded by Manager Billy Rigney with Bobby Thomson back on third base where he played during the "miracle finish" of 1951.

A host of Giant oldtimers had been guests of owner Horace Stoneham at a dinner party last night. The stars of yesteryear were introduced in pre-game ceremonies.

Jack Doyle, 89, the Giants' 1895 manager, headed the list. Others were Larry Doyle, Moose McCormick, Hooks Wiltse, Red Murray, George Burns, Hans Lobert, Rosy Ryan, Rube Marquard, Carl Hubbell, George Davis, Monte Irvin, Sid Gordon, Billy Jurges, Hal Schumacher, Buddy Kerr, Babe Young, Sal Maglie, Henry Thompson and Johnny Rucker.

Although mention of Stoneham's name over the public-address system brought noisy booing, it was a sentimental occasion. Willie Mays, who had two hits, drew roaring cheers.

Billy Rigney, last Giant manager, summed it up when he said:

"It's sort of got me. I'll probably burst out crying any minute."

The Pirates had little regard for the drama of the occasion. They ripped into Giant pitching for 17 hits including Frank Thomas' twenty-third and Johnny Powers' second homers.

In the meantime, Bob Friend held the Giants to six hits. Friend had three hits. So did Roberto Clemente and Powers.

PITTSBURGH					NEW YORK				
	AB	H	O	A		AB	H	O	A
Freese,3b	5	1	2	2	O'C'ell,2b	4	0	5	3
Maz'ski,2b	5	2	3	4	M'ller,rf	4	1	1	1
Groat,ss	5	0	2	2	Mays,cf	4	2	6	1
Skinner,lf	3	1	3	1	Rhodes,lf	3	1	1	0
F.Th's,1b	5	2	11	2	T'son,3b	3	1	0	4
Cl'm'te,cf	4	3	1	1	L'man,1b	3	0	9	0
Powers,rf	3	3	0	0	Sp'cer,ss	3	0	1	2
P't'son,c	5	2	4	1	W'trum,c	2	0	3	0
Friend,p	4	3	1	2	2Sauer	1	0	0	0
					M'zant,p	2	0	3	0
					Antone'i,p	0	0	0	0
					B'clay,p	0	0	0	0
					Crone,p	0	0	0	0
					1J'lonski	0	0	0	0
					Miller,p	0	0	0	0
					3Katt,c	1	1	1	0
Totals	41	17	27	15	Totals	29	6	27	12

1Walked for Crone in sixth.
2Grounded out for Westrum in eighth.
3Singled for Miller in eighth.

Pittsburgh   1 3 0 2 0 1 0 1 1—9
New York   1 0 0 0 0 0 0 0 1—1

Runs—Freese, F. Thomas, Clemente (3), Powers (3), Friend, Mueller. Runs batted in—Skinner, F. Thomas, Peterson (2), Friend (2), Rhodes, Mazeroski, Powers. Two-base hits—Clemente, Powers, Mazeroski. Three-base hit—Skinner. Home runs—F. Thomas, Powers. Stolen base—Freese. Sacrifice fly—Rhodes. Double play—Lockman (unassisted), Skinner, Mazeroski, F. Thomas, Clemente, Peterson, Mazeroski; F. Thomas, Groat, F. Thomas. Left on base—Pittsburgh, 8; New York, 3. Base on balls—Friend, 1; Miller, 2. Strikeouts—Friend, 4; Barclay, 1; Crone, 1; Monzant, 1. Hits—Antonelli, 7 in 2 innings; Barclay, 6 in 3; Crone, 0 in 1; Miller, 3 in 2; Monzant, 1 in 1. Runs and earned runs—Friend, 1-1; Antonelli, 4-4; Barclay, 3-3; Crone, 0-0; Miller, 1-1; Monzant, 1-1. Hit by pitcher—Antonelli (Powers). Wild pitch Miller. Winning pitcher—Friend (14-18). Losing pitcher—Antonelli (12-18). Umpire—Delmore, Donatelli, Smith, Sudol. Time, 2:35. Attendance, 11,606.

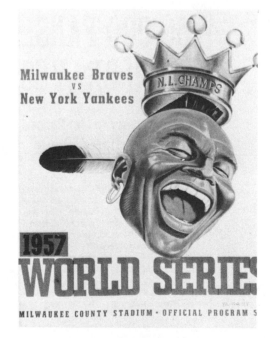

Milwaukee Braves vs New York Yankees

N.L. CHAMPS

1957 WORLD SERIES

MILWAUKEE COUNTY STADIUM · OFFICIAL PROGRAM S

Wide World Photo

TED WILLIAMS　　　　**STAN MUSIAL**

NEW YORK. Sept. 29 (P) Thirty-nine years-old Ted Williams won his fifth American League batting championship and 36-year-old Stan Musial his seventh National League title today and thereby added to their reputation as two of baseball's all-time great hitters.

Williams finished with a .388 average. This was t h e highest big league mark since Ted hit .406 in 1941. The Boston Red Sox's star also became the oldest player ever to capture the championship. Honus Wagner was 37 when he took the National League crown in 1911.

Musial wound up with a .351 average. This enabled the St. Louis Cardinals' first baseman

to tie Rogers Hornsby on the list of all-time NL batting leaders.

Wagner, Pittsburgh's great shortstop, led the senior circuit eight times while Ty Cobb holds the major league record with 12 American League titles.

New Regulation

This was the first season played under the regulation requiring a player to reach 477 times at bat—official and unofficial—to qualify for the championship. Williams, who had a double and single in two trips against the Yankees today, had 420 official at bats and reached the mandatory figure with 120 bases on balls, two sacrifices flies and five hit by pitches. Musial made the grade with his official 502 trips.

BURDETTE'S 3RD VICTORY

World Series Box

New York. Oct. 10 (P)—The official box score of the seventh game of the 1957 World Series

NEW YORK (A)	Ab	R	H	O	A	E	MILWAUKEE (N)	Ab	R	H	O	A	E
Bauer, rf	4	0	1	2	0	0	Hazle, rf	1	1	2	0	0	0
Slaughter, lf	4	0	0	0	0	0	4Pafko, rf	1	0	0	0	0	0
Mantle, cf	4	0	1	2	0	0	Logan, ss	5	1	1	2	4	0
Berra, c	3	0	1	4	1	1	Mathews, 3b	4	1	1	3	4	1
McDougald, ss	4	0	1	2	1	1	Aaron, cf	5	1	2	3	0	0
Kubek, 3b	4	0	1	3	1	1	Covington, lf	5	0	1	2	0	0
Coleman, 2b	4	0	2	4	5	0	Torre, 1b	3	0	0	8	0	0
Collins, 1b	2	0	0	5	0	0	Mantilla, 2b	4	0	1	2	0	0
Sturdivant, p	0	0	0	0	0	0	Crandall, c	4	1	1	4	1	0
3Howard	1	0	0	0	0	0	Burdette, p	3	0	0	0	3	0
Byrne, p	1	0	1	0	0	0							
Larsen, p	0	0	0	0	1	0							
Shantz, p	0	0	0	0	0	0							
1Lumpe	1	0	0	0	0	0							
Ditmar, p	0	0	0	0	0	0							
2Skowron, 1b	3	0	0	3	2	0							
Totals	35	0	7	27	12	3	Totals	34	5	9	27	11	1

1Struck out for Shantz in third
2Hit into force play for Ditmar in fifth
3Struck out for Sturdivant in seventh
4Fouled out for Hazle in eighth

Milwaukee (N)	0	0	1	0	0	0	0	1	0	x—5
New York (A)	0	0	0	0	0	0	0	0	0	—0

Runs batted in—Mathews (2), Aaron, Torre, Crandall. Two-base hits—Bauer, Mathews. Home run—Crandall. Sacrifices—Covington, Burdette, Mathews. Double play—McDougald, Coleman, Skowron. Left on bases—Milwaukee (N), 8, New York (A), 9. Bases on balls—Larsen 1 (Torre), Byrne, 2 (Torre, Burdette), Burdette, 1 (Berra). Struck out—Larsen, 2 (Hazle, Mathews), Ditmar, 1 (Burdette), Sturdivant, 1 (Aaron), Burdette, 3 (Collins, Lumpe, Howard). Hits—Larsen, 3 in 2 1-3 innings, Shantz, 2 in 2-3, Ditmar, 1 in 2, Sturdivant, 2 in 2, Byrne, 1 in 2. Runs and earned runs—Larsen (3-2), Shantz (1-0), Ditmar (0-0), Sturdivant (0-0), Byrne (1-1), Burdette (0-0). Winning pitcher—Burdette. Losing pitcher—Larsen. Umpires—McKinley (A) plate, Donatelli (N) first base, Paparella (A), second base, Conlan (N), third base, Secory (N), left field, Chylak (A), right field. Time 2:34. Attendance 61,207. Receipts (net), $405,102.07.

750,000 FANS HAIL BRAVES

30-Car Caravan Is Forced To Take Different Route

Milwaukee, Oct. 10 (AP) — A crowd of 750,000 persons — with 250,000 of them in the downtown area — lined the parade route of the World Champion Milwaukee Braves tonight.

Police Inspector Rudolph Miller, who made the estimate, said the demonstration was uncanny.

The 30-car caravan of convertibles taking the team to County Stadium had to be turned away from the original planned route through the city. Police said it would have been impossible to open the crowd to let the cars through.

Fans Push Trolleys

Trolley buses that were stalled when their electric power pickup poles left the overhead wires while making sharp turns were pushed through the throng like toys.

Fans refused to budge for motorcycle policemen trying to clear a path.

And when the crowd learned the parade was taking a new route, every vehicle with a driver was put into use. They rode on bumpers and fenders, the tops, and hung through open windows for the ride to the stadium.

Statement Ends Doubt About 1958

NEW YORK. Oct. 8 (/P) —The Brooklyn Dodgers finally made their long-awaited m o v e today. They definitely are going to Los Angeles in 1958.

The official announcement, made at a press conference by public relations director Arthur (Red) Patterson, was so anti-climatic that Walter O'Malley, the club president, didn't even bother to attend. He was at a meeting of the club's board of directors.

Patterson's announcement, contained in one brief printed statement, said simply that in view of the action of the Los Angeles city council yesterday, the Dodger stockholders h a d unanimously agreed to take the necessary steps toward drafting the Los Angeles territory from the Pacific Coast League.

The city council yesterday endorsed, by a 10-4 vote, the proposed contract between t h e city and the National League club which would give O'Malley the 300 - acre Chavez Ravine site for a ball park in exchange for Brooklyn - owned Wrigley Field in Los Angeles.

Thus California is assured of two National League teams for next year and New York w i l l have none. The New York Giants committed themselves last Aug. 19 to move to San Francisco next season.

Spahn Voted Young Award As Season's Best Pitcher

New York, Nov. 28 (/P)—Warren Spahn, ace of the world champion Milwaukee 'Braves and biggest winner in the major leagues last season, was voted the Cy Young Memorial Award today as the top pitcher in baseball.

The brilliant southpaw, whose 21 victories were a prime factor in Milwaukee's first National League pennant, received all but one of the votes of the 16-man panel of baseball writers who participated in the annual poll. The other vote went to Dick Donovan, Chicago White Sox righthander.

Spahn 37 In April

Spahn, who will be 37 next April, thus becomes the second National League pitcher to win the Cy Young Award, instituted last year. Don Newcombe gained the honor in 1956, polling 10 of 16 votes. Spahn had one vote in '56.

By topping 20 victories this season, Spahn joined Hall of Famers Lefty Grove and Eddie Plank, two former American Leaguers, as the only lefthanders to win 20 or more games in eight seasons.

The vote was limited to performance during the regular season without regard to World Series play. This undoubtedly accounts for the failure of Lew Burdette to receive any recognition.

Three Series Victories

Burdette, pitching hero of the World Series, won three games in as many starts. Spahn, the only holdover from the 1948 Braves' series team, won one and lost one. A flu attack prevented him from pitching the finale, setting the stage for Burdette's third victory and second successive shutout over the New York Yankees.

OPEN MINOR ROSTERS TO SELECTION

Players With 4 Years Experience Subject Minus Restriction

By BOB MAISEL
[Sun Staff Correspondent]

Colorado Springs, Colo., Dec. 6—Baseball tonight voted to throw out the bonus rule and then put into baseball law a proposal which calls for the unrestricted draft of four-year players.

It was decided that for the time being, the elimination of the bonus rule would not be retroactive, that a player signed under the old rule must serve out his two years on a major league roster.

Reprinted from
The Baltimore Sun papers

CAMPANELLA BREAKS NECK

Auto Accident May End Career Of Top Catcher

Glen Cove, N.Y., Jan. 28 (AP)—Roy Campanella's brilliant career as one of baseball's greatest catchers appeared at an end today. An auto accident broke his neck and left him temporarily paralyzed.

A seven-man team of surgeons worked over the Negro star of the Dodgers for four hours and 20 minuutes in an attempt to repair the damage to his husky frame and relieve paralysis from the chest down. The operation had been expected to take but two hours.

Future Termed Bleak

Afterwards, Dr. Robert W. Sengstaken, head of the surgical team, termed the operation a success and said the paralysis is expected to disappear. But it may be six weeks before Campanella is up and around.

Dr. Sengstaken said the injury came within an inch of killing the player.

The doctor did not rule out the possibility that Campanella might play baseball again. But the future, nevertheless, was bleak for one of the heaviest hitting catchers in the history of the sport.

Dr. Sengstaken said complete recovery might require months or even years. With age a factor in baseball, Campanella could not spend too much time away from the game if he is to continue.

"In my opinion," the surgeon added, "he would be foolish if he tried to continue playing baseball. But he's not my patient and I won't advise him."

April 19

Davenport's Failure To Touch Third Base Costly In 9th Frame

LOS ANGELES (AP)—A roaring crowd of 78,672 in a gay, picnic mood greeted the Los Angeles Dodgers in their new home Friday and broke the attandance record for any single regular season game ever played in the majors.

The Dodgers rewarded this sprawling mass of humanity with a 6-5 victory over the San Francisco Giants after rookie Jim Davenport forgot to touch third base during a ninth-inning Giant rally.

Although the turnout fell some 8,000 short of the all-time attendance record set in the 1948 World Series at Cleveland, it was the largest in National League history by almost 18,000.

Blue Dodger caps with a bold "LA" on the front dotted the uncovered concrete stands of this football stadium made over into a temporary ballpark. The partisan crowd clutched the Dodgers to their hearts, cheering every pop fly and every Giant strikeout.

There have been more people at a game—86,288 for that fifth game of the 1948 Boston-Cleveland World Series. The New York Yankees and Cleveland also packed in 84,587 at Cleveland for a Sunday doubleheader in 1954.

May 14

With Malice Toward None

By BILL LEE   Sports Editor

THE SEVEN greatest batsmen baseball has known moved their round table chairs Tuesday to make room for Stan Musial, one of the best hitters and finest gentlemen in the game's long history.

In making the 3000th hit of his major league lifetime, Stan The Man did two things. First he joined the limited circle of Ty Cobb, Tris Speaker, Hans Wagner, Eddie Collins, Nap Lajoie, Paul Waner and "Cap" Anson, the only players to achieve 3000 hits since the invention of the box score.

Second, nice guy that he is, Musial gave our boy Moe Drabowsky a sure fire gag to pull on next winter's banquet circuit.

For years Lefty Gomez, a superb pitcher, has been fracturing listeners by switching suddenly to claims of personal hitting prowess.

"I hold the record for the longest home run ever hit to right field in Yankee Stadium," Gomez tells his audience. "Jimmy Foxx hit it off me and it landed in the back row of the third tier."

Now Moe Drabowsky, who numbered public speaking among his courses at Trinity College, can tell them how he should be in the Hall of Fame because he was the pitcher the day Musial got base hit No. 3000. Moe will get a little more fun telling about it next winter than he did thinking about it yesterday afternoon. The hit, a ringing double, launched a rally that beat him and the Cubs.

Musial can feel good about getting the big hit off a pitcher as good as Drabowsky. It could well be that at some future date Moe himself will be knocking politely but firmly on that historic door at Cooperstown.

Reprinted from
The Hartford Courant

July 15

Judge Says Contract Illegal

LOS ANGELES. (AP)—Walter O'Malley's plans for a 12-million dollar Chavez Ravine ball park for his Los Angeles Dodgers were clouded Monday by billows of legal smoke.

Superior Judge Arnold Praeger, ruling on a taxpayer suit, held invalid the contract under which the city would give the ball club land for a fancy stadium.

And he issued a permanent injunction prohibiting the city from carrying out terms of an ordinance covering the contract.

Thus the Dodgers' future again is a question mark. The decision is the latest in a series of hurdles the club has faced in its path toward a permanent park in its new Los Angeles home.

The voters approved the controversial contract last June, and it seemed O'Malley's problems were over. Then came the taxpayer suit, a trial, and today the decision.

It now seems certain there will be a lengthy period of legalistics before O'Malley will know for certain whether he is in or out of the choice Chavez Ravine site, only a mile from civic center.

FINED $250 BY HARRIDGE

Williams Apologizes For Spitting at Fans

CHICAGO, July 25 (P)—Ted Williams today apologized for spitting at the fans during a Red Sox-Athletics game at Kansas City Wednesday night.

A statement released by Red Sox spokesmen in Williams' name said:

"I'm sorry I did it. I was so mad at the park that I lost my temper and afterward I was sorry about it. I'm principally sorry about losing the $250."

Will Harridge, American League president, fined Williams $250 yesterday, saying the Red Sox star's spitting was "conduct detrimental to the best interests of baseball."

Manager Mike Higgins refused to comment as the Red Sox arrived in Chicago for a three-game series with the White Sox.

Williams spat in the general direction of booing fans in Kansas City when they thought he failed to show enough effort after his grounder was snagged by First Baseman Harry Simpson for an unassisted putout.

The night before, Williams really scampered and got to first base after striking out on a wide knuckler that got away from Harry Chiti. And the big outfielder made a valiant try on a subsequent hit-and-run play to avoid being tagged in the baseline on the front end of a double play.

The night of the spitting incident Williams jogged about halfway to first base, then turned and went for the dugout. When the fans opened up with boos, he spat in their direction. That only increased the booing which was carried out at every appearance, even when he slammed a double in the eighth for Boston's only run as the A's won 3-1.

Many of the 12,628 paying customers recalled that Williams was fined $5,000 two years ago for a similar fit of pique in Boston. That fine was imposed by Tom Yawkey, club owner.

Red Sox officials declined to discuss the most recent incident.

Oct. 10

Bob Turley Brilliant In Relief Job

Mound Battle Broken In 8th

By BILL LEE
Courant Sports Editor

MILWAUKEE — The Yankees came from the brink of the grave to win their eighteenth world baseball championship Thursday a sun drenched afternoon.

One defeat short of disaster last Sunday afternoon, the proud Bronx Bombers made the most storied finish of their matchless careers to beat the Milwaukee Braves Thursday 6 to 2.

They had made it three straight victories over the defending champions. They had won four of the last five contests of the 1958 World Series after losing three of the first four.

Only once before in World Series history has any team accomplished this near miracle. The Pittsburgh Pirates beat Washington in 1925 after being down three to one in games.

The Yankees have won more world championships than any team in baseball. This was their eighteenth series triumph against six defeats, but never have they flaunted the odds and brought pride of team and individual effort to the fore to save their reputations the way they've done these past three games of a series the Braves appeared to have signed, sealed and stowed in their foot lockers just four days ago.

Great Relief Pitching

Behind the magnificent 6 2-3 innings of commanding relief pitching Bob Turley worked after the Braves had driven perfect game pitcher Don Larsen out in the third inning, the Yankees hung on grimly in a life and death struggle against the tremendous counter pitching of Milwaukee's Lew Burdette.

Then, in the eighth, the old Yankee brawn came on to destroy Burdette and the Braves. The Milwaukee right hander, who had held the dangerous Bombers to three hits through seven innings, finally met an unhappy fate in the eighth. He had worked with skill and speed to erase the two threats who came up as the inning opened. McDougald was out on a fly to Hank Aaron and Mickey Mantle, who can kill any pitcher with one blow, was caught.

Burdette was almost home free and the score stood at two runs each. But the third out came hard. Yogi Berra laced a double off the right field fence and Elston Howard hammered a clean hit through the middle of the diamond to send Berra racing home with the run that put the Yankees ahead 3 to 2.

That was the ball game, and it must have broken Burdette's heart.

Reprinted from
The Hartford Courant

Sept. 16

Fear George Stirnweiss Train Accident Victim

RED BANK, N.J. (AP)—George (Snuffy) Stirnweiss, 39, former player with the New York Yankees, was feared among those killed when a Jersey Central train fell into Newark Bay Monday.

The Red Bank station agent said Stirnweiss, father of six children, jumped aboard the train just as it was moving out on its last run.

His wife, Jane, fearing the worst, said the last she saw of her husband was when he left home shortly before 9 a.m. She said it was "not like George not to phone if he was all right."

Stirnweiss was employed by Caldwell & Co. in New York, a foreign freight business, and also was director of the New York Journal-American sandlot baseball program. He did not show up at either place Monday.

His children range in age from 17 months to 15 years. Stirnweiss played second base for the Yankees from 1943 through 1950 when he was traded to the old St. Louis Browns.

He finished his active baseball career with Cleveland in 1952. He won the American League batting title in 1945 with a percentage of .309 and in 1944 he led the league in stolen bases with 44.

He had suffered a mild heart attack in June, 1957.

Sept. 21

Homer By Gus Triandos Scores Baltimore Marker

BALTIMORE ⑧ — The American League champion New York Yankees went without a hit or run Saturday against the knuckle balls tossed by 35-year-old Hoyt Wilhelm of the Baltimore Orioles, who won 1-0 on a homer by Catcher Gus Triandos.

Only two Yankees reached base, both on walks, as they swung futilely at Wilhelm's dancing pitches in a drizzle of rain. Eight times, Yankees went down on strikes.

The homer in the seventh inning by Triandos was his 30th of the season. He is tied with Yogi Berra of the Yankees for hitting the most in one year by a catcher.

Wilhelm's no-hit, no-run performance was the second in the major baseball leagues this year. Jim Bunning of Detroit did it on July 20 in beating Boston 2-0.

Don Larsen, pitcher of a perfect World Series game in 1956, started for the Yankees and for six innings he was almost as invincible as Wilhelm.

A bunt single in the first inning by Bob Boyd was the only Oriole hit off Larsen. Two other Orioles reached base on a walk and an error by Bill Skowron.

Shantz For Larsen

Manager Casey Stengel decided six innings was enough for Larsen. It was the pitcher's first game since Aug. 16 when his elbow turned sore.

Bobby Shantz went to the mound for the Yankees and Triandos, a former Yankee, sent his fourth pitch sailing over the 410-foot sign on the center field fence.

That was all Wilhelm needed. The National League castoff who once starred as a great reliever for the New York Giants, hurled himself to glory.

His no-hitter came after two previous frustrating efforts by him since coming to the Orioles from Cleveland on Aug. 23. He lost two games when his balks advanced runners into position to score winning runs.

The right handed pitcher arrived from Cleveland with a 2-8 record but still started against the Yankees this afternoon with

HOYT WILHELM

a remarkably low earned run average of 2.62.

Bobby Richardson worked him for the first walk in the third inning only to be thrown out trying to steal second. Jerry Lumpe got to first the same way in the next inning and became the only Yankee batter to see second when one of Wilhelm's dancing knucklers got by Triandos.

Wilhelm got some defensive help from right fielder Gene Woodling and second baseman Billy Gardner.

Woodling, another ex-Yankee, made a running catch of Norm Siebern's fly in the second inning and Gardner went behind second to snare Siebern's grounder and throw him out in the eighth.

BALTIMORE	ab	r	h	bi	NEW YORK	ab	r	h	bi
Wilms 3b,lf	4	0	1	0	Bauer rf	4	0	0	0
Boyd 1b	4	0	1	0	Lumpe ss	2	0	0	0
Woodling rf	2	0	0	0	Mantle cf	3	0	0	0
Busby cf	1	0	1	0	Skowron 3b	3	0	0	0
Nieman lf	3	0	0	0	Siebern lf	3	0	0	0
Robinson 3b	1	0	0	0	Howard c	3	0	0	0
Triandos c	3	1	1	1	T'rberry 1b	2	0	0	0
Tasby cf,rf	3	0	0	0	aBerra 1b	1	0	0	0
Gardner 2b	3	0	0	0	Richdson 2b	2	0	0	0
Atlman ss	2	0	1	0	Larsen p	2	0	0	0
Miranda ss	0	0	0	0	Shantz p	0	0	0	0
Wilhelm p	3	0	0	0	bSlaughter	1	0	0	0
Totals	29	1	5	1	Totals	26	0	0	0

a — Grounded out for Throneberry in 8th; b—flied out for Shantz in 9th.
Baltimore .... 000 000 10x—1
e. Skowron 2. po-a. New York 24-5.
Baltimore 27-7. lob. New York 1, Baltimore 6.
2b. Williams. hr. Triandos.

PITCHERS	ip	h	r	er	bb	so
Wilhelm (w, 3-10)	9	0	0	0	2	8
Larsen	6	1	0	0	2	2
Shantz (l, 7-6)	2	4	1	1	0	2

pb. Triandos. u. Paparella, Chylak, Tobacchi and Stuart. t. 1:48. a. 10,941.

Baseball World Mourning As Ott Loses Battle for Life

NEW ORLEANS, Nov. 22 (AP) —Mel Ott will be buried today.

Some of the top names in the world of baseball are expected to attend the funeral services this afternoon for the National League's all-time top home-run hitter.

The 49-year-old Ott died yesterday. Physicians had tried for a week to check complications from injuries he received in an automobile collision Friday night a week ago.

Ott went to play for the New York Giants at the age of 16. He stayed for 22 seasons and was named to baseball's Hall of Fame at Cooperstown, N.Y., in 1951 along with Jimmy Foxx. Foxx was one of the two men who hit more homers than Ott's 511. Babe Ruth was the other.

The automobile wreck near Bay St. Louis on the Mississippi Gulf Coast which eventually cost Ott's life also was fatal to the driver of the other car 50-year-old Leslie Curry, sr. Ott's wife, Mildred, was seriously injured.

Wife Still in Hospital

The Otts were pulling onto the highway from a roadside restaurant in their station wagon when the cars crashed. They had gone to inspect a newly purchased cottage at Bay St. Louis.

Mrs. Ott still is under treatment for injuries received in the wreck. She was transferred from a hospital at Gulfport, Miss., to one here last night.

Ott was brought to a New Orleans hospital from Gulfport Thursday when his condition grew worse due to a kidney blockage.

He underwent an eight-hour operation and another was required yesterday when the kidney failed again. He died shortly after noon.

Tris Speaker, 70, Baseball Great, Dies

Whitney, Texas, Dec. 8 (AP)—Tris Speaker, rated by many experts as the best centerfielder in the history of baseball, died today, apparently of a heart attack. The famed "Gray Eagle" was 70.

Burt Howell, a friend, said Speaker, former Cleveland Indians' player and a member of baseball's Hall of Fame, died at his lodge at nearby Lake Whitney.

Speaker collapsed after a fishing trip as he and Charles Caughn, of Hubbard, Texas, pulled their boat into the dock after an afternoon Lake Whitney. Speaker was born in Hubbard, April 4. 1888.

.344 Lifetime Average

Speaker, who compiled a lifetime batting average of .344 in 22 seasons of play in the majors with the Boston Red Sox, Cleveland, Washington and Philadelphia Athletics, had one previous heart attack.

Lifetime Record Of Tris Speaker

Year—Team	Games	B.A.
1907—Red Sox	7	.158
1908—Red Sox	31	.220
1909—Red Sox	143	.309
1910—Red Sox	141	.340
1911—Red Sox	153	.327
1912—Red Sox	153	.383
1913—Red Sox	141	.366
1914—Red Sox	158	.338
1915—Red Sox	150	.322
1916—Indians	151	.386
1917—Indians	142	.352
1918—Indians	127	.319
1919—Indians	134	.296
1920—Indians	150	.388
1921—Indians	132	.362
1922—Indians	131	.378
1923—Indians	150	.380
1924—Indians	135	.344
1925—Indians	117	.389
1926—Indians	150	.304
1927—Senators	141	.327
1928—Athletics	64	.267
	2,789	.344

Haddix Hurls Perfect 12-Inning Game, Loses In 13th

93,103 FANS AT EXHIBITION

Yank-Dodger Crowd In Los Angeles Is Baseball Record

The Yankees led the Dodgers, 6 to 2, after seven innings.

Los Angeles, May 7 (P)—The largest crowd in baseball history—93,103—rose to its feet and gave paralyzed Roy Campanella a mighty ovation tonight.

The greatest catcher the Dodgers ever had was wheeled to second base in a wheel chair just before Los Angeles and the New York Yankees started playing an exhibition game for his benefit.

"This is something I'll never forget," Campanella said over the public address system. "I thank God I'm here living to be able to see it. It's a wonderful thing."

It was estimated Campanella would realize between $50,000 and $75,000 from the game. The Dodgers were giving him their entire share. The Yankees pledged their take to other charities, including sandlot baseball.

"A Great Moment"

National League President Warren Giles was one of the speakers at the pre-game ceremonies.

"This is a great moment for you, Campy," he said. "This tribute to Roy Campanella, to his courage, indicates the tremendous interest you people have in baseball, and your great hearts as well . . . This crowd justifies the faith the National League had in the Dodgers two years ago" (when it permitted the Brooklyn franchise to move here).

Also introduced before the game was Yankee Manager Casey Stengel. He drew almost as big an ovation as Campanella when he trotted briskly onto the field.

First Baseman Bill Skowron of the Yankees pulled a hamstring muscle in his right thigh in the third inning. Yankee Trainer Gus Mauch said Skowron probably will be out of action a week or so.

Skowron suffered the injury when he ran out an infield grounder for a single. He was replaced by Marv Throneberry.

BUCS' HURLER IS BEATEN BY BRAVES, 2-0

Double By Joe Adcock Is Only Hit After Error, Walk

Milwaukee, May 26 (P)—Pittsburgh left-hander Harvey Haddix pitched twelve perfect innings tonight, then lost, 2 to 0, in thirteen innings to Milwaukee on an error, an intentional walk and Joe Adcock's double—the Braves only hit of the game.

Adcock hit a towering drive into the stands in the last half of the thirteenth but got credit for only a double.

Passing Runner Ruled

Umpire Frank Dascoli ruled that Adcock was passing Henry Aaron between second and third and therefore could not get credit for a home run.

Haddix retired 36 men in order before Felix Mantilla got on base on a throwing error in the thirteenth inning. Aaron was walked intentionally and then Adcock blasted his long drive into the stands.

Mantilla, first batter in the thirteenth, became the first Milwaukee base runner when Don Hoak, Pirate third baseman, threw wildly on a routine bounder. Mantilla moved to second on Eddie Mathews's sacrifice. Aaron was purposely passed. Then Adcock broke up the game.

Aaron Stops At Second

Aaron, however, stopped at second base and crossed the pitcher's mound. Adcock thus ran past him and was automatically out. Both then retraced their steps and Aaron's run was ruled valid.

Lew Burdette, of the Braves, in chalking up his eighth victory against two defeats, kept 12 hits well scattered.

Haddix, 33, veteran lefthander acquired by the Pirates from Cincinnati last winter became the first man in modern National League history to pitch a perfect game for nine innings. The last National Leaguer to accomplish the feat was John Ward of Providence in 1880.

From the tenth inning on, Haddix was in a class by himself as the first man ever to pitch a perfect game of more than nine innings. His was even the longest no hitter in history.

Pittsburgh
0 0 0 0 0 0 0 0 0 0 0 0 0 0r. 12h. 1e
Milwaukee
0 0 0 0 0 0 0 0 0 0 0 0 1 2r. 1h. 0e
Haddix and Burgess. Burdette and Crandall. Winning pitcher—Burdette (8-2). Losing pitcher—Haddix (3-3).

CLEVELAND OUTFIELDER BECOMES 3D IN HISTORY TO CLOUT FOUR IN ROW

Defeat Drops Orioles Into Second Place, Game Behind White Sox; Rocky Is Eighth To Get Four Circuits In One Game

By BOB MAISEL

Rocky Colavito became the eighth player in major-league history to hit four home runs in one game, and only the third to do it on successive times at bat, as he led the Cleveland Indians to an 11-to-8 victory over the Orioles last night in Memorial Stadium.

The loss, coupled with Chicago's victory over Washington, dropped the Orioles out of their first-place tie, a position they held for only one day. The Birds are now second, a game behind the White Sox and a half-game in front of Cleveland.

Reprinted from The Baltimore Sun papers

Tigers, Yanks Close Behind

And that rumble you hear just below comes from the Yankees and Tigers, both just a game and a half in back of the Flock.

The story of last night's game is Colavito, the 6-foot-3-inch 190-pound Indian right-fielder who won't reach his twenty-sixth birthday until August 10.

Playing in a park which has yielded fewer home runs than any other in the major leagues since Baltimore returned to the majors, he blasted his way into baseball history by hitting home runs on his last four times at bat.

No. 1 Off Walker

After walking in the first inning, he hit No. 1 off Jerry Walker, the Oriole starter and loser, in the third, got Nos. 2 and 3 off Arnold Portocarrero in the fifth and sixth, and then hit the record tying four-bagger off Ernie Johnson in the ninth.

There was an air of expectation mixed with tension as Colavito stepped to the bat in the ninth. Johnson, who had retired all four men to face him in his short stay on the mound, had not given up a home run this year.

When Colavito connected there was no doubt that he had tied the record. The drive carried far up into the left field stands.

As Colavito circled the bases, the crowd of 15,883 let out a mighty roar in recognition of one of the greatest power displays in baseball history.

Orioles-Indians Box

CLEVELAND	ab.	r.	h.	rbi.	e
Held, ss	5	1	1	0	0
Power, 1b	4	1	0	0	0
Francona, cf	5	2	2	1	0
Colavito, rf	4	5	4	6	0
Minoso, lf	5	1	3	3	0
Jones, 3b	3	0	0	0	0
Strickland, 3b	2	0	1	0	0
Brown, c	4	0	1	0	0
Martin, 2b	3	1	1	1	0
1Webster, 2b	1	0	0	0	0
Bell, p	3	0	0	0	0
Garcia, p	1	0	0	0	0
Totals	40	11	13	11	0

ORIOLES	ab.	r.	h.	rbi.	e
Pearson, cf	3	1	2	0	0
Pilarcik, rf	5	1	1	2	0
Woodling, lf	5	1	3	1	0
Triandos, c	2	0	1	1	0
Ginsberg, c	1	1	0	0	0
Hale, 1b	3	0	0	0	0
Zuverink, p	0	0	0	0	0
2Boyd	1	0	0	0	0
Johnson, p	0	0	0	0	0
3Nieman	1	1	1	0	0
Klaus, 3b	5	0	2	4	0
Carrasquel, ss	5	0	0	0	0
Gardner, 2b	4	1	1	0	0
Walker, p	1	1	1	0	0
Portocarrero, p	1	0	0	0	0
Lockman, 1b	1	1	0	0	0
Totals	38	8	12	8	0

1Popped up for Martin in seventh; 2Flied out for Zuverink in seventh; 3Doubled for Johnson in ninth.

Cleveland	3	1	2	0	1	3	0	0	1	—11
ORIOLES	1	2	0	0	0	0	4	0	1	— 8

Putouts and assists—Cleveland, 27-6; ORIOLES, 27-9. Left on bases—Cleveland, 5; ORIOLES, 8. Two-base hits—Brown, Held, Francona, Klaus, Nieman. Home runs—Minoso, Martin, Colavito 4. Stolen base—Minoso. Sacrificed fly—Triandos.

PITCHING RECORD

	Ip	H	R	Er	Bb	So
Bell (W., 5-5)	6 1/3	8	7	7	4	3
Garcia	2 2/3	4	1	1	0	0
Walker (L., 4-3)	2 1/3	4	6	6	2	1
Portocarrero	3 1/3	7	4	4	1	3
Zuverink	1 1/3	0	0	0	0	0
Johnson	2	2	1	1	0	0

Umpires—Summers, McKinley, Soar, Chylak. Time—2.54. Attendance—15,883.

FINAL STANDINGS

National League

Scores Of Yesterday

Los Angeles, 7; Chicago, 1.
St. Louis, 2-14; San Francisco, 1-8.
Milwaukee, 5; Philadelphia, 2.
Cincinnati, 9; Pittsburgh, 7.

Where They Play Today

Los Angeles at Milwaukee, play-off, Koufax (8-6), Podres (14-9) or McDevitt (10-8) vs. Burdette (21-15) or Willey (5-3).

Standing Of The Clubs

Los Angeles	86	68	.558	
Milwaukee	86	68	.558	
San Francisco	83	71	.539	3
Pittsburgh	78	76	.506	8
Chicago	74	80	.481	12
Cincinnati	74	80	.481	12
St. Louis	71	83	.461	15
Philadelphia	64	90	.416	22

Pirates Beat Reds, 4 To 3, On Two-Run Triple In 12th

Pittsburgh, Sept. 19 (AP) — Bill Mazeroski's two-run triple in the twelfth inning today gave the Pittsburgh Pirates a 4-3 victory over the Cincinnati Redlegs and enabled relief pitcher Elroy Face to pick up his eighteenth victory of the season against one defeat.

Mazeroski, who homered in the third, delivered his game-winning triple with two out. Face had given up three hits and a run to the Redlegs in the top of the twelfth.

Dick Stuart doubled and Don Hoak was hit with a pitched ball to put two on before Mazeroski unloaded.

Cincinnati scored first in the third. Then Mazeroski tied it up with his homer.

In the sixth Vada Pinson, reached first on an error, stole second and scored on Frank Thomas's single to put the Reds ahead again.

Pirates Pull Up Even

The Pirates pulled up even in the eighth when Don Hoak got on on an error, advanced on Bill Virdon's single and scored on a double by pinch hitter Rocky Nelson.

The score remained that way until the Reds pushed over a single run in the twelfth.

CINCINNATI	ab	r	h	rbi
Temple.2b	6	1	2	1
Pinson.cf	6	1	1	1
Bell.rf	5	0	1	0
Rob'son.lf	5	0	3	0
Tho'as.1b	5	0	1	1
Dock'n.1b	0	0	0	0
Jones.3b	4	0	1	0
He'rich.3b	0	0	0	0
2Lynch	1	0	0	0
Cook.3b	0	0	0	0
Bailey.c	4	0	2	0
3Hook	0	0	0	0
Dot'rer.c	0	0	0	0
Kasko.ss	5	1	1	0
New'be.p	5	0	1	0
Nux'all.p	0	0	0	0
Law'nce.p	0	0	0	0
Totals	46	3	13	3

PITTSBURGH	ab	r	h	rbi
Skin'er.lf	5	0	0	0
Groat.ss	5	0	1	0
Cle'ente.rf	5	0	0	0
Stuart.1b	5	1	1	0
Burgess.c	5	0	0	0
Hoak.3b	4	2	0	0
Ma'oski.2b	5	1	2	3
Virdon.cf	4	0	3	0
Hall.p	2	0	0	0
1Nelson	1	0	1	1
Face.p	1	0	0	0
Totals	42	4	8	4

1Doubled for Hall in eighth; 2Lined out for Henrich in eleventh; 3Ran for Bailey in twelfth.

Cincinnati	0	0	1	0	0	1	0	0	0	0	0	1	-3
Pittsburgh	0	0	1	0	0	0	0	1	0	0	0	2	—4

Errors—Burgess 2, Stuart, Kasko, Face. Putouts and assists—Cincinnati 35-12, Pittsburgh 36-11. Double plays—Thomas, Kasko and Temple, Burgess and Mazeroski. Left on base—Cincinnati 8, Pittsburgh 4. Two-base hits—Pinson, Nelson, Groat, Stuart. Three-base hit—Mazeroski. Home run — Mazeroski. Stolen bases — Pinson, Temple. Sacrifice—Bailey.

	Ip	H	R	Er	Bb	So
Hall	8	8	2	1	0	3
Face (W., 18-1)	4	5	1	1	0	1
Newcombe	11 1/3	7	2	1	0	0
Nuxhall	1/3	0	0	0	0	0
xLawrence (L., 7-12)	0	1	2	2	0	0

xPitched to two batters in twelfth.

Hit by pitcher—By Lawrence (Hoak). Umpires—Landes, Burkhart, Venzon, Sudol. Time—2.30. Attendance—8,466.

Jones Hurls No-Hit Ball

CONTEST ENDS IN 8TH INNING

Cardinals Lose As Frisco Hangs On In Flag Race

St. Louis, Sept. 26 (P)—Unpredictable Sam Jones of the still-hopeful San Francisco Giants pitched the second no-hitter of his major league career tonight, throttling the St. Louis Cardinals, 4 to 0, for his twenty-first victory in a game halted in the eighth inning by high winds and heavy rains.

Jones's magnificent effort in the first game of a scheduled twi-night doubleheader kept alive the Giants' thread-thin chance for a tie in the piping hot National League pennant race.

Giants 1½ Games Back

Bill Rigney's Giants now trail the Los Angeles Dodgers and the Milwaukee Braves—in a dead heat for the National League lead—by 1½ games. They still have two to play while the Dodgers and Braves have one each to go tomorrow.

SAN FRANCISCO				ST. LOUIS			
	ab	r	h	rbi		ab	r	h	rbi
Pagan.3b	4	0	1	0	Blasi'e.2b	2	0	0	0
Alou.rf	4	0	0	0	Cunni'm.rf	2	0	0	0
Mays.cf	3	2	2	1	Musial.1b	3	0	0	0
M'C'ey.1b	4	2	2	2	Boyer.3b	3	0	0	0
Cepeda.lf	x2	0	1	1	Cimoli.lf	3	0	0	0
C'p'da.lf	x2	0	1	1	H.Smith.c	2	0	0	0
Sp'cer.2b	3	0	0	0	Flood.cf	2	0	0	0
Br'soud.ss	4	0	0	0	Gram's.ss	1	0	0	0
Schmidt.c	3	0	3	0	Mizell.p	1	0	0	0
S.Jones.p	2	0	0	0	1Shannon	1	0	0	0
					Broglio.p	0	0	0	0
Totals	29	4	9	4	Totals	20	0	0	0

xAwarded first base because of catcher's interference.
1Struck out for Mizell in sixth.

San Francisco .... 1 0 1 0 0 0 2 0—4
St. Louis ...... 0 0 0 0 0 0 0 —0

Errors—Musial, Boyer, H. Smith. Put-outs, assists—San Francisco, 21-8; St. Louis, 23-14. Double plays—Boyer, Blasingame and Musial; Boyer, Grammas and Musial. Left on bases—San Francisco, 7; St. Louis, 2. Two-base hits—Cepeda, Mays. Home runs—Mays, McCovey. Sacrifice—S. Jones, Blasingame.

	Ip	H	R	Er	Bb	So
S. Jones (W., 21-5)	7	0	0	0	2	5
Mizell (L., 13-10)	6	8	2	2	2	0
Broglio	1⅔	1	2	0	0	3

Hit by pitcher—By Mizell (Cepeda). Wild pitch—Mizell. Umpires—Dascoli, Gorman, Secory, Landes. Time—1.51. Attendance—10,000 (estimated).

Braves Top Phils, 5-2, Dodgers Rip Cubs, 7-1, To Tie For N. L. Flag

ALL MILWAUKEE RUNS UNEARNED; BEST-OF-3 PLAYOFF OPENS TODAY

Two-Run Homers By Neal And Roseboro Help Craig Win 11th; Averill Belts 4-Bagger In Fifth For Lone Chicago Score

Braves

Milwaukee, Sept. 27 (P)—The Milwaukee Braves forced a National League pennant playoff with Los Angeles today by thumping the last-place Philadelphia Phillies on five unearned runs, 5 to 2, in the final game of the regular season.

The third playoff in league history will open tomorrow at Milwaukee's County Stadium where the Braves and Dodgers will tangle in the first of their best-of-three series. They will continue at Los Angeles Tuesday and Wednesday, if necessary, thus forcing a delay in the start of the World Series with the Chicago White Sox until Thursday or Friday.

Dodgers

Chicago, Sept. 27 (P)—The Los Angeles Dodgers, who finished seventh last year, tied the Milwaukee Braves for the National League pennant today by closing the regular season with a comparatively easy 7-to-1 victory over the Chicago Cubs.

The Dodgers and Braves meet tomorrow in Milwaukee to open a best-of-three playoff for the right to face the White Sox in the World Series. The second playoff game, and possibly a third, will be played in Los Angeles.

Two-run homers by Charlie Neal and John Roseboro made it easy for Roger Craig to notch his pennant-tying decision which he did with a masterful six-hitter for a final 11-5 record.

PLAYOFF

Dodgers Go Wild With Mantilla's Throw in 12th

LOS ANGELES, Sept. 30 (AP).—The champion Dodgers moved into Chicago today, ready to take on the White Sox for the world championship.

And the Braves, shorn of their National League title, scattered out and headed for their homes.

But the scene in Memorial Coliseum yesterday as the shadows of dusk settled over the place was still a vivid memory to the 36,528 fans gathered in the place, and the millions who watched the drama on television.

Two of the great heroes of the Dodger old guard, First Baseman Gil Hodges and Outfielder Carl Furillo, were all but dismantled by their teammates as the battle came to its quick end in the 12th inning.

Hodges had scored the winning run in the 6-5 victory on Furillo's hit back of second base and Felix Mantilla's wild throw to first base.

The entire Dodger team suddenly became one rolling, tangled mass of happy ballplayers on the grass inside the first-base line.

Congratulated by Haney

Presently Alston excused himself. He showed up, still in uniform and spiked shoes, in the Braves' dressing room to shake hands with Manager Fred Haney.

"You came from behind to win and you deserved it," Haney declared. "Now go after the White Sox."

Haney said he couldn't recall when he had to use four pitchers as he did in the ninth inning—Lew Burdette, Joey Jay, Warren Spahn and Don McMahon.

The Dodgers were down, 5-2, in the ninth when they chased starter Lew Burdette with consecutive singles by Wally Moon, Duke Snider and Hodges. Reliefer McMahon yielded a two-run single to Norm Larker, and Furillo tied it with his long fly off Warren Spahn—a drive on which Hank Aaron made a brilliant catch.

No. 46 for Mathews

The Braves scored off Don Drysdale in the first on Frank Torre's two-run single and added a third run in the second on Snider's throwing error. They knocked out Drysdale in the fifth, when Ed Mathews hit his 46th home run.

Their fifth and final run came in the eighth when Del Crandall tripled and scored on Mantilla's sacrifice fly.

The Dodgers scored a run in the first when Moon singled in Charley Neal, who had tripled. Neal slammed his 19th home run of the season over the leftfield screen in the fourth for the second Dodger run.

The victory went to Stan Williams, sixth Dodger pitcher, who hurled hitless ball for the last three innings. Bob Rush, the fifth Milwaukee pitcher, took the loss.

Even in his greatest hour, Williams was beset by his old enemy — wildness. He got through the 10th inning all right, then fell badly off target. He walked three in the 11th, and had the bases loaded with two out. But he managed to reel across that tightrope when he got Joe Adcock to hit into a forceout. In the 12th, he set the Braves down in order.

DODGERS, 6; BRAVES, 5

MILWAUKEE

	ab	r	h	rbi	po	a
Bruton, cf	6	0	0	0	4	0
Mathews, 3b	4	2	2	1	2	2
Aaron, rf	4	1	3	0	3	0
Torre, 1b	3	0	1	2	10	0
Maye, lf	2	0	0	0	2	0
1Pafko, lf	1	0	0	0	0	0
2Slaughter	1	0	0	0	0	0
Demerit, lf	0	0	0	0	0	0
10Spangler, lf	0	0	0	0	3	0
Logan, ss	3	1	2	0	3	5
Schoendienst, 2b	1	0	0	0	0	0
4Vernon	1	0	0	0	0	0
Cottier, 2b	0	0	0	0	0	0
11Adcock	1	0	0	0	0	0
Avila, 2b	0	0	0	1	0	0
Crandall, c	6	1	1	0	6	1
Mantilla, 2b-ss	5	0	1	1	1	1
Burdette, p	4	0	1	0	0	2
McMahon, p	0	0	0	0	0	0
Spahn, p	0	0	0	0	0	0
Jay, p	1	0	0	0	0	0
Rush, p	1	0	0	0	0	0
Totals	44	5	10	4xx-35	13	

LOS ANGELES

	ab	r	h	rbi	po	a
Gilliam, 3b	5	0	1	0	4	3
Neal, 2b	6	2	3	1	3	3
Moon, rf-lf	6	1	3	1	3	1
Snider, cf	4	0	1	0	1	0
5Lillis	0	0	0	0	0	0
Williams, p	2	0	0	0	0	0
Hodges, 1b	5	2	2	0	11	0
Larker, lf	4	0	2	2	4	0
6Pignatano, c	1	0	1	0	3	0
Roseboro, c	3	0	0	0	5	1
7Furillo, rf	2	0	2	1	0	0
Wills, ss	5	0	1	0	2	5
Drysdale, p	1	0	0	0	1	1
Podres, p	1	0	0	0	0	0
Churn, p	0	0	0	0	0	1
3Demeter	1	0	0	0	0	0
Koufax, p	0	0	0	0	0	0
Labine, p	0	0	0	0	0	0
8Essegian	0	0	0	0	0	0
9Fairly, cf	2	0	0	0	1	0
Totals	48	6	15	5	36	14

1 Flied out for Maye in 5th. 2 Popped out for Pafko in 7th. 3 Lined out for Churn in 8th. 4 Called out on strikes for Schoendienst in 9th. 5 Ran for Snider in 9th. 6 Ran for Larker in 9th. 7 Hit sacrifice fly for Roseboro in 9th. 8 Announced as batter for Labine in 9th. 9 Hit into force play for Essegian in 9th. 10 Walked for Demerit in 11th. 11 Hit into force play for Demerit in 11th.

xx Two out when winning run scored.

MILWAUKEE .... 210 010 010 000—5
LOS ANGELES .. 100 100 003 001—6

E—Snider, Neal, Mantilla 2. DP—Wills to Neal to Hodges, Torre to Logan to Torre. LOB—Milwaukee 13, Los Angeles 11.

2b—Aaron, 3b—Neal, Crandall. HR—Neal, Mathews. SF—Mantilla, Furillo.

	ip	h	r	er
Drysdale	4⅓	6	4	3
Podres	1⅔	1	0	0
Churn	1⅓	1	1	1
Koufax	4	0	0	0
Labine	⅔	0	0	0
Williams	3	0	0	0
xBurdette	8	10	5	5
vMcMahon	0	1	0	0
Spahn	⅔	1	0	0
Jay	2⅓	2	0	0
Rush	1	1	1	1

x Faced three batters in 9th.
v Faced one batter in 9th.

Winner—Williams (5-5). Loser—Rush (5-6).

BB—Drysdale 2 (Mathews, Aaron), Podres 1 (Torre), Koufax 3 (Aaron, Torre, Demerit), Williams 3 (Maye, Torre, Spangler), Jay 1 (Gilliam), Rush 1 (Hodges). SO—Drysdale 3 (Crandall 2, Mantilla), Podres 1 (Burdette), Koufax 1 (Bruton), Labine 1 (Vernon), Williams 3 (Mantilla, Jay, Rush), Burdette 4 (Snider 2, Hodges, Wills), Jay 1 (Williams). HBP—By Jay (Pignatano). WP—Podres. PB—Pignatano. U—Barlick, Boggess, Donatelli, Conlan, Jackowski, Gorman. T—4:06. A—36,528.

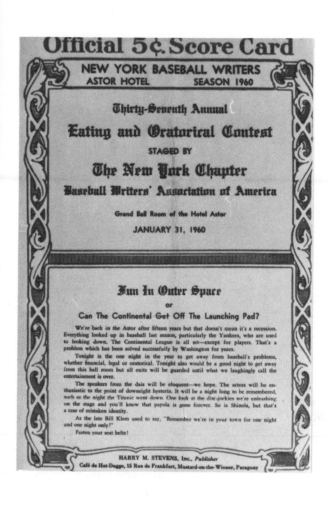

Rigney Fired, Giants Name Tom Sheehan

SAN FRANCISCO, June 18 (AP). — The Giants abruptly fired Manager Bill Rigney today and turned over the job to baseball-wise Tom Sheehan, with a mandate to get the San Francisco club back into National League contention.

If the 66-year-old former head of the Giants' scouting system succeeds, Clubowner Horace Stoneham as much as told him the job was his even into next season.

Rigney's sudden discharge came after the Giants, while only one game out of first place, were trounced three times by the league-leading Pirates.

Jones Pitch 3-Hitter

Cepeda's Triple Single Bat In 3

SAN FRANCISCO, Apr. 12 (AP)—Sad Sam Jones gave the 15-million-dollar Candlestick Park a happy inaugural today, setting down St. Louis on three hits as the San Francisco Giants won their opener, 3-1.

Big Orlando Cepeda crashed a triple and a single his first two times at bat, knocking in all three San Francisco runs before a sellout crowd of 42,269 Each hit came off the first pitch to him by Larry Jackson, Cardinal right hander who was charged with the loss.

Sunny but windy weather prevailed in San Francisco's sparkling new stadium beside the bay. Vice-President Richard M. Nixon described it as "the finest baseball park in America." Gov. Edmund G. Brown, baseball commissioner Ford Frick, and the presidents of both major leagues, were among the notables witnessing the National League opener.

ST. LOUIS (N)	ab r h bi	S. FRANCISCO (N)	ab r h bi
Cunn'gham rf	4 0 0 0	Blas'game 2b	4 1 0 0
Spencer ss	4 0 0 0	Davenport 3b	4 1 1 0
White cf	4 0 2 0	Mays cf	3 1 1 1
Boyer 3b	3 0 0 0	McCovey 1b	4 0 1 0
Musial 1b	3 0 0 0	Cepeda lf	4 0 2 3
Wagan lf	2 0 0 0	Kirkland rf	4 0 1 1
Smith c	2 0 0 0	Bressoud ss	4 0 1 0
a-Nieman	1 0 0 0	Schmidt c	3 0 0 0
Shannon lf	1 0 0 0	Jones p	3 0 0 0
Grammas 2b	2 0 0 0		
b-Sawatski	1 0 0 0		
Jackson p	1 0 0 0		
c-Crowe	1 0 0 0		
Duliba p	0 0 0 0		
Totals	30 1 3 1	**Totals**	30 3 8 5

aStruck out for Smith in eighth.
bPopped out for Grammas in eighth.
cLined out for Jackson in eighth.

St. Louis	000 010 000—1	
San Francisco	200 100 00x—3	

E—Grammas, White. PO—St. Louis 24-9, San Francisco 27-7. DP—Spencer, Grammas and Musial. LOB—St. Louis 3, San Francisco 3.
2B—Mays, McCovey. 3B—Cepeda. HR—Wagner, SS—White, Kirkland (2), Bressoud. S—Davenport.

	IP	H	R	ER	BB	SO
Jackson (L, 0-1)	7	7	3	3	1	3
Duliba	1	1	0	0	1	2
Jones (W, 1-0)	9	3	1	1	1	3

U—Conlan, Donatelli, Burkhart, Vargo.
T—2:21. A—42,269.

5 CITIES FORM 3D BASEBALL BIG LEAGUE

New York, July 27 (P)—A third major baseball league was formed today to operate in 1961 with five founding cities—New York, Houston, Toronto, Denver and Minneapolis-St. Paul. At least three more will be added later.

William Shea, chairman of Mayor Wagner's New York baseball committee, announced at a press conference the founding of the circuit, to be known as the Continental League.

Shea said there will be a minimum of eight cities, and perhaps more, in the league which will play a 154-game schedule. He listed eleven additional cities that had expressed interest. They were Buffalo, Montreal, Atlanta, New Orleans, Miami, Indianapolis, Dallas-Fort Worth, San Diego, Portland, Seattle and San Juan, Puerto Rico.

Franchises By August 18

The new league hopes to have two or more franchises definitely lined up by August 18 when the founders meet with Commissioner Ford Frick's seven-man committee from the existing majors.

"I look forward to the fullest cooperation of the National and American Leagues and expect a program will be initiated at our August 18 meeting to bring the Continental League into the structure of major-league baseball," said Shea. "We are therefore proceeding on the basis of complete and unqualified cooperation of the two existing major leagues."

Frick Has Met With Shea

Frick in his Radio City office said he had been aware that the founders were meeting.

"We are going to sit down and talk with them," he said. "At that time we will discuss the whole situation. Apparently they now have set up their organization."

Frick said he had met with Shea three times and talked to him several times on the phone.

In addition to Frick, the committee includes President Warren Giles of the National League, President Joe Cronin of the American League, National League owners Lou Perini of Milwaukee, and Bob Carpenter of Philadelphia and American League owners Tom Yawkey of Boston and Arnold Johnson of Kansas City.

The Continental League met for the last three days, adopting a constitution and setting up procedures for screening and qualifying other cities for membership. It also made plans to comply with the request from Senator Kefauver to appear before an anti-trust subcommittee in Washington Friday. Each founding city put up $50,000 and reportedly is prepared to invest as much as $2,500,000.

Williams Joins '500' Club at 41

Red Sox Ace Gains Admission With a Two-Run Homer

CLEVELAND, June 17 (AP) —Ted Williams, 41, hit the 500th home run of his major league career tonight. "Sure, it was a thrill; it was one of my goals," he said.

In major league history, only three other players have reached the 500-homer mark.

The Boston Red Sox slugger's eighth home run of the year came in the third inning off Wynn Hawkins of the Cleveland Indian, Willie Tasby, who had singled, was on base.

Ted's smash rose in a low arc through the rainy mist and cleared the left-center-field fence near the 365-foot mark. The blow beat the Indans, 3 1.

Williams said that he hit a slider, and that he knew when his bat met the ball that he had his home run. "It felt wonderful," he added.

Players Greet Him

Williams paused at third base for a handshake with the third-base coach, Billy Herman. When he arrived at home plate, the Splendid Splinter wore a wide grin. Boston players stood on the dugout steps to greet him and pump his hand.

Ted had grounded out on his first time up in the first inning. After he had walked in the seventh, he was replaced by a pinch runner.

While the game still was in progress, Williams said:

"One reason I played this year was to make up for a bad season last year." (He hit 254 last season, and after tonight's game had a .326 batting average.)

The other 500-or-more-homer

Wide World Photo

Ted Williams hits 500th home run of his major league career in the third inning against the Indians at Cleveland.

hitters 'vere Babe Ruth (714), Jimmy Foxx (534) and Mel Ott (511).

Stan Musial of the St. Louis Cardinals is the active player closest to Williams in home runs. Stan has 416, six of them so far this year.

"I hoped at the start of the season to do it this year," Williams said, "but I didn't think I would get the chance, because

of a bad cold early in the season and a leg injury."

Another Feat Recalled

In the pleasure of his excitement tonight, Williams looked back to 1940, his second year in the majors. Asked whether homer No. 500 was his greatest thrill, he said:

"It's nothing like the one I got in 1940 to win the All-Star Game."

Ted Hits Pair For Six RBI In Day Game

BOSTON, Aug. 20 (AP).—Incomparable Ted Williams provided the drama with a pair of three-run homers in the first game today but Baltimore salvaged a split by feating the Red Sox, 6-0, tonight behind Hal Brown's masterful pitching in the second half of a say-night double-header.

Brown, a former Red Sox righthander, allowed his old mates eight singles while keeping the Orioles in the thick of the American League pennant fight, 2½ games behind pacesetting New York.

Williams, who also singled and drew his 2,000th walk, won the daylight half of the competition, 8-6, by belting two tremendous drives for his 514th and 515th major league homers.

Dramatic Rap Ends Colorful Career for Ted

Red Sox Retire Famous No. 9; Jensen to Play

BOSTON, Sept. 29 (AP) — Ted Williams has made an early exit from a brilliant playing career on the wings of his 521st home run and a boisterous good-by.

The Boston slugger's dramatic touch bordered on the uncanny in yesterday's 5-4 victory over Baltimore.

It was the triumphant moment which had been Williams' final goal.

Paid tribute before the game and greeted by volley after volley of cheers during it. Williams came to bat for his final Fenway Park appearance in the eighth inning.

The 10,000-plus customers stood for a minute and a half in demonstration.

Nothing More to Do

As he had done for more than two decades, Williams dug a hole in the batter's box with his right foot, steadily swung his bat—and got a count of one and one.

With the smooth swing which has been his trademark, Ted lined Jack Fisher's next delivery 450 feet into the right-centerfield seats behind the Boston bullpen.

In the dressing room later it was disclosed that Williams had played his last game. He will not appear in the weekend series in New York as at first planned.

"I'm convinced I've quit at the right time," Williams said. "There's nothing more I can do."

Continental League Decides to Quit

Majors Now Plan to Add Four Teams

CHICAGO, Aug. 2 (AP) The Continental League died today, making room for the National and American leagues to add two teams each for 1961.

Walter O'Malley, owner of the Los Angeles Dodgers and chairman of the National League Expansion Committee, said that "we immediately will recommend expansion and that we would like to do it by 1961."

President Branch Rickey of the Continental withdrew his group's immediate bid for recognition as a third major baseball league by agreeing to a plan enabling the American and National leagues to select four clubs from the Continental's potential territory.

Sept. 13

AMERICAN LEAGUE			
	W.	L. Pct.	G.B.
New York	82	56 .594	....
Baltimore	82	58 .586	1
Chicago	81	59 .579	2
WASH'TON.	70	70 .500	13
Cleveland	69	70 .496	13½
Detroit	64	76 .456	19
Boston	61	79 .436	22
Kansas City	49	90 .351	33½

YESTERDAY'S RESULTS

Chicago, 6; Washington, 5. (11 innings.)

Cleveland, 5; Boston, 3.

Detroit, 3; Baltimore, 1.

Kansas City, 12; New York, 3.

Oct. 3

Runnels Takes Title as Yanks Drive to Mark

By the Associated Press

Pete Runnels won his first batting title and a couple of young righthanders, Jim Perry and Chuck Estrada, were the winningest pitchers. The Senators won 73 games, their best total since 1953, and Baltimore's modern-day Orioles finished second, their highest yet.

But the American League champions are the Yankees, and no doubt about it.

With Mickey Mantle winning the home run championship with 40, one more than teammate Roger Maris, who took the RBI title with 112, the Yankees broke their league home run record, gave Manager Casey Stengel his 10th pennant in a dozen years, and finished with a 15-game winning streak—the longest ever for a club headed into the World Series.

Finish With Flourish

The Yankees, their pride stung by last season's third-place finish, bounced back for a 97-57 record, their sixth best under Casey, and crushed Baltimore's surprising bid by winning 19 of their last 21 games. The Yanks wound up with an eight-game margin.

And they finished with a flourish, coming from behind in yesterday's regular season windup for and 8-7 victory over the Red Sox on a two-run homer in the ninth inning by Dale Long.

PITTSBURGH FANS GO WILD

Traffic Jam, Confetti, Jigs Feature Festivities

Pittsburgh, Oct. 13 (P) — The Steel City flipped its lid today—just one second after the Pittsburgh Pirates won the World Series by defeating the New York Yankees, 10-9.

The celebration picked up speed by the minute. Traffic was jammed so badly police threw up their hands in despair.

Confetti, and torn up newspapers littered the streets. Some fans drank beer from bottles they carried from bars. The bars were swamped. Horns tooted, whistles shrilled . . . it was a madhouse.

Girls Distribute Kisses

Police streamed from office buildings. Girls bussed their boy friends. Some of the gals didn't mind kissing anyone — anyone who was a Buc fan.

Police said they would be in for a "rough night." That was the understatement of the year from the indications at dusk.

Some of the delirious fans danced jigs. Others climbed into and on top of cars. Most of them just stood smiling up at the storm of paper coming from office windows and watching the snarled traffic.

Above the honking of horns could be heard the loyal oath of a Pirate fan. "we had 'em all the way." The most typical comment was "isn't it wonderful?" The standard answer — "it sure was."

One man was gallantly attempting to sweep the sidewalk in front of one of the buildings. Making very little progress he smiled and said, "it's worth it after 33 years."

In the city's Oakland section where the ball park is located, another major celebration broke out.

Nelson Signs Autographs

Showers of confetti rained from the University of Pittsburgh's dormitories near Forbes Field. Horns blew and people shouted. Many of those driving had no destination and didn't care.

At least one of the conquering heroes got caught up in the celebration. First Baseman Rocky Nelson, whose car was parked at a service station near the field, signed autographs until he reached his car.

'KNEW IT WAS GOING,' SAYS MAZEROSKI OF SERIES-WINNING HOMER

Pirate Second Baseman Hit Fast Ball; Nelson Explains Play At First In Ninth On Which Yanks Scored Tieing Run

Pittsburgh, Oct. 13 (P)—Champagne bottles popped a merry tune in the Pittsburgh Pirates' dressing room today after their come-from-behind, 10-to-9 victory over the New York Yankees in the final game of the World Series.

The players hugged, they kissed, they danced and they drank champagne. The center of attention was young Billy Mazeroski, whose home run blast won the ball game.

"I hit a fast ball," chortled the Bucs second sacker. "It was the second pitch and I knew it was going all the way as soon as it left my bat."

It took newsmen almost fifteen minutes to get into the jubilant Pirates' dressing room. They took a worse mauling than the players inside.

Lived In Same County

John Galbreath, the Pirates' owner, was the first to work his way through the vast throng of writers to congratulate his team.

"They did a helluva job," he said.

Turning to Harvey Haddix, the left-hander who picked up the victory in relief, Galbreath said:

"This boy and I grew up in the same county — Madison county, Ohio. He was great, simply great."

World Series Box

Pittsburgh, Oct. 13 (P)—The official box score of the seventh game of the 1960 World Series:

NEW YORK (A)

	Ab	R	H	Rbi	Po	A	E
Richardson, 2b	5	2	2	0	2	5	0
Kubek, ss	3	1	0	0	3	2	0
DeMaestri, ss	0	0	0	0	0	0	0
4Long	1	0	1	0	0	0	0
5McDougald, 3b	0	1	0	0	0	0	0
Maris, rf	5	0	0	0	2	0	1
Mantle, cf	5	1	3	2	0	0	0
Berra, lf	4	2	1	4	3	0	0
Skowron, 1b	5	2	2	1	10	2	0
Blanchard, c	4	0	1	1	1	1	0
Boyer, 3b-ss	4	0	1	1	0	3	0
Turley, p	0	0	0	0	0	0	0
Stafford, p	0	0	0	0	0	1	0
1Lopez	1	0	1	0	0	0	0
Shantz, p	3	0	1	0	3	1	0
Coates, p	0	0	0	0	0	0	0
Terry, p	0	0	0	0	0	0	0
Totals	**40**	**9**	**13**	**9**	**24**	**15**	**1**

PITTSBURGH (N)

	Ab	R	H	Rbi	Po	A	E
Virdon, cf	4	1	2	3	0	0	0
Groat, ss	4	1	1	1	3	2	0
Skinner, lf	2	1	0	1	0	0	0
Nelson, 1b	3	1	1	2	7	0	0
Clemente, rf	4	1	1	1	4	0	0
Burgess, c	3	0	2	0	0	0	0
2Christopher	0	0	0	0	0	0	0
Smith, c	1	1	1	3	1	0	0
Hoak, 3b	3	1	0	0	3	2	0
Mazeroski, 2b	4	2	2	1	5	0	0
Law, p	2	0	0	0	0	1	0
Face, p	0	0	0	0	0	1	0
3Cimoli	1	1	1	0	0	0	0
Friend, p	0	0	0	0	0	0	0
Haddix, p	0	0	0	0	0	0	0
Totals	**31**	**10**	**11**	**10**	**27**	**6**	**0**

1Singled for Stafford in third; 2Ran for Burgess in seventh; 3Singled for Face in eighth; 4Singled for DeMaestri in ninth; 5Ran for Long in ninth.

New York (A)	0	0	0	0	1	4	0	2	2—9
Pittsburgh (N)	2	2	0	0	0	0	0	5	1—10

Double plays Stafford, Blanchard and Skowron; Richardson, Kubek and Skowron; Kubek, Richardson and Skowron (None out when winning run scored.) Left on bases New York (A) 6, Pittsburgh (N) 1. Two-base hit Boyer. Home runs– Nelson, Skowron, Berra, Smith, Mazeroski. Sacrifice—Skinner.

	Ip	H	R	Er		Ip	H	R	Er
xxLaw	5	4	3	3	Stafford	1	2	1	1
Face	3	6	4	4	yShantz	5	4	3	3
aFriend	0	2	2	2	Coates	⅔	2	2	2
Haddix (W)	1	1	0	0	zzTerry (L)	⅓	1	1	1
xTurley	1	2	3	3					

xFaced one batter in second.   yFaced three batters in ninth; zzFaced one batter in ninth
xxFaced two batters in sixth.
yFaced three batters in eighth.

Bases on balls—Law 1 (Kubek), Face 1 (Berra), Turley 1 (Skinner), Stafford 1 (Hoak), Shantz 1 (Nelson). Umpires Jackowski (N) plate, Chylak (A) first base, Boggess (N) second base, Stevens (A) third base, Landes (N) left field, Honochick (A) right field. Time 2.36. Attendance – 36,683.

Kubek's Vocal Chord Injured

Pittsburgh, Oct. 13 (P)—Shortstop Tony Kubek, of the New York Yankees, suffered a severely bruised vocal chord in the seventh game of the World Series today and will remain in Pittsburgh's eye and ear hospital overnight for observation.

Kubek was hit on the left side of the neck by a hard hopping ground ball off the bat of Pittsburgh's Bill Virdon in the eighth inning.

"He's resting comfortably and is in real good shape," said Dr. Henry Sherman, who treated Kubek. "There was a little internal bleeding, but not much, and there is some swelling around his neck. But there's nothing to worry about. He'll be okay."

"One thing though, he's going to have a hard time talking for awhile," the doctor said. "Right now, he shouldn't talk anymore than he has too."

Senator Stock Value Disputed

Washington, Oct. 17 (P)—The Internal Revenue Service said today the stock of the Washington baseball club in the American League is worth $350 per share.

The estate of the late Clark C. Griffith contends, in a suit filed before the U.S. tax court, the value should be figured at $65 per share.

Griffith's heirs are contesting a $429,000 tax claim on the value of 4,432 shares left at his death in 1955.

Club President Calvin Griffith said while there had been some shares sold at $400 apiece no large blocks had been sold at that price. This figure would place the total value of the club at seven million dollars, he said, noting the highest price ever paid for a major league franchise was slightly more than five million for the Detroit Tigers three years ago.

Finley Obtains A's and Seeks Minority Stock

CHICAGO, Dec. 20 (AP).—Charles Finley, who yesterday purchased 52 per cent of the Kansas City Athletics, now is aiming for 100 per cent ownership.

The 42-year-old insurance broker put up $1,975,000 for controlling interest of the A's by purchasing the stock held in the estate of the late Arnold Johnson.

Probate Judge Robert Dunne approved Finley's bid. Final court approval of the purchase is contingent on Finley's being accepted by the American League.

Finley, who has been trying to buy a major league club for the last six years, is in position to purchase the remaining 48 per cent of the team's stock.

A Kansas City group, which was outbid by Finley for Johnson's stock, has options to purchase the minority holdings. This group has said it would be willing to let Finley buy the 48 per cent, provided he would keep the club in Kansas City for at least five years.

Finley, who says he wants to buy the remaining stock, estimated it would cost him an additional $1,925,000.

"There will be no problem in getting league approval, and I am not concerned with that," Finley said. "My intentions are to keep the A's permanently in Kansas City and to build a winning ball club. I will spend any reasonable amount of money to get to the first division."

Finley said Joe Gordon definitely will remain as the club's field manager but added that he has given no consideration to Parke Carroll's job as general manager.

CIRCUIT OF TEN TEAMS EXPECTED TO BEGIN ITS OPERATION IN 2 YEARS

Chicago, Oct. 16 (P)—Houston and New York were granted National League franchises today in line with an expansion program to ten teams effective for the 1962 season.

The vote to make Houston and New York the ninth and tenth teams in the National League's first structural change since 1900 were unanimous. The announcement, made by National League President Warren Giles, followed a morning session of the league's club owners. The resolution on Houston and New York was made by Walter O'Malley who, ironically had moved the Dodgers out of Brooklyn to Los Angeles in October of 1957, two months after Horace Stoneham had taken his Giants from New York to San Francisco.

No Concerted Objections

"The resolution was enthusiastically accepted," said O'Malley. "There was no concerted objections although earlier there had been some feeling that along with Houston, the Dallas-Fort Worth territory might be more feasable than New York."

Giles, who said the club owners' action will be finalized at the major league's annual convention in St. Louis in December, termed the addition of New York and Houston as a "giant progressive step toward bringing major league baseball to all four corners of the country."

"This makes us a very solid league geographically," he said enthusiastically.

Doesn't Anticipate Obstacles

"To all intents and purposes," Giles added, "we are now a ten-team league, with operations beginning in 1962. There are certain specifications the new clubs will have to meet, but I have no doubt they will meet the qualifications. I don't anticipate any obstacles."

Giles pointed out that two points must be cleared to pave the way for New York's and Houston's entry. First, a rule must be changed to make New York, currently American League territory, available to the National League. This the N.L. expects to do as soon as possible.

Second, the Houston Sports Association, recipients of the Houston franchise, must acquire the territorial rights from the Houston Buffs of the American Association.

Los Angeles, Minneapolis Enter A.L.

NEW YORK (P) — The American League Wednesday voted to expand to Los Angeles and Minneapolis - St. Paul in 1961, beating the National League to the punch.

Calvin Griffith, was given permission to move his Washington franchise to Minneapolis-St. Paul but new owners will step in to operate a club in Washington.

The names of the new owners in Washington and in Los Angeles will be named within three weeks. Although it was not immediately clear where the Los Angeles club would play, Del Webb, co-owner o fthe New York Yankees and chairman of the league's expansion committe said it probably would be in the Coliseum, sharing the football stadium with the Los Angeles Dodgers.

Joe Cronin President of the league, said another session will be held Nov. 17 "when further forward looking steps for future expansion will be considered." He said the league would expand to 12 clubs "in the near future."

To Play 162 Games

Next year the league will play a 162 - game schedule, each team playing 18 with each other club.

Last week the National League voted to expand to 10 clubs in 1962, adding New York and Houston.

A Dallas - Fort Worth group which had hoped to be voted a franchise Wednesday and possibly Toronto or Buffalo were said to be preferred for future American League additions.

To help stock the two new franchises, Webb said the player limit of each club would be cut from 25 to 23 men. "We must see how this works out before we expand any farther for 1962 to 1963," said Webb.

Pressure had been building up in recent weeks for the American League to make an all out pitch for Los Angeles, which had been grabbed from under its nose by the National League. Brooklyn moved to Los Angeles and New York to San Francisco for the 1958 National League season, vacating New York.

Frank Lane, general manager of the Cleveland Indians, joined forces with a group headed by Dan Topping, president of the Yankees, to push the Los Angeles move.

"We would be silly not to move into Los Angeles," said Cronin just before Wednesday's meeting.

Cronin said general managers were discussing plans for stocking the new Washington and Los Angeles franchises. The members of the 1960 Senators, including home run hitters Harmon Killebrew, Jim Lemon and Bob Allison and pitchers Camilo Pascual and Pedro Ramos will be playing for Minneapolis - St. Paul next season.

Wheelock Whitney, Minneapolis investment man who headed the group that held the franchise in the defunct Continental League, said he was "absolutely elated." "We will be helping Cal (Griffith) if we are financially interested or not," said Whitney.

A's Must Remain for 1961

Cronin said the sale of the Kansas City franchise, expected in the next 20 or 30 days, would not affect the league's lineup. Cronin said the Athletics must remain in the league at least for the 1961 season.

The A's majority stockholder, Arnold Johnson, died last spring and his widow is in the process of making a deal for the club. Ed Vollers, Chicago attorney and secretary if the A's, who is handling the deal, was present at Wednesday's meeting.

Commissioner Ford Frick has said he would cast a vote in favor of adding a second team to those two cities if the two leagues disagreed. Under baseball law the leagues must approve unanimously if a tea mmoves into territory already occupied.

There was no immediate indication that either league would object to the other's move into its territory at New York or Los Angeles.

Webb said the new franchises might be stocked by setting up a disaster plan by which available club would make 10 men available of which no more than three could be taken. That would make 24 men available for the two clubs.

Asked if he was thinking of selling out his interest in the Yankees and taking in the Los Angeles operation, as has been rumored, Webb said, I'll definitely stay in New York."

Commissioner Frick said he had no immediate comment on the expansion move.

Minneapolis To Enlarge Park

Minneapolis already has a ball park that can seat 22,000. This will be expanded to 40,000 capacity before next season.

If the American League club plays in the Coliseum, it will have to share the dates with the Dodgers. The Dodgers have drawn over 90,000 in the Coliseum, primarily a football stadium with a 251-foot left field foul line and a 40-foot screen extending into left center.

It was not determined immediately how records would be rated in a 162-game schedule. There may be a note in the book, designating records made in a 154-game schedule and for others in a 162-game season. That would preserve Babe Ruth's record home run total of 60.

When the two leagues met in late summer and decided to expand, each planned to accept two clubs from the Continental League. The National took in Houston and New York but the American accepted only Minneapolis-St. Paul.

"They should be happy to get three," said Webb who expected no repercussions from the Continental leaguers.

Griffith explaining his move, said, "We got a better deal in Minneapolis and St. Paul. We are being guaranteed about one million attendance a year for five years and a good radio and TV contract."

Yanks Set to Name Houk, Hamey to Succeed Weiss

Stengel Lionized At Dinner Given By N. Y. Writers

NEW YORK, Oct. 20 (AP).—The Yankees will name a new manager today — 41-year-old Ralph Houk.

But never to be forgotten will be the old Yankee manager . . . Casey Stengel, the old man the Yankees dismissed to make room for the younger man in line with the club's new policy —the youth movement.

"The youth movement of America is for kids," blared the 70-year-old Stengel in a speech last night climaxing an emotional evening during which he was given a farewell dinner party by the New York baseball writers.

"Sure I'm old," Stengel challenged an audience that included the 48-year-old Yankee co-owner, Dan Topping, the man who fired him; 65-year-old George Weiss, the general manager who will be the next man to go under the new "youth program" policy of the owners; 58-year-old Roy Hamey, who is slated to succeed Weiss, and 79-year-old Branch Rickey, president of the dormant Continental League.

Spahn Hurls No-Hitter

40-YEAR-OLD TOPS JONES, WINS 290TH

Unearned Run In First Inning Helps Southpaw Repeat Feat

Milwaukee, April 28 ℙ—Milwaukee's southpaw great. Warren Spahn, pitched the second no-hitter of his career for victory No. 290 tonight as the Braves took a 1-to-0 decision from the San Francisco Giants.

Spahn, who was 40 just last Sunday, walked only two men in dazzling the Giants and becoming the second oldest ever to pitch a no-hitter. The immortal Cy Young pitched his third and last no-hitter at the age of 41 in 1908.

The Braves' run was unearned. It came in the first inning on singles by Frank Bolling and Hank Aaron around a passed ball. That was all Spahnie needed in outdueling right-hander Sam Jones.

Shutout King

Spahn, the all-time National League shutout king among lefthanders, boosted his career total to 52, while moving the Braves into first place, replacing the Giants.

In winning his second decision against one defeat this season. Spahn struck out five. He needed flashy fielding help on only a couple of occasions.

In the sixth inning, shortstop Roy McMillan went to his left for a grounder, momentarily bobbled the ball, but fired to first in time to get Jose Pagan.

Spahn Sharp With Glove

Spahn also helped himself with some neat fielding. In the fourth inning, rookie Chuck Hiller walked on four pitches and became the first San Francisco base runner. But he was promptly erased as Spahn got dangerous Harvey Kuenn to hit back to the mound, starting a double play.

Spahn, the last to pitch a no-hitter in the majors, against Philadelphia last September 16, suffered a momentary lapse of control again at the outset of the fifth inning.

He walked Willie McCovey on four pitches. But he then forced Orlando Cepeda to rap back to the mound—and Spahnie once again started a double play.

Used 5 Pitches In Eighth

Spahn needed only five pitches to retire the Giants in the eighth inning. Then he went to the mound in the ninth with the big zero showing for San Francisco on the scoreboard in right center.

Ed Bailey, acquired by the Giants from Cincinnati yesterday, ran the count to 2-2 before striking out on Spahn's ninth pitch for the first out in the final inning.

Then Spahn came up with the play of the game to preserve his no-hitter. Matty Alou, batting for Pagan, dragged a bunt down the first base line. But Spahn got over to the ball in time to nail the speedy rookie.

SAN FRANCISCO	ab	r	h	bi	MILWAUKEE	ab	r	h	bi
Hiller 2b	3	0	0	0	McMillan ss	3	0	0	0
Kuenn 3b	3	0	0	0	Bolling 2b	3	1	2	0
Mays cf	3	0	0	0	Mathews 3b	3	0	0	0
McCovey 1b	2	0	0	0	Aaron rf	3	0	1	1
Cepeda lf	3	0	0	0	Roach lf	4	0	1	0
F. Alou rf	3	0	0	0	Spangler lf	0	0	0	0
Bailey c	3	0	0	0	Adcock 1b	3	0	1	0
Pagan ss	2	0	0	0	Lau c	3	0	0	0
aM. Alou	1	0	0	0	DeMerit rf	1	0	0	0
bASpitzer	1	0	0	0	Spahn p	4	0	0	0
Jones p	2	0	0	0					
Totals	25	0	0	0	Totals	29	1	5	1

a—Grounded out for Pagan in 9th. b—Grounded out for Jones in 9th
San Francisco .... 000 000 000—0
Milwaukee .... 100 000 00x—1
E—McCovey, Lau. PO-A—San Francisco 27-11 Milwaukee 27-11. DP—Spahn. McMillan and Adcock 2 LOB—San Francisco 0, Milwaukee 5. S—McMillan
	IP	H	R	ER	BB	SO
Jones (L, 2-1)	8	5	1	0	3	5
Spahn (W, 2-1)	9	0	0	0	2	5

HP—By Jones (Bolling). PB Bailey 2. U—Donatelli, Burkhart, Pelekoudas, Forman, Conlan. T—2 16. A—8.518.

Willie Matches Feat of 8 Others

MILWAUKEE, April 30 (AP)—Willie Mays became the ninth player in Major League history to hit four home runs in a game as the San Francisco Giants buried the Milwaukee Braves, 14-4, today.

The Giants hit eight homers in the game and thus had 13 in their last two games, tying two major league records. Their two-game total also set a new National League mark.

Even the badly beaten Braves cut in on the record business. Henry Aaron hit two home runs to give the two clubs a total of 10 which equaled the National League high for one game.

Mays, who now has six home runs for the season, hit his four today in five times at bat. He connected off starter Lew Burdette in the first and third innings, Seth Morehead in the sixth and Don McMahon in the eighth. Only Moe Drabowski got him on a line drive to centerfield in the fifth.

Mays drove in eight runs, four shy of the one-game record. He hit one of his home runs with two men on base, two with one on and one with the bases empty.

SAN FRANCISCO	ab	r	h	bi	MILWAUKEE	ab	r	h	bi
Hiller 2b	4	2	3	1	McMillan ss	4	1	1	0
Davenport 3b	4	1	2	0	Bolling 2b	4	1	2	0
Mays cf	5	4	4	8	Mathews 3b	4	0	1	0
McCovey 1b	3	0	0	0	Aaron rf	4	2	2	4
Marshall 1b	2	0	0	0	Roach lf	4	0	1	0
Cepeda lf	5	1	1	1	Adcock 1b	4	0	0	0
M. Alou lf	0	0	0	0	Lau c	3	0	1	0
F. Alou rf	4	1	1	1	McMahon p	0	0	0	0
Bailey c	4	0	0	0	Brunet p	0	0	0	0
Pagan ss	5	3	4	2	cMays	0	0	0	0
Loes p	3	0	0	0	Demeritt rf	4	0	0	0
					Burdette p	1	0	0	0
					Willey p	0	0	0	0
					Drab'sky p	0	0	0	0
					aMartin	1	0	0	0
					Morehead p	1	0	0	0
					M'Kenzie p	0	0	0	0
					bLogan	1	0	0	0
					Taylor c	1	0	0	0
Totals	39	14	14	14	Totals	34	4	8	4

a—Flied out for Drabowski in 5th; b—Fanned for MacKenzie in 7th; c—Walked for Brunet in 9th.
San Francisco ...... 103 304 030—14
Milwaukee .... 300 001 000— 4

E—Mathews. PO-A—San Francisco 27-9, Milwaukee 27-15. DP—Davenport, Hiller and Marshall; Burdette, McMillan and Adcock; Bolling, McMillan and Adcock. LOB—San Francisco 6, Milwaukee 4. 2B—Hiller 2. 3B—Davenport. HR—Mays 4, Pagan 2, Cepeda, F. Alou, Aaron 2. S—Loes 2.

GIANTS PITCHING
	IP	H	R	ER	BB	SO
Loes (W, 2-1)	9	8	4	4	1	3

BRAVES PITCHING
	IP	H	R	ER	BB	SO
x- Burd'e (L, 1-1)	3	5	5	5	0	0
Willey	1	3	2	2	0	0
Drabowsky	1	0	0	0	1	0
Morehead	1	2	4	4	1	1
MacKenzie	1	0	0	0	1	0
McMahon	1	3	3	3	2	0
Brunet	1	0	0	0	0	0

x—Burdette pitched to 1 man in 4th. HBP — By Burdette (Davenport), by MacKenzie (Bailey). U—Pelekoudas, Forman, Conlan, Donatelli, Burkhart. T—2:40. A—13,114.

'Greatest Day Of My Career,' Mays Exclaims

MILWAUKEE, April 30 (AP)—It's the greatest day of my baseball career."

That was Willie Mays' first comment today after tying a major league record by hitting four homers in the San Francisco Giants' 14-4 rout of the Milwaukee Braves.

"Any time a fella hits four homers in one game it should be his greatest day," he said.

Mays, who had gone hitless in seven appearances in two previous games against the Braves, feared he had fallen into a slight slump.

"And I thought it was going deeper," he said. "The last couple of days I didn't hit a ball good at all." The spectacular centerfielder boosted his average to .333 with his tremendous clouts. He has driven in 14 runs and has six homers. His career home run total stands at 285.

Frick Rules On Babe Ruth's Homer Record

NEW YORK, July 17 (AP). Baseball Commissioner Ford Frick ruled today that an American league player who hits more than 60 home runs in his club's first 154 games will be credited with breaking Babe Ruth's record. However, if he hits more than 60 after the 154th game, there will be some distinction in the record books to show the mark was set under a 162-game schedule.

Roger Maris of the New York Yankees has hit 35 home runs and Mickey Mantle of the Yanks has hit 32 through Sunday's games. Maris is 19 games ahead of Ruth's pace and Mantle is eight games ahead.

The Yanks have played 87 games, including one tie game.

YOUTH FANS 6, WALKS 5

Double Play Helps Right-Hander In Debut

Kansas City, June 16 P — Lew Krausse, the Kansas City Athletics $125,000 bonus pitcher, made a sensational big league debut tonight, shutting out the Los Angeles Angels on three hits as the A's won 4 to 0.

The 18-year-old right-hander who was graduated from a Chester (Pa.) high school less than two weeks ago, struck out six and walked five. Four times the Athletics came up with double plays and as a result the Angels had only five men left on the bases.

Leroy Thomas singled for the Angels' first hit off Krausse in the second inning, but Eddie Yost flied out and Ed Sadowski fanned. Leon Wagner drew a one-out base on balls in the fourth but Steve Bilko hit into another double play.

Bilko Singles

In the sixth, after Krausse had walked Ken McBride, to lead off the inning, Albie Pearson flew out and Rocky Bridges grounded into the third double play. Bilko's single to center in the seventh was the second hit off Krausse but with one out Thomas hit into the fourth twin killing.

In the eighth Yost walked for the second time but was doubled up on an attempted steal as Earl Averill struck out for Krausse's fifth victim. Ken Hamlin stroked a ground single but Ken Hunt grounded for the third out.

Shows Poise In 9th

In the ninth inning, the young pitcher showed the poise of a veteran. He struck out dangerous Ted Kluszewski on three pitches for the second out but Wagner walked and Bilko was safe as shortstop Dick Howser fumbled Bilko's grounder. Krausse calmly got Thomas to hit a popup to Bertoia that ended the game.

The largest crowd of the year at Municipal Stadium — 25,869 — watched the celebrated rookie make his first big league appearance in which he also got two hits. His father, Lew Krausse, Sr., was in the stands.

The Athletics scored first in the fourth inning as Norm Siebern doubled home Wes Covington from first base, and they notched three more in the sixth. Jerry Lumpe singled and after Covington grounded out, McBride walked Siebern and Deron Johnson.

Reno Bertoia's single plated Siebern and Lumpe and Johnson scored on Joe Pignatano's sacrifice fly.

McBride was the losing pitcher and the reverse evened his season record at 5-5.

BONUS HISTORY—Bob Bailey (left), an 18-year-old Long Beach, Cal., shortstop became the highest paid bonus player in baseball by signing $175,000 pact with Pittsburgh Pirates. His dad, Paul Bailey, assists him by pouring his favorite breakfast cereal.

Wide World Photo

Pearson cf	ab r h bi	Howser ss	ab r h bi
Pearson cf	4 0 0 0	Howser ss	5 0 0 0
Bridges 2b	3 0 0 0	Stephens cf	3 0 0 0
Klus'ski	1 0 0 0	Lumpe 2b	3 1 2 0
Wagner lf	2 0 0 0	Covingt'n lf	3 1 0 0
Bilko 1b	4 0 1 0	aBauer lf	1 0 0 0
Thomas rf	4 0 1 0	Siebern 1b	3 1 1 1
Yost 3b	1 0 0 0	Johnson rf	3 1 1 0
Sadowski c	2 0 0 0	Bertoia 3b	4 0 1 2
bAverill c	1 0 0 0	Pigtano c	1 0 1 1
Hamlin ss	3 0 1 0	Krausse p	3 0 2 0
McBride p	1 0 0 0		
Moeller p	0 0 0 0		
cHunt	1 0 00		
Kline p	0 0 00		
Totals	27 0 3 0	Totals	29 4 8 4

a—Grounded out for Covington in 7th. b—Struck out for Sadowski in 8th. c—Forced runner for Moeller in 8th. d—Struck out for Bridges in 9th.

Los Angeles .... 000 000 000—0
Kansas City .... 000 103 00x—4

E—McBride. Howser. PO-A—Los Angeles 24-14. Kansas City 27-13. DP—Hamlin, Bridges and Bilko. Howser, Lumpe and Siebern; Lumpe and Siebern; Lumpe; Howser and Siebern. Pignatano and Lumpe. LOB—Los Angeles 5 Kansas City 9. 2B—Siebern. S—Krausse. Lumpe. SF—Pignatano.

	IP	H	R	ER	BB	SO
McBride (L, 5-5)	6 1.3	7	4	4	1	1
Moeller	2-3	0	0	0	0	0
Kline	1	1	0	0	0	0
Krausse (W, 1-0)	9	3	0	0	5	6

HBP By Kline (Pignatano) U—Smith. Soar McKinley, Chylak. T—2 14 A—25,869.

GIANTS BLAST REDS, 14 TO 0

Victors Score 12 Times In Ninth For Record

Cincinnati, Aug. 23 UP—Juan Marichal pitched a three hitter and the onrushing San Francisco Giants erupted for twelve runs in a record ninth inning, hitting five homers, in a 14-to-0 victory tonight over the first place Cincinnati Reds.

Marichal outpitched eighteen-game winner Joey Jay in what had been a brilliant, 1-0 pitching duel into the eighth inning.

But Orlando Cepeda, Felipe Alou, Jim Davenport, Willie Mays and Johnny Orsino touched Jay and relievers Jim Brosnan and Bill Henry for homers in the hectic ninth. The Giants sent fifteen batters to the plate in the ninth and eleven of them got hits.

Tie Major Record

It was only the third time in the majors that five homers had been hit by a team in one inning. The New York Giants did it June 6, 1939, and the Philadelphia Phillies did it June 2, 1949.

The Giants also set a modern major league record for runs in the ninth inning, bettering the previous tops of 11 by several teams in both leagues.

San Francisco				Cincinnati			
	ab r h bi				ab r h bi		
A'l'tit'no 2b	4 2 2 2	Kasko ss	4 0 1 0				
Davenp't 3b	5 1 1 3	Blas'ame 2b	3 0 0 0				
McCovey 1b	4 2 2 2	Pinson cf	3 0 0 0				
Mays cf	5 1 1 2	Robinson rf	3 0 1 0				
Cepeda rf-lf	5 1 1 2	Lynch lf	3 0 0 0				
Bailey lf	3 0 0 0	Coleman 1b	3 0 0 0				
F.Alou rf	2 1 1 1	Freese 3b	3 0 0 0				
Orsino c	2 1 1 1	D.J'hns'n c	3 0 0 0				
Pagan ss	3 1 2 1	aBell	1 0 0 0				
Marichal p	4 1 1 0	Zim'rman c	0 0 0 0				
		Jay p	2 0 0 0				
		Brosnan p	0 0 0 0				
		Henry p	0 0 0 0				
		bPost	3 0 0 0				
Totals	41 14 16 13	Totals					

a—Flied out for Johnson in 8th; b—Reached first on error for Henry in 9th.
San Francisco .... 100 000 2(12)—14—16
Cincinnati .... 000 000 000—0

E—Orsino. Pagan. Blasingame. Freese. PO-A—San Francisco 27-6. Cincinnati 27-8. DP—Pagan and McCovey; Kasko, Blasingame and Coleman. LOB—San Francisco 3. Cincinnati 3. 2B—McCovey. Cepeda. HR—Amalfitano. Davenport. Mays. Cepeda. F. Alou. Orsino.

	IP	H	R	ER	BB	SO
Marichal (W, 13-7)	9	3	0	0	1	6
Jay (L, 18-8)	8 1-3	5	5	5	3	2
Brosnan	1-3	5	5	5	1	0
Henry	1-3	4	4	4	0	1

HBP By Jay (Orsino) U—Barlick. Jackowski. Vargo. Crawford. T—2.30. A—30,827.

Ty Cobb Dies of Cancer at Age of 74; Called Greatest of Baseball's Great

ATLANTA, July 17 (AP) — Tyrus Raymond (Ty) Cobb, described by many as the world's greatest baseball player, died today of cancer. He was 74.

The Georgia Peach, who died in Emory University Hospital, had been treated since December, 1959, for cancer of the prostate gland which had spread to the pelvic bones and the vertebrae, his physician, Dr. R. Hugh Wood, said.

Wood said the hospital and doctors were not allowed to reveal the diagnosis until Cobb's death.

"In addition," the physician reported, Cobb "had diabetes and chronic heart disease. While his general condition had deteriorated in the last two weeks, the end came rather suddenly."

Cobb, whose fabulous baseball career stretched over 20 years, entered the hospital June 5.

The attending physician said Cobb had sunk gradually and was unconscious when the end came. "He died peacefully and without pain," the doctor said.

The doctor said Cobb knew from the start that he had cancer. "At times he was in much pain," he said.

Cobb was born Dec. 18, 1886, near Royston, in northeast Georgia. After playing sandlot ball in his hometown, Cobb made his professional debut at 17 with Augusta, Ga., in the South Atlantic League.

His historic big league career spanned 24 years, 22 with Detroit as an outfielder. He managed the Tigers six years and finished his major league career in 1928 with the Philadelphia Athletics.

Cobb's magic bat and flashing spikes etched more records than any other player to flash across the baseball scene since the big leagues began operating in 1876.

Cobb played 3033 major league games establishing over 90 records. In 24 seasons of grim duels with the pitchers, he hit for a .367 average—nine points higher than Rogers Hornsby, who played for 23 years.

Cobb's sharp thinking extended beyond baseball and into the business world. He put part of his salary, which ranged from $1800 at the start of his big league career to $40,000, into blue-chip stocks and became a millionaire.

Records Held

ATLANTA, July 17 (AP) — Ty Cobb held 16 major league records and shared 5 at the time of his death.

RECORDS STILL UNSURPASSED

Highest percentage, 10 or more seasons—.367.
Most years leading league, percentage—12.
Most consecutive years, leading league, percentage—9.
Most years batting .300 or better—23.
Most games played in major leagues—3033.
Most times at bat, lifetime—11,429.
Most runs scored, lifetime—2244.
Most hits, lifetime—4191.
Most years leading league in hits—8.
Most one-base hits, lifetime—3052.
Most years 200 or more hits—9.
Most times, 5 or more hits, game, lifetime—14.
Most stolen bases, lifetime—892.
Most stolen bases, season—96.
Most total bases, lifetime—5863.
Most triples, lifetime, one league—297.

RECORDS TIED

Most years batting .400 or better—3 (also held by Rogers Hornsby and Jesse Burkett).
Most consecutive years batting .400 or better—2 (also held by Jesse Burkett).
Most years playing 100 or more games—19 (also held by Honus Wagner and Tris Speaker).
Most times 5 hits in a game, season—4 (also held by Willie Keeler and Stan Musial).
Most home runs, two consecutive games—5 (also held by 6 others).

BRAVES' STAR, 40, STOPS CUBS, 2 TO 1

Spahn's 6-Hitter Makes Him 13th to Win 300 and First Since Lefty Grove in '41

MILWAUKEE, Aug. 11 (AP) — Warren Spahn, the Milwaukee Braves' 40-year-old left-handed pitching star, gained his 300th major league victory tonight by defeating the Chicago Cubs, 2-1, with a masterly six-hitter.

Gino Cimoli's third home run of the year, a tremendous blast to left with one out in the eighth inning, broke a 1-1 tie and raised Spahn to the mark reached by only twelve other pitchers.

Spahn became the third left-hander to make the exclusive "300 Club." He is the first to make it since Lefty Grove struggled to his 300th victory while with the Boston Red Sox in 1941.

40,775 See Victory

The largest Milwaukee crowd in three seasons—40,775—turned out to give Spahn a rousing ovation as he was mobbed by team mates after the final out.

Spahn doffed his cap and blew kisses to the fans as he ran happily into the dugout.

Obviously tense despite his seventeen seasons with the Braves, Spahn had runners on base in every inning after the second. He managed to work out of trouble in every inning except the sixth, however.

That's when the Cubs tied it at 1-1 on three singles and prevented the left-handed ace from claiming his fifty-third career shutout.

It was Spahn himself who drove in the Braves' first run with a sacrifice fly in the fifth.

Young Won 511

The "300 Club" is headed by the late Cy Young, whose amazing record of 511 victories from 1890 to 1911 appears untouchable. Young won 289 games in the National League and 222 in the American while pitching for five club in twenty-two years.

Others who won more than 300 are Walter Johnson (416), Christy Mathewson and Grover Cleveland Alexander (373), Kid Nichols (360), Jim Galvin (355), Tim Keefe (345), John Clarkson (328), Eddie Plank (325), Mike Welch (318) and Charles (Hoss) Radbourne (308).

Spahn, Grove and Plank are the only left-handers in the group.

A native of Buffalo and now an off-season rancher in Hartshorne, Okla., Spahn came up to the Braves in 1942. He appeared in only four games without being involved in a decision that year.

He then went into the Army for three years and served in Europe. He was wounded, decorated for bravery and won a battlefield commission in the infantry.

He had an 8-5 record in his first full season with the Braves, in 1946, and then hit the twenty-victory mark for the first time with a 21-10 record in 1947. Since then, Spahn has failed to win twenty in only three seasons—1948, when he was 15—12; 1952, with 14—19, and 1955, with 17—14.

CHICAGO (N)	ab.r.h.rbi	MILWAUKEE (N)	ab.r.h.rbi
Heist, cf	4 0 0 0	Cimoli, cf	4 1 2 1
Zimmer, 2b	4 0 2 0	Bolling, 2b	4 0 0 0
Santo, 3b	3 1 0 0	Mathews, 3b	4 0 1 0
Altman, rf	4 0 1 0	Aaron, rf	4 0 1 0
Williams, lf	4 0 1 0	Adcock, 1b	3 0 0 0
Rodgers, 1b	4 0 1 1	Thomas, lf	3 0 1 0
Kindall, ss	4 0 1 0	Torre, c	4 0 0 0
Bertell, c	3 0 0 0	McMillan, ss	3 0 1 0
aBanks	1 0 0 0		
Curtis, p	3 0 0 0		
bMcAnany	1 0 0 0		
Total	34 1 6 1	Total	27 2 6 2

aSafe on error for Bertell in 9th; bFlied out for Curtis in 9th.

Chicago .... 000 001 000—1
Milwaukee ...... 000 010 01x—2

E—Williams, Bolling, Mathews. A—Chicago 9, Milwaukee 10. DP—McMillan, Bolling, Adcock; Williams, Bertell, Zimmer. LOB—Chicago 8, Milwaukee 4.
HR—Cimoli. SB—Aaron. Sacrifice—Santo. SF—Spahn.

	IP. H. R. ER.BB.SO.
Curtis (L, 7—7)	8 6 2 1 2 6
Spahn (W, 12—12)	9 6 1 1 1 5

Umpires—Crawford, Barlick, Jackowski, Vargo. Time—2:25. Attendance—40,775.

Slugging Oriole Ties Mark With 5th Grand-Slam

By the Associated Press

Take that spotlight off Roger Maris for a moment and turn it on Jim Gentile, Baltimore's slugging first baseman with the grand-slam habit.

Gentile, up among the leaders in home runs and runs batted in but completely overshadowed by Maris' attempt to crack Babe Ruth's record, equaled a major league mark last night by cracking his fifth grand-slam of the season in an 8-6 victory over Chicago.

The slam, Gentile's 44th homer of the year, came off Don Larsen as the Orioles scored seven runs in the fifth to put it away. Chuck Estrada was the beneficiary—just as he had been for Gentile's four previous bases-loaded shots.

Phils Defeat Braves After Dropping 23d in Row

Streak Ends One Game Short of Cleveland's 1899 Mark

MILWAUKEE, Aug. 20 (AP) — The Philadelphia Phillies broke the second longest major league losing streak today in taking the second game of a double-header from Milwaukee, 7—4.

The Phils lost the first game, their twenty-third defeat in a row, 5—2.

The second game not only ended the Phils' losing string, it also broke the Braves' ten-game winning streak—the longest in the National League this season.

John Buzhardt, whose pitching record is now 4-13, broke the losing string that began on July 28. He had been the last Phil hurler to win a game. He went all the way today, allowing nine hits and being backed by thirteen Phil hits.

The victory left the Phillies one short of the record of twenty-four consecutive losses set in 1899 by Cleveland, then in the National League. The Phillies already had erased the modern era major league mark of twenty in a row.

Warren Spahn, who nine days ago had joined the select group of 300-game winners, scored his 302d victory in the opener.

Carlton Willey was the losing pitcher in the second game, but

FIRST GAME

PHILADELPHIA (N.)	ab	r	h	rbi	MILWAUKEE (N.)	ab	r	h	rbi
T. Taylor, 2b	3	0	1	0	Cimoli, cf	5	0	1	0
Callison, lf	4	0	0	0	Bolling, 2b	5	0	1	0
Walls, 3b	3	0	0	0	Mathews, 3b	4	1	2	1
Demeter, rf	4	0	0	0	Aaron, rf	4	0	2	0
Herrera, 1b	2	0	0	0	Adcock, 1b	2	2	0	0
Gonzalez, ss	4	1	0	0	Thomas, lf	4	0	1	2
Malkmus, ss	4	1	1	2	McMillan, ss	4	0	0	0
Kenders, c	4	0	1	0	White, c	4	0	0	0
Short, p	1	0	1	0	Spahn, p	4	0	0	0
Baldschun, p	0	0	0	0					
aC. Smith	1	0	1	0					
Green, p	0	0	0	0					
Total	30	2	5	2	Total	35	5	7	3

aSingled for Baldschun in 7th.

Philadelphia ... 020 000 000—2
Milwaukee ...... 000 230 00x—5

E—Walls, Short, Malkmus. A—Philadelphia 14, Milwaukee 13. DP—Bolling, McMillan, Adcock. LOB—Philadelphia 6, Milwaukee 9. 2B Hits—Kenders, Thomas. HR—Malkmus, Mathews. Sacrifice—Taylor.

	IP.	H.	R.	ER.	BB.	SO.
Short (L, 4-10)	4⅓	6	5	3	2	1
Baldschun	1⅓	1	0	0	1	1
Green	2	0	0	0	0	1
Spahn (W, 14-12)	9	5	2	0	0	0

Wild pitches—Short 2, Baldschun. PB—Kenders 2. Umpire—Boggess, Landes, Forman, Gorman. Time—2:32.

SECOND GAME

PHILADELPHIA (N.)	ab	r	h	rbi	MILWAUKEE (N.)	ab	r	h	rbi
T. Taylor, 2b	4	0	1	2	Maye, rf	4	0	3	1
Callison, lf	5	0	0	0	Bolling, 3b	3	0	0	0
Gonzalez, cf	5	0	1	0	Mathews, 3b	3	0	0	0
Demeter, 1b	5	1	1	0	Aaron, rf	4	1	1	0
Covington, rf	3	1	1	1	Adcock, 1b	4	1	2	1
bWalters	2	0	2	0	Thomas, lf	4	0	0	1
Walls, 3b	5	3	2	0	Torre, c	4	0	1	2
Dalrymple, c	3	1	3	1	McMillan, ss	2	1	1	0
Malkmus, ss	3	1	1	2	cChrisley	0	1	0	0
Buzhardt, p	3	0	1	1	Mantilla, ss	1	0	0	0
					Willey, p	1	0	0	0
					aSpangler	1	0	1	0
					Hendley, p	0	0	0	0
					Nettebart, p	0	0	0	0
					dBoyd	1	0	0	0
					Antonelli, p	0	0	0	0
					eCimoli	1	0	0	0
Total	38	7	13	7	Total	34	4	9	4

aSingled for Willey in 6th; bSingled for Covington in 8th; cWalked for McMillan in 8th; dGrounded out for Nottebart in 8th; eForced runner for Antonelli in 9th.

Philadelphia ... 000 201 040—7
Milwaukee ...... 001 000 111—4

E—None. A—Philadelphia 11, Milwaukee 1. DP—Malkmus, Demeter; Malkmus, T. Taylor, Demeter. LOB—Philadelphia 8, Milwaukee 5.

2B Hits—Buzhardt, Walls. HR—Covington, McMillan, Adcock. SB—T. Taylor. Sacrifice—Buzhardt. SF—Malkmus.

	IP.	H.	R.	ER.	BB.	SO.
Buzhardt (W, 4-13)	9	9	4	2	2	4
Willey (L, 5-7)	6	8	3	3	1	3
Hendley	1⅓	2	2	2	1	0
Nottebart	⅔	2	1	1	0	0
Antonelli	1	1	0	0	0	0

Umpires—Landes, Forman, Gorman, Boggess. Time—2:52. Attendance—24,637.

it wasn't until the Phillies scored four runs off Bob Hendley and Don Nottebart in the eighth inning that they wrapped up the game.

The Braves scored first on Roy McMillan's home run. The Phillies got two in the fourth, one on Wes Covington's homer and one more in the sixth. The Braves matched that in the seventh.

Finally, in the eighth, singles by Don Demeter, Ken Walters, Bob Malkmus and Tony Taylor,

5-2 Loss to Spahn Precedes 7-to-4 Victory in Twin Bill

a walk and Buzhardt's squeeze bunt produced the four big runs.

The Braves scored runs in the eighth and ninth, the latter on Joe Adcock's twenty-sixth homer.

Eddie Mathews' twenty-fifth home run was the margin of victory for Spahn in the first game. He hit it with two out in the fifth and set off a three-run rally that finished Chris Short, the Phil's starter.

Spahn, who today became the twentieth pitcher to work in 600 games, scattered five hits and struck out eight batters. The victory was his fourteenth of the season and fifth in a row. He lost a shutout when Malkmus hit a two-run homer in the second.

Short blanked the Braves until the fourth when Frank Thomas tied the score with a two-run double.

Hits 59th

Roger Gives It Big Try As Yanks Clinch Pennant

By the Associated Press

Roger Maris strode to the plate in the top of the ninth, dug in and fouled the first pitch by knuckleball specialist Hoyt Wilhelm back of the plate. Wilhelm wound up again, let go and Maris tried to check his swing. He couldn't and the ball trickled down the first base line.

On that note last night ended the most serious threat to Babe Ruth's 60 - homer record of 1927 as Maris, who had hit No. 59 in the third inning, failed in his final chance to tie baseball's most prized record under the 154-decision edict of Commissioner Ford Frick.

All eyes were on Maris while he took his final shots at the Babe's mark in Baltimore, where the Yankees went about the job of clinching their 26th American League pennant by whipping the Orioles, 4-2.

In the first inning, Maris lined out to right and there was hardly a stir in the crowd. He tagged Milt Pappas for No. 59 in the third, sending a vicious line drive into the rightfield seats over the 380-foot mark on a 2-1 pitch.

Maris came up in the fourth and struck out against Reliever Dick Hall, then smashed a shot in the seventh off Hall that brought the crowd to its feet as it flew down the rightfield line. It went foul.

Maris got good wood on the next pitch, sending a towering fly to deep right-center that chased rightfielder Earl Robinson back before he grabbed it for the out 20 feet short of the wall. Then came the ninth inning dribbler.

"I wanted to get three good swings whether I hit it or not," Maris said in the dressing room while expressing regret over his last time at bat. "The way it turned out, I didn't get one. I would have liked to have taken a full swing."

Second to Hit 59

Thus Maris joins a long list of homer hammerers who have come within range of Ruth's record, but failed. However, Roger tied Ruth's mark of 59 in 1921, and became only the second man in major league history to hit that many. Jimmy Foxx and Hank Greenberg each hit 58. Maris still has eight games under the expanded schedule in which to match or surpass Ruth's total.

The honor of clinching the Yanks' 11th pennant in the last 13 years went to Ralph Terry (15-3), who got the job done for the second year in a row. He did it with a four-hitter that made Ralph Houk the first rookie manager in 15 years to win a major league flag.

Houk, who succeeded Casey Stengel at the Yankee helm this season, became the first rookie field boss to win since

Ed Dyer took the National League title with the 1946 St. Louis Cardinals. The last American League first-year pilot to do it was Mickey Cochrane of the Detroit Tigers in 1934.

Berra Also Homers

The Yankees wrapped it up with a three-run rally in the third started by Maris' shot off Pappas (12-9). Yogi Berra followed with a homer and a single by Johnny Blanchard and Elston Howard's double finished off the outburst for a 4-0 lead.

The Orioles were able to get to Terry only in the sixth when consecutive singles by Ron Hansen, Hall and Brooks Robinson scored one run. Hall came around from second when Bobby Richardson dropped the ball after Jerry Adair hit into a force out.

The Detroit Tigers remained well ahead of the Orioles in the battle for second place by beating Los Angeles, 6-3, when Chico Fernandez stroked a bases - loaded double that featured a four-run tie-breaking rally in the seventh inning.

Chicago's Ray Herbert defeated Boston, 3-1, with a seven-hitter, and Bobby Del-Greco hit a two-run homer in the ninth that gave Kansas City a 4-2 victory over Cleveland in other games. Minnesota-Washington was rained out.

With New York Mets
Lavagetto, Hemus Join Stengel's Coaching Staff

NEW YORK, Oct. 2 (AP) — Cookie Lavagetto and Solly Hemus, two managers who were fired this season, joined the New York Mets today as coaches under 71-year-old Casey Stengel, who was put out to pasture by the New York Yankees last year.

Manager Stengel introduced his new coaches called to re-introduce the "old perfessor" after a year's absence.

"Attention," shouted Stengel over the noise of tinkling glasses and fractured syntax, "we're giving away a diamond ring to start this thing off."

Everybody laughed but few stopped talking. Stengel, even with a mike, had rugged competition the rest of the way.

"Lavagetto worked for my club (Oakland in 1948) as a player," said Stengel. "He handled Billy Martin and did great work. He did great work for (Chuck) Dressen."

Lavagetto was let out as manager of the Twin Cities and Hemus was released as St. Louis Cardinals manager during the 1961 season. With Stengel on a one-year contract there have been strong reports that Lavagetto is the heir to the throne in 1963.

Why had Stengel decided to return to baseball?

"To help assist Mr. Weiss (George Weiss, Mets president) and see if we can't start and rebuild this thing in a hurry. Five or six owners gave me terrific offers to come back last fall but I decided to lay out a year. After all one year I did lay out (1937), they asked me to.

"Mr. Weiss influenced me by getting on the phone too often. I talked to the ownership and the first thing you know I changed my mind and said 'yes.'"

Did Stengel think he was too old to manage, a young man asked.

"Nobody had to carry me out to take out my pitchers," he said. "No office help or player had to tell me when to make a move. My health is good enough above the shoulders and I have good enough legs to make the mound."

Was this strictly a one-year deal or would Casey stay longer if everything went all right?

"I'll decide myself," he said. "I didn't say I was coming back for 40 years. And not for 10 or 15 or 20 to help rebuild. I am willing to give up my reputation to assist in some way. I'll know when I should quit. I know when I have a pain in the belly or the head."

Stengel, Weiss and the coaches and scouts will go over the list of players eligible to be picked from the other National League teams. The names of all eligible players, except the Cincinnati men who are on the World Series list, were turned over to Weiss today.

The Mets and new Houston club will make their picks the day after the series closes in the city where it ends.

Oct. 1

61st HOMER COMES IN FINALE

Maris' Momentous Blast Wins Share of History

By the Associated Press

Baseball has two home-run kings today—the fabled Babe Ruth and a modern-day counterpart, Roger Maris.

By the decree of Ford Frick, commissioner of baseball, Ruth still wears one crown because nobody has been able to surpass his 60 home runs in the 154-game season of 1927.

However, another will have to be fitted for the blond head of the 27-year-old Maris, who yesterday smashed his 61st home run on the final day of the American League season—which was extended to 162 games this year with expansion to 10 teams.

Each campaign, Ruth's in 1927 with the Yankees and Maris' with the same club 34 years later had one tie in addition to the games played to a decision. But neither homered in the ties.

Hit Off Stallard

The momentous 61st homer was struck by Maris at precisely 2:46 (Washington Time) yesterday off Tracy Stallard, rookie righthander of the Red Sox. It was in the fourth inning and Maris was batting for the second time. In the first inning he had lofted a long fly to leftfield.

Stallard's first pitch to Roger in the fourth was high and outside for a ball. The next was low and inside, almost into the dirt. Plate Umpire Bill Kinneman called it another ball.

Maris, who had vowed earlier he would come out of the dugout swinging, whaled into the next pitch, a fast ball which was rather high and over the plate. He drove the ball into the lower rightfield stands, about 15 rows deep and about 360 feet away. And thus

he became the first man in major league baseball history to hit 61 home runs in a season.

"It was the biggest home run I ever hit," Maris exclaimed later. "I knew it was gone the minute I hit it. I can't explain how I felt. I don't know what I was thinking of as I rounded the bases. My mind was a blank."

Cheers Last 5 Minutes

After Roger had jogged around the bases and ducked into the dugout, the other Yankee players pushed him out on the field, where he twice took bows to a standing ovation of the 23,154 Yankee Stadium fans. They continued their wild cheering for five minutes.

The ball was caught by 19-year-old Sal Durante of Brooklyn, who will receive $5,000 and two trips to the West Coast.

"It's great, great, great," Maris told a horde of reporters, photographers, TV and radio men who crowded around his cubicle in the Yankee clubhouse after the game, which was won by the Yankees on the home run, 1-0.

"It's the greatest thrill I ever had. I thought nothing could match the thrill I got when I hit my 60th (in the Yankees' 159th game), but this beats everything.

"Whether I beat Ruth's record or not is for others to say, but it gives me a wonderful feeling to know that I'm the only man in history to hit 61 home runs. Nobody can take that away from me."

Roger Batted More Often

"Babe Ruth was a big man in baseball, maybe the biggest ever. I'm not saying I am of

his caliber but I'm glad to say I hit more than he did in a season. I'd like to have done it in 154 games but since I didn't, I'm glad now that I did it in 162 games."

A statistical comparison of the two record years shows that Maris was officially at bat 590 times to Ruth's 540. The difference is not that wide in the matter of plate appearances including walks, sacrifices and hit by pitched balls. All told, Ruth went to the plate 692 times in 1927 to Maris' 698 in 1961.

Ruth had 138 walks and 14 sacrifices in addition to his 549 official at bats. Maris drew 95 walks, hit seven sacrifices and was hit six times by pitches.

In total appearances Maris actually reached his 60 before Ruth did. He reached No. 60 in his 684th trip to the plate, while Ruth got No. 60 in his 689th appearance, on the next to last day of the season.

While New York was tuning up for the World Series, opening Wednesday at Yankee Stadium, there was a desperate battle at Kansas City with 10th and last place at stake.

Cash Wins Title

As it turned out, nobody finished 10th. Kansas City beat Washington, 3-2, and the two clubs wound up in a tie for ninth.

Norm Cash won the unofficial batting title with two hits in three at bats for Detroit and a .361 average. Cash hit his 41st homer in the Tigers' 8-3 triumph over Minnesota.

Cleveland announced the firing of Manager Jimmy Dykes at Los Angeles and then defeated the Angels, 8-5, with Coach Mel Harder at the helm.

Oct. 9

Ford Breaks Ruth's Mound Record

Through no fault of his own, Ford was not on the scene of battle to collect the winner's reward.

Ford Twists Ankle

New York's 25-game-winning southpaw ace twisted his right ankle slightly early in the contest; then caromed a painful foul off his own right ankle before bouncing into a double-play in the sixth.

Ford was on the premises long enough, though, to extend one World Series record and create a second new one.

After yielding a single to Chacon, leading off the Redlegs' sixth, Ford was replaced by Coates.

He had completed the required five innings to qualify as the winning pitcher, however. It was his ninth victory in series competition against four defeats. No other hurler ever has won more than seven games in the post-season event.

Ford's Streak At 32

The 5 runless frames, during which he also was tagged for 2 1-baggers by Darrell Johnson and a single by Eddie Kasko, stretched Ford's string of consecutive scoreless World Series innings to 32.

The streak, embracing two shutouts against Pittsburgh last October and last week's 2-to-0 triumph is a new record.

"The old series mark of 29 2-3 scoreless innings was held by the late Babe Ruth, who achieved the feat while a lefthanded pitcher for the Boston Red Sox during the 1916 and 1918 classics against Brooklyn and Chicago.

The Baltimore-born bambino subsequently was sold to New York, where he became the greatest homerun slugger of all-time.

Reprinted from
The Baltimore Sun papers

ONCE-IN-LIFETIME THRILL: ROBINSON

Fame Vote So Excites Family, 'No One Wants To Eat'

Stamford, Conn., Jan. 23 (P)—"It's hard to describe my feelings fully at this time. I am pleased and honored. My family is so excited, no one wants to eat."

This was Jackie Robinson, the first Negro to be elected to the Baseball Hall of Fame, speaking today after he got the news that he had been elected to the diamond shrine.

Robinson, the great Brooklyn Dodgers infielder, was so excited, he spoke in staccato sentences in the living room of his rambling home here.

Afforded Wonderful Things

"Baseball has afforded me a lot of wonderful things," he continued. "It offered me a chance to get a fine position in the business world for one thing. And now this — a once-in-a-lifetime thrill."

The graying Robinson now is vice president of a national restaurant and coffee manufacturing company. In fact, he didn't know about his election to the Hall of Fame until he arrived home from his office.

His wife Rachel, and two of his children were at the door waiting to break the news when he stepped in the door.

Reds Spoil Dodgers' New Park Debut, 6-3

Los Angeles, April 10 (P)—Wally Post spoiled the Dodgers' debut in their fancy new stadium today with a home run—the park's first—that led Cincinnati to a 6-to-3 victory over Los Angeles before 52,564.

The Dodgers, ironically, had elected to walk Frank Robinson to get at Post with two out in the seventh inning and the score tied 2-2.

Hits First Pitch

Post, who had singled twice earlier, drove lefthander Johnny Podres' first pitch over the centerfield wall at the 410-foot mark, scoring Vada Pinson and Robinson ahead of him.

CINCINNATI	ab	r	h	bi	LOS ANGELES	ab	r	h	bi
Kasko ss	5	1	1	0	Wills ss	3	0	0	0
Rojas 2b	3	0	0	0	fHoward	1	0	0	0
aLynch	1	0	0	0	Gilliam 2b	4	1	2	0
Blas'ame 2b	0	0	0	0	Moon lf	4	0	0	0
Pinson cf	4	3	4	1	Snider rf	3	1	2	0
Rob's'n r-lf	4	1	1	0	cT. Davis	1	0	0	0
Post lf	5	1	3	3	Roseboro c	2	0	0	0
Keough rf	0	0	0	0	Fairly 1b	4	0	1	2
Coleman 1b	4	0	1	1	Spencer 3b	4	1	1	0
Harper 3b	4	0	1	1	W. Davis cf	3	0	0	0
Edwards c	4	0	0	0	dWalls	1	0	0	0
Purkey p	4	0	1	0	Podres p	2	0	1	0
Henry p	0	0	0	0	L.Sherry p	0	0	0	0
Brosnan p	0	0	0	0	dHarkness	1	0	0	0
					Perranoski p	0	0	0	0
					eCarey	1	0	1	1
Totals	38	6	14	6	Totals	32	3	8	3

a—Struck out for Rojas in 8th; b—Grounded out for L. Sherry in 8th; c—Grounded into double play for Snider in 8th; d Walked for W. Davis in 9th; e—Singled for Perranoski in 9th. f—Grounded out for Wills in 9th.

Cincinnati .... 100 001 301—6
Los Angeles .... 000 200 001—3

E—None. PO-A—Cincinnati 27-13, Los Angeles 27-8. DP—Wills, Gilliam and Fairly; Harper, Rojas and Coleman; Kasko and Coleman; Blasingame, Kasko and Coleman. LOB—Cincinnati 11, Los Angeles 8. 2B—Kasko, Pinson 2, Fairly, Podres. 3B—Spencer. HR—Post. S—Rojas. SF—Coleman.

	IP	H	R	ER	BB	SO
Purkey (W. 1-0)	7 1-3	6	2	2	3	1
Henry	1 1-3	2	1	1	0	0
Brosnan	1-3	0	0	0	0	0
Podres (L. 0-1)	7 1-3	11	5	5	4	5
L. Sherry	2-3	0	0	0	1	0
Perranoski	1	3	1	0	0	1

HBP—By Henry (Roseboro). U—Barlick, Crawford, Vargo, Harvey. T—2:47. A—52,564.

CARDS ON TOP, 8-1 AS MUSIAL STARS

Stan Gets Record 3,431st Hit in Rout of Dodgers

LOS ANGELES, May 19 (AP)—Stan Musial set a National League career record for hits by getting his 3,431st tonight as the St. Louis Cardinals defeated the Los Angeles Dodgers, 8-1, before 50,103.

Musial, who now holds forty-one National League records, had failed in nine at bats to get the record-setting hit before he singled in the ninth inning off Ron Perranoski, a left-hander.

The crowd gave Musial a standing ovation as he was taken out of the game for a pinch-runner.

The Cardinals' victory moved them to within a game of second-place Los Angeles and kept them five games behind the league-leading San Francisco Giants.

ST. LOUIS (N.)	ab	r	h	rbi	LOS ANGELES (N.)	ab	r	h	rbi
Flood, cf	5	0	2	1	Wills, ss	4	0	0	0
Sch'nd'nst, 2b	5	0	1	0	Gilliam, 3b	4	0	1	0
Grammas, 2b	0	0	0	0	W. Davis, cf	4	0	2	0
Musial, lf	5	1	1	0	T. Davis, lf	4	0	1	0
Boyer, 3b	4	2	1	0	Howard, rf	2	0	0	0
bLandrum, lf	0	1	0	0	Camilli, c	3	1	0	0
White, 1b	3	2	2	0	Moon, 1b	3	0	1	0
Sawatski, c	0	0	0	1	Burright, 2b	3	0	1	1
cOliver, c	0	0	0	1	Drysdale, p	2	0	0	0
Gotay, ss	5	0	1	0	Ortega, p	0	0	0	0
Clemens, rf	4	1	1	2	aWalls	1	0	0	0
Sadecki, p	4	1	0	0	Perranoski, p	0	0	0	0
					dCarey	1	0	0	0
Total	35	8	9	5	Total	31	1	6	1

aHit into force play for Ortega in 7th; bRan for Musial in 9th; cHit sacrifice fly for Sawatski in 9th; dFlied out for Perranowski in 9th.

St. Louis .... 000 410 003—8
Los Angeles ..... 010 000 000—1

E—W. Davis, Moon, Gotay, Wills. A—St. Louis 14, Los Angeles 11. DP—Gotay, Schoendienst, White; Boyer, Schoendienst, White. LOB—St. Louis 8, Los Angeles 8. SB—White 2. Sacrifice fly—Sawatski, Oliver.

	IP	H	R	ER	BB	SO
Sadecki (W. 2-1)	9	6	1	1	5	2
Drysdale (L. 5-3)	4 2-3	5	3	2	3	
Ortega	2 1-3	1	0	0	1	0
Perranoski	2	3	1	1	1	

HBP—By Drysdale (White). Balk Sadecki. Umpires—Smith, Steiner, Boggess, Landes. Time 2:31. Attendance 50,103.

CARDS BEAT GIANTS, 8 TO 4

Musial batted in two runs with his seven hundredth double and a single. Only Ty Cobb and Tris Speaker own more doubles than Stan The Man.

SAN FRANCISCO	ab	r	h	bi	ST. LOUIS	ab	r	h	bi
Kuenn lf	5	0	1	1	Flood cf	5	3	4	0
Pagan ss	5	1	1	0	Javier 2b	5	3	4	3
Mays cf	4	1	1	2	White 1b	5	2	3	1
F. Alou rf	4	1	2	1	Musial lf	4	1	2	2
Cepeda 1b	4	0	1	0	aClemens rf	0	0	0	0
Daven't 3b	4	0	2	0	Boyer 3b	3	1	1	0
Hiller 2b	4	0	2	0	Sawatski c	4	0	1	2
Haller c	2	0	0	0	Gotay ss	4	0	1	0
Perry p	0	0	0	0	Smith lf	2	0	0	0
Bolin p	1	0	0	0	bB'h'nd'net	1	0	0	0
Nieman	1	0	0	0	James lf	0	0	0	0
Larsen p	2	0	1	0	Sadecki p	4	1	1	1
Sanford p	2	0	1	0					
Pig'tano	1	1	0	0					
Totals	36	4	11	4	Totals	37	8	13	9

a—Ran for Musial in 7th; b—Flied out for Smith in 7th; c—Fanned for Bolin in 8th.

San Francisco ... 200 000 100—4
St. Louis .... 300 000 23x—8

E—None. PO-A—San Francisco 24-5, St. Louis 27-19. LOB—San Francisco 7, St. Louis 7.

2B—Kuenn, Musial, Sawatski, Javier, White. HR—Mays, F. Alou, White, Sadecki. S—Haller.

	IP	H	R	ER	BB	SO
Sanford (L. 6-5)	7	9	5	5	3	4
Perry	1-3	2	2	2	0	0
Bolin	2-3	1	1	1	0	1
Larsen	1	1	0	0	0	1
Sadecki (W. 3-3)	9	11	4	4	1	6

Balk Sanford. U—Donatelli, Secory, Venzon, Pryor. T—2:33. A—17,390.

LEFT-HANDER, 26, REPEATS '59 FEAT

Koufax Ties Strikeout Mark He Shared With Feller— Dodgers Hit 3 Homers

CHICAGO, April 24 (AP)—Sandy Koufax of the Los Angeles Dodgers struck out eighteen batters today and matched the modern major league mark he already shared with Bob Feller. The 26-year-old left-hander accomplished the feat in beating the Chicago Cubs, 10—2.

Koufax' effort set a record for a National League day game. The previous mark of seventeen had been shared by Dizzy Dean of the St. Louis Cardinals and Art Mahaffey of the Philadelphia Phillies.

Feller struck out eighteen for the Cleveland Indians in a losing day game against the Detroit Tigers on Oct. 2, 1938, and Koufax did the same against the San Francisco Giants in a night game on Aug. 31, 1959. Each game went nine innings.

The major league record for strikeouts is nineteen. It is shared by Charles Sweeney, who accomplished the feat for Providence against Boston in a National League game on June 7, 1884, and by Hugh Dailey, a one-armed Chicago pitcher who tied the mark in a Union Association game against Boston on July 7 of the same year. The Union Association was organized as a third major league in 1884. It expired after one season.

Although he weakened somewhat in the middle innings, Koufax equaled the strikeout record on 144 pitches, including ninety-six strikes and forty-eight balls.

Koufax, who led the National League in strikeouts last year with 269, increased his total for this season to forty in thirty-two innings.

LOS ANGELES (N.)	ab	r	h	rbi	CHICAGO (N.)	ab	r	h	rbi
Wills, ss	4	1	0	0	Brock, cf	3	0	0	1
Gilliam, 2b,3b	4	1	1	0	Hubbs, 2b	4	0	0	0
Moon, 1b	4	3	3	0	Santo, 3b	4	0	2	0
Harkness, 1b	0	0	0	0	Banks, 1b	4	0	0	0
Snider, rf	3	2	2	3	Williams, lf	4	2	2	1
Fairly, rf	0	0	0	0	Will, rf	3	0	1	0
T. Davis, lf	5	2	2	4	White, ss	3	0	1	0
Roseboro, c	5	0	2	0	Thacker, c	3	0	1	0
W. Davis, cf	3	0	0	1	Cardwell, p	1	0	0	0
Carey, 3b	4	1	2	1	aRodgers	1	0	0	0
cBurright, 2b	1	0	0	0	Balsamo, p	0	0	0	0
Koufax, p	4	0	0	0	bMcKnight	1	0	0	0
					Gerard, p	0	0	0	0
					Elston, p	0	0	0	0
Total	37	10	12	9	dMorhardt	1	0	0	0
					Total	32	2	6	2

aStruck out for Cardwell in 5th; bStruck out for Balsamo in 7th; cRan for Carey in 8th; dStruck out for Elston in 9th.

Los Angeles ..... 021 130 102—10
Chicago .... 000 001 001—2

E—Banks. A—Los Angeles 6, Chicago 12. LOB—Los Angeles 7, Chicago 7. 2B—Roseboro, Santo, Williams. 3B—Snider. HR—Carey, T. Davis, Snider, Williams. SB—Wills, Moon, Burright. Sacrifice—Gilliam. SF—W. Davis.

	IP	H	R	ER	BB	SO
Koufax (W. 3-1)	9	6	2	2	4	18
Cardwell (L. 0-4)	5	7	7	7	1	3
Balsamo	2	2	1	1	2	0
Gerard	1 1-3	2	2	2	0	0
Elston	2-3	1	0	0	0	1

Wild pitch—Cardwell. Balk—Balsamo. Umpires—Boggess, Landes, Smith, Steiner. Time—2:41. Attendance—8,938.

June 25

43 Players Perform In Seven-Hour Battle

ALL STAR SOUVENIR PROGRAM 50¢

WRIGLEY FIELD · CHICAGO 1962

TWO GRAND SLAMS PACE 14-3 TRIUMPH

Four-Run Homers by Allison and Killebrew in Twins' Big First Set a Record

BLOOMINGTON, Minn., July 18 (AP)—The Minnesota Twins scored eleven runs in the first inning today and went on to overwhelm the Cleveland Indians, 14—3.

During the big assault, Bob Allison and Harmon Killebrew became the first major league players to hit grand-slam homers in the same inning. Dick Stigman, making his first start for the Twins after twenty-five relief appearances, coasted to victory.

The Twins sent fourteen batters to the plate in the inning and got seven hits. One was a homer by Earl Battey.

Allison's grand slam was the fifth of his career and his eleventh homer of the season. Battey's homer followed and the Indian starter, Barry Latman, was relieved by Jim Perry.

Killebrew, who had walked ahead of Allison's homer, went to bat a second time in the inning with the bases filled and blasted his four-run homer off Perry. It was his third career grand slam. Allison ended the inning by popping out.

Killebrew hit another homer, his twenty-fourth of the season, with none on in the third.

DODGERS LOSE KOUFAX FOR TWO-WEEK PERIOD

LOS ANGELES, July 19 (P)—Sandy Koufax is on the bench until his talented left hand heals, and the Los Angeles Dodgers' pennant chances are up in the air as a result.

A specialist examined the 26-year-old strikeout king from Brooklyn Wednesday and ordered rest and drugs for Koufax, who was en route to his finest season with a 14-5 record.

There has been unconfirmed speculation that Koufax would be out of action two weeks, or even longer. This means he'll miss at least three or four pitching turns.

The Dodgers currently are in first place by two games in the National League race. They beat Cincinnati 6-5 in 11 innings Wednesday night.

Koufax returned from Los Angeles to Cincinnati Wednesday and was examined by Dr. Travis Winsor, a nationally known authority on vascular disturbances. Dr. Winsor said:

"Koufax is suffering from a diminution in the amount of blood flowing to the index finger of his left hand. He will be put on a series of drugs to expand the arteries in the area.

"His period of inactivity from baseball will depend on immediate and ultimate response to medication."

Reds Down Cubs, 7-5 and 10-3; Hubbs Errs After Setting Mark

Second Baseman Handles 418 Chances Flawlessly Before Second-Game Miscue

CINCINNATI, Sept. 5 (AP) — Joe Nuxhall gave seven hits tonight and drove in two runs while pitching the Cincinnati Reds to a 10-3 victory over the Chicago Cubs in the second game of a double-header.

The Reds made a sweep by winning the opener, 7—5, on Gordon Coleman's tenth-inning homer.

It was Nuxhall's fifth straight victory since he was recalled from San Diego. He struck out seven and walked three before being relieved by Dave Sisler after eight innings.

Ken Hubbs set a major league field record for second basemen by handling 418 successive chances flawlessly before erring on a throw in the eighth inning of the second game. He bettered Bobby Doerr's mark of 414 in the fourth inning of the opener.

Doerr of the Boston Red Sox fielded in seventy-three successive games in 1948 without an error. Hubbs' miscue came seventy-nine games after his last error on June 12.

Sanford Captures 16th in a Row As Giants Down Pirates by 2-0

Alou's Streak Snapped but His 2 Hits Pace Team's 7th Straight Victory

SAN FRANCISCO, Sept. 11 (AP)—Jack Sanford posted his sixteenth straight pitching victory and twenty-second for the season today by blanking Pittsburgh, 2—0. The triumph was the seventh straight for the pennant-contending San Francisco Giants.

Sanford hurled an eight-hitter, gave one walk and struck out three as he continued the longest victory string in the major leagues this season. The husky right-hander lost for the sixth time on June 13 and hasn't been beaten since.

The modern record — nineteen straight triumphs in one season — was set by Rube Marquard of the New York Giants in 1912.

Tom Sturdivant, who had captured five straight, took the loss before a crowd of 10,283 that saw the Giants complete the current home stand.

Felipe Alou paced the San Francisco attack, although missing his bid for a share of the National League's record for consecutive hits. He got two of the Giants' four hits.

Alou grounded out to third in the first inning, ending his string at nine, one short of the mark. But in the fourth he singled and scored. He hit his twenty-fifth homer in the sixth.

Pittsburgh posed threats in the fourth, sixth and eighth. In the fourth Bob Skinner led off with a single, but Smoky Burgess' grounder caromed off Sanford's glove to Chuck Hiller at second for a double play.

The twin killing saved a run, as Robert Clemente singled to center before Donn Clendennon fouled out to end the inning.

With one out in the sixth, Dick Groat tripled and Skinner walked. Burgess, the leading hitter for the Pirates, again hit into a double play.

In the eighth, singles by Bill Mazeroski and Bill Virdon put runners on first and second with one out. But Sanford got Groat on a pop fly and struck out Bob Skinner.

PITTSBURGH (N.)	ab	r	h	rbi		SAN FRANCISCO (N.)	ab	r	h	rbi
Virdon, cf	4	0	2	0		Kuenn, 2b, lf	4	0	0	0
Groat, ss	3	0	1	0		Hiller, 2b	4	0	1	0
Skinner, lf	3	0	1	0		F. Alou, rf	3	2	2	1
Burgess, c	4	0	1	0		McCovey, 2b	3	0	1	0
Clemente, rf	4	0	1	0		Davenport, 3b	3	0	0	0
Clendenon, 1b	3	0	0	0		Mays, cf	3	0	0	0
Schofield, 2b	3	0	0	0		Cepeda, 1b	3	0	0	0
Mazeroski, 2b	3	0	1	0		Haller, c	3	0	0	0
Sturdivant, p	2	0	0	0		Pagan, ss	3	0	0	0
aMarshall	1	0	0	0		Sanford, p	3	0	0	0
Friend, p	1	0	0	0						
Total	33	0	8	0		Total	29	2	4	2

aPopped out for Sturdivant in 8th.

Pittsburgh .... 000 000 000—0
San Francisco ..... 000 101 00x—2

E—Schofield. A—Pittsburgh 8, San Francisco 13. DP—Sanford, Hiller, Cepeda; Pagan, Cepeda. LOB—Pittsburgh 7, San Francisco 3. 2B—Hiller. 3B—Groat. HR—F. Alou. SB—Clendenon, Cepeda.

	IP.	H.	R.	ER.	BB.	SO.
Sturdivant (L, 8-4)	7	4	2	2	0	1
Friend	1	0	0	0	0	0
Sanford (W, 22-6)	9	8	0	0	1	3

PB—Burgess. Umpires—Smith, Steiner, Boggess, Landes. Time—2:04. Attendance—10,283.

CARDS WHIP DODGERS, 12-2

Maury Wills Steals Two Bases For 97 Total

St. Louis, Sept. 23 (AP)—Larry Jackson, a longtime Dodger nemesis, was backed by a fierce fifteen-hit attack today as the St. Louis Cardinals slowed pennant-bound Los Angeles, 12 to 2.

The setback sliced the Dodgers' lead over the Giants to 3½ games, pending the outcome of San Francisco's game in Houston.

Maury Wills, who fell one short of Ty Cobb's record 96 steals based on a 154-decision ruling by Commissioner Ford Frick, swiped two bases in his club's one hundred fifty-sixth decision for a 97 total. Cobb stole his 96 in 156 games, but two were ties.

LOS ANGELES		ST. LOUIS	

a—Ran for Musial in 5th; b—Grounded out for Richert in 7th; c—Struck out for Roebuck in 9th.

Los Angeles ...... 000 000 200—2
St. Louis .... 200 305 00x—12

E—T. Davis. PO-A—Los Angeles 27-7, St. Louis 27-12. DP—Wills and Fairly. LOB—Los Angeles 11, St. Louis 4. 2B—Gilliam, Snider, Flood, White, Boyer, Musial. 3B—White. HR—Jackson. SB—Sawatski.

	IP.	H.	R.	ER.	BB.	SO.
Drysdale (L, 25-8)	3 1-3					
Perranoski						
J. Smith		1-3				
Richert		1-3				
Roebuck						
Jackson (W, 15-11)	9					

Wild pitch—Drysdale (Flood); balk—Jackson (J. Davis). U—Donatelli, Secory, Vargo. Time—2:32. A—20,742.

Cheney Fans 21 Orioles, Senators Win in 16th, 2-1

BALTIMORE (AP) — Tom Cheney of the Washington Senators struck out 21 batters, an all-time major league record, and defeated the Baltimores 2-1 Wednesday night on Bud Zipfel's 16th inning homer.

Zipfel's 6th homer of the season, off Dick Hall, broke up a 1-1 tie which had existed since the 7th inning.

Cheney, a 27-year-old right-hander, entered the game with a 5-8 record. He hurled only three previous complete games this season—and all were shutouts.

His 16-inning performance was the longest pitching stint of the season topping the 15 innings hurled by Al Jackson of the New York Mets in a losing effort.

Cheney topped a record of 19, set back in 1884, and the modern mark of 18 — performed six times since 1906 by four different pitchers. Sandy Koufax of the Los Angeles Dodgers reached the 18 mark — in 9 innings — for the second time on April 24 this season.

Washington scored its first run of Wednesday night's game in the first inning on Ron Stilwell's infield hit, a double by Chuck Hinton and an infield out by Zipfel.

The Orioles tied it at 1-1 in the seventh on a double by Marv Breeding and a pinch single by Charley Lau, who batted for Oriole starter Milt Pappas.

WASHINGTON	ab	r	h	bi		BALTIMORE	ab	r	h	bi
Kennedy ss	6	1	0	0		Adair ss	6	0	2	0
Stilwell 2b	3	1	1	0		Snyder rf	7	0	2	0
b-King	1	0	1	0		Robinsn 3b	5	0	1	0
Cottier 2b	2	0	0	0		Gentile 1b	7	0	1	0
Hinton rf	7	0	1	0		Powell rf	7	0	1	0
Zipfel 1b	7	0	0	0		Nicholson cf	7	0	1	0
Costeen	0	0	0	0		Landrith c	6	0	0	0
Schmidt c	0	0	0	0		e-Brandt	1	0	0	0
Hicks cf	5	0	1	0		Breeding 2b	6	1	1	0
d-Schaive	1	0	0	0		f-Williams	1	0	0	0
Piersall cf	0	0	0	0		Pappas p	2	0	0	0
Lock lf	7	0	1	0		a-Lau	1	0	1	1
Brinkman 3b	5	0	1	0		Hall p	3	0	0	0
Cheney p	6	0	0	0		Hoeft p	0	0	0	0
						Stock p	0	0	0	0
Totals	57	2	10	2		Totals	59	1	10	1

a—Singled for Pappas in 7th; b—singled for Stilwell in 10th; c—ran for Retzer in 6th; d—fouled out for Hicks in 16th; e—flied out for Landrith in 16th; f—struck out for Breeding in 16th.

Balt. .... 000 000 100 000 000 0—1
Wash. .... 100 000 000 000 000 1—2

E, Adair, Breeding; po-a, Washington 48-12, Baltimore 48-16; lob, Washington 13, Baltimore 13.

2b, Hinton, Snyder, Adair, Gentile, Hicks, Breeding; hr, Zipfel; sb, Adair; s, Cheney.

PITCHING	ip	h	r	er	bb	so
Cheney (w, 6-8)	16	10	1	1	4	21
Pappas	7	4	1	1	3	4
Hall (l, 6-6)	8 1-3	5	1	1	1	4
Hoeft	1-3					
Stock	1-3	0	0	0	1	0

wp, Cheney; b, Pappas; u, McKinley, Chylak, Umont, Stewart; t, 3:59; a, 4,098.

Giants-Dodgers Box Score

Los Angeles, Oct. 3 (AP) — The box score of the third National League playoff game of 1962:

SAN FRANCISCO	ab	r	h	rbi	po	a	e		LOS ANGELES	ab	r	h	rbi	po	a	e
Kuenn lf	5	1	2	1	2	0	0		Wills ss	5	1	4	0	2	3	0
Hiller 2b	3	1	0	1	1	0	0		Gilliam 2b-3b	5	0	1	0	3	1	0
bMcCovey	0	0	0	0	0	0	0		Snider lf	3	2	1	0	2	0	0
cBowman 2b	0	1	0	0	4	1	0		Burright 2b	1	0	0	0	3	2	1
F. Alou rf	4	1	1	0	4	0	0		eWalls	1	0	0	0	0	0	0
Mays cf	3	1	1	3	0	0	0		T. Davis 3b-lf	5	1	2	1	1	0	0
Cepeda 1b	4	0	2	1	8	0	0		Moon 1b	3	0	0	0	10	0	0
Bailey c	4	0	2	0	3	1	0		Fairly 1b-rf	0	0	0	0	2	0	0
Davenport 3b	4	0	1	1	2	4	0		Howard rf	4	0	0	0	0	0	0
Pagan ss	5	1	2	0	1	1	1		Harkness 1b	0	0	0	0	0	0	0
Marichal p	2	1	1	0	0	0	1		Roseboro c	3	0	1	0	3	1	1
Larsen p	0	0	0	0	0	1	0		w. Davis cf	3	0	2	0	2	0	0
aM. Alou	1	0	1	0	0	0	0		Podres p	2	0	0	0	0	2	1
dNieman	1	0	0	0	0	0	0		Roebuck p	0	0	0	0	0	1	0
Pierce p	0	0	0	0	0	0	0		Williams p	0	0	0	0	0	0	0
									Perranoski p	0	0	0	0	0	0	0
Totals	36	6	13	4	27	7	3		Totals	35	4	8	3	27	14	4

aSingled for Larsen in ninth.
bWalked for Hiller in ninth.
cRan for McCovey in ninth.
dStruck out for M. Alou in ninth.
eLined out for Burright in ninth.

San Francisco .... 000 200 004—6
Los Angeles .... 000 001 021—4

Double Plays—Gilliam, Wills and Moon; Wills and Moon; Wills, Burright and Fairly. Left on bases—San Francisco, 12; Los Angeles, 8. Two-base hits—Snider, Hiller. Home Run—T. Davis. Stolen bases—Wills 3; T. Davis. Sacrifices—Hiller, Marichal, Fairly. Sacrifice fly—Cepeda.

	Ip.	H.	R.	Er.			Ip.	H.	R.	Er.
yMarichal	7	8	4	3		Roebuck (L, 10-2)	3 1-3	4	4	3
Larsen (W, 5-4)	1	0	0	0		Williams	⅓	0	0	0
Pierce	1	0	0	0		Perranoski	⅓	1	2	1
xPodres										

xFaced three batters in sixth. yFaced one batter in eighth.

Base on balls—Marichal 1 (T. Davis), Larsen 2 (Roseboro, W. Davis), Podres 1 (Mays), Roebuck 3 Mays, McCovey, F. Alou), Williams 2 (Bailey, Davenport). Strikeouts—Marichal 2 (Roseboro, Podres), Larsen 1 (Howard), Perranoski 1 (Nieman). Wild pitch—Williams. Umpires—Boggess (plate), Donatelli (first base), Conlan (second base), Barlick (third base). Time—3:00. Attendance—45,693.

Sept. 28

NATIONAL

	W.	L.	Pct.	G.B.
xLos Angeles	101	61	.623	
xSan Francisco	101	61	.623	
Cincinnati	98	64	.605	3
Pittsburgh	93	68	.578	7
Milwaukee	86	76	.531	15
St. Louis	84	78	.519	17
Philadelphia	81	80	.503	19½
Houston	64	96	.400	36
Chicago	59	103	.356	42
New York	40	120	.250	60

xMeet in a best-of-three play-off to decide the league champion.

SUNDAY'S RESULTS
St. Louis 1, Los Angeles 0.
San Francisco 1, Houston 1.
Chicago 5, New York 1.
Cincinnati 4, Philadelphia 0.
Pittsburgh 4, Milwaukee 3.

Yanks Win Series

By WATSON SPOELSTRA
Detroit News Sports Writer

SAN FRANCISCO, Oct. 17.—Step aside, Casey Stengel.

Ralph Houk is the first manager to win two world championships in his first two seasons on a major league job.

The 43-year-old manager of the New York Yankees defied second guessers in a wild ninth inning before 43,948 spectators yesterday at Candlestick Park where Ralph Terry's superb 1-0 shutout rubbed out the persistence of the San Francisco Giants.

In seven games, the Yankees won their 20th World Series in 40 years. It was New York's 10th championship since Detroit's last American League pennant in 1945.

Reprinted from
The Detroit News

Sudden-Death Clash Deteriorates Into Game Of Errors

By LOU HATTER
[Sun Staff Correspondent]

Los Angeles, Oct. 3—The Los Angeles Dodgers, matchless at the grand collapse, folded like an over-inflated balloon in the ninth inning today and handed the National League pennant to the San Francisco Giants, 6 to 4, in the hectic finale of the 1962 play-offs.

Through the courtesy of two Los Angeles pitchers who couldn't find home plate and a second baseman who couldn't find the baseball, the Giants poured four runs over in the finale frame to win the fourth pennant play-off in National League history.

The weary Giants, who emerged triumphant almost in spite of themselves, thereby salvaged the dubious honor of meeting the healthy, well-rested New York Yankees in the World Series, beginning tomorrow in San Francisco at 3 P.M. (Baltimore time.)

Sudden-Death Duel

This afternoon's incredible struggle was billed as the "sudden-death" duel for a pennant which Los Angeles had all but sewed up one week ago.

For awhile, both teams looked like they had entered into a suicide pact. It appeared that neither desired to oppose the American League titleholders.

The Dodgers tried not once, but twice, to donate the marbles to San Francisco.

The second offer, featuring four bases on balls, a wild pitch, Larry Burright's error and only two rival hits—by Matty Alou and Willie Mays—was grasped like money from home by the greedy Giants in the concluding frame.

25,693 On Hand

Shortly thereafter, Dodger ____ ____ in a Chavez Ravine audience of 25,693, who had been transformed earlier into merry maniacs, went home solemn mourners. For all of Los Angeles, it had been sudden death, indeed.

This fiasco, matching yesterday's come-from-behind 8-to-7 Dodger victory in baseball incompetence, must have had the nation's televiewers tied up in neurotic knots. Seven errors were perpetrated by the gladiators of both teams before the Dodgers finally shot themselves dead.

Three Los Angeles miscues—all on throws — were committed in the third frame, where San Francisco tallied twice with the additional help of singles by Jose Pagan, Harvey Kuenn and Felipe Alou.

Pitcher Johnny Podres, catcher John Roseboro and second baseman Junior Gilliam were guilty of these atrocities while the Dodgers comforted themselves as though they were fighting for last place in the little league.

Reprinted from
The Baltimore Sun papers

End of the Season

NEW YORK

	AB	R	H	RBI	PO	A
Kubek, ss	4	0	1	0	1	5
Richardson, 2b	2	0	0	0	3	0
Tresh, lf	4	0	1	0	6	0
Mantle, cf	3	0	1	0	3	0
Maris, rf	4	0	0	0	0	0
Howard, c	4	0	0	0	5	0
Skowron, 1b	4	1	1	0	6	0
Boyer, 3b	4	0	2	0	2	2
Terry, p	3	0	1	0	1	1
Totals	32	1	7	0	27	3

SAN FRANCISCO

	AB	R	H	RBI	PO	A
F. Alou, rf	4	0	0	0	1	0
Hiller, 2b	4	0	0	0	1	3
Mays, cf	4	0	1	0	1	0
McCovey, lf	4	0	1	0	3	0
Cepeda, 1b	3	0	0	0	12	0
Haller, c	3	0	0	0	5	0
Davenport, 3b	3	0	0	0	3	4
Pagan, ss	2	0	0	0	1	2
aBailey	1	0	0	0	0	0
Bowman, ss	0	0	0	0	0	1
Sanford, p	2	0	1	0	0	1
O'Dell, p	0	0	0	0	0	0
bM. Alou	1	0	1	0	0	0
Totals	31	0	4	0	27	11

a—Fouled out for Pagan in 8th. b—Singled for O'Dell in 9th.

New York (A	000	010	000 -1
San Francisco (N	000	000	000 -0

E—Pagan. DP—Pagan, Hiller and Cepeda; Davenport and Cepeda. LOB—New York (A) 8, San Francisco (N) 4. 2b—Mays. 3b—McCovey.

	IP	H	R	ER
Terry (W)	9	4	0	0
xSanford (L)	7	7	1	1
O'Dell	2	0	0	0

x—Faced three batters in 8th.

BB—Sanford 4 (Richardson 2, Terry, Mantle). SO—Terry 4 (Cepeda 2, F. Alou, Hiller). Sanford 3 (Terry, Mantle, Howard). O'Dell 1 (Terry). U—Landes (N) plate. Honochick (A) first base, Barlick (N) second base, Berry (A) third base, Burkhart (N) left field, Soar (A) right field. T—2:29. A—43,948.

Wide World Photo

SAME PLAY—BUT 7 YEARS APART

The defensive play that won yesterday's game and the World Series for the Yankees was Tom Tresh's running, gloved-hand catch (above) of Willie Mays' seventh-inning drive to the leftfield corner. It was like an echo from the past, a sad echo for the New York club—the seventh game of the 1955 World Series with the then Brooklyn Dodgers in Yankee Stadium. With none out and two Yankees on base in the sixth inning, Brooklyn's Sandy Amoros made a sensational catch (left) of Yogi Berra's drive to the left-field corner and doubled Gil McDougald off first. The Dodgers won the game, 2-0, for their first Series victory. Tresh was a 17-year-old Detroit schoolboy when that catch was made. Had he failed to catch Mays' drive yesterday, it would have put the Giants' centerfielder on second with one out. The next batter, Willie McCovey, smashed a stand-up triple but was stranded on third when Orlando Cepeda struck out.

Jan. 6

Hornsby Funeral Set for Tuesday

AUSTIN, Tex. (UP)—Funeral services will be held in Austin Thursday for Rogers Hornsby, the famed "Raj of Swat," who died yesterday following a heart ailment.

Services here will be at the Weed and Carlson Funeral Home followed by burial at Hornsby Bend, nine miles south of Austin.

Hornsby Bend was settled in 1832 by Reuben Hornsby, a colonist with Stephen F. Austin. The land, on the picturesque Colorado River of Texas, is still in the hands of Reuben Hornsby heirs.

Present and former baseball players, umpires and officials in Texas will be honorary pall-bearers.

Koufax Has No-Hitter, Faces 28

LOS ANGELES, May 11 (AP)— Lefthander Sandy Koufax of the Los Angeles Dodgers pitched the first no-hitter of the major league season tonight, permitting just two base-runners in an 8-0 victory over the San Francisco Giants.

Ed Bailey, a lefthanded batter, spoiled Koufax's bid for the first regular season perfect game in 41 years when he walked on a 3-2 pitch with one out in the eighth inning. Jim Davenport promptly banged into a double play. Koufax had retired the first 22 men to face him and faced only 28 in all.

The second base runner was Willie McCovey, who walked on four pitches with two out in the ninth. Koufax wrapped up the no-hitter by personally throwing out Harvey Kuenn.

Kourfax, who pitched the last National League no-hitter when he blanked the New York Mets at Dodger Stadium last June 30, had only a few anxious moments against the power-hitting Giants.

The play that numbed the 49,807 fans came in the seventh inning when Tommy Davis had to go back to the railing of the left-field stands for Felipe Alou's towering smash.

The last no-hitter in the majors came last Aug. 26 when Jack Kralick of the Minnesota Twins blanked Kansas City 1-0.

The Koufax masterpiece was the third no-hitter since the multimillion-dollar Dodger Stadium was opened in 1962. Bo Belinsky of the Los Angeles blanked Baltimore, 2-0, last May 5 — about six weeks before Koufax's first no-hitter.

Oddly enough, all three came in Saturday night games.

SAN FRANCISCO					LOS ANGELES				
	ab	r	h	bi		ab	r	h	bi
Kuenn lf	4	0	0	0	W. Davis cf	5	1	0	0
F. Alou rf	3	0	0	0	G'l'am 2b-3b	3	2	2	0
Mays cf	3	0	0	0	Fairly 1b	5	0	3	3
Cepeda 1b	3	0	0	0	T. D'v's 3b-lf	4	1	1	0
Bailey c	2	0	0	0	Moon lf	3	2	2	2
D'venport 3b	3	0	0	0	Oliver 2b	1	0	0	0
A'Hitano 2b	3	0	0	0	Howard rf	3	0	0	0
Pagan ss	3	0	0	0	Roseboro c	4	0	2	2
Marichal p	2	0	0	0	Trace'ski ss	4	1	2	0
Pregenzer p	0	0	0	0	Koufax p	3	1	0	0
aMcCovey	0	0	0	0					
Totals	26	0	0	0	Totals	36	8	12	7

a—Walked for Pregenzer in 9th.

San Francisco .... 000 000 000—0
Los Angeles .... 046 003 04x—8

E—None. PO-A—San Francisco 24-11, Los Angeles 27-9. DP—Pregenzer, Pagan and Cepeda; Tracewski, Oliver and Fairly. LOB—San Francisco 1, Los Angeles 8. 2B—Fairly. HR—Moon. SB—Gilliam.

GIANTS PITCHING

	IP	H	R	ER	BB	SO
Marichal L, 4-3	5 1-3	9	4	4	1	3
Pregenzer	2 2-3	3	4	4	4	1

DODGERS PITCHING

	IP	H	R	ER	BB	SO
Koufax W, 4-1	9	0	0	0	2	4

Balk—Pregenzer. U—Walsh, Conlan, Burkhart, Pelekoudas. T—2:13. A—49,807.

WYNN REGISTERS HIS 300TH VICTORY

Right-Hander Goes 5 Innings in 7-4 Triumph After A's Set Back Indians, 6-5

By The Associated Press

KANSAS CITY, July 13— Early Wynn scored his 300th major league pitching victory today as the Cleveland Indians defeated the Kansas City Athletics, 7—4, in the second game of a double-header. The A's won the opener, 6—5.

Wynn, the 14th major league pitcher to win 300, lasted only five innings, the minimum distance a starter has to hurl to be credited with a victory.

The 43-year-old right-hander left after the fifth with the Indians ahead 5-4, and Jerry Walker blanked the A's in the last four innings.

Warren Spahn of the Milwaukee Braves is the only other active major-leaguer in the 300-victory circle.

Wynn, who first pitched in the majors in 1939 with the Washington Senators, reached his goal in his eighth try. He made three attempts last year with the Chicago White Sox and five since he was signed as a free agent by Cleveland last month. He won No. 299 on Sept. 8 of last year.

Wynn, who yielded six hits and struck out three men, set another record when he walked three. His career total of bases on balls now is 1,765, one more than the previous record held by Bob Feller.

Wynn, five times a 20-game winner, has lost 243 games, one this year. He was given a 5-1 lead on a four-run burst in the fifth but yielded three runs in the A's half before retiring.

Mets Win, 7-3, Behind Craig

New York, Aug. 9 (UP) — Jim Hickman crashed a full-count, two-out grand slam home run for the New York Mets in the ninth inning tonight as dour Roger Craig sweated out a 7-3 victory over the Chicago Cubs, breaking his personal eighteen-game losing string that has matched the longest in a season in National League history.

Craig, wearing a big No. 13 on his uniform instead of his usual 38, sat alongside manager Casey Stengel, who gestured wildly with crossed fingers attempting to put a hex on Chicago relief pitcher Lindy McDaniel on the 3-2 pitch to Hickman. Hickman hit a fly ball down the left field line that caught the overhang for a home run.

Craig, who had limited the Cubs to eight hits, was lifted for a pinch hitter with two out in the ninth and the socre tied 3-3.

Tim Harkness, the pinch hitter, drew a walk, loading the bases. Hickman, the lead-off man, followed with his drive off the facade in left and Craig, Casey and the rest of the Mets poured onto the field.

CHICAGO					NEW YORK				
	ab	r	h	bi		ab	r	h	bi
Brock rf	5	1	3	1	Hickman 3b	5	2	1	4
Burton cf	4	0	0	0	Carmel 1b	3	0	1	1
Williams lf	4	1	2	0	Hunt 2b	4	0	0	0
Santo 3b	3	0	1	1	Snider rf	4	0	1	1
Ranew 1b	4	0	0	0	Thomas lf	4	1	2	1
Hubbs 2b	3	0	1	0	Hicks cf	4	1	2	0
Rodgers ss	4	1	1	1	Coleman c	4	0	1	0
Toth p	4	0	0	0	Moran ss	3	2	1	0
McDaniel p	0	0	0	0	Craig p	2	0	0	0
					aHarkness	0	1	0	0
Totals	35	3	8	3	Totals	33	7	9	7

a—Walked for Craig in 9th.

Chicago .... 000 030 000—3
New York .... 000 120 004—7

E—Toth, Snider, Santo. PO-A—Chicago 26-9, New York 27-15. DP—Brock and Ranew. LOB—Chicago 8, New York 4. 2B—Moran. 3B—Brock, Williams. HR—Thomas, Rodgers, Brock, Hickman. S—Craig. SF—Santo.

	IP	H	R	ER	BB	SO
Toth L, 3-7	8 2-3	9	7	7	2	7
McDaniel	0	0	0	0	2	0
Craig W, 3-20	9	8	3	3	1	8

x—Faced two men in 9th.

HBP—By Craig (Hubbs). PB—Bertell. U—Forman, Gorman, Landes, Sudol. T—2:31. A—11,566.

SECOND GAME									
CLEVELAND (A.)					KANSAS CITY (A.)				
	ab	r	h	rbi		ab	r	h	rbi
Francona, lf	5	0	1	0	Tartabull, cf	5	1	1	0
Tasby, lf	0	0	0	0	Causey, ss	5	0	0	0
Howser, ss	5	1	2	0	Lumpe, 2b	4	0	1	3
Kirkland, cf	5	2	1	0	Alusik, rf	3	1	1	1
Alvis, 3b	4	1	0	0	Lau, c	3	0	1	0
Adcock 1b	4	1	1	3	Charles, 3b	2	0	1	0
Adcock 1b	4	1	1	3	Essegian, lf	4	0	0	0
Romano, c	3	1	2	1	Harrelson, 1b	3	1	2	0
Ludlow, rf	2	0	2	2	Drabowsky, p	1	0	1	0
Brown, 2b	4	0	0	0	Willis, p	0	0	0	0
Wynn, p	2	1	1	0	aCimoli	1	0	1	0
cHeld	1	0	1	0	bLaRussa	0	1	0	0
Walker p	0	0	0	0	Fischer, p	0	0	0	0
					dSiebern	1	0	0	0
					Lovrich, p	0	0	0	0
					eEdwards	1	0	0	0
Total	35	7	12	7	Total	33	4	9	4

aSingled for Willis in 5th, bRan for Cimoli in 5th, cDoubled for Wynn in 6th, dStruck out for Fischer in 6th, ePopped up for Lovrich in 9th.

Cleveland .... 010 040 101—7
Kansas City ...... 000 130 000—4

E—Harrelson, A. Cleveland 13, Kansas City 12. DP—Lumpe, Held, Harrelson and Adcock. LOB—Cleveland 8, Kansas City 7. 2B—Hits Lumpe, Held, Lau. 3B—Kirkland. HR—Alusik. SB—Kirkland. SF—Adcock.

	IP	H	R	ER	BB	SO
Wynn (W, 1-1)	5	6	4	4	2	3
Walker	4	3	0	0	4	2
Drabowsky (L, 0-6)	4	8	5	5	5	5
Willis	1-1	0	0	0	0	0
Fischer	1	2	1	1	0	0
Lovrich	3	2	1	1	0	0

Umpires—Knapp, Kinnamon, Umont and Stevens. Time—2:43. Attendance—13,565.

PIRATES TOP CUBS, 7 TO 6

Lynch's Record Pinch Belt In 9th Brings Victory

Chicago, Aug. 20 (AP)—Jerry Lynch set a major league record with his fifteenth career pinch-hit home run in the ninth inning today to give the Pittsburgh Pirates a 7-to-6 victory over the Chicago Cubs. Lynch homered off Lindy McDaniel.

The pinch homer broke the major league record of fourteen, set by George Crowe.

PITTSBURGH					CHICAGO				
	ab	r	h	bi		ab	r	h	bi
Bailey 3b	5	2	2	1	Boris rf	4	0	2	1
Mota lf	4	2	3	0	Gram'as ss	3	0	0	0
Clemente rf	5	0	1	2	Hubbs 2b	4	2	1	0
Mazeski 2b	3	0	1	2	W'liams lf	4	2	1	0
Clende'n 1b	3	0	0	1	Santo 3b	4	0	1	0
Pag'roni c	3	0	1	0	Burton rf	3	0	0	0
Virdon cf	3	0	0	0	Banks 1b	4	0	1	0
Schofield ss	4	1	1	0	Bertell c	4	0	1	0
Gibbon p	1	0	0	0	dRanew c	0	0	0	0
aLogan	1	1	1	0	Rodgers ss	3	0	1	0
Sisk p	0	0	0	0	fBurton	1	0	0	0
Haddix p	0	0	0	0	Brock lf	3	0	1	0
McBean p	0	0	0	0	Ellsworth p	2	0	0	0
cLynch	1	1	1	1	eLandrum	1	0	0	0
Face p	0	0	0	0	McDaniel p	0	0	0	0
Totals	34	7	11	9	Totals		6	11	2

a—Singled for Gibbon in 6th. b—Flied out for Haddix in 7th. c—Hit home run for McBean in 9th. d—Struck out for Bertell in 6th. e—Announced for Rodgers in 6th. f—Walked for Landrum in 6th. x—Burton awarded first base on catcher's interference in 2nd.

Pittsburgh ... 000 003 301—7
Chicago ...... 000 002 202—6

E—Pagliaroni 2, Rodgers. PO-A—Pittsburgh 27-15, Chicago 27-11. DP—Bailey, Mazeroski and Clendenon 2; Hubbs, Rodgers and Banks; Schofield, Mazeroski and Clendenon; Santo, Hubbs and Banks; Hubbs and Banks. LOB—Pittsburgh 5, Chicago 8.

2B—Bailey, Mazeroski. HR—Lynch. 3B—Hubbs. S—Mazeroski. SF—Clendenon.

	IP	H	R	ER	BB	SO
Gibbon	5	4	2	2	1	2
Sisk	1-3					
Haddix	3-3					
McBean (W, 13-3)	2					
Face						
Ellsworth	6	1-3				
McDaniel (L, 8-4)	1 2-3					

WP—Haddix 3. PB—Pagliaroni. U—Harvey, Weyer, Barlick, Vargo. T—2:48. A—15,341.

L.A. LEAD INCREASES TO 3 GAMES

Flag Contenders Lose Second In Row; Lefty Posts 11th Shutout

Race At A Glance

National League

	W.	L.	P.C.	To Play
Los Angeles	93	59	.612	10
St. Louis	91	63	.591	8

St. Louis, Sept. 17 (AP)—Sandy Koufax, Los Angeles' splendid southpaw, hurled a four-hit, 4-to-0 shutout over second-place St. Louis tonight, increasing the Dodgers' National League lead to three games while becoming the first left-hander in major league history to post eleven shutouts in one season.

The fireballing Koufax, the fleet Maury Wills and towering Frank Howard all contributed to another key Dodger victory, the second in a row in this vital three-game series that may determine the National League pennant winner.

Musial Gets First Hit

And for the second night in a row, 42-year-old grandfather Stan Musial, who plans to retire this season, played the spoiler for the only run off Johnny Podres in the Dodgers' 3-to-1 victory Monday night and got the first hit off Koufax in this one—a single to center leading off the seventh inning.

Koufax, winning his twenty-fourth game against only five losses, broke the record for left-hander sset by Carl Hubbell of the New York Giants, who pitched ten shutouts in 1933. Koufax eleventh made him the most prolific shutout pitcher since Grover Cleveland Alexander recorded sixteen for the 1916 Philadelphia Phillies.

Besides Musial's single, the only other hits off Koufax came in the eighth when Tim McCarver blooped a single to short center with one out, Julian Javier singled to left oneo ut later. Koufax then got Dick Groat, the league's leading hitter, to line out to Willie Davis for the inning ending out.

The Box Score

LOS ANGELES					ST. LOUIS				
	ab	r	h	bi		ab	r	h	bi
Wills ss	4	1	2	0	Javier 2b	4	0	1	0
Gilliam 2b	4	1	1	0	Groat ss	4	0	0	0
T. Davis lf	4	0	2	0	Musial lf	4	0	1	0
Howard rf	4	1	2	1	aKolb lf	0	0	0	0
Skowron 1b	4	0	0	0	Schultz p	1	0	0	0
Fairly 1b	0	0	0	0	bBoyer	1	0	0	0
McMullen 3b	4	0	1	0	cK'pole	1	0	0	0
Trac'ski c	4	0	1	0	cWithrow	1	0	0	0
W. Davis cf	4	1	1	1	Flood cf	4	0	0	0
Roseboro c	4	0	1	0	White 1b	4	0	0	0
Koufax p	3	0	0	0	James rf	3	0	0	0
					McCarver c	2	0	1	0
					Simmons p	2	0	0	0
					bShannon	1	0	0	0
Totals	35	4	10	4	Totals	35	0	4	0

a—Ran for Musial in 7th; b—Flied out for Simmons in 8th; c—Grounded out for MacKenzie in 9th.

Los Angeles .... 100 002 001—4
St. Louis .... 000 000 000—0

E—Groat. PO-A—Los Angeles 27-8, St. Louis 27-7. LOB—Los Angeles 6, St. Louis 6.

2B—Gilliam. W. Davis, Roseboro. HR—Howard. 3B—Wills. W. Davis. S—Simmons.

	IP	H	R	ER	BB	SO
Koufax W, 24-5	9	4	0	0	1	4
Simmons L, 14-6						
Schultz						
MacKenzie						

HBP—By Koufax (McCarver). WP—Simmons. U—Gorman, Forman. T—2:54. A—30,650.

Musial Goes Out Way He Came In: With Pair of Hits

ST. LOUIS, Sept. 29 (AP)—Stan Musial, who broke in with the St. Louis Cardinals with two hits 22 years ago, ended his career the same way today in a 14-inning, 3-2 Cardinal victory over the Cincinnati Reds.

Musial got the first hit off the Cincinnati starter, Jim Maloney, a single up the middle in the fourth inning. Then in the sixth he singled after a double by Curt Flood and drove in the first run of the game. Musial then left the game for a pinch runner.

His two hits brought his career total to 3,630 in 3,026 games. He ended with a .331 lifetime batting average. This year he hit .251.

Before the game Musial was given one standing ovation after another by the crowd of 27,576. After civic and baseball officials praised him in brief speeches, the 42-year-old Musial stood at a battery of microphones and said:

"As long as I live I will always remember this day. For me it is both a great joy and a great sorrow. It is a joy because of this wonderful day for me, and it is a sorrow because it is a farewell."

Ken Boyer, captain of the Cardinals, presented Musial with a ring with diamonds arranged in the shape of his uniform number—6. August Busch Jr., the club's president, said the number would be retired.

CINCINNATI (N.)					ST. LOUIS (N.)				
	ab	r	h	rbi		ab	r	h	rbi
Rose, 2b, lf	6	0	3	0	Flood, cf	7	1	2	0
Harper, rf	6	0	0	0	Groat, ss	4	0	0	0
Pinson, lf	1	0	1	0	Maxvill, ss	1	0	1	1
Neal, 2b	0	0	0	0	Musial, lf	3	0	2	1
Robinson, cf, lf	6	0	0	0	aKolb, rf	1	1	0	0
Coleman, 1b	5	1	1	0	uBearnarth	1	0	0	0
Edwards, c	2	0	0	0	Shannon, rf	1	0	0	0
bKeough	1	0	0	0	Boyer, 3b	6	0	4	0
Pavletich, c	3	1	1	0	White, 1b	5	0	2	0
Cardenas, ss	6	0	2	2	James, cf, lf	5	0	0	1
Kasko, 3b	5	0	0	0	McCarver, c	5	0	0	0
Maloney, p	2	0	0	0	Javier, 2b	3	0	0	0
cSkinner	1	0	1	0	fAltman	1	0	1	0
O'Toole, p	0	0	0	0	Buchek, ss	2	0	1	0
dGreen	1	0	0	0	Gibson, p	2	0	0	0
Worthington, p	0	0	0	0	fClemens	1	0	0	0
Henry, p	0	0	0	0	Taylor, p	0	0	0	0
hWalters	1	0	0	0	iSawatski	1	0	0	0
Jay, p	1	0	0	0	Broglio, p	1	1	0	0
Total	51	2	10	2	Total	51	3	13	3

aRan for Musial in 6th, bStruck out for Edwards in 7th; cSingled for Maloney in 8th, dPopped out for O'Toole in 9th, eSingled for Javier in 9th, fWalked for Gibson in 9th, gStruck out for Kolb in 10th, hPopped out for Henry in 11th, iCalled out on strikes for Taylor in 11th.

Cincinnati .. 000 000 002 000 00—2
St. Louis ... 000 002 000 000 01—3

E—Boyer, Groat 2—Cincinnati 13, St. Louis 14. DP—McCarver, Groat, McCarver, Buchek, Maxvill, Neal, Cardenas, Coleman. LOB—Cincinnati 12, St. Louis 13.

2B Hits—Flood, Rose, Maxvill. Sacrifice—Harper. SF—James.

	IP	H	R	ER	BB	SO
Maloney	7	5	2	2	1	11
O'Toole	1	1	0	0	0	0
Worthington	1/3	1	0	0	2	1
Henry	1 2/3	1	0	0	2	0
Jay (L, 7—18)	3 1/3	5	1	1	0	3
Gibson	9	7	2	2	1	0
Taylor	2	1	0	0	2	1
Broglio (W, 18—8)	3	2	0	0	1	2

Wild pitches—Maloney, Gibson, Broglio 2. Umpires—Barlick, Weyer, Vargo, Williams. Time—3:45. Attendance—27,576.

Dodgers Defeat Yankees, 2-1, To Sweep World Series

KOUFAX GAINS 2D WIN OFF WHITEY FORD ON UNEARNED RUN IN 7TH

F. Howard, Mantle Hit Homers; Pepitone's Muff Is Decisive

By LOU HATTER
[Sun Staff Correspondent]

Los Angeles, Oct. 6—The Los Angeles Dodgers this afternoon became the new rulers of the baseball universe by defeating the New York Yankees, 2 to 1, thereby capping an unprecedented four-game World Series sweep of the Bronx Bombers before a howling, bugle-tooting mob of 55,912 Chavez Ravine extroverts.

Sandy Koufax, the raven-haired left-hander who fanned a Series record fifteen Yanks last Wednesday in New York, again was the chief executioner, establishing two additional Series marks and emerging partner to a third en route to his second triumph in the 1963 event.

Sandy Fans Eight

The 27-year-old Koufax struck out eight today and checked the Yankees on six blows while his playmates collected only two off a blameless Whitey Ford.

The pay-off run was delivered to the Dodgers through the courtesy of New York's first sacker, Joe Pepitone, whose seventh-inning muff of a thrown ball enabled Jim Gilliam to scoot all the way to third base.

From there he tagged up and scored following Willie Davis's sacrifice fly to center, unraveling a 1-to-1 tie created by solo homers by the Dodgers' Frank Howard and Mickey Mantle, of the Bombers, in the fifth and seventh frames.

World Series Box

Los Angeles, Oct. 6 (P)—The box score of the fourth game of the the 1963 World Series:

NEW YORK (A)	ab	r	h	rbi	po	a	e
Kubek, ss	4	0	0	0	2	0	0
Richardson, 2b	4	0	2	0	1	4	0
Tresh, lf	4	0	0	0	1	0	0
Mantle, cf	4	1	1	1	4	0	0
E. Howard, c	4	0	2	0	6	1	0
Lopez, rf	4	0	0	0	1	0	0
Pepitone, 1b	3	0	0	0	8	3	1
Boyer, 3b	3	0	0	0	1	0	0
Ford, p	2	0	0	0	2	0	0
aLinz	1	0	1	0	0	0	0
Reniff, p	0	0	0	0	1	0	0
Totals	33	1	6	1	24	11	1

LOS ANGELES (N)	ab	r	h	rbi	po	a	e
Wills, 2b	2	0	0	0	4	0	0
Gilliam, 3b	3	1	0	0	0	0	0
W. Davis, cf	2	0	0	1	2	0	0
T. Davis, lf	3	0	0	0	0	0	0
F. Howard, rf	3	1	2	1	2	0	0
Fairly, rf	0	0	0	0	0	0	0
Skowron, 1b	3	0	0	0	9	1	0
Roseboro, c	3	0	0	0	11	0	0
Tracewski, 2b	3	0	0	0	2	1	1
Koufax, p	2	0	0	0	1	2	0
Totals	24	2	2	2	27	8	1

aSingled for Ford in eighth.

New York (A)	0 0 0 0 0 0 1 0 0—	1
Los Angeles (N)	0 0 0 0 1 0 1 0 x—	2

Double plays—E. Howard and Pepitone; Kubek, Richardson and Pepitone; Tracewski and Skowron. Left on bases—New York (A) 5, Los Angeles (N) 0. Two-base hit—Richardson. Home runs—F. Howard, Mantle. Sacrifice fly—W. Davis.

PITCHING SUMMARY

	Ip.	H.	R.	Er.		Ip.	H.	R.	Er.
Ford (L)	7	2	2	1	Koufax (W)	9	6	1	1
Reniff	1	0	0	0					

Bases on balls—Ford 1 (Wills). Strikeouts—Ford 4 (W. Davis, Wills, Roseboro, Koufax), Koufax 8 (Kubek, Tresh, 2; Pepitone, 2; Boyer, 2; Mantle). Umpires—Crawford (N) plate, Paparella (A) first base, Gorman (N) second base, Japp (A) third base, Rice (A) left field, Venzon (N) right field. Time—1.50. Attendance—55,912.

Ken Hubbs, Rookie of Year in '62, and Friend Die

PROVO, Utah, Feb. 15 (AP) —Ken Hubbs, star second baseman for the Chicago Cubs, and a friend were found dead today in the wreckage of a light plane that crashed on a frozen lake near here.

Mr. Hubbs, 22 years old, was the National League's Rookie of the Year in 1962.

He and his companion, Dennis Dayle, 23, left this north-central Utah town in Mr. Hubbs's single-engined Cessna 172 Thursday morning for their homes in Colton, Calif. The plane got only about five miles.

The wreckage was sighted on Utah Lake, just south of Provo, late this morning by Harlon Bement, state aeronautics director.

Mr. Bement was directing the Utah phase of a three-state aerial search that began yesterday evening when Mr. Hubbs's father reported the plane had failed to arrive in Colton.

Mr. Hubbs and Mr. Doyle were flying home after participating in a basketball tournament at Provo sponsored by the Church of Jesus Christ of Latter-day Saints. Mr. Hubbs bought the plane last year and obtained his pilot's license two weeks ago.

Mr. Hubbs held two major league fielding records, both set in 1962. He played 78 consecutive games without an error and handled 418 chances during the stretch.

He batted .262 in 1962 when he won the Rookie of the Year honor, receiving 19 of a possible 20 votes. His batting average last year was .235.

Mr. Hubbs broke into professional baseball with Morristown of the Appalachian League in 1959 and played with a number of minor league clubs before moving up to the Cubs.

Ex-Red Pilot Hutchinson Succumbs To Cancer At 45

Cincinnati, Nov. 12 (AP) — The manager hasn't been born who could satisfy all of Cincinnati's rabid baseball fans all of the time.

But Fred Hutchinson, who died today in Bradenton, Fla., of cancer, probably came as close to doing it as is humanly possible. He was 45.

JIM UMBRICHT DEAD; PITCHER ON COLTS, 33

HOUSTON, April 8 (AP) — Jim Umbricht, Houston Colt right-handed relief pitcher, died today of cancer. He was 33 years old.

Despite a six-hour operation on March 7, 1963, he was in uniform on opening day last season and before the season ended he compiled a 4-3 record in 76 innings as a relief pitcher. He gave up 52 hits, struck out 48 batters, allowed 21 walks and had a 2.61 earned run average.

The Colts purchased Umbricht from the Pittsburgh Pirates for $50,000 in the National League player pool in 1961. In Houston's first year in the majors, 1962, he had a 4-0 record.

His five-year record at Pittsburgh and Houston was 194 innings in 88 games for a 9-5 record and a 3.06 earned run average.

The athlete was a graduate of the University of Georgia, where he played both baseball and basketball. In 1951 he was named All-Southeastern Conference shortstop.

2-OUT RALLY FINALLY ENDS 8-6 STRUGGLE

S.F. Sweeps Longest Twin Bill Despite Met Triple Play

New York, May 31 (P)—Pinch hitter Del Crandall, batting .191, smashed a two-out ground rule double to right field, scoring Jim Davenport with the tie-breaking run in the 23rd inning and sparking the San Francisco Giants to an 8-to-6 victory over the New York Mets today in the longest game played in major league history on a time basis.

Davenport tripled to the right field corner off Galen Cisco after Cisco retired the first two batters. Cisco walked Cap Peterson intentionally before Crandall batted for relief hurler Gaylord Perry and hit a 1-2 pitch to right. Peterson went to third on the out.

Add Insurance Run

J. Alou then hit an infield dribbler that scored Peterson. Willie Mays ended the inning by forcing Alou at second.

Bob Hendley pitched the 23rd for the Giants and retired the Mets in order.

The game was the second of a doubleheader that consumed 10 hours and 16 minutes. The Giants won the opener, 5-to-3, before 57,037, largest crowd in the majors this season.

Sets Time Record

The time of the game—seven hours and 22 minutes—eclipsed the old mark of seven hours set by New York and Detroit in a 22-inning American League game June 24, 1962.

Only three other games went more innings. The teams however set a major league mark for innings played in one day—32. The previous high was 29 played by Boston and Philadelphia in the American League July 4, 1905. The game also is the longest played in the majors this season.

There were other highlights. The Giants played the game under protest and the Mets executed a triple play among other things.

Manager Al Dark announced in the fifteenth inning the Giants were playing under protest because plate Umpire Ed Sudol refused to check with the first base umpire when the Mets' Chris Cannizzaro walked on a 3-2 pitch.

Manager Ejected

Dark contended Cannizzaro had swung at the pitch and had not checked his swing in time as Sudol ruled. Dark was ejected from the game during the argument.

The triple play, second of the season in the majors, came in the fourteenth after Jesus Alou singled off Larry Bearnarth and Mays walked. Orlando Cepeda, who had rapped six hits in 10 previous at bats in the double-header, lined a smash to shortstop Roy McMillan who grabbed the ball, stepped on second to get Alou and threw to Ed Kranepool, catching Mays.

SAN FRANCISCO	ab	r	h	bi	NEW YORK	ab	r	h	bi
Kuenn lf	5	0	3	1	Kanehl 2b	4	0	1	0
dM. Alou lf	0	0	0	0	McMillan ss	4	0	0	0
Crandall c	4	0	0	0	Gonder c	4	0	0	0
Mays cf	3	1	1	0	Thomas lf	4	0	1	0
Hart 3b	4	1	1	0	cD Smith lf	0	0	0	0
Cepeda 1b	4	2	3	1	Christ'er rf	4	1	1	0
Hiller 2b	2	0	1	0	Kranepl 1b	4	0	1	1
aJ'vnp't 2b	1	0	0	1	Hickman cf	4	1	2	3
J Alou rf	4	1	2	1	C. Smith 3b	3	0	2	0
Garrido ss	4	1	1	0	Jackson p	0	0	0	0
Marichal p	4	0	0	0	Sturdi't p	0	0	0	0
					bAltman	1	0	0	0
					Bearnarth p	0	0	0	0
					eSteph'son	1	0	0	0
Totals	34	5	12	4	Totals	34	3	8	1

a—Hit sacrifice fly for Hiller in 6th; b—Struck out for Sturdivant in 7th; c—Ran for Thomas in 8th; d—Ran for Kuenn in 9th; e—Struck out for Bearnarth in 9th.

San Francisco ..... 000 103 001—5
New York .... 030 000 000—3

E—Hickman, Hart. PO-A—San Francisco 27-10, New York 27-13. DP—Garrido, Davenport and Cepeda; Davenport and Cepeda 6. New York 6. LOB—San Francisco 6, New York 4.

2B—Cepeda, C. Smith. HR—Hickman. SB—Cepeda. S—Crandall, Jackson, Garrido. SF—Davenport.

	IP	H	R	ER	BB	SO
Marichal W 8-1	9	8	3	0	7	2
Hickman L 3-7	5	5	4	4	1	3
Sturdivant	2	2	1	0	2	1
Bearnarth	2	2	1	1	0	1

x—Faced 3 men in 6th.
HBP—By Marichal (C. Smith). U—Burkhart, Sudol, Pryor, Secory. T—2:27.

SAN FRANCISCO	ab	r	h	bi	NEW YORK	ab	r	h	bi
Kuenn lf	5	1	0	0	Kanehl 2b	1	0	0	0
Perry p	3	0	0	0	cGonder	1	0	0	0
jCrandall	1	0	1	1	Samuel 2b	6	0	2	0
Hendley p	0	0	0	0	McMillan ss	11	2	0	0
J Alou rf	10	1	4	2	Thomas lf	4	1	2	0
Mays cf-ss	10	1	1	1	Chr' t pr rf	10	2	3	3
Cepeda 1b	9	1	3	0	Kranepl 1b	11	0	1	0
Haller c	10	1	4	1	Hickman cf	10	1	2	1
Hiller 2b	8	1	1	1	C. Smith 3b	9	0	4	1
Hart 3b	4	0	1	1	Cannzaro c	7	0	1	1
hM.Alou cf-l	6	0	0	0	Wakefield p	0	0	0	0
Garrido ss	4	1	1	1	aAltman	1	0	0	0
fMcCovey	1	0	0	0	bJackson	0	0	0	0
D'vp't ss-3b	4	1	1	1	Anderson p	0	0	0	0
Bolin p	2	0	1	0	Sturdivant p	1	0	0	0
MacK'nzie p	0	0	0	0	dD. Smith	1	0	0	0
Shaw p	0	0	0	0	Larv p	0	0	0	0
gSnider	1	0	0	0	gTaylor	1	0	0	0
Herbel p	0	0	0	0	Bearnarth p	0	0	0	0
iPeterson 3b	4	1	0	0	Cisco p	2	0	0	0
					kSteph'son	1	0	0	0
Totals	71	8	17	8	Totals	83	6	20	6

a—Walked intentionally for Wakefield in 2nd; b—Ran for Altman in 2nd; c—Flied out for Kanehl in 2nd; d—Grounded out for Sturdivant in 5th; e—Struck out for Larv in 7th; f—Struck out for Garrido in 8th; g—Grounded out for Shaw in 9th; h—Grounded out for Herbel in 10th; i—Lined out for Herbel 1 3b; j—Doubled for Perry in 23rd; k—Struck out for Cisco in 23rd.

S.F. ..... 010 002 300 000 000 000 002—8
N.Y. ..... 010 002 300 000 000 000 000—6

E—Garrido, Haller, Cepeda, Cisco. PO-A—San Francisco 69-14, New York 69-31. DP—Perry, Davenport and Cepeda; Davenport and Cepeda, Christopher and Kranepool. Triple play—McMillan and Kranepool. LOB—San Francisco 16, New York 14.

2B—J. Alou, Kranepool, Cepeda, Crandall. 3B—Kranepool, Haller, Davenport. HR—Christopher. S—Herbel, Hiller, C. Smith, Cisco.

	IP	H	R	ER	BB	SO
Bolin	6	2-3	8	4	4	2	2
xMacKenzie	0	1	0	0	0	0
Shaw	1 1-3	1	0	0	0	1
Herbel	6	7	0	0	0	2
Perry, W. 3-1	10	7	0	0	3	9
Hendley	1	0	0	0	0	1
Wakefield	1	3	1	1	0	0
Anderson	2	4	2	2	2	1
Sturdivant	3	2 2-3	3	2	2	0	2
Larv	2	3	0	0	2	2
Bearnarth	3	0	0	0	0	3
Cisco, L 2-5	9	8	2	2	4	4

x—Faced 1 man in 7th.
HBP—By Shaw (Samuel). bvCisco (Cepeda). PB—Cannizzaro. U—Sudol, Pryor, Secory, Burkhart. T—7:23. A—57,037.

SAN FRANCISCO, Feb. 22

SAN FRANCISCO, Feb. 22 (AP)—The first three native Japanese baseball players ever signed by a United States major league club will play in the farm system of the San Francisco Giants this year.

The Giants announced today a deal with the Osaka Hawks of Japan's Pacific League whereby the three young high school stars would come to the United States for at least a year of minor league seasoning.

Many United States major leaguers have gone to Japan to play, but this is the first time that the talent has flowed the other way.

The three youngsters—whose contracts were assigned to the Giants' Fresno farm club of the Class A California League, are Masonari Murakami, a left-handed pitcher; Tatsuhiko Tanaka, a third baseman, and Hiroshi Takahashi, a catcher.

None has had professional experience. They were recommended to the Giants as the best high school players in Japan.

KOUFAX PITCHES HIS 3D NO-HITTER

Dodger Ace Ties Record in 3-0 Victory Over Phils

By The Associated Press

PHILADELPHIA, June 4 — Sandy Koufax of the Los Angeles Dodgers pitched the third no-hit game of his major league career tonight. He allowed only one walk in gaining a 3-0 victory over the Philadelphia Phillies and tied Bob Feller's modern record for no-hitters.

Koufax, a 28-year-old left-handed fireball ace, faced the minimum number of 27 batters in the game. Richie Allen became a base runner, however, when he walked with two strikes on him in the fourth inning. He was thrown out trying to steal.

While becoming the second man to pitch three no-hitters, both since 1900, Koufax struck out 12 batters. By striking out 10 or more men for the 54th time in his career, Sandy tied a record shared by Feller and Rube Waddell.

LOS ANGELES (N.)				PHILADELPHIA (N.)			
	ab.r.h.rbi				ab.r.h.rbi		
W. Davis, cf	4 0 0 0			Rojas, cf	3 0 0 0		
Wills, ss	4 0 1 0			Callison, rf	3 0 0 0		
Gilliam, 3b	4 1 1 0			Allen, 3b	2 0 0 0		
T. Davis, lf	4 1 2 0			Cater, lf	3 0 0 0		
Howard, rf	3 1 1 3			Triandos, c	3 0 0 0		
Fairly, 1b	3 0 1 0			Sievers, 1b	3 0 0 0		
McMullen, 1b	3 0 1 0			Taylor, 2b	3 0 0 0		
Parker, rf	1 0 1 0			Amaro, ss	3 0 0 0		
Camilli, c	4 0 0 0			Short, p	2 0 0 0		
Tracewski, 2b	3 0 1 0			Roebuck, p	0 0 0 0		
Koufax, p	3 0 1 0			Culp, p	0 0 0 0		
				aWine	1 0 0 0		
Total	34 3 9 3			Total	26 0 0 0		

aStruck out for Culp in 9th.

Los Angeles ....000 000 300—3
Philadelphia ....000 000 000—0

E—Allen. A—Los Angeles 8, Philadelphia 13. DP—Taylor, Amaro, Sievers. LOB—Los Angeles 4, Philadelphia 0. 2B Hits—Tracewski, Parker. HR—Howard.

	IP.	H.	R.	ER.	BB.	SO.
Koufax (W. 6—4)	9	0	0	0	1	12
Short (L, 3—3)	6⅔	8	3	3	0	4
Roebuck	⅓	0	0	0	0	0
Culp	2	1	0	0	0	2

Umpires—Vargo, Forman, Jackowski, Crawford. Time—1:55. Attendance—29,709.

Bunning Hurls Perfect Game

PITCHER HAS NO-HITTERS IN 2 CIRCUITS

Becomes First In 42 Years To Win Flawless League Contest

New York, June 21 — Philadelphia's Jim Bunning pitched a perfect game against the New York Mets today, retiring all 27 batters he faced in the Phillies 6-to-0 victory in the first game of a doubleheader.

The Phillies won the second game 8-to-2, increasing their National League lead to two games over San Francisco.

Bunning, who became the first to hurl a winning no-hitter in both the National and American Leagues, also became the first in 42 years to pitch a perfect game in regular season play and win.

Taylor Makes Save

A great defensive play by Tony Taylor, second baseman, in the fifth inning, protected Bunning's perfect game.

Jesse Gonder drove a wicked grounder into the hole between first and second. Taylor made a spectacular diving stop and while on his knees, tossed to John Herrnstein for the out.

In the fourth, Ron Hunt smashed a long drive to right but the ball curved foul by several feet.

The Mets hit only four balls to the outfield. Bob Taylor went to a 3-2 count with two out in the eighth, but Bunning fired a third strike past him.

Bunning also starred at bat, smashing a two-run double in the Phillies' four-run sixth.

PHILADELPHIA				NEW YORK			
	ab.r h.bi				ab.r.h.bi		
Briggs cf	4 1 0 0			Hickman cf	3 0 0 0		
Herrnst'n 1b	4 0 0 0			Hunt 2b	3 0 0 0		
Callison rf	4 1 2 1			Kranep'l 1b	3 0 0 0		
Allen 3b	4 0 1 1			Christo'r rf	3 0 0 0		
Covington lf	2 0 0 0			Gonder c	3 0 0 0		
Wine pr-ss	1 1 0 0			R Taylor lf	3 0 0 0		
Taylor 2b	2 2 1 0			C Smith ss	3 0 0 0		
Rojas ss-lf	3 0 1 0			Samuel 2b	3 0 0 0		
Triandos c	4 1 2 1			A'spro ph	1 0 0 0		
Bunning p	4 0 1 2			Stallard p	1 0 0 0		
				Kanehl ph	1 0 0 0		
				Stephson ph	1 0 0 0		
Totals	32 6 8 6			Totals	27 0 0 0		

Philadelphia ......110 004 000—6
New York ....000 000 000—0

E—None. LOB—Philadelphia 5, New York 0.

2B Triandos, Bunning. HR—Callison 8, Herrnstein, Rojas.

	IP	H	R	ER	BB	SO
Bunning W 7-2	9	0	0	0	0	10
Stallard L 4-9	5⅓	7	6	6	1	3
Wakefield	1⅔	0	0	0	0	0
Sturdivant	2	1	0	0	0	0

WP Sturdivant. T 2:19.

Alvis's Condition Is Improved

Boston, June 27 (UP)—Max Alvis, Cleveland Indians' third baseman, showed improvement today after being stricken with spinal meningitis.

Dr. Thomas Tierney, team physician for the Boston Red Sox, said Alvis had a comfortable night and was improved.

He said Alvis was more comfortable today, with much less pain. The disease is marked by headaches and painful stiffening of the neck.

Alvis became ill yesterday.

He will be hospitalized probably for three weeks, but Dr. Tierney said it is difficult to say when he will be fully recovered.

Alvis's teammates and others who traveled with them to Boston were given sulfa pills as a precaution.

Yogi, Linz Feud

Sour Note Hit On Harmonica

Chicago, Aug. 20 (P)—Manager Yogi Berra of the slumping New York Yankees and infielder Phil Linz became involved in a heated row over Linz's harmonica playing following the team's fourth straight defeat today.

The Yankees were on a bus en route from Comiskey Park to O'Hare Airport. They had just lost, 5 to 0, to the Chicago White Sox and dropped 4½ games off the pace in the American League pennant race.

Linz, sitting in the rear of the bus next to first baseman Joe Pepitone, took out a harmonica and started playing it.

Silence, Then Toot

Berra, in the front of the bus, turned around and shouted, "Put that thing in your pocket!"

There was silence for a second, then a couple of toots on the harmonica.

Berra rushed back toward Linz and yelled, "I said to put it away. You'd think you just won four straight."

Linz appeared startled as Berra rushed toward him, and he flipped the instrument into the air toward him. Berra angrily swatted it with his right hand, and it bounced off Pepitone's right knee.

The harmonica cut the first baseman's knee but not badly. It did, however, require a bandaid.

"Why are you getting on me," Linz asked Berra. "I give a hundred per cent out on the field. I try to win. I should be allowed to do what I want off the field."

Berra replied:

"Play it in your room." Berra also was overheard telling Linz, "I'll take care of you."

Crosetti Interferes

Berra, in his first year as manager, then returned to his seat, bringing on silence.

At this point, Yankee coach Frank Crosetti started yelling at Linz, and Linz shouted back, telling the coach to stay out of the argument.

Crosetti said later the incident was the worst he has seen in his 33 years with the team.

The bus proceeded to the airport where the players, somewhat bewildered by the incident, boarded a plane for Boston where they play Friday night.

CALLISON CONNECTS FOR 3-RUN HOMER OFF RADATZ IN 9TH INNING

Robinson Drives In Two Runs For A.L. With Triple, Also Singles, Stars In Field; Williams, Boyer Hit For Circuit

By Lou Hatter

New York, July 7 John Callison's tie-breaking homer with two mates aboard capped a four-run ninth-inning rally and carried the National League to a 7-to-4 triumph over the Americans in baseball's thirty-fifth All-Star classic here today.

The blast off the right-field auxiliary scoreboard by the Philadelphia Phillies' outfielder followed a walk and stolen base by Willie Mays, Orlando Cepeda's bloop single to right on which first baseman Joe Pepitone's bad-hop peg to the plate enabled Mays to score and an intentional pass to John Edwards.

Struck with dramatic impact off Boston's Dick Radatz after two were out in the final frame, Callison's four-base bomb squared the midseason carnival of the game's super stars at seventeen victories apiece plus one tie.

Reprinted from
The Baltimore Sun papers

Cubs Whip Giants As Jackson Wins

San Francisco, Oct. 4 (AP)—Larry Jackson, winningest pitcher in the majors, breezed to his twenty-fourth victory for the eighth-place Chicago Cubs today, beating the fourth-place San Francisco Giants, 9 to 2.

The Cubs gave Jackson a seven-run cushion in the first three innings, chasing loser Gaylord Perry, 12-11, in the third.

Jackson, who lost eleven, survived some shaky moments in hurling the Cubs to a 9-9 season split with San Francisco. He gave up a fifth-inning sole homer to Willie Mays, the National League leader with 47.

CHICAGO	ab	r	h	bi	SAN FRANCISCO	ab	r	h	bi
Stewart ss	4	1	2	2	M Alou rf	4	0	1	0
Clemens rf	5	0	0	0	Mays cf	4	1	1	1
Williams cf	5	1	1	0	Cardenal cf	0	0	0	0
Santo 3b	4	1	2	0	Cepeda 1b	4	1	2	0
Banks 1b	3	2	2	2	Haller c	2	0	1	0
Cowan cf	1	0	0	0	Hundley c	1	0	0	0
Roe'bella lf	4	2	2	1	Hart 3b	4	0	1	0
C'pbell 2b	4	1	2	2	Peterson lf	4	0	2	1
Bertell c	3	1	1	1	Davenport ss	4	0	1	0
Jackson p	3	0	1	1	Lanier 2b	4	0	0	0
					Perry p	0	0	0	0
					Murakami p	2	0	0	0
					O'Dell p	1	0	0	0
					Kuenn ph	1	0	0	0
Totals	36	9	13	9	Totals	35	2	9	2

Chicago	034 002 000—9
San Francisco	000 110 000—2

E—None. DP Chicago 1, San Francisco 2. LOB—Chicago 3, San Francisco 7. 2B—Campbell, Banks, Haller. HR Mays (47), Stewart (3). SB Stewart. S Jackson. SF Bertell.

	IP	H	R	ER	BB	SO
Jackson W 24-11	9	9	2	2	1	3
Perry L 12-11	2	8	6	6	1	1
Murakami	4	4	3	3	0	2
O'Dell	3	1	0	0	0	0

Perry faced 3 men in 3rd.
T—2:10. A—33,452.

All-Star Box Score

New York, July 7 (AP)—The box score of the 1964 major league All Star baseball game:

AMERICAN LEAGUE	ab	h	h	bi	po	a	NATIONAL	ab	r	h	bi	po	a
Fregosi, ss	4	1	1	1	4	1	Clemente, rf	3	1	1	0	1	0
Oliva, rf	4	0	0	0	0	0	Short, p	0	0	0	0	0	1
Radatz, p	1	0	0	0	0	0	Farrell, p	0	0	0	0	0	0
Mantle, cf	4	1	1	0	2	0	gWhite	1	0	0	0	0	0
Hall, rf	0	0	0	0	0	0	Marichal, p	0	0	0	0	0	0
Killebrew, lf	4	1	3	1	0	0	Groat, ss	3	0	1	1	0	0
Hinton, lf	0	0	0	0	0	0	dCardenas, ss	1	0	0	0	1	0
Allison, 1b	3	0	0	0	9	0	Williams, lf	4	1	1	1	1	0
fPepitone, 1b	0	0	0	0	1	0	Mays, cf	3	1	0	0	7	0
Robinson, 3b	4	0	2	2	1	2	Cepeda, 1b	4	0	1	0	6	0
Richardson, 2b	4	0	1	0	0	4	hFlood	0	1	0	0	0	0
Howard, c	3	1	0	0	9	0	Boyer, 3b	4	1	2	1	0	2
Chance, p	1	0	0	0	0	1	Torre, c	2	0	0	0	5	0
Wyatt, p	0	0	0	0	0	1	Edwards, c	1	1	0	0	5	0
bSiebern	1	0	0	0	0	0	Hunt, 2b	3	0	1	0	1	0
Pascual, p	0	0	0	0	0	1	iAaron	1	0	0	0	0	0
eColavito, rf	2	0	1	0	0	0	Drysdale, p	0	0	0	0	0	3
							aStargell	1	0	0	0	0	0
							Bunning, p	0	0	0	0	0	0
							cCallison, rf	3	1	1	3	0	0
Totals	35	4	9	4	26	10	Totals	34	7	8	6	27	6

a—Grounded out for Drysdale in 3rd; b—Flied out for Wyatt in 5th; c—Popped out for Bunning in 5th; d—Ran for Groat in 5th; e—Doubled for Pascual in 7th; f—Ran for Allison in 8th; g—Struck out for Farrell in 8th; h—Ran for Cepeda in 9th; i—Struck out for Hunt in 9th. x—Two out when winning run scored.

American	1	0	0	0	0	2	1	0	0	—4
National	0	0	0	2	1	0	0	0	4	—7

Error—Pepitone. Left on bases—American, 7; National, 3. Two-base hits—Groat, Colavito. Three-base hit—Robinson. Home runs—Williams, Boyer, Callison. Stolen base—Mays. Sacrifice fly—Fregosi.

	Ip	H	R	Er		Ip	H	R	Er
Chance	3	2	0	0	Bunning	2	2	0	0
Wyatt	1	2	2	2	Short	1	3	2	2
Pascual	2	2	1	1	Farrell	2	2	1	1
Radatz (L)	2 2/3	2	4	4	Marichal (W)	1	0	0	0
Drysdale	3	2	1	0					

Bases on balls—Farrell 1 (Allison), Radatz 2 (Mays, Edwards). Strike outs—Drysdale 3 (Mantle, Allison, Howard), Chance 2 (Clemente, Groat), Bunning 4 (Allison, Richardson, Howard, Fregosi), Short 1 (Oliva), Pascual 1 (Boyer), Farrell 1 (Mantle), Radatz 5 (Edwards, Hunt, White, Cardenas, Aaron), Marichal 1 (Radatz). Hit by pitcher—Farrell (Howard). Wild pitch—Drysdale. Passed ball—Torre. Umpires—Sudol (N), Paparella (A), Secory (N), Chylak (A), Harvey (N), Salerno (A). Time—2,27. Attendance—50,850.

Belinsky Suspended by Angels After Knocking Out a Reporter

WASHINGTON, Aug. 14 (AP) — Bo Belinsky, the controversial Los Angeles Angel pitcher, knocked out a 64-year-old sportswriter, Braven Dyer, today in an early morning dispute over a story that Belinsky planned to quit baseball. Belinsky was immediately suspended from the team indefinitely.

There also were indications that Belinsky might be on his way out of the American League. Club officials said they planned to send him back to Los Angeles as soon as possible.

The incident occurred in a Washington hotel after the Angels arrived late last night for a four-game weekend series.

Dyer, who covers the team for the Los Angeles Times, said he had questioned Belinsky in the lobby about an Associated Press story that the 27-year-old pitcher planned to quit baseball.

Belinsky frequently has said he plans to quit baseball for something that pays more money.

Dyer Phones Paper

Dyer said Belinsky said he had been misquoted in the AP story and gave the writer some comment, and Dyer went to his room to telephone it to his newspaper.

"I had already undressed and gone to bed when Belinsky called me," Dyer said. "He said he had read the AP story and hadn't been misquoted. I told him it was too late to call my paper."

Belinsky then complained about mistreatment by newspapers, Dyer said, and ended by saying, "You come down here and I'll stick your ..... head under the shower."

Dyer, once a star college football player, said, "A writer can't let a player get away with a threat like that. I dressed and went down to his room."

When he got there, Dyer said, "I knocked on the door. We started talking, and that's all I remember."

Dyer said he came to with Manager Bill Rigney and the team trainer working over him.

"It looks like I'm going to be all right," Dyer said, "except right now I've got a little double vision. There is no sign of concussion."

Dyer said he had a great deal of swelling under his left ear, where six stitches were taken, and his right eye was blackened.

Belinsky has been in and out of the headlines since 1962 when he pitched a no-hitter as a rookie, had a string of victories, and made headlines with a series of late-hour incidents.

He had a highly publicized engagement with Mamie Van Doren, the actress, but it was broken off.

An Hawaiian Interlude

After a series of losses, the left-hander was sent down for a time last season to Hawaii in the Pacific Coast League. This year he was off to a good start, but had lost his last three games.

Rigney was quoted as saying: "Belinsky has been suspended without pay. He is no longer with this club. I will get him out of Washington as soon as I can."

Rigney said Belinsky told him:

"Brave came at me. I didn't know why, so I hit him. He must have hit his head against the wall while falling."

Rigney said he found Dyer on the floor, bleeding from his left ear.

"I was scared to death," he said.

Rigney called the trainer, who revived Dyer and called Dr. George Resta, the team physician for the Washington Senators.

Oct. 17

Yanks Fire Yogi Berra; Johnny Keane Quits Cards

EX-ST. LOUIS MANAGER GETS ONE-YEAR PACT AT $45,000 WITH N.Y.

Houk Denies Player Complaints About Berra, Says Bid Was Not Made Until Sunday; Champions' Shake-Up Seen Over

New York, Oct. 20 (AP)—Johnny Keane completed his stunning switch from World Series winner to loser by signing to manage the New York Yankees today, five days after he led the St. Louis Cardinals to victory over the Yanks.

Keane, who will be 52 November 3, was given a one-year contract at a reported $45,000 a year as successor to Yogi Berra, fired last Friday.

Keane said he got more than he did in St. Louis and Ralph Houk, general manager, said he got more than he did in his first year as manager, reportedly $35,-000.

Houk Denies Reports

Houk went to great lengths at a crowded news conference to insist the Yanks never contacted Keane until Sunday night

However, the Associated Press reported Friday night that Keane would get the job.

Houk also denied reports that some Yankee players complained to him about the way Berra was handling the club during the season.

Cards Name Schoendienst

"This was not true and no Yankee player ever discussed such situations with me," said Houk.

Keane had left the Cardinals under dramatic circumstances, handing his resignation to owner Gussie Busch the morning after his World Series triumph. The man who spent 35 years in the Cardinal organization had carried a letter of resignation dated September 28 in his pocket for two weeks

Shortly after Keane had been confirmed as Yankee skipper, Red Schoendienst, one of his former coaches, became Cardinal manager.

GIBSON GOES DISTANCE FOR SECOND VICTORY AS BROCK, K. BOYER HOMER

St. Louis Jumps To 6-0 Lead In First 5 Innings Off Stottlemyre And Downing; Mantle, Linz And Clete Boyer Connect For Losers

By BOB MAISEL
[Sports Editor of The Sun]

St. Louis, Oct. 15—The St. Louis Cardinals, a scrappy team of opportunists who led the National League for only six days during the entire season and did not clinch the pennant until the last day, are the new world champions of baseball.

With everything riding on this seventh game of the World Series, they again let the New York Yankees make the mistakes and capitalized on them, taking a 6-0 lead in the fifth inning, then holding on to win the big one, 7 to 5.

Included in the ten-hit Cardinal attack were home runs by Ken Boyer and Lou Brock, but the hero of it all for the new champions was a tall, lean, loose and lanky right-hander by the name of Bob Gibson, who was the unanimous winner of the sports card awarded to the most valuable player of the series.

Only 2 Days Rest

Working with just 2 days rest, Gibson struck out 9 for a total of 31 in this series, an all time record in World Series play, as he out-pitched Yankee starter Mel Stottlemyre and 4 successors, Al Downing, who failed to retire a batter, Roland Sheldon, Steve Hamilton and Pete Mikkelsen.

Once again the Yankees went to the long ball, but this time their own faulty defense and alert Cardinal play had them so far behind, they couldn't make up the difference.

Mickey Mantle, adding to some of his series records and setting some new ones, hit a 3-run homer in the sixth, to pull the Yankees to within 3 runs, 6-3. And, with Gibson finally showing signs of wear-and-tear in the ninth, Clete Boyer and Phil Linz also homered into the left field stands to make it 7-5.

Card Bullpen Shunned

However, just as he has been throughout most of this series, manager Johnny Keane was reluctant to go to his bullpen.

He stuck with Gibson, and when second baseman Dal Maxvill squeezed Bobby Richardson's high pop fly for the final out, it set off one of the wildest scenes you'd care to see in any ball park

World Series Box

SEVENTH GAME

St. Louis, Oct. 15 (AP)—The box score of the seventh game of the 1964 World Series:

NEW YORK (A)	ab	r	h	rbi	po	a		ST. LOUIS (N)	ab	r	h	rbi	po	a	e
Linz, ss	5	1	2	1	2	0		Flood, cf	5	0	0	0	2	0	0
B. Richardson, 2b	5	1	2	0	1	3		Brock, lf	4	1	2	1	0	0	0
Maris, cf	4	0	1	0	1	0		White, 1b	4	1	2	0	6	0	0
Mantle, rf	4	1	1	3	2	0		K. Boyer, 3b	4	3	3	1	1	2	0
Howard, c	4	0	1	0	6	1		Groat, ss	3	0	1	1	1	3	0
Pepitone, 1b	4	0	0	0	8	2		McCarver, c	2	1	1	1	9	0	0
Tresh, lf	2	0	1	2	0	0		Shannon, rf	4	1	1	0	3	1	0
C. Boyer, 3b	4	1	1	1	5	1		Maxvill, 2b	3	0	1	1	5	3	0
Stottlemyre, p	1	0	0	0	1	1		Gibson, p	4	0	0	0	1	0	
aHegan	0	0	0	0	0	0									
Downing, p	0	0	0	0	0	0									
Sheldon, p	0	0	0	0	0	0									
bLopez	1	0	0	0	0	0									
Hamilton, p	0	0	0	0	0	0									
Mikkelsen, p	0	0	0	0	0	0									
cBlanchard	1	0	0	0	0	0									
Totals	35	5	9	5	24	13	2		Totals	33	7	10	5	27	8	0

aWalked for Stottlemyre in 5th.   cStruck out for Mikkelsen in 9th.
bStruck out for Sheldon in 7th.

| NEW YORK (A) | 0 0 0 0 0 3 0 0 2—5 |
| ST. LOUIS (N) | 0 0 0 3 3 0 1 0 x—7 |

Double play—Groat, Maxvill and White; Shannon and Groat. Left on base—New York (A) 6, St. Louis (N) 6. Two base hit—White, K. Boyer. Home run—Brock, Mantle, K. Boyer, C. Boyer, Linz. Stolen base—Shannon, McCarver. Sacrifice—Maxvill. Sacrifice fly—McCarver.

PITCHING SUMMARY

	Ip	H	R	Er			Ip	H	R	Er
Stottlemyre (L)	4	5	3	3		Hamilton	1⅓	2	1	1
xDowning	0	3	3	3		Mikkelsen	2⅓	0	0	0
Sheldon	2	0	0	0		Gibson (W)	9	9	5	5
xFaced 3 men in fifth.										

Base on balls—Stottlemyre 2 (McCarver, Groat), Gibson 3 (Tresh 2 Hegan). Strike outs—Stottlemyre 2 (K. Boyer, Shannon), Sheldon 2 (Shannon, Maxvill), Hamilton 2 (Brock, White), Gibson 9 (B. Richardson, Mantle, Stottlemyre, Howard 2, C. Boyer, Lopez, Tresh, Blanchard).

Umpires—Secory (N) plate, McKinley (A) first base, Burkhart (N) second base, Soar (A) third base, V. Smith (N) left field, A. Smith (A) right field. Time—2:40. Attendance—30,346.

Berra Signs $40,000 Contract

YOGI IS DUE MONEY FROM YANKEES TOO

To Get Added $25,000; 'Not Bitter' Over Firing, He Says

New York, Nov. 17—Yogi Berra, a Yankee for eighteen years, joined his old boss Casey Stengel today as a coach for the New York Mets. If the 39-year-old ex-catcher can get in shape during spring training he will be a player-coach and pinch hitter.

Fired as Yankee manager the day after he lost the World Series to the St. Louis Cardinals, Berra will benefit by a rare salary arrangement. In addition to the reported $40,000 a year salary from the Mets he will get an additional $25,000 from the Yankees.

Berra said when the Yanks hired him as special field consultant after firing him as manager, that the contract contained an escape clause that gave him permission to take any other offer and still get the $25,000.

Berra "Not Bitter"

"I'm not bitter," said Berra in answer to a question at a mammoth news conference at Shea Stadium. "I had eighteen fine years over there. They took me off the sandlots in St. Louis when the Cardinals and Browns didn't want to sign me.

"They said they wanted to make a change. I had no idea they weren't going to hire me as manager again."

Did Berra want to manage again?

"I don't know," he said. "I worked for Casey for twelve years and I know I can learn a lot more from him. I might "

Houston Hopes to Spray Glare Away

Astrodome Gets Paint Test

HOUSTON, April 20 (AP) — Painters began Tuesday spraying a thin coat of paint on the 4,596 plastic skylights on the $31.6 million Houston Astrodome.

Houston Astros officials hope this will eliminate a glare that forced outfielders to wear batting helmets the only times they attempted to play baseball in the indoor stadium in daylight.

Examination of the first few panels painted indicated success.

A bright sun glared through adjacent unpainted skylights but none appeared to penetrate the painted sections. The painting job will take three days.

The final test will come Friday and Saturday when the Astros work out prior to night games with Pittsburgh.

Roy Hofheinz, president of the Astros, said he believes the Sunday game between Houston and Pittsburgh will be played under ideal conditions.

At least part of the stadium's lights will have to be used because Hofheinz said engineers have estimated the paint coating will reduce the normal level of natural light by 25 to 40 per cent.

Wantz, Angel Pitcher, Dies After Surgery

INGLEWOOD, Calif., May 14 (AP)—Dick Wantz, a relief pitcher for the Los Angeles Angels, died at Daniel Freeman Hospital last night after surgery for a brain tumor.

Wantz, 25 years old, was a 6-foot-5-inch, 190-pound right-hander. He had appeared in only one game this season. He began experiencing severe headaches during a late April series between the Angels and Yankees in New York. When the club moved to Detroit he was hospitalized there for a few days.

He flew here last week and reportedly was feeling much better. But last weekend he was hospitalized, given a spinal tap and X-rays, and the tumor was found.

Wantz lived in nearby Artesia. His wife and a young son survive.

June 9

Baseball Draft Selections

1. Kansas City—Rick Monday, 19-year-old sophomore from Arizona State bats lefthanded. Hit .371 during regular college season.
2. New York Mets—Leslie Rohr, 19, lefthanded pitcher from Billings, Mont. High School. 6-5, 200 pounds.
3. Washington—Joe Coleman, Jr., 17, right-handed pitcher from Natick (Mass.) High School. 6-3, 165 pounds.
4. Houston—Alex Barrett, 18, right-handed shortstop from Atwater High School, Winston, Cal. 6-0, 175 pounds.
5. Boston — Bill Conigliaro, 17, right-handed outfielder-pitcher from Swampscott (Mass.) High School. 6-0, 175 pounds.
6. Chicago Cubs — Richard James, 17, right-handed pitcher from Coffee High School, Florence, Ala. 6-0, 200 pounds.
7. Cleveland—Raymond Fosse, 18, right-handed catcher from Marion (Ill.) High School. 6-3, 210 pounds.
8. Los Angeles Dodgers—John Scott Wyatt, 17, right-handed shortstop from Bakersfield (Cal.) High School. 6-2, 200 pounds.
9. Minnesota—Ed Leon, 18, right-handed shortstop from University of Arizona; home, Tucson, Ariz., 5-11, 165 pounds.
10. Pittsburgh—Douglas Dickerson, 17, outfielder from Ensley High School, Birmingham, Ala., 6-1, 185 pounds.
11. Los Angeles Angels—James Spencer, 17, first baseman from Andover High School, Linthicum, Md., 6-0, 190 pounds.
12. Milwaukee—William Grant, first baseman from Watertown High School, Swampscott, Mass. 6-4, 205 pounds.
13. Detroit — William Lamont, 18, catcher from Hiawatha High School, Kirkland, Ill. 6-1, 190 pounds.
14. San Francisco—Alan Gallagher, 19, third baseman from Santa Clara University and Daly City, Cal., 6-0, 182 pounds.
15. Orioles — Scott McDonald, 18, right-handed pitcher from Marquette High School, Yakima, Wash., 6-1, 195 pounds.
16. Cincinnati—Bernardo Carbo, 17, third baseman from Livonia High School, Garden City, Mich., 5-11, 170 pounds.
17. Chicago White Sox—Kenneth Plesha, 19, catcher from Notre Dame University from McCook, Ill., 5-11, 185 pounds.
18. Philadelphia — John Michael Adamson, 18, right-handed pitcher from Point Loma High School, San Diego, Cal., 6-2, 185 pounds.
19. New York Yankees—William Burbach, 17, right-handed pitcher from Wahlert High School, Dubuque, Iowa; hometown, Dickeyville, Wis., 6-4, 195 pounds.
20. St. Louis—Joe Di Fabio, 21, right-handed pitcher from Delta State College and Crawford, N.J., 5-11, and 195 pounds.

SANTO'S INFIELD BLOW OFF VERSALLES' GLOVE DRIVES MAYS ACROSS

Willie, Torre, Stargell Blast Winners' Circuits; McAuliffe and Killebrew Connect For Americans; Koufax Gets Victory

BY JIM ELLIOT
(Sun Staff Correspondent)

Minneapolis-St. Paul, July 13—Ron Santo's high-bouncing infield single scored the winning run in the seventh inning here today, breaking up a home-run duel as the National League edged the American League, 6 to 5, in the thirty-sixth All-Star baseball game.

The scratch safety off shortstop Zoilo Versalles's glove by the Chicago Cubs' third baseman deprived the American Leaguers of a shot at an underdog victory as they overcame a 5-to-0 lead gained by the National League over the first two innings.

Nationals Lead Series

The triumph, which went to Los Angeles Dodger southpaw Sandy Koufax who was the pitcher of record when the winning run scored, enabled the National League to take the lead in All-Star play for the first time since the mid-season classic began in 1933.

The series now stands at 18-17, Nationals, with one tie.

Maloney Hurls 10-Inning No-Hitter But Loses, 1-0

LEWIS HITS HOMER FOR METS IN 11TH

18 Struck Out By Cincinnati's 25-Year-Old Righthander

Cincinnati, June 14 (AP)—Cincinnati's Jim Maloney pitched a no-hitter for 10 innings but gave up a lead-off home run to Johnny Lewis in the eleventh inning and wound up with a two-hitter as the New York Mets edged the Reds, 1 to 0, tonight.

Maloney, whose feat goes into the record books as a 10-inning no-hitter, allowed only two baserunners and struck out 18 before going into the eleventh.

Ties Strikeout Record

The eighteen strikeouts tied the National League record for strikeonts in an extra-inning game.

Warren Spahn, now with the Mets, reached that figure against Chicago in fifteen innings in 1952.

The fastballing Maloney, who pitched the third one-hitter of his six-year career in his first start this season, worked the count to 2-1 on Lewis, whom he already had fanned three times.

Lewis, however, swung at the next pitch and drove the ball against the upper part of the center field wall for a home run.

McMillan Singles

Maloney then struck out Ron Swoboda for his eighteenth, but Roy McMillan followed with a single to center field. Maloney ended the inning by getting Jesse Conder to hit into a double play.

New York's Larry Bearnarth, who relieved starter Frank Lary in the ninth, got Pete Rose on a fly ball, leading off the Red's 11th and struck out Vade Pinson.

Frank Robinson then singled to center field for Cincinnati's seventh hit, but Gordie Coleman grounded out, ending the game and ending the Mets' 10-game losing streak

STENGEL'S HIP HURT IN FALL

Casey Injured In Fall, Surgery Slated

New York, July 25 (AP) — Casey Stengel, manager of the New York Mets, suffered a fractured left hip in a fall early today on the eve of his 75th birthday party and must undergo surgery.

Stengel was reported in very satisfactory condition at Roosevelt Hospital, but a hospital spokesman said he was in extreme pain and under heavy sedation.

Reporters were not allowed to see him.

Hurt In Fall

His wife, Edna, is scheduled to fly to his side Monday from their home in Glendale, Calif.

Dr. Peter La Motte, the Mets' team physician, said Stengel suffered the injury in a fall getting out of a friend's car early today but was not aware of the seriousness of the injury until he awoke this morning.

Dr. La Motte said that because of Stengel's age the surgery must be considered serious.

Stengel will be 75 Friday, but a celebration for the gnarled old Perfesser was scheduled today between games of a Met doubleheader at Shea Stadium.

Angels Top A's in 13th; Campaneris in 9 Positions

KANSAS CITY, Sept. 8 (AP) —Bert Campaneris of Kansas City played all nine positions tonight, but the California Angels spoiled the feat by beating the Athletics, 5-3, with the help of pitcher John O'Donoghue's wild throw in the 13th inning.

CALIFORNIA (A.)	ab	r	h	bi
Cardenal, cf	6	0	0	1
Pearson, lf	5	2	1	0
Fregosi, ss	5	1	1	0
Adcock, 1b	4	0	2	2
Lopez, pr	0	0	0	0
Power, 1b	0	0	0	0
Smith, ph	1	0	0	0
Dees, 1b	1	0	0	0
Knoop, 2b	3	1	1	0
Kirkpatrick, rf	5	0	2	0
Egan, c	2	0	0	0
Rodgers, c	2	1	0	0
Schaal, 3b	5	0	1	0
Chance, p	4	0	0	0
Lee, p	1	0	0	0
Ranew, ph	1	0	0	0
Totals	45	5	8	3

KANSAS CITY (A.)	ab	r	h	bi
Campaneris, ss, 2b, 3b, lf, cf, rf, 1b, c, p	3	1	0	0
Lachemann, c	2	0	2	0
Tartabull, cf, rf	4	0	0	0
Causey, 2b, ss	5	1	2	0
Charles, 3b, 2b	6	0	1	1
Landis, cf, rf	5	1	1	0
Bryan, c	3	0	1	0
Harrelson, ph	1	0	1	1
Talbot, pr	0	0	0	0
Reynolds, ph	1	0	0	0
Blanchard, ph	1	0	0	0
Schwartz, 1b	2	0	0	0
Hershberger, rf	0	0	0	0
Stahl, rf	3	0	0	0
Clinton, rf	1	0	0	0
Green, 2b	4	0	1	1
Joyce, p	2	0	0	0
Rosario, 1b	3	0	0	0
Totals	46	3	9	3

California	000	000	101	000	2—5
Kansas City	100	000	002	000	0—3

E—Campaneris, Causey, O'Donoghue. DP—Kansas City 1. LOB—California 12, Kansas City 10.

2B—Charles, Adcock, Bryan. SB Campaneris, Kirkpatrick, Tartabull. S—Tartabull, Kirkpatrick. SF—Cardenal.

	IP	H.	R.	ER.	BB.	SO.
Chance	8⅓	5	3	3	2	6
Lee (W, 9-6)	3⅔	4	0	0	3	1
Coates		0	0	0	0	0
*Joyce	6	5	2	1	1	2
Mossi	⅓	0	0	0	0	0
Dickson	⅔	0	0	0	1	1
Campaneris	1	1	1	1	2	1
Monteagudo	1	1	0	0	1	1
Wyatt	2	1	0	0	2	0
**O'Donoghue (L, 8-18)	1	0	2	0	1	0
Segui	1	0	0	0	1	0

*Faced one batter in 7th.
**Faced three batters in 13th.

REDS' ACE FANS 12 IN 1-TO-0 VICTORY

Walks 10 Before Cardenas's Homer Wins Opener—Cubs Take Second Game, 5-4

CHICAGO, Aug. 19 (AP)—Jim Maloney of the Cincinnati Reds pitched the first major league no-hitter of the season today, beating the Chicago Cubs, 1-0, in 10 innings.

The Cubs, however, won the second game of the doubleheader at Wrigley Field, 5-4, on Don Landrum's two-out two-run homer off Billy McCool in the ninth inning.

Leo Cardenas's home run broke up Larry Jackson's pitching duel with Maloney in the opener and brought the 25-year-old right-hander his first no-hit victory.

Maloney pitched 10 innings of no-hit ball against the New York Mets on June 14, but lost when Johnny Lewis hit a homer for the Mets in the 11th. Maloney is the first major leaguer to hurl two extra-inning no-hitters.

Relying mainly on a blazing fast ball and a sharp-breaking curve, Maloney struck out 12 Cubs and issued 10 bases on balls. He also hit one batter with a pitched ball.

2 Balls to the Outfield

Maloney did not allow a ball to be hit out of the infield until Doug Clemens flied to the center fielder, Vada Pinson, in the eighth. Jimmie Stewart also flied to Pinson in the ninth.

Maloney filled the bases with three walks in the third inning, but got out of the jam by getting Billy Williams to bounce out to Pete Rose.

The Cubs threatened again in the eighth and ninth.

Jackson walked to open the eighth, advanced to second on a sacrifice and moved to third on Clemens's fly. Maloney then struck out Ernie Banks after walking Williams intentionally.

The Cubs filled the bases in the ninth on two walks and a hit batter, but Landrum popped to Cardenas to end that threat.

Three One-Hitters

Maloney, who registered his 14th victory against six losses, had pitched one-hitters in each of the last three years including one April 19 this year against the Milwaukee Braves.

The 10 walks by Maloney were the most ever issued in a no-hitter. The 6-foot-2-inch 200-pounder from Fresno, Calif., threw 187 pitches. He had a three-ball count on 15 batters.

Maloney said he wasn't as sharp as when he lost his no-hitter to the Mets, but added:

"I think this was the biggest game of my career. I knew I had the no-hitter going all the way, and I felt good all the way."

FIRST GAME

CINCINNATI (N.)	ab.	r.	h.	bi
Harper, lf	5	0	1	0
Rose, 2b	5	0	1	0
Pinson, cf	3	0	2	0
Robinson, rf	4	0	2	0
Coleman, 1b	4	0	0	0
Keough, 1b	0	0	0	0
Johnson, 3b	4	0	0	0
Edwards, c	4	0	0	0
Cardenas, ss	4	1	1	1
Maloney, p	4	0	2	0
Totals	37	1	9	1

CHICAGO (N.)	ab.	r.	h.	bi
Landrum, cf	4	0	0	0
Clemens, lf	3	0	0	0
Williams, rf	4	0	0	0
Banks, 1b	5	0	0	0
Santo, 3b	3	0	0	0
Bailey, c	2	0	0	0
Beckert, 2b	2	0	0	0
Kessinger, ss	2	0	0	0
Stewart, ss	1	0	0	0
Jackson, p	2	0	0	0
Totals	28	0	0	0

Cincinnati	000	000	000	1 1
Chicago	000	000	000	0-0

E—Banks. DP—Cincinnati 1, Chicago 1. LOB—Cincinnati 7, Chicago 10.

3B—Robinson. HR—Cardenas (9). S—Pinson, Landrum.

	IP	H	R	ER.	BB	SO
Maloney (W 14-6)	10	0	0	0	10	12
Jackson (L. 11-15)	10	9	1	1	0	5

HBP—By Maloney, Santo. T 2:51

Mays Homers As Giants Top Mets by 8-3

17th Circuit Sock Breaks Old Mark Of Ralph Kiner

NEW YORK, Aug. 29 (AP) — Willie Mays slammed a three-run homer, his 41st of the season and a record-breaking 17th in one month, as the San Francisco Giants defeated the New York Mets 8-3 Sunday.

The victory moved the Giants to within 1 and a half games of the National League leading Los Angeles Dodgers, who lost to Philadelphia 13-3.

Mays' homer off starter Jack Fisher climaxed a five-run out-burst in the third inning.

The blow set the league record for homers in a month. Ralph Kiner hit 16 with Pittsburgh in September, 1949. Rudy York of Detroit holds the major league mark of 18.

The homer also was the 494th of Mays' career, putting him alone in fifth place on the all-time list. He had been tied with Lou Gehrig.

SAN FRANCISCO	AB	R	H
M Alou.rf	4	0	1
G'b'lels'n.lf	4	2	1
Mays.cf	5	1	2
McCovey.1b	2	0	0
H'nd'rs n.rf	2	1	1
Hart.3b	3	1	1
Haller.c	2	0	0
Lanier.2b	4	1	2
Fuentes.ss	4	1	1
Bolin.p	2	1	1
Sch'field.ph	1	0	0
M'rak'mi.p	1	0	0
Totals	34	8	10

NEW YORK	AB	R	H
Hunt.2b	3	1	0
Lewis.cf	5	1	1
Kranep'l.1b	5	0	2
Smith.3b	4	0	1
Ch'st'p'r.rf	4	1	2
Steph'a'n.c	2	0	0
Sch'fer.c	1	0	0
Swoboda.lf	3	0	0
M'Millan.ss	4	0	1
Fisher.p	0	0	0
Rich'a'n.p	1	0	0
Hillere.ph	1	0	0
Hchman.ph	1	0	0
Totals	34	3	7

San Francisco	005	000	030—8
New York	000	020	010—3

E—McMillan. DP New York 1. LOB—San Francisco 4. New York 9.

RBI San Francisco: Gabrielson, Mays 3, Hart, Lanier, Bolin. New York: Kranepool, Smith, Christopher. 2B Lanier, Hart, Kranepool, Christopher. HR—Mays (41st), Christopher (5th).

SAN FRANCISCO—PITCHING

	IP	H	R	ER	BB	SO
Bolin (W. 8-4)	6	6	2	2	3	6
Murakami	3	1	1	1	1	6

NEW YORK—PITCHING

	IP	H	R	ER	BB	SO
Fisher (L. 8-17)	2⅓	5	5	5	2	0
Richardson	2⅔	0	0	0	0	3
Moorhead	1	0	0	0	2	1
Eilers	2	4	3	2	1	1
Bethke	1	1	0	0	0	0

HBP By Bolin Hunt. PB Stephenson 2. T 2:47. A 46,033.

Giants Beat Dodgers, 4-3, In Brawl-Spiced Contest

BAT-SWINGING GIANTS—San Francisco shortstop Tito Fuentes (26) swings a bat in defense of Juan Marichal (27) in third-inning rhubarb. Dodger pitcher Sandy Koufax holds catcher John Roseboro after Marichal hit Roseboro with bat.

PITCHER WILL MISS TWO STARTS

Punishment Is Highest Levied By A Loop President

New York, Aug. 23 (AP)—Juan Marichal, ace right-hander for San Francisco's pennant-contend-ing Giants, was suspended today for eight playing days and tagged with a $1,750 fine—the highest ever levied by a league president—for hitting Los Angeles catcher John Roseboro over the head with a bat in a game at San Francisco yesterday.

The announcement of Marichal's record fine and lengthy suspension—the nineteen-game winner figures to miss two pitching turns — was made by National League president Warren Giles at league headquarters in Cincinnati.

Calling Marichal's bat-swinging episode "unprovoked," "obnoxious" and "repugnant," Giles directed that the fine be paid by Marichal or deducted from his salary if the money is advanced to him by the club.

MAYS'S 38TH HOMER GIVES KOUFAX LOSS

Marichal Ejected After Slugging Roseboro With Bat

San Francisco, Aug. 22 (AP)—Willie Mays hit his sixth homer in six games, a three-run shot in the third inning, that carried San Francisco to a 4 to 3 victory over National League leading Los Angeles and Sandy Koufax today minutes after a free-for-all fight erupted.

The Giants' victory further tightened the pennant battle with San Francisco moving into second place one percentage point behind the front-running Dodgers. Milwaukee, beaten by Pittsburgh, dropped into third but is only two percentage points off the pace.

Koufax 21 and 5

Koufax, who lost his first game since July 28 and is 21-5, was pitching to San Francisco's 19-game winner, Juan Marichal, when the fight started.

Marichal, the lead-off batter in the inning, turned and hit Dodger catcher John Roseboro over the head with his bat after Roseboro had returned a pitch to the mound close to Marichal's head.

A free-for-all broke out and lasted 14 minutes. Roseboro left the game bleeding from a cut over his left eyebrow while Marichal was ejected.

Koufax, leading 2-1, went back to work and retired two Giants before running into control difficulty. He walked Jim Davenport and Willie McCovey, and then Mays smashed a fast ball over the left center-field fence.

It was Mays's thirty-eighth homer of the season and his fourteenth this month.

Peterson Homers

Cap Peterson hit a bases-empty homer in the second for the Giants' first run, his third homer of the season and his second off Koufax.

Ron Herbel took over after Marichal was ejected and won his eighth game against six losses.

Maury Wills bunted for a hit leading off the first and went to second on a ground-out. Ron Fairly doubled Wills across.

Wes Parker hit a one-out double in the second and scored a single by Roseboro.

The Dodgers scored their final run in the ninth after Herbel hit Parker with a pitch and Jeff Torborg, Roseboro's replacement, singled. Masanori Murakami then relieved Herbel. Parker scored when Hal Lanier dropped Murakami's throw in an attempted force out at second on John LeJohn's grounder.

But Murakami bore down and got Wills on a pop-up and struck out Jim Gilliam on a called third strike.

LOS ANGELES					SAN FRANCISCO				
	ab	r	h	bi		ab	r	h	bi
Wills ss	5	1	1	0	Fuentes ss	1	0	0	0
Gilliam 3b	4	0	0	0	Davenport 2b	3	1	0	0
W Davis cf	4	0	1	0	McCovey 1b	3	1	0	0
Fairly rf	4	1	1	1	Mays cf	3	1	1	3
Lefebvre 2b	4	0	0	0	Hart lf	3	0	0	0
Johnson lf	4	0	2	0	Peterson rf	4	1	1	1
Parker 1b	3	2	1	0	M Alou rf	1	0	0	0
Roseboro c	3	0	1	1	Lanier 2b	3	0	1	0
Torborg c	1	0	1	0	Bertell c	3	0	0	0
Koufax p	3	0	0	0	Marichal p	0	0	0	0
LeJohn ph	1	0	0	1	Schroder ph	1	0	0	0
					Herbel p	0	0	0	0
Totals	36	3	8	3	**Totals**	28	4	4	4

```
Los Angeles          110 000 001—3
San Francisco        013 000 00x—4
  E Gilliam 2, Lanier. DP Los Angeles
1. LOB Los Angeles 8, San Francisco 5.
  2B Fairly, Parker. HR Peterson (3),
Mays (38). S Davenport.
```

	IP	H	R	ER	BB	SO
Koufax L 21-5	8	4	4	4	4	8
Marichal	⅓	0	1	2	0	0
Herbel W 8-6	8⅔	4	3	1	1	2
Murakami	⅓	0	0	0	0	1

```
  HBP By Herbel (Parker). WP Koufax.
T 2:18. A 42,807.
```

Koufax of Dodgers Hurls Perfect Game

By The Associated Press

LOS ANGELES, Sept. 9—Sandy Koufax of the Los Angeles Dodgers pitched a perfect game tonight in a 1-0 victory over the Chicago Cubs and became the first pitcher in baseball history to pitch four no-hitters in his career.

Outpitching Bob Hendley in a brilliant duel between left-handers, Koufax hurled his fourth no-hitter in four years and surpassed the record for multiple no-hitters held by Bob Feller, Cy Young and Larry Corcoran.

Hendley, who allowed only one hit, yielded a run in the fifth inning when the Dodgers scored without a hit. Lou Johnson walked to open the inning, was sacrificed to second, stole third and raced home when Chris Krug, the catcher, threw wild.

That was enough for the Dodgers, who remained half a game behind San Francisco in the National League pennant race.

The only hit off Hendley—and the only hit of the game—was Johnson's bloop double to right field with two out in the seventh inning.

Koufax, 29 years old, whose career was in jeopardy three years ago because of a circulatory ailment in his pitching hand, retired 27 Cubs in order.

Koufax Strikes Out 14

Koufax struck out 14, lifting his major-league-leading total to 332, as he posted the first perfect game in his 11-year career, the eighth in modern baseball history and only the third in National League annals. Jim Bunning of Philadelphia accomplished the feat last year.

Feller, the long-time Cleveland ace, pitched no-hitters in 1940, 1946 and 1951. Corcoran pitched three pre-1900 no-hitters for the Cubs, in 1880, 1882

and 1884. Young pitched his first no-hitter for Cleveland, which was then in the National League, in 1897, and pitched no-hitters for Boston of the American League in 1904 and 1908.

Koufax, bringing his won-lost record to 22-7, was overpowering with his assortment of fast balls and breaking stuff. He struck out the last six batters he faced and seven of the last nine.

In the eighth he faced two of the Cubs' hardest-hitting players, Ron Santo and Ernie Banks. He struck out both, then ended the inning by fanning Byron Browne, a rookie left fielder.

Tension Mounts

In the ninth as the tension mounted in the crowd of 29,139, Koufax fired a third strike past the young Cubs' catcher, Krug. A pinch-hitter, Joey Amalfitano, also went down swinging—on three pitches. Then it was up to another pinch-hitter, Harvey Kuenn, the former American League batting champion.

Kuenn also went down swinging—and Koufax had his first perfect game.

He also closed in on another of baseball's most spectacular achievements, Feller's strikeout record of 348 in one season. Koufax now is 16 shy of matching that feat.

There were no tough chances for the Dodger fielders as only seven batters hit the ball well enough to get it to the outfield.

The Box Score

CHICAGO (N.)					LOS ANGELES (N.)				
	ab	r	h	bi		ab	r	h	bi
Young, cf	3	0	0	0	Wills, ss	3	0	0	0
Beckert, 2b	3	0	0	0	Gilliam, 3b	3	0	0	0
Williams, rf	3	0	0	0	Kennedy, 3b	0	0	0	0
Santo, 3b	3	0	0	0	Davis, cf	3	0	0	0
Banks, 1b	3	0	0	0	Johnson, lf	2	1	1	0
Browne, lf	3	0	0	0	Fairly, rf	3	0	0	0
Krug, c	3	0	0	0	Lefebvre, 2b	3	0	0	0
Kessinger, ss	2	0	0	0	Tracewski, 2b	0	0	0	0
Amalfitano, ph	1	0	0	0	Parker, 1b	3	0	0	0
Hendley, p	2	0	0	0	Torborg, c	3	0	0	0
Kuenn, ph	1	0	0	0	Koufax, p	2	0	0	0
Totals	27	0	0	0	Totals	24	1	1	0

Chicago   000 000 000—0
Los Angeles   000 010 00x—1

E—Krug. LOB—Chicago 0, Los Angeles 1. 2B—Johnson. SB—Johnson. S—Fairly.

	IP	H	R	ER	BB	SO
Hendley (L, 2-3)	8	1	1	0	1	3
Koufax (W, 22-7)	9	0	0	0	0	14

T—1:43. A—29,139.

PHILS TRIM BRAVES, 4-1

812 See Culp's 10-Hitter Mean 7th Loss In Last 9

Milwaukee, Sept. 20 (AP)—The Philadelphia Phillies capitalized on Wade Blasingame's wildness for four runs in the first inning and beat the Milwaukee Braves, 4-to-1, before the smallest crowd in the city's 13-season National League history.

Only 812 watched the Braves, a strong pennant-contender a few days ago, lose for the seventh time in their last nine games. The club is slated to move to Atlanta next year.

AARON SLAMS TWO HOMERS TO PACE ROUT

	W.	L.	Pct.	G.B.
San Francisco	87	60	.592	....
Cincinnati	84	64	.568	3½
Los Angeles	84	64	.568	3½
Milwaukee	81	66	.551	6
Pittsburgh	80	70	.533	8½
Philadelphia	76	70	.521	10½
St. Louis	73	744	.497	14
Chicago	67	82	.450	21
Houston	61	88	.409	27
New York	47	102	.315	41

Milwaukee, Sept. 17 (AP) — The Milwaukee Braves snapped San Francisco's fourteen-game winning streak tonight, beating the National League-leading Giants and Juan Marichal, 9 to 1, with a ten-hit attack spiked by Hank Aaron's two home runs.

San Francisco's winning streak was the longest in the National League since 1951 when the Giants, then in New York, won sixteen straight en route to the pennant.

The fourth-place Braves, six games off the pace, racked losing pitcher Marichal for five runs and seven hits in the first 3 1-3 innings as they sent theGiants' ace down to his eleventh defeat.

Four Runs In 6th

Aaron did the heaviest damage with his ome runs, smacking is thirtieth—a solo shot—in the first inning and his thirty-first n singled.

Weak-hitting Woody Woodward drove in the other two runs off Marichal, doubling in a run in the second and singling in another in the fourth.

The Braves broke the game wide open in te sixth, scoring four runs on Frank Thomas's second double, two walks, singles by Billy O'Dell and Felipe Alou and Mathew's sacrifice fly.

The victory went to Phil Niekro in his first major league start. He needed relief help from O'Dell in the sixth inning when the Giants loaded the bases wth no one out.

O'Dell got out of te jam without a score, striking out Jack Hiatt and Hal Lanier and getting Orlando Cepeda to pop up.

SAN FRANCISCO					MILWAUKEE				
	ab	r	h	bi		ab	r	h	bi
Schofield, ss	5	0	1	0	f.alou, cf	4	0	1	2
J.Alou, rf	4	0	0	0		3	1	1	1
Mays, cf	4	0	2	0	Aaron, rf	4	2	2	3
Hend'son, cf	0	0	0	0	Carty, lf	3	0	0	0
McCovey, 1b	3	0	0	0	Cline, cf	1	0	0	0
Hart, 3b	2	1	0	0	Oliver, c	1	0	0	0
G'br'ls'n, lf	2	0	1	0	Thomas, 1b	4	2	2	0
Hiatt, c	1	0	0	0	Bolling, 2b	3	2	1	0
Barton, c	1	0	0	0	Wood'rd, ss	3	1	2	2
Haller, c	2	0	0	0	Niekro, p	2	0	0	0
Cepeda, ph	1	0	0	0	O'Dell, p	2	1	1	1
Brown, rf	1	0	1	0					
Lanier, 2b	3	0	1	1					
Peterson, ph	1	0	0	0					
Marichal, p	1	0	0	0					
Perry, p	1	0	1	0					
Daven'p't, 2b	2	0	1	0					
Totals	34	1	8	1	Totals	33	9	10	9

San Francisco   010 000 000—1
Milwaukee   112 104 00x—9

E—None. LOB—San Francisco 9, Milwaukee 3. 2B—Davenport, Brown, Thomas 2. Woodward, Bolling. HR—Aaron 2 (31). SF—mathews.

	IP	H	R	ER	BB	SO
Marichal (L, 22-11)	3 1-3	7	5	5	0	3
Perry	2	2	4	4	2	3
Priddy	2 2-3	1	0	0	0	3
Niekro (W, 2-3)	5	5	1	1	0	4
O'Dell	4	3	0	0	0	4

Niekro faced 3 men in 6th.
PB—Oliver 2 T—2:50. A—6,924.

Satch Hurls Well But A's Lose

Kansas City, Sept. 25 (AP)—The Boston Red Sox were able to collect only one hit in three innings off 60-year-old Satchel Paige but went on to a 5 to 2 victory over Kansas City tonight behind homers by Lee Thomas and Tony Conigliaro.

Paige, undoubtedly the oldest player ever to play in a major league game, started the game for the A's and allowed only a first inning double by Carl Yastrzemski.

The Negro right-hander retired the last seven men he faced in order and then, after taking his warmup pitches at the start of the fourth inning, was replaced by Diego Segui.

Paige was making a return to the majors after a 12-year absence. When he left the lights in the stadium were turned off, matches were lit and the 10,000 in the stands sang a salute.

BOSTON					KANSAS CITY				
	ab	r	h	bi		ab	r	h	bi
Gosger, cf	4	1	1	0	C'panris, ss	4	0	0	0
Jones, 3b	3	0	0	0	Tartabull, cf	4	1	1	0
Malsone, 3b	1	0	0	0	Causey, 2b	3	0	0	0
Yastr'ski, lf	4	1	2	0	Bryan, c	4	0	0	0
C'nigl'ro, rf	3	2	2	2	Green, 2b	4	0	2	1
Thomas, 1b	3	1	1	3	Rosario, 1b	4	0	1	0
Mantilla, 2b	4	0	1	0	H'berger, cf	3	0	0	0
Bressoud, ss	4	0	0	0	Reynolds, lf	3	0	0	0
Ryan, c	4	0	0	0	Paige, p	1	0	0	0
M'b'q'tte, p	4	0	0	0	Segui, p	1	0	0	0
					lahl, ph	1	0	0	0
Totals	34	5	7	4	Totals	32	2	7	2

Boston   000 000 230—5
Kansas City   100 001 000—2

E—Rosario. DP—Boston 1. LOB—Boston 4, Kansas City 4. 2B—Yastrzemski. HR—Thomas, Conigliaro (31).

	IP	H	R	ER	BB	SO
M'b'q'tte (W, 10-18)	9	7	2	2	1	5
Paige	3	1	0	0	0	1
Segui	4	3	2	2	1	4
Mossi (L, 5-7)	1 1-3	1	1	1	1	0
Wyatt	1 1-3	2	2	2	1	1
Aker	1 1-3	0	0	0	0	1

WP—Segui. PB—Bryan 2. T—2:14. A—9,289.

Oct. 2

National League

Standings Of The Teams

	W	L	Pct	G B
Los Angeles	96	65	.596	....
San Francisco	94	67	.584	2
Cincinnati	89	72	.553	7
Pittsburgh	89	72	.553	7
Milwaukee	86	75	.534	10
Philadelphia	83	76	.522	12
St. Louis	79	81	.494	16½
Chicago	72	89	.447	24
Houston	65	96	.404	31
New York	50	110	.313	45½

Koufax Proud, Exhausted In Finest Hour Of Career

Los Angeles, Oct. 2 (AP)—"I feel like I'm 100 years old."

A weary, perspiring, grey-faced Sandy Koufax, speaking just a decibel above a whisper, confided that he had reached the end of his endurance when he retired Dennis Menke, of Milwaukee, for the last out in the ninth inning today.

The putout by left fielder Lou Johnson gave Koufax and the Dodgers a 3-to-1 victory and the National League championship.

Record 382 Whiffs

The brilliant southpaw, too spent to take off his sweat-stained uniform, sat alone in the tiny four-by-eight kitchenette alongside the commissary, where the rest of the Dodgers were celebrating their triumph by dowsing each other with champagne.

"I'm tired, very tired," he murmured. "I don't remember ever being so tired in my life. I don't believe I could have gone on any longer."

The handsome native of Brooklyn had just pitched his twenty-sixth triumph, a four-hitter over the Braves, in which he fanned thirteen to raise his season total to a record 382.

GIANTS TOP REDS, 3-2, LOSE TITLE

San Francisco's Flag Dreams Waft Away On Dodger Win

San Francisco, Oct. 2 (AP)—The San Francisco Giants were eliminated from the National League pennant race today, after hanging on to a slim chance for a tie by edging Cincinnati, 3 to 2, as Willie Mays and Jim Hart rapped key hits in a three-run sixth-inning uprising.

The Giants, however, lost their last opportunity for a tie when the Los Angeles Dodgers defeated Milwaukee, 3-1, and won their third pennant in the last seven years. The Dodgers will meet the American League champion Minnesota Twins in the World Series starting Wednesday.

RICKEY DIES AT AGE 83

Baseball Genius Had Collapsed On November 13

Columbia, Mo., Dec. 9 (AP)—Branch Rickey, a baseball front office genius who master-minded the St. Louis Cardinals to seven national league pennants and five world championships, and the old Brooklyn Dodgers to two pennants, died today. He was 83.

Boone County Hospital reported Rickey died at 10 P.M., a few minutes after Mrs. Rickey and one of their five daughters, had left the hospital after a day-long vigil in the intensive care ward.

Rickey, who had a shrewd ability for picking winning baseball talent, had collapsed November 13 of what doctors termed "an irregularity of the heart."

He had stood to accept membership in the Missouri Sports Hall of Fame, and was reminiscing. "I'm going to tell you a story from the Bible about spiritual courage," when he dropped into his chair, then to the floor.

Rickey was administered oxygen and rushed to a hospital here. He had suffered two known previous heart attacks, in 1958 and 1961.

REDS DROP TO 4TH SPOT

San Francisco Hero Tops Mize Mark Of 1947

San Francisco, Oct. 2 (AP)—Willie Mays set a season high for the Giants by hitting his fifty-second homer today as second-place San Francisco dropped Cincinnati into fourth place in the National League by beating the Reds, 6 to 3.

Mays was taken out of the game immediately after the fourth-inning blast over the left-field fence off Reds's starter and loser Bill McCool. Mays had shared the season record with Johnny Mize, who hit 51 in 1947.

Ken Henderson, the 19-year-old rookie who the Giants believe eventually will take Mays's place in center field, got the last hit off McCool, a two-run single that capped the winning three-run rally in the seventh inning. The hit brought in scorer Dom Zanni.

CINCINNATI	ab	r	h	bi	SAN FRANCISCO	ab	r	h	bi
Harper lf	5	1	0	0	Fuentes ss	4	1	0	0
Rose 2b	1	0	0	0	McCovey 1b	2	0	0	0
Helms 2b	4	0	0	0	Lanier 1b	1	0	0	0
Pinson cf	4	0	1	0	Burda 1b	1	0	0	0
Robison rf	3	0	1	1	Mays cf	3	1	1	1
Johnson 3b	4	1	1	0	Hend'son cf	2	0	1	2
Pavletich c	3	0	1	0	Hart lf	4	2	3	0
Perez 1b	3	0	0	0	J Alou rf	1	0	1	0
Cardenas ss	1	1	1	1	Alou rf	2	0	0	0
Shamsky rf	2	0	0	0	Davenp'rt 3b	4	0	0	0
McCool p	2	0	0	0	Lanier 2b	4	0	1	1
Edwards ph	1	0	1	0	Barton c	4	1	3	1
					Estelle p	1	0	0	0
					Bolin p	3	1	1	0
Totals	33	3	6	2	Totals	35	6	11	5

Cincinnati .... 010 200 000—3
San Francisco ...... 010 200 30x—6
E—Fuentes 2, Johnson. DP—Cincinnati 1. LOB—Cincinnati 11, San Francisco 7. 3B—Lanier, Hart, Cardenas. HR—Mays (52). SF—Cardenas.

	IP	H	R	ER	BB	SO
McCool L.9-10	6	10	6	5	1	4
Zanni	1	0	0	0	0	1
Davidson	1	0	0	0	0	0
Estelle	3 2-3	5	3	1	6	1
Bolin W.1-6	5 1-3	1	0	0	1	9

McCool faced 5 men in 7th. HBP—By McCool, J. Alou. WP—Estelle. T—2:47. A—39,489.

Dec. 10

OFFICIALS HERE ARE JUBILANT

Outfield Slugger Hit 33 Home Runs Last Season

By JIM ELLIOT

"Cannons at the four corners!" an excited Harry Dalton shouted upon completion of a major four-player trade yesterday which brought slugger Frank Robinson to the Orioles from the Cincinnati Reds in exchange for veteran pitcher Milt Pappas, newly-acquired outfielder Dick Simpson and reliefer Jack Baldschun.

It appeared that the dam had burst at Memorial Stadium at 4.30 P.M. yesterday when the Orioles finalized with Cincinnati's Bill DeWitt the deal which provided the Orioles with that truly outstanding star that they had sought unsuccessfully for twelve years.

Gathered in Lee MacPhail's office, which will be turned over to director of player personnel Dalton in five days, were Dalton, outgoing president MacPhail, executive vice president Frank Cashen, vice president Jack Dunn and publicity director Bob Brown, and they all seemed to leap at once.

Dalton's First Deal

This was the first trade to be negotiated by Dalton, appointed to his new position only on Tuesday, and the former director of the Oriole farm system bubbled over with joy.

Frank Robinson, 30 years old, has been one of major-league baseball's great stars since 1956 when the native of Beaumont, Texas, was the unanimous choice for "National League Rookie of the Year" honors.

In 1956, the righthanded Robinson, 6-foot-1 and 187 pounds, slammed 38 home runs which is still the all-time big-league record for a first-year player.

Most Valuable In 1961

And since that year, Robinson in many respects has even bettered his starting performance as he went on to be the "Sophomore of the Year for 1957", made most All-Star teams and capped a sparkling 1961 campaign by being voted the "Most Valuable Player in the National League" while leading Cincinnati to the pennant.

Robinson hasn't slackened his pace since 1956, and last year crashed 33 homers and drove in 113 runs while batting .296 for the Reds, from whose farm system he originally graduated.

PIRATES WIN, FINISH THIRD

Pittsburgh Tops Chicago, 6-3. Passes Cincinnati

Pittsburgh, Oct. 3 ℗—Jim Pagliaroni's two-run, pinch-hit single highlighted a four-run, eighth-inning rally that carried Pittsburgh to a 6-to-3 triumph over the Chicago Cubs today.

The victory, their eleventh in the final thirteen games, vaulted the Pirates into third place in the National League, one game ahead of the Cincinnati Reds, who lost to San Francisco, 6 to 3.

Ron Santo's two-run double in the eighth inning put the Cubs ahead 3-2, but the Pirates rallied in their eighth, starting with Gene Alley's single against Ted Abernathy, making a major league record eighty-third appearance of the season.

Cubs Make Triple Play

After Manny Mota singled, Billy Hoeft replaced Abernathy and gave up a double to Bob Bailey that tied the game. Pagliaroni followed with his two-run single against Lindy McDaniel, and Willie Stargell climaxed the rally with a run-scoring double.

The Cubs tied a major league record when they pulled a triple play, their third of the season.

Like the first two, Bill Faul was pitching for the Cubs.

The play came in the fifth inning after the Pirates had scored a run and had Bill Mazeroski at second and Gene Alley at third.

Del Crandall lined a Faul pitch to first baseman Ernie Banks, who stepped on first for the second out and fired to shortstop Don Kessinger, who completed the triple play by stepping on second, retiring Mazeroski.

CHICAGO	ab	r	h	bi	PITTSBURGH	ab	r	h	bi
Land'm cf	4	1	1	0	B.Bailey 3b	4	1	1	0
Beckert 2b	4	0	1	0	Virdon cf	3	0	0	0
W.l'iams rf	3	2	1	0	Pagl'oni ph	1	0	1	2
Santo 3b	4	0	2	3	Oliver lf	4	0	0	0
Banks 1b	3	0	0	0	Clem'te rf	4	1	2	1
Stewart lf	4	0	1	0	Stargell lf	4	1	1	0
R.novs'y c	4	0	2	0	Clendenon 1b	4	1	1	0
Kes'ger ss	3	0	0	0	Maz'ski 2b	3	0	1	0
Clemens ph	1	0	0	0	Alley ss	3	1	2	1
Faul p	2	0	0	0	Crandall c	2	0	0	0
E.Bailey ph	1	0	0	0	Mota ph	1	0	1	0
Altman ph	1	0	0	0	Spriggs pr	0	0	0	0
					May c	2	0	0	0
					Sisk p	2	0	0	0
					Lynch ph	1	0	0	0
					Rodgers ph	1	0	0	0
Totals	34	3	8	3	Totals	32	6	10	6

Chicago .... 000 100 020—3
Pittsburgh .... 000 010 14x—6

E—Mazeroski, Clendenon. DP—Pittsburgh 1. Triple Play—Chicago 1. LOB—Chicago 6, Pittsburgh 2.
2B—Williams, Beckert, Santo, B Bailey, Stargell. HR—Clemente (10).

	IP	H	R	ER	BB	SO
Faul	7	5	2	2	0	2
Abernathy L.4-6	0	2	2	2	0	0
Hoeft	1-3	1	1	1	0	0
McDaniel	2-3	1	1	1	0	3
Sisk	7 2-3	8	3	2	0	3
Face W.5-2	1-3	0	0	0	1	0
McBean	1	0	0	0	0	1

WP—Sisk. McDaniel. T—2:15. A—26,527.

Yankees Defeat Red Sox, 6 To 4

Boston, Oct. 2 ℗—Mel Stottlemyre became the American League's second 20-game winner today, scattering eight hits as the Yankees trimmed Boston 6 to 4. The victory kept the Yankees one game ahead of seventh-place California.

Stottlemyre, who has lost nine times, gained the victory after he halted a sixth-inning Boston rally by getting Dalton Jones to hit into a force out with the bases loaded.

Tom Tresh singled across two Yankee runs in the first inning, and Hector Lopez belted a two-run homer in the sixth.

NEW YORK	ab	r	h	bi	BOSTON	ab	r	h	bi
Rich'son 2b	5	1	2	1	Schilling 2b	2	0	0	0
White cf	4	1	2	1	Mantilla 2b	3	0	0	0
Tresh lf	3	0	1	2	Jones 3b	5	1	2	0
Howard c	3	0	0	0	Yastrski lf	4	0	0	0
Boyer 3b	3	1	0	0	Cnigl'ro cf	4	0	0	0
H.Lopez rf	4	2	2	2	Thomas 1b	4	2	1	0
Repoz cf	1	0	0	0	Gosger cf	3	0	0	0
Barker 1b	4	0	0	0	Bressoud ss	4	1	2	1
Linz ss	3	1	1	0	Ryan c	3	0	0	0
Kubek ss	1	0	0	0	Bennett p	1	0	0	0
St'l'm're p	4	0	1	0	Green ph	0	0	0	0
					Nixon ph	1	0	1	0
					Wilson pr	0	0	0	0
Totals	35	6	9	6	Totals	33	4	8	4

New York .... 210 002 100—6
Boston .... 101 002 000—4

E—Jones, Bressoud. DP—New York 2. LOB—New York 4, Boston 8.
2B—White, H.Lopez, Richardson, Linz, Bressoud 2. HR—H.Lopez (7), Jones (5). SB—White.

	IP	H	R	ER	BB	SO
St'l'm're W.20-9	9	8	4	4	6	3
Bennett L.5-7	6	7	5	3	1	4
Radatz	3	2	1	1	1	2

T—2:20. A—4,300.

Yanks And Ford Beat Bosox, 11-5

Boston, Oct. 3 ℗—Whitey Ford became the biggest winner in New York Yankee history today, picking up career victory No. 232 as the Yankees whipped Boston, 11 to 5.

Ford was tagged for eleven hits, including homers by Jim Gosger and Carl Yastrzemski, before Pedro Ramos relieved him in the eighth inning.

NEW YORK	ab	r	h	bi	BOSTON	ab	r	h	bi
Rich'son 2b	6	0	1	1	Sch'ling 2b	5	1	1	0
White rf	5	2	2	0	Malzone 3b	4	0	0	0
Tresh lf	5	2	3	0	Yastr'ski lf	4	2	3	2
Mosc'to lf	0	0	0	0	Cnigl'ro rf	4	0	2	2
Howard c	5	1	2	1	Horton 1b	4	0	0	0
Repoz cf	4	1	1	1	Gosger cf	2	1	1	1
Boyer 3b	4	3	2	1	Green cf	2	0	1	0
Kubek ss	4	1	3	3	Bressoud ss	4	0	2	0
Barker 1b	4	1	3	2	Ryan c	3	0	0	0
Ford p	3	0	1	0	Nixon c	1	0	0	0
Ramos p	1	0	0	0	Wilson p	1	0	0	0
					Earley p	1	0	0	0
					Petroc'li ph	1	0	0	0
					Thomas ph	1	0	0	0
Totals	41	11	18	9	Totals	39	5	11	5

New York .... 013 201 103—11
Boston .... 110 000 201—5

E—Boyer, Gosger, Conigliaro. DP—Boston 2. LOB—New York 9, Boston 7.
2B—Boyer, Howard, Barker, Yastrzemski, Malzone. HR—Kubek (5), Gosger (9), Yastrzemski (20). S—Kubek, Ford, Boyer.

	IP	H	R	ER	BB	SO
Ford W.16-13	7	11	5	4	0	4
Ramos	2	0	0	0	0	4
Wilson	2 2-3	7	4	4	1	1
Earley L.0-1	3 1-3	5	3	3	1	3
Duliba	2	3	1	1	0	1
Radatz	1	3	3	3	1	1

Ford faced 1 man in 8th
PB—Howard 2. T—2:30. A—5,933.

Eckert Fields Questions On Assuming Diamond Job

Chicago, Nov. 17 ℗—Retired Air Force Gen. William D. Eckert stepped into his role as commissioner of baseball today with the deftness and poise of a fighter pilot.

Minutes after the announcement of his selection was made, Eckert was bombed with questions ranging from immediate plans to the delicate baseball situation concerning Milwaukee.

Eckert's first answer about Milwaukee was "I am generally familiar with the problem and hope it will be worked out to the satisfaction of the communities concerned."

Frick To The Rescue

Someone pressed the questioning, and outgoing Commissioner Ford Frick interrupted by saying, "Gentlemen, you are not being fair. He cannot answer such questions and shouldn't be subjected to them. The files on Milwaukee are voluminous and have been compiled over a two-year period."

Eckert ended the Milwaukee questioning by saying, "I am not familiar with the legalities of the matter."

Eckert, 56, was nattily attired in a black suit with a gray tie. A slim man at 5-foot-8½ and 160 pounds, Eckert said his immediate duties were to consult with Frick and Frick's staff.

MacPhail Praised

"For the next three months, I will confer with Mr. Frick whom I will ask to assist, advise and officiate at the baseball meetings in Miami next month.

"I will confer with the presidents of the two leagues and learn all I can about their business and their problems," said the new commissioner, a handsome man with thinning grey hair.

Bucs' Hurler Retires First 12 Men In Order

Pittsburgh, Oct. 2 ℗—Don Cardwell allowed only one hit—Vic Roznovsky's two-out single in the fifth inning—as Pittsburgh defeated the Chicago Cubs, 3 to 0, today.

Cardwell, now 13-10, retired the first twelve batters he faced, then walked Ron Santo opening the fifth. Two outs later, Roznovsky singled to right, but Cardwell escaped the jam by getting Don Kessinger on a grounder.

The Pirates scored in the first on Bob Bailey's double and two infield grounders and again in the eighth on a two-run homer by Gene Alley.

CHICAGO	ab	r	h	bi	PITTSBURGH	ab	r	h	bi
Land'm cf	4	0	0	0	Bailey 3b	3	1	1	0
Beckert 2b	4	0	1	0	Virdon cf	4	0	1	0
Williams rf	3	0	0	0	Maz'ski 2b	3	0	0	0
Santo 3b	2	0	0	0	Pagl'oni c	2	0	0	0
Banks 1b	3	0	0	0	Spriggs pr	0	1	0	0
Stewart lf	2	0	0	0	Crandall c	1	0	0	0
Rnovs'y c	3	0	1	0	Alley ss	3	1	1	2
Kes'nger ss	2	0	0	0	Cardwell p	3	0	0	0
Altman ph	1	0	0	0					
Jackson p	1	0	0	0					
Clemens lf	1	0	0	0					
Totals	26	0	1	0	Totals	28	3	5	3

Chicago .... 000 000 000—0
Pittsburgh .... 100 000 02x—3

E—Beckert. DP—Chicago 1, Pittsburgh 2. LOB—Chicago 2, Pittsburgh 4.

	IP	H	R	ER	BB	SO
Jackson L.14-21	7	3	1	1	0	5
Abernathy	1	2	2	2	0	1
Cardwell W.13-10	9	1	0	0	3	3

T—1:45. A—3,262.

DODGERS TAKE SERIES BY DEFEATING TWINS BEHIND KOUFAX, 2-0

L.A. Hurler Fans 10 Going Route As Mates Score Both Runs In 4th On Johnson Homer, Fairly's 2-Bagger And Parker's Single

By LOU HATTER
(Sun Staff Correspondent)

Minneapolis-St. Paul, Oct. 14 — Sandy Koufax, dean of baseball's college of pitching arts and science, presided, 2 to 0, here today as the Los Angeles Dodgers won the decisive seventh game of the 1965 World Series from the Minnesota Twins.

In orderly, unspectacular but thoroughly dominant fashion, the 29-year-old Dodger lefthander authored his second successive shutout of the American League champions and tenth of the season before an equally respectful audience of 50,596.

There was a brief intermission for a hitting clinic in the fourth inning. Lou Johnson caromed a towering home run off the left-field foul pole. Ron Fairly pulled southpaw Jim Kaat's next offering into the right-field corner for two bases and Wes Parker singled Fairly home with a chop over first sacker Don Mincher's head.

Twins Get 3 Hits

This cluster of three Los Angeles blows produced all the scoring of the sunny afternoon and matched Minnesota's total hits off Koufax, who struck out ten enroute to his first ride in a white, convertible Corvette awarded him afterwards as the outstanding player in the sixty-second post-season classic.

Koufax, of course, did not do it all alone. After overcoming an early siege of wildness in the opening frame, where two of his three bases on balls were issued he was indebted especially to the veteran Dodger third baseman, Jim Gilliam, for preservation of the shutout — possibly the victory — in the fifth.

With one retired here, Frank Quilici, the Twins' light-hitting second baseman, doubled to deep left-centerfield.

Rich Rollins batted for Al Worthington — second of five Minnesota hurlers — and walked, after Koufax and a host of other unofficial umpires thought the rival pinch-hitter had been struck out on a two-and-two change-of-pace curve.

Hurley Says Ball Three

Ed Hurley, the official umpire, called it ball three, however, and Koufax still was fuming moments later when Rollins trotted to first. As it turned out, this may have been a blessing in disguise.

Zoilo Versalles, who had singled in the Minnesota third, only to be denied a stolen base when Joe Nossek was called out by Hurley for obstructing catcher John Roseboro's peg, strode next to the plate.

The Twins shortstop rifled a hot grounder along the third-base line — bound apparently for two-base territory in the leftfield corner.

Great Stop For Force

The nimble Gilliam — only three days removed from his thirty-seventh birthday — lunged to his right, however, skillfully backhanded the baseball and, after recovering his balance, stepped on the bag to force Quilici.

Reprinted from
The Baltimore Sun papers

World Series Box

Minneapolis-St. Paul, Minn., Oct. 14 (AP)—Box score of today's seventh game of the 1965 World Series:

LOS ANGELES	ab	r	h	bi	o	a	e	MINNESOTA	ab	r	h	bi	o	a	e
Wills, ss	4	0	0	0	2	4	0	Versalles, ss	4	0	1	0	0	2	0
Gilliam, 3b	5	0	2	0	2	1	0	Nossek, cf	4	0	0	0	0	0	0
Kennedy, 3b	0	0	0	0	0	1	0	Oliva, rf	3	0	0	0	4	0	1
W. Davis, cf	2	0	0	0	1	0	0	Killebrew, 3b	3	0	1	0	2	2	0
Johnson, lf	4	1	1	3	0	0	0	Battey, c	4	0	0	0	8	1	0
Fairly, rf	4	1	1	0	0	0	0	Allison, lf	4	0	0	0	1	0	0
Parker, 1b	4	0	2	1	6	0	0	Mincher, 1b	3	0	0	0	10	0	0
Tracewski, 2b	4	0	0	0	1	0	0	Quilici, 2b	3	0	1	0	1	3	0
Roseboro, c	3	0	1	0	12	0	0	Kaat, p	1	0	0	0	1	1	0
Koufax, p	3	0	0	0	0	1	0	Worthington, p	0	0	0	0	1	1	0
								aRollins	0	0	0	0	0	0	0
								Klippstein, p	0	0	0	0	0	0	0
								Merritt, p	0	0	0	0	0	0	0
								bValdespino	1	0	0	0	0	0	0
								Perry, p	0	0	0	0	0	0	0
Totals	32	2	7	2	27	7	0	Totals	30	0	3	0	27	10	1

aWalked for Worthington in fifth.
bFouled out for Merritt in eighth.

Los Angeles	0	0	0	2	0	0	0	0	0	2
Minnesota	0	0	0	0	0	0	0	0	0	0

Left on bases—Los Angeles, 9; Minnesota, 6. Two-base hits—Roseboro, Fairly, Quilici. Three-base hit—Parker. Home run—Johnson. Sacrifice—W. Davis.

PITCHING SUMMARY

	Ip	H	R	Er		Ip	H	R	Er
Koufax (W)	9	3	0	0	Klippstein	1⅔	2	0	0
Kaat (L)	3	5	2	2	Merritt	1⅓	0	0	0
Worthington	2	0	0	0	Perry	1	0	0	0

Kaat faced three men in 4th.
Bases on balls—Koufax, 3 (Oliva, Killebrew, Rollins); Kaat, 1 (Koufax), Worthington, 1 (Roseboro); Klippstein, 1 (Roseboro); Perry, 1 (Wills). Strikeouts—Koufax, 10 (Versalles, Battey 2, Allison 2, Mincher, Kaat, Oliva 2, Quilici); Kaat, 2 (Wills); Klippstein, 2 (Tracewski, Koufax); Merritt, 1 (Roseboro); Perry, 1 (Koufax). Hit by pitcher—By Klippstein (W. Davis).

Umpires—Hurley (A), plate; Venzon (N), first base; Flaherty (A), second base; Sudol (N), third base; Stewart (A), left field; Vargo (N), right field. Time—2:27. Attendance—50,596.

Dodgers

Minneapolis-St. Paul, Oct. 14 (AP) —As the bedlam subsided in the Los Angeles dressing room today, Dodger owner Walter O'Malley carefully pushed through the crowd, stepping gingerly toward Walt Alston, and throwing his arms around the manager, said:

"Walt, it's getting to be a habit."

"But," replied Alston, "we sure did it the hard way."

That was more indicative of Alston's feelings toward his 1965 World Champions than anything he would say directly when asked to compare the present club with his three other series' winners.

Scratched All Year

"The 1955 one was our first," Alston said, "so that was exciting. Then in 1959 we came from behind to win in a tight race and in 1963 they came back after blowing it the year before.

"This is a club that all year long has had to battle. All year long this team has scratched."

But he would go no farther in making comparisons.

Koufax, Drysdale Sign

PAIR TO GET MORE THAN $210,000

Don Hopes To Throw For Dodgers In Weekend Tilt

Los Angeles, March 30 ⁽ᴬᴾ⁾ — Pitching aces Sandy Koufax and Don Drysdale wrote a happy ending to their cliff-hanger 32-day holdout today by signing with the Los Angeles Dodgers for "more than $210,000."

Dodgers General Manager Buzzy Bavasi declined to disclose the exact figure. He flew into town yesterday to try to bring the two to agreement and said they rejected his "final" offer of $210,-000 — $112,500 for Koufax and $97,500 for Drysdale.

But this morning, he upped the ante enough for them to sign.

The Los Angeles *Herald Examiner* said it learned the settlement figure was $230,000—$120,000 for Sandy and $110,000 for Don.

Pitchers "Both Happy"

Bavasi made the announcement at a news conference with 26-game winner Koufax sitting on one side and 23-game winner Drysdale on the other.

Koufax seemed to summarize the attitude of all when he said: "Let's put it this way. Don and I are both happy."

Bonus Boy Signs With N.Y. Mets

St. Petersburg, Fla., April 4 ⁽ᴬᴾ⁾ — The New York Mets signed George Seaver, a pitcher they won in a draw, today for a bonus estimated at $50,000.

Seaver originally was picked by the Atlanta Braves in the high school and college draft and the University of Southern California star was signed for $40,000 by Richmond, the Braves' farm team in the International League.

However, William Eckert, the baseball commissioner, nullified the deal because Seaver was signed after Southern California started its season this year. Base-ball rules say a player cannot be signed off a college campus once his team has begun play.

The Mets, Philadelphia Phillies and Cleveland Indians then put in a bid for the 21-year-old pitcher from Fresno, Cal., and the Mets won in a draw held by Eckert.

Under the rules, Seaver had to be signed for at least as much as Richmond paid. A spokesman for the Mets said his bonus, with fringe benefits, would amount to about $50,000.

Seaver, who was a high school teammate of Met pitcher Dick Selma, was assigned to Jacksonville of the International League.

Houk Takes Over Club As Yankees Fire Keane

Dan Topping, Jr., Assumes General Manager Role As New Yorkers Skid To Cellar

Anahei, Cal., May 7 ⁽ᴬᴾ⁾—Johnny Keane was fired as manager of the 10th place New York Yankees tonight and general Manager Ralph Houk took over direction of the club.

The move had been rumored—and vehemently denied by the club—for two days before it was announced just before the Yankees took the field against the California Angels.

Houk, a cigar-chomping ex-Marine, led the Yankees to three straight American League pennants before moving upstairs as their general manager in 1963.

Keane, who came to the Yanks a year ago, has had nothing but trouble. The perennial champions slipped to sixth place in 1965 and have been in and out of last place all this season.

The decision was made by Dan Topping, Jr., vice president of the Yankees, and was made known by him in a telegram to Houk, who was with the club.

Topping will take over the duties of general manager.

Keane came to the Yankees in a stunning sequence of events immediately after the 1964 World Series in which his St. Louis Cardinals beat the Yankees.

TWINS BLAST 5 HOME RUNS IN ONE FRAME

Record - Tying Salvos Send Kansas City To 9-4 Defeat

St. Paul-Minneapolis, June 9 ⁽ᴬᴾ⁾ —The Minnesota Twins smashed a record tying five home runs in the seventh inning today, riding the late explosion to a 9-to-4 victory over Kansas City.

The Twins just missed breaking the major league record for most home runs in an inning when Jimmie Hall came within about two feet of clearing the fence after Harmon Killebrew had crashed the fifth homer of the frame.

Minnesota trailed 4-3 going into the big inning after Killebrew's two-run homer in the sixth inning had pulled the Twins back into contention.

Rollins Is Spark

Pinch hitter Rich Rollins started the barrage, connecting off A's starter Catfish Hunter after Earl Battey walked. That put the Twins ahead 5-4.

Zoilo Versalles followed with another homer, finishing Hunter and bringing on Paul Lindblad.

Sandy Valdespino went out, but Tony Oliva tagged Lindblad for the third homer of the rally. Then Don Mincher followed Oliva with the fourth.

Killebrew Again

John Wyatt replaced Lindblad and was greeted by Killebrew's second homer of the game. Hall then narrowly missed.

The five homers in one inning was an American League record. Three National League teams have accomplished the feat, the last time by San Francisco on August 23, 1961.

Ironically, it was against the Athletics in 1964 when the Twins tied the American League record for consecutive homers with four.

CLONINGER HITS 2 GRAND SLAMS

Braves' Pitcher Posts N.L. First; S.F. Loses, 17-3

San Francisco, July 3. (P)—Atlanta pitcher Tony Cloninger became the first National League player ever to hit two grand slam homers in one game today as the Braves crushed the San Francisco Giants, 17 to 3.

Cloninger also singled in a run, and his nine runs batted in for the day set a major league record for a pitcher. Vic Raschi of the New York Yankees drove in seven in 1953 while no National League pitcher ever had driven in more than five.

Wins Ninth Game

Four players have hit two grand slam homers in one game in American League history, but none was a pitcher. The last to accomplish the feat was Jim Gentile, of Baltimore, in 1961.

Besides setting a NL record for grand slams in a game, Cloninger became only the second National League pitcher to hit a pair of homers in a game twice in one season. Don Newcombe of the then Brooklyn Dodgers became the first in 1955.

Besides Gentile, the other players who hit two grand slams in a game were Tony Lazzeri of the New York Yankees in 1936, Jim Tabor of Boston in 1939 and Rudy York of the Red Sox in 1946.

MCCARVER'S TALLY ENDS MOUND DUEL

B. Robinson Sparkles, Richert Loses In 100-Plus Heat

By JIM ELLIOT
[Sun Staff Correspondent]

St. Louis, July 12—Maury Wills, an eighth-inning shortstop replacement, lined a tenth-inning single to right scoring Tim McCarver from second base and breaking up a duel of nine pitchers here today as the National League edged the American League, 2 to 1 in the thirty-seventh All-Star Game.

A crowd of 49,936, largest ever to witness a St. Louis sports event and including Vice President Humphrey, sat in new Busch Memorial Stadium in sweltering 100-degree temperature and cheered mightily when the Dodgers' speedy little infielder drove Cardinal catcher McCarver across with one out in the game's first extra inning.

Reprinted from
The Baltimore Sun papers

TED, CASEY JOIN STARS

Williams, Stengel Inducted Into Hall Of Fame

Cooperstown, N.Y., July 25 (P)—Ted Williams gently chided the baseball writers and Casey Stengel thanked everybody from Kankakee, Ill., to Shea Stadium today as the two newest members were formally inducted into baseball's Hall of Fame.

A record crowd of over 6,000 turned out at Cooper Park to listen to the morning ceremonies preceding the annual Hall of Fame exhibition game between the St. Louis Cardinals and Minnesota Twins.

Baseball Commissioner William D. Eckert, making his first appearance at Cooperstown, introduced the new members to a roar of applause. Eckert said he looked forward to the day when baseball will be the pride, not only of the United States, but of all the world. He said the game "must expand and progress in keeping with the times."

Still No Necktie

Williams, 47, and a few pounds heavier than when he hit .406 in 1941, wore no necktie, as usual. But his white sports shirt was buttoned at the neck as he charmed the listeners, including the writers with whom he had often feuded.

"I find it difficult to say what is really in my heart," he said. "But I know it's the greatest thrill of my life.

"I received 280 odd votes actually 282 of a maximum of 302 from the writers. I know I didn't have 280 close friends among the writers. I know they voted for me because they felt in their minds, and some in their hearts, that I rated it and I want to say to them thank you."

WISCONSIN LOSES SUIT WITH BRAVES

State Supreme Court Reverses Decision Against Club

Madison, Wis., July 27 (P)—Wisconsin's Supreme Court called Milwaukee out today on its bid to stay in baseball, and awarded the vagabond Braves to Atlanta.

In a dramatic 4-to-3 decision, the black-robed justices ruled that baseball is a monopoly, and leaving the city without a major league franchise clearly harmed its economy, but "the State is powerless to deal with it."

In modern times, franchise shifts always have been from cities with two teams.

Dismissal Ordered

The court returned the case to Circuit Judge Elmer W. Roller, of Milwaukee, who had found the National League and its members violated Wisconsin's antitrust laws by approving the Braves' move, and ordered him to dismiss the suit.

The decision, however, actually is only another step in a series that long has seemed destined to be decided ultimately by the United States Supreme Court.

Wisconsin attorney general Bronson C. La Follette, who initiated the State suit, said he would ask the nation's highest tribunal within 30 days to consider a review.

More Action Pending

And a Federal antitrust action, filed in United States District Court earlier last year by Milwaukee, is working its way up a crowded calendar, although it still may be a year away from trial.

Representative Emanuel Celler (D., N.Y.), one of many to comment on today's decision, mentioned Federal action specifically.

"Baseball is not a state monopoly, but a Federal monopoly, and a Federal antitrust suit is long overdue," he told a reporter in Washington. "Baseball now is in violation of the Federal antitrust laws."

All-Star Box Score

St. Louis, July 12 (P)—The box score of the 1966 major league All-Star Baseball game.

AMERICAN	ab	r	h	bi	po	a		NATIONAL	ab	r	h	bi	po	a
McAuliffe ss	3	0	0	0	1	1		Mays cf	4	1	1	0	3	0
Stottlemyre p	0	0	0	0	0	2		Clemente rf	4	0	2	0	2	0
bColavito	0	0	0	0	0	0		Aaron lf	3	0	0	0	0	0
Siebert p	0	0	0	0	0	0		McCovey 1b	3	0	0	0	10	0
Richert p	0	0	0	0	0	1		Santo 3b	3	0	1	0	0	2
Kaline cf	4	0	1	0	1	0		Torre c	3	0	1	0	5	0
Agee cf	0	0	0	0	1	0		McCarver c	1	1	1	0	1	0
F.Robinson rf	4	0	0	0	2	0		Lefebvre 2b	3	0	0	0	4	1
Oliva rf	0	0	0	0	0	0		Hunt 2b	1	0	0	0	0	2
B.Robinson 3b	4	1	3	0	4	1		Cardenas ss	3	0	0	0	2	0
Scott 1b	4	0	0	0	4	1		fStargell	1	0	0	0	0	0
cCash 1b	1	0	0	0	3	0		Wills ss	1	0	1	1	0	0
Freehan c	4	0	1	0	6	0		Koufax p	1	0	0	0	0	1
Battey c	1	0	0	0	4	0		aAllen	1	0	0	0	0	0
Knoop 2b	2	0	0	0	1	1		Bunning p	0	0	0	0	0	0
eRichardson	1	0	0	0	0	0		bAllen	1	0	0	0	0	0
McLain p	0	0	0	0	0	0		Marichal p	0	0	0	0	0	0
Kaat p	0	0	0	0	0	0		gHart	1	0	0	0	0	0
cKillebrew	1	0	0	0	0	0		Perry p	0	0	0	0	0	0
dPepitone ss	2	0	0	0	0	0								
Totals	38	1	6	0x	28	11		Totals	33	2	6	2	30	7

aGrounded out for Koufax in 3rd. bStruck out for Bunning in 5th. cSingled for Kaat in 6th. dRan for Killebrew in 6th. eHit into double play for Scott in 7th. fFouled out for Cardenas in 7th. gGrounded out for Knoop in 8th. hFlied out for Stottlemyre in 8th. Struck out for Marichal in 8th. xOne out when winning run scored.

| American | 0 | 0 | 0 | 0 | 0 | 0 | 1 | 0 | 0 | 0 | —1 |
| National | 0 | 0 | 0 | 0 | 0 | 0 | 0 | 0 | 1 | 1 | —2 |

E—None. DP—McCovey, Cardenas and McCovey. LOB—American, 5; National, 5. 2B—Clemente. 3B—B. Robinson, Hunt.

PITCHING SUMMARY

	ip	h	r	er			ip	h	r	er
McLain	3	1	0	0		Richert (L)		2	1	1
Kaat	2	1	1	1		Koufax	3	1	1	1
Stottlemyre	1	0	0	0		Bunning	2	1	0	0
Siebert	2	0	0	0		Marichal	3	1	0	0
						Perry (W)	2	1	0	0

BB—Perry 1 (Battey), Stottlemyre 1 (McCarver). SO—Koufax 1 (McLain), Bunning 2 (F. Robinson, Knoop), Marichal 2 (McAuliffe, Battey), Perry 1 (Freehan), McLain 1 (Mays, Aaron, Torre), Kaat 1 (Allen), Siebert 1 (Hart).

WP—Koufax, Perry. U. Barlick (N) plate, Umont (A) first base, Vargo (N) second base, Honochick (A) third base, Neudecker (A) left field, Engel (N) right field. T—2:18. A—49,936.

Veteran Tiger Manager Dressen Dies Of Cardiac Arrest At 67

Former Oriole Player And Dodger Pilot Survived Two Previous Heart Attacks

Detroit, Aug. 10 (UP) — Charlie Dressen, manager of the Detroit Tigers who battled back from two heart attacks only to be stricken by a kidney infection, died today.

Dressen, who would have been 68 next month, died of a cardiac arrest, said a spokesman at Ford Hospital.

He had entered the hospital last Sunday for treatment of the kidney infection.

'Sincere Enthusiasm For Game'

"Few remain in baseball who can match his deep knowledge and sincere enthusiasm for the game," said Tigers Owner John E. Fetzer in leading the tributes to Dressen.

Los Angeles Dodgers President Walter O'Malley, who was president when the club was in Brooklyn and won National League pennants in 1952 and 1953 under Dressen, said:

"He was tremendously dedicated to the game of baseball, only yesterday I sent a get-well message to Charlie in the hospital and told him, 'You've licked bigger ones than this. Now pull this game out and get well.'"

"Extremely Grieved"

Frank Skaff, acting manager of the Tigers since another coach, Bob Swift, was stricken with lung cancer, said he and the Tigers were "extremely grieved and heartbroken. Charlie was not only respected as a manager . . . but as a man as well."

Final Standings

	W.	L.	Pct.	G.B.
Los Angeles	95	67	.586	
San Francisco	93	68	.578	1½
Pittsburgh	92	70	.568	3
Philadelphia	87	75	.537	8
Atlanta	85	77	.525	10
St. Louis	83	79	.512	12
Cincinnati	76	84	.475	18
Houston	72	90	.444	23
New York	66	95	.410	28½
Chicago	59	103	.364	36

L.A. SOUTHPAW WINS NIGHTCAP, 6-3, AFTER PHILS TAKE OPENER

Koufax Strikes Out 10, Wins 27th On 7-Hitter; Lefty Forced To Pitch With 2 Days Rest When Dodgers Lose 1st Game, 4-3

Philadelphia, Oct. 2 (P) — The Los Angeles Dodgers clinched their second consecutive National League pennant today, beating Philadelphia, 6-to-3, as Sandy Koufax, pitching for the first time this season with only two days rest, scattered seven hits.

Manager Walter Alston reluctantly called upon his brilliant left-hander to save the day after the Dodgers blew the first game of a doubleheader 4-3 on two throwing errors in the eighth inning.

Little Suspense

With the second-place San Francisco Giants winning, 7-3, in 11 innings over the Pittsburgh Pirates, the Dodgers had to win the second game or send the regular season into an extra day for the second time in baseball history.

The Giants had a postponed game with Cincinnati, which would have been played tomorrow had the Dodgers lost both games to the Phillies and opened the door for San Francisco to tie the race.

There was little suspense in the nightcap, however, especially after the dramatics of the first game.

The only suspense there actually came in the ninth inning. Koufax went into the inning with a four-hit, 6-0 lead, but the Phillies rallied for three runs and had Bill White at second with a no-out, two-run double.

Strikes Out

Koufax, however, bore down and struck out Bob Uecker, got pinch hitter Bobby Wine to ground out and fanned Jack Brandt for his tenth strikeout of the game.

In bringing his record to 27 victories, most of his career, and 9 losses, Koufax duplicated his feat of last year when, working on just two days rest, he pitched a four-hitter as the Dodgers beat Milwaukee on the next-to-last day of the season and clinched the pennant.

The Dodgers championship marks the first time a National League team has won two straight pennants since the Braves did it in 1957 and 1958.

Alston, who now has won six pennants in thirteen years with the Dodgers, had hoped right-hander Don Drysdale would win the opener and clinch the pennant, so Koufax could rest for the opening of the World Series against the American League champion Baltimore Orioles in Los Angeles Wednesday.

L.A. BLANKED BY JUSTER FIFTH TIME

Cardinals' Rookie Allows Four Hits To Win, 2-0

St. Louis, Sept. 28 (P) — Rookie Larry Jaster tied a 50-year-old record for shutouts and threw a roadblock into Los Angeles' drive for the National League pennant tonight by pitching a four hitter as St. Louis defeated the Dodgers 2 to 0.

Jaster, 22-year-old left-hander, shut out the Dodgers for the fifth consecutive time this season. He tied a modern N.L. record held by Grover Alexander, who pitched five shutouts for Philadelphia against Cincinnati in 1916. Alexander's shutouts, however, were not in succession.

Jaster also broke the record of four consecutive shutouts against one team held by Fred Fitzsimmons of the New York Giants, who accomplished the feat against Cincinnati in 1929.

Rookie Ed Spiezio gave Jaster all the help he needed with a two-run double in the fourth inning against loser Don Sutton.

Curt Flood, leading off the fourth, was safe when third baseman Dick Schofield bobbled his grounder and Sutton then walked Tim McCarver.

Spiezio Doubles

Orlando Cepeda struck out and Mike Shannon forced McCarver at second before Spiezio drove both runners home with a line drive double into the left field corner.

Jaster, who has allowed the Dodgers nothing but singles this season, was clipped for two-out hits by Lou Johnson and Tommy Davis in the fourth inning. He then walked Dick Stuart, loading the bases, but got out of the jam by retiring Jim Lefebvre on a soft fly to right field.

In bringing his record to 11-5, Jaster also worked out of a jam in the top of the seventh. Tommy Davis and Schofield singled around a pair of outs, but Jaster struck out pinch hitter Al Ferrara to end the inning.

Sutton, who was charged with his twelfth loss against twelve victories, left for a pinch hitter in the fifth. He allowed only two hits.

Jaster retired the first eleven Dodgers he faced. Los Angeles' lead-off hitter, Maury Wills, bunted to start the game, crossed the bag ahead of the throw but was called out on an appeal play when Umpire Tony Venzon ruled he didn't touch the bag.

BIRD HURLER YIELDS ONLY FOUR BLOWS

Six Errors Made By Dodgers, Three In 5th By W. Davis

By LOU HATTER
(Sun Staff Correspondent)

Los Angeles, Oct. 6 — Baltimore's Jim Palmer became the youngest pitcher ever to hurl a World Series shutout here today, blanking the Los Angeles Dodgers, 6 to 0, to gain a second straight victory for the Orioles in baseball's sixty-third post-season spectacle.

The 20-year-old right-hander, who will become an eligible voter nine days hence, zeroed the defending world champions on four hits, struck out six and walked three—one of these intentionally—before 55,947 Chavez Ravine spectators.

Dodgers Make 6 Errors

It was the first shutout of Palmer's two-year Oriole career, and the Dodgers never had a chance after their normally impeccable defense collapsed behind Sandy Koufax, possibly the most fabulous lefthanded pitcher of all time.

The Orioles capitalized on six Los Angeles errors, tieing a series record, while taking the 1966 road show back to Baltimore for a third, fourth and—if necessary—fifth game, beginning Saturday afternoon at 1 o'clock.

Baltimore's most useful ally was Dodger centerfielder Willie Davis, who muffed two fly balls in the glaring sun and threw still another ball away during the fifth inning, where three unearned Oriole runs decided the score.

Fly Drops In For Triple

Davis's three errors were the most ever committed in one inning by one player in World Series history.

Third baseman Jim Gilliam, right-fielder Ron Fairly and Ron Perranoski—second of four Los Angeles hurlers—also were guilty of misplays. On still another occasion, Davis and Fairly allowed Frank Robinson's fly to deep right-center to drop untouched for a gift triple.

Powell Drives In Run

This set up a fourth Oriole run, driven across also at Koufax's expense in inning No. 6 by Boog Powell's second single of the afternoon.

Baltimore wrapped up the verdict with two final runs in the eighth, where Frank Robinson walked, Brooks Robinson singled, Powell bunted both into scoring zone and Dave Johnson kayoed Perranoski with a hit off the Dodger lefthander's shins.

Johnson's bruising blow drove in Frank Robinson, and the other member of Baltimore's Swish Family Robinson followed when Perranoski flung the baseball into the Baltimore dugout.

ORIOLE FIRST TO WIN TITLE IN 2 MAJORS

New York, Nov. 8 (P)—Frank Robinson of the Baltimore Orioles unanimously was voted the American League's Most Valuable Player today, becoming the first player in baseball history to win the coveted award in both leagues.

In the 35-year history of the award, no other player has been able to achieve M.V.P. distinction in both the American and National leagues.

But Robinson, who won the N.L. version with Cincinnati in 1961, accomplished the feat by gaining the 1966 A.L. award without dissent from the twenty voting members of the Baseball Writers Association of America.

Orioles Sweep First Three

In winning the award, the 31-year-old outfielder led a 1-2-3 Baltimore sweep of the top places, drawing a maximum 280 points to 153 for third baseman Brooks Robinson and 122 for first baseman Boog Powell.

Points were on a basis of 14 for a first-place vote, 9 for second, 8 for third down to 1 point for tenth.

Frank Robinson, who won the American League triple crown of batting while leading the Orioles to the pennant and a four-game sweep of the Los Angeles Dodgers in the World Series, is only the third A.L. player to win the award unanimously and the first in a decade.

World Series Box

ORIOLES	ab	r	h	rbi	po	a
Aparicio, ss	5	0	2	1	4	1
Belefray, lf	5	0	0	0	1	0
F. Robinson, rf	3	2	1	0	1	0
B. Robinson, 3b	4	1	1	0	1	1
Powell, 1b	3	1	2	1	8	0
D Johnson, 2b	4	0	2	1	2	4
Blair, cf	3	1	0	0	4	0
Etchebarren, c	3	1	0	0	6	0
Palmer, p	4	0	0	0	0	2
Totals	34	6	8	3	27	8

DODGERS	ab	r	h	rbi	po	a
Wills, ss	4	0	0	0	3	1
Gilliam, 3b	4	0	0	0	2	3
W. Davis, cf	4	0	0	0	2	0
Fairly, rf	3	0	0	0	3	0
Lefebvre, 2b	3	0	0	0	3	0
L. Johnson, lf	4	0	1	0	1	0
Roseboro, c	4	0	1	0	5	1
Parker, 1b	2	0	1	0	5	1
Koufax, p	2	0	0	0	0	1
Perranoski, p	0	0	0	0	0	1
Regan, p	0	0	0	0	0	0
aT Davis	1	0	1	0	0	0
Brewer, p	0	0	0	0	0	0
Totals	31	0	4	0	27	8

aSingled for Regan in eighth.

Orioles	0 0 0 0 3 1 0 2 0—6
Dodgers	0 0 0 0 0 0 0 0 0—0

Errors—Gilliam, W Davis 3, Fairly, Perranoski. Double Play—Gilliam, Roseboro and Parker. Left on bases—Orioles, 6, Dodgers, 7.
Two-base hits—L. Johnson, Aparicio. Three-base hit—F. Robinson.
Sacrifice—Powell.

PITCHING SUMMARY

	Ip	H	R	Er		Ip	H	R	Er
Palmer (W)	9	4	0	0	Regan	⅔	0	0	0
Koufax (L)	6	6	4	1	Brewer	1	0	0	0
Perranoski	1⅓	2	2	2					

Bases on balls—Palmer, 3 (Fairly, Parker, Lefebvre); Koufax, 2 (F. Robinson, Blair); Perranoski, 1 (F. Robinson); Regan, 1 (Etchebarren). Strikeouts—Palmer, 6 (W. Davis 2, Lefebvre 2, Fairly 2); Koufax, 2 (Etchebarren, Palmer), Perranoski, 1 (Blefary), Regan, 1 (Palmer), Brewer, 1 (Blefary). Wild pitch—Regan, Palmer.

Umpires—Chylak (A) plate; Pelekoudas (N), first base; Rice (A), second base; Steiner (N), third base; Drummond (A), left field, Jackowski (N), right field.

Time—2.26. Attendance—55,947.

Sandy Koufax Retires From Game At Career Peak Due To Arthritis

Los Angeles, Nov. 18 (P)—Sandy Koufax of the Los Angeles Dodgers bowed out of baseball at the peak of his brilliant pitching career today, saying he feared if he continued he may permanently harm his fabled arthritic left arm.

The man many consider the finest hurler in baseball history told a news conference that the pain in his pitching elbow has grown progressively worse since it began three years ago.

No Comment From Club

He began by saying, "A few minutes ago I sent a letter to the Dodgers asking them to put me on the voluntary retired list."

There was no immediate comment from the club.

General manager E. J. Bavasi said earlier that Koufax had told him he was through. That, Bavasi indicated, was that.

Bavasi said the Koufax retirement will seriously handicap the Dodgers in trading at the winter meetings next month.

"I wanted Sandy to wait until after the winter meetings," Bavasi said. "It would have been a big help to the club. But now that I have to go into the meetings without Koufax on our roster, the other clubs will have us right where they want us."

Amazing Record

Koufax, at $125,000 the highest paid pitcher in history, has set an amazing variety of records and won many awards since hurting his arm in 1964.

He said, "I feel I am doing the right thing and I don't regret one minute of the past twelve years. The only regret is leaving baseball."

What will he do? "I have spoken to a few people and a few have spoken to me but at this moment I don't know what I'll do."

Not Unexpected

Koufax, whose lightning fast ball and sweeping curves had for years been the downfall of National League batsmen, said he told Bavasi a month before the end of the 1966 season that it likely was his last year.

Bob Swift Dies; Ex-Tiger Pilot Cancer Victim

Detroit, Oct. 17 (P)—Bob Swift, who three times posted winning records as an acting American League baseball manager but never won the job permanently, died in a Detroit hospital today.

The 51-year-old Swift, who took over the Detroit Tigers twice in the last two years when manager Charlie Dressen suffered heart attacks, was hospitalized shortly after the All-Star Game with what was thought to be a stomach ailment.

It was later diagnosed as lung cancer.

FORMER L.A. STAR HAPPY WITH MOVE

By LOU HATTER
[Sun Staff Correspondent]

Pittsburgh, Dec. 1 — The Los Angeles Dodgers tonight carried out their threat to trade shortstop Maury Wills, who quit the National League champions' recent post-season tour of Japan without authority—pleading a knee injury —and wound up playing his guitar at a Honolulu night club.

The defiant six-time base-stealing king and veteran of a half-dozen All-Star games was swapped to Pittsburgh for infielders Bob Bailey and Gene Michael.

It was the Dodgers' second major deal within 48 hours at baseball's annual winter convention, now in session here. Tuesday, outfielder Tommy Davis and utilityman Derrell Griffith went to the New York Mets in exchange for second baseman Ron Hunt and outfielder Jim Hickman

JOHNNY KEANE DIES IN HOUSTON

Heart Attack Fells Former Big League Manager

Houston, Jan. 6 (AP) — Johnny Keane, the ex-manager of the St. Louis Cardinals and the New York Yankees, died tonight in his Houston home of an acute heart attack. He was 55.

Keane led the Cardinals to a 1964 World Series victory over the Yankees, four games to three. Almost immediately, he gave the Cards his resignation, the Yankees fired Yogi Berra as manager and Keane was Berra's replacement.

Replaced By Houk

When the Yankees plunged to tenth place last May, Ralph Houk replaced Keane as manager.

As the time of his death, Keane was a special assignment scout for the American League California Angeles.

Keane was born in St. Louis, but he was a Houston resident for more than 30 years, playing and managing the Texas League Houston Buffs before moving into the big leagues. He was a third baseman in his playing days.

35 Year Wait

He managed Cardinal farm teams in Rochester, N.Y.; Omaha, Neb., and Columbus before moving up to the parent club as a coach in 1959. A year later, he replaced Solly Hemus as Cardinal manager.

After his 1964 series victory, Keane said, "I waited 35 years for this. That's a long time, but it was worth it. I never dreamed a human being could be this happy."

May 1

BARBER LOSES DESPITE NO-HITTER; TIGERS BEAT BIRDS TWICE, 2-1, 6-4

Wild Lefty Leaves Game With Two Out In 9th After Giving 10 Walks; Belanger's Error Behind Stu Miller Lets In 2d Run

By JIM ELLIOT

Steve Barber and Stu Miller, the latter going the last one-third inning, combined for the second Oriole no-hitter in American League history yesterday at the Stadium, but the Birds amazingly were the losers when Barber's wildness and an error gave the Detroit Tigers two ninth-inning runs and a 2-to-1 triumph.

Bird Box Scores

DETROIT

	ab	r	h	bi	e
Mcauliffe, ss	3	0	0	0	0
Horton, ph	1	0	0	0	0
Lumpe, 2b	2	0	0	0	0
Stanley, cf	2	0	0	0	0
Wert, 3b	3	0	0	0	0
Kaline, rf	4	0	0	1	
Northrup, lf	4	0	0	0	
Freehan, c	1	0	0	0	
Cash, 1b	3	0	0	0	
Tracewski pr-ss	0	1	0	0	
Oyler, ss	2	0	0	0	
Wood lr-1b	0	1	0	0	
Wilson, p	3	0	0	0	
Gladding, p	0	0	0	0	1
Totals	24	2	0	1	

ORIOLES

	ab	r	h	bi	e
Aparicio, ss	3	0	0	1	0
Snyder, lf	4	0	0	0	
F. Robinson, rf	4	0	1	0	0
B. Robinson, 3b	3	0	0	0	0
Epstein, 1b	4	0	0	0	0
Blefary, lf	2	1	0	0	0
Held, 2b	2	0	0	0	0
Haney, c	0	0	0	0	0
Etchebarren, c	2	0	1	0	0
Lau, c-ph	0	0	0	0	0
Belanger pr-2b	0	0	0	0	1
Barber, p	1	0	0	0	0
S. Miller, p	0	0	0	0	0
Totals	25	1	2	1	2

Detroit .... 000 000 002—2
Orioles .... 000 000 010—1

Double Plays—Detroit 1, Orioles 1. Left On Base—Detroit 11, Orioles 4. Stolen Bases—Freehan, F. Robinson. Sacrifices Cash, Oyler, Wert, Wilson, Barber, Held. Sacrifice Fly Aparicio.

PITCHING SUMMARY

	ip	h	r	er	bb	so
Wilson, W. (2-2)	8	2	1	1	4	4
Gladding	1	0	0	0	0	1
Barber, L. (2-1)	8⅔	0	2	1	10	3
S. Miller	⅓	0	0	0	0	0

Hit By Pitcher By Barber (McAuliffe, Freehan). Wild Pitch Barber.
Time—2.38.

BIRDS BOW AS MANTLE HITS 500TH

Homer Off Stu Miller Helps Yanks Gain 6-5 Victory

By JIM ELLIOT
[Sun Staff Correspondent]

New York, May 14—Mickey Mantle crashed his 500th career home run here today, then almost went from hero to goat with an error as the Orioles lost, 6 to 5, in their series finale with the New York Yankees before 18,872 Yankee Stadium fans.

Two were out and the bases empty in the seventh inning when Mantle pulled a 3-and-2 pitch from Stu Miller 375 feet, deep into the lower right-field deck, to put the Yanks on top, 6-to-4.

Oriole Box Score

ORIOLES

	ab	r	h	bi	e
Belanger, ss	5	1	1	1	1
Snyder, cf	4	0	0	0	0
Blefary, lf	3	1	0	0	0
F. Robinson, rf	4	2	2	0	0
Powell, 1b	4	1	2	1	1
B. Robinson, 3b	2	0	0	0	0
Held, 2b	2	0	0	0	0
Lau, ph	1	0	1	2	0
Mil., p	1	0	0	0	0
Blair,	1	0	0	0	0
Fisher, p	0	0	0	0	0
Etch barre, c	4	0	0	0	0
Barber, p	0	0	0	0	0
Bunker, p	1	0	0	0	0
Bowens, ph	1	0	0	0	0
Johnson, 2b	2	0	0	0	0
Totals	34	5	6	4	3

NEW YORK

	ab	r	h	bi	e
Clarke, 2b	3	1	0	0	0
Howser, 3b	4	1	1	0	0
Mantle, 1b	4	1	2	1	1
Howard, c	4	0	0	0	0
Tresh, lf	3	1	0	1	0
Whitaker, rf	3	0	1	2	0
W. Robinson, p	2	0	0	0	0
Pepitone, ph-cf	2	1	2	2	0
Amaro, ss	4	0	2	0	1
Stottlemyre, p	2	0	0	0	0
Womack, p	2	0	0	0	0
Totals	33	5	8	6	2

Baltimore .... 000 004 010—5
New York .... 300 002 10x—6

DP—Orioles 2 LOB—Orioles, New York 6 2B—Powell, Lau. HR—Belanger (1), Pepitone (1), Mantle (4).

Pitching Summary

	IP	H	R	ER	BB	SO
Barber	⅓	2	3	2	1	1
Bunker	4⅔	2	0	0	0	2
Miller (L. 0-4)	2	3	3	1	0	2
Fisher	1	1	0	0	1	0
Stottlemyre	5⅔	5	4	4	3	5
Womack (W. 3-2)	3⅓	1	1	0	0	2

HBP—By Barber (Tresh). T—2.38.
A—18,872.

CUBS TOP METS TWICE, 5-3, 18-9

Adolfo Phillips Cracks 4 Homers In Twinbill

Chicago, June 11 (AP)—Adolfo Phillips slammed four homers and knocked in eight runs today, sparking the Chicago Cubs to 5-to-3 and 18-to-9 victories over the last place New York Mets.

Phillips smashed three homers and knocked in seven runs in the second game route in which a total of 11 homers were hit. This broke the National League game record of 10 and tied the major league mark of 11 set by the New York Yankees and Detroit in 1950.

Randy Hundley hit two homers and Ron Santo and Ernie Banks clubbed one each for the Cubs in the nightcap.

Senators Shade Chisox In Record 22d Inning, 6-5

Washington, June 12 (AP)—Paul Casanova's bases-loaded single in the 22nd inning gave the Washington Senators a 6-5 victory over the Chicago White Sox tonight in the longest night-game in baseball history.

The 6-hour, 38-minute marathon was the longest ever under lights in both innings played and time consumed.

Hank Allen walked with one out in the 22nd and raced to third on Cape Peterson's single. Mike Epstein drew an intentional walk and Casanova, who had bounced into a double play with the bases loaded in the 20th, came through with the winning hit to left.

Bob Humphreys, who pitched the final three innings for Washington, was the winner and John Buzhardt, who came on in the 14th, took the losse.

It broke the night game record of 19 innings. Five previous games had gone 19 innings.

The longest game in major league history for innings was 26 between Boston and Brooklyn in 1921.

N.L. STARS WIN, 2-1, IN 15 INNINGS

Tony Perez Hits Homer To Beat A.L. In Longest Game

Anaheim, July 11 (AP)—Tony Perez's home run in the fifteenth inning of the longest baseball All-Star game ever played gave the National League a record fifth straight victories over the American League, 2 to 1, today.

The Cincinnati Reds' third baseman sent the sellout crowd of 46,309 home for a late dinner when he blasted a pitch by Kansas City's Catfish Hunter 380 feet into the bleachers in left field.

It was a tense battle of fine pitching that broke all records for strikeouts in All-Star play with a total of 30. The twilight game started in searing 91-degree heat and ended in the cool of a fine California evening.

All-Star Game Box Score

NATIONAL	ab	r	h	rbi	po	a
Brock, lf	7	0	1	0	3	0
cMays, ph-cf	4	0	1	0	8	0
Clemente, rf	6	0	1	0	6	0
Aaron, cf-lf	6	0	2	0	5	0
Cepeda, 1b	6	0	1	0	15	0
Allen, 3b	4	1	1	0	1	3
Perez, 3b	3	1	1	1	0	2
Torre, c	2	0	0	0	4	1
Haller, c	1	0	1	0	7	0
bBanks, ph	1	0	0	0	0	0
McCarver, c	2	0	2	0	7	1
Mazeroski, 2b	4	0	0	0	1	0
Drysdale, p	0	0	0	0	0	0
hHelms, ph	1	0	0	0	0	0
Alley, ss	5	0	0	1	2	3
Marichal, p	1	0	0	0	0	1
Jenkins, p	0	0	0	0	0	0
Gibson, p	0	0	0	0	0	1
fWynn, ph	1	0	0	0	0	0
Short, p	0	0	0	0	0	1
iStaub, ph	1	0	1	0	0	0
Cuellar, p	0	0	0	0	0	0
jMoze, ph-3b	0	0	0	0	1	0
Totals	51	2	9	2	45	13

AMERICAN	ab	r	h	rbi	po	a
B. Robinson, 3b	6	1	1	1	0	4
Carew, 2b	3	0	0	0	2	1
McAuliffe, 2b	3	0	0	2	3	0
Oliva, rf	6	0	2	0	4	0
Killebrew, 1b	4	0	0	0	15	0
Conigliaro, rf	6	0	0	0	4	0
Yastrzemski, lf	4	0	3	0	0	0
Freehan, c	6	0	1	0	13	0
aPetrocelli, ss	1	0	0	0	1	0
bMcGlothlin, p	0	0	0	0	0	0
e-Mantle, ph	1	0	0	0	0	0
Peters, p	0	0	0	0	0	1
c-Alvis, ph	1	0	0	0	0	0
Downing, p	0	0	0	0	0	0
g-Agee, pr	0	1	0	0	0	0
Hunter, p	1	0	0	0	0	0
e-Berry, ph	1	0	0	0	0	0
Chance, p	1	0	0	0	1	2
d-Fregosi, ph-ss	4	0	1	0	2	3
Totals	49	1	8	1	45	16

a—Singled for Chance in 3rd. b—Struck out for McGlothlin in 5th.
c—Struck out for Brock in 6th. d—Singled for Peters in 5th. e—Ran for Mincher in 5th. f—Singled for Gibson in 9th. g—Singled for Haller in 10th.

b—Grounded into fielder's choice for Downing in 10th. e—Singled for Short in 11th. f—Flied out for Cuellar in 13th. g—Grounded into double play for Drysdale in 13th. h—Struck out for Hunter in 15th.

National	0	1	0	0	0	0	0	0	0	1—2
American	0	0	0	0	0	0	1	0	0	0—1

Double Play—Robinson, Carew and Killebrew; McAuliffe, Killebrew. Left On Base—National 5, American 7. Two-Base Hits—Yastrzemski, McCarver. Home Runs—Allen, B. Robinson, Perez. Stolen Bases—Aaron, S. Fregosi, Freehan, Mazeroski.

PITCHING SUMMARY

	Ip	H	R	Er
Chance	3	2	1	1
McGlothlin	2	2	0	0
Peters	2	1	0	0
Downing	3	0	0	0
Hunter (L)	5	4	1	1

	Ip	H	R	Er
Marichal	3	2	1	1
Jenkins	3	1	0	0
Gibson	2	1	0	0
Short	1	1	0	0
Cuellar	2	1	0	0
Drysdale (W)	2	0	0	0

Bases on balls—Short (Yastrzemski), Seaver (Yastrzemski). Strikeouts—Marichal 3 (Oliva, Yastrzemski, Freehan), Jenkins, 6 (Killebrew, Conigliaro, Mantle, Fregosi, Carew, Oliva); Gibson, 2 (B. Robinson, Oliva); Drysdale, 2 (Hunter, Killebrew); Seaver, 1 (Berry), Chance, 1 (Clemente); McGlothlin, 2 (Allen, Alley); Peters, 4 (Mays, Clemente, Cepeda, Allen); Downing, 3 (Clemente, Allen); Hunter, 4 (Alley 2, Clemente, Perez).

Time—3:41. Attendance—46,309.

Umpires—Runge (A), Flaherty (N), Secory (N), first base; Dimuro (A), second base; Burkhart (N), third base; Ashford (A), left field; Felsbouches (N), right field.

GIBSON INJURED IN CARDS' LOSS

Breaks Bone In Leg; Bucs Triumph, 6-4

St. Louis July 15 (AP)—Pinch-hitter Jose Pagan drive in the tie-breaking run in the eighth inning tonight, sparking Pittsburgh to a 6-to-4 victory over the St. Louis Cardinals, who lost pitching ace Bob Gibson for up to six weeks with a broken bone in his right leg.

Gibson, struck in the leg by a liner off the bat of Roberto Clemente in the fourth inning, suffered a fractured fibula above his right ankle and doctors estimated he will be sidelined from four to six weeks.

MATHEWS' 500TH HOME RUN

July 16

Astros 8, Giants 6

(Late Friday Game)

HOUSTON	ab	r	h	bi		SAN FRANCISCO	ab	r	h	bi
RJackson ss	5	0	0	0		Cline cf	1	0	1	0
Morgan 2b	4	0	1	0		Perry pr	0	1	0	0
Wynn cf	4	3	2	0		Mays cf	2	0	0	0
Staub rf	5	2	3	1		Dietz c	1	0	0	0
Mathews 1b	4	1	2	3		Davenprt 3b	4	1	2	3
NMiller lf	3	2	1	3		McCovey 1b	5	0	0	1
Asprmnte 3b	4	0	2	0		Hart lf	5	2	2	1
Sherry p	0	0	0	0		Haller c	4	0	0	0
Adlesh c	4	0	0	0		Brown rf	4	0	2	0
Giusti p	4	0	2	1		Lanier ss	4	0	1	1
Lillis 3b	0	0	0	0		Fuentes 2b	4	2	3	0
						Marichal p	1	0	0	0
						Gibbon p	0	0	0	0
						Siebern ph	1	0	0	0
						Bolin p	0	0	0	0
						Henry p	0	0	0	0
						Hiatt ph	0	0	0	0
						Linzy p	0	0	0	0
Total	37	8	13	8		Total	34	6	11	6

Houston	0	0	0	3	0	4	1	0	0—8
SanFrancisco	1	0	1	0	2	1	0	1	0—6

E—Giusti, Morgan. DP—Houston 1, San Francisco 2. LOB—Houston 5, San Francisco 7. 2B—Cline, Staub, 3B—Davenport, Giusti. HR—N.Miller (1), Davenport (4), Mathews (7), Hart (17). SB—Morgan, Fuentes. S—Davenport, Marichal.

	IP	H	R	ER	BB	SO
Giusti (W,4-8)	7	9	5	5	1	4
Sherry	2	2	1	1	1	4
Marichal (L,12-8)	5	10	7	7	1	3
Gibbon	1	1	0	0	0	0
Bolin	1-3	1	1	1	2	0
Henry	1 2-3	2	0	0	0	3
Linzy	1	0	0	0	0	0

WP—Henry. T—2:50. A—14,194.

Services Held In Miami for Jimmy Foxx

Miami, July 25 (AP)—"I've got lots of memories of Jimmy. With that guy, every day was a memory."

It was Rube Walberg talking. He was a teammate of Jimmy Foxx, one of baseball's greatest home run hitters, when Connie Mack's old Philadelphia Athletics dominated the American League in the early 1930s.

AND THE OLD southpaw was here to pay his last respects to Foxx at services in a flower-bedecked funeral chapel packed with friends of the Hall of Fame star.

Foxx, who retired in 1945 after hitting 534 major league home runs, choked to death Friday while having dinner at the home of his brother, Sam. He was 59.

AMONG THE pallbearers was Max Carey, former Pittsburgh and Brooklyn infielder. With Foxx and Ted Williams, Carey was one of three Hall of Famers in the Old Timers Professional Baseball Association of Greater Miami.

The eulogy delivered by the Rev. Jiles Kirkland, pastor of the First Methodist Church of South Miami, was brief.

"His feats and exploits on the baseball diamond are too well known to mention, too many to enumerate," he said. "His name had something of magic to me."

Foxx was buried in Flagler Memorial Cemetery.

NEW TV PACT FOR BASEBALL

NBC Pays $50,000,000 For Three-Year Package

Chicago, Aug. 4 (P)—Organized baseball and the National Broadcasting Co. agreed today on a $50,000,000 three-year television contract.

The package includes the World Series, the All-Star Game and 28 weekly telecasts.

John E. Fetzer of the Detroit Tigers, chairman of the major league television committee, announced the agreement after a day-long negotiating session.

K.C. SUSPENDS LEW KRAUSSE

Finley Forbids Players To Drink On Planes

Kansas City, Aug. 18 (P)—Pitcher Lew Krausse of the Kansas City Athletics was suspended indefinitely without pay today by owner Charles O. Finley and the club was notified that alcoholic drinks no longer will be served to the A's on airlines.

The owner warned the A's he won't tolerate the "shenanigans" of a few.

"Krausse has been suspended indefinitely without pay for conduct unbecoming a major league ball player," Finley announced from his Chicago office. "I will have no further comment on Krausse."

Injured Conigliaro Out Of Flag Drive

Boston, Aug. 19 (P)—Boston Red Sox slugger Tony Conigliaro was reported in satisfactory condition today with a fractured left cheekbone he received last night when struck in the face by a fast ball.

Doctors said he will be out of action for three or four weeks, and it is possible he will not play again in the five weeks remaining in the American League baseball season.

Near Fatal Blow

He was hit just below the protective helmet by a fast ball thrown by Jack Hamilton of the California Angels and carried from the field on a stretcher in the fourth inning of the Red Sox' 3-2 victory at Fenway Park.

"If it had been two inches higher," team physician Dr. Thomas Tierney said, "He would have been dead."

"We're just going day by day," Tierney said, not predicting when Conigliaro would return to action.

TWINS TAKE A.L. LEAD ON CHANCE GEM

Dean's Second August No-Hitter Completes Sweep Of Tribe

Cleveland, Aug. 25 (P)—Minnesota's Dean Chance became the first man in 29 years to pitch two hitless games in one month tonight when he hurled a no-hitter and defeated Cleveland 2-to-1 in the second game of a twi-night doubleheader. The Twins had won the ten-inning opener, 6-to-5.

The sweep gave the Twins possession of first place, in the American League, one half game in front of both Boston and Chicago, who split their twi-night doubleheader.

Just nineteen days ago, Chance had pitched five perfect innings, defeating Boston 2-0 in a rain-shortened game. Although he was credited with a complete game for that performance, organized baseball records list only no-hitters of nine or more innings.

Vander Meer In '38

Johnny Vander Meer, pitching for Cincinnati in 1938, hurled consecutive no-hitters to become the only man in baseball history to perform that feat.

Chance struck out eight but was wild, walking five Cleveland batters, including the first two he faced.

He allowed a run without a hit in the first inning when Lee Maye and Vic Davalillo opened with walks.

An error by Cesar Tovar loaded the bases for the Indians, and then Chance's wild pitch allowed Maye to score.

Sept. 2

Standings Of The Teams

	W	L	Pct	G B
Boston	77	59	.566	
Minnesota	75	58	.564	½
Detroit	74	60	.552	2
Chicago	73	60	.549	2½
California	67	65	.508	8
Washington	64	71	.474	12½
Cleveland	63	72	.467	13½
Orioles	60	71	.458	14½
New York	60	75	.444	16½
Kansas City	55	77	.417	20

Finley Fires Dark, Names Appling To Lead Athletics

Washington, Aug. 20 (P)—Manager Alvin Dark of the Kansas City Athletics, on the verge of signing a new two-year contract, was fired abruptly today in the wake of a feud between the players and owner Charles O. Finley.

Finley, the controversial owner who has averaged a manager per season since he took control of the A's in December, 1960, immediately named veteran coach Luke Appling as interim manager for the remainder of the 1967 season.

A statement issued by the Kansas City players today apparently had a direct bearing on Finley's actions.

After Finley suspended pitcher Lew Krausse for what he described as conduct unbecoming a major league player, the A's held a meeting here and released a statement which accused Finley of undermining the morale of the ball club by using informers to spy on the players.

"We players feel that if Mr. Finley would give his fine coaching staff and excellent manager the authority they deserve these problems would not exist," the statement said.

Shown a copy of the statement late yesterday, Finley was visably shaken and said, "This compels me to withhold the announcement of a two-year Dark contract until further consideration."

By 5.30 A.M. today, Dark was out of a job, having been notified of his dismissal by telephone about one hour after the conclusion of an all-xnight meeting.

The A's held another clubhouse meeting after today's scheduled game with the Senators was postponed by rain and drafted a statement which accepted the blame for Dark's dismissal.

"We players feel a deep personal loss at the firing of Alvin Dark," the statement said. "We feel this action is the result of the public statement of August 19."

Dark in Tears

Dark bade a tearful farewell to the players in D.C. Stadium.

"I'm not upset about being fired," he told A's. "That's part of baseball. I hate to leave you kid . . . good luck. . . ."

Dark tried to continue, but couldn't. Tears streamed down his cheeks as he turned his back and left the clubhouse.

The A's praised Dark, several saying he was the best manager they ever played for. First baseman Ken Harrelson said, "Finley made a big mistake. Te's a menace to baseball."

Asked earlier if the players' statement was the reason for his firing, Dark said:

"I think it was. It definitely did it. I had to back up my players. Everything in their statement was correct."

Finley issued a statement of his own this afternoon, saying he fired Dark because "I am convinced he had lost contro of his players."

National League

Scores Of Yesterday

St. Louis, 5; Atlanta, 2.
Pittsburgh, 10; Houston, 3.
Cincinnati, 10; Chicago, 3.
Los Angeles, 2; New York, 1.
San Francisco, 2; Philadelphia, 1.

Final Standings

	W.	L.	Pct.	G.B.
St. Louis	101	60	.627	
San Francisco	91	71	.562	10½
Chicago	87	74	.540	14
Cincinnati	87	75	.537	14½
Philadelphia	82	80	.506	19½
Pittsburgh	81	81	.500	20½
Atlanta	77	85	.475	24½
Los Angeles	73	89	.451	26½
Houston	69	93	.426	32½
New York	61	101	.377	40½

Giants Nip Reds In 21 Innings, 1-0

Cincinnati, Sept. 1 (P) — Bob Lee walked Dick Groat with the bases loaded in the 21st inning tonight, giving San Francisco a 1-to-0 victory over Cincinnati in the longest night game in National League history.

Gaylord Perry, who pitched 16 innings, and reliever Frank Linzy scattered 12 hits and stopped the Reds cold in the five-hour, 40-minute struggle.

With one out in the twenty-first, Jim Hart singled to center and Ollie Brown doubled to left off Lee, the fourth Cincinnati pitcher. Hal Lanier drew an intentional pass, filling the bases, before Lee walked Groat, forcing in the game's lone run.

It was the longest N.L. night game in both innings and time consumed and the longest 1-0 game on record.

The clubs also tied the mark of 20 scoreless innings, set by the Boston Braves and Pittsburgh Pirates in a 1918 game won by Pittsburgh 2-0 in the twenty-first inning.

Perry, the Giants' starter, went out for a pinch hitter in the seventeenth after scattering 10 hits, striking out 12 and extending his string of consecutive scoreless innings to 29. Linzy allowed two more hits in squaring his record at 6-6.

SAN FRANCISCO	ab	r	h	bi	CINCINNATI	ab	r	h
J Alou lf	9	0	2	0	Harper rf	8	0	0	0
Haller c	9	0	0	0	Pinson cf	9	0	1	0
Mays cf	9	0	2	0	Rose lf	9	0	1	0
McCovey 1b	8	0	0	0	L May 1b	4	0	0	0
Hart 3b	9	1	2	0	Abernthy p	1	0	0	0
Brown rf	9	0	4	0	S Lamsky ph	1	0	0	0
Lanier ss	7	0	1	0	Nottebart p	0	0	0	0
Fuentes 2b	3	0	0	0	Coker pn	1	0	0	0
Davenprt ph	1	0	1	0	Lee p	0	0	0	0
Cline p	0	0	0	0	Edwards ph	1	0	0	0
Groat 2b	3	0	1	1	Perez 3b	9	0	0	0
Perry p	5	0	1	0	Ruiz 3b	4	0	0	0
Hiatt ph	1	0	1	0	Helms 2b	8	0	2	0
Henderson pr	0	0	0	0	Bench c	8	0	0	0
Linzy p	2	0	0	0	Cardenas s	5	0	0	0

San Francisco 000 000 000 000 000 000 001 — 1
Cincinnati 000 000 000 000 000 000 000 — 0

E—None. DP—San Francisco 1. LOB—San Francisco 12, Cincinnati 8. 2B—Brown, May. S—Perry. Helms, WP—Queen. L—Lee. W—Linzy.

Standings Of The Teams

Sept. 25

	W.	L.	Pct.	G.B.
Minnesota	90	67	.573	—
Boston	90	68	.570	½
Chicago	89	68	.567	1
Detroit	88	68	.564	1½
California	80	74	.519	8½
Orioles	73	84	.465	17
Cleveland	73	85	.462	17½
Washington	72	84	.462	17½
New York	67	89	.429	22½
Kansas City	60	95	.387	29

Clemente Paces 10-3 Pirate Win

Pittsburgh, Oct. 1 (P) — Roberto Clemente slugged a two-run triple and a home run today to power Pittsburgh's 10-to-3 triumph over the Houston Astros and earn his fourth National League batting title with a .357 average.

Clemente took titles in 1961, 1964 and 1965. His 209 hits this season gave him the highest batting average in the majors since 1961 when Norm Cash of Detroit hit .361.

Clemente tripled home two runs in the first and rapped a solo home run—his 23rd—in the sixth. It was his 110th run batted in.

Dodgers Edge Mets

Los Angeles, Oct. 1 (P) — Alan Foster and Phil Regan collaborated on a two-hitter today as the Los Angeles Dodgers closed their season with a 2-to-1 victory over the New York Mets.

A two-out error by second baseman Ken Boswell in the eighth inning sent both Los Angeles runs across the plate after the Dodgers filled the bases on a walk and singles by Ron Hunt and John Roseboro.

Regan hurled two hitless innings of relief to pick up the victory as the Dodgers became the first National League team ever to win a pennant one-season and finish eighth the next.

NEW YORK	ab	r	h	bi	LOS ANGELES	ab	r	h
Heise ss	3	0	0	0	W Davis cf	4	0	0	0
Harrelson ss	2	0	0	0	Hunt 2b	4	0	1	0
Boswell 2b	3	0	0	0	W Davis cf	4	0	1	0
Kranepool 1b	3	0	0	0	Ferrara rf	4	0	0	0
Swoboda rf	3	0	0	0	Roseboro c	3	0	1	0
Moock 3b	3	0	0	0	Fairly 1b	3	0	0	0
Otis cf	3	0	0	0	Gabrielso lf	3	0	0	0
Boyer cf	0	0	0	0	Bailey 3b	3	0	0	0
Sullivan c	3	0	0	0	Lefebvre ss	3	0	0	0
Grote c	0	0	0	0	Foster p	2	0	0	0
Frisella p	2	0	0	0	Regan p	0	0	0	0
Seinar p	0	0	0	0					

New York 010 000 000 — 1
Los Angeles 000 000 02x — 2

E—Harrelson. DP—Los Angeles 1. LOB—New York 3, Los Angeles 3. SB—W Davis.

ANGELS END FLAG HOPES OF DETROIT

Beat Tigers, 8-5, In Second Game, Prevent Tie For Pennant

Detroit, Oct. 1 (AP)—Don Mincher's third home run of the day and a two-run triple by Roger Repoz helped California crush Detroit's American League pennant hopes with an 8-to-5 victory over the Tigers in the second game of a season-ending doubleheader.

The Tigers won the first game 6-4, but their bid for a first-place tie with Boston fell short in the nightcap as the Angels stormed from behind to deliver the death blow.

The Red Sox already had clinched at least a tie for the flag by ousting Minnesota 5-3 when the Tigers sent righthander Denny McLain to the mound in the nightcap against the California spoilers.

The Angels, who had stunned Detroit 8-6 in the second game of Saturday's twin bill with a six-run burst in the eighth inning, spotted McLain an early 3-1 edge before seizing the lead in the third inning.

RED SOX TOP TWINS, 5-3, IN FINAL GAME TO CAPTURE PENNANT

American League

Scores Of Yesterday

Orioles, 4; Cleveland, 0.
Boston, 5; Minnesota, 3.
Detroit, 6-5; California, 4-8.
Washington, 4; Chicago, 3.
New York, 4; Kansas City, 3.

Final Standings

	W.	L.	Pct.	G.B.
Boston	92	70	.568	..
Detroit	91	71	.562	1
Minnesota	91	71	.562	1
Chicago	89	73	.549	3
California	84	77	.522	7½
Orioles	76	85	.472	15½
Washington	76	85	.472	15½
Cleveland	75	87	.463	17
New York	72	90	.444	20
Kansas City	62	99	.385	29½

Lonborg Pitches Win For Boston's First Flag Since 1946

BY JIM ELLIOT
(Sun Staff Correspondent)

Boston, Oct. 1 — Fifty-five-year-old Fenway Park erupted in one of the wildest scenes in major league history at 4.33 P.M. today when the Boston Red Sox defeated the Minnesota Twins, 5 to 3, to win Boston's first American League pennant since 1946 on this final day of the season.

Carried from the field by many of the thousands of delirious fans who poured out of the stands from among the 35,770 on hand was Sox righthander Jim Lonborg who, after three years of trying, not only beat the Twins for the first time but went the distance on a seven-hitter.

Lonborg Starts Rally

The celebrating fans didn't wait to discover whether the Detroit Tigers had won a doubleheader from the California Angels today — a feat which would have forced a best-of-three playoff with Boston for the pennant.

But the Angels gave the Red Sox a big helping hand by rallying to beat the Tigers in the nightcap, 8 to 5. This completed the Cinderella story for the Beantowners who finished ninth last season.

The 24-year-old Lonborg, while capturing his twenty-second victory against nine defeats, sparked the decisive five-run, sixth-inning rally when he beat out a perfect bunt as the leadoff batter.

It was Lonborg's second hit of the day and, before the big inning was over the Sox had gathered four hits more. Those blows coupled with two wild pitches, a walk and an error, provided more than enough.

Triple Crown Winner

The big bat in Boston's twelve-hit attack was again Carl Yastrzemski, who yesterday sent the Sox into a first-place tie with a three-run homer in a 6-to-4 victory. Today, he resorted to the single with a two-run one-bagger to wipe out an early 2-to-0 Minnesota advantage.

Yastrzemski went 4-for-4 today with three singles and a double. He raised his batting average to .326 and the two runs batted in gave him 121.

The 28-year-old Yastrzemski, although his homers were equaled by Minnesota's Harmon Killebrew, thus did for Boston what Frank Robinson did for Baltimore last year—won the "triple crown."

Victim of the sudden onslaught which had followed five innings of Boston mistakes and frustration was Dean Chance, Minnesota's big winner who suffered the loss and closed with a 20-14 record.

The Box Score

MINNESOTA	ab	r	h	bi	BOSTON	ab	r	h	bi
Versalles ss	3	0	0	0	Adair 2b	4	1	2	0
Reese lf	1	0	1	0	Andrews 2b	0	0	0	0
Tovar 3b	3	1	0	0	DJones 3b	2	0	0	0
Killebrew 1b	2	2	2	0	Ystrmski lf	4	1	4	2
Oliva rf	3	0	2	0	Harrelson rf	3	0	1	0
Allison lf	4	0	1	1	Tartabull rf	1	1	0	0
Hernandz ss	0	0	0	0	Scott 1b	4	0	0	0
Uh'aendr cf	4	0	1	0	Petrocelli ss	3	0	1	0
Carew 2b	4	0	0	0	RSmith cf	4	0	0	1
Zimmrman c	2	0	0	0	Gibson c	2	0	0	0
Nixon c	1	0	0	0	Siebern ph	1	0	0	0
Rollins ph	1	0	0	0	EHoward c	1	0	1	0
DChance p	2	0	0	0	Lonborg p	4	1	2	0
Worthgtn p	0	0	0	0					
Kosco ph	1	0	0	0					
Roland p	0	0	0	0					
Grant p	0	0	0	0					
Total	31	3	7	1	**Total**	35	5	12	4

Minnesota ..... 1 0 1 0 0 0 1 0 0 — 3
Boston .... 0 0 0 0 5 0 0 x — 5

E. Scott. Yastrzemski. Killebrew. DP-Minnesota 3. Boston 2. LOB Minnesota 5; Boston 7. 2B—Oliva. Yastrzemski.

	IP	H	R	ER	BB	SO
D Chance (L.20-14)	5	6	5	5	0	2
Worthington	1	0	0	0	1	1
Roland	1	3	0	0	0	0
Grant	2	3	0	0	0	1
Lonborg (W.22-9)	9	7	3	1	4	5

WP Worthington (2). T 2:25. A—35,770.

CALIFORNIA	ab	r	h	bi	DETROIT	ab	r	h	bi
LRodrgez 3b	5	0	1	0	Trcewski ss	4	1	3	0
Fregosi ss	4	0	0	0	MAuliffe 2b	4	0	0	0
Hall rf	4	1	1	0	Kaline rf	4	0	1	0
Mincher 1b	4	2	2	3	WHorton lf	4	3	2	3
Reichardt lf	4	0	0	0	Freehan c	3	1	3	1
Repoz cf	3	0	1	0	Wert 3b	4	1	2	1
Rodgers c	4	1	3	1	Mathews 1b	4	0	1	2
Knoop 2b	3	0	0	0	Stanley cf	4	0	0	0
Wright p	1	0	0	0	Sparma p	3	0	0	0
Kelso p	0	0	0	0	Gladding p	1	0	0	0
Skowron ph	1	0	0	0					
JHamilton p	0	0	0	0					
Johnstone ph	1	0	0	0					
Cimino p	0	0	0	0					
Satriano ph	1	0	0	0					
Total	35	4	8	4	**Total**	35	6	12	6

California ... 0 1 0 1 0 0 0 2 0 — 4
Detroit ..... 2 0 3 1 0 0 0 x — 6

E. Sparma. Repoz. McAuliffe. DP-Detroit 2. LOB California 7. Detroit 6. 2B W. Horton. HR—W. Horton (19). Mincher 2 (24). Rodgers (6).

	IP	H	R	ER	BB	SO
Wright (L.5-5)	2 2-3	6	5	2	1	0
Kelso	1-3	0	0	0	0	0
J Hamilton	1	0	0	0	1	0
Cimino	1	1	0	0	0	3
Sparma (W.16-9)	7	7	4	4	2	2
Gladding	2	1	0	0	0	2

HBP Sparma (Fregosi). T 2.24.

CALIFORNIA	ab	r	h	bi	DETROIT	ab	r	h	bi
Repoz cf	5	0	1	2	MAuliffe ss	4	0	2	3
Fregosi ss	4	1	2	1	Lumpe 2b	1	0	1	0
Mincher 1b	5	1	1	2	Trcewski ss	2	0	0	0
Hall rf	5	0	0	0	GBrown ph	1	0	0	0
Reichardt lf	3	3	2	1	Oyler ss	0	0	0	0
Held lf	0	0	0	0	Kaline rf	4	0	2	0
Satriano 3b	4	0	0	0	WHorton lf	4	0	0	0
Rodgers c	3	0	1	1	Mathews 1b	4	1	1	0
Knoop 2b	3	2	1	0	Northrup cf	4	1	1	2
RClark p	0	0	0	0	Freehan c	4	1	2	0
Simmons p	0	0	0	0	Wert 3b	2	2	1	0
Johnstone ph	1	0	1	0	McLain p	0	0	0	0
MGlothlin p	2	1	1	1	Hiller p	0	0	0	0
Rojas p	0	0	0	0	Marshall p	0	0	0	0
Brunet p	0	0	0	0	Wicksham p	0	0	0	0
					Aguirre p	0	0	0	0
					Matchick ph	1	0	0	0
					Lasher p	0	0	0	0
					Cash ph	1	0	0	0
					Dobson p	0	0	0	0
					Lolich p	0	0	0	0
					Green ph	0	0	0	0
					Price ph	1	0	0	0
Total	35	8	10	8	**Total**	33	5	10	5

California .... 0 1 3 3 1 0 0 0 0 — 8
Detroit ...... 0 3 0 0 0 0 2 0 0 — 5

DP California 3. Detroit 1. LOB-California 6. Detroit 5. 2B-Mathews, Fregosi. Reichardt. Freehan. 3B-McAuliffe. Repoz. HR-Reichardt (17). Northrup (10). Mincher (25). SB-Reichardt. S McLain. Rojas.

	IP	H	R	ER	BB	SO
R.Clark	1 2-3	4	3	3	1	1
Simmons	1-3	0	0	0	0	0
MGlothlin (W.12-8)	4 2-3	4	2	2	1	0
Rojas	1 1-3	2	0	0	1	0
Brunet	1	0	0	0	0	0
McLain	2 2-3	4	3	3	0	1
Hiller (L.4-3)	2-3	1	3	3	2	2
Marshall	1-3	2	1	1	0	0
Wickersham	0	0	0	0	0	0
Aguirre	1 1-3	2	1	1	0	1
Lasher	2-3	1	0	0	0	1
Dobson	1-3	0	0	0	1	0
Lolich	1 2-3	0	0	0	1	0

HBP Wickersham (Fregosi). WP Lasher. T 3.12. A- 38,398.

Cardinals Win, 7-2, To Capture Series

Gibson Holds Red Sox To 3 Hits, Matching 2 Records; Lonborg Is Loser

St. Louis right-hander Bob Gibson stopped the Boston Red Sox on three hits at Fenway Park in Boston yesterday as the Cardinals took the seventh and deciding game of the World Series, 7 to 2.

The victory was Gibson's third of the Series and a National League record-matching fifth of his career in World Series competition. All of his five victories, including two against the New York Yankees in 1964, have been complete games, tying another World Series record.

Also Hit Home Run

Gibson heaped insult on the grievous injury he was dealing the Red Sox, losers in only one of six previous World Series appearances, by whacking a home run to deep center field in a two-run fifth inning that gave St. Louis a decisive 4-to-0 lead.

Boston right-hander Jim Lonborg, who had handcuffed the Cards in two earlier outings in the Series, started against Gibson with just two days' rest. A 22-game winner for the American League champions in the regular season, Lonborg allowed all seven Cardinal runs on ten hits in going the first six innings.

Gibson, working on three days' rest, struck out ten and had a no-hitter until George Scott tripled and scored on a throwing error to lead off the fifth. Ironically, it was Scott whom Gibson struck out to end the game.

Cardinal left fielder Lou Brock had a single, double and a walk and stole three bases for a record seven thefts in the seven Series games. St. Louis second baseman Julian Javier contributed a three-run homer and a single.

Reprinted from
The Baltimore Sun papers

Series Box Score

ST. LOUIS (N)

	AB	R	H	BI	PO	A
Brock, lf	4	1	2	0	1	0
Flood, cf	3	1	1	1	0	0
Maris, rf	3	0	2	1	1	0
Cepeda, 1b	5	0	0	0	6	2
McCarver, c	5	1	1	0	12	0
Shannon, 3b	4	1	0	0	0	0
Javier, 2b	4	1	2	3	4	3
Maxvill, ss	4	1	1	0	3	3
Gibson, p	4	1	1	1	0	1
Totals	38	7	10	6	27	9

BOSTON (A)

	AB	R	H	BI	PO	A
Foy, 3b	3	0	0	0	2	3
Moorehead, p	0	0	0	0	0	0
Osinski, p	0	0	0	0	0	0
Brett, p	0	0	0	0	0	0
Andrews, 2b	3	0	0	0	1	2
Yastrzemski, lf	3	0	1	0	2	0
Harrelson, rf	4	0	0	0	0	0
Scott, 1b	4	1	1	0	9	0
R. Smith, cf	3	0	0	0	2	0
Petrocelli, ss	3	1	1	0	3	2
Howard, c	2	0	0	0	4	1
b-Jones, 3b	0	0	0	0	0	0
Lonborg, p	1	0	0	0	0	0
a-Tartabull, ph	1	0	0	0	0	0
Santiago, p	0	0	0	0	0	0
c-Sieborn, ph	1	0	0	0	0	0
R. Gibson, c	0	0	0	0	1	0
Totals	28	2	3	1	27	8

a-Struck out for Lonborg in 6th.
b-Walked for Howard in 8th.
c-Hit into force play for Santiago in 8th.

ST. LOUIS (N) . . 002 023 000—7.
BOSTON (A) . . . . 000 010 010—2

Errors—Javier, Foy. Double Play—Maxvill, Javier and Cepeda. Left On Bases—St. Louis 7; Boston 3. 2B—McCarver, Brock, Petrocelli. 3B—Maxvill, Scott. Home Run—B. Gibson, Javier. SB—Brock 3. S—Andrews. SF—Maris.

PITCHING SUMMARY

	IP	H	R	ER
B. Gibson (Winner)	9	3	2	2
Lonborg (Loser)	6	10	7	6
Santiago	2	0	0	0
Morehead	1/3	0	0	0
Osinski	1/3	0	0	0
Brett	1/3	0	0	0

BB—B. Gibson 3 (Foy, Yastrzemski, Jones), Lonborg 1 (Flood), Morehead 3 (Brock, Flood, Maris). SO—B. Gibson 10 (Harrelson 3, Scott 2, Petrocelli 2, Lonborg, Foy, Andrews, Tartabull), Lonborg 1 (Cepeda), Morehead 1 (Gibson). WP—Lonborg, Gibson.

Time—2.23. Attendance—35,188.

Umpires—Stevens (A) Plate, Barlick (N) First Base, Umont (A) Second Base, Donatelli (N) Third Base, Runge (A) Left Field, Pryor (N) Right Field.

A. L. Approves Transfer Of A's To Oakland, Plans Expansion

Chicago, Oct. 18 (P) — The American League approved tonight transfer of the Kansas City Athletics to Oakland, Cal., effective in 1968, and also added an expansion plan to increase membership to 12 clubs by 1971 with the expansion franchises going to Kansas City and Seattle, Wash.

The awards to the new franchise cities are subject to applicable baseball rules and procedures and, in the case of Seattle, to that city being able to provide suitable stadium facilities.

After 24-Inning Encounter
Astros, Mets Glad for Rest

HOUSTON, April 16 (AP) — The New York Mets and the Houston Astros, the National League's expansion teams of 1962, were thankful today was a day off.

Both teams literally collapsed on locker-room benches after a Monday night record-breaker won by the Astros, 1-0 in 24 innings.

It was the longest night game, in number of innings, ever played in the major leagues and the longest complete game ever in the National. The 23 consecutive scoreless innings also set a record.

Only 3000 of the 14,219 customers were present when the 6 hour and 6 minute marathon ended at 1:37 a.m. CST.

With one out and the bases loaded, Norm Miller scored as Al Weis, the Mets' shortstop, let Bob Aspromonte's double play grounder through him for an error.

Until Miller crossed the plate, Houston had not scored in 35 innings but the victory left the Astros at the top of the League with a 5-1 record.

Weis had played brilliantly for 23 innings, but he sank to his knees from sheer exhaustion as the ball went through his legs. "I just plain blew it," Weis said.

"These long games can really be murder," said Gil Hodges, manager of the Mets. Hodges also was involved in the previous longest night game in the majors. Last year, when he managed the Washington Senators, they defeated the Chicago White Sox, 6-5, in 22 innings on June 12 in Washington. That game lasted 6 hours, 38 minutes.

Ron Swoboda and Tommie Agee of the Mets each went hitless in ten at-bats. Agee's average dropped from .312 to .192, Swoboda's from .385 to .217.

Both teams got 11 hits as Hodges used eight pitchers, one short of a record, and Hatton used five. Wade Blasingame was the winner, Les Rohr the loser.

Miller opened the 24th with a single. A balk by Rohr sent him to second. Jim Wynn was purposely walked and both runners advanced on Rusty Staub's grounder to second base. Hodges ordered another pass, this one to John Bateman, to load the bases. Aspromonte took a two-one count off Rohr and then hit the grounder that got through Weis.

Boston and Brooklyn played a 1-1 tie in 26 innings on May 1, 1920, but the league record for a complete game before Monday night was set May 31, 1964, when San Francisco needed 23 innings to defeat the Mets, 8-6, in seven hours and 31 minutes.

The American League record for the longest complete game also is 24 innings when Philadelphia defeated Boston, 4-1, on Sept. 1, 1906.

NEW YORK	ab r h bi	HOUSTON	ab r h bi
Weis ss	9 0 1 0	RDavis cf	0 0 1 0
Boswell 2b	10 0 1 0	NMiller rf	8 1 1 0
Agee cf	10 0 0 0	Wynn lf	8 0 1 0
Swoboda rf	10 0 0 0	Staub 1b	9 0 2 0
Shemsky lf	4 0 2 0	King c	9 0 1 0
CJones lf	6 0 1 0	Bateman ph	0 0 0 0
Kranpool 1b	8 0 2 0	Aspromnte 3b	9 0 0 0
Buchek 3b	2 0 0 0	Gotay 2b	9 0 2 0
Charles 3b	6 0 1 0	Torres ss	8 0 3 0
Grote c	7 0 2 0	DWilson p	2 0 0 0
Seaver p	3 0 1 0	Thomas ph	1 0 0 0
RTaylor p	0 0 0 0	Buzhardt p	0 0 0 0
Linz ph	1 0 0 0	Rader ph	1 0 0 0
Koonce p	0 0 0 0	Coombs p	0 0 0 0
WShort p	0 0 0 0	Murrell ph	1 0 0 0
Selma p	0 0 0 0	Ray p	2 0 0 0
Bosch ph	1 0 0 0	Blasgme p	2 0 0 0
AJackson p	0 0 0 0		
Harrelson ph	1 0 0 0		
Frisella p	1 0 0 0		
Cardwell ph	0 0 0 0		
Rohr p	0 0 0 0		
Total	79 0 11 0	Total	79 1 11 0

One out when winning run scored.

N.Y.   000 000 000 000 000 000 000 000—0
Houston 000 000 000 000 000 000 000 001—1

E—D.Wilson, Weis. DP—New York 1, Houston 1. LOB—New York 16, Houston 16. 2B—King, Charles. SB—C.Jones, Charles, S—Buchek, N.Miller, Grote, Kranepool, Cardwell.

METS' PITCHING	IP	H	R	ER	BB	SO
Seaver	10	2	0	0	0	3
R.Taylor	1	1	0	0	0	1
Koonce	1-3	1	0	0	0	0
W.Short	1	1	0	0	2	1
Selma	2-3	0	0	0	0	4
A.Jackson	3	1	0	0	0	4
Frisella	5	4	0	0	4	3
Rohr (L,0-1)	2 1-3	1	1	0	4	2

ASTROS' PITCHING	IP	H	R	ER	BB	SO
D.Wilson	9	5	0	0	3	5
Buzhardt	2	0	0	0	0	2
Coombs	2	3	0	0	0	2
Ray	7	2	0	0	1	11
Blasgme (W,1-0)	4	1	0	0	1	3

WP—Seaver, D.Wilson, Rohr. Balk—Rohr. T—6:06. A—14,219.

A'S HUNTER IN PERFECT GAME ROLE

Catfish Sets Down 27 Twins In Order For 4-To-0 Victory

Oakland, May 8 (AP) — Catfish Hunter hurled the American League's first perfect game in regular season play since 1922 tonight and drove in three runs as the Oakland Athletics trimmed Minnesota, 4 to 0.

Hunter, a 22-year-old right-hander in his fourth major league season, set down all 27 batters he faced in stymieing the normally hard-hitting Twins to become the ninth perfect game pitcher in modern baseball history.

Hunter Fans 11

The 6-foot, 192-pound youngster from Hertford, N.C., struck out eleven and needed just one outstanding defensive play — third baseman Sal Bando's stab of a fifth inning grounder by Bob Allison—in tossing the second no-hitter of the young season.

His perfect game gem matched a feat last accomplished by Sandy Koufax, the Los Angeles Dodgers' brilliant southpaw, three years ago against the Chicago Cubs.

Larsen In Series

The last American Leaguer to toss a perfect game was New York Yankees' right-hander Don Larsen, who did it in the 1956 World Series against the Brooklyn Dodgers. But it had been 46 years since Charlie Robertson, of the Chicago White Sox, pitched a perfect game against the Detroit Tigers in a regular season contest.

Hunter completed his classic performance by getting pinch-hitter John Roseboro to ground out, leading off the ninth, striking out Bruce Look and fanning Rich Reese on a 3-2 count after the pinch-hitter had fouled off five straight pitches.

Plates First Run

Locked in a scoreless duel with Minnesota's Dave Boswell for six innings, Hunter gave himself all the offensive help he needed with a run-scoring bunt single in the seventh.

In the eighth, his two-run single capped a three-run wrap-up burst for the A's.

Hunter, who signed with the Athletics for a $75,000 bonus in 1964, was 13-17 last year and missed a month because of an appendectomy. He came into tonight's game with a life-time record of 32-38, including a 2-2 mark this season.

It was the first no-hitter ever hurled by an Oakland pitcher.

MINNESOTA	ab r h bi	OAKLAND	ab r h bi
Tovar 3b	3 0 0 0	Campneris ss	4 0 2 0
Carew 2b	3 0 0 0	RJackson rf	4 0 0 0
Killebrew 1b	3 0 0 0	Bando 3b	3 0 1 0
Oliva rf	3 0 0 0	Webster 1b	4 1 2 0
Uhlaendr cf	3 0 0 0	Donaldson 2b	3 0 0 0
Allison lf	3 0 0 0	Pagliarni c	3 1 0 0
Hernandz ss	2 0 0 0	Monday cf	3 2 2 0
Roseboro ph	1 0 0 0	Rudi lf	3 0 0 0
Look c	3 0 0 0	F.Robsn ph	0 0 0 0
Boswell p	2 0 0 0	Cater lf	0 0 1
Perranoski p	0 0 0 0	Hunter p	4 0 3 3
Reese ph	1 0 0 0		
Total	27 0 0 0	Total	31 4 10 4

Minnesota 000 000 000—0
Oakland   000 000 13x—4

E—Boswell. DP—Minnesota 2. LOB—Minnesota 2, Oakland 0. 2B—Hunter. Monday. 3B—Campaneris.

	IP	H	R	ER	BB	SO
Boswell (L,3-3)	7 2-3	9	4	4	1	4
Perranoski	1-3	1	0	0	1	0
Hunter (W,3-2)	9	0	0	0	0	11

HBP—by Perranoski (Pagliaroni). WP—Boswell (2). T—2:28. A—6,298.

MONTREAL, SAN DIEGO IN BIG LEAGUE

National Loop Awards Franchises. Expansion Set For 1969

Chicago, May 27 (AP) — Montreal and San Diego were awarded National League baseball franchises tonight at the cost of $10,000,000 each, effective for the 1969 season.

Warren Giles, president of the National League, called it "the most important decision the league has made since allowing the New York Giants and Brooklyn Dodgers to move to the West Coast."

"Pros and cons of expansion of all five represented cities were taken into full consideration," said Giles. "It was a very difficult decision."

3 Cities Lose Out

Cities losing out were Buffalo, Dallas-Fort Worth and Milwaukee.

The American League previously admitted Kansas City and Seattle for the 1969 season, expanding to twelve teams.

The N.L. moguls started their meeting at 11:45 A.M. and didn't announce their final decision until 10 P.M.

Giles said the $10 million purchase price for each club included an immediate sharing in the national television game of the week and the World Series television contract.

Giles said the vote accepting San Diego and Montreal followed "I judge sixteen, seventeen or eighteen ballots."

SENATORS DOWN TIGERS, 8 TO 4

Howard Blasts 2 To Set Big League Homer Mark

Detroit, May 18 (AP)—Frank Howard blasted two home runs today, setting a major league record of ten homers in six successive games and leading the Washington Senators to an 8-to-4 victory over the Detroit Tigers.

The towering Washington slugger, major league leader in home runs and runs batted in, connected with the bases empty in the third inning and poled his seventeenth homer of the year with two on in the fifth.

Howard's ten homers in six games broke the mark of seven previously shared by Roger Maris of the New York Yankees and George Kelly, Walker Cooper and Willie Mays, all of the New York Giants.

The record for hitting home runs in successive games is held by Dale Long, who hit eight in eight games for Pittsburgh in May, 1956.

"Without a doubt this is the best spring start I've ever had," said Howard. "I've opened my stance up a little bit and I feel more comfortable at the plate. Right now things are going good. But it could change overnight.

"I don't kid myself," added Howard. "I have a pretty good idea of what I can do. I'm a streak hitter. Show me a guy that's not a streak hitter and I'll show you a Mantle, Mays or Kaline.

"You do it for two weeks and then don't do it again for a month and a half," he said.

Howard said he is beginning to swing the bat as he did when he first came into the major leagues with the Los Angeles Dodgers in the late 1950s.

"I feel I'm swinging the bat as I did when I first came up," he said. "I've been platooned so much—just batting against left-handed pitchers—that I honestly felt I'd forgotten how to hit

Three Good Rips

"Now I'm hitting the ball better and seeing the ball better than I did before," he said. "For the last couple of years I've been trying to get too smart, too scientific at the plate. Now I get three good rips at the ball and you can't ask for more than that."

Howard's homers, and a solo blast by Ken McMullen, backed the tight pitching of Frank Bertaina, who held the American League leading Tigers hitless for five innings and finished with a five-hitter in squaring his record at 2-2.

Mickey Lolich, victim of Howard's two homers, took the loss, his second in four decision.

The Senators scored in the first inning on singles by Del Unser, Sam Bowens and McMullen but Detroit tied the game without benefit of a hit in the second Bill Freehan walked, took second on a wild pitch, moved to third on a fly ball and scored on Dick McAuliffe's sacrifice fly.

Howard's first homer of the day, a shot into the upper right field stands, broke the tie. The 6-foot-7 first baseman drove a Lolich pitch over the left field roof in the fifth following singles by Unser and Bowens.

WASHINGTON	ab r h bi	DETROIT	ab r h bi
Unser cf	5 2 2 0	Stanley 1b	4 1 1 0
Bowens lf	5 1 2 0	Northrup cf	5 0 0 0
F Howard 1b	5 2 3 4	Kaline rf	3 0 0 0
McMulln 3b	5 1 4 2	Freehan c	3 2 3 1
C Petersn rf	5 0 1 0	W Horton lf	4 1 1 2
Hansen ss	4 1 1 0	Wert 3b	4 0 0 0
Casanova c	4 0 0 0	MAuliffe 2b	2 0 0 1
Coggins 2b	4 1 1 0	Oyler ss	3 0 1 0
Bertaina p	4 0 1 2	Lolich p	0 0 0 0
		Dobson p	0 0 0 0
		W La: ph	0 0 0 0
		R Baul p	0 0 0 0
		Warden p	0 0 0 0
		Treewski ph	1 0 0 0
		Hiller p	0 0 0 0
		Price 1b	1 0 0 0
Total	41 8 15 8	Total	30 4 5 4

Washington ... 1 0 1 0 3 2 0 0 1—8
Detroit .... 0 1 0 0 1 0 2 0—4

E Bowens. DP Washington 1 Detroit 1. LOB Washington 6, Detroit 7. 2B Coggins, McMullen, Freehan, Oyler. HR F Howard 2 (17), W Horton (9), McMullen (8). SF McAuliffe.

	IP	H	R	ER	BB	SO
Bertaina (W,2-2)			4	4	7	3
Lolich (L,2-2)	4 1-3	9	5	5	1	3
Dobson	1-3	0	0	0	0	0
R Baul	1 1-3	3	2	2	0	0
Warden	1 2-3	2	1	1	1	0
Hiller	1	1	1	1	0	4

WP—Bertaina. T—2:39. A—13,607.

Drysdale Gets 58 2-3 Shutout Innings Before Skein Ends

Wide World Photo

Los Angeles, June 9 (AP)—Records more than a half-century old have fallen to Los Angeles Dodger right-hander Don Drysdale, feats only less surprising than his prognostication:

"I think the Dodgers can win the pennant."

the pennant," despite the fact his shutout string came to an end last night against the Philadelphia Phillies.

Bedell Bats In Run

Howie Bedell, in his second official time at bat this season, hit a sacrifice fly in the fifth inning to end the string at 58 2-3 innings.

But Drysdale has rewritten the record books. His six straight shutouts are a major league record and when he retired Roberto Pena in the third inning, he also erased the longest shutout winning string of 56 by Walter Johnson of the Washington Senators in 1913.

Los Angeles went on to win the game 5-3 although Drysdale was knocked out in the seventh inning.

He now has won seven straight and the Dodgers, tabbed for the second division, have surged into second place by winning six straight and nine of their last ten games.

"I think all good things have to come to an end," observed the 6-foot-6 veteran in his thirteenth major league season. "I knew it would happen sooner or later. I'm just happy I could break a record. My biggest hope was that we could win the game."

Doc White 89

Asked how long he felt the record of six complete game shutouts and 58 2-3 innings would stand, Big D replied:

"That's hard to say. There is always somebody around who can break a record. This gives everybody a target to shoot at. I wish all the luck and will be the first to congratulate him if I'm still around to do it."

Doc White, who set the previous complete game record at 5, is now 89 and Johnson died years ago.

The inning which broke Drysdale's string saw Tony Taylor single to right leading off and Clay Dalrymple single to center

DON DRYSDALE

sending Taylor to third with none out.

Pena struck out, but pinch hitter Bedell's soft fly was enough to score the run.

Umpire Augie Donatelli at the plate, heedful of San Francisco Manager Herman Franks's charges that Drysdale greased the baseballs, checked Big D's hair at the urging of Phillies' Manager Gene Mauch.

Donatelli told Drysdale not to rub the back of his neck or the front of his cap to make sure no oily preparation was being applied to the baseball in violation of the anti-spitball rule.

PHILADELPHIA	ab r h bi	LOS ANGELES	ab r h bi
Rojas 2b	5 0 2 1	Parker 1b	4 1 2 1
Briggs cf	2 0 0 0	W Davis cf	4 1 0 0
Sutherlnd ph	1 0 0 0	Gabrielsn lf	4 0 1 0
Farrell p	0 0 0 0	Fairey lf	0 0 0 0
Gonzalez lf	4 0 0 0	Haller c	3 1 3 0
Callison rf	3 0 0 0	K Boyer 3b	4 1 2 1
White 1b	4 1 1 1	Fairly rf	4 1 1 1
T Taylor 3b	4 1 1 0	Popovich 2b	4 0 1 0
Dalrymple c	2 1 1 0	Versalles ss	2 0 0 1
R Allen ph	1 0 0 0	Drysdale p	2 0 0 0
Ryan c	0 0 0 0	Aguirre p	1 0 0 0
Pena ss	4 0 0 0		
L Jackson p	1 0 1 0		
Bedell ph	0 0 0 0		
G Jackson p	0 0 0 0		
Lock cf	2 0 0 0		
Total	33 3 6 3	Total	33 5 10 4

Philadelphia ... 0 0 0 0 1 1 1 0 0—3
Los Angeles .... 1 0 0 3 0 0 1 0 x—5

E Pena, Versalles, Fairly. DP Philadelphia 1. LOB Philadelphia 7, Los Angeles 6. 2B Haller. HR White (5), Parker (3). SB W Davis. SF Versalles.

	IP	H	R	ER	BB	SO
L Jackson (L,6-5)	4	6	4	3	1	2
G Jackson	3	4	1	0	0	1
Farrell	1	0	0	0	1	0
Drysdale (W,8-3)	6 1-3	6	3	3	1	2
Aguirre	2 2-3	0	0	0	1	2

T—2:28. A—50,060.

TIANT FANS 19, SETS TWO MARKS

Tribe Hurler Beats Twins, 1-0, In 10 Innings

Cleveland, July 3 (AP)—Luis Tiant struck out nineteen batters tonight, breaking one major league record and tying another, as the Cleveland Indians edged Minnesota 1-to-0 on Joe Azcue's run-scoring single in the tenth inning.

Tiant's total strikeouts fell two short of the major league record for strikeouts in an extra-inning game, but combined with his thirteen strikeouts against Boston last Saturday they broke Sandy Koufax's record of 31 strikeouts in two consecutive games.

Seventh Shutout

That total of 32 plus the 9 Tiant got against Detroit June 23 broke the American League 3-consecutive-game record of 40 set earlier this season by teammate Sam McDowell and ties the major league mark set by Koufax in 1959.

Tiant, in gaining his seventh shutout of the season, climaxed his brilliant performance by striking out the side in the tenth inning after the Twins had runners at first and third with none out.

MINNESOTA	ab	r	h	bi	CLEVELAND	ab	r	h	bi
Tovar 3b	4	0	1	0	Alvis 3b	4	0	0	0
Holt lf	3	0	1	0	I Brown ss	3	0	0	0
Killebrew ph	1	0	0	0	Johnson lf	4	1	1	0
Allison lf	0	0	0	0	Azcue c	4	0	2	1
Uhlaendr cf	4	0	1	0	Cardenal cf	3	0	0	0
Oliva rf	4	0	0	0	Sims 1b	3	0	1	0
Reese 1b	4	0	1	0	Harper rf	3	0	0	0
Quilici 2b	3	0	1	0	Fuller 2b	3	0	0	0
Roseboro c	4	0	1	0	Tiant p	3	0	0	0
Hernandz ss	3	0	0	0					
Rollins ph	1	0	0	0					
RClark 3b	0	0	0	0					
Merritt p	4	0	0	0					
Total	35	0	6	0	Total	30	1	4	1

None out when winning run scored

Minnesota	000	000	000	0—	0
Cleveland	000	000	000	1—	1

E Tovar. LOB Minnesota 6. Cleveland 3. 2B Tovar, Reese. S Quilici.

	IP	H	R	ER	BB	SO
Merritt (L 5-8)	9	4	1	0	1	7
Tiant (W 13-5)	10	6	0	0	0	19

T—3.15. A—21,138.

NATIONALS TAKE 'STAR' CLASH, 1-0

Pitching Dominates As Mays Scores Lone Run In First

By JIM ELLIOT
[Sun Staff Correspondent]

Houston, July 9 — An unearned run scoring on a double play—that's how the National League continued its "hex" over the American League tonight. A first-inning run supplied a 1-to-0, sixth straight National triumph before 48,321 fans in the Astrodome.

Willie Mays, of San Francisco, singled as the first National batter of the night and took second when Harmon Killebrew failed to hold a pickoff throw from pitcher Luis Tiant, of Cleveland.

A 3-2 wild pitch on a walk to St. Louis's Curt Flood enabled Mays to advance to third, and Mays scored while the American infield was turning a double play on Willie McCovey's grounder to second.

All-Star Game Box Score

AMERICAN	Ab	R	H	Rbi	Po	A
Fregosi, ss	3	0	1	0	1	[illegible]
Campaneris, ss	1	0	0	0	1	0
Carew, 2b	3	0	0	0	2	2
Johnson, 2b	1	0	0	0	1	1
[illegible]	[illegible]	[illegible]	[illegible]	[illegible]	[illegible]	[illegible]
Howard, rf	2	0	0	0	0	0
Oliva, rf	1	0	1	0	2	0
Horton, lf	2	0	0	0	1	0
Azcue, c	1	0	0	0	5	0
Killebrew, 1b	1	0	0	0	4	0
Powell, 1b	2	0	0	0	2	0
Freehan, c	2	0	0	0	4	0
McLain, p	0	0	0	0	0	0
McDowell, p	0	0	0	0	0	0
eMantle, ph	1	0	0	0	0	0
Stottlemyre, p	0	0	0	0	0	0
John, p	0	0	0	0	0	0
Robinson, 3b	2	0	0	0	0	1
Wert, 3b	1	0	1	0	1	0
Tiant, p	0	0	0	0	0	0
aHarrelson, ph	1	0	0	0	0	0
Odom, p	0	0	0	0	0	0
Monday, cf	2	0	0	0	0	0
Totals	30	0	3	0	24	10

NATIONAL	Ab	R	H	Rbi	Po	A
Mays, cf	4	1	1	0	0	0
Flood, lf	1	0	0	0	1	0
M. Alou, lf	1	0	1	0	1	0
Javier, 2b	0	0	0	0	0	0
[illegible]	[illegible]	[illegible]	[illegible]	[illegible]	[illegible]	[illegible]
Aaron, rf	3	0	1	0	1	0
Santo, 3b	3	0	1	0	2	0
Perez, 3b	0	0	0	0	0	1
Helms, 2b	3	0	1	0	1	2
Reed, p	0	0	0	0	0	0
Koosman, p	0	0	0	0	0	0
Grote, c	2	0	0	0	3	0
Carlton, p	0	0	0	0	0	1
cStaub, ph	1	0	0	0	0	0
Seaver, p	0	0	0	0	0	0
F. Alou, lf	0	0	0	0	0	0
Kessinger, ss	2	0	0	0	1	2
dWilliams, ph	1	0	0	0	0	0
Cardenas, ss	0	0	0	0	0	1
Drysdale, p	1	0	0	0	0	1
Marichal, p	0	0	0	0	0	0
bHaller, ph-c	2	0	0	0	6	0
Bench, c	0	0	0	0	2	0
Totals	28	1	5	0	27	8

a—Flied out for Tiant in third
b—Flied out for Marichal in fifth.
c—Popped out for Carlton in sixth.
d—Flied out for Kessinger in sixth
e—Struck out for McDowell in eighth.

	1	2	3	4	5	6	7	8	9	R	H	E
AMERICAN	0	0	0	0	0	0	0	0	0—	0	3	1
NATIONAL	1	0	0	0	0	0	0	0	x—	1	5	0

Error—Killebrew; Double Plays—Carew, Fregosi to Killebrew (A). Johnson to Powell (A). Left On Bases—American 3. National 8. Two-base Hits—Fregosi. Helms. Oliva. Wert. Stolen Base—Aaron.

PITCHERS

AMERICAN	ip	h	r	er
Tiant—L	2	2	1	0
Odom	2	0	0	0
McLain	2	1	0	0
McDowell	1	1	0	0
Stottlemyre	1/3	0	0	0
John	2/3	1	0	0

NATIONAL	ip	h	r	er
Drysdale—W	3	1	0	0
Marichal	2	0	0	0
Carlton	1	0	0	0
Seaver	2	2	0	0
Reed	2/3	0	0	0
Koosman	1/3	0	0	0

Base On Balls—Tiant 2 (Flood, Aaron); Odom 2 (Santo, Helms). McLain 2 (Flood. Santo).

Struck Out—Tiant 2 (Grote, Kessinger); Odom 2 (McCovey, Aaron); McLain 1 (McCovey). McDowell 3 (Haller, Mays, McCovey); Stottlemyre 1 (Aaron).

Struck Out—Marichal 3 (Howard, Powell, Freehan); Carlton 1 (Fregosi). Seaver 5 (Yastrzemski, Azcue, Powell, Mantle, Monday), Reed 1 (Johnson). Koosman 1 (Yastrzemski).

Umpires—Crawford (N) plate; Napp (A) first base. Steiner (N) second base. Kinnamon (A) third base; Wendelstedt (N) right field. Odom (A) left field.

Time—3.10. Attendance—48,321.

N.L. AGREES TO DIVISIONAL PLAY FOR '68

Senior Loop Gives In As American League Compromises, Too

By JIM ELLIOT
[Sun Staff Correspondent]

Houston, July 10—The American and National Leagues, against a couple of strong objections lodged especially by the Chicago White Sox, late today accepted the recommendations of Baseball's Executive Council and agreed to uniformity for their 1969 seasons when both leagues expand to twelve clubs.

After all-day individual league meetings, the two major leagues in a 4½-minute joint session agreed to everything which the Executive Council decided upon and recommended in a resolution two weeks ago. It included the following:

1. The National League adopted play in two divisions of six clubs each, which the American League had already decided upon.

162-Game Season

2. The American League went with the National League in adopting a 162-game schedule rather than the 156-game schedule it wanted.

3. Each club will play 18 games with each of the 5 clubs in its division for 90 games, and 12 games with each of the 6 clubs in the other division for 72 more games.

4. The two leagues will start their seasons, to run for 25 weeks and 4 days, on the same date—Monday, April 7—and will close on the same date—Thursday, October 2.

Late World Series

5. Both leagues will start their play-offs, best three-of-five games, between division champions on the same date, Saturday, October 4, and have agreed to a World Series start Saturday, October 11.

"I'm very pleased that both leagues adopted the resolution," said Commissioner William D. Eckert, a member of the Executive Council. "I feel that in the long run, it will be regarded as a long step forward in efforts toward harmony and uniformity."

Joe Cronin, president of the American League, and Warren Giles, president of the National, flanked the commissioner when he made his announcement, and both hastened to add that the resolution had been accepted for the 1969 season only and was subject to review by both leagues.

Divisional Setups

American League alignment has an Eastern Division made up of Baltimore, Boston, Cleveland composed of California, Chicago, Kansas City, Minnesota, Oakland and Seattle.

In the National League, the Eastern Division encompanies Chicago, Montreal, New York, Philadelphia, Pittsburgh and St. Louis. The Western Division takes in Atlanta, Cincinnati, Houston, Los Angeles, San Diego and San Francisco.

The new American League franchises will be located in Kansas City and Seattle. The new National franchises will be in Montreal and San Diego.

Reprinted from
The Baltimore Sun papers

Aaron Joins Elite 500 Homer Set With Game-Winning Four-Master

Atlanta Star Connects Off McCormick And Is Eighth Player To Reach Mark

Atlanta, July 14 (P) — Hank Aaron slammed the 500th home run of his major league career today, drawing a standing ovation from Atlanta Braves' fans as he became the eighth player in baseball history to reach the coveted milestone.

The shot gave the Braves a 4 to 2 victory over the Giants.

The historic homer, struck 14 years after Aaron hit his first as a rookie, came in the third inning of the Braves' game with San Francisco.

The pitcher was left-hander Mike McCormick.

Slugger Not Worried

Aaron, 34, had hit his 498th and 499th homers exactly a week ago. He said he wasn't worried about his 500th "because it'll come."

SAN FRANCISCO					ATLANTA				
	ab	r	h	bi		ab	r	h	bi
Hunt 2b	3	0	0	0	FAlou cf	4	1	1	0
Schroder 2b	2	1	1	0	Millan 2e	4	1	2	0
Cline cf	4	0	1	1	HAaron rf	4	1	2	3
McCovey 1b	3	0	1	0	Torre c	4	0	2	0
Bonds cf	1	0	0	0	TAaron lf	4	0	1	0
Hart 3b	4	0	1	0	DJohnson 1b	4	0	1	0
JAlou lf	4	1	2	0	RJackson ss	4	1	1	0
Marshall rf	1	0	1	0	Martinez 3b	3	0	1	1
Hiatt c	4	0	0	0	Reed p	4	0	1	0
Lanier ss	2	0	1	0	Upshaw p	0	0	0	0
Mays ph	1	0	1	0					
MCormick p	1	0	0	0					
Bolin p	0	0	0	0					
FJohnson ph	1	0	0	0					
Herbel p	0	0	0	0					
Davenprt ph	1	0	0	0					
Gibbon p	0	0	0	0					
Dietz ph	1	0	1	1					
Sadecki pr	0	0	0	0					
Total	36	2	10	2	Total	35	4	12	4

San Francisco   000 000 011—2
Atlanta   003 100 00x—4

E—Hart, Marshall. DP—San Francisco 2, Atlanta 1. LOB—San Francisco 8, Atlanta 8. 2B—RJackson, Lanier, D.Johnson. 3B—Schroder. HR—H.Aaron (19). SB—F.Alou.

	IP	H	R	ER	BB	SO
McCormick (L,6-12)	2 2-3	6	3	3	0	4
Bolin	1 1-3	3	1	1	0	0
Herbel	2	2	0	0	1	0
Gibbon	2	1	0	0	0	0
Reed (W,9-4)	8 1-3	9	2	2	1	4
Upshaw	2-3	1	0	0	0	0

T—2:16. A—34,000.

HANSEN PULLS TRIPLE PLAY

Senator Shortstop's Gem Upstages Indian Win

Cleveland, July 30. (P)—Washington shortstop Ron Hansen pulled an unassisted triple play tonight, but the Indians buried the Senators, 10-1.

The play was the first unassisted triple play in the major leagues in 41 years.

Hansen pulled off the play in the first inning with Cleveland runners on first and second and the hit-and-run on. He grabbed Joe Azcue's line drive, stepped on second to double Dave Nelson and tagged Russ Snyder coming from first.

Seven Other

Seven other players have pulled unassisted triple plays. The last two in 1927 by Chicago Cub shortstop Jim Cooney and Detroit first baseman Johnny Neun.

WASHINGTON					CLEVELAND				
	ab	r	h	bi		ab	r	h	bi
Unser cf	5	0	1	0	Nelson 2b	5	1	2	1
HAllen 2b	4	0	0	0	Snyder rf	2	2	1	0
Alvea lf	4	0	0	0	Azcue c	3	0	0	0
FHoward 1b	4	0	0	0	Cardenal cf	4	2	2	4
McMullin 3b	3	0	0	0	Sims 1b	3	1	1	0
Holtman rf	3	0	0	0	Cardenal cf	4	2	2	4
Casanova c	4	0	1	0	Schnblum lf	0	0	0	0
Hansen ss	4	0	0	0	Maye lf	3	0	2	3
BHoward p	2	0	0	0	Harper rf	0	0	0	1
Haywood p	0	0	0	0	Fuller 3b	3	0	0	0
Epstein ph	1	0	1	0	LBrown ss	4	1	1	0
Humphrey p	0	0	0	0	MDowell p	2	1	1	0
CPeterson ph	1	0	0	0	Paul p	0	0	0	0
Total	34	1	6	1	Total	31	10	12	9

Washington   010 000 000—1
Cleveland   000 260 20x—10

E—McDowell, Hansen. TP—Washington 1. LOB—Washington 9, Cleveland 6. 2B—Maye, L.Brown, Nelson, Cardenal 2. HR—F.Howard (30). S—McDowell. SF—Harper.

	IP	H	R	ER	BB	SO
B.Howard (L,1-6)	4	8	5	5	2	0
Haywood	2	2	3	3	3	1
Humphreys	2	2	2	2	2	1
McDowell (W,11-9)	8	6	1	1	3	9
Paul	1	0	0	0	1	0

PB—Casanova. T—2:49. A—5,937.

ATHLETICS NIP WHITE SOX, 1-0

Wilhelm Appears In 907th Game To Set Mark

Chicago, July 24 (P) — Jim Nash's four-hit pitching and a run-scoring single by Rick Monday gave the Oakland Athletics a 1-to-0 victory over Chicago in the opener of a doubleheader tonight as White Sox reliever Hoyt Wilhelm set an all-time record with the nine hundred and seventh appearance of his career.

Bert Campaneris singled in the fifth inning for his third straight hit, stole second and scored on Monday's two-out single, giving Nash, 7-6, the nod in a duel with Chicago's Tommy John, 7-3.

Wilhelm replaced John in the ninth, breaking Cy Young's major league mark of 906 lifetime pitching appearances, set in 1911.

"I would like to go for 1,000," said Wilhelm. "The knuckler doesn't take too much out of the arm or shoulder so maybe I can keep going. I feel great."

Wilhelm's relief job tonight was his forty-second appearance of the season. In 57 innings he has yielded only nine earned runs for a 1.45 e.r.a.

Between games he was presented with an assortment of gifts in ceremonies at home plate.

FIRST GAME

OAKLAND					CHICAGO				
	ab	r	h	bi		ab	r	h	bi
Cmpaneris ss	4	1	3	0	Aparicio ss	4	0	0	0
Cater 1b	4	0	1	0	McCraw 1b	4	0	0	0
Monday cf	3	0	2	1	Wagner rf	4	0	0	0
Bando 3b	4	0	1	0	Ward 3b	4	0	2	0
RJackson rf	4	0	0	0	Davis lf	2	0	1	0
Rudi lf	3	0	0	0	Josephson c	3	0	0	0
Gosger lf	0	0	0	0	Berry cf	1	0	0	0
Duncan c	3	0	2	0	Nomar 3b	3	0	2	0
Donaldsn 2b	3	0	0	0	John p	3	0	0	0
JNash p	4	0	0	0	Wilhelm p	0	0	0	0
Total	35	1	8	1	Total	29	0	4	0

Oakland   000 010 000—1
Chicago   000 000 000—0

E—McCraw. DP—Chicago 1. LOB—Oakland 6, Chicago 4. SB—Campaneris 2. S—Bando. S—John. DP—

	IP	H	R	ER	BB	SO
J.Nash (W,7-6)	9	4	0	0	0	5
John (L,7-3)	8	8	1	1	0	1
Wilhelm	1	0	0	0	0	0

T—2:18.

Sept. 23

Tovar became the second player in American League history to play all nine positions in the field in one game. Bert Campaneris of the A's, the first to do it, was the first batter Tovar faced.

OAKLAND					MINNESOTA				
	ab	r	h	bi		ab	r	h	bi
Cmpaneris ss	4	0	1	0	Tovar p	3	1	1	0
RJackson rf	4	0	1	0	RonClark 3b	4	0	0	0
Cater 1b	2	0	0	1	Nettles 1b	2	1	0	0
Bando 3b	4	0	0	0	Allison lf	3	0	0	0
Hershbrgr rf	2	0	0	0	Carew 2b	4	0	2	1
Donaldsn ph	1	0	0	0	Holt rf	2	0	1	0
DGreen 2b	4	0	0	0	Hernandz ss	1	0	0	0
Pagliaroni c	4	0	0	0	Reese 1b	2	0	0	0
Monday cf	4	0	0	0	Uhlaendr cf	0	0	0	0
Rudi lf	1	0	0	0	Look c	4	0	1	0
Duncan ph	1	0	1	0	THall p	3	0	0	0
Lewis pr	0	1	0	0	Zimrman c	0	0	0	0
Lindblad p	0	0	0	0	Worthgtn p	0	0	0	0
Total	28	1	3	1	Total	29	2	6	2

Oakland   000 000 010—1
Minnesota   001 010 00x—2

E—D.Green, Pagliaroni, T.Hall. DP—Minnesota 1. LOB—Oakland 6, Minnesota 9. SB—Tovar, Allison. 3B—Allison. SB—Tovar, RonClark. Campaneris. S—Hernandez, Odom, Holt. SF—Cater.

	IP	H	R	ER	BB	SO
Odom (L,15-10)	7	5	2	1	3	5
Lindblad	1	1	0	0	1	0
Tovar	1	0	0	0	1	0
T.Hall (W,2-1)	6 1-3	2	1	1	2	2
Worthington	1 2-3	1	0	0	0	1

HBF—Odom (Nettles). WP—T.Hall. Balk—Tovar. T—2:18. A—11,340.

Gibson Fans 15 But Loses To Pirates, 6-4, In Ninth

St. Louis, Aug. 24 (P)—Bob Gibson struck out fifteen batters but had his consecutive game winning streak snapped at fifteen games today when Pittsburgh scored two unearned runs in the ninth inning for a 6-to-4 victory over the St. Louis Cardinals.

It was the first loss for Gibson, 18-6, since May 22 when San Francisco beat him 3-1.

PITTSBURGH					ST. LOUIS				
	ab	r	h	bi		ab	r	h	bi
Patek ss	3	1	0	0	Brock lf	3	1	1	0
Wills 3b	4	0	1	0	Flood cf	4	0	1	0
MAlou cf	3	1	0	1	Maris rf	4	0	1	1
Clemente rf	4	1	1	0	Cepeda 1b	4	1	1	0
Stargell lf	4	1	2	3	Edwards c	4	0	1	0
Kolb rf	0	1	0	0	Shannon 3b	4	1	1	1
Clendenon 1b	4	1	0	0	Javier 2b	4	0	1	0
Alley 2b	4	0	1	1	MCarver ph	1	0	1	0
JMay p	1	0	0	0	RDavis pr	0	0	0	0
Moose p	1	0	0	0	Maxvill ss	3	1	0	0
Walker p	0	0	0	0	Tolan ph	1	0	0	0
Sisk p	0	0	0	0	Gibson p	3	0	1	1
Jimenez ph	1	0	0	0	Gagliano ph	1	0	0	0
McBean p	1	0	0	0					
Mota ph	1	0	0	0					
Face p	1	0	0	0					
Total	33	6	6	5	Total	35	4	9	3

Pittsburgh .... 000 000 312—6
St. Louis .... 100 300 000—4

E—Cepeda. Maxvill. LOB—Pittsburgh 4, St. Louis 5. 2B—Cepeda, Wills, Stargell. HR—Stargell (21). SB—Brock, Gibson. S—J May. SF—M Alou.

	IP	H	R	ER	BB	SO
Moose	3 2-3	8	4	4	0	1
Walker	0	0	0	0	1	0
Sisk	1 1-3	0	0	0	1	0
M.Bean	2	0	0	0	0	0
Face (W.2-4)	2	1	0	0	0	0
Gibson (L.18-6)	9	6	6	4	2	15

WP—Sisk. T—2.35. A—31,019.

Tigers Rally To Give McLain 30th

Horton's Fly Climaxes Two-Run Comeback In 9th Inning

Detroit, Sept. 14 (P)—Denny McLain won his 30th game as Detroit rallied for two runs in the last of the ninth inning and a 5-to-4 victory over the Oakland Athletics today.

The victory cut Detroit's magic number for clinching the American League pennant to four and made McLain the first 30-game winner in the majors in 34 years.

Two home runs by Reggie Jackson left McLain on the short end of a 4-3 score as the Tigers came to bat in the ninth. Al Kaline batted for McLain, who allowed six hits, and walked.

After Dick McAuliffe fouled out, Mickey Stanley singled to center and Kaline raced to third.

Then, with the infield drawn in, Jim Northrup bounced to first baseman Danny Cater. Kaline broke for the plate and Cater's high throw sailed over catcher Dave Duncan's head, allowing the tying run to score.

With the outfield drawn in, Willie Horton lifted a long drive that soared over the head of left fielder Jim Gosger and Stanley scored the winning run.

McLain raced from the dugout with the rest of the Tigers to embrace Horton.

McLain, who became the first pitcher to win 30 games since Dizzy Dean did it in 1934, was rocked early by the A's but allowed only two hits over the last five innings and struck out ten.

McLain is the thirteenth major league pitcher to win 30 games since baseball's modern era began at the turn of the century.

Dean watched McLain from the stands. Curiously, both Dean and McLain had the same uniform numbers, 17, and were the same age, 24, in their respective 30-game seasons.

Lefty Grove was the last American League pitcher to win 30 games. He posted a 31-4 record for the old Philadelphia Athletics in 1931.

The modern major league record of 41 victories was set by Jack Chesbro, of the New York Highlanders—now the Yankees—in 1904. Ed Walsh, of the Chicago White Sox, the only other modern day pitcher to win 40 games, did it in 1908.

Several pitchers, including Walter Johnson and Cy Young, have won 36 or more games at least twice.

Christy Mathewson, of the old New York Giants, did it four times in six years between 1903 and 1908.

McLain started his streak April 4 when he beat the White Sox at Chicago. He was 15-2 at the All-Star break had a winning streak of nine straight, stopped by Baltimore July 20.

The Orioles beat McLain twice. His other three losses were administered by New York, Cleveland and Chicago.

OAKLAND					DETROIT				
	ab	r	h	bi		ab	r	h	bi
Campaneris ss	4	0	1	1	MAuliffe 2b	5	0	1	0
Monday cf	4	0	1	0	Stanley cf	5	1	2	0
Cater 1b	4	1	2	0	Northrup rf	4	1	0	0
Bando 3b	3	0	0	0	WHorton lf	5	1	2	1
RJackson rf	4	2	2	3	Cash 1b	4	1	2	1
DGreen 2b	4	0	0	0	Freehan c	4	0	0	0
Keough lf	3	0	0	0	Matchick ss	4	0	1	0
Gosger lf	1	0	0	0	Wert 3b	2	0	0	1
Duncan c	2	1	0	0	GBrown ph	1	0	0	0
Dobson p	1	0	0	0	Trcewski 3b	0	0	0	0
Aker p	0	0	0	0	McLain p	1	0	0	0
Lindblad p	0	0	0	0	Kaline ph	0	1	0	0
Donaldson ph	0	0	0	0					
Segui p	1	0	0	0					
Total	30	4	6	4	Total	34	5	9	4

One out when winning run scored.

Oakland .... 000 211 000—4
Detroit .... 000 300 101—5

E—Matchick, Bando, Cater. DP—Detroit 1. LOB—Oakland 2, Detroit 10. HR—R.Jackson 2 (28), Cash (21). S—McLain, Bando, Donaldson.

	IP	H	R	ER	BB	SO
Dobson	3 2-3	4	3	2	3	2
Aker	1	0	0	0	0	0
Lindblad	1-3	0	0	0	0	0
Segui (L.5-5)	4 1-3	5	2	2	1	7
McLain (W.30-5)	9	6	4	4	1	1

WP—Aker. T—3:00. A—33,688.

TWO UMPIRES FIRED BY A.L. PRESIDENT

Salerno, Valentine Say They Were Released For Union Work

Cleveland, Sept. 16 (P)—American League umpires Al Salerno and William Valentine were fired today by League President Joe Cronin and Valentine said it was because they tried to organize an American League umpires' association.

"There's no doubt that we were released from our jobs because of our activities," Valentine said at a news conference.

Salerno added: "I don't care if I never umpire another game

. . . It's very important that this be brought into the open and I hope it will improve conditions for other umpires."

League Confirms Release

In Boston, Bob Holbrook, executive assistant to Cronin, confirmed that both men had been released and both have been paid for the remainder of the season, along with severance pay.

Cronin was reported unavailable for comment in Boston. However, the Cleveland Plain Dealer said Cronin told them in a telephone interview that the two umps were fired, not for union activity, but because he was dissatisfied with their work.

"An umpire's union . . . it's all news to me," Cronin was quoted as saying.

He said "we had planned to make changes at the end of the season. We decided to do it now."

Valentine also said all 40 major league umpires are organizing into one group. The National League umpires already are in the National League Umpires' Association.

HODGES SUFFERED HEART ATTACK

Doctors Diagnose Ailment Of Mets' Skipper

Atlanta, Sept. 25 (P)—Doctors today confirmed that Gil Hodges manager of the New York Mets, has suffered a small heart attack.

Dr. Linton Bishop, a heart specialist, said the result of a second electrocardiogram showed evidence of a "small coronary thrombosis," but described Hodges's condition as good.

A coronary thrombosis is a heart irregularity caused by a blood clot.

Bishop's findings were confirmed by Dr. J. Willis Hurst, chief of medicine at Emory University.

"There is no doubt in my mind that Mr. Hodges will be able to resume fulltime duties in the future," Bishop said.

The doctors advised Mrs. Hodges, who flew from New York to Atlanta early today to be with her husband, that with proper rest and treatment Hodges would be able to resume his duties next spring.

Bishop informed Mets general manager John J. Murphy of Hodges's condition today and told Murphy the manager was well enough to discuss the upcoming National League expansion draft with him.

Murphy said he would consult with Hodges before the draft next month.

The Mets' manager also was well enough to name pitching coach Rube Walker as acting manager for the rest of this season.

Meanwhile, doctors said Hodges was admitted to the hospital last night after he complained of chest pains during a game between the Mets and the Atlanta Braves.

An initial electrocardiogram showed changes in heart pattern, but a diagnosis was withheld pending the second test.

PERRY NO-HITS CARDINALS, 1-0

Gibson Handed Eighth Loss As Giants Triumph

San Francisco, Sept. 17 (AP)—Gaylord Perry of the San Francisco Giants pitched a no-hitter tonight, yielding only walks in the second and eighth innings as he beat Bob Gibson and the St. Louis Cardinals, 1 to 0.

Second baseman Ron Hunt gave Perry, 15-14, the only run he needed with a first-inning home run.

Gibson, ace of the champion Cardinals' pitching staff, allowed only four hits but suffered his eighth defeat. He has won 21 but the Giants have beaten him three times in four 1968 decisions.

Perry, a 30-year-old, 6-foot-4 right-hander in his seventh big league season, struck out nine and allowed only two balls to be hit past the infield. He retired twelve batters on ground balls.

Perry capped his masterpiece by blowing a called third strike past Curt Flood to end the game. He threw 101 pitches. Pinch hitter Lou Brock and Bobby Tolan grounded out for the first two out in the final inning.

ST. LOUIS	ab r h bi	SAN FRANCISCO	ab r h bi
Tolan lf	4 0 0 0	Bonds cf	3 0 1 0
Flood cf	4 0 0 0	Hunt 2b	3 1 1 1
Maris rf	3 0 0 0	Cline lf	3 0 1 0
Cepeda 1b	3 0 0 0	McCovey 1b	3 0 0 0
McCarver c	3 0 0 0	Hart 3b	3 0 0 0
Shannon 3b	2 0 0 0	Davenport 3b	0 0 0 0
Gagliano 2b	2 0 0 0	Marshall rf	2 0 0 0
Maxvill ss	2 0 0 0	Mays cf	1 0 0 0
Edwards ph	1 0 0 0	Dietz c	2 0 0 0
Schofield ss	0 0 0 0	Lanier ss	3 0 1 0
Gibson p	2 0 0 0	Perry p	3 0 0 0
Brock ph	1 0 0 0		
Total	27 0 0 0	Total	26 1 4 1

St. Louis .... 0 0 0 0 0 0 0 0 0—0
San Francisco .. 1 0 0 0 0 0 0 0 x—1

DP—St. Louis 1. LOB—St. Louis 2. San Francisco 4. 2B—Lanier. Bonds. HR—Hunt (2). SB—Bonds. S—Hunt.

	IP	H	R	ER	BB	SO
Gibson (L.21-8)	8	4	1	1	2	10
Perry (W.15-14)	9	0	0	0	2	9

T—1:44. A—9,546.

RAY WASHBURN HURLS NO-HITTER AT GIANTS AS CARDS WIN, 2 TO 0

Gem Comes On Heels Of Masterpiece By Perry Tuesday

San Francisco, Sept. 18 (AP)—Ray Washburn of the St. Louis Cardinals pitched a no-hitter today, stifling the San Francisco Giants, 2 to 0, and helped write major league history with the second masterpiece in as many days at Candlestick Park.

Gaylord Perry of the Giants had no-hit the Cardinals less than 24 hours earlier at Candlestick and it was the first time two no-hitters were pitched in successive games in one ballpark.

Washburn, a sturdily built 30-year-old right-hander, struck out eight and allowed five runners, all of them on walks.

ST. LOUIS	ab r h bi	SAN FRANCISCO	ab r h bi
Brock lf	4 0 0 0	Bonds rf	3 0 0 0
Flood cf	4 0 2 1	Hunt 2b	3 0 0 0
Tolan rf	4 0 1 0	Mays cf	3 0 0 0
Cepeda 1b	3 1 1 0	McCovey 1b	3 0 0 0
Edwards c	4 0 0 0	Hart 3b	3 0 0 0
Shannon 3b	4 0 2 1	Dietz c	3 0 0 0
Gagliano 2b	3 0 0 0	Cline lf	3 0 0 0
Schofield ss	3 1 1 0	Lanier ss	2 0 0 0
Washburn p	3 0 0 0	Schroder ph	1 0 0 0
		Mason ss	0 0 0 0
		Bolin p	2 0 0 0
		Marshall p	0 0 0 0
		Linzy p	0 0 0 0
Total	31 2 7 2	Total	26 0 0 0

St. Louis .... 0 0 0 0 0 1 1 0—2
San Francisco ... 0 0 0 0 0 0 0 0—0

E—Lanier. DP—St. Louis 1. San Francisco 1. LOB—St. Louis 5. San Francisco 4. 2B—Shannon. Schofield. S—Washburn.

	IP	H	R	ER	BB	SO
Washburn (W.13-7)	9	0	0	0	5	8
Bolin (L.9-5)	8	6	2	2	3	5
Linzy	1	1	0	0	0	0

T—2:19. A—4,703.

Gibson Breaks E.R.A. Record

St. Louis, Sept. 27 (AP)—Bob Gibson broke the National League record for lowest earned run average with a six-hit shutout that gave the St. Louis Cardinals a 1-0 victory over the Houston Astros tonight.

Gibson, 22-9, making his last start before the World Series, lowered his E.R.A. to 1.12, breaking the record of 1.22 held by Grover Cleveland Alexander of the Philadelphia Phillies in 1915.

Hub Leonard of Boston holds the major league e.r.a. record of 1.01 for 222 innings set in 1914.

The 33-year-old Cardinal right-hander turned in his thirteenth shutout of the season and struck out eleven.

LEFTHANDER VICTOR OVER BOB GIBSON

By LOU HATTER
[Sun Staff Correspondent]

St. Louis, Oct. 10—Detroit's Mickey Lolich, Jim Northrup, Bill Freehan, and associate heroes affirmed here today that super-Cardinals Bob Gibson and Lou Brock are mere mortals after all while leading the Tigers to baseball's 1968 global championship.

With the plucky Lolich pitching a five-hitter to become only the second left-hander ever to score three victories in a World Series, the American Leaguers defeated St. Louis, 4 to 1, in the showdown seventh game of the sixty-fifth post-season classic.

A two-run triple by Northrup and Freehan's double were the decisive blows that toppled the peerless Gibson and the defending champion Redbirds from the throne under a three-run seventh-inning assault.

Series Box Score

DETROIT (A)

	AB	R	H	BI	PO	A
McAuliffe 2b	4	0	0	0	3	5
Stanley ss-cf	4	0	1	0	1	3
Kaline rf	4	0	0	0	5	0
Cash 1b	4	1	2	0	6	1
bTracewski	0	0	0	0	0	0
Oyler ss	0	0	0	0	0	0
Northrup cf-lf	4	1	2	2	3	0
Freehan c	4	0	1	1	6	1
Wert 3b	4	0	1	1	0	0
Lolich p	3	1	1	0	1	2
Totals	35	4	8	4	27	15

ST. LOUIS (N)

	AB	R	H	BI	PO	A
Brock lf						
Javier 2b						
Flood cf						
Cepeda 1b						
Shannon 3b						
McCarver c						
Maris rf						
Maxvill ss						
aGagliano						
Schofield ss						
Gibson p						
Totals	30	1	5	1	27	8

a—Grounded out for Maxvill in eighth.
b—Ran for Horton in ninth.

Detroit (A) .... 0 0 0 0 0 0 3 0 1—4
St. Louis (N) ...... 0 0 0 0 0 0 1 0 0—1

Error—Northrup. Double Play—Stanley and Cash. Left On Base—Detroit (A) 5, St. Louis (N) 3. Two Base Hit—Freehan. Three Base Hit—Northrup. Home Run—Shannon. Stolen Bases—Flood.

Pitching Summary

	IP	H	R	ER	BB	SO
Lolich (W)	9	5	1	1	3	4
Gibson (L)	9	8	4	4	1	8

Base on Balls: Lolich 3 (McCarver, Cepeda, Brock). Gibson 1 (Wert). Strike Outs: Lolich 4 (Shannon, Maris, Cepeda, Gibson). Gibson 8 (Kaline 2, Horton, Northrup, Wert, Lolich 2, Stanley). Time—2:07. Attendance—54,692. Umpires: Plate: Honochick (American League) First Base: Landes (National League) Second Base: Kinnamon (American League) Third Base: Harvey (National League) Left Field Line: Haller (American League) Right Field Foul Line.

Short Pays 10 Million For Washington Club

By Lou Hatter
[Sun Staff Correspondent]

San Francisco, Dec. 3—The long-awaited sale of the Washington Senators was confirmed, and deal talk finally gave way to deeds at baseball's winter meetings today.

Culminating negotiations which began prior to the world series, Democratic National committee treasurer Robert E. Short, of Minneapolis, purchased the American League club for a sum which, he stated, is "in the area of $10,000,000."

Former Owner Of Lakers

The handsome, 50-year-old Short, a Minneapolis trucking, airline and hotel executive and former owner of the pro basketball Minneapolis Lakers, declared that he has no plans to move the troubled franchise from its present site.

RESIGNATION TURNED IN BY ECKERT

Baseball Commissioner Leaves Amid Talks On Reorganization

By Lou Hatter
[Sun Staff Correspondent]

San Francisco, Dec. 6—Baseball today acknowledged a grave error of three years' duration by accepting the "resignation" of its commissioner William D. Eckert.

League Attorney Bowie Kuhn Named Baseball Commissioner

Compromise Choice To Serve For Term Of One Year

By LOU HATTER
[Sun Staff Correspondent]

Miami Beach, Feb. 4—In its infinite capacity for the unexpected, baseball proceeded late today from "the unknown soldier" to a little-known lawyer as its new high commissioner.

Bowie Kuhn, 42-year-old National League attorney and a native Marylander, became the choice of the 24 major league owners as the game's "pro-tem" chief executive at $100,000 for a one-year period.

The announcement by Cincinnati club president Francis Dale produced hardly less surprise that three years ago when William D. Eckert, a retired Air Force general, emerged from a no-man's land of professional sport as an eminently unqualified successor to Ford Frick.

Eckert resigned under pressure last December 6 in San Francisco after filling three years of his seven-year contract at $65,000 per annum. He is being paid off in full.

Compromise Choice

Kuhn's "unanimous" election today obviously was a compromise. American and National League executives had failed to agree during an all-night December 20-21 stand-off in Chicago on two nominees from an original field of seven—Michael Burke, president of the New York Yankees, and San Francisco Giants' vice president Chub Feeney.

Kuhn, born in Takoma Park, Md., and now a resident of Ridgewood, N.J., said that "my affiliation with the State of Maryland is very deep. Bowie is an old family name you find throughout the state."

His great great grandfather, Robert Bowie, was governor of Maryland during the war of 1812, Kuhn revealed. A great, great uncle, Joseph Kent, also was a former chief executive of the Free State, he recalled.

"Kent is my middle name," he added.

Active Within Baseball

Although his qualifications outside the game's inner sanctum are little known, the 6-foot 5½ inch Kuhn, a 230-pounder, has been active in the legal affairs of baseball since 1950.

It was then that he joined the New York corporate law firm of Willkie, Farr and Gallagher, following his graduation from the University of Virginia school of law.

More recently, Kuhn has been a legal counsel for the owners' player relations committee. That body presently is involved in a pension stalemate over which a spring player strike at this time appears inevitable.

Responding that he is "extremely flattered, honored and delighted to take over this important job," Kuhn announced that he will disassociate himself at once from the committee.

Nats, Williams Reach Terms On Lush, Multi-Year Pact

By LOU HATTER
[Sun Staff Correspondent]

Washington, Feb. 21—Colorful, controversial Ted Williams, one of the greatest hitters in the history of the game, tonight officially terminated an eight-year baseball retirement to become manager of the hapless Washington Senators.

In addition to a five-year contract for an estimated $75,000 annual salary, the onetime Boston Red Sox slugger becomes part-owner of the franchise, purchased recently by Robert Short for a sum in excess of $9 million.

The package with which Short finally lured Williams from his south Florida fishing haunts, following a week of intensive nego-purchase a reported 10 per cent of the Senators stock.

Relaxed, enthusiastic, gracious, even optimistic, the 50-year-old Hall of Famer assumed field leadership of a team which has been mired in the American League's second division for 22 seasons with the comment:

"I can only tell you from the heart I am happy to be here."

When a man has spent a quarter-century in baseball, "he never loses his great liking for the game that has meant so much to him," Williams added.

Short's coup marked the second for this city's long-suffering sports buffs within two weeks. It matches the acquisition of Vince Lombardi, an equally stormy and successful celebrity, as coach and part-owner of the downtrodden Washington Redskins.

Before a battery of microphones, cameras and newsmen, Williams offered no immediate panacea for the problems of the talent-bare Senators.

BASEBALL SIDES AGREE ON PENSION

Owners To Increase Contributions To Appease Players

New York, Feb. 25 (AP)—Major league baseball players won increased pension benefits from the club owners today and the threat of a strike was lifted.

Under the agreement, the owners will raise their contribution to the pension plan, made from television receipts, from $4.1 million in 1968 to $5.45 million yearly for the next three years. Retirement benefits at age 50 for a 10-year player will be increased to $600 monthly from $500.

Improved Benefits

The increased pension contribution makes possible the following improved benefits, the negotiators announced:

"1. Players will qualify for retirement benefits after 4 years of major league service rather than the present 5 years.

"2. Retirement benefits at age 50 will be increased from $50 to $60 a month for each of the first 10 years of active major league service (i.e., $600 a month for a 10-year player). In addition, retirement benefits payable for each year of active major league service from 11 to 20 years will be increased from $10 to $20 a month.

Earlier Retirement

"3. Early retirement will be permitted at age 45 with an actuarial adjustment from the benefits payable on normal retirement at age 50.

"4. A dental program will be established.

"5. Life insurance coverage will be increased to $50,000 for each active player and $25,000 for each presently inactive player who presently inactive player who qualifies for retirement benefits.

"6. Widows' benefits, disability benefits and maternity benefits and other health care benefits will be substantially improved.

"7. Provision will be made to permit a member who has ended his active service as a player to receive a portion of his retirement benefits in a lump sum. Full pension benefits could be reinstated upon appropriate reimbursement to the pension fund."

Mickey Mantle Retires As Player

Slugger Says He Can't Play Like He Would Like To — Number 7 To Be Retired

Fort Lauderdale, Fla., March 1 (AP)—Mickey Mantle, at a loss for words, announced his retirement from baseball today before a packed news conference at the New York Yankees' spring training hotel.

Mike Burke, president of the Yankees, introduced Mantle to reporters, saying the veteran star had "reached a firm conclusion, and I think it's best that he tell it to you himself."

Can't Do What Was Wanted

Then Mantle, dressed in a dark blue turtle neck, light blue slacks and checked jacket, stepped to the rostrum. But instead of making a statement, Mickey said "I'm open for questions."

The first one, of course, was what had he decided.

"I'm not going to play baseball anymore; that's all I know," he said slowly. "I can't play anymore. I don't hit the ball when I need to. I can't steal when I need to. I can't score from second when I need to."

Mantle said he reached the decision after talking with Houk and Burke.

"Ralph said if he was me and at this point he wasn't sure what to do, he'd probably call it off right now, and that's what I'm doing," the outfielder turned first baseman said. Mantle said his outside business interests, which include a chain of country kitchens and clothing stores, also helped him reach a decision.

"I have to appear at all the kitchen openings and there are about 45 sold right now," he explained.

Mantle said he had not current plans to remain with the Yankees organization. "But Mike told me if I ever wanted a job, it was available."

'Hawk' Reverses Field. To Be On Club For Yank Game Tonight, Paul Says

New York, April 22 (AP)—Ken Harrelson, "realizing what I was doing was bad for myself," reversed his decision to retire from baseball and today agreed to report to the Cleveland Indians.

The decision by the Hawk was announced early in the evening after Harrelson and his lawyer, Bob Woolf, met most of the afternoon with general manager Gabe Paul of Cleveland, general manager Dick O'Connell of Boston, baseball commissioner Bowie Kuhn and Joe Cronin, president of the American League.

Paul, making the announcement in the commissioner's office where the meeting was held, said that the slugging outfielder-first baseman would be in uniform tomorrow night for the game against the New York Yankees in Cleveland.

"I Feel Great"

"They made me realize what I was doing was bad for myself and that I should be back in baseball," Harrelson said. "I'm glad to have settled this thing. I feel great. I'm a ballplayer. I want to get back and do my thing."

Attired in one of his mod outfits—blue bellbottom slacks, cowboy boots, white turtleneck sweater, ascot tie, a white belt with a big buckle and a blue long-sleeved jacket—Harrelson added:

"They convinced me the outside opportunities in Cleveland could be the same as in Boston. If we win the pennant in Cleveland I'm sure the same business opportunities would be open to me there. My Boston interests are solid, although my future business in Boston probably would be hurt by not being there.

"I've got gambling blood in me. I'm ready to get out and try. Everything is based on performance."

It was Harrelson's many financial ventures off the field in Boston, said by Woolf to be worth as much as $750,000, that Harrelson cited when he announced his retirement after Boston sent him to Cleveland in a six-player trade Saturday night.

Along with Harrelson, the Red Sox traded left-handed pitchers Dick Ellsworth and Juan Pizarro for catcher Joe Azcue and right-handed pitchers Sonny Siebert and Vicente Romo.

Dodgers Lose, 4-3

LOS ANGELES, June 8 (AP)—The Montreal Expos snapped their losing streak at 20 games—three short of the modern major league record—by edging the Los Angeles Dodgers, 4-3, today. Home runs by Rusty Staub and Mack Jones proved decisive.

Expos Trade Clendenon For Four Met Youngsters

San Francisco, June 15 (AP)—The Montreal Expos swapped veteran first baseman Donn Clendenon to the New York Mets for four minor leaguers today.

Clendenon, who will be 34 on July 15, was traded for infielder Kevin Collins and right-handed pitchers Steve Renko, Bill Carden and Dave Colon.

The Boston Red Sox tonight traded catcher Joe Azcue to the California Angels for Tom Satriano, a catcher and utility infielder.

Azcue, traded to the Red Sox earlier in the season from Cleveland in a deal that involved Ken Harrelson, left the team last week because he was not playing regularly. He said he would retire if not traded and that he would not play for Boston again.

Satriano, 28, is a left-handed batter who hit .259 for the Angels in 41 games this year with one home run and 16 runs batted in. This is his sixth year in the majors.

Clendenon was batting .240 with four home runs and 14 r.b.i.'s in 38 games for Montreal.

Clendenon was involved in the controversial trade for Rusty Staub last winter, refusing to report to Houston and eventually being allowed to play with the Expos.

Collins and Renko were with Tidewater of the International League. The Expos will place Collins on the major league roster, but are undecided about Renko.

Clendenon entered the 1969 season with a .280 lifetime average.

The New York Yankees traded shortstop Tom Tresh to the Detroit Tigers in the biggest deal yesterday. In exchange, the Yankees obtained rookie outfielder Ron Woods.

In a lesser transaction the St. Louis Cardinals dealt pitcher Dennis Ribant to Cincinnati's Indianapolis farm club for pitcher Aurelio Monteagudo who will report to the Cards' Tulsa farm team.

Cincinnati also figured in a Friday transaction when the Reds purchased southpaw pitcher Al Jackson from the New York Mets for an undisclosed amount of cash.

In other Friday deals Atlanta traded catcher Walt Hriniak and two minor leaguers to San Diego for outfielder Tony Gonzalez and the Chicago White Sox traded pitcher Sammy Ellis to Cleveland for pitcher Jack Hamilton.

CINCINNATI STAR FANS 13 BATTERS

Maloney's No-Hitter Is 2d of Career—Chaney Saves It With Great Catch

CINCINNATI, April 30 (AP)—Jim Maloney of the Cincinnati Reds pitched the second no-hitter of his career tonight, overpowering the Houston Astros, 10-0, with a 13-strike-out performance.

Maloney yielded five walks in becoming the second National League to hurl hitless ball this year.

Montreal's Bill Stoneman pitched a no-hitter against the Phillies 13 days ago.

Darrel Chaney, the Reds' shortstop, raced into short left field and made an over-the-shoulder catch of Johnny Edwards's looping fly ball in the sixth inning. That preserved the no-hitter.

Edwards, a former Red, had caught both of the previous games in which Maloney pitched no-hit ball for nine or more innings.

Maloney pitched nine innings of no-hit ball, but lost, 1-0, on a 10th-inning homer by Johnny Lewis of the Mets on June 14. 1965. Then he pitcheu a 10-inning no-hitter to beat the Chicago Cubs, 1-0, on Aug. 19 of the same year.

The 24-year-old right-hander struck out 18 in the first game, equaling the National League record, and 12 in the second game.

Koufax Leads the List

Sandy Koufax leads the list of no-hit pitchers with four. Bob Feller, Cy Young and Larry Corcoran each pitched three.

Maloney, who has 125 career victories, has pitched four one-hitters and eight two-hitters since entering the National League in 1960. He holds the Reds' club record for strike-outs, the 265 he achieved in 1963 when he won 23 games and lost seven.

The Reds, after picking up an unearned run in the first inning, chased the Astro starter, Wade Blasingame, in the fourth inning when they sent 11 batters to the plate while piling up seven runs.

Maloney said he had pitched harder earlier this year, but tonight he "just had better stuff on the ball . . . and they weren't hitting."

It was his third victory this year. He has lost none.

He refused to comment on problems of arm tightening that have plagued him through the season.

"I don't even want to think about it;" he said.

The no-hitter was hardly any different from his others, he said.

"You just walk out there and if you've got a no-hitter you've got one."

HOUSTON (N.)	ab.	r.	h.	bi	CINCINNATI (N.)	ab.	r.	h.	bi
Morgan, 2b	3	0	0	0	Rose, cf	4	2	0	0
Alou, lf	4	0	0	0	Tolan, rf	5	0	3	4
Wynn, cf	2	0	0	0	Johnson, lf	3	1	1	0
Rader, 3b	3	0	0	0	Savage, lf	0	0	0	0
Miller, rf	3	0	0	0	Perez, 3b	4	0	1	0
Menke, ss	2	0	0	0	Bench, c	3	1	1	0
Biefary, 1b	3	0	0	0	May, 1b	3	1	0	1
Edwards, c	3	0	0	0	Helms, 2b	4	2	1	0
Blasingame, p	1	0	0	0	Chaney, ss	4	1	1	2
Ray, p	0	0	0	0	Maloney, p	3	2	1	1
Geronimo, ph	1	0	0	0					
Guinn, p	0	0	0	0					
Geiger, ph	1	0	0	0					
Coombs, p	0	0	0	0					
Total	26	0	0	0	Total	33	10	9	8

Houston . . . . 000 000 000—0
Cincinnati . . . . 100 700 02x—10

E—Menke, Biefary. DP—Houston 1, Cincinnati 1. LOB—Houston 4, Cincinnati 6. 2B—Maloney. 3B—Tolan.

	IP.	H.	R.	ER.	BB.	SO.
Blasingame (L. 0-5)	3⅔	2	7	6	3	2
Ray	1⅓	2	1	1	1	1
Guinn	2	2	0	0	0	3
Coombs	1	3	2	2	0	1
Maloney (W, 3-0)	9	0	0	0	5	13

HBP—By Blasingame (Johnson), (May). Coombs (Johnson). Wild pitch—Blasingame, Ray.
T—2:28. A—3,898.

DON WILSON DOWNS REDS ON NO-HITTER

Duplicates Maloney's Feat In Astros' 4-To-0 Victory

Cincinnati, May 1 (AP)—Lanky Don Wilson hurled the second no-hitter at Crosley Field in 24 hours tonight as the Houston Astros, held hitless by Jim Maloney in their previous start, blanked the Reds, 4 to 0, to snap an eight-game losing streak.

Wilson, a 24-year-old right-hander who pitched a no-hitter against the Atlanta Braves two years ago as a rookie, struck out 13 batters, walked six and hit one on the way to duplicating Maloney's Wednesday night feat.

It was the second time in two seasons that pitchers on opposing teams have fired successive no-hitters in the same park. San Francisco's Gaylord Perry beat St. Louis, 1-0, with a no-hitter last September 17 in a night game at San Francisco and the Cardinals' Ray Washburn came back with a 2-0 no-hit triumph over the Giants the next afternoon.

Third Of Season

Wilson's no-hitter was the third of the current campaign, Montreal's Bill Stoneman having stymied Philadelphia, 7-0, on April 17.

Wilson, a 6-foot-3, 205-pound fastballer, allowed two Cincinnati runners to reach second. Johnny Bench walked and stole second in the second inning and Wilson walked pinch hitter Jim Stewart and Pete Rose in the eighth.

In the ninth, he fanned Tony Perez on a 3-2 pitch and got Bench to fly to center fielder Jim Wynn after falling behind the Reds' catcher 3-1.

Pop Foul

Then Tommy Helms, swinging on the first pitch, lifted a pop foul off the third baseline. Third baseman Doug Rader clutched the ball and the Astros swarmed around Wilson to congratulate him.

Wilson, who went into the game with a 1-3 record and a mediocre 4.13 earned run average, struck out Rose and Bob Tolan in the first inning and fanned Whitfield and Helms in the second after walking Bench.

He retired the hard-hitting Reds in order in the third and fourth, then hit Bench with a fast ball to open the fifth before adding two more strikeouts.

Rose walked in the sixth, and Whitfield drew a pass in the seventh. With Stewart on first in the eighth, catcher Don Bryant dropped Rose's foul pop for an error and the Reds' star drew a walk. But Wilson got Tolan and Alex Johnson on fly balls, ending Cincinnati's final threat.

HOUSTON	ab	r	h	bi	CINCINNATI	ab	r	h	bi
Morgan 2b	[illegible]	[illegible]	[illegible]	[illegible]	Rose cf	[illegible]	[illegible]	[illegible]	[illegible]
JAlou lf	[illegible]	[illegible]	[illegible]	[illegible]	Tolan rf	[illegible]	[illegible]	[illegible]	[illegible]
Wynn cf	[illegible]	[illegible]	[illegible]	[illegible]	AJohnson lf	[illegible]	[illegible]	[illegible]	[illegible]
Rader 3b	[illegible]	[illegible]	[illegible]	[illegible]	Perez 3b	[illegible]	[illegible]	[illegible]	[illegible]
Menke ss	[illegible]	[illegible]	[illegible]	[illegible]	Bench c	[illegible]	[illegible]	[illegible]	[illegible]
NMiller rf	[illegible]	[illegible]	[illegible]	[illegible]	Whitfield 1b	[illegible]	[illegible]	[illegible]	[illegible]
Blefary 1b	[illegible]	[illegible]	[illegible]	[illegible]	Helms 2b	[illegible]	[illegible]	[illegible]	[illegible]
Bryant c	[illegible]	[illegible]	[illegible]	[illegible]	Chaney ss	[illegible]	[illegible]	[illegible]	[illegible]
DWilson p	3	0	0	1	Carroll p	[illegible]	[illegible]	[illegible]	[illegible]
					Stewart ss	[illegible]	[illegible]	[illegible]	[illegible]
					Merritt p	[illegible]	[illegible]	[illegible]	[illegible]
					Ruiz ss	[illegible]	[illegible]	[illegible]	[illegible]
					Beauchp ph	[illegible]	[illegible]	[illegible]	[illegible]
					Noriega p	[illegible]	[illegible]	[illegible]	[illegible]
Total	34	4	9	4	Total	[illegible]	[illegible]	[illegible]	[illegible]

Houston . . . . [illegible]
Cincinnati . . . . [illegible]

E—Helms, Tolan, Bryant. DP—Cincinnati 1. LOB—Houston [illegible], Cincinnati 7. 2B—Menke. 3B—Blefary. HR—Rader (2). SB—Bench. S—Morgan. SF—D.Wilson.

	IP	H	R	ER	BB	SO
D.Wilson (W.2-3)	[illegible]	[illegible]	[illegible]	[illegible]	[illegible]	[illegible]
Merritt (L.1-3)	[illegible]	[illegible]	[illegible]	[illegible]	[illegible]	[illegible]
Carroll	[illegible]	[illegible]	[illegible]	[illegible]	[illegible]	[illegible]
Noriega	[illegible]	[illegible]	[illegible]	[illegible]	[illegible]	[illegible]

HBP—by Merritt (D.Wilson), by D. Wilson (Bench). T—2:[illegible]. A—[illegible].

Phils Suspend Richie Allen After Star Misses Twin Bill

New York, June 24 (AP) — Richie Allen, controversial first baseman of the Philadelphia Phillies, was suspended indefinitely without pay tonight by manager Bob Skinner.

Allen was suspended after he failed to show up at Shea Stadium for tonight's twi-night double-header with the New York Mets.

Asked how long the suspension could last, Skinner replied:

"That's up to Mr. Allen. It depends on what he tells me. The game is too big for this type of thing."

SEAVER PITCHES 4-0 MET VICTORY

Cub Rookie Quall Spoils Bid For Perfect Game

New York, July 9 (AP) — Tom Seaver retired 25 consecutive batters before rookie Jim Qualls's one-out single in the ninth inning ended his bid for a perfect game as the New York Mets defeated the Chicago Cubs 4 to 0 tonight.

Randy Hundley opened the ninth by bunting Seaver s first pitch back to the mound and the pitcher threw him out—the 25th Cub retired in a row. Then Qualls, also swinging at the first pitch, dumped his hit into left field, breaking the spell. Seaver then got the last two batters to end the game.

The one-hitter was Seaver's eighth straight victory and ran his record for the season to 14-3.

Standing Ovation

Seaver, who drove in one of the Mets' runs with a second inning single, got a tremendous, standing ovation from the Shea Stadium crowd of 59,083 when he came to bat in the eighth nining with his perfect game still intact.

After Qualls singled, the fans fell silent for a moment, then cheered Seaver again.

The Mets, who won their seventh straight game and crept within three games of the first place Cubs in the National League East Division race, had a run on opposing starter Ken Holtzman's first three pitches.

Tommie Agee lined the first pitch for a triple into the right field corner and then Bobby Pfeil doubled for the run.

In the second, two Chicago errors and hits by Seaver and Agee produced two more runs.

CHICAGO	ab	r	h	bi	NEW YORK	ab	r	h	bi
Kessinger ss	4	0	0	0	Agee cf	5	1	2	1
Beckert 2b	3	0	0	0	Pfeil 2b	4	0	1	1
BWilliams lf	3	0	0	0	CJones lf	3	1	1	1
Santo 3b	3	0	0	0	Clndenon 1b	4	0	0	0
Banks 1b	3	0	0	0	Charles 3b	4	0	1	0
Spangler rf	3	0	0	0	Garrett 2b	0	0	0	0
Hundley c	3	0	0	0	Swoboda rf	4	0	1	0
Qualls cf	3	0	1	0	Gaspar rf	0	0	0	0
Holtzman p	0	0	0	0	Grote c	4	1	0	0
Aberntthy p	2	0	0	0	Weis ss	4	1	1	0
WSmith ph	1	0	0	0	Seaver p	2	0	1	1
Total	28	0	1	0	Total	34	4	8	4

Chicago 000 000 000—
New York 120 000 10x—4

E—Santo, Kessinger, Beckert LOB—Chicago 1, New York 9. 2B—Pfeil, Agee, Charles. 3B—Agee HR—C.Jones (10). S—Seaver.

	IP	H	R	ER	BB	SO
Holtzman (L.10-5)	1 1-3	4	3	1	0	2
Abernathy	6 2-3	4	1	1	2	2
Seaver (W.14-3)	9	1	0	0	0	11

T—2:02 A—59,083

METS TOP CUBS AND SLICE LEAD

Weis Homer Sparks Win To Leave N.Y. 4½ Out

Chicago, July 15 (P) — Light hitting Al Weis's three-run homer in the fourth inning today led the New York Mets to a 5-to-4 victory over the Chicago Cubs and lifted them to within 4½ games of the National League East leaders before 38,608 at Wrigley Field.

The homer was the first of the season for Weis, who now has five in eight major league seasons spanning 663 games. It came with two outs and followed singles by Art Shamsky and Ed Kranepool.

Weis also singled and scored the Mets' first run in the third after Tommie Agee tripled. Ken Boswell slugged his third homer in the fifth.

Cubs Tie Score

After Weis and Agee had put the Mets ahead, the Cubs tied it in the bottom of the third when Jim Qualls singled, moved to second on a sacrifice, stole third and scored on a sacrifice fly by Don Kessinger.

The Cubs picked up an unearned run in the sixth. Ron Santo singled and came all the way home when Ernie Banks' single went through Agee for an error.

NEW YORK	ab	r	h	bi	CHICAGO	ab	r	h	bi
Agee cf	4	0	1	1	Kessinger ss	3	0	1	1
Boswell 2b	4	1	2	1	Beckert 2b	4	0	0	0
CJones lf	3	0	0	0	BWilliams rf	4	1	1	1
Shamsky rf	3	1	1	0	Santo 3b	4	2	2	1
Caspar rf	0	0	0	0	Banks 1b	4	0	2	0
Garrett 2b	4	0	1	0	WSmith lf	4	0	0	0
Kranepool 1b	4	1	1	0	Hundley c	4	0	0	0
Martin c	4	0	1	0	Qualls cf	4	0	0	0
Weis ss	4	2	2	3	Selma p	0	0	0	0
Gentry p	2	0	0	0	Nye p	1	0	0	0
RTaylor p	1	0	0	0	Spangler ph	1	0	0	0
					Aguirre p	0	0	0	0
Total	33	5	9	5	Total	32	4	8	3

New York .... 0 0 1 3 1 0 0 0 0 — 5
Chicago .... 0 0 1 0 0 1 0 2 0 — 4

E—Agee. DP—New York 1, Chicago 1. LOB—New York 4, Chicago 4. 3B—Agee. HR—Weis (1), Boswell (3), B.Williams (10), Santo (19). SB—Qualls. S—Gentry, Selma. SF—Kessinger.

	IP	H	R	ER	BB	SO
Gentry (W,9-7)	7 2-3	7	4	3	1	4
R Taylor	1 1-3	1	0	0	0	2
Selma (L,9-4)	4 1-3	5	5	5	1	5
Nye	2 2-3	3	0	0	1	3
Aguirre	2	1	0	0	1	3

Save—R.Taylor. T—2:24. A—38,608.

'ROCK' HELPS BIRDS EDGE ROYALS, 4-2

Oliver's Blunder Kills Rally; McNally Ties League Record

By JIM ELLIOT
[Sun Staff Correspondent]

Kansas City, July 30—Dave McNally, with the aid of one of the worst base-running blunders of the year, equalled an American League pitching record tonight as the Orioles beat the Kansas City Royals, 4 to 2, before 13,648 fans.

The Oriole southpaw wasn't around for Bob Oliver's ninth-inning mental lapse, but the eight innings Dave lasted enabled him to capture his 15th straight decision without defeat, his 17th straight going back to last season, and to compile a 29-2 record since last year's All-Star break.

McNally tied Johnny Allen's league record of 17 consecutive victories, set between September 10, 1936, and September 30, 1937, while Allen pitched for Cleveland.

Oriole Box Score

ORIOLES

	ab	r	h	bi
Buford, lf	3	0	1	2
Blair, cf	3	0	1	0
F. Robinson, rf	4	0	1	1
Powell, 1b	4	1	0	0
B. Robinson, 3b	4	1	2	0
Johnson, 2b	4	0	2	0
Hendricks, c	3	0	0	1
Belanger, ss	4	1	1	0
McNally, p	3	1	1	0
TOTALS	32	4	9	4

KANSAS CITY

	ab	r	h	bi
Hernandez, ss	4	0	0	0
Schaal, 3b	4	0	0	0
Foy, 1b	4	1	1	1
Piniella, lf	3	1	3	0
Martinez, c	4	0	0	0
Adair, 2b	3	0	0	0
Drabowsky, p	0	0	0	0
Taylor, ph	1	0	0	0
Oliver, rf	4	0	0	0
Keough, cf	4	0	1	0
Nelson, p	2	0	0	0
Rios, 2b	1	0	0	0
Kirkpatrick, ph	1	0	0	0
TOTALS	35	2	5	2

ORIOLES .... 000 101 200—4
Kansas City ...... 200 000 000—2

Error—Martinez, Belanger. Double play—Orioles 1, Kansas City 1. Left on base—Orioles 4; Kansas City 7. 2-base—Martinez, Buford, Foy. Home run—F. Robinson (26). Stolen base—Foy 2, Belanger. Sacrifice fly—Hendricks.

Pitching Summary

	ip	h	r	er	bb	so
McNally (W,15-0)	8	5	2	2	1	7
Watt	1	0	0	0	0	1
Nelson (L,6-10)	6⅓	7	4	4	2	5
Drabowsky	2⅔	2	0	0	0	3

Wild pitch—McNally. Time—2:06. Attendance—13,648.

Reprinted from
The Baltimore Sun papers

Twins Show Punch Off Field As Martin Knocks Out Boswell

BALTIMORE, Aug. 10 (AP)— Billy Martin, manager of the Minnesota Twins, disclosed today he knocked out Dave Boswell, a Twins' pitcher, during a fight in Detroit last Wednesday after Boswell had socked and kicked Bob Allison, an outfielder with the club.

Boswell, reported to have received 20 stitches to close facial wounds, did not show up for the weekend series against Baltimore, in which the Orioles swept the three games.

The right-hander, who has a 12-9 won-lost record for the American League's Western Division leaders, was sent home to Minnesota today as the Twins went to New York to continue their road trip against the Yankees.

Martin, a scrapper during his playing days on and off the field, had seven stitches taken in his right hand, which was badly swollen. Martin spent most of his major-league career with the Yankees.

Allison was reluctant to talk about the incident, but Martin said the big outfielder had several teeth chipped, sustained a black eye and was kicked in the back.

Martin said the trouble started after Art Fowler, the pitching coach, reported Boswell had not run his normal 18 to 20 laps preceding Wednesday night's game in Detroit, leaving the field after running two.

"I saw Boswell after the game at a restaurant," Martin said, "and told him I wanted to talk to him the next day about the laps.

"At about 11:30 [P.M.], Boswell left the place and said he was on his way, 'to get that squealer, Fowler.'

"Allison went outside to try and stop Boswell, and was standing there with his hands in his pockets when Boswell hit him with a Sunday punch, knocked him down and almost out.

"Both players were being held away from each other when I arrived on the scene. Boswell then ripped right out of his shirt and came after me. He struck me in the temple and in the chest."

Martin said he then got the upper hand and landed "about five of six punches in the stomach, a couple to the head, and when he came off the wall I hit him again. He was out before he hit the ground."

Martin, who said Allison calmed Boswell down earlier this season after Boswell accused a teammate of losing a game, said he would back up any action taken by Calvin Griffith, the club's owner.

"We're trying to win a pennant," Martin said, "not battles."

Don Drysdale Calls It Quits After 14 Years

Los Angeles, Aug. 11 (P)—Big Don Drysdale, the Los Angeles Dodgers' superstar pitcher, plagued by painful arm trouble, announced today his retirement from baseball "for the good of the team."

Sept. 16

CARLTON FANS 19 METS, BUT LOSES

Swoboda Hits Two Homers To Nip Cards, 4-3

St. Louis (P)—Ron Swoboda cracked a pair of two-run homers to power the New York Mets to a 4-to-3 victory over the St. Louis Cards tonight, spoiling a modern major league record 19-strikeout performance by Steve Carlton.

The victory put the Mets 4½ games ahead of the Chicago Cubs, who lost 8-2 at Montreal, in the National League East. The Met's magic number for clinching the divisional title was cut to 11.

3 Held Old Mark

Carlton baffled the Mets on a combination of fast balls and curves in breaking the record set twice by Sandy Koufax, of the Los Angeles Dodgers, and once each by Don Wilson, of Houston, and Bob Feller, of Cleveland.

The 24-year-old left-hander, in his third full season with the Cards, received a standing ovation from the crowd when he completed his string by fanning the Mets in order in the ninth.

Swoboda, victim of two of Carlton's whiffs, lifted the Mets from behind with each of his homers and both came when Carlton had two strikes on him.

NEW YORK					ST. LOUIS				
	ab	r	h	bi		ab	r	h	bi
Harrelson ss	4	0	1	0	Brock lf	4	1	2	0
Otis lf	5	0	0	0	Flood cf	5	2	2	1
Agee cf	5	1	1	0	Pinson rf	4	0	3	1
Clendenon 1b	3	1	1	0	Torre 1b	4	0	1	1
Swoboda rf	4	2	2	4	McCarver c	4	0	0	0
Charles 3b	4	0	0	0	Shannon 3b	4	0	0	0
Grote c	4	0	2	0	Javier 2b	4	0	0	0
Weis 2b	4	0	1	0	Maxvill ss	3	0	0	0
Gentry p	1	0	0	0	B.Browne ph	1	0	0	0
Pfeil ph	1	0	1	0	Carlton p	3	0	0	0
Gosger pr	0	0	0	0	Gagliano ph	1	0	0	0
McGraw p	1	0	0	0	Nossek ph	0	0	0	0
Total	36	4	9	4	Total	37	3	8	3

New York   0 0 0 2 0 0 0 2 0 — 4
St. Louis   0 0 1 0 2 0 0 0 0 — 3

E—Javier, Charles. DP—Clendenon, Harrelson. DP—New York 1. LOB—New York 7, St. Louis. HR—Swoboda 2 (9). SB—Pinson, Brock 2.

	IP	H	R	ER	BB	SO
Gentry						3
McGraw (W,8-3)						3
Carlton (L,16-10)	9	9	4	4	2	19

WP—Carlton. T—2:23. A—13,606.

Rose Keeps Batting Lead

CINCINNATI, Sept. 28 (AP)—Tony Perez cracked his 36th home run of the season today and three Cincinnati pitchers scattered four hits as the Reds downed the Houston Astros, 4-1.

Pete Rose, the defending National League batting champion, went 0 for 3 and his average dropped to .347, but he maintained his lead over Roberto Clemente of the Pirates (.341) and Cleon Jones of the Mets (.340).

Wayne Granger set a major league record, pitching in his 89th game of the season for the Reds.

Perez's homer in the third inning followed a walk to Rose and overcame a 1-0 Houston lead. Denis Menke cracked his 10th home run in the second, the Astros' first hit of the game.

HOUSTON (N.)					CINCINNATI (N.)				
	ab	r	h	bi		ab	r	h	bi
Morgan 2b	3	0	1	0	Rose rf	3	1	0	0
Alou rf	4	0	0	0	Helms 2b	3	1	1	0
Davis lf	2	0	0	0	Tolan cf	3	0	1	0
Rader 3b	4	0	0	0	Perez 3b	4	1	1	2
Watson 1b	3	0	0	0	Bench c	4	0	2	1
Menke ss	4	1	1	1	May 1b	3	0	1	0
Martinez c	3	0	1	0	Johnson lf	1	0	0	0
McFadden pr	0	0	0	0	Stewart cf	2	0	0	1
Edwards c	1	0	0	0	Woodward ss	4	0	1	0
Miller cf	4	0	0	0	Arrigo p	2	0	0	0
Griffin p	2	0	0	0	Carroll p	1	0	0	0
Lampard ph	1	0	0	0	Granger p	0	0	0	0
Bouton p	0	0	0	0					
Blasingame p	0	0	0	0					
Billingham p	0	0	0	0					
Total	31	1	4	1	Total	30	4	8	4

Houston   0 1 0 0 0 0 0 0 0 — 1
Cincinnati   0 0 2 0 0 0 2 0 x — 4

E—Rader, Martinez, Perez. DP—Houston 1, Cincinnati 1. LOB—Houston 7, Cincinnati 10. 2B—Helms, Bench. HR—Menke (10), Perez (36). SB—Morgan, Stewart. S—Carroll.

	IP	H	R	ER	BB	SO
Griffin (L, 11-10)	4	6	3	2	2	5
Bouton	⅓	2	2	2	1	0
Blasingame	⅓	0	0	0	1	1
Billingham	1⅓	0	0	0	1	1
Arrigo (W, 4-7)	5⅓	2	1	0	4	3
Carroll	2⅔	0	0	0	3	1
Granger						

Save—Granger. HBP—by Arrigo (Davis). Wild pitch—Arrigo. T—2:47. A—26,018.

MAYS HOMER TOPS PADRES

Willie's 600th Provides Margin In 4-2 S.F. Win

San Diego, Sept. 22 (P)—Willie Mays came off the bench and broke a seventh-inning tie with his 600th major league homer tonight, giving San Francisco a 4-to-2 victory over San Diego and keeping the Giants a half-game ahead of Atlanta in the National League West.

Mays batted for rookie George Foster after Ron Hunt opened the seventh inning with an infield hit and the 38-year-old outfielder hit rookie Mike Corkin's first pitch an estimated 390 feet into the left center field pavillion to shatter a 2-2 tie.

A San Diego stadium crowd of 4,779 gave Mays a standing ovation as he rounded the bases and he was greeted at home plate by the entire San Francisco bench.

The ball Mays hit into the seats was retrieved by a 15-year-old fan, Al Frolander, Jr. of Carlsbad, Calif., and presented to Mays in the dugout.

13th Of Year

The homer was only the 13th this season for Mays, but made him only the second man ever to hit 600 in a career. Only Babe Ruth with 714 hit more.

Meanwhile, veteran righthander Don McMahon pitched four innings of relief for the Giants to gain his third victory against one loss.

Hunt and Jim Hart singled home second-inning runs to give the Giants a 2-0 lead. However, the Padres fought back to tie it against Ron Bryant and McMahon.

Jose Arcia singled, stole second and scored on a single by Ollie Brown in the third inning. The Padres tied the score in the sixth after Bryant left the game with a pulled muscle in his rib cage. Brown hit a double off McMahon and scored on a triple by Nate Colbert.

4-Time Leader

Mays, who came to the Giants in 1951, has led the majors in homers four times during his career—the last time in 1965 when he whacked 52. That was his best home run season and his production slipped to 37 the next year and then to 22 in 1967 and 23 in 1968.

SAN FRANCISCO					SAN DIEGO				
	ab	r	h	bi		ab	r	h	bi
Fuentes 2b	3	0	1	0	Arcia 2b	3	1	1	0
Davenport 3b	0	0	0	0	Stahl ph	1	0	0	0
Hunt 2b	5	1	2	1	Slocum cf	0	0	0	0
Hart lf	3	0	1	1	R.Pena 3b	4	0	1	0
Foster lf	0	0	0	0	O.Brown rf	4	1	2	1
Mays cf	2	1	1	2	Ferrara lf	4	0	0	0
McCovey 1b	4	0	1	0	Colbert 1b	4	0	2	1
Bonds rf	3	0	1	0	Murrell cf	3	0	1	0
Henderson rf	3	0	1	0	Roberger p	0	0	0	0
Hiatt c	4	0	0	0	Spiezio ph	1	0	0	0
Lanier ss	2	1	1	0	Cannizzaro c	2	0	0	0
Bryant p	1	1	0	0	Roberto c	1	0	0	0
McMahon p	1	0	0	0	Kendall ph	1	0	0	0
					Dean ss	2	0	0	0
					V.Kelly ph	1	0	1	0
					I.Brown ss	0	0	0	0
					Corkins p	2	0	0	0
					Morales cf	1	0	0	0
Total	31	4	9	4	Total	37	2	8	2

San Francisco   0 2 0 0 0 0 2 0 0 — 4
San Diego   0 0 1 0 0 1 0 0 0 — 2

E—Lanier, Murrell. DP—San Francisco 1. LOB—San Francisco 10, San Diego 5. 2B—R.Pena, O.Brown. 3B—Colbert. HR—Mays (13). SB—Arcia. S—Bryant, Fuentes.

	IP	H	R	ER	BB	SO
Bryant	5	4	1	1	0	3
McMahon (W,3-1)	4	4	1	1	3	3
Corkins (L,1-3)	4	4	4	4	4	3
Reberger	3	1	0	0	4	3

T—2:51. A—4,779.

METS BEAT CARDS, 6-0, ON 4-HITTER BY GENTRY TO WIN NL EAST TITLE

Clendenon Hits 2 Homers As Cinderella Team Sets Off New York Celebration On Field By 54,928 Shea Stadium Fans

New York, Sept. 24 (AP)—The incredible, implausible New York Mets clinched the National League's East Division championship tonight, riding two homers by Donn Clendenon and the four-hit pitching of Gary Gentry to a 6-to-0 victory over the St. Louis Cardinals.

Clendenon and Ed Charles walloped home runs in a five-run Met explosion in the first inning and Clendenon connected again in the fifth as Gentry, a rookie righthander, coasted to his 12th victory of the season.

The Impossible Dream

The victory climaxed an impossible dream for the Mets, baseball's Cinderella team. They had never finished higher than ninth in seven previous seasons and avoided a cellar finish last year by just one game.

The Mets spent most of the season in second place and trailed Chicago by 9½ games on August 13. Suddenly, New York caught fire, and the Cubs began losing.

Tonight's victory gave the Mets a 34-10 record since that date.

Overtake Cubs

New York overtook Chicago on September 10, moving into first place for the first time ever. It also marked the first time all season that the Cubs had fallen out of the lead. Until then, Chicago had spent 155 consecutive days in first place.

New York kept the pressure on, winning 11 of the next 15 games, while the Cubs continued to stumble. The Mets clinched a tie for the pennant last night and came to the ballpark today knowing that a Cubs loss to Montreal would wrap up the title.

But while the players were taking batting practice, Chicago's 6-3 victory over the Expos was posted on the scoreboard. That meant, to clinch the title the Mets would have to beat the Cards. They wasted no time doing just that before an uproarious crowd of 54,928.

ST. LOUIS	ab	r	h	bi		NEW YORK	ab	r	h	bi
Brock lf	4	0	2	0		Harrelson ss	3	1	1	0
Flood cf	1	0	0	0		Agee cf	3	1	0	0
Davalillo cf	3	0	1	0		CJones lf	4	0	0	0
Pinson rf	4	0	0	0		Clendenon 1b	3	2	2	4
Torre 1b	4	0	0	0		Swoboda rf	3	1	0	0
McCarver c	3	0	0	0		Charles 3b	4	1	2	2
Shannon 3b	3	0	1	0		Grote c	4	0	2	0
Javier 2b	3	0	0	0		Weis 2b	4	0	0	0
Maxvill ss	1	0	0	0		Gentry p	4	0	0	0
White ph	0	0	0	0						
DaVanon ss	0	0	0	0						
Carlton p	0	0	0	0						
Giusti p	1	0	0	0						
Hague ph	1	0	0	0						
Campisi p	0	0	0	0						
Simmons ph	1	0	0	0						
Grant p	0	0	0	0						
Total	29	0	4	0		Total	32	6	7	6

St. Louis .... 0 0 0 0 0 0 0 0 0—0
New York .... 5 0 0 0 1 0 0 x—6

E—DaVanon. DP—New York 2. LOB—St. Louis 4, New York 6. 2B—Grote. HR—Clendenon 2 (15), Charles (3).

	IP	H	R	ER	BB	SO
Carlton (L,17-11)	1-3	3	5	5	2	1
Giusti	4 2-3	2	1	1	2	2
Campisi	2	0	0	0	1	3
Grant	1	0	0	0	0	0
Gentry (W,12-12)	9	4	0	0	2	5

T—2:02. A—54,928.

Shea Stadium Resembles Moon After Fans' Revelry

New York, Sept. 25 (AP)—The Shea Stadium playing field looked today like the pockmarked, crater-riddled surface of the moon. But there wasn't even an American flag flying to note the historic occasion.

Someone stole that, too.

In one of the most incredible souvenir snatching safaris in baseball history, Shea Stadium was stripped of everything that wasn't tacked down—and a number of things that were—after the New York Mets clinched the National League East pennant last night.

The scene, some 12 hours after the mass revelry that didn't end until some three hours of hysteria had passed, was viewed today by heads groundskeeper John McCarthy with almost total disbelief as he stood on the dugout steps, his hands jammed in his orange nylon windbreaker.

Extensive Damage

"I've been in this business since 1956," McCarthy said, "and I've seen more people get hurt and I've seen more violence. But I've never seen damage to a field to this extent."

The damage was clear to see, the field cleared of the dancing, jumping, howling, screaming fans who had poured out of the stands in celebration after the Mets' 6-0 victory over St. Louis. The fans stormed the field, scaled the walls, climbed the scoreboard in exhilaration.

They celebrated by stealing the American flag in center field and climbing a light tower on which was placed one of their own banners. They celebrated by scribbling the center field walls with graffiti of the affectionate "Love The Mets" type.

They celebrated by littering the playing surface with papers, programs, ice cream containers, beer cans. They celebrated by ripping up 1,000 to 1,500 feet of sod from the playing surface and leaving it pockmarked with craters.

Pieces Of Scoreboard

They celebrated by breaking three wheels off the batting cage and stripping the netting off it. They celebrated by tearing up the all-weather matting in the coaches' boxes behind first and third base. They celebrated by taking pieces of the scoreboard.

And they celebrated by stealing home plate.

"You can't take home plate unless you force it," explained McCarthy. "They forced it.

"It usually takes us four hours to clean up. This time it'll take us four days."

Fortunately, the Mets are headed for Philadelphia before the field has to be used again Monday night for the Mayor's Trophy Game against the once-formidable New York Yankees.

The American flag will be replaced, the center field walls repainted, the field re-sodded, the batting cage will be re-fitted but nothing likely will re-capture the moment that spawned the storm.

It had been building since 1962 when the Mets came into existence, taken to the hearts of New York's baseball fans because of the ineptness represented by such as Marv Throneberry, the intrepid first baseman-outfielder who turned a triple into a single better than anyone in baseball.

All Quiet At Park

And it reached its crescendo at 9:07 P.M. September 24, 1969, when young Gary Gentry got Joe Torre to ground into a game-ending double play. Then it began. It lasted some three hours, and it required the 300 police on hand, plus reinforcements, to finally end it.

But today all was quiet. Manager Gil Hodges was at his Brooklyn home, his phone off the hook. Undoubtedly his two aces, Tom Seaver and Jerry Koosman, will be the keys to a challenge for the National League pennant against the Western winner.

MIRACLE METS STAY HOT AND SWEEP BRAVES, 7-4, FOR FIRST NL PENNANT

Three Home Runs And Brilliant Relief Job By Nolan Ryan Create Bedlam At Shea, Bring Year's 3d Inter-City Meeting

By KEN NIGRO
[Sun Staff Correspondent]

New York, Oct. 6—"Poor Baltimore!" the sign at Shea Stadium read. "First the Jets, then the Knicks, now the Mets."

So it may be. The miracle New Yorkers kept their date with fate this afternoon by slugging three home runs and four doubles in a 7-to-4 destruction of the Atlanta Braves before a thundering crowd of 53,195.

The smashing triumph gave the Mets a 3-0 sweep in the best-of-five National League championship series and catapulted them into their first World Series. It came only eight years after the team was born.

Once again there was an ironic touch to the victory by the former tailenders of baseball. The Mets, who existed all season on their great pitching, banged out 14 hits for a three-game total of 37 against the tattered Braves pitching staff.

Homer Heroes

Even when the Mets did make an out, they hit line drives like they were shot from a cannon and the yells must have been heard all the way in Minnesota where the Orioles were clinching the American League flag.

Included in the barrage were four-baggers by Tommie Agee, Ken Boswell and Wayne Garrett, the red-haired 21-year-old third baseman.

Garrett's homer, only the second of his big league career, was the big one. It came in the fifth with one on and put the Mets ahead for keeps, 5-4.

Garrett also tossed out Tony Gonzalez for the final out in the ninth, setting off an unbelievable demonstration by the frenzied Shea faithful.

Reprinted from
The Baltimore Sun papers

MARTIN IS FIRED AS TWIN PILOT

Failure To Heed Club Policy Causes Ouster

New York, Oct. 13 (P)—Tempestuous Billy Martin, who won battles on and off the field in his first year as a major league manager, lost a war today when he was fired by the Minnesota Twins.

Twins President Calvin Griffith, citing Martin's refusal to follow front office "policy and guidelines," announced the dismissal in New York, where he is attending the World Series. Griffith broke the news to Martin in a phone call to the manager's Minneapolis home.

Phillies Trade Allen To Cards

Philadelphia, Oct. 8 (P) — Rich Allen, the controversial first baseman of the Philadelphia Phillies, was traded to the St. Louis Cardinals today in a seven-player deal that could wind up in the office of the commissioner of baseball.

The Phillies sent Allen to the Cardinals for catcher Tim McCarver, outfielder Curt Flood, relief pitcher Joe Hoerner and utility outfielder Byron Browne. St. Louis also acquired infielder Cookie Rojas and pitcher Jerry Johnson.

The trade, however, had hardly cooled off before the 31-year-old Flood, one of baseball's top defensive outfielders and a consistent hitter, announced he has retired from baseball.

"Once the trade is made it still goes," said a Cardinals spokesman. "The Phillies might throw it into the hands of the commissioner. We're out of it."

General manager John Quinn of the Phillies, who engineered the trade with Bing Devine, his St. Louis counterpart, said he would have no comment on the Flood development until after he has had a chance to talk with the veteran outfielder. Earlier, at a news conference, Quinn had said the only thing guaranteed in the deal was that all players were physically sound.

Allen, the pivotal figure in the deal, was overjoyed at the news. "I'm so glad to be out of here, Philadelphia. Six years in this town is enough for anybody. I'm glad to be away from Quinn and all of them. They treat you like cattle."

Decides To Retire

In a statement released by his public relations agent, Gene Lunn, Flood said: "If I were younger I certainly would enjoy playing for Philadelphia. But under the circumstances, I have decided to retire from organized baseball effective today and remain in St. Louis where I can devote full time to my business interests."

Phillies' owner Bob Carpenter commented, "Richie and the Phillies couldn't put it together," when asked how he felt about the deal. Carpenter said he felt Quinn did "a very exceptional job getting the most talent for Allen."

11-2 VICTORY SENDS BIRDS INTO SERIES

Blair Drives In 5 Runs; Mets Top Braves For NL Flag

By LOU HATTER
[Sun Staff Correspondent]

Minneapolis-St. Paul, Oct. 6—The Orioles won the American League pennant today by demolishing the Minnesota Twins, 11 to 2, concluding a three-game sweep of the first post-season championship series.

The New York Mets completed a sweep of the Atlanta Braves in the National League play-off, 7-4, at Shea Stadium. The Mets will be in Baltimore to open the World Series Saturday.

Before 32,735 mute Metropolitan Stadium spectators, Baltimore romped to its second American League pennant in the last four years on a barrage of 18 hits off a procession of seven rival pitchers.

Palmer Winner

Featured in the assault, on which Jim Palmer coasted to an easy ten-hit victory, were these explosive bat pyrotechnics:

A home run, two doubles and a pair of singles by centerfielder Paul Blair, driving five runs across;

Reprinted from
The Baltimore Sun papers

Mets Take Series With 4th Straight Win, 5-3

New York, Oct. 16 (Special)—The eight-year climb from the cellar to a world championship ended today as the New York Mets completed their demolition of the Orioles, taking their fourth straight Series game, 5-3.

Jerry Koosman suffered a momentary lapse in the third inning when the Orioles hit two home runs for a 3-0 lead, but he finished strong, compiling a five-hitter for his second Series win.

Donn Clendenon, who blasted a two-run homer, and Al Weis, who also hit one, were the Met batting heroes. They got help from Ron Swoboda, whose double in the eighth put the finishing touch on the Orioles

The Orioles' third-inning lead came from home runs by Dave McNally,

with Mark Belanger on base, and Frank Robinson.

Some 57,397 people, constituting the largest crowd ever to witness a game at Shea Stadium, swarmed onto the field after the final out, capping what might be termed the most remarkable surge to the top in baseball history.

World Series Play-By-Play

First Inning

ORIOLES—Buford thrown out. Blair flied out. Swoboda made a nice running catch of F. Robinson's liner. No runs; no hits; no errors.

METS—Agee walked. Harrelson struck out as Agee stole second. Jones flied out, Agee taking third. Clendenon walked. Swoboda struck out. No runs; no hits; no errors.

Second Inning

Powell flied out. B. Robinson thrown out. Johnson singled. Etchebarren forced Johnson at second, Charles to Weis. No runs, one hit, no errors.

METS—Charles thrown out. Grote flied out. Weis lined out. No runs; no hits; no errors.

Third Innings

ORIOLES — Belanger singled. McNally hit the first pitch into the Baltimore bullpen for a home run, scoring behind Belanger. Buford was thrown out. Blair struck out. F. Robinson hit a home run. Powell struck out. Three runs; three hits; no errors.

METS — Koosman doubled. Agee popped out. Harrelson struck out. Jones popped out. No runs; 1 hit; no errors.

Fourth Inning

ORIOLES—B. Robinson flied out. Johnson and Etchebarren thrown out. No runs; no hits; no errors.

METS—Clendenon struck out Swoboda singled. Charles fouled out. Grote forced Swoboda at second, Belanger unassisted. No runs; one hit; no errors.

Fifth Inning

ORIOLES—Belanger flied out. McNally struck out. Swoboda caught Buford's liner. No runs; no hits; no errors.

METS — Weis grounded out. Koosman struck out. Agee singled. Harrelson flied out. No runs; one hit; no errors.

Sixth Inning

ORIOLES—Blair flied out. F. Robinson took a called third strike. Powell singled. B. Robinson lined out. No runs; one hit; no errors.

METS—Jones was hit by a pitch. Clendenon hit a home run, his third of the series. Swoboda lined out. B. Robinson threw out Charles. Belanger threw out Grote. Two runs; one hit; no errors.

Seventh Inning

ORIOLES — Johnson fouled out. Etchebarren struck out. Belanger grounded out. No runs; no hits; no errors.

METS—Weis homered. Koosman struck out. Agee flied out. Harrelson lined out. One run; one hit; no errors.

Eighth Inning

ORIOLES—Curt Motton batted for McNally and grounded out. Buford flied out. Blair grounded out. No runs; no hits; no errors.

METS—Ed Watt now pitching for Baltimore. Jones doubled. Clendenon grounded out. Swoboda doubled, Buford trapping the ball as he attempted to make the catch, Jones scoring. Charles flied out. Grote reached first on Powell's error. When Watt dropped Powell's throw to first for another error, Swoboda scored. Weis struck out. Two runs; two hits; two errors.

Ninth Inning

ORIOLES — F. Robinson walked. Powell forced F. Robinson. Chico Salmon ran for Powell. B. Robinson flied out. Johnson flied out. No runs; no hits; no errors.

Ump Crawford Says Martin Ran Correctly After Bunt

By LOU HATTER

New York, Oct. 16—Umpire Shag Crawford claimed today that J.C. Martin legally had one foot on the first-base foul line when Oriole pitcher Pete Richert's 10th inning throw struck the New York Met runner on the decisive final play of yesterday's fourth World Series game here.

Richert's peg, following Martin's pinch bunt, enabled the tie-breaking run to score from second base for a 2-to-1 New York victory.

Photo Misleading

There was no dispute until a photograph late last night showed Martin running in fair territory and not within a three-foot-wide restraining area in foul ground. The area begins 45 feet from first base.

Martin was running on the fair side of the line when the picture was snapped, just before the baseball caromed off his left wrist. The throw had been intended for Oriole second baseman Dave Johnson, who was covering first.

Prior to this afternoon's concluding 5-3 Oriole loss, at a press conference during which commissioner Bowie Kuhn announced that no fine would be imposed for Baltimore manager Earl Weaver's ejection yesterday, Crawford insisted that the photograph was misleading.

"The play was entirely legitimate," he declared. "The picture was taken while the ball was still in flight. By the time the ball hit Martin, he was on the line."

SERIES SHARE ON SHOESHINE

'Tip' Due Clubhouse Man For Job On Shoes

By KEN NIGRO
[Sun Staff Correspondent]

New York, Oct. 16—In this miracle year of the Mets it seems only right that ever. the clubhouse man should share today in their final World Series triumph.

"I'll have to give him (the clubhouse man) an extra big tip," shouted Cleon Jones in the noisy Met locker room.

"He really gave those shoes a good shine."

Jones was referring to a big play in the sixth inning when he claimed he was hit on the foot by one of Dave McNally's pitches. Umpire Lou DiMuro did not agree and it appeared Jones's protest would go the same way as Frank Robinson's the inning before when the Oriole right fielder insisted he was hit by a pitch.

Hodges Makes Point

But Met manager Gil Hodges came out and asked DiMuro to look at the ball. The umpire did and when he saw the polish on it, he waved Jones to first. Cleon scored a moment later when Donn Clendenon hit a home run and the Mets were on their way to a World Series triumph after seven years of humiliation.

Cronin Welcomes Milwaukee To AL

Jan. 15

Murphy Dies; Took Mets From Depths

From Press Dispatches

New York, N. Y. – Johnny Murphy, 61, general manager of the champion New York Mets, died of a heart attack here Wednesday night.

Murphy had been hospitalized since Dec. 30, when he

Johnny Murphy

suffered an earlier heart attack. He had been believed to be recovering until he was stricken again.

The Mets' rise from the depths to the heights of baseball dated back to the appointments of Gil Hodges as manager and Murphy as general man-

ager in 1967. Murphy, who had been a Met vice president since 1964, was instrumental in luring Hodges from the Washington Senators and acquiring many of the players who helped the Mets win the National League pennant and World Series last year.

Murphy was one of the outstanding relief pitchers in baseball in his playing days with the New York Yankees and Boston Red Sox. He had a lifetime record of 93-53 for 13 seasons in the major leagues and won two games without defeat in World Series competition.

Murphy had nicknames of the "Fordham Fireman," because he had attended Fordham University, and "Grandma," because of his fidgety habits when taking his position on the mound.

When Lefty Gomez, a Yankee pitching star of that era, was asked once how many games he would win, he said, "It depends on how Murphy's arm holds up."

Murphy is survived by his wife, Elizabeth; twin sons, Thomas and John Jr., and three grandsons.

Reprinted from
The Milwaukee Journal

Milwaukee, April 1 (P)—Joe Cronin officially welcomed Milwaukee into the American League today, ending a four-year estrangement between the city and major league baseball.

"On behalf of the American League, I want to convey my sincere congratulations to your organization on its return to baseball," Cronin, American League president, said to the Milwaukee Brewers in a telegram.

"I sincerely hope the fans of Wisconsin will be rewarded with an exciting team," he said.

Allan (Bud) Selig, president of Milwaukee Brewers, Inc., read Cronin's message at a news conference, then said he felt the telegram sealed the move of the Seattle Pilots to Milwaukee.

Lawyers in Seattle still were hammering away in federal bankruptcy court today at the exact wording of the order approving sale of the Pilots to the Brewers for $10.8 million.

After 2½ hours of deliberation before bankruptcy referee Sidney C. Volinn, the hearing was recessed until 1 P.M. tomorrow. At that same hearing Washington State will seek to have all legal restrictions against a joint Seattle and state damage antitrust suit lifted. The suit is against the league, the individual owners and the owners of the Pilots.

Volinn had stayed all legal action so that he could consider the Pilots' petition to have the sale approved. He gave that approval last night.

The only question left after Volinn announced his decision to approve the sale was when he would sign the order. Wallace Aiken, attorney for Pacific Northwest Sports, Inc., the Pilots' owner, asked for an early morning signing because the closing time on the sale was 11 A.M.

However, attorney Elwin Zarwell, the Brewers' representative, said Volinn's decision made the sale final so far as the Brewers were concerned.

Sale papers for the Pilots were signed March 8 and became final today. The American League had approved Milwaukee last week when Volinn cleared the way for owners to vote. Only Volinn's decision stood between Milwaukee and its first baseball team in five years.

Milwaukee has the Brewers. Seattle has an empty stadium and baseball has potentially big trouble on its hands.

William L. Dwyer, special assistant Washington state attorney general, said after the hearing last night the state and Seattle would press their joint $82 million anti-trust damage suit against the American League and Pacific Northwest.

Sens. Warren G. Magnuson and Henry M. Jackson, both Washington Democrats, say they will introduce legislation in the Senate next week taking away baseball's anti-trust immunity. Rep. Brock Adams (D-Wash.) was to introduce similar legislation in the House.

Volinn approved the sale, he said, because the club couldn't meet its debts and continue to operate in Seattle. The only alternative to the sale—an American League takeover—was unfair because the league might be forced to bear deficit spending of as much as $5 million over the next three years, Volinn added.

Angels Ruin Milwaukee's Return To Baseball, 12-0

Milwaukee, April 7 (P)—Andy Messersmith fired a four-hitter and California ruined Milwaukee's return to the major leagues before a crowd of 37,237 today scoring a 12-0 victory.

started in the second inning.

The Angels' long ball attack when Alex Johnson opened with a triple and scored on Jim Spencer's sacrifice fly. The Angels scored three more in the next inning, all with two out.

Sandy Alomar beat out an infield hit starting the rally and Jim Fregosi walked. Then Bill Voss tripled for two runs and scored on a wild pitch.

That finished Brewer starter Lew Krausse and the Angels continued the assault in the fourth, bunching five hits for four more runs. Consecutive doubles by Roger Repoz and Joe Azcue were the key hits in the rally.

Baseball Suspends McLain Until July 1 For 'Gullibility'

Kuhn Says Pitcher Was 'Victim Of Confidence Scheme,' Clears Him Of Gambling

New York, April 1 (AP)—Denny McLain, cited for being bullible and greedy, was suspended until July 1 today by the commissioner of baseball. Bowie Kuhn, after an investigation disclosed that the Detroit Tigers' pitcher had attempted to become a partner of gamblers involved in bookmaking operations.

The action by Mr. Kuhn, who suspended Mr. McLain six weeks ago while he investigated the pitcher's off-the-field activities, also prohibited the former ace of the Detroit staff from appearing at the Tigers' camp or in their clubhouse until the suspension is lifted.

In addition, Mr. McLain was placed on probation with the requirement that he provide the commissioner's office with data on his financial affairs to show that further difficulties do not lead him into a similar situation again.

Mr. McLain, in his first comment on the decision, said: "I can't say I agreed with the decision because I want to play baseball right now."

He spoke in Detroit in a television interview.

"I've never done anything to hurt the game of baseball," he added. "More than anything else, I'm happy there was a decision finally reached. By July 1, Denny McLain will be ready to pitch."

Mr. McLain had flown to Detroit from Lakeland, Fla., where his brother, Tim, had said earlier that there would be no comment until the press conference late tonight.

The cost of the suspension to Mr. McLain, already deep in myriad financial difficulties, is estimated at about $45,000—half his yearly salary—plus the $5,700 Mr. Kuhn said the pitcher was duped out of by the gamblers with whom he was associating.

Mr. Kuhn handed down his decision at a formal press conference in a midtown hotel, ending speculation about Mr. McLain's fate that had existed since February 19 when he suspended the pitcher indefinitely because of his "involvement in 1967 bookmaking activities and associations."

In the six weeks since, Mr. Kuhn said that his investigation had disclosed that Mr. McLain had become involved "with certain gamblers, said to be involved in a bookmaking operation," after playing an engagement at a bar in Flint, Mich., in January, 1967.

"McLain at that time commenced placing basketball bets with this operation," Mr. Kuhn said, "and subsequently he was persuaded to make financial contributions totaling approximately $5,700.

Says He Was Conned

"While McLain believed he had become a partner in this operation and has so admitted to me . . . it would appear that, in fact, he was the victim of a confidence scheme. I would thus conclude that McLain was never a partner and had no proprietary interest in the bookmaking operation.

"The fair inference is that his own gullibility and avarice had permitted him to become a dupe of the gamblers with whom he associated."

Mr. Kuhn said his investigation had not shown any other material facts beyond those—that no evidence exists that Mr. McLain "has been guilty of any misconduct involving baseball or the playing of baseball games."

Mr. Kuhn, however, concluded that Mr. McLain's association with gamblers "was not in the best interests of baseball" and "therefore must be made the subject of discipline." Mr. Kuhn pointed out at the same time, that the suspension was not based on Mr. McLain's "irresponsibility."

The commissioner also said, in answer to questions, that had Mr. McLain actually become a partner in bookmaking operation, it would have been a fact he would have had to consider, "but he was neither a bookmaker nor a partner in the book. He thought he was, but he wasn't. He didn't get a penny out of the entire thing."

Pressed as to what the difference is in attempting to become a bookmaker and actually being one, Mr. Kuhn said:

"I think you have to consider the difference is the same as between murder and attempted murder."

Let Off Easily?

Asked if Mr. McLain were not being let off easily, Mr. Kuhn replied sharply:

"I do not think it [the suspension] is a slap on the wrist. I think a suspension for half-a-year is a very serious matter."

Mr. Kuhn said that Mr. McLain had been notified of the decision by a member of his staff before the press conference. He also revealed that he had disclosed the action he was going to take to President Nixon when they met at the White House yesterday.

"In the President's judgment," Mr. Kurn said, "the decision was a fair one."

Has Not Damaged Image

Mr. Kuhn also said he does not think the McLain case had damaged the public's image of baseball.

"I think the good name of baseball is vindicated by the action I took," he said. "The public tends to receive it in this light: Denny is here and baseball is there. I think the public has viewed the problem as one of avarice."

Mr. McLain has all but agreed with that in several statements he has made since the February 19 ruling.

"I extended myself on business deals and used some bad judgments," Mr. McLain has said. I made a lot of lousy investments."

In Bad Financial Shape

Those investments have so drained Mr. McLain's financial resources—his $90,000-a-year salary plus an estimated $100,000 more in post-season appearance fees, mostly as an organist—that he is immersed in severe money problems.

Cards End Braves' Streak, 6-5

Cardenal's Single Off Wilhelm Caps 4-Run Rally In 9th

Atlanta, May 10 /P—Jose Cardenal's two-run single off Hoyt Wilhelm, who was making the 1,000th pitching appearance of his career, capped a four-run rally in the ninth inning today and gave the St. Louis Cardinals a 6-to-5 victory over Atlanta, snapping the Braves' winning streak at 11 games.

The Cardinals, who had lost five games in a row and nine of their previous 10, trailed 5-2 when Richie Allen opened the ninth with his ninth homer.

Joe Torre's single knocked out Atlanta starter George Stone. Julian Javier and Vic Davalillo poked singles off reliever Bob Priddy, filling the bases and bringing the 46-year-old Wilhelm out of the bullpen.

Wilhelm retired Joe Hague on a ground ball as one run scored, then walked Leron Lee intentionally to refill the bases and set the stage for Cardenal's go-ahead single.

Rico Carty delivered Atlanta's first run with a single, stretching his hitting streak to 28 games.

"That's the way it goes," Wilhelm said in the dressing room almost 30 minutes after the game.

"My arm was feeling pretty good and it (the knuckler) was jumping."

Last night Wilhelm worked three innings and saved a victory for the Braves by fanning Allen and Torre in each the seventh and ninth innings.

"We win a few like that, too," he said. "That's baseball."

Asked if he had any feeling about his 1,000th appearance, Wilhelm said, "Not a hell of a lot."

His first pitch was a ball which plate umpire Ed Sudol took to Wilhelm as a souvenir. Hoyt casually tossed it to the dugout.

ST. LOUIS					ATLANTA				
	ab	r	h	bi		ab	r	h	bi
Cardenal cf	5	0	1	2	SJackson ss	3	0	0	0
CTaylor rf	5	0	0	0	Millan 2b	4	1	1	0
Maxvill ss	0	0	0	0	HAaron rf	4	0	0	0
Brock lf	4	1	1	0	Carty lf	4	1	1	1
RchAllen 3b	4	1	2	1	Lum lf	0	0	0	0
Torre c	4	2	3	2	Cepeda 1b	4	0	0	0
Javier 2b	4	1	2	0	CBoyer 3b	4	1	1	0
Gagliano 1b	3	0	1	0	Gonzalez cf	3	2	2	1
Davalillo rf	1	1	1	0	King c	2	0	1	1
Ramirez ss	3	0	0	0	Didier c	0	0	0	0
Hague 1b	1	0	0	1	Garr ph	1	0	0	0
Torrez p	1	1	1	0	GStone p	3	0	0	0
Rojas ph	1	0	0	0	Priddy p	0	0	0	0
McCool p	0	0	0	0	Wilhelm p	0	0	0	0
JJohnson p	0	0	0	0	Aspromte ph	0	0	0	0
Lee ph	0	0	0	0					
Campisi	0	0	0	0					
Total	37	6	11	6	Total	32	5	6	5

St. Louis ... 0 0 0 2 0 0 0 0 4—6
Atlanta .... 0 0 0 4 0 0 1 0 0—5

DP—Atlanta 1. LOB—St. Louis 5, Atlanta 5. 2B—King. HR—Torre (4), Gonzalez (0), RchAllen (9). SB Brock, S Jackson.

	IP	H	R	ER	BB	SO
Torrez	6	4	1	1	2	3
McCool	2-3	2	1	1	1	0
J Johnson (W,1-0)	1 1-3	0	0	0	0	1
Campisi	1	0	0	0	2	0
G.Stone	8	8	4	4	0	8
Priddy (L,2-1)	0	2	2	2	0	0
Wilhelm	1	1	0	0	1	0

T—2:31. A—23,166.

FRANK'S BAT LIFTS BIRDS TO 12-2 WIN

Ties Mark By Hitting Grand Slams Two Innings In Row

By JIM ELLIOT
(Staff Correspondent)

Washington, June 26—Frank Robinson, the only player ever named most valuable in both major leagues, tonight became the third player in big-league history to crash two grand slam homers in successive innings as the Orioles whipped the Washington Senators, 12 to 2, before 13,194 fans at Robert F. Kennedy Memorial Stadium.

Robinson's tremendous feat completely overshadowed Dave McNally's 7-hitter. McNally became only the second American League pitcher this year to win 11 games while teammate Don Buford had a 4-for-5 night which included his eighth homer of the year.

Coleman Victimized

Robinson first connected off Washington's starting pitcher, right-hander Joe Coleman, in the fifth inning, a 390 foot wallop to the base of the scoreboard in right field.

Then, in the sixth inning, Frank blasted a pitch from southpaw reliever Joe Grzenda into the upper deck in left-center field, a distance measured at 442 feet.

The only players ever to perform the feat previously in the game's 101-year history were Jim Gentile, who did it as an Oriole May 9, 1961, against the Minnesota Twins at Minnesota, and Detroit's Jim Northrup, June 24, 1968.

"Diamond Jim," as Gentile was known, set a club record of nine runs batted across in one game, one more than Robinson, and hit his grand slams in the first and second innings. Northrup hit his in the fifth and sixth innings.

Seventh On List

Robinson became only the seventh player to hit two grand slams in one game. Besides Gentile and Northrup, others to hit two in one game were Tony Lazzeri, Yankees, 1936, Jim Tabor, Red Sox, 1939; Rudy York, Red Sox, 1946, and the only National Leaguer, a pitcher, Tony Cloninger, of Atlanta, in 1966.

Seaver Fans Ten In Row; Mets Win, 2-1

New York, April 22 /P—Tom Seaver tied the major league record with 19 strikeouts and set a record with 10 straight strikeouts today while pitching the New York Mets to a 2-to-1 victory over San Diego.

The 1969 Cy Young Award winner and 25-game winner for the world champions, wiped out the old record for consecutive strikeouts of eight held jointly by four pitchers. He also tied the game record of 19 in a game set by Steve Carlton of the St. Louis Cards against the Mets last September 15.

The Box Score

SAN DIEGO					NEW YORK				
	ab	r	h	bi		ab	r	h	bi
Arcia ss	3	0	0	0	Agee cf	3	1	1	0
Murrell lf	4	0	0	0	Harrelson ss	3	1	1	0
DRoberts p	0	0	0	0	Boswell 2b	3	0	1	1
VKelly 3b	4	0	0	0	CJones lf	3	0	0	0
Gaston cf	4	0	0	0	Shamsky rf	2	0	0	0
Ferrara lf	3	1	1	1	Swoboda lf	1	0	0	0
Colbert 1b	3	0	0	0	Foy 3b	2	0	0	0
Campbell 2b	0	0	1	0	Kranepool 1b	3	0	0	0
Morales rf	3	0	0	0	Grote c	3	0	0	0
Barton c	2	0	0	0	Seaver p	3	0	0	0
Corkins p	2	0	0	0					
Webster ph	1	0	0	0					
Slocum ss	0	0	0	0					
Total	29	1	2	1	Total	27	2	4	2

San Diego ... 0 1 0 0 0 0 0 0 0—1
New York ... 1 0 1 0 0 0 0 0 x—2

LOB—San Diego 3, New York 5. 2B—Boswell. 3B—Harrelson. HR—Ferrara, Agee.

	IP	H	R	ER	BB	SO
Corkins	7	4	2	2	1	5
D.Roberts	1	0	0	0	0	0
Seaver (W,3-0)	9	2	1	1	2	19

T—2:14. A—14,197.

Santo's Hit In 11th Gives Cubs 4-3 Win Over Braves

Chicago, May 12 /P—Ron Santo's scratch single with the bases loaded in the 11th inning gave the Chicago Cubs a 4-to-3 victory over the Atlanta Braves today in a game in which Ernie Banks hit his 500th career home run and Rico Carty stretched his consecutive game hitting streak to 30 games.

Despite Banks's home run in the second inning, the Cubs trailed 3 to 2 in the last of the ninth when Billy Williams hit his 12th home run of the year.

The 39-year-old Banks lined his third homer of the season and No. 500 off a Pat Jarvis 1 to 1 pitch in the second inning with nobody on. The ball barely made the leftfield bleacher section and bounced back onto the field where Carty retrieved it and threw it to the Cub dugout.

Banks doffed his cap to 5,264 screaming fans, and held up the ball, which will be enshrined in the Hall of Fame at Cooperstown, N.Y.

Banks, who hit his first homer of Gerry Staley in St. Louis on September 20, 1953, two days after Chicago bought him from the Kansas City Monarchs, joined eight others in the 500-homer club, headed by Babe Ruth with 714.

Aug. 3

BIRDS HOLD OFF ROYAL RALLY, 10-8

Early 5-0 Spree Helps Cuellar Win No. 15; 5 R.B.I. For Motton

By JIM ELLIOT

The Kansas City Royals took the Orioles right down to the wire last night at the Stadium, actually out-hitting the Birds, 13-12, before losing a major-league record 23d straight time to one opponent.

A crowd of 12,931 watched the Orioles win, 10 to 8, giving Mike Cuellar his 15th triumph against 6 defeats although Mike was long gone when the Orioles upped their all-time victory mark against the expansion club of 1969.

Braves Drop Doubleheader Despite Aaron's 3,000th Hit

Cincinnati, May 17 (P)—Atlanta's Hank Aaron drove in one run with his 3,000th hit and two more with his 570th homer, but the Cincinnati Reds nipped the Braves, 7 to 6, on pitcher Don Gullett's run-scoring single in the 12th inning, completing a doubleheader sweep today.

Aaron, hitless in four trips to the plate in the first game, drove in a first-inning run with his 3,000th hit, an infield single behind second base. The game was held up while Stan Musial, last of eight other major leaguers to reach the 3,000 milestone, and Braves' president William Bartholmay presented the ball to Aaron.

Standing Ovation

The crowd of 33,217—largest at Crosley Field in 23 years—gave the Braves' 36-year-old slugger a standing ovation.

In the third, Felix Millan singled and Aaron tagged Reds' starter Wayne Simpson for his 16th homer of the season giving Atlanta a 3-0 lead.

The slugging outfielder from Mobile, Ala., whose 569 home runs place him third on the all-time long ball list, is the first player ever to collect both 3,000 hits and 500 homers.

Signed by the then Boston Braves in 1951 for $10,000 after sparkling as a teenager for the Indianapolis Clowns of the old Negro American League, Aaron made it to the majors in 1954, the Braves' second season in Milwaukee. He got his first hit April 15 off Vic Raschi of St. Louis.

```
ATLANTA           CINCINNATI
         ab r h bi           ab r h bi
SJackson ss 7 0 1 0  Rose rf   7 1 1 1
Millan 2b  6 3 2 0  Woodward 2b 4 0 1 0
HAaron rf  5 2 3 3  Chaney 2b  3 0 1 0
Carty lf   3 0 0 0  Gullet p   1 0 1 1
Gonzalez lf 2 1 0 0  Perez 3b  7 2 5 0
Cepeda 1b  6 0 1 1  Bench cf  7 2 2 2
Lum cf     6 0 0 0  LMay 1b   6 1 3 5
CBoyer 3b  5 0 2 0  McRae lf  3 0 0 0
Lidier c   6 0 0 0  Tolan cf  5 0 1 0
GStone p   3 0 0 0  Corrales c 2 0 0 0
Wilhelm p  0 0 0 0  Stewart lf 3 0 0 0
Carr ph    1 0 0 0  Concepcion ss 7 1 2 0
Kline p    0 0 0 0  Simpson p  2 0 0 0
Jaster p   1 0 0 0  JWatt ph   1 0 0 0
King ph    1 0 0 0  Granger p  1 0 0 0
Neibauer p 0 0 0 0  Helms ph   1 0 9 0
                    Carroll p  0 0 0 0
                    Bravo lf   0 0 0 0
Total     52 6 9 4  Total     59 7 17 7
One out when winning run scored.
Atlanta      102 000  00 300 000 — 6
Cincinnati   000 002 010 300 001 — 7
E—Concepcion, C.Boyer, Chaney,
Perez. DP—Atlanta (1), Cincinnati 3.
LOB—Atlanta 11, Cincinnati 15. 2B—
Perez, L.May, Tolan. 3B—Concepcion.
HR—HAaron (16), Rose (6), Bench (11),
L.May (11). SB—Perez, Tolan. S—Milan,
Bravo.
              IP  H R ER BB SO
G.Stone       7   9  3  3  1  9
Wilhelm       1   0  0  0  1  2
Kline         2   3  3  3  0  0
Jaster        2   2  0  0  1  1
Neibauer (L,0-2) 2-3 3  1  1  3  2
Simpson       4   4  3  2  2  4
Granger       3   4  2  1  4  1
Carroll       3   1  0  0  0  0
Gullet (W,2-0) 2   0  0  0  2  0
HBP—by Simpson (Cepeda). T—5:55.
A—33,217.
```

Flood Loses Battle With Reserve Rules

Attorneys Promise To Press Court Action; Kuhn Hopes Player Returns To Game

New York, Aug. 12 (P)—Curt Flood lost his suit against baseball today when a federal judge upheld the legality of the sport's controversial reserve system and suggested any change should be made through player-owner negotiations.

In handing down his decision two months after the trial in open court ended, Judge Irving Ben Cooper denied Mr. Flood's bid for an injunction and for damages in the $4.1 million anti-trust suit that was brought after he was traded by the St. Louis Cardinals to the Philadelphia Phillies.

"An Appeal, Of Course"

"There will, of course, be an appeal," said Allan Zerman, one of Mr. Flood's attorneys.

Before the trial it was expected appeals could possibly take the case all the way to the United States Supreme Court.

BOUTON GETS REPRIMAND

Baseball Chief Displeased With Pitcher's Book

New York, June 1 (P)—Pitcher Jim Bouton had his wrist slapped today by Baseball Commissioner Bowie Kuhn for writing the controversial book, "Ball Four."

Kuhn met with the Houston Astros' right-hander for two hours and afterward told newsmen. "I advised Mr. Bouton of my displeasure with these writings and have warned him against future writings of this character."

He added, "Under all the circumstances, I have concluded that no other action was necessary."

Miller Attends Meeting

Bouton was accompanied by Marvin Miller, executive director of the Major League Baseball Players Association, and Dick Moss, an association lawyer.

While they met, youngsters demonstrated outside the commissioner's office with signs reading, "Kuhn Stop Repression and Harassment," "Jim Bouton Must Not Be Repressed," and, "No Punishment For Exposing The Truth."

Bouton's book, co-authored with Leonard Schecter, editor of Look Magazine, concerned his playing days with the New York Yankees. He made personal disclosures of many players, including superstar Mickey Mantle.

Excerpts In Magazine

Although the book has not yet been released, excerpts of it appeared in Look. Bouton told newsmen after the hearing that it was from the magazine articles that Kuhn took the action for he had not read the entire manuscript.

Upon first appearing before newsmen after the meeting, Bouton said, "No comment." Then he opened up. Would he be writing another book?

"I have no plans to write any more books," he said.

Was he sorry about "Ball Four?"

"Absolutely not. I'm glad I wrote the book."

Wouldn't this publicity help sales?

"That would be nice."

What did he think about the demonstration?

"Terrific."

Bouton also said he "expected there might be some opposition" to the story when he wrote it, but didn't expect any disciplinary action from Astro officials.

He said he would rejoin the team in Houston tomorrow for a night game at the Astrodome.

Was he keeping any diaries lately?

"No comment," he said. "I guess I'm entitled to a few no comments."

McLain Out Rest Of Season

New York, Sept. 9 (P)—Pitcher Denny McLain was in more hot water today when baseball commissioner Bowie Kuhn suspended him again, this time for the rest of the 1970 season.

Kuhn said McLain's latest penalty—his third suspension this year—did not stem from involvement with gamblers, which kept him on the sidelines until July 1. Nor did it stem from his August 28 dousing of two Detroit sportswriters with ice water, for which the Tigers slapped him with a one-week suspension.

All Kuhn would say was that "certain new allegations have been brought to my attention, including allegations regarding McLain's conduct with respect to the Detroit management and information that on occasions McLain has carried a gun."

After 3½ hours of meetings with McLain, his lawyer and officials of the Detroit ball club and baseball, Kuhn announced the new suspension, which he said was "pending further proceedings, which by agreement of counsel will not take place before the end of the season."

San Francisco, July 18 (P)— Willie Mays's 3,000th major league hit—a second inning single off Mike Wegener—overshadowed Gaylord Perry's four-hit pitching today in the San Francisco Giants' 10-to-1 victory over the Montreal Expos.

Mays, who became the 10th major leaguer in baseball history to collect 3,000 hits, also singled in the sixth before leaving the game and receiving a standing ovation from a Ball Day crowd of 28,879.

He hit an 0-2 pitch through the left side of the Montreal infield with two out in the second to reach the milestone.

Mays is in his 19th season and heading toward his best year since 1966, when he had 37 homers, 103 runs batted in and a .288 batting average. His two hits today raised his season's average to .278 and he picked up his 51st r.b.i. of the year.

"I feel that I'm running faster now than I have in the last three years, especially in the field," he said

The Giants promised every fan a free pass to another Giant game and also announced that Mays's son, Michael, would receive a four-year college scholarship in commemoration of his father's 3,000th hit.

```
          MONTREAL        SAN FRANCISCO
              ab r h bi        ab r h bi
Staehle 2b    3 0 1 0   Bonds rf   3 3 1 1
Jones lf      2 0 0 0   Hunt 2b    4 1 0 0
Shaun cf      1 0 0 0   Mays cf    4 1 2 1
Fairey cf     3 0 1 0   BTaylor p  1 0 0 0
Bateman c     4 0 1 0   Dietz c    3 0 1 1
Laboy 3b      3 0 0 0   Hart 3b    2 2 2 0
Wine ss       1 0 0 0   Fuentes 3b 0 0 0 0
Brand ss      2 0 0 0   FJohnson lf 3 1 0 0
Wegener p     1 0 0 0   Lanier ss  4 0 2 2
Fairey ph     0 1 0 0   McCovey 1b 5 1 2 1
Dillman p     0 0 0 0   Perry p    4 2 2 2
Bailey ph     1 0 0 0
McGinn p      0 0 0 0
Total        30 1 4 1   Total      36 10 12 11
```

Montreal   0 0 0 0 0 1 0 0 0—1
San Francisco   0 5 1 0 0 2 0 0 x—10

E—Bateman, Wine. DP—Montreal 2, San Francisco 1. LOB—Montreal 5, San Francisco 7. 2B—Lanier 2, McCovey, Staehle, Perry. Bonds. Fairly. HR—Perry (1). SB—Bonds. SF—Dietz.

```
               IP  H  R ER BB SO
Wegener (L,1-3) 5  7  8  4  3  4
Dillman        2  4  2  2  1  2
McGinn         1  1  0  0  0  1
Perry (W,14-8) 9  4  1  1  2  2
```

HBP—by Wegener (Hunt), by Perry (Fairey). T—2:07. A—28,879.

Minor Leaguers Work Play-Off Opener In NL

By KEN NIGRO

Pittsburgh, Oct. 3 — It was a strange sight. The umpires at home plate were having the ground rules explained to them instead of vice versa

It all came about as a result of a full-scale strike by the major league umpires who set up picket lines today outside of Three Rivers Stadium. They are seeking higher wages in post-season games and decided to strike when the baseball owners would not meet their demands yesterday at a meeting in Chicago.

Four minor league umpires— John Grimsley, Fred Blandford, Hank Morgenweck and George Grygiel—were brought in to work this afternoon's National League Championship Series opener but what would happen tomorrow was a moot question.

Sympathy Walkout

There were indications of a sympathy walkout by maintenance personnel at the park including ushers, ticket-takers and sellers and electricians.

The six umpires who were supposed to work the game— Nick Colosi, Bob Engel, Doug Harvey, Stan Landes, Paul Pryor and Harry Wendelstedt— all were picketing along with Tony Venzon, Frank Dezelan and Ed Vargo. They carried signs which read, "Major League Umpires on Strike for Higher Wages."

UMPIRES 'SETTLE' WITH BASEBALL

Strike Ends After One Day, Talks To Continue

By KEN NIGRO

Pittsburgh, Oct. 4—The first strike of its kind in the history of sports was "settled" today when the major league baseball umpires agreed to go back to work after a one-day walkout.

Actually, it was more of an armistice than a settlement. The umpires accepted baseball's original offer of $3,000 per man for the play-offs and $7,000 per man for the World Series. This represents a $500 increase from last year.

TOLAN HERO AGAIN FOR CINCINNATI

Pirates Beaten, 3-2, In NL Play-Off For Clincher

By KEN NIGRO
Sun Staff Correspondent

Cincinnati, Oct. 5 The Cincinnati Reds pushed across a run in the eighth inning today and edged the Pittsburgh Pirates, 3 to 2, to win the National League pennant.

The victory gave the Reds a three-game sweep in the best-of-five series and put them into the World Series for the first time since 1961. But today's win, like the other two, did not come as the result of the awesome power the Reds had demonstrated all through the season. Instead, it was some clutch pitching from an underrated pitching staff that enabled them to stay close until Bobby Tolan knocked home the tie-breaking run with a two-out single.

"Who would have thought," said frustrated Pirate manager Danny Murtaugh, "that we would hold them to nine runs in three games and yet lose all three.

Vida Blue Pitches No-Hitter As A's Blank Twins, 6-0

Oakland, Sept. 21 (P)—Oakland rookie Vida Blue, a fastballing 21-year-old left-hander, tossed a no-hitter at the Minnesota Twins tonight and the A's trimmed the American League West leaders, 6 to 0.

The Twins, who needed a victory to clinch the West title, were stopped by the six-footer from Mansfield, La., whose best pitch was a fastball mixed with a sharp breaking curve.

With a crowd of 4,284 roaring its approval, Blue calmly went out in the ninth and struck out leadoff batter Danny Thompson on four pitches. Pinch-hitter Bob Allison struck out swinging on a 2-2 pitch and Cesar Tovar fouled out to Mincher.

Blue, recalled from the minors 18 days ago, twirled a one-hitter only 10 days ago in beating Kansas City in his second start.

Tonight the lefty missed a perfect game when he allowed the Twins their only runner—a fourth inning two-out walk to Harmon Killebrew. He struck out nine.

The A's jumped on Jim Perry, for a first inning run on Bert Campaneris' triple, who scored on a double play bouncer, and wrapped it up in the eighth keyed by Campaneris' three-run homer as the A's scored five runs.

```
         MINNESOTA        OAKLAND
            ab r h bi        ab r h bi
Tovar cf    4 0 0 0   Campaneris ss 5 2 2 3
Cardenas ss 3 0 0 0   Rudi lf      2 0 1 0
Killebrew 1b 3 0 0 0   Hovley cf   2 0 1 0
Oliva rf    3 0 0 0   FAlou rf    4 0 1 0
Alyea lf    3 0 0 0   Mincher 1b  3 1 2 0
Holt cf     0 0 0 0   Bando 3b    3 1 1 0
Repick 3b   3 0 0 0   RJackson cf 3 0 0 0
Mitterwald c 3 0 0 0   Tenace c   2 1 0 0
Thompson 2b 3 0 0 0   DGreen 2b   4 1 1 1
JPerry p    2 0 0 0   Blue p      2 0 0 0
Allison ph  1 0 0 0
Total      27 0 0 0   Total      30 6 9 4
```

Minnesota   0 0 0 0 0 0 0 0 0—0
Oakland   1 0 0 0 0 0 0 5 x—6

E—Thompson. DP—Minnesota 2. LOB—Minnesota 1, Oakland 8. 2B—FAlou. 3B—Campaneris. HR—Campaneris (21). S—Blue.

```
              IP  H  R ER BB SO
JPerry (L,23-12) 8  9  6  2  5  3
Blue (W,2-1)   9  0  0  0  1  9
```

HBP—by JPerry (Mincher), by JPerry (Bando). T—2:21. A—4,284.

Oct. 5

BIRDS WHIP TWINS, 6-1, FOR SWEEP

Palmer's Seven-Hitter Gives Baltimore 2d Straight AL Title

By LOU HATTER

Baltimre's second successive American League pennant and third in the last five years became a reality at Memorial Stadium yesterday, when Jim Palmer pitched the Orioles to a 6-to-1 triumph over the Minnesota Twins.

The victory before 27,608 elated partisan fans on a delightfully sunny afternoon achieved a repeat of last October's championship three-game sweep of the Western Division titlists. It was never in doubt.

By romping away again with the Eastern crown by 15 games, then trimming the Twins three in a row once more, the Orioles now qualify undisputedly for the 1970 World Series.

Reprinted from
The Baltimore Sun papers

FLOOD GOES TO SENATORS IN 3-1 DEAL

Normal Pact Indicated; Phils Get Goosen, Martin, Terpko

Washington, Nov. 3 (P—Controversial Curt Flood officially became a member of the Washington Senators today in a 3-for-1 trade, assuring his return to baseball after court battle against the reserve clause.

The announcement of Flood's signing was imminent after the Senators acquired his contract from Philadelphia in a deal that sent first baseman Greg Goosen, outfielder-first baseman Gene Martin and pitcher Jeff Terpko to the Phillies.

Not Known If He Signed

The Senators' announcement did not indicate whether Flood had signed his contract but it was believed the 32-year-old outfielder would soon put his signature on the normal pact containing the reserve clause.

Robert Short, Senators' owner, announced during the World Series that he had obtained the right to negotiate with Flood, who sat out this past season atfer he was traded from St. Louis to Philadelphia and instituted a $4.1 million suit against baseball.

Short and Flood apparently had agreed to the terms of the contract, calling for a salary estimated at about $110,000 a year, nearly 10 days ago but had to iron out other legal difficulties.

Flood, who said he was a victim of the reserve clause and that the St. Louis-Philadelphia trade violated his rights, lost the first phase of the suit when a federal judge ruled against him and in favor of baseball's defendants. An appeal is pending.

The reserve clause prohibits a player from negotiating with any team except the one which holds his contract.

Flood indicated last week he would sign with Washington because, "like everybody else, I've had some business reverses and I need the money—but I still think the reserve clause stinks."

"5 Kids To Support"

He said: "I'm paying alimony and I've got five kids to support. That's enough to drive any man back into the game."

Flood hit .293 during his 14 major-league seasons. He played in three World Series and in three All-Star games.

Goosen and Terpko were assigned immediately to the Eugene (Ore.) club in the Pacific Coast League.

Goosen, 25, who hit .241 in 41 games with Milwaukee and Washington, was sent outright to Philadelphia's No. 1 farm club. Terpko, 20, 6-10 with Pittsfield, was assigned to Eugene on a conditional basis. The Phillies have up to 3 days after the opening of the 1971 season to make a determination Terpko or they would get the rights to negotiate for another player.

Reds Are Early Series Favorite

Las Vegas, Nev., Oct. 5 (P—Cincinnati is an 11-10 favorite to beat Baltimore in the World Series and 11-10 to take the first game, according to Jimmy (The Greek) Snyder, Las Vegas oddsmaker.

Snyder called it a "toss-up series" and gave Cincinnati the edge only because the Reds play the first two games of the best-of-seven series at home, starting Saturday.

"This is probably the closest series odds in history," he said.

He also quoted odds of 12-1 against Cincinnati sweeping four straight games, and 15-1 against Baltimore winning four in a row.

McLain Is Traded To Washington In Eight-Man Swap

Brinkman, Rodriguez, 2 Hurlers Sent To Tigers

Cincinnati, Oct. 9 (P— Troubled Denny McLain was reinstated and traded by Detroit to the Washington Senators today, actions that came after psychiatric tests showed the controversial pitcher "not ill" but "was subject to emotional stress."

'TEAMS SIMILAR', SAYS PETE ROSE

Birds, Reds Are The Best For World Series

By KEN NIGRO

Cincinnati, Oct. 5—"This is the way it should be," said Pete Rose "the Big Red Machine against the big, bad Birds."

In addition to being a vital cog in Cincinnati's attack, Rose also likes to give nicknames. It was he who started this Big Red Machine business.

"I bought a 1934 Ford early this year and I called it the Little Red Machine," Rose explained after he had helped the Reds edge Pittsburgh and win the National League pennant. "Then when we started playing so well, we naturally became the Big Red Machine."

Cuellar Is Familiar

"I really feel that the best two teams will be playing in the series," he added. "I think we're similar in a lot of ways. We're both good up the middle with good hitting and pitching. Their starters might be a little better but I think we have the edge in the bullpen."

Rose of course has faced Mike Cuellar before but he is totally unfamiliar with the other Oriole pitchers.

"That's why I'm glad it's a seven-game series," he said. "It might take me awhile to get used to their guys. Although I hope not too long."

Rose had an interesting observation about Cuellar who pitched in the National League for the Houston Astros before going to the Birds two years ago.

"It'll be good to hit off Mike in the daytime," he said. "He's got that good screwball and there's something about the rotation of the ball that makes it tougher to follow at night. Look at Juan Marichal (the San Francisco Giants' pitcher). I think he was something like 14-1 last year at night."

But as good as Cuellar, Dave McNally and Jim Palmer figure to be, Rose should manage his fair share of hits. This afternoon he contributed a big single in the eighth that sent Ty Cline to second. Bobby Tolan followed with another single to deliver the tie-breaking run.

"I thought Moose made a good pitch," Rose said, "it was a slider on the inside."

Reprinted from
The Baltimore Sun papers

WORLD SERIES — BALTIMORE (AL) 4   CINCINNATI (NL) 1

LINE SCORES

TEAM	1	2	3	4	5	6	7	8	9	10	11	12	R	H	E
Game 1 October 10 at Cincinnati															
BAL (AL)	0	0	0		2	1	0		1	0	0		4	7	2
CIN (NL)	1	0	2		0	0	0		0	0	0		3	6	0

Palmer, Richert (9)   Nolan, Carroll (7)

Game 2 October 11 at Cincinnati															
BAL	0	0	0		1	5	0		0	0	0		6	10	2
CIN	3	0	1		0	0	1		0	0	0		5	7	0

Cuellar, Phoebus (3)   McGlothin, Wilcox (5),
Drabowsky (5), Lopez (7)   Carroll (5), Gullett (8)
Hall (7)

Game 3 October 13 at Baltimore															
CIN	0	1	0		0	0	0		2	0	0		3	9	0
BAL	2	0	1		0	1	4		1	0	X		9	10	1

Cloninger, Granger (6),   McNally
Gullett (7)

Game 4 October 14 at Baltimore															
CIN	0	1	1		0	1	0		0	3	0		6	8	0
BAL	0	1	3		0	0	1		0	0	0		5	8	0

Nolan, Gullett (3),   Palmer, Watt (8),
Carroll (6)   Drabowsky (9)

Game 5 October 15 at Baltimore															
CIN	3	0	0		0	0	0		0	0	0		3	6	0
BAL	2	2	2		0	1	0		0	2	X		9	15	0

Merritt, Granger (2), Wilcox (3),   Cuellar
Cloninger (5), Washburn (7),
Carroll (9)

COMPOSITE BATTING

NAME	POS	G	AB	R	H	2B	3B	HR	RBI	BA
Baltimore (AL)										
Totals		5	171	33	50	7	0	10	32	.292
F. Robinson	OF	5	22	5	6	0	0	2	4	.273
B. Robinson	3B	5	21	5	9	2	0	2	6	.429
Blair	OF	5	19	5	9	1	0	0	3	.474
Belanger	SS	5	19	0	2	0	0	0	1	.105
Powell	1B	5	17	6	5	1	0	2	5	.294
Johnson	2B	5	16	2	5	2	0	0	2	.313
Buford	OF	4	15	3	4	0	0	1	1	.267
Hendricks	C	3	11	1	4	1	0	1	4	.364
Etchebarren	C	2	7	1	1	0	0	0	0	.143
Palmer	P	2	7	1	1	0	0	0	0	.143
Rettenmund	OF	2	5	2	2	0	0	1	2	.400
McNally	P	1	4	1	1	0	0	1	4	.250
Cuellar	P	2	4	0	0	0	0	0	0	.000
Salmon	PH	1	1	1	1	0	0	0	0	1.000
Crowley	PH	1	1	0	0	0	0	0	0	.000
Drabowsky	P	2	1	0	0	0	0	0	0	.000
Hall	P	1	1	0	0	0	0	0	0	.000
Lopez	P	1	0	0	0	0	0	0	0	.000

Phoebus P 0-0, Richert P 0-0, Watt P 0-0

NAME	POS	G	AB	R	H	2B	3B	HR	RBI	BA
Cincinnati (NL)										
Totals		5	164	20	35	6	1	5	20	.213
Rose	OF	5	20	2	5	1	0	1	2	.250
Bench	C	5	19	3	4	0	0	1	3	.211
Tolan	OF	5	19	5	4	1	0	1	1	.211
May	1B	5	18	6	7	2	0	2	8	.389
Helms	2B	5	18	1	4	0	0	0	0	.222
Perez	3B	5	18	2	1	0	0	0	0	.056
McRae	OF	3	11	1	5	2	0	0	3	.455
Concepcion	SS	3	9	0	3	0	1	0	3	.333
Carbo	OF	4	8	0	0	0	0	0	0	.000
Woodward	SS	4	5	0	1	0	0	0	0	.200
Cline	PH	3	3	0	1	0	0	0	0	.333
Nolan	P	2	3	0	0	0	0	0	0	.000
Bravo	PH	4	2	0	0	0	0	0	0	.000
Stewart	PH	2	2	0	0	0	0	0	0	.000
Cloninger	P	2	2	0	0	0	0	0	0	.000
McGlothin	P	1	2	0	0	0	0	0	0	.000
Chaney	SS	3	1	0	0	0	0	0	0	.000
Corrales	PH	1	1	0	0	0	0	0	0	.000
Carroll	P	4	1	0	0	0	0	0	0	.000
Gullett	P	3	1	0	0	0	0	0	0	.000

Merritt P 0-1, Granger P 0-0, Wilcox P 0-0, Washburn P 0-0

COMPOSITE PITCHING

NAME	G	IP	H	BB	SO	W	L	SV	ERA
Baltimore (AL)									
Totals	5	45	35	15	23	4	1	2	3.40
Palmer	2	15.2	11	9	9	1	0	0	4.60
Cuellar	2	11.1	10	2	5	1	0	0	3.18
McNally	1	9	9	2	5	1	0	0	3.00
Drabowsky	2	3.1	2	1	4	0	0	0	2.70
Hall	1	2.1	0	0	0	0	0	0	0.00
Phoebus	1	1.2	1	0	0	1	0	0	0.00
Watt	1	1	2	1	3	0	1	0	9.00
Lopez	1	.1	0	0	0	0	0	0	0.00
Richert	1	.1	0	0	0	0	0	1	0.00

NAME	G	IP	H	BB	SO	W	L	SV	ERA
Cincinnati (NL)									
Totals	5	43	50	20	33	1	4	0	6.70
Nolan	2	9.1	9	3	9	0	1	0	7.71
Carroll	4	9	5	2	11	1	0	0	0.00
Cloninger	2	7.1	10	5	4	0	1	0	7.36
Gullett	3	6.2	5	4	4	0	0	0	1.35
McGlothin	1	4.1	6	2	2	0	0	0	8.31
Wilcox	2	2	3	0	2	0	1	0	9.00
Granger	2	1.1	7	1	1	0	0	0	33.75
Merritt	1	1.2	3	1	0	0	1	0	21.60
Washburn	1	1.1	2	2	0	0	0	0	13.50

Reprinted from
The Sports Encyclopedia: BASEBALL

'Ageless' Paige Is Enshrined

New York, Feb. 9 (AP)—Satchel Paige, the ageless pitching marvel whose exploits have made him part of American baseball folklore, doggedly maintained today "I don't feel segregated" after his election to the Hall of Fame in a special category honoring Negro League stars.

"I heard they had a place for me," Paige said slowly and distinctly. "I'm proud wherever they put me in the Hall of Fame. Every year I played, I said that was my best year. I know this is my best year."

The question of Paige's feelings in response to his designation as the first black player to be honored in this manner—criticized by some for separating blacks and whites — virtually dwarfed the proceedings presided over by commissioner Bowie Kuhn.

No Harsh Feelings

But, despite persistent prodding by media representatives, Paige never once uttered a word criticizing his selectin by the method announced only last week. And Kuhn underscored the fact that Paige will be fully accepted as a Hall of Famer.

"Technically he's not in the Hall of Fame," the commissioner acknowledged. "But realistically the Hall of Fame is a state of mind—and I thiink the fans feel that way."

Paige is not eligible for selection to the Hall of Fame as a major leaguer since he does not fulfill the requirement of having played 10 years in the majors—a requirement which none of the old stars of the Negro Leagues can meet.

But besides emphasizing his pleasure at being selected, Paige pointed out he has never been bitter toward the sport because black players were prohibited from playing in the majors until Jackie Robinson broke the color line in 1947.

Flood Left Trail Of Clues Before Jumping Senators

Washington, April 28 (AP)—There were a few clues that Curt Flood would leave the Washington Senators and head for Europe, but no one thought he'd do it.

Pitcher Casey Cox may have been the last Senator to see Flood before he quit the team Tuesday before the Washington-Minnesota game. The two had dinner together the night before.

"He talked about some things going wrong, but there was no indication he would do something like this," Cox said.

One of Flood's closest friends on the team is first baseman Mike Epstein, who called his departure a personal tragedy.

Flood, Epstein Close

"I've never been closer to a ball player in my career," Epstein said. "When I first heard he'd left, I felt he'd be back. But then after I thought about it, I'm sure he won't. He's an extremely proud man."

Epstein recalled Flood telling him Sunday, as the two shagged flies in the outfield: "things are closing in on me."

Having no idea Flood was contemplating leaving, Epstein attempted to console him by saying: "Life is like baseball. You have a slump and you get out of it."

Clubhouse Clue

Clubhouse manager Fred Baxter also received a clue Sunday but didn't think much of it at the time. Flood paid him and his helpers for the services they provide the team.

"I remember thinking, 'why is he doing this?' because they usually pay on the 15th and 30th," said Baxter, who added that he forgot about it when Flood showed up Monday night. "Now everything seems to fall into place."

Flood's departure shocked the Senators, especially owner Bob Short, who lured the once-great player out of self-imposed exile to join Washington for a $110,000-a-year salary.

Quit Following '69 Trade

The 33-year old Flood quit baseball in 1969 when he was traded by St. Louis, for whom he toiled 12 years, to the Philadelphia Phillies. He took his .293 lifetime batting average and moved to Copenhagen, Denmark. Meanwhile, he sued baseball and its reserve clause for $3.5 million.

He lost his case in the U.S. Court of Appeals in New York and is expected to appeal to the U.S. Supreme Court.

Flood's teammates of a few weeks feel that his failure to hit well had little, if anything, to do with his final decision.

GIANTS' RALLY NIPS BRAVES, 6-5

S.F. Wins In 10th Despite Aaron's 600th Homer

Atlanta, April 28 (AP) — Hank Aaron's 600th career home run helped Atlanta build an early lead but the San Francisco Giants came back to nip the Braves, 6-to-5, tonight on Willie May's run-scoring single in the 10th inning.

SAN FRANCISCO	ab	r	h	bi	ATLANTA	ab	r	h	bi
Bonds rf	5	1	2	0	SJackson cf	5	0	1	0
Foster rf	1	0	0	0	Garr lf	5	2	4	1
Speier ss	6	2	3	0	HAaron rf	5	2	2	3
Mays cf	6	1	4	2	Cepeda 1b	3	0	0	0
McCovey 1b	4	1	1	2	Lum rf	2	0	0	0
Dietz c	5	0	2	2	Millan 2b	5	0	3	1
Hendersn lf	2	0	0	0	King c	4	0	0	0
Fuentes 2b	4	0	1	0	EWilliams 3b	4	0	0	0
Hamilton p	0	0	0	0	MPeres ss	4	1	1	0
McMahon p	0	0	0	0	Reed p	2	0	0	0
FJohnson ph	1	0	0	0	Garrido ph	1	0	0	0
Cumbrlnd p	1	0	0	0	Priddy p	1	0	0	0
JJohnson p	0	0	0	0					
Lander p	0	0	0	0					
Perry p	3	0	0	0					
Gallagher 2b	2	0	0	0					
Total	43	6	14	6	Total	41	5	11	5

San Francisco   0 0 3 0 1 0 1 0 0 1— 6
Atlanta   2 0 2 0 0 1 0 0 0 0— 5

E—Perry. LOB—San Francisco 13, Atlanta 8. 2B—H.Aaron, Mays. 3B—M.Peres. HR—H Aaron (8), McCovey (3). SB—Henderson, Millan 2. SF—McCovey.

	IP	H	R	ER	BB	SO
Perry	6 2-3	5	5	5	1	5
Hamilton	1	0	0	0	1	0
McMahon	1-3	0	0	0	0	0
Cumbrlnd (W,2-0)	2	2	0	0	0	1
J Johnson	7	5	5	3	1	0
Reed	7	9	5	5	1	4
Priddy (L,0-1)	3	5	1	1	0	2

T—3:04. A—13,404.

DODGERS TOP BUCS, 7 TO 5

Stargell Sets Record With 11th April Homer

Pittsburgh, April 28 (AP)—Pinch-hitter Jim Lefebvre keyed a four-run seventh inning rally with a bases loaded single as the Los Angeles Dodgers came from behind to defeat the Pittsburgh Pirates, 7 to 5, tonight despite a record-setting home run by Willie Stargell.

Stargell crashed a ninth inning homer for the Pirates, setting an all-time mark of 11 in the month of April.

LOS ANGELES	ab	r	h	bi	PITTSBURGH	ab	r	h	bi
Wills ss	4	0	0	0	Cash 2b	3	1	1	0
Buckner rf	2	0	1	0	Clines cf	4	1	1	0
Mota rf	2	0	0	0	Davalillo cf	1	0	0	0
WDavis cf	4	0	0	1	Clemente rf	4	0	1	1
WParker 1b	3	0	1	0	Stargell lf	4	1	3	2
Haller c	4	2	1	0	RRobrtsn 1b	3	0	0	1
Garvey 3b	4	2	1	0	Sanguillin c	4	0	0	0
Crawford lf	3	2	1	1	Pagan 3b	4	0	1	1
Russell 2b	4	1	1	0	Alley ss	4	0	1	0
Osteen p	1	0	0	0	Ellis p	3	0	0	0
Vance p	1	0	0	0	Veale p	1	0	0	0
Lefebvre ph	1	0	1	2	Grant p	0	0	0	0
Mikkelsn p	0	0	0	1	Hebner ph	1	0	0	0
					JNelson p	0	0	0	0
Total	35	7	9	7	Total	40	3	13	5

Los Angeles   0 0 0 0 3 0 0 4 0 — 7
Pittsburgh   0 1 1 0 0 0 0 0 2 — 5

E—W.Parker, W.Davis, Garvey 2, Ellis. Pagan. DP—Los Angeles 1. LOB—Los Angeles 7, Pittsburgh 10. 2B—Mota 2, Cash. HR—Hebner (1), Stargell (11). S—Wills. SF—W.Davis.

	IP	H	R	ER	BB	SO
Osteen	3 1-3	7	3	3	1	1
Vance (W,2-0)	3 2-3	3	0	0	0	1
Mikkelsen	2	3	2	1	1	0
Ellis (L,2-3)	7	6	3	2	0	5
Veale	1	1	0	0	3	1
Grant	1	1	1	1	0	1
J.Nelson						

Save—Mikkelsen. WP—Osteen. T—2:46. A—6,318.

CUB PITCHER NO-HITS REDS

Holtzman Posts 2d Classic With 1-0 Victory

Cincinnati, June 3 (P)—Left-hander Ken Holtzman, of the Chicago Cubs, pitched the first no-hitter of the 1971 baseball season tonight, beating the Cincinnati Reds, 1 to 0.

Holtzman, who pitched a no-hitter for the Cubs two years ago against the Atlanta Braves, overcame periods of wildness for his classic, and stifled the Reds, mostly on ground balls.

Big Hitter Silenced

In order to nail down his no-hitter in the ninth, Holtzman had to face the top of the Reds' powerful batting order.

Hal McRae made the first out, flying out to John Callison on a 1-0 pitch. Then Tommy Helms struck out on a 1-2 pitch after fouling off one ball.

That brought up slugger Lee May, who ran the court to two balls and two strikes before striking out to end the game.

Holtzman scored the game's only run in the third inning when he led off and reached first base on Tony Perez's throwing error. The pitcher moved up on Don Kessinger's infield out and then scored on Glenn Beckert's line single to right center.

There were four major league no-hitters last season, two in each league.

CHICAGO					CINCINNATI				
	ab	r	h	bi		ab	r	h	bi
Kessinger ss	4	0	1	0	McRae lf	3	0	0	0
Beckert 2b	4	0	2	1	Helms 2b	4	0	0	0
BWilliams lf	4	0	1	0	LMay 1b	3	0	0	0
Santo 3b	4	0	0	0	Bench c	3	0	0	0
Pepitone 1b	4	0	1	0	TPere 3b	3	0	0	0
BDavis cf	4	0	0	0	Foster cf	3	0	0	0
Callison rf	3	0	1	0	Bradford rf	1	0	0	0
DBreeden c	3	0	0	0	Concepcn ss	3	0	0	0
Holtzman p	3	1	0	0	Nolan p	2	0	0	0
					Ferrara ph	1	0	0	0
					Gibbon p	0	0	0	0
Total	33	1	6	1	Total	26	0	0	0

Chicago .... 0 0 1 0 0 0 0 0 0—1
Cincinnati .... 0 0 0 0 0 0 0 0 0—0
E—T.Perez. DP—Chicago 1. LOB—Chicago 5, Cincinnati 3. SB—Kessinger.

	IP	H	R	ER	BB	SO
Holtzman (W, 3-6)	9	0	0	0	4	6
Nolan (L, 3-6)	8	5	1	0	0	3
Gibbon	1	1	0	0	0	0

WP—Holtzman. T—1:55. A—11,731.

ANGELS SUSPEND ALEX JOHNSON

'Patience Exhausted,' Says Walsh In Announcement

Anaheim June 26 (P)—Controversial Alex Johnson, the 1970 American League batting champion, was suspended indefinitely without pay today by the California Angels for, "Failure to give his best efforts to the winning of games with which he is concerned."

The announcement was made by the club's home office. The Angels, 32-42 in the American League West, lost a ten-inning 4-3 decision to the White Sox in Chicago this afternoon.

A club official said the suspencion came 10 days after Johnson was given an official warning by general manager Dick Walsh.

"Walsh and Alex met the day after the trading deadline and he was placed on formal notice," said the official.

Out Of Patience

Walsh said Johnson was "in constant violation of club rules and regulations," but he did not specify which rules.

"It is tragic that a player of his talent has not applied himself. We waited this long in hopes of salvaging the individual. I have exhausted my patience," said Walsh.

If the suspension last longer than 10 days, the player may have his case automatically reviewed by the commissioner.

Johnson, benched numerous times this season by field manager Lefty Phillips for lack of hustle, hs criticized fellow players for not allowing him to play his game. He, in turn, was faulted by teammates for his poor team attitude.

Accused Ruiz

Early this month, Johnson accused teammate Chico Ruiz of pulling a gun on him in the clubhouse. a charge that was vehemently denied by Ruiz. Baseball commissioner Bowie Kuhn has said he will investigate the incident.

Aug. 11

TWINS BOW TO ORIOLES IN 10TH, 4-3

Rettenmund's HR Wins Game; Killebrew Hits 500th

By JIM ELLIOT
Sun Staff Correspondent

Harmon Killebrew crashed the 500th and 501st home runs of his long career here last night, but the 33d homer of Merv Rettenmund's short big-league lifetime gave the Orioles a 10-inning, 4-to-3 victory over the Minnesota Twins in their series opener.

A Metropolitan Stadium crowd of 15,881 stood and cheered loud and long when Killebrew became the 10th player in major-league history to reach the 500 mark with his 13th homer of the year with two out in the first inning. It was only his second in the past seven weeks.

Reprinted from
The Baltimore Sun papers

Aug. 27

Carty Fears Eye Damage

Atlanta, (P)—Atlanta Braves outfielder Rico Carty, who led the National League in hitting last season, said yesterday his right eye probably has been damaged permanently as a result of an altercation involving three Atlanta policemen.

The policemen have been suspended without pay and Police Chief Herbert Jenkins commented, "This case involved the worst case of misconduct of a police officer I've ever seen."

'Terrible Thing'

Jenkins said the matter would be taken to a Fulton County grand jury for investigation, and that the suspended policemen also would be brought before the Aldermanic Police Committee.

"It's inexcusable," Jenkins said. "It's a terrible thing. If I had had the authority, I'd have fired them."

Mayor Sam Massell called it "apparently an incident of blatant brutality."

Carty commented on the possible damage to his eye in response to questions at a news conference in the offices of the Braves yesterday. He has not played this year because of other injuries.

Sept. 22

Short Gets Permission To Move Senators

Boston (P)—Owner Bob Short of the financially troubled Washington Senators was given American League approval late last night to move his franchise to the Dallas-Fort Worth area.

The announcement came at the end of a 12½-hour meeting of American League club owners.

The vote was 10-2 with the Baltimore Orioles and Chicago White Sox opposing the shift, to take effect at the start of the 1972 season.

Stadium Holds 22,000

League President Joe Cronin said the transfer was conditional that the league "must be satisfied with proper facilities."

The stadium, located in Arlington, Tex., between Dallas and Fort Worth, now seats approximately 22,000. Under terms of the transfer approval, the stadium must seat 35,000 by 1972 and 45,000 by 1973, both promised by Texas officials.

The approval also calls for a satisfactory lease to be worked out and indemnities for the Texas League club now in the stadium.

The owners approved the move after a marathon session in which a Washington group led by that city's president of the Board of Trade, Joseph Danzansky, offered to purchase the Senators for $9.4 million, the same amount Short paid for the club in 1968.

Cronin Is Sad

Cronin said the American League and Baseball Commissioner Bowie Kuhn "had worked very hard, very diligently, to find a proper buyer.

"Being an old Washington ball player, I feel very sad that there was no other alternative, but it is with pleasure that we welcome Dallas-Fort Worth."

Kuhn called it, "indeed a sad day for Washington . . . but equally a great day for Dallas-Fort Worth."

The commissioner said that efforts had been made to find "a purchaser for the club in Washington who could provide sufficient working capital."

Short, sober despite an apparent victory to recoup losses which he claims have amounted to more than $3 million, said it had been impossible "to find a solution to the problems I was beset by in Washington.

"It is not easy to confess failure publicly, but I do so," Short said.

Cronin said there was "no change in the financial structure" as a result of the move. "Mr. Short is owner of Dallas-Fort Worth."

Kuhn said that "if it's possible to find another club for Washington, it would be a very fine thing."

Mayor Tom Vandergriff of Arlington, who led the fight for a major league franchise with Mayors Wes Wise of Dallas and R. M. Stovall of Fort Worth, said this was "one of the most decisive, forward-looking days in baseball history.

"We want to be a contributing partner in making the league stronger," Vandergriff said. "We are confident we'll become one of the most successful franchises in baseball."

Sept. 26

McLain Loses 22d

Boston (P)—Rookie Rick Miller drove in two runs and Juan Beniquez scored one and knocked in another, leading the Boston Red Sox to a 6-to-3 victory over the Washington Senators yesterday.

Denny McLain lost his 22d game for the Senators.

WASHINGTON					BOSTON				
	ab	r	h	bi		ab	r	h	bi
Maddox cf	5	1	2	0	Griffin 2b	5	1	1	0
DNelson 3b	5	0	2	0	Beniquez ss	3	1	2	1
FHoward 1b	4	1	1	2	Ogilvie lf	4	0	0	0
Billings c	3	1	1	0	RSmith cf	3	1	0	1
Burroughs lf	3	0	1	0	Petrocelli 3b	3	2	2	0
Unser rf	4	0	0	0	Cooper 1b	3	1	2	1
Harrah ss	4	0	0	0	RMiller rf	3	0	2	1
Ragland 2b	4	0	1	0	Fisk c	4	0	2	1
McLain p	1	0	0	1	Curtis p	4	0	1	0
Riddleber p	0	0	0	0					
Casanova ph	1	0	0	0					
Shellenbk p	0	0	0	0					
Bittner ph	0	0	0	0					
Total	34	3	8	3	Total	32	6	12	5

Washington .... 0 1 0 0 0 0 2 0 0 — 3
Boston .... 0 2 1 0 1 2 0 0 x — 6

DP—Washington 1, Boston 1. LOB—Washington 8, Boston 7. 2B—R Miller 2, Maddox. HR—F Howard (25). SB—Beniquez 2, D Nelson, Griffin. SF—Cooper.

	IP	H	R	ER	BB	SO
McLain (L-10-22)	5	7	5	5	3	3
Riddleberger	1	2	1	0	0	0
Shellenback	2	3	0	0	1	0
Curtis (W 2-2)	9	8	3	3	4	6

Sept. 14

FRANK HITS 500TH AS BIRDS SPLIT

Orioles Take Opener From Tigers On McNally's 19th Win

BY LOU HATTER

Frank Robinson became the 11th player in baseball history to hit 500 career home runs last night when the Oriole super-star clouted one in each game as Baltimore split a double-header with Detroit.

Robinson's first of the evening gave Dave McNally a three-run sendoff in the first inning of the opener, and the veteran southpaw coasted to his 19th victory, 9 to 1.

The second game was long beyond recall when Robinson lofted lifetime four-bagger No. 500 into Memorial Stadium's left-field seats off Tiger left-hander Fred Scherman in the final frame with Boog Powell aboard to render the nightcap a slightly more respectable 10-to-5 defeat.

Standing Ovation

Baltimore's 36-year-old Mr. Clout drew a standing ovation from the remnants of an original crowd of 13,292. He responded to chats of "We Want Robinson, We Want Robinson," by emerging from the dugout, grinning happily, and waved his cap after receiving the back-slapping congratulations of his teammates there.

With his 25th homer of the 1971 season, Robinson thus joined the game's distinguished "500 Club," in which only 10 had attained membership since 1876 prior to last night's twin-bill here.

Reprinted from
The Baltimore Sun papers

Sept. 27

BIRDS ROLL AS PALMER GAINS 20TH

Indians Clubbed, 5-0: Club Matches Mark Set In 1920

By KEN NIGRO
Sun Staff Correspondent

Cleveland—Jim Palmer yesterday became the fourth Baltimore pitcher to win 20 games, blanking the Cleveland Indians, 5 to 0, on a three-hitter.

In joining Dave McNally, Mike Cuellar and Pat Dobson in the 20-victory column, Palmer was overpowering. The tall right-hander also contributed a run-scoring double in the seventh as the Birds broke open a scoreless duel with three runs. Brooks Robinson's single produced two more in the eighth.

It was only the second time in major league history that four pitchers on one club had won 20 or more games in a single season.

Finished Second

In 1920, Urban Faber (23), Claude Williams (22), Dickie Kerr (21) and Ed Cicotte (21) turned the trick for the Chicago White Sox who somehow still contrived to finish second that year. It later was discovered that two of the hurlers were involved in the infamous Black Sox scandal.

The victory enabled the Orioles to sweep the four-game series from the sad Indians who went over the century mark with their 101st defeat. Earl Weaver's crew also stretched its winning streak to eight.

Reprinted from
The Baltimore Sun papers

Nov. 24

Nats become Rangers

Arlington, Tex. (AP)—The Dallas-Fort Worth major league baseball club adopted the name Texas Rangers yesterday and announced that Ted Williams would return as manager for the 1972 American League season.

Arlington mayor Tommy Vandergriff and club owner Bob Short, who moved his team here from Washington, D.C., made the dual announcement at a luncheon viewed as a "birthday party" of sorts for the former Senators.

Williams, who managed the Senators last year, was not present at the luncheon.

It was also disclosed that the Dallas Chamber of Commerce has approved a resolution to rename Turnpike Stadium Vandergriff Stadium. It was Vandergriff who was instrumental in persuading club owners to bring the franchise to Texas.

Vandergriff, master of ceremonies of the luncheon, said, "We feel our region will be good for the American League."

American League president Joe Cronin told the audience that in Vandergriff they had a "most persuasive mayor" whom he said "thoroughly convinced the owners that this was really major league territory."

Short told a news conference after the luncheon that "at or about one million people" attending would be necessary for the club to break even.

He also said ticket prices will be "something less than the average in Washington," adding that the price will be similar to that of such clubs as Atlanta, St. Louis, Kansas City and Houston.

Concerning club personnel, Short said, "We've got a better pitching staff than people give us credit for." And he said his club has "tremendous, young talent."

He admitted, however that, "We do need help and Williams is going to be out shopping for it."

Short predicted that controversial pitcher Denny McLain and power-hitting Frank Howard will be in the lineup next spring but he pointed out that a club seeking help might trade any member of the team.

Oct. 16

F. Robinson says 'never' to managing

By JIM ELLIOT

Ernie Banks, Maury Wills, Junior Gilliam, Willie Mays, Hank Aaron—all of you gentlemen, move up a notch. Frank Robinson is no longer desirous of becoming a major-league baseball manager, let alone be the first black ever to manage in the big leagues.

For several years, most learned people in baseball have named Robinson as most likely to become the first black man ever to pilot a major-league team, and Frank himself, was receptive to the idea.

"I've changed my mind," the Oriole slugger said yesterday, after his workout at the Stadium preparatory to playing in the sixth game of the 1971 World Series against Pittsburgh here today.

Reprinted from
The Baltimore Sun papers

Pittsburgh wins World Series in 7 as Oriole bats fail

By JIM ELLIOT

Baltimore's Orioles no longer are the world champions. They reigned a year and two days, until yesterday when they were dethroned by the Pittsburgh Pirates in the seventh game of the 1971 World Series, 2 to 1.

A roaring Memorial Stadium crowd of 47,291 saw the Pirates become only the sixth team in the 68-year history of the World Series to lose the first two games and come on to triumph.

And it was Steve Blass, the 29-year old son of a plumber from Canaan, Conn., who for the second time within six days held the Orioles to one run over the nine-inning distance to gain a pitching victory.

The 6-foot, 170-pound, right-hander last Tuesday stopped the Orioles on a 3-hitter, 5 to 1, for Pittsburgh's first victory. Yesterday, it was a 4 hitter as the Orioles' bats continued to slump through a fifth straight game, during which span they could muster only 21 hits.

Reprinted from
The Baltimore Sun papers

World Series Box

PITTSBURGH	ab	r	h	bi	ORIOLES	ab	r	h	bi
Cash, 2b	4	0	0	0	Buford, lf	3	0	1	1
Clines, cf	4	0	0	0	DJohnson, 2b	4	0	1	0
Clemente, rf	4	1	1	1	JPowell, 1b	4	0	0	0
B.Robertson, 1b	4	0	1	0	F.Robinsn, rf	4	0	0	0
Sanguilln, c	4	0	2	0	Rettenmd, cf	4	0	0	0
Stargell, lf	4	1	1	0	B.Robnsn, 3b	2	0	0	0
Pagan, 3b	3	0	1	0	Hendricks, c	3	1	2	0
Hernandz, ss	3	0	0	0	Belanger, ss	3	0	0	0
Blass, p	3	0	0	0	Cuellar, p	2	0	0	0
					Shopay, ph	1	0	0	0
					P.Dobson, p	0	0	0	0
					McNally, p	0	0	0	0
Total	33	2	6	2	Total	29	1	4	1

Pittsburgh .... 0 0 0 1 0 0 0 1 0—2
ORIOLES .... 0 0 0 0 0 0 0 1 0—1

Error—B. Robertson. Double play—Pittsburgh 1. Left on base—Pittsburgh 4. Orioles 4. Two-base hit—Hendricks. Pagan. Home run—Clemente (2). Sacrifice—Shopay.

PITCHING SUMMARY

	IP	H	R	ER	BB	SO
Blass (W, 2-0)	9	4	1	1	2	5
Cuellar (L, 0-2)	8	4	2	1	2	6
P. Dobson	2-3	2	0	0	0	1
McNally	1-3	0	0	0	0	0

Time—2.10. Attendance—47,291.

Reprinted from
The Baltimore Sun papers

Police seal city center

Pittsburgh (P)—An estimated 40,000 persons rioted in the downtown area last night after the Pittsburgh Pirates won the World Series. Police, exasperated after a series of lesser crowd-control measures failed, swept into more militant sections of the crowd and made scores of arrests.

Early checks with area hospitals showed at least 100 persons injured, some seriously. There was no immediate figure on arrests, but a police spokesman said it would easily run into the hundreds.

The rioting erupted from what began as a boisterous but not violent victory celebration in honor of the Pirates' World Series win. At that point, police estimated that 100,000 persons were involved.

But the celebration soon exploded. There was widespread bottle-throwing and stoning, and police ordered the downtown area sealed off.

Cars were overturned and burned. Bonfires were set, and telephone booths were ripped apart and scattered in the streets. There was nude dancing and heavy drinking in the streets, and police reported at least a dozen rapes.

Ordered to disperse

So wild was the outburst that the Pirates canceled a planned midtown victory parade. But some players showed up downtown anyway, and were mobbed.

Using bullhorns, police ordered the crowds to disperse, saying: "You are ordered to clear this area. The parade has been canceled, so let's go home."

But the crowds roared disapproval, and soon rocks and bottles filled the air. About 100 police took part in the first sweep, moving head first into the crowd and trying to force it up Liberty avenue.

Dogs were brought in, and where the jeering demonstrators refused to move, police used billy clubs liberally.

March 17

Pie Traynor, Pirate great, dies at 72

Pittsburgh (AP)—Harold (Pie) Traynor, Hall of Fame third baseman with the Pittsburgh Pirates during the 1920s and 30s, died yesterday. He was 72.

The idol of Forbes Field fans posted a lifetime batting average of .320 for his 17 playing seasons. He succeeded George Gibson as Pittsburgh manager in 1934 and resigned in 1939. He later became a radio announcer for the Pirates.

Hero of a legend

In 1958 he underwent an operation to remove a small tumor in his chest which doctors said apparently resulted from his being hit with the ball during his active career. He entered the hospital on July 9 and was discharged an August 5.

Traynor, big and angular, played far behind the third base bag and constantly scooped up balls hit to his right. This led to a legend of his era coined by a baseball writer.

Praised by McGraw

"The batsman smashed a double down the third base line and was thrown out by Traynor."

In 1929 the famed John McGraw, manager of the Giants, praised Traynor.

"If I were to pick the greatest team player in baseball today," McGraw said, "and I have some of the greats on my own club, I would have to pick Pie Traynor."

April 3

Strike talks at standstill

New York (AP)—Striking major league baseball players continued to scatter to their homes yesterday while representatives of both sides met here to discuss the pension dispute that threatens to delay the opening of the 1972 season scheduled for Wednesday.

At the same time, opinion was divided among the players as to whether the strike really was necessary, and among the owners as to how long it might last.

And one owner, Bill Bartholemay of the Atlanta Braves, said that "every effort will be made" to field a team on opening day, even if it means using minor leaguers.

Negotiators for both sides met yesterday for the second straight day and reported no progress in their 90-minute talks. John Gaherin, representing the owners, said he and Marvin Miller, executive director of the striking Players Association, had agreed to talk again today.

"The situation remains the same," said Gaherin following yesterday's talks. "There is no progress toward a settlement. We will meet again tomorrow."

June 11

Braves win as Aaron hits 649th

Philadelphia (AP) — Hank Aaron hammered the 649th home run of his career and his 14th grand slam to help the Atlanta Braves wallopu the Philadelphia Phillies, 15-to-3, last night.

The home run, Aaron's 10th of the season, moved him into second place head of New York's Willie Mays on the all-time list and enabled him to tie the late Gil Hodges for the National League lead in career grand slams.

Aaron connected in the sixth, the Braves' only hit of the inning, against reliever Wayne Twitchell. Marty Perez opened the inning with a walk and reached second when Twitchell threw away Tom Kelley's bunt. Ralph Garr walked and Aaron then lined a 2-1 pitch over the left field fence.

ATLANTA	ab	r	h	bi	PHILADELPHIA	ab	r	h	bi
Millan 2b	3	0	0	0	Doyle 2b	5	0	0	0
OsBrown lf	1	1	0	0	Gamble rf	3	1	1	0
Garr rf	3	4	2	0	Montanez cf	4	1	1	0
HAaron 1b	3	2	1	4	Luzinski lf	2	0	0	0
Cepeda 1b	2	0	0	0	Hutton 1b	3	0	1	0
Carty lf	3	2	1	1	Money 3b	0	0	0	0
Garrido 2b	1	0	0	1	Harmon 3b	4	0	1	1
EWilliams 3b	4	3	2	4	MCarver c	3	1	2	0
Lum cf	6	0	3	2	Koegel c	1	0	0	0
Casanova c	5	0	1	1	Bowa ss	4	0	0	0
MPerez ss	4	2	3	0	Fryman p	1	0	0	0
TKelley p	4	1	1	0	Freed ph	1	0	0	0
					Twitchell p	0	0	0	0
					Browne ph	1	0	0	0
					Selma p	0	0	0	0
					RStone ph	1	0	0	0
Total	41	15	14	13	Total	33	3	6	1

Atlanta .... 3 0 2 0 2 4 0 2 2—15
Philadelphia ... 0 0 0 1 0 0 0 2 0— 3
E—H.Aaron, Casanova, Lum 2. Twitchell, Koegel. DP—Philadelphia 1. LOB—Atlanta 9, Philadelphia 7. 2B—Lum, Casanova 5. 3B—Lum. HR—E.Williams (5), H.Aaron (10). SB—Garr.

	IP	H	R	ER	BB	SO
T.Kelley (W,4-5)	9	6	3	1	4	8
Fryman (L,2-6)	4	7	5	5	2	0
Twitchell	3	4	6	5	3	1
Selma	2	3	4	4	4	2

WP—T.Kelley, Twitchell, Selma. Balk—Fryman. PB—McCarver. T—2:33. A—23,242.

April 3

Gil Hodges, Mets' pilot, dies at 47

West Palm Beach, Fla. (AP)—Gil Hodges, the one-time star of the old Brooklyn Dodgers who managed the New York Mets to baseball's world championship in 1969, collapsed and died yesterday.

Hodges had just finished a golf match at the Ramada Inn course and was strolling back to his motel room with companions when he slumped to the ground.

He was rushed to the Good Samaritan Hospital, where he was admitted at 5.25 P.M. (EST). He died 20 minutes later.

Death apparently was caused by a heart attack, a hospital spokesman said.

Hodges would have been 48 tomorrow, just one day before the scheduled start of the 1972 major league baseball season.

He was playing golf because the Met's scheduled exhibition game here with the Montreal Expos had been canceled by the strike of major league baseball players.

April 14

Baseball strike is settled; season begins tomorrow

By The Associated Press

The major league baseball strike ended in its 13th day yesterday when the owners and players agreed to start the 1972 season tomorrow without rescheduling any of the 86 games postponed by the player walkout.

The end of the strike came after day-long discussions between the owners, meeting in Chicago, and the Players' Association, in New York, that resulted in a three-part proposal made by the owners and accepted by the players.

The proposal was that the season start tomorrow, none of the postponed games be made-up and no money be paid the players for the games postponed during the first general strike in the 103-year history of the sport.

Announcement of the settlement was made simultaneously in New York, by Marvin Miller, executive director of the players' association, and, in Chicago, by Commissioner Bowie Kuhn.

Miller immediately hailed it as a triumph for the players.

"Clearly the players have triumphed in something that few people thought they could or would do," Miller asserted. "They have stood together."

Miller also insisted that "this could have been settled last Sunday," emphasizing that there never was a "back pay issue. It all came about because the owners wanted to reschedule all the games. The players never asked for back pay."

"I'm delighted to have this over," said Kuhn. "I hope we've all learned a lesson. I will work with people in baseball for procedures to prevent this sort of thing in the future. Nobody wants it again—neither the players, the clubs nor the fans.

"It's inevitable that there will be hard feelings," Kuhn acknowledged. "My job is to hold them to a minimum. I did so in this meeting and will do so with the players. Who won? Nobody. The players suffered. The clubs suffered. Baseball suffered."

Because of the fact that games postponed will not be rescheduled, the season now will range from 153 games for some teams to 156 games for other teams. Division winners will be determined on the basis of won-lost percentage.

Under terms of the over-all settlement, the owners also will contribute $500,000 to the players' pension fund and $400,000 to the health care fund in addition to the annual $5.4 million contribution they already had been making.

May 12

'Say Hey,' Willie's back home

New York (AP)—Willie Mays, a living legend with the Giants for two decades, returned to New York yesterday as a member of the Mets and immediately disclaimed any role as a prima donna of special status.

"The Mets have a good team—they're not going to keep me out there just because I'm Willie Mays," the 41-year-old superstar said after being dealt to the Mets by San Francisco for a promising minor league pitcher and an undisclosed sum of cash.

"I'm not going to be something on display. I have to play ball. If used in the right way, I think I can do a good job for the Mets," he added.

The announcement of the trade, on again and off again during the last week, was made following a poorly kept secret meeting among M. Donald Grant, chairman of the board of the Mets; Horace Stoneham, owner of the Giants; Bob Scheffing, Mets' general manager, and Yogi Berra, the Mets' manager.

May 3

Blue brings long holdout to end by signing A's $63,000 contract

Boston (P)—Vida Blue, the Oakland A's young southpaw pitching sensation, got a whopping pay increase yesterday as he ended a long holdout and igned a 1972 contract.

Blue, who received $14,750 last year as he won the American League's Most Valuable Player and Cy Young awards in his first full season with the A's, signed an agreement for $63,000.

However, the 22-year-old left-hander fell short of his goal. He originally asked $115,000, then lowered his demands to $92,000.

Blue, who flew to Boston late Monday night, kept baseball Commissioner Bowie Kuhn, American League President Joe Cronin and A's owner Charlie Finley waiting for nearly 1½ hours.

He signed during a 15-minute meeting at league headquarters and then appeared at a news conference before joining the A's for a scheduled night game with the Boston Red Sox.

"I'm signed, I'm happy, I'm ready to play," Blue said. "I think the team has a uniform for me, but I don't know."

Club has uniform

"We have one," Finley assured him.

Blue, who had a 24-8 record and was a big gate attraction around the league in 1971, said he had been doing "a lot of running," but probably will need "three or four weeks" before "he'll be in condition to pitch.

"Vida will remain with the club during the conditioning program," Finley said. "Manager Dick Williams will map the program."

Told of Williams's prediction that Blue will win 20 games this year despite the late start, Vida said:

"I'll be lucky if I win 10. I'll take what I can get."

Finley said he and the A's were looking forward to Blue returning to the mound "and start winning."

"However," Finley added, "the number of wins isn't really the most important thing. The big point is just having him back with us. We hope he wins, but we're not going to rush him into anything."

Kuhn announced that Blue's agreement provides $50,000 salary, a $5,000 bonus for his 1971 performance and $8,000 "for any possible liability under a contingent four-year college scholarship" which was part of Blue's original bonus arrangement when he signed in 1967.

Ordinarily, a major league player's salary does not start until he's ready to play. However, Finley said that as part of his offer at a meeting in Chicago last Thursday, Blue's salary would be pro-rated starting April 27.

Kuhn said he was "very happy" that an agreement had been reached and "I congratulate Vida and Charlie both for concessions they have made."

Blue was relaxed and at ease, tieless with a knit shirt open at his neck, as he sat between Kuhn and Finley. The commissioner and Finley appeared tense at times.

The negotiations appeared to fall through last Friday when Blue refused to sign an announcement of the contract's details. Kuhn stepped in the next day and, using what he called his general powers to act "in the best interests of baseball," ordered Finley to keep the offer open.

Finley threatened to withdraw the offer, charging the commissioner had "arbitrarily involved himself and forced himself" into the salary dispute.

Asked after Blue's signing about his criticism of the commissioner, Finley replied tersely: "No comment."

Blue's attorney, Robert J. Gerst of Los Angeles, did not accompany the pitcher to Boston. However, he said Monday night "we're not happy, but we're satisfied."

Gerst added:

"We'll be back next year."

Oct. 1

Clemente hits 3,000, Bucs win

Pittsburgh (P)—Robert Clemente's 3,000th career base hit, a leadoff double in the fourth inning, touched off a three-run Pittsburgh rally that moved the Pirates to a 5-to-0 victory over the New York Mets yesterday.

The game was halted after Clemente's ringing double and he was presented with the baseball as the crowd at Three Rivers Stadium gave him a standing ovation.

NEW YORK	ab	r	h	bi	PITTSBURGH	ab	r	h	bi
WGarrett 3b	4	0	0	0	Goggin 2b	4	0	2	0
Boswell 2b	4	0	1	0	Stennett cf	4	0	0	0
Milner lf	3	0	0	0	Clemente rf	2	1	1	0
Staub rf	3	0	0	0	Davalillo rf	1	0	0	0
Rauch p	0	0	0	0	Mazroski ph	1	0	0	0
Marshall ph	1	0	0	0	Stargell 1b	3	1	1	1
Kranpool 1b	3	0	1	0	Zisk lf	1	2	0	0
Fregosi ss	3	0	0	0	Sanguillen c	3	1	1	1
Schneck cf	3	0	0	0	Pagan 3b	3	0	0	0
Dyer c	3	0	0	0	JHrnands ss	3	0	1	2
Nolan c	2	0	0	0	Ellis p	3	0	1	0
Matlack p	2	0	0	0	Clines ph	1	0	0	0
Hahn rf	0	0	0	0	BJohnson p	0	0	0	0
Total	49	0	2	0	Total	28	5	8	3

New York 0 0 0 0 0 0 0 0 0—0
Pittsburgh 0 0 0 3 2 0 0 0 x—5
E—WGarrett. DP—New York 1. LOB—New York 5, Pittsburgh 4. 2B—Clemente. 3B—J. Hernandez.

	IP	H	R	ER	BB	SO
Matlack (L,14-10)	6	5	5	5	3	5
Rauch	2	1	0	0	0	4
Ellis (W,15-7)	9	2	0	0	2	4
B.Johnson	3	1	0	0	1	3

Save—B.Johnson (3). PB—Dyer, Nolan.
T—2:10. A—13,117.

Oct. 4

Carlton wins 27th, Phils blast Cubs

Chicago (P)—Steve Carlton won his 27th game and Don Money and Greg Luzinski hit back-to-back home runs in both the third and fifth innings as the Philadelphia Phillies beat the Chicago Cubs, 11 to 1, yesterday.

Bill Robinson started the Phillies to their first six-homer game of the season by hitting his eighth after Luzinski's single in the second. Left-hander Dan McGinn, making only his second 1972 start, was the victim of the Phillies rapid start.

Larry Bowa doubled to open the third, then Money and Luzinski hit their first pair of home runs. Lefty Larry Gura was the Cubs' second pitcher when Money hit his 15th homer of the season and Luzinski followed with his 18th.

PHILADELPHIA	ab	r	h	bi	CHICAGO	ab	r	h	bi
Harmon 2b	5	1	2	1	North cf	5	0	1	0
Bowa ss	5	2	2	1	Hiser rf	5	0	0	0
Money 3b	3	2	2	3	Tyrone lf	4	0	0	0
Schmidt 3b	1	1	1	0	Fanzone 3b	4	1	1	0
Luzinski lf	4	3	3	2	Bourque 1b	4	0	2	1
Montanez 1b	3	0	0	0	Rudolph c	4	0	2	0
Lis ph	1	0	0	1	Montreuil 2b	2	0	0	0
Freed rf	5	0	1	0	Rosello ss	4	0	1	0
WRobinson cf	4	1	1	2	McGinn p	0	0	0	0
Bateman c	4	0	1	0	Kessinger ph	1	0	0	0
Carlton p	3	1	1	0	Gura p	0	0	0	0
					Becker! ph	1	0	1	0
					Compton p	0	0	0	0
					Popovich ph	1	0	0	0
					Decker p	0	0	0	0
					Hundley ph	1	0	1	0
					Larock pr	0	0	0	0
Total	38	11	14	10	Total	36	1	9	1

Montreuil awarded first on catcher's interference.
Philadelphia 0 2 4 0 2 0 2 1 0—11
Chicago 0 0 0 0 0 0 0 1 0—1
E—Rosello, Bateman. DP—Chicago 1. LOB—Philadelphia 4, Chicago 10. 2B—Bowa, Bourque. HR—W.Robinson (8), Money 2 (15), Luzinski 2 (18), Harmon (2). S—Carlton.

	IP	H	R	ER	BB	SO
Carlton (W,27-10)	9	9	1	1	1	7
McGinn (L,0-5)	3	8	6	6	1	1
Gura	3	3	3	3	1	3
Compton	2	2	1	1	1	1
Decker	1	1	1	1	1	1

WP—Gura. T—2:07. A—2,751.

June 20

Flood loses suit

Baseball keeps antitrust status

Washington (P)—The Supreme Court yesterday extended baseball's unique exemption from antitrust laws in a 5-to-3 ruling against Curt Flood.

Rolling off the names of 87 oldtime players and witty lyrical references to "Casey At The Bat," Justice Harry A. Blackmun said he recognizes that the immunity is an aberration. But he said any change in the 50-year tradition, established by Justice Oliver Wendell Holmes, would have to come from Congress and not the courts.

Will keep reserve system

As a result, baseball will be able to retain its special reserve system, which binds a ballplayer to the team that owns his contract. Other sports, partly impelled by judicial decisions, have loosened these bonds and given players some freedom to choose the team for which they will play.

Justice Blackmun said Congress apparently has no quarrel with baseball's special status since it has adopted none of the more than 50 bills introduced in the last two decades to change the system.

"I think the decision is constructive in its recognition that baseball has developed its present structure in reliance on past court decisions," said Bowie Kuhn, the baseball commissioner. "The decision opens the way for renewed collective bargaining on the reserve system after the 1972 season."

"We will continue"

"We will continue in our efforts to remedy the inequities in baseball's present reserve system through collective bargaining," said Marvin Miller, the executive director of the Major League Players Association, the union that supported Mr. Flood in his long legal battle.

Reds edge Bucs for NL flag

By KEN NIGRO
Sun Staff Correspondent

Cincinnati—It was a very short-lived dynasty. Pittsburgh's one-year reign as baseball's World Champions ended yesterday in incredible fashion as the Cincinnati Reds scored the winning run on a wild pitch in the ninth inning for a heart-pounding 4-to-3 victory.

For sheer drama and excitement, this was one great baseball game. It had 41,887 fans at rain-soaked Riverfront Stadium on their feet all through the unbelievable ninth as Cincinnati first tied the score on Johnny Bench's leadoff homer and then won the whole thing many minutes later when pinch runner George Foster streaked home as relief pitcher Bob Moose uncorked a wild pitch.

The sensational victory gave the Reds the National League pennant and advanced them to the World Series for the second time in three years.

The game which was delayed 1 hour and 28 minutes by rains was filled with a thousand different angles but in the end, everything boiled down to one little wild pitch that long will be remembered as the biggest in baseball history.

Couldn't believe it

"It was just unbelievable," said Moose who normally is a great control pitcher. "The ball just seemed to bounce straight up and then I saw it roll back to the screen. I couldn't believe it."

Foster could, though, and so could Cincinnati third base coach Alex Grammas.

"We were ready for anything," Grammas said. "I told George to be alert, that Moose would throw that slider and that it might bounce. When he went, I was right behind him. We went step for step."

Oct. 25

Robinson, baseball star, dies at 53

Stamford, Conn. (P)—Jackie Robinson, who broke major league baseball's racial barrier with the old Brooklyn Dodgers, died yesterday of heart disease. He was 53 years old.

Mr. Robinson, who was nearly blind from diabetes, suffered an early morning attack at his 14-room home in this suburb of New York city. At 7.10 A.M. he was pronounced dead on arrival at Stamford Hospital.

Mr. Robinson's ailments were no secrets—the heart problems that felled him briefly in 1968; the diabetes that had impaired his eyesight.

Still, death came as a shock to those who recalled him as a daring baserunner, clutch hitter and the man who opened the big league gates to blacks. In 1962, he became the first black to be elected to the Baseball Hall of Fame.

President Nixon said, "This nation to which he gave so much in his lifetime will miss Jackie Robinson, but his example will continue to inspire us for years to come."

Mr. Nixon, who selected Mr. Robinson last summer to his personal all-time baseball team, added, "His courage, his sense of brotherhood and his brilliance on the playing field brought a new human dimension not only to the game of baseball but to every area of American life where black and white people work side by side."

Mr. Nixon said last year that Mr. Robinson was "the greatest athlete I ever saw."

Dodgers Swap Sizemore For Richie Allen

. Los Angeles. Oct. 5 .P—The Los Angeles Dodgers today traded 1969 rookie-of-the-year Ted Sizemore and catcher Bob Stinson to the St. Louis Cardinals for heavy hitting Richie Allen.

Sizemore started 1969 as a shortstop and was moved to second base when Maury Wills rejoined the club following a Montreal trade.

The Dodgers finished this season with Bill Graberkewitz playing second base and Steve Garvey at third.

Grabarkewitz had played third most of the season with Garvey at Spokane. but Garvey played 36 games for the Dodgers batting .269.

He was the opening day third baseman. was optioned to Spokane and then finished the season with the National League club.

Grabarkewitz batted .289 with 17 home runs and 86 r.b.i.

Cards Build Defense

During his rookie year in 1969, the 5-10, 170-pound Sizemore, a product of the University of Michigan. batted .306 in 96 games with 34 r.b.i.

In St. Louis. Cardinal general manager Bing Devine said he conferred with Allen this morning.

"He and I talked this morning. and I told him he did everything we had expected of him." Devine said.

"It was just that the club wasn't balanced enough and it wasn't to be that he could stay with us. The vital aspect was defense."

The Cardinals. Devine said. had decided some time back to leave veteran catcher Joe Torre at his new position. third base. and had been pleased with the progress of Joe Hague at first.

Oct. 13

Compassionate Williams consoles lost, lonely, crying young Tiger fan

Detroit (P—Dick Williams wound up celebrating "the biggest game of all our careers" by comforting a tiny, sobbing Detroit Tigers fan yesterday.

The Oakland manager broke away from the bedlam of the A's dressing room after their 2-to-1 victory over Detroit pushed them into the World Series to say a few words of kindness to a lost boy.

"Root for your home team all the time. I know you're sorry the Tigers lost, but wait here and your brother will be along shortly." Williams told the teary, freckle-faced lad. But the boy slipped outside the locker room and hurried away.

Inside, the Oakland players were still whooping, singing and swigging champagne to celebrate their triumph. More than an hour after Tony Taylor flied to George Hendrick in center field to end the struggle on the field, the A's were still in full uniform or half clad.

"They are tears of happiness." Oakland owner Charles Finley told newsmen as drops of champagne trickled down his cheeks.

"We were all tense." Williams said. "That's not saying we choked. This was the greatest win we ever had in the biggest game of all our careers. But Wednesday (when

Oakland lost 4-3 in 10 innings) was the toughest loss we ever had. So. we rebounded."

The manager praised Vida Blue. who shut out the Tigers on three hits after relieving starter John Odom in the sixth. because "he showed me something today. Our man Blue will pitch in the series."

Williams added that Blue has "worked hard for me. Everything I've asked him to do. he has done and done well. His contract dispute is between him and Mr. Finley."

Blue sat on a stool with his chest bare and said he had expected to start in the playoffs. He contended Wednesday

that Williams was under Finley's orders not to use him as a play-off starter.

"But me not starting isn't my complaint. It's not being told. Nobody has come to me. They kept away from me like it was a cardinal sin to tell me."

The pitcher. who slumped to a 6-10 regular season mark after winning 24 games in 1971. refused to call yesterday's job his best performance of the season. "There've been other days like today.

"It was just another ball game. We still have seven more ball games. I'm not really excited."

Oct. 13

Campaneris to play: AP

Cincinnati .P — Bert Campaneris will be permitted to play for the Oakland Athletics in the World Series. The Associated Press learned late last night.

Baseball Commissioner Bowie Kuhn will formally announce his decision on Campaneris today. The Oakland shortstop was suspended for the final three games of the American League play-offs after a bat-throwing incident in last Sunday's game with Detroit.

Kuhn won't let Campaneris off scot free. it was learned. There was speculation that he could be fined or may be suspended for a portion of the start of the 1973 season.

Oct. 23

A's nip Reds, 3 to 2, win World Series

Oct. 13

Odom, Blue pitch A's to first flag, 2-1

By LOU HATTER
Sun Staff Correspondent

Detroit—The Oakland Athletics won their first American League pennant here yesterday, edging Detroit, 2 to 1, in the final 1972 play-off game behind the five-hit tandem pitching of Blue Moon Odom and Vida Blue.

Gene Tenace singled the decisive unearned run across in the fourth inning following a disputed safe ruling at first base, where Tiger shortstop Dick McAuliffe's throwing error pulled Norm Cash's foot off the bag.

The Athletics, beaten three straight by Baltimore in last October's play-off, advanced into the World Series, beginning tomorrow, against the Cincinnati Reds in the new National League champions' Riverfront Stadium.

Tenace's single to left off Detroit southpaw Woodie Fryman drove George Hendrick home from second base. The latter had advanced on Sal Bando's sacrifice bunt.

The A's catcher thus acquitted himself of an opening-inning passed ball that set up the Bengals' lone tally

With McAuliffe and Duke Sims aboard on a single to right and a walk, Tenace muffed a high, inside Odom fastball. Both runners moved into the scoring zone, and McAuliffe scooted across while Bill Freehan was grounding out to shortstop Dal Maxvill.

Oakland's triumph before 50,276 partisans may have been costly.

Reggie Jackson, who clouted 25 regular-season homers, suffered a pulled hamstring muscle of the left thigh while stealing home with the tieing run in the second frame on the front end of a double theft with Mike Epstein.

The A's slugging centerfielder was on crutches during the frenzied post-game clubhouse celebration. His World Series status remained extremely doubtful. Hendrick replaced Jackson following his damaging slide under Freehan on the relay back to the plate from Detroit's second baseman, Tony Taylor.

The box score

OAKLAND	ab	r	h	bi	DETROIT	ab	r	h	bi
MAlou rf	2	0	1	0	MAuliffe ss	4	1	1	0
Maxvill ss	4	0	0	0	Kaline rf	4	0	0	0
Rudi lf	5	0	0	0	Sims lf	3	0	0	0
RJackson cf	0	1	0	0	Freehan c	4	0	0	1
Hendrick cf	3	1	0	0	Cash 1b	4	0	1	0
Bando 3b	3	0	1	0	JNiekro pr	0	0	0	0
Epstein 1b	3	0	0	0	Northrup cf	2	0	2	0
Tenace c	3	0	1	1	MStanley ph	1	0	0	0
DGreen 2b	1	0	0	0	TTaylor 2b	4	0	0	0
Odom p	2	0	1	0	ARodrgez 3b	3	0	0	0
Blue p	1	0	0	0	Fryman p	2	0	0	0
					WHorton ph	1	0	1	0
					Knox pr	0	0	0	0
					Hiller p	0	0	0	0
Total	29	2	4	1	Total	32	1	5	1

Oakland ... 0 1 0 1 0 0 0 0 0 — 2
Detroit ... 1 0 0 0 0 0 0 0 0 — 1

E—McAuliffe Sims. DP—Detroit 1. LOB—Oakland 6, Detroit 7. 2B—Odom. SB—R.Jackson 2. Epstein. S—Bando, M.Alou.

	IP	H	R	ER	BB	SO
Odom (W.2-0)	5	2	1	0	2	3
Blue	4	3	0	0	0	3
Fryman (L.0-2)	8	4	2	1	1	3
Hiller	1	0	0	0	1	0

Save—Blue (1). HBP—by Fryman (Epstein), by Fryman (M.Alou). WP—Odom. Balk—Fryman. PB—Tenace T—2:48 A 50,276.

Solid hurling, Tenace's bat pace victory

By JIM ELLIOT
Sun Staff Correspondent

Cincinnati — Charles O. Finley's 12-year-old dream of a World Series victory came true yesterday when the controversial owner's Oakland Athletics squeezed by the Cincinnati Reds, 3 to 2, in the seventh game of the 1972 baseball classic, the most closely fought in its 69-year history.

A man was grabbed by police outside Riverfront Stadium Saturday, possessing a gun he repeatedly planned to use to shoot Gene Tenace, catcher of the Athletics, if Tenace homered. Tenace had hammered a record-tying four homers in the first five games.

Nothing was said about singles and doubles, however, and it was a run-scoring first-inning single and a sixth-inning r.b.i. double by the 26-year-old Tenace, from Lucasville, Ohio, which brought him recognition as the hero of the Series and winner of the car accompanying the honor.

Back-to-Back doubles by Tenace and Oakland captain Sal Bando supplied two runs in the sixth, and when the A's lead held up to the end, Finley and his wife jumped atop the Oakland dugout and kissed. They were joined by manager Dick Williams and wife, who proved copycats.

Sharing the top laurels in the windup were four Oakland pitchers who limited Cincinnati's so-called Big Red Machine to four hits for a fourth victory by one run.

Two of Cincinnati's three victories also were by a single tally, making this Series the first to have more than four games decided by one run.

Jan. 1

Baseball Star Killed Flying Earthquake Aid

From News Dispatches

Wide World Photo

SAN JUAN, P.R. — Pittsburgh Pirates outfielder Roberto Clemente died in the crash of a DC7 plane on a relief mission to earthquake-stricken Nicaragua shortly after takeoff from Puerto Rico late yesterday, a spokesman for the Puerto Rican Port Authority said today.

The spokesman said Clemente was one of five persons aboard the four-engine propeller-driven plane, which developed engine trouble on takeoff and was trying to return to the airport when it crashed just off the coast.

Coast Guard spokesmen said they found chunks of wreckage but no survivors.

Clemente, 38, headed Puerto Rico's relief efforts for quake survivors at Managua. He was named to the post Christmas Eve.

A port authority official said the other occupants of the plane were pilot Jerry Geisel; copilot and owner Arthur Rivera, a private air-cargo operator; flight engineer Rafael Macias, and another passenger, identified only by his last name, Lozano.

Throughout the night, two

ROBERTO CLEMENTE

Coast Guard helicopters, a patrol boat and a buoy tender searched vainly for survivors one to two miles north of the San Juan airport.

Clemente's wife, Vera Cristina, and his father, Melchor, watched the operation from a nearby beach.

Amadee Chardon of the airport communications department at San Juan International said the plane went down at 9.22 p.m. It was loaded with medicine, food and relief supplies for the survivors of the devastating earthquake at Managua Dec. 23.

Sources at San Juan International said the DC7 plunged into the ocean as it made a sharp left bank while climbing after takeoff, a normal procedure for aircraft leaving from the field.

Clemente, born Aug. 18, 1934, in Puerto Rico, completed his 18th season with the Pirates in 1972.

Last season, he became the 11th man in baseball history to reach 3,000 hits for a baseball career.

Clemente had compiled a lifetime batting average of over .300. He won four National League batting titles and hit over .300 13 times.

Last season, he batted .312 in 102 games.

In 1971, he batted .414 in the World Series against the Baltimore Orioles and was named the outstanding performer in the series, won by the Pirates.

He won the National League's Most Valuable Player award in 1966 and was selected to the league's all-star team 12 times.

March 13

Hall of Famer Frisch succumbs at age 74

Wilmington, Del. (AP)—Frankie Frisch, the manager of St. Louis' 1930's "Gas House Gang" who played his way into baseball's Hall of Fame, died yesterday a month after he was injured in an automobile accident.

Frisch, 74, died at the Wilmington Medical Center of cardiac arrest. He had been in critical condition since February 8 when his car slammed into an embankment near Elkton, Md., after the rear tire blew out.

Frisch, elected to the Hall of Fame in 1947, compiled a .316 batting average during a 19-year career with the New York Giants and St. Louis Cardinals. He whacked 2,880 hits before quitting at the end of the 1937 season.

Frisch went on to gain additional fame as manager of the dashing St. Louis Cardinals' "Gas House Gang" that won the 1934 World Series in Frankie's first full season.

He ended his 33-year association with the major leagues in 1951 when he resigned as manager of the Chicago Cubs. For a few seasons after that, the raspy-voiced Frisch was heard as a baseball broadcaster.

April 15

A.L. OPENERS
New Rule Unveiled

While most of the baseball world worried about the weather today in Cincinnati where the Reds, the San Francisco Giants and rain are scheduled to open the major league season, the American League is preparing to unveil its designated hitters tomorrow.

There are five American League openers tomorrow along with five in the National League. But since three of those AL games are at night, the first look at the DH rule will come during the game at Boston between the Red Sox and New York Yankees. It starts 45 minutes before Milwaukee at Baltimore.

"I USED the rule and had good success with it at Louisville in the International League before I came to Boston," Eddie Kasko, manager of the Red Sox, said. "I didn't like it then, but what's the sense of complaining now?"

The rule calls for a player to bat in place of the pitcher during the entire game. The American League adopted the rule for a trial period of three seasons. The National League turned it down.

The Red Sox, according to Kasko, plan to use Orlando Cepeda as their DH.

"We got Cepeda (from Oakland) for that role," he said, "because of our ball park."

Cepeda, still hobbling from his fourth knee operation in five years, will bat in the fifth position in the order.

"I never was much of a pinch hitter in the National League," he said, "but so far things have been working out okay for me as the DH."

IN PITTSBURGH, there will be emotions of a different sort tomorrow when the Pirates play the Cardinals. Before the game the No. 21 jersey worn by the late Roberto Clemente will be retired in a special pre-game ceremony.

The Pirates also will wear a special shoulder patch above the traditional black stripe on their sleeves. It will bear No. 21 as a tribute to the outfielder who perished in a plane crash.

Taking his place in rightfield will be Manny Sanguillen, the regular catcher for the past four seasons.

Reprinted from
The Washington Star-News

July 16

'2 Good Games' Both No-Hitters

Special to the Star-News

DETROIT — Nolan Ryan of the California Angels, only the fourth pitcher in baseball history to record two no-hitters in a single season, was calm and objective about his accomplishment.

"It's nice to have my name linked with such great pitchers," Ryan said yesterday, after the historic 6-0 victory over the Detroit Tigers, "but I'm just me. You throw it over the plate with enough stuff on it and not many hitters are going to hurt you."

And, he added, "I needed this because I wasn't pitching well."

Ryan is now in the company of double no-hit pitchers Johnny Vander Meer (1938), Allie Reynolds (1951) and Virgil Trucks (1952).

IT WAS Ryan's second no-hitter in two months — the first was against Kansas City — and he struck out 17, one short of matching Bob Feller's American League record and two short of the major league record shared by Steve Carlton and Tom Seaver. The 17 strikeouts were also the most ever in a no-hit game.

"I was 'up' more than I have been because of the way we've been losing . . . I wanted to throw a shutout," he said.

"So I've thrown two good games," Ryan said of his 1973 gems. "But look at my record. I'm 11-11. I can't look back and say 1973 was my best year just because I pitched two no-hitters.

"I haven't pitched as well as last year and I feel I have to improve myself. I feel for this club to stay in the pennant race I have to do the job I'm capable of doing in the second half of the season."

A LONG delay, due to a five-run Angel eighth inning, caused Ryan's arm to stiffen somewhat. He only struck out one batter the last two innings.

After the first seven innings, Ryan seemed a cinch to break the league's nine-inning strikeout record of 18, set in 1938 by Feller of the Indians.

"There'll be another day," Ryan said.

THAT WOULD have added insult to injury for the Tigers, who had won the first three games of the series and were on a five-game winning streak. They also were the victims of a no-hitter by Kansas City's Steve Busby April 27.

The 17 strikeouts matched Ryan's career high. He had 17 against Minnesota last Sept. 30 which tied the league mark of a nine-inning night game.

He has 220 so far this season in 189 innings. Last year he led the major leagues with 329 strikeouts in 284 innings. Add to this some more phenomenal facts. It was the 12th time this season and the 43rd time in his career that he's struck out 10 or more batters in a game.

"That was the best I've ever seen anybody pitch," exclaimed the Tigers' Dick McAuliffe, who was joined by fellow left-handed hitter Duke Sims in striking out three times against Ryan. Sims said almost the same thing: "That's the best I've ever seen."

THE CLOSEST thing to a hit was a rising line drive by designated hitter Gates Brown with one out in the ninth. Shortstop Rudy Meoli moved back to the edge of the grass when Brown came to bat and didn't move closer to second base as most shortstops usually do against pull-hitting lefthander Brown. Meoli made a leaping catch.

"He had everything," Detroit Manager Billy Martin moaned.

"He always pitches good against us," said Brown who kept muttering: "He threw super stuff, super stuff, super stuff . . . ."

ANGELS 6, TIGERS 0

CALIFORNIA	ab	r	h	bi	DETROIT	ab	r	h	bi
Alomar 2b	5	0	2	0	Northrup lf	4	0	0	0
Pinson rf	4	0	0	1	MStanley cf	3	0	0	0
McCraw lf	2	0	0	0	GBrown dh	2	0	0	0
Llenas ph	1	0	1	2	Cash 1b	4	0	0	0
Stanton lf	0	1	0	0	Sims c	3	0	0	0
Epstein 1b	3	1	1	0	MAuliffe 2b	3	0	0	0
ROliver dh	3	1	1	1	Sharon rf	3	0	0	0
Berry cf	3	0	0	0	ARodrgez 3b	3	0	0	0
Gallagher 3b	4	0	2	2	EBrnkmnss	3	0	0	0
Meoli ss	4	1	1	0	JPerry p	0	0	0	0
Kusnyer c	3	2	1	0	Scherman p	0	0	0	0
NRyan p	0	0	0	0	BMiller p	0	0	0	0
					farmer p				
Total	32	6	9	6	Total	27	0	0	0

California   001 000 050— 6
Detroit   000 000 000— 0

DP—Detroit 2. LOB—California 5, Detroit 4. 2B—Epstein, Meoli. SF—Pinson.

	IP	H	R	ER	BB	SO
N.Ryan (W,11-11)	9	0	0	0	4	17
J.Perry (L,9-9)	7 1-3	5	3	3	3	2
Scherman	1-3	0	0	0	0	0
BMiller	0	2	3	3	1	0
Farmer	1 1-3	2	0	0	1	0

T—2:21. A—41,411.

Reprinted from
The Washington Star-News

Aaron hits 700th home run but Phils whip Braves, 8 to 4

Atlanta (AP)—The Philadelphia Phillies overcame Hank Aaron's 700th career home run last night with a three-run rally in the sixth inning for an 8-to-4 triumph over the Atlanta Braves.

The 39-year-old Aaron hit a two-run homer in the third inning off left-hander Ken Brett, giving the Braves a 4-2 lead. It was Aaron's 27th of the baseball season as he pursues his march toward Babe Ruth's all-time mark of 714.

The Braves' 20-year veteran stroked a 1-1 fast ball 10 rows deep into the left-center field stands at Atlanta Stadium.

The 18-year-old fan who caught the ball, Robert Winborne, of Atlanta, was given 700 silver dollars in a brief ceremony with Aaron later in the Braves' clubhouse.

Aaron had singled in the opening inning to run his hitting streak to nine consecutive games. In that span he has hit six home runs and driven in 14 runs. He is batting .256 with 52 r.b.i. for the year.

The Phils went ahead to stay in the sixth off loser Ron Schueler, 5-5. Their three-run uprising was capped by Bob Boone's sacrifice fly after Jose Pagan knocked in the tying runs with a bases-loaded single.

The Braves scored twice in the second inning, keyed by a run-scoring grounder and Ralph Garr's r.b.i. single off Brett.

The Phils opened the scoring in the top of the second on Larry Bowa's run-scoring infield hit. They added another in the third on Bill Robinson's 12th home run of the season. Boone hit his fifth homer in a three-run ninth inning.

The crowd of 16,236 gave Aaron a two-minute standing ovation in Atlanta Stadium and the veteran had to take two bows in front of the Braves' dugout.

On July 21, 1934, Ruth's next-to-last season, he had 701 home runs but added his 702d the following day.

The homer was Aaron's 1,372d extra-base hit, leaving him only five behind Stan Musial's all-time record in that category.

"I wanted to hit No. 700 before the All-Star break," Aaron said to a packed audience of newsmen, photographers and television cameras.

"That sounds a little better, only 14 to go," said the 39-year-old Aaron. "I don't feel any special thrill. It's just a number. The only real one is THE one."

"It was a fast ball, down and in," Aaron said of his memorable homer as champagne was passed around to his teammates in a steamy dressing room.

"I felt it was going out," he said. "After hitting some 600, you kind of know when they're going."

"I'm just glad it went up in the stands and that I hit it before the home folks," he said. "Yes, I knew it was out of the ball park. I was just hoping some kid would catch it."

Brett, now 9-3 in his best of four major league seasons, said he was thinking about No. 700, "but I wasn't going to worry about it as long as I won. I wasn't going to pitch around him because of that guy behind him, Dusty Baker. I think he's one of the best hitters in baseball.

"There's no substitute for winning," Brett added. "The score was 8-4 in our favor. If he had hit four home runs, I couldn't care. We would have won."

PHILADELPHIA	ab	r	h	bi	ATLANTA	ab	r	h	bi
BRobinson rf	4	1	1	2	Garr rf	4	0	1	1
Doyle 2b	5	1	1	0	MPerez ss	4	0	1	0
Montanez 1b	4	1	1	0	Evans 3b	4	1	1	0
Lusinski lf	4	1	2	0	HAaron lf	4	1	2	2
Unser cf	4	1	0	0	Baker cf	4	1	0	0
Pagan 3b	4	0	1	2	DeJohnsn 2b	3	0	0	0
Boone c	3	1	1	1	Dietz 1b	3	1	1	0
Bowa ss	4	1	3	1	BJackson ph	1	0	0	0
Brett p	3	0	0	0	Casanova c	2	1	1	0
Brandon p	0	1	0	0	Tepedino ph	1	0	0	0
					Schueler p	1	0	0	0
					Lum ph	1	0	0	0
					Devine p	0	0	0	0
Total	35	8	11	7	Total	34	4	7	4

Philadelphia   011 003 003— 8
Atlanta   022 000 000— 4

E—Montanez, Evans, Baker, DeJohnson. DP—Atlanta 1. LOB—Philadelphia 6, Atlanta 5. 2B—Casanova, Evans, Montanez. HR—B.Robinson (12), H.Aaron (27), Boone (5). SB—Bowa. S—B.Robinson. SF—Boone.

	IP	H	R	ER	BB	SO
Brett (W,9-3)	7	7	4	4	2	1
Brandon	2	0	0	0	0	0
Schueler (L,5-5)	8 1-3	10	8	6	3	7
Devine	2-3	1	0	0	1	0

Save—Brandon (1). WP—Brett, Schueler. T—2:24. A—16,236.

Sept. 28

RYAN'S SONG

California's Nolan Ryan stood motionless on the mound last night as the scoreboard in center field proclaimed his 383rd strikeout and the fans gave him a four-minute ovation. His total surpasses the seasonal major league all-time record held by Sandy Koufax. No 383, Ryan's 16th of the game, came in the 11th inning and the victim was Minnesota's Rich Reese. To make it all sweeter, Ryan recorded his 21st victory of the season as the Angels rallied to win 5-4.

Reprinted from
The Washington Star-News

Sept. 22

Hiller sets record as Tigers top Bosox

Detroit — John Hiller set a major league baseball record with his 38th save of the season last night as the Detroit Tigers dumped the Boston Red Sox, 5-to-1.

Sept. 26

Mays takes final bow

New York — A choked-up Willie Mays bade farewell to baseball after being lavished with costly gifts last night and said, "In my heart, I am a sad man.

"Just to hear you cheer like this for me and not to be able to do anything about it makes me a very sad man," he said.

"This is my farewell. You don't know what is going on inside of me tonight."

The 42-year-old all-time star announced his retirement from the game less than a week ago, saying he felt he was not physically able to continue the grind.

Honored by old teammates, former rivals, prominent dignitaries of sports and government, and a sellout crowd of more than 50,000 in Shea Stadium, the boyish, enthusiastic superstar from the cornfields of Alabama could not restrain his emotion as he thanked everyone for their thoughtfulness.

Once, he turned toward the bench of the New York Mets, embroiled in a fight for the National League East pennant and said in a quivering voice:

"Forgive me, I know it is as hard on you as it is on me."

He apologized for delaying the game with the Montreal Expos and thanked Mets' officials for enduring him despite a .211 batting average.

"That proves I was loved all over the world," he said.

Oct. 2

METS: 'You Gotta Believe'

By Bruce Keidan
Special to The Star-News

CHICAGO — When it was finally over and champagne was flowing in the locker room of the Beer-and-a-Shot Division champions of the National League, it was left to Rusty Staub to sum up the incredible saga of the 1973 New York Mets.

"Anybody who tries to be realistic about this baseball team," said the Mets' right fielder, "is making a serious mistake."

It was not realistic but surrealistic, the Eastern Division race and the division title clinched by the Mets here yesterday with a 6-4 victory over the Chicago Cubs.

Surrealistic and high camp and terribly improbable, but here it is in black and white for baseball historians of the future to read and ponder.

WHEN RELIEVER Tug McGraw came to the mound in the seventh inning to save the two remaining runs of the lead the Mets had built for starter Tom Seaver, New York gained its 82d victory of the season, against 79 defeats! That record—final because the second game of the scheduled doubleheader was canceled because of wet grounds and irrelevance — was enough to give the Mets a final margin of 1½ games over second-place St. Louis, the only other team in the six-team division that managed to avoid a losing record.

Just 82 victories, a simple majority, and the Mets have earned the right to meet the Western Division-champion Cincinnati Reds in the best-of-five league-championship playoffs beginning Saturday. The Reds, by contrast, won 99 games. Only two teams in their division won fewer than 82 games. By further contrast, the Mets won exactly 83 games in each of their previous three seasons — and finished in third place all three years.

"Cheap champions," they will be called, one-eyed kings in the land of the blind. But despite the mediocre record that made them titlists, the Mets are one hell of a baseball team right now.

Reprinted from
The Washington Star-News

"Remember," said Manager Yogi Berra, who also led the 1964 New York Yankees to a pennant, "this team was in last place until the last day of August. We were only 6½ games out (of first), but we had to leapfrog over five teams."

THEY DID it in part because those five other teams showed a remarkable disinclination to play winning baseball and in part because they personally buried the other championship pretenders in head-to-head play down the stretch. They won 23 of their last 32 games, all of them against Eastern rivals.

"There's only been two times when I've had my regular club" Berra pointed out, referring to his two-year term as manager of the Mets. "That was the beginning of last year and the end of this year. And both times we've been in first place."

And it is true. The Mets led last season until Staub suffered a fractured wrist that kept him out entirely and a platoon of his co-workers suffered lesser injuries that limited both their playing time and effectiveness. This season, shortstop Bud Harrelson and catcher Jerry Grote both were injured in May, and the Mets' defense up the middle collapsed. Both missed two months of the season on the disabled list. And McGraw, who was never disabled, spent two months in a private purgatory where batters abused him almost as they pleased.

Now, however, both Harrelson and Grote are sound. McGraw, an 0-6 pitcher on August 21, finished with a 5-6 record and 25 saves—including four victims, 12 saves and no losses in his last 17 outings. And he has contributed the slogan that has become the team's creed: "You gotta believe!"

"WE BELIEVED in ourselves," said left fielder Cleon Jones, whose second-inning home run off Cub starter Burt Hooton launched the Mets to their title-clinching victory. "We know this club didn't have the talent, the bench strength of the 1969 (Mets) team (that won the World series). But we were proud of ourselves and we believed in ourselves."

Only Berra wasn't sure. "When we got it up to 5-0 in the fifth inning today, I felt pretty good," he said. "But when they (the Cubs) came back, I was worried. I didn't believe we'd won until we got the last out."

He had cause for concern. The Cubs rocked Seaver for two runs on four hits in their half of the fifth, then responded to an unearned New York run in the seventh with two more runs on Rick Monday's 26th homer of the season with none out in the same inning. Suddenly, the drizzling rain and gray skies over Wrigley Field became a mood. If the Cubs could rally to win, another game would be necessary. The possiblity of a first-place tie still existed.

But McGraw was there and McGraw believed. He entered then and proceeded to make believers of the Cubs by checking them on one hit, an infield single, the rest of the way.

"IT WAS different," Berra would say. "I played for 14 World Series teams (as a Yankee). It seemed like on those teams, the beginning of September, the players would call a meeting and say, 'Let's go. We need a new wing on the house. A new car or something.' And then we'd pull away from the other teams. It was never like this."

In all the history of baseball, hardly anything was quite like this Beer-and-a-Shot Division pennant race.

Oct. 9

Mets crush Reds, 9 to 2, as brawl erupts and fans toss debris on field

By KEN NIGRO
Sun Staff Correspondent

New York—It wasn't much of a game, but what a fight.

The New York Mets and Cincinnati Reds forgot about baseball for a brief spell yesterday and engaged in a wild free-for-all that caused the umpires to suspend play for a few minutes.

The brawl, which emptied both dugouts and bullpens, came in the fifth inning and interrupted what had been a laugher for the Mets. When order finally was restored, New York went on to pound the dazed Reds into submission, 9 to 2.

The victory, sparked by Rusty Staub, who drove in four runs with a pair of homers, gave the big Met machine a two-games-to-one lead in the play-off for the National League pennant.

Then came the brawl

But for once, the final score was anticlimactic compared to the battle in the top of the fifth inning.

It all started when Pete Rose, Cincinnati's aggressive left fielder, slid hard into second base as Bud Harrelson was completing the relay to first for an inning-ending double play. The two exchanged words and then Rose, who weighs 200 pounds, began pushing the lightweight New York shortstop, who is listed at 150 pounds but looks even lighter.

With that, all hell broke loose. Players swarmed onto the field and the second base area soon resembled a boxing arena. When the original fight was broken up, relief pitchers Pedro Borbon and Buzz Capra went at it.

When that fight, too, ended, Borbon marched off the field wearing a Met cap.

But the trouble had only just begun. When the Red's took the field in the bottom of the fifth, the fans in the left field stands started pelting the area with every object imaginable. The Cincinnati pitchers in the bullpen had to run for cover. One object actually hit Gary Nolan and he slumped to his knees.

Rose and other Reds retaliated by throwing the objects back in the stands.

Some fans, meanwhile, made menacing moves toward the Cincinnati dugout, but police lined up on the roof and held them back.

Finally, with two outs in the bottom of the fifth, a bottle of whisky sailed past Rose's ear. That was enough for Reds' manager Sparky Anderson, who waved his team off the field.

Suddenly, Shea Stadium was an eerie sight—there was a full house in the stands but not a player in sight. Chub Feeney, National League president, came out from the stands to talk to the umpires while Mets' manager Yogi Berra and a delegation of players went out to left field to plead with their boisterous fans to maintain their sanity.

All the suspense in this one ended in the second inning when the amazing New Yorkers erupted for five runs on four hits. Staub's three-run blast capped the uprising and came off lanky southpaw Tom Hall, who has been the Mets' favorite pigeon all through this series.

Oct. 9

Rain shuts out Orioles, A's; 3d game today

By LOU HATTER
Sun Staff Correspondent

Oakland, Calif.— A wet pitch from climate-control headquarters washed out yesterday's third game of the American League Championship series, delaying a southpaw mound match here between Mike Cuellar, of the Orioles, and Oakland's Ken Holtzman until 3.30 P.M. today.

In consultation with his umpire crew, American League president Joe Cronin announced the postponement 23 minutes before the scheduled starting time.

Inspection of Oakland Coliseum's soggy outfield, the muddy infield despite its protective tarpaulin, related hazards for the players and a forecast of continuing rain until nearly dusk dictated the decision, according to Tom Monahan, a league spokesman.

A's are angered

While physical combat was reserved exclusively yesterday for the Cincinnati Reds-New York Mets National League play-off games, Athletics' club owner Charlie Finley and his manager, Dick Williams, accepted the ruling reluctantly and bitterly.

Neither were consulted. Nor was Baltimore general manager Frank Cashen or Oriole manager Earl Weaver.

In the presence of newsmen on a clubhouse ramp, the volatile Finley sounded off harshly at Cronin, with whom the former's spats have been numerous.

With a crowd of close to 40,000 anticipated following Sunday's 6-to-3 bombardment of the Orioles in Baltimore, squaring the best-of-five pennant showdown at one victory apiece, Finley asserted angrily:

"It was grossly unfair to the fans to call the game so early. According to my weather report, it wasn't even raining across the bay in San Francisco."

Oct. 16

Kuhn reinstates Andrews

New York *P*—Baseball commissioner Bowie Kuhn slapped Oakland A's owner Charles O. Finley on the wrists yesterday and slapped second baseman Mike Andrews back on the rebellious A's World Series squad,

Andrews, supposedly suffering from a shoulder ailment, was placed on the disabled list Sunday, an action which Marvin Miller, executive director of the Major League Baseball Players Association, called "highly suspicious" and which Andrews's teammates and Kuhn labeled embarrassing—and worse.

Andrews committed two 12th-inning errors Sunday which gave the New York Mets four runs and a 10-7 victory that squared the series at one game apiece. Less than two hours later, he was on the disabled list while his teammates were flying to New York for last night's third game.

Finley had requested that the A's be given permission to replace Andrews with Manny Trillo. "There is no basis to grant the request and it is accordingly denied," Kuhn replied.

"I might add that the handling of this matter had the unfortunate effect of unfairly embarrassing a player who has given many years of able service to professional baseball.

"It is my determination that Andrews remains a full-fledged member of the Oakland World Series squad," Kuhn added.

"There is no suggestion that this condition Andrews's shoulder has changed or worsened since the series began, or has been injured in this series. The fact that Andrews was used in game No. 2 by the Oakland club appears to indicate to the contrary."

Finley said the A's would abide by the commissioner's decision.

In a team meeting before the game, the A's were told that Andrews was on his way to New York.

Pitcher Darold Knowles said it wasn't known if the infielder would rejoin the team, or merely was coming to tell his side of the story.

Plans to retire

Pitcher Rollie Fingers said emphatically, "We want him back. He's a great guy to be around, the kind of guy who'd help you out in any jam."

Andrews has indicated he plans to retire from baseball after this year. Finley said yesterday that if Andrews returned to uniform he will not play in the remaining World Series games.

Oct. 22

Campaneris, Jackson HR's win 7th game

BY LOU HATTER
Sun Staff Correspondent

Oakland, Calif.—Demonstrating anew that disunity sometimes breeds strength, the Oakland Athletics upstaged their perpetually controversial owner, Charlie Finley, yesterday and won a second successive global baseball championship.

Powered by a pair of two-run third-inning homers by Bert Campaneris and Reggie Jackson, the irrepressible A's—wracked by dissension, discord and near-rebellion earlier last week—rose up and whipped the New York Mets, 5 to 2, in the final game of an unforgettable 1973 World Series.

While Oakland thereby became the first team to capture the inter-league classic two years in a row since the 1961-1962 New York Yankees, it also lost a respected leader.

Williams confirms resignation

Immediately following the triumph that also featured an insurance r.b.i. single by Joe Rudi, Dick Williams officially confirmed his resignation as manager after guiding the Athletics to three American League West titles, two pennants and yesterday's World Series repeat during a three-year tenure here.

Less than one week ago, the latter feat appeared to be an impossibility.

The A's had been ripped internally over Finley's high-handed treatment of Mike Andrews, perhaps the most-publicized substitute in history. William's intention to quit was a loosely guarded secret. His players had swung bamboo bats against superior New York pitching and butchered the ball as though equipped with cast-iron gloves. Their wives were in a clamor over miserable seating arrangements at New York's Shea Stadium.

What is more, last night it was revealed that Jackson had been playing under threats on his life since one week before Oakland's pennant play-off conquest of the Orioles, during which the league's home-run and runs-batted-in king collected only three hits.

Notwithstanding these and other distractions and dilemmas, it was Jackson who rallied the embattled A's from a 2-to-3 deficit to their eventual successive successes here Saturday and yesterday before a 49,333 sellout crowd at Oakland Coliseum.

Jackson most valuable player

For those heroics—a pair of run-scoring doubles and a single in the 3-to-1 sixth-game verdict, plus his four-base bomb in the finale—Jackson afterward was acclaimed "most valuable player" of the 70th post-season tournament.

Campaneris qualified as a valid candidate, also. He scored the marginal run of the A's 2-to-1 decision in game No. 1, then singled for an 11-inning 3-to-2 victory in New York last Tuesday, was a horror to the Mets again in baseball's 1973 curtain call yesterday.

Dec. 21

Cronin frees Houk from Yankees, binds Williams to A's

Boston (P)—American League president Joe Cronin ruled yesterday that Oakland manager Dick Williams is not free to manage the New York Yankees but that Yankee manager Ralph Houk can go to Detroit to lead the Tigers.

In what were expected to be historic baseball decisions, Cronin reasoned that the Yankees had given Houk his release but that Oakland owner Charles O. Finley had not formally released Williams so that he was not entitled to sign with the Yankees.

No appeal to Kuhn

Cronin did say that if the Yankees and A's work out a deal, Williams could go to New York under a contract he signed with the Yanks last week.

Unless a private settlement can be reached, Cronin said, Williams's contract with Oakland, which has two years to run, is valid.

Cronin said there could be no appeal of his decision to baseball commissioner Bowie Kuhn.

"Based upon the entire record, I find the New York club did not have the right to sign Dick Williams and, thus, I refuse to approve his contract with the New York club," Cronin said after sitting as judge and jury in two days of formal hearings.

In the case of Houk, Cronin ruled that the manager's contract with Detroit is valid. He noted that the Yankees had drawn up a news release announcing Houk's resignation, with two years to go on a New York contract, on the final day of the 1973 season.

However, he said, the Williams case was different. Williams, with two years left on a contract with Finley, announced his resignation after leading the A's to the World Series championship.

At that time, Finley said on national television that Williams had his blessing. Later, Finley demanded player compensation for the loss of his manager. He praised Williams and said the A's would suffer "irreparable injury" by the defection of the manager.

Finley later praised the decision by Cronin for "putting a stop to this garbage of managers and coaches in all sports failing to honor a contract."

"There never was any question in my mind over the validity of the contract that I had with Williams and neither was there any question in my mind of the eventual ruling of Joe Cronin," he said.

Finley was asked if he now would be willing to make a trade with the Yankees.

"My name is Charles O. Finley and not Santa Claus," he said. "Tell 'em to go look under some other Christmas tree."

"We are unhappy about it, certainly," a Yankees spokesman said of Cronin's ruling.

However, the Yankees and Williams had no other comment, pending talks with their attorneys.

"I think baseball has learned something from this," said Cronin.

Kuhn orders Aaron to start

NEW YORK (AP) — Hank Aaron apparently will be in the Atlanta Braves' opening day line-up after all.

That became a near certainty Monday when Baseball Commissioner Bowie Kuhn disapproved the Braves' announced plan to have the 40-year old slugger sit out the opening three-game series in Cincinnati April 4-6-7 and go after Babe Ruth's all-time record of 714 home runs in Atlanta when the Braves open at home April 8.

In a terse statement, Kuhn virtually ordered the Braves to have Aaron in the starting lineup for at least two of the Cincinnati games.

The Braves' slugger has 713 lifetime home runs, one behind Ruth.

Aaron said he had no comment on Kuhn's ruling, but added:

"I've said all I can say about it. I may have something to say later, but he's the commissioner of baseball, I suppose, and I have to abide by the rules."

Bill Bartholomay, the Braves' chairman of the board, was unavailable for comment, as was Atlanta Manager Eddie Mathews.

"I have had a number of discussions with Bill Bartholomay about his February announcement regarding Henry Aaron," Kuhn said. "Although he has advanced some substantial arguments in support of his announcement, he has not been able to persuade me that the procedure he wishes to follow is good for baseball.

"As a result, I have advised him that I am disapproving the announcement and that, barring disability, I will expect the Braves to use Aaron in the opening series in Cincinnati in accordance with the pattern of his use in 1973, when he started approximately two of every three Braves games."

Aaron started two of the first three games last season against Houston and appeared in 120 games, some of them as a pinch hitter. He batted .301 with 40 homers and 96 runs batted in.

At the Braves' training camp in West Palm Beach, Fla., Don Davidson, assistant to Bartholomay, said the club's reaction was "no comment."

"Bartholomay is traveling at the present time, but the 'nmcomment' holds for both me and Eddie Mathews," Davidson said.

However, Eddie Robinson, vice president of the Braves, said he was surprised by Kuhn's statement.

"Bill Bartholomay and I have talked since the ruling today," he said, "and I think there will be a comment forthcoming, but not at this time. We may have a statement, but not now. It's a ticklish thing, and I think we should be prepared before we make a statement."

3 Oriole stars take salaries to arbitration

By CAMERON C. SNYDER

Pitcher Dave McNally, centerfielder Paul Blair and second baseman Bobby Grich of the Orioles, were among the four dozen major league baseball players who yesterday invoked the sport's new arbitration procedure to settle 1974 contract differences.

As the deadline for taking salary disputes to binding arbitration passed, the Major League Players Association said it would take perhaps two more days to determine exactly how many athletes had chosen to let an impartial third party determine their salaries this year.

Meanwhile, the first arbitration hearing was held, with Harry H. Platt, a Detroit lawyer and labor arbitrator, meeting with pitcher Dick Woodson and the Minnesota Twins for over four hours.

Historic event

Terming the session "an historic occasion," Platt said he would render his finding before the end of the week.

Never before has a player had an alternative to sitting out part of a relatively brief career—about six years for the average major leaguer—in order to put pressure on his owner to meet or approach his salary demands.

Under the contract negotiated by the players association and team owners, an arbitrator must choose either the salary demand of the player or the offer made by his team, a condition expected to compel both sides to name reasonable and defendable final wage figures.

The arbitrator has 72 hours after the hearing to make his decision. The arbitration process is a voluntary one in that players may choose instead to continue negotiating on their own as they have in the past. The hearings on arbitrations filed by yesterday's deadline will be completed February 22.

The first Oriole arbitration, according to executive vice-president and general manager Frank Cashen, is scheduled for Thursday, February 21, in New York with McNally.

McNally said yesterday that there is a $10,000 spread between what he wants and what the Orioles have offered. McNally's salary was around $105,000 last season when he posted a 17-17 record with an earned-run average of 3.25.

Hank's Pop: I Knew He Would Hit It Today

Cincinnati, April 4 (AP) — "I knew Henry would hit one today. The weather was so warm," said Hank Aaron's father, Herbert Sr., after watching the Atlanta slugger match Babe Ruth's home run record.

Mrs. Aaron: 'Nerve-Wracking'

"I knew it was out when it left the bat," the 65 year-old retired Mobile, Ala., shipyard worker said of his son's historic first-inning homer Thursday in Riverfront Stadium. It tied Ruth's mark of 714.

The elder Aaron sat with another son, Herbert Jr., and Hank's wife, Billye, in a box adjacent to the Atlanta dugout as the blow gave the Braves a 3-0 lead over the Cincinnati Reds in the 1974 baseball opener.

"This sure is nerve-wracking," said Mrs. Aaron, an Atlanta television hostess who married the 40-year-old Braves' slugger last December.

Mrs. Aaron, wearing a tan suit over a green blouse and with a green, brown and tan bandana covering her hair, greeted her husband's homer off Jack Billingham with mixed emotions.

"He'll be damned if he breaks Ruth's record and he'll be damned if he doesn't," she said.

Before Aaron returned to swarming teammates in the Atlanta dugout he went to his family's box. His wife, tears streaming down her cheeks, leaned over and kissed him.

Brother Herbert Was Confident

Hank's brother, Herbert Jr., also was confident Aaron would at least equal the Babe's fabled record in the opener.

"I did expect it here," said the 42-year-old maintenance engineer. "I just had a feeling."

His brother also thinks Hank should be in the lineup for the second and third games of the opening series Saturday and Sunday.

"He should play. It's part of his job," Herbert Jr. said.

* * *

Cincinnati, April 4 (AP) — Hank Aaron wasn't outwardly showing any signs of nervousness during batting practice today before the major league baseball opener between the Atlanta Braves and Cincinnati Reds.

Aaron did, however, express some concern about it to teammate Dave Johnson after he had taken a few cuts in the batting cage.

"Look like I'm swinging the bat all right?" Aaron whispered to Johnson.

"Yes, kid, you look okay," Johnson replied.

"I look nervous?" Aaron asked.

"Yep," Johnson replied.

Reprinted from
The Baltimore Sun papers

Aaron Hammers No. 715 And Moves Ahead of Ruth

Some Facts and Figures On Home Run No. 715

ATLANTA, April 8 (AP)—The facts and figures on Henry Aaron's 715th home run, breaking Babe Ruth's record:

Date—April 8, 1974.

Site—Atlanta Stadium..

Inning—Fourth.

Time—9:07 P.M., Eastern Daylight Time.

Opposing pitcher—Al Downing, Los Angeles Dodgers.

Men on base—One.

Score—3-1, Los Angeles.

Distance — 400 feet (approximate).

Direction—Left-center field.

Weather—Overcast, windy and cool, occasional drizzle, 62 degrees.

Count—One ball, no strikes.

Outs—None.

Type of pitch—Fastball.

LOS ANGELES (N.)	ab.	r.	h.	bi.	ATLANTA (N.)	ab.	r.	h.	bi.
Lopes, 2b	2	1	0	0	Garr, rf	3	0	0	1
Lacy, 2b	1	0	0	0	Lum, 1b	5	0	0	1
Buckner, lf	3	0	1	0	Evans.....				
Wynn, cf	4	0	1	2	Evans, 3b	4	1	0	0
Ferguson, c	4	0	0	0	Aaron, lf	3	2	1	2
Crawford, rf	4	1	1	u	Office, cf	0	0	0	0
Cey, 3b	4	0	1	1	Baker, cf	2	1	1	0
Garvey, 1b	4	1	1	0	Johnson, 2b	3	1	1	0
Russell, ss	4	0	1	0	Foster, 2b	0	0	0	0
Downing, p	1	1	1	1	Correll, c	4	1	0	0
Marshall, p	1	0	0	0	Robinson, ss	0	0	0	0
Joshua, ph	1	0	0	0	Tepedino, ph	0	0	0	1
Hobgh, p	0	0	0	0	Perez, ss	2	1	1	0
Mota, ph	1	0	0	0	Reed, p	2	0	0	0
					Oates, ph	1	0	0	1
Total	34	4	7	4	Capra, p	0	0	0	0
					Total	29	7	4	6

Los Angeles .... 003 001 000—4
Atlanta .... 010 402 00x—7

E—Buckner, Cey, Russell 2, Lopes, Ferguson. LOB—Los Angeles 5, Atlanta 7. 2B—Baker, Russell, Wynn. HR—Aaron (2). S—Garr. SF—Garr.

	IP.	H.	R.	ER.	BB.	SO.
Downing, (L, 0-1)	3	2	5	2	4	2
Marshall	3	2	2	1	1	1
Hough	2	0	0	0	2	1
Reed (W, 1-0)	6	7	4	4	1	4
Capra	3	0	0	0	1	6

Save—Capra (1). Wild pitch—Reed. PB—Ferguson. T—2:27. A—53,775.

Aaron Is Congratulated By Nixon After Homer

ATLANTA, (AP) — President Nixon telephoned congratulations to Henry Aaron shortly after the 40-year-old slugger smashed his record 715th career home run.

Donald Davidson, the traveling secretary of the Braves, said Aaron was in left field when the call came through but Manager Eddie Mathews sent word he would let Aaron take the call between innings.

Aaron talked with the President, Davidson said, during the bottom of the sixth inning.

An Old-Timer Reacts

SHANNON, Miss., April 8 (AP)—Al Downing should not be embarrassed that he gave up Hank Aaron's 715th home run, the pitcher who served up the last two homers to Babe Ruth said tonight.

"I've never been embarrassed that Ruth hit the home runs off me," said Guy Bush, now a Shannon farmer. "And I don't imagine the pitcher Aaron hit one off tonight is embarrassed."

Bush, 73 years old, was watching on television as Aaron broke Ruth's homer record, set at 714 when the Babe hit two off Bush in 1935 while Bush was pitching for Pittsburgh and Ruth for the Boston Braves.

"He was going to hit it sooner or later, and I'm glad he hit it now," Bush said.

Kuhn Misses Homer 715 For a Date in Cleveland

CLEVELAND, April 8 (AP)—The baseball commissioner, Bowie Kuhn, did not see Henry Aaron become baseball's home run king.

"I wish I could have been there, but I'm thrilled for him," Kuhn said tonight, after Aaron hit No. 715, breaking Babe Ruth's mark. "I'm proud of him. He's one of the greatest we have ever seen."

Kuhn was at a dinner here when Aaron hit the homer on his second time at bat in Atlanta. The Indians were scheduled to have their home opener against the Milwaukee Brewery tomorrow but Snow has already forced postponement of the game until Wednesday.

"I had no commitment to be there [Atlanta]," Kuhn said. "I was invited both to Atlanta and Cleveland and I decided to accept the invitation here since I was in Cincinnati and fortunate to participate on the day Aaron hit his 714th home run."

Streaker Unawed By Aaron's Homer

CINCINNATI, April 4 (AP)—An unidentified male came up with his own version of the current streaking craze today at the major league baseball opener in Riverfront Stadium, in which Henry Aaron hit his 714th career home run to tie Babe Ruth.

The man, in his mid-20s, took off his clothes in the upper left-field bleachers and jumped up and down near his seat during the Cincinnati Reds-Atlanta Braves game.

"The crowd booed police when they started after him," said a photographer who took the streaker's picture. "Then when the police stopped, the crowd cheered."

Cincinnati's left fielder, Pete Rose, said he watched the incident from his position. "He was even signing autographs," said Rose, who scored the winning run in a 7-6, 11-inning victory.

April 11

Kroc apologizes for berating team

SAN DIEGO (AP) — Ray Kroc said Wednesday night he "talked without thinking" in berating his San Diego Padres over the public address system at San Diego stadium.

"Certainly I'll make a public apology," the Padres' owner said in a telephone interview from Hollywood, where he stopped on the way back to his Florida home. 'I used a bad choice of words and I'm sorry."

The interview was published in Thursday's San Diego Union.

Kroc, the McDonald's hamburger tycoon who bought the Padres this year, took to the loudspeaker during the team's home opener and fourth straight loss Tuesday night and apologized to the fans for "the stupidest ballplaying I've ever seen."

The statement brought a bitter reaction from players on the Padres and the visiting Houston Astros, and an apology was demanded by Baseball Commissioner Bowie Kuhn and National League President Chub Feeney.

June 4

Aaron's Ex-Wife Seeks Increase in Payments

ATLANTA (AP) — Hank Aaron's former wife filed a petition in Superior Court here Monday seeking a ten-fold increase in the alimony and child support payments she receives from the Braves' baseball star.

Mrs. Barbara Aaron said in her petition that the Atlanta Braves slugger was earning about $100,000 a year when they were divorced in February of 1971, but that Aaron now earns "in excess of one million dollars per year."

"Since his income has gone up 10 times," Mrs. Aaron's attorneys said it would be reasonable to increase his payments from the current total of $1,600 per month to $16,000 per month.

Aaron now pays $200 a month in support of each of his four children and $800 a month in alimony, a total of $1,600.

Aaron married his second wife, Billye, last fall.

June 5

Indians forfeit to Texas after fans disrupt play

Cleveland (AP)—Last night's baseball game between the Texas Rangers and the Cleveland Indians was forfeited to the Rangers with the score tied, 5-to-5, in the bottom of the ninth inning when unruly Cleveland fans poured onto the field after the Indians scored the tying run.

The game goes into the books as a 9-to-0 Texas victory, but all records count.

As soon as pinch hitter Ed Crosby, who had singled in the first run of the 2-run rally, crossed the plate with the tying run on John Lowenstein's sacrifice fly, a slew of youngsters ran out into center field.

Players in the Texas dugout ran out onto the field, a half-dozen armed with bats, and began chasing the youngsters.

More spectators poured onto the field and a series of fights ensued with the players. Then Cleveland players joined in.

The game was halted earlier in the sixth inning and again in the seventh as some of the fans in the crowd of 25,134 threw firecrackers, tennis balls and beer cups onto the field and numerous youngsters, one woman and one streaker ran onto the playing area on a promotion night that featured beer for 10 cents.

The last forfeited game was on the final day of the 1971 season in Washington. It was the last home game for the Washington Senators before they moved to Texas.

June 5

Record Belt By Aaron Beats Phils

PHILADELPHIA (AP) — Hank Aaron belted his 16th career grand slam home run Tuesday night, a National League record, to highlight a six-run seventh inning that carried the Atlanta Braves to a 7-3 victory over the Philadelphia Phillies.

The homer was the 10th of the baseball season for Aaron and 723rd regular season homer of his career. The 16 grand slams put Aaron one ahead of Willie McCovey on the National League list. Lou Gehrig, New York Yankee great, holds the major league record with 23.

It was also Aaron's 731st home run overall, including World Series and All-Star games, a major league record. He had been tied with Babe Ruth at 730.

Aaron greeted reliever Eddie Watt with his grand slam over the left field wall. Paul Casanova's run-scoring single accounted for the final run of the inning.

ATLANTA				PHILADELPHIA			
	ab	r	h bi		ab	r	h bi
Garr rf	5	1	1 1	DCash 2b	4	0	1 1
Evans 3b	2	1	0 0	Bowa ss	4	0	0 0
Lum cf	5	2	3 1	Schmidt 3b	3	1	1 0
Aaron lf	3	1	1 4	Luzinski lf	4	0	0 0
Office cf	1	0	0 0	Unser cf	3	1	1 1
DJohnsn 1b	3	1	0 0	Grbkwtz ph	1	0	0 0
MPerez 2b	5	0	0 0	Mcntanez 1b	4	0	1 1
Casanova c	4	0	2 1	MAndrsn rf	3	1	1 0
CRobinsn ss	4	1	2 0	Boone c	3	0	1 0
Harrison p	2	0	0 0	Schueler p	2	0	1 0
NMiller ph	1	0	0 0	Watt p	0	0	0 0
MJFrell ph	1	0	0 0	Scarce p	0	0	0 0
House p	0	0	0 0	BRobinsn ph	1	0	0 0
				Culver p	0	0	0 0
Total	36	7	9 7	Total	32	3	7 3

Atlanta   100 000 600— 7
Philadelphia   010 100 010— 3

E—D.Cash, Bowa. DP—Atlanta 1, Philadelphia 2. LOB—Atlanta 8, Philadelphia 3. 2B—Lum. HR—Lum (4), Unser (4), Aaron (10).

	IP	H	R	ER	BB	SO
Harrison (W,4-6)	6	4	2	2	1	1
House	3	3	1	1	0	4
Schueler (L,3-6)	6 1-3	7	5	5	4	3
Watt	1-3	2	2	2	0	0
Scarce	1 1-3	0	0	0	1	1
Culver	1	0	0	0	0	1

Save—House (2). HBP—by Watt (DaJohnson). WP—Watt. T—2:26. A—17,197.

June 16

Ryan Fans 19 In 15

ANAHEIM (AP) — Fireballing Nolan Ryan struck out 19 Boston batters in a 15-inning marathon and came close to establishing two records—most strikeouts in an extra-inning game and a personal mark for number of pitches in a single game.

The Angels won the game Friday night 4-3 on Denny Doyle's run-scoring double.

When Ryan left the mound, he was only two strikeouts short of the record for an extra-inning game. Ex-Washington pitcher Tom Cheney fanned 21 Baltimore Orioles in a 16-inning game on Sept. 12, 1962.

Last season the right-hander had 383 strikeouts, breaking the major league record held by Sandy Koufax of the Los Angeles Dodgers.

Meanwhile, Ryan also was shooting for another record, which resulted in an unusual conversation when Angels' Manager Bob Winkles told Ryan in the 12th inning: "That's it."

"But I haven't broken my record yet," Ryan said. "Just one more inning, okay?"

Record? What record, demanded Winkles.

Ryan beamed: "Most pitches in a game."

So he got another inning—but still fell short of his "record" for most pitches in a single game.

June 20

Scott ruins Busby's bid

By The Associated Press

George Scott ruined a perfectly good evening for Steve Busby Wednesday night.

The Milwaukee first baseman walked on a 3-2 count, Busby's rare moment of imperfection, and thus spoiled a perfect game by the Kansas City pitcher.

Scott was the only baserunner Busby allowed during a 2-0 no-hitter, first of the 1974 baseball season and the second of his brief career.

"I didn't make a whole lot of bad pitches and made them hit the ball," said Busby, who received excellent fielding support en route to his beauty.

Two catches by right fielder Al Cowens and a sparkling play by second baseman Cookie Rojas preserved the no-hitter.

June 28

Williams Returns

ANAHEIM (AP) — Dick Williams, who led the Oakland A's to victory in the past two World Series, is leaving his exile from baseball next Monday to manage the California Angels because the offer was "so tremendous I couldn't turn it down."

Williams, 45, agreed to serve with the Angels through the 1977 American League season for what is believed to be at least $100,000 a year. He succeeds Bobby Winkles, fired earlier Thursday as the Angels, 30-44, languished in last place in the Western Division.

"I'm quite happy they called me and I'm quite happy to be returning to baseball," Williams said from his Riviera Beach, Fla., home. He has been in private business since A's owner Charles O. Finley blocked his being hired as manager of the New York Yankees.

Williams quit the A's after the 1973 World Series and Finley, after allowing the Angels to approach Williams, requested the lifting of a court injunction in San Francisco that prevented Williams from managing any team except Oakland through 1975.

The fiery field leader said he missed baseball, but when asked if he would have taken any offer, he said, "No sir! Definitely not."

July 18

Bob Gibson fans 3,000th batter

St. Louis ⚘ — George Foster's 2-run double in the 12th inning gave the Cincinnati Reds a 6-to-4 victory over the St. Louis Cardinals last night in a game that featured Bob Gibson's 3,000th career strikeout.

A walk to Darrel Chaney and a single by Dave Concepcion preceded Foster's game-winning hit.

The durable St. Louis right-hander became only the second pitcher in major league baseball history to reach the 3,000-strikeout plateau when he fanned Cesar Geronimo on a high fastball in the second inning.

Gibson, who struck out four batters before leaving the game after 7 innings, moved into an elite class with the immortal Walter Johnson, who had 3,508 strikeouts in his career.

A Busch Stadium crowd of 28,743 roared its approval and accorded the veteran pitcher a standing ovation as he strolled to the dugout at the inning's completion.

CINCINNATI	ab r h bi	ST LOUIS	ab r
Geronimo cf	7 0 1 0	Brock lf	4 0 1 0
Rose lf	3 0 1 0	Heidemn ss	3 0 0 0
Morgan 2b	3 0 0 0	Tyson ss	3 0 0 0
Beach c	6 0 1 1	McBride cf	4 0 0 0
TPerez 1b	6 0 1 0	Ksmith rf	4 1 0 0
Driessen 3b	3 2 1 0	Simmons 1b	4 1 0 0
Gagliano ph	0 0 0 0	Torre 3b	4 1 1 3
Chaney 3b	1 1 0 0	McCrr c	2 0 0 0
Concepcion ss	3 2 3 0	Hill c	2 0 0 0
Griffey rf	7 0 1 2	Hentzlmn 2b	3 0 0 0
GFoster rf	3 0 1 2	JCruz ph	1 0 0 0
TCarroll p	2 0 1 0	Davanon 2b	1 0 0 0
Crowley ph	1 0 1 1	Gibson p	2 0 0 0
Hall p	0 0 0 0	Mriendez ph	1 0 0 0
Kosco ph	1 0 0 0	Hrabosky p	0 0 0
Carroll p	0 0 0 0	Garman p	0 0 0 0
Rettenund ph	1 0 0 0	Dwyer ph	1 0 0 0
McEnany p	0 0 0 0	Folkers p	0 0 0 0
Gullett ph	1 0 0 0	Pena p	0 0 0 0
Borbon p	0 0 0 0	Reitz ph	1 0 1 0
		Forsch pr	0 0 0 0
Total	49 6 14 6	Total	40 4 5 4

Cincinnati   110 101 000 003— 6
St. Louis   031 000 000 000— 4

E—Gibson, Simmons, Morgan 2. DP—Cincinnati 1, LOB—Cincinnati 13, St. Louis 7. 2B—Driessen, Griffey, TPerez, GFoster. HR—Torre (6), R Smith (13). SB—Morgan.

	IP	H	R	ER	BB	SO
TCarroll	5	3	4	4	6	3
Hall	2	0	0	0	0	0
Carroll	3	1	0	0	0	1
McEnany (W 1-0)	1	0	0	0	0	1
Borbon	1	1	0	0	0	0
Gibson	7	10	4	3	2	4
Hrabosky	1 1-3	0	0	0	1	0
Garman	2 2-3	1	0	0	1	3
Folkers (L 2-1)	1 1-3	2	2	2	2	1
Pena	2-3	1	0	0	0	0

WP—Borbon. PB—Hill. T—3.02. A—28,743.

Pirate Farmhand Killed in a Game

SALEM, Va., Aug. 22 (AP) —Alfredo Edmead, an 18-year-old rightfielder of the Salem Pirates, was killed tonight in a collision with a teammate during the Pirates' Carolina League game with Rocky Mount.

Edmead, a Puerto Rico native who was the youngest player for Salem, a Pittsburgh Pirate farm club, collided in the sixth inning with the Salem second baseman, Pablo Cruz, on a short fly to right field.

Both players were rushed to a hospital, and Edmead was pronounced dead on arrival. The cause of death was listed as a massive skull fracture. Cruz injured a knee and is out for the year.

Aug. 16

Indians Clip Twins, 4 to 2

CLEVELAND (AP) — Frank Duffy's two-out, bases-loaded single provided two runs and Gaylord Perry gained his 16th victory as the Cleveland Indians defeated the Minnesota Twins 4-2 in American League baseball Thursday night.

Perry, 16-7, who won 15 consecutive games earlier this season but has been trying to get No. 16 since July 3, allowed five hits.

The Indians took a 1-0 lead in the third inning when Tom McCraw scored on a fielder's choice. The Twins tied the game in the fourth when Tony Oliva hit his 11th home run of the season.

MINNESOTA	ab r h bi	CLEVELAND	ab r h bi
Brye cf	4 0 1 0	Lowenstn 3b	3 0 0 0
Braun 3b	2 0 0 0	Lee lf	4 0 0 0
Hisle lf	3 0 0 0	Hendrick cf	4 0 1 0
Darwin rf	4 0 0 0	Torres cf	0 1 0 0
Oliva dh	4 1 1 1	Spikes rf	3 0 0 0
Holt 1b	3 0 0 0	Ellis c	3 0 0 0
Carew ph	1 0 0 0	Gahble dh	1 1 0 0
Terrell 2b	4 1 1 0	Lis dh	0 0 0 0
Thompsn ss	4 0 2 1	Alvarado pr	0 0 0 0
Brgman c	3 0 0 0	McCraw 1b	2 1 2 1
Blyleven p	0 0 0 0	Duffy ss	3 0 1 2
Burgmeier p	0 0 0 0	Brohamr 2b	3 0 0 1
		GPerry p	0 0 0 0
		Buskey p	0 0 0 0
Total	32 2 5 2	Total	26 4 5 4

Minnesota   000 100 100— 2
Cleveland   001 002 01x— 4

E—Lowenstein 2. DP—Cleveland 2. LOB—Minnesota 6, Cleveland 7. 2B—McCraw, Ellis, Thompson, Hendrick. HR—Oliva (11). S—Duffy, Braun, Ellis. SF—McCraw.

	IP	H	R	ER	BB	SO
Blyleven (L,11-14)	7 1-3	5	4	4	4	4
Burgmeier	2-3	0	0	0	1	0
G.Perry (W,16-7)	7	5	2	2	2	2
Buskey	2	0	0	0	0	0

Save—Buskey (13). HBP—by Blyleven (Spikes). WP—Blyleven. PB—Borgmann, Ellis. T—2:23. A—11,920.

Marshall Dips Foe In Red

Sept. 9

The Associated Press

Mike Marshall, making his recordbreaking 93rd appearance of the season, came on in the eighth inning to snuff out a Cincinnati rally, then struck out the side in the ninth to preserve the Los Angeles Dodgers' 7-4 victory over the Reds.

The victory gave the Dodgers two out of three in their weekend series against the Reds and put them 3½ games ahead of the second-place Reds.

Marshall pitched in all three games of the series to break his own record of 92 appearances in one season, set with the Montreal Expos last year. He also broke a record for innings pitched in one season by a reliever. He now has 180-2-3, surpassing his former mark of 179.

Brock Breaks Record

ST. LOUIS, Sept. 10 (AP)—Lou Brock stole second base in the seventh inning of the Cardinals' game against the Philadelphia Phillies tonight and set a major league record of 105 stolen bases for one season.

Brock's theft, his second of the game, came during the Cards' 142d game and his 134th. It eclipsed the previous record of 104 set by the Los Angeles Dodgers' Maury Wills in 1962.

His first steal came in the opening inning following a single to left before an enthusiastic Busch Stadium crowd of 27,285.

Brock led off the seventh with a single to left. Following the steal, Brock's teammates and photographers poured onto the field and Brock was presented with the historic base that he stole.

The game was stopped and Brock, who addressed the crowd, embraced the Cards' second baseman, Ted Sizemore, an injured player who usually bats behind him.

In a salute to his throng of admirers, the 35-year-old outfielder said, "The left-field fans probably knew I was going to steal 105 before I did. They were behind me all the way."

Among those who saluted Brock was James (Cool Papa) Bell, a former Negro League star who was inducted into the Hall of Fame last month. Bell, a speedster in his playing days, went onto the field to congratulate the man who now owns the single season base-stealing record.

Brock, who had vowed to set the record before a home crowd, remained at first base for only one pitch before each steal.

He broke rapidly in the first inning as Philadelphia's right-hander, Dick Ruthven, fired to the plate and reached second base well ahead of the throw.

In the seventh, Brock waited until the count was 0-1 and streaked to second, once again well ahead of the catcher's wide throw to the bag.

The thefts by Brock, who has been thrown out 28 times, also lifted him to 740 for his career, eclipsing the previous record of 738 set by Max Carey of the Pittsburgh Pirates in 1929, his final season in the majors.

Only Ty Cobb, who has 892, and Eddie Collins, who had 743, stole more bases during their careers.

Brock, who has stolen 14 bases in 15 games this season against the Phillies, broke Carey's mark in the first inning after singling.

Sept. 11

ST. LOUIS	ab	r	h	bi	NEW YORK	ab	r	h	bi
Brock lf	9	0			Harrelsn ss	7	0	0	0
Sizemre 2b	10	1	1	0	Millan 2b	10	1	4	0
Smith rf	8	0	1	0	Jones lf	9	2	3	2
Torre 1b	9	0	2	1	Milner 1b	10	0	2	1
Simmons c	3	0	1	0	Garrett 3b	10	0	0	0
McBride cf	10	1	4	0	Schneck cf	11	0	2	0
Reitz 3b	10	1	4	2	Ayala rf	2	0	1	0
Tyson ss	2	0	0	0	Dyer c	9	0	2	0
Forsch p	1	0	0	0	Koosman p	2	0	0	0
Godby lf	2	0	0	0	Boswell 3b	4	0	0	0
Herndon pr	0	1	0	0	Webb p	0	0	0	0
Hill c	1	0	0	0	Pembrtn ph	1	0	1	0
Schnblm ph	1	0	0	0	Hahn cf	6	0	0	0
Billngs c	5	0	1	0	Gosger ph	0	0	0	0
Hrnandz ph	1	0	0	0	Boisclr pr	0	0	0	0
Folkers p	0	0	0	0	Hodges c	0	0	0	0
Cruz ph	1	0	0	0	Martnz ph	1	0	0	0
Bare p	0	0	0	0	Krnpool ph	1	0	0	0
Osteen p	4	0	0	0	Theodor ph	1	0	0	0
Siebert p	1	0	0	0	Apodaca p	1	0	0	0
Melndz ph	1	0	0	0	Cram p	3	0	1	0
Garman p	0	0	0	0	Staub ph	1	0	0	0
Hunt ph	1	0	0	0					
Hrbsky p	0	0	0	0					
Dwyer ph	1	0	0	0					
Heidman ss	6	0	3	0					
Totals	86	4	18	3	Totals	89	3	16	3

St. Louis 100 000 002 000 000 000 000 000 1—4
New York 100 020 000 000 000 000 000 000 0—3

E—Tyson, Schneck, Dyer, Osteen, Webb, Hodges. DP—St. Louis 1, New York 1. LOB—St. Louis 19, New York 25. 2B—Milner, Schneck (2). HR—Jones (13), Reitz (6). SB—McBride. S—Koosman, Forsch, Millan, McBride, Jones.

	IP	H	R	ER	BB	SO
Forsch	6	5	3	2	4	3
Garman	2	0	0	0	0	2
Hrabosky	3	2	0	0	0	3
Folkers	2	3	0	0	1	2
Bare	1-3	0	0	0	1	0
Osteen	9 1-3	4	0	0	2	5
Siebert (W,8-8)	2 1-3	2	0	0	3	1
Koosman	9	5	3	3	4	5
Parker	3	2	0	0	0	0
Miller	1	1	0	0	1	1
Apodaca	3	2	0	0	1	1
Cram	8	7	0	0	2	4
Webb (L,0-1)	1	1	1	0	0	1

HBP—by Koosman (Tyson), by Parker (Dwyer). WP—Forsch, Koosman, Cram. PB—Simmons. T—7:04. A—13,460.

Hiller Sets AL Mark

Sept. 13

DETROIT (AP) — Tom Veryzer belted a two-run homer in the 10th inning and relief pitcher John Hiller notched a record-breaking 17th victory as the Detroit Tigers beat the Milwaukee Brewers 9-7 Thursday night.

Veryzer smashed his gamewinning homer into the upper deck of the left field seats off Tom Murphy, 8-8, with Leon Roberts on second base.

Roberts had led off the inning with an infield hit and was sacrificed to second base before Veryzer hit his first major league homer.

Hiller, 17-10, broke the American League record of 16 victories by a reliever, set by Boston's Dick Radatz in 1964. Elroy Face holds the National League mark with 18 in 1959.

MILWAUKEE	ab	r	h	bi	DETROIT	ab	r	h	bi
Money 3b	4	2	1	0	LeFlore cf	5	0	1	0
Berry cf	5	0	2	3	Suthrlnd 2b	4	1	1	0
Scott 1b	5	0	0	0	Kaline dh	4	2	1	0
Briggs lf	5	2	3	1	Ogilvie lf	3	2	2	2
Porter c	5	1	1	2	Freehan c	4	1	1	3
Lezcano rf	4	0	1	1	Sanders 1b	5	1	1	0
Hegan dh	2	0	0	0	Roberts rf	5	1	2	2
TJohnsn ss	5	1	1	0	ARdrgez 3b	4	0	1	0
Lind 2b	3	1	1	0	EBrnkmn ss	1	0	0	0
Colborn p	0	0	0	0	Coleman p	0	0	0	0
Mitchell dh	2	0	1	0	GBrown ph	0	0	0	0
Castro p	0	0	0	0	Knox pr	0	0	0	0
Murphy p	0	0	0	0	LaMont c	0	0	0	0
					Veryzer ss	3	1	1	2
					Lmnczyk p	0	0	0	0
					Hiller p	0	0	0	0
Totals	40	7	11	7	Totals	38	9	13	9

Milwaukee 002 140 000 0—7
Detroit 000 302 200 2—9
One out when winning run scored

E—Roberts, Freehan. DP—Detroit 2. LOB—Milwaukee 7, Detroit 8. 2B—TJohnson, Berry, Sanders 2, Roberts, Ogilvie. 3B—Briggs. HR—Porter (11), Freehan (14), Veryzer (1). S—Sutherland, A. Rodriguez.

	IP	H	R	ER	BB	SO
Colborn	5 2-3	4	5	5	1	0
Castro	1	3	2	2	0	0
Murphy (L,8-8)	2 2-3	6	2	2	2	0
Coleman	4 2-3	6	6	3	2	0
Lmnczyk	2 1-3	3	1	1	0	1
Hiller (17-10)	3	1	0	0	1	2

HBP—by Colborn (Kaline, Brinkmn). A—5,006. T—2:43.

Sept. 18

Cards Top Bucs In 13th Inning, 2-1

PITTSBURGH (AP) — Larcenous Lou Brock stole his 109th base of the season and the 744th of his career, second highest total in major league history, then scored the winning run on Ted Simmons' sacrifice fly in the 13th inning, giving the St. Louis Cardinals a 2-1 victory over the Pittsburgh Pirates Tuesday night.

The victory, St. Louis' sixth in a row, put the first-place Cards 2½ games ahead of the slumping Pirates—who now have lost six straight—in the National League East pennant race.

After Brock opened the 13th with a single off Jerry Reuss, 15-10, who went the distance for Pittsburgh, the fleet Cardinal outfielder swiped second. Reuss had thrown over to frst base six times before the theft.

Ted Sizemore moved Brock to third with a sacrifice, then Reggie Smith was walked intentionally and Simmons hit his decisive sacrifice fly.

Brock, the major leagues' single-season stolen base champion, stole his 108th base of the year, in the 10th inning, tying him with Eddie Collins for second place on the all-time list with 743. The stolen base in the 13th put Brock ahead of Collins.

The Cardinals, who have beaten Pittsburgh in 10 of 13 meetings. tied the score 1-1 in the seventh. Simmons rapped a two-out single, took second on a balk and Torre drove him home with a double down the left field line.

Pittsburgh jumped to a 1-0 lead in the first inning when Al Oliver homered off Cardinal starter Bob Gibson.

Gibson worked the first nine innings before he was taken out for a pinch hitter in the 10th. He allowed only five hits—none after the fourth inning.

ST LOUIS					PITTSBURGH				
	ab	r	h	bi		ab	r	h	bi
Brock lf	6	1	1.	0	Stennett 2b	6	0	0	0
Sizemore 2b	4	0	0	0	Hebner 3b	6	0	1	0
RSmith rf	5	0	1	0	AOliver cf	5	1	1	1
Simmons c	4	1	1	1	Stargell lf	5	0	1	0
Torre 1b	6	0	1	1	Zisk rf	4	0	0	0
McBride cf	4	0	1	0	Sanguilln c	5	0	1	0
Reitz 3b	5	0	0	0	Krkpatrik 1b	3	0	1	0
Tyson ss	2	0	1	0	Macha ph	1	0	0	0
Heidemn ss	3	0	1	0	BRobrtsn 1b	1	0	0	0
Gibson p	2	0	0	0	Taveras ss	4	0	0	0
Hunt ph	1	0	1	0	Clines ph	1	0	1	0
Herndon pr	0	0	0	0	Reuss p	4	0	0	0
Hrabosky p	1	0	0	0	Howe ph	1	0	0	0
Total	43	2	8	2	Total	45	1	5	1

Cards   000 000 100 000 1— 2
Pirates   100 000 000 000 0— 1

E—Reuss, Tyson, A.Oliver, Sanguillen, Torre. DP—St. Louis 1, Pittsburgh 1 LOB—St. Louis 9, Pittsburgh 7. 2B—Torre. HR—A.Oliver (9). SB—Brock 2. S—Sizemore. SF—Simmons.

	IP	H	R	ER	BB	SO
Gibson	9	5	1	1	1	1
Hrabosky (W,7-1)	4	0	0	0	1	6
Reuss (L,15-10)	13	8	2	2	5	11

Balk—Reuss. T—3:17. A—21,458.

Sept. 30

Giants Offered Move By Finley

SAN FRANCISCO (AP) — Oakland A's owner Charles O. Finley recently offered San Francisco Giants President Horace C. Stoneham $3 million to move his baseball team to another city, the San Francisco Examiner reported Sunday.

The Associated Press was unable to reach either Finley or Stoneham Sunday for comment.

The report said Stoneham rejected Finley's offer, and when Finley asked how much Stoneham would pay him to leave the area, the Giants' owner replied: "Not one cent."

The A's, despite winning a fourth straight American League West title this season, have drawn barely 800,000 fans. The Giants, fifth in the National League West, have the lowest attendance in major league baseball, just over 500,000.

Sept. 26

Kaline Congratulated By President Ford

BALTIMORE (AP) — Al Kaline, the 12th player in major league history to record 3,000 base hits, received a congratulatory telephone call Wednesday night from President Ford.

Kaline, 39, a Detroit Tiger designated hitter, reached the milestone in Tuesday night's game against the Baltimore Orioles. He received the call from Ford about an hour before another game here Wednesday night.

"He congratulated me and said he was happy for me," Kaline said, "and told me to be sure and stop in and see him when I was in Washington."

DETROIT					BALTIMORE				
	ab	r	h	bi		ab	r	h	bi
Leflore cf	5	1	2	1	Coggins rf	3	1	2	0
Suthrland 2b	4	0	2	0	Cabell 1b	2	0	1	0
Kaline dh	4	0	2	1	Blair cf	5	0	2	0
Freehan c	3	0	0	0	Grich 2b	3	0	0	0
Sanders 1b	3	0	1	0	TDavis dh	4	1	2	0
Roberts rf	4	0	0	0	JPowell 1b	2	0	1	0
Meyer lf	4	0	0	0	Northrup rf	0	0	0	0
ARodrgez 3b	3	1	1	0	Oliver ph	1	0	0	0
Oglivie ph	1	0	0	0	Baylor lf	4	1	2	1
EBrnkmn ss	2	2	1	2	BRobinsn 3b	3	1	1	1
GBrown ph	1	0	0	0	Hendrcks c	2	0	0	0
Ruhle p	0	0	0	0	Etchebrn c	2	0	1	1
Hiller p	0	0	0	0	Belanger ss	4	1	1	0
					McNally p	0	0	0	0
					BReynlds p	0	0	0	0
Total	34	4	9	4	Total	35	5	13	3

Detroit   001 001 200— 4
Baltimore   000 021 02x— 5

E—Leflore. DP—Detroit 1, Baltimore 1. LOB—Detroit 6, Baltimore 9. 2B—Leflore 2, Blair, Kaline, Baylor, B.Robinson. HR—E.Brinkman (14). SB—Baylor. S—Freehan, J.Powell.

	IP	H	R	ER	BB	SO
Ruhle	5 1-3	9	3	1	0	0
Hiller (L,17-12)	2 2-3	4	2	2	2	1
McNally	6 2-3	8	4	4	2	4
BReynlds (W,7-5)	2 1-3	1	0	0	0	3

WP—Hiller. T—2:33. A—11,492.

Kaline Joins Select Group

DETROIT (AP) — Al Kaline is the 12th player in major league baseball history to reach the 3,000-hit level. Here is a list of the 12 (Name, total hits, years played, year reached 3,000, teams):

Ty Cobb, 4,191, 1905-28, 1921, Tigers, Athletics.

Stan Musial, 3,630, 1941-63, 1958, Cardinals.

Hank Aaron, 3,594, 1954-1974, 1970, Braves.

Tris Speaker, 3.515, 1907-28, 1925, Red Sox, Indians, Senators, Athletics.

Honus Wagner, 3,430, 1897-1917, 1914, Louisville, Pirates.

Eddie Collins, 3,310, 1906-30, 1925, Athletics, White Sox.

Willie Mays, 3,283, 1951-73, 1970, Giants, Mets.

Nap Lajoie, 3,251, 1896-16, 1914, Phillies, Athletics, Indians.

Paul Waner, 3,152, 1926-45, 1942, Pirates, Dodgers, Braves, Yankees.

Cap Anson, 3,041, 1876-97, 1897, Cubs.

Roberto Clemente, 3,000, 1955-172, Pirates.

Al Kaline, 3,000, 1953-1974, Tigers.

Chronologically

Anson, Cubs, 1897.

Wagner, Pirates, 1914.

Lajoie, Indians, 1914.

Cobb, Tigers, 1921.

Speaker, Indians, 1925.

Collins, White Sox, 1925.

Waner, Braves, 1942.

Musial, Cardinals, 1958.

Aaron, Braves, 1970.

Mays, Giants, 1970.

Clemente, Pirates, 1972.

Kaline, Tigers, 1974.

Sept. 29

Nolan Ryan Hurls Third No-Hitter

ANAHEIM (AP) — Nolan Ryan had his fastball blazing Saturday night and pitched the third no-hitter of his career, hurling the California Angels to a 4-0 victory over the Minnesota Twins.

The fireballing right-hander became only the fifth pitcher in major league baseball history to hurl three no-hitters.

Ryan joined Sandy Koufax of Los Angeles, who had four nohitters, Larry Corcoran of the Chicago Cubs, Jim Maloney of Cincinnati and Bob Feller of Cleveland, who had three apiece, in the select circle.

It was the third no-hitter of the 1974 season, all of them coming in the American League.

The 27-year-old Ryan struck out 15 batters and walked eight en route to his 22nd triumph against 16 defeats. He struck out the side in both the first and second innings.

Ryan's previous no-hitters were May 15th, 1973—a 3-0 decision over the Kansas City Royals—and July 15, 1973—a 6-0 victory over the Detroit Tigers.

The previous no-hit efforts this season were earned by Kansas City's Steve Busby who stopped Milwaukee June 19th and Cleveland's Dick Bosman who turned the trick against Oakland exactly one month later.

Morris Nettles backed Ryan with a run-scoring single in the third off loser Joe Decker, 16-14, and a two-run single in the fourth.

MINNESOTA	ab r h bi	CALIFORNIA	ab r h bi
Brye cf	2 0 0 0	MNettls cf	4 1 2 3
Carew 2b	2 0 0 0	DDoyle 2b	4 0 1 0
Braun 3b	3 0 0 0	Bochte 1b	3 0 0 1
Darwin rf	4 0 0 0	Lahoud dh	4 0 1 0
Oliva dh	3 0 0 0	Stanton rf	4 0 1 0
Pisle lf	3 0 0 0	Chalk 3b	2 1 0 0
Bourque 1b	3 0 0 0	Balaz lf	2 1 1 0
Killebrew ph	0 0 0 0	Meoli ss	2 1 1 0
Terrell pr	0 0 0 0	Egan c	2 0 0 0
Gomez ss	2 0 0 0	NRyan p	0 0 0 0
Soderholm ss	2 0 0 0		
Borgman c	3 0 0 0		
Decker p	0 0 0 0		
Butler p	0 0 0 0		
Total	27 0 0 0	Total	27 4 7 4

Minnesota   000 000 000— 0
California   002 200 00x— 4

E—Braun. LOB—Minnesota 8, California 4. 2B—Meoli, Balaz. SB—M. Nettles. S—Egan. SF—Bochte.

	IP	H	R	ER	BB	SO
Decker (L,16-14)	2 2-3	4	2	1	0	1
Butler	5 1-3	3	2	2	3	8
N. Ryan (W,22-16)	9	0	0	0	8	15

T—2:22. A—10,872.

Oct. 3

Fergy Hits, Texas Wins

BLOOMINGTON, MINN. (AP) — Ferguson Jenkins, the first American League pitcher to be in the starting lineup as a batter this season, singled to break up a no-hitter and came around to score in the Rangers' 2-1 victory over the Twins.

Jenkins, 25-12, who was allowed to hit for himself as Texas Manager Billy Martin did not use a designated hitter in the season finale, got the Rangers first hit of the game with an infield single in the sixth inning off rookie right-hander Jim Hughes and later scored the first run of the game on Jim Spencer's single.

TEXAS	ab r h bi	MINNESOTA	ab r h bi
DNelson 2b	2 0 0 0	Brye cf	4 0 1 0
Randle lf	2 0 0 0	Braun lf	4 0 0 0
Biones lf	2 0 0 0	Oliva dh	4 0 0 0
Spencer 1b	3 0 1 1	Kusick 1b	4 0 1 0
Hargrove 1b	1 0 0 0	Soderholm 3b	4 1 1 1
Grieve rf	4 1 1 1	Hisle rf	3 0 0 0
Howel 3b	4 0 0 0	Killebrew ph	1 0 0 0
Lovitto cf	3 0 0 0	Thompson ss	3 0 1 0
Harrah ss	0 0 0 0	Gomez 2b	3 0 0 0
McKanin ph	3 0 0 0	Roof c	3 0 0 0
Sundberg c	1 0 0 0	Hughes p	0 0 0 0
Jenkins p	2 1 1 0		
Cubbage ph	1 0 0 0		
Foucault p	0 0 0 0		
Total	28 2 3 2	Total	32 1 5 1

Texas   000 001 100— 2
Minnesota   000 000 100— 1

DP—Minnesota 1. LOB—Texas 3, Minnesota 5. 2B—Brye. HR—Grieve (2), Soderholm (10). SB—Sundberg. S—D. Nelson.

	IP	H	R	ER	BB	SO
Jenkins (W,25-12)	7	5	1	1	1	4
Foucault	2	0	0	0	0	1
Hughes (L,0-2)	9	3	2	2	3	7

WP—Hughes. Balk—Hughes. T—1:59.

Tiger Star Denies Fans Last Hurrah

DETROIT (AP)—Al Kaline bowed out after 22 seasons as a Detroit Tiger in a flourish of boos he heard from the clubhouse in the fifth inning of the Tigers' 5-4 loss yesterday to Baltimore.

The boos weren't directed at Kaline but at Mgr. Ralph Houk for replacing the 39-year-old designated hitter with Ben Oglivie.

There was a meager crowd at Tiger Stadium—much smaller than the paid attendance announced at 4,671.

But the fans, many of whom undoubtedly went to the otherwise meaningless game just to watch Kaline close his illustrious career, booed and jeered loudly when Oglivie batted both in the fifth and eighth innings.

"I didn't know if I should play or not. I've got a bad left shoulder and couldn't swing very well," Kaline said.

"Everybody wanted to see me hit my 400th home run but no way could I swing hard enough to hit a home run.

"I could have played but I could only punch the ball."

Houk said he left the decision on whether to play up to Kaline.

"It's not that big a thing." Houk said. "The guy couldn't go out there again . . . He's given 100 percent every day all year.

"When he came in the dugout the second time after batting in the third he said 'that's it.' "

Kaline, who last week became only the 12th player to reach 3000 career hits, took a third strike in the first inning.

Then, in what proved to be his final trip to the plate—although the fans expected it to come later—he hit a sinking liner to Al Bumbry in leftfield.

"I'm glad it's over I really am," Kaline said smiling. "I don't think I'll miss it. I may miss spring training."

After the World Series he will go to Dunedin, Fla., to work as a special hitting and outfield instructor with Detroit's team in the Florida Instructional League.

He plans to do much the same thing occasionally next season in Detroit but will not go on the road.

"I purposely want to stay away from baseball for a year," he said. "I want to stay away from travel and see how I'll react. I'll make up my mind in a year or two and see if I want to get back into it."

Kaline finished with 3007 hits. His last was a single Tuesday. No. 3000 was a double a week earlier in Baltimore, his home town.

He signed for a bonus of some $40,000 in 1953 out of Southern High School in Baltimore and played with the Tigers for his whole career.

His first hit was a single through shortstop against Luis Aloma in the eighth inning of a 14-4 loss in Chicago to the White Sox, July 8, 1953.

He finished his career among the major league and AL leaders in numerous categories. He hit 399 homers, 498 doubles and 75 triples.

Oct. 4

Indians name Frank Robinson manager

CLEVELAND (AP) — Frank Robinson, one of the game's greatest stars for nearly two decades, is expected to make baseball history Thursday when he is named manager of the Cleveland Indians — the first black manager in the major leagues.

The Cleveland Indians are expected to name Robinson as a replacement for the fired Ken Aspromonte.

"I didn't chase this job and I haven't heard that I'm going to be the manager," insisted Robinson Tuesday. "But certainly I hope I will. I want to be a big league manager.

"It isn't just becoming the first black. I want the job. I want to manage."

Robinson's appointment will come 27 years after Jackie Robinson became the first black ballplayer. Since then, many black men, including Robinson, have been mentioned for a managerial post but, somehow, none of them were ever hired.

"If it's true, it's fantastic," said former Dodger star Maury Wills, another of those mentioned frequently as a possible manager. "But I won't believe it till I see it.

"My heart is still thumping," said Braves' home run king Hank Aaron, after hearing the news in Atlanta. "I think I'll go out and celebrate."

The Indians picked up Robinson and his estimated $180,000-a-year salary from the California Angels in September. He has been used mostly as a designated hitter and will probably continue as a player-manager next season. Lou Boudreau of Cleveland and then Boston was the last player-manager almost 20 years ago.

The Indians also hold the distinction of having the first black player in the American League — outfielder Larry Doby, who joined the team late in the 1947 campaign. Ironically, Doby, now a Cleveland coach, is expected to be released when Robinson assumes command.

Robinson, the only man named Most Valuable Player in both leagues, began his major league career with Cincinnati in 1956. He won the National League MVP with the Reds in 1961 and five years later, won it in the American League with Baltimore when he captured the triple crown with 49 home runs, 122 runs batted in and a .316 average.

He was traded to Los Angeles in 1972 and to Calfiornia last year.

He carried a .298 lifetime average into the current season and has a career total of 573 home runs, placing him fourth on the all-time list behind Aaron, Babe Ruth and Willie Mays.

Aspromonte, who many feel did a fine job with the Indians this year, will be handling the club for the final time tonight when it finishes up in Boston. He has been kept in the dark about the Robinson developments.

"I don't know anything," said Aspromonte. "Nobody tells me a thing. I'm going to Cleveland, pack up and close my house and then go home to Silver Spring, Md."

Oct. 3

Braves Win, Aaron Hits 733rd HR

ATLANTA (AP) — Hank Aaron, baseball's all time home run king, lined a solo shot over the left-field fence in his final at-bat of the 1974 season and Phil Neikro pitched a four-hitter to become a 20-game winner as the Atlanta Braves battered the Cincinnati Reds 13-0 Wednesday night.

The homer was Aaron's 20th this 6ear and the 733rd of his career. He had been hitless in two previous at-bats before connecting off right-handed rookie reliever Rawly Eastwick.

Niekro, 20-13, gave up two infield singles to Dave Concepcion and Dan Driessen and clean hits by Pete Rose and Ken Griffey. Andy Meesersmith of the Los Angeles Dodgers is the only other 20-game winner in the National League.

The Braves jumped on Tom Carroll, 4-3, for four runs in the first inning behind a three-run double by Vic Correll.

Mike Lum rapped his 11th homer of the year in tte third, a blast over the right-field fence that followed a walk to Aaron, then he singled for a run and Neikro doubled for two in the Braves' six-run eighth that wrapped up the rout.

CINCINNATI	ab	r	h	bi	ATLANTA	ab	r	h	bi
Rose pf	3	0	1	0	Garr rf	5	2	2	0
Armbstr lf	1	0	0	0	MPerez 2b	4	1	0	
Griffey rf	4	0	1	0	Evans b	4	1	2	2
Concepcn ss	4	0	1	0	Aaron lf	3	2	1	1
Crowley 1b	2	0	0	0	Office cf	1	1	0	1
Freed 1b	1	0	0	0	Baker cf	4	0	0	0
Driessen 3b	2	0	0	0	Murrell rf	1	1	1	0
Knight 3b	2	0	1	0	Lum 1b	3	3	2	3
GFoster cf	3	0	0	0	Correll c	4	1	2	3
Plummr c	3	0	0	0	CRobinsn ss	4	0	1	1
Kennedy 2b	2	0	0	0	PNiekro p	5	0	1	2
TCcarroll p	1	0	0	0					
Morgan ph	1	0	0	0					
Eastwick p	0	0	0	0					
Bench ph	1	0	0	0					
Baney p	0	0	0	0					
Total	30	0	4	0	Total	38	13	13	13

Cincinnati   000 000 000— 0
Atlanta   402 000 16x—13

E—Evans, TCarroll. DP—Atlanta 1. LOB—Cincinnati 6, Atlanta 9. 2B—Correll, P.Niekro. HR—Lum (11), Aaron (20).

	IP	H	R	ER	BB	SO
TCarroll (L,4-3)	4	4	6	3	5	1
Eastwick	3	3	1	1	1	2
Baney	1	6	6	6	2	0
PNiekro (W,20-13)	9	4	0	0	3	3

T—2:15. A—11,081.

Andrews Sues

Oakland, Oct. 10 (AP)—Mike Andrews, the utility infielder temporarily dropped by the Oakland A's during the 1973 World Series, filed a $2.5-million lawsuit today against A's owner Charles O. Finley and Dr. Harry R. Walker, a team physician.

The suit filed in Alameda County Superior Court asked $1 million in damages and $1.5 million in punitive damages, alleging the 31-year-old Andrews, who did not play major league baseball this year, "has been held up to public scorn, contempt, ridicule and disgrace" because of his treatment during last year's World Series.

Andrews was at his home in Peabody, Mass., today but would not answer telephone calls. His wife said he had been advised not to discuss the suit.

Andrews made two errors at second base in the 12th inning of the second World Series game, which the A's lost 10-7 to the Mets, and Finley asked him to undergo a physical examination after the game.

Dr. Walker, who examined Andrews, signed a letter saying the infielder "was unable to play his position" because of a bad shoulder and Andrews was left behind when the A's flew to New York.

The A's asked permission to replace Andrews with infielder Manny Trillo, but Commissioner Bowie Kuhn turned down the request and ordered Andrews reinstated.

Andrews rejoined the team in New York after going from Oakland to his home near Boston.

After the World Series, which Oakland won in seven games, Andrews was placed on waivers by the A's and, when no other team claimed him, was released by Oakland.

Attorneys Robert S. Gottesman

of San Francisco and Harold Meixler of Boston filed the suit in behalf of Andrews, alleging libel and slander.

It alleged that Andrews had been unable to find employment as a ball player this season and has suffered "severe mental anguish and emotional distress."

Andrews also signed the doctor's letter, which was sent to Kuhn, but said in a New York news conference during the Series that he first told Finley: "I couldn't sign it because it was a lie."

Andrews said he finally signed when he became convinced "if I didn't sign I'd never be in an A's uniform again."

Other Oakland Players were angry when they learned of Andrews' plight. He had become a popular member of the team, although he had joined the A's only midway in the season after being picked up as a free agent.

Manager Dick Williams, who had managed Andrews several years earlier with the Boston Red Sox, told the A's he was in sympathy with them and Andrews.

Andrews' suit against Finley said the A's owner caused distribution of copies of the doctor's letter to Kuhn and that publication of the letter damaged Andrews' "good name, fame and reputation as a professional ball player."

Nov. 7

Marshall wins Cy Young

Associated Press

LOS ANGELES — Mike Marshall, first relief pitcher ever to win the Cy Young Award, says he will weigh his future until next March before telling the Dodgers whether he will pitch in 1975.

"I simply will weigh the various ingredients, my family, my academic pursuits, my feelings, and baseball at that time, then make my decision, not before."

Marshall was named to the National League's top pitching honor yesterday after appearing in a record 106 games during the regular season.

The 31-year-old righthander, whose relations with the press have never been of the best, nevertheless received 17 first place votes of the 24 ballots cast to give him an easy win over teammate Andy Messersmith.

Nov. 6

Sam Rice's Letter Reveals The Truth

COOPERSTOWN, N.Y. (AP) — The truth finally has come out about one of the most disputed plays in World Series history: Right fielder Sam Rice of the Washington Senators did indeed catch a line drive by Pittsburgh's Earl Smith while tumbling into the bleacher seats during the third game of the 1925 Series.

The details of the controversial play were revealed in a letter to the Baseball Hall of Fame left by Rice to be opened after his death. Rice, inducted into the Hall of Fame in 1963 by the special Old Timers Committee, died on Oct. 13 at the age of 84.

The letter said in part, "The ball was a line drive headed for the bleachers toward right center...I turned slightly to my right and had the ball in view all the way...about 15 feet from bleachers I jumped as high as I could and back handed and the ball hit the center of pocket in glove (I had a death grip on it)

"My feet hit the barrier...and I toppled over on my stomach into first row of bleachers...at no time did I lose possession of the ball."

It was ruled that Rice had caught the ball although there was doubt about it. The game, played Oct. 10, 1925, was won by the Senators 4-3, but Pittsburgh won the series, four games to three.

Rice wrote the letter July 26, 1965—nearly 40 years after the game—and entrusted it with Paul S. Kerr, president of the National Baseball Hall of Fame and Museum.

Rice was elected to the Hall in recognition of his .322 lifetime batting average, including 2,987 hits, and stolen base exploits during his total of 20 years with the Senators and Cleveland Indians.

Not only was he the fielding star of the 1925 Series, but he led both teams with 12 hits.

Finley Lights Way for Dark's Return

By Eric Prewitt

Oakland, Oct. 18 (AP)—The A's celebrated their third consecutive World Series title and parted their controversial ways today with a rallying cry of "keep it alive in '75" and an invitation for Alvin Dark to return as manager.

"Alvin Dark has done an exceptionally great job, and if he wants it, the job is his next year," A's owner Charles O. Finley told a crowd which cheered the team at the end of a parade through downtown Oakland.

However, the Chicago Daily News reported that Dark had enough of Finley's imposing ways and would not be back next year. If that is the case and Dark would neither confirm nor deny that it was—it would be the second year in a row that a manager had walked out on Finley after winning the World Series. Dick Williams did it last year.

"I've got nothng to resign from," Dark said. "My contract has run out."

The manager, who was fired by Finley in Kansas City seven years ago, said he hasn't made up his mind about 1975 and added, "I won't express myself until after I've talked to Mr. Finley."

Finley expressed himself clearly about the NL champion Dodgers, Series losers in five games, when he said at today's ceremonies. "We beat the cockiest team in baseball."

The owner, his voice slightly hoarse from five games' worth of cheering, yelled into the microphone on a park bandstand that "the Dodgers have got only one player who could play on our team."

He meant Steve Garvey, who won the respect of the A's with a .381 BA and his clubhouse visit Thursday night to congratulate the Oakland team after its 3-2 fifth game victory.

Finley's remark also was intended for Dodger Bill Buckner, who said during the Series that only three of the A's could start for the Dodgers. Finley read that remark to his team in a pre-game dressing room meeting. The A's later hinted that Buckner, who was a goat in the final game, might learn a little humility from the incident.

The new A's slogan was first brought up by catcher Ray Fosse in a Thursday night post-game celebration when he yelled, "Keep it alive in '75."

It's a natural follow-up to "Once More in '74," the motto Finley came up with before the A's started their successful drive this year to a third straight world championship.

Only five A's players—Catfish Hunter, Vida Blue, Blue Moon Odom, Paul Lindblad and Darold Knowles missed the parade.

"There's nothing I like better than a parade in Oakland this time of year," said reliever Rollie Fingers, who rode in an antique automobile but will pick up a new car next week as the World Series' Most Valuable Player.

Oct. 31

AL votes Hunter Cy Young award

Associated Press

NEW YORK — Catfish Hunter, ace of the world champion Oakland pitching staff, was named winner of the American League Cy Young Award yesterday.

Hunter totaled 90 points in voting by a 24-member panel of the Baseball Writers Association of America, and easily defeated Ferguson Jenkins of the Rangers, who finished with 75.

The A's ace was the only pitcher named on each of the 24 ballots and received 12 first-place votes to 10 for Jenkins.

Nolan Ryan of the Angels was third with 28 points and one first-place vote. The other first-place ballot went to Cleveland's Gaylord Perry, who tied with Luis Tiant of Boston with eight points. Baltimore's Mike Cuellar had six and reliever John Hiller of the Detroit Tigers had one, completing the voting.

Oct. 26

Baseball Not Ready For Pay TV

WASHINGTON (AP) Baseball Commissioner Bowie Kuhn said yesterday it would be unthinkable for professional baseball to let the lure of pay cable TV "jeopardize our relationships with our broadcast friends."

Over-the-air television broadcast of games is too important in drawing fans to the ball parks, Kuhn told the Federal Communications Commission.

He said it's unrealistic to think "baseball is poised to dive into the pot of gold" of pay cable TV.

Dec. 18

Vida Blue Named In Paternity Suit

OAKLAND (AP) — Oakland Athletics pitcher Vida Blue was named Tuesday in a paternity suit filed in Alameda County Superior Court by 20-year-old Patricia Duncan, a college student.

The Alameda College student charged that Blue is the father of her daughter, Joy Blue, born in Oakland Oct. 17. She demanded the court declare Blue the father and award her monthly support for the child.

She claimed Blue has refused to support the child since birth.

Oct. 22

Alston Signs Another Pact With Dodgers

LOS ANGELES (AP) — Walter Alston, the man who turned a seeming lack of outward forcefulness into one of his greatest assets, has signed his 22nd one-year contract to manage the Dodgers.

The Dodgers announced the signing Monday as Alston, 62, a one-time farmer and schoolteacher, drove from Los Angeles to his winter home in rural Darrtown, Ohio.

Only four managers have won more pennants than Alston, who won his seventh this year before his Dodgers lost the World Series to Oakland.

And only two men, Connie Mack and John McGraw, have managed the same team for a longer period than Alston.

Mack piloted the Philadelphia Athletics for 50 years and McGraw led the New York Giants for 31.

Alston's credentials as a major league manager were not always totally accepted. When he was first named to the job in 1953—without any previous major league managing experience—many, including some of his players, thought the even-tempered Alston was not tough enough to get the job done.

Nov. 20

MVP Honors To Burroughs, Rudi Second

NEW YORK (AP) — Jeff Burroughs, the Texas Rangers' fence-breaking outfielder, was named the American League's Most Valuable Player today.

Burroughs, a 23-year-old who played only his second year in the big leagues in 1974, won handily over Oakland outfielder Joe Rudi to become the first player from an expansion club to win the coveted award.

The beefy slugger, who batted in a league-leading total of 118 runs, hit 25 homers and fashioned a .301 batting average, was the only player named on all 24 ballots by the Baseball Writers Association of America.

The writers, consisting of two in each of the American League cities, gave Burroughs 10 first-place votes and a total

of 248 points. Rudi had 5½ votes for first and 161½ points overall.

Two of Rudi's teammates at Oakland followed in the voting as third baseman Sal Bando had 143½ points for third place and outfielder Reggie Jackson 119 for fourth.

In fifth place was pitcher Ferguson Jenkins of the Texas Rangers with 118 points. "Catfish" Hunter, the A's Cy Young winner this season, was sixth with 107 points, giving the 1-2 teams in the American League West a sweep of the top six positions.

Nov. 14

Brock bitter with scribes

ST. LOUIS (AP) — Lou Brock is bitter. And he admits it.

After outrunning baseballs all season for a record 118 stolen bases, the St. Louis Cardinal outfielder finished second to Steve Garvey Tuesday in the race for the National League's Most Valuable Player.

"If I steal a thousand bases next year and they offer me the MVP, I wouldn't accept it," Brock said. "They (the voting writers) have been consistent. They have been showing consistent bad judgment for three years."

Cincinnati outfielder Pete Rose was the National League's MVP in 1973, while Reds catcher Johnnny Bench won the award in 1972.

Garvey, the Los Angeles Dodgers first baseman, received 270 points to Brock's 233. Garvey also garnered 13 first-place votes, while Brock drew eight.

The 35-year-old Brock had been generally favored to win the annual award, with the Dodgers' vote expected to be split between Garvey, pitcher Mike Marshall and Jim Wynn.

Brock, in addition to breaking Maury Wills' season

record of 104 stolen bases, batted .306 and scored 105 runs. Garvey, 25, hit .312, smacked 21 home runs and drove in 112 runs.

"It's really hard to understand how they voted," said St. Louis Manager Red Schoendienst. "Not that the other guy (Garvey) didn't have a good year, but I don't know what else anyone could ask Brock to do."

Cardinals Coach Vern Benson added: "I'd hate to think where we'd have been without Lou. He obviously kept us in the race."

Brock had so anticipated winning the award he had set up a news conference in Chicago Tuesday afternoon which was canceled when Garvey was named the winner.

In Chicago to film a documentary on his life and arrange groundwork for a book, Brock declined to talk to local baseball writers. But he did make a brief reference to the MVP result on a Chicago television program.

"My hat's off to him (Garvey)," Brock told sportscaster Johnny Morris on WMAQ TV, but then Brock added "I'm not pleased."

Torre MVP Of Japan Trip

Shizuoka, Japan, Nov. 20 (AP) —Joe Torre, obtained in a trade after the World Series, has been one of the brightest stars in the Mets rocky tour of Japan.

Torre, who slammed five home runs in the 18-game Japanese tour, was named the Most Valuable Player of the tour.

Despite's Torre's three - run homer the Mets dropped a 7-4 game to Tokyo's Yomiuri Giants.

It was the Giants' sixth victory against three losses and two ties with the Mets. Overall, the Mets compiled a 9-7-2 record in Japan.

Nov. 15

First appearance
Milwaukee welcomes Aaron

MILWAUKEE (AP) — Hank Aaron has yet to hit a baseball for the Milwaukee Brewers, but the all-time home run king already has made a profound impact on his return to the city where he began his quest for stardom 21 years ago.

"I want to end my career here. My main challenge is to come back and bring a championship to this city that I love so dearly," Aaron said Thursday in his first appearance here since the Brewers obtained him in a trade with the Atlanta Braves Nov. 2.

Brewers' president Bud Selig announced that Aaron, who will be 41 Feb. 5, had signed a two-year contract as a player. Manager Del Crandall said Aaron will be used primarily as a designated hitter.

The news conference, described as the largest ever held here, was considered momentous enough to be televised locally live. The dozens of newsmen were joined by admiring dignitaries — including former Wisconsin Gov. Warren P. Knowles — and many cheered as Aaron entered the conference room at the towntown hotel.

Aaron, who hit 398 of his record 733 home runs for the old Milwaukee Braves from 1954 through 1965, said he was confident he could improve on his 1974 figures of a .268 batting average and 20 home runs.

He said the pressure of trying to surpass Babe Ruth's previous record of 714 career homers was past, and that not having to play in the field every day should help his stamina.

But Crandall and others pointed to Aaron's potential leadership value to the team. American League president Lee MacPhail said Aaron should boost attendance not only here, but in AL cities where he never has played.

"I'm delighted and so are all the other 11 clubs in our league," MacPhail said. "A couple of years ago a few of us worked quite hard to sell the concept of the designated hitter. Today, all those people will be recompensed a thousand-fold for getting the DH rule through."

Aaron said one of his reasons for asking to leave the Braves and the National League, which does not have the DH rule, was to be able to play without the strain of regular outfield duty.

Ticket director Dick Hackett said the trade has produced "stacks of mail inquiring about season tickets.

"It's unbelievable," he said. "We get letters from little old ladies, little kids, saying 'God bless you for bringing Hank Aaron back.'"

Selig declined to discuss Aaron's contract, other than to call it "an extraordinary contract for an extraordinary athlete."

Aaron reportedly earned $200,000 annually under his expired three-year contract with Atlanta.

Selig also declined to say whether Aaron has been promised a front office job with the Brewers, who have been without a general manager since Jim Wilson resigned in August.

Dec. 26

Dick Allen Passes Trainers' Exam

PHILADELPHIA (AP) — Baseball star Dick Allen has become a licensed thoroughbred trainer.

The American League home run champion, who recently was traded from the Chicago White Sox to the National League's Atlanta Braves, passed his trainer's examination Tuesday at Keystone Race Track.

Allen left immediately after the examination, but a friend said the slugger has seven race horses on his farm. The friend said Allen had to get back to the farm because of a help shortage.

"He's doing all the work, cleaning out stalls and everything," the friend said.

Donald H. Shanklin, steward at Keystone, reported Allen passed the standard written test for trainers.

"He was very adequately prepared," Shanklin said. "He really seems dedicated and has put quite a bit of money into racing. I think he'll be a fine addition to the sport."

Allen owns all the horses he'll be training. In addition to the seven on the farm, he has four quartered at Keystone. Two of his horses ran Nov. 11, a 3-year-old named Getting Ready finishing seventh and a 2-year-old called Pisces' Dream running fifth.

The 32-year-old Allen, who said he was retiring from baseball when he left the White Sox in mid-September, has declined to sign with the Braves. However, he has never officially submitted a letter of retirement from the game.

"Everybody said I'm retired except me," Allen proclaimed last month. "I'm only retired if they don't want me back. I'm going to play somewhere next year, even if it's Jenkintown (a Philadelphia suburb)." He even hinted at playing in Japan.

But after he was dealt by the White Sox to the Braves, he sent a telegram to the Atlanta club, declining their contract offer, at least for the time being.

Steinbrenner Suspended

NEW YORK (AP) — Commissioner Bowie Kuhn suspended one of baseball's principal owners Wednesday, barring New York Yankee boss George M. Steinbrenner from operation of his club for the next two years.

The action was a consequence of Steinbrenner's conviction and subsequent $15,000 fine for making illegal political campaign contributions to former President Richard M. Nixon and others through his Cleveland-based American Ship Building Company.

Steinbrenner was visibly upset at Kuhn's decision, and persons close to him in Cleveland said he could be expected to challenge Kuhn's order in court.

In a statement accompanying his decision, Kuhn said his action was taken to preserve public confidence in baseball.

"An essential element of a professional team sport is the public's confidence in its integrity," he said. "If the public does not believe that a sport is honest, it would be impossible for the sport to succeed.

"We have taken elaborate precautions over the years to insure insofar as we possibly can the honesty of professional baseball and the public's confidence in that honesty."

Steinbrenner headed a group of investors which purchased the Yankees from the Columbia Broadcasting System on Jan. 3, 1973. Just over 15 months later, on April 5, 1974, he was indicted by a federal grand jury investigating Watergate-related charges for allegedly making illegal campaign contributions from corporate funds.

In August, with the Yankees in the thick of the American League East Division championship race, Steinbrenner pleaded guilty, admitting the contributions had been made and that he influenced some of his shipbuilding company's employes to make false statements to federal investigators and a federal grand jury.

"Attempting to influence employees to behave dishonestly is the kind of misconduct which, if ignored by baseball, would undermine the public's confidence in our game," said Kuhn.

In his decision, the commissioner said he was acting in the best interest of the game and declared Steinbrenner "ineligible and incompetent, for the specified period, to manage, or advise in the management of the affairs of the New York Yankees."

The order does not prohibit Steinbrenner from continuing as owner of the team. Officials in the commissioner's office said they did not know if it would prohibit him from sharing in any profits.

Kuhn warned that violation of his order may be grounds for further action.

Steinbrenner expressed shock and disappointment at the commissioner's decision.

Dec. 6

Spitball Regulation Toughened

NEW ORLEANS (AP) — Organized baseball continued its crackdown against spitball pitchers Thursday by announcing that, if a pitcher had any foreign substance on his person or in his possession, he would be ejected from the game.

Previously a pitcher had to be caught applying a foreign substance—such as saliva, sandpaper or grease—to the ball to be thrown out of a game.

Johnny Johnson, chairman of baseball's Playing Rules Committee, also said that a filled or doctored bat would be illegal and, if used, the player would be ejected from the game and suspended for three days by the league president.

Dec. 19

Hooper Dies at 87; Put Ruth in Outfield

SANTA CRUZ, Calif. (AP) — Harry Hooper, the skillful outfielder who followed former Boston Red Sox teammates Babe Ruth and Tris Speaker into Baseball's Hall of Fame, died Wednesday at age 87.

"He was the oldest living member of the Hall of Fame. I don't know who has that distinction now," Hooper's son, Harry Jr., said.

Hooper, voted into the Hall of Fame in 1971, was considered one of the top right fielders and leadoff batters in the game. He batted .281 over his 17-year big league career which began with the Red Sox in 1909 and ended in 1925 with the Chicago White Sox. He got on base 3,602 times and stole 375 bases.

But his greatest contribution may have been his part in talking Red Sox Manager Ed Barrow into using Ruth, who started his career as a pitcher, in the outfield.

"Ruth wanted to play every day. Barrow said he would be the laughing stock of baseball if he put the best left-handed pitcher in the league in the outfield. I told him that the big crowds were turning out to see the Babe hit, not pitch," Hooper said in a 1973 interview.

Ruth, whose greatest days were with the New York Yankees, went on to hit a record 714 home runs. Ruth, Speaker and Hooper were together in Boston in 1914 and 1915.

Hooper underwent surgery Nov. 29 for a circulatory problem and died early Wednesday at Dominican Hospital in Santa Cruz. His home was nearby Capitola.

"He'd been duck hunting just three weeks ago. He retired as postmaster of Capitola in 1952, but he was a very active fisherman, hunter and conservationist," Harry Hooper Jr. said. "He's pretty much recovered surgery. He died kind of from old age, I'd say."

Other survivors include a son, John of Baytown, Tex., who waged a letter-writing campaign to Hall of Fame electors on behalf of his father four years ago, and a daughter, Marie Strain of Burlingame, Calif.

Dec. 31

Hunter Picks Yankees for $3.5 Million

NEW YORK (AP) — Jim (Catfish) Hunter and the New York Yankees announced New Year's Eve they had agreed to contract terms, which The Associated Press learned would exceed $3.5 million and make Hunter the highest paid player in the sport's 105-year history.

The 8:15 p.m. announcement in snowy, holiday-festive New York ended the most celebrated free agency in baseball history and one of the three or four most expensive bidding wars American sport has known.

Hunter, the 28-year-old right-handed ace of the Oakland A's pitching staff, was declared a free agent 15 days ago because owner Charles O. Finley failed to live up to his contract. Hunter was present at a news conference called by the Yankees to annouce the contract agreement.

Yankee President Gabe Paul, who hopes the addition of Hunter, baseball's winningest pitcher the last five years, will return the New York team to their former days of greatness, made the official announcement.

The AP learned from highly placed baseball sources that Hunter and his attorneys had requested a package deal calling for a five-year playing contract that would total $3.75 million and pay Hunter $2.5 million in salary, bonus and retirement benefits.

The source said the proposal called for a $1 million bonus for Hunter, a five-year contract at $200,000 per year, a 10-year retirement plan at $50,000 a year, a $1-million life insurance policy for Hunter, a $25,000 policy for each of his two children and $200,000 in attorneys' fees.

High baseball sources said Tuesday night that it was a package very similar to this one which was being discussed in the final hours of negotiations Tuesday afternoon in Ahoskie, N.C., where the contract agreement was reached between the Yankees, Hunter and his four attorneys.

With this decision, reached 15 days after an arbitration panel had declared him a free agent, Hunter closed the books on one of the most bizarre chapters in baseball's 105-year history.

And he gave sweet revenge to the Yankees and owner George M. Steinbrenner. The Yankees were prohibited last year from signing former Oakland Manager Dick Williams, and Steinbrenner just recently was suspended from baseball after being convicted of making illegal political campaign contributions.

Dec. 19

Judge Denies Finley Bid

OAKLAND (AP) — A judge refused Wednesday to grant Oakland Athletics' owner Charles O. Finley a temporary restraining order to halt other major league baseball clubs from bidding for the services of ace pitcher Catfish Hunter.

After an informal hearing in his chamber which lasted nearly an hour, Alamada County Superior Court Judge Spurgeon Avakian refused a restraining order and set Jan. 3 for a hearing of the case on its merits before Judge George W. Phillips Jr., who becomes presiding judge next month.

Dec. 25

ST. LOUIS (AP) — St. Louis Cardinal speedster Lou Brock, who stole a record 118 bases during the 1974 baseball season, today was named Sports Man of the Year by the Sporting News.

Brock beat out such candidates as tennis star Jimmy Connors, Los Angeles Dodger relief pitcher Mike Marshall and golfer Johnny Miller in a vote by the Sporting News staff.

The 35-year-old Brock, who finished second to Dodger first baseman Steve Garvey in the National League's Most Valuable Player voting, batted .306 in leading the Cardinals to a second-place finish in the NL Eastern Division.

Brock's 1974 base stealing performance gave him 753 lifetime thefts, third behind Billy Hamilton (937) and Ty Cobb (892), and represented his fourth straight NL stolen base crown and the eighth of his career.